GENERAL HISTORY OF AFRICA · VI

Africa in the Nineteenth Century until the 1880s

Unesco General History of Africa

UNESCO International Scientific Committee for the Drafting of a General History of Africa

GENERAL HISTORY OF AFRICA · VI

Africa in the Nineteenth Century until the 1880s

EDITOR J.F.ADE AJAYI

HEINEMANN · CALIFORNIA · UNESCO

First published 1989 by the
United Nations Educational, Scientific
and Cultural Organization,
7 Place de Fontenoy, 75700 Paris

and

Heinemann International
a division of Heinemann Educational Books Ltd
Halley Court, Jordan Hill, Oxford OX2 8EJ
P.M.B. 5205, Ibadan, P.O. Box 54314, Nairobi
P.O. Box 10103, Village Post Office, Gaborone
OXFORD LONDON EDINBURGH
MELBOURNE AUCKLAND SYDNEY
IBADAN NAIROBI GABORONE
KINGSTON PORTSMOUTH NH (USA)
SINGAPORE MADRID

First published 1989
in the United States of America by the
University of California Press
2120 Berkeley Way, Berkeley
California 94720, United States of America

Heinemann International ISBN 0 435 94812 1

Unesco ISBN 92 3 101712 8

University in California Press ISBN 0 520 03917 3

The ideas and opinions expressed in this book are those of the authors and do not necessarily represent the views of Unesco.

The designation employed and the presentation of material throughout the publication do not imply the expression of any opinion whatsoever on the part of Unesco concerning the legal status of any country, territory, city or area or of its authorities, or concerning its frontiers or boundaries

Filmset in 11 pt Monophoto Ehrhardt by
Butler & Tanner Ltd, Frome and London

Printed in Great Britain by
Butler & Tanner Ltd, Frome and London

Contents

M. OMOLEWA worked as editorial assistant to the volume editor.

Note on chronology

It has been agreed to adopt the following method for writing dates. With regard to prehistory, dates may be written in two different ways.

One way is by reference to the present era, that is, dates BP (before present), the reference year being +1950; all dates are negative in relation to +1950.

The other way is by reference to the beginning of the Christian era. Dates are represented in relation to the Christian era by a simple + or − sign before the date. When referring to centuries, the terms BC and AD are replaced by 'before the Christian era' and 'of the Christian era'.

Some examples are as follows:

(i) 2300 BP = −350

(ii) 2900 BC = −2900
AD 1800 = +1800

(iii) 5th century BC = 5th century before the Christian era
3rd century AD = 3rd century of the Christian era

Key for Maps

BAULE	Ethnic Groups
NYUMI	States
DIAFUNU	Regions
Gambia	Rivers
⚔	Battlesites
▲	Mountains
■	Monastic headquarters of religious order
●	Site of town
⊙	Site of City

List of Figures

List of Plates

Acknowledgements for plates

Ade Ajayi, J. F. and Crowder, M. (eds), *Historical Atlas of Africa*, Longman, London, 1985, © Longman, London. Fig. 3.1, vol. II (1st edn.), Longman, London, 1974, 22.1

Allen and Thompson, *Narrative of an Expedition*, London, 1848, 27.4*

al-Rafei, Abdel-Rahman., *Açr Mohammad ʿAlī*, Dar al-Nahdal al-Micriyyah, Cairo, 1930, 13.2 (4th edn.), 1982, Dar el-Maaref, Cairo, © Judge Helmy Shahin, 13.3

al-Rafei, Abdel-Rahman, *Thawrat Arabi wal-Ihtelal al-Biritani*, Dar al-Nahdal al-Micriyyah, Cairo, 1937 (original photo published in *The Cutaphic*, London, 1882), 13.5

Archives du Ministère des Affaires éstrangères, Paris, by kind permission of H. Exc. the Minister of Foreign Affairs of the French Republic, Fig. 4.1

Arhin, K., by kind permission of the Asantehene of Ghana, 25.1

Arnot, F. S., *Bihé and Garengaze*, J. E. Hawkins and Co. Ltd., 1893, 12.8*

© *Arts of Asia*, Hong Kong, March–April 1978, p. 89, 28.1

Barbour, N., *Morocco*, Thames and Hudson, 1965, Editions du Seuil, Paris, 19.3

Barth, H., *Travel and Discoveries in Northern and Central Africa*, Longman, London, 1857, 20.5*

Basel Mission Archive, 25.8

Batran, A., 23.1

Bennet, N. R. and Brooks G. E. (eds), *New England Merchants in Africa: A History through documents, 1802–1865*, Boston University Press, Boston, 1965, © Peabody Museum of Salem, photo by Mark Sexton, 9.2

Bennett, N. R., *Mirambo of Tanzania*, Oxford University Press, New York, 1971, © National Museums of Tanzania, Dar-es-Salaam, 10.3

Binger, L., *Du Niger au Golfe de Guinée*, Hachette, Paris, 1892, 24.3a*, by kind permission of the Bodleian Library (shelf no: 710.11. s.8/1) vol. I, p. 463, 25.4(b), vol. I. p. 17, 25.5*, 25.6**, vol. II, 25.7*

Bowdich, T. E., *A Mission From Cape Coast Castle to Ashantee*, John Murray, London, 1819, 25.2*, 25.3*

Brooks, G., *The Kru Mariner in the Nineteenth Century*, Liberian Studies Association, Newark, NJ, 1972 (original from J. L. Wilson, *Western Africa*, New York, 1856), 24.3b*

Burton, R., *The Lake Region of Central Africa*, Longman, Green, Longman and Roberts, London, 1860, vol. II, p. 80 and 278, © Royal Geographical Society, London, 10.1, 10.2

Burton, R., *First Footsteps in East Africa*, Routledge and Kegan Paul Ltd, London, 1894, photo reproduced by Sasor Publisher, London, 15.3, British Library reproduction, 28.2

Cameron, V. L., *Across Africa*, Daldy, Isbister and Co, London, 1877, vol. I, p. 352, 12.1*

Cerulli, E., *Somalia. Scritti vari editi ed inediti*, © Instituto Poligrafico e Zecca dello Stato, Rome, 1957, vol. I, p. xi, 9.1*
Church Missionary Gleaner, 1855, 26.2*
Collection Bibliothèque Générale et Archives, Rabat 18.2
Corry, J., *Observations Upon the Windward Coast*, Frank Cass Publishers, London, 1807, 24.1*
de Chassiron, Ch., *Aperçu pittoresque de la Régence de Tunis, Imprimerie de Bénard, Paris, 1849*, 17.3**
Denham, Clapperton and Oudney, *Narrative of Travels and Discoveries in Northern and Central Africa*, London, 1826, 22.3*, 22.4*
Deschamps, H., *Histoire de Madagascar*, Berger-Levrault, Paris, 1960, 16.4** (all rights reserved)
Ellis, W., *Three Visits to Madagascar*, J. Murray, London, 1858, front cover photograph, by kind permission of the British Library, 16.1, 16.6, 16.7
Evans Pritchard, E., *The Sanusiya of Cyrenaica*, Oxford University Press, Oxford, 1949, © Oxford University Press, 17.4*
Fagg, W. B. and Pemberton III, J. (ed. Holcombe, Bryce), *Yoruba Sculpture of West Africa*, New York, 1962, © National Museum, Lagos, 26.1
French National Museums, 17.5
Frey, Colonel, *Côte Occidentale d'Afrique*, Flammarion, Paris, 1890, 20.1*
Gamitto, A. C. P. (tr. I. Cunnison), *King Kazembe*, Atica, Lisbon, 1960, © Atica, Lisbon, 12.4*
Harris, W. C., *The Highlands of Aethiopia*, Longman, London, 1844, 15.6
Hinderer, A., *Seventeen Years in Yorubaland*, London, 1872, British Library, London, 26.3
Holt, P. M. and Daly, M., *History of the Sudan*, Weidenfeld and Nicolson, London, 1979, by kind permission of The National Trust, Kingston Lacy, Bankes Mss, 14.1, by kind permission of George Weidenfeld and Nicolson Ltd, London, 14.2, © BBC Hulton Picture Library, 14.7
Ikime, O., *Merchant Prince of the Niger Delta: the rise and fall of Nana Olomu, Last Governor of the Benin River*, Heinemann, London, 1968, 27.2
Institut fondamental d'Afrique Noire (I.F.A.N.), Dakar, 23.2, 23.3
Johnston, H. H., *British Central Africa*, Greenwood Press, London, 1897, 3.1*
Johnston, H. H., *British Central Africa*, Methuen and Co, London, 1897, p. 92, 8.1*, p. 93, 8.2*, p. 421, 8.3*
Julien, Ch. A., *Histoire de l'Algérie contemporaine: conquete et colonisation*, Presses Universitaires de France, Paris, 1964, 17.1**, 17.2**, 19.2(a–b)**
Laroui, A., *Origines sociales et culturelles du nationalisme marocain*, Maspéro, Paris, 1977, 18.3
Lefebvre, T., *Voyage en Abyssinie, (1845–54)*, Paris, photos reproduced by Sasor Publisher, 15.1, 15.2
Ling Roth, H., *Great Benin, Its Custom, Art and Horrors*, Kings and Sons, Halifax, 1903, (original from *Globus*, 1897, vol. I, p. xxii), 26.4, 26.5*, 27.1*
Mage, E., *Voyage dans le Soudan occidental*, Hachette, Paris, 1868, © Hachette, Paris, 23.4, 23.5
Magyar, L., *Reisen in Süd Afrika in den Jahren 1849 bis 1857*, Pest and Leipzig, 1859, 12.5*, 12.6*

M'Bokolo, E., *Noirs et Blancs en Afrique équatoriale*, Editions de l'Ecole des Hautes Etudes en sciences sociales, Paris, 1981 (Photographs reproduced from du Belley, Griffon, 'le Gabon', *Le Tour du Monde*, 1865), 27.5, 27.6

Miers, S., *Britain and the Ending of the Slave Trade*, Longman, London, 1975, © The Illustrated London News Picture Library, 4.2

Mollien, G., *Travels in the Interior of Africa*, London, 1820, 24.2*

Museum of the Institute of Ethiopian Studies, Addis Ababa, 15.7

Museum of Toulouse, © Jean Dieuzaide, Toulouse, 18.1

Museum of Versailles, Photothèque, Groupe Presses de la Cité, Paris, 19.1

Mutibwa, Ph., *The Malagasy and the Europeans*, Longman, London, 1974, Direction de la Presse et de la Publication, Ministère de l'Information, Madagascar, 16.2 (a–f), 16.3

Nachtigal, G., (tr. and ed. Fisher, A. G. B. and H. J.), *Sahara and Sudan*, Hurst, London, 1974, vol. I, © Hurst, London, 20.2*, 20.3*, vol. II, 1980, 22.2 (a–c)*, 22.5*

© National Army Museum, London, 7.1

Nigerian Information Service Centre, Embassy of Nigeria, Paris, 27.3

Omer-Cooper, J., *The Zulu Aftermath*, Longman, London, 1966 (original from Gardiner, A. F., *Narrative of a Journey to the Zoolu country*, London, 1836), © Slide Centre Ltd, 1.1 (original from Livingstone, D. and C., *Narrative of an Expedition to the Zambezi*, John Murray Publishers, London, 1865), 8.4*

Petherick, J. and K., *Travels in Central Africa*, Tinsley Brothers, London, 1869, 14.5*

Photothèque, Groupe Presses de la Cité, Paris, 19.4

Photothèque, Musée de l'Homme, Paris, © 26.6 (a–b)

Pogge, P., *Im Reiche des Muata Jamvo*, Berlin, 1880, 12.10*

Porter, A. T., *Creoledom*, Oxford University Press, Oxford, 1963, by kind permission of the Foreign and Commonwealth Office Library, 3.3

Raison-Jourde, F., *Les Souverains de Madagascar*, Karthala, Paris, 1983, Fonds Grandidier du Musée des Collections scientifiques. Tsimbazaza, Antananarivo 16.5

Rassam, H., *Narrative of a British Mission to Theodore, King of Abyssinia*, Murray, London, 1869, photos reproduced by Sasor Publisher, London, 15.4, 15.5

Roger Viollet, H., © Harlingue-Viollet, Paris, 28.4

Rohlfs, G., *Meine Mission nach Abessinien*, Leipzig, 1882, photo reproduced by Sasor Publisher, London, 15.8

Saunders, C., *Black Leaders in African History*, Heinemann, London, 1978 (original from John Aitken Chalmers, *Tiyo Soga, A Page of South African Mission Work* (1st edn), 1877), 3.2

Schweinfurth, G., *The Heart of Africa*, Sampson, Low, Marston, Low and Searle, London, 1873, vol. I, frontispiece, 12.3*, 14.3*, 14.4*, 14.6*

Snouk Hurgronje, C., *Mekka in the latter part of the nineteenth century: daily life, customs and learning: the Muslims of the East-Indian Archipelago*, E. J. Brill, Leiden, 1970, © E. J. Brill, 28.3*

Stanley, H. M., *Through the Dark Continent*, Sampson, Low, Marston, Low and Searle, London, 1878, vol. I, p. 89, 11.1*, 11.2*, p. 474, 11.3*, p. 332, 11.4*

Sullivan, G. L. *Dhow chasing in Zanzibar Waters*, Frank Cass Publishers, London, 1873, © Frank Cass Publishers, 4.1*

Tabler, E. C., *Trade and Travel in Early Barotseland*, Chatto and Windus, London, 1963 (original from Dr Emil Holub, *Seven Years in South Africa, vol. II*, Samson, Low, Marston, Searle and Ribbington, London, 1881), 8.5*, 8.6*

© The Mansell Collection Ltd, London, 13.4

© The Tate Gallery, London, 13.1

Vansina, J., *Art History in Africa*, Longman, London, 1984, © Staatl. Museum für Völkerkunde, Munich, 6.1, © Photo Institut des Musées Nationaux du Zaire (IMNZ), no. 73.381.1, 73.381.2, 70.8.2 (left to right), 12.2 © The Walters Art Gallery, Baltimore, 12.7, © Museum für Völkerkunde, Berlin, 12.9, © Werner Forman Archive, London,. 20.4, © Frobenius Institut, 25.4(a)

* by kind permission of the Syndics of Cambridge University Library.

**by kind permission of the Bibliothèque Nationale, Paris.

We regret that we have been unable to trace the copyright holders of plates 22.1, 27.5, 27.6 and would welcome any information enabling us to do so.

Preface

AMADOU-MAHTAR M'BOW

Director-General of Unesco (1974–1987)

For a long time, all kinds of myths and prejudices concealed the true history of Africa from the world at large. African societies were looked upon as societies that could have no history. In spite of important work done by such pioneers as Leo Frobenius, Maurice Delafosse and Arturo Labriola, as early as the first decades of this century, a great many non-African experts could not rid themselves of certain preconceptions and argued that the lack of written sources and documents made it impossible to engage in any scientific study of such societies.

Although the *Iliad* and *Odyssey* were rightly regarded as essential sources for the history of ancient Greece, African oral tradition, the collective memory of peoples which holds the thread of many events marking their lives, was rejected as worthless. In writing the history of a large part of Africa, the only sources used were from outside the continent, and the final product gave a picture not so much of the paths actually taken by the African peoples as of those that the authors thought they must have taken. Since the European Middle Ages were often used as a yardstick, modes of production, social relations and political institutions were visualized only by reference to the European past.

In fact, there was a refusal to see Africans as the creators of original cultures which flowered and survived over the centuries in patterns of their own making and which historians are unable to grasp unless they forgo their prejudices and rethink their approach.

Furthermore, the continent of Africa was hardly ever looked upon as a historical entity. On the contrary, emphasis was laid on everything likely to lend credence to the idea that a split had existed, from time immemorial, between a 'white Africa' and a 'black Africa', each unaware of the other's existence. The Sahara was often presented as an impenetrable space preventing any intermingling of ethnic groups and peoples or any exchange of goods, beliefs, customs and ideas between the societies that had grown up on either side of the desert. Hermetic frontiers were drawn between the civilizations and Ancient Egypt and Nubia and those of the peoples south of the Sahara.

It is true that the history of Africa north of the Sahara has been more closely linked with that of the Mediterranean basin than has the history of sub-Saharan Africa, but it is now widely recognized that the various civilizations of the African continent, for all their differing languages and cultures, represent, to a greater or lesser degree, the historical offshoots of a set of peoples and societies united by bonds centuries old.

Another phenomenon which did great disservice to the objective study of the African past was the appearance, with the slave trade and colonization, of racial stereotypes which bred contempt and lack of understanding and became so deep-rooted that they distorted even the basic concepts of historiography. From the time when the notions of 'white' and 'black' were used as generic labels by the colonialists, who were regarded as superior, the colonized Africans had to struggle against both economic and psychological enslavement. Africans were identifiable by the colour of their skin, they had become a kind of merchandise, they were earmarked for hard labour and eventually, in the minds of those dominating them, they came to symbolize an imaginary and allegedly inferior *Negro* race. This pattern of spurious identification relegated the history of the African peoples in many minds to the rank of ethno-history, in which appreciation of the historical and cultural facts was bound to be warped.

The situation has changed significantly since the end of the Second World War and in particular since the African countries became independent and began to take an active part in the life of the international community and in the mutual exchanges that are its *raison d'être*. An increasing number of historians has endeavoured to tackle the study of Africa with a more rigorous, objective and open-minded outlook by using – with all due precautions – actual African sources. In exercising their right to take the historical initiative, Africans themselves have felt a deep-seated need to re-establish the historical authenticity of their societies on solid foundations.

In this context, the importance of the eight-volume *General History of Africa*, which Unesco is publishing, speaks for itself.

The experts from many countries working on this project began by laying down the theoretical and methodological basis for the *History*. They have been at pains to call in question the over-simplifications arising from a linear and restrictive conception of world history and to re-establish the true facts wherever necessary and possible. They have endeavoured to highlight the historical data that give a clearer picture of the evolution of the different peoples of Africa in their specific socio-cultural setting.

To tackle this huge task, made all the more complex and difficult by the vast range of sources and the fact that documents were widely scattered, Unesco has had to proceed by stages. The first stage, from 1965 to 1969, was devoted to gathering documentation and planning the work. Operational assignments were conducted in the field and included campaigns to collect oral traditions, the creation of regional documentation centres for oral traditions, the collection of unpublished manuscripts in

Arabic and Ajami (African languages written in Arabic script), the compilation of archival inventories and the preparation of a *Guide to the Sources of the History of Africa*, culled from the archives and libraries of the countries of Europe and later published in eleven volumes. In addition, meetings were organized to enable experts from Africa and other continents to discuss questions of methodology and lay down the broad lines for the project after careful examination of the available sources.

The second stage, which lasted from 1969 to 1971, was devoted to shaping the *History* and linking its different parts. The purpose of the international meetings of experts held in Paris in 1969 and Addia Ababa in 1970 was to study and define the problems involved in drafting and publishing the *History*; presentation in eight volumes, the principal edition in English, French and Arabic, translation into African languages such as Kiswahili, Hausa, Fulani, Yoruba or Lingala, prospective versions in German, Russian, Portuguese, Spanish and Chinese, as well as abridged editions designed for a wide African and international public.[1]

The third stage has involved actual drafting and publication. This began with the appointment of the 39-member International Scientific Committee, two-thirds African and one-third non-African, which assumes intellectual responsibility for the *History*.

The method used is interdisciplinary and is based on a multi-faceted approach and a wide variety of sources. The first among these is archaeology, which holds many of the keys to the history of African cultures and civilizations. Thanks to archeology, it is now acknowledged that Africa was very probably the cradle of mankind and the scene – in the neolithic period – of one of the first technological revolutions in history. Archaeology has also shown that Egypt was the setting for one of the most brilliant ancient civilizations of the world. But another very important source is oral tradition, which, after being long despised, has now emerged as an invaluable instrument for discovering the history of Africa, making it possible to follow the movements of its different peoples in both space and time, to understand the African vision of the world from the inside and to grasp the original features of the values on which the cultures and institutions of the continent are based.

We are indebted to the International Scientific Committee in charge of this *General History of Africa*, and to its Rapporteur and the editors and authors of the various volumes and chapters, for having shed a new light on the African past in its authentic and all-encompassing form and for having avoided any dogmatism in the study of essential issues. Among these issues we might cite: the slave trade, that 'endlessly bleeding wound', which was responsible for one of the cruellest mass deportations in the history of mankind, which sapped the African continent of its life-blood

1. Volumes I and II have been published in Arabic, Spanish, Korean, Portuguese, Chinese and Italian; Volume IV in Arabic, Portuguese and Spanish; Volume VII in Spanish.

while contributing significantly to the economic and commerical expansion of Europe; colonization, with all the effects it had on population, economics, psychology and culture; relations between Africa south of the Sahara and the Arab world; and, finally, the process of decolonization and nation-building which mobilized the intelligence and passion of people still alive and sometimes still active today. All these issues have been broached with a concern for honesty and rigour which is not the least of the *History*'s merits. By taking stock of our knowledge of Africa, putting forward a variety of viewpoints on African cultures and offering a new reading of history, the *History* has the signal advantage of showing up the light and shade and of openly portraying the differences of opinion that may exist between scholars.

By demonstrating the inadequacy of the methodological approaches which have long been used in research on Africa, this *History* calls for a new and careful study of the twofold problem areas of historiography and cultural identity, which are united by links of reciprocity. Like any historical work of value, the *History* paves the way for a great deal of further research on a variety of topics.

It is for this reason that the International Scientific Committee, in close collaboration with Unesco, decided to embark on additional studies in an attempt to go deeper into a number of issues which will permit a clearer understanding of certain aspects of the African past. The findings being published in the series 'Unesco Studies and Documents – General History of Africa'[2] will prove a useful supplement to the *History*, as will the works planned on aspects of national or subregional history.

The *General History* sheds light both on the historical unity of Africa and also its relations with the other continents, particularly the Americas and the Caribbean. For a long time, the creative manifestations of the descendants of Africans in the Americas were lumped together by some historians as a heterogeneous collection of *Africanisms*. Needless to say, this is not the attitude of the authors of the *History*, in which the resistance of the slaves shipped to America, the constant and massive participation of the descendants of Africans in the struggles for the initial indepedence of America and in national liberation movements, are rightly perceived for what they were: vigorous assertions of identity, which helped forge the universal concept of mankind. Although the phenomenon may vary in different places, it is now quite clear that ways of feeling, thinking, dreaming

2. The following eleven volumes have already been published in this series: *The peopling of ancient Egypt and the deciphering of Meroitic script; The African slave trade from the fifteenth to the nineteenth century; Historial relations across the Indian Ocean; The historiography of Southern Africa; The decolonization of Africa: Southern Africa and the Horn of Africa; African ethnonyms and toponyms; Historical and socio-cultural relations between black Africa and the Arab world from 1935 to the present; The methodology of contemporary African History; The Educational Process and Historiography in Africa; Africa and the Second World War; Libya Antiqua.*

and acting in certain nations of the western hemisphere have been marked by their African heritage. The cultural inheritance of Africa is visible everywhere, from the southern United States to northern Brazil, across the Caribbean and on the Pacific seaboard. In certain places it even underpins the cultural identity of some of the most important elements of the population.

The *History* also clearly brings out Africa's relations with southern Asia across the Indian Ocean and the African contributions to other civilizations through mutual exchanges.

I am convinced that the efforts of the peoples of Africa to conquer or strengthen their independence, secure their development and assert their cultural characteristics, must be rooted in historical awareness renewed, keenly felt and taken up by each succeeding generation.

My own background, the experience I gained as a teacher and as chairman, from the early days of independence, of the first commission set up to reform history and geography curricula in some of the countries of West and Central Africa, taught me how necessary it was for the education of young people and for the information of the public at large to have a history book produced by scholars with inside knowledge of the problems and hopes of Africa and with the ability to apprehend the continent in its entirety.

For all these reasons, Unesco's goal will be to ensure that this *General History of Africa* is widely disseminated in a large number of languages and is used as a basis for producing children's books, school textbooks and radio and television programmes. Young people, whether schoolchildren or students, and adults in Africa and elsewhere will thus be able to form a truer picture of the African continent's past and the factors that explain it, as well as a fairer understanding of its cultural heritage and its contribution to the general progress of mankind. The *History* should thus contribute to improved international cooperation and stronger solidarity among peoples in their aspirations to justice, progress and peace. This is, at least, my most cherished hope.

It remains for me to express my deep gratitude to the members of the International Scientific Committee, the Rapporteur, the different volume editors, the authors and all those who have collaborated in this tremendous undertaking. The work they have accomplished and the contribution they have made plainly go to show how people from different backgrounds but all imbued with the same spirit of goodwill and enthusiasm in the service of universal truth can, within the international framework provided by Unesco, bring to fruition a project of considerable scientific and cultural import. My thanks also go to the organizations and governments whose generosity has made it possible for Unesco to publish this *History* in different languages and thus ensure that it will have the worldwide impact it deserves and thereby serve the international community as a whole.

Description of the Project

B. A. OGOT*

President, International Scientific Committee for the Drafting of a General History of Africa (1978–1983)

The General Conference of Unesco at its 16th Session instructed the Director-General to undertake the drafting of a *General History of Africa*. The enormous task of implementing the project was entrusted to an International Scientific Committee which was established by the Executive Board in 1970. This Committee, under the Statutes adopted by the Executive Board of Unesco in 1971, is composed of thirty-nine members (two-thirds of whom are African and one-third non-African) serving in their personal capacity and appointed by the Director-General of Unesco for the duration of the Committee's mandate.

The first task of the Committee was to define the principal characteristics of the work. These were defined at the first session of the Committee as follows:

(a) Although aiming at the highest possible scientific level, the history does not seek to be exhaustive and is a work of synthesis avoiding dogmatism. In many respects, it is a statement of problems showing the present state of knowledge and the main trends in research, and it does not hesitate to show divergencies of views where these exist. In this way, it prepares the ground for future work.

(b) Africa is considered in this work as a totality. The aim is to show the historical relationships between the various parts of the continent, too frequently subdivided in works published to date. Africa's historical connections with the other continents receive due attention, these connections being analysed in terms of mutual exchanges and multilateral influences, bringing out, in its appropriate light, Africa's contribution to the history of mankind.

(c) *The General History of Africa* is, in particular, a history of ideas and civilizations, societies and institutions. It is based on a wide variety of sources, including oral tradition and art forms.

(d) The *History* is viewed essentially from the inside. Although a scholarly

* During the Sixth Plenary Session of the International Scientific Committee for the Drafting of a General History of Africa (Brazzaville, 1983), an election of the new Bureau was held and Professor Ogot was replaced by Professor Albert Adu Boahen.

work, it is also, in large measure, a faithful reflection of the way in which African authors view their own civilization. While prepared in an international framework and drawing to the full on the present stock of scientific knowledge, it should also be a vitally important element in the recognition of the African heritage and should bring out the factors making for unity in the continent. This effort to view things from within is the novel feature of the project and should, in addition to its scientific quality, give it great topical significance. By showing the true face of Africa, the *History* could, in an era absorbed in economic and technical struggles, offer a particular conception of human values.

The Committee has decided to present the work covering over three million years of African history in eight volumes, each containing about eight hundred pages of text with illustrations, photographs, maps and line drawings.

A chief editor, assisted if necessary by one or two co-editors, is responsible for the preparation of each volume. The editors are elected by the Committee either from among its members or from outside by a two-thirds majority. They are responsible for preparing the volumes in accordance with the decisions and plans adopted by the Committee. On scientific matters, they are accountable to the Committee or, between two sessions of the Committee, to its Bureau for the contents of the volumes, the final version of the texts, the illustrations and, in general, for all scientific and technical aspects of the *History*. The Bureau ultimately approves the final manuscript. When it considers the manuscript ready for publication, it transmits it to the Director-General of Unesco. Thus the Committee, or the Bureau between committee sessions, remains fully in charge of the project.

Each volume consists of some thirty chapters. Each chapter is the work of a principal author assisted, if necessary, by one or two collaborators. The authors are selected by the Committee on the basis of their *curricula vitae*. Preference is given to African authors, provided they have requisite qualifications. Special effort is also made to ensure, as far as possible, that all regions of the continent, as well as other regions having historical or cultural ties with Africa, are equitably represented among the authors.

When the editor of a volume has approved texts of chapters, they are then sent to all members of the Committee for criticism. In addition, the text of the volume editor is submitted for examination to a Reading Committee, set up within the International Scientific Committee on the basis of the members' fields of competence. The Reading Committee analyses the chapters from the standpoint of both substance and form. The Bureau then gives final approval to the manuscripts.

Such a seemingly long and involved procedure has proved necessary, since it provides the best possible guarantee of the scientific objectivity of the *General History of Africa*. There have, in fact, been instances when the

Bureau has rejected manuscripts or insisted on major revisions or even reassigned the drafting of a chapter to another author. Occasionally, specialists in a particular period of history or in a particular question are consulted to put the finishing touches to a volume.

The work will be published first in a hard-cover edition in English, French and Arabic, and later in paperback editions in the same languages. An abridged version in English and French will serve as a basis for translation into African languages. The Committee has chosen Kiswahili and Hausa as the first African languages into which the work will be translated.

Also, every effort will be made to ensure publication of the *General History of Africa* in other languages of wide international currency such as Chinese, Portuguese, Russian, German, Italian, Spanish, Japanese, etc.

It is thus evident that this is a gigantic task which constitutes an immense challenge to African historians and to the scholarly community at large, as well as to Unesco under whose auspices the work is being done. For the writing of a continental history of Africa, covering the last three million years, using the highest canons of scholarship and involving, as it must do, scholars drawn from diverse countries, cultures, ideologies and historical traditions, is surely a complex undertaking. It constitutes a continental, international and interdisciplinary project of great proportions.

In conclusion, I would like to underline the significance of this work for Africa and for the world. At a time when the peoples of Africa are striving towards unity and greater cooperation in shaping their individual destinies, a proper understanding of Africa's past, with an awareness of common ties among Africans and between Africa and other continents, should not only be a major contribution towards mutual understanding among the people of the earth, but also a source of knowledge of a cultural heritage that belongs to all mankind.

1

Africa at the beginning of the nineteenth century: issues and prospects

J. F. A. AJAYI

Perspective

This volume attempts a survey of African history in the nineteenth century before the European Scramble and the establishment of colonial rule. This 'precolonial century',[1] as it has been called, has loomed rather large in the post-Second World War effort to reinterpret African history, of which effort the Unesco *General History of Africa* may be regarded as a climax. Once it was accepted that change in African history did not originate with the colonial period, considerable attention began to be paid to the preceding century. Major events and changes with revolutionary import during the century, such as the reforms of Muḥammad ʿAlī in Egypt, the reunification of Ethiopia under the emperors Téwodros and Menelik, the Mfecane of the Sotho–Nguni states in Southern and Central Africa, the *djihād* movements in West Africa, have been the subject of various scholarly works and are all dealt with in the following chapters. Nevertheless, the general characteristics of the nineteenth century, and the significance of the century as a whole in the historiography of Africa, remain controversial.

In the first place, because of the relative abundance of reliable oral material and the new written sources produced by the expanding scale of European activities in Africa in the period – such as accounts of European travellers, missionaries, traders, and government consular and other agents penetrating into the interior of the continent, often for the first time – the nineteenth century in many parts of Africa is better known and better researched than earlier periods. There has been a tendency, similar to what happens in oral tradition, to telescope all significant change in the whole precolonial history of Africa into the favoured period of the nineteenth century. Fortunately, other volumes of the Unesco *General History* have already dealt with the dynamics of change in Africa in the earlier periods. The 'myth' of static Africa has thus already been exploded. Unfortunately, the corollary has persisted in the assumption that change in the nineteenth century was necessarily different from change in earlier periods and can

1. P. Curtin, S. Feierman, L. Thompson and J. Vansina, 1978, p. 362.

only be explained by reference to factors that did not previously exist. It is therefore important here to examine the extent to which the changes taking place in the nineteenth century were a continuation of changes already taking place in the eighteenth century, and to what extent they were due to new factors associated with the expanding scale of European activities and increasing integration of African economies into the world system.

The tendency to explain change in Africa in the 'precolonial century' unduly, if not exclusively, in terms of the expanding scale of European activities constitutes the second issue in the historiography of the period. The increasing integration of African economies into the world system is often treated not merely as a major factor leading to change but in fact as the dominant theme of African history in the period. The nineteenth century is discussed not only as the prelude to the colonial period but essentially as its beginning. In accordance with the late Dr K. O. Dike's dictum of 'trade and politics' – that 'the history of modern West Africa is largely the history of five centuries of trade with European nations'[2] – changes in the overseas trade and trade routes, and the internal network of markets and long-distance trading that fed the overseas trade have for too long been perceived as the major, if not the sole, dynamic factor in African history in the nineteenth century. Thus, the changes in Egypt are explained by the impact of Napoleon Bonaparte, rather than by the complex of internal factors dating back to the eighteenth century that produced a national movement that rallied round the Albanian Muḥammad ʿAlī's efforts to set Egyptian renaissance against Ottoman attempts to reimpose direct rule. Similarly, the Mfecane is explained vaguely as a reaction to the European presence, either in terms of pressure on the eastern frontier of the Cape Colony or a desire to profit from the Portuguese trade in Delagoa Bay, rather than in terms of the internal dynamics of northern Nguni society. The conjuncture of these remarkable events at the beginning of the century with the *dj̲ihād* movements in West Africa and new stirrings in Ethiopia is considered remarkable, and seems to require a global explanation.[3] But rather than seek for such explanation in the dynamics of

2. K. O. Dike, 1956, p. 1. This dictum was of course an exaggeration, even in terms of Dike's own analysis of the Niger Delta in the nineteenth century, which emphasized the internal factors of change. For a critique of the 'trade and politics' thesis, see S. I. Mudenge, 1974, p. 373 – 'Once the presence of external trade has been established, its consequences are then assumed: analysis of its actual impact on the political system and its relationship to internal production and consumption in the given polity becomes unnecessary, and all effort is expended in explaining the organization of trade routes and marketing and the types of goods involved.'

3. Cf. the tentative view of I. Hrbek in 1965 (published in 1968): 'It is surprising how many far-reaching events took place in Africa between 1805 and 1820; though they were unrelated to each other, they form a distinct trend in African history'. He listed the 'Fulbe revolutions' of West Africa; 'the rise of the Zulu'; 'the rise of Buganda'; 'the foundation of Modern Egypt by Muḥammad ʿAlī's; 'the unification of Imerina on Madagascar'; 'the rise

African societies, the industrialization of Europe and the impact of the world economy on Africa has provided too facile an alternative hypothesis.

It is therefore necessary in this introductory chapter to focus attention on Africa at the beginning of the nineteenth century, to survey the general characteristics and tendencies of the period, the nature and extent of continuities with the past, the innovations and new departures, and the tendencies for the future. It is only by tackling this problem at the beginning of the volume that we can hope at the end to be in a position to consider the nature of African development during the century and the extent to which the European factor is to be regarded as 'a necessary precondition of the development of African societies, technical, cultural and moral',[4] or the predominant cause of African underdevelopment.

Demography and population movements

By 1800, the main linguistic and cultural divisions of the African population had long been established in their various locations, claiming rights over their own portions of the land mass.[5] Indeed, for most parts of Africa, the process was complete by the sixteenth century and, by the nineteenth century, varying degrees of consolidation had taken place and stability had been established. Only in the Horn of Africa, East Africa (outside the central highlands of the Great Lakes region) and in Madagascar were major migrations into relatively underpopulated areas still continuing into the seventeenth and eighteenth centuries, and even in those places stability in the sense of mastery over the land space had been achieved by the beginning of the nineteenth century.

This is to use the term migration in the sense of extraordinary movements of significant numbers of people over wide areas of time and space. However, in another sense mobility of people in the process of earning their livelihood continued, either as pastoralists involved in transhumance; or crop farmers alternating between land under cultivation and land left fallow; or hunters and gatherers roaming over defined areas for animals or honey or even palm fruits; or fishermen following the movement of fish according to different seasons; or specialist craftsmen such as blacksmiths or traders pursuing their occupation in enclave colonies in distant places. Movements of this sort should, however, be regarded as regular flows of population that usually did not involve permanent abandonment of

of Omani hegemony on the East African coast'; and 'the abolition of the slave trade'. See I. Hrbek, 1968, pp. 47–8. Historians now reaching for a continental synthesis too easily find a common explanation in the progressive integration of Africa into the world-economy.

4. T. Hodgkin, 1976, p. 11, referring to the point of view of what he calls 'imperialist administrator-scholars'.

5. This section draws heavily on Unesco, *General History of Africa*, Vol. V, ch. 3 and Vol. VII, ch. 18.

locations or displacement of people and the movement of significant numbers over long distances or long periods of time. However, population pressure relative to the pattern of land use, perhaps arising from normal increase over a period of relative prosperity, or immigration due to war and the collapse of existing state systems, or to prolonged drought, pestilence or other ecological disaster in a neighbouring area could set off a process of expansion by drift. The nineteenth century was to witness several such movements. Some were triggered off by movements that began before 1800, as in the case of the Fang in the forest belt of Equatorial Africa; others developed as a result of nineteenth-century changes in trading opportunities and patterns as among the Chokwe of Angola. The most spectacular movements were associated with the decline or rise of state systems, and could be either on a local basis as in the case of the aftermath of the collapse of Old Ọyọ in the Yoruba area of western Nigeria, or on a subcontinental basis as in the aftermath of the Mfecane among the northern Nguni of Natal in Southern Africa. Such movements often necessitated the occupation and cultivation of areas hitherto regarded as relatively inferior land, and the development of techniques and new crops suitable for such new environments.

The figure of 100 million is usually given as an estimate of the total population of Africa at the beginning of the nineteenth century. This is partly an arbitrary figure and partly based on projections back from the meagre demographic data of the post-1950 period. The actual figure may have been very different. However, the crucial historical issues concern the demographic trends and the interaction between the trends and the systems of political economy, the regional distribution of population relative to land resources and agricultural practice.

The general assumption of demographers is that, given existing agricultural systems, technologies and patterns of health care and diseases causing excessive infant mortality, the overall population could not have been expanding much. Normally, a rise of 0.5 per cent per annum (compared with the current 2.5 to 3.5), that is to say 50 more births than deaths per thousand annually, could have been expected. That would have doubled the population within a millennium. Given the stability of the population in North Africa, and the intensive agriculture and irrigation in the fertile areas and oases, there was a steady increase of population in periods of prosperity, but this seems to have been balanced by periods of drought and plague, and the population barely remained stable. In the grasslands of the Sudanic zone of West Africa, Central and Southern Africa, the populations were constantly adapting their techniques and achieving a symbiosis between pastoralists and agriculturists, or developing systems of mixed agriculture capable of sustaining a rising population. Similarly, in the more forested areas, systems of agriculture were developed which sustained increases in the population, and by the eighteenth century high densities were achieved in some areas such as the Lower Casamance, the

Igbo country in south-eastern Nigeria, the Cameroon grasslands and the Great Lakes region of East Africa.

However, in addition to the occasional natural disasters, the loss of population through the slave trade and the devastating wars associated with it, especially the loss of women of childbearing age over such a long period, was such that the overall population of Africa declined in the seventeenth and eighteenth centuries, though the loss was unevenly distributed, falling most harshly on those less able to defend themselves, and being concentrated in that period in West and West-Central Africa.

The effects of this loss of population are still to be fully explored, and remain a subject of speculation and of active controversy.[6] Although the rapid expansion of population against the background of inelastic resources and stagnant, or diminishing, productivity is today regarded as one of the most prominent features of underdevelopment,[7] that is so in the context of a structurally dependent economy. In the freer economies of the early nineteenth century, underpopulation was definitely a factor of underdevelopment. It is true that some economies appear to have gained something from the slave trade when compared with their neighbours: they managed to remain resilient by exploiting the weakness of their neighbours, thus sustaining their relative prosperity long enough to build up stable systems of political economy in which the challenge of rising population generated increased productivity and further development. But even such communities must have suffered from the impoverishment of their neighbours and the instability on their borders. No one could have escaped the overall depressive and traumatic social and economic effects of the massive loss of population through the slave trade and the attendant wars.[8] The slave trade seems to provide the best explanation of why in most of Africa, of all continents, the political and economic structures at the beginning of the nineteenth century seem to have remained unstable and fragile. There appears to have been a perpetual ebb and flow in the frontiers of state systems, and in the rise and fall of administrative centres. Much of the land appears not to have been put to optimum use even by the standards of available technology and land use.

The nineteenth century brought no sudden change in the overall demographic situation. The campaign against the slave trade was slow to make its mark. The initial effect was more to concentrate the export of slaves on fewer ports than to reduce the total output significantly, but the reduction did eventually come, slowly at first and fairly dramatically after 1850. However, as the numbers involved in the trans-Atlantic trade diminished, the export to Zanzibar and the Indian Ocean increased. What is more, the rise of alternative export trade vastly increased the demand for domestic

6. See J. E. Inikori (ed.), 1982a, especially pp. 29–36 of J. E. Inikori, 1982b.
7. L. Valensi, 1977, p. 286.
8. J. E. Inikori, 1982b, pp. 51–60.

slaves for use as labour in the procurement and transportation of ivory, palm oil, groundnuts, beeswax, cloves and, later, wild rubber and cotton. Thus the nineteenth century saw a significant increase in the internal slave trade and the demand for slave labour, with the ruinous effects of the processes of procurement. It is argued that before 1830 in Angola, and for some time after 1880 in Central and East Africa, the population was declining in some places by as much as half within a generation. However, abolition eventually stopped the massive exportation of Africans abroad and it would appear that for the first time since the seventeenth century, the overall demographic trend for the continent as a whole in the early nineteenth century was a rising one,[9] with the curve steepening between 1850 and 1880, then declining somewhat on the initial impact of colonial rule, before resuming the upward curve, at first gently and then more dramatically from the 1930s onwards. This population increase in the early nineteenth century, a result of both internal and external factors, became a significant factor of change, especially in areas like Southern and East Africa that had experienced little or no slave trade in the eighteenth century.

Increased European interest

Whatever doubts there may be about the actual population of Africa in 1800 and the effects of a possible upward turn in the demographic curve at the beginning of the nineteenth century, there can be no such doubt about the increase in European interest, though the effects of this increasing interest as a factor of change in African history may have been exaggerated.

The interest first manifested itself towards the end of the eighteenth century in expeditions to obtain more accurate information about the main geographical features such as the sources of the principal rivers, the location of mountains and lakes, distribution of population, leading states and markets, and the main agricultural and industrial products. Next, the French Revolutionary and Napoleonic wars in Europe and the efforts, notably of Britain as the leading maritime power to contain the expansionism of France, spilled over to Africa. The French occupied Alexandria and Cairo in Egypt as the gateway to the Far East. The British seized the Dutch colony at the Cape of Good Hope. Thereafter, the increasingly triumphant British naval power found in the growing abolitionist movement a mission providing all necessary opportunities for intervention in Africa. In 1807 the British government prohibited the slave trade to British traders and converted the freed-slave settlement in Freetown into a Crown Colony and a base for a West Africa-wide naval campaign against the slave trade. The French were expelled from Egypt, but continued to seek commercial advantages and in other ways to profit from the weakness of the tottering Ottoman empire in North Africa, using the campaign against

9. Unesco, *General History of Africa*, Vol. VII, ch. 18; also J. C. Caldwell, 1977, p. 9.

piracy in the Maghrib as an excuse. Following their defeat, the French were obliged to join the abolitionist movement and this too provided a reason for showing more interest in the coastal bases and trading stations in West Africa. Thus the abolitionist and missionary factors, and the search for alternative items of trade in place of the discredited trade in slaves were introduced into the politics of nineteenth-century Africa.

It is important not to exaggerate the extent of European power in Africa at the beginning of the nineteenth century, or the rate at which Europeans acquired 'possessions' or penetrated inland before 1850. The Portuguese made extensive claims both in Angola and in Mozambique. They had established military outposts and *prazos* (agricultural estates) in the interior, and from time to time they controlled the area from Loje, south of Cuanza, as far east as Kassanje, apart from trading posts on the coast between Ambriz and Moçâmedes. In Mozambique their effective control was by 1800 limited to Mozambique Island; elsewhere they depended more on Brazilian and mulatto merchants than on Portuguese officials. The increased demand for slaves in the late eighteenth and early nineteenth century had shifted attention from the *prazo* system, and the security of the trade routes depended more on the *pombeiros* (barefoot mulatto merchants), bearing Brazilian trade-goods and surviving only on the good will of African rulers and merchants.[10] The French had revived their trading posts in Senegambia after 1815, notably Saint-Louis and Gorée. Their venture to establish an agricultural farm in Waalo with a military post in Bakel to protect it had been a failure. In North Africa, they seized Algiers in 1830. They spent the next twenty years overcoming the resistance of the Algerians, notably the movement led by Amir 'Abd al-Ḳādir. The British had established Freetown and the agricultural villages on the neighbouring peninsula as centres for the acculturation of freed slaves into a Creole culture. With the increasing prosperity and expansion of the Creoles to Bathurst (now Banjul), Badagry, Lagos and beyond, British commercial and missionary influence was spreading along the coast and at one or two points like Abẹokuta began to penetrate into the interior around 1850. On the Gold Coast (now Ghana), the British still shared the trade with the Danes and the Dutch, and took measures to resist Asante (Ashanti) efforts to dominate the coast, notably by exploiting the Fante fear of Asante domination and encouraging the Fante to act together under British tutelage. In Southern Africa, though the attempt to settle British farmers in Natal was not successful, the Cape Colony was expanding largely through the rebellious *trekboers* who seceded into the interior and obliged the British rulers to follow after them, if only to save the *trekboers* from extermination by the new African states, while appearing to act as mediators or effective rulers. But, up to 1850, South Africa remained a colony of poor farmers,

10. A. F. Isaacman, 1976, pp. 8–11.

divided internally and often at the mercy of their African neighbours who were no less divided.

Various attempts to imitate the British success in Freetown ranged from the American settlement in Liberia, the French settlement of Libreville in what is now Gabon, and the other British settlement, Freretown, in East Africa. Increasing British and French interests in India and the Indian Ocean – in Aden, Mauritius, Madagascar and the new sultanate of Zanzibar – were soon to have their repercussions on East Africa. It needs to be emphasized, however, that the Euro/American presence was waterborne and coast-centred. It made no appreciable penetration into the interior of the continent before 1850, whereas the major events in Africa in the early nineteenth century – the Ethiopian revival, the Mfecane, the West African *djihād*s – were initiated from the interior of the continent, although Muḥammad ʿAlī's reforms in Egypt were a notable exception.

The missionary factor made a substantial contribution to the spectacular British success in Freetown. Responding to the challenge of the new opportunities, German missionaries, mostly from the Basel Mission but with a few from the Bremen Mission, overcame their pietist hesitation and became involved in the politics of development in a British colony. They and their British colleagues found more opportunities as farm managers, linguists, teachers, builders, and promoters of commercial enterprises than as preachers. A number of mission stations were established, and leading individual missionaries became deeply involved in local political and racial conflicts; nevertheless, nothing like the Freetown success was achieved. Elsewhere, missionary organizations were being founded, and a few pioneer mission stations established in which preliminary educational efforts and linguistic studies were being undertaken that would yield fruit later. However, as a significant factor of change in Africa, Christian missions belonged to the second rather than the first half of the nineteenth century. In 1850, David Livingstone was still on his first missionary journey. The Holy Ghost Fathers were founded in 1847, and the White Fathers in 1863.

European trading influence spread much more quickly and more widely than missionary influence in the first half of the nineteenth century. This was largely because the new European trade was an outgrowth of the pre-nineteenth-century slave trade. The legitimate trade was pioneered by former slave-traders and often even by practising slave-traders. It is important to emphasize this because the structure of the new trade was very similar to that of the old. There was to be an increasing monetization of the trade in the latter part of the century but, in the first half, the trade in palm oil, groundnuts (peanuts), ivory and cloves depended on the internal slave trade and the trust system: that is, the advance of trade goods on credit to the bigger African traders, thus necessitating measures to protect the investment and to guarantee delivery of goods. As long as European traders remained on the coast and African traders brought goods to them there, or coastal African middlemen took goods on credit to the interior to negotiate for and bring produce back to the coast, or *pombeiros* and Arab and Swahili traders did the same, the new trade was conducted within the existing pre-nineteenth-century structure. More Africans were involved in the collection of palm fruits, gum arabic, honey, and even ivory than had been in the procurement and sale of slaves to Europeans. Increasingly, also, in the major trading areas on the coast and along the trade routes, there were subtle changes in the composition and method of recruiting the political elite among the African populations. Notably, events of the nineteenth century favoured the rise to prominence of warrior groups seeking to share political power. Some of the creoles also became substantial traders and their numbers and importance were to increase into the 1870s. But the rapidity and the extent of social mobility should not be exaggerated. The traditional rulers and chiefs did not easily surrender their privileges. Rather, wherever possible, they brought in a few warriors to strengthen their position, and occasionally relied on the odd European or creole traders. The warrior or creole merchant seeking a share in chiefly privileges had to compete for it within the existing structures. They recruited a large following of slaves and clients, acquired wealth and tried to use it to buy their way into positions of influence and power. Thus, the diversification of the items of trade without substantial modification of the pattern of trade did not produce the economic and social revolution expected, at least not in the first half of the nineteenth century.

The European trade was expanding rapidly.[11] However, this expansion was made possible by and was dependent upon the pre-existing patterns of local and regional trade. A number of issues arise from this that should be emphasized. One was that the pattern of local and regional trade was of course far more dependent on the internal dynamics of the African communities – particularly the systems of production in agriculture, crafts and manufacture – than on the stimulation coming from outside. The second was that, compared with the internal trade, the external trade – at least initially – was secondary in the life of the majority of African peoples. It was nevertheless important because it brought in the critical factor from outside that might have made the difference in the fortunes of those who controlled it and those who did not. It is not easy to draw up a sliding scale of its growth in relative importance as a source of revenue to the African rulers, or as a source of essential commodities that could not be obtained elsewhere. The most important of such essential commodities was, for most African states, firearms. The European policy of seeking to control the trade in firearms in their own self-interest tended to make trade as a possible source of firearms far more important in the estimation of

11. A useful summary but with a focus on the whole precolonial century can be found in P. Curtin, S. Feierman, L. Thompson and J. Vansina, 1978, especially pp. 369–76, 419–43.

many a ruler than it actually was, since the possession of guns did not everywhere confer military superiority.

A third issue arising from the growth of the external trade is its importance, on the sliding scale, not only relative to internal local and regional trade, but also relative to agriculture. Whatever importance particular rulers might have attached to the external trade, there can be no doubt that throughout the early nineteenth century it remained peripheral to agriculture in terms of the total activity of African peoples. As employers of labour, providers of basic needs such as food, clothing and shelter and as the sources of raw materials for crafts and manufactures, etc., it is inexplicable that the agricultural systems should be treated as if they were less important than trade generally, and, more specifically, external trade.

Agricultural systems

It should be emphasized that at the beginning of the nineteenth century the basis of the economy of all African communities was food production, through a variety of systems of crop farming, rearing of animals, fishing, hunting, or combinations of these. All other activities, including trade, politics, religion, crafts, building, mining, or manufacturing, were secondary to and could not have been carried on without agriculture.[12] Not only were agricultural systems central to the economic lives of the masses of African peoples; to a large extent they also provide a basis for understanding the structure of social relations within the communities, the pattern of authority, the relations with their neighbours and their response to external factors of trade and other interactions. It is therefore surprising that historians have tended to take the agricultural base of African societies for granted while concentrating on the factor of external trade.[13]

Most of the available studies of nineteenth-century agricultural systems in Africa look at them from the standpoint of colonial economies. They tend to be theoretical and ideological, contributing more to the debate about underdevelopment than to an understanding of the historical development of African agriculture in the early nineteenth century. They view African agricultural systems uniformly as sustaining 'natural economies', witnessing the penetration of capital in the mercantilist period, as a prelude to the development of peripheral capitalism in the colonial period. There are only a handful of studies based on empirical data that show how particular agricultural communities in different parts of Africa functioned and developed in the early nineteenth century. They do not yet provide a basis for regional surveys of African agriculture, let alone a continental synthesis. However, they do provide necessary insights for re-examining

12. D. Beach, 1977, p. 40, referring specifically to the Shona.

13. See P. J. Shea, 1978, p. 94: 'Trade and production are obviously interrelated, but I would argue that production must receive priority attention.'

the main characteristics of the agricultural base of African societies and the factors of historical change operating within them.

A study of some village communities in Tunisia from the mid-eighteenth to the mid-nineteenth century[14] highlights features primarily of the areas under Ottoman influence in the first instance, but also with Africa-wide significance – features such as land tenure, family patterns of production and exchange, pressures from central government with demands for taxes in return for protection but few social services, and the constant health hazards, including periodic epidemics of plague, cholera and smallpox. The study deliberately focuses on the period between 1750 and 1850 in order to emphasize continuity and to stress that the roots of the weaknesses of Tunisian political economy lay in the eighteenth rather than in the nineteenth century, when they could have been attributed to the factor of European intervention. Leaving aside the controversy over the effects of outside interference for the moment, and the fact that there were a variety of forms and patterns even in the Maghrib and Egypt, not to mention the whole of Africa, the main features of the Tunisian experience deserve to be discussed in the wider continental context.

Land tenure in the Tunisian villages in the early nineteenth century was governed by Islamic law, but capable of a variety of interpretations both in theory and in practice at the different levels of the central government, local *ḳāʿid*s, and the individual families concerned. Because of the intensive nature of the 'oasis' agriculture practised, land, even in the rural areas, had a potential economic value greater than in other parts of Africa where a less intensive form of agriculture was practised. There was consequently greater pressure for a recurrent realization of the commercial value of landholdings. Nevertheless, the essential fact was that at the beginning of the nineteenth century private property rights in land were generally not recognized. This was the basic difference compared with European feudalism. In Tunisia, as in other parts of Africa, land belonged to the community or to the king as trustee of the community. At the local level, the *ḳāʿid* or the relevant chief allocated it for use. There was sometimes competition for the control of the right to allocate. Neighbouring communities, even those paying tax or tribute to the same overlord, could struggle over the use or the right to allocate the use of particular pieces of land, but the basic assumption was that land could not be bought or sold. The nineteenth century was to accelerate the pace of change, especially with European intervention, and the growth of enclosure and estate agriculture, which encouraged the pressure for making the commercialization of land general. The central government, while upholding the theory of the legal basis of land tenure, sometimes tried to convert the commercial value of land to profit; just as families in financial difficulty were sometimes anxious to offer land, at least temporarily, as security for loans. But such adaptations

14. L. Valensi, 1977.

of the eighteenth-century system of agriculture came slowly, and rarely challenged the basic theory of land tenure.

Again, while we hardly need to emphasize the variety of patterns of production in different ecological zones of Africa – in the details of land-holding and inheritance, the basic tools of farming, the crops planted, the land use, division of labour between men and women, specialization between one community and another in terms of crops, crop-farming and animal husbandry, etc. – there is another feature of the Tunisian experience relevant to Africa as a whole. This is the extent to which it is misleading to persist in describing African agricultural systems as 'subsistence', or sustaining 'natural economies'. These terms were initially justified on the mistaken notion that African rural communities were static, 'tribal', 'self-contained' or 'almost self-contained.'[15] As empirical evidence has been gathered to disprove this view of isolated communities, it appears that some protagonists of the view that African agriculture had a subsistence character, while conceding the prevalence of the circulation of goods and services, are now defining subsistence in ideological terms. They claim that African farmers were subsistence farmers, not peasants, on the grounds that though they might have bought and sold, their predominant motive was not profit. They define peasants as 'small agricultural producers who intend to make a living by *selling* part of their crops and herds', and they consider that peasantization is necessarily the result of 'the impact of new markets' and the profit motive.[16] What the Tunisian experience highlights is that African agricultural systems in the early nineteenth century were such that the different communities could not be regarded as self-contained. There was a variety of crops according to the variety of soils, family traditions and individual preferences and specialized skills. Crop farming, crafts and animal husbandry went together in a variety of patterns that encouraged exchange as the means by which families made up their essential needs. Each family gave up part of its surplus in return for what it needed but did not produce, and saved the remainder of its produce for years of drought and other calamities.

There was no region of Africa so remote that the rural communities in the early nineteenth century could have been described as completely self-sufficient and self-contained. In his study of Womunafu's career in Bunafu, D. W. Cohen has shown how even such 'a small and isolated community could be supplied with goods and services that only specialists offered or that derived only from remote centers of extraction and manufacture'.[17] This was a remote part of northern Busoga described by Cohen as hitherto an 'unadministered zone' into which migrated a number of individual

15. E. P. Scott, 1978, especially pp. 449–53, where the footnotes review the lengthy debate on subsistence agriculture versus exchange, and 'formal' versus 'substantive' forms of exchange.

16. R. Palmer and N. Parsons, 1977b, pp. 2–5.

17. D. W. Cohen, 1977, p. 48; see also Fig. 11.2, below.

leaders and their followers and lineage groups at the end of the eighteenth century and in the early nineteenth century. This migration was part of the final stages of the drift of the Luo migrations from the headwaters of the Nile, joined by groups displaced from the northern shores of Lake Victoria and from small states like Luuka as a result of the pressures of the expanding kingdom of Buganda. They sought relatively underpopulated areas away from existing power structures and they lived in dispersed homesteads, not in nucleated villages. Formal markets for regular exchange did not exist. Through intermarriage, ritual and other forms of interaction, a sense of community emerged. After a period of rivalry, some overall authority also began to be recognized, but the family homestead remained the centre of their lives. In the words of Cohen:

> the dispersal of compounds . . . provides a context for the emergence and maintenance of heroic traditions centered on the clearing of the land, and this in turn constitutes the basis for maintaining, within the lineage of the clearer of the land, eternal rights to, and control over, the land. There is an enduring ideal that each man is master of his compound in the same sense that a king is master of his domain. The common man's estate is an enclosed world, with or without fence; and within the boundary marking off his land, he is lord.[18]

We need not go into detail here about the evolution of some form of supra-lineage authority out of the rival traditions of the different antecedents of the lineages that settled in Bunafu. What needs to be emphasized is that at the beginning of the nineteenth century the individual household there was the unit of production and unit of land holding. But, however remote and enclosed, the household even in Bunafu was not self-sufficient. Within two generations, there developed a network of social and cultural relationships through which goods and services circulated with remarkable efficiency. New migrants like the *mukama* Womunafu and his entourage brought a stock of goods, skills and new technologies; the demand for specialized goods like ironware, especially farming implements, pottery and salt led to occasional fairs to which people brought their surplus produce such as barkcloth, skins and live animals in exchange; others took their produce to the locations of known specialist craftsmen like blacksmiths, fishermen and potters. Similarly, goods and services circulated through payments for rituals and worship, or in payment of bride price and other social dues, and even in raiding, stealing and kidnapping. As Cohen has put it, his study 'offers a series of images of a regional economy of the unadministered zone in the early nineteenth century structured not upon the "channeled effect" associated with international and interregional trade but structured, rather, upon a remarkably extensive and thickly knit network of circulation, distribution and redistribution.'[19]

18. D. W. Cohen, 1977, p. 43.
19. ibid, p. 47–8.

The nineteenth century brought changes, new pressures and opportunities even for the people in Bunafu, as in other places. As the family expanded, land hitherto regarded as marginal began to be cultivated. New crops hitherto regarded with caution were experimented with and some became new staples. The 'economic horizon' of the villagers expanded as the traffic strengthened the links that stretched from the villages to the coastal ports and overseas markets. Expansion of trade brought social and political changes. Initially, it tended to strengthen the position of chiefs who found it easier to accumulate wealth from taxing trade in salt, iron and copper, not to mention ivory, beeswax and palm oil, than from tribute in agricultural produce and customary labour. At the same time the profits of trade could not be so easily monopolized. Several individuals moved away from their customary locations to seek their fortunes, and social mobility was thus facilitated. But these changes were slow and represented not so much innovation as expansion of tendencies and patterns already evident by the eighteenth century. Thus the causal effect of the external trade should not be exaggerated. As J.L. Vellut has emphasized, the nineteenth century was not just 'the history of the ebb and flow of the world economy as experienced by ... Africa', but also 'the slow-moving ... history of diversification in making use of natural resources.'[20] It is essential to emphasize this internal factor on which the external came to impinge and which shaped the response of African peoples to the external factors. As Cohen has shown in his chapter on the Great Lakes region – hitherto studied only as a collection of centralized states responding to external forces – 'the nineteenth century was not simply a world of states, large and small. It was also a world in which individuals and households were in innumerable small, sometimes undramatic ways, altering their orientations to state authority, to service, to production, and to the market.'[21]

The agricultural system around the ancient city of Kano in northern Nigeria at the beginning of the nineteenth century provides interesting similarities and contrasts with the world of Bunafu in the 'unadministered zone' of northern Busoga. For one thing, the market played a stronger role in the economy, since Kano was a well-established centre of local, regional and international trade based in part on major and highly successful industrial activity in the manufacture, dyeing and distribution of textiles, and the tanning of leather. Yet it would be misleading to concentrate on the channel effects of the markets and trade routes and to ignore the network of social and cultural relations on which the markets and the trade routes depended. Similarly, in Kano, there was the influence of Islam, and the much greater role of the ruler and the ruling class and merchants of the walled city in the management of the economy. And yet in Kano, as

20. See p. 295 below.
21. See p. 292 below.

in Bunafu and the village communities of Tunisia, the bulk of agricultural production not only of basic essentials but also of a variety of cottons and dyes was in the hands of commoners in the rural areas among whom the household was the unit of production. As Abdulahi Mahadi has observed in a recent study, the head of a household in the Kano area, the *maigida*, was 'like a ruler of a town'. He fed, clothed and met social obligations of members; he determined the size of land and the type of crops to be cultivated each year; how much time to spend on the collective household farm (*gandu*; plur., *gandaye*), and how much on individual private farms (*gayauni*; sing., *gayauna*). There was no clear division of labour between men and women, all members participated in planting: while men made the holes and inserted the seeds, women and children filled them up; while both men and women took part in weeding, children minded sheep, goats and other domestic animals; while men harvested, women gathered the bundles to central depots. Apart from the network of social and cultural relationships, some of which involved sharing labour and exchanging produce, there was the institution of *gayya* (communal work) – organized at the village level on a voluntary basis, but with conscientious participation a mark of good citizenship – to provide additional labour at the time of planting, harvesting, housebuilding, and other major enterprises.[22]

As mentioned above, compared with Bunafu, the state in Kano in the person of the *amīr* and his delegated officials played a more active role in the management of the economy and in the life of the rural communities. In this, Kano was more like Tunisia. The *amīr* was recognized as the owner of the land. He could regulate the acquisition, use and disposal of land. He could deprive people of the use of their land for wilful disobedience, failure to pay prescribed taxes, or habitual anti-social behaviour like stealing. At the same time, it was part of his responsibilities to guarantee security of tenure to subjects in good standing, with the result that heads of households generally believed that they 'owned' their land. It was realized, however, that such security of tenure did not include the right to alienate the land, though leasing and subletting were generally allowed. Based on the concept of the *amīr* as owner of the land, enterprising rulers had actively encouraged immigration of groups with a variety of agricultural and industrial skills from Borno, Azben, Nupe and other places, settling them in different parts, offering inducements to resettle the original population. The ruler, as well as leading officials and merchants, were granted estates where they used the labour of slaves and clients for crop farming, breeding livestock and industrial production. Additional labour was recruited through the *gayya* system of voluntary labour.

The success of the *djihād* at the beginning of the nineteenth century brought important changes to the political economy of Kano. In particular, it brought the application of the *sharī'a* (the Islamic legal system) to land

22. A. Mahadi, 1982, especially ch. 6.

tenure, and under the caliphate the state intensified various measures to promote industrial and commercial prosperity. What needs to be emphasized here is that the eighteenth-century agricultural system remained the basis of the new political economy. In the words of Mahadi, 'there was no fundamental departure from the pre-nineteenth century land tenure system. The elements of continuity predominated over those of change.'[23] The *sharīʿa* allowed the *amīr* to give out land, thus permitting commercialization of land but 'Kano still regarded commercialization as illegal.' It seems that the most noticeable effect of the *sharīʿa* on land tenure was to encourage fragmentation of the *gandaye* into individual family holdings on inheritance, thus reducing the size of agricultural units among commoners. At the same time, there was remarkable expansion of estate agriculture by the ruling and commercial elite, thus increasing land shortage, especially around Kano and other urban centres. This encouraged farming in more distant places, and more commoners abandoned agriculture to concentrate on crafts and industrial production or became clients dependent on the ruling and commercial elite for earning their living.

Patterns of authority

Kano and Bunafu thus represented two different models of the way in which the power structure affected agricultural development in Africa in the early nineteenth century, one where authority was centralized and structured, the other where it was diffuse and informal. This is not a distinction between 'state' and 'stateless' societies as anthropologists have earlier suggested. In Bunafu, not only was there a sense of government and authority, some of the migrants came with traditions of structured hierarchical political systems from which they were fleeing, but which they still drew upon in the rivalries that accompanied the emergence of a new authority system in Bunafu. Others also carried with them belief in the power of a the *mukama*, a charismatic prince chosen and possessed by the god, or the efficacy of ritual firelighting from royal hearths, to affect fertility and harvests. As Vellut has argued, instead of the state–stateless dichotomy, we should think of two modes of power structures:

> the hierarchical, well-defined order based on the payment of tribute which was that of the kingdoms; and, at the other extreme, the more egalitarian and informal type of government by councils of elders and notables.
>
> These two models were complementary, and in practice there were many kinds of intermediate situations, waverings and compromises. The realities of the environment and of economic activity, as well as historical circumstances and even personal considerations, determined whether the prevailing type of organization tended towards the mon-

23. A. Mahadi, 1982, pp. 566–7.

archical model, with its qualities of order and security, or towards the more flexible, less authoritarian democratic ideal.[24]

It should be added that the state system was not always the most effective framework of order. Cutting across the lineage system of non-centralized societies, a variety of integrative institutions developed in the religious, judicial and economic fields which could function as an overall framework of order or replace a disintegrating state-system.[25] The *poro* and similar associations in Upper Guinea, or various so-called 'secret societies' in the Cross river and equatorial forest areas of the Cameroons and Gabon are examples. In the case of the Aro, it was the widespread influence of a set of oracles, managed through a network of Aro colonies and local 'secret societies', that provided a judicial and economic basis of integration over a wide section of Igboland. Economic changes in the nineteenth century affected the pattern of authority not only in terms of the structures of the state systems, but often in strengthening such existing non-political integrative structures as well.

The events of the early nineteenth century indicate a tendency towards centralized power structures, with the authority of the king becoming more effective than ever before. While the sprawling empires such as the Lunda complexes of states, or Old Ọyọ or the Mossi empire of the Mogho-Naaba were disintegrating, new, smaller, and more authoritarian states emerged in their place. While Muḥammad 'Alī succeeded in making his power in Egypt stronger, and thus further weakened the Ottoman empire, his vision and his son's effort to build an Afro-Arab empire in its place did not succeed. 'Uthmān dan Fodio (Usman dan Fodio) succeeded in making the Sokoto caliphate a sprawling empire, but effective political power was devolved to the *amīrs*. More than any of these, the Mfecane set off a chain of events that encouraged the formation of a series of compact centralized kingdoms not only in Southern but also in Central and even East Africa. In probing the causes of Mfecane, L. D. Ngcongco has shown the centrality of the system of agriculture in the political economy of the northern Nguni, and the role of the state in adapting society to respond to the changing needs of the agricultural system.

Over the years, the northern Nguni had developed a system of mixed farming. They lived in dispersed settlements, different from the nucleated villages of the Sotho–Tswana. In their family homesteads, the patrilineal head lived usually with two or three wives, each wife and her children in a separate house. The men looked after cattle and did some hunting; the women planted crops. The pattern of land use allowed for the cattle to have access both to sweet and sour pastures:

24. See pp. 316–20 below.
25. J. Oriji, 1982.

> in the spring and early summer, Nguni herders could drive their herds to graze on the upland sourveld pastures, and from the middle of the summer season they would move their stock down to the sweet grasses at the bottom of the river valleys. Climatic variations had also made it possible for these farmers to select the environment most suitable for the cultivation of either sorghum, millet or maize.[26]

Maize, which was introduced sometime in the eighteenth century, had by the early nineteenth century replaced other traditional crops as the staple diet. These factors seem to have brought in relative prosperity and a rising population. This, in turn, sharpened competition for land and created social and political tension. There was a hierarchy of rulers, paramount and tributary kings. The royal homestead was larger, providing for communal activities whether ritual, cultural or military. It would appear that the paramount rulers of the northern Nguni took over the Sotho–Tswana practice of centralized initiation rites. They went further to use initiation rites to recruit young men and women for communal labour, and later also to recruit into military brigades; the brigades of young men being camped at the royal homestead, sometimes for as long as ten years before being released to go and marry and farm. This also served as a method of family planning and population control. As the competition for land grew into all-out wars, these age regiments were deployed more and more for military purposes.

Internal initiatives

Thus the Mfecane, which is recognized as one of the major factors of revolutionary change in nineteenth-century Africa, can best be explained in terms of pre-nineteenth-century social and economic development adapted to changing situations. Efforts to find a blanket explanation for the Mfecane in terms of the European presence at the Cape, or the approaching capitalist pastoralism of the *trekboers*, or the mercantilist force of Portuguese trade in Delagoa Bay have not stood the test of close scrutiny in the light of available evidence. The main initiatives in the Mfecane came from within Africa. This is also true of the other major events of the early nineteenth century, such as Muḥammad ʿAlī's reforms in Egypt, and the *d̲j̲ihād* movements in West Africa.

The national movement which brought Muḥammad ʿAlī to power, and which he shrewdly manoeuvred in order to lead and inspire it, has often been attributed to the galvanizing effect of Napoleon and his 'Egyptian Mission'. However, as A. Abdel-Malek has shown below,[27] this is a mistaken view: 'Eighteenth-century Egypt is now seen as the laboratory from which the new Egypt emerged.' It was the national feeling nurtured among

26. See p. 94 below.
27. See Chapter 13 below.

PLATE 1.1 *Ceremonial dance at Mbelebele, a military camp of the Zulu in 1836*

the Egyptian elite in the major towns, especially Cairo and Alexandria, and among the *shaykhs* and *'ulamā'* at Islamic centres like al-Azhar which provoked the revolts of October 1798 and April 1800 against the French, weakened their position and forced their withdrawal. It was also this movement that frustrated the attempt of the pro-Ottoman Mamluks to re-establish their power over Egypt. It was this national feeling that provided the context for Muḥammad 'Alī's reforms, and his ambition and that of his son to make the Egyptian government truly national, independent both of the Ottoman and the Europeans, and at the head of an Afro-Arab empire.

This groping for renewal and reform is just as discernible in the activities of various rulers who faced the challenges of the Mfecane, of those seeking to re-establish imperial order in Ethiopia, or those of the *shaykhs* of the Western and Central Sudan looking to the traditions of Islam for ideas of a new social and political order. Largely because of the writings of the *djihād* leaders and European travellers, we know enough about the complex of forces and ideas that produced the series of revolutionary movements starting from Futa Toro, Futa Jallon and Bondu in the eighteenth century and stretching to the Sokoto, Massina and Dinguiraye *djihāds* in the nineteenth. We therefore do not need to speculate about the possible contribution to that complex of forces and ideas of European mercantilist influence in the days of the slave trade or capitalist influence in the days of abolition and journeys of discovery. The initiative for the *djihād* movements came from within. The *djihād* states took a great interest in promoting agriculture, partly through traditional household production, partly also through estates worked by slave or client labour. They also promoted industrial manufacture and trade. They improved trade routes and offered protection to traders and merchants. By far the greatest portion of the traffic on the routes was for local and regional exchange. But the *djihād* leaders also promoted trans-Saharan trade routes and the pilgrimage route to the Eastern Sudan, the Nile Valley and Mecca. Evidence is building up that these internal trading initiatives had developed trade routes that permitted trans-continental traffic before the new European trade of the nineteenth century.[28] The Europeans, of course, were quick to note the results of these internal initiatives and were attracted to the possibility of profiting from them.

Because we do not have the advantage of similar writings on the areas further south, the temptation has been greater to speculate on the possible or probable effects of Old Ọyọ's participation in the slave trade through the Ẹgbado country and Porto Novo in the eighteenth century.[29] But such speculation, and other hypotheses on the possible effects of abolition have

28. See, for example, P. Curtin, S. Feierman, L. Thompson and J. Vansina, 1978, ch. 14.

29. R. Law, 1977, especially pp. 217–36, has reviewed the evidence thoroughly but seems predisposed to exaggerate the influence of trade generally, especially the slave trade, in the economy of Old Ọyọ, e.g. p. 255: 'The collapse of the volume of slave exports in the

so far failed to explain the collapse of the empire structurally in its economic, political, religious and social bases, and the widespread experimentation with various political and religious ideas for new structures and systems in the nineteenth century. It is more likely that, as in the *djihād* states, the seeds of collapse came from internal discontent and yearning for reform, and the actual collapse owed more to the penetration of Islamic ideas and the direct impact of the Sokoto *djihād* than to the slave trade and/or abolition. The consequent wars, population movements, colonization of new areas hitherto regarded as marginal such as the coastal swamps, the rise of new towns and markets, and the spirit of reform and experimentation, created new opportunities that the Europeans came to exploit rather than to set in motion.

This groping for renewal, then, will explain why so many African rulers in the course of the nineteenth century from Egypt and Tunisia to Madagascar and Lesotho, Abẹokuta and Fanteland, suspicious as they were of European intentions, nevertheless risked cautious collaboration with European traders, adventurers or missionaries as a way of importing European technology to assist their work of development. It was not only Egypt that experienced a sense of renaissance. The nineteenth century may well be called the 'African Age of Improvement',[30] in which the urge for improvement dominated the scene, but the urge came from within. The rulers tried to exploit increased European activities to achieve improvement but were to end up being exploited and frustrated in the search for renaissance.

Conclusion

The early nineteenth century introduced new factors of change into African history, notably the new interest of Europeans not merely in trade but also in intervening directly in the social and economic life of African peoples. This brought with it a campaign to learn more about the peoples of and resources available in the interior of the continent, a campaign to stop the slave trade, to encourage the export of certain crops, with missionaries seeking to convert to Christian ways of living, and traders pressing to go into the interior to trade. All these brought new economic opportunities and challenges. The centres of the new trade did not always coincide with the centres of the pre-nineteenth-century trade. The new sources of trade and wealth, and essential commodities such as firearms, became objects of competition between different states or interest groups within states. This new trade greatly expanded commercial activity, not only through its own

1790s is likely to have cut deep into the *Alafin*'s revenues, and Awole may have responded by stepping up demands for taxes from within the kingdom.'

30. A. G. Hopkins, 1980, used this phrase as the title of his Inaugural Lecture, with a focus on the objective of African economic history generally, rather than trends in the nineteenth century specifically.

traffic, but even more in stimulating existing traffic. However, the extent to which the new trade was a continuation of pre-nineteenth-century trade should be emphasized, as should the extent to which it was pioneered and sustained by the same peoples and structures that sustained the slave trade; how much it depended on internal slave trade and slave labour; and thus how much it was based on the existing power structures and internal network of social and economic relations, trade routes and, above all, agricultural systems.

In view of this, we should not distort the pattern of development in the early nineteenth century by antedating the predominance of European power and influence to control initiatives for change in African history. In the early nineteenth century, the factors of continuity with the eighteenth century and the factors of change internal to the continent far exceeded in importance the factors of change coming from outside.

2 Africa and the world-economy

I. WALLERSTEIN

From 'luxury' to 'essential' trading patterns

The great transformation of Africa's economic relations with the wider world did not occur with the late nineteenth-century partition by European powers. Rather, conversely, the partition of Africa was a consequence of the transformation of Africa's economic relations with the wider world, and in particular with Europe, a transformation that took place in a period beginning approximately in 1750 and culminated in the extensive European direct colonization of the last decades of the nineteenth century.

There had long been trading networks in various parts of Africa, and many of these networks had extended beyond the frontiers of the African continent – across the Indian Ocean, the Mediterranean, and the Atlantic.[1] By and large, these extra-continental trading links constituted the same kind of 'long-distance trade' as that which had been well known for millennia in Asia and Europe as well. Such long-distance trade involved the exchange of so-called luxury products, that is products that were usually small in bulk and high in profit per unit of size. The production of such items for exchange tended to involve a small proportion of the manpower of the originating zones and probably a small proportion of the total value produced in these zones. In these senses, 'luxury' trade was 'non-essential' trade in that its interruption or cessation did not require any basic reorganization of productive processes in the originating zones. The two zones whose products were thus exchanged could not therefore be said to have been located in a single social division of labour.[2]

The modes of trade in the Indian Ocean arena did not seem to change very much in the period between 1500 and 1800. The intrusion first of the Portuguese and later of other Europeans into this maritime zone changed the personnel somewhat, but hardly the nature or extent of this trade. Even

1. A. G. Hopkins, 1973, p. vi, notes the existence of 'clusters of inter-connected economies in which trade was widespread, regular, and of great antiquity.'

2. I have previously elaborated on the sense in which Africa's external trade prior to 1750 could be considered such a 'luxury' trade. See I. Wallerstein, 1973, 1976.

the personnel was less changed than is often thought. As late as the 1750s in Mozambique, whose littoral had been colonized by the Portuguese, there seemed to be more Gujerati/Indian merchants than Portuguese in residence. Important changes seem to have occurred only in the second half of the eighteenth century, with the collapse of the Mughal empire and the rise of British India, as well as with the rise of the Omani Arabs on the Swahili coast.[3]

The traditional compartmentalization between largely non-commercialized agricultural production and the long-distance trade in non-agricultural (luxury) products remained the rule even in those cases where there were small European agricultural settler communities, such as the *prazeros* in the Zambezi valley or the Boers on the Cape coast.

The one zone in which the economic situation was somewhat different was those parts of West and Central Africa where communities had begun to participate in the slave trade. The slave trade was of course a product of, and a key element in, the construction of the European-centred capitalist world-economy that had come into existence *c.* 1450. By the seventeenth century this capitalist world-economy included as part of its peripheral production areas the 'extended' Caribbean zone of the Americas. In this zone, the expanding plantation systems (especially sugar, but also tobacco, cotton, and other products) came to depend increasingly for their manpower on slaves who were 'captured' in West and Central Africa and transported across the Atlantic.

Should this long-distance trade in slaves be classified as 'luxury' trade or as trade in 'essentials'? Can it be said to have involved the 'production' of manpower for the capitalist world-economy? And should therefore the 'producing' zones be seen as peripheral areas of this capitalist world-economy? There is no simple answer to these queries. In terms of numbers exported there was an upward curve in the slave trade from 1450 to 1800, with a significant increase *c.* 1650. The numbers by 1750 were about triple those of 1650.[4]

It is clear that, at some point, the slave-dealers were no longer 'foraging' for persons to be enslaved but had begun to be engaged in systematic

3. See E. A. Alpers, 1975.

4. For some figures, see P. D. Curtin, 1969, Tables 33, 34, 65, 67 and Figure 26. While Curtin's figures in absolute terms have been the subject of much vigorous debate, there has been less controversy about the shape of his growth curve. See the debate between J. E. Inikori, 1976a, 1976b and P. D. Curtin, 1976; see also the summary of the scholarly evidence plus the new synthesis by P. E. Lovejoy, 1982. Lovejoy alters the curve slightly, but not fundamentally.

It should also be noted that the total curve for Africa masks a geographic shift. The Angolan coast was involved in a major way as of the sixteenth century, the Bight of Benin only as of *c.* 1650, the Gold Coast as of *c.* 1700, the Bight of Biafra as of *c.* 1740. The Sierra Leone coast, involved early, was a significant exporter only as of the middle of the eighteenth century. South-east Africa became a major source only in the nineteenth century.

procedures for obtaining their quarry. At some point, therefore, production and political systems in West and Central Africa began to be adjusted as a function of these now continuing economic ties. When such 'adjustment' could be said to have occurred to a significant degree – 1650, 1700, 1750 – is hard to say, although I tend to feel a later date is more plausible than an earlier one.[5] What is true, as we shall argue, is that the very shift of slave-trading from a 'luxury' to an 'essential' trade undermined its *economic* viability, since it meant that the costs of reproduction had thereupon to be included in the overall profitability calculations of the remuneration of labour services in the capitalist world-economy, since, in all 'essential' trade, production costs include 'opportunity costs'.

As long as Africa was 'outside' the world-economy, the 'cost' of a slave to the slave-owner was the expense of procurement plus maintenance plus supervision (prorated for his/her life as a slave) divided by total work output during his/her life as a slave. The 'benefit' to the world-economy was essentially the surplus value produced by the slave minus the 'cost'. Once Africa was 'inside' the world-economy, that is, was producing on its soil commodities that were part of the division of labour of the world-economy, then someone who was a slave was not something else, for example a free peasant producer or a wage-labourer. Therefore, although the 'cost' of the slave remained the same perhaps for the slave-owner, the 'benefit' had to be recalculated from the point of view of the world-economy as a whole. The numerator of the equation had to take into account the 'alternative' accumulation from some other use of the individual. It may be that he/she would have produced still more net surplus value if not enslaved. Furthermore, and crucially, the denominator changed since the years of reproduction, formerly usually outside these calculations, were now part of them. Therefore, the net accumulation from the slave years was reduced while the net accumulation if not enslaved remained the same. Ergo, the calculus was less favourable to slavery, from the point of view of the accumulation process in the world-economy as a whole.

Nonetheless, it was not these changing economic implications of the slave trade that would have the greatest impact on Africa's future development but a more fundamental process that was occurring within the capitalist world-economy. The first long economic and geographic expansion of the capitalist world-economy had occurred between 1450 and 1600–50. In that period, no part of Africa could be said to have been part of this historical system. The period 1600/50–1730/50 was, for the capitalist world-economy, a period of relative stagnation, of taking a breath, of consolidation, primarily within the geographic zones that had already been included in the sixteenth century. It was still largely true at this time that no part of

5. For an argument that the 'slave trade era' involved, as of *c.* 1650, the 'production' of slaves, and that therefore the period 1650–1800 marked something different from and in-between luxury trade and the later trade in essentials, see S. Daget, 1980.

Africa could be said to have been incorporated into this system (with the reservations noted about the changing structure of the slave trade).[6]

Capitalist expansion

However, about 1730–50, for reasons internal to the functioning of the capitalist world-economy, Africa resumed its economic and geographical expansion. In the next hundred years, it would incorporate into its production network five new major geographical areas hitherto external to the capitalist world-economy: Russia, the Ottoman empire, India, the 'further' zones of the Americas (Canada, western North America, the southern cone of South America), as well as (northern, western, and southern) Africa. It is the story of the incorporation of this fifth zone that is our subject.

From the point of view of the Europe-based capitalist world-economy, all five zones of expansion shared certain features. They were all at the geographic perimeters of the previous boundaries. They were all zones with which Europe was already in contact via long-distance 'luxury' trade. They were all potential production zones of primary products that could utilize low-cost labour.

But of course these five zones were also disparate in many ways. Their ecologies were quite different and therefore the nature of their products and the costs of production from the point of view of the incorporating world-economy were different. The political systems in place were also quite varied. At one extreme there were the world-empires, like the Russian empire and the Ottoman empire; extensive economies with a single, bureaucratized political superstructure. At the other extreme were the 'further' zones of the Americas, thinly populated, non-agricultural economies, not linked one to the other, with multiple, often acephalous, political structures. In the first case, incorporation into the world-economy involved the 'incorporators' coming to terms with existing political systems and somehow transforming them into state-structures contained within and constrained by the interstate system. In the second case, incoporation involved for the 'incorporators' creating new (often colonial) political structures that were capable of organizing production and participating in the interstate system. Crudely speaking, in the first case, existing state structures were 'weakened'; in the second case, new 'stronger' ones were created. In both cases, the resulting political structures were those of peripheral zones, 'weak' in relation to the 'strong' state-structures of the core zones of the capitalist world-economy.

The process of incorporation in Africa stood in between these two extremes. There were multiple existing political structures. Some of them were relatively strong and bureaucratized; others were virtually acephalous.

6. For a detailed analysis of the capitalist world-economy in the period 1450–1750, see I. Wallerstein, 1974, 1980.

Africa in no sense constituted a single 'economy'. However, in many particular areas, there did exist regional 'economies' that transcended single political units. From the point of view of the 'incorporators', some of the existing political structures had to be 'weakened' (as was true for the Russian, Ottoman, and Mughal empires). But in other places, new political authorities had to be created, ones that were strong enough to ensure the smooth functioning of transformed economic processes. Eventually, as we know, totally new, colonial political systems were created almost everywhere, but not for the most part immediately.

'Incorporation' into the world-economy involves essentially two processes. The first and primary one is the transformation of some significant segment of production processes such that they become part of the integrated set of production processes that constitute the social division of labour in the world-economy. The second is the transformation of the political structures such that they become 'states' which are part of and constrained by the rules and workings of the interstate system, these states then being strong enough to facilitate the relatively free flow of the factors of production within the world-economy but not strong enough to interfere with them, at least to interfere with them more than for limited periods and in limited ways. It is our contention that such incorporation occurred for northern, western, and southern Africa in the period after 1750 (and ending *c.* 1900), but that eastern Africa did not begin to be incorporated until *c.* 1850 or even 1875.[7]

Incorporation was a slow, steady process; it did not occur dramatically overnight. At any point within the incorporation process an observer would note the continuity of older patterns of agricultural production, their statistical dominance. The older norms and values would seem relatively intact. It is easy therefore to play down the significance of what was occurring. What changed, however, were four things: some production was beginning to be oriented systematically to a market which was that of the capitalist world-economy; this production was that of 'essentials' from the point of view of the world-economy; for this production one needed to recruit (or impress) a workforce, which therefore led to new labour-supply structures; and this production was generally profitable to those who controlled it locally, and therefore attracted still others to participate in it. Incorporation merely began this process, but if the quadruple combination of production oriented to a world market, production of essentials, restruc-

7. 'Incorporation' is to be distinguished from 'peripheralization'. One involves the broadening of capitalist development; the other its deepening. In any given zone, incorporation precedes peripheralization. The latter started *c.* 1875/1900 for most of northern, western, southern Africa; perhaps *c.* 1920 for eastern Africa. The process is still going on. Often when it is argued that Africa was not part of the world-economy until the twentieth century, what is meant is that peripheralization had not yet occurred. For a brief discussion of the distinction and the relation between the two processes, see T. K. Hopkins and I. Wallerstein, 1982.

turing of the labour-force, and profitability exist, then we have the economic base of incorporation with its political consequences. It should be underlined that Africa did not choose to be incorporated into the world-economy. No region ever did. Incorporation was an exogenously originated process, which was resisted. African resistance was not inefficacious; it delayed the onset of incorporation and slowed it down. But at some point the balance of force was against the resisters. Local 'agency' did not cease at that point. The local struggles for power continued, more or less along the paths already laid down. They merely operated within new and usually different systemic constraints than prior to incorporation. Local agency never ceased in Africa, or anywhere else for that matter.

Since much of Africa's 'international' commerce prior to this point was in the slave-trade, and incorporation was accompanied by the abolition of the slave trade, incorporation has often been discussed as the shift from the slave trade to 'legitimate' commerce. To use this ideological language of the period is however to be somewhat misleading, as can be seen if we look at northern or southern Africa, not to speak of those non-African parts of the world which were incorporated at the same time into the capitalist world-economy. The decline of the slave trade, important as it was, was secondary to the generalized need of the capitalist world-economy for new areas of low-cost *production*, as part of the general expansion of its level of economic activity and rate of accumulation.

Incorporation of Egypt and the Maghrib

This process can be seen most clearly if we do not start the discussion, as is usually done, with the case of the western coast of Africa. We shall begin rather with the case of Egypt. Prior to 1730, Egypt's production was part of the division of labour in the Ottoman world-empire. Egypt served as one of the granaries of this historical system as well as a major transit point in long-distance intercontinental luxury trade. In the second half of the eighteenth century, the internal contradictions of the Egyptian system, combined with a decline in demand for prior exports, had led to a fiscal crisis of the Egyptian state structure, and consequently to an increase in taxation, which thereupon led to peasant resistance through abandonment of lands. At the very same time, the expanding capitalist world-economy was seeking to include Egyptian production within its network. This effort was made concrete in the active military competition of France and England at the end of the eighteenth century to control the region. The Egyptian response took the form of the coming to power of Muḥammad ʿAlī and his attempt to 'modernize' Egypt.

In economic terms, this 'modernization' involved the establishment of a stable export of an agricultural good. For various reasons having to do with the comparative ecology and political structures of the capitalist world-economy, long-staple cotton was a better option for Egypt than wheat. But the large-scale production of cotton required a change not only in the irrigation system but also in the social relations of production. Muḥammad ʿAlī installed a state monopoly of trade with direct collection of taxes by salaried bureaucrats. This led to increasingly regulated control over peasant production practices, and impressment for work on infrastructure and for military service. Eventually this was converted into corvée labour on private large estates, whose extent grew from about 10 per cent of the arable land in 1818 to about 45 per cent by 1844. This process was further intensified after the death of Muḥammad ʿAlī, continuing the expropriation of the peasantry, and culminating in the major peasant-supported ʿUrabist revolt in 1881–2, itself one of the factors leading to the establishment of British colonial rule. The entire transformation of the productive process resulted in the creation of a sizeable stratum of landless rural workers, direct supervision of agricultural work, and a significant increase in total work time required of the peasantry.[8]

The process was different in the Maghrib. On the one hand, it can be argued that there was a continuous attempt to incorporate the Maghrib (and particularly Morocco) into the capitalist world-economy from its very origins in the late fifteenth century.[9] On the other hand, there seems to be little evidence of a significant change in production relations in this region until the mid-nineteenth century or even later. Between 1450 and 1830 a good deal of the trans-Mediterranean links of the Maghrib and Europe (but not all) were mediated by the phenomenon of privateering, which in some ways can be assimilated economically to long-distance luxury trade, with the same ambiguities that the eighteenth-century West African slave trade exhibited. Unlike the latter, however, privateering declined in the eighteenth century and a more commercial form of interchange came, somewhat spasmodically, to dominate the Mediterranean trade, especially in Morocco and Tunisia.[10] Already in the second half of the eighteenth century, Morocco was producing industrial and food crops, animal products, and even mineral ore for export to Europe, and this increased significantly after 1820.[11] It is probably because Algeria was most resistant to this economic incorporation that it was subjected so early to conquest at a period of time when the expansion of European political rule in Africa was not yet the norm.

8. For more details, see A. R. Richards, 1977.

9. See A. Laroui, 1975, pp. 29–33; D. Seddon, 1978, p. 66.

10. A. Laroui says of eighteenth-century Tunisia that its evolution was in some ways parallel to that later undertaken by Egypt. 'Tunisia was the pathbreaker, but in the next century drew inspiration from the enlightened despotism of Muḥammad ʿAlī'. A. Laroui, 1975, p. 43.

11. See D. Seddon, 1978, pp. 69–71.

The West African pattern

One of the factors that enabled the Maghrib to maintain for so long this ambiguous relationship with the capitalist world-economy (half in, half out) was the large role the trans-Saharan trade played in North Africa's economic life. Precisely because the Maghrib served as the transit and transfer nexus of what was in effect an indirect long-distance trade between the Sahelian zones and Europe, there was less pressure on it to create new loci of export-oriented production on its own territory. There are conflicting views on the degree to which the trans-Saharan trade continued to be important in the period 1750–1880.[12] It is clear, however, that late nineteenth-century colonization eliminated the economic significance of these ancient trade routes, and simultaneously therefore withdrew the 'protective cover' for the Maghrib of its entrepôt role.

The rise of so-called legitimate trade in West Africa in the nineteenth century has been a central theme of historiography for some time now. What was important was not, however, the increase in the quantity of trade or even its changing content in terms of the items traded, but the transformation of productive structures that followed therefrom and the political consequences of such changes in the relations of production. This was a process that started before the British efforts to abolish the slave trade, since these efforts were themselves a parallel outcome of the expansion of the capitalist world-economy; to be sure the transformation of productive structures in West Africa was accelerated by abolition.[13]

The 'classic' and in some ways the most successful of the new products, now amply documented, was that of palm oil in the Niger delta area. This production at first co-existed with the slave trade,[14] and later flourished on its own, until the boom came to an end in 1861, and finally declined at the end of the century.[15] The palm-oil trade similarly expanded in the Gold

12. A. A. Boahen, 1964, p. 131, says that nineteenth-century trade was 'but a fraction of its former value', while, C. W. Newbury, 1966, argues that, far from declining, the trade actually increased, reaching a peak in 1875.

13. C. Chamberlin, 1979, pp. 420–1, in criticizing the term 'legitimate trade', says that in addition to its Eurocentrism, it 'suggests that abolition caused the changeover from slave to non-slave exports, when in fact the transition pre-dated and post-dated the key British [abolition] measure of 1807.'

He finds the relevant consideration to be Europe's need of raw materials and points out the 'extraordinary demands on production' involved in the new amounts of palm oil, timber, and rubber exported. 'Many producers became involved in the harvest of the new commodities over wide areas.'

14. See A. J. H. Latham, 1978. See also C. Coquery-Vidrovitch and H. Moniot, 1974, p. 108: 'Unlike for European nations, the slave trade and legitimate commerce were not two contradictory activities for Africans. On the contrary, their complementarity up to the 1860s facilitated the evolution.'

15. See A. G. Hopkins, 1973, p. 133.

Coast (now Ghana), though to a lesser degree,[16] and in Dahomey (now the Republic of Benin) where the slave trade had been of such great importance that the local population might be said to have been effectively incorporated already via the slave trade.[17]

A second major new product was groundnuts (peanuts), whose export-oriented production began on the Upper Guinea coast in the 1830s, and spread out westward to Senegambia.[18] Rubber was a third major product, although trade in it started much later and in part to compensate for the decline in the demand for palm oil.[19] The late slave-trade period and the subsequent expansion of cash-crop production in coastal or near-coastal zones in turn stimulated an economic expansion in the Central Sudanic zone of West Africa (livestock, potash, agricultural products, leather goods).[20]

To be sure, not all attempts at creating new forms of cash-crop production succeeded. In particular it seems that direct European involvement was counterproductive, as in the failed efforts at agricultural colonization in Waalo between 1819 and 1831,[21] and in the various efforts in Senegal, the southern Gold Coast, and Nigeria later on.[22] It was not that European personnel began to loom larger on the African scene; rather, the important change was that Europeans were largely displacing African merchants from

16. See A. A. Boahen, 1975, p. 91. On Nigeria's advantages over the Gold Coast as a palm-oil producer, see S. D. Neumark, 1954, p. 60.

17. See I. A. Akinjogbin, 1967, p. 141: 'From 1767 onwards the long-term implications of Tegbesu's economic settlement became the dominant issues in the national life of Dahomey. By making the slave trade the basis of the economy of Dahomey, Tegbesu had placed the kingdom at the mercy of external factors which the Dahomeans could neither control nor even influence.' See also D. Ronen, 1971 and J. E. Inikori, 1977.

The shift from the slave trade to palm oil strengthened the hand of private as against royal merchants (R. Law, 1977) and increased the importance of the northern savanna trade, as it did for Asante (Ashanti). See J. F. Munro, 1976, p. 46. But most of all, it caused fundamental changes more in the production than in the commercial arena. 'The bulking up, transporting and storage of commodities like palm oil and groundnuts, and the breaking down of imported goods into the quantities needed for many small producers, required more manpower than the trade in slaves'. See J. F. Munro, 1976, 47.

18. See G. E. Brooks, 1975, who emphasizes the quickness with which African cultivators responded to the high European (especially French) demand. See also B. Mouser, 1973, 1975.

19. See R. E. Dumett, 1971.

20. See P. E. Lovejoy, 1974, pp. 571–2: 'Economic growth which had begun after 1750 continued through the nineteenth century . . . [T]he century before colonial rule was a time of relative prosperity.' Lovejoy emphasizes the fact that far more bulk products were flowing between the coastal zone (including European re-exports) and the Central Sudan than has been hitherto recognized.

21. See B. Barry, 1972, pp. 237–58.

22. See J. F. A. Ajayi and B. O. Oloruntimehin, 1976, p. 211. A. G. Hopkins, 1973, p. 138, argues: 'The promoters [of these experiments] found that they were unable to compete in international markets, partly, it is interesting to note, because of the high cost of free African labour.'

the role of those in the port areas who purchased bulk items from traders who went into the interior and shipped them overseas, and vice-versa.[23]

New export-oriented production necessarily implied new imports. The import of various European manufactures, particularly from Great Britain, multiplied throughout the nineteenth century. For example, cotton-goods imports, already the leading import in the eighteenth century, went up fifty times between 1815 and 1850, and seven times more by 1891.[24] West African manufacturers adjusted to this massive inflow as had other peoples of other regions being incorporated into the world-economy. In part the local manufactures were displaced; in part they resisted the competition by design specialization and retreated into production for more limited markets.[25]

Southern Africa

In southern Africa the process of incorporation was once again somewhat different, both because there was no slave-exporting and because of the presence of a white-settler community. Despite the fact that the Boers in the Cape Colony in the eighteenth century were Europeans living in a European colony, it is hard to argue that they were in a meaningful sense an integrated segment of the capitalist world-economy.[26]

The change of regime that occurred as a result of the Napoleonic Wars was of course the local consequence of Britain's new hegemony in the

23. See C. Chamberlin, 1979, p. 423. As for the internal trading roles, as G. I. Jones, 1963, p. 82, says of the Niger delta region, 'whether they liked it or not the European traders had ... to conform to the African trading organization'.

24. See C. W. Newbury, 1972. See also A. G. Hopkins, 1973, p. 129.

25. See J. E. Flint, 1974, pp. 388–9 and E. Reynolds, 1974a, p. 70.

26. M. F. Katzen, 1969, p. 193, observes that despite the multiple efforts of the Dutch authorities from Van Riebeeck on to create export-oriented production, 'the only Cape exports before 1778 were a trickle of hunting products (ivory, pelts, ostrich feathers, and so on), and wheat, wine and brandy in the eighteenth century'. Even the latter was very limited: 'Wine was produced for sale only two or three days' journey from Cape Town, grain somewhat further afield ... The VOC regarded the Cape essentially as a refreshment station, to be run as economically as possible' (p. 202). J. F. Munro, 1975, p. 56, for the period prior to 1806, distinguishes between the zone in a radius of 50–60 miles from Cape Town, 'where wheat and wine were produced for the maritime market', and other subsistence-oriented agrarian zones plus the settlement frontier of the pastoral eastern Cape, which maintained 'tenuous links with Cape Town's maritime commerce ...'

A. Atmore and S. Marks, 1974, p. 110, indeed asserted even of nineteenth-century southern Africa that 'without the continuous injection of technological skills from the metropolis itself or from the metropolitan enclave at the Cape', it is possible that the Afrikaners 'would have become merged with the majority population of [the] various [African] societies, as did the Portuguese *prazeros* in the Zambesi valley, or the half-caste Griqua on the Orange river'. But, of course, that is just the point. In the nineteenth century, they were willy-nilly incorporated into the world-economy, and their behaviour was a function of this reality.

world-economy. This political shift, however, itself reflected the long upturn and expansion of the world-economy. The British basically lost little time in beginning to restructure production processes so as to incorporate effectively the region. They increased shipping markedly, brought in new British colonists, and developed commercial sheep-rearing such that by the mid-1840s the Cape Colony had become a significant locus of production for the world-economy.[27] Later, Natal became a locus of sugar production on plantations using indentured Indian labour.

In the eighteenth century the white farmers utilized the labour of Khoi-Khoi and the so-called Coloureds, largely in the form of slave labour. The British brought formal emancipation. The expanding and changing economy led to the Great Trek of the Boers, with the British essentially following from the rear, and with active movement of Zulu and other Nguni peoples.[28] The outcome was an acute struggle for control of the land and of labour in production that was oriented to the world market. In the Cape Colony, an African peasant agriculture came into existence alongside white-owned farms using African tenant-labourers.[29]

Nothing similar to this occurred in the Angola region in this period despite the even longer history of European links. Rather, the slave trade and the ivory trade continued apace, the process of acquisition reaching further and further into the interior, eroding various existing political structures.[30] The abolition of the slave trade led to attempts to create a white-settler plantation sector, which prospered briefly during the cotton boom of the 1860s, but ultimately failed, as had similar attempts in West Africa.[31] No significant African cash-crop production was initiated.

Delayed incorporation of eastern Africa

The eastern coast of Africa was also still relatively outside the capitalist world-economy. Its primary external links had been across the Indian Ocean. Still, India and to a lesser extent south-western Asia were now themselves being incorporated into the capitalist world-economy. The slave trade expanded in this region in the nineteenth century, however, precisely because eastern Africa was still an external arena. Nonetheless, it served there, as it had in west-central Africa, as a dynamic disruptive and reconstructing force. The island of Zanzibar was incorporated into the world-

27. See J. F. Munro, 1976, pp. 56–60.

28. Previously, it had only been in Zuurveld in the 1780s and 1790s that 'substantial political and economic pressures were put upon Nguni societies by white colonists' (C. Bundy, 1979, p. 29).

29. See ibid., pp. 44 ff.

30. See D. Birmingham, 1976, pp. 267–9 and J.-L. Vellut, 1975, pp. 134–5. Vellut believes this increased the interior's dependence on the world-economy. See also W. G. Clarence-Smith and R. Moorsom, 1975.

31. See J. F. Munro, 1976, pp. 51–2; W. G. Clarence-Smith, 1979, pp. 14–15.

economy via its dominant role in the world market for cloves by the mid-nineteenth century, which involved the establishment of a plantation system.[32] Sugar plantations were created on Mauritius, and Madagascar developed rice and beef production for export to Mauritius.[33] It was, however, the Scramble for Africa which later spilled over into eastern Africa and precipitated the kind of change of which it was the result elsewhere in Africa.

The transformation of production structures could not have occurred in isolation from a transformation of the political structures that facilitated the economic changes and sought to legitimize them. But what precisely was the link? I. Hrbek remarked some time ago on the importance of the years 1805–20 in African history. He observed the simultaneity of the following events: the Western Sudanese *djihād* of ʿUthmān dan Fodio (Usman dan Fodio) (and other Islamic revolutions), the rise of the Zulu under Shaka, the eclipse of Bunyoro and the rise of Buganda in the interlacustrine region, the Fulbe (Fulani, Peul) revolutions in the Western Sudan, the modernizing regime of Muḥammad ʿAlī in Egypt, the unification of the Imerina on Madagascar under Radama I, and the rise of Omani hegemony under Sayyid Saʿīd. He observed that 'all these processes were going on in "contact" zones and were due to some extent to external impact and influence.'[34]

Implications of incorporation

There is no need to exaggerate the role of external forces in African state-building. The internal forces were the primary mechanism of political evolution and the existing logics of development account for most of the particular details. Furthermore states were constructed in this same era which were quite remote from the world-economy as, for example, the Rozvi.[35] Also it is quite obvious, by looking at the West African states, that there is an imperfect connection between participation in the slave-trade and state-formation. If the two went hand to hand for Dahomey and Ọyọ, in Benin we had the formation of a strong state without such participation, and the inverse was true for the Niger delta.[36]

The point, however, is a different one. It is that involvement in the world-economy required political structures that ensured the functioning of the economy; its commerce, its production, its labour-force supply.

32. See F. Cooper, 1977, pp. 47–79.

33. Indeed, it was British interest in securing this production for Mauritian demand that led to British support, via the Treaty of 1817, for Madagascan independence against the French designs. See P. M. Mutibwa, 1972, p. 39.

34. I. Hrbek, 1968, p. 48. See also A. Wilson, 1972, on the expansion of the Luba Lomani empire in this period.

35. See S. I. Mudenge, 1974.

36. A. G. Hopkins, 1973, pp. 105–6, discusses this.

The outside pressure was to have such structures.[37] Where the existing structures performed the necessary functions, for whatever reason, there was little pressure to change them. But, of course, the involvement in the world-economy increased the economic importance to given internal producers of sympathetic political structures. It is the internal producers who pressed to change the structures.[38] This led to various kinds of turmoil, which were of limited benefit to other participants in the world-economy. The latter in turn pressed for political stabilization, which took the form of creating states which participated in and were therefore constrained by the interstate system.[39] Ultimately, as we know, this led in most of Africa to the creation of colonial states. The abolition of the slave trade was a crucial political and economic event in this process. As plantation slavery and the slave trade were phenomena deriving from the operation of the capitalist world-economy, so was the abolition of the slave trade and of plantation slavery. I do not wish here to re-open the question of the importance of the abolitionists as a pressure group in this process. They of course existed and were part of the process. But the fact that such a pressure group existed and played a role in the process is not an explanation of the process but one of the aspects of it that needs to be explained.

Plantation slavery depended for its economic viability on reducing its total costs below a certain level, which depended heavily on the fact that recruitment to slave status was principally by means other than demographic reproduction. We have already suggested that the very process of expanding the quantity of slaves 'recruited' began to transform the economic character of the slave trade in western Africa, increasing the 'opportunity costs' of slave-trading and thereby affecting the rate of world accumulation.

This general phenomenon combined with a more narrow British concern.

37. W. K. Hancock, 1942, p. 163, expressed this view, with the eyes of an external participant wishing to involve Africans in the world-economy. He noted that mere economic pressures were insufficient: '[T]he political problem proved itself a stubborn one. European traders in West Africa discovered very early that their business – even though Africans participated eagerly in it – demanded the shelter of a *pax* which African society was too weak to build.' Too weak to build, sometimes, perhaps; but also too strong to allow to be built, at other times.

38. This is the essential message of K. O. Dike's classic work. He notes (1956, p. 11): 'With abolition the radical change in the economic sphere soon wrought corresponding changes in the social and political planes'; cf. C. Chamberlin, 1979, 430. See also the analysis of Dahomey's internal politics in J. C. Yoder, 1974. A. G. Hopkins, 1973, p. 143 speaks of a 'crisis of the aristocracy in nineteenth-century West Africa ... stemming from a contradiction between past and present relations of production'; that is, from the shift from slave-trading to cash-cropping. He indicates the variation in the ability of particular political structures to weather the crisis intact.

39. P. Ehrensaft, 1972, traces successive British interventions in West Africa; A. S. Kanya-Forster, 1969, ch. 2, does the same for France. B. M. Magubane, 1979, ch. 2, traces the picture in South Africa.

The comparative productivity of sugar plantations in British West Indian territories declined throughout the eighteenth century.[40] A major zone of alternative production available was in British India.[41] This zone, however, was an area of existing dense agricultural production, where true slavery would have been economically too costly (if one wished to enslave the indigenous population) or politically too difficult (if one wished to import others). Hence the slave trade seemed to be less immediately useful for the production of sugar and other plantation crops in British zones while being counter-indicated if one wished to encourage cash-crop production in western Africa. Britain was at this point the hegemonic power in the world-system and was therefore in a politico-military position to carry out abolition.[42]

Hence the interests of all accumulators in the capitalist world-economy as a collective class combined with the more specific interest of British accumulators as a sub-class in creating a political climate in which abolition could become public policy.[43] It was of course opposed by the subset of

40. See W.A. Green, 1974, p. 247: 'British action in West Africa in the decades before 1850 was dictated largely by West Indian requirements.' On the argument that 'overproduction' in sugar was a crucial element behind abolition of the slave trade, see E. Williams, 1966, pp. 149–50 and D.H. Porter, 1970, pp. 142–3. *Per contra*, see R. Anstey, 1975, p. 386.

41. On the link between abolitionists and East India sugar production, see E. Williams, 1966, pp. 183–8.

Indian sugar became a major item on the British scene in 1791, following the crisis caused by the revolution in Santo Domingo. A considerable amount was sold between 1794 and 1800, see J.P. Marshall, 1968, pp. 88–9. The West India sugar lobby then succeeded in restoring the high tariff and imports from India declined. Still it was felt that, barring the tariff, 'despite the higher freight, the East Indies could undersell the West' (C.N. Parkinson, 1937, p. 85). What happened then? Given the fact that 'the bigger financiers clearly had a foot in both camps' (ibid., p. 86), the resulting Parliamentary decisions might be seen as a compromise: the West Indian lobby lost on abolition but won on the East Indian tariff. When the duties were finally equalized in 1836, Bengal sugar plantation exports showed a phenomenal rise; see K.N. Chaudhuri, 1966, Table 1, p. 347.

A word should be added about one more sugar-producing area, this one in Africa: Mauritius. The British duty was lifted in 1826 and sugar rapidly dominated all island production. Slavery was in theory abolished in 1835 and slaves were replaced by Indian contract labourers. Nonetheless an illegal slave trade continued to flourish. These slaves, however, came from the external arena, East Africa. See B. Benedict, 1965, pp. 12–19; E.A. Alpers, 1975, p. 214.

42. That is not to say that British efforts were instantaneously successful or pursued with vehemence from the outset. S. Daget, 1979, p. 436, notes that 'English repression [of the slave trade] did not seriously hamper the economics of the French slave trade' before 1831. J.F. Munro, 1976, p. 43, argues that it was not until the 1850s that the Atlantic slave trade dwindled to 'insignificance'.

43. See B.K. Drake, 1976, pp. 86–7. Finally, one should not leave out of the equation the 'cooperation' of the African end of the slave-trading operation, as C. Coquery-Vidrovitch and H. Moniot, 1974, p. 311, remind us: '"Legitimate" trade triumphed, to be sure, because Europe found in it a more solid basis [for trade], but also because the merchant structures of a number of African states lent themselves to it readily. In other words, the

accumulators who were negatively affected by this change. It was also, it should be added, a policy that was enforced in a flexible manner. Where the plantations were non-British but direct supply zones for British manufacturing interests, Great Britain tended to 'condone' slavery. One instance was the American South. A second was Cuba and Brazil, which continued through most of the nineteenth century to obtain slaves from the still permitted trade 'south of the line', where the economies of the slave trade remained different, as we indicated above.[44]

The nineteenth century up to Partition was, it has been argued, the era of 'informal empire' or the 'imperialism of free trade'. J. Gallagher and R. Robinson summed up this analysis: 'By informal means if possible, or by formal annexations when necessary, British paramountcy was steadily upheld.'[45] Free trade is a term too easily thrown around. We should be clear that traders tend to favour free trade if they have a competitive advantage in the market and tend to see ways of restraining free trade if and when they do not. Hence the fact that the role of the chartered companies in eighteenth-century West Africa was less than in the seventeenth century has led some historians to speak of the rise of free trade. The very process of dismantling of the monopoly powers of chartered companies was however 'a gradual one', we are told; the shift to free trade 'was therefore somewhat limited'; and the explanation of the shift resided primarily in 'practical business reasons', to wit, the lower overhead costs and greater flexibility of response to an expanding slave-trade market.[46] As for the nineteenth-century era of even freer trade, it has been argued that it rather represented a serious restriction of free trade under the ideology of 'legitimate commerce'.[47]

Britain's championship of the doctrine of free trade in Africa was the ideological reflection of her worldwide hegemony, of those 'halcyon days' in which Britain's manufactures outcompeted those of all her rivals and her navy could enforce 'a freedom of access to the markets of the world unparalleled before or since.'[48] Britain's traders triumphed over all their competitors: over the Boers in southern Africa,[49] over the African merchants in West Africa,[50] over the French.[51]

second partner in Atlantic trade, the African, if he did not play a decisive role, was nonetheless an actor in it, adapted himself, and extracted profit from the market, in short, behaved like a responsible party in the affair.'

44. See A. G. Hopkins, 1973, p. 113; D. Eltis, 1979, p. 297. P. D. Curtin's figures, 1969, pp. 240, 247, for Brazil show that the bulk of the slaves came from Mozambique and Angola. The same seems to be true for Cuba. Abolition also did not affect the essentially 'luxury' trans-Saharan slave trade. See R. A. Austen, 1979.

45. J. Gallagher and R. Robinson, 1953.

46. A. G. Hopkins, 1973, pp. 93–4.

47. See D. D. Laitin, 1982.

48. J. S. Galbraith, 1970, pp. 34–5.

49. A. Atmore and S. Marks, 1974, p. 120, note of nineteenth-century southern Africa:

The ultimate decline of Britain's advantage had nothing to do with developments in the periphery of the world-economy. It was simply the consequence of the rise of the competitive qualities of manufactures elsewhere: in France, in Germany, in the USA. The depression of 1873 detonated the active political challenge to British hegemony; in Africa as all over the world.[52] By 1879 the structure of African informal empire was crumbling; by 1900 most of Africa was colonized.[53]

Conclusion

We have thus argued that the period from 1750 on should be seen as one involving the incorporation of (at least northern, western, and southern) Africa into a particular historical system, that of the capitalist world-economy, and that Partition represented not the beginning but the culmination of this process. What, however, of the view that 'the role of trade generally and the slave trade in particular ... has been grossly

'So long as Britain maintained its monopoly of the area – and by the mid-century there was little evidence of other contestants – and so long as the territories remained underdeveloped and controllable by informal means, there seemed little need of formal empire'.

J. Gallagher (and R. Robinson, 1953, p. 3) remind us that the absence of formal empire was in fact far from total. There was the British annexation of Natal in 1843, keeping the Boers out of Delagoa Bay in 1860 and 1868 and out of St Lucia Bay in 1861 and 1866, as well as British blocking of the union of the two Boer republics in 1860. These various efforts maintained the Boer republics in a state of 'dependence on British ports' in the mid-century period.

50. At first in this period it is true that West Africa's 'merchant groups served as Europe's [largely Britain's] economic and political intermediaries.' (S. B. Kaplow, 1978, p. 20). But their position as large-scale intermediaries was steadily undermined, see, for example, E. Reynolds, 1974b and 1975. Even the collapse of the cowrie currency should be read as the collapse of an independent financial base for the West African merchant class, see O. A. Nwani, 1975; A. G. Hopkins, 1970.

51. 'The history of the *Exclusif* [France's attempt to maintain mercantilist constraints on West African trade] was the history of its long agony': B. Schnapper, 1959, p. 151. Britain had two simple advantages over France, says Schnapper: more capital, and cheaper textiles to sell.

52. It is no mere coincidence that French protectionism in Senegal dates from 1873. See C. W. Newbury, 1968, p. 345.

53. I have previously analyzed this in I. Wallerstein, 1970, p. 403, where I argued: 'To challenge effectively the British economic hegemony in the world, the other industrializing powers needed, or felt they needed, larger markets for their industries and access to raw materials. Thus started the scramble for Africa; and once it had started, Britain had no choice but to join in or be the loser.'

It is not that Britain faced no previous losses from its policies before the 1880s. Indeed R. Olaniyan, 1974, p. 37, talking of the 1860s, speaks of how Britain's 'half-hearted protection yielded humiliating harvests', but its previous 'losses' were not sufficiently heavy to lead to a massive shift in policy.

exaggerated'?[54] Or the linked argument that the increase in cash-cropping in West Africa did not constitute a social revolution because it occurred initially within the existing African political, economic, and social systems, which 'proved able to meet the changing demands of the coastal trade [in the period of 'legitimate' commerce] through adaptation rather than revolution'?[55]

It is not wrong to say that many, even perhaps most, African systems 'adapted' to the new exigencies. Some of course were broken, and ultimately virtually all were placed under colonial rule. But adaptation is the point, not the counterpoint. Adaptation was usually all that was required; nothing more, but nothing less. The adaptation to a new social framework of action was the consequence of Africa's incorporation into a particular historical system, the capitalist world-economy, at a particular moment in time.

54. J. F. A. Ajayi and R. S. Smith, 1971, p. 124. See also R. A. Austen, 1970; *per contra*, A. G. Hopkins, 1973, p. 124.

55. J. F. A. Ajayi and B. O. Oloruntimehin, 1976, p. 214. This argument that we had economic change but not social change is curiously the inverse of that of A. C. Unomah and J. B. Webster, 1976, p. 298, in the same volume who stress the change in the 'social life of East African peoples'. See also C. Coquery-Vidrovitch, 1971, p. 121, who stresses that the key transformations in Dahomey – wage-labour and private property – did not date simply from the period of colonial rule.

3

New trends and processes in Africa in the nineteenth century

A. A. BOAHEN

Not necessarily in terms of originality but rather in those of tempo, scale and impact, the first eight decades of the nineteenth century witnessed many new trends and processes. Indeed, it is the combination of these three features that makes the period in question so revolutionary and marks it out as the end of old Africa and the beginning of modern Africa. This chapter will attempt to analyse these new trends and processes, assess their impact and consider what would have happened had there not been European colonial intervention during the last two decades of that century.

New demographic trends

The first of the new trends was demographic. The nineteenth century saw the most revolutionary socio-economic change in Africa, namely, the abolition and suppression of the slave trade. By the end of the period under review and for reasons that are discussed elsewhere in this volume, the slave trade was a thing of the past. While abolition did not cause any sudden change in the rate of population growth, there is no doubt that the general tendency was one of gradual increase rather than, as hitherto, decline, especially during the last three decades of the period under review.

But growth was not the only change affecting population. What was even more dramatic was its redistribution, which took the form of internal migrations and movements. Typical examples of these dramatic internal migrations of the period were those of the Nguni in Southern and Central Africa, the Chokwe in Central Africa, the Azande in East Africa, the Fang in Equatorial Africa and the Yoruba in West Africa. The Nguni migrations, as will be seen later, resulted in the spread of the Nguni section of the Bantu peoples from the Natal region into different parts of South, Central and East Africa. Though the Nguni incursions caused a great deal of devastation, destruction and untold suffering, there were also some positive results. The Nguni conquered and absorbed new peoples to form new nations such as the Ndebele and the Sotho. By using the military and political systems and ideas developed by the Zulu, the Nguni also formed new kingdoms such as Gaza, Swazi, Ndebele, Sotho and Pedi. These kingdoms, were, in the words of J. D. Omer-Cooper, 'militarist, highly centralized and administered under the king by commoner *indunas* rather than royal relatives.'[1] Moreover, the presence of the Nguni inspired state-building activities among some of the peoples whom they invaded. For instance, the Holoholo living on the eastern shore of Lake Tanganyika adopted the Nguni military tactics to build a strong kingdom. The Hehe of southern Tanganyika, who were divided into over thirty independent chiefdoms, also came together as a result of the Nguni incursions, and, using Nguni military regiments, weapons and field tactics, succeeded in conquering the neighbouring peoples such as the Sangu and the Bena and in forming a large Hehe kingdom.

In West Africa, mainly for political reasons, the Yoruba migrated virtually *en masse* from the open grassland areas of northern Yorubaland into the forest areas to the south. These movements resulted in the formation of new communities such as Ibadan, Abẹokuta, Ọyọ, Iwo, Modakẹkẹ and Ṣagamu. Like the Nguni, the Yoruba also embarked on various political and constitutional experiments in answer to the political and ecological challenges posed by their new environment. These experiments resulted in 'Ijaye's military dictatorship, Ibadan's republicanism, Abẹokuta's federalism and the confederalism of the Ekiti Parapọ'.[2] The population map of south-western Nigeria as we know it today dates from these movements. It was also in the nineteenth century that the great migrations of the Fang and their relatives, the Bulu, Beti and Pahoain occurred from the savanna regions of the southern part of modern Cameroon into the forest areas as far as the hinterland and coastal areas of Gabon.[3]

Islamic revolutions

Far more revolutionary were the new trends in the social fields, and in no sphere was this more so than in that of religion. As is well known, the diffusion of Islam from Arabia into Africa began as early as the seventh century. However, outside North Africa and the Nile Valley, until about the very end of the eighteenth century, this diffusion had been on the whole rather spasmodic and, with a few exceptions such as the Almoravids, peaceful and mainly through trading activities. Right from the very first decade of the nineteenth century, however, this diffusion took on a very militant and dynamic form especially in north-western Africa. Nothing shows the tempo and scale of this better than the fact that in the savanna belt of West Africa, known as the Western Sudan, whereas there were only two major *dj̲ihād*s throughout the eighteenth century, one in Futa Jallon in the 1720s and the other in Futa Toro in the 1770s, as many as four major *dj̲ihād*s, and several minor ones, broke out during the period under

1. J. D. Omer-Cooper, 1976a, pp. 350–1.
2. O. Ikime, (ed.), 1980, p. 307.
3. P. Curtin, S. Feierman, L. Thompson and J. Vansina, 1978, pp. 423–4.

review. The major ones were the *djihād* of 'Uthmān dan Fodio (Usman dan Fodio) in Hausaland in 1804, that of Seku Ahmadu (Aḥmad Lobbo) in Massina in 1818, that of al-Hadjdj 'Umar in the Bambara area from 1852 and that of Samori Ture in the 1870s.[4]

One fascinating feature of these Islamic revolutions apart from that of Samori was that they were led by the Torodbe (the clerical wing of the Fulbe [Fulani, Peul] people) who were found living across the whole of the Western Sudan. The revolutions were thus the answer of the Torodbe or Fulani Muslim clerics to the crisis created in the Western Sudan by political oppression, social injustice and illegal taxation on the one hand and the decline and weakening of Islam on the other. The aims of the leaders of these revolutions were 'to convert Islam from the level of personal beliefs to one of communal law . . . to shake off the remnants of traditional customs and to create a theocratic empire where Islamic laws and practices would prevail.'[5] The revolution of Samori in the 1870s was the most successful and the most important of the many rebellions organized from the 1840s onwards by the Joola (Dyula), that Islamized and educated trading section of the Soninke. Details of the activities of Samori Ture are given in Chapter 24 below. Suffice it to state here that though Samori was far less educated and less fanatical than the earlier *djihād* leaders, there is no doubt that until the mid-1880s he aimed at converting people to Islam and using it as an integrating force.

These Islamic revolutions or *djihād*s had very far-reaching political and social consequences. Politically, they resulted in the creation of huge empires such as the Sokoto caliphate which, by the 1820s, covered almost the whole of the former Northern Region and parts of the former Western Region of Nigeria; the Massina empire which dominated the area of the Niger bend until its incorporation into al-Hadjdj 'Umar's empire, which stretched from the headwaters of the Senegal and Gambia rivers to Timbuktu; and the huge empire of Samori Ture which extended from the northern parts of modern Sierra Leone and Guinea to Bamako, and included the important Joola trading and Islamic centre of Kankan.[6] These revolutions also resulted in the replacement of the old Hausa and Soninke ruling elites by a new elite of predominantly Fulbe and Joola clerics. It thus signified a fundamental shift in the focus of political authority in the Western Sudan. 'Uthmān dan Fodio's *djihād* also resulted in the revival and strengthening of the old kingdom of Borno thanks mainly to the activities of Shaykh Muḥammad al-Kanēmi, a devout Kanēmbu Muslim

4. M. Hiskett, 1976; see also Chapters 20, 21 and 24 below.
5. J. F. A. Ajayi, 1965, p. 1. See also M. Last, 1974.
6. See Chapter 24 below and also P. Curtin, S. Feierman, L. Thompson and J. Vansina, 1978, pp. 388–90.

called in by the rulers of Borno to assist them against the forces of ʿUthmān dan Fodio and his son Muḥammad Bello.

But even more far-reaching were the social consequences of these revolutions. In the first place, as a result of the educational and proselytizing activities of these *djihād* leaders and their supporters and military leaders, most of whom were good Muslim scholars, Islam was not only purified but also transformed from a religion of the towns into that of the rural areas also. Moreover, while the first two leaders belonged to the Ḳādirīyya order, al-Hadjdj ʿUmar belonged to the relatively new Tijāniyya, which appealed more to the ordinary people. Al-Hadjdj ʿUmar therefore succeeded in winning a huge following and it is significant that there are more Tijāniyya followers in West Africa today than those of the Ḳādirīyya order. Thirdly, with the emphasis of all the three *djihād* leaders on education and learning, the level of Islamic scholarship and literacy was greatly raised during the nineteenth century. Finally, as a result of these *djihāds*, a common feeling of Islamic solidarity grew right across the Sudānic belt which has remained to this day.

It should be added in conclusion that the *djihād* leaders and their flag-bearers did not entirely succeed in establishing the true caliphate ruled in accordance with the *sharīʿa* in the Western Sudan. Rather, they had to compromise with some of the existing socio-political institutions and realities. What therefore emerged in the end was not uniform and unadulterated Islamic culture and society but rather a Fulbe–Hausa culture in Hausaland and a Fulbe–Mande culture in the area of the Niger bend, though both were heavily impregnated with the tenets of Islam and the teachings of the founding fathers.

Islam also gained ground in other parts of Africa, especially in Cyrenaica and the eastern Sahara in present-day Libya and, later, in the northern parts of modern Sudan thanks to the activities of the Sanūsī and Mahdī respectively, and finally in the interior parts of eastern Africa and especially in Buganda following the activities of Arab and Swahili traders.[7]

Christian missionary activities

No less revolutionary and lasting in its impact was the other contemporaneous religious revolution that was taking place elsewhere in Africa, namely, the Christian missionary revolution. Though attempts at the planting of Christianity in the areas to the south of the Western Sudan reach as far back as the era of the Portuguese explorations in the fifteenth century, there was hardly any trace of the Christian religion left by the turn of the eighteenth century. However, from about the last decade of that century and especially during the first five decades of the nineteenth century, the situation underwent a revolutionary change. Primarily because

7. R. O. Collins and R. L. Tignor, 1967, pp. 16–18; A. A. Boahen, 1964, pp. 110–17.

of the evangelical revival in Europe associated with John Wesley, and the anti-slavery and humanitarian spirit of the age, born out of radical philosophies typified by the American and French revolutions, the attempt to plant and spread Christianity assumed the same dynamic if not militant form that characterized Islamic expansion in the Western Sudan. Here, initially, instead of the Ḳu'rān and the Sword, the Bible, the plough and commerce were the means resorted to, and the active agents were not *djihād* leaders, clerics and their flag-bearers but a host of missionary societies, formed and based in Europe and America, and their African agents in Africa. Thus, whereas by 1800 there were only three missionary societies operating in the whole of West Africa, namely, the Society for the Propagation of the Gospel (SPG), the Wesleyan Missionary Society (WMS) and the Glasgow and Scottish Missionary Society, by 1840 only four decades later, there were more than fifteen such societies at work. These societies included the Church Missionary Society (CMS), the North German or Bremen Missionary Society, the Basel Evangelical Missionary Society of Switzerland, the United Presbyterian Church of Scotland and the Society of African Missions from France. During the next three decades, more than ten other societies joined from the USA.

In East and Central Africa, by as late as 1850 only a single society, the Church Missionary Society, was operating. By the time of David Livingstone's death in 1873 there were two others, namely, the Universities Mission to Central Africa (UMCA) formed in 1857 to establish 'centres of Christianity and civilization for the promotion of true religion, agriculture and lawful commerce' in response to a passionate appeal to the British public in a speech delivered at Cambridge University by Livingstone in that year, and the Society of the Holy Ghost, a Catholic order formed in France in 1868.[8] It was the travels, publicity and manner of death of Livingstone that precipitated the religious revolution in East and Central Africa. Within four years as many as five missions entered the field. These were the Livingstone Mission formed by the Free Church of Scotland in 1875; the Blantyre Mission formed by the established Church of Scotland in 1876 to work in modern Malawi; the London Missionary Society (LMS) which, in response to a letter from the explorer and journalist, H. M. Stanley to the *Daily Telegraph* inviting missions to reach for Buganda, extended its work from South Africa to present-day Tanzania; and the Catholic White Fathers, who followed the CMS into Buganda two years later.[9] Thus, by the end of our period, the missionary revolution was well under way also in East and Central Africa.

But even more widespread and successful were missionary activities in Southern Africa. By the end of the Napoleonic Wars, there were only two

8. R. Oliver, 1965, p. 13.

9. A. J. Wills, 1964, pp. 82–97; R. Oliver, 1965, pp. 1–48; N. R. Bennett, 1968, pp. 231–5.

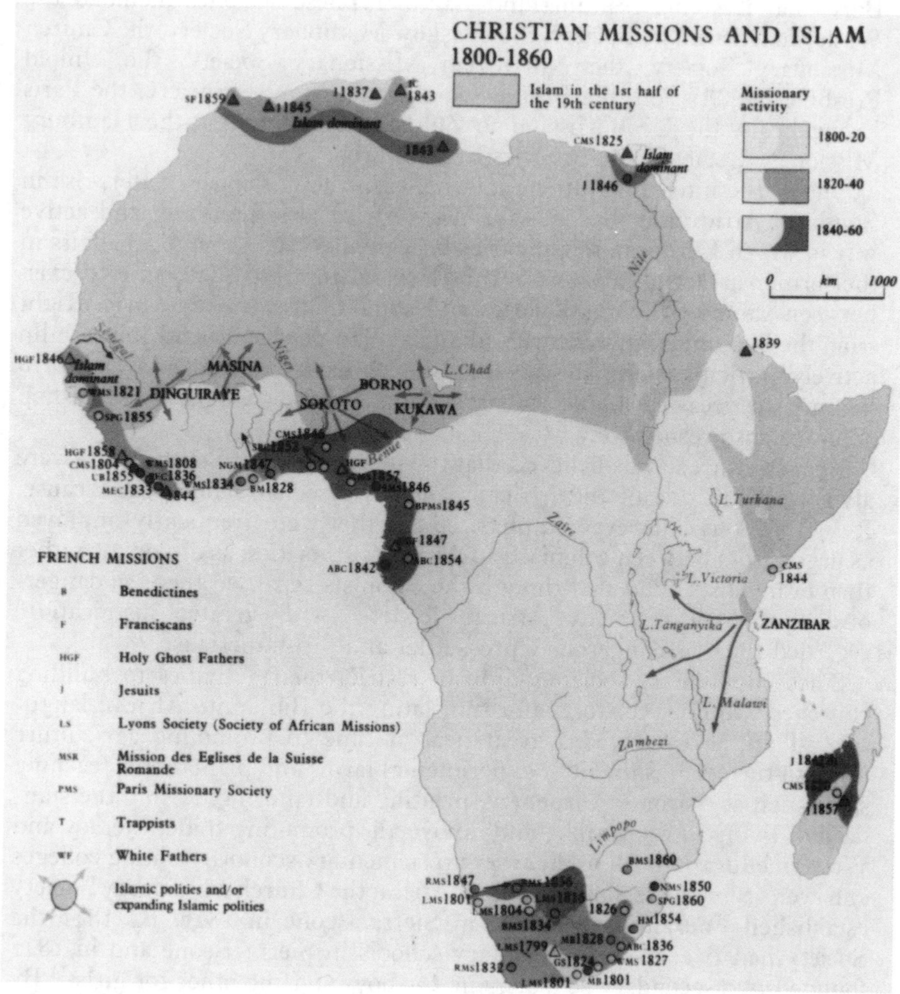

FIG. 3.1 *Christian missions and Islam, 1800–60* (*Source: J. F. Ade Ajayi and M. Crowder* (*eds*) Historical Atlas of Africa, *Longman, London, 1985*)

missionary societies operating in the whole area. These were the Moravian Mission, which entered the Cape for the first time in 1737, withdrew only six years later and did not return until 1792; and the London Missionary Society, which appeared at the Cape for the first ime in 1799.[10] But from 1816, many societies from Britain, Europe and the USA, Protestant as well as Catholic, entered not only the Cape, but also Natal and the Transvaal. By the 1860s, they had penetrated as far north as the areas of modern

10. E. Roux, 1964, pp. 25–6; E. A. Walker, 1957, pp. 92–3, 144–6, 173–5.

Botswana, Lesotho, Namibia and Zambia. These societies included the Wesleyan Missionary Society, the Glasgow Missionary Society, the Church Missionary Society, the Norwegian Missionary Society, the United Presbyterian Mission, the Berlin Society, the Rhenish Society, the Paris Evangelicals, the USA Mission to Zululand and Mosega, the Hamburg Missionary Society and the Swiss Free Church.[11]

One of the interesting differences between the missionary enterprise in Southern Africa and that in, say, West Africa was the direct and active way in which European missionaries became involved in political affairs in the former area and, above all, the close relationship that came to exist between some of the missionaries and some of the African kings. Right from the beginning, missionaries like J. T. Van der Kemp and John Philip actively participated in politics while Lobengula, Lewanika and Cetshwayo became the great friends of Robert Moffat, François Coillard and Bishop John Colenso respectively.[12]

At first, it used to be believed that the missionaries in South Africa were always on the side of the Africans and always championed their cause. Recent work has, however, emphasized that they were 'frequently employed as negotiators between colonial and African authorities, as diplomats rather than evangelists', and that though the colonists regarded them as dangerously pro-African, many African leaders (with greater justification) regarded them as dangerously pro-settler and pro-imperialist.[13]

These missionary societies did not restrict their activities to building churches, winning converts and translating the Bible into African languages. They also devoted a great deal of time to promoting agriculture through the establishment of experimental farms and plantations, teaching skills such as masonry, carpentry, printing and tailoring, raising the standard of living of the people, and, above all, promoting trade, literacy and Western education. All of them set up elementary schools, training colleges and even secondary schools. In West Africa, the Church Missionary Society established Fourah Bay College in Sierra Leone in 1827. By 1841 the Society had twenty-one elementary schools in Sierra Leone and in 1842 founded two secondary schools, one for boys and the other for girls.[14] By 1846, the Wesleyans had also established four girls' schools and twenty boys' schools in the Gold Coast and in 1876 opened their first secondary school, the Wesleyan High School, now known as Mfantsipim School. The CMS also established a Grammar School in Lagos in 1859, while the

11. E. A. Walker, 1957, pp. 133, 144–6, 178; E. Roux, 1964, pp. 24–31. C. P. Groves, 1954, Vol. 2, pp. 118–61; D. Denoon, 1973, pp. 26–9, 67–81, 80–90; H. W. Langworthy, 1972, pp. 82–115.

12. D. Denoon, 1973, pp. 96–7; C. P. Groves, 1954, Vol. 2, pp. 252, 274; E. Roux, 1964, pp. 25–32.

13. D. Denoon, 1973, p. 65.

14. A. A. Boahen, 1966, pp. 118–23.

Wesleyans opened the Methodist Boys' High School in 1879.[15] It should be emphasized that schools were not founded only on the coast, but also in some of the inland towns.

PLATE 3.1 *The Church of Scotland Mission's church at Blantyre (Malawi)*

In East and Central Africa, at Livingstone there was a school with an enrolment of 400 students by 1890 as well as a workshop and a printing press 'which was perpetually turning out primers and translations of the Scriptures, tales and easy lessons in geography and natural history in Nyanja, Tonga, Nguni, Nyakyusa and Nkonde'.[16] By 1835, the LMS reported that it had 4000 children in its schools in Madagascar, and by 1894, 137 000 of the population of the Merina highlands of Madagascar were estimated as registered in Protestant schools. This proportion was 'similar to that of Western Europe at the same time'.[17]

In Southern Africa, even greater attention was paid to education than in other parts of Africa, thanks partly to the grants-in-aid that were given by the governments of the Cape and Natal during the period. It would appear that the educational activities of the missionaries had been far more

15. J. F. A. Ajayi, 1965, pp. 152–6.
16. R. Oliver, 1965, p. 62.
17. P. Curtin, S. Feierman, L. Thompson and J. Vansina, 1978, p. 414.

successful than their evangelical activities by 1870.[18] Not only had many elementary or village schools been established but, from as early as the 1840s, teacher-training and secondary institutions were founded. The Glasgow Missionary Society, for instance, established a seminary at Lovedale in Natal in July 1841 to which an industrial department was attached. This taught masonry, carpentry, waggon-making and smithing, and from 1861 on, printing and book-binding.[19] The Roman Catholics had also established a convent of the Sisters of the Holy Family with a boarding school, primary school and home of refuge in Natal and another one in the Orange Free State by 1877. In 1868, the French missionaries established a teacher training institute at Amanzimtote and a seminary for girls at Inanda in Natal in the mid-1860s, and in 1880 the Anglicans established the St Albans College among the Zulu.[20]

Probably even more far-reaching than that of the Islamic revolution was the impact of this Christian religious revolution on African societies. This was most obvious in the manner of life of the converted Africans. Apart from acquiring various technical skills, the Africans gained access to European medical ideas, however rudimentary, while the traditional styles of architecture were improved upon and the wearing of Western-type clothing became more common.[21] Also, by condemning polygamy, belief in ancestors, traditional gods and witchcraft, the missionaries weakened the traditional basis of African societies as well as family relationships.

Another effect of the introduction of the new religion was religious pluralism and, with it, the division of African societies into rival and competing factions. First, African societies became divided into converts and non-converts or what in South Africa became known as the 'red' people and the 'school' people.[22] Furthermore, just as Islam caused the division of its converts and adherents into Ḳādirīyya and Tijāniyya factions, so Christianity crystallized the 'school' people into Catholic, Methodist, Anglican, Lutheran, Congregational and Presbyterian groups. Whereas in many areas in Africa, this polarization did not cause any serious social tensions and animosities, in other areas, particularly Buganda and Madagascar, it did, as will be seen in subsequent chapters.

Emergence of the Western-educated elite

The greatest social impact of the missionary revolution, however, was the emergence of an educated elite in Africa. From the 1850s onwards, as a result largely of the educational activities of the missionary societies already

18. L. Thompson, 1969a, pp. 335, 385.
19. C. P. Groves, 1954, Vol. 2, pp. 135–6; M. Wilson, 1969b, pp. 261–2; L. Thompson, 1969a, p. 335.
20. C. P. Groves, 1954, Vol. 2, pp. 261–5.
21. M. Wilson, 1969b, pp. 266–7.
22. ibid., p. 265; M. Wilson, 1971, pp. 74–5.

discussed, a class of Africans educated mainly in English and French began to appear first on the coast and then steadily inland. The regions that saw the greatest development of this phenomenon were undoubtedly South Africa and West Africa.

According to Leo Kuper, as many as 3448 African students passed through the Lovedale Missionary Institution alone between 1841 when it was opened and December 1896. Of these, 'over seven hundred were in professional occupations, mostly teachers but including also eight law agents, two law clerks, one physician, and two editors or journalists; almost one hundred were clerks and interpreters, about one hundred and seventy artisans and over six hundred labourers and farmers.'[23] It should not be forgotten that Lovedale was not the only such institution; there were others in the Cape and Natal. Many of the products of these institutions, as will be seen later, were to play a leading role in the mass religious movement among the Bantu in the 1880s and especially the 1890s. Among them were Tiyo Soga, in 1856 the first Xhosa to be ordained a minister of the Free Church of Scotland; Nehemiah Tile, who studied theology at the Healdtown Institution; Reverend Kanyome, a Cape Bantu clergyman; James M. Dwane, born in 1841 and ordained in 1881; and Mangena M. Mokone.[24] Probably the most influential was to be John Tengo Javabu, who was born in 1859, attended the Healdtown Institution (like Nehemiah Tile), gained the teacher's certificate in 1875, and in 1883 became the first African to pass the matriculation examination. In 1884, he founded the first Bantu newspaper (*Imvo Zabantsundu*) and was to play a prominent role in Cape politics between the 1890s and 1910s.[25]

Viewed in relation to the entire black population in South Africa, the number of the Western-educated elite that had emerged by 1880 was exceedingly small. Even smaller was the elite in East and Central Africa by that date. In Tanganyika, for instance, the first African priest of the Universities Mission to Central Africa, Cecil Majaliwa, was not ordained until as late as 1890, the second not until 1894 and the third not until 1898.[26] In Kenya, it was not until the early decades of this century that a significant elite which played an active part in local politics – men like John Owale, R. Omulo, J. Okwiri, Harry Thuku, James Beauttah, Hesse Kariuku, John Muchuchu, not to mention Jomo Kenyatta – emerged.[27] This was undoubtedly because the educational activities of the missionary societies did not really get going until after the period under review.

It was in West Africa that a relatively large number of members of an educated elite had emerged by 1880 and the country that produced the

23. L. Kuper, 1971, pp. 433–4.
24. E. Roux, 1964, pp. 78–80; E. A. Walker, 1957, pp. 521–2.
25. E. Roux, 1964, pp. 53–77; E. A. Walker, 1957, pp. 394–5, 536.
26. J. Iliffe, 1979, pp. 216–19.
27. B. A. Ogot, 1968, pp. 266–70.

PLATE 3.2 *Tiyo Soga*

first significant number was Sierra Leone. Indeed, it was the Creoles, as the educated people of Sierra Leone came to be called, who pioneered most of the missionary and educational activities in the other parts of West Africa. Three typical examples were James Africanus Horton who was born in 1835 in Sierra Leone, trained in Britain as a doctor from 1853 to 1859 and entered the West African Medical Service as a Staff Assistant Surgeon; Samuel Ajayi Crowther who was one of the first products of Fourah Bay College and the first African to be ordained as a Bishop of the Anglican Church; and James Johnson, that fiery intellectual and evangelist.[28] Others included Broughton Davies, who qualified as a doctor in 1859, and Samuel Lewis, the lawyer, the first African to receive a knighthood.[29] Liberia also produced a few intellectuals, among whom was Edward Wilmot Blyden, who was born in the West Indies. Slightly larger were the numbers in Nigeria and the Gold Coast. In Nigeria, the elite included people like Essien Ukpabio, D. B. Vincent (later known as Mojola Agbebi), H. E. Macaulay, G. W. Johnson, R. B. Blaize and J. A. Otunba Payne.[30] The Gold Coast elite of the 1870s and 1880s included J. A. Solomon, E. J. Fynn, J. P. Brown, J. de Graft Hayford, A. W. Parker, T. Laing, J. H. Brew and John Mensah Sarbah.[31]

28. E. A. Ayandele, 1966, pp. 185–96; J. F. A. Ajayi, 1965.
29. C. M. Fyle, 1981, pp. 74–6.
30. E. A. Ayandele, 1966, pp. 58–9, 192–200.
31. F. L. Bartels, 1965, pp. 72–100.

PLATE 3.3 *Charlotte Village School, Sierra Leone, c. 1885*

Moreover, in West Africa as to some extent in the Portuguese areas of Mozambique and Angola, while some members of the educated elite entered the professions as civil servants, teachers, catechists, ministers and church agents – by 1885 according to the latest account, the Wesleyans had 15 African ministers, 43 catechists, 259 preachers and 79 teachers in the Gold Coast[32] – the majority entered the commercial field as independent traders and operated on credit provided by the foreign companies and resident traders. It was the latter, described as the 'aspirant bourgeoisie' by Susan Kaplow,[33] who, as will be seen later, pushed the frontiers of retail trade in the Gold Coast, Sierra Leone and Nigeria further and further inland during the period under review. As one report from the Gold Coast put it, by 1850, the young men had gone to reside in the interior as traders and clerks and it was they who were 'causing a great increase in the consumption of the manufactures of Great Britain and are widely extending commerce and civilisation amongst the native population'.[34] Similar social developments took place in Madagascar and in Central and East Africa. Thus, by the end of the period under review a new rung had been added to the social ladder in Africa, an educated elite which had become divided

32. M. McCarthy, 1983, pp. 110–11.
33. S. B. Kaplow, 1977, pp. 313–33.
34. Quoted in M. McCarthy, 1983, p. 126.

into a professional class of doctors, ministers, teachers, catechists and agents and an aspirant bourgeoisie or entrepreneur group, as some would prefer to call them, of educated traders and merchants.

Ethiopianism

There were two unique and interesting consequences of the emergence of this educated elite in Africa. First was the rise of Ethiopianism, an African religious and political nationalist movement. This, secondly, embodied an intellectual revolution, especially in South and West Africa. It should be emphasized that until as late as the 1850s those educated Africans who entered the professions were treated as equals by the whites and were given appointments commensurate with their educational qualifications and experience. Many of the African educated elite sincerely believed that Africa could only be civilized by the application of European learning, technology and religion. But the decades after the 1850s saw 'the emergence of pseudo-scientific thought in Europe and America which interpreted society in terms of fixed racial categories in which the Negro was assigned a very lowly place'.[35] These racist ideas were given very wide publicity during the second half of the century by the writings of people like Arthur de Gobineau, Sir Richard Burton and Winwood Reade. These ideas came to be accepted by the generality of European missionaries and administrators in Africa, who began to discriminate against the educated Africans in favour of whites, both in Church and government. It was principally this racial discrimination practised against the educated Africans by the white missionaries and the consequent sense of humiliation and indignation that gave rise to the religious and political nationalist movement that became known as Ethiopianism, a term coined from the Biblical verse, 'Ethiopia shall soon stretch out her hands unto God'.[36] Following similar movements of independency shown by Nova Scotians in Sierra Leone at the beginning of the century, this movement aimed at establishing Christian churches under the control of Africans themselves and in tune with African cultures and traditions. It began in South Africa probably early in the 1860s. It reached its maturity in the 1880s with the formation of the first break-away Ethiopian or African independent Church in South Africa in 1884 by the Tembu Wesleyan minister, Nehemiah Tile, and in West Africa by a group of Nigerian church leaders of the Southern Baptist Mission (American) in 1888.[37] It is significant that while Tile expressed his wish 'to adapt the message of the Church to the Heritage of the Tembu' he also added that 'as the Queen of England was the Head of the English Church,

35. J.A. Horton, 1969, p. xvii (Introduction by G. Shepperson); P.D. Curtin, 1964, pp. 28–57; R. July, 1967, pp. 212–13.

36. G. Shepperson and T. Price, 1958, pp. 72–4.

37. ibid., pp. 72–4; G. Shepperson, 1968; E. Roux, 1964, pp. 77–80; B.G. Sundkler, 1961, pp. 38–47; D.B. Barrett, 1968, pp. 18–24; T. Hodgkin, 1956, pp. 98–114.

so the Paramount Chief of the Tembu should be the *summus episcopus* of the new religious organization'.[38] T. B. Vincent, later known as Mojola Agbebi, one of the leaders of the first secessionist movement in Nigeria, declared in 1889 that 'to render Christianity indigenous to Africa, it must be watered by native hands, pruned with the native hatchet, and tended with native earth ... It is a curse if we intend for ever to hold at the apron strings of foreign teachers, doing the baby for aye.' He also talked of infusing into his converts 'individuality of Race, congregational independence, self-support and self-government ... the retention of Native names, native dress, healthful Native customs and habits, and the use of the native language in worship'.[39] From South Africa, Ethiopianism spread throughout East and Central Africa and became an extremely powerful phenomenon during the last two decades of the nineteenth century and the first two of the twentieth.

In West Africa, however, the educated elite did not stop short at political action. They also set themselves the task of refuting and disproving racist ideas and practices in a series of articles, pamphlets, books and speeches, and it was this that gave rise to the second of the unique processes of the period, namely, the intellectual revolution and the accompanying birth of African racial consciousness, pan-Africanism and the concept of the African personality. The pioneers of this revolution in West Africa were undoubtedly James Africanus Horton (1835–83) and Edward Wilmot Blyden (1832–1912). Among the works of Horton on the themes in question were *Political Economy of British Western Africa*, with *the requirements of the several colonies and settlements: An African view of the Negro place in Nature* (1865); *West African Countries and Peoples: A Vindication of the African Race* (1868); and *Letters on the Political Condition of the Gold Coast* (1870). In *West African Countries and Peoples*, Horton refuted the idea of inherent racial inferiority of the black man by arguing that the difference in the stages of civilization between whites and blacks arose 'entirely from the influence of external circumstances'. To those who moved from the assumption of racial inferiority of the black to the assumption that he would ultimately disappear from the face of the earth in the face of white power, Horton argued:

> we find that wherever the African race has been carried to ... they increase, no matter under what depressing and burdensome yoke they may suffer; from which it may be safely inferred that the African people is a permanent and enduring people, and the fancies of those who had determined their destruction will go in the same limbo as the now almost defunct American slavery.[40]

38. Quoted by T. Hodgkin, 1956, p. 100.
39. Quoted by E. A. Ayandele, 1966, p. 200.
40. J. A. Horton, 1969, p. 69; see also R. July, 1967, pp. 110–29; for a more detailed biography of J. A. Horton, see C. Fyfe, 1972.

Finally, in answer to the proposition that the black was incapable of improvement, he argued: 'Africans are not incapable of improvement, but that by the assistance of good and able men they are destined to figure in the course of time, and to take a prominent part in the history of the civilized world'.[41] Again in his *Letters on the Political Condition of the Gold Coast*, Horton wrote in the Preface:

> 'Rome was not built in a day;' the proudest kingdom in Europe was once in a state of barbarism perhaps worse than now exists amongst the tribes chiefly inhabiting the West Coast of Africa; and it is an incontrovertible axiom that what has been done can again be done. If Europe, therefore, has been raised to her present pitch of civilization by progressive advancement, Africa too, with a guarantee of the civilization of the north, will rise into equal importance.[42]

Horton not only condemned racism but was also one of the earliest advocates of pan-Africanism. As George Shepperson has shown, this pan-Africanist spirit was born during his studies in Britain in reaction to pseudo-scientific racist theories, for it was there that he added the name Africanus to his two other names James Beale, and in most of his subsequent writings, he signed himself simply as Africanus Horton.[43] Finally, it should be pointed out that Horton was not only interested in racial and cultural issues but also in political independence. Indeed, in writing his *West African Countries and Peoples*, his aims were not only to 'disprove many of the fallacious doctrines and statements of anthropologists (detrimental to the interests of the African race)', but also to establish 'the requirements necessary for establishing that self-government recommended by the Committee of the House of Commons, 1865'.[44]

Even more prolific, more radical and perhaps better known was Horton's contemporary, Edward Wilmot Blyden.[45] Though born in St Thomas in the West Indies, he migrated at an early age to Liberia where he studied, lived and worked as a lecturer and diplomat till his death at the age of 80. He published numerous books and pamphlets and delivered many speeches in Europe and America, all in condemnation of the racist theories of the day. Among those published during the period under review were *African Colonization* (1862), *Vindication of the Negro Race* (1857), *A Voice from Bleeding Africa on Behalf of Her Exiled Children* (1856), *Hope for Africa* (1861), *From West Africa to Palestine* (1873), and *Christianity, Islam and the Negro Race* (1887). In these works he also advocated 'Africa for the Africans', pan-Africanism, the African personality, Islam and polygamy

41. J. A. Horton, 1969, pp. ix–x.
42. J. A. Horton, 1970, p. i.
43. J. A. Horton, 1969, p. xvii (Introduction).
44. ibid., p. vii (Preface).
45. For further details, see H. L. Lynch, 1967; J. S. Coleman, 1958, pp. 106–7, 175–6, 183–4; R. July, 1967, pp. 208–33.

which were to him more in keeping with African personality, insisted on the purity and integrity of the black race and therefore condemned mixed marriages, championed Ethiopianism and, above all, preached racial pride. In an article published in 1874, he praised the Mande and Fulbe peoples, who were Muslims and were developing the idea of a national and social order without the aid or hindrance of foreigners. Blyden concluded:

> During all the years which have elapsed since the commencement of modern progress, the African race has filled a very humble and subordinate part in the work of human civilization. But the march of events is developing the interesting fact that there is a career before this people which no other people can enter upon. There is a peculiar work for them to accomplish, both in the land of their bondage, and in the land of their fathers, which no other people can achieve. With the present prospects and privileges before his race – with the chances of arduous work, noble suffering, and magnificent achievement before them – I would rather be a member of this race than a Greek in the time of Alexander, a Roman in the Augustin period, or an Anglo-Saxon in the nineteenth century.[46]

It was also Blyden who in his famous speech to the American Colonization Society in May 1880 gave great publicity to the phrase 'Ethiopia Stretching Out her Hands Unto God' and equated Ethiopian with African; and it was he who first used the term 'African personality' in his lecture delivered on 19 May 1893 in Freetown when he described the African Race as 'a Great Race – great in its vitality, in its power of endurance and its prospect of perpetuity'. He continued:

> It is sad to think that there are some Africans, especially among those who have enjoyed the advantages of foreign training, who are so blind to the radical facts of humanity as to say, 'Let us do away with the sentiment of Race. Let us do away with our African personality and be if possible in another Race ... Preach this doctrine as much as you like, no one will do it, for no one *can* do it, for when you have done away with your personality, you have done away with yourselves ... the duty of every man, of every race is to contend for its individuality – to keep and develop it ... Therefore, honour and love your Race ... If you are not yourself, if you surrender your personality, you have nothing left to give to the world ...[47]

Another great leader of the intellectual revolution of the time was undoubtedly that fiery Yoruba-Creole evangelist, James Johnson (*c.* 1836–1917). Like Horton, he was born and educated in Sierra Leone at the Freetown Grammar School and Fourah Bay College and taught in that institution from 1860 to 1863. He then joined the Church Missionary

46. Quoted in H. S. Wilson, 1969, pp. 239–40.
47. ibid., pp. 249–50.

Society which transferred him to Nigeria in 1874 where he was put in charge first of the famous Breadfruit Church in Lagos. In 1876, he was appointed as the Superintendent of all CMS stations in the interior of Yorubaland until 1880 when he was removed simply because he was 'a black man'.[48] In his sermons, letters and articles, James Johnson not only advocated Nigerian nationalism but also Ethiopianism which, in West Africa, never became the anti-government and secessionist doctrine that it was in South and Central Africa but became identified with Africa, with the eulogization and romanticization of the achievements of the Negro race as well as a struggle for power and position not only in Church government but also in the civil service.

Like Blyden, but unlike Samuel Ajayi Crowther, James Johnson advocated 'Africa for the Africans', while he also popularized the concept of Ethiopianism in his sermons and writings.[49] Unlike his contemporary Crowther, he also passionately believed in and advocated the evangelization of Africa by Africans and vigorously and vehemently condemned the doctrine of black racial inferiority then being advocated. He believed that there should be an independent African Church that would abolish all sectarianism, embrace all African Christians 'and make of them all one African whole'.[50] He insisted that the African Church was to be staffed at all levels by Africans since 'European missionaries could not identify themselves with African racial ambitions and idiosyncracies'. Indeed, he argued that the European presence would prevent the full development of Africans by destroying such qualities as 'the superior physique, the manly independence, the courage and bravery, the daring and self-reliance, and the readiness to face difficulties' found among Africans who had not come into contact with Europeans.[51] When he was accused in 1881 of being anti-white, Johnson replied:

> With the missionaries of the present day an independent thought in an African and a clear enunciation of his convictions are a great crime. He has no right to them: he must always see with other people's eyes and swear by other people's opinions: he must not manifest any patriotic sentiments; he must denude himself of manhood and of every vestige of racial feeling and fling away his individuality and distinctiveness to make peaceable existence with them possible and secure favourable recommendations to the Society.[52]

In the light of such views, is it surprising that the European missionaries became so scared of him and engineered his removal from the interior of Yorubaland in 1880.

48. E. A. Ayandele, 1966, pp. 195–6; R. July, 1967, pp. 197–207.
49. E. A. Ayandele, 1966, p. 187.
50. ibid, p. 187.
51. Quoted by E. A. Ayandele, 1966, p. 191.
52. Quoted by E. A. Ayandele, 1966, p. 191.

Similar intellectual activities went on in other parts of Africa especially in Angola and, as will be seen below, in Egypt and the other Barbary states as is evident from the writings of Egyptian scholars, such as Shaykh Rifā'a al-Ṭahṭāwi (1801–73.)[53]

From the views of these educated Africans, the level of scholarship and learning displayed in their writings, the sophistication of their argumentation, the bite of their logic and, finally, from the sheer volume of their articles, publications and correspondence, there is no doubt that a veritable intellectual revolution occurred in West Africa in particular and Africa in general. This resulted in the birth of Ethiopianism, pan-Africanism and the ideology of African personality, the movement for religious and political independence, and the development of a new consciousness of pride and confidence in black peoples.

New political trends

Besides the demographic and religious revolutions, two other trends became discernible in Africa during the period under review. These were political and economic. The main new political trends that typified the period were ever-increasing centralization, modernization or renaissance, some constitutional initiatives and experimentation, the integration of some of the new educated elite into the old political structures and, finally, the confrontation between the Africans and the Europeans.

Though it is a fact that some of the old empires such as Asante and Ọyọ in West Africa and the Luba empire in Central Africa broke up, there is no doubt that the more widespread political trend in Africa during the period was towards greater centralization. Certainly, the Sokoto empire, the Massina empire, the empire of al-Hadjdj 'Umar and, above all, that of Samori were typical examples of the centralizing tendencies in nineteenth-century African politics. The Nguni migrations had the same result, as has been pointed out already. Other typical examples of centralization can be found in Ethiopia, Madagascar and Buganda.

At the beginning of the nineteenth century, both Ethiopia and Madagascar consisted of a series of independent rival states. However, as will be seen below,[54] by the end of our period, the former had been united mainly through military conquest under the leadership of one of the central states of Shoa, whose king, Menelik II, assumed the title of Emperor of the united kingdom in 1889. At the same time, and using the same methods, the central Imerina kingdom under the inspired leadership of King Andrianaimpoinimerina (1782–1810) and his successors subdued and absorbed virtually all the states of the northern, eastern and central parts of that island. Both of these conquests were followed by attempts to impose the

53. See Unesco, *General History of Africa*, Vol. VII, ch. 21; and Chapter 13 below.
54. See Chapters 15 and 16 below.

language and culture of those central states on the others with a view to building a truly national state, and these processes were continued in the decades after the close of our period.

In West Africa, two completely new states, the products of the humanitarian, abolitionist and racist campaigns of the period, Sierra Leone and Liberia, were also formed in 1787 and 1820 respectively, while Libreville was founded in Equatorial Africa. Here again, by the end of our period, the first two states had been able not only to absorb a number of independent states inland, but had also succeeded in developing into nation-states each with its own culture and language, Creole in one case and Americo-Liberian in the other. In this exercise, the Sierra Leoneans were undoubtedly much more successful than the Liberians, since the culture that they evolved was not simply an importation from elsewhere but rather a synthesis of African, Nova Scotian and British elements moulded by the environmental conditions of Freetown and its surrounding areas.[55] It was the products of this dynamic culture, the Creoles, who played such a decisive role in the missionary and intellectual revolutions in West Africa. A similar process of expansion and centralization occurred in Egypt, as well as in the Great Lakes region where Buganda, Burundi and Bunyoro expanded the range of their power and influence, mainly in an attempt to control the means of production and exchange.

Besides these centralizing trends, another interesting and in this case a completely new nineteenth-century phenomenon was that of modernization or, as some would call it, renaissance. Euro-African contacts, which until the beginning of our period had been confined largely to the coastal peripheries, were, in the period under review, steadily extended inland as a result of the Industrial Revolution, largely through the efforts first of explorers, then traders and, finally, missionaries. This steady extension of European contacts and influence inland included not only guns and powder, but also railways, telegraphs, agricultural and mining machinery, the printing press, technical education and, above all, finance capital. These new developments created opportunities, but also challenges and dangers. Among the most novel and interesting features of African history during the period were the initiatives and reactions of African rulers and advisers in the face of these opportunities and challenges. It would appear that in most cases the approach of the Africans was not simply one of blind imitation or wholesale substitution but rather one of adaptation and synthesis. Instances of this process of modernization in Africa are legion.[56] Egypt built its first printing press at Būlāķ, Cairo, in 1822; the first printing press was established in Portuguese Luanda in 1841; the first modern mines were opened in Algeria in 1845 and in the Gold Coast in the 1870s. Some of the states, such as Ethiopia and Tunisia, embarked on public works;

55. For further details, see L. Spitzer, 1974; A. Porter, 1963.
56. See Chapters 13, 15, 16 and 17 below.

nearly all the Barbary states, as well as Egypt reformed their monetary systems. Other states, such as Egypt, set up textile and cotton mills, saw mills, glassworks and paper mills, all during the reign of Muḥammad ʿAlī.

But more interesting and of far-reaching consequence was the modernization process in the military sphere. In the face of steady European encroachment, many African states, especially in North and West Africa, modernized the organization, training, equipment and recruitment of their armies. As will be seen in later chapters, Morocco, for instance, set up at Fez an engineering school to train artillery men, surveyors, and cartographers and sent soldiers abroad for training. Tunisia under Aḥmad Bey not only reorganized its army on the lines of a Western army and adopted Western techniques and methods but also set up factories to produce modern guns and other military equipment. Ethiopia under Téwodros and Menelik also abolished its unpaid levies, replacing them with a well-equipped army of professional soldiers and set up factories to produce cannon and mortars. Finally, Samori Ture also reformed and modernized his army and equipped it with some of the latest weapons of the day. It was these reforms that enabled both Samori Ture and Menelik to hold out for so long against the imperial powers during the last two decades of the century. However, as some of the later chapters will show, this modernization process was undertaken through loans raised mainly in Europe at high interest rates, and this prepared the ground or provided the excuse for the imperialist takeover at the end of our period.

Modernization also took place in the constitutional field. There is no doubt that in many states in Africa, partly as a result of the large increase in the number of the educated elite and the *ʿulamāʾ*, who naturally began to demand a say in the administration of their countries, a number of political and constitutional experiments were embarked upon. In fact, the Fulbe *djihād* of the first half of the nineteenth century could also be described as the militant political answer to this confrontation between the new educated elite of the *ʿulamāʾ* and the traditional ruling elite, while the Joola rebellions of the second half of the nineteenth century could be regarded, as indeed Yves Person has shown, as a revolt of the educated mercantile class against the conservative ruling elite.[57] In other parts of Africa, especially on the west coast, this confrontation was not resolved in such a militant and violent way, but rather in more constitutional approaches. Indeed, during the period under review, the educated elite did not seek to replace the old aristocracy as the national leaders of the people as they were to do in the 1920s and 1930s but rather sought accommodation within the system and co-operation with them. In this connection, we have already referred to the constitutional experiments that followed the Yoruba migrations. However, nothing illustrates this trend better than the Constitution of the

57. See Chapter 24.

Fante Confederation of the Gold Coast, drawn up in 1874. Articles 4, 5 and 6 of that Constitution read:[58]

> That there shall be elected a president, vice-president, secretary, under-secretary, treasurer and assistant-treasurer.
>
> That the president be elected from the body of kings, and be proclaimed king-president of the Fanti Confederation.
>
> That the vice-president, secretary and under-secretary, treasurer and assistant-treasurer, who shall constitute the ministry, be men of education and position.

The objects of the Fante Confederation as stated in this Constitution were no less interesting and significant. These were to promote friendly intercourse between and to unite all the kings and chiefs of Fante for offensive purposes against their common enemy; to make 'good and substantial roads throughout all the interior districts included in the Confederation' which were to be 'fifteen feet broad, with good gutters on either side'; and establish schools for the education of all children within the Confederation and 'to obtain the service of efficient school-masters'. Others were to promote agricultural and industrial pursuits and introduce 'such new plants as may hereafter become sources of profitable commerce to the country' and, finally, to develop and facilitate the working of the mineral and other resources of the country. Particular emphasis was placed on the promotion of education of both sexes and on industrial training. As Clause 22 put it,

> That normal schools be attached to each national school for the express purpose of educating and instructing the scholars as carpenters, masons, sawyers, joiners, agriculturists, smiths, architects, builders, etc.

The progressive and modern nature of the objectives of the Confederation are truly astonishing while the spirit of harmonious co-operation between the educated elite and the traditional rulers pervading the Constitution was really revolutionary. Had this bold co-operative effort, which was very much inspired by the writings of Africanus Horton, been allowed to materialize and the plans implemented, the course not only of the history of the Gold Coast but probably the whole of British West Africa would have been different. But for reasons to be discussed later, the British had killed this bold and interesting initiative stone-dead by 1873.[59]

A similar constitutional experiment was that of the Egba United Board of Management formed at Abẹokuta. According to Africanus Horton, its express purpose was that 'of directing the native government, of forwarding civilization, and promoting the spread of Christianity, as well as of pro-

58. H. S. Wilson, 1969, p. 214; for the full text see pp. 213–18.

59. See Chapter 25 below.

tecting the property of European merchants and British subjects'.[60] A third example was the constitution for the kingdom of the Grebo, which, as Person points out, was set up in imitation of the Fante Confederation.

It should be evident from all this that in the political as in the religious and demographic fields, really fundamental changes were taking place and the roots of many of the basic issues of today – the relationship between the educated elite and the traditional rulers, the problems of socio-economic development, the idea of political independence, the concept and practice of pan-Africanism and the phenomenon of racial discrimination – can be found during the period under review.

New economic trends

In the economic as in the other fields, some new trends became discernible during our period. The most radical change was the well-known one of the abolition and suppression of the slave trade and its replacement by export agriculture which has wrongly, but in a typically Eurocentric manner, been termed legitimate trade. Radical in its impact as it was, this change was rather slow in coming. Indeed, in East and Central Africa, as will be seen below, the first six decades of the century saw the expansion and intensification of that inhuman traffic.[61] It was not until the very end of the period under review that export agriculture completely replaced the slave trade.

Very well-known as this change was, its real significance has been lost on many scholars. It was not the change-over from the so-called illegitimate to the so-called legitimate trade but, rather, the fundamental shift in the distribution of incomes from the ruling aristocratic elite to the ordinary people that was significant. Since the slave trade, which constituted the principal source of income, was a monopoly of the kings and their military leaders and advisers, the bulk of the income went to them. But with its replacement by natural products such as palm oil, groundnuts, cotton, gum, honey, beeswax, kola nuts, etc., which could be produced or collected by the ordinary people, and especially those living in the rural areas, a steady redistribution of income ensued, leading to the rise of a new set of rich people in not only the urban and market centres but also in the rural areas. The roots of the present-day phenomenon of rural capitalism can be traced to this period.

Another consequence of the development of this export agriculture was the steady integration into the capitalist world-economy not only of the external economy of Africa, but also its internal or rural economy. Unfortunately, nowhere in Africa was this fundamental change in the mode of production accompanied by a corresponding change in the means of

60. J. A. Horton, 1969, pp. 151–3.
61. See Chapter 4 below.

production. In other words, the change to export agriculture was not accompanied by a technological change in the means of production nor in the industrial processing of the products prior to exportation. Africa was therefore unable during the period to develop an economy that could stand up against the capitalist and industrialized economy of Europe, hence the tragedy that befell it in the following decades.

Another interesting economic change in the nineteenth century, also often ignored by scholars, was the completion of the commercial unification of Africa. In spite of long-established trade routes across the Sahara and across Dārfūr to the Nile Valley, until the beginning of the nineteenth century there were hardly any transcontinental commercial routes linking Central and East Africa or linking Central and North Africa. It was only in the nineteenth century, and even then only from about the third decade onwards, that Central, East and North Africa became inextricably linked by great commercial highways. These were the result of the activities of the Arabs, Swahili, Yao, Nyamwezi and Kamba of East Africa, the Arabs of Egypt and Sudan, and the Tio, Ovimbundu and Chokwe of Central Africa. The outcome of all this was not only the commercial unification of Africa and an increase in intra-African contacts, not only a tremendous increase in the number of African entrepreneurs, middlemen and traders, but above all the progressive opening up of the hinterland of Africa to European and Arab/Swahili influence and manufactured goods with the tragic consequences that have been referred to and that will be discussed in greater detail in Volume VII of the Unesco *General History*.

Conclusion

The last question to be considered very briefly, then, is what would have happened had there not been any colonial interlude? It needs no prophet or soothsayer to see that had there been no such interlude, most of the new trends would have continued. Politically, the trend towards greater and greater centralization would have continued, and this would have ultimately resulted in the evolution of more natural nation-states and political entities than those that resulted from the European scramble and partition of Africa. Constitutional experiments such as those of the Fante Confederation and the Egba United Board would probably have succeeded, and the co-operation between the educated elite and the traditional ruling aristocracies, which in the colonial and neo-colonial contexts has still proved elusive, would probably by now have become an established practice. In the social field, the expansion of Christianity and Islam would have continued, as in fact it did during the colonial period. However, instead of slowing down, the pace of the spread of Western education and the introduction of technical schools and polytechnics would have increased, as is evident from the programme of the Fante Confederation and the educational reforms in nineteenth-century Egypt. Furthermore, following the great continental commercial highways, intra-African contacts and communication would have grown and Africa would have become more inward-looking and self-reliant. Above all, the feeling of racial identity, pan-Africanism and the slogans of Ethiopianism and 'Africa for Africans' would have gained momentum and brought about the ideological and spiritual, if not the political unity of the continent. But alas, the colonial interlude put an end to all these healthy and fascinating 'straws in the wind'.

From the above, it is quite evident that the nineteenth century was indeed a very dynamic and revolutionary century. It saw the development of many new trends and processes whose impact clearly signifies the end of the old and the beginning of the modern Africa. The period also clearly demonstrates the ability of Africans to face up to new challenges, to show initiatives, to adopt and adapt new techniques and new ideas, and to cope with new environmental situations. It is equally evident that African achievements in the political and social fields, and especially in the intellectual field, were far greater than in the economic field. By the end of the period under review, most African states were enjoying autonomous and sovereign existence, while intellectually and academically Africans had proved that they were not unequal to their European critics. Unfortunately, these undoubted social, intellectual and political achievements were nowhere matched by a comparable achievement in the technological and economic fields. Africans could not therefore develop the economic and technological base that could have enabled them to stand up to the strong imperialist storm that swept through the continent from our period onwards. Herein lies the fundamental cause of the tragedy of partition, conquest and the establishment of colonial rule that became the fate of Africa from the end of our period onwards.

4 The abolition of the slave trade

S. DAGET

This chapter does not attempt to assess the magnitude of each of the changes that the nineteenth century brought to Africa. It makes no claim to be a survey of the entire slave-trade phenomenon and, for instance, refers only in passing to the trans-Saharan and the Arab trade, which merit analysis by specialists in those fields. It outlines in broad terms the difficulties encountered by the Western world in abolishing the trade in black slaves, mostly bound for plantations on the American side of the Atlantic, and briefly sets out the circumstances under which the trade came virtually to an end, indicating some of the consequences that this entailed. A great deal of research is still needed in order to obtain a clearer view of the whole phenomenon, and emphasis should be laid on the study of oral tradition as being the main source of information.

African participation in the trade had never been general. Some of the hinterland peoples were quite unaware of it. Some coastal societies destroyed slave ships and held their crews to ransom. Others had their political and class structure overturned by it. Others again drew strength from the authoritarian and exclusivist nature of the system, and in those cases black and white interests coincided in a flourishing business. Some African producers and distributors of exportable manpower did well out of this branch of the coastal economy and foreign trade. During the eighteenth century they bartered nearly 7 million human beings for approximately 300 million piastres-worth of merchandise specific to the 'Guinea trade', including perhaps 80 million firearms. In the same period, the trans-Saharan trade accounted for the deportation of over 700 000 individuals and the Indian Ocean trade for about 200 000. At the end of the Middle Passage the slave-traders exchanged the 6 million Africans who had survived the voyage – 40 per cent of them women and children – against the produce of slave labour, which sold increasingly well on the European side of the Atlantic. Nevertheless some European intellectuals, their principles and finer feelings outraged, condemned the eating of sugar dyed with the blood of the 'forgotten men of the universe', and called for the abolition of the trade.

Abolitionist ideology was not African in inspiration. It was directed against the world of Atlantic slave-owners and slave-traders, before any interest was shown in the effects of the trans-Saharan or Arab trade. The forms it took rested on a foundation of moral philosophy whose efficacy as a driving force was very limited. Yet, for half a century, the anti-slavery movement and 'civilized' Africa officially backed mounting Western pressure on the West African coast. Around 1860, the West began establishing for good a presence on the coast that had hitherto been sporadic, secondary and sometimes prohibited. Similar trends developed in North and East Africa from 1830 until the end of the century.

The Western impetus for abolition

Throughout the eighteenth century, as they polished up their definition of the universal human right to liberty and the pursuit of happiness, anthropologists, philosophers and theologians came up against the case of the African and his condition in the world. Their thinking led them to modify the ideas commonly accepted until then about the African black and the American slave, and they transformed the brute beast of burden into a moral and social being. Their slogan, 'The Negro is a man', implicitly impugned the generally held view about the propriety, legality and usefulness of selling black Africans. Their humanitarian arguments led to a demand for abolition, since the balance sheet of the trade consisted, as they saw it, entirely of debits.

It bled the states that encouraged and subsidized it; it killed tens of thousands of whites and hundreds of thousands of blacks; and it took people who were both producers and consumers away from their lands and reduced them to slavery in America, i.e. to ciphers. It prevented the diversification of trade on the African coast. It perpetuated barbarism in the black continent – this being the view of the only Westerners credited with knowing about Africa, the slave-traders. While denouncing the scourge, abolitionists did not seek or expect to convert black traders or white pro-slavers straightaway. They put forward a programme for the regeneration of Africa through Christianity, civilization, and normal trade, and proposed rational stages for its implementation: public opinion in the Christian world to be changed, the so-called 'civilized' governments to be persuaded to adopt official positions, and the Atlantic trade to be legally abolished.

In France in the eighteenth century the *Grande Encyclopédie* and the works of the Abbé Raynal, with revisions by Diderot, taught bourgeois revolutionaries a disgust for slavery. This current of lofty secular thought supported from a distance the ideals of the Société des Amis des Noirs (Society of Friends of the Blacks), which was rumoured to be in the pay of the British. There, revolutionaries were sensitive neither to the realities of the slave trade nor to the need for popular support for their new ideology. In Britain, on the other hand, ordinary folk were educated in philanthropy through theological exposition based on a vigorous evangelical revival. The

American Quakers, having themselves forsworn dealing in slaves, had already persuaded British Quakers to join the British movement for abolition.[1] At the same time political circles were subjected to indoctrination. The Clapham Sect was the spearhead of this two-pronged attack, and spoke up for it year after year in the House of Commons through the mouth of William Wilberforce. The fight against the array of obstacles set up by slave-owners and traders lasted twenty years, but on 25 March 1807 Britain abolished the trade. This was the second official abolition, following that of Denmark in 1802. In 1808 the USA gave general effect to the Quakers' individual decisions. This movement by governments to adopt the humanitarian cause was championed by Britain, whose slave-traders had shipped some 1 600 000 Africans to its American colonies during the previous century.

The hagiography that portrays humanitarian revolution as opening 'one of the noblest pages in English history' received a severe blow in 1944 from an analysis written from the standpoint of historical materialism. According to Eric Williams, abolition represented primarily the working out of the economic imperatives of Britain as a budding industrial country.[2] It is true that this seminal approach did not entirely deny the role played by moral philosophy and an idealistic and triumphant humanitarianism. Nonetheless, it drew attention to certain serious contradictions between the theories and the realities. Among the most prominent leaders of the abolitionist movement there were many bankers (the same was true of the French Société des Amis des Noirs), which showed that the capitalist class had much to gain from having the trade abolished. The theories of the abolitionists at the time proved powerless against the reality of the very strong current of trade to flourishing slave plantations in Cuba and Brazil. Nor were the so-called humanitarian forces capable of controlling the effects of the standardization of import duties on sugar, which ultimately led, as was to be expected at a time when the mechanization of plantations was still far from complete, to an increase in the demand for black manpower. Perhaps the chief merit of Williams's stimulating thesis was to provoke further research, as the economic debate still continues. Thus, Seymour Drescher has set about demonstrating that abolition was 'econocide', and Roger Anstey argued that British philanthropy was rooted in faith and benevolence.[3] There is perhaps less disagreement among historians as to the political factors involved in abolition.

Proposals for collective abolition, put forward by Britain in 1787 and again in 1807, came to nothing. In 1810 Portugal made some vague promises in return for the entry of its goods to the British market. With the ending of the Napoleonic Wars a world was crumbling in ruins. The peace of 1815

1. R. Anstey, 1975, ch. 9 *passim*.
2. E. Williams, 1944, *passim*.
3. S. Drescher, 1976, p. 427; R. Anstey, 1975, chs 1 and 2 *passim*.

opened the Mediterranean, the Indian Ocean and the Atlantic to maritime trade; and to the transport of slaves. At the Congress of Vienna, British diplomacy sought an explicit condemnation of the trade, but all it obtained was an empty, procrastinatory declaration, reaffirmed at Verona. From 1841, this pretence of official abolitionist morality gave the British Foreign Office and the Admiralty all the authority they needed for their combined strategies in regard to the international slave trade. This was a radical three-point plan of action: domestic legislation making it illegal for nationals of the country concerned to engage in the traffic; bilateral treaties giving navies the reciprocal right to search and seize at sea merchant vessels of either contracting nation caught in the illegal trade; and collaboration through mixed commissions, empowered to adjudicate on captured slave ships and set free the slaves found on board. The same provisions were also applicable in the Indian Ocean, especially between Mauritius and Bourbon (the island now known as Réunion).

This plan appealed to a section of the public with liberal–philanthropic leanings. Moreover, not every national economy could afford to ignore British customers or British goods. And for governments in difficulties requiring London's support, an abolitionist gesture was as good as genuine co-operation. On the other hand, the English plan was bound to attract opposition from interests likely to be damaged by forcible suppression. States opposed it in the name of their national sovereignty, for the right of search and joint commissions presupposed a partial surrender of that sovereignty. They saw abolition as an aspect of the wicked machinations of the British in their bid for world hegemony, backed by the absolute superiority of the Royal Navy. They opposed it on the grounds of the damage that would be done to navies, colonies and national trading interests. Portugal, Spain, the USA and France used and distributed cotton, sugar, coffee and tobacco produced on slave plantations dependent on the import of Africans into Brazil, Cuba, the Southern States of the USA and the West Indies. Shipping agents were directly concerned: they also attracted investment, and provided employment for small local sectors of the economy that made a profit out of the trade.

Denmark, the Netherlands and Sweden, which still practised slavery in some of their smaller colonies, subscribed to reciprocal suppression.[4] In return for substantial indemnities, Spain and Portugal agreed to it in 1817. But Portugal reserved to herself the right to trade legally south of the Equator, and this only came to an end in 1842 under the threat of severe military sanctions from Britain. Spain strengthened her anti-slavery legislation and her agreements with London, but Cuba continued the trade until 1866, the year of the third abolition law in Spain. The Cortes, the Council of State and the Treasury all gave way before the threat of secession

4. S. E. Green-Pedersen, 1976; E. Ekman, 1976; P. C. Emmer, 1976.

by the island's planters.[5] A conditional promise by the British of *de jure* recognition for Brazil induced the new empire to conclude the 1826 suppression treaty; but even so the Brazilian trade increased until 1850. It stopped in the following year; but this was not simply because the Royal Navy violated Brazil's territorial waters to clear them of slave ships. Coffee depended on the British market, the *fazendeiros* were bankrupting themselves to pay their debts to the slave-dealers, and the white inhabitants were worried about an increase in the black population.[6]

Politically stronger states reacted differently to British pressure. France, eager for prestige, maintained its freedom of action by a pretence at legislation and by naval suppression patrols which remained innocuous in home waters for as long as they did on the coast. Between 1815 and 1830 the French illicit trade fitted out 729 slaving expeditions for the west and east coasts of Africa. But when it became clear that such operations no longer benefited French ports either financially or socially, the government signed a reciprocal search agreement. Another reason was that the monarchy that emerged after the 1830 revolution felt it desirable to gain Britain's goodwill.[7] This volte-face by the French resulted in several small countries acceding to the 1831–3 agreements. Britain took the opportunity to renew its attempts to internationalize the issue, and extended its naval suppression to cover the whole of the Atlantic and Indian oceans. An 'equipment' clause in the treaties allowed the seizure of ships obviously equipped for the slave traffic, even though not carrying human cargoes. But the slave ships of the USA remained exempt. For forty years American diplomacy managed to evade any serious commitment. In 1820 the trade was legally equated with piracy; in 1842 came the compromise of 'checking the flag', which protected the Americans from British suppressive action; and 80-gun suppression squadrons served to safeguard national pride whilst at the same time remaining mere formalities. In the 1840s the Southern planters called for the legal reopening of the trade, and meanwhile took to breeding slaves for the home market on special ranches.[8] During the Civil War the Lincoln administration committed itself to the right of search, which had been in abeyance since 1820. The American trade then stopped.

Thus for half a century the proliferation and accumulation of documents testify mainly to the emptiness of the undertakings entered into. Throughout all this avalanche of words, Africa and the Africans were hardly ever mentioned, just as though they did not exist. Shipping agents benefited from the illicit trade, making bigger profits than during the period of legally protected trade,[9] while the slave plantations stockpiled manpower.

5. A. F. Corwin, 1967.
6. L. Bethell, 1970, chs 11 and 12.
7. S. Daget, 1983.
8. E. D. Genovese, 1968, pp. 131–2.
9. P. E. Leveen, 1971, p. 27, Table 3. Also R. Anstey, 1976, personal communication.

The planters resisted abolition for different reasons. Impervious to the doctrines put about by abolitionist bodies, they considered only racial stereotypes and assumptions: abolition would not help 'the brutish race of slaves to improve its lot'.[10] The social prestige attaching to the ownership of slaves and the demographic habits brought about by the absence of white immigration helped to prolong the system. Above all, the planters' opposition was reinforced by the contradiction between the growing demand in the West for the products of slave labour and the prohibition on the import of the labour regarded as essential for increasing the supply of these products. Exports of Brazilian coffee grew tenfold between 1817 and 1835, and tripled again by 1850. Exports of Cuban sugar quadrupled between 1830 and 1864.[11] In 1846 Britain's free-trade measures, by standardizing import duties on sugar for the British market, seemingly subsidized the produce of the slave estates. Historians differ as to the effects of this innovation in producing a recrudescence of the slave trade.[12] But in Cuba, where the trade was on the decline, imports of new slaves in the decade 1851–60 were 67 per cent higher than in 1821–30. During the five years that the standardization of import duties continued in Britain, imports of slaves into Brazil increased by 84 per cent compared with the previous five years, 1841–5.[13] It paid the American plantation owner to import fresh manpower so long as its purchase price was below $600 a head. This remained true until 1860.[14]

The process of suppression

It was not only on the West African coast that warships operated. At the London conference in 1816, French proposals for measures to be taken against the so-called 'Barbary' slave-traders were rejected as an attempt to divert attention from the need for urgency in taking repressive military action in the Atlantic. But in 1823 France enacted an order prohibiting her ships from transporting slaves across the Mediterranean. This step was taken in a political context of little relevance to the slave-trade issue in itself: the war with Spain, the liberation of the Greeks, support for Muḥammad 'Alī's Egypt – in short, as part of an attempt to gain supremacy over the whole of the landlocked Mediterranean, which was under way even before France decided on direct intervention in Algeria. For the time being,

10. Quoted in S. Daget, 1973.

11. L. Bethell, 1970, p. 73, note 4 and p. 284; F. W. Knight, 1970, p. 44.

12. F. W. Knight, 1970, p. 55 does not believe the measure made any difference. For a contrary view, see P. E. Leveen, 1971, pp. 78–80; H. Temperley, 1972, p. 164; D. R. Murray, 1971, p. 146.

13. D. R. Murray, 1971, pp. 141–7. Cf. H. S. Klein, 1976, pp. 67–89; L. Bethell, 1970, Appendix pp. 388–95.

14. P. E. Leveen, 1971, pp. 10, 72 and ff.; F. W. Knight, 1970, p. 29; cf. A. F. Corwin, 1967, pp. 135–44.

Britain seemed to have lost the lead. However, the activities of the warships produced no visible results. Military efforts at suppression were more effective in some parts of the Indian Ocean, especially between Mauritius, Madagascar and Réunion where British ships succeeded in capturing French slave ships. It also seems that some British ships from Mauritius had mounted slaving expeditions to Madagascar where Tamatave was under the control of the chieftain Jean-René. In the event of the 'international' seizure of a ship, the matter was settled by returning the ship after confiscating the African slaves on board. When a national vessel made the seizure, the slave ship was brought to court for adjudication, but that does not mean that the slaves on board were freed. Usually, they simply disappeared – that is to say, they were dispersed on the plantations – for the customs authorities had long turned a blind eye to such activities.

The French captured a number of their own slave ships in American waters, and brought them to court at Guadeloupe and Martinique. On instructions from Paris, which was obsessed with the idea of colonizing Guyana, the confiscated slaves were escorted to Cayenne. When suppression was called for under bilateral treaties, it was the slave ships and not the slave-traders on whom sentence was pronounced by the Mixed Commissions. The effectiveness of the commissions on the American side of the Atlantic depended on the attitude prevailing in the slave plantations. In Cuba, out of 714 slave ships captured between 1819 and 1845, the Hispano–British Commission condemned only 45. When bounties for ships seized were awarded to the sailors of the Spanish local squadron, fifty vessels were arrested during the last ten years of the trade. The results achieved by the commissions in Surinam and Brazil were no better.[15] Only one out of every five slave-trading vessels was captured in American waters, despite the fact that around 1840 nearly seventy warships of different nationalities were assigned to suppression duties there.

On the West African coast the numbers were smaller. The Dutch, Portuguese and American naval squadrons operated spasmodically; the American squadron was often under the command of Southerners, and it was based on Cape Verde, a long way from the centre of the traffic. Such were the conditions at the time of the founding of Liberia and, so far as the fleeting appearance of cruisers was concerned, they remained so until 1842. The treaty with the British stipulated the presence of four or five warships, but that remained purely theoretical. Between 1839 and 1859 two American slave ships were seized with their cargoes. In 1860 there were seven arrests, the slaves from which helped to populate Liberia.

Two naval squadrons – those of Britain and France – were in continuous operation. France set up its squadron in 1818, and it remained independent

15. D.R. Murray, 1971, *passim*; P.C. Emmer, 1976, pp. 245–51; L. Bethell, 1970, pp. 200–13.

until 1831. Based on Gorée, which had ceased since 1823–4 to be a distribution centre for the slave trade, between three and seven warships would set out to search for slave ships, but they took no suppressive action for the first four years of operation. This was because there was uncertainty as to the government's real intentions. London accused the French of deserting their principles and their duty. French abolitionists accused the Navy Ministry of collusion with slave-owning interests. In 1825 the Ministry reacted by offering a bounty of 100 francs a head for confiscated slaves. Some thirty slave ships were seized at sea and taken to court, bringing the number of those on which sentence was passed to the hundred mark. In theory this should have saved some thousands of Africans from slavery in the Americas but, in the event, when they were not shipped to Cayenne, Senegal took them as 'enlisted' labourers for public works in the colony. The agreements of 1831–3 were bedevilled by national pride and rivalry between the parties.[16] The French Navy tried to increase the number of its anti-slave-trade cruisers comparable to that of the Royal Navy. By 1838 the number of French ships had risen from three to six, and in 1843–4 there were fourteen on each side. In 1845, as an indirect consequence of Anglo-American agreement, the Anglo-French treaties were amended and the number of ships assigned to suppression duties was fixed at twenty-six for each party. From then on, counting the five men-of-war of the American squadron and the six Portuguese ships off the Congo, a real naval task force seemed to be mobilized against the trade. In 1849 France waived certain obligations that it was unable to fulfil. For seven years the Second Empire promoted the 'free enlistment' of African manpower. This was a slave trade in disguise, such as some British and Dutch men practised on their own account. The French naval squadron had done no suppression to speak of; but it had shown the French flag along the coast, which was perhaps its main object.

The British Admiralty shouldered the job of humanitarian policing, but without enthusiasm. Its material resources increased from three warships to twenty-six; but they were ill-adapted for this specialized task. They drew too much water to sail up the rivers, and had to put off long-boats, which were vulnerable to attack from the slave-trading stations and boats lying in wait for them. They were so slow that they were outstripped at sea by the light brigs, and later by the Americans' clippers. For want of steamships, the colonial administration of Sierra Leone started by buying a few of the condemned ships, assigning them to suppression duties on account of their sea-going qualities. The squadron was based and victualled in the Sierra Leone and at the Gold Coast forts, and its leave station was Ascension Island. Offers to Spain to buy Fernando Po, in order the better to carry out suppression in the Bight of Biafra, came to nothing.

16. S. Daget, 1981, *passim*.

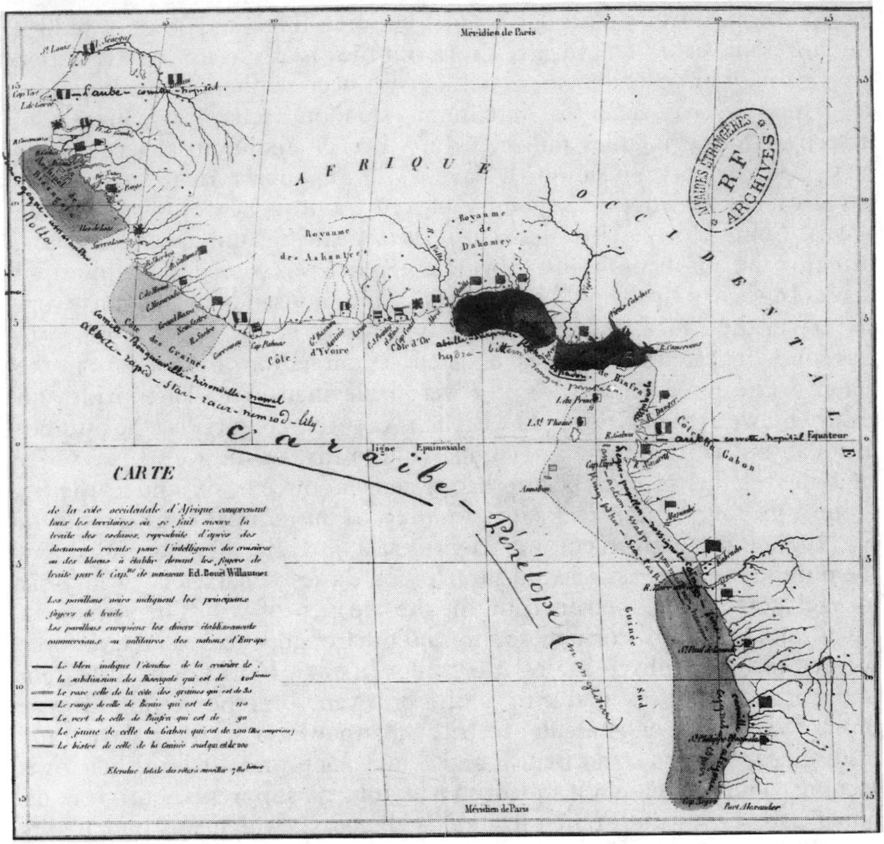

FIG. 4.1 *Map of the west coast of Africa including all the territories where the slave trade is still carried on, reproduced from recent documents for the information of patrols and blockades to be mounted off slaving centres by Captain E. Bouët Willaumez* (*Source*: Mémoires et documents Afrique 30, *p. 415*)

Effective suppression depended on the human factor. The British sailors, indoctrinated from London, were for abolition heart and soul. They also had a power complex, which on occasion led the Royal Navy to disobey Admiralty orders in the name of humanity and treat international maritime law with contempt. The navy illegally searched and seized French and American vessels in advance of the bilateral treaties, thus setting in train a chain of protests and diplomatic reparations. The offering of a capture bounty, initially at a very high figure, led to accusations that British sailors were more interested in the reward for seizing a ship than in the condition of the Africans packed tight on board. There was in fact high mortality among the slaves between the seizure of a ship and their being freed at Sierra Leone, St Helena or Mauritius. Deaths also occurred among the seamen, either from sickness or in the course of their duties: there were some murderous fights between cruisers and slave ships.[17]

The slave ships took shrewd advantage of the confusion that prevailed in the international field so far as suppression was concerned. On the coast their intelligence about the movements of cruisers was good, and they managed to evade them perhaps four times out of five. They behaved like pirates, flying false flags and using forged ships' papers bought in the West Indies. Notwithstanding the law, they often escaped punishment. Once the suppression treaties were strengthened they threw off their disguise: French papers were no protection after 1831, nor Portuguese after 1842. But the maintenance of American sovereignty effectively protected slave-trading under the US flag until 1862.

The reaction to these subterfuges was an increase in violence. Cruiser captains and local governors of Western settlements spontaneously resorted to a particular type of armed action. They mounted overland punitive expeditions,[18] especially where African political power seemed to be unorganized. In Liberia the Governor, the Reverend Jehudi Ashmun, moved against the trading stations at Cape Mount. Near Sierra Leone, in 1825, a campaign by Governor Turner cleared the islands and the peninsula for a time; and above all it brought a long strip of the coast under permanent British tutelage. These were commando operations, and they were repeated against the Gallinas and then at Sherbro and Rio Pongos. South of the Equator, slave ships in the 'Portuguese' waters off Cabinda and Ambriz were systematically shelled. The expeditions were rounded off by setting fire to the barracoons and the African brokers' villages, which were very quickly rebuilt a short distance away. The impounded slaves were freed and sent to Sierra Leone, the Gambia or Mauritius, for the sake of the bounties. Some of them settled down. Many joined the black colonial forces. Others were offered employment as freely enlisted workers in the West Indies.[19]

On the ground that they had eradicated the evil 'by the roots',[20] in France and Britain these operations were regarded as decisive. They introduced two new techniques: the signing of 'treaties' with local rulers on the coast, who undertook to put down the slave trade in the territories under their control (these treaties were in some cases imposed and their terms dictated rather than negotiated); and, secondly, suppression by means of a standing blockade of the main export centres, which was the beginning of a policy of diplomacy by armed intervention. The decade 1841–50 was crucial for the west coast of Africa, which until then remained the home base of the slave trade.

17. C. Lloyd, 1949, passim; S. Daget, 1975.
18. C. Lloyd, 1949, pp. 93–100.
19. C. Fyfe, 1962; J. U. J. Asiegbu, 1969.
20. C. Lloyd, 1949; P. J. Staudenraus, 1961; C. Fyfe, 1962.

It was also an important decade for the trans-Saharan slave trade. In spite of the efforts of the abolitionist Consul Warrington, Britain was largely indifferent to the trade towards North Africa. In theory, all the participants in the trade, with the exception of Morocco, were under the control of the Turks of Constantinople. In practice, however, the provinces had long considered the suzerainty of the Ḳāramānlī to be of little consequence and tended to act independently. The French military conquest of the Regency of Algiers in 1830 turned into colonization from 1842 onwards, and the white settlers had little desire to employ slave labour. Caught between French and British pressures, the neighbouring Regency of Tunis abolished the trade between 1840 and 1842. Further east, the Regency of Tripoli had more obstacles to overcome because it had to obtain the consent of chieftains in the hinterland, some of whom were powerful middlemen in the trade in slaves from Borno or Sokoto. In 1842, Shaykh ʿAbd al-Djalil, who dominated the Fezzān from his stronghold at Murzuk, did agree to the abolition of the trade, but he was murdered. Turkey had re-established direct rule over Tripoli and Cyrenaica in 1835 and it was thenceforth clear that the effective abolition of the trade depended on the Turkish attitude towards it. The Sultan of Constantinople banned the trade in 1857, but it was not really interrupted anywhere, not even in Egypt, in spite of the growing Western influence. In 1870, the German traveller Georg Schweinfurth, who had arrived from 'the heart of Africa', wondered what kind of assistance abolition of the trade was likely to receive from the Khedive.[21] Morocco was a case apart. It was the only country in the Maghrib regarded by the Europeans as a power to be reckoned with, and diplomatic initiatives and humanitarian coaxings were unavailing there until 1887. At a time when the Atlantic slave trade was beginning to show signs of waning, the trans-Saharan trade could still rely on secure routes for the export and distribution of slaves. They ran, on one hand, to Morocco, which was importing from 3500 to 4000 black Africans a year in the middle of the nineteenth century and 500 a year as late as the 1880s,[22] and, on the other, to the Red Sea and the Middle East, which we shall consider in more detail later. The West had no means of suppressing the trans-Saharan slave trade, which was entirely in the hands of Africans, because it did not extend beyond the boundaries of Africa.

Abolitionists argued that without buyers of slaves there would be no sellers. Supporters of slavery reversed the order of the terms, arguing that without a supply of slaves from Africa there would be no demand for them in the West: their consciences were clear, in the light of the tacit complicity of Africa itself.

21. G. Schweinfurth, 1873, ch. IX; A. A. Boahen, 1964; J. L. Miège, 1961–3, Vol. 3; F. Renault, 1980.

22. J. L. Miège, 1961–3, Vol 3; F. Renault, 1980.

African reactions

Between 1787 and 1807, i.e. in the period immediately preceding abolition by the West, more than a million Africans were transported to the Americas. To this figure must be added about 15 per cent who died during the Atlantic passage, and an unknown number of deaths caused by the journey to the coast and during local slave-producing operations by African 'fishers of men'.[23]

Abolition certainly did not immediately disrupt the vitality of the export market on the coast. Indecisiveness by the abolitionists left Portugal and Brazil to carry on the illicit trade south of the Equator at their leisure, and exportation was sometimes as high as in the eighteenth century. Though seriously combated after 1842, the trade did not die out on the Loango Coast until the end of the century.[24] North of the Equator, extension of the abolition order to the European settlements brought about the closure of traditional trading centres in Senegambia, Sierra Leone, Liberia and the Gold Coast. But the political authority of the settlements was weak, and abolition was not really effective beyond their boundaries. Sometimes Western slave-traders continued to operate in the vicinity. Gradually they disappeared, the production and distribution of exportable manpower was in the hands of Africans.

On the borders of Sierra Leone the configuration was an advantage to busy English, Spanish and mulatto-owned slave factories at Rio Nuñez and Rio Pongos in the north-west and on the Gallinas river in the south-east. The production areas, though sometimes 400–500 km distant, were mostly near the coast. Transactions were personal between local chiefs, caravaneers, brokers and agents. In Dahomey, on the other hand, the slave trade was one of the mainstays of the ruling house, which delegated the running of it to its chief vassals. In 1818 King Gezo, who was in debt to the Brazilian mulatto Francisco Felix Da Souza, appointed Da Souza as *chacha*, a 'white-man's chief' who acted as an economic adviser and administrator of the Whydah trade. This office survived the death of the first *chacha* in 1849 and was inherited by Da Souza's son. It was management on a grand scale: the *chacha*s kept a stock of Western goods, offset bookkeeping debits and credits, prepared cargoes in advance to facilitate speedy loading, collected taxes, checked the movements of white foreigners, and provided entertainment for their customers. This economic apparatus was capable of being adapted to other types of produce. Produce for the slave trade, which was in the hands of the chiefs, was secured by annual military expeditions, not always victorious, against the neighbouring countries, principally the Yoruba. It also came from the Central Sudan – whence captives were distributed, moreover, to the north and to Egypt – by

23. R. Thomas and R. Bean, 1974.
24. G. Dupré and A. Massala, 1975, p. 1468.

caravans, which split up their loads at the border: the blacks earmarked for export, who were strong, were kept aside and incorporated in the ordinary porterage teams.[25] Further east, from Badagry to the borders of the kingdom of Benin, prolonged strife among the Yoruba people glutted the Whydah market. Local rulers and the black and white slave-traders of the lagoons supplied the heavy demand from the Portuguese and Brazilians, who made the best part of their fortune out of it before turning their hands to other kinds of trade.[26]

East of Cape Formosa, among the rivers of the Niger delta from the Nun to Old Calabar, the slave trade was still run by the remarkable machinery that came into play in the last third of the eighteenth century, though this was already being applied to other types of trade that were carried on simultaneously. Local priests and dignitaries, the Arochukwu oracle, the 'Canoe Houses' and the Ekpe society, ran a market which accounted for half the slave trade north of the Equator: about 200 000 individuals. Produce came in from Sokoto, Benue, Nupe, north-western Cameroon and the inner delta area, procured by the traditional methods: warring, kidnapping, in settlement of debts, payment of protection tribute, community purges, straightforward purchase on the market, and straightforward gift. It was taken via chains of dealers, or the usual supply channels, to the distribution points.[27] There again, transactions were governed by well-tried procedures. The price per slave had been fixed in advance in the local money of account, the copper bar, equivalent to a specific quantity of goods – the same as in earlier periods. In 1825 and 1829 men and women were worth 67 bars, and the price went down as low as 45 or 50. In terms of the value of the landed cargo, the price per slave was 33 Spanish dollars, of which 8–10 per cent went to the distributors by way of commission. At Duke Town, Duke Ephraim's city in Old Calabar, the heads of other more or less rival houses, Egbo Eyo, Tom Honesty and Ogan Henshaw, helped to make up cargoes with slaves or foodstuffs. Forty thousand yams cost 2000 bars, the price of forty slaves. Around 1830 the biggest share of the trade was reputedly carried on at Bonny.[28]

Estimates of the volume of the slave trade during the sixty years of the abolitionist period can only be in terms of orders of magnitude. From 1807 to 1867, between Senegal and Mozambique, 4000 European and American ships carried out perhaps 5000 slaving expeditions, representing a displacement of 1 000 000 metric tonnes. Goods to the value of roughly sixty million piastres or dollars were bartered for a total of 1 900 000 Africans actually put on board at the export points. Of these, most probably 80 per

25. C. Coquery-Vidrovitch, 1971, pp. 109–11; P. Manning, 1979; M. Adamu, 1979.
26. P. Verger, 1968, chs 11, 12.
27. K.O. Dike, 1956; P. Curtin, 1969, esp. pp. 254–5; M. Adamu, 1979.
28. S. Daget, 1983, see, *inter alia*, the ships *Le Charles*, 1825 and *Le Jules*, 1829.

cent were loaded south of the Equator.[29] Between the beginning of the century and the 1880s, the trans-Saharan trade and the Arab trade exported 1 200 000 and 800 000[30] black Africans respectively, individuals who had been captured in the vast belt stretching from the Bambara country in the west to southern Mozambique.

Cliometricians, sociologists and historians agree that the slave trade was a complete catastrophe for Africa. Their learned observation endorses the popular view. But the proposition needs explanation. Humanitarianism is a Western ideology, and it is unlikely to have found any place in the minds of African distributors of the time – with very rare exceptions. But this does not mean that they were constitutionally incapable of giving up the trade, as Western supporters of slavery maintained. The continuance of the supply of exportable manpower from Africa can be logically explained in economic terms. That the distributors were black and the exporters white is irrelevant: it was a paying proposition, profitable to both trading partners, whose sole object was to make money. That was the situation at the grass roots. The continuance of the supply is to be explained in terms of the efficient working of an integrated system: and what Africans were resisting was the disruption of this system. For one thing, it would have ruined the established business of the distributors,[31] who had no other prospects, to say nothing of the chain of repercussions it would have set off on the social and political structure, both locally and further afield. In other words, so long as the barter system between the hinterland and the coast, and the coast's foreign trade, had no clear alternative to the slave trade, opposition by African slave-traders to its suppression was dictated strictly by the imperative needs to avoid commercial chaos.[32] The supposed complicity of the African distributors was no more than a reflex reaction to the immediate economic situation. This also explains the fall in the selling price of exportable manpower: it was the market's defence against growing pressure from the forces of suppression. The latter thus helped to contribute to an unsatisfactory situation. This argument needs to be modified when the exportation of Africans to the north or east is considered. While the economic interests of the slave hunters and distributors are self-evident in this case too, it is hard to see what kind of economic compensation accrued to the countries that were plundered. Certain individuals with strong personalities were able to consolidate their power, men like Tippu Tip, for instance, or Rabeh. But any benefits that may have been conferred on the regions under their control still have to be identified by specialists.

29. P. D. Curtin, 1969, Tables 76, 77.
30. R. A. Austen, Tables 2.8, 2.9.
31. G. N. Uzoigwe, 1973, p. 201.
32. G. N. Uzoigwe, 1973; B. O. Oloruntimehin, 1972, p. 40, says 'a real crisis of adjustment'.

Sierra Leone and Liberia

One cliometrician has indicated that suppression saved 657 000 people from slavery in America.[33] Another specialist considers this figure to be far too high and has reduced it to 40 000 for the period from 1821 to 1843.[34] Estimates of the number of slave ships captured by the anti-slavery squadrons are not much more precise. It may reasonably be put at somewhere between 1000 and 1200 men-of-war, about a quarter of the probable total of the number of expeditions carried out in the illegal trade.[35] The courts of the British Vice-Admiralty, the French courts, the American squadrons and, above all, the Mixed Commissions (which, having served their purpose, were disbanded between 1867 and 1870) freed about 160 000 Africans.

Being known to all as slaves, i.e. chattels, their freeing did not happen of its own accord: it required a decision by the naval or colonial authorities, or by the commissions, to relieve them of their slave status. Several thousand freed slaves, severed from their roots, led a precarious and threatened existence in the very heart of the Brazilian and Cuban slave plantations, posing the problem of their social and economic integration.[36] A few hundred acquired a dubious status in the French settlements in Guyana, Senegal and Gabon. Others acquired a genuine political existence, as in Liberia and Sierra Leone. At Freetown, the 94 329 men, women and children registered on the books of the Liberated African Department[37] provided the first original, positive indications as to how the various questions arising in connection with the suppression of the slave trade could be answered.

In 1808 the British Crown took over Sierra Leone, with the object of partly redeeming the failure of the philanthropic settlement founded twenty years earlier on the three principles of the anti-slavery movement, Christianity, civilization and trade. In three waves of voluntary settlement, 2089 former slaves and fugitives from England, Nova Scotia and Jamaica had colonized the north-east of the peninsula. These foreigners got on badly with their African neighbours. The French, in addition, ravaged their plantations. Some of the settlers intrigued for personal power. The climate and the unhealthy surroundings took a heavy toll of the settlers. Worst of all, the Company entrusted with the administration declared itself unable to keep its promises in regard to landownership rights. By 1802 the pioneer stock had been reduced to 1406. The colony was saved by the humanitarian, abolitionist function which was given to it in 1808. By 1811 the population

33. P. E. Leveen, 1971, p. 75.
34. D. Eltis, 1977.
35. C. Lloyd, 1949, Appendix A; S. Daget, 1983, *passim*.
36. A. F. Corwin, 1967, p. 166; F. W. Knight, 1970, p. 29; L. Bethell, 1970, pp. 380–3.
37. R. Meyer-Heiselberg, 1967, *passim*; J. U. J. Asiegbu, 1969, Appendix VII.

had risen to 4000. After twenty years of official existence as a colony there were 21 000 Africans living in the mountain villages and at Freetown. By 1850 the town had 16 950 inhabitants and the interior nearly 40 000. There were eighty-nine whites. By that time new arrivals were finding themselves among the third generation of free citizens of a largely self-governing state.

The first generation had coped with the problems of creating a viable new society from scratch. Between 1816 and 1823 the impetus came from the Governor, Sir Charles MacCarthy, an administrator and builder with the soul of a missionary. The continual growth of the population, and its eagerness to put down roots, made improvement of the amenities imperative. As the seat of the colonial government and the naval Vice-Admiralty, the victualling base for the naval patrol, and the official liberation centre for the Mixed Commissions, Freetown and the interior could count on a more or less regular injection of subsidies. MacCarthy improved the early villages and built new ones, where new arrivals were adopted and settled down among brothers. Vague European notions of model communities contrasted with African values, ways of life and traditional activities. Land and property in the town appreciated in value, and craft industries and trade opened the way to personal prosperity. Around 1828 enterprising individuals secured the entrée to the coast's new type of economy. In 1831 the colony was opened to foreign trade. The standard of British governors and the level of British subsidies fell. The Sierra Leoneans were to take charge of their own affairs, subject to remaining within the colonial framework. Throughout this teething period Western influence, including that of the missionaries, was crucial.

The British upper and ruling classes financed the churches and the smaller denominations, whose personnel had had no training whatsoever in anti-slavery or missionary work. Sierra Leone became their training ground. In addition to spreading Christianity and civilization the missions had to fight the slave trade, especially at Rio Pongos. But local slave-traders suspected these people of spying for the colonial government: they set fire to buildings of the Church Missionary Society who abandoned the field. In the colony itself, where political authority was conscious of its humanitarian mission, the missionaries were not unconscious of politics. MacCarthy put them in charge of the villages of freed slaves. In the civil administration, despite acute personal and doctrinal rivalries, the co-operation of powerful personalities with the government achieved sound long-term results. Schools were opened, and scores of different ethnic groups rubbed shoulders in them, through the intermediary of English, from which a national language developed. Though religious syncretism was not achieved, at any rate Christianity, traditional African religions and Islam co-existed at close quarters.

The second generation solved the problems of growth. Liberated Africans began to occupy high positions, first in competition with and then alongside the old founding stock. Initially there was neither perfect harmony nor complete integration between the two groups: the earlier inhabitants tried to maintain a class distinction. During the peak twenty years of slave-trade suppression, the situation was further complicated by the arrival of 2000 people a year. Despite gaps caused by mortality, not all of them could be assimilated. Some of them were recruited into the British army. One in every ten emigrated to the Gambia under compulsion. An official emigration scheme to the West Indies was set up, in theory offering freedom of decision and guaranteeing repatriation. But the planned nature of the scheme was too reminiscent of the horrors of the past. The liberated Africans preferred the hardships of the bush or the security of the traditional villages. On the other hand, with the help of the missionaries several thousand returned to their original areas, mainly the Yoruba country, where they told of their experiences and the skills they had acquired.

From the economic point of view, a spectacular 'boom' could not be expected. By 1827, however, an embryonic development process had started. The main emphasis was laid, at first, on the production of food, and especially of rice, but efforts were also directed towards the cultivation of export crops and the exploitation of local natural resources: in the first category there were sugar, ginger and indigo, and in the second there were coffee and exotic timber. An indigenous variety of coffee had been discovered in the early days of the settlement and was cultivated systematically. In 1835, this was beginning to provide an economic argument for allocating more funds for putting an end to the peripheral Rio Nuñez or Gallinas slave trade: in just eighteen months, a trading house in London had received almost 65 000 kg of coffee, which confirmed the need to protect the people engaged in growing and marketing the crop. Sierra Leonean companies established for the purpose of exporting timber, especially a variety of teak, were beginning to prosper. Here again, the main interest lay in the creation of a reliable economic substitute for the slave trade: in 1824 fifty Western ships loaded 200 000 dollars' worth of timber in the Sierra Leone estuary.[38] Favourable conditions combined to create a certain amount of wealth (it can hardly be described as capital) within the colony. Its ships began to ply the waters along the West African coast as far as the Bight of Biafra. Foreign ships were thenceforth able to put in safely to ports in the estuary for the purpose of the legitimate trade so earnestly desired by the abolitionists. However, the significance of this 'take-off' should not be exaggerated: it simply showed that the experiment was viable, with a minimum of administrative support from the European metropolis.

All things considered, the British government's action in 1853 in making the Sierra Leoneans subjects of the Crown represented implicit recognition of the fact that a heterogeneous medley of cultures had been welded

38. Public Records at Fourah Bay College, Freetown, and British Parliamentary Papers, Correspondence returns, West Africa, 1812–74, pp. 135–46; C. Fyfe, 1962, see 'timber'.

together into a viable Creole society. A 'civilized' nation had been created not according to some Utopian European model but by the strength of its own genius.[39] The part that was obviously played by the British anti-slavery movement left intact the character of an African solution.

The experience of Liberia was only slightly different. In law, the settlement established by the American Colonization Society at Cape Mesurado in 1821 was a piece of private enterprise. The federal government of the USA had no hand in it; but it did set up a temporary office there without any governmental functions, whose staff became members of the society. It handed over to the settlement the Africans freed by the naval patrol, thus helping to populate the country. The creation of Liberia was the result of philanthropic and civilizing aspirations, but also of a desire to mitigate the expansion of the black population in the USA, which was regarded as dangerous.

A mere handful of settlers defended their settlement against opposition from the local chiefs. The latter disputed that they had given up either their lands or their sovereignty, and also the black foreigners' aim of cutting down the main overseas commercial activity carried on in the area, namely the slave trade. The Reverend Jehudi Ashmun stood up to this opposition with 450 settlers, 200 of whom were liberated Africans. This defensive action proved the saving of the settlement; and in 1824 it was given the name of Liberia, with Monrovia as its main centre. A political charter was drawn up in the USA and administered by the local governor according to his own interpretation of it. When ships arrived, whether American or not, Ashmun set them to trading legally in ivory, timber, skins and oil in return for traditional Western goods. This trade is said to have begun to show a profit in 1826, but this is doubtful. By 1830, in addition to 260 liberated Africans, the settlement comprised 1160 settlers, mostly slaves from the Southern plantations manumitted by their owners for propaganda or pioneering reasons. There were few free-born American blacks: they were to arrive later. The Colonization Society's American policy was ambivalent: to Northerners it stressed the evangelical advantages of repatriation, while to Southerners it held out the glowing prospect that in getting rid of blacks they were purifying their own society.

The factors that made for the success of Liberia were of three kinds. In the first place, other colonization societies grew out of the original one and founded three more settlements, at Bassa Cove, Sinoe and Cape Palmas: the last, named Maryland, being incorporated in the country's territory only in 1856. There was self-government in the sense that the American societies were subordinated to the settlements and not the other way round. The inhabitants showed courage in an environment that was hostile both ecologically and politically. The land was not very fertile, and had been

39. C. Fyfe, 1962; J. Peterson, 1969, *passim*; J. U. J. Asiegbu, 1969; J. F. A. Ajayi, 1965, ch. 2; S. Jakobsson, 1972.

worked by archaic methods. There was no business and no capital, and free men's labour was expensive. But there were engineers who knew how to build in concrete. The settlements on the coast drove out the slave-traders and stopped the trade. The aim of philanthropists and colonizers was achieved. The second factor was the personal qualities of the people in charge. Their background was Anglican and English-speaking; they were well fitted for the life they had chosen, but they were realists; and they planted the seeds of a new nation. The constitution that Thomas Buchanan brought from the USA in 1839 was remodelled to suit the specific case of Liberia. John B. Russwurm, the Governor of Maryland from 1836 to 1851, brought into being a land which racialism could not reach. J. J. Roberts, Governor of Liberia from 1841 and then President from 1847 to 1856, showed himself to be a statesman. The scene was set for de facto independence.

It was a challenge by the British to the country's legal existence that led to *de jure* independence. British seamen and traders contested the attributes of sovereignty assumed by Monrovia, such as control of trade, taxation and a national flag. The dispute had arisen on the economic plane, but the reply came at international diplomatic level when the USA enlightened Britain about the nature of its relationship with the settlements: Liberia was not an American colony, although it had US support. It was Governor Roberts who persuaded the settlers to overcome their pusillanimity and demonstrate their political maturity. By a simple but peremptory declaration of independence, Liberia was enrolled among the sovereign powers on 26 July 1847, and the first African republic was born. Under the constitution establishing the legislature, executive and judiciary, nationality was open only to citizens of black race. Around 1860, 6000 of them were manumitted slaves, 5700 were slaves freed by the American naval patrol, 4500 had been born free in the USA, and 1000 had purchased their freedom. The republic had still to assert its authority on its own soil, fight the French system of 'free enlistment', defend its frontiers and enlarge its territory.[40] All that was still in the future.

As regards the period we are considering, it cannot be said that Liberia was as well developed economically as Sierra Leone. The French naval officer, Edouard Bouët-Willaumez, who was in command of the anti-slave-trade squadron, sailed along the Liberian coast on several occasions. He was struck by the poverty of the inhabitants.[41] This economic appraisal contrasted with the qualitative appraisal made during the same period by the American Horatio Bridge, according to whom Liberia deserved to be known as the 'black man's paradise'.[42] Each of these views is coloured, however, by the personality of the individual who expressed it: they are

40. P. J. Staudenraus, 1961; J. C. Nardin, 1965.
41. L. E. Bouët-Willaumez, 1845, ch. 4, pp. 90–2.
42. H. Bridge, 1845, ch. 20.

the views of white men imbued with the spreading of colonialist mentality. In terms of historical significance, it would probably be irrational and certainly anachronistic to present the experiments made in Sierra Leone and Liberia in the nineteenth century as precursors of the independence movements of the twentieth century. But the birth of the idea that new African nations could be created on a coast ravaged by 250 years of unbridled slave-trading and the materialization of that idea, were prodigious events in themselves.

While it pointed the way ahead, the experience of Sierra Leone and Liberia fell short of satisfying the new generations of abolitionists. The anti-slavery movement was divided as to the methods and priorities to be adopted for the purpose of dismantling American slavery and the African slave trade. The failure of a philanthropic settlement on the Niger, sponsored by T. F. Buxton in 1841, brought criticism of the lack of success of abolition and a denunciation of the total failure of suppression. However, these rearguard critics were fighting an uphill battle, for despite official reluctance, the idea of colonization societies was gaining ground in private circles. Above all, the coast north of the Equator was wide open to innovations.

Protecting new trade

The naval squadrons were less concerned about suppression than about their task of protecting the 'legitimate' trade of their own nationals. From the first decades of the nineteenth century the coast met American, British and French demand for African natural products, and these purchases increased. In 1838, Bouët-Willaumez, later Governor of Senegal and the forerunner of colonization, ordered a systematic survey to be carried out of the possibilities for trade between Senegal and Gabon. Although it gave poor returns, trade other than in slaves developed in parallel and not in competition with the slave trade. The competition was between the Western nations, and they eventually arrived at an informal apportionment of spheres of economic interest to which African rulers did not object. France was predominant north of Sierra Leone and at some points on the Ivory Coast and in Gabon, where she set up Libreville in imitation of Freetown.[43] Americans and Europeans came to the coast and were tolerated in what was in effect a British economic enclave. Change was in the air. The industrial and technological revolutions in Britain and France were ushering in the modern age, and it was also on the way in other countries. It created new needs, the most important of which, from the coast's point of view, was for oils, as lubricants for machinery and the raw material of soap

43. B. Schnapper, 1961; H. Brunschwig, 1963, esp. ch. 7; H. Deschamps, 1965; E. M'Bokolo, 1981.

and lamp fuel. The products of African oil-bearing plants thus established themselves in Western markets.

The coast had always exported palm oil, but in minute quantities. Imports into Britain rose from 982 metric tonnes in 1814 to 21 000 tonnes in 1844, levelled off for ten years or so, and then doubled by 1870. France imported an average of 4000 tonnes a year between 1847 and 1856 and 2000 tons in the following decade. She compensated by importing an average of 8000 tonnes of groundnuts a year from Senegal and the Gambia plus 25 000 tonnes of 'tulucoona' nuts for the manufacture of household soap; these imports were worth 35 million gold francs in 1870. Something that had long been an abstract Utopian ideal – an alternative to the slave trade, a substitute for trade in men – had at last materialized. It remained to develop production on an industrial scale; and this took no longer than it had taken the Cuban and Brazilian plantations to reach full production of sugar and coffee. The main producing areas corresponded to the best slave-exporting areas, from Dahomey[44] to the rivers of the Niger delta and Cameroon. One of the essential features of the changeover was that manpower was mobilized on land that had been internally colonized. This admittedly meant that production was by means of a form of slavery, but within an African social and economic context. In fact the energetic development of this economic novelty did not immediately disrupt the traditional economy: slave trade and oil trade co-existed side by side. A more extensive system of barter began to radiate into the interior. On the coast the same agents for the Western trade still kept their grip on the market: they understood purchasing, gave credit, circulated traditional currencies, and introduced metal coinage. The increase in the number of people competing for trade upset the internal balance and led to a realignment of forces.[45] These economic changes were accelerated by religious and cultural factors causing distortions, which were never very far removed from politics, which helped, however, to put an end to the trade.

A small number of men and women from the Protestant and Roman Catholic missions became important agents of Western influence. In Senegal, an apostolic prefecture still managing to survive after the French reoccupation of 1817, Mother Javouhey defined the first task of the apostolate as the training of an African clergy. The education given to the children of Christians and some non-Christian Africans could not stand up against the Ḳu'rān schools. Islam grew in stature as the century progressed.

In 1844 Mgr. Bessieux, who had had experience in Liberia, set up the Saint-Cœur de Marie mission in Gabon. Calling the local beliefs 'absurd inventions', he strove to convert and baptize, but did little in the way of teaching, being more concerned with conversions than with the converted. Success went to the American Mission under the Reverend Wilson. At

44. C. Coquery-Vidrovitch, 1971.
45. K.O. Dike, 1956; K.K. Nair, 1972, ch. 2.

Dakar, in the Lebu Republic, personal friendships and respect for the local culture – the result of instructions to be 'Negroes among Negroes'[46] did not make up for the mission's rather feeble otherworldliness, which tended to cut it off from reality. With no practical solutions to offer, the missionary realized that he could avail little against a highly Africanized and keenly propagated Islam. He set about training an elite, even if it meant alienating its members from their own culture and cutting them off from their roots. At Grand Bassam the African ruler refused to admit the mission. At Whydah the apostolic vicariate entrusted to the African missions of Lyons was set up in 1868. Its first school opened its doors in 1873, as did the one at Porto-Novo, which was already under French tutelage.

Buxton's ideas were fermenting among the Protestant missions, and with the success of Sierra Leone and the liberated Africans they gained able apologists in the field. Some of these were professionals like Samuel Ajayi Crowther, who was enslaved at 15, liberated, and became a pastor, bishop and nation-builder. Others were engaged in legitimate trade. Most were emigrants returning to their areas of origin, where they helped the missions and prepared the ground for them. The missionaries themselves settled on the littoral between the Gold Coast and Cameroon, except in the kingdom of Benin and found themselves among peoples that were devoutly religious but faced with political 'crises of adjustment'. They arrived at Badagry in 1842, at Whydah in 1843 and at Calabar in 1846. Their bridgehead in the interior was the large town of Abẹokuta, in the new Ẹgba country.

Unlike the Roman Catholic ones, the Protestant missions sought temporal influence. They conceived of the Christianity they were propagating as a whole that included education, culture, class affiliation and political choice. They spread arithmetic and spoken and written English among people who had long been self-taught. Specialists came from Sierra Leone to teach architecture, printing and medicine. Learning belonged to the people who attended the missions, and the advantages that came from taking part made them into a privileged class. But they conformed to a pattern already familiar to the local chiefs, not all of whom approved. Some, however, paraded a superficial Westernization in their dress, their homes, their food and drink and their way of life. The missions' purpose was to create a middle class in order to cream off an elite, which would then be trained on Western lines, and would secure and expand the two-way flow of trade to and from the coast. The spread of civilization would be an incidental by-product which the palm-oil trade, limited to coastal transactions, could not achieve on its own.[47]

Thus the Protestant missions, very much of this world, took on the role of reformers, which included interfering in political and military strategy. The Abẹokuta missionaries suggested to England the making of a road to

46. Quoted by P. Brasseur, 1975a, p. 264, note 22; 1975b.
47. J. F. A. Ajayi, 1969; K. K. Nair, 1972.

the sea, in order to speed up the barter trade – and the delivery of war material. They invoked the technical help of British troops against Dahomey. At Calabar their influence in the city-states secured by agreement the ending of local customs that they considered objectionable. From their position of strength, the missions did not object to the rival intrusion of Western administrations, but counterbalanced it by siding with or against the established trade. Around 1850 the missions, together with the traders and the political administration, became involved in an irreversible process leading to an early form of colonial rule. The appointment of consuls with expansionist views went hand in hand with armed blockades and the establishment of protectorates. The excuse given by international diplomacy was always that such actions were aimed at the radical and final suppression of the slave trade. Humanitarian methods had become the instruments of economic, military and political power.

Conclusion

At this point, we can attempt to establish a kind of chronology of the decline in the slave trade, bearing in mind that it was nowhere completely extinguished in this period.

The trade had ended in 1824 in Senegal and Gorée, the headquarters of the French anti-slave-trade naval station. The influence and progress of Sierra Leone began to have a beneficial effect in that region around 1830, but sporadic operations continued in the Rio Pongos and Rio Nuñez areas until 1866–7. Between 1848 and 1850 independent Liberia sought the assistance of French warships against the international slave ships and refused to continue provisioning the slaving system, which was disguised as a 'free enlistment' system. The Ivory Coast and the Gold Coast had remained relatively unscathed by the illegal trade throughout the abolitionist period: Ivory Coast researchers have shown that although some slaving activities persisted, they were not intended to supply the ships plying the coast but to meet regional or inter-regional domestic demand and there is evidence for this view in records preserved in the archives. Further east, from Whydah to Lagos, the situation was more confused. Slave-trade transactions or 'free enlistment' operations were still taking place in the years 1853–5 and went on even until 1860. In some cases, the Africans were embarked on very large-capacity steamships; the *Nordaqui*, for instance, carried an unprecedented cargo of 1600 slaves. Nevertheless, the convergent diplomatic efforts and the coercive policies of France and Britain eventually succeeded in curbing the slave trade. Between Benin and Gabon a widely applied policy of concluding treaties and promoting land occupation projects had the effect of severely impeding the traffic in slaves. The Anglo-Portuguese treaty of 1842, which at last enforced the right to search slave ships south of the Equator, had similar effects in the area stretching from the Congo as far as the Portuguese colony of Angola.

PLATE 4.1 *A group of Oromo women on board HMS* Daphne *in 1867 after being liberated from an East African slave-trading dhow*

PLATE 4.2 *Released slaves on the Universities' Mission estate at Mbweni near Zanzibar – paying wages*

It was only gradually, however, at different speeds in different sections of the coast, that the trade declined until it died out almost entirely between 1860 and 1870.

In 1867, the French admiral, Fleuriot de Langle stated after a voyage of inspection that he was favourably impressed by what he saw 'apart from a few exceptions'. His report serves, however, to underline the serious problem raised by the revival of slave-trading on the East coast of Africa. During the period 1860–70, between 30 000 and 35 000 slaves arrived in the ports controlled by Zanzibar: some were kept on the spot to work in the clove plantations. The remainder were sent as far as Somaliland and Oman; around 1870 Oman was importing 13 000 slaves a year, some of whom travelled on to the Persian Gulf and Persia, Mesopotamia or Baluchistan and India.[48] In 1873, a treaty between Britain and the Sultan of Zanzibar introduced the right of search, including the authorization to seize Arab dhows, but it did not have much impact, just as the Anglo-Portuguese treaty of 1842 had had little effect on the Mozambique slave trade to the Comoro Islands and Madagascar. As François Renault says, the slave trade really disappeared from these endless coastlines and vast tracts of land only with the advent of the colonial administrations,[49] considerably later, therefore, than the termination of the Atlantic trade. This delay can probably be explained by the fact that the Western abolitionists had not been made fully aware of the effects of the Arab trade until David Livingstone discovered them in the course of his explorations. Allowance must also be made for the time it took, after that point, to rouse the conscience of the West.

Thus in contrast to the arguments put forward on national and individual grounds by Western supporters of slavery, the abolitionist doctrine introduced the notions of treating African slaves as men and of opening Africa to the world. Around 1870 it achieved its aims: apart from rare exceptions, the Atlantic slave trade was at an end. This outcome was not the unilateral achievement of the West, which for a long time dragged its feet and even now was still not altogether convinced that the means expended in the cause of universal morality would pay off. In a way, an equal effort was made by the Africans of the hinterland and the coast. In difficult domestic circumstances, they managed at one and the same time to resist economic disintegration and to adjust rapidly to innovation. The African reaction to the abolitionist hypothesis showed tremendous adaptability and speed. For the time being, this was as important a factor in achieving abolition as were Western decisions. As for the new approach by the West, it stemmed from the white man's inability to conceive of the existence of values other than his own. His interest in African civilization was that of a scientist in a laboratory specimen. After a century of the battle for abolition, the con-

48. F. Renault, and Daget, S. 1980; R. Coupland, 1939.
49. F. Renault, and Daget, S. 1980, pp. 43–69.

science of the West was clear: and hence it felt free to impose its own values, by force if need be. Not everything was on the debit side. Changes did occur, and cracks appeared in the structure, so that it often crumbled away or was torn down, leaving clear the way ahead.

5 The Mfecane and the rise of new African states

L. D. NGCONGCO

We are already familiar with how iron-working and iron-using societies of Bantu-speaking migrants who also kept cattle and grew crops established themselves in several parts of Southern Africa south of the Limpopo from about the middle to the later centuries of the first Christian millennium.[1] On entering the region south of the Limpopo the Sotho–Tswana branch of the southern Bantu tended to keep to the plateau west of the Lebombo–Drakensberg line of mountain ranges, while the Nguni-speaking groups migrated into the narrow corridor between these mountain ranges and the Indian Ocean.

For some ten to fifteen centuries before the end of the nineteenth century, these Bantu-speaking communities had developed in this region south of the Limpopo a flourishing Iron Age civilization characterized by a congeries of small states under the political control of established royal lineages and dynasties. Generally speaking these states were peopled by iron-smelting and iron-using farmers, who also produced crops – chiefly sorghum and millets – and engaged in some hunting as well as bartering and long-distance trade.[2]

The first decades of the nineteenth century witnessed the eruption of a tremendous social and political revolution that tore apart as well as rebuilt the prevailing state system in Bantu-speaking Southern Africa and beyond, as well as transforming the nature and the quality of the lives of many communities from as far afield as the vicinity of Zululand in Natal up to southern Tanzania. This revolution, referred to as the Mfecane (crushing) in Nguni languages, is also known as Difaqane (hammering) in Sotho–Tswana.

During the Mfecane, old states were defeated, conquered and annexed to others. Some states were uprooted from their traditional localities and forced to re-establish themselves in new areas. Many were weakened and impoverished in the process. In some cases traditional ruling dynasties were supplanted, while in other instances whole village populations were annihilated or taken into captivity. Yet this same revolution saw the rise

1. D. W. Phillipson, 1969; R. R. Inskeep, 1969, pp. 31–9.
2. M. Wilson, 1969a; R. J. Mason, 1973; L. Ngcongco, 1982, pp. 23–9.

of large-scale centralized kingdoms in several parts of Southern Africa. It also gave rise to new 'empires' and kingdoms served by new bureaucracies and military organizations.[3]

The Mfecane resulted in the depopulation of substantial parts of Southern Africa, and thereby facilitated the subsequent dispossession of African land by white migrant settler communities. Not only did these Boer farmers establish themselves on the choicest portion of African land, they also embarked immediately on systematic campaigns of spoliation of African herds and the enslavement of Africans under the device euphemistically referred to as 'apprenticeship'.

Within the African states themselves the Mfecane had a profound impact. It taxed the ingenuity of African political leaders and forced them to adapt their military tactics as well as their skills in political organization and statecraft. In some ways the Mfecane appears undoubtedly to have been a cataclysmic event with negative results; but looked at differently it can be viewed as a development of a positive and creative nature that took generations to unfold. Some of the states it gave rise to have survived to the present and form part of today's international community of nations. Taking into account the overall scope of the Mfecane's wide-ranging span of activities, the variety of kingdoms and diversity of peoples whose destinies were touched by the ebb and flow of its sweeping drama, and the fundamental character and the quality of the changes wrought within the fabric of most of these polities, one must conclude that the Mfecane has until recently been the most neglected subject in Southern African historiography, and agree with J. D. Omer-Cooper that it 'positively dwarfs the Great Trek'.[4]

This chapter is concerned with the nature of the revolution that started among the northern Nguni and was made famous by the military activities and socio-political transformations engineered by the Zulu king, Shaka, and continued in one way or another by some of his former generals or contemporaries over a wide terrain in Southern and even East Africa. In order to understand fully what lay behind this great revolution, it is essential to take a close look at the physical environment of the northern Nguni region and understand the adaptation of societies to changes in their physical environment as well as see how their own activities helped shape the environment in which they lived and to which they responded. At the same time it is important to note how rulers of some Nguni states contrived to control both production and reproduction processes in order to ensure the surplus labour on which depended the strength of the king and the independence of the state.

3. T.R.H. Davenport, 1978, p. 56; D. Denoon, 1973, pp. 23–4, 32–3; J.D. Omer-Cooper, 1966, ch. 12.

4. J.D. Omer-Cooper, 1966, p. 4.

The country and farming practices of the northern Nguni

Centuries of settlement and farming by the communities of the northern Nguni area led to considerable adaptation by these farmers to the physical environment in their area of settlement.

The land of the northern Nguni or proto-Zulu can for convenience's sake be designated as the area lying south of the Phongolo (Pongolo) and north of the Thukela (Tugela) rivers and roughly bounded by the valley of the Mzinyathi (Buffalo) in the west.[5] It is a region of high relief into which several rivers have cut deep valleys. The major river systems of the area are the Thukela, Mhlatuze, Mfolozi, Mkuze and Phongolo. These, together with their tributaries, cut deep into the surrounding high-lying ground. Between these major rivers the ground often rises to a height of about 1000 m above the river valleys themselves.[6] These river valleys extend westwards deep into the interior of the country.

As a result of this high relief the region experiences a considerable variation of rainfall and temperature over relatively short distances. Likewise the vegetation varies considerably, creating 'a number of different vegetation types interlacing through the country'.[7] The entry into the region and settlement of crop-producing and stock-raising farmers of necessity brought human interference with the natural vegetation of the area.

In a work focusing on the effects of human settlement on the physical environment in all of Southern Africa, the ecologist J. P. H. Acocks maintains that the vegetation of most of the area between the Drakensberg and the Indian Ocean was probably 'forest and scrub-forest', while low-lying valleys contained tracts of savanna.[8] From the earliest times of their settlement in the region, proto-Zulu Nguni farmers using slash-and-burn methods devastated, and in the process substantially changed, the natural patterns of the vegetation. Over one and a half centuries the fire, iron hoe and axe of the Nguni farmer had driven the forest back to the crests of the high ridges, and bush had been confined to the wettest slopes along the watercourses.[9] Through these methods farmers increased the area of the savanna-type vegetation to their own advantage.

Guy argues that where the scrub-forest had been removed it had given place to grasses spreading from the depth of the river valleys, with the wooded elements being reduced by regular burning, a process that favoured the grass understorey.[10] Centuries-long manipulation of the vegetation eventually resulted in a complex pattern of vegetation changes that

5. J. Guy, 1980.
6. ibid.
7. ibid.
8. J. P. H. Acocks, 1953.
9. J. Guy, 1977.
10. ibid., p. 4.

produced an interlacing of 'sourveld' and 'sweetveld' grazing, determined largely by the amount of rainfall as well as the topography of the area.[11]

In the higher-rainfall areas, the grass tends to be of the sourveld variety. This is a variety whose nutritive value and palatability is at its highest soon after the first spring rains and in the early months of the summer season. But the food value and palatability of sourveld grass decreases as it matures. Sourveld, therefore, tends to provide grazing for roughly four months of the year before it begins to lose both its food value and palatability. Sweetveld, on the other hand, tends to be rather more characteristic of the drier parts of the country, where it is usually found in association with scattered trees in savanna vegetation types of which it generally forms the understorey. Although sparse and easily damaged, sweetveld grass retains its palatability and food value throughout the dry season. Sweetveld is therefore particularly important as winter grazing. Between these two extremes of sweet and sourveld grazing can be found transitional belts of mixed veld capable of supporting grazing for some six to eight months in the year.[12]

While other parts of Southern Africa such as the areas occupied by the Sotho–Tswana communities of what is now the Transvaal highveld did also have considerable tracts of sweetveld coverage, such areas nevertheless lacked the river system of the northern Nguni area, which ensured that the low rainfall parts of the region had the paradoxical feature of being dry, but well-watered.[13] Also, on the highveld tracts of sweetveld, pasturage often occurred in association with tsetse fly, which causes sleeping sickness in man and animals alike.

Further the pre-colonial farmers of the highveld did not have the advantage of similar patterns of interlacing tracts of sweet and sourveld such as characterized the rangelands of the northern Nguni region. The settlement patterns of the Sotho–Tswana with their separate villages, arable lands and cattle posts may be said to have reflected a form of spatial organization suited to the availability of much more vast and open country by comparison with that of the northern Nguni. Sotho–Tswana societies, while cattle-keeping and crop-cultivating, did not appear to have been exposed to the pressure of dense settlement that ultimately came to face the leaders of the larger states in the region of the northern Nguni. Their close settlement (as opposed to the scattered settlement of the Nguni) had more to do with aggregation of whole communities near the few and sparse water sources than with pressure of population density.

For as long as there was a careful balance maintained between the growth of both human and cattle populations on the one hand, and access to the various types of grazing on the other, there appeared to be no serious threat

11. ibid.
12. J. Guy, 1980, p. 7.
13. ibid.

to the stability of the region. But towards the latter part of the eighteenth century a limit seems to have been reached to the capacity of human action to expand resources of land for cultivation and grazing. Population increase, influenced somewhat by the adoption of maize as one of the principal crops in the region, seems to have placed an enormous strain on the customary access to land and related resources.[14]

Although the narrow corridor between the Drakensberg Mountains and the Indian Ocean always imposed definite physical limits to the expansion potential of communities living in that area, the northern Nguni chiefdoms did enjoy a number of advantages peculiar to the region. For generations, in fact centuries, they had enjoyed the advantages of a beneficent physical environment which they had learnt to exploit skilfully. In the spring and early summer, Nguni herders could drive their herds to graze on the upland sourveld pastures, and from the middle of the summer season they would move their stock down to the sweet grasses at the bottom of the river valleys. Climatic variations had also made it possible for these farmers to select the environment most suitable for the cultivation of either sorghum, millet or maize. As we now know maize was introduced in that region some time in the eighteenth century and it quickly replaced other traditional food crops as the staple diet. In an area of very good rainfall this substitution of maize as the basic food item may have given a boost to population and thereby increased pressure on the land. This could have contributed to increasing restlessness and violence as the numerous small states in the region began struggling and competing seriously for dwindling resources.

These changing conditions in the area of the northern Nguni may have been exacerbated by a severe famine known as Madlathule, whose eruption is estimated to have occurred somewhere between the last decade of the eighteenth and the first decade of the nineteenth century.[15] *Inter alia* this terrible famine is said to have been characterized by roving bands of starving people who pounced on food stores. While the chronology of the Madlathule famine is uncertain, it is significant that it is thought to have occurred close to another famine in the land of the Basotho that is said to have resulted in widespread cannibalism.

The structure of northern Nguni society

That Zulu modes of farming and production resulted in a steady increase of the population in that region can no longer be doubted. There is hardly any evidence suggesting that population increase might have been due to large-scale migration into the region. The increase must therefore have been a result of natural growth unrelieved by any increase in land and other important resources. As communities found it increasingly difficult

14. S. Marks, 1967a; M. Gluckman, 1963, p. 166.
15. J. Guy, 1980, pp. 9, 15; A. T. Bryant, 1929, pp. 63–88.

to engage in time-worn practices of shifting their stock from one pasture to another or to convert more scrub-forest into savanna, some embarked on forceful appropriation of land and pasture previously claimed by others.

Some of the rulers of these small states had begun to adopt strategies designed to control production as well as reproduction. In order to understand this process, one has to take a close look at the structure of Nguni society in the pre-colonial period. The society was divided into thousands of commoner homesteads each under a patrilineal head. Generally speaking the head of each homestead had two to three wives, depending on his rank in society. Each of the wives and her children lived in her own house. Each wife and her children produced food for their own subsistence needs. Usually there was division of labour according to sex: the males handled cattle production and engaged in hunting, while the females were mainly responsible for crop production.

The royal homesteads, of which there might be several in each state, were organized differently. In addition to the normal production activities performed by the members of each house, including their relatives and retainers, the various royal homesteads also developed, especially from the late eighteenth century onwards, into military barracks. Male regiments recruited from the different parts of the country lived at these barracks and there performed services for the king, including crop production. Members of female regiments were not stationed at these military villages but remained in the homesteads of their own fathers. Until the king gave permission for them to do so, neither male nor female members of the regiments could marry. They could stay as long as ten years in a regiment before being released to marry. Apart from other things, this practice of the kings of the northern Nguni states controlled both the rate of production and reproduction.

It is not clear when this development started among the northern Nguni. It has now become usual to associate the start of such changes with the rule of Dingiswayo of the Mthethwa, and their perfection with the rule of Shaka of the Zulu.[16] For centuries before the advent of these changes it had been more common among the Sotho–Tswana than among the Nguni to handle initiation as a group and political affair. That this very significant change may have been linked to important changes in Nguni socio-economic life appears likely. It is also possible that when the larger states began to expand, they incorporated pockets of Sotho communities whose form of organization of initiation may have been adopted by the northern Nguni rulers for purposes of political control.

A careful consideration of both the ecological factors and the nature of social organization and production in the country of the northern Nguni suggests strongly that, from the last quarter of the eighteenth century to

16. S. Marks, 1967b, p. 532, for the view that the state-construction process began earlier among the Hlubi, Ngwane and Nolwande.

the first decades of the nineteenth century, population explosion had intensified a struggle for dwindling resources that had been building up over several generations. The population explosion factor was first articulated by Max Gluckman and has since been supported by several other writers.[17] It now appears indisputable that the growth of population and its accompanying feature of land shortage must have contributed significantly to the violence that was generated in the northern Nguni region during the early nineteenth century.

Other explanations have been put forward for the revolution known as the Mfecane or Difaqane. While some of these explanations have struck the critical reader as fairly tenable or even plausible, others have sounded quite wild and patently fanciful. According to one view, for example, the internal reorganization and military reforms that laid the foundations for the large nation-states such as the Mthethwa and Zulu, were due to the founders imitating Europeans. Dingiswayo in particular was said to have consciously emulated Europeans he had observed during his wanderings before he became ruler.[18] It is hardly necessary to pay any more attention to this blatantly racist opinion than simply to endorse the strictures of one critic who described such ideas as attempts by their propagators to 'derive reflected glory from Zulu achievement', and went on to assert that such claims cannot be substantiated on any evidence whatsoever.[19] It has further been pointed out that there is hardly any similarity between the states organized by Dingiswayo and Shaka and the contemporary European polities of the region.

The gradual but purposeful eastward thrust of the eighteenth-century Boer immigrant farmer (*trekboer*) from the western part of the Cape and the resultant barrier it placed before the opposite advance of southern Nguni pastoralists has been suggested as another factor to explain the origins of the Mfecane. It has been argued that this eighteenth-century migration of Boer pastoralists created pressure of land shortage by blocking the path for the natural expansion of the southern Nguni pastoralists and thereby created a crisis further back among the northern Nguni.[20] While the factor of population pressure among the Nguni in general is without doubt an important one, and therefore tends to be quite persuasive, its linking to the eastward *trekboer* migration from the Cape Colony leaves unanswered the question why the social revolution sparked off by such

17. M. Gluckman, 1963, p. 166; J. D. Omer-Cooper, 1966, chs 1 and 2.

18. Henry Flynn in a paper written in about 1939 first aired the questionable notion that Dingiswayo's innovations were probably due to his association with white people, especially one Dr Cowan (see J. Bird (ed.), 1888, Vol. 1, pp. 62–3). Later A. J. Bryant, 1929, p. 94, underlined this baseless speculation in a manner suggestive of the now thoroughly discredited 'Hamitic hypothesis'. These writers set the tone for a whole line of uncritical followers who subsequently repeated the false tradition as an established fact.

19. D. Denoon, 1973, p. 19.

20. R. Oliver and J. D. Fage, 1962, p. 163.

population pressure did not break out among the southern Nguni or Xhosa states immediately blocked by the *trekboers*. Posed in this form, the population pressure argument raises a further problem. It faces us with the need to demonstrate convincingly that until the *trekboers* migrated up to the Great Fish river towards the middle of the eighteenth century, overcrowding among the northern Nguni, that is those living north of the Thukela river, could or often was alleviated by displaced groups hiving off from that area and migrating southward through the settled communities of Xhosa-speaking Nguni in search of *lebensraum*, and settling among them or in lands further south. In this respect, it appears that the physical barrier presented by the Drakensberg may in fact have proven less of an obstacle than the mass of densely settled Xhosa-speaking communities living south of present-day Natal.[21]

An interesting and important explanation is related to a desire by the large states of the northern Nguni areas to control trade, mainly in ivory, with the Portuguese-controlled port of Delagoa Bay on the east coast. This hypothesis was first advanced by Monica Wilson and has received support from Allan Smith.[22] Well before the end of the eighteenth century, states like those of the Hlubi Ndwandwe and Ngwane had been participating in trade with the Portuguese, mainly through Tsonga middlemen. On his accession to the Mthethwa throne, Dingiswayo did open up an ivory trade route with Delagoa Bay, conquering in the process several clans to open up his access to the Indian Ocean port.[23] Dingiswayo's efforts appear to have been matched by those of Zwide and Sobhuza, who also attempted to expand along the Phongolo river in order to establish a foothold on the trade with Delagoa Bay.[24] Although some scholars have raised doubts about the importance of the trade factor as an incentive for transformation of small states into large states, the matter is still very much in debate.

It is, however, difficult to take very seriously explanations based on the characters or personal qualities of the leaders of the revolution. It is more instructive to attempt to understand why leaders like Dingiswayo, Shaka and Mzilikazi and others like them rose and flourished at the same time and around the same general area. This line of enquiry might help us to avoid the danger of mythologizing the role of some principal actors in this great human drama and more reasonably perceive them as products of a particular socio-economic environment.

Towards the end of the eighteenth century, therefore, and especially during the early years of the nineteenth century, a combination of factors centring largely on increasing shortage of land as a result of increased population brought about unrest that later erupted in violence in most of

21. J. D. Omer-Cooper, 1966, p. 169.
22. M. Wilson, 1958, p. 172; A. Smith, 1969.
23. A. T. Bryant, 1929, p. 97; A. Smith, 1969, pp. 182–3.
24. A. T. Bryant, 1929; A. Smith, 1969, p. 185.

the northern Nguni states. Very crucial and revolutionary changes in the social and cultural fabric of whole societies there had been gradually taking place. Disturbed conditions in the war-infested region compelled one state after another to modify or abandon time-honoured practices like cattle-herding on a loan basis and traditional ceremonies such as initiation along with circumcision, where it was felt that continued adherence to them would hinder appropriate and efficient responses to the exigencies of a rapidly changing situation. For instance, male initiation, which included circumcision and seclusion for long periods of up to six months, could at critical moments keep out of commission hundreds of youths who might be required for military service. Consequently, changes and adaptations to social customs and traditional practices led to innovations in military techniques and to modernization in military organization. Among the great innovators and modernizers of this period were Zwide of the Ndwandwe, Dingiswayo of the Mthethwa and Shaka of the Zulu.[25]

In the series of wars that these numerous Nguni states engaged in, the forced migrations consequent upon them or the conquests, annexations and incorporations resulting from them, three powerful groups emerged dominant in the region. The first were the Ngwane–Dlamini (who later became the Swazi) under Sobhuza, living on the Phongolo river. Between the Phongolo river, the Mfolozi river and the Indian Ocean lived the second powerful group, namely the Ndwandwe confederacy under King Zwide. To their west were smaller chiefdoms such as the Khumalo. To the south of this group lay the third powerful group, the Mthethwa confederacy ruled by Dingiswayo. They occupied roughly the triangle between the Indian Ocean, the lower Mfolozi and Mhlathuze rivers.[26]

The rulers of these three large states were, in essence, paramount kings exacting tribute from a congeries of smaller states, chieftaincies and clans. Generally, the subordinate states enjoyed considerable autonomy in matters of day-to-day living, while recognizing the suzerain control of the paramount authority in such important issues as 'first fruits' rituals, initiation ceremonies, payment of tribute and the waging of war.

The first round in the struggle for supremacy involved Sobhuza's Ngwane-Dlamini and Zwide's Ndwandwe who were vying for control of the fertile Phongolo valley maize lands. The Ndwandwe state, which came into prominence before the middle decades of the eighteenth century, had originally been part of a large cluster of Embo-Nguni chiefdoms that had been migrating southwards from the Thembe kingdom in the hinterland of Delagoa Bay towards the latter part of the seventeenth century. Together with other offshoots of Embo-Nguni, such as the Ngwane, Dlamini and Hlubi, they finally settled in the valley of the Phongolo, at a time when they were ruled by either Langa II or his predecessor Xaba. The Ndwandwe

25. J. D. Omer-Cooper, 1966, p. 27; J. Bird, 1888, Vol. 1.
26. A. T. Bryant, 1929, p. 160.

built their main settlement on the ema-Gudu foothills overlooking the southern Phongolo valley. It was here in their new home that the Ndwandwe rulers embarked on a policy of gradually extending their political control through the subjugation of several smaller chiefdoms found in the neighbourhood. These small states included some Ngwane and Ntungwa communities in the Phongolo valley as well as a collection of Khumalo clans under Mashobane. Here also, as their state flourished and prospered, they took the appellation of Ndwandwe, in order to distinguish themselves from other Embo-Nguni, some of whom had settled on the northern bank of the Phongolo and others to the west of the Ndwandwe chiefdom.[27]

The political authority of the Ndwandwe rulers increased enormously as they brought one small state after another under their suzerainty. Under the rulers Langa II and his son Zwide, the borders of the state extended to both sides of the Phongolo river in the north and southwards as far as the valley of the Black Mfolozi; and from near the Ngome forest in the west towards St Lucia Bay in the Indian Ocean.[28] The Ndwandwe rulers were thus the first Nguni rulers to bring about the type of transformation that created a large state from the numerous petty chiefdoms of the region. Through the skilful exploitation of old customs and practices and the organization of these to serve new purposes, coupled with the ruthless use of military force where necessary, the Ndwandwe rulers succeeded in building up a powerful confederacy around the Usuthu–Phongolo confluence, collecting tribute from many smaller Nguni chiefdoms in the region.

Zwide succeeded to the Ndwandwe throne around 1790 and reached the peak of his rule about the same time as Dingiswayo of the neighbouring and rival Mthethwa confederacy.[29] The greater share of building the powerful Ndwandwe confederacy had fallen on his shoulders. But it is important to recognize that he built upon foundations laid by his father and grandfather, and that in doing so he exploited institutions, customs and practices already in vogue in much of the region even among the Sotho–Tswana west of the Drakensberg.

Like several other Nguni states in the region, the Ndwandwe kingdom depended a great deal on the deployment of military regiments recruited through the traditional initiation of males and females of approximately the same age group. For males the age-set initiation was accompanied by circumcision. Indications are that Zwide and his predecessors may have been among the first Nguni rulers to perceive some political significance in the 'Sotho–Tswana' practice of co-ordinating and controlling circumcision and related initiation rites on a community or chiefdom-wide

27. ibid., pp. 158–61.
28. ibid, p. 160.
29. ibid.

rather than an individual family basis. Thereafter it was easy to extend the principle. While subject chiefs could continue to rule their own people, they could no longer organize and preside over initiation ceremonies of their own as in the past. These ceremonies were henceforth to be organized from the centre, and youths from all parts of the Ndwandwe-ruled communities would be made members of national age-regiments.[30] This of course would in future facilitate deployment of such age-regiments in military activities.

Apart from the use of age-regiments to weld together the different parts of their 'national' state, the Ndwandwe rulers appear also to have relied on the extensive use of magico-religious influence in order to enhance their own authority and to help create the mystique of an all-powerful and invincible monarch. In addition to the more traditional annual 'first fruits' ceremonies, Zwide, in particular, deployed the services of an impressive array of medicine men and royal magicians, news of whom helped to spread the fear of Zwide's power throughout many of the surrounding chiefdoms. Zwide also used diplomatic marriages to build or temper his relationship with some of the states of the region. Thus, he gave his sister Ntombazana as a bride to the Mthethwa ruler, Dingiswayo. Similar considerations may have induced him ultimately to agree to one of his daughters, Thandile, marrying Sobhuza of the Ngwane (Swazi), among which people she became popularly known as Lazidze, the daughter of Zwide.

That Zwide had no intention of allowing such diplomatic marriages to stand in the way of his expansionist policy became evident when Sobhuza revived his claim to the use of fertile arable lands in the Phongolo valley. Zwide responded by attacking Sobhuza's capital on the southern border of Swaziland.[31] After several contests the Ndwandwe army emerged victorious, expelling Sobhuza's followers from the Phongolo valley and driving them in a northerly direction. There, among the mountains of what is now Swaziland, Sobhuza (also known as Somhlolo) laid the foundations of the Swazi nation.

The Swazi

The nuclear Ngwane group comprised an aggregation of clans of Embo-Nguni as well as pockets of Ntungwa-Nguni stock plus some Tsonga clans under the leadership of Dlamini royal lineages. It was these clans, welded together as the first stratum of Ngwane society in the Shiselweni district, that became known as *bemdzabuko* or true Swazi.[32] In the central part of what is present-day Swaziland Sobhuza brought under his political control several other clans found in the vicinity. These were mainly of Sotho

30. J. D. Omer-Cooper, 1966.
31. J. S. M. Matsebula, 1972, pp. 15–16; H. Kuper, 1947, p. 13; J. D. Omer-Cooper, 1966, pp. 29, 49; A. T. Bryant, 1964.
32. J. S. M. Matsebula, 1972; H. Kuper, 1947, p. 14.

(Pedi) stock but had intermingled with small pockets of Embo-Nguni and Ntungwa-Nguni communities. The Sotho communities that Sobhuza integrated into his own kingdom had a fairly well-developed age-regiment system. To distinguish these newer Swazi from those who migrated from the south they were generally referred to as *ema-khandzambili* (those found ahead).[33]

Even before they were expelled from the Phongolo valley, Sobhuza's people had, like those of Dingiswayo, adopted the age-set system. This rendered the integration of the new communities of central Swaziland with the rest of his subjects much easier than it would otherwise have been. Like the Sotho communities, the Swazi age-sets functioned as military regiments only in time of war. The youth of the conquered clans were incorporated into the Ngwane initiation system and made to fight in the same regiments alongside their conquerors,[34] while the chiefs of these Sotho communities were not destroyed but were, in fact, allowed a considerable degree of autonomy in local affairs. Although the Sotho clans at first occupied a somewhat inferior position in Ngwane society, as time progressed and as they demonstrated their loyalty to the state beyond doubt, they were accorded the same treatment as the Nguni members of the Swazi state.

Sobhuza did not only lighten the yoke of subjection on the conquered Sotho clans by allowing their chiefs much local autonomy as well as providing for considerable room for mobility of Sotho youths in the Swazi army; he also sought to consolidate his own position and ensure the safety of his new kingdom by maintaining amicable relations with his neighbours. Although Zwide had expelled him from his former domicile and pursued him into the modern Swaziland, Sobhuza kept friendly relations with the Ndwandwe and attempted to cement that friendship by marrying one of Zwide's daughters as his *nkosikati* (senior wife). To placate Shaka of the Zulu, Sobhuza sent a tribute of young girls to him, including princesses of the royal blood. Even though Shaka killed some of these women when they became pregnant, Sobhuza continued his policy of conciliation.[35] As a result, his kingdom enjoyed relative immunity from the depredations of Shaka's regiments.

Sobhuza died in 1840 and was succeeded by his son Mswazi (Mswati) after whom the Ngwane-Dlamini people became known as Swazi. Like his father before him, Mswati had to defend the new state against successive invasions from the south, apart from revolts from within. First, Mswati who was comparatively young at the death of his father had to contend with several attempts calculated to frustrate his attempt to rule. To start with, there was the rebellion of Fokoti, who mustered considerable support

33. ibid.
34. H. Kuper, 1947, pp. 15–17; H. Beemer, 1937.
35. J. D. Omer-Cooper, 1966, p. 50.

in southern Swaziland, but Mswati was saved by Malunge's rallying of royal regiments in his favour.

After Fokoti's rebellion, Mswati made efforts to strengthen his position, such as in greater centralization of the age-regiments, the creation of a more extensive network of royal villages and the reorganization of the *incwala* (first-fruits) ceremony in the direction of increased royal absolution. However, these reforms did not prevent another son of Sobhuza, the regent Malambule, from rebelling in 1846 shortly after Mswati had graduated through the circumcision rite. The rebellion implicated white missionaries as well as agents of Zulu imperialism. In the end Mswati was obliged to ally with Transvaal Boers in order to quell the danger of invasion by the Zulu forces of Mpande. The treaty that helped to deliver the Swazi from the jaws of the Zulu dragon was signed on 26 July 1846.[36]

A key figure in the defeat of the Malambule insurrection was another brother of Mswati, Somcuba (Somquba). The status he enjoyed as Sobhuza's first-born son was enhanced by the part he played in quelling the Malambule uprising as well as in negotiating the treaty of 1846 with the Boers of Ohrigstad. About 1849, however, Somcuba began his own rebellion against Mswati. This culminated in efforts to build a rival state through the 'amalgamation of Pai and Sotho clanlets in the Crocodile river region',[37] and Somcuba's usurpation of royal prerogatives by practising his own *incwala* ceremonies. By 1856 Mswati's campaigns against the rebel and the support of the Lydenburg Boers had resulted in the killing of Somcuba, a new treaty of cession with the Boers of Lydenburg,[38] and the restoration of normal conditions in the region.

Mswati's domestic policy was more successful than his foreign adventures. He embarked on a policy of diplomatic marriages with 'princesses' chosen from many of the ruling lineages of communities recently integrated into Swazi society. At the same time he bestowed Swazi royal brides on chieftains of the various clans and lineages. Swazi commoners were also quick to emulate Mswati's practices thus bringing about great changes through extensive intermarriage. The effect was to wipe out the ethnic divisions between the various elements of Swazi society.[39]

The Mthethwa

The expulsion of the Ngwane-Dlamini from the Phongolo valley left Zwide of the Ndwandwe and Dingiswayo of the Mthethwa to confront each other in the northern Nguni country. Zwide himself had become king of the Ndwandwe around 1790. He appears to have been responsible for building

36. J. S. M. Matsebula, 1972; A. T. Bryant, 1929, pp. 325–8; H. Kuper, 1947, pp. 19–20.

37. J. A. I. Agar-Hamilton, 1928, pp. 60–1; H. Kuper, 1947, p. 20.

38. H. Kuper, 1947; G. M. Theal, 1908–11, Vol. 4, p. 456.

39. H. Beemer, 1937.

a powerful Ndwandwe state based on the collection of tribute from subject polities, the use of an army based on age-regiments, the myth of a sacred kingship organized around the annual *incwala* first-fruits ceremonies and the control of trade routes with Delagoa Bay.

The Mthethwa kingdom had become famous under Dingiswayo, son of Jobe and grandson of Kayi (who may generally be regarded as founder of the Mthethwa kingdom).[40] Like the Ndwandwe, Ngwane, and later the Zulu states, the power of the Mthethwa was also built on tribute collecting, cattle-raiding and an army based on age-regiments. The Mthethwa also traded extensively with Delagoa Bay.

As has already been pointed out, the age-regiments were being deployed generally throughout the major Nguni states of the region and most of the Nguni states appear to have been influenced by Pedi and other Sotho groups in the vicinity.[41] But Dingiswayo seems to have brought his usual thoroughness and imagination to the reorganization of what was a fairly general practice in the area. He terminated the circumcision rite that used to accompany the formation of age-grades in order to do away with the period of seclusion necessitated by such rites. He adopted the chest-and-horns formation for his army. Dingiswayo also formed an alliance with the Maputo kingdom at Delagoa Bay. In subsequently conquering and incorporating the Qwabe state, Dingiswayo is said to have been assisted by soldiers armed with guns from his allied kingdom of Maputo, and not, as Fynn stated, a company of soldiers sent by the Portuguese.[42] Dingiswayo's Mthethwa kingdom collected tribute from more than thirty chiefdoms in the region, including a small chiefdom under Senzangakhona, namely the Zulu state. Subsequently Shaka, a son of Senzangakhona, became a general in Dingiswayo's army.

The Zulu

Mthethwa expansion under Dingiswayo had been checked by Zwide and his Ndwandwe regiments. Several wars had been fought by the rival armies. In 1818 Dingiswayo was captured by Zwide and killed. Because of the personal character of Dingiswayo's rule, his death created a vacuum in the leadership of the Mthethwa. Shaka, who had been rising fast in Dingiswayo's esteem (and had with his help become head of the small Zulu chiefdom) now quickly stepped into the breach. He replaced Dingiswayo as head of the Mthethwa confederacy of chiefdoms. He had, in effect, inherited the Mthethwa 'empire'. But in the same way that Bismarck was to ensure that Germany was absorbed into Prussia, Shaka 'incorporated' the Mthethwa empire into the Zulu state, thus making the Mthethwa part

40. T. Shepstone in J. Bird, 1888, Vol. 1, pp. 160–4; A. T. Bryant, 1929, p. 95.
41. J. D. Omer-Cooper, 1969, pp. 211–13.
42. A. Smith, 1969, p. 184.

of the Zulu nation. He did, however, allow the Mthethwa traditional system of government to continue under a minor son of Dingiswayo with a regent subservient to himself as the Zulu monarch.[43] In dealing with other groups, however, Shaka appears to have insisted on total incorporation rather than mere suzerainty.

Even while he was only head of the Zulu state and subservient to Dingiswayo, Shaka had already started reorganizing his army. This process of rationalizing social institutions for military purposes was now carried to a logical conclusion. Shaka also revolutionized the military techniques themselves. The long throwing spear was replaced by a short broad-bladed stabbing spear that was much more effective in close-up fighting after the enemy had lost the long throwing spear or javelin. Zulu fighting men now carried long shields, discarded sandals and went barefoot for greater speed and mobility. Like Dingiswayo before him, Shaka kept a permanent army of regiments drawn from men under 40 years of age. Unlike Dingiswayo, he kept these regiments in military barracks where they were maintained by the state and led a life of celibacy until they were discharged from military service. Because they were maintained in barracks, Shaka's regiments were well drilled and efficient and always ready for emergencies.[44]

Shaka's army was instructed in several military tactics of which the 'cow-horns' formation was only the most spectacular. The army was trained to be hardy and ruthless in dealing with the enemy. Unlike Sobhuza or Dingiswayo, Shaka often wiped out the ruling elites of the conquered peoples and sought total incorporation of captured groups into the Zulu system with members of the Zulu royal family replacing the original rulers. Sometimes the chiefs of the larger groups were recognized by being allowed a free hand in the local control of their own peoples.

It was while Shaka was involved in the critical wars for the domination of what later became Zululand that he developed and perfected some of the techniques and tactics referred to above. This drive to bring all groups in the region of northern Nguni under his own control brought Shaka into direct conflict with Zwide's Ndwandwe, whom he defeated in two successive battles in 1819 and 1820.[45]

Shaka's defeat of the Ndwandwe army at Mhlatuze meant not only a disastrous military defeat for Zwide himself but also a collapse of the Ndwandwe state, a loose confederacy that had been built up through systematic subordination of small states in the Mkuze and Phongolo valleys. Fragments of the Ndwandwe state under the leadership of Zwide's erstwhile generals fled panic-stricken northwards into what is now Mozambique. The leaders of these splinter groups were Soshangane, Zwangendaba

43. A. T. Bryant, 1929, pp. 158–67, 202–3; E. A. Ritter, 1955, pp. 113–16.
44. J. D. Omer-Cooper, 1966, pp. 35–7.
45. L. Thompson, 1969a, p. 344; E. A. Ritter, 1955, pp. 129–49.

and Nqaba. The bulk of the Ndwandwe, now effectively subjugated, remained under Sikunyane as a tributary state of the Zulu sovereign.[46]

The Gaza

Soshangane was the first of Zwide's generals to break away, taking with him a small following. He established himself in Tsonga country not far from Delagoa Bay where he seems to have had little difficulty in defeating and placing under his rule several small groups like the Manyika, the Ndau and Chopi, whom he incorporated among his own followers. In Mozambique, Soshangane's followers were generally referred to as Shangana after himself. There he began building his own kingdom, which he called Gaza. His regiments were sent on expeditions in all directions, capturing young men and women, cattle and grain. The economic power of the Gaza kingdom was based firmly upon the control of the trade between the interior and the Portuguese coastal settlements of Delagoa Bay.[47] This trade had been going on since the time of the pre-Gaza states at a time when Delagoa Bay, though a Portuguese trading post, nevertheless attracted the trading vessels of other foreign nations such as the English and Austrians.[48] Delagoa Bay served mainly as an outlet for ivory and other trade goods exported from Nyaka's kingdom, the Thembe and Maputo states.[49]

The new Gaza kingdom thus took control of trade that touched much of Natal and probably even the eastern frontier of the Cape Colony.[50] But the Gaza kingdom put too heavy a reliance on military expeditions and warfare. From his capital of Chaimaite on the middle Sabi, Soshangane's regiments fought the surrounding chiefdoms and harassed eastern Shona states. The brunt of these attacks fell on the peoples of southern Mozambique, especially the Tsonga.[51] There was a strengthening of the Nguni element in Gaza society when in 1826 Soshangane's people were joined by Ndwandwe remnants from northern Zululand after Shaka had defeated Sikunyane, the son of Zwide.[52]

It was into the familiar Zulu-type state that the conquered Tsonga communities were incorporated. In extent the Gaza state stretched from the lower Zambezi to just south of the Limpopo. The authority of the king was backed by an army based on the age-regiment system and used the military techniques of the Zulu army. The original Nguni group from the south formed a kind of socially superior class known as 'ba-Nguni', while

46. J. D. Omer-Cooper, 1966, pp. 57–8; H. Fynn in J. Bird, 1888, Vol. 1, pp. 86–90.
47. A. T. Bryant, 1929, p. 313; J. D. Omer-Cooper, 1966, ch. 4.
48. A. Smith, 1969, pp. 176–7.
49. S. Marks, 1967b.
50. A. Smith, 1969, p. 169.
51. J. Stevenson-Hamilton, 1929, p. 169.
52. J. D. Omer-Cooper, 1966, p. 57.

the newly incorporated citizens were referred to as 'ba-Tshangane'. In contrast with many founders of Mfecane-inspired states, Soshangane did not use his age-regiments to unify subject communities with his nuclear Nguni group. J. D. Omer-Cooper states that they were kept in regiments of their own distinct from those of the Nguni group but placed under 'ba-Nguni' officers. It is also suggested that they were considered to be expendable and on the battlefield were invariably put in the front line.[53]

The Ndebele

Mzilikazi, the founder of the Ndebele state, was the son of Mashobane, the head of a small Khumalo chiefdom on the Black Mfolozi river, paying tribute to the Ndwandwe monarch Zwide. Born in 1796, Mzilikazi became ruler of his people when in 1818 Zwide had Mashobane killed, suspecting him of betrayal. As the son of Mashobane's senior wife (who was a daughter of Zwide), Mzilikazi, the heir-apparent, was duly installed head of the Khumalo chiefdom by Zwide.

Soon after Shaka's victory over Zwide at the battle of the White Mfolozi, Mzilikazi deserted his grandfather Zwide and transferred his allegiance to Shaka. Sent by Shaka on an expedition against a neighbouring Sotho group in 1822, Mzilikazi defied Shaka by refusing to deliver the captured cattle. He then repulsed a Zulu regiment sent to punish him. He had gathered his Khumalo people on the top of Ntumbane hill. A second regiment was able to dislodge Mzilikazi from his supposedly impregnable fortress and also delivered a heavy punishment to the Khumalo regiments. Mzilikazi escaped over the Drakensberg Mountains with a considerably reduced following of some 200 men, women and children. In the words of one writer: 'Largely shorn of women, children and livestock and backed by a few hundred foot-soldiers armed with hand-weapons, Mzilikazi stood on the threshold of a twenty-year odyssey which was to take him over 1500 miles through many strange lands'.

Mzilikazi managed to evade pursuing Zulu regiments as he cut his path of escape among several small-scale Sotho groups on the highveld. On his way across the Vaal river he captured cattle, men, women and children. He was also joined by pockets of Nguni who had earlier crossed over the Drakensberg to live among the Sotho communities of the highveld. In 1824 Mzilikazi settled on the Olifants river in country generally occupied by the Pedi, a Sotho–Tswana group who until 1820 had been ruled by Thulare. His settlement was called Ekupumleni. Mzilikazi's military campaigns against the Pedi and other Sotho groups, mainly of what is now the eastern and northern Transvaal, not only enormously increased his herds but also swelled the numbers of his followers through conquest and capture as well as through accommodating refugees from Shaka. On the

53. J. Stevenson-Hamilton, 1929, p. 169.

Transvaal highveld, occupied predominantly by Sotho–Tswana communities, Mzilikazi's Nguni followers were called Ndebele. By 1825 Ndebele regiments were fighting Sotho–Tswana communities all over the highveld, even as far west as eastern Botswana. In two to three years Mzilikazi's kingdom had become the most powerful and richest on the highveld.

It was the news of Mzilikazi's wealth that attracted bands of adventurers; plunderers such as those led by Moletsane of the Taung (whose settlement was on the Vaal river) and Jan Bloem's gun-firing and mounted half-caste raiders who had for some time been harrying several African states in Transorangia. These raided Mzilikazi's enormous cattle posts not far from the Vaal river and helped themselves to his vast herds.[54] This, and occasional harassment by Zulu regiments, plus the threat of a possible attack from Zwangendaba and Nqaba[55] – both former generals of Zwide – persuaded him in 1827 to move his capital to the northern slopes of the Magaliesberg Mountains, near the source of the Odi (Crocodile) river. This was in the heart of the Kwena and Kgatla country in what is now the Transvaal Province of South Africa. There, near the site of the present city of Pretoria, Mzilikazi built his new headquarters, called Mhlahlandlela, from which his regiments systematically attacked the Kwena and Kgatla states of the central Transvaal for some five to seven years. His regiments went on expeditions northwards beyond the Limpopo river, southwards beyond the Vaal river and westwards as far as the fringes of the Kalahari Desert. At Mhlahlandlela, Mzilikazi also laid the basis for effective nation-building around the capital and its satellite settlements of Gabeni and Nkungwini. But even at his new home Mzilikazi found no repose. Jan Bloem's armed Koranna, reinforced by some Sotho–Tswana regiments, attacked his cattle posts in 1828, looting thousands of cattle and killing the herds. Mzilikazi's regiments that had been on duty elsewhere quickly caught up with the southward-moving raiders as they were leaving Ndebele territory, killed most of the raiders and recaptured any cattle. A year later an attack on his cattle posts by a strong Griqua and Sotho force under the leadership of Barend Barends was similarly frustrated. But Mzilikazi still dreaded the possibility of another Zulu attack. In 1832 he moved his settlement westwards to Mosega on the Madikwe (Marico) river. From this new base he attacked most of the Tswana groups in the western Transvaal and those in present-day Botswana until he was defeated and driven out of Mosega by a joint force of Boers, Tswana and Griqua in 1837.[56]

Mzilikazi now went to build his headquarters at Bulawayo. His regiments gained reasonably easy control over the Kalanga and Shona chieftaincies

54. J. D. Omer-Cooper, 1966, ch. 9.
55. ibid.
56. L. Ngcongco, 1982, pp. 161–71.

of the region. The power of Shona states had been sapped by the earlier battles against the Zwangendaba and Nxaba Nguni. From Bulawayo Ndebele regiments frequently attacked the Shona in order to capture cattle. Many Shona chiefdoms submitted as tribute-paying vassal states, while others put up a stout resistance. Some Shona, especially those east of the Sabi and Hunyani rivers, never really came under Ndebele authority. But the Kalanga chieftaincies were scattered and the inhabitants incorporated into Ndebele society. Some were obliged to migrate southwards and in a south-westerly direction into present-day Botswana.

In his new home Mzilikazi felt less threatened by powerful enemies. He therefore spent less time on military expeditions, and more and more on the consolidation of his kingdom. But as the Ndebele state was essentially expansionist and militarist it still needed to ensure a steady inflow of tribute in the form of cattle, grain, iron tools and weapons, personal ornaments and leather goods, or the provision of labour and services. Regiments accordingly continued to be sent out to the north and east among the Shona-speaking communities as well as some of the Sotho–Tswana states in the south. Some Tswana, like Bakaa, were left with some of Mzilikazi's herds to look after.[57] In 1842, for example, the Ngwato king, Sekgoma defeated an invading Ndebele regiment. In the following year Mzilikazi's tribute-gatherers were killed by the Ngwato.[58] Either because the militarist streak in Mzilikazi's character was gradually fading away or because he considered it less of a priority to do so at that point in time, Mzilikazi surprisingly took no action to punish this Ngwato insult until twenty years later.

Mzilikazi appeared keener to avenge his defeat on the Zambezi at the hands of Sebetwane's Kololo in 1839. Against them he despatched two powerful expeditions, one in 1845 and the other five years later. Both ended disastrously, putting an end to any further designs on so formidable an enemy. On the other hand, in 1847 the Ndebele were surprised by an invasion by a Boer Commando under Hendrik Potgieter, aided by Pedi auxiliaries. The expedition proved utterly abortive. As he had done to Griqua and Koranna raiders some twenty years earlier, Mzilikazi sent a regiment in pursuit of the apparently successful raiders, who had captured thousands of Ndebele cattle. The crack Zwangendaba regiment caught up with the raiders as they were camping for the night. The Pedi guards were massacred and the cattle recaptured.

For a whole decade after 1850 Mzilikazi fought no major war. Anxious to cement good ties with Europeans, he signed a treaty with Boers in 1852 permitting them to hunt in his country. Mzilikazi also received three visits,

57. A. Sillery, 1952, p. 118.

58. R.K. Rasmussen, 1977, p. 35; A. Sillery, 1952, p. 118, gives the date 1838 for this incident.

in 1854, 1857 and 1860, from the missionary Robert Moffat.[59] These visits paved the way for the entry of Europeans into the Ndebele kingdom. Moffat also secured, in particular, Mzilikazi's consent to missionaries operating in his country.[60] After this, Europeans began entering Ndebele kingdom in ever-increasing numbers. There were hunters, traders, and missionaries – all harbingers of Rhodes and the British South Africa Company.[61] This was particularly so after the ancient Tati gold diggings of the Kalanga had become known to Europeans in 1867.[62] By then Mzilikazi was already a very sick man. He died early in September 1868.

The Ndebele kingdom was a militarist state. When it was established in what is today Zimbabwe a pattern of statecraft that had been evolving in the Transvaal blossomed into full maturity. In building his kingdom, Mzilikazi replicated some of the features of the Zulu empire of which his own Khumalo polity had been only a tiny part. He employed the age-regiment as his essential instrument for absorbing conquered peoples and for cutting across the social strata that ultimately developed north of the Limpopo.

After 1840, Ndebele society comprised three such strata. The first layer was made up of the parent groups of original followers of Mzilikazi from the Natal–Zululand area and others who joined him south of the Vaal. They were known as the Zansi people. Next in prestige came those who were incorporated during migrations north of the Vaal, predominantly Sotho–Tswana peoples. They were known as E-Nhla. The lowest group in the hierarchy were the Hole, made up of those conquered in the country north of the Limpopo.[63] The prestigious social position of the Zansi encouraged the other groups to strive consciously to emulate their way of living, speak their language and adopt their culture. Intermarriage between the members of these social 'classes' was frowned upon.[64] But as individuals became more proficient in speaking Sindebele and distinguished themselves in war, they became socially acceptable and could even rise in the army. The age-regiment system had the effect of cutting across these social classes and made for quicker absorption of the conquered youth. It helped to assimilate such youths into Ndebele customs, the Sindebele language and loyalty to Mzilikazi.

The position of the king was crucial in binding the different groups of subjects together. This was reflected in the annual first-fruits (*incwala*) ceremony. More than any other ritual this ceremony dramatized the central role of the king's person in the life of the nation. In the words of one

59. R. Moffat, 1945, Vol. 1, p. 225.
60. J. D. Omer-Cooper, 1966, p. 153.
61. ibid., p. 152.
62. L. Thompson, 1969b, p. 446.
63. A. J. B. Hughes, 1956.
64. ibid.

anthropologist,[65] the first-fruits ceremony ritualizes the king and served as a device for protecting the whole community 'by allaying the evil forces which might harm their ruler and consolidating the political nation around him'.[66] The ceremony was attended by all his subjects and was held at his capital.[67] As the theoretical owner of all the cattle in the Ndebele kingdom, Mzilikazi was in a position to control the ability of his subjects to contract marriages. In addition to the control of the national herd, Mzilikazi also had under his care all the captured maidens. This meant that he controlled both the economic productive as well as the biological reproductive potential of his subjects. He himself became attached to a large number of his subjects through marriage.

Since the Ndebele kingdom was a conquest state, the organization of its vast army significantly overlapped with, and somewhat overshadowed, the political and administrative organization of the state. This army, numbering some 20 000 in the latter years of Mzilikazi's reign, was divided into regimental units, all overseen by regimental *indunas* or commanders. These in turn were under the supervision of four divisional *indunas*, with Mzilikazi himself at the apex of the system.

Nearly all adult men formed part of the army, and therefore belonged to regiments. These regiments lived in regimental towns. Married members of a regiment were allowed to live in the regimental town with their wives and servants. They constituted a kind of reserve force that could be called up in an emergency. Sons were enrolled in the same regiments as their fathers. Thus, instead of youths being recruited into a single regiment from all the communities forming part of the state (as was the case among the Sotho–Tswana), membership of a regimental town became hereditary. Occasionally, when population growth warranted it, Mzilikazi would select youths from the various regimental towns to form a new regiment which would be placed under its own *induna* who would then be permitted to build a new regimental town. Each regimental town was under the supervision of both its *induna* and one of Mizilikazi's queens.

It is essential to note, however, that while the regimental system operated in this manner for the purpose of absorbing the youth, not all the conquered people lived in the regimental towns. There were ordinary villages of conquered persons leading their traditional life styles in the midst of the whole Ndebele kingdom. But these were generally attached to regimental towns.

Finally, in the Ndebele kingdom Mzilikazi himself was the focus of all political power. He appointed all the *indunas* or headmen of villages and received detailed reports from them. Mzilikazi travelled frequently among the various regimental towns and made surprise visits in order to inspect

65. H. Kuper, quoted in T. R. H. Davenport, 1978, p. 45.
66. ibid.
67. R. K. Rasmussen, 1977.

the progress of affairs in the satellite towns. Within a relatively short time he had built a well-founded kingdom, in which conquered peoples – some only associated with the state rather than being an integral part of it – had embraced the Ndebele language and culture. On the other hand, the Ndebele also became devotees of the Shona Mwari/Mlimo religion characterized by an oracular priesthood or spirit mediums.[68]

The Sotho

The kingdom of Lesotho was another new state born out of the turmoil of the Mfecane. It was welded together out of a series of small autonomous Sotho-speaking communities that were scattered widely over the plains stretching north and west of the Drakensberg Mountains. Most of these communities comprised several clans and lineages belonging to Kwena and Fokeng groups of Sotho–Tswana societies.

The internecine wars unleashed by the campaigns of the Hlubi and Ngwane against these Sotho-speaking communities of the Transorangian highveld provided a suitable outlet for Moshoeshoe's talent for leadership and organization. Moshoeshoe was the son of a comparatively obscure chieftain of the small Mokoteli clan, a junior branch of one of the Kwena chiefdoms in the region. Recorded tradition attributes some of Moshoeshoe's achievement to the tutelage and influence of an eminent 'philosopher king' of the Sotho world, one Mohlomi, ruler of the Monaheng, another branch of the Kwena confederacy of chiefdoms on the highveld. Mohlomi's wisdom and reputation as a rainmaker had earned him tremendous respect among the Sotho-speaking states of Transorangia. His extensive travels among them, and the numerous diplomatic marriages he contracted with the daughters of many of the rulers, are considered by some to have prepared the way for the subsequent unification of these states by Moshoeshoe.[69]

It is possible, however, to exaggerate the influence of the wise Mohlomi on Moshoeshoe's character and achievement. It should be readily recognized that Moshoeshoe was himself endowed with unmistakable leadership qualities. First noticed in the initiatives he took among his age-mates during their initiation, these qualities now came to be clearly demonstrated when the incursions of the Hlubi and Ngwane resulted in a general collapse of most of the Sotho chiefdoms in Transorangia.[70] Early in his career, Moshoeshoe perceived the defensive potential of flat-topped mountains. He accordingly established himself, his family, and some of his age-mates on such a mountain fortress, Butha-Buthe mountain, and fortified the

68. ibid.; A. J. Wills, 1967, p. 155.
69. J. D. Omer-Cooper, 1966, p. 99; D. F. Ellenberger, 1912.
70. L. Thompson, 1969b, p. 399.

narrow passes giving access to the summit with stone walls punctuated by lookout huts situated at vantage points.[71]

Using this mountain fortress as a base, Moshoeshoe was able to mount raids against some of his neighbours, as well as to defend his people against the Tlokwa of Mma-Nthatisi whom he defeated at the 'Battle of the Pots'. But when the Tlokwa returned in 1824 and laid a prolonged siege on Butha-Buthe mountain, the stubborn resistance of Moshoeshoe's people nearly collapsed from exhaustion and starvation. They were rescued by the appearance of an Ngwane army[72] that attacked the Tlokwa, causing them to abandon the siege. Later that year Moshoeshoe moved his people southward through cannibal-infested country[73] to a new mountain fortress that had been earlier identified by his scouts. This new mountain fortress, called Thaba Bosiu, on the Little Caledon river, was easier to defend. Moshoeshoe, his father and some of his closest followers built their houses on the summit of this flat-topped mountain – about 500 ha in extent with good grazing 'and a fair supply of perennial spring water'.[74] Considerable work was done to fortify the various approaches to Thaba Bosiu.[75]

Feeling secure on his well-nigh impregnable mountain, Moshoeshoe now concentrated on the task of building a new nation out of the remnants of many broken peoples. He quickly subdued None, chief of the Bamantsane, whom he found in occupation of the land around Thaba Bosiu. Meanwhile, several groups – Sotho and Nguni – came to Moshoeshoe to seek refuge under his rule. He placed some under the supervision of his brothers, later also under his sons. Larger groups such as the Baphuthi under Moorosi, the Bataung under Moletsane, and the Barolong under Moroka, he allowed to remain under the local administration of their own traditional rulers as long as they recognized his paramountcy.

In dealing with the threat of powerful and dangerous neighbours, Moshoeshoe employed the tactic of cultivating their friendship by sending them tribute. Thus he protected himself from the attacks of Ama-Ngwane by paying tribute regularly to Matiwane. At the same time he sent a tribute of blue crane feathers to Shaka. Ultimately, the Basotho became alarmed at the possibility of the Ngwane remaining in the vicinity indefinitely. At Moshoeshoe's instance, therefore, the Ngwane were attacked by a Zulu army in 1827 and severely mauled, but not driven out of the area of Transorangia. In retaliation, Matiwane's Ngwane attacked Moshoeshoe on his mountain stronghold of Thaba Bosiu in July 1827, but they were beaten and driven back.[76] The defeat of the much-dreaded Ngwane of Matiwane spread Moshoeshoe's fame far and wide. Most of the Ngwane went into

71. J. D. Omer-Cooper, 1966, pp. 100–1.
72. ibid., p. 101.
73. D. F. Ellenberger, 1912, p. 146.
74. L. Thompson, 1969b, p. 399.
75. G. Tylden, 1950, p. 5; D. Ellenberger, 1912, p. 147.
76. J. D. Omer-Cooper, 1966, p. 102.

the present-day Transkei and were defeated at Mbolompo. More broken groups now flocked to Moshoeshoe. His victory over the Ngwane had demonstrated the wisdom of his choice of Thaba Bosiu as capital.

To add to his reputation, Moshoeshoe sent armies in association with the Baung of Moletsane against groups like the Thembu to raid for cattle. In a counter-attack, Moshoeshoe's people beat off the invasion by Sekonyela's regiments and put an end for quite a while to Tlokwa harassment. Another test of the strength of Moshoeshoe's mountain capital was administered by Ndebele regiments sent into Transorangia on a punitive expedition against Moletsane and his Taung.[77] The Ndebele army entered Lesotho and attempted to storm Thaba Bosiu. They were beaten back and forced to withdraw. Diplomatically, Moshoeshoe sent the retreating army a small herd of slaughter cattle as a gift, begging for peace and saying he was convinced that starvation must have driven them to attack him. The Ndebele went away with tremendous respect for the great mountain king, and never returned to attack him again.[78] Once more, the success of Moshoeshoe's defensive tactics against such a redoubtable foe as the Ndebele reverberated throughout the Sotho-speaking world. This success enormously increased Moshoeshoe's prestige. It also clearly demonstrated his defensive strategy, namely to fight his powerful enemies when necessary and to conciliate wherever possible.[79]

No sooner had the Ndebele danger receded than Moshoeshoe's kingdom had to face a new scourge. This appeared in the form of a series of attacks on Sotho villages by bands of mounted and armed raiders. These Griqua and Koranna banditti had started harrying the Basotho early in 1830. Their attacks now became frequent and more alarming. The intensive wars in Transorangia had weakened and impoverished most of the states in the region. Moshoeshoe's kingdom was a striking exception especially in terms of the number of cattle held by the Basotho. Griqua and Koranna raiders descended on their villages and herds with lightning speed. They attacked in small companies, but being mounted they enjoyed superior mobility. They were also armed with muskets of greater range than any kind of throwing spear. They were good shots and specialized in sudden attacks on their victims. The Basotho responded by organizing counter-ambushes and night raids on the camps of the Griqua and Koranna bandits. They killed the people and captured their horses and guns. In time, the Basotho bred an indigenous horse, the 'Basotho pony' and turned themselves into 'a nation of mounted gunmen'.[80] This was a tremendous development in defensive nation-building.

Through a Christian Griqua man, Adam Krotz, Moshoeshoe made

77. E. Casalis, 1861, pp. 22–4; L. Thompson, 1969b, p. 400.
78. J. D. Omer-Cooper, 1966, p. 103; L. Thompson, 1969b, p. 400.
79. G. Tylden, 1950, pp. 8–10; L. Thompson, 1969b, p. 400.
80. J. D. Omer-Cooper, 1966, p. 104.

contact with white missionaries. In 1833 he sent cattle to the Philippolis mission station 'to buy missionary'. His request coincided with the arrival of a small party of French missionaries whose hopes to start work among the Bahurutshe were frustrated by news of Mzilikazi's harassment of the Bahurutshe and other neighbouring Tswana peoples.[81] These French missionaries were persuaded that it was providential that they should instead commence their labours among the Basotho of Moshoeshoe. He settled them at Makhoarane, which the missionaries named Morija. Other mission stations were opened shortly at Beersheba and Mekuatling. Missionaries were brought into the Sotho kingdom as a defensive move. They were supposed to help Moshoeshoe defend his kingdom by offering him the best advice, and by assisting him to acquire firearms as well as establish contact with powerful white governments with whom Moshoeshoe could establish ties of friendship and alliance.

The effect of Moshoeshoe's nation-building technique could be seen in the accretion to his kingdom of several groups dislodged from their own home areas by the disturbed conditions of the Mfecane. The Batlhaping under Lepui came to settle under French missionaries at Bethulie mission station. In 1836 the Bataung of Moletsane came to live at Beersheba before migrating two years later to Mekuatling, while in 1833 the Barolong of Moroka were allowed to live at Thaba Nchu with their Wesleyan missionaries. Subsequently Thembu immigrants fleeing from the effects of the Sixth Frontier War sought the protection of Moshoeshoe.

The 1830s saw the intensification of Boer encroachment on Sotho-occupied territory. This reached its peak after 1836, the year of the Boer exodus commonly referred to as 'The Great Trek'. Numerous clashes ensued between the encroaching Boer and dispossessed Basotho farmers. While some of the conflicts were the result of disputes over land, others were the result of counter-claims to cattle ownership, and differences over labour questions. The frequency and the growing intensity of these conflicts drew forth the reluctant intervention of the British government which, after attempting two abortive solutions,[82] threw in the sponge by recognizing an independent Boer republic in the heart of Moshoeshoe's country. To add insult to injury, the Bloemfontein Convention, by which Great Britain legitimized Boer expropriation of Sotho territory, included as one of its provisions an article that banned the sale of arms and ammunition to the Basotho and other black states while the Boers themselves could freely purchase such requirements.

It is therefore hardly surprising that the Orange Free State republic embarked upon an aggressive expansionist foreign policy that threatened

81. J.D. Omer-Cooper, 1966.

82. Such solutions were the Treaty System of 1843–5, as part of which a treaty was signed with Moshoeshoe in 1845; and the creation of a Boer enclave under British administration entitled Orange River Sovereignty in 1848.

to undo all the work of Moshoeshoe and, in its desperate bid to reach the sea at Port St Johns,[83] annihilate the very kingdom of Lesotho. The Basotho had to fight two wars in 1858 and 1865 against the Orange Free State before their country was taken over on behalf of Her Majesty's Government by Governor Wodehouse.

Moshoeshoe's plea for the annexation of his country by the Queen's government was a defensive move in the preservation of the nation that he had worked so hard to build. It was done to prevent the incorporation of his kingdom into the Boer republic of the Orange Free State. By the time Moshoeshoe died in March 1870 he had not only saved his kingdom from disintegration, he had also created the basis for an independent state that has survived to the present.

The Kololo

The Kololo were Bafokeng of the Patsa branch. Before the outbreak of the Mfecane they lived near Kurutlele mountain on the left bank of the Vet (Tikoane) river. Their neighbours were the Bataung of Moletsane.[84] A sudden attack upon them by the Mma-Nthatisi Tlokwa, and the capture of nearly all their stock, uprooted these Fokeng Patsa. They fled poverty-stricken across the Vaal river where their numbers were increased by the accretion of another and larger group of Bafokeng.[85] Many small Sotho communities, fleeing from the wars of the Hlubi and Ngwane, had crossed the Vaal river and left the area of Transorangia. Sebetwane, a prince of the Patsa house, now took over the leadership of the combined Fokeng group.

Sebetwane's followers wandered extensively in search of a new home, and cattle to replace their lost herds. Their travels took them westwards towards the country of the Batlhaping. In that area they encountered two other dislodged and wandering groups, the Baphuting and the Bahlakwana. After an initial skirmish between the Fokeng and Phuting, the three groups subsequently joined forces in a combined attack on the Tlhaping capital of Dithakong on 26 June 1823.[86] Robert Moffat, an agent of the London Missionary Society who had been resident at Kuruman among the Batlhaping, procured the assistance of the pro-missionary Griqua captains at Griquatown, and the co-operation of other half-caste leaders at nearby centres. A mounted force of one-hundred gunmen was quickly assembled and despatched to help defend Dithakong.

On the day of the battle the invaders were heavily defeated and driven back with great slaughter. They were put to flight by the guns of the

83. G. Tylden, 1950; D. Ellenberger, 1912, p. 306.

84. E. W. Smith, 1956, p. 50.

85. This group of Fokeng had earlier been attacked by Moletsane's Taung and stripped of their cattle (see D. Ellenberger, 1912).

86. J. D. Omer-Cooper, 1966, p. 94; E. W. Smith, 1956, pp. 52–3.

Griqua horsemen.[87] After this disastrous defeat at the battle of Dithakong the mixed horde broke up. The Phuthing and Hlakoane moved in an easterly direction,[88] while Sebetwane led his followers, now renamed Makololo, northwards through the country of the Barolong.

In his campaigns against the various sections of the Barolong, Sebetwane is said to have teamed up with that veteran raider Moletsane, chief of the Baung.[89] They extended their campaigns to the Hurutshe where they sacked and destroyed the Hurutshe capital, Kaditshwene (Kureechane), scattered the inhabitants, and slew the regent Diutlwileng. Next, these two allied groups fought the Kgatla-Kgafela near the confluence of the Api and Crocodile rivers,[90] but their campaigns in that neighbourhood drew forth the attack of Mzilikazi's army upon them, presumably because they had encroached upon what the Ndebele considered their own sphere of operations.[91] Sebetwane and Moletsane now separated, the latter moving south towards Matlwase (Makassie).[92]

The Makololo now went on to attack the larger section of the divided Kwena kingdom at Borithe, under Moruakgomo. The Bakwera had been weakened by dynastic strife and split into three sections.[93] Subsequently Sebetwane turned upon the Bangwaketse, who were the strongest of the Tswana states in the region. They defeated them at Iosabanyana in 1824, where their old fighter king, Makaba II, was also slain. Sebetwane fell upon the Kwena once more, flushed out remaining pockets of resistance from the fastnesses of Dithejwane, and captured large numbers of cattle. He then settled down at Dithubaruba, the former Kwena capital, in what seemed to have been intended as a permanent, or at least a prolonged settlement. But the following year, 1826, a skilfully executed surprise attack by the Ngwaketse king, Sebego, son of the late Makaba II, defeated Sebetwane and expelled him from the Dithejwane Hills with much loss of life and nearly all the cattle the Kololo had.[94]

Once more Sebetwane and his poverty-stricken Kololo followers were forced to set out on their travels. In their northward wanderings, they twice fought with the Ngwato under Kgari, defeating them and relieving them of much of their cattle. But on their journey to Lake Ngami, they lost their way in the desert and were forced to abandon many of the Ngwato cattle.[95] But once they reached the country of the Batawana in the vicinity

87. R. Moffat and M. Moffat, 1951, pp. 87–8, 91–7.
88. S. Broadbent, 1865, pp. 128–33.
89. J. D. Omer-Cooper, 1966.
90. ibid., p. 116; D. Ellenberger, 1912, p. 308.
91. D. Livingstone, 1857, p. 85.
92. S. Broadbent, 1865, pp. 128–33.
93. A. Sillery, 1954.
94. A. G. Bain, 1949, pp. 51–71.
95. D. Livingstone, 1857, p. 85.

of Lake Ngami, they easily defeated the inhabitants and dispossessed them of their stock.[96]

Sebetwane now attempted to cross the Kalahari Desert in order to reach the west coast. Defeated by desert conditions and by the stiff resistance of some desert communities,[97] he was forced to return to Lake Ngami. Moving northwards he once more fought and defeated the Batawana and took over their new town and their government. The Tawana later broke away and returned to their original home near Lake Ngami.[98] After an arduous journey the Makololo settled near the confluence of the Zambezi and the Kafue rivers. They had hardly settled before they had to fight back invasions from Nguni regiments. One was from Nqaba, the leader of the Msene Nguni. The other two were attacks by Mzilikazi's Ndebele, who had also been wandering along the Zambezi river in search of a new home.

Sebetwane and his Kololo succeeded in warding off all those invasions. But the experience persuaded them to move their settlement further west on the Kafue plateau. As was the case among the Kwena, in the land of the Tswana, Sebetwane's triumph over the Lozi was facilitated by the civil strife then raging in that kingdom because of a succession dispute. Sebetwane conquered the Lozi, except for a small group that fled into exile under the leadership of some members of the royal family.[99]

Having successfully disposed of the Ndebele threat, Sebetwane now settled down to consolidate his new kingdom. His military prowess, demonstrated in the manner in which he handled the Nguni and, particularly, the Ndebele invasions, tremendously increased his prestige and presented him in the eyes of many communities of the area as a leader worth following.

Under Sebetwane's rule the Kololo state flourished significantly. He tackled the challenge of building national unity with vigour and imagination. He fostered unity by taking wives from among the Lozi as well as the other conquered peoples, and encouraged his closest Kololo followers to do the same. Sebetwane insisted that all the subjects in his state were the children of the king. Sebetwane retained many Lozi chiefs in their offices and replaced royals who had fled with new Lozi functionaries. Some Lozi chiefs were co-opted onto Sebetwane's council and were regularly consulted by him.[100]

Sebetwane did not impose the Sotho age-mate initiation on the Lozi or any of his other conquered subjects. But he saw to it that the Kololo language was spoken throughout his kingdom. He respected the Lozi political system and did not replace it, but he allowed it where possible to exist side by side with the new Kololo system until the two grew into each

96. J.D. Omer-Cooper, 1966, p. 119; D. Ellenberger, 1912, p. 310.
97. D. Livingstone, 1852, pp. 163–73.
98. J.D. Omer-Cooper, 1966, p. 119.
99. ibid., p. 121.
100. D.E. Needham, 1974.

other and merged. However, socially and politically the Kololo figured as a ruling aristocracy. Sebetwane pioneered an original system of local administration whereby villages were grouped into 'provinces' or, at least, 'districts'. Kololo functionaries were placed in charge of such administrative units to administer and collect tribute from the subject peoples. Part of the tribute was appropriated by the king and part was distributed. In every village Sebetwane placed at least two Kololo families as lords of the land.[101]

Whereas Lozi tradition and religion had required the king to seclude himself from the people, Sebetwane made himself accessible to all his people, irrespective of social, political or economic status. In this way he not only proved to be truly the father of all his people but, what was more, he fundamentally changed the character of Lozi kingship. When he died in July 1851 most of his subjects, including the Lozi, had come to regard themselves as Makololo. He was succeeded by Sekeletu.

Lozi royals like Masiku and Sepopa, who had fled up the Leambye river when Sebetwane conquered the Lozi state, had only maintained there a kind of government in exile and worked hard to keep the flame of Lozi 'nationalism' flickering steadily. Sekeletu's iron yoke served only to fan this smouldering fire into a roaring blaze. His death in 1864, and the even greater cruelty of his successors, provided the signal for Lozi rebellion. Sepopa led an army against the Makololo. It was joined by people on the plain and on the Toka plateau. The Kololo were defeated, their rule overthrown and the Lozi dynasty was restored.[102]

On his journeys to Angola and down the Zambezi, Livingstone had recruited Kololo porters. When he returned the majority to their home country in 1860 some sixteen of them remained behind in the Shire valley. They had married local women and wished to build their homes there. These young men possessed guns, and had also acquired much experience of Kololo methods of military and political organization. They were generally imbued with pride in the achievements of the Kololo state. They organized the Manganja peoples of the Shire valley into several chiefdoms of stockaded villages, and made themselves rulers over them. At the time, the Manganja were subject to cruel and ravaging raids by slave-traders. These Kololo chiefdoms defended the Manganja against the Nguni, Yao and Portuguese slavers. The villages were later grouped into two kingdoms under Molokwa and Kasisi, the ablest of these leaders. They distributed other Kololo as chiefs over the local Manganja at strategic points in the valley. They welcomed the Livingstonia mission and co-operated with it. Ultimately the Kololo established cordial relations with the Yao, but the Nguni remained a problem. The influence of these Kololo chiefs of the Shire endured despite strong Nguni harassment until the colonial partition in the 1890s.

101. D.E. Needham, 1974.
102. J.D. Omer-Cooper, 1966, p. 124.

Trans-Zambezi Nguni states

After the defeat of the Ndwandwe at the battle of Mhlatuze, splinters of that confederacy were scattered in all directions. Zwangendaba and Nqaba (Nxaba) led their Nguni followers into southern Mozambique not far from Delagoa Bay, where Soshangane had preceded them, and was in the process of establishing his kingdom. In a three-cornered struggle for supremacy, Soshangane successively defeated both Zwide and Nqaba, forcing them out of the area. He subsequently consolidated the organization of his kingdom at the expense of the local Tsonga peoples.

Zwangendaba and his Jere Nguni followers crossed the Limpopo into Rozwi country, fighting most of the Shona states of the region, and in the process destroying the Changamire empire. Not far from the present city of Bulawayo, at Thaba Zika Mambo, Zwangendaba's regiments engaged the Rozwi army, defeated them and killed the last Mambo, Chirisamhuru. Zwangendaba then led his Nguni regiments across the Zambezi into Nsenga country. They crossed the Zambezi near Zumbo on 20 November 1835.[103]

Pressing northwards west of Lake Malawi, Zwangendaba's Nguni fought many wars against the Chewa and Tumbuka communities, taking many captives and resting for a few years at one place before moving on. They continued their northward march until they reached Mapupo on the Fipa plateau, between the northern end of Lake Malawi and the southern end of Lake Tanganyika.[104] Their numbers had been immensely increased by fresh recruits from the many people they had defeated on their long journey.

After Zwangendaba's death, in about 1848, his Nguni split into several factions. These engaged in separate campaigns of invasion against many states in the area. Their operations extended as far north as the southern shores of Lake Victoria and as far east as the Indian Ocean. From Mozambique, Nqaba also led his Msene Nguni into the area of present-day Zimbabwe. They emulated their Jere Nguni predecessors in the upheavals they created with their successive military campaigns against one group or another in the region. In a brief skirmish between Zwangendaba's Jere and Nqaba's Msene Nguni the latter had the upper hand. They subsequently moved in a westerly direction towards the country of the Lozi. There, in a battle against Sebetwane's Kololo, the Nguni of Nqaba were defeated and dispersed, and their leader was slain.[105]

The Maseko Nguni, under their leader Ngwane, also migrated into Zimbabwe from Mozambique, crossing the Zambezi between Sena and Tete in 1839. Passing through southern Malawi and around the southern tip of Lake Malawi, the Maseko penetrated south-eastern Tanzania. There,

103. R. Gray, 1965; L. Thompson, 1969a, p. 347; D.R. Hunt, 1931, p. 284.
104. J.D. Omer-Cooper, 1966, pp. 123–4.
105. E.W. Smith, 1956, p. 71.

in the Songea district, they established a powerful state under Mputa, the successor of Ngwane.[106]

Conclusion

In retrospect, it becomes clear that the Mfecane was the result of radical socio-political changes in most of the northern Nguni states. It was triggered by a combination of population explosion and land shortage, as well as dendro-climatological changes that adversely affected the delicate ecological balance between the patterns of sweet and sourveld pastures on the one hand and the pressures on these by a steadily growing human and cattle population. This critical situation appears to have been exacerbated by the Madlathule drought, which seems to have intensified the intense struggle in that region for rapidly dwindling resources. There is an indication that the influence of and competition for a burgeoning trade in imported goods brought in through the port of Delagoa Bay may also have weighed more than scholars have hitherto been willing to consider.

It is, however, equally clear that the impetus for these important changes that so immensely revolutionized the political and military organization of these Nguni states derived entirely from internal sources. The Zulu revolution was certainly not a result of the transplantation or wholesale adaptation to local conditions of ideas gleaned from external sources. But the Zulu successor states – Swazi, Gaza, Ndebele, and the various Nguni polities – all carried with them the essential features of the revolutionary Zulu state organization, namely, a formidable military machine based on the age-regiment system. In all these states the regimental system became the central or main institution used for the purpose of welding together disparate ethnic entities in the new states.

The Sotho-type kingdoms like those of Moshoeshoe and, to a certain extent, Sebetwane, while they did make use of age-mate circumcision among their original core or founding groups, did not extend to or impose the system on newly incorporated communities, for the purpose of keeping the nation-state together. They appear to have relied more on such devices as diplomatic marriages and proconsular-type supervision (whether by the traditional rulers of such incorporated states or by members of the conquering royal families), permitting considerable local autonomy and making use of extensive consultative mechanisms, whether direct or through individuals and councils.

The Mfecane revolution brought about the genesis of new states in Southern, Central and East Africa. The Zulu kingdom rose out of the ashes of the Mthethwa and Ndwandwe confederacies, as well as from the debris of numerous pre-Mfecane Nguni chiefdoms of the Zululand–Natal region. Today the Zulu kingdom survives as a truncated and considerably reduced

106. J. D. Omer-Cooper, 1966, p. 73.

base for one of South Africa's Bantustans. The kingdoms of Swaziland and Lesotho have survived from the pre-colonial creations of Sobhuza and Moshoeshoe respectively as islands of sanity in a sea of racialism. Today they are respected members of the international comity of nations. Mzilikazi's Ndebele kingdom survived for only half a century before succumbing to the wave of British chartered company colonization then sweeping whole regions of Southern and East Africa during the high point of European imperialist expansion. The Kololo kingdom of Sebetwane proved to be not much more than a personal creation that disintegrated quickly in the hands of less capable successors. It therefore did not long survive the death of its founder.

While the Mfecane created new polities, it also resulted in many small states disappearing, some temporarily (e.g. the Batawana state of Moremi I and the Luyi (Lozi) kingdom) and others permanently, e.g. the Hlubi, Ngwane, Mthethwa, Ndwandwe, Zizi Bhele and numerous others. Some chiefdoms or states were broken into fragments and considerably weakened by the Mfecane. This happened particularly among the Tswana states. A few states in the heart of the Mfecane operational area emerged unscathed, and could even be said to have been strengthened by the turmoil of the Mfecane, e.g. the Pedi, Tlhaping and Tlharo.

It seems possible to divide the Mfecane states into several categories. There were the aggressive militarist–offensive states. The Zulu, Ndebele and Gaza kingdoms appear to have been fairly good examples of this genre. To this group may also be added the various Nguni states of the trans-Zambezi region. These states, which employed the military machine to conquer and subdue others, tended also to rely on the edge of the sword or the barrel of the gun to maintain the allegiance of subordinate polities. Their expansionist or imperialistic policies required that they keep professional or semi-professional armies on a permanent basis in 'barracks' or military villages. Regiments were required to embark on regular tax- or tribute-gathering expeditions at outlying parts of the kingdom. These armies were built on the age-regiments, which in the Ndebele and Zulu cases were the essential instruments for the absorption of conquered youths. The Gaza state did enrol conquered youths in age-regiments but kept these segregated from those of the 'Nguni' youths, even though the regimental leaders were drawn from the conquering ruling group. Thus in the Gaza state, the regiments did not contribute to building national unity. Because of the blatant discrimination against the 'ba-Tshangane', as the conquered Tsonga were called, they were not assimilated into the Gaza state. This, more than any other factor, accounted for the weakness of the Gaza conquest state and its ultimate collapse under the Portuguese onslaught. Conquest states tended to draw their state bureaucracies from commoner and military rather than royalist members. In the Ndebele state, regimental commanders not only supervised their regiments but also together with one of Mzilikazi's queens represented him in their regimental town.

Examples of Mfecane states building defensive nations were the kingdoms of Lesotho, Swazi and, to a certain extent, the Kololo. In these states, age-mate initiation, although practised, was not exploited as an instrument for incorporating youths from conquered communities. These states were not essentially militaristic or expansionist. The campaigns they fought were either considered defensive, or essential for defining or delimiting the geographical boundaries of the state, or imperative for acquiring wealth in cattle. The founders of these states put much emphasis on strong defensible positions. Moshoeshoe built his capital on a flat-topped mountain (*ghobosheane*), Sobhuza located his capitals in inaccessible mountain areas, while Sebetwane chose the Kafue flood plain with its treacherous islands, a location that proved disastrous to unsuspecting enemies.

These defensive kingdoms did not maintain standing armies. Initiation age-mates functioned as military units in times of war. The kings intermarried extensively with their subjects to forge closer ties, especially with leading families, both in the core group and among the newly incorporated communities. Cattle were needed in order that they might be loaned out (the *mafisa* system) to favoured citizens or even whole chiefdoms. Consultation and local autonomy were much used to keep the disparate elements happy. These defensive states also attracted missionaries and strove hard to acquire guns and ammunition for defensive purposes. Even the conquest states ultimately admitted missionaries.

All these Mfecane states were founded on kinship as the basic social matrix on which the state was finally shaped. So was the institution of kingship. Both conquest and defensive states exploited the first-fruits ceremony as a ritual to stengthen the monarchy. With the evolution of the African state system of the Mfecane period the importance of kinship ties gradually gave way to service, functionality and territoriality. Some states, like the Kololo, insisted on a language policy for the whole kingdom. Others, like the Ndebele, did not impose a language policy but proficiency in the language of the rulers could be a golden key with which individuals could unlock doors to the corridors of power. Even after the Kololo kingdom had formally ceased to exist, the language and culture of the Kololo endured. In the Ndebele state, likewise, many Kalanga and Shona became acculturated Ndebele.

Finally it should be observed that the many wars of the Mfecane period did considerably reduce African populations in, for instance, the areas of Natal and the Orange Free State. In a way the Mfecane could be said to have weakened many African states and to have rendered them less prepared to cope with or withstand a second and more destructive Mfecane, namely that unleashed by the Boer farmers who now encroached upon African lands with impunity, seizing not only land but also cattle and children.

The Mfecane also redistributed African populations in Southern Africa. It produced greater concentrations in certain places and left 'open spaces' in others. It also gave rise to a galaxy of talented leaders such as Shaka,

Mzilikazi, Sobhuza, Zwangendaba and Sebetwane. As Omer-Cooper correctly observed, these men

> demonstrated not only courage, powers of leadership and military skill but [also] the capacity for original thought and action; the ability to devise or adopt new institutions and new techniques to solve new problems; the statesmanship to rise above a narrow tribal point of view. They demonstrated the capacity of the Bantu to respond to challenges and that the traditional tribal education had a far less cramping effect on the development of human personality than some have supposed.[107]

107. J. D. Omer-Cooper, 1966, p. 180.

6

The impact of the Mfecane on the Cape Colony

E. K. MASHINGAIDZE

Introduction

The rise of the Zulu nation under Shaka during the first quarter of the nineteenth century was followed by widespread wars and disturbances in Southern Africa. Among the most affected were the Nguni-speaking and Sotho-speaking peoples of the region who still remember the destruction and the period during which it happened as Mfecane (Nguni) and Lifaqane/Difaqane (Sotho).[1] This movement, which rapidly spread beyond the region to as far north as the southern shores of Lake Victoria, was as significant to Southern Africa's subsequent historical developments as the spread of the reformist spirit among the Fulbe (Fulani, Peul) people and the accompanying *djihād*s which this spirit inspired were to historical developments in the Western Sudan during the same period. Like the Fulbe *djihād*s, the Mfecane transformed most Southern African societies in ways no other movement had done since the start of the Iron Age in the region. This chapter analyses the impact of the Mfecane upon the Cape Colony.[2]

The original area of the Mfecane was not the Cape but the country of the northern Nguni peoples in present-day Natal. It must be noted that although the outbreak of the Mfecane appears to have been a sudden occurrence, the fermentation causing the explosion was itself a long process building up over generations. The process entailed, among other things, the transformation of cattle-keeping and agricultural Nguni peoples from small polities based on the clan to larger states. The emergence of large-scale states, it appears, was a result of the need to cope with an increasing shortage of pastures and agricultural land. By the end of the eighteenth century the process had resulted in the rise of the Ndwandwe, Ngwane, Mthethwa and other larger chiefdoms under powerful military leaders. In order to protect and promote the interests of their people, the leaders were

1. W. G. A. Mears, 1970, p. 5
2. Comprehensive studies of the Mfecane have been made by J. D. Omer-Cooper, 1966, 1969; L. Thompson, 1969b; W. F. Lye, 1967.

extending control over the territories of weaker neighbours. Thus, by the mid-1820s, small chiefdoms could hardly maintain their independence and separate identities.

The Cape Colony on the eve of the Mfecane

Three things need to be done before we look at the Cape Colony on the eve of the Mfecane. First, we must provide a working definition of the Cape Colony. Then we need to give a brief picture of the population distribution and the relationships between the various groups. Finally a word has to be said about the economic situation in the Colony.

Defining the Cape Colony is rendered more difficult by the fact that the frontiers of the Colony were never static. The eastern boundary, especially, was notoriously fluid and unreliable.[3] For example, while in 1771 it was roughly the Gamtoos river, eight years later in 1779 it had been moved further, to the Great Fish river, where it still remained on the eve of the Mfecane. The Great Fish river was, therefore, roughly the dividing line between the whites to the south and west and the blacks to the east and north of it. The majority of the Africans were people generally known collectively as Cape Nguni,[4] also sometimes called southern Nguni,[5] inhabiting the territory between the Keiskamma and the Umzimkulu. The Cape Nguni fell into three broad groups: the Xhosa, Thembu and Mpondo.[6] Robin Derricourt's broad classification includes the Mpondomise and the Bomvana among the main groups.[7] The neighbours of the Cape Nguni were the Khoisan, most of whom were found west of the Kei river.

In this chapter the Cape Colony will be defined to include the territory inhabited by the whites as well as that occupied by the Africans west of the Great Fish as far as the Umzimkulu. This definition has been justified by the socio-economic patterns and the nature of new relationships which emerged after, and as a result of, the Mfecane, as will be seen.

On the whole, the relationships between the various Nguni-speaking peoples were relatively peaceful. The same could be said about the relationships between the Nguni and their Khoisan neighbours. This is not, however, to suggest that conflicts did not exist between the two groups or, for that matter, between the various Nguni peoples. For instance, Nguni–Khoisan clashes were frequent, especially in the area between the Upper

3. It has been described elsewhere as the 'moving frontier'. See W. M. Freund, 1974.
4. J. J. Van Warmelo, 1935, p. 60.
5. The names 'Cape Nguni' and 'southern Nguni' are, in fact, geographical and are applied to the Nguni-speaking peoples whose homes were south of the Umzimkulu. The Nguni speakers, north of that river, are known as 'Natal Nguni' or, simply, 'northern Nguni'.
6. J. J. Van Warmelo, 1935, p. 60.
7. R. Derricourt, 1974.

Kei and the Amathole to the north-west of the Transkei.[8] Conflicts were usually sparked off by the stock-raiding activities of the San, which provoked reprisal raids by the Nguni. It must be said, however, that such conflicts, whether between the Nguni and the Khoisan, or between Nguni chiefdoms, were usually fairly localized and controlled.

The so-called eastern frontier of the Cape was, however, a zone of black–white tension and often open conflict, and for this several factors were responsible. First, it must be borne in mind that for centuries Nguni-speaking communities had been slowly moving south-westwards from the Natal area. On the other hand white expansion in the opposite direction had been taking place since 1652, when Jan van Riebeeck founded a Dutch settlement at the Cape. The two movements were bound to clash somewhere. They clashed in what South African historiography used to refer to as 'Kaffir Wars'.

Secondly, the Fish river, although recognized by the Cape government as the boundary, was often violated by the people whom it was meant to separate and keep apart. The colonists, especially cattle-farmers, violated it in search of grazing. The Africans, on the other hand, had never had any intention of recognizing, let alone respecting, this boundary, because when it was proclaimed by the Cape government many Xhosa communities had long been established along the Fish river and to the west of it. The frontier zone was regarded by many Xhosa as part of their ancestral lands of which they had been deprived by the ever-expanding Colony. For this reason, therefore, many Xhosa continued to graze and water their herds across the Fish and in defiance of the Cape government. Xhosa hunters also continued to hunt west of the Fish river.

The third reason why the eastern boundary line continued to be a zone of black–white tension and violence was that the two racial groups were pursuing similar economic activities such as, for example, cattle-farming and agriculture, which were staple industries on either side of the frontier. Coupled with this were the conflicting land tenure systems.

Finally, in the eighteenth century and up to the early nineteenth century, Nguni expansion south-westwards was necessitated by a real dilemma created by developments in northern Nguniland. These developments made it impossible for Cape Nguni to expand north-eastwards.

Because they formed the vanguard of the Cape Nguni's westward and southward expansion, the Xhosa automatically bore the brunt of black–white conflict on the border. As a result the Xhosa have not only been by far the most written about, they have also been the most abused and the most hated of the Cape Nguni peoples of the region in Cape colonial historiography.[9]

8. R. Derricourt, 1974, p. 49.

9. In fact the Eastern Cape Frontier Wars are generally known as 'Kaffir Wars' in South African history books. The Xhosa were thought to be 'savages who only understood force

PLATE 6.1 *Dolls representing a San man and woman on sale in Cape Town, early nineteenth century.*

As already said, the Xhosa, who did not recognize the Fish as a boundary, simply crossed it at will to graze their cattle and sheep. Such boundary 'violations' were sometimes accompanied by cattle-rustling, to which the Cape colonists often responded with organized retaliatory raids into Xhosa areas, arguing that such action was necessary for them to retrieve their property. It was not unusual, however, for the activities of the colonial commandos to exceed the stated objectives.

It is clear, therefore, that black–white relationships in the region were not peaceful on the eve of the Mfecane. We should now turn to the economic situation of the Cape Colony on the eve of the Mfecane.

Economic situation and prospects

It must be noted that when the news of general unrest in Natal, the Caledon Valley area and the Highveld was received in the Cape Colony in 1822–3 many colonists had been there for just over two years. Among these were British settlers who had been brought to the Cape in 1820 to boost the Colony's scanty and predominantly Dutch population. Most of these nearly 5000 settlers had been sent to the new district of Albany where they held about 40 ha (100 acres) each. Although they may not have realized it, one of the main considerations for the establishment of the Albany settlement, as far as Governor Somerset was concerned, was that the settlers would assist with the defence and stabilization of the notorious Eastern Frontier.

The Cape Colony's economic situation and prospects had never been bright. The dangerous military situation on the frontier was simply aggravating the economic problems. The 1820 settlers were in a worse situation than the Dutch farmers living in the old districts of the Colony. By 1823, there were already indications that agriculture, expected to be Albany's staple economic activity and the main source of livelihood, was going to be a huge flop. To start with, many of the new farmers were not qualified to do the work for which they had been brought to Africa. There was also a general complaint that the holdings were too small. Then came floods in 1822 that destroyed all the crops. Many farmers had abandoned their land by 1823 and those that still held on had lost their original enthusiasm and were broken in spirit. With the small amounts of capital they had brought from Britain rapidly dwindling, many were either heavily in debt to the government for rations or were facing destitution. Excessive drinking was on the increase as many a broken heart sought to drown its worries and sorrows.[10]

With just about a third of the original number of the farmers still on their plots in 1823 and facing formidable odds, the whole future of the

and punishment'; C. W. De Kiewiet, 1968, p. 51. The Xhosa were also thought to be incorrigible cattle thieves who should be fought; E. A. Walker, 1968, pp. 116–19.

10. G. Butler, 1974, p. 176; E. A. Walker, 1968, p. 157.

Albany settlement as an agricultural venture was highly doubtful. As already pointed out, the rest of the farmers had abandoned their holdings, some opting for other forms of employment in urban centres, or setting themselves up as independent traders, and many more taking to cattle-farming.

A much more serious problem facing farmers in the old settlements and in the Albany District was shortage of unskilled labour. Even in this respect, however, the 1820 settlers were worse off than the old colonists. While old colonists could employ Xhosa, Khoisan or even slave labour, the 1820 settlers were not allowed any of these forms of labour.[11] The farmers of 'Anglostan', as G. Butler called Albany, were expected to use free labour from Britain. However, most of such labourers brought from Britain had deserted their masters on arrival in South Africa and had gone to urban centres where prospects were thought to be brighter. Desperate efforts were being made to encourage further migration to the Colony. Of those who responded to the call to migrate to the Cape Colony, most of them Irish workers, only a very insignificant trickle actually reached the Eastern Frontier Districts. Many bought their freedom on arrival at the Cape, and sought careers elsewhere. In the circumstances, therefore, the new settlers were compelled to rely on themselves, their wives and children to do 'the most menial tasks' normally reserved for labourers and slaves.[12] All these hardships were aggravated by the need for the farmers and all able-bodied people to go from time to time to the Eastern Frontier for defence duties.

In an effort to alleviate the financial hardships of the distressed settler farmers, some people formed an organization known as the Society for the Relief of the Distressed Settlers to raise funds for them. The Society did raise money, so that by 1824 it could assist some farmers with much-needed capital. But, as already mentioned, no financial assistance could solve the two chronic problems vexing the Colony; labour shortage and the volatile situation of the Eastern Frontier. These problems had not yet been solved when, in about 1822–3, the effects of the Mfecane reached the Cape Colony from across the Orange river and from Natal.

The coming of the Mfecane

The details of events in the northern Nguni territory, the Caledon valley area and the Highveld do not concern us here.[13] Of interest to this chapter is to see how the waves of events in Natal, the Caledon valley and the Highveld engulfed the Cape Nguni area and the Cape Colony proper. An attempt will be made to identify new social forms, relations between the various groups in the region, and any socio-economic patterns emerging

11. ibid., p. 157.
12. G. Butler, 1974, p. 178; G. M. Theal, 1891, pp. 238–9.
13. Such details are the subject of Chapter 5, above. Also see Note 2 above.

various groups in the region, and any socio-economic patterns emerging as a result of the Mfecane.

As already pointed out, the original centre of the Mfecane was in Natal among the northern Nguni-speakers. The exact causes of the Mfecane are not known. It would appear, however, that the population of this area had been steadily growing over the generations. Apparently this trend had, by contemporary methods of land use, led to overcrowding. In response to this apparent pressure on the land, new methods of political organization were tried. By the last decades of the eighteenth century, a number of strong chiefdoms had emerged, the best known of which were those of the Ndwandwe, the Ngwane, and the Mthethwa. Within the first two decades of the nineteenth century all these chiefdoms, including the Zulu, had been transformed into formidable military states under semi-monarchical leaders: Zwide, Sobhuza, Dingiswayo and Shaka respectively.

Had the new state system not been accompanied by a revolution in military methods and strategy, the tension and open violent conflicts characterizing relations among northern Nguni states from around 1815 on would not have led to large-scale wars. It is also possible that without the efficient military strategy such as was employed later by the various northern Nguni armies and, especially by the Zulu, the waves of events would not have gone beyond northern Nguniland.

As far as is known, the first major open conflict began in 1815 between Zwide's Ndwandwe and Sobhuza's Ngwane. The Ngwane were defeated and forced to flee across the Phongolo (Pongola) river where they laid the foundations of the Swazi nation. According to J. D. Omer-Cooper this conflict marked the beginning of the Mfecane. With Sobhuza's departure, a conflict between Zwide and Dingiswayo was almost inevitable. Indeed, towards the end of 1817, the expected clash between the Ndwandwe and the Mthethwa took place. Dingiswayo, king of the Mthethwa, was killed in this war, leaving his people demoralized, scattered and leaderless.

The Ndwandwe would have gained full victory and mastery over the whole territory between the Thukela (Tugela) and the Phongolo, following the fall of Dingiswayo, but for a new power which had been rising under Dingiswayo's patronage. This was Shaka, son of Senzangakhona, the chief of a then very insignificant Zulu group. As a youth, Shaka had been trained in one of Dingiswayo's Mthethwa regiments. Because of his intelligence and initiative he had been rapidly promoted to high ranks in the army. At the time of the clash between the Ndwandwe and the Mthethwa not only was Shaka a high official in the Mthethwa army, he had also succeeded his father as chief of the small Zulu group, then under the Mthethwa. After the death of Dingiswayo at the hands of Zwide, Shaka and his Zulu emerged as the only centre of serious resistance against Zwide and his Ndwandwe. Shaka prepared himself for a decisive showdown with Zwide by bringing under his control several chiefdoms including the now demoralized Mthethwa. He also perfected his new military methods and conscripted into his army all the youth who had reached the age to enter the initiation school. The initiation school had been abolished and replaced with military training for youths.

The celebrated war with Zwide's Ndwandwe came in 1818 and the Ndwandwe were decisively defeated after a number of campaigns. Omer-Cooper has rightly described the defeat of the Ndwandwe as a turning point in both Shaka's career and in the history of the Mfecane.[14] With no serious opposition in the northern Nguni territory, Shaka continued the campaigns of building his Zulu military state. The chief vehicle of Zulu expansion was military conquest and the incorporation of defeated chiefdoms into the Zulu nation. Many smaller chiefdoms were brought under Zulu rule. But many more also managed to avoid Shaka's clutches by fleeing their homes in the Natal region. Within a few years of the fall of Zwide in 1818, a welter of defeated and displaced chiefdoms, families and individuals had been forced to flee from their home areas westwards across the Drakensberg onto the Highveld, where they set in motion waves of migrations as areas were devastated and homes and crops destroyed. Other displaced northern Nguni elements struck southwards across the Thukela and the Umzimkulu. By 1822–3 the effect of the movement of insecure, hungry and destitute people from the north-east had reached Pondoland and Thembuland, striking terror and destruction wherever the fugitives went. By 1823 Pondoland in particular was all excitement because of northern Nguni immigrants. The northern Thembu, under their chief, Ngoza, had settled there briefly before moving back to Zululand. In so-called Nomansland, west of Pondoland, were Mdingi's Bhele who were later joined by the Wushe and the Bhaca under Madikane. Then came the Zulu invasion of Pondoland in 1823–4. Although Faku very wisely restrained his people from attacking the Zulu, all the same the invaders drove away many Pondo cattle.

As reports of happenings in Pondoland reached the Cape colonists, among whom the northern Nguni refugees, wandering marauders and invaders were known as the 'Fetcane', the Cape Colony was also being entered from the north by groups of refugees. Unlike the so-called Fetcane, the refugees entering the Colony had lost their group cohesion and identity. Like the former, they were also destitute, demoralized, hungry and insecure. The 'Mantatees'[15] or 'Bechuanas', as they were generally called,

14. J. D. Omer-Cooper, 1966, p. 33.

15. The terms 'Mantatees' (also spelt 'Mantatis') and 'Fetcane', as used by white colonists, early writers and Cape government officials, need brief explanations. As used by these people, the terms apply to agents of the Mfecane. The name 'Mantatees' as used by people like Robert Moffat, for instance, collectively refers to such groups as the Phuthing, Hlakoana and Fokeng marauders who fell upon the Thlaping capital of Dithakong in 1823. Calling these people 'Mantatees' is, of course, misleading as these people had no connection with Mma Nthatisi, the Tlokoa chieftainess. Later the term was again misleadingly used to refer to Tswana- and Sotho-speaking refugees drifting into the Cape Colony from across

had run away from the Caledon valley area and Transorangia, after the invasions of the Ngwane and the Hlubi and the devastating effects of the activities of the Tlokoa under their chieftainess, Mma Ntatisi. Some had come from as far north as the Vaal river and beyond, having been disturbed by the ever-expanding waves of the Mfecane. Many of the Tswana refugees had fled their areas in Botswana after the attack on the Tlhaping capital of Dithakong by the Phuting, Hlakoana and the Fokeng in 1823.

The refugees poured into such districts as Graaff-Reinet and Albany. They were not a military threat as they were unarmed and without chiefs. All they were looking for was support and protection.

The Cape's initial response, 1823–8

The response of the Cape colonial government and that of the colonists to the influx of the refugees must be considered and understood against the background of the two most pressing needs of the Cape Colony on the eve of the Mfecane; border security and cheap labour. The question of labour, in particular, had made many prospective farmers decide to abandon agriculture and opt for other forms of employment.

It soon became clear to the frightened and anxious farmers in the Graaff-Reinet and Albany areas that the hundreds of so-called Mantatees and Bechuana (Tswana) drifting from across the Orange river were not likely to create security problems for them. If anything, their gentle and almost timid-looking faces, and the fact that most of them had lost their cohesion and group loyalty encouraged the colonists to think that the Sotho and Tswana refugees would make 'docile and willing servants'[16] and satisfy one of the Colony's most critical wants. This assumption was correct, as gradually the destructive effects of the Mfecane in the interior were proving to be extremely beneficial to the Cape Colony. Indeed, the governor decided in 1823 that the refugees should be apprenticed to interested colonists as labourers for a minimum period of seven years.[17] The farmers in the Graaff-Reinet and Albany districts in particular found the decision beneficial as they had not had any labourers.

Contemporary opinion as to the quality of the Sotho and Tswana workers is not unanimous. In 1834, the Cape naturalist and explorer, Dr Andrew Smith, found that some of the farmers had thought their servants 'low' and many of them 'extremely covetous, nay even dishonest, and all very

---

the Orange and the Caledon, especially after Dithakong. 'Fetcane' or 'Mfecane' on the other hand, if applied to people, generally referred to northern Nguni invaders, e.g. the Zulu and the Ngwane of Matiwane. See J.D. Omer-Cooper, 1966, pp. 93–6; W.G.A. Mears, 1970, pp. 5–13; L. Thompson, 1969b p. 393; G. Butler, 1974, p. 182; H.H. Dugmore, 1958, p. 44.

16. See, for example, pictures (and captions) of two so-called Mantatees in G. Butler, 1974, p. 228, also pp. 181–2.

17. G.M. Theal, 1891, p. 240; G. Butler, 1974, p. 182; W.F. Lye (ed.), 1975, p. 20.

lazy'.[18] On the other hand, another explorer, George Thompson, found that 'the distribution of some hundreds of refugee Mantatees among the most reputable families, as servants and herdsmen' had proved a 'great advantage'.[19] Thompson's view does not however differ from Andrew Smith's independent opinion and observation, that in spite of what the farmers said about their servants, the presence of the Sotho and Tswana in the Colony was 'desirable inasmuch as they . . . supplied the deficiency of servants created by the circumstances of the Hottentots having of late years preferred other vocations to the service of the farmers'.[20] In fact, most Khoi people of the Cape had either drifted to urban centres or were living under the protection of Christian missions to avoid the humiliation of having to work for the people who had grabbed their ancestral lands.

It is not possible to give exact figures of Tswana–Sotho destitutes who were given temporary asylum in the Cape Colony. Possibly, we are speaking in terms of several hundreds, if not thousands. Moreover, the influx went on for as long as the disturbances in the interior continued, and it was not until the late 1820s that some Tswana and Sotho refugees began to return to their countries. The volume of returnees increased round about the mid-1830s after peace and stability had been established by such rulers as Moshoeshoe, founder of the Sotho nation.[21] The first five years of the Mfecane seem to have seen more refugees entering the Colony. George Thompson is reported to have said that there were 1000 Sotho and Tswana refugees in the Colony by 1826.[22] This was about three years after the influx into the Colony started.

Whatever numbers were involved, several points are indisputable. First, as already pointed out, the scourge of the peoples of Natal, the Caledon and the Orange valleys and the Highveld areas was, ironically, the blessing of the Cape Colony, bringing as it did cheap labour into an agricultural community that was on the point of collapse for lack of labour. The timely arrival of this source of labour gave a fresh impulse to the agricultural industry of the Colony's Eastern Districts. Secondly, the influx of refugees was bound to generate socio-economic patterns that were to alter the character of the Colony. For instance, it is said that in Albany and Graaff-Reinet the 'all-white phase' of the settlements, during which white farmers, their wives and children had been compelled to do the most menial tasks, was ended by the arrival of African labourers. This change, we are told, had been completed by the late 1820s.[23] The change undermined one of the fundamental principles underlying the founding of 'Anglostan' or Albany, that of white settler self-reliance. From then on, the importance

18. W. F. Lye (ed.), 1975, p. 21.
19. Quoted in G. Butler, 1974, p. 182.
20. W. F. Lye (ed.) 1975, p. 21
21. W. F. Lye, 1969, p. 203.
22. ibid., pp. 202–3, citing G. Thompson.
23. G. Butler, 1974, p. 181.

of black labour in the Colony's economic development was very firmly entrenched.

The third indisputable point about the Tswana–Sotho influx into the Colony is that it made cheap labour more readily available. This in turn undermined a second principle of the Albany and Graaff-Reinet settlements: that of intensive farming. For instance, partly because of pressure from the farmers for more land, and partly because of the availability of cheap labour, the 100-acre farms were extended into larger holdings in 1825.[24]

For their part, the Tswana and the Sotho also benefited from the temporary sojourn in the Colony. First, they were allowed to establish homes on their employers' property. Secondly, according to the terms of their 'apprenticeship', they were to be remunerated in animals and other such valuables.[25] In this way many of them acquired personal property that they were allowed to take back to their countries.

The presence of Sotho and Tswana in the Cape Colony did not, however, solve the other pressing want of the Colony. It did not in any way change the nature of the relationships between the colonists and their southern Nguni neighbours. Tension, open conflict on the border, cattle-lifting, retaliatory commando raids all continued.

This picture of black–white relationships in the Colony, however, must be qualified lest the reader is left with the impression that no areas of peaceful intercourse existed. There was, in spite of disputes and fights over grazing and hunting rights, a desire by both black and white for the promotion of commercial relations, because each of the groups had access to certain things that the other did not have. For example, the Xhosa had ivory, horns, hides, beef and gum for which there was a high demand from the colonial traders. The Xhosa needed copper, beads, buttons, guns, gunpowder and spiritous liquors, especially brandy, which only the colonial traders could supply. Thus, in spite of the hostilities between the Africans and the colonists, a system of barter existed. No form of control, military or legislative, could stop this. In fact, ever since the meeting of black and white on the Eastern Frontier, commercial intercourse had continued between them, and in defiance of government policy. Strict government control of the border only succeeded in encouraging co-operation between black and white in a system of smuggling.

Indeed, it was because of the flourishing smuggling business that the Acting Governor, Sir Rufane Donkin, decided in 1821 to regularize commercial relationships between the Colony and the Xhosa.[26] His idea was that a regularly held fair or even fairs should be instituted on the Keiskamma. Although the Governor opposed the idea at first, he also later accepted the

24. Farms were enlarged in 1825, according to G. M. Theal, 1891, p. 239.
25. W. F. Lye (ed.), 1975.
26. G. Butler, 1974, p. 197.

realities of the situation and a fair was established at Fort Willshire. The fair, which began as an annual occasion, quickly developed into a quarterly, a monthly and, by 1824, a weekly market,[27] where scores of colonial traders and thousands of Xhosa traders met to exchange their wares. Male and female African traders travelled to Willshire from as far away as the area between the Keiskamma and the Kei rivers,[28] bringing horns, ivory, hides, gum and beef and taking back beads, buttons, brass wire, brandy and a variety of European manufactures.

The Willshire fair must also be seen as a meeting point, and the market day as an occasion to allow experimentation with meaningful communication between black and white. Indeed, in the process of bargaining everybody tried hard to make himself understood by speaking the languages of trading partners. In Dugmore's words, 'strange Kaffer was spoken . . . and strange Dutch and English too'.[29]

The Willshire market was, however, a façade, although perhaps a necessary one. It could not conceal the realities of black and white relationships. Indeed, it must be emphasized that Willshire itself was first and foremost a defence post on a violent frontier, with everything about it bearing testimony to this fact. The market day was permeated with a military atmosphere in that the 'motley throng of black, and white, and brown' was, to quote Dugmore again, varied by 'the red, green, and the blue uniforms of "Line", Rifles and Artillery'.

No matter how successful commercial intercourse between black and white was, it could therefore never persuade the Xhosa to forget the ancestral lands now in white colonial hands. Indeed, while black and white were busy trading at Willshire before the watchful eye of the law, far away in Xhosa-land illicit firearms trading was also flourishing between white smugglers and Xhosa buyers. The Xhosa were acquiring guns in preparation for an armed confrontation between black and white that they knew was sure to erupt. In fact the war did come in 1834–5 and it was not the last one, nor was it the first. Yet another reminder of the violent realities of Xhosa–colonist relations was that just as commercial activities were going on at Willshire and in far-off Xhosa-land, lonely white travellers and European herdboys tending their parents' cattle were being killed by disgruntled Xhosa.[30]

27. G. M. Theal, 1891, p. 237.
28. H. H. Dugmore, 1958.
29. In the course of hard bargaining Dutch- and English-speaking traders tried to express themselves in Xhosa while the Xhosa traders also tried to express themselves in the two European languages.
30. For example, the sons of Garbett and Sloman, the Clay Pit victims, the Irish Party etc. were among victims of Xhosa anger.

External threat and black–white concerted response

It is clear so far that up to 1828 the events of the Mfecane had not very seriously threatened the stability and equilibrium of black–white relationships in the Cape. As already seen, Tswana and Sotho refugees who drifted into the white section of the colony from 1823 on were soon absorbed into its economic life. In the north-east, Faku's Mpondo had almost single-handedly prevented Shaka's regiments from advancing beyond Pondoland.

This situation, however, changed in 1828. A different class of fugitives suddenly appeared in the trans-Kei part of the Cape and, unlike the Sotho and Tswana refugees, they struck terror among the Thembu and the neighbouring Xhosa of Hintsa. They were also different in that, unlike the Sotho and Tswana, they still retained their political cohesion, loyalty and military capability almost intact. These were the Ngwane under Matiwane, a seasoned warrior who had already terrorized several states, including Moshoeshoe's Sotho.

The Ngwane, who now included Hlubi elements, crossed the Orange river from Lesotho and entered Thembu-land some time between January and February 1828. Their arrival coincided with that of Shaka's regiments in Pondoland, an event that was already creating a great deal of sensation among colonists, Thembu and Xhosa. Thus the whole area from the Eastern Districts to the Umzimvubu in the north-east was buzzing with rumours about the 'Fetcane' or 'Mfecane',[31] as the Zulu regiments were called.[32] Shaka's regiments in Pondoland were trying to penetrate further south in a bid to open the way to the Cape, with which Shaka had wanted to establish diplomatic contacts. Although they were determined to fight any southern Nguni state that stood in their way, the Zulu were, however, under strict instructions to avoid clashes with the British.

To go back to the Ngwane. As soon as they entered Thembu country they were met by an advance party of Cape colonial forces which was under the impression that they were the Zulu. A skirmish ensued but its results were inconclusive. Preparations were made for a major and decisive battle, and for this Governor Somerset, Hintsa, the Gcaleka chief and Vusani, the Thembu chief, co-operated. A combined force of British troops, colonial burghers, Xhosa and Thembu regiments was mustered for the final show-down, which took place at Mbholompo, where the Ngwane were thoroughly defeated and many were killed. Some of the survivors joined the Thembu and the Xhosa to increase the Mfengu element in these areas. Others fled back to Lesotho with Matiwane and were allowed to settle in Lesotho by Moshoeshoe I. However, homesickness compelled Matiwane and his

31. See Note 15 above.

32. Reports about Zulu presence were no idle rumours as a Zulu regiment was already advancing southwards through Pondoland.

followers to go back to Natal. On his return, however, Matiwane was killed by Dingane, who had by that time succeeded Shaka as the Zulu ruler.

The decisive defeat of the Ngwane at Mbholompo resulted in the effective elimination of one of the strongest and most destructive agents of the Mfecane. In fact, after Mbholompo the Colony and the areas of the Xhosa and the Thembu were free from any serious external threat. It should also be noted that concerted action against Matiwane's Ngwane meant the formation of a temporary alliance of the British, the Xhosa and the Thembu. This, of course, necessitated the suspension of British–Xhosa hostilities.

Now, while concerted action between Xhosa and Thembu is explicable, British involvement is not so easy to explain. What then were the considerations lying behind British involvement? Their territory was in no immediate danger of being invaded by the Ngwane. Moreover, even if they were still under the impression that the invaders of Thembu country were Shaka's Zulu, Shaka had never given them any reason to fear an invasion from him. Did they perhaps fear that continued unrest in Thembu-land might spread to the Xhosa area and force desperate Xhosa to flee westwards into the Eastern Districts and thereby create a sensation among the farmers? Or, as has been suggested elsewhere, was British involvement a calculated gesture motivated by diplomatic considerations rather than by fears of an invasion? Such a view would suggest that it was thought in Cape government and white settler circles that military assistance given to the Xhosa and the Thembu would make the Xhosa forget the ancestral lands in European hands and thereby contribute towards friendly black–white relationships.

Whatever reasons there were for British involvement in the 'Fetcane' campaigns of 1828, one important point has to be mentioned. The fight against Matiwane is an example of one instance when black and white buried the hatchet to face a common enemy. We can only conclude that in spite of the tension and open conflicts that characterized Xhosa–settler relations there was in the Cape some stability and equilibrium which in 1828 both black and white felt was being threatened by an external force and needed to be defended.

The emergence of the Mfengu

One of the most important and enduring results of the Mfecane was the emergence of new social units or political states as the displaced and scattered victims of the widespread disturbances regrouped themselves, often in new areas and different environments. In most cases, the new groups were made up of diverse elements who, thanks to the leadership qualities of certain individuals, were brought together into identifiable polities. The Swazi, the Gaza and the Ndebele are good examples of such polities. Many survivors of the wars either joined such leaders to increase the membership of the emerging political states or they were absorbed into already existing polities. That is how, for instance, Moshoeshoe built a big Basotho nation.

Many more survivors drifted about, leaderless, insecure and destitute and, although they were welcomed by certain chiefs, were never completely assimilated by the host communities.[33] Such were the diverse elements, mainly from Natal, who entered the Cape Nguni territory. They arrived in ones and in groups, large and small, some straight from the northern Nguni area and others via the Caledon valley area. Because they were destitute and hungry, their career was one of begging – *ukufenguza* – from which the name, *amaMfengu* (Fingo), was derived. It seems that the name was given to them by their Thembu, Xhosa and Mpondo hosts. This name is therefore collectively applied to those refugees or immigrants from the northern Nguni territory, mainly though not exclusively, Hlubi, Bhele, Ngwane and Zizi, who were given a new home in the Cape Nguni area after having been displaced and scattered by the Mfecane.[34] These fugitives began drifting into the Cape area almost at the start of wars in the northern Nguni area and the volume of immigrants increased during the period between 1822 and 1828. The defeat of Matiwane's Ngwane in 1828, by a joint British–Xhosa and Thembu force, resulted in many Ngwane survivors joining the already growing Mfengu population in the Cape Nguni area.

The response of the Thembu, Xhosa and Mpondo rulers to the requests of the fugitives was positive. They received them kindly as subjects and provided their immediate wants such as land, food and cattle. According to custom, although the ownership of the cattle continued to rest with the host chiefs, the Mfengu settlers were entitled to the milk from the cows and they could use the cattle in any domestic tasks.

Because most of the Mfengu were hard-working, many of them were settled within a short time and they also raised property of their own. They produced enough food and even surplus for exchange. One of the things that the Mfengu were good at growing was tobacco, which they exchanged for livestock. They also participated in the frontier trade with the colonists and were very successful in this.[35]

Although on the whole the Mfengu living in Pondoland and in Thembuland seem to have been happy, and many of them were soon integrated into the host communities, the Mfengu in the Xhosa area continued to feel discriminated against. For this reason, the process of integration in the Xhosa area was not successful. True, the Mfengu soon learnt to speak their hosts' language, though with an accent, but because they continued to see

33. See eyewitness account by one of the participants, B. Bowker (1810–1907) in G. Butler, 1974, pp. 252–4; also in H. H. Dugmore, 1958, p. 4 and J. D. Omer-Cooper, 1966, p. 92.

34. As a rule the definition does not include voluntary immigrants from Natal who settled in Cape Nguni territory after the Mfecane. See also, J. J. Van Warmelo, 1935, p. 65.

35. J. Ayliff and J. Whiteside, 1962, p. 20.

themselves, and were also regarded by the Xhosa, as a separate group and as subject people, complete integration was never achieved.

The failure of complete assimilation of the Mfengu to the Xhosa created hostile relations between the two groups and further complicated the already tense Xhosa–British relations. As mentioned above, Xhosa–Mfengu relations were originally warm and would have promoted the integration of the Mfengu into the host society. However, the relations between the two began to sour and the Mfengu started to look for alternative and more favourable circumstances. What exactly led to the souring of the relations between the Xhosa and Mfengu is not known, although it is clear that external forces exploited the failure of the integration process by exaggerating and perpetuating whatever cultural, political and economic differences existed between them. The most important of the divisive external factors were the Wesleyan Methodist Missionary Society, the white settlers and the Cape Colony government.

The Wesleyan Methodist Missionary Society had been working among the Gcaleka Xhosa since July 1827, when William Shaw was allowed by Hintsa to establish a mission in his area. Following the negotiation, a mission had been established at Butterworth, near Hintsa's capital, by W. J. Shrewsbury. Though not very enthusiastic about the mission, Hintsa protected it and Shrewsbury and his wife. He also allowed the Mfengu to attend services.[36]

The appearance of the Wesleyan missionaries on the scene at this time was bound to interfere with the processes of assimilation and integration that had been initiated by the settlement of the Mfengu in the Xhosa area. The attitude of the individual missionary to Mfengu grievances, real and/or imagined would be crucial. The Mfengu felt themselves discriminated against, politically oppressed and economically exploited by their Xhosa hosts. It was this ruler–subject relationship between the Xhosa and the Mfengu that was to be exaggerated into a 'master and slave relationship' by John Ayliff, Shrewsbury's successor, and later endorsed by Cape government officials. This slavery myth, together with another one – that the Mfecane had completely destroyed the Mfengu as a military force – had a number of effects and implications for Xhosa–Mfengu relations according to R. A. Moyer.[37] First, they represented the Mfengu as pitiable objects deserving the sympathies of the Cape government, the missionaries and humanitarians. Secondly, because they exaggerated the military incapacity of the Mfengu and their 'oppression' by the Xhosa, the two myths made both the missionaries and the government feel that they had an obligation to champion the rights of the Mfengu and to 'deliver' them from Xhosa 'bondage'. Thirdly, the two myths seem to have been readily swallowed by the Mfengu, who continued to regard themselves as apart from the

36. J. Ayliff and J. Whiteside, 1962, p. 20.
37. R. A. Moyer, 1974.

Xhosa. For this reason, not only did they begin to see the missionaries, the government and the colonists as liberators but they also tended to identify their own interests, aspirations and hopes, fears and anxieties with those of the external groups.

The external forces had their own ulterior motives in promoting the two myths, of course. The more the Mfengu saw themselves as oppressed and exploited, the more they would depend on the missionaries for the articulation of their case. The Mfengu would be expected to reciprocate missionary assistance by being more receptive to Christian teaching. The more the Mfengu saw themselves as being economically exploited by the Xhosa, the easier they would be to recruit as cheap farm labour.

Even more serious still, as long as the Mfengu saw themselves as apart from the Xhosa and identified their interests and anxieties with those of the British colony, they were bound to physically move away from the Xhosa and join the British colony at the earliest opportunity. This opportunity was eventually provided by the Sixth Frontier War (1834–5) when the Mfengu had to decide what position to adopt in a war that they at first regarded as a conflict between the British and the Xhosa. A meeting held immediately after the outbreak of the war resolved as follows: first that no Mfengu would take part in the invasion of the Colony; secondly, that as far as possible the Mfengu should defend and protect missionaries and traders; and, thirdly, that the Mfengu should act as British intelligence agents conveying security messages from John Ayliff to the British army commander, keeping him and his forces informed about the movements and intentions of the Xhosa forces.

Indeed, from the beginning of the war in December 1834 to May 1835, when they left the Xhosa area to go and settle in British-controlled territory, the Mfengu had done a great deal of intelligence work for the British army and against the Xhosa. Not only did they convey messages between Ayliff and the army commander, they also reported the activities of the Gaika and Gcaleka Xhosa to Ayliff at Butterworth. Ayliff in turn kept the magistrate/civil commissioner at Grahamstown well posted about developments in the Xhosa area. Mfengu couriers regularly travelled the 240 km between Grahamstown and Xhosa territory.[38] Although most of the secret activities were done at night, Hintsa, the Gcaleka ruler, soon discovered them and was determined to end Mfengu treachery.

Within weeks of the start of the war many isolated white centres were destroyed by the Xhosa who also killed a number of farmers and traders. Governor Benjamin D'Urban was compelled to go to the war zone to see for himself and to organize the defence of the British Colony. It was while the Governor was camping near Butterworth that Ayliff and his Mfengu protégés asked him to declare the Mfengu British subjects as a means of their 'deliverance' from Xhosa 'bondage'. The request was granted on 3

38. J. Ayliff and J. Whiteside, 1962, pp. 23–4.

May 1835 and the Mfengu, not less than 16 000 men, women and children with about 15 000 cattle and many thousands of goats all belonging to the Xhosa chiefs, left the Xhosa area escorted by British troops.[39] The trek began on 9 May and it effectively ended the processes of assimilation and integration that had been in progress since the arrival of the Mfengu in the Xhosa area. The long trek ended on 14 May when every person and animal had crossed the Keiskamma into the 'promised land': the Peddie District set aside for the Mfengu by Governor D'Urban. After the formal handing over of the land to the eight Mfengu chiefs, every man was required to vow that he would be faithful to God and loyal to the British king, and would co-operate with the missionaries by sending his children to them to be taught. The Mfengu would not forget the 'bondage' from which the Cape government and the missionaries had 'delivered' them.

The evacuation of the Mfengu from the Xhosa area came in the middle of the Sixth Frontier War and, as already pointed out, it was conditional on the Mfengu carrying out certain undertakings. For instance, they were expected to assist the British against the Xhosa, which they did immediately after their arrival in the new land. About 500 Mfengu joined the British army and were largely responsible for dislodging the Xhosa from the Buffalo River valley, guarding all the crossings into the Colony, and retrieving stolen cattle from the Xhosa area.

Another condition of their 'deliverance' was that they would provide cheap labour for the Colony, a very welcome idea, especially at the time when many Tswana and Sotho were returning to their countries, having completed their apprenticeship and seeing that peace was returning to their own countries.[40] Regarding co-operation with the missionaries, the Mfengu were willing for their children to be taught by missionaries and many adults themselves attended church services.

Above all, the evacuation of the Mfengu from Xhosa territory had been calculated to weaken the Xhosa in future conflicts with the whites. The area in which the Mfengu were settled was conveniently selected to be a buffer zone between the Xhosa and the British Colony.

Conclusion

The Mfecane brought about military, political, social, economic and in some cases, even cultural changes to the peoples of the various parts of Africa which it affected. The severity or otherwise of the impact of the Mfecane depended very much upon such factors as, for example, the agents of the movement and their objectives, on the one hand, and, on the other, local factors such as the military, the political and social conditions.

As we have seen, three kinds of victims of the Mfecane entered the area

39. ibid, pp. 28–9.
40. See 17 above.

defined as the Cape Colony. These were the hungry and destitute refugees – Sotho, Tswana and northern Nguni – who came in search of food, protection and support. Most of the Tswana and Sotho were apprenticed to the colonial farmers, while Natal Nguni fugitives were offered protection and food by the Xhosa, Thembu and Mpondo rulers. The second kind were Shaka's Zulu regiments, which invaded Pondoland but, because of Mpondo resistance, could not penetrate it. The third were people other than the Zulu who were equally strong and destructive, such as the Northern Thembu of Ngoza and Matiwane's Ngwane. Ngoza's Thembu entered Pondoland in 1822–3 but, like the Zulu after them, did not get beyond the Umzimvubu, again because of Mpondo resistance.

The only serious force that seems to have gone further south was the Ngwane of Matiwane, who created such a sensation in the whole area from the Umzimvubu to the Gamtoos when they suddenly appeared in Thembuland from Lesotho. Because they were mistaken for Shaka's Zulu, and because they were seen as a threat to the stability and equilibrium obtaining in the Colony, in spite of Xhosa–white border clashes, the Ngwane were fought by a combined British, Xhosa and Thembu force. Whatever military impact the Ngwane invasion might have had was short-lived, as they were quickly and effectively defeated by the combined force. British–Xhosa–Thembu military unity, which had been brought about by the need to defend common interests against an external threat, was also short-lived, as it ended on the disappearance of the Ngwane menace.

It would appear, however, that the economic, social and cultural impact of the Mfecane was more impressive and durable than either the military or the political results. This is all the more interesting because the groups that were instrumental in the cultural, economic and social impact were the weakest of the agents, namely the helpless, militarily innocuous Tswana, Sotho and Mfengu destitutes and beggars. As already seen, it was the timely arrival of the Tswana and Sotho refugees in 1823 that saved the agricultural settlement of Albany and Graaff-Reinet from a disastrous collapse for lack of cheap labour. The availability of labour was also to lead to the undermining of white settler self-reliance and intensive agriculture; the principles on which the two agricultural settlements had been originally founded. The arrival of the Mfengu in the Peddie District in 1835 was to ensure an endless flow of cheap labour for the farmers.

Because of their northern Nguni origin, and also because of their numbers, the Mfengu were, potentially, a political, social and cultural force. But their political impact upon their Cape Nguni hosts was weakened by their withdrawal from the Xhosa area in 1835 to go and settle with the colonists. As British subjects, they fought Britain's wars against the Xhosa. Whatever achievements or otherwise were made in these wars tended to be associated with the British and not with the Mfengu. For example, although Mfengu participation and sacrifice in the wars of 1834–5, 1846 and 1851–3 against the Xhosa were just as important as those of the colonial soldiers, these wars remain an Anglo–Xhosa affair, with the Mfengu occupying a peripheral position.

The Mfengu cultural impact upon the Cape Nguni and the white settlers is not easy to assess. Moreover, culturally, the Cape Nguni and the Natal Nguni were very similar. There is one area, however, in which the Mfengu impact was significant. Because they accepted Christianity, Western education, European agriculture and European employment much earlier than Cape Nguni people, the Mfengu were to play a major role as agents of modernization among other African societies in the Cape. They provided the first African teachers, evangelists, agricultural demonstrators and secretaries.

7 The British, Boers and Africans in South Africa, 1850–80

N. BHEBE

In the period 1850 to 1880 South Africa remained simply a geographical expression with no political significance. It was divided into British colonies, Boer republics and African states. Up to the 1870s Britain, which claimed supremacy in the subcontinent, hesitated from translating its claims into reality by taking over the political control of the whole region. Many of the British officials on the spot urged the British government to do so, arguing that the best way to meet British interests and at the same time be fair to the various peoples of South Africa was to bring the whole area under British rule. Successive British governments shied away from such responsibilities because of the expenses involved. It was indeed a potentially costly enterprise, because it meant conquering what looked like a multitude of African states, subduing the Boer republics (which were wedded to their independence), persuading the British colonies to join up with these states, and finally subsidizing the administration of the then very poor country. But from the 1870s onwards, with the onset of the European 'New Imperialism', the discoveries of diamonds and gold as well as the concomitant expanding British investments in the region, the British changed their minds and energetically sought to extend their hegemony throughout the subcontinent. By the end of the period, the British had conquered and annexed many African societies, afforded protection to others and humbled by force of arms the most recalcitrant and powerful of them – the Zulu. The British efforts to control more firmly the South African societies had further led them to war with the Boers. Because of these wars and their aftermath (arrangements involving either outright annexation or loose sovereignty) Britain could justifiably claim, among other European powers, at least by 1881, to have a hold on South Africa that was something more than simply a sphere of influence. Within South Africa, the period saw the British colonies acquiring a measure of self-rule, the Boers consolidating their unity, and the Africans progressively losing their land and sovereignty to both the Boers and the British.

British withdrawal from the interior

The 1850s opened with a British withdrawal from the interior of South

Africa. The energetic and overconfident Governor and High Commissioner, Sir Harry Smith, who assumed office in 1847, had within a short time of his arrival extended British rule in South Africa in a most dramatic manner. Convinced of the peaceful and stabilizing effects of British rule and the need to bring the 'benefits' of British industrial and cultural achievement to the Africans, he annexed the Xhosa country between the Keiskamma and the Kei rivers, calling it British Kaffraria, and the whole territory of the mixed population of Boers and Africans between the Orange and Vaal rivers, which became known as the Orange River Sovereignty. Smith was quite optimistic that the new responsibilities would not be a financial burden to the British, because the administrative costs of the new acquisitions would be met from local revenues. Subsequent events proved him totally wrong. His policy produced wars that were costly in money, lives and destruction of property, simply because the Boers were opposed to the annexation while the Africans rejected his 'civilizing' measures and revolted against the loss of their lands and sovereignty.

The first to launch an armed resistance were the Boers, under the leadership of Andries Pretorius, who in 1848 raised a commando of 12 000 soldiers and chased the British Resident (Major Harry Warden) and his other officials out of the Orange River Sovereignty. The Boers were unable to sustain their victory because they soon dispersed, leaving Pretorius with a tiny force that was easily defeated by Smith on 29 August 1848.

After restoring the British administration and assigning to it a small force to back it up, Smith dashed back to the Cape. He left Warden with the tricky and potentially explosive task of drawing up boundaries among the rival territorial claimants of the Orange River Sovereignty. The contestants were the powerful kingdom of Moshoeshoe, the lesser states of the Taung, Tlokwa, Rolong of Moletsane, Sikonyela and Moroka respectively, and the Boers, Kora and Griqua. Moshoeshoe's kingdom was growing very rapidly through the admission of refugees escaping the demands imposed upon them by the intrusive Boers. He therefore needed for his people's occupation most of the lands along the Caledon river valley, right from its junction with the Orange river to its headwaters. As Moshoeshoe's expansive people infiltrated into these fertile and arable northern and western frontiers of their country, they clashed violently with their neighbours, who prized the same lands. The British tried to resolve these conflicts by drawing up boundaries. But Warden worsened the situation, as his boundaries favoured the Boers and the smaller states at the expense of the Sotho of Moshoeshoe. Besides, the announcement of boundaries was itself sufficient to trigger off an intense competition for land occupation among all the population groups, which in turn led to increased livestock raids.

The whole crisis put Moshoeshoe in a difficult position in which he could only survive by sitting on the fence. He did not want to antagonize the British, who now ruled the Boers, because they were powerful and, in

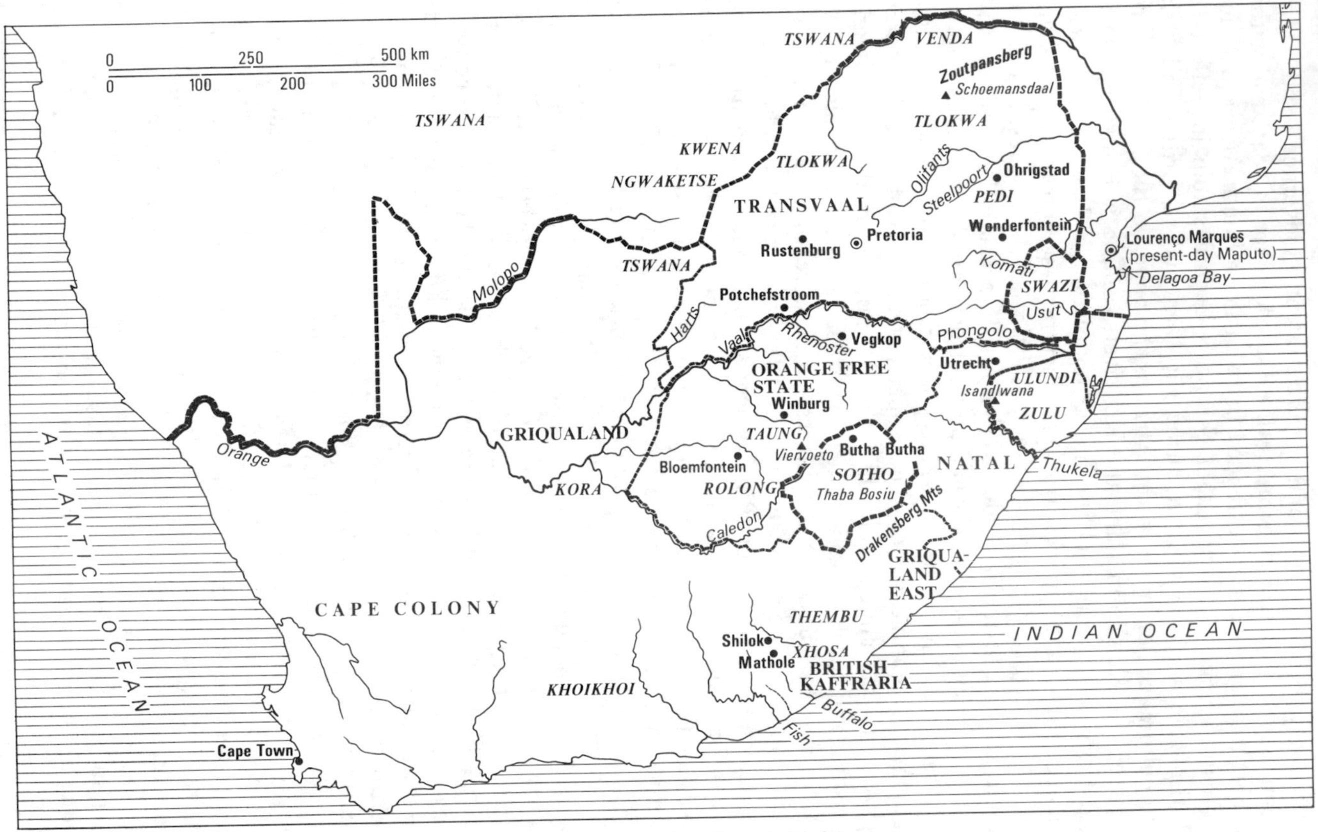

FIG. 7.1 *Map of South Africa showing the states and peoples, 1850–80 (after N. Bhebe)*

the event of a war with his white neighbours, he wanted to be able to count on British support. But the British embarrassed him. He had welcomed them in the region, expecting them to restrain the Boers from gobbling up his lands. Yet now the Boers took up his lands with the connivance of the British. Indeed, his people criticized him severely for what they saw as his collaboration with the British in giving away parts of their country. In the circumstances he could not effectively check his subjects from violating the Warden boundaries. All he could do was to rebuke his subjects, who disregarded the new borders at the same time as Moshoeshoe took every opportunity to protest to the British officials against the unfair boundaries. His people simply ignored his chidings, settled where they wanted and carried out livestock raids and counter-raids into neighbouring states.

Warden, the British Resident, could not bring about peace in the area either. His military force was inadequate, and he chose to ignore Moshoeshoe's territorial claims. When he created a boundary for the Tlokwa, Warden struck a blow at the Sotho of Moshoeshoe's national integrity, because they were constantly awaiting a propitious moment to destroy the Tlokwa, their object being to recover lands taken away from them by the Tlokwa when Moshoeshoe's kingdom had still been weak. Warden even forced a boundary on the Taung of Moletsane, who had never asked for it because they knew the land they occupied belonged to Moshoeshoe. Similarly, Moshoeshoe and his people could never countenance such recent intruders as the Kora of Taaibosch being generously provided with land by Warden. Warden's aim, on the other hand, was to try to weaken Moshoeshoe's kingdom at the same time as he wooed the support of the smaller states to overcome the British military weakness in the region.[1]

Indeed, when the war broke out following numerous incidents of livestock raids and counter-raids between the Taung and the Tlokwa, Warden was able to muster a sizeable force from the few Boers who cared to support him, the Griqua Rolong, as well as the Kora and come to the aid of the Tlokwa. He dispersed the Taung army at the Viervoet hills and crowned his victory by looting 3468 head of cattle, as well as goats and sheep. The redoubtable Moshoeshoe joined the struggle on the side of his allies, the Taung of Moletsane, and together they inflicted a crushing defeat on Warden and his African allies, causing a collapse of the British administration in the Orange River Sovereignty in June 1851.[2]

Warden could not secure much help from the local Boers and the British in Cape Colony. The Boers either looked for assistance from their kith and kin across the Vaal river or tried to reach a peaceful settlement with the victors, Moshoeshoe and Moletsane. In the Cape Colony the British forces were pinned down by the Xhosa in the war that had been raging since

1. P. Sanders, 1975, pp. 149–50, and p. 159.
2. ibid., ch. 14.

December 1850. In fact it was these two wars on the eastern front and the Orange River Sovereignty that compelled the British to abandon Smith's expansionist policy in South Africa.

The causes of the Anglo–Xhosa war of 1850–3 lay in Smith's efforts to deprive the Xhosa of their independence. In 1848 he took away vast Xhosa territories by annexing to the Cape Colony the area between the Fish and Keiskamma rivers and then declaring a separate British Colony of Kaffraria between the Keiskamma and Kei rivers. Many Xhosa were prevented from settling in their former lands west of the Keiskamma, which were now parcelled out to the Mfengu 'loyalists' and white farmers. In Kaffraria itself, the Xhosa were split up and allotted 'reserves', while their chiefs' powers were severely circumscribed by the supervision of imposed white magistrates. Such customs as *labola* (bridewealth) and accusations of witchcraft were outlawed as being contrary to British justice. Moreover, the white magistrates knew very little of the Cape Laws and nothing of the Xhosa legal system, with the result that they followed their personal instincts in reviewing Xhosa cases submitted to them. The members of the 500-strong African police force that backed the magistrates were untrained, and so proud to carry out the white man's orders that they became overbearing towards their people. All these grievances forced the Xhosa to try and rid themselves of British rule.

Smith sparked off the war by his rough handling of the chief and, indeed, disregard of the people's attachment to their institutional authorities. He summoned the paramount chief, Sandile, to a meeting in King William's Town. Sandile refused to go because a few years previously the British had treacherously arrested him after he had responded to a similar summons. Smith deposed him and tried to impose in his place a white chief and Sandile's mother, both of whom were rejected by the Xhosa. Smith then outlawed Sandile and tried to apprehend him by force. By December 1850 the Xhosa had had enough of the British Governor's interference in their lives and began to attack British forces and military installations in the area. They wiped out a number of military villages.

Sandile's cause received wide support from neighbouring Africans. East of the Kei river he got the moral support of his brethren under Sarili's paramountcy. Many members of the African police and Cape Coloured Mounted Riflemen deserted and joined Sandile's forces. The Khoikhoi and some of the Thembu also fought on Sandile's side. The result was that many white farmers and Africans who sided with the British were killed, their livestock captured and immovable property destroyed. Meanwhile Smith relied on local African allies because the Cape Colony white farmers were not willing to fight his war. Even with more reinforcements he received from the British government in March 1852, Smith failed to crush the Xhosa rising. The war was only brought to an end by his successor, Sir George Cathcart, who enlisted the support of the Cape white farmers by promising to give them a part of the cattle looted during the campaign.

Indeed when the Xhosa were defeated in October 1852, both the Xhosa of Sandile and those of Sarili – who lived east of the Kei and had mostly accorded moral support to their fighting western brethren – lost vast herds of cattle to the British.[3]

The expensive Anglo–Xhosa war and the complete disruption of the British administration in the Orange River Sovereignty caused the British to recoil from Smith's forward policy. They appointed two commissioners, Major William Hogge and Charles Owen, to go and arrange for a British disengagement from the area north of the Orange river. In order to deal effectively with the situation in the Orange River Sovereignty, without interference from the Boers north of the Vaal river, the commissioners bought off the latter by guaranteeing their independence. Andries Pretorius managed to raise from the scattered and factionally torn Boers of the Transvaal a delegation that hammered out a settlement with the British and concluded the Sand River Convention on 17 January 1852.

Under the Sand River Convention, the British recognized the independence of the Transvaal and unilaterally abrogated any treaties of alliance with the African states to the north of the Vaal river. The Transvaal bound itself not to meddle in the affairs of the British colonies and not to engage in slavery and the slave trade. The British and the Transvaal Boers further agreed to exclude the African societies on both sides of the Vaal from their firearms and ammunitions markets, while permitting the Boers free access to the British arms markets.[4] Needless to say, even though the Africans used clandestine means and 'unscrupulous' British arms dealers to obtain some guns, the Anglo–Boer arms embargo effectively prevented the African states from stockpiling large arsenals and, indeed, from purchasing the latest military equipment available in the British and other European markets. In short, by this agreement the whites guaranteed themselves military superiority over the Africans and made the conquest of the latter by the former technically inevitable.

With the Transvaal out of the way, the commissioners turned their attention to the Orange River Sovereignty. However, Cathcart, the new High Commissioner, wanted to patch up British military prestige, which lay in tatters in the eyes of the Africans, by striking a telling blow to Moshoeshoe's kingdom. With a large force of infantry and cavalry, he met Moshoeshoe at Platberg on 15 December 1852 and delivered an ultimatum that was impossible to fulfil. Moshoeshoe was ordered to produce within three days 1000 horses and 10 000 cattle, which would be used as compensation for the Boer property lost during the Warden war and also to finance Cathcart's own current expensive expedition. When Moshoeshoe failed to meet the deadline and pleaded for more time, Cathcart ignored

3. E. A. Walker, 1957, pp. 250–4; C. Brownlee, 1896, pp. 306–19; M. Wilson, 1969b, p. 256.
4. E. A. Walker, 1957, pp. 252–3; L. Thompson, 1969b, pp. 420–1.

the King's excuses and ordered an invasion of what is today Lesotho. But he met with such stiff resistance from the Lesotho infantry and cavalry that he was only too willing and relieved to withdraw when Moshoeshoe displayed a diplomatically submissive posture in a letter dated 20 December 1852. Moshoeshoe beseeched the High Commissioner to be content with the loot of over 5000 cattle which the Governor's troops had managed to capture. The King confessed himself sufficiently punished and indeed well impressed by the power of the British and therefore begged for peace. He would also in future try to prevent his people from causing disorder. On receipt of the letter the following day, the Governor with his mauled army (thirty-eight dead and fifteen wounded) quickly pulled out of the dangerous kingdom.[5]

Cathcart's experience of the Sovereignty quagmire added to the British conviction that the region could only be retained at a high cost. Sir George Clerk was therefore sent out to go and complete the British withdrawal from north of the Orange river. Getting wind of the impending British departure, Moshoeshoe prepared for the certain long struggle ahead with the Boers by destroying their potential allies, the Tlokwa, Griqua, and Kora in the north-west of his kingdom. All the southern Sotho around his kingdom now fell under his rule, except Moroka's chiefdom, whose population had been whittled down anyway to only 1000 people during the previous war.

In the meantime Clerk managed with some difficulty to assemble some Boers who were prepared to negotiate independence with him, and on 23 February 1854 concluded the Bloemfontein Convention, which was more or less along the same lines as the Sand River Convention. The Convention gave the Boers complete independence. The British renounced any alliances with the African rulers to the north of the Orange river, except Adam Kok. Even Adam Kok's treaty, which had restricted the amount of land the Boers could purchase in his country, was eventually amended in such a way that enabled the whites to buy off all his lands. Clerk also refused to be drawn by Moshoeshoe into any discussions concerning the boundary between the Orange River Sovereignty (soon to be called the Orange Free State) and his kingdom.[6] In their withdrawal the British therefore opened the way for Adam Kok's land dispossession by the white farmers, as well as for territorial clashes between the Boers and the Sotho.

On the eastern front of the Cape Colony, Cathcart was primarily concerned to prevent the Xhosa from disturbing the peace. After the 1850–3 war he regarded many of Sandile's Xhosa, the Thembu and Khoikhoi as rebels and, therefore, confiscated their lands west of the Keiskamma, in the White Kei and Kat river valleys, the foothills of the Mathole and

5. P. Sanders, 1975, pp. 185–93; E. A. Walker, 1957, pp. 254–5; L. Thompson, 1969b, pp. 421–2.
6. P. Sanders, 1975, pp. 200–1.

around the British military villages. The confiscated lands were sold to the white farmers and also given to the Mfengu 'loyalists'. In this way he hoped to neutralize the area so that it could be a buffer between the predominantly black east and the white Cape Colony in the west. Cathcart also changed the political aspects of Smith's policy. Where Smith had severely curtailed the powers of the Xhosa chiefs, Cathcart left them to exercise unlimited jurisdiction over their people in the crowded 'reserves' and reduced the British magistrates to 'mere diplomatic agents without power'.[7]

When Cathcart bade farewell to South Africa in 1854, the British had withdrawn from the interior, leaving the Boers and Africans to their own devices. Even British Kaffraria, which they chose to hang on to, was not considered a 'normal' colony to be developed in the interests of its own people and of Britain. Instead, it was regarded as an aspect of the Cape Colony's defence system, a territory where nothing more seemed worthy of attention than what was required for British logistical needs. The British government was simply in a mood to do only what was needed to guarantee its possession of the naval base on the Cape peninsula. It seemed possible to achieve this by denying the weak and disunited Boers independent access to the sea through the retention of the Cape Colony and Natal. The two white colonies were also to be maintained with as little cost to the mother country as possible by granting them a measure of self-rule so that they would agree to shoulder the greater part of the expenses of their own administration and defence. The result was that the Cape Colony was granted a constitution with parliamentary institutions in 1853 and Natal, initially annexed in 1845 as a district of the Cape Colony, was separated and given its own Legislative Council in 1856.

The Cape Colony and Natal before 1870

The need to economize was not, however, the only reason that prompted the British government to grant representative institutions to the Cape Colony in 1853.[8] The Cape constitution was born in the atmosphere of the British abandonment of the mercantilist system and the adoption of free trade. In Britain both the Manchester and Wakefield schools, which featured prominently in the discussions relating to colonial policies, advocated, for opposite views, the granting of self-rule to the colonies. And Lord Grey, the Colonial Secretary who initiated the process of granting self-government in the Cape Colony in 1846, was in fact a free-trader. Furthermore, the Cape colonists themselves were instrumental in bringing about self-rule, because for many years they petitioned the British govern-

7. E. A. Walker, 1957, p. 286.

8. S. Trapido, 1964, pp. 37–54; E. A. Walker, 1957, pp. 233–45; T. R. H. Davenport, 1969, pp. 321–4; C. F. J. Muller (ed.), 1975, pp. 183–4.

ment to give them representative institutions. They were not even silenced by the Legislative Council made up of the governor, officials and nominated unofficial members, which was established in 1834. Thus a combination of colonial pressures, free-trade principles, and the need to economize, forced the British to grant the Cape Colony a measure of self-rule.

The 1853 constitution was framed in such a way that it protected the interests of the rich English merchants, who were a minority, at the same time as it permitted limited political participation of the majority: poor Boers, Coloureds and Africans. This was achieved by means of the property qualifications for the franchise and membership of the two houses of parliament. Only the wealthy could be elected to the upper house, because qualification for election rested on being an enfranchised British subject and having unencumbered property worth £2000, or encumbered property worth £4000. The franchise and membership of the lower house were open to any male British subject having property worth £25 or a salary of £50 per annum. This permitted a few Boers and Coloureds to vote. But the use of English as the official language in parliament, barred from standing for election about 70 per cent of the rural Boers, who even as late as the 1870s could hardly speak the language.[9]

Two issues dominated the Cape parliament, the demand for the partition of the Colony and the conflicts between the executive and the legislative authorities. The eastern Cape districts were predominantly English-speaking and therefore wanted to be separated from the western, predominantly Dutch-speaking districts because of fear of being dominated. The constitution produced conflicts by its attempt to combine autocracy and democracy. It provided for no responsible ministers, rather, bureaucrats who headed departments were appointed by the Colonial Secretary and were responsible to the Governor. The Governor initiated policies that were then discussed and voted on by the two houses. For the constitution to work, it depended on the personality of the particular governor and the economic situation of the colony. Sir George Grey, who was Governor in a period of relative economic prosperity (1854–62) and was tactful in his dealings with the Cape parliamentarians, incurred no serious conflicts with the two houses. But Sir Philip Wodehouse, his successor (1862–72) was authoritarian, high-handed, and overly insensitive to the separatist feelings of the easterners and found himself confronted by bitter factions and generally hostile houses which were ready to fight with their only weapon: refusal to vote him new taxes. His problems were aggravated by the economic depression of the 1860s, which resulted in huge government deficits. The frequent constitutional crises at the Cape were only partially resolved by the granting of responsible government in 1872. But even then the Governor's powers and functions continued to cause clashes between himself and the Cape cabinet.

9. F. A. Van Jaarsveld, 1975, pp. 154–7.

It was during the rule of Governor Sir George Grey and his successor, Sir Philip Wodehouse, that the Xhosa of Kaffraria on the Ciskei lost their independence completely. Grey in particular put enormous pressure on the Xhosa of the Ciskei because of his so-called civilizing policy. He created what has been termed 'a chequerboard of black and white' by planting white settlers among the Xhosa. He also reduced the powers of the Xhosa chiefs, limiting their responsibilities to civil cases, while the white magistrates did everything else. Chiefs were given salaries so that they could give up the right to fines, which were thereafter collected by the British officials. A hut tax was imposed to help pay for the administration of the Colony. The people were forced to work on public works for low wages. The labour and financial demands, combined with population pressures caused by vast numbers of white settlers, compelled the Xhosa to seek millenarian solutions to their problem of subjugation. Although direct imperial pressures fell heavily on the Xhosa of Sandile and their Thembu neighbours, the Xhosa of Sarili to the east of the Kei river (in what is now the Transkei) suffered enormous population pressures as a result of the continuous immigration of refugees who either voluntarily tried to escape direct British exploitation and oppression or were actually driven out of the west on the pretext that they were rebellious.

The Xhosa, together with the Thembu, resorted to religious solutions in 1856–7. In March 1856 a girl by the name of Nongqause, who was apparently under the religious tutelage of Mhlakaza, one of the advisers of Chief Sarili, prophesied that if the people killed all their cattle, destroyed their grain stores, and did not plant any crops that year, a whirlwind would come and blow the English oppressors into the sea. Besides, their heroes would rise from the dead and bring vast herds of cattle, huge quantities of grain, and even white men's manufactured goods. The message was obeyed by the Xhosa and the Thembu, and when the appointed day came nothing happened. Large numbers of people died of starvation on both sides of the Kei in 1857. Many of the Xhosa in the Ciskei streamed to the Cape Colony to seek employment among the whites as the only means of survival. The whole episode makes little sense and people have tried to look for hidden explanations without success. E. A. Walker was convinced that Moshoeshoe, who wanted to divert the British from the Orange Free State, where he confronted the Boers, engineered the Xhosa into their suicidal move so that in desperation they would rise against the British.[10] Some people think that it was a white man's plot meant of course to lead the Xhosa into self-destruction. Little or no evidence exists to support either of these views. Perhaps Monica Wilson is right in interpreting the cattle-killing among the Xhosa just like the many, millenarian movements that have taken place in Europe, America and elsewhere in Africa. It was a movement, Wilson

10. E. A. Walker, 1957, p. 289.

tells us, in which people sought to rid themselves of foreign domination and to recover their lands from the white settlers.[11]

In the meantime Grey had taken advantage of the cattle-killing episode and its consequent weakening of the Xhosa and the Thembu. He confiscated large pieces of land from many of Sandile's chiefs whom he suspected of plotting an uprising against the British. The dispossessed chiefs and the people of Sarili were then all driven right across the Mbashe river so that an empty zone patrolled by the British police remained between the Kei and Mbashe rivers. He also encouraged white immigrants to settle on the confiscated lands. The black and white population was then ruled as a separate district with its own lieutenant-governor. In 1865 Wodehouse found the Ciskei too poor and too expensive to run as a separate colony and annexed it to the Cape Colony.

During the period before 1870, the Natal whites also made some constitutional progress. Within a few years of its annexation, many Boers returned to the highveld across the Drakensberg Mountains, in protest against British failure to recognize their land claims, the British African policy, and the new political arrangements, which excluded them completely from any participation. At the same time, Natal had a large African population, many of them returnees from exile whence they had been driven during the Mfecane.

The initial difficulties facing the weak colonial administration in Natal concerned the government of the Africans. The solutions were provided by the 1846 commission and elaborated upon over the years by Theophilus Shepstone, the Diplomatic Agent and Secretary for African Affairs (1853–75). The 1846 commission recommended the setting aside of reserves or locations for African settlement, and by 1860 land amounting to 2 million acres (810 000 ha) had been delineated for that purpose. However, the locations were situated mostly in the rugged, barren and wild parts of Natal, which were unsuitable for agriculture. The commission made other recommendations, such as provision for African education, administration of each location by a white officer backed by a black and white police force and the enforcement of the Roman-Dutch law in the place of the African laws. In view of the amount of money required to implement some of these recommendations, they were never effected. As a result, African education remained largely, if not exclusively, the responsibility of the ill-financed and ill-equipped missionaries, while the administration was done by Shepstone.

Fluent in the Nguni languages and having lived among the Xhosa, Shepstone was able to establish some working relationship with the African communities. All the Africans living in the reserves were placed under chiefs and headmen, and where the latter did not exist, new ones were created. African laws, except those concerning witchcraft, were permitted to operate. To finance his administration, Shepstone imposed a hut tax

11. M. Wilson, 1969b, pp. 256–60; see also C. Brownlee, 1896, pp. 135–70.

collectable in cash or cattle (which could be sold to the white farmers for cash). His administration was consistently attacked by the white settlers because, they argued, it made the Africans economically self-sufficient and therefore prevented them from becoming labourers on the farms and plantations. But Shepstone did not lock up the Africans in locations because he loved them. Rather, he clearly saw that coercive measures to produce labourers would only result in resistance, which the comparatively weak Natal colonial administration could not possibly cope with. The settlers who criticized him seem to have ignored the contribution of Africans to the profits of large landowners who subsisted on the rentals of over half the black population living as squatters on white farms, and to the colony's revenues in the form of the hut tax. In fact what Shepstone had done was to produce a cheap administration that afforded the white colonial society opportunities to exploit both the Africans and their natural resources in comparative peace and security.[12]

The white society was mostly of British origin. After the drain by Boer emigration the white population increased steadily as a result of immigration by British subjects escaping from the social problems accompanying the economic crisis of 1847–51. Financed by speculators, some 5000 white settlers left Britain for Natal in this period. By 1870 the whites in Natal numbered 18 000. The increase in the number of white settlers went hand in hand with constitutional changes. In 1856 Natal was made a separate colony and granted a Legislative Council. The franchise was made colour-blind, so that male British subjects owning at the minimum immovable property worth £50 or renting property worth £50 at an annual rate of £10 could vote. But the whites made it impossible for the Africans to qualify for the vote. A law passed in 1865 allowed literate Africans with some property to petition the lieutenant-governor to exempt them from African customary laws. The lieutenant-governor could turn down the application, even though the African might have the necessary qualifications. Then, to qualify for the vote, the exempted African had to show that he had resided in Natal for seven years, and put in an application supported by three enfranchised whites, and endorsed by a magistrate or any acceptable white official. The lieutenant-governor again had the discretion to turn down such a petition. The result was that, up to 1903–5, only three Africans had qualified for the vote in Natal and Zululand.[13]

Economically, Natal came to rely on the sugar industry, which required intensive use of human labour. Efforts to compel Africans to supply the necessary labour came to nothing, because of the poor working conditions and low wages offered by the planters. The Natal planters, assisted by their government, resorted to the importation of Indian labourers. The scheme was arranged in such a way that at the end of a ten-year period of working

12. E. H. Brookes, 1974, pp. 41–57; J. Guy, 1980, pp. 41–4.
13. E. H. Brookes, 1974, pp. 55–7; E. H. Brookes and C. de B. Webb, 1965, pp. 75–7.

in Natal, the Indian labourer had the option of either returning to India with his passage paid or exchanging his passage fees for a land grant and remaining in Natal permanently. The first Indians arrived under that scheme in 1860 and towards the end of the 1860s there were 6000 of them in Natal; many of these opted to remain in South Africa permanently. Because of Indian labour, the Natal sugar industry became established and indeed expanded until by 1870–71 it was the colony's biggest item of export trade.

It is clear, therefore, that by the beginning of the 1870s political power both in Natal and the Cape Colony was slowly devolving to the white settlers by means of constitutional arrangements. In the Cape Colony, where there was a majority of non-English-speaking whites, the constitution had to prescribe qualifications beyond financial ones in order to maintain power in English hands. Both in Natal and the Cape Colony Africans were herded into reserves where they were taxed in order to compel them to become labourers in the white enterprises and also in order to pay for their own administration. Even though there were financial constraints, the intention was always there to proletarianize the Africans through industrial education, as well as by breaking down their social cohesion through stripping the chiefs of their powers, the imposition of European laws, limiting the amount of land available for their use and, above all, through the activities of Christian missionaries.

The Boer republics before 1870

As the two British colonies thus made constitutional progress and, with British imperial assistance, established mechanisms for guaranteeing white political supremacy and economic deprivation and exploitation of the blacks in the 1850s and 1860s, the Boers also tried to achieve internal unity and to subjugate the African communities of the interior. When the British retreated from the north of the Orange river, the Boers were divided into numerous groups. The main division was along the Vaal river, causing two Boer republics to eventually emerge – the Orange Free State in the south and the Transvaal (South African Republic) in the north.

In 1854, when the Bloemfontein Convention was signed, perhaps many people in the Orange Free State wanted independence, but very few were prepared for it. Apart from poverty, ignorance, military weakness, and lack of administrative infrastructure, the Free State government dreaded its powerful neighbour, the Sotho kingdom of Moshoeshoe, with whom it had no settled border. The Orange Free State also suffered from a fundamental division that caused it for many years to waver between joining the Cape Colony in the south or amalgamating with its sister republic in the north. In this way the Orange Free State exposed itself to frequent interference from both directions.

The division was primarily between the *trekboer*s and the *voortrekker*s.

The former were the Boers who went across the Orange river in search of land before the Great Trek. They settled mostly in the south of what later became the Orange Free State. Whenever they were embroiled in wars with their African neighbours, they tended to look to the south for assistance. They were reinforced by British merchants and land speculators who settled in Bloemfontein during the brief period of annexation. Quite different from this group, variously called 'loyalists' or 're-annexationists', were the Boers living in the north-east of the republic, mostly in and around the Winburg district. These were the products of the Great Trek, men and women who had left the Cape Colony out of bitterness against the British government. These *voortrekkers*, 'faithful *maatschappijers*' or republican patriots, as they are variously called, always stood for complete independence from the British and when in trouble turned to the Transvaal for assistance.[14] This division explains in part the way the Orange Free State was easily goaded by Sir George Grey, the federalist Governor and High Commissioner, to toy with the idea of joining the Cape Colony in 1858; why the Free Staters voted the Transvaal President, Marthius Wessels Pretorius, to be their own president (1860–3); and why the Orange Free State remained neutral in the Anglo–Boer War (1880–1). Despite all these weaknesses, the Orange Free State achieved some semblance of statehood much quicker than the Transvaal. The same committee that negotiated independence with the British arranged for the election of the first government and produced a draft constitution based on the American one. The government had an executive president and a *volksraad* (legislative authority). The Boers did not try to disguise their racism by means of high material franchise qualifications as in the British colonies; the blacks were totally excluded from the country's citizenship and therefore from the franchise. Only whites who had lived in the country for six months were made citizens, and every white man who had registered for military service could vote.[15]

The first President, Josias P. Hoffman, did not remain long in power because he was considered too friendly to Moshoeshoe and the English settlers. He was therefore compelled to resign and Johannes Nicolaas Boshof, who had extensive administrative experience and stood for the complete independence of the republic, was elected. He created a strong civil service and organized state finances on a firm basis.[16] Nevertheless, Boshof's presidency was marked by instability arising out of border disputes with Lesotho, and out of tensions between the *maatschappijers* and the loyalists, resulting in the dual intervention of Sir George Grey and Pretorius. In October 1855 Sir George Grey intervened and managed to bring together Moshoeshoe and Boshof to sign an agreement on the procedures

14. F. A. Van Jaarsveld, 1961, p. 29.
15. L. Thompson, 1969b, pp. 429–30; C. F. J. Muller, 1975, pp. 233–5.
16. C. F. J. Muller, 1975, p. 255.

for settling disputes between their peoples. No border was fixed, and Moshoeshoe later said he only signed the treaty out of respect for Sir George Grey.[17] He thus did nothing to restrain his people from quarrelling with the Boers. Still afflicted by border problems, Boshof had to confront Pretorius, who wanted to unite the two Boer republics. Driven by a misconception that the majority of the Free Staters desired amalgamation with their northern brethren, and claiming to have inherited the leadership of the Free State from his father, Andries Pretorius entered Bloemfontein on 22 February 1857 and on the next day declared his intention to take over the state and outlawed the Boshof government. Rejecting his claims, the Boshof government deported him and charged his supporters with sedition. This provoked the mobilization of commandos on both sides of the Vaal river, which confronted each other on the opposite banks of the Rhenoster river on 25 May. Pretorius had banked on many *maatschappijer*s deserting Boshof and joining his army. To his surprise, not only were there not many people defecting to his side, but he now also had a further and more dangerous enemy in his rear, Stephanus Schöeman, the Zoutpansberg Commandant, with whom he competed for the leadership of the Transvaal, and who had formed an alliance with the Free State. Scared that he would be completely annihilated, Pretorius agreed to sign an agreement by which both republics acknowledged each other's autonomy on 1 June 1857.[18] The abortive civil war, however, exposed only too clearly the deep divisions among the Boers.

The agreement did not remove the tensions among the three factions which had emerged in the Orange Free State, consisting of the 'loyalists', who were for re-annexation to the Cape Colony, the supporters of Boshof who stood for Orange Free State independence, and the unionists who wanted incorporation into the Transvaal. The tensions reached such a pitch that Boshof was forced into a tactical resignation in February 1858 and, when he withdrew his resignation, several members of the *volksraad* left in protest. Coupled with the internal disputes were the increasing border quarrels with Lesotho. Boshof decided to check the border disputes by invading Lesotho in March 1858. By converging on Thaba Bosiu, Moshoeshoe's stronghold, the Boer commandos left their rear exposed, which was then raided by the Lesotho army. The Boers abandoned the struggle as they went back home to defend their families and property. The military weakness of the Orange Free State, which was exposed by the half-hearted invasion of Lesotho, had already been acknowledged by Boshof even before the war when he requested military assistance from both Pretorius and Sir George Grey.[19] Grey responded by arranging a

17. G. M. Theal, 1900, pp. 16–18.
18. G. M. Theal, 1900, pp. 40–5.
19. G. M. Theal, 1900, pp. 50–60; P. Sanders, 1975, pp. 203–36; L. Thompson, 1969b, p. 432.

meeting between Moshoeshoe and Boshof and on 29 September 1858 both sides signed the Treaty of Aliwal North which confirmed the Warden boundary.[20]

Pretorius, on the other hand, found a chance to renew his efforts to unify the two Boer republics. The Transvaal made it clear that it could only assist the Orange Free State in return for the latter's absorption by the Transvaal. The prospect of unity between the two republics alarmed Grey, who was already contemplating federating the individual republics with the British colonies. As early as 1857 Grey had come to the conclusion that Britain had made a mistake by pulling out of the interior of South Africa. He therefore started calling for the abrogation of the conventions and for the re-establishment of British rule under some form of federation. He feared that fragmentation of the whites weakened them in the face of the ubiquitous African states. He feared that the Boer republics might unite and enter into relations with foreign powers, thereby threatening the British colonies and Britain's retention of vital naval bases. Besides, he thought, the numerous Boer conflicts with the African states were potentially dangerous, as they could spill over into the British colonies. Grey therefore moved swiftly to smother the Boers' plans of unification by informing them that if they united Britain would feel itself free from the obligations of the conventions and therefore start negotiating alliances with the African states and even sell them guns. The Transvaal therefore retreated to the north of the Vaal river to safeguard its independence, leaving Grey to encourage the Free State to take steps towards unity with the Cape Colony. But when he tried to encourage the Cape parliament to discuss the Free State offer of unity, the British government removed him from South Africa in June 1859.

With the collapse of the federation scheme, Boshof and his supporters, who had been enthusiastic about re-annexation, were discredited and the president resigned. This strengthened the unionists and they elected Pretorius as president. But the desire of the Orange Free State for unity was not matched by similar sentiments in the Transvaal, where the fear of the cancellation of the Sand River Convention and re-annexation by the British predominated. The Transvaal *volksraad* forced Pretorius to resign his presidency in the Transvaal, but he continued for another three years to work through his supporters there for unity. By 1863 Pretorius had failed even in the Orange Free State and he retired to his home republic.

The unsuccessful experiments of unity with either the Cape or the Transvaal made the Free Staters turn to themselves in shaping their national destiny. They elected as their president Johannes Henricus Brand, a lawyer and experienced parliamentarian from the Cape, who was to rule them for twenty-five years. But before looking at the Free State relations

20. P. Sanders, 1975, pp. 233–41.

with their neighbours during Brand's rule, it is necessary to consider how the Transvaal transformed itself into a state.

The Transvaal took longer than the Orange Free State to attain recognizable features of a state. The Boers to the north of the Vaal river were widely dispersed and further divided by religious differences. M. W. Pretorius, who took over from his father in 1853 and, as we have seen, ceaselessly fought to unite the two republics on either side of the Vaal river, was the chief champion of the unification of the Transvaal as well. He contended with such separatist groups as the Zoutpansbergers, centred around the Schoemansdaal village in the north; the Lydenburgers and W. F. Joubert in the east; and the Boers of the Utrecht district along the Buffalo river. The biggest group was that of Pretorius himself in the Potchefstroom Marico-Rustenburg area.

Some form of unity was established in 1849 through the adoption of the Thirty-three Articles of 1844 as a constitution.[21] The articles were nothing more than rules concerning the administration of justice, election of the members of the *volksraad* as well as general laws. The biggest flaw of the articles was their failure to separate legislative functions from executive ones – so that the *volksraad* tried to exercise both. Moreover, since the state had no capital, the *volksraad* met in different villages and invariably failed to form a quorum, so that local non-members had to be co-opted. Pretorius strove for a proper constitution providing for a legislature and an executive. On this he clashed with the Lydenburgers, who were extremely suspicious of a one-man executive, such as the presidency, lest he should become an autocrat.

These differences were worsened by the religious quarrels. To sever their connections completely, Pretorius urged the Potchefstroom community to split from the Cape Synod of the Nederduitse Gereformeerde Kerk (Dutch Reformed Church) and they formed the independent Nederduitse Hervormde Kerk (NHK) whose pastors were to be recruited from the Netherlands. The Lydenburgers stuck to their connections with the Cape Colony, while a further splinter Church called the Gereformeerde Kerk van Suid-Afrika emerged from the NHK. Its distinguishing characteristic was a refusal by its members to sing hymns in church.

Despite all these differences, a draft constitution providing for a president, legislature, judiciary, and army authority was produced in January 1857. The *volksraad*, which was dominated by Pretorius's followers, elected him the president and the Zoutpansberg leader, Johannes Schöeman, commandant-general. Schoeman rejected both the constitution and the army post and raised a commando to attack Pretorius's supporters in the Rustenburg district. War was avoided when both sides agreed to choose a committee to amend the constitution in accordance with the wishes of the Zoutpansbergers. With the approval of the constitution in 1858,

21. G. M. Theal, 1900, pp. 413–17, for an English translation of the articles.

Pretorius and Schöeman became the president and commandant-general respectively, while the Lydenburgers were persuaded to join the republic in 1860.

But Pretorius plunged the nascent republic into chaos when, as we have seen, he accepted the presidency of the Orange Free State. Fearful of jeopardizing the Transvaal's independence, the *volksraad* asked Pretorius to choose between one of the presidencies, and he resigned from the Transvaal. However he continued to work through Schöeman and the people of Potchefstroom, his staunchest supporters. These set up a committee of their own with powers and functions that rivalled those of the *volksraad*. The *volksraad* in turn appointed its own president and commandant-general and both governments claimed to rule the republic. Peace only returned to the Transvaal when Pretorius resigned from the Orange Free State and was re-elected President of the Transvaal in 1864. He ruled the Transvaal until he was forced to resign for his mishandling of the republic's claims to the diamond fields in the 1870s.

Boer relations with the Africans before 1870

In both the Transvaal and the Orange Free State, many African communities had either been destroyed and absorbed into the Mfecane fugitive states, such as the Ndebele kingdom of Mzilikazi, or forced to seek refuge in the difficult and easily defended parts of the country. Located in such places, resourceful leaders, such as Moshoeshoe, were able to build large followings out of displaced refugees and to emerge as powerful nations in the 1840s, when the Ndebele were expelled from the region by the Boers. Such states, as already seen in the case of Lesotho, were strong enough to contend with both the intruding Boers and the British.

After the expulsion of the Ndebele, many small chiefdoms that had submitted to Mzilikazi but had not been fully incorporated into his nation, together with others that had eluded the Ndebele by moving out of the range of their frequent raids reoccupied their erstwhile territories. Many of these peoples were overwhelmed and incorporated into the Boer states before they could build up their means of resistance. These were the Africans who suffered direct economic exploitation by the Boers. Exploitation was built into the citizenship, labour and other laws enacted by the Boers. The Transvaal constitution, for instance, rejected any notions of equality between black and white. To rule out any possibility of effective African resistance, the incorporated peoples were prohibited from possessing firearms or horses and they were forced to carry passes supplied by their employers or government officials at all times. Each farmer was entitled to keep a number of African families on his farm, who supplied him with regular free labour. 'With regard to natives living within the European area under direct protection of the Boers, the furnishing of regular labour supply would be regarded as payment for the land which had been assigned to them.'[22]

The Africans who did not live on the farms were put under chiefs and the different chiefdoms were allotted a location or reserve. The locations were widely dispersed, and each of them was placed as near as possible to a white farming area. This was meant to divide the Africans so as to preclude any concerted uprisings, as well as to ensure that every white farmer had easy access to a black labour reservoir. Each chief paid tax in cattle and labour. Indeed, one of the important duties of the *landdrost*s (magistrates) and *fieldcornet*s (ward military commanders) was to collect labourers from the chiefs in their districts and distribute them among the white farmers on a one-year contract basis. The chiefs were further expected to supply men to assist the Boers in times of war.

The Transvaal, moreover, practised the controversial system of apprenticeship, which had been carried over from the Cape Colony. African children captured in wars were distributed to farmers, for whom they worked until they were 25 years old (boys) or 21 (girls). In return for insignificant payments or favours, incorporated African parents were at first persuaded and later pressured to offer their children to farmers to be raised as apprentices. It was not uncommon for the Boers to organize commando raids on neighbouring African states purely for the purposes of capturing children. Even though the Transvaal laws prohibited the sale of these children from one farmer to another, the whole system smacked of slavery and was denounced by the missionaries and traders as such.[23]

The Boers claimed the Transvaal and its people by right of their conquest and expulsion of the Ndebele. They therefore felt themselves entitled to demand submission and services from all Africans to the south of the Limpopo. These impositions were stiffly resisted by the Tswana in the west, the Sotho and Venda in the north and the Pedi in the east. For instance, the Kwena of Sechele around Dimawe and the Ngwaketse of chief Gaseitsiwe around Kenye used guns bought from missionaries and traders to resist the Boers. In this way they were able to maintain their independence so that their territories were used by missionaries and traders who were not permitted to pass through the Transvaal on their way to the north.

In the east the Pedi resisted the military poundings of the Ohrigstad-Lydenburg Boers until a border was drawn between the two communities along the Steelport river in 1857. At the same time the Pedi quickly learned the importance and effectiveness of guns in warfare, particularly when used in combination with their Lulu mountain fortresses. As early as the 1850s they therefore strove to build large stocks of firearms by purchasing them

22. W. Kistner, 1952, p. 213.

23. L. Thompson, 1969b, pp. 435–7; for the Cape Colonial system in the earlier years, see A. Atmore and S. Marks, 1974, p. 116.

from traders and working for them as migrant labourers in Natal, the Cape Colony and, when the diamond mines were opened, Griqualand West.[24]

In the north it was the Venda, the Transvaal Ndebele and Sotho who resisted the Boer expansion. In 1854, for instance, the people of the Sotho chief Makapane east of the Watberg ranges killed twelve members of a white hunting party under the leadership of the Boer military commander, Hermanus Potgieter. These whites behaved in an overbearing manner to Chief Makapane, apparently 'demanding oxen and sheep for slaughter without payment, and forcing blacks to give them several children for slaves.'[25] Whatever the specific reasons, it was clear that Makapane wanted to keep his country clear of the whites, perhaps for fear of competition in ivory hunting. The killing of the white hunters signalled a fairly general attack on white settlements south of the Zoutpansberg. The Boer communities in the area and even those as far south as Potchefstroom and Rustenburg all sheltered their families in laagers. A large Boer commando of 500 troops was raised from all the Transvaal districts, except Lydenburg, and it invaded the Makapane chiefdom under the joint command of P. Potgieter and President Pretorius. Warned of the approaching invasion, the Sotho retreated into their nearby cave and made ready to fire on the approaching enemy. Effectively checked from flushing out the Sotho, the Boers blocked the entrance of the cave with wood and stones and guarded it against anybody trying to escape for twenty-five days. It was estimated that 900 of Makapane's people were killed trying to escape and that more than double that number perished in the cave from starvation and thirst.[26]

The Boers retired, convinced that the massacre would serve as a deterrent to further resistance from the Sotho and Venda of the north. But in 1859 another rising occurred, this time a little further north, around the Boer village of Schoemansdaal. The Boer administration in that village imposed heavy demands on the local Africans, by supporting rebels, exacting tribute and waging unprovoked wars on the chiefdoms in order to capture slaves. Although the Africans were defeated, the Boer administration thereafter lost control of the blacks.

By the 1860s the Venda of Zoutpansberg had incorporated firearms into their military and hunting techniques. Their country teemed with elephants and was therefore frequently visited by white hunters and traders. Many of the Venda entered the service of the hunters and acquired marksmanship and skills to maintain guns. As the elephant zone receded into the tsetse-fly zone of the Limpopo valley, hunting on horseback, at which the whites were adept, gave way to hunting on foot. The latter was done by the Africans, who were loaned guns by white merchants and were called *swart-*

24. P. Delius, 1980.
25. G. M. Theal, 1900, p. 27.
26. ibid., pp. 23–31.

skuts (black shots or black marksmen). Many of these guns were in the end not returned to their white owners but were in fact used to drive the Boer settlers out of the Schoemansdaal settlement. In fact, one of the leaders of the uprising of 1867, the Venda chief Makhado, was a former *swart-skut*. The 1867 uprising was so effective that the Boers abandoned the Zoutpansberg district.[27]

Meanwhile the Boers of the Orange Free State dealt mostly with the Southern Sotho of Moshoeshoe, the Rolong of Moroka and the Griqua of Adam Kok. The latter ceased to be a factor in 1861 when he sold his land rights to the Orange Free State and migrated to Nomansland and founded another East Griqualand. Moroka too remained a faithful client of the Orange Free State.

The Sotho of Moshoeshoe remained determined to resist the Boer expansion. Even though the king had signed the Treaty of Aliwal North in 1858, implying his acceptance of the Warden boundary, he had no intention of enforcing it on his people, who contined to violate the border. However, by the 1860s the balance of power was tipping in favour of the Boers. The king was old and losing control, particularly over his sons, who were already vying with each other for the succession. The Free State on the other hand was growing in strength. The economy was becoming healthy as the farmers strove to improve their livestock, the products of which found easy markets in Natal and the Cape Colony. Its population was expanding as the result of immigration from the colonies. By the 1860s the Free Staters, too, had a fair amount of commitment to their independence to the extent that President Brand could count on them to fight a prolonged war with patriotic zeal. Consequently, when the 1865 war broke out following numerous border violations on both sides, the Boers were able to sustain a ruthless campaign against Lesotho, while it was the Sotho who showed signs of disunity. Molapo, Moshoeshoe's son, governing the northern part of the country, concluded a separate peace treaty with the Boers. Such lack of unity forced Moshoeshoe to sign the Treaty of Thaba Bosiu in 1866 under which he lost a great deal of his arable lands to the Orange Free State. But Moshoeshoe did this only to gain time to reorganize his people; in 1867 another war broke out and dragged on until the British intervened.

As early as 1861 Moshoeshoe had asked for British protection and repeated the request in 1865 through Sir Philip Wodehouse, the Governor and High Commissioner. Wodehouse was in favour of British expansion in South Africa and saw the annexation of Lesotho as a step in the right direction. Thus, at the same time as he was persuading the British government to accede to Moshoeshoe's request, he was also taking steps to cut off arms supplies to the Boers to ensure that the Orange Free State would not be able to take over Lesotho. When the British government

27. L. Thompson, 1969b, pp. 440–2; R. Wagner, 1980, pp. 330–6.

agreed to take Lesotho, Wodehouse annexed it as a Crown Colony on 12 March 1868.

British expansion in South Africa 1870–80

The annexation of Lesotho represented a change in the British policy of withdrawal from territory north of the Orange river. The change became even more apparent with the disallowing of Transvaal territorial expansion in 1868 and the annexation of Griqualand West in 1871. British expansion coincided with the era of mineral discoveries in Southern Africa. In 1867 a diamond was picked up at Hope Town in the Cape Colony, and the following year alluvial and dry digging for diamonds started along the Vaal river towards its junction with the Orange river. In 1868 an elephant hunter called Henry Hartley and Carl Mauch, a geologist, reported the existence of gold deposits between the Ndebele and Ngwato countries as well as in Mashonaland. Even though the gold discoveries proved largely illusory, they initially aroused a great deal of interest both in South Africa and Britain, while diamond mining grew rapidly into a major South African industry.

President Pretorius, whose state seemed chronically poor, saw a chance of pulling it out of its predicament by enlarging its borders in such a way that it encompassed most of the known mineral deposits and had an outlet to the sea. In April 1868 he announced that his republic stretched north and west to Lake Ngami and east to include a small section of the coast line south of Delagoa Bay. The Portuguese, who had the tiny village of Maputo near Delagoa Bay, and the British missionaries and traders whose road to Central Africa was threatened, all protested vigorously and put pressure on the government to prevent the Boer expansion. By 1869 Pretorius had given up his territorial ambitions.

The discovery of diamonds meanwhile sparked off territorial disputes among the Transvaal, Orange Free State, Waterboer's Griqualand West, the Rolong and the Tlhaping. The Transvaal and the Orange Free State claims clashed in the area between the Harts and the Vaal rivers, so that President Brand withdrew in favour of President Pretorius of the Transvaal. Pretorius and the African states submitted their cases for arbitration by the Lieutenant-Governor of Natal, Robert Keate, and Pretorius lost his case to the Africans. Brand, on the other hand, pleaded to have his territorial conflicts with Griqualand West submitted for arbitration. This was rejected by the British, for fear of having their position as the paramount power in Southern Africa challenged. Waterboer then applied for British protection, and Britain annexed not only Griqualand West but also the rest of the diamond fields on 27 October 1871.

The declaration of a protectorate over Lesotho, which Brand believed was timed to prevent its conquest and absorption by the Boers, the limitations imposed on the Transvaal's territorial aggrandizement, and the snatching away of the diamond fields, all embittered the Boers to the extent that for many years to come the British forfeited their co-operation and indeed also reinforced the Boer determination to resist being brought back under British hegemony by physical force. This ensuing era of fresh British expansion in Southern Africa has generated much discussion among historians. Antony Atmore and Shula Marks[28] in particular have summarized succinctly the current interpretations and have gone on to offer some new ideas which, in turn, have generated further research.[29]

Atmore and Marks argue that the scholars who have relied most heavily on 'the official record' such as R. Robinson and J. Gallagher, broadly recognize the importance of economic factors in explaining late nineteenth-century British imperialism, 'but veer sharply away from any further and more precise economic analysis of the events they portray, whether in South Africa or elsewhere.' Instead, the 'official mind' historians see British expansion, in the final analysis, as occurring when policy-makers are drawn irresistibly into the African (including the South African) interior to stop 'crises or emergencies' on the 'frontier' or 'periphery' of their formal colonial holdings or informal empire. However, what is omitted, Atmore and Marks point out, is the thorough analysis of these crises, which in the end proved so crucial for the creation of the British empire. In fact, when these crises are explored, they reveal that they were actually 'related to the break-down of indigenous authorities under the weight of the demands of an increasingly industrialized Britain.' In the early nineteenth century these pressures occurred mostly on the eastern front in South Africa, where the informal agents of industrialized Britain – the missionaries, traders, and administrators – were active. But with mineral discoveries in the interior in the late nineteenth century, the demands of industrialized Britain rapidly shifted there and were imposed upon both the African states and the Boer republics. Thus, although the strategic importance of the Cape on the sea route to India continued to influence British imperial policy in South Africa in the late nineteenth century, expanding British economic interests in the subcontinent weighed preponderantly.

These British interests demanded vast supplies of African labour that could not be secured if Africans retained their independence and economic self-sufficiency. Their kingdoms therefore had to be smashed and their people proletarianized. The rapid industrialization of South Africa called for the subordination of the white states as well. The reason was that both the colonies and the Boer republics were incapable 'of successfully performing the role of collaborators'. What followed this assessment was an extremely 'complex and confused situation', in which, among other

28. A. Atmore and S. Marks, 1974; see also C. de B. Webb, 1981, which distinguishes Marks and Atmore's 'radical' interpretations from those of the 'conservatives' and 'liberals'.

29. See for instance the collected papers and illuminating Introduction in S. Marks and A. Atmore (eds.), 1980.

things, the British government sought to secure its interests by promoting a subordinate confederation in South Africa. Again, 'official mind' historians, the best example of them in this case being C. F. Goodfellow,[30] have explained the genesis and operation of the confederation policy – which reached its climax in the annexation of the Transvaal, initiated the fall of the Zulu kingdom, and led to the destruction of the Pedi state – in terms of the personalities of the British Colonial Secretary, Lord Carnarvon, and the Governor and High Commissioner, Sir Bartle Frere. Atmore and Marks argue that, though this may well have been true, the solutions offered by the confederation policy satisfied almost uniquely British interests and socio-economic imperatives in South Africa.

It is therefore possible that the Transvaal may have been annexed to release the African labour locked up by the pass laws of 1873 and 1874 so that workers could flow freely to the diamond mines and railway construction in the Cape Colony. Besides, the Transvaal obstructed the free flow of African labour by permitting the activities of British and colonial land speculators who subsisted on profits from rents paid by the African farm squatters. The squatters had little intention of selling their labour to the miners and other white employers because they had sufficient land to produce crops for their own consumption and for sale in order to pay taxes. For these reasons the Transvaal, like the Zulu kingdom whose military system held up labour supplies, had to go.

Indeed, Norman Etherington[31] goes a long way to substantiating the views of Atmore and Marks when he shows that after the discovery of diamonds, African labour was drawn from all over the subcontinent, including what are today Mozambique and Zimbabwe, and that the Transvaal, Orange Free State and the Zulu kingdom obstructed its free flow. Moreover, Shepstone, the key source of information in the 1870s for British policy-makers and operators, was not only concerned about immediate solutions to the problem of securing African labour for the British capitalists, but looked further to see the solution to the whole problem as lying in a federation of the white states with a common African policy. Clearly, therefore, some accounts of British imperialism in South Africa have neglected the growing economic importance of the region to Britain, a situation which became increasingly apparent at the end of the 1860s with the discovery of diamonds and reports of gold deposits, and most evident in the 1880s when gold began to be mined in the Witwatersrand.

Between 1871 and 1874, however, the British government tried to secure a federation of the South African states and thereby to guarantee the security of its interests in South Africa by means of persuasion. When Britain granted the Cape Colony responsible government, it was with the hope that the Colony would take over the Lesotho labour reservoir and the

30. C. F. Goodfellow, 1966.
31. N. Etherington, 1979.

diamond-rich Griqualand West so that the Cape would emerge as the most powerful state and draw to itself the rest of the white settlements. To the disappointment of the British, the Cape government agreed to annex Lesotho but turned down the offer of Griqualand West. The offer was refused because the Cape had a large Boer population that sympathized with the republics, which never gave up their claims to the diamond fields. By the middle of 1873, Lord Kimberley, the Colonial Secretary, confessed that the quarrels over the diamond mines stood in the way of a South African confederation and stopped pressing for it.[32]

Lord Carnarvon, who succeeded Kimberley in February 1874, resuscitated the federation policy and officially launched it on 4 May 1875. It seemed to be the only antidote to the festering ills of South Africa, which were epitomized by Griqualand West, where labour supplies were desperately short, imperial expenses on defence and administration high, territorial disputes deafening, and guns easily obtained by the Africans who then, in defence of their independence, turned the same firearms on the white men. Then there was the unsolved Langalibalele uprising, whose handling by the Natal whites exposed the dangerous weakness of the individual white states in confronting Africans with easy access to guns.

In 1873 Langalibalele of the Hlubi refused to register the guns that his people had procured – mostly from the diamond fields – and this was interpreted by the Natal government as an act of rebellion. Shepstone and the Lieutenant-Governor raised an army to invade his kingdom, but the Hlubi chief escaped to Lesotho, where he was betrayed by Molapo, the Sotho chief, and handed back to his enemies. In the only encounter that took place with the Hlubi and their neighbours, the Natal troops ran away and in the process some of them were killed. But the Natal government in the end dealt with the Hlubi in a most cowardly and vindictive manner. Even before the Chief, Langalibalele, was apprehended, the government inflicted measures that were disproportionate to the crime committed. His chiefdom was erased, his cattle and horses impounded, his land taken away and his subjects distributed to farmers as indentured labourers. When finally the chief was summarily tried and found guilty, he was banished for life and imprisoned on Robben Island.

It was quite clear to the British government, which was also impressed by the arguments of the Anglican Bishop, John William Colenso, the only stout defender of the Hlubi chief, that injustices done to the Hlubi were the result of the excessive dread of the blacks held by the whites. Actual contacts made by Langalibalele with the Sotho, Ndebele, and Zulu before the rising, or rumours of them, further raised the spectre of a general African uprising against the balkanized whites in South Africa. Advised by Shepstone and others, Lord Carnarvon saw federation as the only answer to the 'terrible labyrinth' of South Africa.[33]

32. C. W. De Kiewiet, 1937, ch. 2; C. F. Goodfellow, 1966, ch. 3.

33. E. H. Brookes and C. de B. Webb, 1965, pp. 113–20; N. A. Etherington, 1979, pp. 246–7; N. A. Etherington, 1981, pp. 34–7.

As a first step, Lord Carnarvon secured the appointment of Sir Garnet Wolseley, recently returned from Kumasi where he had defeated the Asante, to deal with the Natal difficulties. Wolseley was instructed to gain control of African affairs for the Crown and to delay responsible government for the whites in preparation for a South African federation.[34] Since peaceful approaches would be pursued, Carnarvon became conciliatory to the Boers by dangling a settlement of the diamond fields disputes. In 1875 he proposed a conference of the colonies and republics where minor issues such as a common African policy and territorial misunderstandings would be discussed as a prelude to the main issue of confederation. The mistake Carnarvon made was to suggest the names of the delegates and, in fact, he blundered gravely when he appeared to support the division of the Cape Colony by inviting the secessionist and leader of the opposition, John Paterson, as representative of the easterners and the Prime Minister, John Charles Molteno, as representative of the westerners. The result was that the Cape Colony and the republics, which were still aggrieved at the loss of the diamond fields, refused to participate, leaving Natal and Griqualand West as the only willing ones.

After this fiasco, Carnarvon called another conference in London in August 1876. The conference was again a failure. President Brand of the Orange Free State negotiated a settlement of his claim to the diamond fields and received £90 000 as compensation but then refused to be drawn into discussions concerning federation. Highly sensitive to imperial interference and jealously guarding the responsible status of his country, Prime Minister Molteno, who happened to be in London at the time, also refused to attend the conference, saying he had no mandate from his government to do so. Only Griqualand and Natal came to the conference, so nothing could be accomplished. This second failure drove Carnarvon 'as far as his impatience, his patriotism, and his *amour propre* would allow.'[35] He resolved to use more forceful measures to unite South Africa.

Lord Carnarvon's first target was the Transvaal. His chance came when he received a telegram in September 1876 from the High Commissioner which exaggerated the predicament of the Transvaal at the hands of the Pedi of Sekhukhune.[36] The Transvaal had gone to war with the Pedi in May 1876 for a number of reasons. In the 1860s and early 1870s, the Pedi population and power grew rapidly. Many neighbouring African societies that wished to escape the labour demands and taxes imposed on them by the Boers attached themselves to the Pedi kingdom, while others were coerced into doing so. As already pointed out, the Pedi were also actively building up their firearms supplies. The Pedi population expansion immediately deprived the Boers of labour supplies, as their territorial

34. C. F. Goodfellow, 1966, p. 62.
35. ibid., p. 110.
36. ibid., p. 114.

extensions took them into the disputed areas, where they clashed with the Lydenburgers. Matters came to a head when the Pedi prince, Johannes Dinkwanyane, prevented a Boer from occupying a piece of land and again when a Pedi contingent forced the African residents of a Berlin mission station to abandon it. The Transvaal President, J. J. Burgers, who was looking for loans to build a railway to the sea, wanted to crush the Pedi disturbances as a way of building up the confidence of investors in his republic. Burgers could also not ignore the Lydenburgers' call for firm action against their 'troublesome' Pedi neighbours and he therefore led the republic to war.[37]

With the assistance of the Swazi, Burgers launched a three-pronged attack on Sekhukhune's Lulu mountain fortress. The Lydenburgers and the Swazi carried out their operations from the east where the first target was the stronghold of prince Dinkwanyane. Meanwhile, Burgers' commando swept its way from the west, the plan being that the two forces, together with a third, would ultimately converge on Sekhukhune. Because of the half-hearted show put up by the Boers, who left the Swazi to do most of the fighting and to sustain heavy casualties, the latter abandoned the struggle. As soon as the Swazi left, Boer morale crumbled very quickly and they started to desert before they could make any assault on Sekhukhune's fortress. Undermining Boer patriotism were their several grievances against Burgers, whom they accused of heresy, a wrong education policy and poor economic planning. Moreover, the Boers from the western districts were not as committed as the eastern Lydenburgers to the struggle against the Pedi because they were not directly affected by Pedi pressures and resistance and there did not seem to be any personal gain expected from the war.[38].

After Burgers' withdrawal, the local Boers continued to harass Sekhukhune, and, because it was the planting season, he agreed to negotiate a truce. Philip Bonner rightly points out that in that war neither the Boers nor the Pedi were defeated, 'the situation had reached a stalemate, with neither side holding any decisive advantage.'[39] It was only in 1879 that the British, with their Swazi allies, managed to overpower the Pedi kingdom and to capture Sekhukhune.[40]

The British, however, took the 1876 Boer fiasco to be a thorough defeat and a signal for the impending collapse of the Transvaal. Carnarvon appointed Shepstone to be the Special Commissioner for the Transvaal and on 9 October 1876 empowered him to take over the republic with or without the consent of its *volksraad*. Various motives for the annexation of the Transvaal have been suggested. The Transvaal was known to contain

37. P. Bonner, 1983, pp. 137–40.
38. ibid., p. 143.
39. ibid., p. 144.
40. L. Thompson, 1971, p. 282.

mineral deposits that made it potentially the richest part of South Africa. The Transvaal blocked the free flow of labour from within Transvaal and from the neighbouring regions. The Transvaal government was also threatening to build a railway to Delagoa Bay so that it could not only be independent of the British colonial harbours but also threaten British supremacy by entering into relations with foreign powers. Carnarvon further calculated that the annexation of the Transvaal would result in the encirclement of the Orange Free State and therefore force the latter to come to terms. Shepstone's take-over of the Transvaal on 12 April 1877, though clumsy and not calculated to conciliate the Boers, was relatively simple because the republic was bankrupt and its president unpopular.[41] Having annexed it, Carnarvon appointed Sir Bartle Frere as the Governor and High Commissioner to carry his 'scheme of federation into effect.'[42]

Frere's task was far from easy. The Cape Colony refused to take the lead in the confederation movement; its leaders regarded the British efforts to encourage it to do so as unwanted interference with its responsible status. The Orange Free State was also against being dragged into the union. When in 1878 Frere invited its leaders to a conference to discuss the issue, President Brand replied that the republic was doing so well in every sphere of life that its leaders could not contemplate the loss of its independence. The Transvaal could have been forced to unite with the other states under the annexation arrangements. But Shepstone's administration failed to conciliate the Boers, so that they remained as wedded as ever to the idea of disannexation. Besides, Shepstone himself became so embroiled in the Transvaal–Zululand border disputes that when he was requested to offer his opinion on confederation in 1878 he replied that he had 'scarcely been able to think sufficiently of it to give you my opinion', and asked for 'a little free breathing'.[43] Only Natal was willing to confer on the issue. Consequently Carnarvon was forced to resign on a matter unrelated to South Africa in January 1878 when his federation dream was nowhere near realization.

From the standpoint of securing British interests in Southern Africa, Frere was an ideal choice with the right vision. He wanted to impose a South African confederation built 'upon European self-government and the subjugation and civilization of the Africans'.[44] 'Subjugation' and 'civilization' meant basically the transformation of the African societies into labour reservoirs for British and colonial enterprises, and markets for industrialized Britain, while 'European self-government' would safeguard British capitalist investments. Frere decided that the African aspect of the confederation should be dealt with first. His vision encompassed the whole

41. C. F. J. Muller, (ed.), 1975, pp. 263–4.
42. C. F. Goodfellow, 1966, p. 123.
43. ibid., p. 147.
44. ibid., p. 155.

subcontinent, so that the Tswana, the Xhosa, Zulu, Ndebele and Shona societies all had to be annexed by declaring protectorates or by conquest.

Of immediate and practical significance was Zululand, whose border disputes with the Transvaal could be utilized to manufacture a *casus belli*. The disputed territory was an appropriate issue for Frere, and indeed the Colonial Office, in that it entangled Natal, Zululand and the Transvaal and involved Shepstone, who had always nursed grand ambitions around it. Its history dated to as far back as the 1850s. In 1856 Cetshwayo had gone some way towards guaranteeing the next Zulu succession for himself by annihilating Mbulazi, a possible contender, and his faction. Thereafter Cetshwayo co-ruled with Mpande, before the latter's death in 1872. But Cetshwayo still feared another of Mpande's sons, Mkungu, who lived in Natal under the protection of Bishop Colenso and Shepstone. His fears seemed to materialize in the 1860s when there were rumours of a possible Natal invasion of Zululand, and these spread to the Transvaal and were taken advantage of by some Transvaalers. In 1861 some Transvaal Boers sent messages to Cetshwayo purporting to confirm the rumours and then offering to guarantee his succession and later his coronation in return for land in the territory under dispute. Cetshwayo made empty promises which he never bothered to follow up.

At the same time, Shepstone, who had since the 1850s yearned to found a black kingdom with a white administration that was self-financing, and free from settler interference, now saw a chance of realizing his ambition in the disputed territory. As soon as he got wind of the Boer communications with the Zulu, he rushed to Cetshwayo and on behalf of the Natal government confirmed him as the Zulu heir apparent. From this point on, however, the Boers took up farms in the Utrecht district, the disputed territory. The Zulu refrained from throwing them out by force but turned to the British government to take over the Utrecht district so that it would form a buffer against the Transvaal.

For years Shepstone urged the British government to accept the Zulu offer, arguing that it would serve to settle the excess Natal black population and prevent the Transvaal from reaching the sea through Zululand. Shepstone's idea became even more significant in the 1870s, the years of labour shortages in Natal, the Cape Colony and Griqualand West. It was soon discovered that migrant labour routes ran through the Transvaal, Zululand, and the disputed territory. Since both states interfered with the routes, a Shepstone kingdom between them would become the safest corridor. For as long as Shepstone had his eyes on his possible black state, he supported Cetshwayo's territorial claims against the Transvaal, because he needed the Zulu king's co-operation. Indeed that was why he attended Cetshwayo's coronation in 1873.

Moreover, Shepstone believed strongly that if Britain wanted to control all the African states in Southern Africa it had to start by controlling and influencing the Zulu kingdom. But once Shepstone became the ruler of the Transvaal he changed sides and began to support the territorial claims of the Boers. The reason was perfectly simple: 'Now he had only to uphold the Transvaal claims in order to secure the corridor free of charge.'[45] The only danger to his objective, indeed to the peace of the whole subcontinent, remained the Zulu kingdom, which had to be destroyed. In this, Frere and the Colonial Office, which had taken up Shepstone's views in 1874, concurred.

When Shepstone sailed to Natal in 1878 his aim was not to go and settle the territorial dispute but to use the whole issue to force a war on Cetshwayo. The Commission set up on 26 February 1878 by Sir Henry Bulwer, the Lieutenant-Governor of Natal, had recommended a boundary that was favourable to the Zulu. But Frere's proposed implementation was simply calculated to provoke strong Zulu objections in that the Boer farmers on the Zulu side of the boundary were not to be evicted.

The second issue Frere clutched at was that of Chief Sirayo. The sons of Sirayo pursued two wives of the chief into Natal on 28 July 1878 and brought them back to Zululand where they were tried and executed. The Natal government protested to Cetshwayo that some of his subjects had violated the Natal border, and demanded that Sirayo's sons be sent over to Natal for trial. Cetshwayo's response was to send a fine of £50 and to apologize for the rash and irresponsible behaviour of the youths. Frere took the matter up in December 1878 and demanded 500 head of cattle from Cetshwayo for defying the Natal government and that the Sirayo culprits should be handed over. When war broke out, Cetshwayo was still trying to collect the cattle to pay the fine.

Then in September 1878 two Natal whites strayed into Zululand and were roughly handled by the Zulu border guards, but they were not injured. Frere blew the whole event out of proportion by saying it was 'a most serious insult and outrage and should be severely punished.'[46] Besides, Frere claimed that Cetshwayo had scared the missionaries out of his kingdom and that he must let them go back to their stations unmolested. Most likely the missionaries had left on the advice of Shepstone, who knew of the impending war, just as he had done in 1877.[47]

On 11 December 1878 the full ultimatum was delivered to the Zulu representatives. It demanded the dismantling of the Zulu army, acceptance of a British resident, reinstatement of all the missionaries, and payment of fines from the various alleged violations of the Natal border and persons.[48] The ultimatum was simply impossible to meet within the specified twenty to thirty days. When the time expired, the British forces under Lieutenant-General Lord Chelmsford invaded the Zulu kingdom on 10 January 1879.

45. N. A. Etherington, 1981, p. 41.
46. E. H. Brookes and C. de B. Webb, 1965, p. 133.
47. N. A. Etherington, 1981, p. 42.
48. E. Brookes and C. de B. Webb, 1965, p. 134.

Chelmsford's army consisted of 15 000 soldiers, many of whom were Africans drafted in Natal, while Cetshwayo's force probably numbered 45 000. The major advantage enjoyed by the British was their firearms, which were most effective when used in combination with such defensive measures as trenches, walls of waggons or sandbags. The Zulu, on the other hand, fought with spears and shields and had a limited number of guns which they had not yet integrated fully into their military technology and training. The shields were useless against bullets. The spears were devastatingly lethal in close combat, but the Zulu were not allowed to profit from this advantage by the British army, which fired at them from a long distance. The result was that in nearly all the battles the Zulu suffered enormous casualties while striving to get near their enemies. It was only at Isandhlwana on 22 January 1879 that the Zulu tackled a British column in the open and thoroughly beat it. The fighting, however, came to an end on 7 July 1879 when Chelmsford defeated the Zulu at Ulundi. Cetshwayo was hunted down, captured in August and then shipped off to Cape Town for imprisonment.

As Jeff Guy argues, the Ulundi defeat did not lead to the destruction of the Zulu kingdom. What finally destroyed the kingdom were the political arrangements made by Sir Garnet Wolseley, who was appointed High Commissioner for South Eastern Africa with supreme authority, both civil and military, over Natal, the Transvaal and Zululand; he took over from Lord Chelmsford on 4 July 1879. He did not annex Zululand but split the kingdom into thirteen independent chiefdoms. Some of the new chiefs found it almost impossible to govern because of the resistance put up by many leading personalities of the pre-war period who were denied positions in the new political dispensation. The new chiefs resorted to ruling by violence, leading to the killing of many people and general disorder in the country. The result was a civil war which raged well into the 1880s.[49]

Meanwhile, none of the objectives for which the Zulu war had been fought were realized. It had been fought primarily as a prelude to incorporating the African states into a federation, but the results went in opposite directions. Frere, the moving spirit on the spot behind the scheme was, as we have seen, superseded by Wolseley who was sent to make peace even at the expense of federation. Besides, the Zulu war was followed by the Anglo-Boer War (1880–1) and the Cape–Lesotho War (1880–1), which sealed the death of the federation scheme.

The Boers in the Transvaal never accepted the loss of their independence, and for three years they tried all peaceful means to persuade the British to pull out. The Boer resolve to recapture power from the British solidified with each failure of their pacific effort. In 1877 they sent a deputation to London to go and protest against annexation. Lord Carnarvon adamantly

49. J. J. Guy, 1980, chs 3, 4, 5; J. J. Guy, 1981.

refused to consider dis-annexation but was prepared to discuss Boer self-rule within a South African confederation. Paul Kruger, the most important delegate, requested a referendum in which the Boers would decide what form of government they wanted under the British Crown but flatly refused to have anything to do with the confederation.[50] When the delegates reported the results of their fruitless mission at a rally in Pretoria at the end of 1877, many Boers demanded armed resistance. But the leaders seemed convinced that if the results of a referendum showed conclusively that the Boers were against annexation, Carnarvon would grant them their independence. A referendum was duly conducted, and by a vast majority the Boers rejected British rule.

A second delegation was sent to London to go and elaborate on the Boer views to the Colonial Secretary, Sir Michael Hicks Beach, who had succeeded Lord Carnarvon. The new Colonial Secretary again refused to give up the Transvaal. When the delegation reported back at a huge gathering, the cry for a war of liberation was heard again, only this time louder than before. But still the leaders insisted on exhausting all the peaceful means of achieving independence. But before dispersing they sent an emissary to go and confer with Frere, who was in Natal, and at the same time they vowed solemnly to strive unto death for the restoration of their republic. Frere came up to the Transvaal and met the Boers but he still emphasized that they could obtain self-rule and economic aid under the Crown and nothing else. He also agreed to forward a fresh petition to the British government but nothing came of this either.

Further, in March 1879, Shepstone was replaced by Owen Lanyon, whose understanding of the Transvaal was limited, and Frere by Wolseley, a military man who believed not in diplomacy but in brute force. The actions of both officials helped to harden the Boer determination to try to regain their independence by force. On 15 December 1879 a large rally attended by over 6000 Boers was held at Wonderfontein and resolved to discard peaceful methods of seeking independence, to reject the status of British subjects, and to set up as soon as possible a republican government. Wolseley arrested those he considered to be ringleaders and only released them on bail. At that point the Boers began to pin their hopes on the new Liberal Government in Britain whose leader, Gladstone, while in opposition, had spoken sympathetically of the Transvaal's need for independence. However, when they asked him to live up to his promises, Gladstone, like his predecessors, informed the Boers that all they could hope for was self-government within a confederation.

By December 1880 the patience of the Boers had run out and they unilaterally reinstituted their republican government, which was to operate for a while from the new capital of Heidelberg. The provisional government was headed by Paul Kruger, Piet Joubert and M.W. Pretorius. On 16

50. C.F. Goodfellow, 1966, pp. 141–4.

PLATE 7.1 *Boer commandos*, c. *1880*

December war broke out when Lanyon refused to give up the administration of the Transvaal peacefully. The war was fought throughout the rest of December and into January, until on 27 February 1881 the Boers scored their decisive victory against the British at Amajuba hills.

The peace settlement came in the form of the Pretoria Convention, signed in August 1881. In the settlement, even though the British failed in their supreme objective of federating the Transvaal with the other colonies and the Orange Free State, they gained control of African labour in that a resident would be stationed in Pretoria to supervise Boer African administration. Secondly, overall British imperial supremacy in the Transvaal was guaranteed through British control of the republic's external relations as well as the British right to station and move military forces and equipment freely about in the Transvaal in time of war. The Boers obtained self-government, which indeed proved to be a stepping stone to greater freedom. Further negotiations produced the London Convention of 27 February 1884 under which Britain relinquished its control over the Africans, but retained control of the republic's foreign relations.[51]

51. C.F.J. Muller (ed.), 1975, pp. 264–72; C.F. Goodfellow, 1966, pp. 198–213; L. Thompson, 1971b; F.A. Van Jaarsveld, 1961.

Just as the imperial forces were struggling to crush the Boer uprising, the Cape colonial forces were fighting the Sotho in a war that broke out on 13 September 1880. Just like the first Anglo–Boer War, the Lesotho armed conflict was intimately related to the British efforts to achieve a South African confederation. Both the Cape colonial government and the British officials at the Cape wanted to disarm the African states as a first step to federation. And it was the Sotho rejection of unilateral disarmament that led to the Cape–Sotho War of 1880–1.

Since 1872 Lesotho had come under the Cape colonial administration. Indeed as part of the efforts to bring South Africa into a union, Gordon Sprigg, the Cape Prime Minister who had replaced Molteno, had colluded with Frere to have the Peace Preservation Bill passed by the Cape Parliament in 1878. The legislation empowered the government to order the Africans in the Cape Colony to surrender their guns in return for compensation. The law was initially not to apply to Lesotho; but Sprigg, who was aware of the large quantities of guns in Sotho hands, decided to extend it to that kingdom.

To the Sotho, guns had considerable social, political and economic significance. The guns were bought with wages earned at the diamond mines, and as such represented an enormous investment in labour. The Sotho also valued their guns because they might be used in future to defend their kingdom, as the long history of their struggle with the Orange Free State had only too clearly taught them. The possession of a gun by a man further signified the passage from childhood to adulthood among the Sotho. The Sotho also suspected that the Cape government did not fully trust them. Besides, the chiefs suspected that the Cape government wanted to weaken them so as to turn them into slaves. There were further measures that drove the Sotho into armed resistance. In 1879 the Cape Colony proposed to alienate the Qluthing district to white farmers as a punishment for its Sotho chief, Moorosi, who had recently rebelled. Such action was in complete violation of the British promises to Moshoeshoe that no part of his country would be alienated. Moreover, the Cape government also announced that the hut tax would be increased to £1. This was utterly unacceptable to the Sotho in view of the recent Cape move to appropriate £12 000 from the Lesotho account to the Cape Colony.

The Sotho tried to come to an understanding with the Cape Colony by peaceful means. They protested to Sprigg when he twice came over to their country to discuss most of these issues with them; they sent petitions to the governor and the Queen of England; they sent delegates to Cape Town to go and lobby the parliamentarians, but all these efforts came to nothing.

Meanwhile power in Lesotho shifted from the king, now called Paramount Chief, Litsie, to the chiefs. The king was getting too old and, though opposed to the disarmament and other Cape colonial measures, was extremely fearful of the adverse effects of an armed resistance that might drive out the British and expose the kingdom to the Orange Free State.

He therefore moved out of step with the popular clamour for armed struggle and called for peaceful protests. The result was that the majority supported chiefs Lerotholi, Masopha and Joel, who all vowed to oppose the Cape government measures by violence and encouraged their people to punish the supporters of the colonial administration by destroying and confiscating their property and disobeying the magistrates.

On 13 September 1880 the Cape moved its forces into Lesotho; war then broke out and continued for seven months. For the Cape government, the war expenses escalated dramatically and hit the unacceptable level of £3 000 000. At this point Sir Hercules Robinson, the new Governor and High Commissioner, began anxiously to seek peace with the Sotho. The Sotho were also tired of the war at the end of seven months and therefore sued for peace. It was a propitious moment for the Governor to make his Award of 29 April 1881. The Award still called for surrender of the guns in return for compensation; but added that the people could retain them as long as they licensed them. A complete amnesty was offered, but a fine of 5000 head of cattle had to be paid by the 'rebels' for compensating the 'loyalists' and traders who had lost property during the war. On the whole, therefore, the Sotho had won the war since they had fought primarily for the retention of their guns. The prestige and power of the chiefs, who had led the successful war, increased enormously at the expense of the king, who had vacillated at a moment when the country needed leadership of uncompromising militancy. Moreover, the Cape government decided to implement its new policy through the chiefs. It was indeed a double victory for the Sotho chiefs.[52]

The Lesotho victory, the non-annexation of the Zulu kingdom and the granting of self-rule to the Transvaal marked the end of the British efforts to federate the region by force. For the time being the British government contented itself with controlling the various parts of South Africa loosely, mostly by means of stationing residents who monitored the situation. Britain would renew its efforts to gain much firmer control after the discovery of gold in the mid-1880s. From the point of view of the Africans, Britain had done much to reduce their independence. On the eastern front the Ciskei with its large Xhosa, Mfengu, and Khoikhoi population was firmly subordinated to the Cape Colony and so too were the Sotho, even though the latter enjoyed a large measure of internal freedom. Griqualand West had also lost its sovereignty. The Zulu and the Pedi were launched on the road to self-destruction. The arrest of Sekhukhune and the installation of his rival, Mampuru, guaranteed that that kingdom would be torn apart by factional fights and therefore ensure its subordination to the Transvaal.

52. S. Burman, 1981, chs 9–12.

8 The countries of the Zambezi basin

A. F. ISAACMAN

This chapter[1] examines the broad patterns of change that occurred during the first three-quarters of the nineteenth century in Central Africa, an area encompassing the present-day nations of Malawi, Mozambique, and Zambia. Special emphasis is placed on the Zambezi valley region, an important zone of economic and cultural exchange and the homeland of many of the principal Shona- and Lunda-related states. Rather than merely describing the history of the various precolonial kingdoms, we shall examine the region as a whole, with special attention to the changes brought about by the progressive incorporation of the region into the world capitalist economy and by the Nguni–Sotho diaspora. Together these events altered the political map of Central Africa and precipitated widespread economic and social transformations. Despite the focus on these extra-regional factors the indigenous societies were by no means static, and each society's internal configuration helped to condition both the initial pattern of interaction with the alien merchants and invaders and the ultimate direction of change. An introductory overview of Central Africa at the end of the eighteenth century is included in order to place the subsequent developments within their appropriate historical perspective. Similarly, the chapter concludes with a brief examination of the region on the eve of the European 'Scramble', since the changes that transpired during the nineteenth century carried important implications for the subsequent pattern of Central African response to European imperialism.

On the eve of the nineteenth century

Although nineteenth-century economic changes and the Nguni–Sotho invasions, commonly known as the Mfecane, had a dramatic impact on Central Africa, these events can be viewed as part of a broader pattern of political and economic change that antedated the nineteenth century.[2]

1. This chapter was commissioned in 1975 and completed in early 1976 and updated in 1981. I would like to thank Barbara Isaacman, James Johnson and Paul Lovejoy for their penetrating criticism of an earlier draft of this manuscript.

2. J. D. Omer-Cooper, 1966, for example, argues that these events created a disjuncture in the history of Central Africa.

Throughout the preceding centuries, migrations, state formation and the development of long-distance trading systems had altered Central African societies. What was unique about the nineteenth century was not change itself but the relatively rapid rate of change and the far-reaching implications that it carried.

Well before the nineteenth century the Zambezi valley and surrounding regions had undergone a major political revolution. Successive Shona and Lunda groups had established their pre-eminence over most of the territory previously occupied by relatively small-scale agricultural societies. While fringe areas such as the Tonga of southern Mozambique or the Tumbuka and lakeside Tonga of contemporary Malawi managed to maintain their autonomy, most of the indigenous societies were swept into either the Shona or Lunda state system.

The process of state formation probably occurred first in the region south of the Zambezi river. By the beginning of the sixteenth century, Shona-speaking immigrants coming from contemporary Zimbabwe had imposed their rule over the region stretching southwards from the margins of the Zambezi to the Sabi river. At the apex of this powerful kingdom was the Mwenemutapa, from whom the Shona empire derived its name. Although subsequent wars, which reduced the power of the Mwenemutapa, enabled several provincial leaders to secede and create autonomous kingdoms, Shona hegemony continued throughout the region. The most powerful of these independent Shona states – Barue, Manica, Quiteve and Changamire – maintained effective control over south-central Mozambique until the nineteenth century. Within this zone the only foreign incursion occurred along the southern margins of the Zambezi river. There, Portuguese and Goan settlers and traders established crown estates, or *prazos da coroa*, which were nominally incorporated into Lisbon's colonial empire.[3]

The expansion of Lunda-related peoples from the Katanga region began somewhat later and had not yet reached its completion by the first decades of the nineteenth century. The Lozi, first of the Lunda immigrants, had settled in the fertile Zambezi flood plains two centuries earlier. They were followed in quick succession by settlers who established the kingdoms of Kalonga and Undi in what is now Malawi, and to the west the progenitors of the Lala, Senga and Bemba states. By 1740 the last of the major Lunda immigrants – Mwata Kazembe – had settled in the Luapula region. Throughout the rest of the century the Lunda consolidated their holdings and extended their frontiers by both diplomatic and military activities. By 1800 a number of the Lunda-related states, such as Undi, Kalonga and Lozi, had reached their apogee, while others – like the Bemba – were still in the process of expansion.[4]

3. For a discussion of the Zambezi *prazos*, see A. Isaacman, 1972a; M. D. D. Newitt, 1973a.
4. For a summary of the Lunda expansion, see H. W. Langworthy, 1973, pp. 16–27.

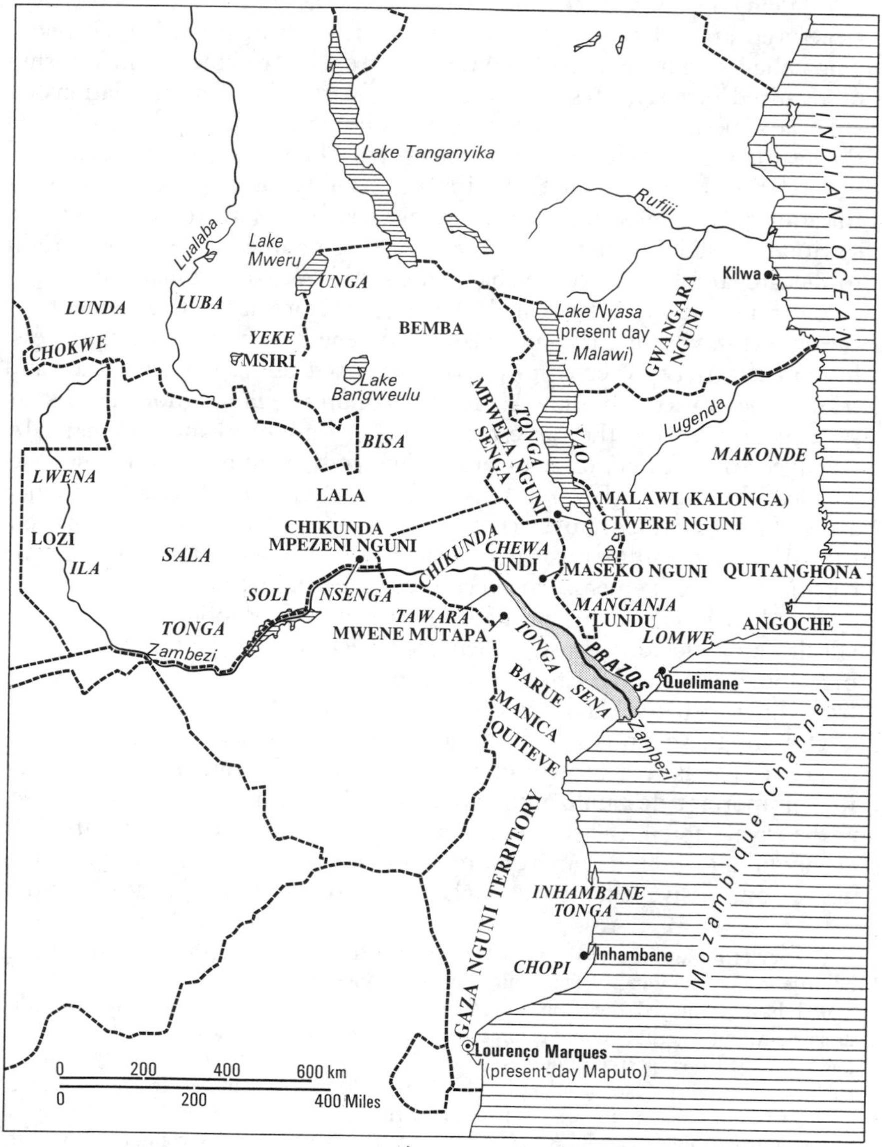

FIG. 8.1 *Peoples and politics of Central Africa,* c. *1800–80* (*after A. F. Isaacman*)

Allowing for differences in detail, the Shona and Lunda states were structured around similar organizational principles. At the apex stood a king believed to have sacred qualities that were either inherent in kingship or acquired through rites of investiture. The ruler's intimate relationship with the supernatural, sanctified by spirit mediums and cult priests, ensured the health and well-being of his subjects and the fertility of the land. The interrelationship between kingship and fertility underpinned the mystification of the ruler and reinforced his position as symbolic owner and spiritual guardian of the land. As a result, he retained the exclusive right to allocate land, which was the basis of control over subordinate chiefs and other subjects and underpinned a cycle of reciprocity. In repayment for the opportunity to use the king's land and benefit from his divine prowess, his subjects were expected to provide specified taxes, labour service and tribute that varied from one kingdom to another. Throughout both state systems, moreover, the largest tusk of a dead elephant automatically belonged to the monarch as owner of the land. In some societies, such as Manica, the Lunda of Kazembe, and Undi, the monarch also maintained a theoretical monopoly over commerce, while in Changamire's kingdom the ruler was the ultimate owner of most cattle.[5] These tribute, labour and commercial arrangements enhanced the power and wealth of the monarch, who redistributed to his principal lieutenants a portion of the surplus which he extracted, to ensure their continued loyalty. In this respect the precolonial central African states organized the flow of scarce resources from the dominated classes to the dominant class.[6]

Despite these unifying rituals and institutions, a number of factors militated against the growth of highly centralized kingdoms. Among the most important destabilizing factors were the recurring succession crises at the royal capital, the reluctance of outlying officials to subordinate their economic and political interests to those of the central authority, revolts against oppressive leaders who violated the 'rule of law', the lack of ethnic

5. For a critique of the 'trade and politics thesis', as well as a discussion of the significance of cattle in the kingdom of Changamire, see S. I. Mudenge, 1974.

6. I have employed the term 'dominant class' to refer to the surplus-appropriating aristocracy and its religious and commercial allies who governed the Central African states and controlled their scarce resources. The absence of historically specific analysis of pre-capitalist Central African economies and, in particular, the lack of detailed reconstruction of 'who produced what for whom' (the social relations of production in Marxist terms), makes it impossible to delineate with any certainty the exact class configuration of the states under examination. Before such a synthetic analysis can be undertaken, rigorous investigation of specific polities is needed to determine how the dominant class maintained and reproduced its access to scarce resources, the degree and manner in which it controlled and extracted labour and the extent to which these processes helped to shape the development of distinct class interests and class consciousness.

The works of C. Coquery-Vidrovitch, 1972; C. Meillassoux, 1974; E. Terray, 1972 and M. Godelier, 1975, though not in total agreement, represent an important theoretical breakthrough for an analysis of class formation.

and cultural homogeneity, and the absence of a standing army to police the vast regions of the kingdom. The result was an irregular, though recurring, pattern of conflict and secession. Thus, the Shona states of Barue, Manica, Quiteve and Changamire all asserted their independence from the Mwenemutapa only to be faced with the same problems within their own homelands.[7] A similar pattern characterized the area north of the Zambezi, especially in the Malawian kingdoms of Kalonga, Undi and Lundu.[8] The fragility of many states should not mask the durability of more-localized kinship and community networks which provided a bedrock of social loyalties and assistance in times of need.[9]

Just as far-reaching political changes antedated the nineteenth century, so complex trading networks operated throughout the region well before the nineteenth-century expansion. Despite tendencies by historians and anthropologists to characterize the indigenous societies as 'subsistence oriented', commerce in such basic commodities as iron, salt, cloth and grain was a regular feature of the indigenous economies and complemented the local agricultural sector.[10] Thus while most Sena were predominantly farmers, a small group of weavers regularly exported their cloth several hundred kilometres to the Zumbo region and the Chewa homelands where it was in great demand.[11] Similarly, Bisa traders engaged in large-scale commerce in iron throughout the eighteenth century,[12] the Chewa of Kasungu used their salt surplus to acquire Tumbuka hoes,[13] and the Lozi national economy was based on the exchange of cattle, fish and a variety of manufactured and agricultural products between different regions of the kingdom.[14] What still requires detailed investigation is not whether the exchange of surplus occurred but rather the character of the productive system that generated the surplus.

This pattern of local and inter-regional commerce, buttressed by a limited mining and manufacturing sector, helped to shape and sustain trade between the interior and the coast. Although the data are fragmentary, it is clear that throughout the seventeenth and eighteenth centuries an international network built upon localized trading provided commodities for the Indian Ocean ports dominated by Indian and Muslim merchant capital. Among the most important were ivory from the Luangwa valley and adjacent Undi territory, gold from the mines in the kingdoms of

7. A. Isaacman, 1973; S. I. Mudenge, 1974; H. H. K. Bhila, 1972; D. Beach, 1980.
8. H. W. Langworthy, 1971; K. M. Phiri, 1975, pp. 78–80.
9. Within the kinship system inequalities also existed; male elders tended to accumulate and control scarce resources at the expense of junior male relatives and women. See C. Meillassoux, 1981.
10. K. M. Phiri, 1975, pp. 109–37; A. D. Roberts, 1970a.
11. A. Isaacman, 1972a, p. 73.
12. A. D. Roberts, 1970a, p. 723.
13. K. M. Phiri, 1975, p. 111.
14. G. L. Caplan, 1970, pp. 6–7.

Manica and Changamire and just north of Tete, and copper from the Kafue region.[15] The scale of this trade seems to have been relatively small and somewhat irregular until the last two decades of the eighteenth century. The eastward thrust of the Lunda of Kazembe and their commercial alliance with the Bisa, the intensified activities of Yao merchants from the coast, and the commercial expansion of the Chikunda traders from the Zambezi *prazos* dramatically increased the level of exports to the Indian Ocean entrepôts. All three groups acquired substantial quantities of ivory and slaves for the world market, setting the stage for the progressive incorporation into the larger world economy, which was based almost entirely on the exchange of these two commodities for European manufactured goods.[16]

Transformation in the political and economic systems often generated parallel changes in the social and ethnic composition of Central African societies. The immigration of alien Shona- and Lunda-related peoples resulted in widespread intermarriage and even the emergence of entirely new ethnic groups, such as the Sena, Zambezi Tonga, and Goba.[17] The immigrants generally succeeded in imposing their core institutions and values upon the local population. The spread of the Lunda social mechanism of perpetual kinship and positional succession throughout much of the region north of the Zambezi, for example, altered the basic structure of kinship and carried profound implications for the transmission of kingship.[18] Of similar significance was the spread of the Shona Mwari cult and the supporting system of national ancestor spirits (*mhondoro*) throughout the southern tier of the Zambezi. The simultaneous introduction of the Shona language and symbol system in conjunction with the spread of Mwari must have fundamentally altered the cosmology of the indigenous inhabitants.[19] Culture change, however, was not unidirectional. Although this problem needs to be studied in depth, it is clear that both the Shona and Lunda conquerors borrowed cultural elements from the indigenous societies, often creating new syncretic forms. The Chewa and Lundu cults of Makewana and Mbona seem to represent such a hybrid,[20] as does the division between land chief and political chief that characterized the rule of the Lunda of Kazembe over the Shila.[21]

By the end of the eighteenth century Central Africa had undergone a

15. A.D. Roberts, 1970a, p.717; S.I. Mudenge, 1974, pp. 384–90; A.F. Isaacman, 1972a, pp. 75–85; H.H.K. Bhila, 1972.

16. E.A. Alpers, 1975, pp. 172–208; A.D. Roberts, 1970a, pp. 727–8; K.M. Phiri, 1975, pp. 109–26.

17. A.F. Isaacman, 1972a, p.4; C.S. Lancaster, 1974.

18. For a discussion of perpetual kinship and positional succession, see J. Vansina, 1966, p.82.

19. See D.P. Abraham, 1966; T.O. Ranger, 1973.

20. T.O. Ranger, 1973; M. Schoffeleers, 1972a, 1972b; H.W. Langworthy, 1971, p.9.

21. I. Cunnison, 1959, pp. 180–4.

dynamic phase in its historical development. Migrations and conquests in the preceding centuries had altered the political and cultural map of the region, while the scale of trade had increased substantially. These changes, in turn, often generated tensions between the dominant and the dominated and between different commercial interests competing for the region's scarce resources. Thus, despite the tendency towards political centralization, conditions remained relatively fluid and could be exploited by alien merchants and a new wave of conquering immigrants

The slave trade and incorporation into the capitalist world economy

Unprecedented commercial penetration from the East African coast during the nineteenth century resulted in the incorporation of most of Central Africa into the capitalist world economy. As in the case of West Africa, the slave trade figured prominently in the process by which the region, especially north of the Zambezi river, became part of the periphery of the international trading system. Despite some basic similarities, there were important differences. Many of the captives were exported to the Indian Ocean plantation system, Madagascar and the Middle East rather than to the New World. There was also the very significant role of the ivory trade, and the fact that the far-reaching changes accompanying this involvement in international trade were compressed into a much shorter time-frame. Moreover, the level of violence that accompanied the slave trade was probably higher in Central Africa, creating unprecedented fragmentation and rural dislocation. While some Central African trading societies, or at least the dominant class within them, benefited in the short run through their participation in the ivory and slave trade, they ultimately became subordinate to and dependent upon the international trading system whose centres of decision-making lay outside Africa.[22]

Several factors operated simultaneously to expand the slave trade during the first half of the nineteenth century. As a result of the resurgence of the plantation system in north-eastern Brazil and the subsequent development of sugar estates in Cuba, slave-traders in appreciable numbers from the West Indies and Latin America began to visit Mozambican ports where captives were generally cheaper than in West Africa and the limited British naval force far less intimidating.[23] Simultaneously, French planters on the islands of Bourbon (now called Réunion), Seychelles and the Mascarenes, as well as the rulers of Madagascar, intensified their demand for slaves. The most significant stimulant, however, was the development of clove

22. See Chapter 2 above; also, I. Wallerstein, 1976; E. A. Alpers, 1975, pp. 264–7.

23. E. A. Alpers, 1967, pp. 4–12; A. F. Isaacman, 1972a, pp. 85–94; K. M. Phiri, 1975, p. 130.

plantations on the islands of Zanzibar and Pemba shortly after the turn of the century.[24]

Conditions within Central Africa facilitated the growing demand for slave labour. Bisa, Yao and Chikunda trade networks already linked the interior to the coastal markets of Kilwa, Mozambique Island and Quelimane. Despite their initial emphasis on ivory, the inland traders had always brought a small but steady supply of slaves to these international entrepôts. The use of captives as ivory porters facilitated the addition of a larger slave component without disrupting the commerce in elephant tusks. On the contrary, ivory exports also increased substantially as African merchants tried to satisfy the new markets in Britain and the USA as well as their traditional Asian clients.[25]

As the demand for cheap labour and ivory skyrocketed, Yao, Bisa and Chikunda merchants expanded their commercial empires. The Yao penetrated into the Lake Nyasa region during the first half of the century and, after 1850, entered the Shire valley in search of new markets among the Manganja and Chewa. Simultaneously, they established commercial ties to the Indian Ocean port of Ibo, which became a major export centre. The Chikunda, initially in the service of Afro-Portuguese and Afro-Goan *prazeros,* extended their commercial contacts from the area immediately north of the Zambezi to the Luangwa valley and south into what is now Zimbabwe, while the Bisa intensified their operations in the territory between the Shire and Luapula valleys. All three groups continued to emphasize the ivory component of the trade as well and in the case of the Bisa traders it remained the dominant export commodity.[26]

By the middle of the nineteenth century Central Africa had become a major supplier of slaves. Annual exports from Quelimane to Brazil, for example, had increased by 400 per cent between 1800 and 1835.[27] The newly developed port of Ibo on Mozambique Island, and Kilwa, were doing a booming business, while the post-1844 resurgence of the sultanate of Angoche was directly related to its entrance into the slave trade, and even the southern Mozambican ports of Inhambane and Lourenço Marques, largely ignored by European slavers, became important secondary entrepôts.[28] Zanzibar remained the principal recipient of these captives, with annual imports increasing from 10 000 per annum in 1810 to at least 20 000 in 1850.[29] Paralleling this growth was a proportionate increase in ivory exports.[30]

24. ibid.; E. A. Alpers, 1975, pp. 209–18; A. M. H. Sheriff, 1971.
25. R. W. Beachey, 1967.
26. K. M. Phiri, 1975, pp. 117–30; E. A. Alpers, 1975, pp. 209–63; A. D. Roberts, 1973, pp. 189–93; Y. B. Abdallah, 1973, pp. 29–31.
27. A. F. Isaacman, 1972a, p. 92.
28. E. A. Alpers, 1967, pp. 10–12; M. D. D. Newitt, 1973b; P. Harries, 1981.
29. E. A. Alpers, 1967, pp. 10–12.
30. R. W. Beachey, 1967; K. M. Phiri, 1975, pp. 117–26; E. A. Alpers, 1975, p. 234.

As the involvement of Angoche suggests, the economic pre-eminence of the Yao, Chikunda and Bisa did not go unchallenged for long. A number of African as well as alien merchants rapidly entered into the competition for slaves and ivory. Coastal Makua chiefs and aspiring merchants, for example, began both to exploit the populous hinterland and to prevent their Yao rivals from sending caravans across Makua territory to Mozambique Island. By the middle of the nineteenth century they were able to replace the Yao as the major supplier of slaves to Mozambique Island.[31] Arab and Swahili traders, often linked directly to the Zanzibar plantation economy, also became prominent. In some cases, they established permanent communities in the interior, as did Jumbe of Khota Khota, located on the western shores of Lake Malawi. More commonly, however, the coastal entrepreneurs outfitted caravans that were sent to important inland markets where slaves and ivory were readily accessible. From contemporary Tanzania came the Nyamwezi traders, the most important of whom, Msiri, imposed his commercial and political hegemony throughout eastern Lunda.[32] By the middle of the century, news of the potential profits had filtered westward to Angola, motivating Mambari traders to initiate commercial relations with the Lozi and their Kololo overlords.[33] In short, increasing international demands for bond labour meant that much of the region north of the Zambezi became a labour reserve in which the principal activity became the 'production' of slaves.

The intensified competition among the traders and their virtual monopoly of modern weapons thus dramatically altered the character of the slave trade in the period after 1840. Whereas most slaves had probably been obtained through legal commerce in the preceding period, raiding and conquest replaced it as the dominant mode of acquisition. According to Chikunda traditions, for example, in the earlier phase of the slave trade they were able to purchase Nsenga, Chewa and Tonga slaves, many of whom were originally criminals, social outcasts or strangers. Subsequently, however, they used coercive tactics to satisfy the coastal demand.[34] Similarly, Yao itinerant traders initially exploited their access to cheap cloth and iron hoes to achieve a pre-eminent commercial position, but external pressures during the second half of the century motivated them to exert military pressure in the Shire valley in order to ensure their economic hegemony.[35] Makua participation in the slave trade underwent a parallel transformation while force had always been a component of the Arab-Swahili strategy.[36]

31. E. A. Alpers, 1975, pp. 219–29.
32. J. Vansina, 1966, pp. 227–31.
33. E. Flint, 1970.
34. A. F. Isaacman, 1976, pp. 24–5.
35. K. M. Phiri, 1975, pp. 147–50; E. A. Alpers, 1969.
36. E. A. Alpers, 1975, pp. 219–28; K. M. Phiri, 1975, pp. 139–45; H. W. Langworthy, n.d.

PLATE 8.1 *Jumbe of Khota Khota*

To ensure a constant supply of captives and ivory, a number of trading groups carved out sizeable conquest states. Although differing in detail, these polities shared common characteristics that shaped their historical development. All these alien overlords relied heavily on European weapons to impose their hegemony and maintain their pre-eminence. These sophisticated weapons were acquired in exchange for captives in an updated version of the gun–slave cycle. Once firmly entrenched, the alien ruling classes expanded the frontiers of their empire; while the amount of force varied, coercion was the dominant mechanism of incorporation. The new acquisitions provided additional sources of slaves and ivory, which were used to increase the size of their arsenals, thereby enabling further expansion. Although politically independent, these conquest states were an indirect, or secondary, extension of European economic and military power into the interior.

This pattern of commercial penetration, conquest and state formation occurred along the entire margin of the Zambezi river and in the adjacent Luangwa valley. After 1840 a large number of Chewa, Tonga, Tawara, Nsenga and Soli chieftaincies were forcibly absorbed by the conquest states, which were dominated by Afro-Portuguese and Afro-Goan warlords and their Chikunda subordinates. Of these, the most important were Massangano, Makanga and the Zumbo states of Kanyemba and Matakenya.[37] A similar phenomenon occurred at an accelerated rate to the north, reaching its high point in the 1870s. As mentioned earlier, Yao merchant-chiefs, like Mataka, Makanjila and Mpona, imposed their hegemony over much of the Shire valley, Arab traders established political enclaves in the Lake Nyasa region and the Yeke leader, Msiri, gained control over the western provinces of the Lunda kingdom of Kazembe.[38] In short, throughout a large region the slave trade brought to power new dominant classes whose authority rested on the exploitation and intimidation of the indigenous population.

Even when the slavers did not impose themselves as political overlords, their predatory raids and ability to exploit internal cleavages within many polities in the region often eroded the authority of the indigenous aristocracy. By circumventing the royal trade monopoly, Arab and Swahili merchants established a base of local power within the Lunda kingdom of Kazembe. In 1872 they intervened directly in Lunda politics, helping to arrange for the assassination of Kazembe Muonga Sunkutu and the selection of a more pliant successor.[39] Similarly, the combination of Chikunda and Swahili incursions and their commercial alliances with outlying chieftaincies eroded Undi's position throughout the nineteenth century and

37. A. F. Isaacman, 1976, pp. 22–48.

38. J. Vansina, 1966, pp. 227–31; E. A. Alpers, 1969, pp. 413–16; H. W. Langworthy, n.d., pp. 14–18; K. M. Phiri, 1975, pp. 140–5; Y. B. Abdallah, 1973, pp. 40–60.

39. I. Cunnison, 1966, pp. 235–6; A. D. Roberts, 1973, p. 199.

PLATE 8.2 *Arab traders of the northern Lake Malawi region*

caused the ultimate decline of the kingdom by 1880.[40] Other alien merchants precipitated an armed confrontation between the Senga leader Kambamo and his arch-rival Tembu in order to gain additional captives for export.[41] To the south, Chikunda bands exploited their military skills into prominent economic and political positions by allying with victorious factions within Senga and Sala society.[42]

The impact of the slave-traders on the political fortunes of the indigenous aristocracy was not uniform. In some cases the dominant class emerged stronger as a result of economic and military ties to the slave-traders. Consider relations between the Bemba rulers and the Arab and Swahili traders. Under the leadership of Chileshe Chipela the Bemba had just completed a phase of territorial expansion and political centralization when the foreign traders entered their homeland around 1860. As a result, the

40. H. W. Langworthy, 1971, pp. 18–21.
41. H. W. Langworthy, n.d., pp. 20–1.
42. B. Stefaniszyn, and H. de Santana, 1960, p. 364; W. V. Brelsford, 1956, p. 58.

Bemba kingdom was far more unified and powerful than most states in the region. The geographical position of the Bemba, somewhat removed from the principal trade routes, precluded the growth of a large and potentially seditious merchant community within the core of their kingdom. Equally important, there was no incentive for the Arab and Swahili traders to adopt a hostile posture since the Bemba were not economic rivals. Most of the royal families' wealth came from raiding and tribute in the form of ivory and slaves and they were happy to exchange them for the cloth and other imported goods provided by the coastal merchants. This economic complementarity fostered a harmonious relationship and simultaneously enhanced the internal position of the Bemba aristocracy, which used the foreign commodities to recruit new followers and strengthen their links to subordinate chiefs. The continued demand for captives and ivory also fuelled a new expansionist phase from 1860 to 1880, during which Bemba forces conquered most of contemporary north-eastern Zambia. Thus, through ties to foreign merchants, the Bemba rulers gained unprecedented regional power while accumulating a substantial amount of wealth.[43]

As in the case of the Bemba, other local chiefs and merchants entered into alliances with the slave-traders that proved extremely beneficial. Throughout the 1870s the Chewa chief, Mwase Kasungu, whose territory straddled the Lake Malawi–Katanga trade route, provided food for the Arab caravans in exchange for guns. These weapons enabled him to withstand the subsequent Mbwela Nguni invasions.[44] Economic considerations also motivated Arab and Swahili protection of the Senga chiefs, who were important suppliers of ivory.[45] Similar factors help explain Chikunda alliances with the Ambo against the Bemba, and assistance that they provided the Nsenga against the Soli, which occurred in the decade preceding the 'Scramble'.[46] In all these cases, it is clear that the aliens' strategy was to prevent the expansion of a commercial or political rival in order to maintain their own respective spheres of influence.

Ironically, those rulers and merchants engaged in the quest for additional captives occasionally became victims of the political and social upheavals generated by the slave trade. In several instances, they overstepped their authority and enslaved their own subjects or neighbours in order to maintain the flow of wealth and weapons upon which their power rested. The Makua aristocracy pursued such a self-destructive strategy. Until the 1850s the Makua had been the principal exporters of slaves to Mozambique Island. One by-product of their predatory activities was a large-scale migration of the victimized societies. Faced with a diminished labour pool

43. A.D. Roberts, 1973, pp. 164–214.
44. K.M. Phiri, 1975, pp. 143–5; H.W. Langworthy, n.d., pp. 12–13.
45. H.W. Langworthy, n.d., pp. 18–21.
46. W.V. Brelsford, 1956, p. 64; B. Stefaniszyn and H. de Santana, 1960, p. 64; K.M. Phiri, 1975, p. 150.

the Makua rulers began raiding each other and enslaving their own subjects in order to maintain the profitable slave trade on which they had become totally dependent. Within two decades the Makua were badly fragmented, leaving them easy prey to subsequent Portuguese invasions.[47] The Afro-Portuguese *prazero* community exhibited a similar myopic desire for profits which precipitated the rapid demise of the *prazo* system. As in the case of the Makua chiefs, the *prazeros* violated their historic charter and began to enslave people living on their lands when they could no longer acquire captives from the interior. In reaction to these excesses the indigenous population either revolted and drove the *prazeros* off the land or fled into the interior, depriving the estate owner of his traditional source of tribute. The effect, in either case, was the destruction of most *prazos* by 1830, and those that managed to survive suffered from recurring famines that so debilitated the indigenous population that they proved no match for the attacks of the subsequent decades. Fifty years later the Gwemba, Nsenga and Tawara rose up against their *mestizo* (Afro-Portuguese and Afro-Asian) and Chikunda overlords who had been enslaving them and exporting them to the coast.[48]

The Shona-dominated region, stretching from the southern margins of the Zambezi to the Inhambane hinterland, became a secondary source of slaves, as did the Delagoa Bay area to the south. Within this broad zone there were only small pockets of alien commercial penetration, most notably Chikunda conquests along the southern margins of the Zambezi river, and occasional forays by Portuguese and African traders linked to commercial interests at the ports of Inhambane and Lourenço Marques (present-day Maputo). These activities, which antedated the nineteenth century, were sporadic and on a very limited scale.[49]

A combination of demographic, commercial and political factors explains the unwillingness or inability of the slave-traders to exploit this southern tier of the Zambezi valley to any appreciable degree. The lower population density meant that there was a smaller pool of potential captives to draw on than in the region to the north, to which the traders had easy access. In addition, the Shona states had ample supplies of gold and ivory which they exported for European goods. Thus, the only way the alien merchants could acquire an appreciable number of captives was through force, and the powerful Shona states were able to repel most raids. The defeat which the army of the Mwenemutapa inflicted on a Portuguese force in 1807 and the repeated Barue and Manica attacks on the Europeans demonstrated where the balance of power lay. While the Gaza Nguni, who imposed their hegemony over much of the southern region in the period after 1830, did

47. E. A. Alpers, 1975, p. 225.

48. A. F. Isaacman, 1972a, pp. 114–23.

49. ibid., pp. 89–92; A. Smith, 1969, pp. 176–7; A. Lobato, 1948, pp. 7–8; P. Harries, 1981, pp. 312–18.

participate in the international slave trade, the blockade by the British naval squadron of the ports of Lourenço Marques and Inhambane after 1850 made the trade increasingly problematic and ultimately unprofitable. Within a decade the Gaza aristocracy and regional merchants had ceased their involvement in the maritime slave trade, preferring to utilize their captives internally.[50]

Although additional research is needed, preliminary evidence suggests that a similar shift occurred throughout much of Central Africa. One by-product of the declining international demand for slaves in the second half of the century was the transformation of captives from export commodities to corvée labourers. There are several documented cases of slaves previously earmarked for export who were pressed into local production. Slave labour figured prominently among the Gaza, Makua, Lozi, Gwemba, Makonde and Chikunda, among others. In the latter two cases the reliance on captives enabled free men to collect ivory, wax and rubber for overseas export. The Lozi aristocracy and landlords also used slaves to dig canals and ditches in order to bring fertile marshy soil into cultivation. By the last quarter of the century it was estimated that a quarter of the Lozi population were slaves. Similarly, Nguni dynamism was premised upon their ability to incorporate and extract surplus from their large pool of captives.[51]

Allowing for local variations, a broad pattern of economic dislocation resulting from the slave trade is nevertheless discernible. The violent disruption of much of the rural economy, the export of many of the most productive members of the indigenous societies, the inadvertent introduction of highly contagious diseases, and the growing dependence of the Central African economy on the world trading system intensified the process of underdevelopment. It is true that this process was accompanied by the dissemination of new crops such as tobacco, maize, rice and cassava, the introduction of modest technological innovations like the Chikunda traps, granaries, and weapons, and the expansion of some local industry. But these were relatively insignificant developments when placed in juxtaposition to the economic retardation of the region as a whole.[52]

Little needs to be said about the unprecedented level of destruction that

50. P. Harries, 1981, pp. 312–18.

51. L. Gann, 1972, pp. 188–92; E. Flint, 1970, pp. 73–9; P. Harries, 1981; W.G. Clarence-Smith, 1979b; P.D. Curtin, S. Feierman, L. Thompson and J. Vansina, 1978, p. 403; T.I. Matthews, 1981, pp. 23–4.

While slavery had been a feature of many Central African societies before the slave trade, preliminary evidence suggests a growing tendency to acquire captives to extract surplus which the aristocracy used to maintain its privileged position. To the extent that slaves acquired as corvée labourers tended to become chattel, the nature of slavery often changed from earlier forms which emphasized the reproductive role and the use of slaves primarily to expand the size of the kinship network.

52. G. Hartwig and K.D. Patterson (eds), 1978; A.D. Roberts, 1970a, pp. 734–6; B. Reynolds, 1968, p. 17, and p. 59; J. Vansina, 1978.

PLATE 8.3 *A 'Ruga-Ruga' (slave- raider)*

accompanied the raids and the expansionist activities of the slave-traders. Fields were ravished, entire villages destroyed and survivors often compelled to flee their homelands and resettle in inaccessible, unproductive locations. One nineteenth-century traveller recalled the effect of the Yao raids in the 1860s against the Manganja:

> A number of the Manganja went with them. Everywhere they saw sad signs of the war – villages burnt, gardens uncared for, the beautiful land about them rapidly becoming desert. About midday they came upon a large party of Ajawa [Yao], who were just returning from a successful raid. The smoke of burning villages was seen in the distance. A long train of captives carried the plunder, and their bitter cry was heard, even above the triumphant utterances of the Ajawa women, who came out ... to welcome back the visitors.[53]

Chikunda forays in the homelands of the Chewa, Tonga and Nsenga and as far north as the Lunda of Kazembe, and Arab-Swahili attacks against the people living in the Lake Malawi area produced similar turmoil and decay.[54] In the most extreme instances, entire regions were depopulated. One British official recanted in 1861 that 'An Arab who lately returned from Lake Nyasa informed me that he travelled for seventeen days through a country covered with ruined towns and villages ... where no living soul is to be seen.'[55]

This loss of many of the most productive members of the society reinforced the rural dislocation. Although the evidence is uneven, data from the Zambezi region, the Shire valley and the Lake Malawi region suggest that famines recurred with great regularity,[56] which often necessitated the exchange of slaves for food, further intensifying the population drain. Whatever the case, the unstable conditions and threats of new raids prevented the resurgence of the rural economy.

Famines and psychological stress also left the uprooted and malnourished vulnerable to infectious diseases carried by the coastal traders. Diseases common to the Indian Ocean communities, such as smallpox and cholera, but uncommon to the Central African interior, whose population lacked any natural immunity, had a devastating effect. Epidemics of both smallpox and cholera ravaged large portions of the region stretching from the present-day Tanzania–Malawi border to southern Mozambique. In the late 1850s one European explorer noted that 'The most dangerous epidemic is ... small-pox which ... sweeps at times like a storm over the land.'[57] Documented epidemics of smallpox swept parts of Mozambique in 1834, 1836 and 1862, and were reported in the interior throughout the period from

53. H. Rowley, 1867, pp. 112–13.
54. F. Selous, 1893, p. 48.
55. Cited in R. Coupland, 1939, p. 140.
56. A. F. Isaacman, 1972a, pp. 114–24; E. A. Alpers, 1967, p. 20.
57. R. Burton quoted in G. W. Hartwig, 1978, p. 26.

1850 to 1880.[58] Sleeping sickness, probably related to changes in the disease environment as a result of forest clearance and the hunting of game, also struck much of the area under investigation.[59]

The high mortality and its debilitating effects further reduced rural productivity which, in turn, intensified the spiral of malnourishment and disease. The tendency of surviving communities to relocate in overcrowded stockaded villages, whose soils proved incapable of supporting them, further aggravated this problem. The epidemics had at least two other disruptive effects. Evidence suggests that they led to a sharp increase in witchcraft accusations and social upheavals. There are also suggestions that the privileged in a number of societies sought additional captives to compensate for demographic losses, thereby further augmenting the intensity of the slave trade.[60]

While it might be argued that African trading societies, or at least the aristocracy and merchants within them, benefited at the expense of their weaker neighbours, the evidence suggests that the advantages which these groups enjoyed were short-term and made them excessively dependent on the capitalist world economy. At a minimum, the great commercial states lost their economic autonomy. To maintain their pre-eminent positions they had to expect not only that the coastal demand for ivory and slaves would continue despite growing British pressures, but also that they could acquire sufficient supplies of both commodities. In extreme cases, such as the Makua, the failure to maintain the external supply of slaves resulted in internal conflict and self-destruction. More commonly, the competition for captive labour generated intense hostility among and within trading factions. There are numerous examples of wars among the Chikunda bands, Yao chiefs and Swahili trading groups.[61] The dependence on European arms and alien intermediaries often left the indigenous trading communities quite vulnerable. The Portuguese, for example, exploited their role as suppliers of weapons to pressure the Chikunda bands to recognize Lisbon's limited authority over their territory.[62] Similarly, the Sena began to rely so heavily on their Arab allies that they jeopardized their sovereign status.[63] Even the powerful Bemba were not totally immune to pressures from Arab and Swahili traders.[64]

Moreover, with the abolition of the slave trade, those classes or strata within them who profited from the trade – the aristocracy, merchants, warlords and landlords – searched desperately for new commodities such

58. R. Burton; J. R. Dias, 1981; G. Liesegang, n.d.
59. J. R. Dias, 1981.
60. G. Hartwig, 1978, pp. 25–31.
61. A. F. Isaacman, 1976, pp. 37–8; Y. B. Abdallah, 1973, pp. 52–4; K. M. Phiri, 1975, pp. 144–6; E. A. Alpers, 1969, pp. 413–14.
62. A. F. Isaacman, 1976, pp. 31–5.
63. H. W. Langworthy, n.d., pp. 20–1.
64. A. D. Roberts, 1973, p. 268.

as wax, coffee, groundnuts, and vegetable oils which they could extract from their subordinates or acquire through commerce in order to ensure a constant supply of European consumer goods and weapons necessary to maintain their privileged position. In some regions this legitimate commerce offered new opportunities for aspiring itinerant traders to accumulate capital and for the growth of peasant agriculture. To the extent that particular classes or strata successfully made this transition, they merely perpetuated or extended their dependent position in a world economy over which they had no control.

Viewed from a somewhat different perspective, the unequal value of commodities exchanged reflects the fragile position of the region within the larger international trading system. As E. A. Alpers has noted, 'What Africans received in exchange for ivory, even though it had little intrinsic value in their own societies, were goods that in no way equalled the value placed on ivory by the merchant capitalists of India, Europe and America.'[65] This discrepancy was particularly acute in the sale of captives. In return for the lost labour power, the Central African societies received a variety of inexpensive perishable commodities and weapons of destruction, neither of which compensated for the depletion of the work force. Similarly, when Africans hunted ivory they were exhausting a limited resource and were not receiving capital goods that expanded the productive base of their societies. Recent research suggests that they were not only distorting their economies but also destroying the ecology.

As the region was becoming progressively impoverished, disparities in wealth and social equality became more pronounced. Although more detailed research is needed to determine the character of the production systems and the allocation of surplus in specific Central African societies, it is clear that the dominant aristocracy, often allied with all or a fraction of the merchant class, was the principal beneficiary. The emergence of the powerful Yao chiefs, Makanjila and Mataka, testifies to the growing political and social differentiation within these societies, as do the desperate efforts of the Makua rulers to remain in power.[66] A similar phenomenon occurred in the sultanates of Angoche and Quitanghona and in the Chikunda and Arab-Swahili conquest states, where a small political-commercial class prevailed despite growing opposition and periodic revolts. The extent to which popular discontent surfaced more frequently during the second half of the century suggests growing class antagonisms as did slave uprisings in Lozi society and on the *prazos*.[67]

In other instances trading interests, independent of the rulers, were able to dominate commerce and undercut the position of the political authorities.

65. E. A. Alpers, 1975, p. 266.

66. Y. B. Abdallah, 1973, pp. 40–60; E. A. Alpers, 1975, pp. 228–9.

67. N. Hafkin, 1973, pp. 253–80, and pp. 311–59; A. F. Isaacman, 1976, pp. 23–30; K. M. Phiri, 1975, pp. 140–6.

Perhaps the two best examples of this power shift occurred in the northern states of Undi and Kazembe. In both cases alliances between local merchants and foreign traders facilitated the circumvention of the royal monopoly and drastically weakened the position of the respective national leaders.[68] A similar pattern occurred in the kingdom of Kassanje, located in the adjacent territory of Angola. There the local matrilineages were able to gain control of the slave trade, at the expense of the royal family, leading to the rapid fragmentation of the state.[69]

One by-product of greater commercial interaction was the substantial amount of cultural borrowing that occurred between different societies. The direction of change varied appreciably, depending on such factors as the nature and duration of contact between the trading groups and the host population. Where interaction was substantial, three broad patterns of acculturation occurred. In several instances, isolated bands of merchants and raiders became totally absorbed into the local society, as in the case of the Chikunda hunters, who were incorporated into Nsenga, Ambo and valley Tonga communities.[70] In sharply contrasting situations, the aliens profoundly altered the host culture. The Chewa subjects of Khota Khota, for example, absorbed aspects of Islam into their religion, adopted Swahili names, Swahili words and phrases, and underwent a major restructuring of their social system.[71] Similarly, many Yao traders converted to Islam and adopted coastal cultural patterns as a result of their contact with the Arabs. Their participation in long-distance trade also led to the growth of urban centres and the development of rituals and prohibitions designed to ensure the fidelity of Yao women while their husbands were in the interior,[72] suggesting that change also occurred as societies modified internal structures to meet new external conditions. In addition to these two patterns of acculturation, there are indications that the fluid conditions facilitated the development of new ethnic and cultural groups. Several of the bands of Chikunda broke away from the decaying *prazo* system around the middle of the century and organized autonomous communities in the Luangwa valley. Attracting followers from a variety of disparate ethnic groups, they evolved a culture incorporating diverse Malawian and Shona institutions and values.[73] A parallel phenomenon occurred in the area of what is now eastern Zaire where the Manyema were transformed from a disparate band of slavers into a coherent social and cultural group.[74]

68. H.W. Langworthy, 1971, pp. 18–21; I. Cunnison, 1966, pp. 235–6; J. Vansina, 1966, pp. 227–31.
69. J.C. Miller, 1973, pp. 23–6.
70. W.V. Brelsford, 1956, pp. 60–2.
71. K.M. Phiri, 1975, pp. 140–6; H.W. Langworthy, n.d., p. 23; M.E. Page, 1974, pp. 88–9.
72. E.A. Alpers, 1972, pp. 172–96; E.A. Alpers, 1969, pp. 417–20.
73. A.F. Isaacman, 1972b, pp. 454–61.
74. M. Page, 1974, pp. 69–84.

The impact of the Nguni and Kololo invasions

Like the progressive incorporation of Central Africa into the world capitalist system, the Nguni and Sotho invasions beginning in the 1820s represented a continuation of ongoing processes but in new forms and on an unprecedented scale.[75] The diaspora of Southern African peoples falls within the larger pattern of migrations and state formation that had begun several centuries earlier. In some cases the immigrants conquered groups that had managed to remain outside the sphere of the Shona or Lunda state systems. The Gaza Nguni domination of the Tonga of southern Mozambique illustrates this phenomenon. Often, the invaders imposed their hegemony over existing kingdoms. Whatever the case, the new conquest states encompassed an appreciable part of contemporary Mozambique, Malawi and Zambia and were organized around a set of unique military and centralized political institutions.

Three waves of immigrants swept into Central Africa during the middle decades of the nineteenth century. The first were the Nguni followers of Soshangane who carved out the Gaza Nguni empire, stretching north from southern Mozambique to the Zambezi river and extending west into present-day Zimbabwe. Soshangane's defeat of his arch-rival Zwangendaba in 1831 compelled the latter to migrate across the middle Zambezi, where he ultimately settled at Mapupo between Lake Malawi and Lake Tanganyika. At approximately the same time, Kololo immigrants of Sotho descent under the direction of Sebetwane migrated across the Tswana homelands and the middle Zambezi region before settling among the Lozi, whom they conquered.

Although each of the migrating groups will be treated separately in this chapter, they exhibited certain common characteristics. All were motivated by similar incentives to flee their historic homelands, faced similar problems in their trek northwards and benefited from the weapons and military strategy that they borrowed directly or indirectly from the Zulu. The groups had all suffered from the expansionist activities of their neighbours – the Gaza and Zwangendaba at the hands of Shaka and the Kololo from the raids of the Tlokwa – and faced the prospect of losing their herds and being annihilated. Because these conflicts had substantially reduced their membership, they were forced to incorporate a great number of aliens if they were to become a viable military and political force. The adoption of the Zulu short stabbing spear and the development of superior martial skills facilitated the acquisition of captives and the development of conquest

75. Recent work by Philip Bonner, Jeffrey Guy, David Hedges, and Henry Slater has suggested that nineteenth-century state-building processes associated with Nguni-Sotho expansion had their antecedents in political changes and consolidation of the power of chief and elders in the preceding period. See articles in S. Marks and A. Atmore (eds), 1980; D. Hedges, 1978.

states, although their pre-eminence did not go unchallenged. It also enabled them to seize large herds which carried important social and religious as well as economic significance within Nguni and Sotho societies. Thus, in terms of their expansion and acquisition of wealth, access to new weapons was as critical to the Nguni and Sotho as it was to the Chikunda, Yao and Arab-Swahili slave-traders.

Fearing an attack by the Zulu, Soshangane and his Gaza Nguni followers had moved northwards from the area north of the Thukela (Tugela) river into the Delagoa Bay region by 1821. Here they met only limited resistance from the Chopi, who were organized into relatively small chieftaincies, and from the Portuguese who maintained only a nominal presence at the port of Lourenço Marques. Within a year or two, the Gaza Nguni had extended their domain to the Inhambane hinterland, even as their ranks were swollen by additional Nguni of Ndwandwe descent whom Shaka had defeated in 1826.

Despite these initial gains, Soshangane faced a number of threats, not the least of which were attacks from the Zulu, whose army remained in relatively close proximity. After military confrontations in 1828, Soshangane relocated the core of his kingdom in the middle Sabi, outside the range of Shaka's army, but this placed his forces in direct conflict with the Nguni of Zwangendaba, whom they defeated in a series of battles in 1831.

PLATE 8.4 *Soshangane's Shangana arrive at Shapanga to collect the annual tribute from the Portuguese*

These victories enabled Soshangane to consolidate his southern holdings and expand his frontiers. Gaza forces then moved westward into present-day Zimbabwe, where Soshangane built his capital at Chaimaite, and northwards into the Zambezi valley. By the middle of the 1830s Gaza armies were raiding the Shona kingdoms of Manica, Quiteve, and Barue as well as the surviving *prazos* along the Zambezi river. Rather than attempt to incorporate this vast region into his empire, the Gaza leader was content to plunder the Shona states and to collect tribute from the *prazeros* and Portuguese officials residing in the towns of Sena and Tete.[76]

The core of Soshangane's empire was southern Mozambique and the adjacent areas to the west. There the subject peoples were treated harshly and compelled to pay heavy taxes and provide young men for the Soshangane age-regiments. Unlike the strategy of the Zwangendaba Nguni, no efforts were made to incorporate the Tonga and Chopi recruits into Gaza society. Rather than blurring cultural and ethnic differences as occurred in other Nguni societies, the segregated age-regiments ruled by Nguni officers symbolized the inferiority of the indigenous population. Tensions between the oppressed majority and the Nguni aristocracy surfaced periodically. For example, several Tonga chieftaincies tried to regain their freedom by migrating outside the sphere of Gaza rule. Individual Chopi and Tonga polities forged alliances with the Portuguese, whom they hoped would act as a compelling force. Among the Nguni it was commonly believed that their subjects sought revenge by bewitching Soshangane and causing his death.[77]

As the Gaza were imposing their hegemony, Zwangendaba and his followers embarked on a twenty-year trek in search of an appropriate homeland. During this period they contested with the Gaza for control of the Delagoa Bay area, administered the final blow to the fragmented Rozwi empire of Changamire, temporarily settled among the Nsenga and plundered the western margin of Lake Malawi before finally settling at Mapupo. At every phase of their migration they assimilated new followers. The problem of manpower was particularly acute because the original group of 300 was hardly a viable political or military unit and many of the women and children were killed in the conflict with Soshangane. Like the Gaza, they initially sought to expand their following by incorporating only individuals and fragmented groups of Nguni descent, thus ensuring that the dominant culture and language would prevail. As they moved further from the Nguni homelands, however, Zwangendaba realized that aliens would have to be assimilated to ensure the survival of his relatively small band.

Unlike the Zulu or Gaza Nguni, therefore, Zwangendaba and his advisers incorporated a multitude of disparate people into their ranks. Individuals were attached to specific Nguni families with whom they formed quasi-kin

76. G. Liesegang, 1964, pp. 47–50; J.D. Omer-Cooper, 1966, pp. 59–60; M.D.D. Newitt, 1973, pp. 223–4; A.F. Isaacman, 1972a, pp. 122–3.
77. J.D. Omer-Cooper, 1966, pp. 59–60.

relationships that tended to blur their captive status. At the appropriate age, the young adoptees were placed into Nguni age-regiments which were important socializing institutions. Depending on their military prowess, the foreign-born recruits could acquire substantial amounts of plunder, high rank and status. The rapid expansion of the Zwangendaba Nguni thus provided a wide variety of opportunities, and facilitated the upward mobility of many aliens who simultaneously adopted Nguni culture and shifted their primordial loyalty.[78] That the vast majority, estimated at 90 per cent, of the Nguni who settled at Mapupo in the 1840s were originally of foreign descent, demonstrates the success of Zwangendaba's assimilationist policy.[79]

Paralleling this incorporation was the creation of a highly centralized political structure capable of governing the expansive polity. The Nguni concept of kingship shifted from one based on seniority and limited authority within a loose cluster of related villages to one in which the ruler was the personification of the state and its ultimate authority. Simultaneously, the age-regiments were transformed into the military arm of the king, whose leaders were appointed by and made responsible to Zwangendaba. Because the age-regiments were not initially coterminous with the territorial segments of the kingdom, provincial leaders lacked the military capacity to secede. By the death of Zwangendaba, the Nguni state had become a major power in Central Africa.[80]

Zwangendaba's death marked the end of the expansive phase of Nguni development. The succession dispute was particularly bitter and resulted in the fragmentation of the kingdom into several major and numerous minor segments. The expansionist designs of the independent sections were severely restricted both by the powerful indigenous states, such as the Bemba, Lunda and Fipa to the north, and the growing presence of well-armed Arab-Swahili, Yao and Chikunda forces.

Nevertheless, by eventually selecting targets among the weaker polities to the south, two of the Zwangendaba offshoots were able to carve out substantial domains by 1870. The Mpezeni Nguni took advantage of the impotence of the Nsenga chieftaincies, which had not fully recovered from Zwangendaba's raids, to impose their authority over the south-western portion of the tsetse fly-free Malawian plateau in what is now the Fort Jameson region. The Mbwela established their domain in territory that formerly belonged to the Tumbuka, Tonga and Henga. In both cases, their ranks were swollen by other age-regiments who subsequently joined the newly created states. As the Mpezeni were gaining new adherents, a former slave of Nsenga descent, Ciwere Ndhlou, who had become a prominent military officer, declared his independence and organized an independent

78. T. Spear, 1972, pp. 9–13; J. D. Omer-Cooper, 1966, pp. 64–72.
79. T. Spear, 1972, p. 11.
80. ibid., pp. 9–13; J. D. Omer-Cooper, 1966, pp. 64–72.

kingdom bearing his name in contemporary Dowa district. In addition to these three segments, the Gwangara, another segment of the defunct Zwangendaba state, moved into Tanzania where they defeated the Maseko Nguni, who fled southward across the Rovuma and settled in the highland country of the Kirk Range in the late 1860s.[81]

The migration of the Kololo followed the broad pattern of Zwangendaba's Nguni. Fleeing northward from Dithakong, the Kololo encountered a number of hostile peoples, including the Tswana and Ndebele, who defeated them. Continued threats from the Ndebele convinced Sebetwane to cross the Zambezi river and move westwards, arriving on the frontier of the Lozi kingdom around 1835.

Despite their ostensible power, the Lozi were particularly vulnerable. The death of Mulambwa, who had ruled for nearly fifty years, not only created a leadership vacuum but also precipitated an intense struggle within the core of the kingdom. Moreover, antipathy towards the Lozi aristocracy was particularly acute in the outlying provinces among the subject peoples who were not prepared to defend the alien and authoritarian Lozi regime from foreign invasion. Thus, when the Kololo attacked, they faced opposition from only one segment of the royal family and within four years they had conquered the vast Lozi kingdom.[82]

Once in power the Kololo faced the delicate problem of incorporating the more numerous Lozi and their former subjects into Sotho society while maintaining their dominant position. Their mutually unintelligible languages and the very different cultural systems complicated this process of social and political integration. To fuse the disparate elements within the kingdom, Sebetwane entered into a number of marriage alliances with prominent indigenous authorities, encouraged people throughout the state to adopt Kololo as the national language, refused to allow his Kololo followers to become a dominant minority, spared the lives of the Lozi royal family and publicly declared that 'all are children of the king'. Accompanying these symbolic gestures were specific policies which brought Lozi into Sebetwane's government and ensured that a number of indigenous rulers were allowed to maintain their positions in the reorganized territorial administration.[83]

Sebetwane's incorporative policy enjoyed considerable success in the first instance. Kololo quickly became the lingua franca for much of the kingdom, and Lozi living along the flood plains of the Zambezi began to adopt the nomenclature Kololo. They demonstrated their loyalty by defending the polity against successive attacks by the Naba Nguni and Ndebele. The victory against the Ndebele secured the south-western border

81. T. Spear, 1972, pp. 15–19; J. D. Omer-Cooper, 1966, pp. 72–85; K. Rennie, 1966, pp. 303–6.
82. J. D. Omer-Cooper, 1966, pp. 120–2; M. Mainga, 1973, pp. 65–88.
83. G. Caplan, 1970, pp. 10–11; J. D. Omer-Cooper, 1966, pp. 123–4.

and enabled Sebetwane to shift his attention towards the continued consolidation of the kingdom and the acquisition of weapons from Angolan traders to bolster the state's military capacity.[84]

Ultimately, several factors frustrated the assimilationist strategy. The death of Sebetwane in 1863 precipitated a bitter struggle for the throne that divided the Kololo community. This conflict demonstrated the fragility of the Kololo, whose numbers had already been diminished by their susceptibility to malaria. Operating from a position of relative weakness, Sekeletu, the new king, nevertheless reversed his father's policy of accommodation and imposed an authoritarian anti-Lozi regime. He forced the Lozi out of the administration, terminated marriage alliances with prominent local families and allowed his Kololo subordinates to become a dominant minority. Predictably, in 1864, the Lozi rebelled under the leadership of exiled members of the royal family. Within weeks they had liberated their homelands and killed virtually all the Kololo men.[85]

The popular uprising did not totally eliminate Kololo influence in the Zambezi valley. Several years earlier a small group of Kololo had accompanied David Livingstone in his eastern journey down the Zambezi and had settled among the Manganja. Their adamant opposition to the slave trade and their reputation as soldiers quickly contributed to their popularity. With the aid of European weapons provided by Livingstone, the Kololo repelled the predatory activities of both the Yao and the coastal Arabs, to the relief of their Manganja hosts.[86]

Under the leadership of Maluka and Ramukkan, the Kololo rapidly assumed a more active role in the politics of the Shire region. With the assistance of Manganja allies, the Kololo defeated a number of prominent chiefs and the reigning Lundu Tsagonja, who was the titular owner of all the Manganja land. This process of conquest and incorporation took several years, but by 1870 they had established a Kololo state divided into six regions, each of whose leaders enjoyed a great deal of autonomy. For the next two decades the Kololo remained the dominant force in the strategically located Shire valley.[87]

The realignment of the political map of Central Africa represents the most far-reaching effect of the Nguni–Sotho diaspora. The immigrants organized several new kingdoms that dominated an appreciable part of the region. In the process they not only incorporated a number of localized polities but did irreparable damage to several major states, most notably the Rozwi, Undi and Lundu. The structure of the Nguni states, and to a lesser degree the Kololo, constituted a substantial departure from earlier political forms. The new polities were smaller in scale, denser in population

84. G. Caplan, 1970, pp. 12–13.
85. ibid.; M. Mainga, 1973, pp. 105–28.
86. W. H. J. Rangley, 1959, pp. 59–98; A. F. Isaacman, 1976, p. 23.
87. ibid.; E. Mandala, 1977.

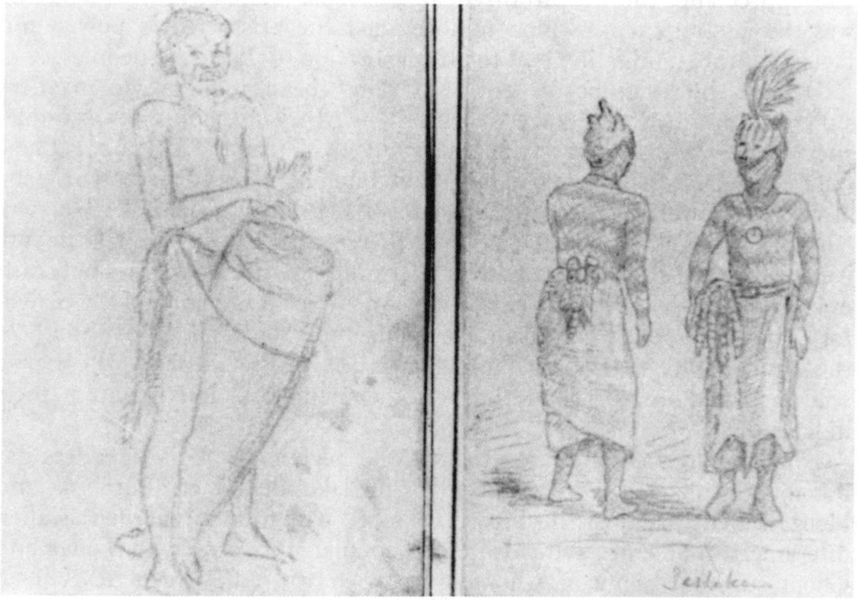

PLATE 8.5 *Drummer and dancers at the court of Sipopa, ruler of the Lozi, 1875*

PLATE 8.6 *Sipopa, one of the leaders of the Lozi rebellion against the Kololo in 1864 and ruler of the Lozi until 1876*

and appreciably more centralized. Their most distinctive characteristic was the age-regiment, which underpinned the aristocracy's power and facilitated the domination and the incorporation of disparate peoples.

Despite their significant territorial gains the South African invaders suffered a number of military setbacks. The Mpezeni Nguni, for example, spent almost a decade periodically trying to defeat the Bemba.[88] Their failure reflected the more generalized inability of Nguni offshoots to penetrate the territory of the powerful states living north of the Lake Malawi–Rovuma region. With the exception of the Gwangara, the Nguni segments were compelled to turn southward where they met some surprisingly stiff opposition. Both the Chewa chieftaincy of Mwase Kasungu and the Senga, for example, repelled Nguni incursions in the 1860s and 1870s. South of the Zambezi, Gaza raiders faced continued resistance from the Barue who managed to withstand the periodic incursions and maintain their independence.[89]

Even within the conquered regions the hegemony of the invaders did not go unchallenged. During the 1870s the lakeside Tonga, Tumbuka and Henga rebelled against the Mbwela Nguni, whom they regarded as alien interlopers. The Gaza state also faced popular uprisings from Tonga and Chopi subjects, some of whom even allied with the Portuguese in an effort to gain their independence. The Lozi organized the most successful insurrection, driving out the Kololo and liberating their homelands.[90]

Inextricably related to the process of Nguni state formation were the profound social and cultural transformations that occurred throughout the region. Despite the incorporation of thousands of captives and subject peoples, the rate and pattern of acculturation varied substantially from one subject group to another. As a rule, the process of assimilation was most rapid during the expansive phase of the migration rather than in the later sedentary stage when the power and prestige of the immigrants was tarnished, the plunder more limited and the host population more numerous. Thus, the Zwangendaba Nguni increased their numbers by geometric proportions as they moved through the fragmented polities on their northward trek, but the autonomous segments were far less successful once they had settled in their new homelands. A similar phenomenon occurred among the Kololo.

The actual pattern of acculturation also differed from one contact situation to another. At one extreme, exemplified by the Zwangendaba Nguni, the dominated population adopted the culture and identity of the invaders. At the other extreme were the Kololo immigrants, who established their ascendancy over the Manganja, but were totally absorbed into the sub-

88. H. W. Langworthy, 1972, p. 92.

89. A. F. Isaacman, 1976, pp. 8–9, 49.

90. T. Spear, 1972, p. 28; K. Rennie, 1966, pp. 310–11; G. Caplan, 1970, pp. 10–12; D. L. Wheeler, 1968, p. 587.

ordinate society.[91] Between these two poles were the more common examples of cross-fertilization leading, in some cases, to the formation of syncretic cultures. Even the vanquished Kololo left their impact on the Lozi, who adopted their language and important governmental institutions.[92] Within the Mpezeni kingdom, on the other hand, all the political elements of the new society were of South African derivation while non-political cultural elements such as land inheritance, marital patterns, female circumcision and language were heavily influenced by the indigenous Nsenga tradition.[93] This bifurcation is not surprising since the Mpezeni kingdom was controlled by political and military institutions designed to ensure the pre-eminence of the Nguni. Spatial and demographic considerations seem initially to have determined the extent of cultural borrowing within the Mbwela Nguni state; in the core of the kingdom where the Nguni were more numerous, the Tonga and Tumbuka adopted most aspects of the alien culture, but towards the outlying provinces the rate of borrowing diminished proportionately. This general pattern is complicated somewhat by the Nguni adoption of Tumbuka as the national language and the subsequent Tumbuka cultural renaissance, which suggests that many of the subject people only superficially adopted Nguni culture.[94]

Although a discussion of the effects which the Mfecane had on the existing patterns of social stratification is conspicuously absent from the literature, fragmentary evidence suggests the growth of new classes within the Nguni kingdoms. During the expansive phase, a military aristocracy consisting of the regimental commanders and their principal subordinates emerged. Their power was based primarily upon the tribute and plunder which they acquired – especially the herds of cattle and captives, some of which they redistributed to their followers. From an economic perspective, their pre-eminent position closely paralleled that of the surplus-appropriating aristocracy who governed the neighbouring conquest states and controlled the ivory and slave trade.

As the Nguni groups settled north of the Zambezi, the opportunities for plunder were more limited. While the military leaders continued to exact tribute from their subjects, they began to exploit their slaves in order to ensure a continued source of wealth. Rather than incorporating captives and strangers and providing them with opportunities for upward mobility, there are indications that many were reduced to a permanent state of bondage. The Mbwela, Maseko and Mpezeni aristocracy all kept appreciable numbers of slaves (*abafo*) to work their fields. Other slaves served as hunters and iron workers for their masters.[95] The convergence of ethnicity

91. W. H. J. Rangley, 1959, pp. 59–98; A. F. Isaacman, 1976.
92. G. Caplan, 1976.
93. J. A. Barnes, 1951, pp. 2–18; T. Spear, 1972, pp. 23–6.
94. T. Spear, 1972, pp. 29–32; H. L. Vail, 1972, pp. 161–2.
95. K. M. Phiri, 1975, pp. 154–6.

and class factors suggests that the subsequent resistance to the Nguni should not be analysed exclusively in ethnic terms.

The Nguni and Sotho immigrants primarily played only an indirect role in the slave trade. While their military campaigns undoubtedly facilitated Arab and Swahili plundering, there is little evidence that they developed a commercial alliance with the slave-traders on a regular basis. Of all the major Nguni and Kololo leaders, only Mpezeni, Soshangane, Sebetwane and the Maseko chief, Chikuse, exported slaves and in all four cases the transactions were limited in scale and sporadic.[96] In general, they chose to utilize captives internally and thereby enhance their political and economic position rather than to sell the slaves to any of the trading communities. Nevertheless, their predatory activities created significant dislocation within many societies. For those communities north of the Zambezi who suffered most heavily from the raids of the slave traders, the Nguni attacks aggravated the problems of rural stagnation and intensified the process of underdevelopment.

On the eve of the 'Scramble'

During the first three quarters of the nineteenth century, Central Africa underwent an extensive transformation. The emergence of new ethnic groups, increased cultural exchange and intensified class cleavages are expressions of this far-reaching change. The incorporation of much of the region into the world economy impeded rural growth and intensified economic dependency. The territorial ambition of the slave-traders and their Nguni-Kololo counterparts simultaneously precipitated a dramatic realignment of political power within the region. In short, on the eve of the 'Scramble' conditions within Central Africa were extremely fluid. In addition, the prevailing political fragmentation, ethnic and regional particularism and internal strife, in part reflecting growing class antagonisms, placed serious constraints on the capacity of most African societies to resist European imperialism.

By 1875 there were very few indigenous regional powers. To a certain extent this power vacuum reflected the past inability of many Central African societies to organize or sustain a centralized political system. Many of the Lunda and Shona states had also undergone a process of political fractionalization. North of the Zambezi, the slave trade intensified internal rivalries in the kingdoms of the Lunda of Kazembe, Undi, Kalonga and Lundu that left them vulnerable to the seditious activities and attacks of the slave traders and their Nguni counterparts. To the south, cleavages within the Shona aristocracy, coupled with the devastating raids of the Zwangendaba and Gaza Nguni, substantially weakened the regional powers. The incursions of Zwangendaba, for example, are generally

96. E. Flint, 1970, pp. 73–9; H. W. Langworthy, n.d., pp. 34–7.

credited with destroying the badly divided Rozwi kingdom of Changamire, while the division of the Barue state into two competing factions, coupled with the debilitating Gaza raids, enabled the Goan adventurer Gouveia to usurp temporarily the Barue throne around 1875.[97]

Gouveia's success was part of a larger process by which Yao, Arab-Swahili, Chikunda and Nguni invaders took advantage of the power vacuum to impose conquest states. While these new military states were undoubtedly stronger than the polities they had vanquished, the subject peoples often perceived them as alien interlopers and resented their authoritarian rule. As a result, the leaders were compelled to intensify their coercive practices, which heightened the level of hostility and increased the frequency of insurrections. The revolts of the lakeside Tonga, Tumbuka and Henga against the Mbwela Nguni, and of the Tonga and Chopi against the Gaza, demonstrate the growing antipathy of the oppressed. A similar spirit of defiance motivated the Tawara and Tonga to periodically challenge the Afro-Portuguese and their Chikunda allies, who had carved out large territorial holdings along the southern margin of the Zambezi. The Swahili ruler, who governed the coastal sultanates of Angoche and Quitanghona, faced similar opposition. Such animosity did not lend itself to a unified struggle against the Europeans. On the contrary, many of the subject peoples subsequently refused to assist the alien rulers; others actually aided the Europeans whom they perceived as 'liberators'.[98]

The dependence of the slave-trading states on European weapons and markets further compromised their autonomy. In the first instance they were particularly vulnerable to external pressures, as suggested by the willingness of the Afro-Portuguese and Chikunda to serve as Lisbon's imperial agents. Ultimately, changing conditions within the world capitalist economy provoked opposition to their participation in the slave trade and, together with growing European imperial ambitions, set the stage for an intensive conflict.

While most Central African societies were becoming more vulnerable as the century progressed, there were a few cases in which external threats or temporary foreign annexation ultimately strengthened political and military capabilities. The Bemba kingdom, in part responding to the Nguni incursions, completed a dual process of political centralization and territorial expansion during the period after 1850. By the eve of the 'Scramble', the kingdom had reached its apogee and, had it not been for the untimely death of Mwamba III, it might have proved as formidable an opponent to the European invaders as it had been to the Nguni.[99] Similarly, the liberated Lozi kingdom under the rule of Lewanika was appreciably stronger and

97. A. F. Isaacman, 1976, pp. 48–52.
98. A. Dachs, 1972, pp. 288–9; J. T. Botelho, 1921, pp. 469–504.
99. A. D. Roberts, 1973, p. 217.

better organized than it had been during the pre-Kololo period.[100] The resurgence of the kingdom of the Mwenemutapa during the second half of the nineteenth century also demonstrates that fluid conditions could enable a state whose power had atrophied to regain its pre-eminence.[101] But these examples were the exception. On balance, the changes of the nineteenth century tended to favour subsequent European imperialist activities.

100. M. M. Bull, 1972, pp. 463–72.
101. T. O. Ranger, 1963, pp. 1–3.

9 The East African coast and hinterland, 1800–45

A. I. SALIM

Coastal communities, *c.* 1800

The period under review witnessed some very significant developments and changes in the socio-economic and political status of the people of the East African coast and its hinterland. The advent of the Omani Arab hegemony was an important factor in these changes. In order to appreciate the nature and extent of these changes, a survey of the politico-economic pattern prevailing on the coast in about 1800 is important.

One significant overall political factor was the high degree of autonomy enjoyed by the coastal communities under indigenous leaders. The final expulsion by 1728 of the Portuguese, south of the Rovuma river, with the aid of the Omani, was not followed immediately by the placing of an effective, comprehensive Omani authority on the coast. At the turn of the century, the Omani presence was significantly evident in only three main centres: Mombasa, Zanzibar and Kilwa. Even in Mombasa, the Omani Mazrui family had come to assume an autonomous status which, in time, encouraged its members to demonstrate virtual defiance of the Busaʿidi dynasty ruling in Muscat. They were able to maintain this autonomy with the cooperation of the Swahili *shaykh*s of the Ithnaashara Taifa (Twelve Nations) which were subdivided into two federations: the Thelaatha Taifa (Three Nations) and the Tissa Taifa (Nine Nations). The leaders of these Swahili groups participated noticeably in the administration of Mombasa. As late as 1857, two decades after the overthrow of the Mazrui, Richard Burton was to remark on this Swahili participation.[1]

In 1799, an Omani governor (*wālī*), who was a kinsman of the ruler (*imām*) of Muscat, was appointed to Zanzibar in succession to Yaqut, an Ethiopian eunuch and freed slave, who possessed large estates in Oman. At first, the indigenous ruler, the *mwenyi mkuu* – with his regalia of office, two drums and two *siwa*s or horns – worked side by side with the Omani governor to administer his people.[2] One of his most important duties was

1. R. Burton, 1872, p. 40.
2. J. M. Gray, 1962, p. 160, notes the reference by American observers to the 'King' and 'princes' of Zanzibar ruling side by side with the Omani governor.

the collection of tax imposed by the Omani on the indigenous Wa-Hadimu and Wa-Tumbatu, who lived by agriculture, fishing, and other maritime pursuits. As Zanzibar was preferred more and more by the Omani as a centre of power and economic development on the East African littoral, the *mwenyi mkuu* lost more and more political authority, whilst his people also lost more and more land to Omani settlers, who began to take over the fertile areas north and east of Zanzibar town.

When in the 1780s the Imām of Muscat's brother attempted to use Kilwa Kisiwani, then under the rule of an indigenous Shirazi sultan, as a base for his rebellion against his brother, the Imām took the determined step, in 1785, of sending an expedition to the island. This expedition left behind a small garrison to prevent any further possible subversion. This Omani presence on the island was also calculated to benefit economically from the French slave trade already established there. Even so, the local sultan for some time retained his title and one-fifth of the custom dues. He exercised his authority with the help of notables from the island itself and from the opposite mainland settlements, as far south as Cape Delgado, where the Kilwa sultan enjoyed an indeterminate degree of overlordship.[3] The economic decline of Kilwa Kisiwani was speeded up by the emergence of the mainland settlement of Kilwa Kivinje, which began to attract the bulk of the slave and ivory trade away from Kilwa Kisiwani early in the nineteenth century.

Around 1800 the rest of the East African coast was ruled by leading Swahili families, as were many of the offshore islands. In the Mafia archipelago and its three main settlements – Kisimani, Chole and Kua – several notable families, among them the Shatri, exercised real authority. The people's sympathy for Kilwa Kisawani's resistance to Omani power during the last quarter of the eighteenth century prevented the imposition of an Omani presence in the archipelago similar to the garrison left behind in Kilwa.

Similarly, the coast between Kilwa and Mombasa was still free of an Omani presence by 1800. Traditional administration, exercised by local leaders – *jumbe*s and *diwani*s – predominated in such settlements as Sadani, Pangani, Mtangata, Tanga, Vanga and Vumba Kuu. The *jumbe* or *diwani*, possessing the usual regalia of office – the *siwa* (horn), the drums and umbrella – carried out such functions as settling disputes, pronouncing judgements, and imposing fines with the help of subordinate officials, the *shaha*, the *mwenyi mkuu* and the *amiri*, who came from prominent local clans. Customary law was mixed with Islamic law in the administrative and judicial processes.

In this area of the coast between Kilwa and Mombasa the most important settlement was Vumba Kuu, situated between Vanga and Gasi on the

3. E. A. Alpers, 1975, pp. 190–1.

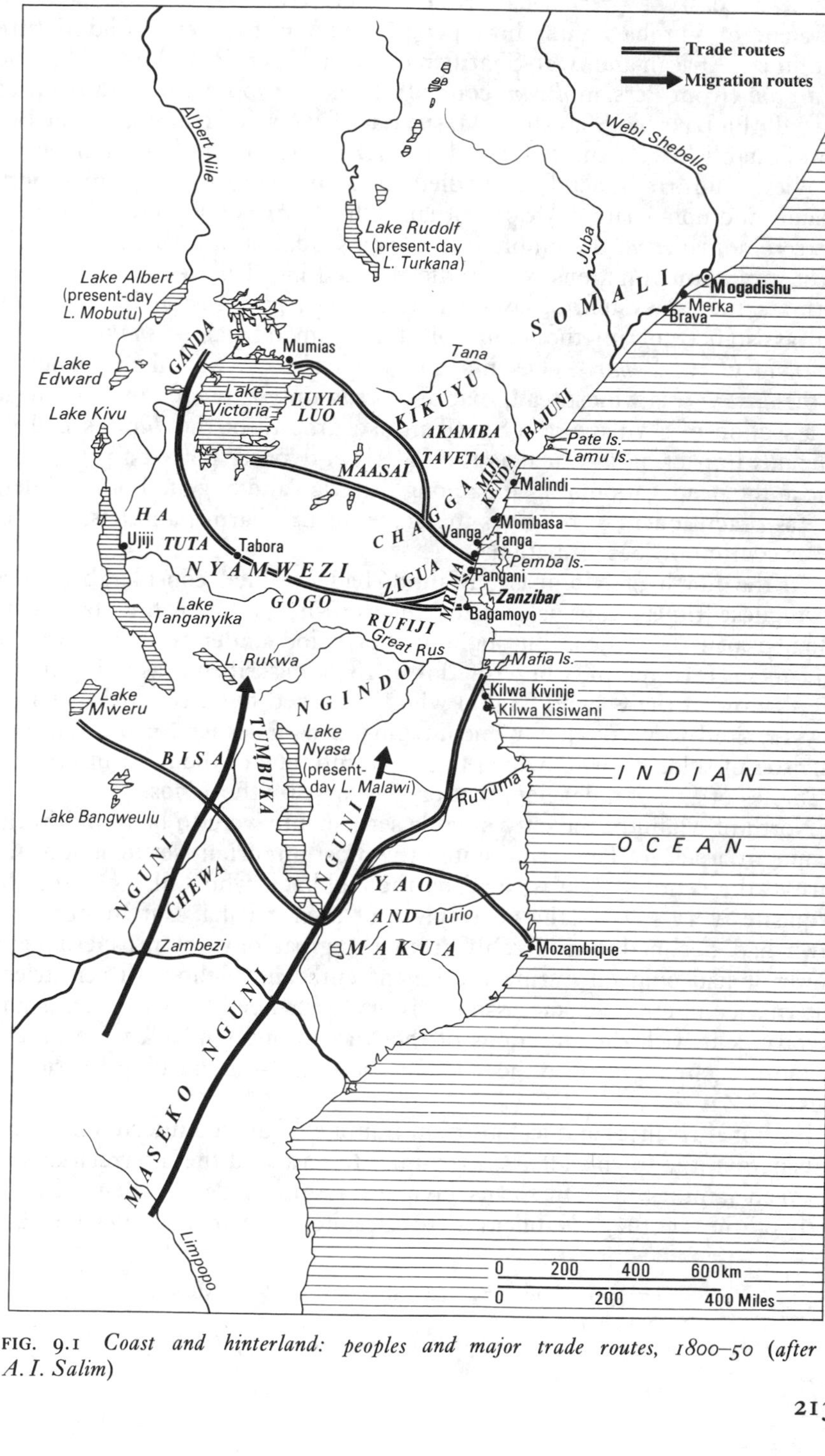

FIG. 9.1 *Coast and hinterland: peoples and major trade routes, 1800–50 (after A. I. Salim)*

southern coast of present-day Kenya. Here, there had developed the diwanate of Vumba Kuu, whose people, the Vumba, were an admixture of Shirazi, African and Arab Sharīfian elements. Its rulers adopted the title of *diwani* (from Persian *divan*, council). From *c.* 1700, with the advent of Sayyid Abū Bakr bin Shaykh Al-Masila Ba-Alawi from Hadramawt, the Ba-Alawi established a dynasty formed through intermarriage with indigenous families. Vumba statecraft embodied in its investiture ceremonies both Islamic and non-Islamic African rituals. The *diwani*'s regalia of office were the ceremonial *siwa*, the umbrella, wooden sandals and turban. Again, his most important functions were judicial – settling disputes in accordance with a syncretic system of laws – part-Islamic, part-customary. He, too, had assistance to run the affairs of state from officials – *shaha*, *waziri*, *mwenyi mkuu* and *amiri* – chosen from notable clans. Whilst the jurisdiction of the *diwani* was widespread, that of a *jumbe* only extended over a village or a section of a village. the Sharīfian background of the *diwani*s had its religious impact, in as much as the Ba-Alawi dynasty played a prominent role in the propagation of Islam among the Digo and Segeju, both as rulers and as practitioners of religious medicine, using charms, amulets, etc., in the execution of these functions.[4]

To the north of Mombasa, Malindi had declined considerably since Portuguese times, especially after the transfer of its ruling family to Mombasa in the 1590s. Throughout the period under review, it was to remain so. J. L. Krapf, who visited it in 1848, described it as living under the shadow of the Oromo (Galla) who threatened the area.[5] It was left to Seyyid Saʿīd to revive it, by encouraging Omani settlers, protected by a garrison of soldiers, who helped to turn it into one of the most impressive examples of agrarian development on the coast by the 1870s.

North of Malindi, the only notable settlements were to be found in the Lamu archipelago. Pate represented the most important settlement at the turn of the century. It was ruled by the Nabhani, who still possessed the exquisite ivory *siwa* as the centrepiece of their regalia. But by 1800 the town had declined considerably from the great days of prosperity and power it had enjoyed during the seventeenth and eighteenth centuries.[6] Internal conflicts over succession, rivalry with neighbouring Lamu and involvement with the ambitions of the Mazrui of Mombasa were to lead to more decline and pave the way for the island-state's subordination to Busaʿidi Zanzibar.

Factional rivalries and jealousies in Lamu encouraged interference from outsiders in the town's affairs. Proximity to Pate and the interrelationship between families in both towns involved Lamu in Pate's affairs. By the turn of the century, Nabhani Pate, despite its economic decline, still

4. A. I. Salim, 1973, pp. 29–30; for a detailed study, see W. F. McKay, 1975.
5. J. L. Krapf, 1865, p. 152.
6. See W. Hichens (ed.), 1939, and J. de V. Allen (ed.), 1977, for details.

considered Lamu subordinate to it, but Lamu's leading families thought otherwise. This uneasy relationship forced the two to take opposite sides in the wider dispute between the Mazrui of Mombasa and the Busaʿidi. As will be seen, the outcome was the subordination of both to Zanzibar. Siyu, the other settlement on Pate Island, managed to maintain an independent status beyond the period under consideration, thanks to the determined spirit of independence displayed by its ruler, Bwana Mataka.

The mainland opposite the Lamu archipelago, northwards to the Somali-inhabited regions, was settled by the Bajuni people, whose allegiance was to their own chiefs. Zanzibari control was never really felt here even beyond the period under consideration. A predominantly maritime economy was pursued by the Bajuni. Fishing, mangrove-pole cutting, collection and sale of cowrie shells, tortoise shells and ambergris, supplemented trade in cattle with the neighbouring Somali and Oromo.[7] As the slave trade later grew in importance on the coast, the Bajuni participated in it, shipping slaves to the neighbouring Benadir ports.

During the period under review, the Benadir coast was predominantly self-governing, with centres like Mogadishu, Merka, Brava (Barawa) and Warsheikh being run by local Somali *shaykh*s who welcomed some Arab and Indian participation in the trade of the townships. But even after the establishment of the Zanzibari Omani sultanate, the Benadir ports maintained a great deal of political autonomy.[8] It was not until 1842 that Seyyid Saʿīd appointed a representative at Mogadishu at the request of the Somali chiefs, who were more interested in promoting economic ties with, and acquiring a certain degree of protection from Saʿīd in the event of invasion from marauders in the Somali hinterland than in subordinating themselves to Zanzibar. It was a mutually convenient relationship, since Saʿīd merely expected his man at Mogadishu to monitor commercial traffic and supervise tax collection.[9] That is to say the ambitions of Saʿīd were economic, not political.

The Omani sultanate

The growth and development of the Omani sultanate on the East African littoral was based on those essentially economic ambitions of Seyyid Saʿīd, who rightly considered himself a merchant prince first and foremost. Certain politico-economic factors at home in Oman and abroad on the East coast of Africa contributed to the genesis and development of the Omani sultanate on the coastal strip. The economy of Oman expanded considerably towards the end of the eighteenth century. Using a neutral flag, the Omani exploited the Napoleonic Wars to capture a good share of the carrying

7. J. L. Krapf, 1860, p. 114.
8. See M. Guillain, 1856, Vol. 2, pp. 527–30.
9. ibid.

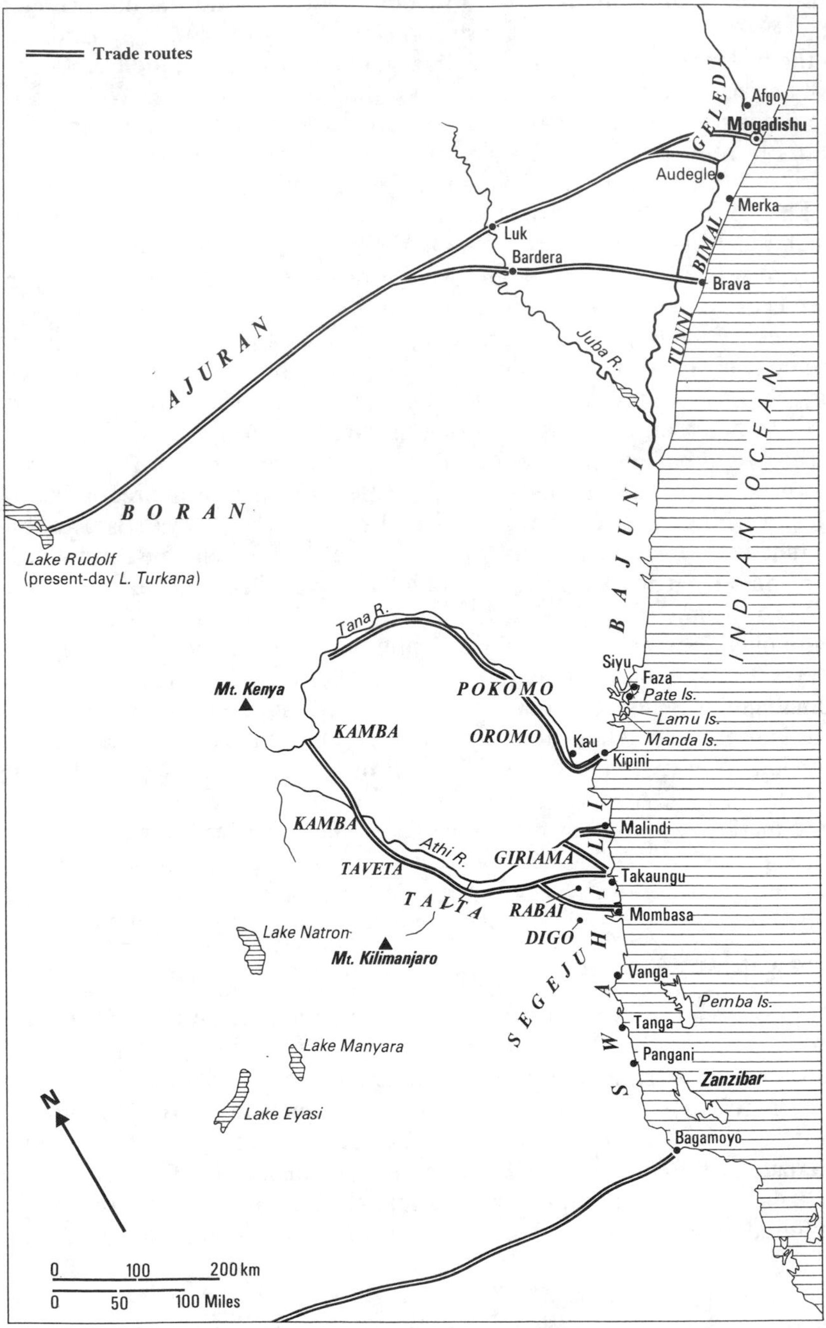

FIG. 9.2 *Northern coast and hinterland: trade routes,* c. *1850 (after A. I. Salim)*

PLATE 9.1 *Pressing sesame oil in Mogadishu, 1847*

trade in the Indian Ocean and neighbouring waters, leading to complaints by British merchants that they were being overshadowed by Oman's expanded merchant shipping. By the turn of the century, the Omani ruler, Sultan bin Aḥmed, had signed commercial agreements that gave his country profitable contacts with the coasts of many regions surrounding the Indian Ocean – Ethiopia, Shiraz, Sind and Batavia (Djakarta) – while his representatives on thc East African coast were sending him revenue worth 40 000 Maria Theresa dollars annually by 1802.[10]

When Saʿīd bin Sultan succeeded his father as imām in 1806, he shrewdly maintained the policy of neutrality towards Britain and France. He signed a commercial treaty with Ile de France (now Mauritius) in 1807. Britain, aware of the strategic importance of Muscat, felt compelled to acquiesce in this policy of neutrality and helped Saʿīd gain stability at home by assisting him in his war against destabilizing forces such as the Gawassim and the Wahhābīs. A stable home front gave Saʿīd time and resources to turn more confidently toward the East African coast.

The factors that focused his attention on the coast were economic and political. He was aware of the economic potential of the coast; he wished

10. C. S. Nicholls, 1971, p. 99. This source has been particularly useful in tracing the growth of Omani power on the East African coast.

to turn the local dynastic quarrels to his political advantage, and step in to counter growing European interest in the area. The Omani' concern about French ambitions to carve a wider sphere of influence was a contributory factor in the decision to place a governor at Kilwa in 1785. In 1801, Pate had invited the British to establish a fort to protect it from French designs in return for half the produce of that island town.[11] This, plus reports of subsequent visits by British ships, may have persuaded Saʿīd to make his presence and influence on the coast more substantial.

Subsequent political and military ventures are more familiar. Saʿīd decided to involve himself in Swahili political conflicts, particularly those in which the Mazrui were playing a hand. Pate's internal crisis of succession had led to Mazrui involvement. By 1811, a pro-Mazrui sultan ruled Pate, while his rival was held hostage by the Mazrui in Mombasa and the rival's supporters were given refuge in Lamu. The stage was thus set for a confrontation between Lamu and Pate, which was supported by the Mazrui. 1812/13 witnessed one of the most celebrated military encounters in Swahili history, the Battle of Shela, when a joint Pate-Mazrui force landed on Lamu island at the village of Shela with a view to bringing Lamu to heel. The invaders were thoroughly beaten and Pate's illusions about maintaining an overlordship in Lamu were finally shattered.

It was fear of reprisals that prompted Lamu to ask Saʿīd for support and protection. The invitation was accepted and a Busaʿidi governor and a garrison were despatched to the island, not only to counter further Mazrui-Pate threats, but also to prevent any further extension of Mazrui influence, which would undermine the burgeoning Busaʿidi influence; the Mazrui were then ensconced in Mombasa and enjoyed influence in Pemba and Pate, while the Busaʿidi had only Zanzibar and Kilwa.

From a defensive position, Saʿīd moved on to the offensive to reduce Mazrui influence and rule, and thus enhance his own. He established a faction of his own in Pate. The leader of this faction became sultan on the death of the pro-Mazrui ruler; and when this pro-Busaʿidi ruler died in 1822, Saʿīd and his governor in Lamu fought the Mazrui and their new candidate, Fumoluti, and succeeded in installing a sultan amenable to the Busaʿidi and establishing a garrison in Pate to protect their interest there. Thus, by 1822, Saʿīd had turned the political tide in his favour in the two most important points in the Lamu archipelago at the time, Lamu and Pate. In the same year, he challenged the Mazrui in Pemba. Acting at the request of an anti-Mazrui faction in Pemba, which had sent two representatives to Muscat to seek support against the Mazrui, the Busaʿidi took advantage of the absence of the Mazrui governor in Mombasa to take over Pemba in 1823. The Mazrui attempt to regain Pemba failed.

Thus, within a decade of turning his attention seriously towards the

11. C. S. Nicholls, pp. 120–1. Captain T. Smee was sent by the British Bombay Council to inquire into the economic possibilities of East Africa.

PLATE 9.2 *Saʿīd bin Sultan, Sultan of Zanzibar (1804–56)*

Swahili coast, Saʿīd had achieved for himself and his dynasty a commanding position and made his erstwhile rivals, the Mazrui, feel acutely vulnerable. It was this feeling that led the Mazrui to treat with the British naval officer, Captain W. F. Owen, and facilitate the declaration of a British protectorate over Mombasa in 1824.

British official policy towards Owen's action was somewhat ambiguous. While the declaration of a protectorate was not renounced, it was not enthusiastically welcomed. Omani–British relations dampened any enthusiasm there might have been otherwise. Owen had hoped and planned that Mombasa could be used as a base to fight the slave trade. Britain had planned to work for the curtailment of the trade through Saʿīd and, in 1822, had signed the Moresby treaty with him for this purpose. Now Owen's support for his rivals, the Mazrui, put the British in a diplomatic spot.

The protectorate, as it turned out, was short-lived. It ended in 1826 not only because the British government finally decided that Saʿīd was the man to work with, but also because the Mazrui themselves had become disenchanted with it. They were unhappy about the undue interference of British officers with their internal government; they were none too happy about sharing their custom dues with them and about the restrictions placed on their importation of slaves. And, of course, the British had failed to help them regain their lost possessions.

Although the protectorate ended in 1826, it was another decade before Saʿīd succeeded in subduing the Mazrui. In 1828, a Busaʿidi force managed to occupy Fort Jesus, but, after some months, Saʿīd's garrison was besieged and forced to withdraw. Two subsequent expeditions – in 1829 and 1833 – failed, largely because of support for the Mazrui from the two Swahili groups, the Three Nations and the Nine Nations. Saʿīd finally succeeded when, as elsewhere in Pate and Pemba, internal division occurred. Two factions arose among the Mazrui. The able and popular ruler, Salīm bin Aḥmed, died in 1835. His successor alienated the S͟hayk͟hs of the Three Nations. Saʿīd was invited once again by a dissatisfied group. His expedition this time (1837) faced no opposition. The Mazrui surrendered and Saʿīd won his most coveted prize, Mombasa. As elsewhere, acknowledgement of the Busaʿidi overlordship was accompanied by a significant degree of autonomy. Thus in Mombasa, Saʿīd's governor shared administrative responsibility with the S͟hayk͟hs of the Three Nations and the Nine Nations.

Coast-hinterland trade relations

By the time Mombasa fell to him, Saʿīd seems to have already made up his mind to move his capital from Oman to Zanzibar. It was to be in many ways a momentous decision affecting his own fortune and the fortunes of the coast as a whole. Extremely fertile and blessed with an excellent harbour, Zanzibar was also strategically placed opposite the Mrima coast, which by then had become the major outlet for the most important items of trade coming from the hinterland, ivory and slaves. Good revenue from this trade had begun to reflect itself in the coffers of the sultan even before he made his decision to make it his capital. His *wālī* (governor) had already started nurturing Zanzibar's paramountcy by ordering all foreign traders to deal only with Zanzibar, banning all direct contact with the Mrima.[12]

> Zanzibar soon outstripped the other coastal towns in economic and political development. Within a short period, Seyyid Saʿīd's business acumen and his liberal and far-sighted policies made Zanzibar the

12. ibid., pp. 80–1.

> greatest single emporium on the western shore of the Indian Ocean. It became the most important market on the east coast for ivory, slaves, cloves, gum copal, cowries and agricultural products, and the greatest importer of Indian, American and European manufactured goods – cottons, beads, wires, chains, muskets, gun-powder, china, earthenware, glass, knives, axes. Its status was enhanced by the international recognition it received in the form of commercial and consular agreements which the Sultan signed with America (1837), Britain (1839), France (1844) and, in time, some German states.[13]

Of all the items of trade noted above, ivory and slaves proved the most profitable to the Omani sultanate, owing to the increased demand for them overseas and, in the case of slaves, locally. During the first three or four decades of the nineteenth century, ivory and slaves reached the coast through the commercial networks established with the littoral by hinterland peoples, predominantly the Yao. E. A. Alpers stresses the importance of ivory in Zanzibar's trading pattern at the turn of the century.[14] It dominated the long-distance trade of East-Central Africa and was the major pre-occupation of most Yao. Attracted by higher prices, the Yao shifted their ivory away from the Mozambican coast towards Zanzibar's coast, its main outlet being Kilwa Kivinje.

One should distinguish here between Kilwa Kisiwani, the island town of that name and Kilwa Kivinje, now used by the Yao in their ivory trade. Kilwa Kisiwani declined significantly by the third decade of the nineteenth century because of internal dissensions and unfavourable environmental conditions. Instead, the village of Kilwa Kivinje, 27 km away on the mainland to the north, emerged as the principal trading centre. As early as 1819, an Omani governor had been placed there to promote the trade and exploit it. Alpers considers the rise of Kilwa Kivinje to be symbolic of the growing economic integration of coast and hinterland.[15] The town's rise and prosperity, he argues, owed as much to its role as a market and to Zanzibari initiative as to the inland peoples who brought down their trade goods to it:

> One of the most important factors in the rise of Kilwa Kivinje to prominence in the trade of East Africa was the contribution made by individuals from the far interior, like the Masaninga Yao adventurer, Mwinyi Mkwinda, who settled at Kilwa Kivinje during the late 18th century.

Thus the caravan trade between the coast and the hinterland was initiated by Africans. The Yao were joined by the Bisa in the carrying trade between the Lake Nyasa area and the coast. According to Alpers, competition between the Yao and the Bisa forced the former to concentrate more on

13. A. I. Salim, 1973, pp. 15–16.
14. E. A. Alpers, 1973, pp. 175–85.
15. ibid., p. 236.

the slave trade to make more profit because the Bisa undercut the ivory price and thus made themselves more welcome at Kilwa. During the first half of the nineteenth century, the ivory trade was probably as important as the slave trade, if not more so. Both the Bisa and the Yao brought down the ivory and slaves to Kilwa whence they were shipped to Zanzibar. By 1850, Kilwa Kivinje had become the most important town on the coast between Mozambique and Zanzibar, the export point of not only ivory and slaves but also other products, such as rice, gum copal, and tobacco. But it was to ivory and slaves that the town owed its economic importance at this time.

The interior peoples who were enslaved were often from groups who were themselves slave-traders, e.g. Yao, Bisa, Makua and Ngindu. Most slaves were acquired as a result of warfare or raids. These raids might not have necessarily been motivated specifically for the acquisition of slaves. Captives from such conflicts were subsequently traded for coastal goods such as cloth. Inland peoples kept slaves for their own use. Sometimes a slave changed masters several times before reaching the coast.[16] According to Alpers, groups of slaves would pass in this manner from the interior to the coast or to one of the inland caravan centres of one of the Yao chiefs like Mponda, Makanjila and Mataka. There, they would be assembled and, in larger numbers, taken down to the coast.

The trading activities of the Yao, the Bisa and others who exploited the Lake Nyasa region were parallelled further north by those of the Nyamwezi, the Kamba and the Miji Kenda. Foreign goods had found their way inland into Tanzania as early as the eighteenth century through regional exchange. This development stimulated elephant-hunting for ivory to be exchanged for these foreign goods. The Sumbwa and Nyamwezi thus came to make their own contacts with the coast around 1800, travelling through Ugogo.[17] This contact led to a commercial network between Unyamwezi and the coast and the blazing of new caravan routes to link the coast and hinterland.

The first non-African caravan to reach Unyamwezi did so in 1824. In 1831, Lief bin Saʿīd, who was half-Arab, half-Nyamwezi, marched inland to Lake Tanganyika and sent his own caravan inland in 1837. In 1841 an Arab caravan crossed Lake Tanganyika to reach Kazembe. By the end of the period under discussion (1845) coastal traders had reached Buganda, where they were welcomed by the Kabaka not only for commercial, but also for military reasons, since the guns he could acquire from them would be useful in conflicts with his neighbours. Rising prices of ivory and slaves were the main incentive behind this push into the interior.[18]

Further north, increased demand for ivory and other goods at the coast

16. E. A. Alpers, 1973, pp. 240–1.

17. J. Illife, 1979, p. 41.

18. ibid., p. 42, notes that ivory prices at Surat, western India, doubled between 1804 and 1808; at Zanzibar they increased sixfold between the 1820s and 1890s.

intensified Miji Kenda regional trade with the Kamba by the beginning of the nineteenth century. The Miji Kenda had by then already established a network of trade with the Swahili, the Waata, the Vanga and the Oromo at border markets. Thus, the Digo exchanged sorghum, sesame, coconuts and other goods for cloth, fish, wire and beads with the Swahili at the Digo market of Mtawe on the mainland south of Mombasa. They had established trade with Shambaa in tobacco, which they sold to the Giriama. The 1830s and 1840s witnessed Vumba-Digo caravans moving inland from Vanga to Taveta, Chaga, Samburu and eventually as far as Lake Victoria.

The Giriama developed their own long-distance trade inland with the Kamba by the end of the eighteenth century. They had been the main suppliers of ivory to the coast even earlier. The ivory was acquired through hunting and barter with the Waata and Oromo. As demand for it rose and local sources of supply began to run dry towards the end of the eighteenth century, the Giriama were encouraged to travel inland, thus pioneering the first caravan journeys to the Kamba of Kitui. The Giriama used the Rabai as intermediaries between them and the Swahili. They virtually monopolized the caravan trade with the Kamba until the 1830s, when Kamba caravans began to eliminate their intermediary role.

Socio-economic effects of expanding trade

The expansion of the Kamba beyond the fertile highlands of Mbooni to the less fertile lowland areas such as Kitui by the early nineteenth century had necessitated socio-economic adjustment and adaptability. Hunting, pastoralism and the barter trade were resorted to in the less fertile areas to maintain subsistence. The system known as *kuthuua* ('search for food') developed. It inevitably led to a barter trade with neighbours like the Kikuyu, Embu and Maasai. With the arrival of the Giriama, this regional Kamba trade network extended to the coast. By the 1820s the Kamba were fitting out their own caravans to travel to the coast, involving more and more people as the potential of the trade became more evident. Kamba caravans dominated the long-distance trade in the northern sector of the East African hinterland during the 1830s, 1840s and 1850s until – as had happened earlier in the southern (Tanganyikan) hinterland – they were supplanted by the Arab and Swahili caravans, which were bigger and better armed, and which moved decisively inland from the late 1850s onward. These coast-hinterland trade relations were to have some significant results. For example the Miji Kenda system of living in enclosed or fortified settlements – *kaya* – was undermined. After 1830, the incentive to pursue commercial activities and opportunities forced many Digo, Giriama, Rabai and Duruma to abandon living in their *kaya*s and establish themselves in the surrounding areas.

This dispersal in search of trading opportunities and better pastures undermined not only the corporate life of the *kaya* but also the authority of the elders. Instead, life became centred on a smaller segment of society, the sub-clan or the lineage. The age-set also died out since dispersal made meetings in the *kaya* for initiation ceremonies increasingly problematic. There arose among the Miji Kenda and the Kamba wealthy individuals who used wealth acquired from trade to build for themselves a following and influence.

An example of such individuals was the Giriama named Ngonyo, who parallelled his father's trade relations with the Swahili, Oromo, Waata and Kamba and built for himself a substantial village bringing together these disparate elements who constituted his following. He thus paved the way for his recognition later as headman by the British. Another example is the Digo leader, Mwakikonge, who established a monopoly of trade with the Vumba and utilized the wealth gained therefrom to develop personal alliances, his own following and even his own court at Dzombo, adopting the title of *kubo*.

The Kamba had their own 'big men' (*andu anene*) who acquired power and influence through wealth accrued from trade. The most notable example was Kivui Mwenda, who gained prominence as a result of the long-distance trade between the coast and Ukambani in the 1820s and 1830s.[19] The sizes of caravans grew bigger as this trade developed. Kivui's caravans had some three hundred men. His network of allies covered Kitui Kamba, Embu and Miji Kenda, extending down to Mombasa, whose governor was a trading partner.

A similar pattern of hinterland–coastal commercial relations may be discerned as having already been well-established by the early decades of the nineteenth century beyond the Swahili–Miji Kenda coast in the north. Lamu had replaced Pate as the most important commercial port in the Lamu archipelago by the early years of the nineteenth century. By this time, a veritable system of plantation agriculture had been established by Lamu's inhabitants on the opposite mainland – the Konde system.[20] At the same time, traders from the archipelago ventured inland from such points as Kau and Kipini, on the Ozi river, up the Tana river to trade with the Pokomo and Oromo in livestock, ivory and agricultural produce.

A significant commercial network linked the Benadir towns on the Somali coast – Brava, Merka and Mogadishu – with the interior. In the course of the nineteenth century, the Benadir ports were joined to points in southern Ethiopia and present-day northern Kenya as far as Lake Rudolph (present-day Lake Turkana). Key points on this extensive network of caravan routes were Luk (Lugh) and Bardera on the Juba river. Somali and Boran traders brought ivory, livestock and occasionally slaves to these towns, from where they were conveyed to market towns near the coast, such as Afgoy, in the neighbourhood of Mogadishu and Audegle, near

19. For details, consult R. Cummings, 1975; on the Miji Kenda, consult T. Spear, 1974.
20. Consult M. Ylvisaker, 1975 and 1983.

Merka. Eventually these goods reached these Benadir ports. Other Somali groups, such as the Bimal, Geledi and Tunni supplied the port towns with agricultural goods grown in the fertile Webi Shebelle valley, and also acted as agents for Somali traders in the hinterland.

These commercial relations, based upon the caravan trade linking each different segment of the East African coast with its hinterland, were to have a gradual socio-cultural impact, already noticeable by the end of the period under review (1845), but which was to develop more significantly during the second half of the century. The rise of individualism and the emergence of a few individuals who amassed wealth (however transient), influence, and prestige outside the traditional social framework has already been touched upon. Far more prevalent was the custom of acquiring foreign wives. This phenomenon became noticeable for example, among the Digo and the Rabai during the nineteenth century as an extension of their commercial relations. In this way, blood-brotherhoods were established between Miji Kenda, Oromo, Kamba and Swahili. There was also a noticeable adoption of new ritual practices resulting from interaction between these groups in eastern Kenya; 'New methods of healing and divining, of controlling rainfall, and of spirit possession spread throughout Kenya as individual cultural practices became amalgamated into regional patterns'[21] in the course of the nineteenth century.

The dynamics of socio-economic changes brought about cultural changes in the coastal towns and among some groups in the interior. With the growth of the caravan trade, the populations of these towns became bigger and more ethnically variegated. There was an influx of new Arab, upcountry African and, more noticeably, slave elements in these towns. The growing use of plantation and domestic slaves and the concomitant widespread practice of concubinage led to greater Afro–Arab and Afro–Swahili ethnic and cultural interaction and integration even within the ruling Omani aristocracy, indeed even within the Sultan's palace. Most of Saʿīd's wives were African, and his children spoke Kiswahili rather than Arabic. All Saʿīd's successors as sultans during the nineteenth century were born of slave women. The attempt to preserve an Arab identity in these circumstances became harder, as many foreign visitors were to observe.

As time passed, there were noticeable cultural differences between the 'raw' Omani or Yemeni Arab and his settled Swahilized or Africanized counterpart in the Swahili towns. The former became distinguished as a *Mmanga* or *M-Shihiri* respectively. The coming of Busaʿidi overlordship, and the new human influx from upcountry and the Yemen, helped to break down pre-existing patterns of urban stratification and stimulated the evolution of new ones, e.g. in Lamu.[22] By the 1850s, of Zanzibar's 150 000

21. T. Spear, 1981, p. 131.
22. See A. El-Zein, 1979 and A. H. Prins, 1971.

inhabitants, some 60 000 were slaves.[23] The Mazrui, displaced from Mombasa in 1837, established themselves in Gasi to the south of their former city-state, and at Takaungu to the north, where they interacted closely with the Digo and the Giriama respectively. Many of them were initiated as Giriama elders. Ngonyo became a blood-brother with many of them. Slaves were imported from Zanzibar and the Mrima. The Mazrui developed Gasi and Takaungu as new politico-economic bases, using Digo and Giriama allies to further this aim.

These changes along the coast were parallelled by those taking place in the hinterland, where many groups experienced 'enlargement of scale' in differing degrees arising from their contact with, and participation in, the long-distance trade. Coastal material culture came to be copied or adopted. Thus, the Swahili long shirt, *kanzu*, became more commonly seen and worn as far inland as Buganda. The Yao chief, Mataka, mentioned above, boasted of his attempts to transform his area into a replica of a coastal settlement. He rebuilt his capital in coastal style, beautifying it with mango trees.[24] Other African rulers were later to do the same, such as Kimweri's son, Semboja, the chief of Mazinde, who dressed in Arab style and admired Swahili cooking; and the Haya ruler, the Rumanyika of Karagwe, whose palace was furnished with luxury goods acquired from the coast via the caravan trade, including stuffed birds, mirrors and clocks.

The first half of the nineteenth century witnessed the implanting of the first seeds of Islam in the hinterland. Islam began to win converts not only among chiefly families, but also for the first time it began to penetrate into the rural areas. Nearest the coast, the Digo and Segeju were the most receptive to the faith. Among the other Miji Kenda, it was not to have any noticeable impact until the last quarter of the century. It won acceptance among the Baganda soon after the arrival of the Arab trader-cum-missionary, Aḥmed bin Ibrāhīm in 1844.[25] By the time Christian missionaries arrived in Buganda in the 1870s, Kabaka Mutesa was already observing Islamic rituals such as fasting, and many mosques had been built. By that time, too, the influence of Islam was observed on a more modest scale in Bonde, in Uzigua and on the Makonde plateau.

Where it had been accepted, Islam tended to be in a syncretic form. At the same time, there were societies that incorporated Islamic elements into their own traditional religion or introduced coastal practices, personages and spirits into their religious rituals. Thus, some Kamba spirits had Swahili names; the Zanzibar Sultan, Barghash, had his name mentioned in Sukuma rituals.[26]

Kiswahili as a language spread more extensively than Islam in the

23. J. Iliffe, 1979, p. 42.
24. ibid., p. 78.
25. See A. Oded, 1974 and A. B. Kasozi, 1974.
26. J. Iliffe, 1979, p. 79.

hinterland, especially that of Tanganyika. By the 1850s, Burton found it spoken widely by Sagara and Gogo and noted that almost every inland ethnic group had someone who could speak it.[27]

Apart from this coastal cultural impact on the hinterland, however limited it was during the first half of the nineteenth century, there was also cultural mingling among hinterland groups. However, there was also considerable resistance to coastal traders and their culture among some of the hinterland groups, especially those remote from the caravan routes. Indeed, important developments took place in the hinterland, independent of the caravan trade or which were at best only remotely affected by it. There were many interior societies that did not consider commercial interaction with the coast necessary for their economic life.

Thus, during the first half of the nineteenth century, the Kikuyu were still expanding their area of settlement in the fertile, forested region of the central highlands of present-day Kenya. Abundance of food led to an increasing population and a barter trade in the surplus produce with their neighbours such as the Kamba. To some extent this also happened with the Maasai, who helped to confine the Kikuyu to the forested areas which the latter gradually cleared as their expanding population needed more room and food. The Kikuyu, like the Kamba, had no centralized political system. Families on one ridge were generally independent of those living on another ridge under their own leader, although relations did exist between some groups, and some leaders did attempt, by force, to extend their authority to encompass other groups. Kikuyu commercial activities were more localized and never reached the coast. Even when the Swahili-Arab caravans found their way into the interior in the second half of the nineteenth century, the Kikuyu showed a distinct lack of interest in establishing any significant trade ties with them.

By 1800, the Maasai's legendary power had significantly declined. This section of the Plains Nilotes group had reached the limits of their expansion. They had also become divided into pastoralists, who occupied the Rift Valley plains between central Tanganyika and central Kenya, and the smaller agriculturist group – the Iloikop or Wa-Kwavi – who settled in the area between Mt Kilimanjaro and the Highlands of present-day Kenya. The history of the Maasai during the period under study is dominated by the struggle between these two groups at one level and by further civil strife between the various *laibons* vying for leadership at another level.

This civil conflict drove groups of Maasai in different directions in the hinterland, a notable factor which inhibited an earlier penetration of this section of the interior by Arab and Swahili traders. Groups of Wa-Kwavi raided as far east as the environs of Mombasa. In 1837, a skirmish took place between Wa-Kwavi and an Arab-Swahili party that met them outside the town. The latter was badly mauled in the encounter. Contemporary

27. ibid.

sources, such as the missionary J. L. Krapf, refer to the recurrent threat posed by the Wa-Kwavi to the Miji Kenda, which justified the defensive aspects of the *kaya* system.

West of the Rift Valley, movement and settlement of peoples took place in the Great Lakes region. These evolved into the Bantu-speaking groups such as the Abaluyia, the Baganda, the Basoga etc., and the Nilotic groups, such as the Luo, the Acholi and others. The first half of the nineteenth century witnessed a continuation of movement, settlement and interaction in that region, as well as a crystallization of diverse political systems within different groups that lent them some relatively distinct identity. For example, in the case of Buganda, a centralized state developed, headed by the ruler (the *kabaka*), with his insignias of office – drums, stools and spears, and his body of counsellors, the *lukiko*. By the nineteenth century, Buganda, which had hitherto been dominated by Bunyoro, became more powerful and expansionist.

By contrast, the Bantu-speaking groups on the eastern shores of Lake Victoria evolved no centralized state (except for the Wanga kingdom). Instead, each clan established its own political and social unit. Clan elders appointed a wise one amongst themselves to administer its affairs under the title of *omwami*, *omukali*, *omukasa*, etc.[28] The Wanga kingdom, which already had a ritual king, the *nabongo*, by the nineteenth century, had started life as a modest chieftainship. The growth of the state is attributed to adroit leadership, which gave the Wanga a significant advantage over their neighbours and, with the passage of time, a significant degree of domination over many of them. The kingdom was to establish relations with the coastal traders when they moved inland from the coastal area during the second half of the nineteenth century. *Nabongo* Mumia hoped to use them to bolster up his declining kingdom in return for giving them a commercial base.

The first half of the nineteenth century also witnessed an important historical development that was to have far-reaching political consequences: the Nguni invasion of the Tanganyikan hinterland. The Nguni invasion, like the long-distance trade, was to have negative as well as positive effects on interior societies. Politically, the two processes led to state formation or consolidation in some areas and to political disintegration in others. These developments concerning the Nguni took place during the second half of the nineteenth century, that is beyond the period under review.

Omani international trade

The survey has shown that there was a very wide spectrum of reactions to the long-distance trade among inland polities, just as there was a wide spectrum of consequences – social, political and economic – arising from

28. G. S. Were, 1968, p. 195.

it affecting these inland societies. The Tanganyika hinterland was generally more affected by these relations with the coast than the Kenyan one during the period under consideration.

One may now note several other important developments that took place on the coast during this period. An important and far-reaching economic policy adopted by Saʿīd bin Sultan was his encouragement of Indian enterprise and settlement. Asian commercial relations with the East African coast predate the nineteenth century, but there was no particularly noticeable Asian presence in Zanzibar or the mainland coast. Saʿīd admired Asian business acumen and expertise and decided that Asians would be useful in the commercial development and exploitation of his empire. By 1804, the custom house collection in Zanzibar had been farmed out to an Asian merchant. By 1811, an appreciable number of Asians had taken residence in Saʿīd's capital. It was the beginning of their crucial and, soon, their dominant role as customs agents, middlemen, financiers or moneylenders and wholesale traders. While the growth of Asian settlement in Zanzibar and some mainland towns won them no political leverage or influence, it did give them a dominant and unsurpassed economic position. For example, Jairam Sewji gained considerable wealth during the period (1834–53) when the customs were farmed out to him, as did Taria Topan after him. Though their own income increased as custom dues rose over the years, invariably the sultans of Zanzibar remained in debt to the chief Asian customs farmers. At another level, Asian capital and goods became crucial for Arab and Swahili caravans. Inevitably, a considerably larger share of the profits from the caravan trade went to the Asian middleman and Asian financier.

Another noteworthy step taken by Saʿīd that was to prove to be a landmark in the area's economic history was his introduction of clove-growing in Zanzibar, giving his island capital near-complete domination of the international market for the crop by 1850.[29] It was to be the beginning of the plantation economy that was to supplement the dhow trade and the caravan trade of the coastal people. The littoral's fertility, especially that of Zanzibar, had been noted early by Saʿīd. Indeed, it was one of the main reasons behind the transfer of his capital to the island. Until the advent of cloves, coconut products were the only exports from Zanzibar, while Pemba was historically an exporter of rice. The first shoots of the clove tree were brought to Zanzibar from Réunion by an Omani Arab, Saleh bin Haramil al-Abry, who is said to have either grown Zanzibar's first clove trees or given the shoots to the sultan. Saʿīd developed the clove industry, and became initially its major exporter. Using slave labour to farm some forty-five plantations, he was producing two-thirds of the 8000 frasilas (a frasila is about 35 pounds) exported from Zanzibar by 1840. Bombay, a leading consumer of cloves, imported $29 000 worth of cloves from Zanzibar in

29. No source on Zanzibari history can omit a reference to cloves. The latest is F. Cooper, 1977, which provides a good survey of clove-growing in Zanzibar and Pemba.

1837–8. 'Five years later, imports from Zanzibar totalled $97 000, dwarfing all other sources'.[30]

The last decade under consideration (1835–45) witnessed the expansion of clove-growing by Saʿīd's fellow Omani Arabs in Zanzibar and Pemba, to the neglect of crops like coconuts and rice. Some who had begun life as caravan traders switched to the clove plantation industry, so that by the 1840s the leading Omani families in Zanzibar and Pemba had become clove cultivators. The clove industry was a major incentive for the slave trade, since much labour was required during the growing and harvesting season. It also encouraged the acquisition of large areas of land. Various methods were used to acquire this land; taking over vacant land in the two islands, paying token rent to the indigenous inhabitants, purchase and, as increased profitability was sensed, expropriation. In this way, Omani Arabs acquired clove plantations in northern and western Zanzibar, while its Wahadimu inhabitants were reduced to cultivating subsistence crops and small-scale cash crops in the southern and eastern parts of the island.[31] In Pemba, on the other hand, Arab plantations were interspersed with the farms of the indigenous Wa-Pemba who also grew cloves, though on a smaller scale. Better relations developed here between the two groups, since land grievances were better contained under the Pemba arrangement.

The commercial treaties Saʿīd signed with the USA, Britain, France and the German states were important contributions to the rise and development of Zanzibar's commercial 'empire' in East Africa. Relations with the USA significantly favoured the commercial development of Zanzibar. The treaty was signed in 1833 when Saʿīd was involved in his economic development plans, so that the American presence stimulated those plans by providing an important market. The treaty provided the Americans with very favourable terms: 5 per cent duty on American goods imported into East Africa and no duties on East African goods purchased by the Americans. American shipping in East African waters increased significantly after the treaty was signed. The Americans carried away goods such as ivory, gum copal, and, as the industry grew, cloves in large quantities. They imported into Zanzibar sugar, beads, brassware, guns and gunpowder and the cotton cloth that became famous in East Africa as 'Merekani' (American). American sales rose from $100 000 in 1838 to $550 000 at the time of Saʿīd's death in 1856, with American cotton imports showing the greatest increase.[32]

The USA became the most important Western nation to trade in East African waters, commercially overshadowing the British. It was indeed this fear of being overshadowed by the Americans that spurred the British to

30. F. Cooper, 1977, p. 51.

31. ibid., p. 58, adds, 'this unequal ethnic division of land became a major source of tension in the twentieth century'.

32. C. S. Nicholls, 1971, p. 332.

sign a similar treaty with Saʿīd in 1839. Even so, British commercial interests – apart from those of British Asian subjects – and the British share in the East African trade, actually declined during this period. After initial reservations, Saʿīd signed a treaty with the French in 1844. The British had encouraged Saʿīd's apprehensions of French designs. After the establishment of a French consulate in Zanzibar in 1844, Anglo-French rivalry continued intermittently, and Saʿīd was compelled to use his utmost sagacity to maintain a neutral stance or to play one side against the other. His need for British military support in Oman, however, helped to boost British political significance. Starting with Atkins Hamerton, the British consul came to enjoy and was at times even able to impose a significant degree of influence over the Busaʿidi Sultan-Imām. The American consul, Ward, even noted after a conversation with Hamerton in 1851 that soon the British planned to take over the East African coast. This British political influence more than compensated for the declining British share in the East African trade.[33]

It was Hamerton who, after two years of negotiations, persuaded Saʿīd, in 1847, to sign what became known as the Hamerton Treaty, banning the export of slaves beyond the sultan's East African dominions. The expanding clove plantation industry and the slave export trade had led to an increase in the East African slave trade. Estimates of the traffic in human cargoes during the nineteenth century have never been reliable. Latter-day scholars have tended to consider figures given by contemporary nineteenth-century sources – European visitors, naval officers, missionaries and explorers – as exaggerated. But they differ in their own estimates. E. A. Alpers[34] challenges C. S. Nicholls's figure of 20 000 traded annually. He notes that A. M. H. Sheriff[35] errs on the conservative side when he arrives at a figure of only 2500 slaves a year during the 1830s (basing the figure on importation into Muscat, Kharaq and Basra) since he seems to underestimate the importance of domestic slaves by concentrating on slaves used in the date plantations in the Persian Gulf area. But F. Cooper gives no figures of his own. He merely notes that the slave export trade from Zanzibar to the Gulf was profitable business throughout the first half of the nineteenth century. The Hamerton agreement proved to be decidedly inadequate in curtailing local and overseas demand for slaves.

Saʿīd is credited with having set in motion a series of economic and commercial policies that not only turned Zanzibar into the most important commercial emporium on the East African coast – importing manufactured goods from India, Europe and the USA, and exporting cloves, ivory, slaves, rhinoceros horns, gum copal and other goods – but also, inevitably, with tying East Africa's economy to the chariot wheel of the Western capitalist

33. ibid., p. 187.
34. F. Cooper, 1977, p. 43; E. A. Alpers, 1973, pp. 185–93.
35. A. M. H. Sheriff, 1971.

system, which enriched the Asian, European and American merchants at the expense of the indigenous East African societies, thus leading to their underdevelopment.

Under this merchant capitalist system, the human and material resources of East African societies were exploited through the unequal exchange that became entrenched between the parasitic foreign merchants based in Zanzibar on the one hand, and the coastal and hinterland peoples on the other.

The very sizeable profits obtained were expatriated to Europe, the USA and India and hardly ever invested in the physical or technological development of East Africa. The imported goods, exchanged for East African products like ivory, were inexpensive consumable items that were useless for capital development. The importation of some of them even undermined local industries, such as the textile industries of Lamu and the Benadir ports which were hard hit by Asian and, later, American cottons.

At the same time, the slave export trade and the inter-group fighting and raids associated with it reduced manpower capital in the hinterland of Tanganyika and contributed to the region's underdevelopment[36] and to its 'progress towards an inevitable dead end'.[37]

Conclusion

During the period under consideration (1800–45), the East African coast and hinterland was composed of city-states and interior societies virtually independent of one another politically, and involved in regional and local trade, and, in the case of the coastal people in trans-oceanic trade.

With the advent of Busaʿidi rule, some nominal allegiance was paid by most of the coastal towns to Zanzibar, although in effect local chiefs wielded real power. The period witnessed the growth of the long-distance caravan trade, which was initiated by inland African groups, such as the Yao and the Nyamwezi. Increased demand for ivory, slaves and other goods, however, acted as a strong stimulant for Arab and Swahili caravans moving inland.

The long-distance trade was to have its social, economic and cultural impact on many hinterland societies, though by no means all. Islam and the Swahili language spread inland, the latter more significantly than the former. Christian missionaries were to come after 1845. At the same time, other important developments took place in the hinterland independent of the caravan trade that were to have their own major impact. Notable

36. There is a sizeable literature on this subject. Consult, for example, W. Rodney, 1972; J. Iliffe, 1979, pp. 67–77; R. Gray and D. Birmingham (eds), 1970; B. Swai, 1984; A. M. H. Sheriff, 1971; and T. Spear, 1981.

37. J. Iliffe, 1979, p. 76, quoting A. D. Roberts, 1970b.

among these was the Nguni invasion, especially in its consequences for the formation of new states and the disintegration of existing ones.

Finally, it has been noted that the creation and development of the Zanzibari commercial empire led to a very unequal exchange between the representatives of oriental and Western capitalism – the Asian, European and American merchants – and the indigenous peoples of the coast and hinterland, whereby the former benefited disproportionately from the international trade they fostered, developed and controlled. This contributed in turn to underdevelopment in East Africa.

10 The East African coast and hinterland, 1845–80

I. N. KIMAMBO

In Chapter 9 it has been shown that by the first quarter of the nineteenth century most of the societies of the East African hinterland were developing independently. They were certainly not stagnant, as some anthropological descriptions would tend to suggest. States of varying sizes had been established from the Great Lakes region to western, central and north-eastern Tanzania. Pastoral and agricultural communities had established themselves in the highlands and rift valley regions. Changes were taking place in many of these societies; people were still moving into agriculturally less attractive, hitherto unpopulated areas, while the influence of more recent movements like those of the Luo and the Maasai were still to be fully absorbed by their neighbours. Only the immediate coastal region and the islands of Zanzibar and Pemba had been drawn into the international economic system. By the early 1840s two separate invasions had begun to take place in East Africa: the first was the trade invasion which was to draw the interior into the international economic system, and the second was the Nguni invasion from Southern Africa, which was the cause of various movements and adjustments in the existing societies. Two other factors were also important in this period: the struggle between the Maasai groups and the growing European interests and pressures in East Africa. This chapter examines briefly these factors in the period between 1845 and 1884.

Omani penetration and the expansion of trade

The shifting of Omani political and commercial interests from Oman to Zanzibar and Pemba and more indirectly to the other coastal city-states has been discussed in Chapter 9. The roots for the growth of a commercial empire penetrating the interior of East Africa were also laid in the early part of the nineteenth century. By the 1840s the trade in ivory and slaves was expanding rapidly and was drawing the interior into the trading network already established on the coast.

There is a tendency to consider ivory and slaves as interconnected commodities of trade since in most cases they came from the same region and also since slaves could be employed to carry ivory. But the importance of this superficial inter-relationship has been exaggerated. Clearly, for long-distance trade, both ivory and slaves had to be exchanged for other bulky commodities, such as cloth, wire and beads which also had to be transported.

A much more important inter-relationship centres on the fact that both commodities were involved in an international commercial system that was drawing East Africa into a subordinate role, and in turn influencing the development of trade in East Africa in the period prior to the establishment of colonialism. The fact is that East Africa was already drawn into the capitalist economic system prior to the actual establishment of colonial rule.

The expansion of the slave trade into the interior depended on the establishment of a plantation economy, firstly on the French-dominated islands of Mauritius and Réunion, but more significantly in the clove plantations of Zanzibar and Pemba. By the time Sayyid Saʿīd had transferred his economic interest to East Africa, the slave traffic to Mauritius had been reduced by British intervention and the island had even been taken over by them in 1810. But Seyyid Saʿīd encouraged the expansion of clove and coconut plantations in Zanzibar and Pemba. By the time he transferred his capital to Zanzibar in the 1840s, clove plantations were already the dominant economic activity and were mostly operated by slave labour. This created a class of landowners, originally mainly Arabs, but by the 1860s including indigenous Shirazi and Indians as well. By the 1860s it is estimated that the islands of Zanzibar and Pemba were absorbing about 10 000 slaves per annum. This was in addition to those supplied to other markets (largely Arab) abroad. It has been estimated that by the 1860s the Zanzibar market alone was handling as many as 70 000 slaves per annum and that the heaviest traffic started after 1840.[1] Although these figures may have been greatly exaggerated, they do indicate that the slave trade has increased tremendously by the middle of the nineteenth century.

The second commercial commodity exported from East Africa was ivory. In Chapter 9 we saw how its market was beginning to expand in the first decades of the nineteenth century due to increased demand in the industrialized West, apart from the traditional market in India. Previously Europe and the USA had obtained their ivory from West Africa. The demand for East African ivory, however, increased when it was discovered that it was of better quality (softer) and therefore more suitable for making luxury goods, such as combs, billiard balls and piano keys, which the richer classes were demanding. All British efforts to control this trade directly from East Africa failed because Indian merchants were already well entrenched in conducting the trade through Bombay from where it was re-exported to Europe. Only a few American traders were able to establish themselves gradually in Zanzibar as the most important Western traders, although they remained heavily dependent on the Indian merchants.

1. E. A. Alpers, 1967, p. 11. See also E. A. Alpers, 1974, p. 236.

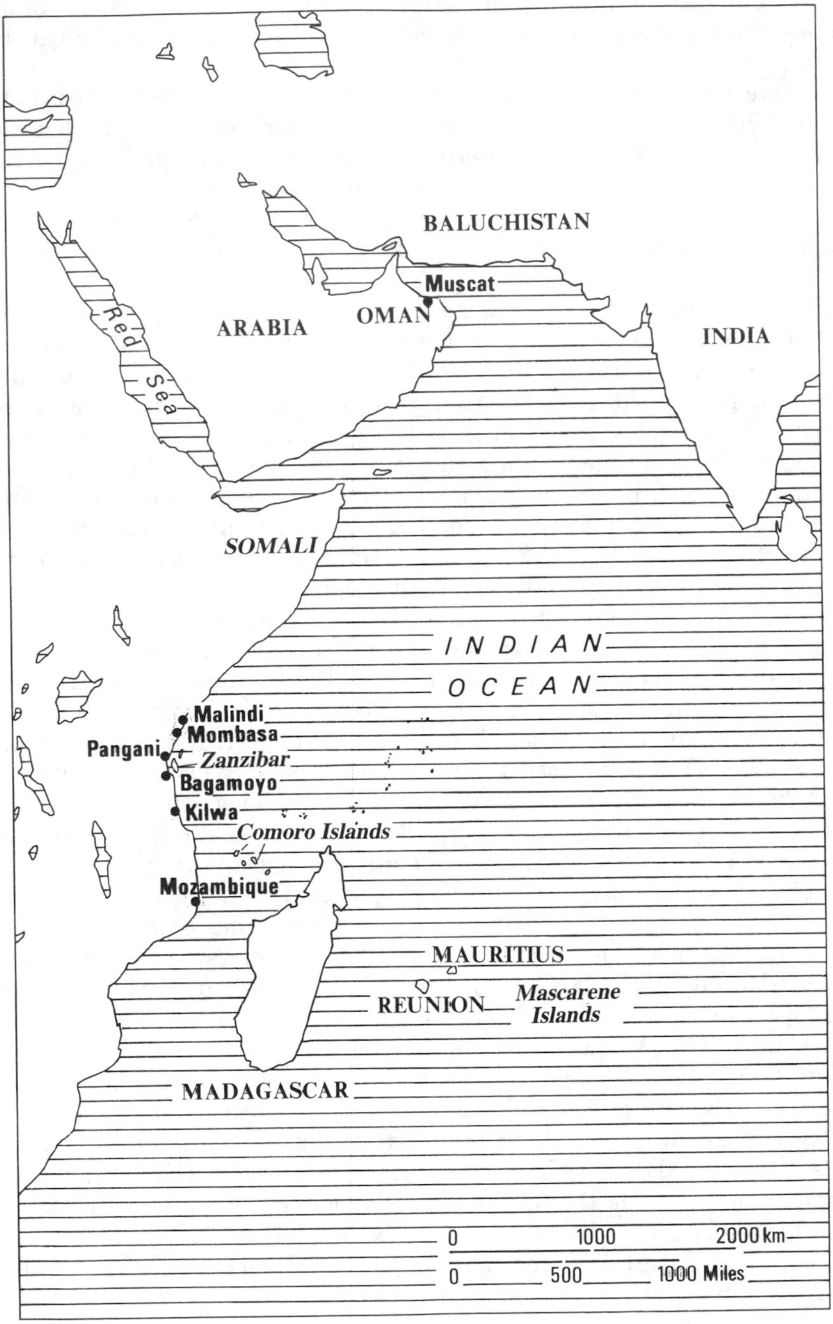

FIG. 10.1 *The Indian Ocean in the nineteenth century (from P. Curtin, S. Feierman, L. Thompson and J. Vansina,* African History, *1978, p. 394)*

Clearly, the terms of long-distance trade in both ivory and slaves were quite favourable to those involved in exploiting the commodities. Consequently, long-distance trade routes radiated from the coastal towns (such as Kilwa, Bagamoyo, Pangani, Tanga and Mombasa) to various points in the interior. As a result, by the 1870s most of present-day Tanzania, Kenya, Uganda, eastern Zaire, northern Zambia, Malawi and northern Mozambique had become part of a vast hinterland connected with Zanzibar through these coastal towns and therefore integrated to varying degrees into the international trading network.

It is tempting to consider this growth of long-distance trade as an unfortunate episode in which the Africans were helpless victims. Certainly in its degrading effects on human life, the slave trade had much disastrous personal and moral impact on East African societies. But the long-distance trade, in all its aspects, had a much greater impact in influencing the actual development of the societies involved. The Africans were by no means spectators of this process. As we shall demonstrate in the following examples, in many cases it was the Africans who seized the initiative in establishing trade relations with the coast. Yet, it is difficult to assess adequately the overall economic impact of this trade invasion on African societies. It is easier to recognize certain discernible contributions brought into the interior by this coastal penetration, such as new crops like maize and rice, and cultural impact represented by the spread of Islam and more significantly by the spread of the Swahili language. But economically how was the East African affected?

Philip Curtin, assessing the impact of a similar kind of trade involvement in the Senegambia region, concluded:

> The data are easily accurate enough to support the generalization that, in spite of the probability of strong contrary swings in wartime, the net barter terms of trade shifted consistently in favor of Senegambia over a period of nearly two centuries. Even if the accuracy of the estimates is no closer to reality than half or double, the overall shift to Senegambia's advantage from the 1680's to the 1830's would have been within the range of fivefold to twentyfold. Or, as a median estimate, the Senegambians at the end of the period received about ten times as much as they had received 150 years earlier for the same quantity of goods exported.[2]

Unfortunately no such data are available for East Africa. R. Coupland, compiling some statistics for Zanzibar and some coastal centres, was able to show, for example, that by 1876 Kilwa was making £120 000 profit yearly, and that between 1869 and 1876 customs revenue in Zanzibar had risen from £65 000 to over £100 000 per annum.[3] This would seem to indicate that a study similar to that of Senegambia could be undertaken

2. P. D. Curtin, 1975, p. 340.
3. R. Coupland, 1939, p. 227, pp. 319–20. See also J. M. Gray, 1963, p. 241.

for at least Zanzibar itself. But such a study would probably tell us very little about the numerous societies of the hinterland that were involved in commercial activities. It is known that by the 1870s the plantation economy, using slave labour, had begun to spread to the mainland coast and to the interior along the caravan routes, mainly in order to supply the food (grain) required to feed both the rich and the labouring sections of the population on the islands of Zanzibar and Pemba, and to feed the large caravan expeditions to and from the hinterland.[4] But this does not give us a complete picture. Furthermore, even if a complete picture could be obtained, a demonstration that the African producer was getting more at a particular time than he was getting previously would not change the exploitative nature of the international capitalist trading system of the time. In fact the coastal traders and their African allies were but middlemen for European traders who were getting the largest share of the profits. The African producer was being exploited by both the middlemen and the European traders. The situation becomes worse in terms of comparison when the product is a human being! In addition we can say that, by being drawn into the world economy on unfavourable terms, the East Africans diverted their energies from developing their own economies for their own purpose to supply raw materials and labour in exchange for foreign-manufactured goods (mainly luxury items) that only benefited certain groups of people in society. In some of these societies the trade had the effect of killing or retarding some of the local industries producing similar items, such as the bark-cloth in the Lake region and the hand-woven cloth industry in south-western Tanzania.

This integration of the vast area of the eastern African hinterland with the coast was not achieved merely by extending new trade routes from the coast to the interior, nor was it simply a result of Arab and Swahili penetration into the interior. To be sure, it involved transformation and assimilation of pre-existing regional trading networks. Thus, for the sake of clarity, we shall discuss the long-distance trade routes in four regions: the Kilwa hinterland routes, the central Tanzanian routes, the Pangani valley route and the Mombasa hinterland routes.

The Kilwa hinterland routes

The Kilwa hinterland routes were probably the oldest of those leading into the East African interior, having been stimulated by the late eighteenth-century demand for slaves in the French-dominated islands. The contact between the whole region of Lake Nyasa and Kilwa was relatively easy because travellers could pass through fairly fertile and inhabited land. This land was controlled by the Yao, who were responsible for transporting ivory, wax and slaves to Kilwa. The Yao continued to play an important part in this trade even during the peak period in the nineteenth century.

4. A. Smith, 1963, p. 296.

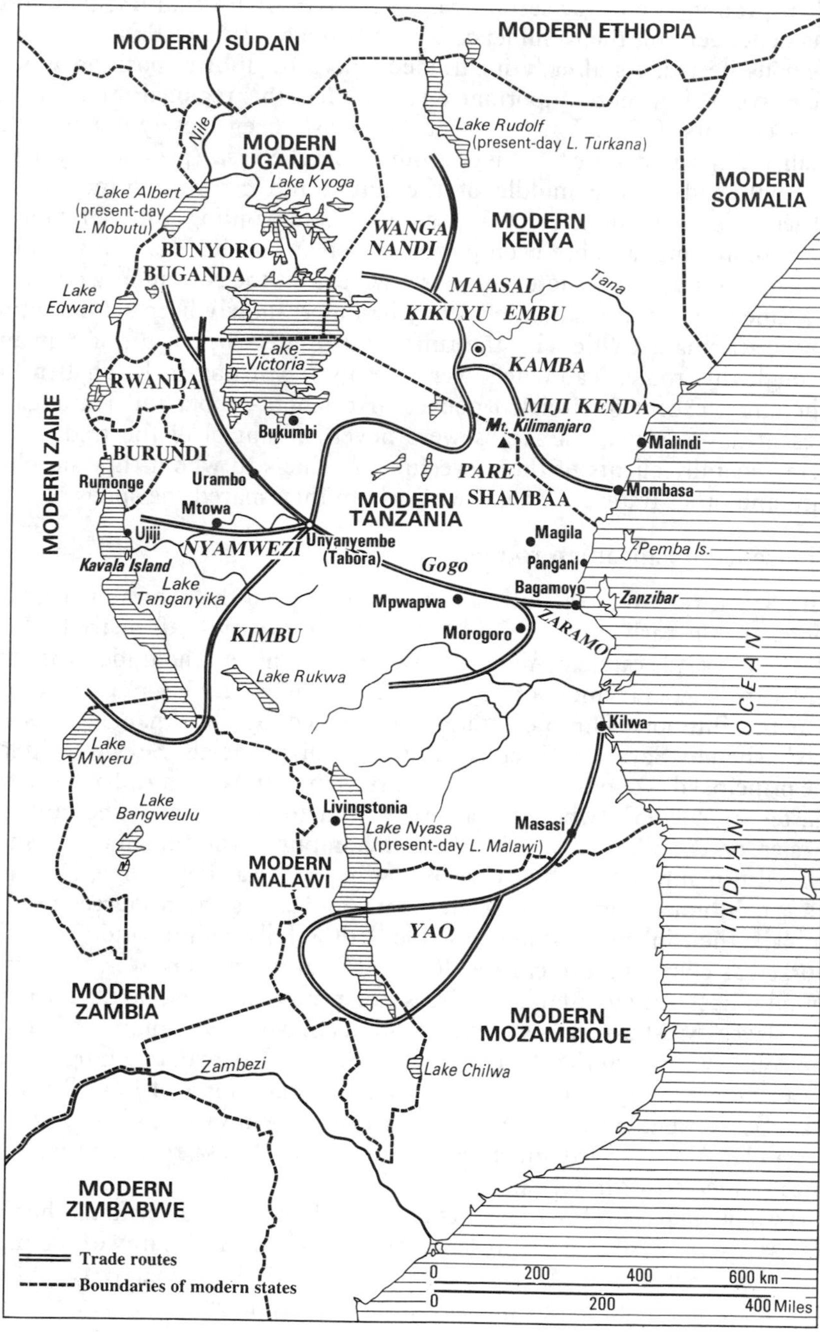

FIG. 10.2 *Trade in nineteenth-century East Africa (adapted from P. Curtin, S. Feierman, L. Thompson and J. Vansina,* African History, *1978, p. 399)*

Their prominence in the second half of the nineteenth century, therefore, was dependent on their eminence in the regional trade of this area in the previous period. As already mentioned, the geographical position was in their favour. But more important was the effect this regional trade had on the society itself. The Yao, who had previously been loosely organized in small groups under petty chiefs around Lake Nyasa (present-day Lake Malawi), had by the middle of the nineteenth century formed larger settlements under chiefs playing a more commanding role. Previously much more emphasis has been put on the effects of the Nguni invasion in causing this transformation. But, as shown below, the Nguni invasion came at a time when stratification in society had more clearly been set in motion by the trading activities. By the time Arab traders began to push inland through this route, Yao chiefs were simply too strong to be challenged. Therefore, except for isolated pockets like Khota-Khota and Karonga in present-day Malawi, the Arabs were never in control of the trade; they were generally clients of the powerful Yao chiefs to whom they supplied guns and other trade goods and with whom they shared the spoils.[5]

The central Tanzanian routes

The Nyamwezi were the most important group on the central Tanzanian routes. In the early years of the nineteenth century most of the trade along these routes was carried on by Nyamwezi caravans. As the trade expanded under the encouragement of Seyyid Saʿīd, Arab traders began to penetrate into the interior. This penetration was aided by the financing system established by Seyyid Saʿīd assisted by his Indian officials. Seyyid Saʿīd left the principal direction of economic affairs in the hands of an Indian customs master in Zanzibar who paid a yearly sum to the sultan. The customs master, on the other hand, with the collaboration of the Indian community who also manned the other coastal stations (Kilwa, Bagamoyo, Pangani, Tanga, Mombasa, etc), advanced to caravan leaders the resources needed to make their inland ventures possible. In the Kilwa hinterland the Arabs worked as clients of Yao chiefs. On the central routes, however, the Arabs found it necessary to establish centres to serve as collecting points for ivory and slaves. Most caravans started from Bagamoyo or Sadani, passed across the country through the Zaramo, Kami, Sagara, Luguru, and Gogo to the Nyamwezi country and further on to Ujiji on the shores of Lake Tanganyika. Some went even further, into Zaire and northwards to Karagwe and Buganda. A southward route went to the Lake Nyasa region to join the ones connected with Kilwa.

Two principal Arab settlements developed on the trade centres: the first was at Unyanyembe, near present-day Tabora in the Nyamwezi country and the other was at Ujiji on the shores of Lake Tanganyika. These settlements differed in one main respect: in Unyanyembe the Arabs made

5. A. Smith, 1963, p. 286.

a settlement resembling a colony among the Nyamwezi, while in Ujiji they were more or less incorporated into the Ha state.[6] Thus, in Unyanyembe the Arabs were an independent community competing for trade with Nyamwezi traders, among whom were the rulers of the numerous Nyamwezi chiefdoms. The Nyamwezi called this group of traders (Nyamwezi and Arabs alike) *bandewa*.[7] They were all struggling to get a share in the long-distance trade. This explains why there were constant conflicts between the Nyamwezi rulers and the Arabs. It also explains the struggles between various rulers of Nyamwezi states; struggles that resulted in new political and social alignments that greatly affected the Nyamwezi people.

On the other hand the Arabs of Ujiji took advantage of the Ha political organization in which Ujiji was part of a larger Ha state whose centre was also far away from Ujiji itself. The Arabs were therefore in an outlying area of the state and could easily be incorporated in a way profitable to both sides.

The Pangani valley route

Unlike the southern and central routes, the Pangani valley route was not specifically controlled by one group of people. It is true that at the beginning, between 1836 and 1862 (when Kimweri ye Nyumbai, the great ruler of the Shambaa kingdom died), the Zigula played a leading role in the development of trade in the area. In about 1836 there was a devastating famine,[8] which caused many Zigula to sell themselves as slaves in order to survive. It is reported that some of them were carried to Somalia by Brava (Barawa) traders where they retained their language to the twentieth century.[9] The majority of them, however, crossed over to Zanzibar where they were employed as slaves in the plantations. Some of them managed to return to their country; there is a story of a group that escaped and returned to the Zigula country safely:

> According to a well-concerted plan a large party of the conspirators assembled one moonlit night on one of the plantations. They made their way thence to the seashore to the north of Zanzibar roadstead. Arriving there in the early hours of the morning, they boarded a number of dhows, surprised and killed or overpowered the members of the crew, raised anchor, made sail and crossed to the mainland.[10]

6. See N. R. Bennett, 1974, pp. 213–21.
7. See A. C. Unomah, 1972.
8. R. F. Burton, 1860, Vol. 1, p. 125. Burton said in 1860 that the famine took place 'about twenty years ago'. J. L. Krapf, 1860, pp. 256–7, reported a similar famine in Mombasa in the same period.
9. S. Feierman, 1974, p. 137.
10. J. M. Gray, 1962, p. 141.

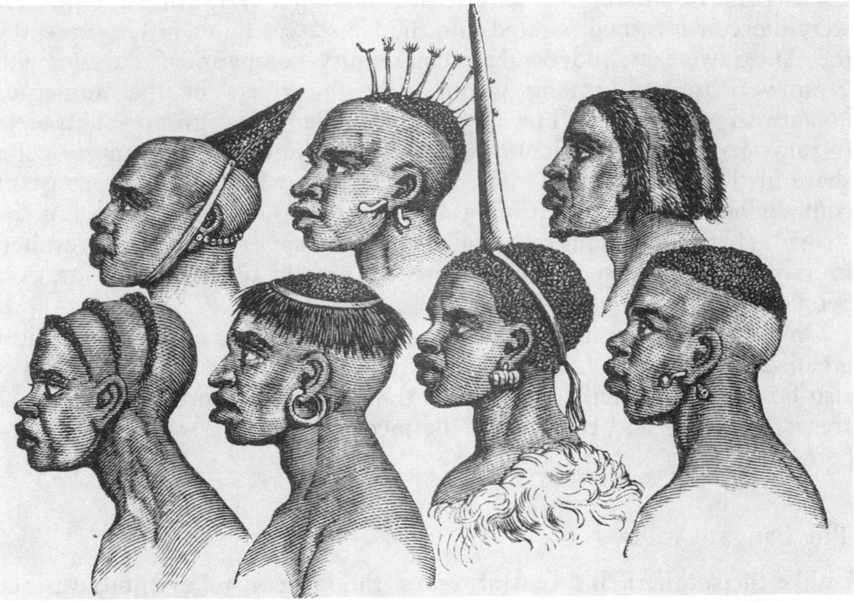

PLATE 10.1 *Nyamwezi hairstyles and head-dresses*

PLATE 10.2 *Nyamwezi traders on the road*

Those who returned had gained an education on the value of the long-distance trade in slaves and ivory. They were the ones who pioneered trade activities in the Pangani valley. Kimweri's capital in the Shambaa mountains was far away from the plains and he was therefore slow to take advantage of the new system of international trade, despite the stability of his kingdom based on political control through territorial chiefs and tribute system. By the time he died in the 1860s it was his son, Semboja, the ruler of the western district bordering the Zigula, who had taken advantage of the situation and moved his capital to the plains at Mazinde.

But neither Semboja nor the Zigula traders had fully explored the Pangani valley route to the interior. Most of the trade stations were limited to the Shambaa and Pare plains, although some individuals ventured far away from the region, e.g. Kisabengo, who established a state near present-day Morogoro.

It was the Arab and Swahili traders from the coast who ventured inland to the Chagga country in Kilimanjaro and beyond to Kenya. On the Pare mountains there were a number of small states but, like the Shambaa, they were all located on the mountains far away from the caravan route.

Most of the coastal traders who went into the Pangani valley had to establish direct contacts with individual rulers or their subordinates in order to establish trading centres. This tended to encourage rivalry among the rulers of numerous small states on the Pare mountains and Kilimanjaro and also between these rulers and their subordinates. We shall examine the socio-political outcome of this rivalry later.

The Mombasa hinterland routes

The Mombasa hinterland was controlled by the Kamba, although by the 1880s they had lost control of the main route to the Arab and Swahili traders. This main route passed through the Ukambani country itself and moved towards the Kenya highlands and beyond to the Lake Victoria shores and onwards to Uganda. The other route moved towards Mount Kilimanjaro and joined up with the Pangani valley route. This second route, like the Pangani route, seems to have been under the control of the coastal traders.

Most writers have accepted J. L. Krapf's suggestion for dating long-distance trade by the Kamba from the famine of 1836.[11] But, as shown elsewhere in this volume, the Kamba predominance in trade did not arise overnight. There is enough evidence to suggest that the Kamba had dominated a regional trading network for over a century before the conventional date.[12] However, the conventional date is relevant in that it denotes the second stage of Kamba trading activity which brought them into the international trading network of the time; the stage at which ivory and other local materials were being exchanged for imported goods. Krapf described this when he made his journeys into Ukambani country in 1848–9: 'The Swahili purvey to the Wakamba cotton fabrics (Americano), blue calico, glass beads, copper, salt, luaha, blue vitriol (zinc), etc., and receive in exchange chiefly cattle and ivory'.[13] By the 1840s, therefore, Kamba

11. See, for example, K. G. Lindblom, 1920, pp. 339–40; D. A. Low, 1963, p. 314.
12. I. N. Kimambo, 1974, p. 207; 1970, p. 18.
13. J. L. Krapf, 1860, p. 248.

weekly caravans to the coast, carrying ivory estimated to weigh from 300 to 400 frasilas were reported.[14] Krapf estimated that each Kamba caravan consisted of as many as 300 to 400 persons.[15] By the mid-nineteenth century, Kamba trading parties were visiting not only their Kikuyu neighbours, but also places far beyond the Mount Kenya region: Mau, Gusii, Lake Baringo and Samburu country.

It appears that in the latter part of the nineteenth century, Arab and Swahili traders were strongly in control of the Kamba trade route.[16] This was because, having pushed through the Maasai country using the Kilimanjaro route (at a time when Maasai power was heavily affected by wars and epidemics), the coastal traders had been able to gain control of the sources of ivory. At this time, trade in slaves (which had not been prominent under the Kamba) seems to have become more important. Kamba traditions picture this as the most disruptive period in their history: disruptive famine led to inter-lineage conflicts that were used by ambitious members of society to sell weaker ones to Arabs.[17] Kamba traditions, therefore, rightly indicate the relationship between the decline of trade in goods in which they themselves played a major part and the rise of the system of profiteering in persons in which the Arabs and Swahili traders played a prominent role.

The effects of long-distance trade on East African societies

At this stage we can look back and review the effect of this intrusion of long-distance trade into East African societies. First of all it is necessary to realize that not all East African societies were in direct contact with the trading network. Trading activities required stable centres and naturally such centres tended to be capitals or areas protected by strong rulers. That is why the constructive effect of the nineteenth-century trade was more noticeable in centralized societies. Non-centralized societies were in many cases more vulnerable because they could easily be raided by those organized on a larger scale. Pastoral societies were generally an exception during this period. This was the period when Maasai-speaking people were engaged in wars among themselves and with other pastoralists and, as we shall discuss later, they formed a buffer region against slave raiding in a large part of Kenya and northern Tanzania.

In general terms we can say that long-distance trade affected the material base on which the society was organized. Although it is generally agreed that control of ritual was the main basis for authority in African societies, it is also recognized that large-scale organizations of states occurred where

14. C. Guillain, 1856, Vol. 2, p. 211. According to Charles Rechenbach's *Swahili–English Dictionary*, one *frasila* is equivalent to about 16kg or 35lb.
15. J. L. Krapf, 1860, p. 248.
16. J. Thomson, 1885, pp. 272–5.
17. See K. A. Jackson, 1972.

the material base was sufficient to maintain a military force and a state bureaucracy. Thus the difference in the size of states in many places where centralized state organization was found in East Africa could be related to the economic strength deriving from the environment. Large states in the Great Lakes region could be maintained by the surplus food raised from the stable agricultural environment supporting bananas as well as grain and livestock. As one moves south of Lake Victoria, rainfall decreases and the economy could only support states of smaller scale. The scale tended to increase in the highland regions, such as the Usambara and Pare mountains and to some extent in Kilimanjaro. In some of the large kingdoms of the interlacustrine region, rulers became stronger by increasing their material base for maintaining their kingdoms through the long-distance trade.[18] Besides traditional weapons, guns were added in their military organization, and imported goods such as cloth and beads could be used to pay for services in addition to foodstuff collected as tribute. But the attraction of the imported goods also increased dangers of instability since it could encourage independent actions by subordinate rulers and thus weaken the kingdom. That is why many kings attempted to keep this long-distance trade strictly under their personal control.

It was in the small-scale state systems that the effect of the imported goods was clearly seen. These covered a large part of Tanzania and, on a smaller scale, western Kenya. Traditional rulers who were able to control the trade were also able to accumulate the imported goods with which to build up a large army and to expand administrative machinery. Weaker states were either raided for slaves or annexed to form larger entities. In these areas the effect was either constructive in that it enabled certain rulers to build up bigger kingdoms in areas previously supporting smaller states, or destructive in the sense that it encouraged rebellion, which in turn destroyed the unity of the states that existed. Despite this generalization, the effect of the long-distance trade was generally destructive. There is no need to detail here the evils of the trade in human beings. But even the value of the material base built on imported goods was deceptive. Most of these goods were luxury items: beads, bracelets and other ornaments. What was useful was cloth, but even this competed with local sources of production which were eventually destroyed. Worse still, the trade in luxury goods and the general violence caused by the need to raid other societies in order to maintain the trade, meant neglect of subsistence agriculture. It is unlikely that the new structure could have been maintained even if colonialism had not intervened. In fact few of the large states built up during this period survived intact to the 1890s.

In order to illustrate this general picture it will be necessary to look briefly at the three caravan-route regions. In discussing the Kamba, we noticed how even their control of trade declined when raiding for slaves

18. Rwanda and Burundi are the exceptions, see note 31.

became prominent. The Kamba were a non-centralized society. The long-distance trade probably encouraged an enlargement of scale of various traditional institutions, beginning with kinship, village age-group and defence organizations. But none of these became the basis for a centralized state structure. In the whole of Kenya, only in the western region did the coastal trade lead directly to an enlarged and centralized political system. This was in the kingdom of Wanga among the Luyia people.

Before one of its greatest rulers, named Shiundu, came to power in the middle of the nineteenth century, the kingdom of Wanga had remained small and was constantly harassed by its pastoralist neighbours. But Shiundu is said to have effectively overcome the instability and by the time he was succeeded by his son Mumia in 1882, the kingdom had expanded beyond its borders. Although G. S. Were has explained that the idea of a large Wanga empire was created during the colonial period as a British strategy for imposing colonial rule on the area by using the kingdom of Wanga as an agent, he nevertheless agrees that Wanga's 'real influence and authority' had expanded to at least two neighbouring areas, Kisa and Buholo.[19] The rulers of Wanga gained power in this period because of two factors: the use of Maasai mercenaries and the presence of Swahili traders at the capital. The first factor arose out of the Maasai wars to be discussed later, while the second was the result of successful penetration by coastal traders, possibly earlier through Buganda and Busoga and later through the Kilimanjaro and Kamba routes.

Both Shiundu and Mumia welcomed coastal traders to their capital. This gave them access to guns with which to arm their military forces. From the Wanga capital raids on neighbouring peoples could be organized. In 1883, Joseph Thomson described a raid that had taken place five years earlier:

> The traders had lost a few men through murder or otherwise. In revenge for this the traders, five years prior to our arrival, had resolved to 'tengeneze' the native (make them behave). For this purpose a combined caravan of some 1,500 men stationed at Kwa-Sundu [later Mumia] was marched upon them. Dividing into sections, they entered the district at different points, and crossed it, devastating every village on the way, killing thousands of men and women, committing the most horrible atrocities, such as ripping up women with child, making great bonfires and throwing children into them, while the small boys and girls were captured as slaves.[20]

Most of the other people of the north-central interior of East Africa were less affected by this international trade. They had less direct or even indirect dealings with the foreigners from the coast; in fact in many cases they were unwilling to welcome these foreigners into their societies,

19. G. S. Were, 1967, p. 125.
20. J. Thomson, 1885, p. 306.

although they were willing to sell foodstuffs to caravans on the stopping stations. One major explanation for this is that the region as a whole had experienced an extended period of violence caused by Maasai wars and the leaders had therefore learned to protect their societies by being more sensitive to outsiders.

The effects of long-distance trade in the Pangani valley were basically destructive. Prior to the trade invasion, a number of states had developed in the region, two of which had become fairly large kingdoms. These were the Shambaa kingdom, which by the mid-nineteenth century was under Kimweri, and the lesser-known Gweno kingdom on the North Pare mountains. The other smaller states were scattered on the South Pare mountains and on the slopes of Mount Kilimanjaro. All these states were located on the mountains, while the caravan routes passed through the plains along the Pangani river valley. Consequently the rulers of these states were less able to control the coastal traders and therefore less able to monopolize the imported goods. Subordinate rulers nearer the caravan route were in a better position to attract Arab and Swahili traders to their districts before they reached the state capitals. The effect of this was clear: rulers who had the support of the traders could build up well-armed groups and disobey the capital. This encouraged a lot of fighting within and among these states. Most of them broke up into smaller states.

The Shambaa kingdom, which had covered the whole region from the Usambara mountains to the coast, was already in trouble before Kimweri's death in the 1860s. One of his sons, Semboja, who was the ruler of the western district, had moved his capital to Mazinde on the plains where he could be in direct contact with traders going into the interior. In this way he was able to build up military capacity and influence greater than those of other district rulers. When Kimweri died, it was Semboja who was to decide who should occupy the throne, which he himself did not want to occupy, having realized that power had moved away from the traditional centre. From the 1870s to the period of colonial invasion in the 1890s, Usambara was full of violence caused by the weakness in the centre. Most of the outlying areas of the kingdom became independent.

The same kind of thing happened to the Pare states. The Gweno kingdom was, by the 1880s, reduced to a number of states and the smaller states of South Pare were segmented further. In Kilimanjaro, however, the continuous inter-state wars tended to produce a temporary union of states which at times seemed as if it would bring all the Chagga together under one ruler. But these were short-lived successes. In the 1880s two strong chiefdoms had become of regional importance, Kibosho under Sina, and Moshi under Rindi or Mandara. Both states were accessible to the coastal traders. Their rulers tried their best to attract these foreigners to their capitals and used their presence and the goods they brought (especially guns) to increase their powers. Periodically each of these states was able to control a number of other Chagga states, but such larger entities were not able to survive long.

The only people in the Pangani valley who seem to have been strengthened by the coastal trade were the Zigula who were discussed earlier. The Zigula had never been brought under the Shambaa kingdom. But because of their control of trade with the coast, many Zigula built up political hegemonies that had not existed before. By the middle of the nineteenth century, the Zigula had come to dominate the whole region between Pangani and Bagamoyo. Several Zigula achieved considerable power and were able to build up new states. Some of these did not last long, but the one founded by Kisabengo near the present-day Morogoro survived to the period of German invasion. Kisabengo is described by Burton as a Zigula who made himself leader of a group of runaway slaves on the coast.[21] By doing so he angered the Sultan of Zanzibar and so he moved further inland in order to protect himself. In Morogoro he was received by one of the ritual leaders of the Luguru. He built his fortified capital near the caravan route and imposed heavy tolls on caravans going to Tabora. Kisabengo's town was described by H. M. Stanley in 1871 as having several thousand inhabitants protected by high stone walls and watchtowers and finely carved wooden gates.[22]

In western Tanzania there was rivalry both among the African chiefs of the numerous small states and among the Arabs settled there, and also between alliances of African chiefs and certain Arab traders. However, the only example of an up-country station where the Arabs were dominant was in the Manyema country across Lake Tanganyika. In western Tanzania they were too weak to replace the African chiefs. It was only in the late 1880s that certain Arabs threatened by European colonization, began to consider establishing their own territorial authority.[23]

African rulers sought to gain a share of the profits of the long-distance trade by supplying ivory and slaves to the traders or (for those who could control territory on the caravan route) by imposing heavy tolls on the trading caravans. For this purpose, they had to build up their power by collecting around them groups of followers armed with guns and ammunition accumulated from the trade. The rivalry for control of trade increased the social disruption and this was further intensified by population movements caused by the contemporaneous Nguni (also referred to as Ngoni in some of the literature) invasion. The consequent instability increased the number of people who were ready to follow enterprising leaders. In western Tanzania such warriors of fortune were known as *ruga-ruga* and were mainly drawn from war-captives, runaway slaves, deserting porters, social outcasts and young men who would have normally performed military

21. R. F. Burton, 1860, p. 85 and p. 88.
22. H. M. Stanley, 1872, pp. 115–16.
23. A. D. Roberts, 1969, p. 73; N. R. Bennett, 1974, p. 218.

service. Such armies were, nevertheless, held together by 'a certain *esprit de corps* and by an iron discipline that was closely modelled on the Nguni warbands'.[24]

Supported by such armies, a number of traditional leaders in western Tanzania carved out new dominions for themselves. Some of them even went outside their own localities to establish empires. In the 1850s, for example, Ngalengwa (later called Msiri), son of a Musumbwa headman, followed the copper traders' route to Katanga where he built up a considerable empire.[25] In Unyanyembe itself, there were rivalries among members of the ruling family, intensified by Arab support for one contender for the throne against another. In the 1860s the Arabs managed to have Mnwa Sele deposed and replaced by Mkasiwa, and Mnwa Sele's brother Simba left Unyanyembe to set up his kingdom among the Konongo to the south-west of Tabora. Another member of the chiefly family in Unyanyembe called Nyungu ya Mawe left his country in 1874 to establish a well-organized kingdom among the Wakimbu to the south-west of the Wanyamwezi. Besides such rulers who went away from their traditional states to subdue a number of small states to form larger ones, there were also examples of states that expanded because of the increased power of their rulers. Mirambo's state is the most striking example, but there were many others. Mtinginya of Usongo in north-eastern Unyamwezi was a hereditary ruler who took advantage of the trade route to Karagwe and Buganda to strengthen and expand his state. Even Isike, the successor of Mkasiwa in Unyanyembe, became powerful enough to offer the Arabs and later the Germans a great deal of resistance.

To illustrate how far changed conditions and opportunities brought about real changes in Nyamwezi patterns of government, we should examine briefly two of the largest states built up during the time: those of Mirambo and Nyungu ya Mawe. The two 'empires' had striking differences in their patterns of organization although they were both born out of the same conditions we have just described. Mirambo was a ruler of the small state of Uyowa to the west of Tabora. It is believed that he was probably captured in his youth by the Nguni when they invaded western Tanzania and that while he was with them he came to understand fully the possibilities of Nguni military organization. In the 1860s, using a small group of warriors, he gained control of a number of states surrounding Uyowa. Between 1870 and his death in 1884 he led many campaigns that greatly expanded the area under his control. As Jan Vansina has pointed out, his state extended 'to Buha and Burundi, to the Vinza and Tongwe in the west, to the Pimbwe and Konongo in the south, to the Nyaturu, Iramba

24. A. D. Roberts, 1969, p. 74.

25. For information on the Msiri empire, see J. Vansina, 1966, pp. 227–35. For earlier sources, see F. J. Arnot, 1889, and A. Verbeken, 1956.

and Sukuma in the east, and to the Sukuma and Sumbwa in the north'.[26] He gained control of the trade route between Tabora and Ujiji and in 1876 obliged the Arabs of Tabora to pay tribute to him when using the route. Mirambo is known to have sent embassies to Mutesa of Buganda in 1876 and 1881 in his attempt to control the Buganda route. He also made direct contacts with the coast in order to obtain guns directly when the Arabs tried to prevent him from getting them. He was quick in recognizing potential sources of new power: he welcomed missionaries to his capital and sought contacts with the British Consul in Zanzibar.

Mirambo's method of control in his 'empire' was based on the imposition of military power on the traditional system. Conquered rulers were required to acknowledge his over-rule by occasionally sending him tributes of ivory and young men for his army. Where there was resistance from a traditional ruler, Mirambo removed him and replaced him with a more submissive member of the same ruling family. Where a conquered province was near a powerful kingdom, Mirambo kept armed men of his own there. But his main method of control was that of keeping his army constantly on the move to intimidate both his neighbours and his subjects.

Nyungu ya Mawe's 'empire' was better integrated than that of Mirambo. Nyungu ya Mawe, like Mirambo, used the *ruga-ruga* to establish himself among the Kimbu. Between 1870 and 1880 he campaigned from his base in Kiwele and gained control of the trade route to the coast east of Tabora and the southbound route from Tabora to Ufipa and Lake Tanganyika. Among the conquered states Nyungu posted his own officials called *vatwale*, who were directly responsible to him. In his 'empire' the real rulers were no longer the traditional chiefs but the appointed *vatwale*. It was the duty of these officials to collect and forward to Nyungu all the ivory obtained in the kingdom. The area under each appointed official consisted of a number of traditional states. Therefore the Kimbu traditional states, numbering about thirty, were ruled by about six or seven *vatwale*.[27]

Mirambo and Nyungu ya Mawe were contemporaries. Both built up polities based on the changed material conditions of the late nineteenth century. Both Nyungu and Mirambo died in 1884. Because Nyungu made innovations in the administrative structure of his 'empire', when he died it survived until it was dismantled by the colonialists. On the other hand, Mirambo's 'empire' broke up into its constituent states simply because there was no successor who could maintain the strong army required to keep it together.

In examining the consequences of the expansion of long-distance trade to the interior we have avoided discussing two major regions. The first is the Great Lakes region which is the subject of Chapter 11. Perhaps it would suffice here to note that by the middle of the nineteenth century,

26. J. Vansina, 1966, p. 75.
27. A. Shorter, 1969, p. 19.

PLATE 10.3 *Mirambo in 1882 or 1883*

there were many kingdoms of varying sizes in the area. Some of them were large and powerful while others were small and weak. But all of them had participated in a regional trade network whose routes connected most of the major capitals. It was into this regional trade network that the international trade from the East African coast was to be absorbed. In the second half of the nineteenth century, the most powerful of these kingdoms were probably Buganda, Bunyoro and Burundi. But there were many others less powerful, including Busoga, Toro, the Ankole states (Nkore, Buhweju and Bunyaruguru),[28] Karagwe, the Buhaya states and Buzinza.

Traders from the coast had reached Buganda as early as 1844.[29] In the 1850s Burton noted that some coastal traders had been there for about ten years, and ten years later Stanley reported some coastal traders who had been in the region for as long as twenty years without going back to the coast.[30] It would appear, therefore, that Buganda was the earliest centre of trade in the region. But soon the coastal traders were able to visit the other capitals. The exception here would be Rwanda and Burundi, where the rulers were able to keep coastal traders out of their region and develop successful tactics for coping with the guns used by their adversaries.[31] On the other hand, the rulers of Bunyoro were also struggling to attract traders to their capital. In the 1870s the king of Bunyoro, Kabarega, was trying to compete with Buganda in making direct contacts with Zanzibar, while at the same time trying to attract the 'Khartoumers' (traders coming down the Nile) who were raiding widely among the non-centralized societies bordering the kingdom on the northern side.[32] It was Buganda under Mutesa (1856–84) which seems to have gained most from the coastal trade. A centralized government with a disciplined bureaucracy had been established earlier. But the traffic in guns which Mutesa kept under his personal control further strengthened the centralized system. Buganda seems to have concentrated its attention more on the international trade than the regional network. Mutesa's raids on Busoga to the east, and his attacks on his western neighbours (Bunyoro, Toro, Nkore, Buhaya and Buzinza) ensured Buganda's predominance in the trade. At times, Mutesa even sought to control both Karagwe and Buzinza to ensure that coastal caravans could get to his capital without problems.

Clearly, in the Great Lakes region some of the larger kingdoms were greatly strengthened by their connections with the coastal traders. The acquisition of firearms, especially, increased their capability to raid others.

28. Ankole is a colonial creation. Previously the unit contained a number of states.

29. J. M. Gray, 1947, pp. 80–2.

30. R. F. Burton, 1860, Vol. 1, p. 173; H. M. Stanley, 1878, Vol. 1, p. 455.

31. The best source on Burundi during the second half of the nineteenth century is at the moment probably R. Botte, 1982, pp. 271–317. There is also a general description of Burundi in E. Mworoha, 1977, pp. 133–209. On Rwanda, A. Kagame, 1963, is an improvement on his earlier work, 1961.

32. D. A. Low, 1963, p. 337.

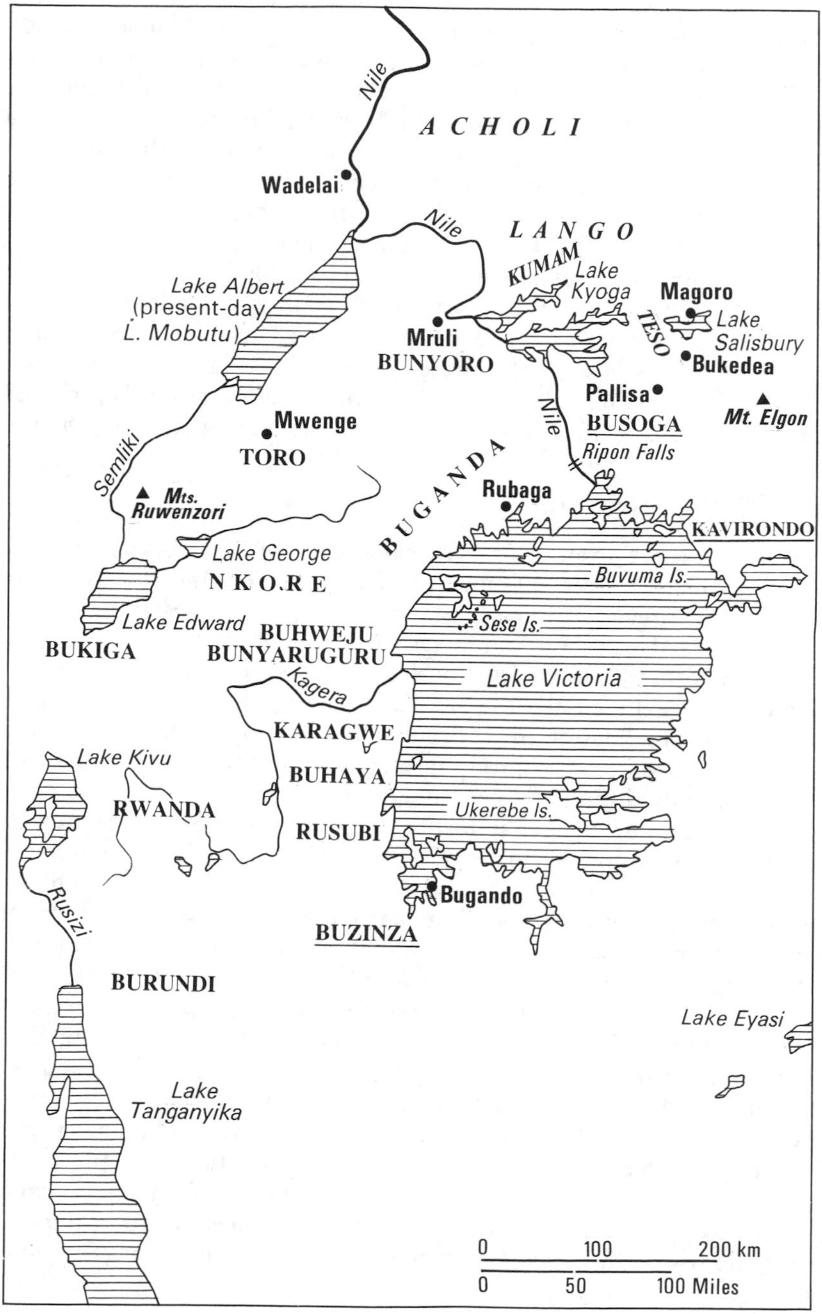

FIG. 10.3 *The Great Lakes region, 1840–84 (adapted from R. Oliver and G. Mathew (eds),* History of East Africa, *1963, vol. I, p. 299)*

As they raided, they accumulated cattle, hoes, ivory and captives; the last two could be sold to coastal traders for all kinds of luxury goods including textiles, bracelets, beads, tableware and, above all, firearms. Larger states could raid smaller ones, but all of them raided the neighbouring non-centralized communities, who suffered the most. The exception of Rwanda and Burundi (already mentioned) shows that it was possible to form an alternative strategy in dealing with this penetration of trade. Their strength came not from acquisition of guns but from their ability to maintain stability and unity in the densely populated mountain environment. Their extensive wars and raids during the period enabled them to accumulate wealth in a situation in which ivory and captives were irrelevant.

The second region we have deliberately omitted in this section is southern Tanzania. This is because the consequences of long-distance trade in this region are best considered along with the consequences of another intruding influence, i.e. that of the Nguni, to which we should now turn our attention.

The Nguni invasion

The Nguni came from South Africa where they had been part of the Nguni-speaking peoples of northern Zululand. Having fled from their homeland in about 1820 to escape the rising power of Shaka, the Nguni warriors moved northwards under their leader Zwangendaba. For about fifteen years they wandered in southern Mozambique and adjacent areas before crossing the Zambezi in 1835 on their march northwards until they reached the Fipa plateau in western Tanzania early in the 1840s. By this time what had started as a group of warriors had become an armed nation of over a hundred thousand people on the march.[33]

At this stage it would be interesting to ask ourselves how this spectacular growth of the Nguni people was accomplished. In order to answer this question one has to go back to the Zulu homeland. Shaka had built up a highly centralized military state organized according to two overlapping principles: one based on lineage and the other on military regiments. According to the first principle, the king was at the top of the pyramid of authority and below him there were segments of lineages consisting of the king's wives and their children and dependents. The segments tended to split and multiply at each generation as they grew larger. The youth, on the other hand, were organized into age-regiments cutting across territorial and lineage lines and directly controlled by the king. This meant that a foreigner could easily be absorbed as he gradually entered into the dynamic structure of the society through both the lineage and the age-regiment. Shaka also introduced changes in military techniques, the most important being the use of the short stabbing spear which made the age-regiments very efficient fighting units.

33. For a detailed account, see J. D. Omer-Cooper, 1966, 1969 and P. H. Gulliver, 1955.

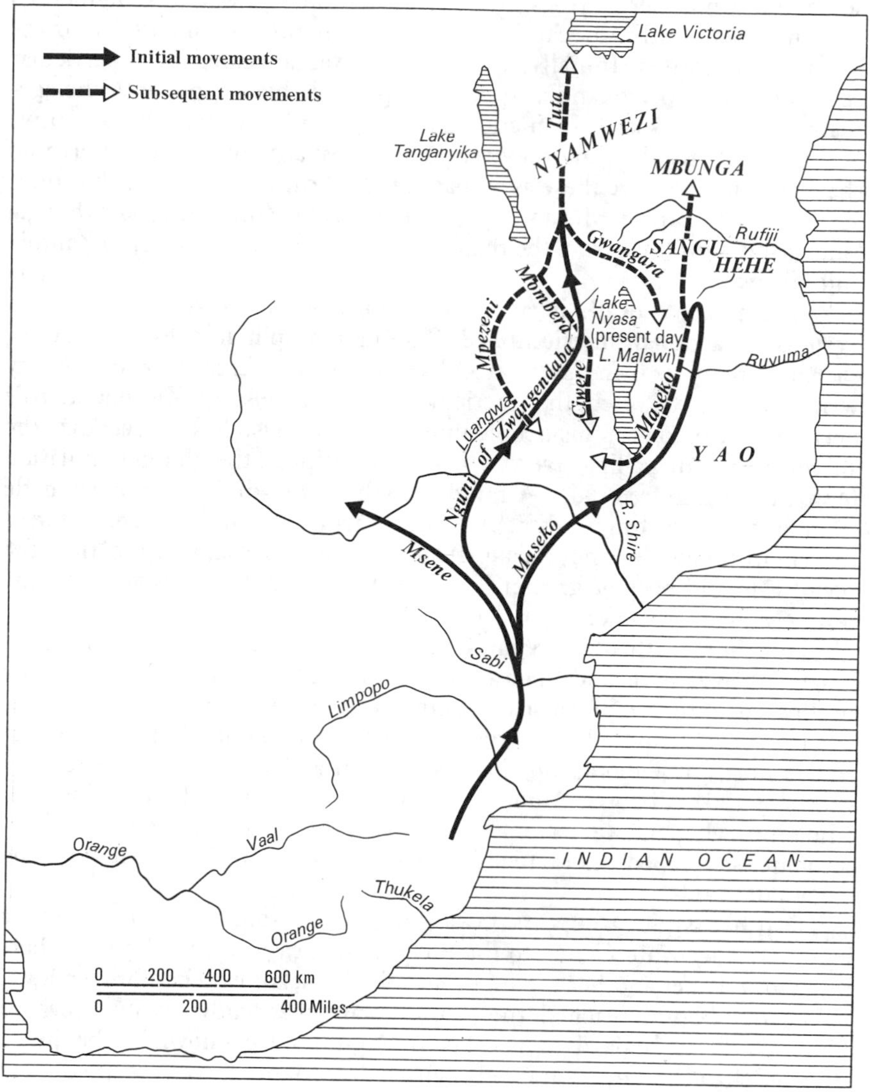

FIG. 10.4 *Northward migration routes of Zwangendaba's Nguni, the Maseko Nguni and the Msene (from J. D. Omer-Cooper,* The Zulu Aftermath, *1966, p. 66)*

Having inherited this dynamic social system, the Nguni were able to build up a well-unified people out of the people they encountered on their movement northwards. Their superior military organization enabled them to survive by raiding other people as they moved. Theirs was, of necessity, a predatory life, although at several places where resources allowed they settled for a number of years. As they moved on, the warriors augmented their numbers with war captives who were in turn assimilated into the Nguni social order. Initially, each captive was allocated to a particular segment of the society and as quickly as possible he was put into the age-regiments where social distinction between a 'true Nguni' and a captive was minimal. By the time they reached the Fipa plateau, the majority of the Nguni nation were these assimilated people captured from such groups as the Thonga from Mozambique, Shona from Zimbabwe, and Senga, Chewa and Tumbuka from the region north of the Zambezi river in Zambia and Malawi.

Zwangendaba's death in about 1848 initiated succession rivalry, and eventually factionalism triumphed. The nation split into five kingdoms, each moving in its own direction and settling in a different territory. Many writers have attributed this factionalism to the loss of Zwangendaba's peculiar ability to keep his people united. But one also has to recognize the spectacular 'snowballing' growth that had multiplied the Nguni population more than a hundredfold.[34] A rapid growth of this kind would have made centralized control more difficult. And bearing in mind the character of the environment on the Fipa plateau, one can perhaps argue that the population had become greater than the environment could sustain by the time Zwangendaba died.

Three out of the five Nguni factions moved south and established kingdoms in Zambia and Malawi. The fourth, known as the Tuta, pressed northwards into the Nyamwezi country, where its members raided villages and upset the Arab trade route between Tabora and Ujiji. They eventually settled north of Tabora, but their raids went as far north as the southern shores of Lake Victoria. Among the Nyamwezi captured by the Tuta was Mirambo who, as we have noted, having learned the Nguni military techniques, escaped to organize his own forces out of the refugees fleeing from Tuta raids.

The other Nguni group, the Gwangara, moved south-east from the Fipa plateau, under Zulu Gama, to the Songea area, east of Lake Nyasa. There its members met another Nguni group, the Maseko, who had broken away before the Nguni reached the Zambezi and had moved into southern Tanzania from Malawi. The Maseko Nguni were known to be much stronger than the Gwangara and their leader, Maputo, was accepted as an overlord of both groups. However, this alliance did not last long, for rivalries between them soon broke into open war and the Gwangara eventually defeated the Maseko Nguni and drove them south across the Ruvuma river. The Ndendeule, an absorbed group, tried to establish a successor state, but were finally defeated by the Gwangara and driven into the Kilombero valley where they established the Mbunga kingdom in the 1860s.

34. A. M. H. Sheriff, 1980, p. 33.

The Gwangara themselves split into two kingdoms, one under Chipeta who formed the Mshope kingdom, and the other under Mtakano Chabruma, who established the Njelu kingdom. The former settled north of Songea while the latter moved further south. Most writers have emphasized the way in which these two kingdoms terrorized by their raiding the whole region between Lake Nyasa and the coast until the German period. However, A. M. H. Sheriff has more recently shown how misleading this interpretation can be; for,

> it would appear that if the Ngoni had continued to lead a predatory life, 'like a swarm of locusts forced to continue advancing as it destroys its own livelihood', they would not have been able to settle down. It is therefore very likely that once they settled in the Songea area, the pattern of their economy must have changed to a more orderly exploitation of the local agricultural resources, using the indigenous people more effectively as cultivators while the Ngoni cared for their huge herds of cattle. With the allocation of agricultural activities to the conquered people on a more permanent basis, the latter's social status was bound to be affected, assimilated into the Ngoni society but not to the same extent as the captives had been during the migration. Raiding continued at the periphery of the Ngoni state but to a more limited extent, which would have provided much less opportunity to the subjects to show their valour and to capture their own captives with which to build up their social status.[35]

Therefore, in terms of emphasis, the first and most obvious legacy of the Nguni invasion was the creation of Nguni states on Tanzanian soil. The two Nguni kingdoms continued to exist as strong entities well into the colonial period. Their role during the Maji Maji war against the Germans is a prominent epic of the early colonial history of Tanzania. The second legacy of the invasion was the introduction of Nguni military techniques, which were adopted by a number of Tanzanian societies. There was a time when it was believed that the need to defend themselves against the Nguni had prompted such groups as the Hehe and the Sangu to use Nguni military techniques and build up centralized political entities. But recent research[36] has indicated that this assumption is incorrect since centralization had started in both cases before the Nguni invasion. What is true is that the Nguni military techniques did strengthen the societies that adopted them and made them capable of facing the conditions of the time, including the effects of the slave trade. Besides the need for self-defence against the Nguni themselves and against the slave-raiders, some of the societies were able to use the techniques to build up large states, as in the case of Mirambo, already discussed, and the Sangu and the Hehe in the southern region.

35. ibid., p. 34.
36. A. Redmayne, 1968a, p. 426; 1968b.

The Sangu were the first to learn Nguni military techniques. In the 1860s and 1870s they dominated most of the southern highlands under their leader, Merere; but from 1875 onwards they were overshadowed by the Hehe, who learned the Nguni military techniques through the Sangu themselves. Merere lost most of the Sangu territory to the Hehe under their leader, Mwinyigumba. It was the Hehe who were able to fight protracted wars against the Gwangara Nguni between 1878 and 1881 without victory on either side. From this time onwards, the Hehe remained a dominant force under Mwinyigumba's son, Mkwawa, who offered the Germans what was probably the stiffest military resistance in Tanzania.

For southern Tanzania, therefore, there were a variety of social and political changes introduced during the second half of the nineteenth century. Some of these changes had started as a result of the widened contacts brought by the long-distance trade, but were accelerated by the Nguni invasion. By the time of the colonial invasion in the 1880s, southern Tanzania, which before the middle of the century was mainly inhabited by societies organized only on lineage lines, had come to possess some of the most powerful kingdoms, such as the Nguni kingdoms, the Hehe and the Sangu.

The Maasai

Earlier in this chapter we alluded to the Maasai as a force affecting the history of the north-eastern interior of East Africa in the second half of the nineteenth century. The main reason for this was not expansion, for the Maasai had, by the end of the eighteenth century, passed their years of expansion.[37] Their attempt to move southwards in the first decades of the nineteenth century is said to have been effectively checked by the Gogo and the Hehe.[38] By the mid-nineteenth century, therefore, the pastoral Maasai controlled the grasslands in the rift valley between central Tanzania and central Kenya while a number of agricultural Maasai (Iloikop or Wa-Kwavi) groups bordered them on the eastern side between Mount Kilimanjaro and the Kenya Highlands and on the western side.

What happened to alter the situation towards the end of the century? The answer is to be sought in the long series of civil wars that occurred during the mid-nineteenth century. The reasons for these wars are still unknown, but several factors can be suggested as having contributed to the situation. Some writers have tended to emphasize the lack of opportunity for a warlike people to expand. 'Thus thwarted, the Maasai turned their aggressiveness inward.'[39] Yet, the picture of the Maasai as warlike people is not borne out by detailed study of their society, as shown below. The

37. E. A. Alpers, 1974, p. 241.
38. J. Thomson, 1885, p. 414.
39. E. A. Alpers, 1974, p. 241

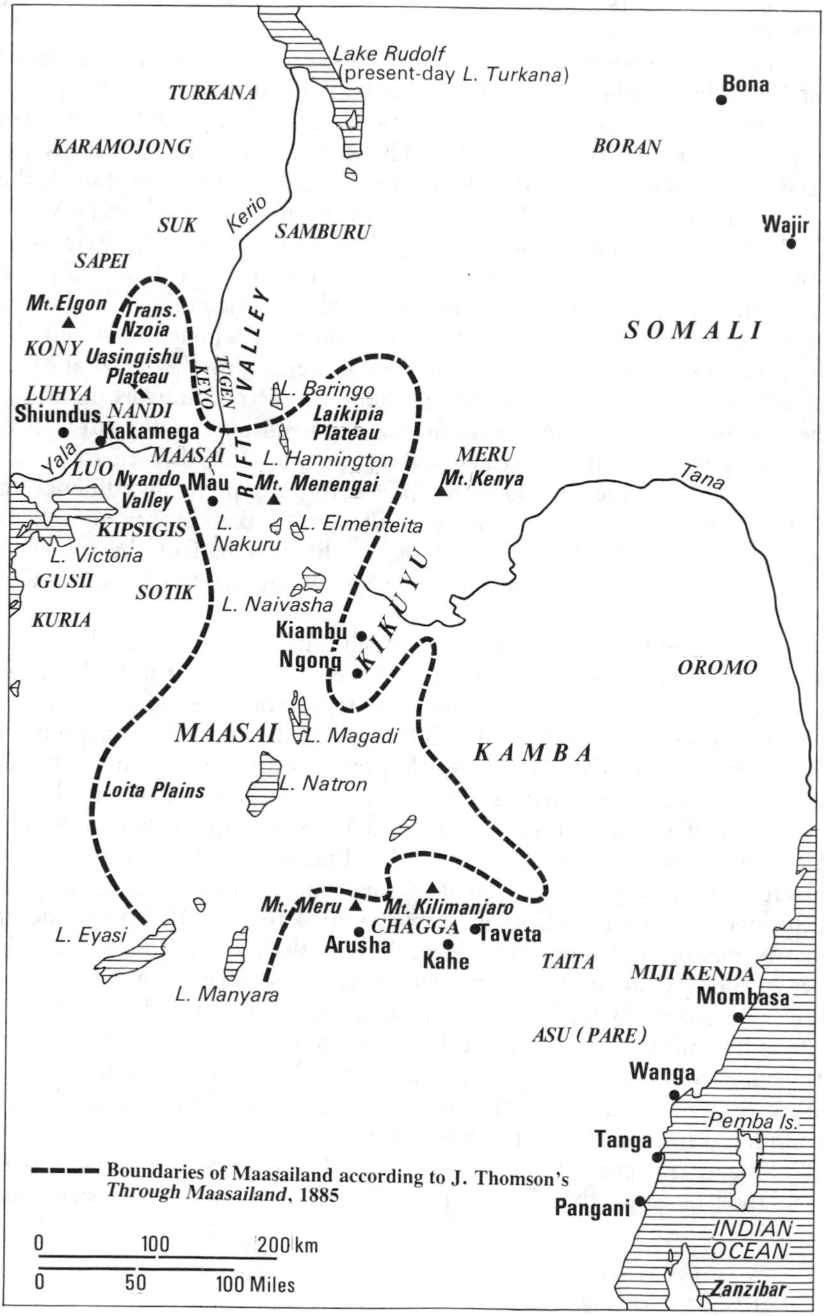

FIG. 10.5 *The Maasai and their neighbours, 1840–84 (from R. Oliver and G. Mathew (eds),* History of East Africa, *1963, Vol. I, p. 298)*

contributary factors can, therefore, be seen by looking at the civil wars themselves.

Until recently our knowledge of the civil wars came from a study carried out by A. H. Jacobs among the Maasai in the first half of the 1960s.[40] According to this study the civil wars were basically conflicts between groups of pastoral and agricultural (Iloikop) Maasai. Both groups were Maasai-speaking, but the latter had taken to agriculture in addition to their main pastoral occupation. From the point of view of the pastoral Maasai, the Iloikop were inferior since they had taken up a different style of life. From the first half of the century, the pastoral Maasai had acquired greater unity through the evolution of a stronger ritual office of the *oloiboni* and therefore they had a central figure who could be widely consulted. Yet, there was no unified political organization either within the pastoral Maasai or within the Iloikop. Jacobs interpreted Maasai traditions as pointing to the transformation of the ritual office as the beginning of the rift between the two groups of the Maasai-speaking people. For, before the rise of Subet, who was the first known *oloiboni* to gain political influence, the pastoral Maasai ritual expert was consulted by Iloikop groups as well. But during Subet's period (covering most of the first half of the nineteenth century to 1864 when he was succeeded by Mbatian), the Iloikop are said to have acquired their own *oloiboni*.

A more recent study by John L. Berntsen[41] has indicated that the division between the two groups of pastoral Maasai and agricultural Maasai was never permanent. In his own opinion, to try to interpret Maasai history in terms of pastoralists versus agriculturalists 'leads one into insurmountable contradictions. All the Maasai people were pastoralists before a battle or a series of raids; loss of cattle and loss of their access to the pasture lands of the Rift Valley region forced some groups to supplement their subsistence by turning to non-pastoral sources.'[42] This means that the picture of nineteenth-century Maasai society was much more complicated than explained by earlier studies, i.e. some groups known as Iloikop at one time may be pastoralists at another, depending on their ability to replenish their herds and regain access to rich pasture lands. Yet, as a result of the nineteenth-century wars, more Maasai groups were pushed away from the rift valley and their semi-pastoral life continued into the colonial period.[43] In order to avoid confusion, we shall view these wars in terms of group alliances whose aim was the control of cattle and pasture lands, both considered to be important to pastoral life.

The actual causes of conflict may have been varied. The first series of wars took place on the Uasin Gishu plateau. This may have been caused

40. A. H. Jacobs, 1965.
41. J. L. Berntsen, 1979.
42. ibid.
43. The Arusha are a good example. See P. H. Gulliver, 1963.

by pressure on grazing land. The pastoral Maasai in the Rift Valley wanted to use the good grassland on the plateau, which was being used by another Maasai group known as the Uasin Gishu. The latter were supported by a number of other Maasai-speaking groups living on the plateau. Eventually, the Uasin Gishu were driven out of the plateau and pushed to other areas. We have already seen how some of them were used to strengthen the kingdom of Wanga before the arrival of coastal traders.

The second series of wars started after the famous famine of 1836, which is known to have affected many parts of East Africa. It appears, therefore, that many raids were undertaken at this time in order to replenish herds lost during the drought. Strife took place in all parts of Maasailand. In the south the Rift Valley Maasai raided groups living further east towards the Pangani river. They succeeded in pushing these groups out of Kibaya, Shambarai and Naberera and forced them to settle east of the Pangani river, the Kilimanjaro lowlands and Taveta. The settlement of the Arusha on the slopes of Mount Meru is also supposed to have taken place at this time. In the north, there were raids against the Laikipia. But the major conflict took place from 1860 to 1864 between the Purko and the Losegalai who lived between Lake Nakuru and the Mau escarpment. A number of the Losegalai fled to the Kipsigis and the Nandi territories. According to traditions collected by Jacobs,[44] these Maasai refugees were responsible for introducing the *oloiboni*-like office to the Nandi, where it was known as *orkoiyot*. This initiated the rise of Nandi power at a time when that of their Maasai neighbours was declining.

The end of the second series also concluded an era of Maasai history, for it ended the period of predominantly Maasai control of the Uasin Gishu plateau and heralded the growth in importance there of other Nilotic groups, such as the Nandi and the Kipsigis. It was this weakening of Maasai control of the plateau that made it easier for coastal traders to use the Kenya caravan routes which they had previously avoided.

The final series of Maasai wars also centred on the northern plateaux. Mbatian had succeeded Subet as ritual leader in the mid-1860s.[45] Various alliances were formed, the Purko and the Kisongo pastoral groups, the Laikipia with a number of Iloikop groups, i.e. those who had been pushed out of the good grazing lands and were forced to be semi-agriculturalists as well as pastoralists. By 1884, the pastoral groups had attained pre-eminence and the Iloikop groups had been scattered in many directions.

It can be said, therefore, that the effect of the long series of wars was to eliminate the powerful Maasai groups, especially on the northern plateaux. Their survivors were widely scattered as a result of the wars: from the

44. A. H. Jacobs, 1965.

45. A. H. Jacobs, 1965, using age-set chronology, suggests that Subet died in 1864. D. A. Low, 1963, p. 306, on the other hand, quoting a number of sources puts Mbatian's succession in 1866.

Kilimanjaro lowlands to Taveta, down the Pare and Shambaa plains in the Pangani valley, from Arusha down to the southern Maasai Steppe towards the coast. These were the groups which came to be known as Iloikop or Wa-Kwavi in the existing literature on the Maasai. Most of those dispersed further north and westwards were absorbed by other groups.

On the side of the pastoral Maasai, the picture of victory may be misleading. Certainly the land occupied by them was also reduced as a result of the wars. They no longer inhabited the regions east of Mount Kilimanjaro and the Uasin Gishu and Laikipia plateaux. Most of the Rift Valley, plains and open plateaux alike remained under their control but with a greatly reduced population. What finally affected the power of the pastoral Maasai severely were the human and animal diseases that infected the region after the prolonged wars. The large areas covered in the raids brought the Maasai into contact with many other groups and made it possible for infectious and unaccustomed diseases to be passed on from other groups. In 1869, for example, the Maasai lost a large number of people from cholera contracted from the Samburu.[46] The worst scourge came in the 1880s when a serious outbreak of smallpox coincided with a pleuro-pneumonia epidemic that decimated Maasai herds. It was these human and animal epidemics, rather than the wars themselves, that finally weakened the Maasai and made their reputed ferocity hardly noticeable at the time of the imposition of colonial rule.

Increased European pressures

Direct European pressures in East Africa between 1845 and 1884 revolved around four interlinked activities: the abolition of the slave trade, propagation of Christianity, geographical exploration and the establishment of 'legitimate commerce'. These four activities were interlinked in the sense that they were a product of the European capitalist expansion coming out of the Industrial Revolution. This developed new productive capacities that made slave labour less profitable and therefore produced new attitudes towards the slave trade. The so-called humanitarian spirit had already successfully persuaded Western countries to abolish the Atlantic slave trade and by the 1840s attention had been directed to the East African slave trade. Likewise, the evangelical movement associated with the humanitarian forces was, by the mid-nineteenth century, turning towards East Africa, partly because geographical exploration (itself a product of this new spirit of scientific curiosity and evangelism) was revealing challenging opportunities for action against the evils of the Arab slave trade through missionary work and through the establishment of 'legitimate commerce'.

The words 'legitimate commerce' were used to refer to trade in commodities other than human beings. However, we saw how ivory became

46. D. A. Low, 1963, p. 308.

one of the most important commodities for international trade in East Africa during the period under discussion. After the transfer of Seyyid Saʿīd's capital from Oman to Zanzibar, the major Western powers of the time – Britain, the USA and France – established trade missions in Zanzibar. Yet, as we have already seen, most of the ivory trade still passed through Bombay before going to Europe because of the predominance of Indian merchants in the East African trade. Nevertheless, in terms of Western imperialism, the East African trade was already within the informal empire[47] of the West under the leadership of the British, whether operating directly from Zanzibar or indirectly through Bombay. Agents of American and German (Hamburg) firms dealing in cheap calico and hardware respectively carried a smaller volume of trade than that controlled by the Indian merchants.[48] This kind of commercial relationship continued undisturbed until near the end of the period under discussion.

The British government concentrated its efforts on stopping the slave trade. Prior to the 1840s the British had in vain attempted to limit the scope within which slaves might be carried in the area under the control of the sultan of Oman. In 1841 Colonel Atkins Hamerton was appointed British consul in Zanzibar. For a number of years his efforts were directed towards reaching a new agreement with the sultan of Zanzibar, who had moved his capital from Oman in 1840. As a result of these efforts the Hamerton Treaty of 1845 was signed. It sought to restrict the slave trade to the sultan's possessions. Even if the treaty could have been enforced, its effect would have been very limited as long as the sultan's empire extended from East Africa to the Arabian peninsula. Furthermore, the unwillingness of the sultan to see the trade stopped made the enforcement of the treaty difficult. When Seyyid Saʿīd died in 1856, and his empire was divided into two parts, Seyyid Majid who inherited the East African half was just as reluctant to give up the slave trade. He even thought of strengthening his control over the trade by building a new capital on the mainland coast, a place called 'Haven of Peace' (Dar es Salaam), but the project was still uncompleted when he died in 1870. Efforts to abolish the Arab slave trade did not succeed until 1873 when, through intensified diplomacy and threat, the British were able to make Majid's successor, Seyyid Barghash, issue a decree prohibiting all trade in slaves by sea.

Why was it so difficult to get the sultan of Zanzibar to agree to stop the slave trade? The answer is obvious if one bears in mind the nature of the expanding plantation economy in Zanzibar and Pemba. Its dependence on slave labour meant that restriction on the procurement of slaves would limit its growth. It is known that plantation agriculture continued to expand after the decree of 1873.[49] As slave-trading was still legal on the mainland

47. R. Robinson and J. Gallagher, 1961, p. 51.

48. R. Oliver, 1952, pp. 1–2.

49. F. Cooper, 1977, p. 54, reports that in 1877, as many as 1000 Omanis emigrated from Oman to Zanzibar.

coast, traders were able to transport slaves a long distance along the coast between Kilwa and Mombasa or even Malindi and smuggle them to Zanzibar, and especially Pemba, in small vessels at night in order to avoid the British naval patrol. Even after the slave trade was prohibited on the mainland in 1876, neither the sultan nor the British were in a position to enforce the decree effectively. The clove plantations on the islands had increased demand for food production on the mainland coast, especially grain. Thus, a number of plantations producing grain with slave labour had sprung up all along the coast between Pangani and Malindi. It was therefore impossible during this time to distinguish slaves intended for sale from those intended for use on these plantations.[50] To make things worse, this was the time when internal strife in many parts of the hinterland was producing large numbers of captives. The traders could easily invent new ways of evading the sultan's soldiers and the British naval patrol. A number of new concealed stations sprang up all along the coast between Pangani and Mombasa, from which small dhows could slip off at night and reach Pemba unnoticed. It is therefore clear that the slave trade remained a major activity well into the colonial period.

The European trade missions and the naval patrol against slave traders were limited to Zanzibar and the coastal areas. Although Europeans could no doubt obtain from Arab traders a few stories about places far away from the coast, the vast hinterland remained unknown to them. Gradually, however, events were to turn the attention of the humanitarians and the evangelicals to East Africa. Until 1856 their main interest was still focused on the trans-Atlantic trade. But as more became known about the horrors of the East African slave trade, European public attention was more and more drawn to the region.

It was David Livingstone's travels in East and Central Africa, more than anything else, that started the process. In 1856 he completed his second journey across Central Africa from Angola to the Zambezi delta. Prior to this period, the Church Missionary Society had sent three German missionaries to start work in East Africa. Johann Krapf arrived in Mombasa in 1844 and was followed by J. Rebmann in 1846 and by J. J. Erhardt in 1849. Their mission station was established at Rabai near Mombasa. By 1856 Rebmann had crossed the Nyika plain to Kilimanjaro to become the first European to see the mountain, and Krapf had gone farther south to visit the Shambaa kingdom of Kimweri and then northwards to the Kamba country where he was the first European to be shown Mount Kenya. Erhardt and Krapf also travelled farther south to the mouth of the Ruvuma and later, after spending some time in Tanga, Erhardt was able to publish a map of East Africa containing a mass of information he had gathered on the coast about the interior, including the Great Lakes,

50. F. Cooper, 1977, p. 126.

which he represented as an inland sea. Erhardt's 'map was to be the main inspiration of Burton and Speke in their expedition of 1858'.[51]

This first group of missionaries acted as pioneers; they gathered considerable information that was extremely valuable to those who followed them. Yet their information hardly came to the attention of the general public and it was only when Livingstone began his attacks on the Arab slave trade in speeches and writings that the popular imagination was caught. In the spirit of the capitalist free-trade conviction of his time, Livingstone was emphasizing the power of commerce, which, he believed, would integrate the vast interior with Christian Europe, thus relieving Africans of the poverty and humiliation caused by the slave trade. He therefore concentrated on travelling in search of navigable rivers, or what he called the 'open path for commerce and Christianity'.[52] The publication of his *Missionary Travels*[53] in 1857, together with his personal appeals, inspired the formation of the Universities Mission to Central Africa (UMCA) by a group of English High Churchmen. The UMCA attempted to follow Livingstone's ideas by trying to enter the Zambezi region, only to find that neither the Zambezi nor the Ruvuma had navigable entries. After the initial problems, the mission had to move to Zanzibar to concentrate instead on freed slaves.

The question of freed slaves attracted the attention of all missionary societies working in East Africa. Between 1858 and 1873 the CMS, UMCA and the Holy Ghost Fathers were all involved. The CMS continued to work at Rabai near Mombasa, where freed slaves from Bombay were sent to assist Rebmann. The UMCA was located in Zanzibar while the Holy Ghost Fathers worked in Bagamoyo. None of these societies had succeeded in carrying out Livingstone's mission of opening the interior for commerce and Christianity. Nevertheless, the work had begun. For, while the missions were beginning to take root on the coast, the interior of East Africa was being explored by Europeans who had been inspired by the initial efforts of these missionaries. In 1858 Burton and Speke had set out to find Erhardt's 'Sea of Unyamwezi'.[54] They reached Lake Tanganyika and Speke also visited the southern shores of Lake Victoria. In 1862 Speke returned with Grant to explore Lake Victoria, and also located the outflow of the Nile. While following the White Nile they met Samuel Baker, who had come up the river from the sea. Later Livingstone himself was to return once more to the heart of Africa, adding more to what had already been revealed. The explorations had a tremendous effect on the missionary invasion. The existence of the big lakes immediately seemed to prove the validity of Livingstone's plan. All major British missionary societies that

51. R. Oliver, 1952, p. 7.
52. ibid., p. 27.
53. D. Livingstone, 1857.
54. R. Oliver, 1952, p. 27.

were working in East Africa wanted to place steamers on these inland waterways. The most important stimulus derived from these explorations sprang from their revelations about the extent and character of the Arab slave trade. For it became clear that the interior was not as inaccessible as Krapf had thought of Kenya or as the UMCA missionaries had thought of the Lower Shire. Certainly caravan routes penetrated the whole interior and human cargo was getting to the coast through them. Even more significant was the revelation of what this trade implied for the lives of the Africans.

After Livingstone's death greater zeal was roused among British missionary societies. The impact of his public funeral ceremony in Westminster Abbey touched almost every pulpit and stimulated popular support for missionary work. As a result, the Scottish Free Church plunged for the first time into missionary work in Central Africa. In 1875 its first expedition penetrated the Zambezi and the Shire and planted a station at Blantyre on Lake Nyasa. The other missionary societies already at work on the coast expanded their efforts rapidly. In 1875 the UMCA started a station at Magila on the mainland in what was part of Kimweri's empire of Usambara, and in 1876 established a station in the southern region of Tanzania at Masasi. Meanwhile, Stanley, an Anglo-American journalist, adventurer and explorer, who had previously been commissioned to look for Livingstone, had completed a second journey to explore the region further. In 1875 his letter about the possibilities for missionary work in Buganda appeared in the *Daily Telegraph*. This stimulated a number of British churchmen to offer funds for missionary work. As a result, the CMS expanded from Freretown in Rabai near Mombasa and established a station at Mpwapwa in the middle of Tanzania in 1876 from where missionaries were able to reach Mutesa's capital the following year. Livingstone's own home society, the London Missionary Society, soon decided to follow his steps and, stimulated by a specific offer of funds, decided to go to Lake Tanganyika, the region where Livingstone spent his last years. From 1877 onwards the London Missionary Society established a number of stations near Lake Tanganyika; Ujiji, Urambo, Kavala Island and Mtowa. Unfortunately work at these stations had to be abandoned because the climate and German political interests proved too hostile for the missionaries. The Society eventually re-established its base in the British sphere of influence in Rhodesia.

Unlike the Protestants, Roman Catholic missionary activities owed their stimulus during the same period to the vision and energies of one individual, Cardinal Lavigerie, who was appointed the Archbishop of Algiers in 1867. A year later, he founded the Société de Notre-Dame d'Afrique, later known as the White Fathers. Its aim was to work in 'Central Africa' as 'the religious counterpart of the African International Association, working within the same geographical limits, from ten degrees north to twenty degrees south of the Equator, and placing its stations within reach of those of the lay organization, so that mutual assistance could be rendered.'[55] The Society's first station in East Africa was established at Tabora in 1878. The Holy Ghost Fathers, who had preceded it ten years earlier at Bagamoyo, had concentrated on establishing colonies for freed slaves rather than expanding mission stations. Thus, by the time the White Fathers started invading the interior, the Holy Ghost Fathers had only gone as far as Morogoro where they established a station 'about a hundred miles inland at Mhonda'.[56]

From Tabora a number of White Fathers went north to establish a station at Bukumbi on the southern shores of Lake Victoria and thence to Buganda. When they arrived at King Mutesa's court they found that the CMS missionary, Alexander M. Mackay, had preceded them by several months and that the Muslims 'had been in the country for several years, and a number of the Chiefs had accepted the faith'.[57] This was the beginning of religious rivalry between the Muslims and Christians on the one hand, and between Protestants and Catholics on the other. Mutesa was able to control these rivalries by balancing one group against the other, but, after his death in 1884, the rivalries were to influence greatly what was happening at the court.

Another group of White Fathers left Tabora and went westwards to set up a mission station at Ujiji in 1879 and from there to Rumonge in Burundi, some 120km south of the present Bujumbura, but the station was abandoned in 1881 after the massacre of three missionaries there. 'The White Fathers were not able to return to their mission for almost fifty years'.[58] In 1885 the White Fathers took over two stations near Ujiji, which had been established by the African International Association after King Leopold of Belgium had decided to concentrate his efforts in the Congo Free State.

Until 1884, therefore, European pressures in the East African hinterland were mainly exerted by missionary societies. Even where there existed commercial activities, they were offshoots of missionary work. Two such examples existed. The first was the Livingstonia Central African Trading Company, which was associated with Scottish missionary activities in the Lake Nyasa region. Its aim was said to be that of supplying the mission station at Blantyre with necessities through running steamships in the waterways of the region and also that of bringing ivory for commerce at a price that would undercut the Arab merchants using slave labour for porterage. The second example is also associated with the Scottish Free Church. A member of the Church, William Mackinnon, who owned the British India Steam Navigation Company, started running ships to Zanzibar in 1872. A few years later he was able to convince the sultan of

55. ibid., pp. 46–7.
56. J. M. Gray, 1963, p. 244.
57. G. D. Kittler, 1961, p. 161.
58. ibid., p. 157.

Zanzibar to approve his plan for building roads to Lake Nyasa and Lake Victoria. Although the roads were not built, it was these plans that matured into the more imperialistic organization known as the British East Africa Company during the partition period.

Missionary work, during the period under discussion, was in its pioneering phase. On the surface it may appear to have made little impact on African societies but, when examined more carefully, it will be found to have already exerted considerable impact. Missionary societies in East Africa were in fact more powerful during this period because they did not have to face the restraints imposed by colonial governments in later periods. As Roland Oliver puts it:

> The missions became a power in the land, and not a spiritual power only. In Buganda, as at Zanzibar, the native political authority was firmly enough established to include the stranger within its protection. Elsewhere even the missionary who set out with a few dozen porters and tried to settle in a native village had to set up what amounted to a small independent state.[59]

The early mission stations were also heavily influenced by their concentration on establishing colonies for freed slaves. Whether the colonies were on the coast (like Freretown or Bagamoyo) or further inland (like Masasi, Blantyre, Mpwapwa, Tabora or Ujiji), the main intention was to build near the slave caravans and to use freed slaves as a nucleus of the mission colonies. This was consistent with the intention to fight the Arab slave trade. But, in fact, the stations became theocratic states that could even attract political exiles, fugitive slaves and misfits in the societies in which they were situated.[60] In this way, the mission stations were increasing the weakness of those societies already weakened by the economic pressures of the time and thus reducing their ability to oppose the imposition of colonial rule. In a more general way, it can be said that missionary societies were also the pioneers for colonial rule. Most of the 300 Europeans who had lived on the mainland before 1884 were connected with missionary activities.[61] Even where they were effectively controlled by a local ruler, the existence of a European mission station with its cultural impact opened the way for a colonial claim during the partition period.

As we have already mentioned, during the period under discussion East Africa was part of a large informal empire under British control. Towards the end of this period, however, the rise of Germany as a major Western power was beginning to increase the competition that already existed. Outside the East African sphere, tensions caused by this competition were already beginning to appear. When King Leopold called an international conference in Brussels in 1876 'to discuss methods of peaceful and co-

59. R. Oliver, 1952, p. 50.
60. ibid.
61. ibid., p. 49.

operative action to develop legitimate commerce and attack the slave trade',[62] the rivalry was already appearing on the surface. The international conference eventually broke up into jealous national sub-committees and Leopold went ahead with establishing his personal empire in the Congo. The most significant action of the period was the British occupation of Egypt in 1882. For the British the action was justified because of the strategic position of Egypt (with the Suez Canal and the Nile) for British interests in India and East Africa, although East Africa was considered of less importance. But the international reaction to this occupation included a series of colonial annexations by Germany: South West Africa in April 1884 and Cameroon in July of the same year. In West Africa Germany and France were beginning to stand together to challenge the British position on the Niger. The 'high tide of imperialism' had begun to flow. When Bismark convened the Berlin Conference in November 1884, the process of partitioning Africa had already started. In East Africa Carl Peters had already arrived in Zanzibar under the auspices of his Gesellschaft für Deutsche Kolonisation (German Colonization Society) and had gone inland to negotiate treaties. The British kept hoping that strengthening Seyyid Barghash's authority on the mainland would be enough to protect their interests without direct colonization.

62. J. Flint, 1963, p. 362.

11 Peoples and states of the Great Lakes region

D. W. COHEN

Introduction

During the first half of the eighteenth century, the king of Buganda, Kabaka Mawanda, sought to bring under his control the rich regions to the east of the central administered zone of his kingdom. He launched a major military campaign. The campaign had some immediate success and Mawanda installed one of his generals to bring the region of the Kyaggwe entirely under the administration of the Buganda kingdom. At several points, however, Kabaka Mawanda's governor in Kyaggwe met resistance. And his successors saw sections of Kyaggwe slip under the influence of Buganda's north-western neighbour, Bunyoro, and the immense Mabira forest of Kyaggwe was closed to the penetration of the Buganda state. By the end of the eighteenth century, the Mabira, directly east and not 45 km from the Ganda heartland, had become a reserve for forces of opposition to the Buganda courts, a place of exile, a haven of refuge. For countless individuals within and without the kingdom, the dark galleries of the Mabira held the promise of a reversal of fortunes.

Towards the close of the eighteenth century, Kakungulu fled the domain of his father, the Ganda king, Semakokiro, whose great-grandfather was Mawanda's brother. Kakungulu found refuge and support in the Mabira. From there, he and his followers organized a patchwork of alliances with states around the frontiers of Buganda and then launched a series of attacks to gain the throne of his father. Kakungulu never captured Semakokiro's throne. But his activities increased the turbulence around the older administrative zones of Buganda, gave the Ganda circle of leaders greater incentives to punish and incorporate regions of opposition to the east and to the west, and may have reinforced the violent character of relations between Buganda and its neighbours.

Kakungulu was not the first individual to attempt to convert a community of refuge in the Mabira into a force of insurgency. In looking to the Mabira, Kakungulu was taking a leaf from the book of tactics of his very own father, Semakokiro. Perhaps some thirty or forty years earlier,

Semakokiro sought to recover his fortunes in the Mabira, taking with him a powerful retinue of support. His exile was a long one.

From our perspective today, Semakokiro's community of exiles in the Mabira has the appearance of a state in formation. The process of formation of a state based in the Mabira was, in this instance, interrupted by its own success in gathering support. Semakokiro succeeded eventually in overthrowing his brother Junju and was seated on the Ganda throne as Kabaka. In looking back through Kakungulu's refuge in the Mabira and to his father Semakokiro's exile before him, one is reminded of the immense, durable, and powerful community organized around the Ganda general and administrator Semei Kakungulu during his 'exile' in eastern Uganda in the early twentieth century,[1] and of the tense and complex character of relations among rulers and their adjutants that typified the political life of the Buganda kingdom in the late nineteenth and early twentieth centuries.

The story of Kakungulu and Semakokiro in the Mabira, located in time towards the close of the eighteenth century, offers historians several paths of entry into the extraordinarily rich and complex nineteenth-century history of the Great Lakes region. One path provides the observer with a view of the state in the Lakes region as still evolving, still incorporating new terrains and peoples within the reach of their authority, the picture of the Lakes region state as a relatively young complex of institutions. A second path offers the observer a view of considerable turbulence as an eighteenth-century backdrop to the nineteenth century. Rulers faced solid opposition from within their domains and from outside. Tenure in office could be brief, providing precious little time to construct ruling coalitions or to build working administrations. The ruler's own brothers and sons were foci of revolt. A third path suggests that the domains or kingdoms of the region were not enclosed social and political units. There was considerable interaction across political frontiers. The lives of rulers and the quality of life for the members of courts and subjects were contingent on the character of relations among states. A fourth path of 'observation' takes us into the little-known and little-understood social and political terrain away from the courts and the capitals of the region and towards some first, faint appreciation of what the Lakes region state meant in the lives of people in the region, how far it reached into domestic lives and production, into trade and exchange, into religious thought and practice.

The Great Lakes region is today, and was in the nineteenth century, a densely populated, well-watered region of eastern and central Africa. The region extends from the Kyoga basin of northern and eastern present-day Uganda and the Mount Elgon foothills and Winam Gulf of western Kenya to the eastern uplands of the Zaire river watershed of eastern present-day Zaire and to the shores of Lake Tanganyika. The Great Lakes region is a historical and cultural area (as well as the physical juncture of two great

1. M. Twaddle, 1966, pp. 25–38.

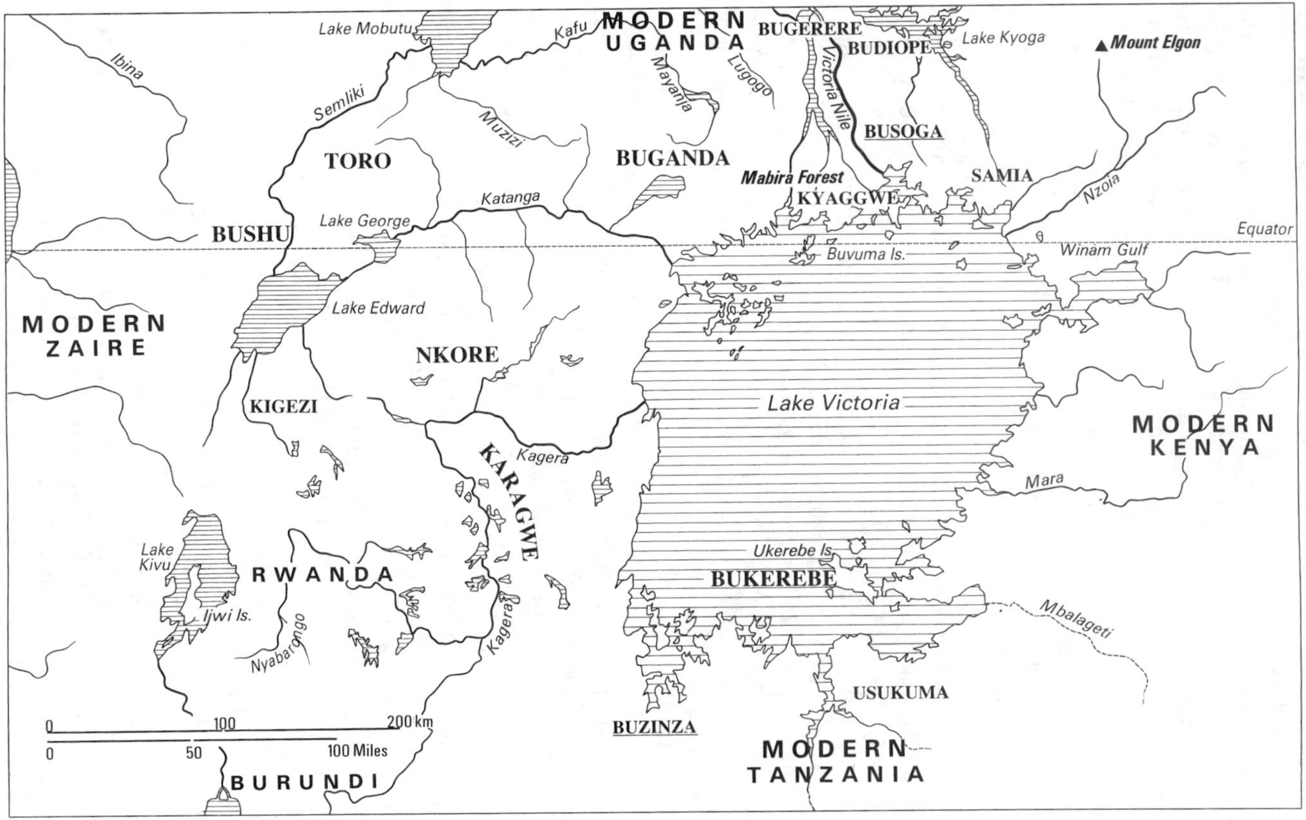

FIG. 11.1 *The Great Lakes region (after D. Cohen)*

watersheds) defined by language, continuous in cultural forms, and, most prominently, characterized by the general shared patterns of precolonial political organization. The Lakes region state conformed to certain region-specific elements of political culture, structural principles, and authoritarian ideology, which touched and sometimes enclosed social formations marked by 'caste', class, and multi-ethnic compositions.

The political order

The Great Lakes region was, at the beginning of the nineteenth century, and seven or eight decades later when European pressures began to affect directly the fortunes of both individuals and states in the area, an agglomeration of small and large, of weak and strong, yet superficially similar, states. The Lakes region kingdom is defined as the domain organized around a ruler, drawing status from association with a dynastic lineage, supported by a court of aides and councillors, the domain organized by a hierarchic array of appointed officials, artisans, and lordly princes.

The traditional focus of students of the region on formal political elements and offices[2] gives special 'voice' to the insurgent activities of Semakokiro, Kakungulu, and the thousands of folk who joined them in exile and rebellion. The story of Semakokiro and Kakungulu and of their exiles draws attention to the potential forces of opposition to existing authority and to the existing capitals in the region and helps us escape rigid concepts of the domain of politics. The Great Lakes state was not – at the outset of the nineteenth century, or later, or earlier – simply an assemblage of king and court and country, or a coupling of political culture, administrative orders, and structure. Semakokiro and Kakungulu relay to us that the state domain was defined, in an important sense, by conflict from within and from without.

The political order of the Lakes Plateau region was extensively transformed in the nineteenth century through the elaboration of two major trends. One was the growing cohesion and power at the centres of a number of states, through the accumulations of labour and trade goods, through the growth of bureaucratic institutions, through the resolution of old divisive processes, and through the control and management of new influences and forces entering the region.

The second trend was the decisive expansion of power of three or four states – Buganda, Rwanda, Burundi, and eventually, Bunyoro, during its period of revival – at the expense of other states. These two trends were closely intertwined. The success of these four major kingdoms during the nineteenth century rested upon the reorganization of administration

2. Understandably so, given the prime attention of anthropologists and historians on the political histories of the kingdoms of the region and the disappointingly small amount of work done on precolonial economic history in the region.

towards stronger central control, the quelling of long-persistent civil strife by the elimination of opposition and by the extroversion of internal conflicts through expansionary and tribute-gathering campaigns, the enlargement of domains through conquests of new areas, the capture and incorporation of sections of regional production and trade, and the integration of new elements and forces entering the wider region.

A signal of this wholesale change in these major domains from the eighteenth to the nineteenth century is noted in looking at the duration of reign-length of the nineteenth-century rulers of Buganda, Rwanda, Burundi, and Bunyoro. In Buganda, Kamanya ruled thirty to thirty-five years, beginning in the first years of the century. Suna followed Kamanya and ruled twenty years. Mutesa followed Suna and ruled twenty-eight years. By comparison, eleven kabakas ruled Buganda in the eighteenth century and a considerable proportion of these eleven were murdered or removed from office. An eighteenth-century 'era of princes' had been transformed into an 'era of long reigns', and Kamanya, Suna, and Mutesa each had the breathing space to organize an initial control, to limit opposition from contending princes and factions, and move to expand the resources of the state.

In Rwanda, a similar 'era of long reigns' supplanted a pattern of abbreviated tenure in the previous era. Mwami Yuhi Gahindiro assumed power in the last decade of the eighteenth century and ruled for more than thirty years. His successor, Mutara Rwogera, ruled for about three decades, and Mutara's successor, Kigeri Rwabugiri, ruled for nearly four decades until his death in 1895.

In Burundi, there were only two rulers in the nineteenth century, Ntare II Rugamba, who is thought to have been placed on the Burundi stool in the last years of the eighteenth century, and Mwezi II Gisabo, who ruled from the mid-nineteenth century until his death in 1908. It is thought that four different kings ruled Burundi in the eighteenth century. In Bunyoro, such a pattern of long reigns is less clear for the nineteenth century, though the long reign of Mukama Kabarega, from about 1870 to his removal by imperial agency in 1899, was part and parcel of the revival of the power and regional influence of Bunyoro in the second half of the nineteenth century.

There is a circular effect to be recognized in the presentation of the evidence of long reigns in the nineteenth century. Time gave rulers, their courts, and their clients, opportunities to construct stronger and more durable networks of authority and more secure administrations. Time gave rulers and administrations opportunities to routinize the circulation of rewards, payments, and offices, and provided many folk away from the courts with assurances that opportunity and security lay with participation in the present regime rather than in opposition to it. Conversely, these effects assured the rulers, courts, and big men of the nineteenth century more time and opportunity to continue the elaboration of their power and

PLATE 11.1 *Buganda in 1875: The Kabaka's Capital*

PLATE 11.2 *Kabaka Mutesa with chiefs and officials*

administration. Sequences of long reigns made more likely the carriage of coalitions and routines formed during one reign into the next. Legitimacy and authority in the Lakes Plateau state were established not simply through an accession ritual. Legitimacy and authority must be seen to have been constructed over time through the section-by-section erection of lattices of social relations. Participation in the state involved the play of institutions of marriage, service, and clientage, and it involved opening new lands for production, building new circuits of exchange, and expanding provisioning of the capitals. These elements could only be built over time.

Buganda, Rwanda, Burundi, and Bunyoro were, over most of the nineteenth century, the most expansive states in the region, and the developments within those states in the nineteenth century had the most demonstrative effect on the shape of the region in the twentieth century. But there were, in the wider region, more than two hundred other domains, virtually all with political institutions similar to those of the larger kingdoms. Some of these smaller states went through processes of political transformation in the nineteenth century, enhancing power within their own immediate arena. Others lost control of the centrifugal forces within and became dependencies of distant organizing centres. The capitals and courts of the major kingdoms began to attract dissidents and insurgents from nearby states, and these adventurous visitors sought assistance from their more powerful hosts in overthrowing authority in their home area. Repeated hundreds of times, these initiatives contributed to the weakening of the smaller states and the expansion of influence of the larger ones.

From the middle of the nineteenth century, the distinction between larger and smaller domains became greater, as the major states in the region gathered in the new resources from outside the region – trade goods, including firearms, European, Arab, and Swahili merchants and adventurers, and Christian and Islamic missionaries. The smaller domains of the Lakes Plateau came more and more to resemble 'gardens' to be cultivated for servants, slaves, and tribute by the larger kingdoms, or simply as tramping grounds for the mobile forces from within and without the region.

Production and extraction

This last observation moves us some way from the view of the region simply as a political terrain. We begin to observe that, in the nineteenth century, the predominant 'business of the state' was the aggregation of production and exchange, whether this process of accumulation was evolving within the framework of the old domain or whether evolving beyond the effective administrative boundaries of the state. The control of production and exchange was very much at issue as states such as Rwanda, Buganda, Burundi, and Bunyoro enlarged their domains and expanded their range of influence in the nineteenth century.

Earlier, note was made of Mawanda's programme of expansion into

Kyaggwe. This eighteenth-century move was directed at productive regions lying beyond the control of the Buganda kingdom. Kyaggwe held bark-cloth, iron ore and iron-working artisans, and it held access to the productive islands of the northern Lake Victoria area. The Buvuma Islands, offshore from Kyaggwe, were well linked into the trading networks of the eastern Lake Victoria area. The aggregation of productive forces, materials, skills, labour, and access to, or control over, the nodes of regional trade circuits were among the main items of business of the precolonial Lakes Plateau state.

Extractions from routinely administered areas and extractions from outside the domain brought wealth into the courts and fed the governing regime. In the nineteenth century, extractions of tribute, with the opposed resistance to the extractions of the state, linked regions of production and regions of consumption in a broad network of 'conflict-driven' relations, while overlaying and affecting – and often deforming – the precolonial market networks that spanned the Lakes Plateau region. The interplay of state extraction and the resistance of producers and producing areas to coercion by the tribute-taking state is most apparent, in the nineteenth century, in the domain of food production, food exchange, and food consumption. Paradoxically, within this region of apparent, and much noted, abundance, the control of supplies of food appears to have moved to the centre of relations among states and relations between the state and producers.[3]

In the routinely administered zones of the region's kingdoms, specialized and non-specialized production generated foodstuffs, along with arrays of other goods, for the courts and capitals. The collections by the state were both regular and irregular in terms of period. Contributions to the courts and capitals were expected from season to season. On the other hand, particular occasions, such as the sending off of military expeditions, various court ceremonies and entertainments, and intermittent food shortages, occasioned special collections of foodstuffs for redistribution through the courts and capitals.

In Buganda, it appears that a form of governmental farm evolved under appointed officials who were charged with responsibility for provisioning the courts of specific chiefs and for provisioning the palace of the kabaka.[4] In Rwanda, Nkore, Karagwe, and Burundi, royal herds – part of the stock of wealth of the state – provided meat, fats, milk, and butter for the coteries of lords, officials, and their clienteles and their households. All this production was, essentially, 'administered production'; that is, organized

3. This is taken up in some detail in D. W. Cohen, 1983. Material presented here is drawn from that study, presented in June 1981 to a conference organized in Naivasha, Kenya by the United Nations University.

4. It is hoped that a paper will soon be finished on this subject. The outlines of this pattern of provisioning are glimpsed through the screen of a number of sources.

and regulated by the state. Administrative farms were capable of producing immense supplies of foods and beverages at relatively short notice. There is an implication that production levels were geared high to meet momentary demands and that there was, by necessity, an overcapacity in the catering organizations.[5]

PLATE 11.3 *Treasure house, and regalia of King Rumanyika of Karagwe*

Programmes of extraction extended beyond these specialized food production sections into external arenas and into 'tribute-taking'. There may be value in viewing the economic activities of the state on a continuum. The transition in extraction from occasional collection towards regularized collections may have marked the process of incorporation of frontier areas and entirely new areas of production into the Lakes region state. An example of a pattern of collection falling along the middle of such a continuum is the extraction of production from central Busoga by agents of Buganda.[6] These were not regularly administered extractions but they were sufficiently controlled and routine to require no military force and to

5. J. Tosh, 1980, p. 9, has, in a recent article, directed attention to the means by which significant surpluses of food were achieved in pre-colonial Africa and challenges the view that the surpluses which supported specialist artisans, hunters, trading caravans, and courts were just the normal surplus of subsistence production.

6. The Buganda collection are treated in S. Kiwanuka, 1972, pp. 139–53; J. Kasirye, 1959; F. P. B. Nayenga, 1976; D. W. Cohen, 1977.

enable them to produce foodstuffs in a prepared form in enormous amounts. There is a suggestion of prior notification and prior preparation. In these extractions from central Busoga, the most common commodity extracted was dried bananas (Lusoga: *mutere*) transported both as meal and as sun-dried cakes. The routine and frequent tribute collection from a specific area would have forced production in the tributary zone far beyond the expected consumption requirements of the producers themselves. In a sense, this tributary zone production encompassed 'defensive surpluses'. Such surpluses would have given the impression to early European travellers in the region of unending abundance and self-sufficiency of the little producer,[7] alongside the more familiar image of sumptuous conditions in the courts. What these travellers would have missed was the structure of 'defensive surplus' in which the effective costs of production of whatever 'reciprocal' goods and services the tribute-taking state offered its tributary zones were transferred to the tribute-producers. These 'defensive surpluses' did not provide security to the producers themselves, for the tribute-taking state in the nineteenth-century Great Lakes region was well positioned to seize these surpluses if they were, for whatever reason, withheld.

Another example located near the middle of our continuum of types of extraction was the collection of fine salt from the Lake George salt source, taken off to the remote, yet regulative (and sometimes protective) courts of Toro and Bunyoro.[8] Further along the continuum were the irregular and unexpected collections of tribute from more remote regions.[9] Here, one might postulate that such foods as *mutere* and other foods and beverages requiring considerable effort in harvest, preparation, and transport were much less significant. In these remote zones, extractions appear to have been more military in character. Armed bands, if not major expeditions, tramped through an area, gathering available stocks of tribute, especially cattle and humans, but also artisans' and marketeers' stocks of ironware and bark-cloth. This was predacity on an immense scale. One military expedition organized in Buganda moved into Busoga, camping in one area for several months. Smaller collection parties were sent hither and yon. In this case, the sources suggest that the tribute-collecting army from Buganda was stationed in the country long enough to force up the production and preparation of foodstuffs and preparation beyond the typical military booty. The tribute taken was consumed by the occupying expeditionary force and some was eventually returned to the courts of Buganda. What almost certainly happened in this case was that the Ganda army remained in Busoga too briefly to stimulate or force a permanent expansion in the production of foodstuffs and other commodities in the region they occupied.

7. For example, see F.D. Lugard, 1893, Vol. 1, p. 366; H.H. Johnston, 1902, Vol. 1, p. 248, and H.M. Stanley, 1880, pp. 142–3.
8. E.M. Kamuhangire, 1972a, 1972b.
9. D.W. Cohen, 1977, pp. 73–80.

But they were there long enough to dismantle a substantial part of the productive organization of central Busoga – which would require many years to recover. Similar large-scale tribute-gathering expeditions were organized from the capital region of Rwanda in the nineteenth century, organized to extract valuable commodities and cattle from the unadministered areas to the north and west, including those around the western shores of Lake Kivu.[10] In time, both production and marketing in these areas were stultified and Rwanda had to look still further afield for new sources of production.

One element of these military expeditions was the establishment of fairly stable transit routes into the target regions. In south-western Busoga, two or three polities were essentially provisioning stations for the Buganda expeditions. These small states were able to produce army provisions in immense quantities at short notice. These provisioning states apparently drew supplies from contiguous areas. By the 1860s, areas just to the north of the Buganda transit route were abandoned. They ceased to offer any productive capacity for the provisioning states, for the Buganda kingdom, or for a resident population.[11] Over several decades, the large-scale tribute extraction organized by the larger kingdoms, such as Buganda, would have had the effect of establishing a significant distinction between areas in which external demand for foodstuffs stimulated production and areas in which external demand weakened or destroyed productive organization.

Sources on the nineteenth century indicate that the extractive programmes of the major kingdoms in the region were actively resisted in the areas of production. In northern and eastern Busoga, Buganda military expeditions were resisted, and occasionally turned back, in the nineteenth century. To expand its collections from the rich areas to the east, Buganda welcomed opportunities to acquire firearms, actively involved itself in local civil conflicts, inserting dependent princes on the stools of a number of states, increased the scale of its military expeditions, and moved farther afield as extractions from the old productive zones collapsed. Resistance to Buganda extractions in the Buvuma Islands was witnessed by H. M. Stanley during his visit to Buganda in 1875.[12] The peoples and polities along the western and north-western frontier of the Rwanda state resisted Rwandan extractions through much of the nineteenth century.[13]

10. D. S. Newbury, 1975, pp. 155–73; Anon., nd; M. C. Newbury, 1975.
11. This is briefly discussed in D. W. Cohen, 1977, pp. 116–77. It is pursued in the present writer's forthcoming study of Busoga, 1700–1900.
12. H. M. Stanley, 1880, pp. 304–42.
13. See note 10 above.

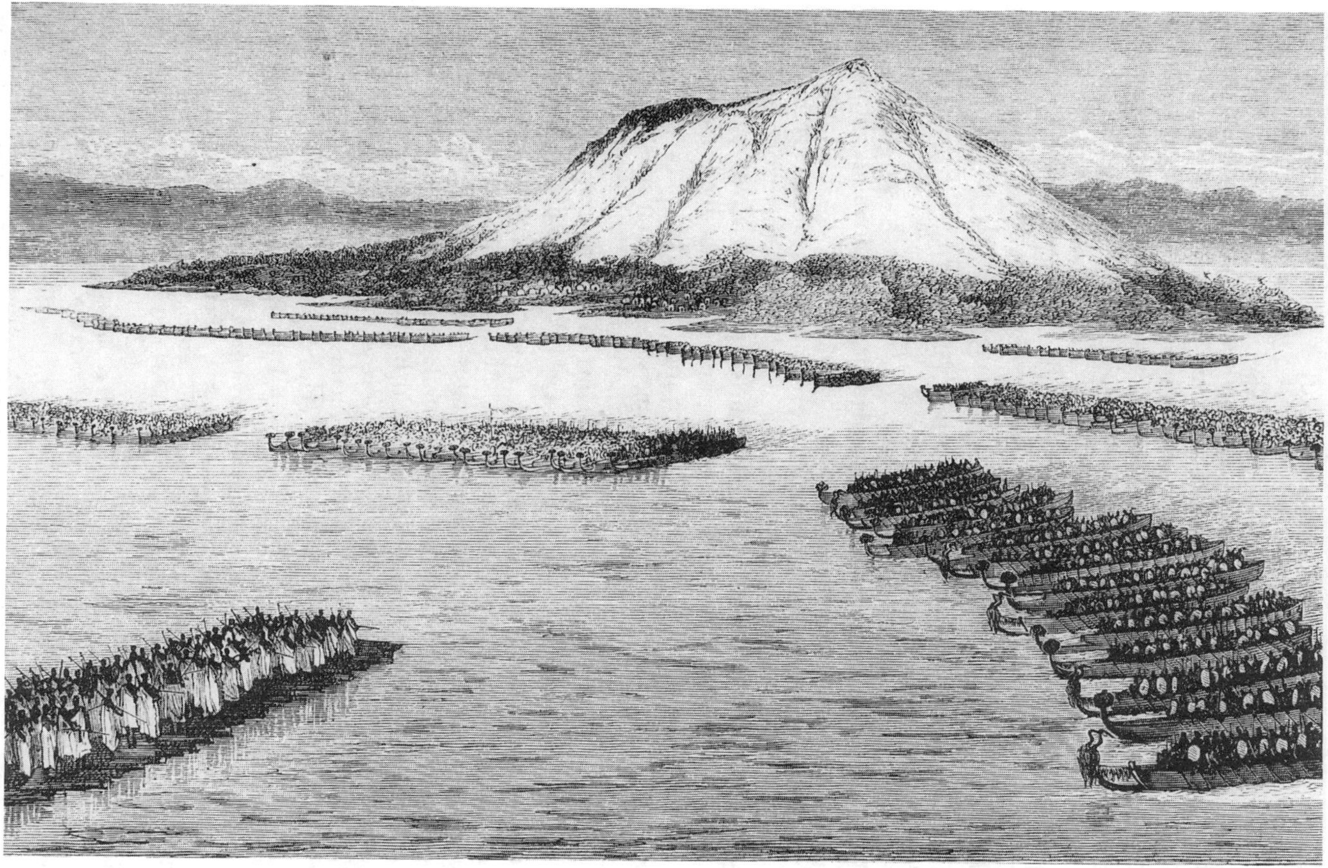

PLATE 11.4 *Naval battle on Lake Victoria between the Baganda and the people of the Buvuma Islands, 1875*

Coercion, violence and the market

The effects of resistance to the almost insatiable demands of the larger states in the Lakes region in the nineteenth century included the decline of productivity in nearby tributary areas and the consequent shift back to the courts of some of the costs of surplus production of foodstuffs – since more elaborate means had to be evolved to maintain the high levels of tribute from beyond the regular producing areas within the existing domains. Resistance, of course, raised the levels of violence in the wider region and resistance appears to have destabilized long-operating trade and market routines organized around and through Lakes Victoria, Kyoga, Lutanzige and Kivu, along with the salt lakes of south-western present-day Uganda, which had generated surpluses and had organized exchanges over a very long period.[14] We can draw a simple portrait of the region in the nineteenth century that highlights the much increased competition between two systems of regional exchange, one based on military force and political coercion, the other based on the market. In the third quarter of the nineteenth century, the Great Lakes region experienced the refinement of the system of coercion rather more than, and at the expense of, the system of marketing. Leaders and courts appear to have abandoned a dependence on markets for the intra-regional supply of goods.

In the nineteenth century, productive areas of the Lakes region became targets of two or three tribute-collecting states simultaneously and they thus became arenas of intense conflict. Both the older Bunyoro state and the newer Toro kingdom forwarded claims to tribute from the saltworks of south-western present-day Uganda. The salt wealth of these two states rose and fell periodically in the century.[15] The Budiope area of northern Busoga and the Bugerere area to the west of the Nile became simultaneous targets of the Buganda and Bunyoro states, which sought to capture the grain, tubers, cattle, bananas, and manufactures from these areas. The resistance of Bugerere and Budiope held back the incorporation of their production into the Buganda and Bunyoro states throughout most of the century.[16] Needless to say, the simultaneous invasion of these productive areas by Buganda and Bunyoro was a central part of the wider conflict of

14. Three interlayering or overlapping circuits of market exchange are noted in the pre-colonial Lakes Plateau region: an eastern lake circuit extending from the Buvuma Islands east and south around Lake Victoria into Usukuma; a Bunyoro–Kyoga circuit extending from Mount Elgon westwards into the grasslands of western Uganda; and a Kivu circuit, extending from the rimland of the present-day Zaire forest around the lakes of the Western rift into Burundi, Rwanda, and the western grasslands of present-day Uganda. See Fig. 11.2. For valuable work on the trade circuits of the region, see J. Tosh, 1970; A. D. Roberts, 1970b; C. M. Good, 1972; B. Turyahikayo-Rugyeme, 1976; E. M. Kamuhangire, 1976; D. Newbury, 1980; J. P. Chrétien, 1981.

15. E. M. Kamuhangire, 1972b.

16. The situation of Bugerere is most instructive. A brief, clear discussion is presented by A. F. Robertson, 1978, pp. 45–7.

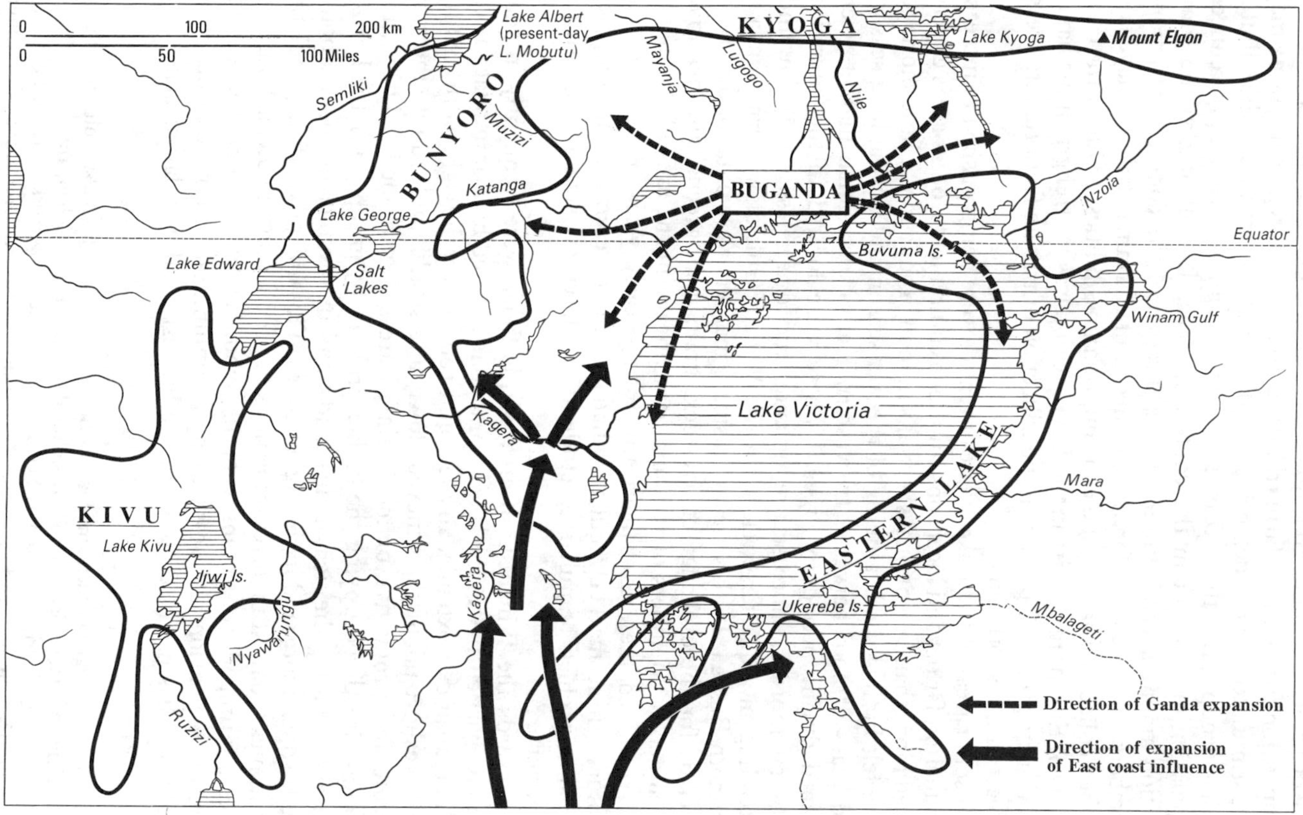

FIG. 11.2 *Trade circuits of the Great Lakes region (after D. Cohen)*

Bunyoro and Buganda over much of the century. In some areas, the competition for 'rights to farm tribute' among several regional powers may have stimulated various defensive and alliance strategies among the tribute-paying groups. In other areas, such conflicts may have simply reduced population and output in the contested arena. In still others, the competition among several powers for resources and the competition among members of the courts for the privileges of 'farming' tribute may have pushed collections far beyond consumption possibilities.[17] One of the early effects of European activity in the Lakes region was to strengthen the hands of the major regional powers in the collection of tribute from remote areas, at least in the short run.

If some areas of the Lakes Plateau region were being pushed to increase production far beyond local consumption requirements, other areas experienced more than exceptional shortfalls in food production. These shortages were felt both at the beginning of the wet season and during long seasons and years of poor harvests. In western Kenya, occasional markets were opened during periods of crisis.[18] These were located in the interstices between moister, more secure uplands and drier, less secure lowlands extending in a quarter-circle from the Winam Gulf of western Kenya to southern Busoga. In this area, occasional markets were organized in times of crisis for the exchange of livestock, grain, fish, greens, and manufactured goods. Members of the dominant lineage in the area of the market site regulated these exchanges and by the early years of the twentieth century, these market regulators had begun to resemble the 'big men' or 'almost chiefs' familiar to students of different parts of the African continent.

Towards the Winam Gulf area, staple foods were frequently in short supply, particularly in the lake littoral zone affected by a unimodal pattern of rainfall and an extended dry season. From at least the eighteenth century, the lakeshore populations moved slowly and steadily upland into the more secure and productive bimodal rainfall areas, constrained only by those groups already occupying the higher ground, by groups over the horizon routinely raiding the rich, higher lands, and by insufficient organization to wedge open more land in the higher zones. This uplands shift in population continues today. It involves transitions in production and diet among those pressing upland, the compression of population in the higher elevations, and the expansion of Luo-speaking communities. The process of upland migration has produced some of the highest rural population densities in

17. Court intrigue in such kingdoms as Buganda may have been a stimulus to extractive campaigns in remote places in the pre-colonial era. See D. W. Cohen, 1983.

18. M. J. Hay, 1975, pp. 100–1. See also the forthcoming work of L. D. Schiller, on Gem and Kano in western Kenya, and R. Herring, 'The Jolue Before 1900', forthcoming. The present writer, working in Siaya, and Priscilla O. Were, working in Samia, have collected some supporting evidence.

Africa in the twentieth century, contributing to the exhaustion of soil and the depletion of forest and woodland reserves.[19]

Those who did not migrate upland continued to suffer the shortfalls of a fragile agricultural system. The occasional markets offered some relief, permitting the exchange of cattle, grazed in the lowlands, for grain and root crops grown more successfully at the higher elevations. Since, in the lowlands, the period of hunger was also the period of heaviest labour demand for cultivating and sowing of grains in the first rains, the occasional markets provided a means of overcoming rather quickly the excessively long dry season or an earlier short harvest. Cattle maintained by the people of the lowlands constituted, through regional exchange, the means of agricultural and nutritional continuity. The so-called 'cattle complex' had an immediate logic for the lowland people, providing them with a means of accumulation of convertible wealth.

Trading circuits

Fragile agriculture in Rwanda was offset by inter-zonal, inter-ethnic, and inter-class exchange.[20] Complementarities in production and consumption among regions of surplus and regions of shortfall created a network of communication, exchange, and interaction that reinforced the broader field upon which the Rwandan state was organized. Such routine exchanges may have permitted the retention of specialized local economies, as well as ethnic-specific or class-specific dietary patterns, reinforcing the social class distinctions in the western Lakes Plateau region.

Rwanda participated in wider extractions through the frequent raiding of rich areas to the north, north-west, and west, and some of these areas were brought under Rwanda's regular administration during the nineteenth century. Rwanda also participated in a trade system centred on Lake Kivu. Woven bracelets manufactured in Butembo – to the west of Lake Kivu – were carried by traders into the markets along the Lake Kivu littoral and the markets on the island of Ijwi. These *butega* of Butembo began to acquire the characteristics of a currency and, by the second half of the nineteenth century, were widely used in exchange in the Kivu zone, enriching marketeers from Ijwi, and bracelet manufacturers in Butembo, while making possible exchanges of cattle, foodstuffs, and other goods over a wide region of Kivu and Rwanda, with the effect, perhaps, of stimulating production throughout the area.[21]

There is evidence of similar growth in an exchange circuit connecting

19. More work needs to be done on twentieth-century social and economic processes in western Kenya, with particular attention to demography, rural economy, and public health. For similar processes in Tanzania, see H. Kjekshus, 1977.

20. H. L. Vis, C. Yourassowsky and H. van der Borght, 1975.

21. L. S. Newbury, nd.

areas on the eastern side of Lake Victoria. There was, first of all, an extensive network of exchange in foodstuffs and other commodities in place by the beginning of the nineteenth century. It had probably been active for centuries. This circuit connected the coasts of Buganda and southern Busoga and the Buvuma Islands in the north with the shores and 'interior' of present-day western Kenya and with the south lake regions of Buzinza, Usukuma, and Unyamwezi, in present-day Tanzania. Apparently central to the nineteenth-century configuration of this circuit was the agricultural revolution which has been noted as coming to the Bukerebe island state in the south lake area in the late eighteenth century or early nineteenth century.[22] The Bukerebe state organized the production of several new crops, including maize and cassava, and introduced to regional production new strains of sorghum and millet. Institutional changes – including the organization of unfree labour (introduced by trade from the mainland) – generated a substantial leap in output. Mainland areas offered markets for Bukerebe's surpluses of food, and Buzinza metalware and Usukuma cattle were sucked into the regional trade circuit through Bukerebe. The peoples of Buzinza and Usukuma looked to the Bukerebe surpluses and the Bukerebe marketeers as means of resolution of periodic shortfalls in the local food supply. Occasionally, it seems, this dependence led to accusations against Bukerebe traders of profiteering from the misery of Usukuma farmers by simply raising the prices of Bukerebe food transported to Usukuma during famines.[23]

If Bukerebe traders held a predominant middleman position in the south, Basuba intermediaries dominated transport and exchange along the more northerly reaches of this eastern lake trade circuit. With exceptional skill and courage, the Basuba navigated the Lake Victoria waters, transporting salt, slaves, dried bananas, grain, beans, livestock, fish, and iron over a great area, connecting the Bukerebe markets in the south to the south Busoga and Buvuma markets in the north.[24]

The monopoly of exchange that the Basuba developed over the northern sectors of the eastern lake system in the nineteenth century rather paralleled the monopolies developed by Bagabo and Bashingo traders in the region of the salt lakes in western present-day Uganda.[25] Each of these groups constructed a well-organized exchange diaspora encompassing political control over production and marketing of salt under the remote licence and protection of the Nyoro and Toro courts. In both the salt lakes and eastern lake circuit, the exchange diaspora evolved its monopoly away from the regular purview of the Lakes Plateau state, did not utilize the model of the state in evolving its marketing network, and only came to accom-

22. G. W. Hartwig, 1976, pp. 62–83, 104–11.
23. ibid., p. 107.
24. M. Kenny, 1979.
25. E. M. Kamuhangire, 1972b.

modate the demands of states of the region when, occasionally, their regions of production, their markets, and their fleets came under attack.

The Bukerebe trading system – the southern sector of the eastern lake circuit – was sufficiently attractive to other trading groups to encourage Waswahili and Arab traders operating in the Unyamwezi area to draw up the filaments of Bukerebe carriage and exchange. Then, through encouraging the production of slaves and ivory in the Bukerebe market area, these newcomers ultimately eclipsed the Bukerebe traders and their food-based exchange system in the south lake region. It was through this southern displacement that Waswahili and Arab traders and their merchandise first touched the Great Lakes region. The merchandise, first, then the traders after, plunged into the markets and states of the Lakes Plateau, moving along the same deeply cut routes west of Lake Victoria that were utilized by the salt lakes traders. Perhaps more important than the merchandise they introduced was the market for slaves and ivory they carried into the central part of the Lakes region. Firearms were exchanged for slaves and ivory. Eventually, Islamic and Christian teachers and European explorers, adventurers, and agents followed these same footpaths as the traders, creating new forces of change in the wider Lakes Plateau region.

While the east coast traffic was extending northward through the western grasslands towards the populations and capitals around the northern side of Lake Victoria, navies from Buganda began to cut away sections of the Suba and Bukerebe monopolies to the east and south, introducing the possibility of active, direct relations between the Buganda heartland and Arab and Waswahili traders on the southern side of the lake. Thus, while Bukerebe influence was being displaced from the south by parties from Unyamwezi and the east coast, Bukerebe influence was being supplanted from the east and north by Buganda's expansionist programmes. An interesting contrast can be drawn between Buganda and Ukerebe in the nineteenth century. As in Bukerebe, Buganda agriculture had been transformed, at one point, towards the production of quite exceptional surpluses of foodstuffs. Unlike Buganda's surpluses, however, the Bukerebe surpluses were destined for areas of quite extreme scarcity, yet areas that could produce what Bukerebe required and was unable to produce itself. In Buganda, surplus production served as social and political aliment within the state, rather than as a stock of wealth to be exchanged in areas of complementary production. Further, the well-developed transport organization created by the Bukerebe state and by the Basuba was deeply cut by Buganda penetration, but this was a penetration by military force rather than by a new marketing organization.

There was, in the nineteenth century, another extensive exchange network centring on the general Bunyoro area, extending to the north and north-west into the Acholi region and West Nile, to the east through the Lake Kyoga area to the slopes of Mount Elgon, and to the south-west through the salt lakes into the Kivu area. Ironware and salt were the evident mainstays of this trading circuit, yet foodstuffs and livestock were probably crucial to the elaboration and maintenance of the system. In one zone north of Lake Kyoga, the Langi produced planned surpluses of food, particularly sesame, for trade.[26] In the nineteenth century, this sesame was destined for Bunyoro to the west, for exchange for iron hoes, which in turn contributed to the expansion of sesame production in the Lango area. Careful study has shown that such surplus production probably involved an array of innovations and refinements in production, land use, cropping, planting and sowing cycles, and labour, in order to maximize output.[27] Here was something of an agricultural transformation, in some ways comparable to that evolving nearly simultaneously in Bukerebe and still another in the Ijwi Islands of Lake Kivu.[28]

One might postulate that individuals and groups participating in the exchange circuit of western present-day Uganda saw the readiness of the Langi to increase sesame output for the market in the nineteenth century as a means of, first, stimulating the trade in ironware to the east – overcoming the precedence in that area of the ironware produced in Samia near the Lake Victoria coast (close by the present Kenya–Uganda border) and thereby stimulating further growth of iron production in Bunyoro; second, forging deeper inter-regional relations between Bunyoro and Lango, relations, perhaps, of dependence or unequal exchange; and, third, creating wealth through the expansion of such commerce, which would in the second half of the nineteenth century pull in valuable ivory from the north-western foothills of Mount Elgon.

Throughout the first three-quarters of the nineteenth century, the western present-day Uganda exchange circuit was the basis of influence of the Bunyoro heartland over a very broad region, even during the periods when conflicts internal to the Bunyoro state enveloped and weakened the power of Bunyoro's monarchs. In such areas as Busoga, there were, in the nineteenth century, reorientations of exchange from the older Lake Victoria markets to the more recently established sites of regular exchange in the Lake Kyoga basin, with Nyoro iron pushing back Samia iron from the markets of northern and north-eastern Busoga. The Lake Kyoga basin attracted new settlement in the nineteenth century, with production from these areas oriented to the Nyoro market. This expansion of the Kyoga circuit complemented the process of population shift northwards in Busoga and allowed a much-harassed population to move farther from the arena of Buganda tribute-gathering adventures. Later, this arm of the Bunyoro or western trade circuit extending through the Kyoga region was quite

26. J. Tosh, 1978.

27. The implication here is that this was a social revolution, worked out by household, or community by community, in the reorganization of social relations of work, task definition, and time.

28. See G. W. Hartwig, 1976, for Bukerebe; and L. S. Newbury, nd, for Ijwi.

resilient in the face of British pressure to convert the population to cotton production.

In the west, the Lake Kyoga trade joined with the trade that passed through the grasslands of western present-day Uganda and centred on the salt production of the south-west present-day Uganda lakes. Agents of the Bunyoro kingdom, and of its tributaries, levied taxes on the production, carriage, and marketing of goods, foodstuffs, and livestock, and with these entered the market on their own account.[29] The rulers of Bunyoro and Toro played robust roles within the exchange economy of the western part of the Lakes region without destroying the routines of traffic and exchange. While some of the historical literature on western present-day Uganda portrays Bunyoro as a pastoralist kingdom and warfare state, it appears that the Bunyoro state was extensively integrated in the regional market, and very dependent on conditions in that market for supplies to its courts and for articulation of control and sway in remote areas. By contrast, Buganda in the nineteenth century looks like the classic warfare or tribute state with no reconciliation between the processes of elaborating a complex internal bureaucracy on the one hand and elaborating the infrastructure of external markets on the other.

If it can be said that in the nineteenth century the activities of the Buganda state tended to deform or destroy sub-regional market activities in the Lakes region, it can also be said that at the same time Buganda began to participate more actively in what might be termed international exchanges extending from the Victoria lake-shores to the East African coast. The differences between Buganda and Bunyoro in respect to existing market opportunities in the nineteenth century are perhaps not so simply perceived after all. The key difference may be located in how each state utilized varying strategies to take advantage of distinct *levels* of market activity in the region. While Bunyoro participated within the regional market system in ways that strengthened and extended the system, Buganda routinely sought military solutions to its perceived shortages of local commodities and services. At the same time Buganda joined the broader international market steadily reaching into the Lakes region from the East African coast, participating in ways that strengthened and extended the east coast system into the interior, managing, to a remarkable extent, to exclude Bunyoro from participating in this 'higher-level' system of exchange. Indeed, in the last decade of the century, Buganda managed to array the forces associated with the east coast market directly against Bunyoro, with the result both of reducing Bunyoro's influence in the region forever and of cutting away the 'northern factor' – Anglo-Egyptian and Sudanic interests – from the region.

Central to this 'higher-level' exchange system extending down from the Great Lakes region to the East African coast was the exchange of ivory

29. E. M. Kamuhangire, 1972b.

and slaves, gathered in the Lakes region, for firearms imported from the coast through the Zanzibari trade network. Carried along with the firearms were small quantities of goods destined for, essentially, aristocratic consumption, including textiles, bangles, tableware, and, later, books. For much of the century, the Buganda court was able to control the distribution of such imports within the kingdom and beyond, increasing the sway of the court (and therefore the influence of all the outsiders who visited there) in the life of the wider society. Importantly, tastes were 'extroverted' in a period preceding the penetration of the region by Europeans, since the Baganda managed, sometimes consciously, sometimes unconsciously, the incorporation of their society in the general imperium of the United Kingdom.

Growth of inequalities and tension

In the last quarter of the nineteenth century, new tastes and consumption pressures from below the aristocratic elements facilitated European influence in the life not only of Buganda, but also of most of the wider region. For some fifty years, firearms acquired by the most powerful states had increased their advantages over tributary areas and, as elsewhere in Africa, had permitted the concentration of politico-military power in the hands of narrowed sections of the region's population. Inequalities, most notable in slave-gathering expeditions but everywhere important, hardened throughout the Great Lakes region in the last few decades of the century. Thus, when Europeans entered into the region's life in some numbers, their support was sought not only by the strong, and increasingly powerful centres, but also by the weak and helpless.

If the eighteenth century was seen to close around the many efforts of parties and forces here and there to resist and overthrow the rulers of states in the Lakes Plateau, so also we see evidence of a new wave of resistance and conflict in the last two or three decades of the nineteenth century. Evidently, in the last third of the century, people were restive over the growing force and command concentrated in the capital regions and the distributed provincial courts of the Lakes Plateau kingdoms. East and west of Buganda, small states resisted many of the tributary campaigns of the Buganda state. In 1875, H. M. Stanley witnessed the disaster of Buganda's campaign against the Buvuma Islands. Even where the larger state brought swift defeat to its target region, parties in the tributaries sabotaged the regular deliveries of tribute to the conqueror.[30] In Bunyoro, Rwanda, and Buganda, and in the small Busoga states, common folk resisted the exactions of the capitals and courts, often by moving to areas more remote from the reach of routine collection, or to areas offering greater opportunities for acquiring land, office, and authority, or, as in the present-day Kenya–

30. This is spoken of in a number of Buganda and Busoga sources.

Uganda borderland, through concentrating and entrenching their settlements as defensive villages.

In the Busoga area, there are thousands of stories of little migrations from state to state, common folk seeking refuge or new opportunities, and there are stories of individuals moving through several domains in a single lifetime. The stories suggest that 'opportunity-seeking' had, by the second quarter of the nineteenth century, come to redefine the relations of individual and household to the state in respect to land, service, and authority.[31] The nineteenth-century context was one of considerable individual and small-group mobility in Busoga. The court, as one opportunity niche, held a focal position in the lives of people whether in a particular domain or outside it, but this focality did not ensure the court's authority. Indeed, throughout the nineteenth century, the typical Busoga court was undermined in its efforts to sustain its authority or to expand its domain by the readiness of countless individuals to abandon their patrons and land so as to seek more attractive opportunities elsewhere. It is possible that during this period, and over issues such as these, an evolved concept of 'state' or 'kingdom' became a significant part of popular discourse. To an extent, this pattern of response of the wider community to authority may have balanced off the growth of force at the capitals through the monopolization of firearms and the arming of courtiers. Here and there, this distancing of central political authority may have facilitated significant shifts in market relations and productive activities; in particular, local spheres of economic activity became significantly detached from the apparatus of the state.

It is clear that, during the nineteenth century, resistance to organized political authority often meant enhancing, sometimes for only a short period, the authority of religious institutions. This tended to reinforce opposition between religious and political authority here and there across the Lakes region. The small community organized around the possessed child Womunafu in the Bunafu area of Busoga in the nineteenth century is an example of such opposition, or competition, among different complexes of authority. In Bunafu, the enclosure of Womunafu was for several decades outside of, and opposed to, the political world around. Yet, the ideas and institutions upon which Womunafu's authority was based were extensively shared by the political capitals nearby.[32] In Bushu, in the western part of the region, the competition between religious and political bases of authority was, to a considerable extent, resolved in the nineteenth century through the integration of opposed elements into a collection of ritual chiefships.[33] In Rwanda, in Bunyoro, and in south-western present-day Uganda, *kubandwa* ideas and organization had long provided complexes of opposition to the authority of political capitals, a critically important

31. See D. W. Cohen, forthcoming.
32. D. W. Cohen, 1977.
33. R. M. Packard, 1981.

plane opposed to the principles and activities of the state and from which the penetration of the state was substantially excluded. At times, *kubandwa* organizations were sufficiently strong to challenge and overthrow existing political authority. In the nineteenth century, perhaps the most substantial of all known *kubandwa* movements focused on the female deity Nyabingi. The Nyabingi movement emerged in opposition to the Rwanda state, which was formalizing its influence beyond the old administrative region in the Rwanda centre, particularly extending to the north and to the west. In the present-day Zaire–Uganda borderland, in Kigezi, and in parts of Nkore, followers of Nyabingi organized resistance to the extension of the Rwanda state into their worlds. Towards the end of the nineteenth century, Nyabingi became a focus of resistance to political authority more generally and to European colonial activity as it was felt by peoples of the region.[34]

Conclusion

The Great Lakes region in the nineteenth century was not so much a neat matrix of centralized polities as a large arena of conflict and struggle among varying interests and forces evolving both within and beyond the particular complex of polities. At one level, states competed for the control of tributary agricultural zones, and specialized resources such as salt, cattle, and iron, as well as access to, and control over, systems and channels of distribution. The competition was not only between states but also between states and organizations and enterprises constructed very differently from the polities of the area.

At another level, common folk here and there across the region sought to define through both participation and resistance the political, social, and economic space in which to pursue security and opportunity. For individuals and households across the region, the nineteenth-century state in the Lakes region often showed more of its extractive than its protective face. The responses of peoples throughout the region varied according to their limitations and opportunities. They included the reorientation of production and marketing away from the demands of the state, the evacuation of areas under excessive pressure from outside, the joining of new religious communities, the search for secure refuges, and the support of efforts to overthrow existing authority. The world of the Great Lakes region in the nineteenth century was not simply a world of states, large and small. It was also a world in which individuals and households were in innumerable small, sometimes undramatic ways, altering their orientations to state authority, to service, to production, and to the market.

Our line of vision into the domain of everyday life in the nineteenth-century Lakes region is considerably obscured by the passage of time. But the lines of change and the forces of change noted throughout the region

34. I. Berger, 1981.

in production and consumption, in commerce, in the relations among states, and in the relations between common folk and the courts, brought significant tensions into the relations of everyday life, penetrating the household, and setting in motion a chain of pressures and changes many of which would be read, in later decades, as consequences of European colonialism.

12

The Congo* Basin and Angola

J. L. VELLUT

The area with which we are concerned is broadly bounded by the Atlantic coast on the west, Lake Tanganyika and the Nile–Zaire ridge on the east, the Ubangui savannas on the north, and the plateau separating the Zaire and Zambezi basins to the south. The period we shall deal with cannot be limited to a single theme. Contrary to the common belief, the history of the years 1800–80 is not a matter only or mainly of long-distance trade and links with the outside world (the economy of Central African communities at this period was still based more on production than on trade). Nor can the precolonial nineteenth century be regarded as an era of widespread violence, because of the slave trade, civil strife, etc.: the commonplace belief that Africa was racked by incessant 'tribal warfare' overlooks the basic fact that the bulk of the peoples in the area led peaceful lives as producers, steadily improving their farming methods, bettering their environment and exporting the produce of food-gathering. Finally, the history of the nineteenth century is not to be reduced to purely political history concerned with despotic kingdoms and states: if there is a political feature common to the Central African communities of the period around 1800, it is more likely to be the much disputed quest for equilibrium and accommodation between powers derived from different sources.

An historical account of nineteenth-century Central Africa must in fact satisfy several requirements. It must describe the ordinary life and aspirations of the societies in this enormous area at the time. This would bring out the continuity between the 1800s and the more distant past: the changes, although noticeable, were slow.

At the same time, the history of Central Africa in the nineteenth century is characterized by breaks with the past. After all, in the years 1800–80 the area was more a part of the world trading network than ever before. The impact of the world economic situation, or of some specific sectors of it, was making itself felt: in some areas it influenced social and political history, giving a noticeable impetus to trade and offering new opportunities for stockpiling, while in others it restricted the process. The beginnings of a

* The name of the River Zaire customary in the nineteenth-century documents has been adopted in this chapter.

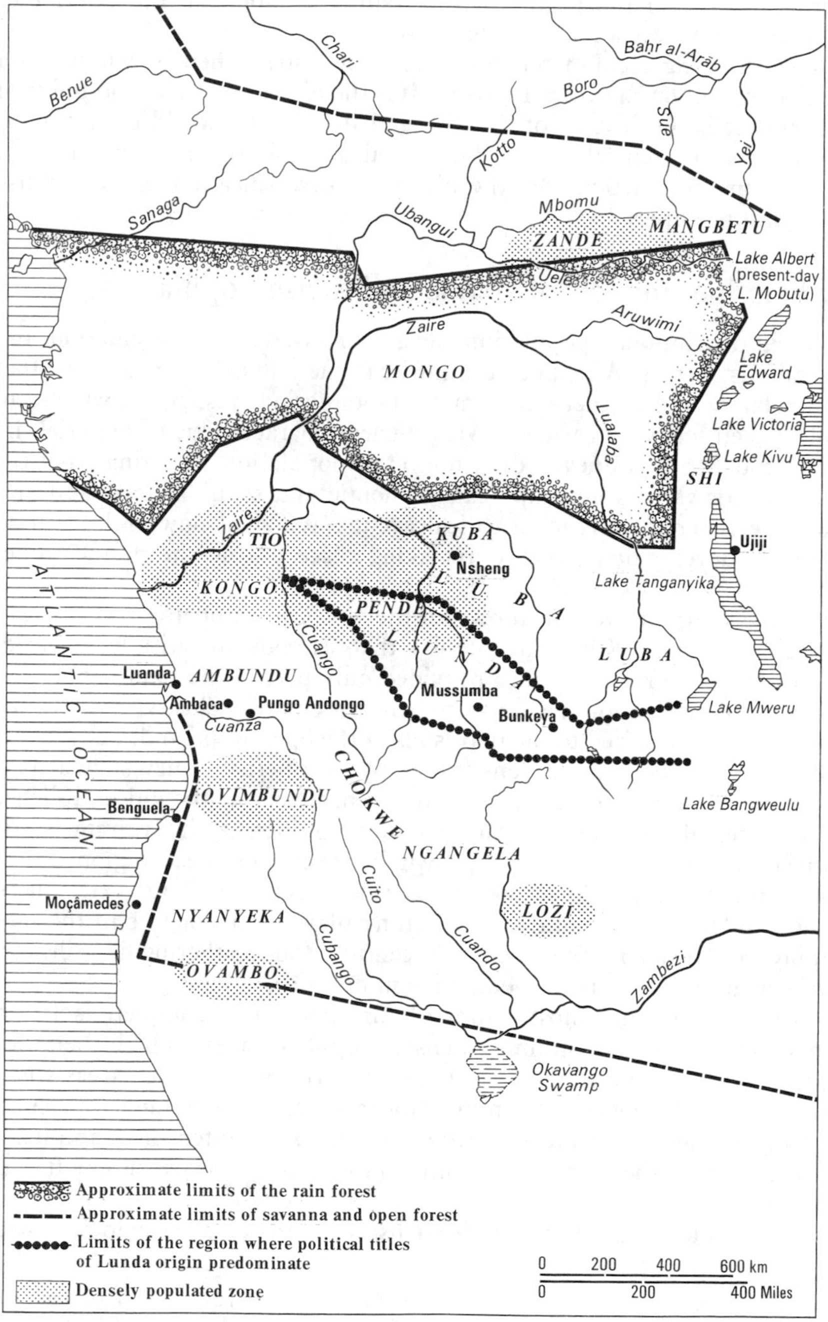

FIG. 12.1 *West Central Africa in the nineteenth century (after J. L. Vellut)*

European grip on the profits of the trading economy in the interior of Central Africa were already evident.

The following account centres around these main themes, which left a special imprint on the years 1800–80. It is the history of social and political changes. It is the history of the ebb and flow of the world economy, as experienced by Central Africa. There is also the slow-moving history of a civilization and, particularly, the history of diversification in making use of natural resources.

Production: models of sparse and dense populations

In their distribution, population behaviour, systems of production and aspirations, Central African communities in the years 1800–80 showed that they retained traits inherited from a remote period, vestiges of which can still be seen today. A basic and very ancient characteristic of material life in Central Africa is uneven distribution of population, resulting from the operation of various geographical, economic and social factors, and also from the repercussions of historical events. We shall now endeavour to trace the developments that were taking place during the period under consideration.

To the south of the rain-forest, in the vast area of open forest (*miombo* in Zaire, *mato de panda* in Angola) that extends to latitude 16–17°S, nineteenth-century agriculture provided only part of the food supply, for agricultural production was far from being intensive.[1] This type of farming was the one best suited to the poor soils of the open woodland, but it could only support a population density low by twentieth-century standards (a maximum of 8 per sq km). In the nineteenth century the old-established African cereals – eleusine ('finger millet'), millets and sorghum – still formed the bulk of the crops grown in several of these regions. As a complement to agriculture, food-gathering (nutrition plants, caterpillars, honey, rodents, etc.), hunting and fishing played a major role in the food supply: and even in the twentieth century food-gathering is still very widespread in these open woodland communities.

Sparse populations most commonly did not live in complete isolation. They were in contact with more densely populated areas, which shed their excess population on to the neighbouring territories. In some areas where the space available was very limited (for instance in the immediate vicinity of watercourses), agriculture became diversified and intensified, and led to polarization of the population, often near capital towns or chieftaincy centres.

The remote origin of these more densely populated areas coincides with

1. These open forests are the vestiges of old dry forest climaxes (*muhulu*). They are characterized by a high proportion of Zambezian species. See the works of F. Malaisse, especially F. Malaisse *et al*, 1972.

PLATE 12.1 *A village in Manyema, a north-eastern province of the Luba Empire, in the 1870s*

the expansion of agriculture in Central Africa. Thanks to archaeology, and later to the earliest written documents, some of these ancient areas can be identified, such as the settlement in what in the nineteenth century was an area of Luba chiefdoms in the Lualaba valley, or again in the Kongo region. For Angola we have some information (of a more recent period) from the missionaries or from tax records. At the beginning of the nineteenth century, for instance, on the very rough basis of recruitment into the armed forces, the Luanda authorities thought that the main centres of density were among the Ambundu in the Golungo and Ambaca areas (population: 60 000 and 37 000 respectively), and among the Ovimbundu of Bailundu (56 000) and Bié ('over 30 000').[2] In Zaire the high-density 'corridor' straddling the 5°S parallel, at the junction of the rain-forest and the savanna, was not demarcated until well into the twentieth century.[3]

Despite the absence of accurate data, several indications suggest that the development of densely populated areas became clear relatively recently, and that the nineteenth century in fact represented the peak of a trend that began only a few centuries earlier. Iron-working, a feature of Bantu agricultural systems, only became widespread from the fifteenth century onwards. Oral historical sources in Central Africa all agree in regarding the seventeenth and eighteenth centuries as a turning-point for the savanna and Great Lakes peoples: new lands were colonized, dynasties were founded, political titles proliferated and so on. Lastly, all the high-density centres in the region known in the nineteenth century had enriched their agriculture by the introduction of American varieties. This innovation led to an increase in yields, as arable land was used more intensively (in several high-density areas there were two or three harvests a year), and high-yield plants were introduced (e.g. cassava).

The chronology of these changes obviously cannot be traced in detail: depending on the region, they might have extended over more than two centuries (1600–1850). This is a rough estimate that can be pinpointed by some landmarks. Around 1800 all the American varieties (maize, cassava, sweet potatoes, beans, etc.) had no doubt not been adopted everywhere in the same way, but no area seems to have ignored them altogether. Moreover in some cases American plants had become so integrated that they were no longer regarded as foreign imports. Thus in the Kongo region we have for the lower Zaire river the first systematic inventory of a Central African flora (Tuckey expedition, 1818), which confirms the widespread use of the American varieties. In the colonial period, a detailed inventory of Kongo agriculture noted that several American imports (groundnuts, sweet potatoes, etc.) were perceived in the oral culture as of local origin as were

2. J. C. Feo Cardozo, 1825, p. 352 *et seq.* These figures are very doubtful. Towards 1850, L. Magyar gave a very different estimate of the Ovimbundu population (1 220 000). The location of the principal densely populated areas in well-known regions is, however, more reliable.

3. See P. Gourou, 1955.

yams or *voandzou*.[4] Elsewhere, however, proverbs and rites still serve as reminders that the foundation of African agriculture antedated the American borrowings in the eighteenth and nineteenth centuries. There is a Mongo proverb *bonkúfo áfókité ngàmomá* ('sweet cassava never becomes like yam'), i.e., a foreigner never knows the language and customs like a native.[5]

Demography, society and politics in high-density areas

The development of more-complex agricultural communities had important consequences for the demography of Central Africa. It is generally considered that communities that gradually take up agriculture and animal husbandry continue for a long time to show a low annual growth rate (between 0.05 and 0.10 per cent), which is fairly close to the known growth rate of hunting and food-gathering communities. On the other hand, communities with a more diversified agriculture have a much higher annual growth rate, put between 0.10 and 0.15 per cent. Figures for a difficult natural environment like that of Africa are unknown: but they are no doubt not very far from this model. Spread over more than two centuries, an increase of this order in the growth rate would have had a considerable effect on the overall population of Central Africa.[6]

Compared with twentieth-century growth rates these figures admittedly seem low. The fact is that in early African communities the death rate remained high. For the nineteenth century the main causes of death are known, but it is impossible to determine the extent of each one's contribution to the total.

First, there were historical factors, especially the slave trade and its attendant violence. While the manpower drain of the slave trade to America was sharply reduced as from the 1850s, the Swahili and Arab trade took over to the east and north of our area. Figures can be given of *overall* losses for the whole of Central Africa,[7] but it is unlikely that it will ever be possible to give a geographical breakdown, especially as the continual movement of groups and individuals spread the impact of the slave trade far and wide.

4. V. Drachoussoff, 1947.
5. *Proverbes Mongo*, No. 489, quoted in G. Hulstaert, 1976.
6. The historical analysis of African demography is still in its infancy. For the moment we have to make do with plausible growth rates based on the natality and mortality rates of societies with similar types of economic and social organization. For the Kongo region, a historian suggested an annual growth rate of about 0.20 per cent in the seventeenth century, and probably less in the eighteenth and nineteenth centuries (?): J. Thornton, 1977.
7. In the region under study, the Manyema and the Lomami basins were affected by the Swahili slave trade. Some authors put at 1.75 million the total number of slaves taken from the whole of Central and East Africa and exported from the continent by Swahili slave-traders between 1800 and 1870. J.D. Fage, 1975.

There were also ecological and epidemiological factors. The nineteenth century certainly saw the beginnings of medical progress in Central Africa, such as better knowledge of endemic diseases, use of vaccination and more general use of quinine. But this progress remained confined to the circles visited by traders from Angola or the Swahili coast. By and large the changes were too limited to defeat the major endemic diseases or epidemic outbreaks.[8]

Hence growth in the nineteenth century was still slow; but it was doubtless more pronounced than before, for it started from the relatively high base level achieved by the population of the area. As in the past, excess population was absorbed by movement elsewhere or by settlement in the savanna or the open forest, following a method of expansion that has left profound traces in the folk memory in the shape of traditions about 'migrations'. Excess population was also absorbed by areas practising a more diversified form of agriculture, and hence able, as P. Gourou puts it, to 'capitalize their surplus population'. Here a more sedentary type of settlement finally succeeded in overcoming the hostility of environments that had been gradually broken in down the ages, and from now on became favourable to human occupation.[9]

This material history and the political and social history of the area both throw light on each other, with no one-way determining influence. In some cases a high-density area would develop as a base for hierarchical political organizations. This is what happened in the case of two high-density areas, Mangbetu and Zande, in north-eastern Zaire. In the Mbomu valley and as far south as the Vela, the Zande area was a relatively high-density area in the nineteenth century despite murderous wars (in the 1870s Georg Schweinfurth put its population density at 40 per sq km). The agrarian system of the Zande was older than the military power of the Avungara, who only began to unify the area at the end of the eighteenth century. Under their rule, however, the term Zande became synonymous with subject-farmers; and they developed a high-yield agriculture capable of feeding a population which grew all the more rapidly because of the accumulation of captives and dependents resulting from the raiding and slave-trading of the warrior-aristocracy.

In the hilly areas to the west and east of Lake Kivu the nineteenth century was a time when new land was colonized. This is what happened with the Shi, and in Burundi and Rwanda. Shi agriculture in particular

8. Our knowledge of epidemic outbreaks is still sketchy. Only the smallpox outbreak of 1864–5 is relatively well documented; it spread from Luanda into Golungo, Bié, the Kongo country, and as far as Namibia; it may have caused as many as 25 000 deaths in a single year: D. Wheeler, 1964. A journey made to the *mussumba* (the capital of the Lunda empire) in 1885–6 afforded Carvalho an opportunity to collect information on smallpox in the region. He stated that smallpox was particularly rife after outbreaks of war, owing to the habit of leaving corpses unburied.

9. P. Gourou, 1971, pp. 89–90.

retained several plant varieties from the agricultural system formerly practised in the region, such as eleusine, sorghum and taro. However, by the nineteenth century at the latest it had absorbed American crops: an inventory of twentieth-century Shi farming noted thirty-two varieties of beans

PLATE 12.2 *Nineteenth-century royal drums from the Kuba kingdom*

and four varieties of sweet potatoes known before the colonial period.[10] The nineteenth century was also the period when the Shi developed chiefdoms or small states. P. Gourou and J. Vansina observed in other contexts (Rwanda and Kuba) that political factors can speed up population growth and also intensify production. Higher-yield agriculture is found to

10. J.B. Cuypers, 1970.

be necessary to feed the clients, dependents and captives who concentrate in the capital towns or chiefdoms. This political factor may have operated in the case of the Shi in the nineteenth century.

It is, thus, not a one-way process: population growth made possible by the production of increasing surpluses calls in turn for further expansion of production. This sometimes happened at the price of an erosion of political power. In the western part of Zaire there are several examples of areas that became in the nineteenth century population reservoirs fed by heavy immigration; but the power of the chiefs weakened whilst stockpiling by clan or lineage leaders and even by enterprising individuals was what really counted. In this way population growth was accompanied by radical changes in the structure of society.

Thus, a pioneer frontier area developed in the nineteenth century to the west of the Luba heartland (i.e. west of the area between the Busimaie and Lubilash rivers). These immigrants came as individuals, small groups or lineages. They did not obliterate all traces of former settlers, but where there had previously been a great variety of clan loyalties, the nineteenth century saw the gradual development of a sense of sharing the same civilization, language, and political organizations, usually in small chiefdoms. A feeling of ethnic identity grew out of this shared historical experience, in which increases in population and agricultural productivity, and also encouragement of individual enterprise, played a key role. During the same period, in small high-density areas on the upper Tshikapa and the upper Kasai, there were many young Chokwe who were prepared to leave their villages and the burdensome power of the chiefs and take to the open forest, hunting elephants, setting up hives and collecting the honey and wax. Because of their skill with plants, particularly cassava, which can tolerate poor soils, the women who went with them were able to start growing crops: these women often came from small Lunda settlements along the tributaries of the Luembe, the Tshikapa, etc.

The assimilation of Lunda women into Chokwe society illustrates a phenomenon that was widespread throughout the 'matrilineal belt': descendants of female captives were members not of their mother's clan (this was the privilege of the free-born), but of their father's. There were many of these descendants of slaves everywhere: among the Kongo they were the *bana ba nzo* (children of the house), among the Chokwe the *ana a tshihunda* (children of the village), and among the Pende of Kwilu they even make up the majority of members of rich and powerful clans.[11] Genealogical trees show that the practice of assimilating captives was very common in the nineteenth century.

11. The assimilation of dependents is studied by L. de Sousberghe, 1961.

The conquest of poor soils

Political factors and social aspirations help to explain the fact that high-density areas sometimes attracted immigration and sometimes, contrariwise, acted as emigration centres and contributed to the settlement of marginal or sparsely populated areas. Moreover the conquest of relatively poor soils represents one of nineteenth-century African agriculture's greatest triumphs. Coupled with stockbreeding, it made possible the consolidation of human settlement, for example, in the difficult regions of southern Angola.

This is sandy, arid country characterized by irregular rainfall. Southern Angolan societies were split up into a great variety of peoples distinguished from each other by their terrain and the varying importance they attached to agriculture and stockbreeding. Ethnic solidarity among the peoples of this region resulted from sharing a common historical experience; that is, both political experience in the form of states that developed from the end of the eighteenth century onwards and also economic experience dictated by environmental similarities. All these peoples, of whom the Kwanyama[12] are the most numerous, have come to be known as the Ovambo. Next among the Ovambo, but much smaller, come the Ndongo, Kwambi, etc. They all live in the Cuvelai river basin, in an area bounded by the Cunene and the Cubango (Okavango). The rise of the Cuvelai and the flooding of the grassy savannas enabled the Ovambo to overcome the drought and make the inhabited areas of the region described by nineteenth-century travellers look like gardens. The Ovambo irrigated and, thanks to their livestock, also manured their farms.

Just as in other high-density areas, the transition to a more intensive type of agriculture in the nineteenth century was facilitated by the assimilation of immigrants and especially of captives taken during raiding expeditions into the lands lying to the south of the Ovimbundu highlands. Although certain American plants, such as groundnuts, beans and a little maize, were known, American plant varieties had not found their way here to the same extent as in the centre of Angola. Millet and sorghum remained the staple crops, being drought-resistant. Royal power was closely linked to the system of production. The king was the 'rainmaker' and also responsible for sharing out the land and organizing river damming and other irrigation works.[13]

As a result of such development, we can say that the long-standing disparities in population distribution were probably accentuated in the nineteenth century. The creation of a surplus from an increase in agricultural production led to relatively rapid increase of population in certain

12. In 1845, the first scholarly traveller in the region, B. J. Brochade, put their number at 120 000.

13. The most authoritative work on the region is still C. Estermann, 1956–61. For a useful survey of the subject as regards the situation in the nineteenth century, see: W. G. Clarence-Smith and R. Moorson, 1975.

areas such as Ovambo, Ovimbundu, Luba, the whole area in Zaire some 5° south of the Equator, etc. This, in turn, led to migratory movements away from other areas. This was further heightened by the varying effects of social and economic factors. Some economic factors encouraged the practice of gathering, such as the collection of ivory and wax by the Chokwe and this promoted the dispersion of people in the forest. Other economic factors, as often happened in river valleys for example, helped bring together a mixed population to create centres of trade and population concentration. Next to production, therefore, we must assess the degree of influence that world trade and economy had on the Central African region.

Central Africa in the fluctuating world economy of the nineteenth century

During the centuries that saw the gradual establishment of a system in which agriculture, stock-breeding, fishing and gathering were the main productive activities, a trade sector always existed in Central Africa, playing a more or less important role according to historical circumstances. Generally speaking, the difficulty and cost of transport restricted trading transactions for a long time to a few major products that were much in demand, such as salt, iron, prestige goods (copper, raffia fabrics, etc.), whereas agricultural produce was rarely carried over great distances.

The rise of a world-wide market economy, which began in the sixteenth century, gradually affected the organization of economic life in ever-widening areas of Central Africa. Here again, the nineteenth century is part of a continuous process, that of unequal trade relationships with the capitalist world. However, from the 1850s, great changes began to take place. Slaves gradually ceased to be Central Africa's principal 'export' to the outside world. Trade expanded in the main products obtained from a gathering-based economy: ivory, wax, copal, oil and coffee. The growth of this market economy is undeniable: the value of goods passing through Angolan ports increased sevenfold between 1844 and 1881; the cash turnover of the Luanda branch of the Banco Nacional Ultramarino increased tenfold between 1865 and 1876. In the early 1870s, however, the value of exports derived from these products was still only twice that derived from the export of slaves in the 1820s.[14]

The volume of these major African products reaching world markets was dependent on the way in which communications and trade networks functioned within the continent. These networks, with their staging posts, trade conventions and currencies, in turn defined the major economic zones on the nineteenth-century map of Central Africa, amounting to new

14. Economic statistics on nineteenth-century Angola are to be found in numerous separate publications. For some basic facts see R. J. Hammond, 1966, more especially pp. 73–4, and its bibliography.

'frontiers' that overlaid and modified the former political and economic divisions of the region.

These new economic zones were dominated by the demands of the nerve centres of the nineteenth-century world economy. Each of them had its own historical traditions and political and social characteristics. Nonetheless, they all had one thing in common, namely that they transformed important aspects of the old African economic system, linking it more or less loosely to the world economy.

Economic zones and trading networks

During the period 1800–80, four main economic zones can be identified in Central Africa. Two were characterized by the important role played in them by Muslim traders. In the north-eastern part of the region, there were outposts of traders from Cairo, the Red Sea and Khartoum, who scoured the Baḥr al-Ghazāl and the area south of the Vela. This network developed as a result of commercial and military expeditions sent into the

PLATE 12.3 *King Munza of Mangbetu in 1870*

PLATE 12.4 *Kazembe in 1831*

Sudan and Dārfūr by the ruler of Egypt, Muḥammad ʿAlī. By about 1850, the Egyptians had reached the Baḥr al-Ghazāl, where Egyptian, Coptic and European traders adopted the techniques perfected since the eighteenth century by the troops of the sultans of Darfur. They built *zeribas*, forts or just thorn-bush reinforcements which they used as bases during barter operations or forays. A European traveller, Georg Schweinfurth, accompanied some of these traders in the 1870s and left a valuable account of the Zande and Mangbetu kingdoms at the time when they first established regular contacts with Sudanese traders.

The Sudanese network had certain distinctive features, in particular the division of influence between state monopolies and private trade, the systematic use of force, mainly through the recruitment of local mercenaries, and a policy of developing plantations for trade, particularly in cotton. These objectives and methods helped inspire the King of the Belgians, Leopold II, when he embarked on establishing a trading empire for himself in the Zaire basin.

Since the 1860s, whole areas of the Central Africa region had also been incorporated in a trading network with bases in the ports and warehouses on the Swahili coast, in places such as Zanzibar and Bagamoyo, on the Indian Ocean. The Swahili routes which went into the region east of Lomami comprised two major groups of tracks. One was a 'corridor' passing through Unyanyembe in the central part of present-day Tanzania and crossing Lake Tanganyika from places such as Ujiji; the other led to the Luapula-Moero region either from Lake Malawi or from south-western Tanzania.

The Swahili network had long been characterized by small caravans stopping at the courts of influential chiefs, the Lunda chief, Kazembe, for example. In the 1870s, however, trading principalities began to develop. The most famous of them was that of Tippu Tip, established at Kasongo in 1875, and it dominated long-distance trade in the Sankuru and the Luba 'empire'. It was through this network that the Swahili country was able to become the first base for colonial penetration into the eastern part of Central Africa.

The two other networks that spread across Central Africa were centred around the outposts of European traders on the Atlantic coast: the Portuguese centres in Luanda, Benguela and Moçâmedes, or the Dutch, French and English trading stations on the lower Zaire river and along the northern coast of Angola. This latter region relied for its supplies mainly on the Kongo trade and on the river trade. The Kongo trade was itself based on the Kwango-Kwilu communities where Kituba, the Kongo local language, was being widely used.

The river trade developed during the second half of the nineteenth century, superseding the old overland routes. The people living along the river, particularly those settled near the Ubangui–Zaire confluence or on the Zaire itself, at the level of the Equator, held exclusive sway over the waterborne trade, as they alone possessed and used canoes. These different groups disseminated the Babangi language, which became the *lingua franca* of the equatorial region, a language that was later adopted by colonizers.

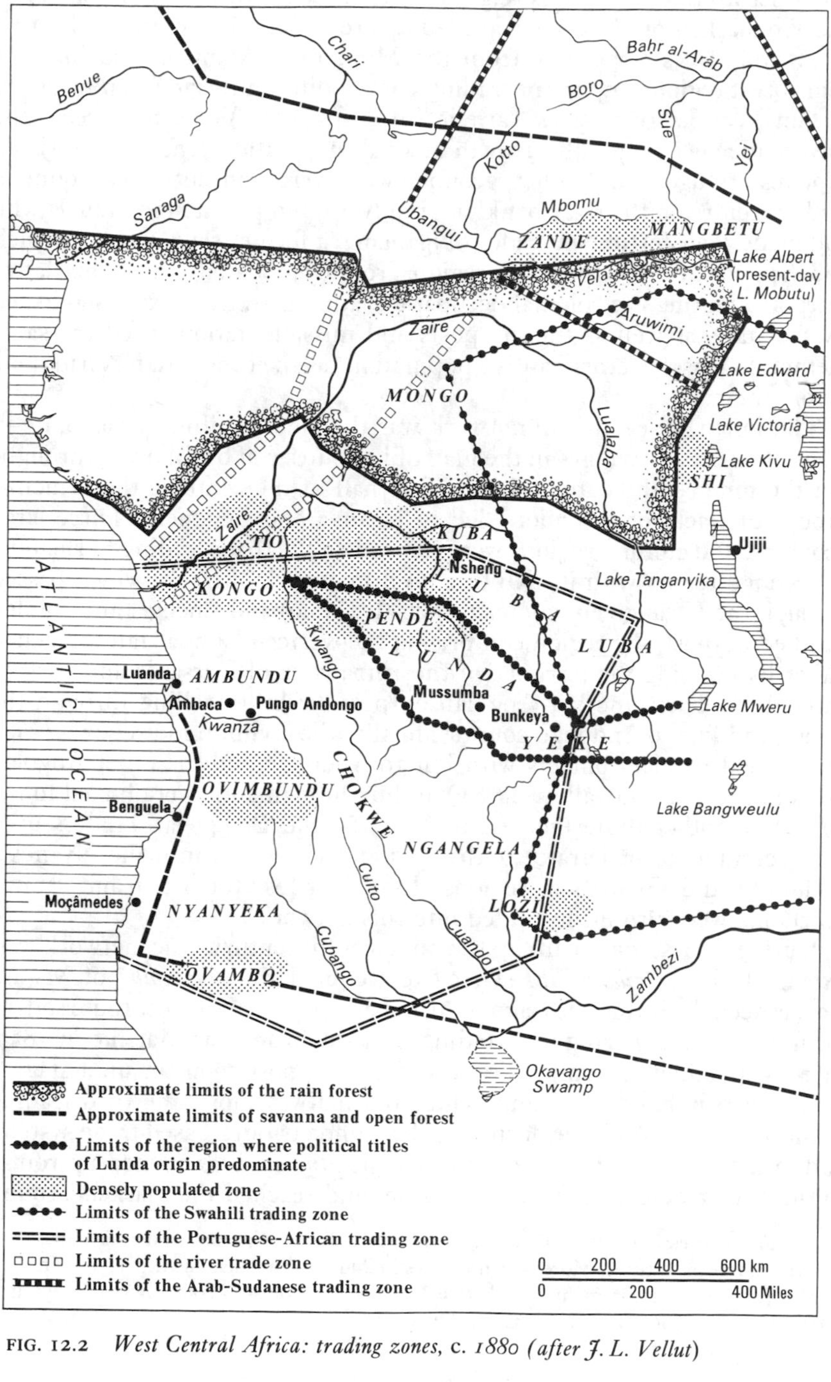

FIG. 12.2 *West Central Africa: trading zones,* c. *1880 (after J. L. Vellut)*

They set up trading centres (e.g. Lukolele), went down the river as far as the Tio markets on the Pool, travelled upstream into the interior, collecting ivory and slaves, especially from the Mongo. They introduced into the rain-forest regions important trading commodities hitherto unknown such as guns, copper rings, new varieties of crops, etc. As we have seen, the slave trade encouraged the growth of small population centres comprising captives, refugees and other groups, who were concentrated around a trading centre on the river bank, or simply around private individuals who had made their fortune in trade.[15] Ngaliema, a former slave who grew rich and held sway over the Pool region around 1880, falls into this latter category. During the colonial occupation, administrative bases established by the state, as well as trading posts and mission stations used the same method to mass together captive populations as the canoe traders had done before them.

The Portuguese–African network was the oldest and most elaborate in Central Africa.[16] Changes in the map of its routes can be followed throughout the nineteenth century. In the first half of the century, the principal groups of tracks or 'corridors' led to Luanda and Benguela. Three large economic and cultural regions were centred on the roads leading to Luanda: the Kongo region with its 'Mubire' (Vili) network of tracks which passed through the Kwango chiefdoms (especially Holo) and Encoge, an Angolan fortified outpost; the region comprising the western Lunda states, reached either by crossing the territory of the Imbangala of Kassanje and passing through Ambaca, another Angolan outpost, or by travelling through the Songo and Pungo Andongo country; finally, the Ovimbundu region, which maintained regular contacts with Pungo Andongo and the other Angolan posts in the Kwanza valley. The Ovimbundu highlands were linked to the coast by another route that led to Caconda and Benguela. Traders used this 'corridor' to penetrate southwards and eastwards into the Nyaneka, Nkhumbi and Guanguela regions. In the 1840s, the Luyi and Lunda kingdoms were also incorporated into this network.

During the second half of the nineteenth century, the network was extended. The *Ambaquistas* started to frequent the *mussumba* of Mwant Yav, especially during the reign of Muteba. They used a direct route setting off from the new Portuguese trading post established at Malanje in 1857, thereby avoiding Kassanje. Traders from this post soon set up a staging post near Kimbundu, a Lunda chiefdom halfway along the road leading to the *mussumba*. With the decline of the Lunda tribute-based trade system, and in the wake of Chokwe expansion, the *Ambaquistas* opened up routes to the Lulua valley, in the Luba region, and reached the markets around

15. The expression 'big river trade' was coined by G. Sautter who was the first to describe its main features. More recent studies include: J. Vansina, 1973; R. Tonnoir, 1970 and B. Jewsiewicki's commentary, *L'administration coloniale et la tradition*; with regard to the Giribuma, see R. Tonnoir, 1974; G. Hulstaert, 1976.

16. J. L. Vellut, 1972.

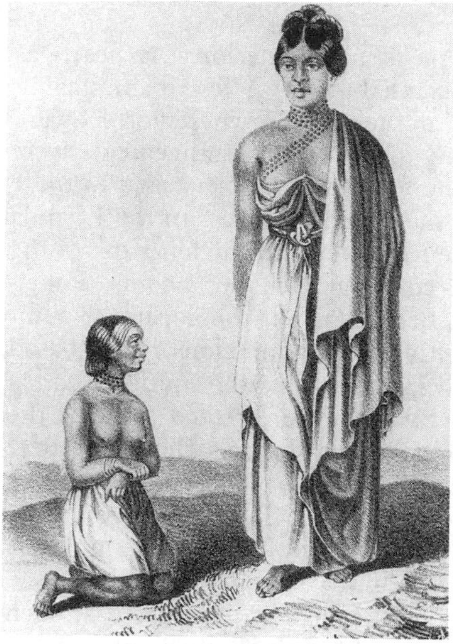

PLATE 12.5 *Kimbundu woman of the chiefly class with her slave-girl, in the 1850s*

PLATE 12.6 *Kimbundu warrior with woman of the chiefly class, in the 1850s*

Kuba. There, they faced competition from the Ovimbundu caravans which, in the 1870s, bypassed the Kalagne Lunda state and traded with the Luba states, buying the slaves which they then sold to the Kuba, who supplied large quantities of ivory.

The order of importance of the commercial centres situated in the major economic zones that were based on the trade economy system can be determined according to the complexity and diversity of the functions they fulfilled in the predominating economy: giving credit to traders, providing storage facilities, packing and equipping trading expeditions, etc. Luanda, followed by Benguela and, in the second half of the century, Moçâmedes, were the centres of the most complex operations and the headquarters of the principal trading firms. Nineteenth-century Luanda had architectural features and institutions characteristic of Portuguese tropical towns in Brazil, Africa and India. But it was also a town possessed of originality in which the Portuguese element was often dominated by Creole and African culture. Here, fortunes were quickly made and as quickly lost. A traveller who visited the town in the 1840s described the governor's ball, where he met a woman decked out in gold and jewels, who had come to Luanda as a mere slave, a man who had arrived at the coast as a prisoner aboard a slave ship and another whose childhood was spent in the crowded backstreets of Lisbon's slums.[17]

In about 1850, none of the Angolan posts in the interior were nearly as big as Luanda, with its 6000 to 10 000 inhabitants. A few main staging posts were situated along the 'corridors' in the interior, where porters were paid off, new ones were recruited, many of the credit arrangements were made, etc. Most of the mulattos and the few Europeans engaged in trade with the interior were concentrated in these small centres. In the Luanda hinterland, Dondo was a leading centre for trade with the left bank of the Kwanza, and it expanded during the coffee and rubber booms; Pungo Andongo was another important place, because it was the departure point for traders travelling to the Lunda chiefdoms and a junction of land-based communications between Benguela and Luanda.[18] To the south, Caconda occupied a similar position, but its activities were directed towards the peoples south of the Ovimbundu highlands and towards Bié. The latter kingdom was an important secondary centre of the network, where porters were changed, goods bought and credit arranged. It had a Portuguese-African colony of about a hundred people, mainly Africans or mulattos (Mbundus from Golungo, *Ambaquistas,* 'Mambari' from Bié, etc.).

Finally, the network of the tribute-based economy terminated at such centres as the *mussumba*, Bunkeya, or capitals of small chiefdoms or the markets of non-centralized communities. Such termini were centres of active transactions.

A system of this type was characterized by increasingly marked contrasts between areas that monopolized profitable operations – centralization of large quantities of products, handling and marketing operations – and those where there were fewer opportunities to accumulate wealth. The more fortunate regions had quite a different appearance from the others: arms, textiles and domestic slaves were plentiful there and rare elsewhere. As we shall see, during periods of economic recession the Portuguese tried to monopolize the profits of the network by eliminating African 'middlemen', whereas during periods of economic growth most of the trade in the interior was carried on by Africans.

During the nineteenth century, the network had to adapt to certain major trade cycles. Up to the 1840s the slave trade was by far the most important Portuguese-African activity. This last peak period was in fact the most disastrous in the history of the Angolan slave trade. It is estimated that from 1780 to 1830, between 15 000 and 20 000 slaves were exported annually from Central African ports (from the Loango coast to the south of Angola). Brazil was the main importer and Angola the principal supplier. It was Angolan slave labour that made it possible to expand the coffee-

17. The German doctor, G. Tams, who visited Luanda in 1841, quoted by A. Stamm, 1972.

18. J. C. Feo Cardozo, 1825, p. 355.

PLATE 12.7 *Mid-nineteenth-century carved tusk from the Loango coast of Congo/Angola showing scenes from trade and Europeans*

plantation economy of Rio de Janeiro and São Paulo in the nineteenth century. On the whole, the Atlantic slave trade, even the clandestine operations, died out in the course of the 1850s, although in the lower Zaire river area it survived outside Portuguese control until the disappearance of the last of the slave markets in Latin America towards the end of the 1860s.

During the remainder of the century, exports from Angola were limited to a few agricultural products (such as coffee and sugar) and especially, products obtained by gathering – mostly wax and ivory – though during the last three decades of the century a greater variety of exported products were gathered, such as wild coffee, copal, palm oil and, later, more importantly, natural rubber.

The development of Africa's major economic zones not only changed the conditions affecting the accumulation of wealth, but also aggravated social oppression. As in the Zaire river region and the Arab and Swahili zones, the Portuguese-African zones favoured the growth of a sector of production based on slave labour. Certainly this type of production had not been unknown in the tribute-based economies of the savanna: slaves

PLATE 12.8 *A caravan of Ovimbundu traders resting*

worked the fields of the leading political families of the *mussumba*, for example. But, in the nineteenth century, the accumulation of captives by certain privileged groups often coincided with the rapid growth of a market-related sector of the economy rather than with economic expansion due to increased payments of tribute-money. We have seen the result in the role played by 'domestic slaves' in the demographic and agricultural expansion of some of the communities in the region, such as the Kongo, Ovimbundu, and Ovambo.

In Angolan colonial society, the slave trade was likewise linked to the capitalist market economy, and had grown to sizeable proportions by the second half of the nineteenth century. In spite of certain legal technicalities – slavery was formally abolished in Angola in 1878 – a slave labour sector was certainly the basis of the boom in cotton, plantation coffee, and especially sugar-cane production. At the end of the period under review, brandy distillation from Angolan sugar cane was the main object of trade with the *sertão*. Slave labour also met the demands of the labour market rising from the beginning of white settlement in the regions to the south of the Ovimbundu highlands.

Portuguese imperialism in Angola

The existence of major trading zones in Central Africa and the nature of their relations with the world economy provide the key to the history of imperialism in this region in the nineteenth century. During this period, in Central Africa at least, financial imperialism had not yet made its appearance, but new forms of trade-based imperialism developed. Over the span of the century, it is possible to identify a number of broad phases in the expansion and contraction of Portuguese possessions in Angola, reflecting the hesitations of the Portuguese governors of the colony between two different conceptions of hegemony over the African trading economy. Thus the new Portuguese imperialists could choose to exercise a purely commercial form of domination, with minimal administrative and military occupation, its only avowed aim being to promote the circulation of goods in collaboration with a large, active African trading community. Alternatively, Portugal could attempt to incorporate the African colonies in its own economic system, while protecting national trade, but more significantly, perhaps, opening up a new market for Portugal's budding industries. The second alternative implied consolidating occupation of the colony, curbing the role of African middlemen to the advantage of colonial traders, diversifying the colony's production of raw materials and securing a market for the new manufactures from the mother country, essentially through a policy aimed at the political and administrative unification of Portugal and its African 'provinces'. Another aspect of this policy of assimilation was the tendency to encourage 'white' settlers in southern Angola.

These two trends, towards contraction or territorial expansion, alternated throughout the nineteenth century, like the swing of a pendulum, since they were bound up with the economic situation and structural changes in the Portuguese economy. Events certainly played their part, and the military setbacks inflicted on the Portuguese by the Africans go some way towards explaining the ebb of colonial occupation during the period 1862–72. Personalities also influenced developments; certain governors were associated with an aggressive policy of maximum occupation, others with a retreat to coastal bases. However, these factors do not assume their real significance unless they are placed in the context of world economic developments, particularly in so far as they affected the Portuguese economy. Indeed, Portuguese imperialism did not escape the general rules of colonial expansion in the nineteenth century.[19]

The determination of the protectionists to ensure that Portugal and its colonies were united in an economic system independent of the great industrial powers was reflected in the first attempts to set up a white colony in the south of Angola, beginning on the coast at Moçâmedes, and at Huíla in the Nyaneka country. The spirit of conquest was still uppermost in the 1850s, with sustained Portuguese efforts to occupy territory and eliminate competition from African traders, in particular the Imbangala and the Kongo. Not until 1860 or thereabouts, following some years of thriving trade, was a turning-point reached, with the Portuguese increasingly adopting a policy of withdrawal. From 1862 to 1875, the colonial power continued to retreat, suffering a series of military defeats at Cassanga in 1862, and in the Dembo country in 1871–2, which the government at Luanda did not seek to avenge. By the early 1870s the withdrawal was complete. The colonial power in Angola had fallen back to the coast, and Africans were rapidly gaining control of trade in the *sertão*. Silva Porto, the leading *sertanejo* of the Bié area, lost his entire fortune in this period under the pressure of competition from the Ovimbundu traders. Angola entered a period of rapid growth in trade: between 1867 and 1873, tonnage shipped down the Kwanza from Dondo increased sevenfold.

Soon, however, the Portuguese colonialists embarked on a new phase of territorial expansion. Following a slackening of world trade from 1873 onwards, competition between the various foreign powers for a slice of the 'African cake'[20] grew increasingly fierce, and in Angola this period began with a severe recession following a prolonged drought and a credit crisis (1874–6). At the same time, work was beginning on the construction of the railway from Luanda to the interior; attempts were being made through diplomatic agreements to stave off the threat from the new arrivals in Central Africa; and the first Portuguese 'explorers' were setting out in the wake of the German and British travellers to be seen in Luanda and in the interior. Central Africa was approaching a major turning-point in its history.

19. This view is not accepted by D. Wheeler and R. Pélissier, 1971, pp. 51–83. The authors give a purely political explanation for the fluctuating fortunes of Portuguese penetration in Angola. This is also the line taken by R. J. Hammond, 1969.

20. The expression is Leopold II's and is quoted, among others, by J. Stengers, 1962, p. 490.

Society and power in Central Africa (*c.* 1800–80)

The political and social history of Central Africa in the nineteenth century should first be seen in the context of an ancient tradition. As far back as the oral and written sources go, we see that the societies living in the region hesitated between two power structures: the hierarchical, well-defined order based on the payment of tribute, which was that of the kingdoms and, at the other extreme, the more egalitarian and informal type of government by councils of elders and notables.[21]

These two models were complementary, and in practice there were many different kinds of intermediate situations, waverings and compromises. The realities of the environment and of economic activity, as well as historical circumstances and even personal considerations, determined whether the prevailing type of organization tended towards the monarchical model, with its qualities of order and security, or towards the more flexible, less authoritarian democratic ideal.

In the period under study here, we find in Central Africa some examples of administrative systems with stable, permanent hierarchical structures that were capable of concentrating quite large populations at specific centres or capitals. But such cases were not the most common, for a combination of several factors was necessary before a political title and a state structure could emerge. A tribute-based economy which was the material basis for the organization of a state required a fairly strong agricultural sector. Even so, agriculture alone afforded rather inadequate opportunities for the accumulation of wealth. More could be appropriated by levying taxes on the production of salt, copper and iron, in addition to tribute claimed in the course of conquests and raids. Lastly, tributes were collected from the trading sector. The power of chiefs thus relied on the existence of markets, exchange and communication networks, which made it possible to impose monopolies or various forms of taxation and other tolls.

Growth or decline in any one of these economic sectors was a factor in the expansion or erosion in the power of states or chiefdoms in the nineteenth century, just as in earlier times. What is peculiar to the nineteenth century is the social mobility in these communities, which made for rapid access to positions previously held by chiefs, or simply encouraged the enterprise of particular individuals, either within a monarchical system or through the channels of clan and lineage. Monopolies and the levying of tribute failed to halt the expansion of trade during the nineteenth century and trade often thrived at the expense of the material power of the political aristocracies.

In addition to these material factors, however, there existed ritual aspects of power, represented by insignia and charms against enemies both within

21. For a sound analysis of the concept of power in two societies of the western savannas, namely the Kongo and the Tio, see the respective studies of W. McGaffey, 1970, and J. Vansina, 1973.

and without. How did the exercise of ritual and mystical power develop at a time of rapid reversals in the military and economic fortunes of these societies? Until historians have turned their attention to this question, our understanding of the history of the region must remain incomplete and confined within terms of reference that fail to reflect the deep aspirations of the ancient societies of Central Africa.

State-organized societies

A number of ancient kingdoms survived the upheavals of the nineteenth century. One of these was the Lunda state of Kalagne, which reached its zenith in the first half of the nineteenth century and subsequently entered a period of decline, from the 1870s onwards. Originally, Kalagne was identified with a densely populated area that lay almost entirely in a territory situated to the east of the Lulua, between latitudes 8°S and 9°S, and longitudes 23°E and 24°E. Although at first concentrated along the waterways, in particular the Kalagne river, groups of Lunda emigrated to neighbouring regions during the eighteenth and nineteenth centuries. New political units were founded as a result of these migrations, but the exodus was also due to a desire to escape the efforts of the chiefs to appropriate captive manpower. This explains the origin of the Lunda settlements in the Chokwe and Luval areas to the south of the state of Kalagne at the beginning of the nineteenth century.

The highest Lunda title was that of Mwant Yav. It originated in the Kalagne valley and, by the eighteenth century at the latest, it was at the centre of a political network that embraced in the symbolic language of perpetual kinship numerous Lunda chiefdoms, between the Kwango in the west and the Luapula in the east.

One of the great reigns of the Kalagne dynasty in the nineteenth century was that of Nawej (*c.* 1820–52). Under him, the power of the Mwant Yav increased. Nawej was held in fear for the vengeance and forced tribute he exacted from unruly chiefs, either by force of arms or through the unscrupulous use of witch-doctors. Although he preferred bows and arrows for hunting, it was in Nawej's reign that Lunda warriors first began to use firearms from Angola (*lazarinas*). At his invitation, the Chokwe hunters had begun to operate on Lunda territory, using firearms and gradually driving the elephants northwards. Some Chokwe visitors came to the capital around 1840, bringing firearms and gunpowder, and some settled on Lunda territory. Nawej tried hard to maintain good relations between the two peoples, but to no avail. Rivalry soon sprang up between Lunda and Chokwe political families.

The Imbangala of Kassanje had been regular visitors to the *mussumba* since the beginnings of the Mwant Yav dynasty. But the most significant development of Nawej's reign was the rapid increase in trading over long distances, still with the Imbangala, but before long also with the

PLATE 12.9 *A Chokwe carving of Chibinda Ilunga, the legendary founder of the Lunda empire. The carving is probably nineteenth-century*

Ovimbundu and 'Mambari'. As late as the end of the century, people still talked about the caravans that used to arrive to do business for Dona Ana Joaquina (Na Andembo), a wealthy merchant lady of Luanda, and the royal caravans sent by Nawej to Dona Ana at Luanda or to the 'Jaga' of Kassanje.

Nevertheless, Nawej had a bad reputation with the traders, who reproached him with interminable delays in repaying debts and his readiness to find excuses to confiscate goods. His direct descendants were very numer ous, and before long the pretenders to the throne began to whisper that Nawej had had his fair share of state power and that the time had come for younger men to take their turn. He died during an illness, smothered by his 'brother' Mulaj, who seized his bracelet – the insignia of power (*lukano*) – and was acknowledged as the new Mwant Yav. The following years were marked by internal dissensions, temporarily quieted by the long reign of Muteba (*c.* 1857–73). In those years of peace, the great caravans would stay over in the *mussumba* during the rainy season, receiving friendly treatment from the Mwant Yav.

From the reign of Mwant Yav Muteba onwards, colonies of Mbundu travellers stayed at the *mussumba*. Those people were natives of the Ambaca area (*Ambaquistas*). The founder of the first of these colonies, Lourenço Bezerra, known to the Lunda by the nickname Lufuma (*c.* 1850–83), was a native of the Golungo. He settled in the *mussumba* in about 1850 and spent some thirty years at the court of the Mwant Yav, and for a long time benefited by Muteba's favourable attitude towards the Angolan traders. In 1869, Lufuma's colony established itself in the immediate vicinity of Luambata, Muteba's new *mussumba,* and introduced Mbundu agriculture and stockbreeding into the region. The Mwant Yav took a keen personal interest in these fields, which grew plants imported from Brazil and Portugal (rice, maize, tobacco, etc.) as well as the staple African crops. The Angolans of Luambata also became craftsmen (metalworkers, weavers, potters, scribes, etc.). The colony traded alongside the Lunda families on a tribute basis. All transactions went through Lufuma. Over the years, Lufuma had built up a clientele of captives, redeemed slaves, etc., whom he took with him when he finally returned to the Malange region for good in 1882. During the years 1800–80, the colony was thus a major centre of trading activity controlled by the aristocratic families of the Lunda court and the Angolan businessmen, who were bound to the region by many marriage ties and were themselves practising the tribute-based trade methods prevalent in the area. Lufuma had in fact become a titled Lunda dignitary, as is shown by his role in the life of the court: it was he, for example, who organized the funeral of the Lukonkesh of Mwant Yav Muteba.

The Chokwe expansion continued through the 1870s. Fleeing their villages and their chiefs, on the pretext of witchcraft, tied as they were to a gathering-type economy, searching for ivory, wax and later rubber, incorporating captive women and young men into their patrilineal families, the Chokwe were soon strong enough to eclipse the power of the Lunda chiefs in the region between the Tshikapa and Kasai rivers. The Lunda villages and chiefdoms in this region broke up and scattered. It was a period of decline for the long-established aristocratic Lunda power. The trend was accentuated by dissension within the *mussumba*: the head of an important political family, Shanam, allied himself with the Chokwe and seized power with their support. He took the name of Mwant Yav Mbumba. His reign was a time of violence, and he continued to use the Chokwe as a threat against Lunda vassals. After his death in 1883, Chokwe warriors seeking to avenge him succeeded in obtaining the *lukano* for Mushidi, one of Mbumba's sons, who had been adopted and raised by a Chokwe family.

The chiefdoms and the fragmentation of power

Despite the far-reaching social changes in the Lunda–Chokwe region in the last quarter of the nineteenth century, the Lunda aristocracy did not die out completely. Elsewhere, states broke up according to various patterns: some states, which had been centralized, split into groupings of chiefdoms, informally united but subject to no common centre; others became even more decentralized, with a tendency in some cases towards the disappearance of the power of the chiefs.

The region to the south of the Ovimbundu highlands in Angola falls into the category of groupings of large chiefdoms. The dominant cultural group on the plateau, broadly termed the Nyanyeka-Nkhumbi, consisted of several ethnic groups: Nyanyeka, Otyilenge, Nkhumbi, etc. In the nineteenth century, some of the chiefdoms in the region were, in fact, the remains of former kingdoms. One such was Mwila, a Nyanyeka kingdom, which dominated the entire Huíla region in the eighteenth century and broke up towards the middle of the nineteenth century with the succession of Jau, which soon disintegrated in its turn. In the eighteenth century Mwila had entered into contact with Caconda and Portuguese Angola. It was the most densely populated part of the Nyanyeka land, and the scene of repeated Portuguese attempts to establish white settlers there in the 1840s, at the cost of many military confrontations. The Nyanyeka chiefdoms, especially Mwila, and later Ngambwe, became trading centres for wax, ivory and livestock, supplying the whole of southern Angola in the second half of the nineteenth century. Although trade itself contributed to the political break-up of the region, raids and plundering expeditions often favoured the swift rise to power of adventurers or newcomers. From the 1840s onwards, traders and petty warlords, often armed, scoured the entire region, carving out territories of their own and establishing strongholds for their following of captives (*servicais*), refugees and adventurers, where man and beast took refuge from violence behind thorn palisades.

Another example of the process of disintegration is provided by the

PLATE 12.10 *Mwant Yav Mbumba*

Luba 'empire', which spanned a vast area between the Lomami, the Lualaba and the western side of Lake Tanganyika. At the height of its expansion, during the first half of the nineteenth century, the military authority of the most prestigious Luba state – that of the Mulopwe with its capital, *kitenta* and the court – was directed against many chiefdoms, which for the most part already shared the Luba concept of power – the *bulopwe* – as the prerogative of chiefs born of the royal blood of the founders, Kongolo and Kalala Ilunga.

The structure proved to be short-lived and a prey to the fluctuating military fortunes of the various political families. During the reign of the Mulopwe Kasongo Kalombo (*c.* 1870–80), its political superstructure began to give way to the pressure exercised in particular by trading caravans from the Swahili area or from Angola. This commercial penetration merely fanned the flames of dissensions between different political leaders on the one hand, and on the other, between the political chiefs themselves and between the latter and chiefs of families which owned land and domains. By the end of the period, the Luba states and chiefdoms had become almost entirely autonomous.[22]

Adventurers, traders, condottieri: the new masters

The power of the *bulopwe* is one of the most ancient and illustrious in the history of the savanna peoples. Elsewhere in the region in the nineteenth century, we see the title of chief being assumed, with great frequency and new forms of power appearing. Either the role of chief had become obsolete (as in certain Kongo or Mbundu groups), or the expansion of trade had led to polarization around enterprising groups or individuals. Examples of this process can be found throughout Central Africa, both in societies with and without chiefs. In the rain-forest of the Central Basin, for example, certain traders succeeded in accumulating slaves, arms, copper, etc. For the most part, they were canoe-traders living on the banks of the Zaire river, who had grown rich by the slave trade. Indeed the history of the kingdom of Msiri begins with a series of trading expeditions.

Towards the middle of the nineteenth century, Sumbwa travellers from what is now Tanzania came to trade with the chiefs of the Lunda, Luba, Aushi, etc. of the Luapula valley and surrounding country. These traders were attracted by ivory, abundant in the region, and copper, worked in the west of the kingdom of Kazembe. In about 1885, Ngelengwa Mwenda, the son of one of these travellers, who had accompanied his father on his expeditions, settled in the territory of chief Katanga, a major centre of

22. Colonial administrators who adopted the theories of indirect administration and were anxious in the middle of the twentieth century to 'reconstitute' hypothetical past empires tended to overestimate the degree of centralization prevailing in the Luba states. For a survey of this question see A. Wilson, 1972.

copper production, densely populated for that part of the world.[23] During this period Arab, Swahili, Nyamweze and Ovimbundu trading expeditions visited the region in great numbers, seeking to expand their trade in copper, ivory and slaves.

Mwenda was perhaps the best known of these traders who succeeded in exploiting the differences among the ruling clans and could command a large and well enough equipped army to be able to settle in a chosen area, attract a large population to the capital and base their power on a following of trusted associates, fellow adventurers, relatives, local political families or simply enterprising individuals of whatever origin. Having established himself in Katanga's country, Mwenda began to offer his services to opposing political factions. Helped by Ovimbundu traders, he intervened in disputes between the Sanga, Lunda, Luba and other chiefs of the region. The most successful of these ventures was his interference in the dispute among pretenders to the throne of Kazembe. Here again, arms from the Bié area played a significant part and contributed to his rise.

By 1880, Mwenda had succeeded in setting up a state of his own. Taking the title and the insignia of *Mwami*, well known in his native country, he founded his capital at Bunkeya in the Lufira valley. At this time most of the chiefs in the region were associated with the power of the Mwant Yav (Lunda) or the Mulopwe (Luba). Mwenda drew many of them into his own empire and succeeded in making them accept his insignia (*kilungu*). Bunkeya became an important centre for all who sought to gain by associating with Mwenda. Mwenda himself became known as Msiri, a name that appears to have been of local origin, derived from *mushidi* (meaning land in Sanga and Luba), the owner of the land.

The women closest to Msiri included at one time a young Swahili girl from a place near Pweto and two mulattos from Angola, symbolizing the role played by the kingdom of Msiri in the trading networks. Known as Garaganja to the Angolans, Katanga to the Swahili, it became a clearing house for trade in Central Africa from Zanzibar to Benguela and from Luba country to the outposts of the Portuguese in Mozambique or the Arabs on Lake Malawi.

A much feared chief and a product of his age, Msiri could be both munificent and implacable, conforming to the stereotype of the chief or the aristocrat. Sometimes he could be cruel. The execution of one of his wives, Masengo, gave the signal for the long Sanga revolt against the Yeke state. The rising continued to rage until after the death of Msiri,[24] when it was eventually put down by the arms of the colonial power.

23. An Arab traveller, Said ben Habib, described this population in the middle of the century. It had more inhabitants than the capital of Kazembe; there was abundant food on the market and local cotton was spun for making clothes. Quoted by F. Bontinck, 1974, p. 12.

24. Msiri died a violent death at the hand of a European on 20 December 1891. The murderer was immediately executed by one of Msiri's sons. The main eye-witness accounts

Conclusion

At the close of this brief survey, can we draw any tentative conclusions? Some are perhaps suggested by the economic history of Central Africa as it developed through the nineteenth century. Conditions affecting the accumulation of wealth and dependents altered in the course of the century as a result of the rise of more-densely populated areas, advances in productivity in agriculture and the various crafts, and the rapid expansion of certain sectors of economic activity. Trade, in particular, was developing constantly in tune with the economic situation and supply and demand as regards the various commodities, and in many societies it contributed powerfully to the beginnings of social stratification.

While various forms of servitude were widespread during this period, it would be rash to speak of 'social classes'. The gradually deepening social differences have too often fallen into the familiar pattern of established political institutions or ethnic and clan solidarity for us to be able to use the concept of 'class'. One age-old function, that of political chief, proved to be particularly malleable in the face of changing circumstances. There had been times in the past history of the region when the office of chief had been liable to fall into the hands of groups or individuals, ranging from visionaries to upstarts or simply adventurers. In the nineteenth century this trend was accentuated, with traditional political office either increasingly based on trade, taken over by upstarts or else replaced by newly created titles.

The institution of chief in the nineteenth century thus continued to be shaped by a long tradition; yet the period lent it new characteristics. In particular, the position of chief seems to have been more unstable than it had been in the old days. The nineteenth century was a period when political fortunes were rapidly won and as rapidly lost. Change came too suddenly, and the autonomous history of the region was too brutally interrupted at the end of the century to allow for great states to emerge. Complex hierarchies and regional divisions were not typical features of the state in Central Africa as it developed in the nineteenth century; the region tended to appear as a network of chiefdoms, a 'horizontal' pattern of communities rather than a 'vertical' territorially based hierarchy.

However, an impression of the political history of the years 1800–80 solely in terms of the fragmentation of Central Africa would be misleading. It was a time when boundaries were no longer being defined primarily by political forces,[25] and the historian is forced to take into account the growth of vast economic regions reaching far beyond the boundaries set by ethnic cohesion or political organization.

of life in Bunkeya before the colonial conquest are those of Ivens and Arnot; F. A. Oliveira Martins (ed.), 1952, pp. 366–83; F. S. Arnot, 1889.

25. J. Vansina, 1976.

The broad lines of the social and economic history of Central Africa in the nineteenth century are gradually beginning to appear: history as it was lived and experienced by the societies of the time, the history of their aspirations, the history of change in mentalities, each in itself a vast unexplored field, all questions which Africa today is duty bound to ask of its past in order better to understand its present.[26]

26. This study owes much to the inspiration drawn from years of work with Bogumil Jewsiewicki, former professor at the National University of Zaire.

13 The renaissance of Egypt, 1805–81

A. ABDEL-MALEK

The impact of Europe: acculturation or renaissance?

Since the Second World War, the Egyptian school of history and historical sociology, supported by innovative Western publications, has clearly demonstrated that eighteenth-century Egypt was not simply a time of silence and self-effacement after three centuries of alienating Ottoman domination.[1]

It has also made clear that the choice of Muḥammad ʿAlī to occupy the post of *wālī* (Viceroy) in 1805 was due to the direct action of both the masses of Cairo and Alexandria and the traditional elites of the period, the *ʿulamāʾ*, the *shaykhs* and leading figures in the towns.[2] It was this year, 1805, that saw the restoration of an autonomous, modern Egyptian state and signalled the beginning of the modern era in Egypt, and not, as traditional colonial historiography would have us believe, the 'Egyptian Expedition', the military invasion led by Napoleon Bonaparte from 1798 to 1801 on the initiative of the Directory, following the wars in Italy. This expedition was a major venture in the struggle against the British empire. As Napoleon himself said, 'It shall expel the English from all their possessions in the East that it attacks, and more especially, shall destroy all their trading posts on the Red Sea coast ... [In view of] The vile treachery whereby England took possession of the Cape of Good Hope having rendered access to the Indies by the usual route very difficult for the vessels of the Republic, our Republican forces must therefore secure another route ...' At the same time, research was carried out in Egypt by the 'scientific mission' and this brought with it the fruits of the age of encyclopaedic Enlightenment and of the patterns of 'polytechnical' thought that were soon to be applied in France and Europe: *The Description of Egypt*,[3] a monumental work in twenty volumes, summarizes this impressive undertaking.

1. M. al-Sharqāwī, 1958; P. Gran, 1979.
2. Cf., essentially, the works of A.-R. al-Rāfeʿī, 1951; L. Bréhier, 1901; A. A. Mustafa, 1965; M. Sabry, 1930; M. S. Ghorbal, 1928; A. F. S. Wahidah, 1950; H. H. Dodwell, 1931.
3. J. C. Herold, 1962, provides a vivid and interesting description, to be compared with

Eighteenth-century Egypt is now seen as the laboratory from which the new Egypt emerged. First came the attempt by ʿAlī Bey al-Kabīr to forge national unity by reducing the number of different feudal systems controlled by the Mamlūks in the delta of Lower Egypt. Then came the first signs of the *aggiornamento* of fundamental Islam undertaken by Shaykh Ḥassan al-Attar; and then the concentration in the towns, and not only in Cairo, of the surplus value derived from the land which a group of traders and scholars with hegemonistic leanings believed should be placed at the disposal of what was later to be known as a 'national effort'. The French expedition was an unparallelled venture that was later to enable the French to strengthen their position in the Levant following their conquest of North Africa. It also enabled them to be seen as the standard-bearers of revolutionary Europe in vast areas of sub-Saharan Africa. Contemporary Egyptian historians, *inter alia*, ʿAbd al-Raḥmān al-Djabartī and Niqōla al-Turk, took an entirely different view: 'The French occupation improved the standing of the lower classes, retailers, street porters, craftsmen, donkey-drivers, stable-boys, pimps and prostitutes'.[4] In short, the riff-raff were happy because they were free, whereas the elite and the middle classes were subjected to all kinds of aggravations due to the suspension of imports and exports.

In the light of this, the underlying reasons for the two Cairo revolts became clear. The first revolt, from 21 to 24 October 1798, having begun with the *shaykh*s and notables of Cairo, extended into the towns and countryside. Two thousand people were killed, ten *shaykh*s were beheaded and the consultative *dīwān* was suspended. The second revolt was much more serious and lasted from 20 March to 21 April 1800. It was led by the *pāsha*s, who still strongly supported the Porte, and by the *shaykh*s of al-Azhar, who provoked sweeping and extremely severe repressive measures. The centrist group, forerunners of the general tendency of the national movement, whose leaders included the *shaykh*s, Khalīl al-Bakrī, ʿAbdallāh al-Sharḳaī and ʿAbd al-Raḥmān al-Djabartī, sent a conciliatory message to General Menou stressing the need for friendly relations between the 'two nations'. The battles of the Pyramids and of Aboukīr and the evacuation of the French invasion force in 1801 were at last to give the nascent Egyptian national movement the opportunity to crystallize, or, in other words, to acquire a social power base. Undoubtedly, this was initially a movement seeking autonomy from the Ottoman empire. But in the nineteenth century, its fiery aspiration for full national independence was to shine like a beacon throughout the Orient, the Mediterranean and Africa, and leave its mark on the world order and the empires of its time.

Between the French evacuation and the appointment of Muḥammad ʿAlī

the work of ʿAbd al-Raḥmān al-Djabartī (1754–1825), the exemplary historiographer of that epoch.

4. N. Turc, 1950, p. 45.

as walī, the country had once again become an Ottoman province. The second Cairo revolt, which resulted in the decisive weakening of French positions, strengthened the local leadership, which tended to favour the Ottoman empire and the *mamlūk*s. Although 'Omar Makram's authority was growing, he could still not steer power in the direction of the new political class in Egypt, the *'ulamā'*, notables and merchants. This was because the army was still controlled by its former masters; the plans of the 'Independent Brothers' had been buried with their leader, General Ya'kūb, who died on the ship taking him to Europe; and, finally, because any possible alternative put forward by the *shaykh*s of the *dīwān*, who had a difficult choice to make in troubled times, when the air was thick with intrigue and plots, had been neutralized. The status of Egypt in 1805 was that of a *wilāya*, a province of the Ottoman empire. The geopolitical situation of the country severely limited its room for manoeuvre. But the essential elements were already in place: a central authority, based on a small but effective military force and, more especially, a genuine mandate representing a national consensus of notables, *'ulamā'*, and the merchants of the time, supported by the people of the towns and large provincial population centres.

For the future, it was thus to be a question as always, of manoeuvre within the iron yoke of geopolitics. As Djamāl Ḥamdān brilliantly demonstrated in his monumental work on *The Personality of Egypt*, this meant that the new rulers had to understand the 'genius of the topographical locus'.

The founding of the modern independent national Egyptian state and the empire under Muḥammad 'Alī and Ismā'īl

The 'Coptic Legion' of General Ya'ḳūb (1800–1) and the proclamation by his supporters, the 'Independent Brothers', of the very concept of an 'Independent Egypt' derived from French influence in opposition to British supremacy. With the departure of the French expedition the movement crumbled. The plans and political career of Muḥammad 'Alī were a different story altogether. His primary object was to give Egypt the military, political, economic and cultural institutions that would make it the driving force behind the reconstitution of a new Islamic empire to replace senescent Turkey. From the start, his plans took into consideration the twin dimensions – Egyptian and Islamic – of Egyptian identity. His campaigns and those of Ibrāhīm were to project Egypt, at one and the same time, as an Islamic, Arab and African country. Having wrested power for himself with the support of the *'ulamā'*, the mob and his faithful Albanians, he had first to take the measure of the land of which he was as yet the uncertain master.

Britain supported the *mamlūk* party, which was led by Muḥammad al-Alfī bey, and in 1806 called on the Porte to remove Muḥammad 'Alī from

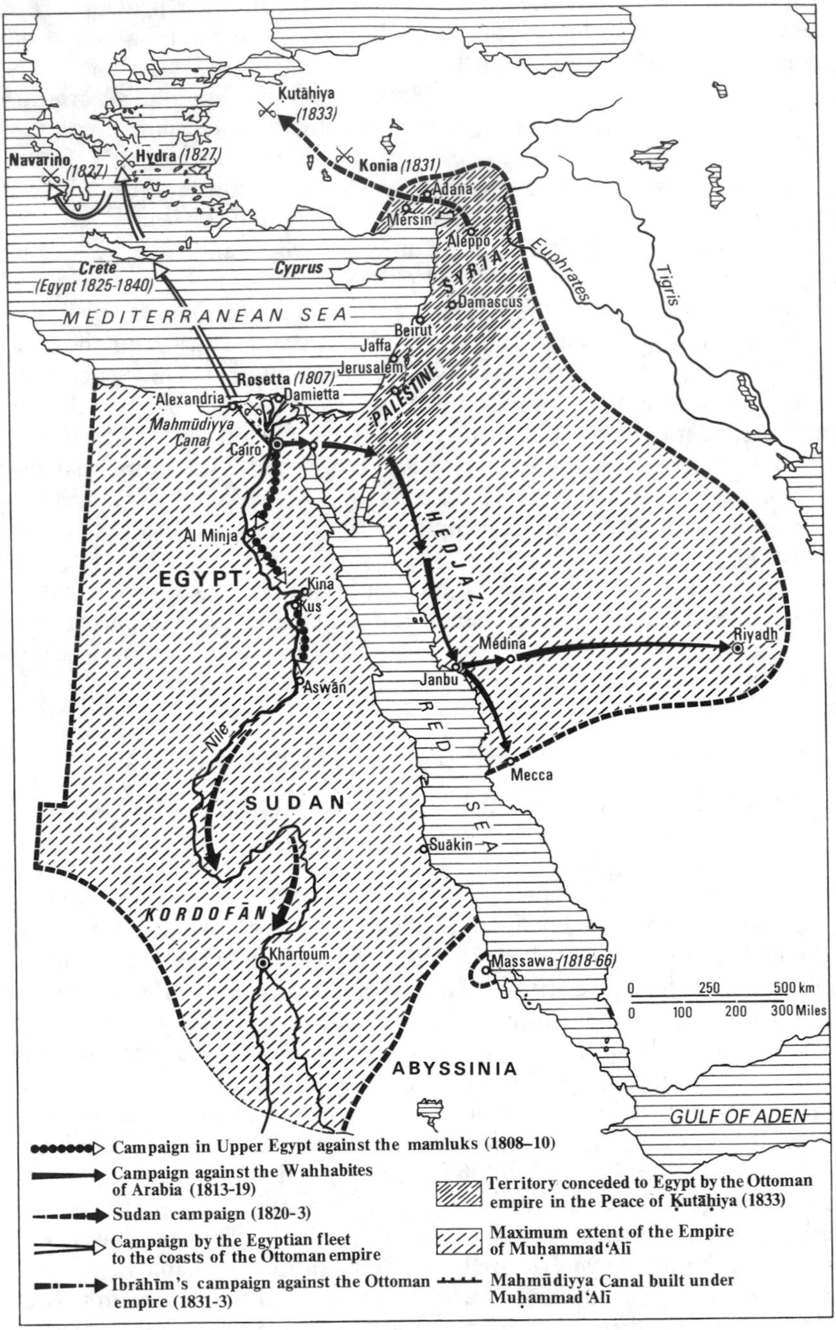

FIG. 13.1 *The Egyptian Empire of Muhammad ʿAlī (1804–49) (after A. Abdel-Malek)*

office. In 1807, the British attempted a direct invasion of Egypt, but were defeated by the Egyptians at Rāshid (Rosetta) on 31 March. Muḥammad ʿAlī, who was reputedly taking advantage of the support of leading public figures, and especially that of ʿOmar Makram, decided to put an end to the *mamlūks*' stranglehold on Upper Egypt, particularly as they were the allies of the British. Between June 1808 and August 1810 he conquered Upper Egypt, and on 1 March 1811, in the massacre of the Citadel, finally eliminated the leaders of the rebel movement, who stood as obstacles both to centralized authority and also to the future plans of the new viceroy.

Until the fall of Napoleon, the geopolitical situation remained basically the same. But from 1815 Britain's influence grew and other countries entered the ring, among them the Austria of Metternich. Having brought the *mamlūks* to heel, Muḥammad ʿAlī undertook the construction of the empire and the great task of national revival.

What was Muḥammad ʿAlī's conception of independence? And how did autonomy within the empire fit into this framework? On 28 November 1810, Muḥammad ʿAlī secretly conferred with the French consul, Drovetti, and suggested that France help Egypt throw off Ottoman domination. Only three days earlier, he had asked Istanbul to grant Egypt, a mere province (*wilāya – eyālet*), the status of *odjak*, with the same degree of autonomy as contemporary Algiers. He then sent his army into Arabia (1813–19), and into the Sudan (1820–3), with the ultimate objective of occupying Ethiopia. However, the British government, which the Egyptian ruler had been flattering, turned against him because he had penetrated three British spheres of influence – the Red Sea, the Persian Gulf and Ethiopia – all of which were indispensable to the security of the route to India. In point of fact, the situation was more complex. 'From the Persian Gulf to the Libyan Desert, from Sudan to the Mediterranean, and on both sides of the Red Sea, a Napoleonic or rather Pharaonic Empire extends over five million square kilometres.' And this at the very time Ottoman power was declining. The 'Egyptian question' seemed likely to supplant the 'Eastern question', thanks to the existence of a great civilizing force in North Africa.[5]

The first clash occurred in 1827 on the two Greek islands of Hydra and Spezzia, where the powerful fleet of Muḥammad ʿAlī and the army of his son Ibrāhīm had massed, coming to the assistance of the Ottoman empire. Negotiations were begun in Alexandria between Colonel Cradock, London's special envoy, and Muḥammad ʿAlī and his assistants. The subject was none other than the independence of Egypt on the basis of its position of strength at that specific time vis-à-vis the Porte. Muḥammad ʿAlī, a good strategist, tried at the eleventh hour to avoid an armed confrontation. But the Sultan's stubborn refusal led directly to the destruction at Navarino, on 20 October 1827, of the Egyptian fleet, which was itself an integral part of the Ottoman battle fleet.

5. E. Driault, 1925.

PLATE 13.1 *Muḥammad ʿAlī (painting by Sir David Wilkie)*

As France, until then a friend, had withdrawn its support, Muḥammad ʿAlī fell back on the Ottoman empire, submitting to the Porte on 12 December a plan of revival that bore the hallmark of statesmanship:

PLATE 13.2 *Ibrāhīm, Muḥammad ʿAlī's son and leading general*

> There can be no doubt that the need for revival is acutely felt in all Islamic countries. Our nation in its present state of apathy is living like cattle. I beseech you: let us leave aside selfishness, quick temper and overzealousness, and devote some thought to the distressing and poverty-stricken state in which Islamic nations now find themselves. Let us go back to the wisdom of yesterday and make a peace which will be more like a truce . . .
>
> It would be a thousand times better for us to live and serve our fatherland and our religion in this way . . . The time has come for me and my son to devote ourselves to the service of the state and of Islam . . .[6]

What followed is well known: the Porte's refusal; the increasingly ambitious designs of the Viceroy within the Arab world under the influence of Ibrāhīm; the war between Turkey and Egypt marked by the great

6. Letter to Cheijh Effendi, 12 December 1827, quoted in M. Sabry, 1930, pp. 153–5.

victories of Ibrāhīm at Konia, Ḳutāḥiya, Naṣībīn; the intervention by the powers, which were intent on eliminating Muḥammad ʿAlī. The latter's from 1831 to 1840 brought him to the gates of Istanbul. The 'holy alliance' of all the European powers saved the government of the Sultan in order the better to destroy the only Islamic state able, on the one hand, to oppose European colonial expansion and, on the other, to assume responsibility for the revival, modernization and renaissance of the provinces of the Ottoman empire.

The check imposed on Ibrāhīm's military activities by his father, at Ḳutāḥiya at the gates of Istanbul, led the former to harden his position. A letter he wrote to his father on the eve of the negotiations made this extremely clear:

> I believe that *independence* must be one of the first points to be discussed and resolved with the two negotiators. For me this is the most crucial question. The cession of the three districts of Anatolia, Alaîa and Cilicia and the Island of Cyprus and finally, the annexation of Egypt and possibly Tunisia and Tripolitania must constitute our minimum demands, from which we must not desist at any price; our essential interests demand this. Firstly, we have to be firm and resolute on the subject of your independence so as to consolidate our position and surround it with guarantees for the future. For without independence our efforts would all be in vain and we should remain under the yoke of this treacherous power which is continually weighing us down with its ridiculous requirements and demands for money. We must now free ourselves from this intolerable burden and seek our only salvation in independence...[7]

Thus, there were two possible roads to the status of an independent nation for Egypt; Muḥammad ʿAlī's goal of autonomy within the Turkish empire bordering on independence, and the vision of Ibrāhīm who sought nothing less than complete independence, with Egypt as the head and the heart of an Arab empire.

In this great enterprise of Muḥammad ʿAlī and his son, Ibrāhīm's outlook began to diverge from that of his father. Contact with the *fallāḥīn* (peasant) soldiers who spoke the same national language, Arabic, as the provinces of the Near East that they both conquered and liberated made Ibrāhīm more conscious of the Arab character of Islamic Egypt and, above all, the urgent necessity of forging the instrument of its renaissance, namely, an army based on advanced technology and cast in the Arab mould. As he was to declare at Acre in 1831: 'I have two objectives, the first and most important of which is to preserve Egypt's eternal honour and restore its past glory...' Before the attack at Homs, he threatened to tear the Ottoman army to

7. Letter of 3 February 1833, quoted in M. Sabry, 1930, pp. 227–8; G. Khankī, 1948, gives the date as 20 January 1833.

shreds 'in order to strengthen Egypt's position even further, ensure it an even more glorious destiny and enhance its honour and prestige'. At the siege of Acre, writing to Pückler-Muskau, Ibrāhīm proclaimed: 'It is impossible for any army in the world to show a greater spirit of endurance and bravery; whenever a case of indecision or cowardice was noted in the army, it was invariably among the Turkish officers, I do not know of any examples of this occurring among Arabs'. And finally to his father he declared, 'I have been living with these men for twenty years now and can state positively that for any three hundred Turks out of a thousand who are known for their loyalty, there are seven hundred Egyptians. Unless you are apprehensive of their habit of occasionally revolting against the established government...'[8] The pan-Arab factor was actively involved in the process of consolidating the modern Egyptian state as long as progress was being made, but it disappeared with Ibrāhīm after 1840.

After 'Abbās I (1849–54), who agreed to everything short of government by a European country, Ismā'īl expressed the national problem in terms of independence and sovereignty. His intention was to reduce his country's dependence on Turkey by negotiation, and then make it an autonomous and stable state with the institutions of self-government to be developed later. Ismā'īl was successful in having the *firmān* of 27 May and 15 June 1866 and that of June 1867 promulgated. The first two established direct hereditary succession to the throne of Egypt from father to son according to the right of primogeniture and in keeping with the 'same mode of succession which obtained in most European dynasties', but in a 'complete break with the traditions of the Islamic world'.[9]

The *firmān* of 8 June 1867 created a new title, that of *khedive*, for Ismā'īl and his successors, the better to distinguish them from the other viceroys. It granted the *khedive* of Egypt the right to promulgate *tanẓīmāt*, administrative ordinances, and conventions with foreign countries (customs, postal services, transport, the policing of foreigners, etc.) which, while not having the full status of international treaties, still conferred the effective right to negotiate economic agreements. The culmination came on 8 June 1873. Egypt – for the first time defined in the *firmān* of that date as a 'state' and no longer as a 'province' – was assured of the continuity of the *khedive*'s power on the terms then obtaining.

According to Sabry, the reconstruction of the Egyptian empire was, on the one hand in line with 'the idea of building a powerful independent state' and 'acquiring by money' what Muḥammad 'Alī had vainly tried to obtain by force, while on the other, it also satisfied the need to 'open up through expansion in Africa this possibility of achieving fame and freedom which would allow it to regain its sense of nationhood and to develop some of its dormant capacities'. Ismā'īl thought that by using the new Egyptian

8. Quoted by Prince H. Pückler-Muskau in M. Sabry, 1930, pp. 469–71.
9. Texts quoted in A. Sammarco, 1935, Vol. 4, pp. 196–7.

corps of army officers to extend Egyptian territory down to the Equator, he could somehow secure an ultimate and inaccessible refuge for his country's independence in the heart of the continent. Initially at least, this expansion into the heart of the African continent was opposed neither by Turkey nor by Britain.

The infrastructure of the new empire, after leaving out some battleships delivered to Turkey and merchant ships able to cater for all Egypt's commercial needs, comprised a war fleet of average strength, eighteen forts, a good telephone and telegraph service, and the beginnings of a railway that was planned to reach Khartoum and Suākin. This Egyptian military expansion brought aspects of European civilization to the Sudan and also to Somalia, Harar, the Equatorial Province, Bunyoro and Buganda. The liberal press in Europe was full of praise. Most of the African populations also seemed to have been favourably disposed. But the enterprise, which reached its peak between 1872 and 1879, was to end in failure.

Ismā'īl gave in on the question of the military high command, thinking that this would induce Britain to tolerate his African enterprise. He accomplished nothing comparable to Muḥammad 'Alī's successes in the economic and, more importantly, industrial spheres. Although efficiently officered, the army was commanded by foreigners, and, after the Treaty of London, it no longer had a powerful industrial infrastructure to rely on. Egypt was no longer able to maintain its independence and modern economic development. None the less, Ismā'īl's motto, in its various formulations, still continues to ring in our ears: 'The peoples of the regions where the Nile has its sources must, from now on, be friends and allies of His Highness the Khedive'.[10]

Concurrently with the implementation of this great national enterprise, the representative and subsequently constitutionalist movement took root and reached its zenith under Ismā'īl. Already, on 5 October 1798, Bonaparte had convened a General Assembly of notables which had termed itself *al-dīwān al-'ām*. Under Muḥammad 'Alī, although the creation of the different institutions of a modern state was to involve actively the entire country, the watchword was efficiency and order rather than a popular mandate. A new consultative body, the *madjlis al-mushāwara* was set up in 1829. It comprised 156 members – *inter alia* 23 senior civil servants and *'ulamā'*, 24 provincial *ma'mūrs* and 99 provincial notables and *shaykhs*. Ibrāhīm was its chairman.

A special assembly, *al-madjlis al-'umūmī*, was constituted in 1847 at Alexandria to resolve the problems of that city. In 1832 a council of the leading public figures comprising twenty-two people was constituted in Syria.[11]

10. M. Sabry, 1933, pp. 383–9; A.-R. al-Rafe'ī, 1948, pp. 104–96; R. Robinson and J. Gallagher, 1961, pp. 2–3, 59, 122–33.

11. On the evolution of constitutionalism in Egypt, see G. Douin, 1933–41, pp. 298–301; P. Ravisse, 1896, p. 9; A.-R. al-Rafe'ī, 1948a, pp. 81–4; J. M. Landau, 1953, p. 9;

In 1834, Shaykh Rifā-ʿa al-Ṭahṭāwī published the first edition of his reflections on the French Revolution entitled *Takhliṣ al-ibrīz ilā Talkhīṣ Bārīz*. It signalled the birth and crystallization of modern Egyptian political and social thought. Its contribution to reflection on 'the fatherland' and the 'nation' was substantial. It bears essentially on the two concepts of 'freedom' and 'secularity' viewed both in their theoretical and practical dimensions. Ṭahṭāwī very skilfully combines arguments drawn from the entire history of Egyptian civilization, with particular reference to the Copts, and that of Islam with particular reference to the Caliph ʿUmar, with the lessons of the French Revolution, to reach the conclusion that only a constitution or charter based on the social contract and not handed down by the sovereign could constitute the basis of a civilized society.[12] Under ʿAbbās I, Ṭahṭāwī was exiled to the Sudan. Saʿīd set up a body akin to a council of state which comprised nine members, the function of which was consultative. It was not until about August 1864 that the constitutionalist movement seemed to be coming to life again.

Two texts – *al-lā'ihah al-asāsiyyah* (the fundamental statute) and *al-lā'ihah al-nizāmiyyah* (the law setting forth the powers of the assembly of delegates) – were promulgated on 22 October 1866 and combined in 'statutes' whereby the *madjlis shūrā al-nuwwāb* (consultative council, assembly of deputies) was constituted. Article I of the first text defined the nature of the new assembly as follows: 'The task of the Assembly shall be to deliberate on the higher interests of the country. It shall also have to take decisions on the projects which the government shall consider as falling within its scope and in respect of which it shall give its opinion, which shall then be submitted to His Highness the Viceroy for his approval'.

There was a preponderance of village leaders in the Assembly – at the expense of intellectuals returning from training abroad – and a marked and continual increase in the number of them being appointed to administrative posts, including that of *mudīr*. The support this group gave to Ismāʿīl during the last years of his reign, and then to the revolution staged by the army, reveals the village leaders as the most representative body in the political life of the period, and as elements of an emerging indigenous bourgeoisie who, in addition, controlled most of the country.

The year 1875 was the turning point. Faced with the increasing penetration of the European powers following the opening of the Isthmus of Suez, Khedive Ismāʿīl became locked in a struggle that was to lead to his downfall and exile in 1879.

D. M. Wallace, 1883, pp. 209–13; J. C. McCoan, 1887, p. 115; G. Baer, 1961, p. 127, n. 37; Baron de Malortie, 1882, p. 214.

12. R. al-Ṭahṭāwī, 1834.

PLATE 13.3 *Shaykh Rifā-ʿa al-Ṭahṭāwī*

The economy, society and culture: the dialectics of modernity and tradition

Towards economic autarchy

The first point to emphasize is that Muḥammad ʿAlī created a national economy in Egypt to replace the uncoordinated local economies that still obtained in most contemporary oriental countries. The existence of a unified national decision-making centre for economic policy was the logical outcome of the thousands of years of Egypt's history. The autarchic economy set up by Muḥammad ʿAlī was to help further his plans of founding a modern Egyptian national state at the heart of an empire. Despite the setback of 1840, Ismāʿīl was able to return to the route mapped out by Muḥammad ʿAlī. The pressure of international big business followed by its penetration, and, finally, the occupation of Egypt in 1882, were to affect this basic situation in two very significant ways. They led, first, to the creation of a single national market – thanks largely to the major efforts undertaken by Ismāʿīl – and, secondly, to the integration of the Egyptian economy into the international economic system through the contracting of loans and, above all, the cotton monoculture.

The work of Muḥammad ʿAlī deserves closer scrutiny. Muḥammad ʿAlī was alone among contemporary Eastern Islamic rulers in considering economics as underpinning politics, and this is what made this canny Albanian officer a statesman. The state he planned to establish was defined initially in 1805 as an ethnic formation centred around a powerful and efficient army, itself buttressed by a self-supporting modern economy.[13]

From 1818 to 1830, he created important industrial units: the munitions and ordnance factories at the Citadel, which reached their apogee in 1828 under Adham bey; the munitions factory at the Arsenal; the gun factory at Ḥūḍ al Marṣūd (1821) which included five gunpowder factories producing 15 874 *ḳantārs* (1 ḳantār = 45 kg) in 1833; the navy arsenal at Alexandria, built in 1829 by Lefébure de Cerisy who had succeeded the brilliant master-craftsman Hadj ʿUmar; finally, the dry dock built by Mougel in 1844. This infrastructure filled Field-Marshal Marmont and Clot Bey with wonder. In the sphere of 'civilian' industry, thirty textile and cotton mills were set up in Upper and Lower Egypt. The Cairo factories supplied factories in the provinces with machines, tools, spare parts, building materials and technicians to repair plant.

This industrial production met the needs of the country both in import substitution and profits of the order of 100 per cent accruing to the national treasury. Three wool mills were built at Būlāḳ, Damanhūr and Fuwwa, together with a large silk factory at Khurunfīsh (1816) and many flax mills throughout the country; three sugar refineries; seventeen indigo factories; two large glassworks; the Rosetta tannery (1827); the Cairo paper mill (1834); and, finally, the six saltpetre works built by the Frenchman Haīm. But this infrastructure suffered from an inherent weakness which was to check the industrialization process a century later. The country lacked the essential minerals, iron and coal, and thus had difficulty in obtaining sufficient power to drive its machines.

'Our goal is not to make profit, but to train our people in the use of industrial techniques', Muḥammad ʿAlī told J. Bowring, who had come to put the case for an agricultural Egypt. Egyptian historiographers have now begun to devote attention to this aspect of the work of the founder of the dynasty which was to survive until ousted on 26 July 1952.

13. See A. Abdel-Malek, 1969, pp. 23, 32, 65, 108; and more detailed studies in A.-R. al-Rafeʿī, 1951; G. Baer, 1962; R. al-Barāwī and M. Ḥamza ʿElīsh, 1944; A. Linant de Bellefonds, 1872–3, p. 3; J. Bowring, 1840; F. Djirdjis, 1958; M. F. Lihītā, 1944; G. Michailidis, 1950; H. Thiers, 1867; F. de Lesseps, 1869; M. K. Moursy, 1914; H. A. B. Rivlin, 1961; J. Tagher, 1949; M. Fahmy, 1954; A. E. Crouchley, 1938; A. A. A. al-Gritly, 1948; A. Abdel-Malek, 1962; H. Khallaf, 1962; C. P. Issawi, 1966; M. S. Ghurbāl, 1944; A. A. Ḥaṭṭāb, 1935.

The Treaty of London, which was signed by the European powers and Turkey on 15 July 1840, was to make it possible to curb this great drive by Egypt to build an independent economy, and its terms condemned the Ottoman empire, as it then was, to general decadence. Thus ended the monopoly established by Muḥammad ʿAlī. Egypt was now open to the penetration of foreign capital, which imposed distortions on the Egyptian economy. The dependence on cultivation of a single crop, cotton, obviously had a damaging effect on the entire Egyptian economy. The cutting of a canal across the isthmus of Suez completed the integration of the Egyptian economy into the world system and led directly to the military occupation of 1882. In this case, integration meant that Egypt was completely at the mercy of world prices and the vicissitudes of the international economic situation from which Egypt was isolated, especially after 1879, when it was deprived of its power to make sovereign decisions.

Another type of distortion resulted from uneven development; Lower Egypt was favoured at the expense of Upper Egypt. It is true that most of the arable land was to be found in the Nile delta, which sustained the large towns. The towns were at the heart of the process of economic, social, political and cultural modernization. An indigenous ruling class, formed by the leading landowners, progressively emerged with the development of the capitalist sector based on the establishment of private ownership of land. The interests of this ruling class were divided between the towns and the countryside on the one hand, and, on the other, the national and the international economy, including external trade, and particularly the sale of cotton.

This symbiosis at the top, as it were, created very strong organic links between the hinterland and the towns. Certain population groups were moving from the countryside to the towns. Here, the term hinterland is used specifically to describe the south, i.e. Upper Egypt. For while Alexandria, looking towards Europe, played a leading economic role, especially from the reign of Saʿīd until the end of the century, Cairo also, situated in the heart of Egypt, controlled the Delta where most of the country's wealth was created and where most of its population lived. To both Cairo and Alexandria, Upper Egypt, particularly under the pressure of foreign finance, became the veritable hinterland.

Agriculture and land use

Agriculture itself quite naturally took pride of place in the economic reforms. At the end of the eighteenth century, all the land, apart from the *wakf*, was in the hands of the *multazim* whose main task was to collect and transmit the revenues owed by their respective village, or villages, to the central or provincial treasury. However, the extent of the rights of usufruct that had been gradually acquired by the *multazim*, usually benefiting his family (to the point that 'State ownership was little more than a farce'), made the formation of the modern and centralized state of which Muḥammad ʿAlī dreamed impossible. All he could do was to endeavour to minimize the scattering and dispersion of the income from the land. The two million *feddāns* (1 *feddān* = 0.56 ha) of arable land in Egypt in 1805 were divided into six categories: 200 000 *feddāns* of *abʿādiyya* or *shiflik* land allocated by Muḥammad ʿAlī to members of his family, and civil and military officers, which were exempt from land taxes; the lands of the *mamlūks* at the Citadel (1811), about 100 000 *feddāns* which on their liquidation in Upper Egypt (1812) were converted into *awsiya* land, granted as compensation to the *mamlūks*, so as not to deprive their families of all resources; the land of the *shaykhs*, or *masmūḥ al-mashāyekh wal-maṣāteb* – 4 per cent of the arable area of each village, 154 000 *feddāns* in all, which had been given to the *ʿulamā*ʾ, who also performed the function of *multazims*; the *rizḳa* land, 6000 *feddāns*, not subject to tax, which had been given as presents to foreign experts working in Egypt; the *athar* land which remained available and was given to the *fallāḥīn*; finally, the *ʿerbān* land on which Muḥammad ʿAlī wished the Beduins to settle. This policy and land allocation made the Viceroy appear to his contemporaries 'as the violator of acquired rights, the destroyer of prosperous businesses, one who takes what belongs to others and deprives them of their means of subsistence'. However, in the words of Shafīḳ Ghurbāl, it was a question of 'emerging from chaos, poverty and hunger and striving towards order, abundance, wealth and strength'.

When considered from the point of view of land ownership alone, the situation appears more complex. True, the general trend was towards order, the Egyptian economy being at the time, generally speaking, state-managed and autarchic. While it is overstating the case to maintain, as does Muḥammad Kāmel Mursī, that the land was registered, at that time, in the name of the *fallāḥīn* individually, since the greater part remained effectively state property, Ibrāhīm ʿAmer more correctly sees this system as a form of transition: 'Before Muḥammad ʿAlī, the real estate *régime* in Egypt and the social system it supported were typical of an "Oriental feudalism", . . . the organization of farming at the time of Muḥammad ʿAlī was a temporary phenomenon, a transitional stage between feudalism and capitalism.'[14] It is necessary to emphasize that the development of the large private estates characteristic of modern Egypt began in the period of Muḥammad ʿAlī. The reason for their introduction, however, was not the desire to create a new class of landowners, but to facilitate administration and tax collection to the benefit of the government and the new ruling class.

There are other facts which deserve to be made clear. It was Muḥammad ʿAlī who diversified the crops and, in particular, from 1821 onwards inten-

14. Ibrāhīm ʿAmer explains the difference between Oriental feudalism and European feudalism as 'the absence of private property in the form of land and central state control of land ownership.'

sified the growing of cotton, on the advice of Jumel who gave his name to the new variety of long-staple cotton. The Jumel cotton along with the American 'Sea Island' type afforded the state – with its monopoly of foreign trade – an appreciable income, since in 1845 the crop amounted to 424 995 *ḳantārs*, produced on 212 473 *feddāns*, an increase of 400 per cent in twenty years. Of this, a maximum of 80 000 *ḳantārs* went to Egyptian spinning mills, leaving 344 995 *ḳantārs* for export. The experts were unanimous in their praise for the Viceroy's policy of agricultural modernization: 'First of all, [he] supplied the capital that was needed to transform the Egyptian agricultural economy from a subsistence economy to a cash crop economy and he did this without sacrificing the production of cereals, upon which the Egyptian agricultural economy had always been based'.[15]

The Viceroy described himself as being primarily 'a farmer and a merchant', especially in talking to foreign observers. He used the word farmer in the sense of the Pharaohs; lords of the 'hydraulic society' of which Egypt offered the most compact and striking example throughout the ages. He used the corvée to have thirty-six canals and drains dug, the best known being the Maḥmūdiyya canal; blocked up the Pharʿawniyya, which was unusable, and put up fifteen bridges and twenty-three dams on the Nile, including the big dam at the Delta, *al-ḳanatir al-khayriyya*, not to mention numerous repair works. Such efforts were concentrated on Lower Egypt. There seems to have been a slackening off towards the end of the reign just when the commission appointed in 1838 recommended an extremely ambitious plan for irrigating 3 800 000 *feddāns*. Muḥammad ʿAlī hesitated to devote a considerable part of his resources in men and materials to building new dams when the economic, political and military offensive of the European powers had begun to take shape.[16]

It was no accident that it was the British who carried out Muḥammad ʿAlī's ambitious project after their occupation of Egypt. Technically, the conclusion drawn was that the achievements of Muḥammad ʿAlī in irrigation seem less impressive when compared with those of other major periods of Egyptian history. Nevertheless, shrewd observers of the period make no mistake: the issue was not only a question of modernization, or of town-and-country planning, but of ensuring 'Egypt's independence of other countries' as John Bowring, the British commissioner in Egypt, correctly diagnosed.

The period 1840–79 was one of transition, from an economy bearing the strong imprint of 'Oriental feudalism' to a 'backward capitalist economy of predominantly agrarian colonial type', dominated by the state, which rediscovered and developed Muḥammad ʿAlī's desire for modernization.

15. H. A. B. Rivlin, 1961, pp. 169–70.

16. Dr Clot bey was the only foreigner to be aware of the problem, for both contemporaries and researchers today – in particular, Bowring and Rivlin – confine themselves to technical considerations and do not explain this phenomenon.

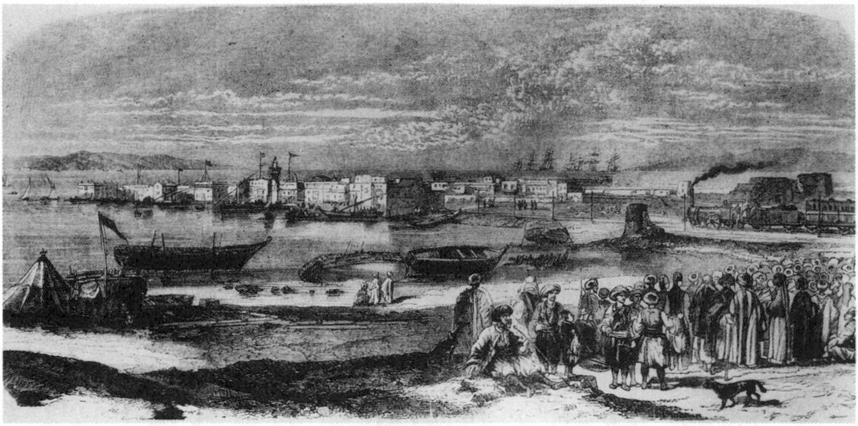

PLATE 13.4 *The arrival of the first train on the railway between Cairo and Suez 14 December 1858*

In fact, the policy of monopoly, which dealt a severe blow to the privileges of the former feudality and concentrated the land, amongst other things, in the hands of the Viceroy, prepared the way for the private ownership of land, its usufruct being the first step. In 1846, a decree enabled land held in usufruct to be mortgaged. In 1854, the transfer of usufruct property deeds had to be conducted in the courts. The law of 5 August 1858, issued by Saʿīd, formally instituted the right to private ownership of land, on various terms (clause 25) beginning with the right of inheritance. Between 1858 and 1871, a number of successive measures assimilated *rizḳa, awsiya* and *abʿādiyya* land to *kharādj* land, which had been the object of these reforms. By 1880, almost all landowners held their land outright. The area of arable land rose from 3 856 226 *feddān*s in 1840 to 4 758 474 *feddān*s in 1882 thanks to the major works of land improvement and infrastructure undertaken mainly under Ismāʿīl.

There has for some time now been a clearer understanding of the effectiveness of Ismāʿīl's use of foreign loans in developing capital works, many of which had an impact on the rural areas. This process began with ʿAbbās who in 1851 granted George Stephenson a contract for the construction of the first railway, which was to link Alexandria with Cairo. Under Saʿīd, Kafr al-Zayyāt, Tantā and Suez were linked to the capital. The construction of the big dry dock at Suez, and the cleaning-out of the Maḥmūdiyya canal were also undertaken on his initiative. Egypt thus became once again the meeting point between the Mediterranean and the Red Sea.

On the basis of the Beardsley report, A. E. Crouchley estimated Ismāʿīl's total expenditure on major works at £E. 51 394 000. During his reign 112 canals extending over 8400 miles were built, the excavation for this, when compared with that necessary for the Suez Canal, being in a proportion of 165 to 100. Several thousands of miles of canals were also dredged and 430 bridges were built. Alexandria became the best port in the Mediterranean. Fifteen lighthouses were built on the two coasts; 1500 km of railway; 5200 km of telegraph lines, plus 2000 km in the Sudan, and sixty-four sugar refineries. He also re-established the postal service, after a period of chaos under Saʿīd. In 1874, Egypt signed the agreements of the First International Postal Congress in Berne. The introduction of sewers, the improvement of the streets of Cairo and Alexandria, the supply of fresh water and lighting to several districts and the modernization of Cairo as a whole on the Paris model were amongst the many municipal works which complemented the major works on infrastructure.

The first social group to emerge as a class in the rural areas was that of the big landowners. During the first stage – from 23 March 1840 to 24 December 1866 – the holding of *ʿuhda* (tax-free lands given in the first instance in usufruct, which gradually became *de facto* property) was restricted to Muḥammad ʿAlī's family and to dignitaries. Of the total, then estimated at 1 200 000 *feddān*s, a quarter was owned by the viceroy's family, and the remainder formed the basis of the big estates to come: Salīm al-Salihdār pasha was given the villages of al-Balynāna and Fad͟hara; the al-Shawāribī family owned 4000 *feddān*s (out of 7000) at Ḳalyūb at the end of the century; Al-Sayyed Abāza pasha was given some twenty villages in Sharḳiyya and still owned fifteen of them, totalling 6000 *feddān*s, on his death in 1876; Badrāwī pasha held Samannūd, some 1400 *feddān*s. The transition to full private ownership was not deliberately sought; it appears that Muḥammad ʿAlī's successors had the *de facto* situation ratified in return for payment of the taxes owned by the *fallāḥīn* who worked on the lands. A second group of landowners was allocated the fallow land, *abʿadiyya*, *abʿadiyya*, which covered an area of between 750 000 and 1 million *feddān*s at the end of Muḥammad ʿAlī's reign, mostly in the two provinces of G͟harbiyya and Beḥeira: Muḥammad S͟harīf pasha, Daramallī pasha, all governors or ministers, were the main beneficiaries. G. Baer points out that it was, however, the *jiflik* lands – the lands 'given' by the sovereign – mainly composed of villages that had been abandoned because of heavy taxation and thus transferred to the royal family, that formed the main part of the big estates. A large proportion of the million *feddān*s which were the property of the khedive's family in 1878 were *jiflik* lands; it was Ismāʿīl who distributed the greater part of these gifts between 1867 and 1876.

Two decrees issued by Saʿīd, on 30 September and 11 October 1854, divided all land into two categories; *ʿushūriyya* (which included the three types described above, as well as the *awsiya* land, the area of which was insignificant) and *k͟harād͟jiyya*, that is the land that remained outside the framework of the large farm-holdings. In fact, Y. Artin and Lord Cromer considered *ʿushūriyya* land to be synonymous with large holdings; its area rose from 636 177 *feddāns* in 1863 to 1 423 987 in 1891, or from 14.5 per cent to 28.8 per cent of the cultivated land, whereas the area of *kharādjiyya* land fluctuated between 3 759 125 and 3 543 529 *feddāns*, that is a fall from 85.5 per cent to 71.2 per cent over the same period.

The earliest available statistics of landownership indicated that in 1894, 11 900 big landowners (with more than 50 *feddāns*) owned 2 243 000 *feddāns* or 44 per cent of the total farmland. The million *feddāns* belonging to the khedive's family in 1878 were distinctly more than its 664 000 *feddāns* in 1844; Ismā'īl had appropriated much of the new land, which he divided into Dā'ira al-Saniyya land (503 699 *feddāns* in 1880) and lands which were the property of the state (425 729 *feddāns* in 1878). As we know, the state-owned lands had to be sold in 1878 to cover the Rothschild loan but the khedive had taken the precaution of distributing a large proportion of them to his relatives before that date; later, measures were also taken that enabled this group to buy back some of the state property. Thus:

> while the dual role of the Egyptian sovereign as owner of state land and of his own lands ended at the end of the reign of Ismā'īl ... the reigning member of the family (khedive, sultan or king) continued to be almost always the biggest landowner. But, in theory – and to a large extent in practice – he no longer had at his disposal a vast reserve of state lands to increase his personal property ... Similarly, the royal family, as a whole, and thanks to its *wakfs*, as well as to its great wealth which enabled it to buy still more land, maintained its prominent place, which dates from the nineteenth century, amongst Egyptian land-holders.

These big landowners were, quite naturally, to be recruited from the high dignitaries of the regime, officers, some village notables, some Beduin chiefs, *'ulamā'* and Copts. The broader landownership position is indicated in Table 13.1.

Information gathered on the socio-economic status of the village *'ūmdas* and *shaykhs* is also very revealing. The end of the era of the monopoly and the emergence of private ownership of land under Sa'īd appreciably reduced the size of this category of rural dignitaries who were previously the stewards of the *multazims*, and always the representatives of central power vis-à-vis the *fallāḥīn*. However, Ismā'īl reinforced their authority: 'this office falls to the biggest landowner', wrote the correspondent of *The Times*, D. Mackenzie Wallace; 'Alī Mubārak pasha's encyclopedia confirms this, and supplies the family names of the *'ūmdas* (Al-Sharīf, Al-Hawwārī, Al-Gayyār, 'Abd el-Hakk, Shi'īr, Al-'Ukalī, Siyāgh, Al-Wakīl, Al-'Itribī, Al-Shirī'ī, etc.) These were the kulaks of Egypt whom the proconsulate of Cromer was to hesitate to use as a power base in the countryside. Their relative weight in the rural areas, at the time of the 1894 census, was a result of the gains acquired under Ismā'īl: the distribution of land, the granting of loans to poor *fallāḥīn*, the renting of their own lands, and

TABLE 13.1 *Egyptian landownership by size of holdings, 1894 and 1914*

Year	Number	%	Area	%
	Big landowners (more than 50 *feddāns*)			
1894	11 900	1.3	2 243 500	44
1914	12 480	0.8	2 396 940	43.9
	Average landowners (5–10 *feddāns*)			
1894	141 070	15.4	1 756 100	34.3
1914	132 600	8.5	1 638 000	30
	Small landowners (less than 5 *feddāns*)			
1894	761 300	83.3	1 113 000	21.7
1914	1 414 920	91.7	1 425 060	26.1

NOTE: The most striking feature does seem to be the fragmentation of property at the turn of the century. The causes for this are numerous: the effects of the Islamic inheritance law; intense demographic growth; the law (December 1912) making the seizure of holdings of 5 *feddāns* illegal. In fact, small landholdings are as much a result of the fragmentation, which is entirely relative, of large holdings, as they are of that of average-sized ones.

commercial transactions with the towns in particular. As the numbers of relatively rich peasants grew in the rural areas so also did the number of *fallāḥīn* families with less than 3 *feddāns* – the amount required for subsistence – and other landless people 'without an occupation'. This process of pauperization was to become even more rapid in the colonial period. Whereas ʿAbbas I backed the Beduins against a possible alliance of *shaykhs* and *fallāḥīn*, and Saʿid sought to reduce the political power of the village dignitaries, Ismāʿīl on the contrary leaned heavily on them; the members of the first consultative assembly of Deputies in 1866 were chosen in large part from among the *shaykhs*; A. R. al-Rāfiʿī estimates the number of *ʿumdas* who sat amongst the seventy-four to seventy-five delegates in 1866, 1870 and 1876 at between fifty-eight and sixty-four; and, Ismāʿīl appointed a great many to the office of *mūdīr* (governor) in opposition to the Turkish-Albanian aristocracy. Quite naturally, these men supported the ʿUrābī revolution in 1882 and rallied the *fallāḥīn* to the national cause.

Cultural development

The development of culture from the admittedly unsuccessful beginnings of acculturation up to the emergence of an authentic philosophy of national culture deserves to be considered a major achievement in its own right. Once again, as throughout Egypt's seven-thousand year history, it was the state which was responsible for the initial planning and the training of officials, and which provided the driving force. The imposing figure of Shaykh Rifāʿa al-Ṭahṭāwī (1801–73) was central to this process. With him the Middle Ages drew to a close in Egypt, as in other countries of the Arab world.

He preached the beginning of a new era, characterized by the reconquest of identity, which is the principal objective of societies and civilizations during the 'nationalist' phase. Such a renaissance can only be brought about within the national framework, with the help of radical thought and a critical approach to both the national heritage and foreign ideas so that 'the fatherland can become the scene of our collective happiness which we will achieve through freedom, thought and the factory'. His masterpiece, *Manāhedj al-albāb al-Miṣriyya fi mabāhedj al-ādāb al-ʿaṣriyya* ('The paths of Egyptian hearts to the joys of the modern way of life'), published in 1869, marked the point at which nationalist thought started moving towards socialism:

> It is work that confers value on all things which do not exist outside it ... Work thus plays a key role in the acquisition of wealth: it is through work that man harnesses the energies of animals and their spontaneous industry, which are then directed into channels beneficial to members of the fatherland...
>
> All the virtues which the believer must display in his behaviour towards his fellow believers are also mandatory for all members of the fatherland, given the reciprocal duties and the patriotic fraternity – not to mention the religious fraternity – which unite them. All those who are united within the same fatherland have a moral obligation to work together so as to better the condition of their fatherland and to add to its honour, its greatness, its wealth and prosperity. This wealth can only be created if social relationships are stable and work is carried out in the public interest. This work should be equally divided between the members of the fatherland so that everyone can then be justly proud of their nation. When injustice, cowardice, falsehood and contempt disappear, then positive values and blessings will abound among them and will usher in an era of collective happiness...[17]

The earliest students to be trained in Europe (chiefly in France, soon followed by England, Austria, Italy, the German States and later the USA), could not, of themselves, provide a framework for the whole country's educational system nor satisfy all its requirements. But with hindsight, when compared with measures taken in the same area by the British colonial rulers, the achievements of this period seem most impressive. Two distinct types of education were available: one traditional and classical, based on Egypt's heritage, and the other modern, to meet the requirements of the military state and the ongoing cultural renaissance. The network of advanced educational institutions of Muḥammad ʿAlī's time, which was unique in the contemporary non-Western world, was later extended and reinforced by the institution of a fully fledged system of national education under Ismāʿīl. This was largely due to the efforts of ʿAli Mubārak and occurred after the hiatus during which European and American religious

17. R. R. al-Ṭahṭāwi, 1869.

missions took root under cover of imperialist penetration in spite of dogged opposition by the Coptic Church. As a result of all these initiatives and thought, within half a century Egypt could boast of an educational system that was both modern and national in character, the main elements of a university of high academic standard, a diversified network of scientific institutions, and an educational curriculum based on modern humanist, scientific and rationalist values. As one would expect, it was in this last area that the most serious obstacles were encountered, which proves yet again that it is easier to change institutions than attitudes.

The conjunction of mission schools with the rise to prominence of new elite groups, as well as the emergence of new social strata, especially in the towns, gave rise to a powerful press and publishing movement. This from the creation of the official gazette *al-Waḳāʾiʿ al-Miṣriyya* (1828), was instigated and managed by the state but did, however, leave room for private initiative – *al-Ahrām* was founded in 1876.

The fact is that Egypt was alone among all the provinces of the Ottoman empire in offering an asylum for intellectuals, thinkers, writers and publicists persecuted by the Porte. It was indeed the best of all refuges, not only Eastern and Islamic, but also intimately involved in the modern European movement, a place where intellectuals could meet and engage in creative work, the only modern Oriental state with an advanced material, technical and economic infrastructure. Since the coming to power of Muḥammad ʿAlī, Egypt had made a great effort to establish a modern state, end four centuries of decadence, and build up an advanced economy supported by an efficient and powerful army. This effort, which was continued by Ismāʿīl under infinitely more difficult conditions, produced a ferment of ideas and dynamic social and political movements. As a result, the Arabic press, both Egyptian and Syro-Lebanese, official and private, flourished in an environment that stimulated national feelings and was propitious to the interplay of ideas and cultural renewal. This represents an essential contribution of Egypt to the progress of education, the press, publishing and of enlightenment generally in the Arab and Islamic world during a period that was later to be seen as one of gestation for national revolution and renaissance.

The methodology of history moved very rapidly towards a scientific approach. Its field of application stretched beyond Egypt to cover the great events sweeping the world; in particular the modern world of competing spheres of influence and, specifically, Europe which represented the most immediate threat. The transition from the concept of *umma* to *waṭan* from the 'community of believers' to the 'fatherland' in the strict sense of the term mirrored, from an ideological standpoint, the political effort made by Egypt to disengage itself from Turkey and become autonomous.

The idea of independence did not evolve along the same lines as that of the concept of the fatherland. The oscillation between a more or less self-centred autonomy and a desire for real independence and imperial ambitions formed part of the problem of defining Egypt's national personality, within an institutional framework, and in the context of the struggle of rival European powers to divide the world between them. The imperfections of the conceptual and ideological bases of analysis, while very real, were of secondary importance: the difficulty lay elsewhere. The thrust and parry of a direct dialectical two-sided confrontation being more or less impossible, three or more strategies had to be brought into play, the protagonists always being Egypt, France and Britain, not forgetting Turkey. Egypt thus had to seek within itself sources of strength and justifications for self-legitimization.

Imitation of the West in the name of 'reform' was quickly seen as a superficial pursuit, a mirror of the possible as opposed to the feasible. It affected dress, town planning, music, in the form of opera and martial tunes, the theatre especially and the first attempts at novel-writing. Everyday life in its personal and private aspects was not considered inviolable. Hence the initiative of the Coptic Patriarch, Kyrollos, and Ṭahṭāwī to provide educational and vocational schemes for girls. Those who had the task of promoting the national renaissance of modern Egypt were faced with the task of reshaping family life, the primordial mould forming that haven of trust and love within which the nation perpetuated itself. Still, the *salons* and the desire for innovation in personal life could in no way mask the effort to reawaken the state as a national entity. Nor could they drown, even for a moment, the country's authentic voice, apprehended through sayings, proverbs and customs, which saw imitation as a dispossession of thousands of years of history. Such dispossession was unthinkable, given the attachment of each Egyptian to the immemorial soil. Popular sensitivity therefore started expressing itself in forms and formulations that emphasized the need for viable intermediaries.

Geopolitics and compradors

The dissolution of the state of Muḥammad 'Alī which began with the Treaty of London in 1840 was the prelude to the penetration into Egypt of European big business supported by the 'compradors' of the time. To the view that the reign of 'Abbās I was one of 'silence and terror' in the face of the European threat, Muḥammad Sabry has replied:

> It must be admitted that the viceroy's vigilant policy erected a barrier against the mass influx of Europeans into Egypt. And thanks largely to the regulations restricting domestic trading, this policy also prevented Europeans, Greeks for the most part, from going into the hinterland, leaving the two cities of Alexandria and Cairo to spread out into rural areas and trade with ignorant peasants. In this way 'Abbās was able to check, but not completely eliminate, the evil which was to spread very rapidly during the 'consular era' under his successor[18]

18. M. Sabry, 1933.

The concession granted on 30 November 1854 by Sā'īd (1854–63) to his childhood friend Ferdinand de Lesseps for the construction of the Suez Canal, which was officially notified by the *firmān* of 19 May 1855, marked the beginning of European big-business penetration into Egypt. It was Napoleon III himself who was the driving force behind the transformation of the Société d'Etudes du Canal de Suez, founded on 27 November 1846 by three groups of ten members each, representing Great Britain, France and Austria, into the Organisation du conseil d'administration de la compagnie universelle du Canal de Suez, set up on 30 November 1854. This, as Napoleon told Enfantin, was 'so that its organization by businessmen would help the statesmen in their diplomatic negotiations'. Enfantin was soon excluded from the project in favour of de Lesseps alone, who took repeated advantage of his friendship with Sa'īd to wring all kinds of concessions from him. De Lesseps contracted more and more foreign loans. When Sa'īd died on 18 January 1863, Egypt's debt ran to 367 million francs (£E 14 313 000) according to the most widely accepted estimation, while M. F. Lihītā gives the figure of £E 16 308 075. Moreover, Sa'īd parted with the Wādī estates of 10 000 ha for a ridiculously low price. This estate comprised Tall al-Kibīr, the key to Egypt, with four inland canals between the Nile and Lake Timsāḥ, three houses and adjoining buildings, and warehouses spreading over an area of 10 000 sq m at Būlāḳ.

In his address on 20 January 1863 to the consular corps in the Cairo Citadel, Ismā'īl stated his intention of abolishing the corvée. 'Nobody is more in favour of the canal than I am', he said a little later, 'but I want the canal to belong to Egypt and not Egypt to the canal'. At the same time, the major drive to develop the national economy, the diplomatic missions and military operations undertaken outside the country in Mexico, Crete and Africa on behalf of the Porte, and to establish an Egyptian empire in Africa, added enormously to Egypt's debt. Its growth pattern is very revealing: as the country got deeper into debt, the terms of loans became more and more draconian. A total of eight loans, including Sa'īd's, were contracted between 1862 and 1873. In actual fact, the 1868 loan was not available for repaying the floating debt, as it was used instead to finance current expenses, including the Canal inauguration ceremonies. Ismā'īl Ṣaddīḳ then devised what was known as the *muḳābala* law (1871): against payment of a sum equal to six annual instalments of the land tax, landowners had their property rights confirmed and were entitled to a 50 per cent reduction of the tax in perpetuity. This law was in force from 1871 to 1877.

The bankruptcy that hung over Turkey in 1874 limited Ismā'īl's room for manoeuvre. In order to meet the deadline of 1 December 1875, he negotiated the sale of 177 642 shares in the Canal, first with his French creditors and then with Britain. On 25 November, the British Prime Minister, Disraeli, with Rothschild's support, bought all the shares in question, i.e. all Egypt's holdings in the Canal company for the paltry sum of £3 976 580.

The foreign residents, who increased in number from 3000 in 1836 to 112 568 in 1897, acted initially as a spearhead, and after 1882 as auxiliaries of the occupation forces. This group, according to M. Sabry, was composed mainly of delinquents, counterfeiters, jailbirds, nabobs and adventurers of all kinds. According to D. S. Landes, they included the best and worst in the European and Mediterranean world: 'bankers and usurers, merchants and thieves, staid English brokers and mercurial Levantine peddlers, proper clerks for the offices of the Peninsular and Oriental; painted harlots for the Square of the Consuls in Alexandria, dedicated scholars for the temples of Abydos and Karnak; cut-throats and confidence men for the alleys of Cairo.[19]

The wholesale trade and imports and exports were almost entirely in the hands of foreigners, mainly English, Greek, Italian and German; only six or seven out of several hundred importers in 1908 were Egyptians. The retail and small wholesale trade was controlled by foreigners, mostly Greeks, Levantines and Jews. Local moneylending and banks were mostly run, in alliance or association with European banks, by Jews, the '*néo-devorants*' – Cattaui, Ménaché, Suarés, Sursock, Adda, Harari, Salvago, Aghion, Sinadino, Ismalun. They operated alongside Greeks, Italians and Syrians and, later, Egyptians. The craftsmen, tradesmen and artisans were Mediterraneans and Levantines. British subjects, half of whom came from Cyprus, Malta and other colonies, were either soldiers, civil servants or cotton merchants. In 1897, 64 per cent of the indigenous working population, as against 0.7 per cent of foreigners, were working in the agricultural sector. Conversely, industrial and business activities occupied 50 per cent of the foreign working population, as compared with 17 per cent of Egyptians.

By 1919, 1488 foreign landowners possessed over 50 *feddāns* making a total of 583 463 *feddāns*, i.e. an average of 400 *feddāns* each, whereas Egypt's leading landowners could only boast an average of 150 *feddāns* each. The average salary per head of foreigners amounted to £E 85 as against £E 9.5 for Egyptians, not to mention foreign companies active in the country and the loans contracted abroad. In 1822, the Mixed Courts were set up in an effort to reduce the scope for financial and administrative disorder.

The Egyptian Revolution: 1881–2

Throughout the nineteenth century, and more particularly after the strategic break of 1840, the Egyptian bourgeoisie rose to prominence within the straitjacket imposed by burgeoning imperialism. It was accompanied by the establishment of a truly national culture of which the chief architects as we have seen, were Ṭahṭāwī and A. Mubārak. At the same time an army was created which became the most powerful in Africa and was led by

19. D. S. Landes, 1958.

polytechnicians and scientists who were past masters of long-term strategy.

The final years of Ismāʿīl's reign saw the emergence of a group that was encouraged by the Khedive himself. This was the 'Ḥilwān Group' (Sharīf, Ismāʿīl Rāgheb, ʿUmar Loutfī, Sultān pasha, Colonels Aḥmād ʿUrābī, ʿAbd al-ʿAl Ḥilmī and ʿAlī Fahmī; Mahmūd Sāmī al-Bārūdī, Sulaymān Abāẓa, Hasan al-Shiriʿī, Mahmūd Fahmī pasha), which, like the secret meetings of groups of officers in the Egyptian army, began to have an effect in 1876. Their activities led to the 'National Programme' which was put before the Assembly on 2 April 1879 by sixty members of parliament with the support of senior religious leaders. The meetings also resulted in the first manifesto signed by the National Party, on 4 November 1879, and the memorandum drawn up jointly by Muḥammad ʿAbduh and W. S. Blunt, on 18 December 1881. At the time these were viewed primarily as protest and constitutionalist movements. But the National Party drew on the support of the army, the last resort. The Party gradually came to work with the country's most influential groups. It recognized the role of the army in the national revolution and took religion, i.e. Islam, as the framework for political life.

These coalescing national groups came up against the European powers, led on this occasion by Britain, strongly supported by France. Under the pretext that heinous plots had caused the riots and a number of deaths in Alexandria on 11 June 1882, the European powers met in Constantinople on 23 June to discuss the 'Egyptian Question' again. They decided to intervene militarily. The British fleet, commanded by Admiral Seymour, bombarded Alexandria on 11 July 1882, causing considerable loss of life and the fire of Alexandria on 12 July. This action was a prelude to the military invasion, the objective of which was to destroy the national movement's spearhead, the army. Indeed, on 9 September 1881 the commanding officers of the three active army brigades had, at the head of all their troops, personally handed to the Khedive Tawfīḳ, in his palace at ʿAbdīn, the demands of the National Party, on behalf of the entire nation. The British invasion resulted in the destruction of the Egyptian army, mostly at the battle of al-Tall al-Kābīr on 13 September 1882, where Brigadier General Muḥammad Ebeīd was killed at the head of his troops and thereby became the unburied hero of the defeated revolution. A large number of pashas, centred around Muḥammad Sultān Pasha, threw in their lot with the occupation forces. Aḥmād ʿUrābī and his companions were cashiered from the army and exiled to Ceylon. The long night of the occupation had begun; although, for months to come, almost a whole year in fact, the *fallāḥīn* continued to take sporadic group action in order to keep the legend of ʿUrābī and his companions alive.

The most outstanding feature of the period between the forced abdication of Ismāʿīl (1879) and the British military occupation was the extreme and accelerated radicalization of the Egyptian national movement and its ideology. The issue of national renaissance was perceived and sometimes

PLATE 13.5 *The bombardment of Alexandria, July 1882*

expressed in explicit terms. Resistance to economic and political penetration by the European powers dominated the national consciousness and determined its themes and modes of expression. With the military occupation began a period which came to an end formally with the 1954 evacuation and, in reality, with the reconquest of Suez in 1956.

To evaluate the achievements of this period of failed revolution, let us consider, first, the revival of Islamic thought. The reversal of 1840 and the occupation could not fail to have their effect on whole groups of people whose awareness had been heightened by Islam. The group of thinkers working within social groups associated with the traditional sectors of the economy and with traditional institutions felt the inhumanity of this historical marginalization more acutely than those involved with modernist sectors of the economy of the period. Their theoreticians, and foremost among them Muḥammad ʿAbduh, diligently sought the reasons for, and the keys to understanding this situation in the heart of the most influential of the country's national and cultural traditions, that of Islam. They saw the religion and ideology of the nineteenth century as no longer those that the Prophet Muḥammad had instituted. The distorted traditions and exegesis of long centuries of decadence and dependence were all that was left: Islam was no longer Islam. The source of the national decadence was thus to be found in that distortion, and the key to any viable future for an Islamic country was to be sought in the return to fundamental principles.

There was room in the suggested reforms for reason or, to be more exact, common sense, but it had to be contained within the religious framework. This was a pragmatic approach, allowing for interaction with the modern world, but ruling out theorizing. Social dialectics, in whatever form, were excluded in the name of the unity of the *umma*, as was historicism, given that the primacy of the past was a fundamental principle. This Islamic fundamentalism seems to have provided the basic tenets of the theology and the essential characteristics that were applied to the political and social dimensions of the national revival.

The radicals were to be found elsewhere. They took root in the same soil, but only, it is true, among certain sectors. Islam nourished both tendencies and Al-Azhar often accepted and moulded both sides, but only during the initial phase. At the time, Ṭahṭāwī was a spokesman rather than a leader. The vanguard of the national movement – the 'Hilwān group' which claimed 'Urābī as its leader – was guided by liberal, independentist and constitutionalist principles. This approach of cautious pragmatism was quite acceptable despite the temporary revolutionary explosion. The vanguard of the classes that were rising to social prominence, and which were either poorly structured or in the process of formation, quite naturally donned an eclectic ideological armour, for they were as yet incapable of the critical discrimination necessary for all synthesis. Superficial eclecticism was thus temporarily preferred to analysis, and revolutionary unanimity to clear definition in terms of principles and classes. It was at this time that, notwithstanding Ṭahṭāwī, the ideology of liberal modernism became an ambiguous slogan.

In the gloom of that period, during the long night of the occupation, whose weight was particularly crushing during this first phase, one man, 'Abdallāh al-Nadīm (1843–96), emerges, a legendary figure. Everything found its focus in him: thought and action, rhetoric and practical effectiveness, classicism and modernity. His main contribution lay essentially in the inculcation of nationalist principles and ideas that had until then been the prerogative of the various elites into the lowly masses living in the towns and rural areas. Journalist, orator, political organizer, playwright, historian, theoretician and outstanding practitioner of dialectal Arabic, 'Abdallāh al-Nadīm was the real originator of the revolutionary populism which, from the columns of his successive newspapers *Al-Tankīt wa'l-Tabkīt* and *Al-Tā'ef* and the activities of the Islamic Benevolence Society, succeeded in rousing public opinion. As he declared, 'I have proclaimed love for the soldiers and the necessity of relying on their support. I have called on the masses to join with them ... '. And, in his appeal of 20 July 1882, at the time of the revolution led by 'Urābī:

> Inhabitants of Egypt! The English say that Egypt is the fortress of the Arab countries and that he who enters that fortress at the same time gains control of the Muslim countries. Rise up in defence of your fatherland. Stand firm, and safeguard this fortress of Muslim

> countries. You have a holy and just war to wage in the name of Allāh in order to preserve this great religion and drive off an enemy who wants to penetrate with his men and cavalry into the country of God, into the holy *Kaʿba*, through your country, with the support of the Khedive who has sold the nation in order to ingratiate himself with the English and given away the lands of Islam in exchange for the protection given to him by the English!

After the defeat, his last newspaper *Al-Ustādh*, which saw itself as the crucible for radicalization of the national ideology, the springboard for patriotic revival and the record-keeper of the long night which was to lead, in 1892, to the resurgence of the national movement around the National Party, declared:

> In short, the most drastic remedy is cauterization by fire. The situation has come to a head. If we can mend this torn fabric, if we can rely on each other, if Egyptians, Syrians, Arabs and Turks can speak with a single voice for the Orient, then we can say to Europe: 'We are ourselves and you are what you are'. But if we continue as we are, contradicting each other, capitulating, turning for help to one outsider after the other, then Europe will be entitled to drive us out of our countries and up to the mountaintops. And after having abandoned us with the wild beasts, to say to us 'If you had been like us, you would have acted like us'.

A period of nine years of underground activity, the first in the history of the Egyptian national movement and one which set a precedent, made Nadīm the spokesman for the *fallāḥīn* masses. One of the few of the rebel *fallāḥīn* of the time to survive, al-Ḥadj ʿUthmān Shuʿīb, wrote in his invaluable recollections, published eighty-four years later, in 1966,

> The country did not remain silent. There were many uprisings that were murderously suppressed by the sultans, the kings and the English. How many young people were lost in this way to no avail...! Then came Gamāl. He avenged ʿUrābī, he avenged the *fallāḥīn*; he drove out the sultan and the English. The one thing that displeases me is the photograph of ʿUrābī. Where are his hands, where is his great stature? And where, his sword?

During the long night that every occupation brings with it, in a bleak atmosphere of abdication and compromise, faced with the terror which descended on the country, a confused Nadīm proclaimed the accession of the masses to the controls of the revolution, which was to set the scene for the future.

The impact of Egypt: The 'other side of the river'

Before making a final assessment, we must first of all answer one fundamental question: what is the explanation for this renaissance at a time of crisis; and then, the blotting out of what for the period was a dazzling breakthrough, the cutting short of a process that is still remembered with regret by the Arab world and by Africa?

First and foremost, there was the crushing weight of geopolitical factors from the beginning to the end of the entire process, which proved more powerful than that of internal factors, which also had a fundamental role to play. If we represent the matrix of 'social dialectics' by two circles, an external, exogenous, circle, and an internal, endogenous, circle, it seems that for Egypt, that tortured country which was the meeting place of the Orient and the West, and of the three continents of Africa, Asia and Europe, the external circle, the circle of geopolitics, did control the whole process.

Moreover, the blows dealt to the first phase of the Egyptian renaissance from the great naval battles in the Mediterranean and the Treaty of London of 1840 to the military occupation of 1882, the massive influx of capital and foreign settlers, the gradual dismantling of the independence and nation-building movement, left Egypt little time – and this brings us to the heart of the endogenous circle of 'social dialectics' – to develop a coherent system of national thought that could withstand foreign penetration; and, at the same time, to give the nation's overall policy a realistic and appropriate structure. The main thrusts of Egyptian thought, liberal modernism on the one hand and Islamic fundamentalism on the other, did not endeavour to join forces until the mid-twentieth century. The nineteenth century was one of projects, of unsatisfactory compromises, of impossible mergers. Hence the nation's permeability, for the modernism derived from acculturation was easily confused with a well thought-out national modernity, and the 'Western wave' could easily isolate the different constituent factors and the principal formations of the Egyptian national movement.

The repercussions of the first stage of the Egyptian renaissance were to make themselves felt beyond the country's borders. Sudan, Ethiopia, the Horn of Africa and the region of the Great Lakes in Central Africa, were to learn from the experience of a renascent Egypt at grips with the forces of imperialism. In the Maghrib, the renaissance of political Islam and the great popular movements of armed resistance to colonial penetration were continually turning for inspiration to the various aspects of the Egyptian effort. The Treaty of Berlin codified the partition of Africa in 1884–5. This Treaty was designed, in large measure, to effect the rationalized and legalized dismemberment of the great continent, whose awakening threatened what was then the 'world order', the hegemonic order of the major powers.

Still further afield, the work of Muḥammad ʿAlī was to be an object lesson for the team set up in 1868 by Emperor Meiji to foster the Japanese restoration. Here the geopolitical situation was the reverse. Secure, thanks to the surrounding seas and continental masses until the irruption of Commodore Perry, Japan remained much more in control of its national and cultural cohesion and was thus able to set about the task of modernization free of the vice-like grip of geopolitics – until Hiroshima and Nagasaki. Here, the impact of the Japanese victory over the Russians at Tsushima (1905) on the awakening national consciousness and the National Party of Muṣṭafā Kāmal and Muḥammad Farīd in Egypt at the turn of the twentieth century is worth remembering. Meanwhile, the constitutional reform effected by the *Tanẓimāt*s in Turkey, situated between the Arab world and Japan, was directly and explicitly based on reforms carried out in Egypt: last ditch efforts by the Ottoman Caliphate, which were later to be taken over and rationalized by *Ittiḥād wa Taraqqī* and the Young Turks of Enver Pasha and Mustafa Kamal (Ataturk).

Thus, we are moving towards a better appreciation of the Egyptian national renaissance which, although in a state of crisis, was to become, objectively, a contributory factor in the resurgence of Africa, Asia and the Middle East from 1805 until the 1955 Bandung Conference.

14 The Sudan in the nineteenth century

H. A. IBRAHIM
with a contribution on the Southern Sudan by
B. A. OGOT

Arab migrations into the eastern Sudan – roughly the present Sudan minus the Southern Region – started as early as the ninth century and reached their peak in the fourteenth century. Through gradual and peaceful means the Arabs infiltrated the country and spread their culture, religion and influence among its Christian and traditionalist societies.[1] By the early sixteenth century the Eastern Sudan was ruled predominantly by two Muslim sultanates: the Fundj and the Fūr. While the Fūr sultans, who descended from a distinguished Sudanese family – the Kayra – ruled Dārfūr until 1874, their counterparts in Sennār capitulated to the Turkish rulers in 1821.[2] The Fundj sultanate had suffered from extensive dynastic rivalries, particularly between its founders, the Fundj and ʿAbdallāb, and subsequently between different hostile groups of the Hamadj who had controlled its destiny since the 1760s. The upshot of all this was the final disintegration of the sultanate by the early nineteenth century into some weak and hostile shaykhdoms.[3] The resultant chaos and local warfare gave the Viceroy of Egypt, Muḥammad ʿAlī, an opportunity that he was impatiently awaiting to add the Sudan to his domains in 1820–1. Thus started the first colonial era, one that dominated the Sudan for over sixty years.

The term 'Egyptian' is often used to describe this colonial period in the history of the Sudan. But, if at all, it should be used with discretion. The Sudan was not conquered or ruled by Egyptians as we know them today, but by a 'Turkish-speaking body whose members had dominated Egypt since medieval times'. With few exceptions, the true Egyptians – people of the Lower Nile – were not given senior political or military posts in Egypt or in the conquered Sudan, but were assigned junior posts in the administration and the army. Hence the Sudanese, and Europeans as well, called the rulers of the country Turks 'for the Sudan was Egyptian only in the sense that it was a dependency of the Ottoman province of Egypt'.[4]

1. For a detailed study of this subject, see Y. F. Hasan, 1967.
2. P. M. Holt, 1973, p. 67.
3. For details see Unesco, *General History of Africa*, Vol. V, ch. 7.
4. R. Hill, 1966, p. 1.

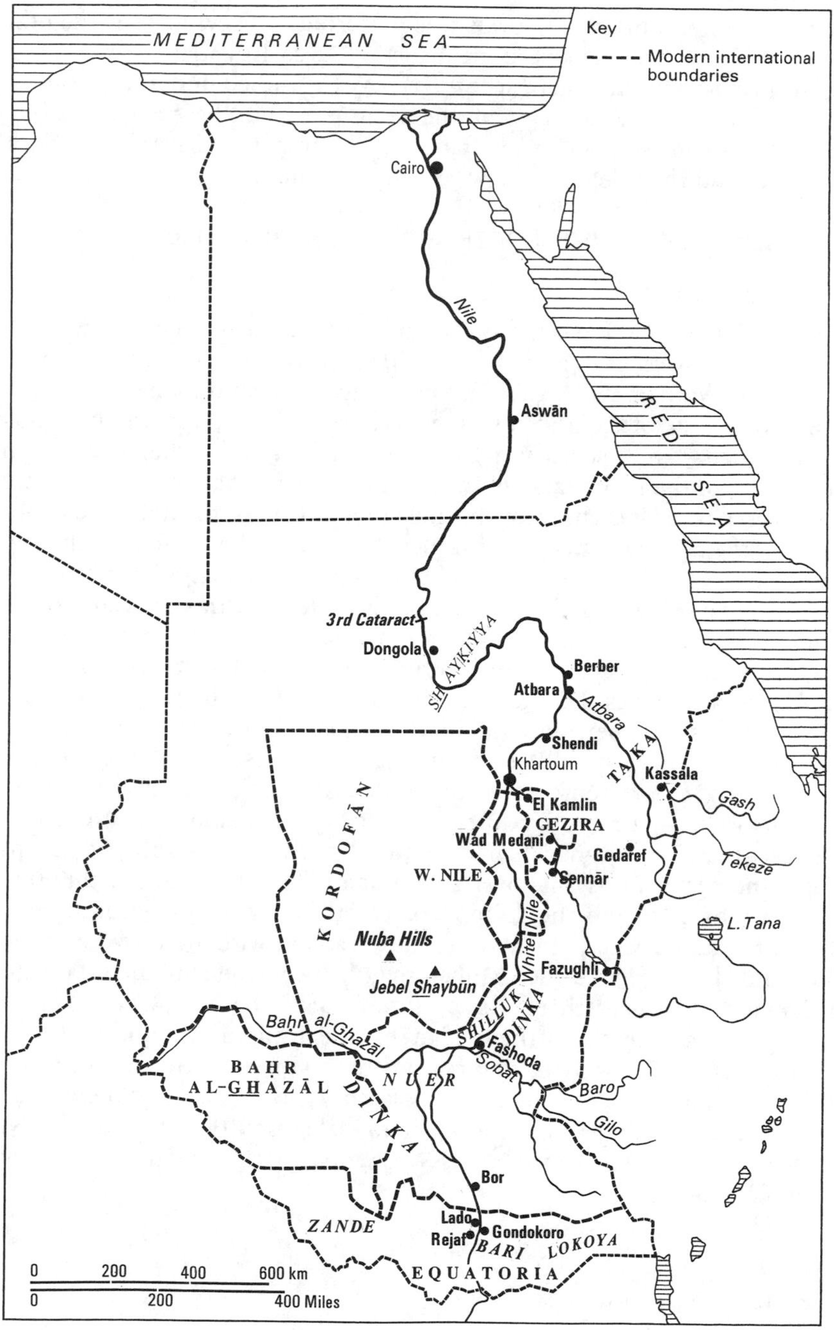

FIG. 14.1 *The Sudan under Turkish rule, 1820–81 (after H. A. Ibrahim)*

In this chapter Turkīyya (Turkish) is preferred to 'Egyptian' or the other commonly used, but awkward, neologism 'Turco-Egyptian'.

Turkish rule in the Sudan (1821–85) may be studied under the following three headings: the strategy of the conquest and the response of the northern Sudanese people; resistance to the imperial drive in the South 1840–80, and the role of the new regime in modernizing the Sudan.

The strategy of the conquest and the response of the northern Sudanese

The strategy of the Turkish invasion of the Sudan has been the subject of much controversy among historians. According to some Egyptian historians, Muḥammad 'Alī's primary objective behind what they called the 'opening up' of the Sudan was the welfare of the country and its people. Muḥammad 'Alī – so they argue – was so sorry for the deteriorating conditions of the inhabitants of the Fundj sultanate that he decided to step in by force to save them from this misery and hardship, and subsequently to unite the Sudanese people with their brothers in Egypt in a strong state that would work for the 'welfare' of both peoples.[5] Some Egyptian historians have even asserted that Muḥammad 'Alī undertook this invasion 'on the request of the Sudanese people themselves'[6] as represented by some notables who approached him in Cairo and urged him to do this. Some Sudanese dignitaries did do this, but it is reasonable to assume that their motive was strictly personal and related to some dynastic rivalries that they had with the rulers of the Fundj sultanate. Consequently they should not be assumed to have represented the Sudanese people as such.

A distinguished Egyptian historian, the late Muḥammad Fu'ād Shukri, claimed that Muḥammad 'Alī's conquest had firmly established Egypt's 'legal and historical rights' over the Sudan. The dissolution of the Fundj sultanate by 1820 and the disappearance of the legitimate authority of its sultan made the Sudan, in Shukri's view, 'a land without a sovereign'[7] – a 'no man's land'. Hence once Muḥammad 'Alī controlled it and established a strong government there, Egypt automatically became, after 1821, the undisputed sovereign of the Sudan by the right of conquest.[8] One of Muḥammad 'Alī's fundamental reasons for visiting the Sudan in 1838–9,[9] Shukri claimed, was to propagate this theory – the 'theory of the vacuum' as he called it – and to depend on it to 'safeguard the unity of the Nile Valley', i.e. to keep its two parts – Egypt and the Sudan – under one political system.[10]

5. M.F. Shukri, 1948, p. 23.
6. M.A. al-Jābrī, n.d., p. 18.
7. M.F. Shukri, 1946, p. 18.
8. ibid., pp. 38–9.
9. For a study of this visit, see H.A. Ibrāhīm, 1980a, 1980b.
10. M.F. Shukri, 1958, p. 13.

This claim to Egyptian sovereignty over the Sudan dominated Egyptian and Sudanese politics – until the 1950s. Shukri seems to have been politically motivated to support the advocates of the unity of the Nile Valley against their counterparts who wanted an independent Sudan. It should also be added that the sultan of Sennār, though he had become a mere figurehead by 1820, remained until that time the legal sovereign of the country. Moreover, Egypt could not assume sovereignty over the Sudan by the right of conquest, as the invasion was undertaken in the name of the Ottoman sultan, and Egypt itself continued to be an Ottoman province until 1914 at least. In any case the Fundj sultanate could not be equated with the Sudan as a whole.

The 'welfare hypothesis' to explain the Egyptian invasion has also been challenged in recent studies by Sudanese scholars.[11] Depending on a wide range of archival material, these studies demonstrate that Muḥammad 'Alī's primary objective was the exploitation of Sudanese human and economic resources to achieve his extensive ambitions in Egypt and abroad.

Anxious to consolidate his independence in Egypt and to build an empire at the expense of the Ottoman emperor, Muḥammad 'Alī just before the conquest of the Sudan had embarked on the formation of a strong modern army. While at first ruling out for many reasons the conscription of the Egyptian *fallāḥin* (peasants),[12] he hoped to recruit twenty or thirty thousand Sudanese Africans in his *niẓam-i-jedīd* ('new organization'). More of them were also needed in his numerous agricultural and industrial enterprises in Egypt. Muḥammad 'Alī had therefore kept urging his commanders in the Sudan to intensify their *ghazuas* – armed slave raids – and to send the greatest possible number of Africans to the camp specially made for them at Aswān. He stressed in a directive that this was the most important reason for undertaking the 'difficulties and expenditure of the conquest', and in another he described this inhuman practice as his 'utmost desire irrespective of the means used to do it'.[13]

Though hardly a year passed until 1838 without at least one or more *ghazuas* for the blacks in the Nuba hills and beyond Fazughli, the supply of black slaves ran short of the demand. Muḥammad 'Alī's hope to swell the black army of his dreams 'was pure optimism based on no thorough survey of the slave reservoir in the Sudan'.[14] The Sudanese blacks had, moreover, stubbornly resisted the *ghazuas* and some of them had even committed suicide to avoid the humiliating life of slavery. Many of those captured were lost *en route*, while others died at Aswān of fever, dysentery, chills

11. See for example, H. A. Ibrāhīm, 1973 and B. K. Ḥumayda, 1973.
12. Being an alien, Muḥammad 'Alī had perhaps felt that a national army would endanger his position in Egypt. Other reasons were presumably the reluctance of the *fallāḥīn* to join the military service and Muḥammad 'Alī's desire to spare their efforts for agricultural development in Egypt.
13. Quoted in H. A. Ibrāhīm, 1973, p. 25.
14. R. Hill, 1966, p. 25.

PLATE 14.1 *Sennār in 1821: the capital of the Old Fundji sultanate at the time of the Turco-Egyptian invasion*

PLATE 14.2 *An encampment of Turco-Egyptian slave-raiders in the Kordofān*

and homesickness. Faced with this drastic failure, Muḥammad 'Alī finally conscripted the *fallāḥīn* in substantial numbers, and soon discovered that they 'made some of the best regular infantry in the Middle East'.[15]

Even those blacks who were recruited for government military service in the Sudan itself showed disobedience and a lack of interest. While some fled from the service, others raised arms against the government. Perhaps the most important of those risings was that of Medani in 1844. In

15. R. Hill, 1966, p. 7.

reaction to injustice and humiliation Sudanese soldiers conspired to revolt simultaneously in four places: Khartoum, Sennār, Kamlin and Medani. But those of Medani rose before the scheduled time, killed some of their Turkish officers, and fled to Sennār to continue the revolt there. It was only with great difficulty that the government suppressed the rising.[16]

Equally important was Muḥammad ʿAlī's desire to exploit Sudanese minerals, particularly gold. On his assumption of power in 1805, Egypt was one of the poorest provinces of the Ottoman empire, if not the poorest. Hence Muḥammad ʿAlī's drive was also intended to find a quick source of revenue to achieve his internal and external aspirations. Being obsessed from early manhood to old age with the illusion that gold was to be found in abundance in the Sudan, he made strenuous effort to discover it, particularly in the Fazughli area and around Djabal Shaybūn. Apart from stressing to his commanders the urgency of gold-prospecting, Muḥammad ʿAlī sometimes sent mining experts to the Sudan, e.g. the Austrian Rosseger and his own engineer Boreani. Finally, in 1838–9, at the age of seventy, he travelled all the way from Cairo to Fazughli to supervise the mining the mining activities there. But his three-week stay was disappointing. Government mining activities had not only failed to provide gold but had also consumed much from the meagre resources of the Egyptian treasury.

The Turkish imperialists were, however, more successful in expanding agriculture in the Sudan. They sent Egyptian agricultural experts who improved irrigation systems, developed existing crops, planted new ones, and effectively combated pests and plagues, particularly locusts. Veterinary doctors were appointed to look after the animals and experts were despatched from Egypt to teach the Sudanese the preservation of hides and skins. The conquest had, moreover, given greater security to northern Sudanese and Egyptian traders and made possible the eventual introduction of European commerce.[17]

But this prosperity in agricultural and animal wealth was presumably not employed to cater for the welfare of the Sudanese people. Instead, the government was mainly concerned with exporting wealth to Egypt. Muḥammad ʿAlī had throughout his reign imposed a strict state monopoly on almost all of the country's products and exports. Consequently, considerable quantities of Sudanese products – indigo, gum, ivory, etc. – were exported to Egypt. Similarly, throughout the Turkish rule the Sudan was Egypt's cheapest source of livestock. In spite of the difficulties of moving them down the Nile, with raids by thieving nomads, and a lack of organized feeding and watering arrangements, a steady flow of cattle arrived each year in Egypt. Animal products such as hides and hair were also sent.[18]

The Sudanese people had not experienced the payment of regular taxes

16. H. A. Ibrāhīm, 1973, pp. 92–4.
17. R. Hill, 1966, p. 50.
18. H. A. Ibrāhīm, 1973, pp. 135–54.

during the time of the Fundj sultanate, and the burden of the government was then light, particularly on the poor. But, in striving to mobilize and exploit all Sudanese resources, the Turkish administrators extended the Egyptian system of taxation to the Sudan, with suitable modifications. By applying this altogether new system of taxation, they inevitably disrupted the economic life of the people. What made matters worse were the brutal means used by the *bāzbuzq* – irregular soldiers – to collect the heavy taxes, and the frequent insistence of the government that they should be paid in cash, though the common usage of coins was still restricted to merchants and townspeople.

The reaction of the people was immediate and usually violent. Some deserted their lands and *saḳias* (waterwheels) to flee to the Ethiopian border or to the west. But many others rose in numerous and disparate tax revolts that took place throughout the Turkīyya. Perhaps the most violent of these was the Sudanese revolt of 1822.

Ignoring the traditional Sudanese taxation system, the Coptic financial intendant Ḥana al-Ṭawīl imposed heavy taxes on the peoples of the Gezira and Berber in 1821. But they rose in violent protest in February 1822, attacking and killing members of the isolated detachments of Egyptian troops. From Shendi to Sennār the people fled by the thousand to the borders of Ethiopia, to the valley of Atbara and to the region of Gedaref. To avoid a large scale revolt, Ismāʿīl, Muḥammad ʿAlī's son and his commander-in-chief in Sennār hurried back from Fazughli to the Gezira. Through conciliation and a revised assessment of the taxes, he temporarily calmed the situation. But Ismāʿīl himself soon committed a disastrous blunder. On his way from the Sudan to Egypt, he stopped at Shendi, and demanded an outrageous contribution from the Jaʿliyīn people: 30 000 dollars and 6000 slaves within two days.[19] Nimir, the *mak* (chief) of the local Jaʿliyīn, protested that his people could not afford what was demanded. Ismāʿīl arrogantly hit Nimir across the face with his pipe. To avenge this humiliation, Nimir conspired with his men to burn Ismāʿīl and all his staff alive at Shendi in late October 1822. Subsequently the revolt spread to other regions and caused extensive loss in life and property.[20] Though a rising of despair, without proper leadership, this revolt was an early warning to the invaders that resistance to their rule was entrenched in the hearts of many Sudanese.

Oppressive taxation and maladministration had also provoked widespread resistance to the short-lived Turkish rule in Dārfūr.[21] Anxious to restore their ancient rule, the remaining members of the Kayra family mobilized Fūr resistance against the colonizers. The most popular and largest of those revolts was that of Amīr Harūn in 1877. For three years

19. R. Hill, 1966, p. 16.
20. M. Shibayka, 1957, pp. 33–5.
21. See below, pp. 371–2.

Harūn continued to harass the intruders and could probably have ended their rule had he not been killed in 1880. His relative, ʿAbdallāh Dūd Banga, however, continued the struggle from his fortified military camp in the Nuba mountains.[22] Faced with this gallant resistance, the Turks were unable to consolidate their rule until the people of Dārfūr, in active co-operation with the Mahdī, finally overthrew it in 1884.

The Sudanese military also had their share in resisting the first colonial era. Several military incidents and risings took place in some northern towns: Medani, Sennār, Obeid, Suākin. But the most serious military revolt took place in Kassala in 1865. Infuriated by the suspension of pay, the Sudanese fourth regiment in Kassala defied the instruction of its Turkish officers, attacked and killed some of them, and besieged the town for twenty-six days. The revolt inflicted some damage in life and property and seriously undermined the Turkish administration in the whole Kassala province. Perhaps it was the most serious challenge that the imperialist had faced in the country for over thirty years. Nevertheless, through deception and diplomacy, the government finally suppressed the revolt. The soldiers surrendered their arms after a vague promise of a general pardon, but the survivors were either executed or sent to long terms of imprisonment.[23] The khedive had also directed that the Sudanese regiments in the Sudan be reduced to three and the rest sent to Egypt.

Resistance to the imperial drive in the South, 1821–80

Up to the beginning of Turkish rule in the Sudan in 1821, the political and economic powers of the Muslim northern Sudan states and Southern Sudan peoples were comparable, if not evenly balanced. But the nineteenth century, especially the second half of it, was to be catastrophic for the people of southern Sudan. It was a period of great material loss and humiliation, a 'period of chaos' as it is popularly remembered in southern Sudan. F. M. Deng, himself a Jieṅ from southern Sudan, has written that it was a period identified in the memories of the southerners 'with the wars of slavery and conquest waged against them by waves of invaders whom they hardly distinguished, except by the use of such varied terms as the Arabs, the Turks, the Egyptians, the Ansars, or the Dongolawis'.[24]

When Muḥammad ʿAlī invaded the Sudan in 1821, he divided the country into provinces and districts under Egyptian and Turkish officers who were placed under a governor-general based at the newly founded town of Khartoum. As noted above, the primary function of the alien regime was to collect revenue in the form of tribute and slaves to swell the ranks of the Egyptian army. Frequent raids were made along the White Nile for the purpose of capturing slaves, and from 1840 the traffic in human

22. M. M. al-Hasan, n.d., pp. 35–40.
23. N. Shouqair, 1967, pp. 545–53.
24. F. M. Deng, 1978, p. 150.

lives reached enormous proportions. The slavers' private armies were armed with guns and huge parcels of land were farmed out to the merchants who found a rich return for their investments amongst the peoples of southern Sudan. The commercial network developed by Muḥammad ʿAlī had certain distinctive features. The traders built *zeribas* (forts), an idea which they borrowed from Dārfūr, whose sultans had practised it since the eighteenth century. The forts were used as bases for barter operations and for conducting forays into the neighbouring areas. Other distinctive features of the network were the division of influence between state monopolies and private trade, the systematic use of force, mainly through the recruitment of local mercenaries, a policy of developing plantations for trade, especially in cotton. The Baggara, for instance, were supposed to pay these taxes in cattle to the governor of Kordofān. Those who could not, or would not, were allowed to pay taxes in slaves. They therefore raided the Jieṅ for slaves.

Futhermore, there were the European merchants who were demanding from the Turkish government that the Sudanese ivory markets be thrown open to free trade. When later the European traders were faced with lower profit margins, they decided to pay their Arab retainers in slaves rather than in cash, and this intensified the slave trade. Kaka in northern Shillukland soon emerged as a major slave market, especially for slaves coming from the southern *zeribas*. The boom at Kaka was partly connected with the abolition of the slave trade in the Turkish-controlled Sudan in 1854. It became the main slave market of the White Nile, and its immigrant population swelled rapidly. The activities of the freebooter, Muḥammad al-Khāyr, a Dongalawi by birth, who moved to Kaka from Taqali in 1854, may also have facilitated the transformation of Kaka into a slave market.[25] It is estimated that by 1860, an average of 2000 slaves were being sold annually at Kaka and, to acquire this number, Khāyr and his slave gangs were terrorizing the whole Shilluk countryside.[26]

The southerners refused to co-operate with the traders and actively resisted their presence in their land. The wars that were waged against the intruders are too many and too diversified to be enumerated here. Only a few need be mentioned as illustration.

The Bari people were the first to seize an opportunity to attack the invaders. In 1854, they attacked a French trading mission, killing two of its men and wounding several others. Shortly afterwards another extremely violent battle took place between about 5000 Bari and another trading mission led by Vaudeny, the Sardinian vice-consul. Vaudeny, his Turkish deputy, and many of his men were killed. Bari chiefs who showed any tendency to collaborate with the intruders were also attacked. Chief Nyagilo, for example, had his authority undermined and property

25. R. Gray, 1970, pp. 76–8.
26. J. Frost, 1974, p. 216.

PLATE 14.3 *Khartoum merchants' boats on an affluent of the Baḥr al-Ghazāl in northern Dinka country*

PLATE 14.4 *A traders'* zeriba *at Mvolo with a Dinka settlement outside its walls*

destroyed. He fled to Gondokoro, but was hunted down and killed there in 1859 by groups of Bari armed youth.[27]

The traders were driven eastwards into the hostile land of the Lokoya. When, in 1860, in reaction to an assault on 5 foreigners, the traders sent a force of 150 soldiers, the Lokoya killed 120 of them and wounded many of the rest.[28]

The northern Shilluk were equally active against the traders in the White Nile. But the immigrants moving into Kaka in particular and northern Shillukland in general, were not all traders. Many of them were refugees escaping from the Turkish rule. The period between 1840 and 1860 'saw a steady stream of refugees from the Turco-Egyptian north entering Shilluk territory. Many of these were Selim Baggara; but there were malcontents from the Muslim Sudan'.[29] The relations between the immigrants and the Shilluk remained amicable until 1860, when the *reth* (king) could no longer control the trading system that had developed in his kingdom, but which was dominated and eventually controlled by foreigners.

Reth Kwatker expelled many Arab traders from his kingdom in 1860. Muḥammad al-Kh̲āyr replied by attacking the Shilluk with 200 Baggara cavalry, over 1000 riflemen and thirteen boats. Fashoda, the royal capital, was destroyed. John and Kate Petherick, who were in the region at this time, gave an eyewitness account of the consequences of this attack. By 1862, they say, Shillukland from Aba Island to the mouth of the Sobat was 'in a very disturbed state', and 'the once-powerful Shillooks have been scattered far and wide'.[30] Kate Petherick noted in her diary: 'Passed an old ruined village of the Shillooks called Kaka; there were at least 600 deserted *tookuls*. Last year [they] were driven from their homes. They were an industrious people, and cultivated grain to a large extent.[31] Later they saw one of al-Kh̲āyr's expeditions that had captured 500 slaves and 12 000 head of cattle.[32]

The Shilluk decided to fight back. A raid by al-Kh̲āyr's marauders was repulsed and about seventy of his Baggara were killed. In 1863, the Shilluk forced the traders to retreat into the interior and al-Kh̲āyr was tracked down and killed. Thus, the relationship between the Shilluk and the Turkish government deteriorated rapidly. The Shilluk had to pay heavy cattle taxes and supply slaves to serve as soldiers for the expanding Sudanese garrison.

By 1868 the protracted conflict had become a full-scale war. In November of that year, a force of 2000 troops sent to subdue the Shilluk met with fierce resistance and the results were inconclusive. The administration then

27. R. Gray, 1970, p. 44.
28. ibid., p. 56.
29. P. Mercer, 1971, p. 420.
30. J. Petherick and K. Petherick, 1869, Vol. 1, p. 990.
31. ibid., p. 96.
32. ibid., p. 97.

PLATE 14.5 *A Shilluk village after a slave raid*

decided to levy an annual tribute of £15 000 upon the Shilluk and Jieŋ̇. Deep resentment was felt throughout the country. As if this was not enough, the Turkish government had decided in 1871 to extend the cultivation of cotton in southern Sudan. By 1874 about 5000 to 6000 ha of cotton, sugar cane and maize was under cultivation in the Fashoda area. This agricultural work, which earned the alien government £300 000 in cotton taxes in that year, had only been possible through the use of forced labour.[33]

The Shilluk rebelled. They killed ninety government troops and reinforcements had to be rushed from Khartoum to quell the rebellion. But the Shilluk were now determined to fight for their freedom. *Reth* Ajaŋ̇ refused to collaborate, and he was murdered by the Arabs in 1874, who then tried to rule without a *reth*. In October of the following year, thousands of Shilluk attacked the government posts at Kaka and Fashoda. Only fourteen soldiers at Kaka survived. More reinforcements arrived in 1876 from Khartoum, armed with Remington rifles. Thousands of Shilluk were slaughtered, and by April of that year, the area between Kaka and Fashoda was considered 'pacified'. The Shilluk were disarmed and large numbers of them were conscripted into the army and sent to Cairo. To add insult to injury, Fashoda was turned into a slave market, where government forces sold the slaves they captured to the Jallāba,[34] in order to recover the annual tax of £12 500. Shilluk population, both bovine and human, was dwindling

33. J. Frost, 1974 for most of the details in this paragraph.
34. On the Jallāba, see below p. 373.

rapidly. Small wonder that bridewealth, which had previously been twenty to thirty cows, was reduced to one cow during the period from 1860 to 1900.

Of all the peoples of the southern Sudan, many weak and defenceless groups could only put up a feeble, if not futile, resistance to the traders' raids. Many were either enslaved or killed in battles, with the result that several groups 'nearly vanished as cohesive political or social units'.[35] The Jienġ and Noath were perhaps best able to protect themselves against those raids by retreating with their cattle into the inaccessible swamps. Being accustomed to warfare, they often inflicted severe defeats on the raiding forces.

Further south were the Zande who, under the leadership of the proud and aristocratic Avungara dynasty, had founded a centralized state in the eighteenth century. Their strong political system was part of the reason why they were able to withstand the slavers' assaults. A Zande chief called Ndoruma was even able to capture a *zeriba* that Abū Ḳurūn, a slave-trader, had established in Zandeland. Subsequently, in 1870, he defeated an enemy force 2000 strong, killed Abū Ḳurūn and several of his men, and confiscated a hundred loads of ammunition.[36]

While none of Muḥammad ʿAlī's two immediate successors (ʿAbbās and Saʿīd, 1848–63) wished to emulate his foreign adventures, the ambitious Khedive Ismāʿīl (1863–79) 'was intrigued by expansion in any direction but particularly up the Nile into the vast hinterland of the southern Sudan'.[37] By taxing and discriminating against the already weakened European traders, Ismāʿīl gradually exerted Turkish authority over the Nile trade. By 1867 European traders were forced to leave the Sudan and from that time on no longer played a role in its commercial life, the control of which fell to Turks and Arabs from Egypt and the northern Sudan. Free from any local European control, Ismāʿīl advanced up the Nile to build for himself an African empire. The suppression of slavery and slave trade was given as a justification for this imperial expansion.[38]

This Turkish attempt to annex Equatoria was under the command of two British officers: Samuel Baker (1869–73) and Charles George Gordon (1874–6 and 1877–9). In spite of their extensive use of violence and their lavish equipment, Baker and Gordon were unable to extend Turkish administration in Equatoria beyond a few scattered posts. While governor-general of the Sudan (1877–9) Gordon himself finally abandoned the Turkish advance in Equatoria. His successor, the German Edouard Carl Oscar Theodor Schnitzer (1840–92), commonly known as Amīn Pasha, inherited only a weak and disorderly Turkish presence, and he was conse-

35. R. Collins, 1975, p. 18.
36. R. Gray, 1970, pp. 64–5.
37. R. Collins, 1975, p. 19.
38. For a study of the question of slavery and the slave trade see: M. F. Shukri, 1937; A. I. M. Ali, 1972; B. K. Ḥumayda, 1973, pp. 254–316.

PLATE 14.6 *A Zande minstrel*

quently forced to abandon it altogether and to withdraw to the east coast in 1889.[39]

Baker's attempts to secure the co-operation of the Africans were futile, as the tradition of resistance to foreigners was already deeply rooted in the southern Sudan. Immediately after his arrival at Gondokoro in 1874, Baker faced the open hostility of the Bari people and their chief, Alloron. They refused to sell him corn and destroyed that which his men cultivated. Though rivals of Alloron, the Beliman Bari and the Lokoya people joined in these operations.[40] The Moogie Bari killed twenty-eight soldiers, harassed the caravans passing through their territory, and infected their neighbours in the west bank with this hostile attitude.

Baker moved up the Nile to Patiko in Acholi in northern Uganda. Here he transformed all the local traders' posts in the area into government stations and recruited into his government forces many of the Danaḳla (or Dongolawi, as they were generally known by the local people because many of them originally came from the Dongola region), who were mercenary soldiers attached to the Arab traders. Such a policy made it difficult for the local people to distinguish between the Khartoum traders and the Turkish government. Baker then rushed westwards into Bunyoro, where he hoped to enlist the support of Kabarega. But he was once more disappointed, and Kabarega was even reported to have conspired to poison the entire mission. Against great odds, Baker finally retreated to Patiko in August 1872.[41]

In 1873, Gordon was appointed governor-general of Equatoria Province to consolidate the achievements of Baker. According to the terms of his commission, he was to build forts, open communications to the south, establish good relations with, and administration over, the local peoples, and regulate the slave trade in the southern Sudan.[42]

After an initial tactical submission to Gordon, the Moogie Bari reopened hostilities and for more than a week there was fighting on both banks of the Nile. It culminated in a battle at which the Moogie defeated a detachment of over forty men, all but four of whom were killed, including their leader Linant de Bellefonds. Had not the river prevented the Moogie from following up this success, Gordon's whole force would have probably been destroyed.[43]

Gordon's advance southwards in the equatorial kingdoms was also a failure. Rather than recognize Turkish sovereignty over his kingdom, as Gordon naively hoped he would do, Mutesa of Buganda mobilized a powerful army against the invaders. In Mutesa, Gordon was 'confronted with an African ruler who combined the inherited political wisdom of an

39. For the career of Amīn Pasha, see I. R. Smith, 1972.
40. R. Gray, 1970, p. 96.
41. S. W. Baker, 1879, pp. 272–3; R. Gray, 1970, pp. 84–104; N. Shouqair, 1967, p. 562.
42. See P. Crabites, 1933, pp. 28–30.
43. R. Gray, 1970, pp. 110–11.

ancient and firmly established dynasty with a remarkably acute appreciation of the role which diplomacy and evasion could play in the task of protecting the independence of his country.'[44] The apparently friendly envoys sent to meet Gordon were spies despatched to report on the strength and movements of the enemy. Nur Bey, who was sent by Gordon to annex Buganda, soon discovered that the shrewd Mutesa had cornered him in his capital Rubaga, thus rendering him completely impotent and dependent for his survival on the good will of Mutesa. This forced Gordon in 1876 to order an immediate withdrawal northward to Lado. Subsequently, the Jieṅ and Noath, under the leadership of a prophet called Donluly, besieged the government garrison at Bor. By 1885 the Bari chief Bego had exterminated this garrison and attacked Lado and Rejaf.[45] For all practical purposes the Turkish advance in Equatoria had by that time come to a disastrous end.

The Turkish colonial advance in Baḥr al-Ghazāl had come up against the greatest of the region's slave traders, al-Zubayr Raḥama Manṣūr,[46] a northern Sudanese who had built for himself a vast trading empire there. He defeated a government expedition and killed its leader in 1872. Confronted with this fait accompli, Khedive Ismāʿīl officially recognized Zubayr as the governor of Baḥr al-Ghazāl. But the adventurous Zubayr looked beyond the frontiers of Baḥr al-Ghazāl to Dārfūr, an untapped source of slaves. Sultan Ibrāhīm mobilized the Fūr army and people and put up a gallant resistance against the invaders. But he was finally defeated and killed at the battle of Manwāshī in 1874, and Dārfūr was thus annexed to the Turkish regime.[47]

Though Khedive Ismāʿīl had subsequently arrested Zubayr in Cairo, and inaugurated measures to break his power in Baḥr al-Ghazāl, the Arab slave-traders rallied behind his son Ṣulaymān. They proclaimed their intention of conquering all of the southern Sudan and then marching on to Khartoum, but they were eventually defeated.

Nevertheless the Turks were unable to establish effective rule in Baḥr al-Ghazāl. This was largely due to the resistance of the African peoples there, who considered the Turks as nothing but new colonizers who should be evicted once and for all. By 1883 the Jieṅ chiefs actively co-operated with the Mahdist forces to overthrow the Turkish regime in Baḥr al-Ghazāl on the clear understanding that they would be left free in their land.[48]

The advent of the Turkish administration had indeed brought an end to widespread slave-raiding in the Sudan, particularly in the south. But the new imperialists were never able to persuade the African peoples there accept their rule. In fact, they increasingly employed force to repress the numerous risings against their domination. Consequently, chiefs and people

44. ibid., p. 117.
45. ibid., p. 161.
46. For Zubayr's own account of his career, see N. Shouqair, 1967, pp. 568–99.
47. ibid.
48. P. M. Holt, 1970, pp. 78–80.

were killed, their cattle were seized, and their crops were destroyed. Like previous invaders, the Turks had further disrupted the society of the southern Sudan until the resistance movement ultimately succeeded in its declared objective of ending Turkish colonialism in this region of Africa.

Modernization and reaction in the nineteenth-century Sudan

The Turkish adventure in the Sudan was thus largely unsuccessful, yet it is generally agreed that modern Sudanese history starts with the Turkish conquest of the country in 1820–21. By the defeat of Sennār and Kordofān in that year the nucleus of what is now the Democratic Republic of the Sudan was founded. Turkish control of the northern and central Sudan was rounded off in 1841 by the conquest of al-Taka – the region of Khūr al-Ḳāsh and the Red Sea Hills.[49] Dārfūr, Equatoria, Baḥr al-Ghazāl, and the Red Sea coast were all incorporated in the modern Sudan during the reign of Khedive Ismāʿīl. On the eve of the Mahdia the Sudan had thus formed an immense block of territory extending from the second cataract to the equatorial lakes and from the Red Sea to Dārfūr.[50]

Apart from uniting the Sudan in its present frontiers, the Turkish regime had also started the process of modernization. By modernization we mean 'the introduction of methods of political and economic organisation and techniques of production, transport, and communications, derived from those employed in European states – all of which substantially modified the structure of the antecedent traditional society'.[51]

The three chief technical innovations of the Turkīyya were firearms, steamers, and the electric telegraph, which was extended to the Sudan during the reign of Khedive Ismāʿīl. Though known in the Sudan by the second half of the seventeenth century at the latest, handguns were not used on any large scale. The superiority of the armaments of the Turkish troops was crucial in overcoming the resistance of the Sudanese. Steamships were first used on the Egyptian Nile in about 1828, but they were not brought into Sudanese waters for another generation. By the 1860s and 1870s a substantial fleet had been established there, maintained by a dockyard at Khartoum.[52]

Firearms and steamers played a vital role in the southward drive of the Turkish imperialists. While tentative and hesitant at first, this imperial expansion was later greatly facilitated by these two inventions. For they enabled the colonizers and their Sudanese collaborators to overcome the

49. P. M. Holt, 1970, p. 3.

50. Besides the Sudan proper, the Turkish Sudan comprised the Eritrean and Somali districts.

51. P. M. Holt, 1973, p. 135.

52. R. Hill, 1965, pp. 2–5.

two principal obstacles to their advance up the White Nile: the obstinate resistance of the southerners and the immense barrier of the Sudd, which blocked the approach to both the equatorial Nile and the Baḥr al-Ghazāl.

The opening up of the south offered new opportunities to a particular sector of the northern society, subsequently known as al-Jallāba. While only a few of them had visited the south before the Turkish conquest, many began to rush there subsequently, particularly after the Upper Nile and Baḥr al-Ghazāl became more accessible to traders from the north. They went originally as servants and armed retainers of alien merchants, but had gradually acquired increasing responsibility and power on their own. Though accelerating the process of Arabization and Islamization in the south, the Jallāba's frequent resort to violence and their contemptuous attitude towards the southerners had, no doubt, nurtured the distrust and fear that still dominates the relations between the northern and southern parts of the country.

Turkish imperialism had established a new administrative system in the Sudan. Its machinery was oppressive, corrupt and incompetent and the Turkish administrators were of low quality, but in contrast to the previous types of government to which the country was accustomed, it was highly centralized. At the head of the administration was normally a single governor-general who bore the Turco–Persian title *ḥukumdār* (colloquially pronounced *hikimdar*).[53] Even during the brief periods in which the governor-generalship was abolished, as was the case in 1843 and 1882,[54] Sudanese provinces were placed directly under a department in Cairo. Though some Sudanese who collaborated with the imperial regime were given junior administrative posts, it was made clear to them that they were mere agents of a central authority that could appoint and dismiss them at will.

The army, particularly the regular infantry (*djihādīyya*),[55] and improvements in communications were important instruments for the colonial government's power of control. Though the colonizers did not embark on a serious road and rail construction programme, the steamers and telegraph networks made an important contribution to centralization. Armed with these instruments, the Turkish administrators largely succeeded in maintaining public security, in repressing the restive Sudanese, and, above all, in forcing the payment of taxes.

The religious life of northern Sudanese society was also greatly affected by changes resulting from imperial rule. Though both the Turks and the Sudanese were loyal to Islam as such, there was a great gulf between the

53. P. M. Holt, 1970, p. 14.

54. Being aware that the remoteness of Khartoum from Cairo might offer temptations to the ambitious, the viceroys made these attempts at decentralization to prevent the excessive accumulation of power and influence in the hands of a governor-general.

55. Both the southerners and the Nūba, usually of slave origin, were conscripted into the *djihādīyya*. Besides this force, there were the Shāiḳia irregulars who had largely replaced the alien irregulars who had come into the Sudan at the time of the conquest.

PLATE 14.7 *Turco-Egyptian administrative consolidation and modernization: the Ḥukumdār's palace at Khartoum with a paddle steamer on the river*

official Sunnite Islam of the Turkish administration and the personal indigenous ṣūfī Islam of the Sudanese that had developed since the Fundj period. In the Sudan, as in Egypt and the Ottoman empire generally, it was the policy of the rulers to establish a secular state in which Islamic institutions as such would have a minimal role. Consequently the ṣūfī Islam of the Sudan, which already had a profound grip on the rulers and the ruled,[56] was bound to suffer severe blows. The imperial administration increasingly undermined the prestige of its leadership, which consisted of the hereditary teachers (*faḳīs*) of the ṣūfī orders. This was in the main done through the promotion of orthodox Islam. By maintaining a hierarchy of *ḳāḍīs* and *muftīs*, and facilitating the education of Sudanese *'ulamā'* at al-Azhar, the colonizers confronted the *faḳīs* with a rival group 'more orthodox and alien in its outlook, and more directly dependent on the government'. By the end of the first imperial era, the prestige of the traditional religious leaders had, therefore 'undergone considerable diminution'.[57] This was indeed a major factor that persuaded them to oppose the imperial government and actively support the Mahdī's efforts to overthrow it.

The process of modernization was accompanied and fostered by an increasing number of foreign visitors, both Europeans and Americans. While very few Europeans had visited the Sudan before 1820, the Turkish

56. During the Fundj period the *faḳīs* were even more effective than the sultans and other political leaders as a focus of stability and continuity.

57. P. M. Holt, 1973, p. 140.

conquest opened up the country to foreign visitors who came as travellers, traders and missionaries, as well as experts, consultants and employees of the administration. Western employees of the government, who were rapidly introduced into the service, particularly during the decade preceding the outbreak of the Mahdia, made an impact on Sudanese society both in the Arabized north and in the south. Being alien in language, customs and religion, their presence created tension among the mass of the Sudanese people.[58] This excessive employment of Europeans in posts for which they were usually unfitted in fact provoked Sudanese resentment to such a pitch that xenophobia became generalized. The Mahdī's declared intention of freeing the country from alien and Christian control therefore found a ready and enthusiastic support from the populace.

Conclusion

The extensive drive of the Turkish imperialists to exploit Sudanese resources, as well as the socio-economic and technological innovations that they introduced, had profoundly shaken the traditional Sudanese society and created widespread discontent. This provoked many uprisings and revolts. Though some of these represented a serious challenge to the colonizers, none commanded enough popular support to enable it to overthrow the government. In the Sudan, as elsewhere, discontent alone could not create a revolutionary situation, which had to be accompanied by a revolutionary ideology, a revolutionary army, and above all, a revolutionary leadership. It was only when the Mahdī provided this in 1885 that the Sudanese rose *en masse* in the Mahdist revolution that ended the Turkīyya, produced an independent Sudan, and at the same time confronted advancing British imperial rule. At least that was the situation in northern Sudan.

In the south, however, slave raiding, pillage and rapine continued unabated. The Mahdist government plundered the south for conscripts into its own army. Bitter memories were engendered which tended to discredit both the Arabs and Islam in the eyes of the Africans in the post-Mahdist period. What had been a socio-economic structure of domination in the Nile Valley was gradually transformed into a racial structure of domination. This, in turn, led to a racial ideology of resistance among the Africans in southern Sudan.

58. See, for example, P. Santi and R. Hill (eds), 1980, p. 145.

15

Ethiopia and Somalia

R. PANKHURST
with some notes on Somali history supplied by
L. V. CASSANELLI

The situation of Ethiopia in the first decades of the century

The nineteenth century dawned on one of the most difficult periods in Ethiopia's history. The once centralized Christian state, much of which had been overrun by the Oromo (Galla)[1] had declined almost to dissolution. Though emperors still held nominal sovereignty, thus giving a semblance of unity, they were mere puppets of the feudal lords. The latter had become virtually independent, and were constantly skirmishing among themselves. Fighting was so extensive that several provinces, including Bagemder, site of the capital, were seriously impoverished. Many peasants, faced with the soldiers' exactions, had left their farms to seek their fortunes with one lord or another, or even as robbers. Agriculture was neglected, and caravans became smaller and less frequent than formerly. The population of Gondar, the only urban agglomeration of any size, was much reduced, and there was less demand for the craftsmen's produce, while the decline in royal patronage led to the commissioning of fewer works of art. The disorganization of economic, political and social life made a deep impression on Ethiopian chroniclers. Abandoning their flattery of the monarch they showered praises on the warlords, but could not avoid sighs for the old imperial greatness. One scribe, Abagaz Sa'una, writing in Geʿez, the traditional literary Semitic language, moaned that power had been usurped by upstarts, for lords had 'become serfs and serfs lords'. Noting that there were then four living monarchs bereft of authority he exclaimed that they had been:

> scattered like dust in the face of the wind. Woe is me! My stomach is agitated and my intestines torn because of your being injured, O my lords. What does it profit the kingdom which has been snatched away by the hands of serfs?[2]

1. This important ethnic group was traditionally referred to by its Amhara neighbours as Galla, a term used in the written sources of our period, but also sometimes locally used with a derogatory connotation. In recent years, increasing preference has been given to the indigenous name Oromo, which tends to be favoured by the modern educated generation.
2. W. Blundell, 1922, pp. 187–8, 191, 470–1, 477.

The decline of imperial authority, and the triumph of regional feudalism, caused this to be referred to by Ethiopian historians as the period of the *Masafent*,[3] literally 'judges', an allusion to the time in the Book of Judges when 'there was no king of Israel: every man did that which was right in his own eyes.[4]

The Christian highlands

The Christian highlands, the core of the empire, were now divided into three independent states, Tigré, Amhara and Shoa, besides several smaller political units.

Tigré, the heartland of the ancient Axumite kingdom, was the northernmost and most powerful. The population, which was mainly Christian, but with a sizeable Muslim minority in the east and south, spoke a Semitic language, Tigrinya. The rulers of the province, because of its proximity to the coast, had acquired considerable wealth from taxes on trade and, through it, many more firearms than were available in other areas.

The province was controlled at the beginning of the century by Ras Walda Sellasé (1795–1816) of Endarta, an important district overlooking the Afar, or Danakil, Depression from which most of Ethiopia derived *amolé*, or bars of rock salt, used for consumption and as 'primitive money'.[5] This chief, formerly the *balgada*, or official in charge of salt caravans, was the son of a general of Ras Mika él Sehul, a Tigré ruler who in the previous century had been master of Gondar and the maker and destroyer of kings. Ras Walda Sellasé, scarcely less powerful than his father's former lord, ruled a vast domain stretching from the edge of the highlands within sight of the Red Sea, to the high Samén mountains less than a hundred kilometres from Gondar. Walda Sellasé, who governed in accordance with long established custom, impressed the British traveller Henry Salt who observed that the chief was 'distinguished ... for his intrepidity and firmness', and adds: 'all crimes, differences and disputes, of however important or trifling a nature, are referred to his determination, all rights of inheritance are decided according to his will, and most wars are carried on by himself in person'.[6] Walda Sellasé, the most powerful chief in the country, wanted to wrest guardianship of the nominal emperor from the Yajju Oromo dynasty then in control of Amhara, and sought to rally the nobles of Tigré for this purpose. As ruler of a region near the coast he was moreover interested in access to the sea, and, through it, to the technically advanced countries of Europe. He expressed his 'utmost wish',

3. Guèbrè Sellasié, 1930–2, Vol. 1, p. 204.
4. Judges XXI, 25. See E. Ullendorff, 1960, p. 82.
5. R. K. P. Pankhurst, 1968, pp. 460–4.
6. H. Salt, 1814, pp. 325, 328, 330. See also J. Kolmodin, 1912–15, pp. 97–8.

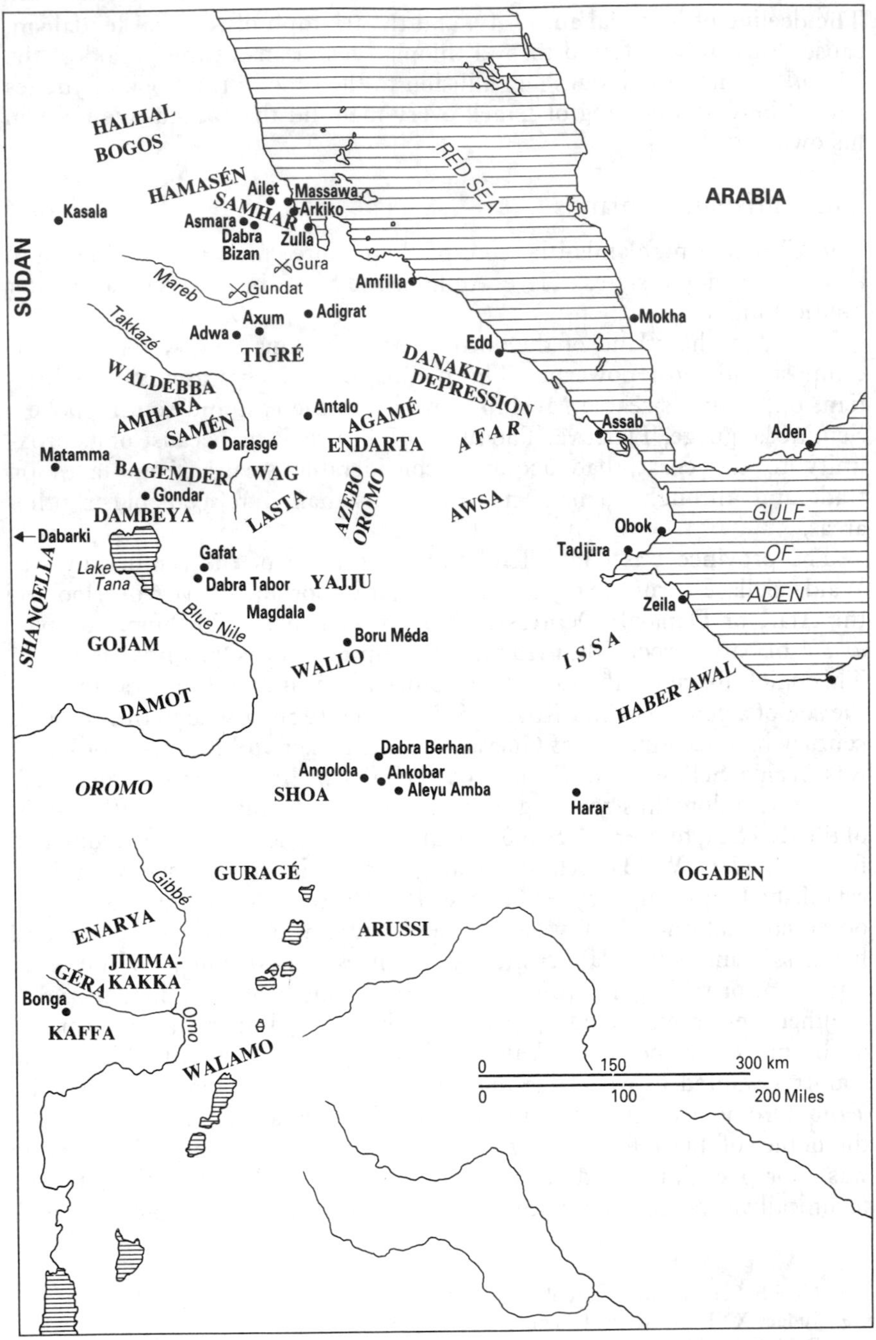

FIG. 15.1 *Ethiopia in the early nineteenth century (after R. Pankhurst)*

Salt reports, to encourage contacts with Britain, but argued that it would be 'useless' to 'interfere' with the Muslims at the coast as long as they had control of the Red Sea.[7] He wrote to George III of Britain in 1810 requesting firearms, and help in obtaining an *abuna*, or Metropolitan, it being the long-established custom to import such ecclesiastics from the Coptic clergy of Egypt.

Walda Sellasé's death in 1816 was followed by a fierce succession struggle. The eventual victor was Dajazmach Sabagadis (1822–31) of Agamé, another important province on the route from the salt depression, who despatched Salt's servant, William Coffin, to Britain in 1827 with a request for military and technical aid. The British sent a consignment of arms, but it was intercepted by the Egyptians at the port of Massawa. Sabagadis later fought against the Yajju, but was captured and executed. Ras Webé (1839–55) of Samén succeeded, after much fighting, in gaining control of Tigré, and later, despite many rebellions, of the highlands as far as Gondar. Alive to the value of foreign contacts he obtained a small quantity of firearms and technicians from France. Proclaiming his intention of installing as Emperor at Gondar a pretender called Takla Giyorgis, he marched against Ras 'Alī, the Yajju ruler of Bagemder, whom he met in battle near the latter's capital, Dabra Tabor, in 1842. Webé's riflemen won the day, but the victorious chief was captured while celebrating. He was released on payment of a ransom, and returned to Tigré. He again came into conflict with Ras 'Alī in 1843–4, but, faced by rebellion in Tigré and by the seizure of Massawa by Egypt, he submitted to the Yajju chief. Despite such setbacks he remained one of the most powerful, and enlightened, rulers of Ethiopia.[8]

Amhara, the second main division of the empire, lay to the north-west. Its population, which was largely Christian, though with a significant number of Muslims, spoke Amharic, the most widespread of the Semitic languages of Ethiopia. The region was based on the important province of Bagemder, whose rulers at times also controlled Dambeya and Gojam to the south. Amhara owed much of its significance to its control of the imperial capital, Gondar. However, being far from the coast, the rulers of Amhara depended for firearms on supplies brought in from the Red Sea through the Sudan or through Tigré whose rulers were reluctant to permit their import.

At the beginning of the century Amhara was ruled by Aligaz Gwangui (1788–1803), brother of 'Alī Gwangui, a Yajju Oromo Muslim who had adopted Christianity for political reasons, but was supported by the Muslims. Aligaz was succeeded by his nephew Gugsa Mersa (1803–25)

7. H. Salt, 1814, pp. 383–4.

8. For a brief contemporary history of Tigré see M. Parkyns, 1854, Vol. 2, pp. 88–120. See also C. Conti Rossini, 1947; and, on Webé, J. Kolmodin, 1912–15, pp. 110, 116–17, 119–20.

PLATE 15.1 *Dajazmach Webé of Tigré*

who established his capital at Dabra Tabor, extended his domains to eastern Gojam, and attempted to destroy the power of the nobility by declaring the nationalization of their land.[9] Islam gained steadily in the ensuing decades. Gugsa's son and successor Ras Yeman (1825–8) sided with the Muslims against the Christians, while Yeman's nephew Ali Alula (1831–

9. C. Conti Rossini, 1921; R. K. P. Pankhurst, 1968, p. 137.

53) shared power with his mother Empress Manan, a Christian convert from Islam, several of whose Muslim relatives became provincial governors. Pilgrimage to the tomb of the sixteenth-century Muslim conqueror, Aḥmad Gragn was revived.[10]

To the south of Amhara, and isolated by Lake Tana and the elbow of the Abbay or Blue Nile, lay Gojam, a virtually independent province whose population was Amharic-speaking and almost entirely Christian. The area had been unified in the late eighteenth century by Ras Haylu (d. 1784–5), whose descendants were long to struggle among themselves. His son Ras Mared (d. 1821) was thus opposed by Dajazmach Zawdé, an Oromo from Damot who had married the latter's sister, and the conflict was inherited by their respective sons and grandsons. These rivalries played into the hands of the Yajju dynasty, for the Gojamé princes of the province, as a modern scholar states, were 'no match' for the Yajju who were, on the other hand, never altogether able to dislodge the Gojamés or to maintain appointees from outside.[11]

Shoa, the third main unit of the empire, was situated in the south-east. Its central highlands were inhabited principally by Amharic-speaking Christians, while the south and west were occupied by Oromo traditionalists and Muslims, with Muslim Afars to the east. The province had been isolated by the expansion of the Oromo, which had enabled its rulers to gain independence from their overlords at Gondar. Though linked by a trade route to that city, Shoa in fact had more important economic ties, through the Afar and Somali lowlands with the Gulf of Aden ports of Tajurah and Zeila and the emporium of Harar. Through these routes a succession of rulers of Shoa obtained small but growing quantities of firearms with which they conquered the neighbouring Oromo who lacked such weapons. This expansion gave Shoa control of trade with territories further inland that were rich in gold, ivory, coffee, spices and slaves.

Shoa had been ruled since the late seventeenth century by a dynasty of its own.[12] The first chief in the nineteenth century, Asfa Wassan (1775–1808) whose name, significantly, meant 'expand the frontier', had his capital at Ankobar. He fought fiercely to capture Oromo land, reorganized the tax system, and severed the last links of vassalage to Gondar.[13] His son, Wasan Sagad (1808–13), who assumed the high-ranking title of *ras*, conducted further expeditions against the Oromo, and co-operated with Ras Walda Sellasé of Tigré in raids against Wallo and Yajju. He followed a policy of toleration and, though attempting to Amharize and Christianize

10. J. S. Trimingham, 1952, pp. 110–11.
11. C. Conti Rossini, 1947; Takla Yasus, nd; Fantahun Birhane, 1973, p. 11.
12. H. Salt, 1814, pp. 494–6. See also R. Perini, 1905, pp. 210–11.
13. C. F. X. Rochet d'Héricourt, 1841, p. 212; 1846, p. 243; A. Cecchi, 1886–7, Vol. 1, pp. 242–3; G. Guèbrè Sellassié, 1930–2, Vol. 1, pp. 60–6.

the Oromo, he appointed a number of them, as well as other Muslims, to positions of state.[14]

Wasan Sagad's son Sahla Sellasé (1813–47) was the first Shoan potentate to claim the rank of *negus*, or king, and claimed also to rule 'Yefat, the Galla people, and Guragé'. Residing partly at Ankobar and partly at Angolola, then recently seized from the Oromo, he maintained a tolerant attitude towards the Oromo and Muslims, and established dynastic marriages with them. Developing a system which the British envoy, Captain W. C. Harris, described as 'entirely feudal',[15] he obtained larger numbers of firearms than his predecessors, and encroached further towards the fertile lands to the south and west. This enabled him to attract caravans from Enarya, Kaffa, Gojam, Damot and other regions.[16] His desire for firearms led him into relations with foreign powers. In 1839 he requested a French traveller, Rochet d'Héricourt, to obtain rifles in Paris, and wrote to the British East India Company to declare:

> God has given me a good and large kingdom, but arts and science have not yet come to my country, as they have to yours. May it therefore please you to assist me, particularly in sending guns, cannons, and other things which I have not in my country.[17]

Sahla Sellasé received diplomatic missions from both Britain and France, and signed treaties of friendship and commerce with them, in 1841 and 1843, respectively. Harris, who brought a gift of firearms, quotes him as declaring that 'a few more muskets would render me a match for all my enemies'.[18] During his reign Shoa enjoyed peace, which contrasted favourably with the war-torn northern provinces. The peasants, according to the French Saint Simonians, E. Combes and M. Tamasier, 'having nothing to fear from the looting of the soldiers', devoted themselves 'with greater energy to the cultivation of their lands, certain to harvest after having sown'.[19] The death of Sahla Sellasé, like that of several of his forebears, was, however, followed by a major Oromo uprising. This was quelled with difficulty by his son Hayla Malakot (1847–55), a weak monarch whose reign witnessed much disorder.[20]

14. C. F. X. Rochet d'Héricourt, 1841, p. 212; 1846, p. 243; A. Cecchi, 1886–7, Vol. 1, pp. 242–4; G. Guèbrè Sellassié, 1930–2, Vol. 1, pp. 67–9. On the early history of Shoa see also D. N. Levine, 1965, pp. 21–38; V. Stitz, 1974, pp. 64–126, 349–50.

15. W. C. Harris, 1844, Vol. 2, pp. 177–8. See also C. Johnston, 1844, Vol. 2, p. 18; A. Cecchi, 1886–7, Vol. 1, p. 244; G. Guèbrè Sellassié, 1930–2, Vol. 1, pp. 70–7.

16. India Office Records, London, Bombay Secret Proceedings, 2060 G. Paragraph 23.

17. C. W. Isenberg and J. L. Krapf, 1843, p. 251.

18. India Office Records, London, Bombay Secret Proceedings, Vol. 3, p. 489; W. C. Harris, 1844.

19. E. Combes and M. Tamasier, 1838, Vol. 2, p. 346.

20. A. Cecchi, 1886–7, Vol. 1, pp. 250–6; G. Guèbrè Sellassié, 1930–2, Vol. 1, pp. 77–84.

PLATE 15.2 *King Sahla Sellasé of Shoa*

The port of Massawa

Beyond the confines of the empire the region was also fragmented, and in many areas distracted by inter-ethnic fighting.

Massawa, an island off the Red Sea coast, and the nearby mainland port of Arkiko, which together handled most of the trade of northern Ethiopia,[21] constituted a distinct cultural unit. The inhabitants, like those of the neighbouring Samhar plain, were Muslims who spoke Tigré, a Semitic tongue related to Geʿez. Contacts with Arabia had also given Arabic extensive currency, but the presence of merchants and soldiers of many races produced a babel of tongues. The area was the scene of conflict between four main interests: first, the Ottoman empire, which had seized Massawa in 1557, establishing a garrison whose descendants constituted a small but powerful occupation force; secondly, Egypt, whose rulers on several occasions purchased or usurped sovereignty on behalf of the Ottoman state; thirdly, a local aristocratic family, descended from the Ottoman troops and local Belaw, based at Arkiko and headed by the *na'ib*, literally 'deputy', who was nominally in charge only of the coast, but exercised a stranglehold over Massawa, which was dependent on him for drinking-water and all its commerce; and, fourthly the governors of Tigré, who, regarding the ports as indispensable for access to the sea, claimed historic rights there, but, though dominating the trade of the interior, took only intermittent action to enforce their claims.

Effective control of the ports at the beginning of the century was divided

21. R. K. P. Pankhurst, 1961, pp. 339–46; 1968, pp. 357–91.

between the Turkish garrison and the *na'ib* who, in the absence of any Ottoman governor, had made himself *de facto* ruler of Massawa, and spoke of 'the gate of Ḥabash as his'.[22] Such pretensions were resented by Walda Sellasé of Tigré, who 'expressed much displeasure', sent a military force against the *na'ib*, and would have 'cut off all communication' had the latter not 'appeased him'.[23] In an attempt to break the *na'ib*'s power, a British nobleman, Lord Valentia, advocated the purchase by his government of an island in the nearby bay of Zulla, but nothing came of the plan.[24]

The *na'ib*'s paramountcy ended in 1813–14 when the ruler of Egypt, Muḥammed 'Alī, seized Massawa on behalf of the Ottomans. His soldier son, Ibrāhīm, was appointed by the Porte as governor of Ḥidjāz and Abyssinia, but the latter portion of the title, though expressive of Muḥammad 'Alī's ambitions, was a fiction, for Egypt's rule was limited to the island, and even there scarcely effective. In 1826 the *na'ib*, using his control over Massawa's water supply, forced the intruders to withdraw, and, despite the continued presence of the garrison, again dominated the area.[25] The Egyptian evacuation aroused the dormant Ethiopian interest. Sabagadis of Tigré requested King George IV of Britain to 'take the port of Mussowa, and give it to us or keep it',[26] but the British government refused.

Muḥammad 'Alī seized Massawa again in 1833, but withdrew in 1841. At about this time Webé of Tigré sent an embassy to King Louis-Philippe of France offering the nearby bay of Amfilla in return for firearms and support for his claim to the coast, but the French were unwilling to co-operate.[27] The *na'ib* took advantage of Webé's defeat at Dabra Tabor in 1842 to encroach into the district of Hamasén, whereupon Webé carried out a *razzia* into the Samhar plain in 1843–4. Two years later he offered Arkiko to the French government, but this proposal too was not accepted. Muḥammad 'Alī regained suzerainty over Massawa in 1846, in return for an annual payment to the Turks of 20 000 Maria Theresa dollars. In the following year his soldiers took over the island, and shortly afterwards attacked Arkiko, burnt it to the ground, and built a fort on the mainland. The *na'ib* became their puppet. Determined to establish control over the whole region, they called upon the coastal rulers as far as the Somali port of Berbera to submit to them. Webé, infuriated, again despatched an army into Samhar in 1843. His men pillaged Arkiko, but, unable to capture Massawa, withdrew. He addressed a dramatic appeal to Queen Victoria in which he claimed that his predecessors had formerly 'governed all the coast of the Red Sea' and requested her to prevent his enemies from 'setting foot

22. G. Valentia, 1811, Vol. 3, p. 252.
23. ibid., Vol. 3, p. 40.
24. ibid., Vol. 3, pp. 261–78.
25. R. K. P. Pankhurst, 1964b, pp. 38–9.
26. Public Record Office, Kew, England, FO 1/2.
27. Public Record Office, Kew, England, FO 1/3; T. Lefèbvre, 1845–54, Vol. 1, pp. 103–4.

on the mainland',[28] but the British refused. His expedition nevertheless demonstrated Tigré's interest in the coast, and revealed the probability of further intervention should the Egyptians attempt to encroach on the hinterland.

The Afar lowlands

To the south-east of Massawa the arid lowlands were occupied by the Afar, a Kushitic-speaking nomadic people, who at the beginning of the century were ruled by the inland sultanate of Awsa. Established a century earlier when the Asaimara or 'red' Afar, occupied the fertile Awsa valley, the sultanate was governed by Sultan Ijdahis whose main rivals were the Adoimara, or 'white' Afar, to the south. His death around 1810 led to confusion in which the Adoimara sacked Awsa, and forced his successor to share power with them. Their growing strength was reinforced by the rise of Shoa, whose expanding trade resulted in the emergence of the port of Tadjūra.[29]

The Danakil coast acquired international interest after the British occupation of Aden in 1839. In the following year an officer of the British East India Company, Captain Moresby, purchased an offshore island from the sultan of Tadjūra for 'ten bags of rice'. The chief also signed a document engaging 'at all times to respect and regard the friendly advice' of the British, and 'not to enter into any other Treaty or Bond with any other European nation or person' without British approval.[30] Two Frenchmen, Combes and Broquand, acting for a French company, the Société Nanto-Bordelaise, soon afterwards bought the coastal village of Edd from its local chief for 1800 Maria Theresa dollars, only to discover that its exposed position made it unsuitable for a port.[31]

The Somali and the Horn of Africa

Further to the east, the desert lowlands on the Gulf of Aden were inhabited by Muslim Somali, who spoke another Kushitic tongue and had long been under Arab influence. Zeila, a port handling the trade of Shoa, the Ogaden, and Harar, had since 1630 been a dependency of the Arab port of Mokha whose rulers had farmed it out to a succession of Arab *amīrs* whose authority, however, scarcely extended beyond the town.[32] The rest of the coastal strip belonged to nomadic Somali who also claimed ownership of Berbera, a virtually uninhabited port that burst into life every winter when caravans from the interior arrived to exchange their goods for manufactures

28. Great Britain, 1868, p. 30.
29. M. Abir, 1968, pp. 23–4. See also I. M. Lewis, 1955, pp. 155–60.
30. E. Hertslet, 1894, Vol. 1, p. 275; Vol. 2, p. 382.
31. P. V. Ferret and J. G. Galinier, 1847–8, Vol. 2, pp. 436–7; R. K. P. Pankhurst, 1966b, pp. 203–18.
32. J. S. Trimingham, 1952, p. 97.

imported by merchants from Arabia, the Persian Gulf and India.[33] The fair was so important that a popular saying held that 'He who commands at Berbera, holds the beard of Harar in his hands'.[34]

The importance of the northern Somali coast was not lost on Muḥammad ʿAlī, who seized Berbera in 1821, but abandoned it on account of local opposition. A decade or so later the Egyptians resumed their interest in the area, but withdrew in 1841 whereupon the governorship of Zeila was purchased by an ambitious Somali merchant, Ḥādjdjī ʿAlī Shermerki. Anxious to monopolize the commerce of the region, he seized Berbera and encouraged Issa groups from the interior to attack caravans bound for Tadjūra. His increasing power was, however, resented by the *amīr* of Harar, who encouraged the Haber Awal Somali to oppose the occupation of Berbera. Shermerki responded by inciting other Somali to close the route to Berbera and to depose the *amīr*, but the Haber Awal drove his men from the port in 1852. He attempted to blockade it but the British at Aden obliged him to desist, and he was arrested by the Ottoman authorities at Mecca in 1855. Zeila was then given to Abū Bakar, an Afar slave-trader from the Tadjūra area.[35]

The coast from Bender Ziada on the Gulf of Aden to Illig on the Indian Ocean was part of the Majerteyn sultanate, which may have been established as early as the fifteenth century. This sultanate of semi-nomadic people derived most of its meagre revenues from the export of incense and aromatic wood. A long tradition of seafaring along the rugged coast provided the region's nomadic residents with an alternative source of income. By the nineteenth century, the sultan's authority over the interior clans was nominal at best. In 1839, the sultan signed a treaty at Aden with the British that provided him with an annual stipend in exchange for his assistance in protecting the lives and property of British seamen shipwrecked off his coast.[36]

Further south the Benadir, or Somali-inhabited Indian Ocean coast, was at the beginning of the century a protectorate of Oman, but became independent of it in the 1820s as a result of British East India Company intervention, after which the area passed under the suzerainty of the Sultan of Zanzibar whose representative resided at the port of Brava (Barawa).

The port of Mogadishu (Mogadiscio) was practically autonomous; as C. Guillain noted, the Zanzibar sultans' authority, like their customs officials, came and went with the monsoons.[37] The hinterland of Mogadishu was controlled by the Geledi clan, whose sultans contracted alliances with many other clans in the region between the Shebelle and Juba rivers. Through

33. R. Burton, 1894, Vol. 1, pp. 71–4; R. K. P. Pankhurst, 1968, pp. 421–4.
34. R. Burton, 1894, Vol. 2, p. 28.
35. ibid, Vol. 1, pp. 11–15; M. Abir, 1968, pp. 14–15.
36. I. M. Lewis, 1965, p. 38; M. Pirone, 1961, Vol. 2, pp. 66–8, 87–8.
37. C. Guillain, 1856, Vol. 3, pp. 185–6; I. M. Lewis, 1965, pp. 37–9.

much of the century, the Geledi alliance dominated the ivory trade that ran from Luk (Lugh) on the upper Juba to Mogadishu; the Geledi sultans also collected tribute from the agricultural clans along the lower Shebelle valley as far south as Brava. Only the powerful Bimal clan, situated in the hinterland of Merka, succeeded in resisting Geledi hegemony.[38] The sultans of Zanzibar, in the meantime, were forced to respect the authority of the Geledi rulers. Power in the Benadir was thus shared in a delicate equilibrium; when, for example, the sultan of Zanzibar sought to construct a fort in Mogadishu in 1870, he had to obtain the approval of Sultan Aḥmed Yūsuf of the Geledi.[39]

A major event that is still vividly remembered in the oral traditions of the southern Somali was the Bardera *djihād*, a militant movement of Islamic reform launched from the religious settlement of Bardera on the Juba river in the late 1830s. The reformers sought to impose their version of an Islamic theocracy on the peoples of southern Somalia, and even succeeded in subduing the coastal town of Brava in 1840. In 1843, however, the Geledi sultan, Yūsuf Muḥammad, gathered his allies from the area between the Shebelle and the Juba and led a massive expedition against the reformers. The settlement of Bardera was besieged and burned to the ground, and Sultan Yūsuf became for a time the most powerful leader in southern Somalia.[40] In the second half of the nineteenth century, a number of Islamic orders – the Ḳādirīyya, Aḥmadiyya, and Salihiyya – began to penetrate the Somali interior, and religious settlements sprang up throughout the countryside.[41]

Finally, beginning in the early part of the century, the last great wave of Somali migrations carried nomads from the Ogaden plains toward the Juba river and beyond. Some of these pastoral nomads took part in the Bardera *djihād* and eventually pushed across the Juba, where they came into conflict with the Oromo. The latter were ultimately forced toward the Tana river, where the British found them when they occupied the East African Protectorate.[42]

The emporium of Harar

Inland from the Somali coast, in the highlands, stood the walled Muslim city of Harar whose inhabitants spoke Adaré, a Semitic language not known elsewhere. The town had for several centuries been an independent state ruled by an *amīr* who wielded such extensive powers that the British

38. On two separate occasions, in 1848 and again in 1878, Bimal warriors were responsible for the death of Geledi sultans on the battlefield. C. Guillain, 1856, Vol. 3, pp. 445–6; G. Revoil, 1885, pp. 26–7.

39. G. Revoil, 1885, p. 22; I. M. Lewis, 1965, p. 38.

40. L. V. Cassanelli, 1982, pp. 135–46.

41. ibid., pp. 194–7; E. Cerulli, 1957, Vol. 1, pp. 187–95.

42. L. V. Cassanelli, 1982, pp. 29–30.

traveller Richard Burton exclaimed, 'The government of Harar is the Amir'.[43]

The emporium of Shoa, Arussi, Guragé, and the Ogaden, the town coined its own money, and did a flourishing trade in coffee, *chat* (a narcotic leaf), saffron, hides and skins, ivory and slaves, besides textiles and other imported goods. Harar, which had many mosques and Muslim shrines, and was a centre of Ḳurʿānic scholarship visited by Arab *shaykh*s, exerted strong religious and cultural influence on the nearby Kūshitic-speaking Qottu Oromo, as well as among some of the Somali. Both groups had intermarried with the Harari nobility, and in some cases their leaders sought recognition from the *amīr*s.

By the early nineteenth century the city was torn by internal strife and under strong pressure from the Oromo, but its perspicacious *amīr*, Aḥmād ibn Muḥammad (1794–1821), held his enemies at bay. His death was, however, followed by strife within his family, as a result of which the Oromo and, to a lesser extent, the Somali, seized land in the vicinity of the city, which survived only through the strength of its walls, its handful of artillery and small band of musketeers.[44]

The Guragé region and Kaffa

Further inland again lay the Guragé region, whose inhabitants spoke a Semitic language, and were divided between those of the west who had been Christian since the Middle Ages, and those to the east who had adopted Islam. Though once governed by a local dynasty, the area had by the early nineteenth century come under the rule of seven independent clans known as the *sabat bét*, or seven houses, whose lack of unity made them an easy prey to slave-raiders, and facilitated their annexation by Sahla Sellasé of Shoa.[45]

To the south-west of the Ethiopian region, in fertile well-wooded highland country lay the old kingdom of Kaffa, a traditionalist state that spoke its own Katicho language. The area, the source of valuable exports, among them civet, ivory, slaves, and coffee, which grew wild, had been largely isolated by Oromo expansion; but in the eighteenth century had made inroads into the territories of its neighbours. By 1820, its king, Hotti Gaotscho, ruled northwards and eastwards as far as the Gibbé and Omo rivers.[46]

43. R. Burton, 1894, Vol. 2, p. 20.

44. E. Cerulli, 1942, pp. 1–20; M. Abir, 1968, pp. 10–11; S. Tedeschi, 1874, pp. 481–500; J. S. Trimingham, 1952, p. 110. For a description of Harar in the middle of the century, see also R. Burton, 1894, Vol. 2, pp. 13–29.

45. W. A. Shack, 1966, pp. 16–17; P. Lebel, 1974, pp. 104–5.

46. F. J. Bieber, 1920–3, Vol. 1., pp. 89–90; A. Cecchi, 1886–7, Vol. 2, pp. 483–91; G. W. B. Huntingford, 1955, pp. 104–5; A. Onneken, 1956.

The Oromo states

The regions south of the Blue Nile were inhabited by traditionalist Oromo, who, early in the century, were in a state of political flux. The old egalitarian *gada* system involving rule by rotating age-groups was challenged by rich and powerful military leaders, often known by the title of *abba dula* or 'father of war', who began to claim life-long authority and the right to establish dynasties. In the first decades of the century, three Oromo monarchies emerged: Enarya (also known as Limmu), Goma, and Guma to the west.[47] Enarya, the most powerful, was ruled by Bofu, an able chief who, to strengthen his power, accepted the advice of Muslim merchants and embraced Islam. He was succeeded by his son Ibsa, or Abba Bagibo (1825–61), who forged dynastic alliances with neighbouring ruling houses and obtained a number of matchlock guns from Gojam, which gave him an impregnable position. During his long reign trade, mainly in slaves,

PLATE 15.3 *Amīr Aḥmād ibn Muḥammad of Harar, 1794–1821*

gold, ivory and civet, flourished, and the kingdom became rich and powerful, though the expansion of Shoa later severed the trade route to Harar and the ports of the Gulf of Aden, and Abba Bagibo's death was followed by the rapid decline of the polity he had built.

The more southerly kingdoms of Jimma-Kakka also known as Jimma Abba Jifar, and of Gera, to the south-west, came into existence a few years

47. For a chronicle of Guma, see E. Cerulli, 1922, pp. 148–62.

after the emergence of Enarya. Jimma-Kakka, the most enduring Oromo monarchy, was founded by Abba Magal, a man of the Hirmata region, who conducted a series of victorious expeditions that were continued by his sons, one of whom, Abba Jifar Sana, originally held the title of *abba dula*, but after adopting Islam in 1830, proclaimed himself *moti*, or king (1830–55), and effected many political and administrative innovations. His successor Abba Reba (1855–9) alienated the neighbouring Oromo rulers, who united and killed him in battle in 1859. The state then passed under the control of Abba Jifar Sana's brother Abba Boko (1859–62) who expanded Islam, and ordered the building of mosques in all his provinces, while his son and successor Abba Gommol (1862–78) further extended the realm.[48]

The area covered by this chapter thus constituted a galaxy of states and polities, each moving in its own orbit, but significantly affecting, and affected by, the other entities in the constellation. Each ruler kept a watchful eye on his neighbours but would often exchange gifts and courtesies with them unless actually at war. Dynastic marriages were made whenever practicable, though these only occasionally crossed barriers of religion. Commerce, on the other hand, made little distinction between faiths, and trade routes linked traditionalist, Christian and Muslim localities. Ethnic and linguistic communities remained largely distinct, but there was much cross-fertilization of cultures. This was true not only of the Ethiopian highlands and the Red Sea coastlands, but also further south along the Somali–Oromo frontier where later nineteenth-century travellers reported the existence of bilingual trading communities.[49]

The unifying efforts of Emperor Téwodros II

The disunity of the first half of the century gave way in the second to two notable attempts at reunification, the first by Dajazmach Kassa Heyku, the future Emperor Téwodros II, or Theodore, of Ethiopia, whose reign put an end to the era of the *Masafent*.

Born *c.* 1820, Kassa was the son of a chief of Qwara, on the borders of the Sudan, whose destitute widow had been obliged to make a living by selling *kosso*, the Ethiopian medicine for tapeworm. Brought up in a monastery, Kassa became a freelance soldier, made himself master of Qwara and assumed the title of Dajazmach. Empress Manan, mother of Ras ʿAlī, the Yajju ruler of Bagemder, attempted to win his support by marrying him to her granddaughter, Tawabech, but he rebelled, pillaged Dambeya, and defeated the commander despatched against 'the *kosso* vendor's son' as he had disdainfully been called. Kassa occupied Gondar in 1847, and later captured the Empress. He released her only when Ras ʿAlī recognized

48. A. Cecchi, 1886–7, Vol. 2, pp. 156–7, 238–40, 266–7, 537–42; G. W. B. Huntingford, 1955, p. 20; M. Abir, 1965, pp. 205–19; H. S. Lewis, 1965, pp. 24–41, 44.
49. U. Ferrandi, 1903, p. 316, n.1.

him as chief of the western frontier area. This triumph over the Yajju, whose pro-Muslim policy had alienated many Amhara Christians, enhanced Kassa's following. In 1848, he attacked the Egyptians in the Sudan, and advanced to less than a hundred kilometres from Sennar. However, because of the potency of Egyptian firearms he was unable to capture it. Following reconciliation, he served Ras Ali until 1852 when he again revolted. The Ras proclaimed the transfer of Kassa's lands to Dajazmach Goshu Zawdé, the ruler of Gojam, who set off to crush the upstart. Kassa, however, easily defeated the Gojamé, and attempted to reconcile himself with Ali, but the latter marched with Dajazmach Webé of Tigré against him. Kassa routed their combined armies in 1853, and burnt Ali's capital, Dabra Tabor, after which he defeated the Ras at Ayshal in Gojam. This battle marked the end of the Yajju dynasty and closed the era of the *Masafent*. The victorious chief's sole remaining rivals in north Ethiopia were Goshu's son, Dajazmach Beru of Gojam and Webé of Tigré. Kassa attacked and captured the former in 1854, after which he assumed the title of *negus*. In the following year he marched against Webé in Samén, and defeated him at Darasgé where he captured no less than 7000 firearms.[50] He then had himself crowned as emperor, and chose the throne name Téwodros, a significant appellation as it was prophesied that a monarch of that name would rule righteously, eradicate Islam, and capture Jerusalem.[51]

The character and aspirations of the new emperor are graphically portrayed by a British observer, Consul Plowden, who declared in 1855 that Téwodros believed himself a 'destined monarch' and was 'capable of great things, good or evil ... He is just, hearing in person the poorest peasant; he has stopped the system of bribes; he has by his own example ... discouraged polygamy and concubinage; he has forbidden the Slave Trade, and has tranquillized the whole country'.[52] The consul depicted Téwodros as a visionary, and observed:

> He is persuaded that he is destined to restore the glories of Ethiopian Empire, and to achieve great conquests; of untiring energy, both mental and bodily, his personal and moral daring are boundless. The latter is well proved by his severity towards his soldiers, even when these, pressed by hunger, are mutinous, and he is in front of a powerful foe; more so even by his pressing reforms on a country so little used to any yoke ... and his suppression of the power of the great feudal Chiefs at a moment when any inferior man would have sought to conciliate them as the stepping-stones to Empire ...
>
> The arduous task of breaking the power of the great feudal Chiefs – a task achieved in Europe only during the reign of many consecutive Kings – he has commenced by chaining almost all who were dangerous ... He has placed the soldiers of the different provinces under the

50. C. Conti Rossini, 1947, pp. 392–6; S. Rubenson, 1966, pp. 35–45.
51. On the Téwodros prophesy, see R. K. P. Pankhurst, 1974.
52. Great Britain, 1868, pp. 143–4.

PLATE 15.4 *Emperor Téwodros inspecting road-building*

> command of his own trusty followers, to whom he has given high titles, but no power to judge or punish; thus, in fact, creating generals in place of feudal Chieftains . . .
>
> As regards commerce, he has put an end to a number of vexatious exactions, and has ordered that duties shall be levied only at three places in his dominions . . . he intends also to disarm the people, and to establish a regular standing army, armed with muskets only, having declared that he will convert swords and lances into ploughshares and reaping-hooks and cause a plough-ox to be sold dearer than the noblest war horse . . .
>
> Some of his ideas may be imperfect, others impracticable; but a man who . . . has done so much and contemplates such large designs, cannot be regarded as of an ordinary stamp.[53]

Téwodros proved a notable unifier, innovator, and reformer.[54] After his coronation he marched into Wallo, and seized the natural mountain fortress of Magdala which was to become his capital. Later in the year he overran Shoa, the last Christian province outside his control, and appointed Hayla Mikaʿél, a brother of the deceased King Hayla Malakot, as his governor, and took the latter's son Menilek away as hostage.

Realizing he could control the country only by military means, Téwodros decided to reorganize his army. His experience with the Egyptians, wrote a British traveller, Henry Dufton, convinced him that the 'primitive mode of warfare' would have to be 'superseded'.[55] He therefore sought to replace unpaid feudal levies, who ravaged the countryside without being very effective on the battlefield, by a well-equipped army of professional soldiers. As early as 1853 he was reported to have 'disciplined his army',[56] with the help of some Turks, and also made use of a British adventurer, John Bell.[57] Téwodros adopted the practice of giving his soldiers 'sums of money' to accustom them to the idea of regular pay,[58] and marshalled his men into regiments, by mixing up those from several provinces, 'thus striking a mighty blow against the feudal system, under which the men clustered round the Chief of their native district'.[59] He established granaries for the army, and ordered his soldiers to purchase their food instead of harassing the peasants, though this prohibition was difficult to enforce.[60]

Téwodros, determined to increase his firepower, attempted, with the

53. Great Britain, 1868, pp. 150–1.
54. For various views of Téwodros see A. d'Abbadie, 1868a, 1868b; T. Noldeke, 1892, pp. 257–84; C. J. Jaenem, 1966, pp. 25–56; D. Crummey, 1969, pp. 457–69; M. Morgan, 1969, pp. 245–69.
55. H. Dufton, 1867, p. 138.
56. Great Britain, 1868, p. 76.
57. H. Dufton, 1867, pp. 183–4.
58. Great Britain, 1868, p. 150.
59. ibid., p. 166.
60. M. Moreno, 1962, pp. 160–1.

help of foreign merchants, to import arms,[61] but this was difficult as the Egyptians in the Sudan and the Turks at Massawa were both hostile, and the rulers of Tigré, which was largely outside his control, were also jealous of allowing the passage of weapons. He therefore conceived the plan of compelling missionaries and other foreign craftsmen to manufacture guns. In 1855 he accepted an offer by Samuel Gobat, the Protestant bishop of Jerusalem, to send him a group of workmen-missionaries from the Chrischona Institute near Basle in Switzerland. When they presented gifts of Bibles, Téwodros declared that he 'would have been more pleased with a box of English gunpowder'.[62] Realizing the value of the craftsmen, however, he treated them kindly, and settled them at Gafat near his capital Dabra Tabor. They were later joined by a French gunsmith and a Polish deserter from the Russian army.[63] In 1861 Téwodros ordered the foreigners to construct a cannon, mortars and bomb-shells.[64] The missionaries at first demurred, but the Emperor insisted, and imprisoned their servants until their masters consented. 'In their perplexity, they could not do otherwise than promise to try', and it was not long before Dabra Tabor saw cannon balls 'soaring up into the air and bursting with a loud crash which made the hills resound with a thousand echoes'.[65] Téwodros presented the craftsmen with shirts of honour, horses and mules with gold and silver trappings, and one thousand Maria Theresa dollars each, and then ordered the casting of still larger weapons. Eventually he asked for a cannon capable of discharging a 1000 pound shell. This gun, which was called 'Sebastapol', weighed seven tons and required five hundred people to pull it. The Emperor declared the day of its casting one of the happiest of his life. He also contemplated 'sending to England and France some of his more intelligent subjects, to learn useful arts and manufactures'.[66]

Conscious of the need to move his forces with the greatest possible rapidity, Téwodros set his European craftsmen to work on road construction.[67] The manual work was unpopular with the soldiers, who despised such labour, but the monarch himself set the example, and according to a British observer, Henry Blanc, 'from early dawn to late at night ... was himself at work; with his own hands he removed stones, levelled the ground and helped to fill in ravines. No one could leave so long as he was there himself'. The task 'would have driven any other man to despair', but Téwodros 'little by little made a road creditable even to a European engineer'.[68] His roads were designed to link Dabra Tabor with Gondar,

61. H. M. Stanley, 1871, p. 273; R. K. P. Pankhurst, 1972, p. 92.
62. C. T. Beke, 1867, p. 259.
63. H. Dufton, 1867, pp. 81–3.
64. ibid., pp. 83–4.
65. ibid., pp. 84–5.
66. Ibid., p. 138.
67. Great Britain, 1868, p. 189.
68. H. Blanc, 1868, p. 344.

PLATE 15.5 *Emperor Téwodros's great cannon 'Sebastopol'*

Gojam and Magdala, in extremely mountainous country. Clements Markham, another British observer, describes the road to Magdala as 'a most remarkable work, a monument of dogged and unconquerable resolution'.[69]

Though a man of war, Téwodros was keenly interested in the pacification of his war-torn land. He issued an edict in 1855 that 'everyone should return to his lawful vocation, the merchant to his trade, and the farmer to his plough'.[70] He also sought to eradicate banditry. On one occasion a group of robbers came to him armed to the teeth, asking him to confirm their right to exercise the occupation of their fathers. Without suspicion he asked what this was, to which they insolently replied 'Highway robbery'. 'Your profession', he answered, 'is dangerous, and agriculture is more profitable. Go down into the plain and cultivate it ... I will myself give you oxen and ploughs'. The men proving obdurate, he gave them a later appointment, and when they again refused to listen, had his soldiers shoot and hack them to death. Such severity, according to the French traveller Guillaume Lejean, brought peace, and the trade routes, until then blood-stained by brigands and civil war, became as safe as those of France or Germany.[71] Téwodros, anxious to weld his empire together, also sought to eliminate religious differences. He ordered the Muslims in his dominions,

69. C. R. Markham, 1869, pp. 295–6.
70. G. Lejean, 1865, p. 63.
71. C. Mondon-Vidailhet, nd, pp. 23–4; G. Lejean, 1865, pp. 63–4, 67.

Plowden notes, 'to become Christian within the year', and expelled all Roman Catholics.[72] He was later quoted as declaring that if he did not 'make Gallas and Amharas eat together at the same table' he should no longer be called a Christian.[73] In order to consolidate his control of Tigré, his first wife having died, he married Terunash, or Teruwarq, daughter of his old enemy, Dajazmach Webé.[74]

The reforming monarch also turned his attention to the Church, whose head, Abuna Salama, he had imprisoned as early as 1857. Téwodros sought to reduce the number of clergy, to curtail ecclesiastical land, and to make the priests dependent on state salaries.[75] These measures were strenuously

PLATE 15.6 *Ethiopian churchmen in the 1840s*

opposed by the clergy.[76] In the long run, hostility from the priests, coupled with that of the provincial nobles, turned much of the population against him. According to the Swedish historian, Sven Rubenson, this was 'probably the single most important cause of his failure'.[77]

Provincial opposition in fact proved impossible to break. The first

72. Great Britain, 1868, p. 143. See also p. 172.
73. M. Moreno, 1962, p. 162.
74. S. Rubenson, 1966, p. 56.
75. R. K. P. Pankhurst, 1968, p. 143.
76. D. Dufton, 1867, p. 140.
77. S. Rubenson, 1966, p. 72.

challenge came from Tigré, where a dissident chief, Agaw Negusé, attempted in 1856 to obtain the protection of France, and offered to accept a Roman Catholic, Bishop de Jacobis, as abuna. In 1859, Negusé ceded the port of Zulla in return for French military assistance[78] but fear of offending the British prevented the French from ratifying the agreement,[79] and Negusé was routed in 1860.

The latter years of the reign were, however, a period of greater difficulties. There were constant rebellions, notably by Amadé Bashir in Wallo where Téwodros fought a determined war, while in Shoa, Bezabeh, a local prince, declared his independence. Gojam came under the control of a rebel noble, Tedia Gwalu, while another chief, Tiso Gobasé, seized Gondar, and Wagshum Gobasé, son of the former ruler of Lasta, revolted there. No less serious, Menelik, heir to the throne of Shoa, escaped from Magdala in 1865, and proclaimed himself an independent sovereign. Faced with ever mounting opposition, Téwodros had recourse to violence. He burnt Gondar in 1864 and sacked it, as well as neighbouring Dambeya, in 1866, when his soldiers destroyed most of the old capital's churches. Processional crosses, manuscripts and other valuables were carried off to Dabra Tabor, and many brass and silver objects were melted down to make cannon. Hundreds of persons were executed. Such violence, which stands in stark contrast to Téwodros's likeable characteristics, such as his love of children,[80] caused Markham to liken him to Peter the Great of Russia.[81]

Conflict with Britain

The last years of Téwodros's reign were clouded by a bizarre dispute with Britain. Faced by increasing opposition in his empire, and the need for technical assistance from Europe, he despatched letters to Queen Victoria and Emperor Napoleon III of France in 1862, proposing to send them embassies. The letter to Queen Victoria, which sparked off the conflict, declared:

> My fathers the Emperors having forgotten our Creator, He handed over their Kingdom to the Gallas and Turks. But God created me, lifted me out of the dust, and restored this Empire to my rule ... By His power I drove away the Gallas. But for the Turks, I have told them to leave the land of my ancestors. They refuse. I am going to wrestle with them.

Explaining that the Turks had prevented him sending an embassy he declared that he wished Queen Victoria to arrange for its 'safe passage'.[82]

78. S. Russel, 1884; J. Kolmodin, 1912–15, pp. 139–43, 145–6.
79. G. Douin, 1936–41, Vol. 3, Part I, pp. 248–9.
80. H. Dufton, 1868, p. 106.
81. C. R. Markham, 1869, p. 293. See also D. Crummey, 1971, pp. 107–25.
82. Great Britain, 1868, p. 225.

Consul Cameron, the British representative, forwarded this appeal to London, reporting that its author had asked him to procure engineers and doctors from England, and observed that there 'need be no fear of bad treatment' as the missionaries working for the monarch were 'very liberally' treated.[83] The two letters reached London in mid-February, but were not considered of importance. No reply was vouchsafed to the Emperor's, while Cameron's remained unanswered until late April when the British Foreign Secretary, Earl Russell, returned an unsympathetic response.[84] The British government, he later observed, felt that 'considering the short tenure of power of Abyssinian Kings' it was desirable 'to withdraw as much as possible from Abyssinian engagements, Abyssinian Alliances, and British interference in Abyssinia'.[85]

As time passed and his letter remained unanswered Téwodros became impatient. He was irritated that the British government showed no interest in Ethiopia, the more so as he knew the French had supported the rebel Negusé, and felt that his royal dignity had been slighted. Cameron made matters worse by visiting the Egyptian side of the Sudan border, and exchanging courtesies with officials there, thus giving the impression that he sided with an enemy then overrunning Ethiopia.[86] Russell's letter to Cameron confirmed the Emperor's fears, for it brusquely stated, 'it is not desirable for Her Majesty's Agents to meddle in the Affairs of Abyssinia', and that the consul should return to Massawa, and remain there 'until further notice'.[87] The British government, it seemed, was breaking off diplomatic relations with Ethiopia and transferring support to Egypt and the Turks in Massawa. Shortly afterwards Téwodros learnt that a missionary, Henry Stern, had published unfavourable remarks about him, among them the accusation that missionaries were tried and sentenced to confinement. Not long afterwards, in November, Cameron's secretary, Kerens, arrived with a letter from Earl Russell's secretary, reminding the consul of his instructions to return to Massawa, and adding that he was only consul at the port, and had 'no Representative character in Abyssinia'.[88]

Téwodros's anger was intensified by a gift which Kerens brought – a carpet on which was represented a turbanned soldier, attacking a lion, and behind him a mounted European. Téwodros interpreted the animal to signify himself; the soldier, the Egyptians and the horseman, the French, supporting the Egyptians. 'But where,' he exclaimed, 'are the English to back up the Lion?'[89] His conclusion that Britain was abandoning him to

83. Great Britain, 1868, pp. 223–4.
84. ibid., p. 229.
85. ibid., p. 396.
86. C. T. Beke, 1867, pp. 93–4.
87. Great Britain, 1868, p. 229.
88. ibid., pp. 236–43.
89. C. T. Beke, 1867, pp. 124–5.

Egypt was no wild assumption, for Britain was anxious to be on friendly terms with Egypt, which produced 70 million kg of cotton a year,[90] at a time when world supplies were short as a result of the American Civil War. When the head of the Ethiopian convent maintained since the Middle Ages[91] in Jerusalem arrived with news that Egyptian Coptic priests had endeavoured to seize the convent, but that the British representative had been reluctant to intervene on Ethiopia's side,[92] Téwodros became enraged and reacted in January 1864 by putting Cameron and his party in chains.

News that the consul had been forbidden to leave Ethiopia had meanwhile alarmed the British government. The Emperor's long-forgotten letter was taken from the files, and a reply was quickly drawn up and entrusted to Hormuzd Rassam, the British Assistant Resident in Aden. After much delay Rassam reached the Emperor's camp in February 1866. Téwodros's position had by then seriously deteriorated. T. M. Flad reported that 'the whole country' was 'in a most disturbed condition, rebels rising everywhere',[93] while C. D. Cameron had prophesied that the state was 'on the eve of dissolution'.[94] Téwodros nevertheless gave Rassam a warm welcome,[95] and released Cameron, Stern and the other European prisoners. Shortly afterwards, however, he arrested Rassam and the other foreigners, apparently in the hope of forcing the British government to listen to his request for foreign workers. He then sent Flad to England, in April, to obtain two gunsmiths and an artillery officer, as well as several other artisans, and a blast steam-engine for his foundry and a gunpowder-mill.[96]

Initially, the detention of Rassam and his colleagues had the effect Téwodros desired. In July 1866 the British representative in Egypt observed that the release of the captives would depend 'very much' on the 'amount of satisfaction' the Emperor would receive,[97] and in August the British Political Resident in Aden, Lieutenant-Colonel Merewether, declared that the government should meet the monarch's requests 'frankly and most liberally'.[98] Such reasoning was accepted by the government, which agreed to Téwodros's request in less than a week.[99] A few days later, however, news was received from Flad's wife that Téwodros had again imprisoned the captives. Relations with the foreigners had in fact taken a

90. ibid., p. 35.
91. For the history of the Ethiopian association with Jerusalem, see E. Cerulli, 1957.
92. C. T. Beke, 1867, pp. 129–34.
93. Great Britain, 1868, p. 348.
94. ibid., p. 351.
95. H. Rassam, 1869, Vol. 2, p. 45.
96. Great Britain, 1868, p. 478. See also H. Rassam, 1869, Vol. 2, pp. 102–3.
97. Great Britain, 1868, p. 484.
98. ibid, p. 492.
99. ibid., p. 503. See also R. K. P. Pankhurst, 1968, pp. 217–35.

turn for the worse. Rassam, in trying to arrange for the departure of the prisoners, had aroused the ruler's anger which had been further intensified by a report that a British company had a contract to construct a railway in the Sudan designed to assist in the invasion of Ethiopia. Téwodros had accordingly ordered the captives to be taken to the fortress of Magdala. Flad reacted by advising the British government to abandon its plan of despatching the workmen to the Emperor, 'because the release of the prisoners would, I fear, not be obtained. Most likely he would go on requiring other things from the British Government to which they never could surrender ... I deem it advisable that Her Majesty's Government should at once use stronger terms'.[100] The Emperor's policy thus miscarried. 'The imprisonment of Mr Rassam', wrote Merewether, was 'so great an outrage and insult' to Britain that the original plan was 'rendered impossible'.[101] It was decided that the workmen should go to Massawa, but not be sent inland until the prisoners had been released and actually reached the port. The monarch, however, declared he would not free them until the workmen arrived at his court.

Téwodros was no longer the powerful ruler he had been only a few years earlier, for he had lost almost the whole country except for Bagemder, Waala, Dalanta and some minor areas.[102] His position, Merewether reported in January 1867, was 'becoming most desperate', his power was 'rapidly diminishing', and unless he made 'some brilliant stroke worthy of his earlier career, his rule will come to an end within the next few months'.[103] The British, aware of their enemy's declining strength, decided in July on military intervention. An expedition from India led by the Commander-in-Chief of the Bombay Army, Lieutenant-General Sir Robert Napier, landed at Zulla in October in preference to the more obvious port of Massawa, which would have been defended by the Ottoman empire. Téwodros meanwhile made desperate efforts to prepare for the impending trial of strength. Abandoning Dabra Tabor, which he put to flames, he had his cannons dragged to Magdala, almost the only place still under his control, where he planned to face the enemy.

The British force, composed of 12 000 fighting men, two-thirds of them Indian and partly armed with breech-loading rifles never yet used in war, advanced inland without opposition. The invaders received co-operation in Tigré from Dajazmach Kassa, the future Emperor Yohannes IV, while Wagshum Gobasé of Lasta and King Menelik of Shoa were both sympathetic. The first and only real battle was fought at Arogé, below Magdala, on Good Friday 10 April, a day of fasting in Ethiopia. The British inflicted heavy casualties on Téwodros's men, whose untried artillery was not

100. Great Britain, 1868, p. 508.
101. ibid., pp. 509–10.
102. S. Rubenson, 1966, p. 81.
103. Great Britain, 1868, p. 550.

effectively used.[104] Napier, though without instructions as to how to treat the Ethiopian monarch, sent him an ultimatum declaring that if he would 'submit to the Queen of England', and deliver all the Europeans 'this day in the British Camp', he would be guaranteed 'honourable treatment'.[105] Unwilling to accept such humiliation, Téwodros replied with a proud letter which constituted his last testament. Addressing himself to his people he enquired, 'Will it always be thus that you flee before the enemy when I myself, by the power of God, go not forth with you to encourage you?' Turning to the British he declared that his countrymen had turned their backs on him and had hated him because he had imposed taxes on them and sought to bring them under military discipline. On the outcome of the battle he exclaimed:

> My followers, who loved me, were frightened by one bullet, and fled in spite of my commands . . .
>
> Believing myself to be a great lord, I gave you battle: but, by reason of the worthlessness of my artillery, all my pains were as nought.
>
> The people of my country, by taunting me with having embraced the religion of the Franks, and by saying that I had become a Musselman, and in ten different ways, had provoked me to anger against them. Out of what I have done of evil towards them may God bring good. His will be done. I had intended, if God had so decreed, to conquer the whole world; and it was my desire to die if my purpose could not be fulfilled. Since the day of my birth till now no man has dared to lay hands on me . . . I had hoped, after subduing all my enemies in Abyssinia, to land my army against Jerusalem, and expel from it the Turks. A warrior who has dandled strong men in his arms like infants will never suffer himself to be dandled in the arms of others.[106]

After writing this remarkable letter Téwodros held his pistol to his head in an attempt to kill himself, but his soldiers snatched the weapon from his hand. He then released Rassam, Cameron, and the missionaries, but continued to detain their wives and children, and several other Europeans. On the following day he sent Napier a peace offering of 1000 cows and 500 sheep, and, learning that it was accepted, freed the remaining hostages. Napier, on hearing the 'magnitude and nature' of Téwodros's gift, decided however, to refuse it. The Emperor, realizing that this implied continued hostilities, attempted to flee, but changed his mind, and returned to Magdala.

104. For the histories of the war see K. St. C. Wilkins, 1870; T. J. Holland and H. M. Hozier, 1870; H. M. Stanley, 1871; C. R. Markham, 1869; A. J. Shepherd, 1868. H. M. Hozier, 1869; F. Myatt, 1970.

105. C. R. Markham, 1869, p. 327.

106. ibid., pp. 330–1.

Though the captives had been released, and the objective of the expedition accomplished,[107] the British launched an assault on Magdala on 13 April. Téwodros's army possessed 3000 'tolerably good' muzzle-loaders and 1000 matchlocks, besides 28 cannon, and 9 brass mortars, the latter locally made 'with neat inscriptions in Amharic'.[108] This ordnance, according to Captain Mozie, was 'much superior' to that of the British, and 'had it not been deserted by its gunners, must have caused much loss to the assailants'.[109] As it was, Téwodros soon saw that resistance was in vain, and dismissed his followers, exclaiming: 'It is finished! Sooner than fall into his hands I will kill myself'. He then placed his pistol to his mouth, and pulled the trigger.[110]

The British, having accomplished their mission, prepared to depart. They had never had any intention of remaining, and had promised to withdraw as soon as the dispute with Téwodros was resolved. It was only on that understanding that the Turks had allowed them to land at the coast, and Kassa to allow their passage through Tigré. Before leaving, they destroyed Magdala fortress and most of its cannon, and took away Téwdros's young son Alamayehu, at the request of his mother,[111] and some four hundred manuscripts, a part of those the Emperor had gathered to establish a library.[112] The last act of the expedition was to reward Kassa of Tigré by giving him 12 heavy guns, 752 muskets and a supply of ammunition. These were to play a major rôle in the ensuing struggle for power.

The advent of France at Obok and Italy at Assab

The second half of the nineteenth century witnessed growing French interest in the port of Obok. In 1856 the port was purchased by M. Lambert, the French Consul in Aden.[113] No effective occupation resulted, but a new treaty was signed in 1862 when four Afar chiefs ceded the territory to France for 10 000 Maria Theresa dollars and bound themselves 'conjointly and separately' to reject any overtures which had 'not received the assent of the Government of his Majesty the Emperor of the French'.[114] Though couched in grandiose terms, the agreement was not highly regarded on the spot. A British observer, Consul Walker, reported that the principal chief 'after receiving the money disappeared, and his successor did not countenance the claim or right of the French to purchase this site of land,

107. See R. K. P. Pankhurst, 1973a, pp. 189–203; C. Jeśman, 1966, pp. 94–151.
108. C. R. Markham, 1869, p. 240.
109. T. J. Hozier, 1869, p. 240.
110. C. R. Markham, 1869, p. 352.
111. R. K. P. Pankhurst, 1973b, pp. 17–42.
112. Lord Amulree, 1970, pp. 8–15.
113. P. Soleillet, 1886, p. 23.
114. E. Hertslet, 1894, Vol. 1, pp. 269–70.

PLATE 15.7 *Emperor Téwodros committing suicide in front of Sir Robert Napier (a modern interpretation)*

nor of the Chief to dispose of it', while the few huts erected by the French 'after their departure were thrown into the sea'.[115]

European interest in the area was enhanced by the opening of the Suez Canal in November 1869. In the same month an Italian Lazarist missionary, Giuseppe Sapeto, purchased the port of Assab on behalf of the Italian Ministry of Marine from two Afar sultans for 6000 Maria Theresa dollars. Returning in March of the following year as representative of the Italian Rubattino shipping company, he found the vendors dissatisfied with the price. A new treaty was accordingly concluded by which the two chiefs, who had been joined by a third, received a further 8100 Maria Theresa dollars, while another chief was persuaded to lease a nearby island for ten

115. Great Britain, 1868, pp. 231–2.

years at an annual rent of 100 dollars with right of purchase for 2000 rupees, or about 1000 dollars.[116] These developments laid the basis for Italian contacts with Shoa in the late 1870s and early 1880s.

Emperor Yohannes and the forging of Ethiopian unity

The death of Téwodros had left Ethiopia divided and without an emperor. Three rival personalities held power in different areas. Menelik had made himself King of Shoa, while Ras Gobasé, who emerged as ruler of Amhara, Wag and Lasta, was crowned Emperor and assumed the name of Takia Giorgis in 1868. The third personality, Kassa of Tigré was, however, the most powerful, in part because of the gift of arms he had received from the British. In 1871 Gobasé set out to capture Adwa, the capital of Tigré, but Kassa defeated him in July, and was crowned Emperor Yohannes IV at Axum in January 1872.[117]

The new Emperor, who was destined to achieve greater effective unification than Téwodros, did so by adopting a more conciliatory policy towards the provincial nobility,[118] and by presenting himself as the friend and protector of the clergy. Before his coronation he succeeded in obtaining an *abuna* from Egypt, and later made contact with the Ethiopian community at Jerusalem and sent them funds of which they were badly in need. He built numerous churches, notably at Adwa and Magdala, gave extensive lands to the Church at the ancient city of Axum, and renewed a grant to the monastery of Dabra Bizan overlooking the Red Sea.[119] Having converted his own wife, Halima, from Islam before marrying her, he attempted the mass baptism of Muslims,[120] particularly among the Azebo Oromo, and persecuted Roman Catholic converts.[121] Anxious to purify religious practices, he forbade the practice of witchcraft, and, in accordance with the opposition of the Ethiopian Church to tobacco, prohibited smoking and the taking of snuff.[122] He was, on the other hand, keen to innovate in the military field, imported firearms, and employed a British officer, John Kirkham, to train his soldiers.[123]

During the first part of his reign Yohannes was confronted by strong pressure from Egypt, then the most powerful state on the African continent,

116. Italy, Ministero degli Affari Esteri, 1906, Vol. 1, pp. 25–8. See also G. Douin, 1936–41, Vol. 3, Part II, pp. 240–9.

117. W. Mc. E. Dye, 1880, p. 473. See also Zewde Gabre-Sellassie, 1975, pp. 17–53.

118. G. Rohlfs, 1885, p. 58. See also Zewde Gabre-Sellassie, 1975, pp. 16, pp. 250–7.

119. Zewde Gabre-Sellassie, 1975, pp. 33–4; R. Perini, 1905, p. 85; L. Villari, 1938; G. W. B. Huntingford, 1965, p. 79; R. K. P. Pankhurst, 1966c, pp. 100–1.

120. J. S. Trimingham, 1952, p. 122; Zewde Gabre-Sellassie, 1975, pp. 94–100.

121. On the religious policy of Yohannes see Gabira Madihin Kidana, 1972.

122. Mangestu Lamma, 1959, p. 52; A. B. Wylde, 1901, p. 44; R. K. P. Pankhurst, 1968, p. 5.

123. E. A. De Cosson, 1877, Vol. 2, p. 64.

PLATE 15.8 *Emperor Yohannes IV*

whose ill-fated Khedive, Ismāʿīl, was building an empire in the Sudan and hoped to annex much of Ethiopia. The stage for conflict was set in May 1868 when the Ottoman sultan transferred Massawa once more to the rule of Egypt. Having occupied the port the Egyptians seized Zulla, and stopped the import of arms into Ethiopia. In the spring of 1872, Werber Munzinger, a Swiss adventurer in Egyptian service, took possession of Bogos and Halhal, two Ethiopian districts on the Sudan border,[124] and the chief of Ailet, inland from Massawa, sold his district to the Egyptian government. Faced with these encroachments Yohannes despatched Kirkham to England in September with a letter for Queen Victoria appealing for help against Egyptian expansion. Kirkham later wrote to the Queen on the Emperor's behalf to draw attention to 'the injustice' of Ethiopia's possessing no port through which it could communicate with the 'Christian powers

124. A.B. Wylde, 1901, pp. 22–3; G. Rohlfs, 1885, p. 43; G. Douin, 1936–41, Vol. 3, Part II, pp. 337–44.

of Europe', and added that if the European powers would secure it 'an outlet to the Red Sea', Yohannes was prepared to enter into 'the most liberal treaties of commerce' with them.[125] Such appeals, however, met with no more support from London than those of earlier times.[126]

Yohannes, anxious for closer foreign contacts, appointed an Englishman, Henry King, as consul in London[127] and, realizing the strength of the anti-slavery movement, informed the British that he intended to eradicate the slave trade by executing merchants engaged in it. The sale of slaves had long been prohibited by the Ethiopian legal code, the *Fetha Nagast*, but the injunction had applied solely to Christians, not to Muslim merchants.[128]

The Egyptians, having established themselves on the southern Red Sea coast, were meanwhile expanding into the Gulf of Aden area. In the winter of 1873–4 they temporarily seized Berbera, and in the following winter established a permanent occupation both there and at Zeila.[129] They then thrust inland and seized Harar in October. Amīr Muḥammad ibn ʿAlī, who had recently come to power there, was unable to resist.[130]

Having acquired a foothold to the east, the Egyptians determined to annex northern Ethiopia as far as the Mareb river. They despatched a force of 2500 men led by an Egyptian nobleman, Arekel Bey; a Danish officer, officer, Colonel Arendrup; and an Austrian, Count Zichy, equipped with modern Remington breechloading rifles and field guns. Yohannes, learning that the intruders had advanced to Asmara, ordered the call to arms to be sounded throughout his kingdom.[131] Vast numbers of men volunteered for a war that they regarded as a Crusade against the encroachment of Islam. Yohannes thus assembled perhaps 70 000 armed men. The decisive battle was fought at Gundat on 15 November 1875, when the Emperor's army attacked the invaders and almost completely annihilated them. Arekel and Arendrup were both killed, and Zichy mortally wounded, while Yohannes captured 2500 Remington rifles, 14 pieces of artillery, and 20 000 Maria Theresa dollars. The Egyptians had meanwhile sent another column inland from Tadjūra which was intercepted by the local Afar who killed its commander, Munzinger, and many of his men.[132]

Ismāʿīl determined to avenge these disasters. In February 1876 a much larger, well supplied army of 20 000 men commanded by Rhatib Pasha; the Khedive's son, Hassan Pasha; and an American officer, General Loring, advanced inland. Yohannes responded by summoning Christians once

125. Public Record Office, Kew, FO 1/27, to Foreign Office, 13 May 1873.
126. G. Douin, 1936–41, Vol. 3, Part II, pp. 378–87, 403–9.
127. J. de Coursac, 1926, pp. 107–18.
128. P. Tzadue, 1968, pp. 175–8.
129. G. Douin, 1936–41, Vol. 3, Part II, pp. 266–79; Part IIIA, pp. 547–55, 583–602.
130. ibid., Vol. 3, Part IIIA, pp. 602–7; J. S. Trimingham, 1952, pp. 120–2.
131. W. Mc. E. Dye, 1880, p. 135.
132. A. B. Wylde, 1901, pp. 23–5; G. Douin, 1936–41, Vol. 3, Part II, pp. 745–1075; Zewde Gabre-Sellassie, 1975, pp. 61–5.

more to rally against the enemies of their faith. The Egyptians, though armed with Remington rifles and Krupp field guns, were again outnumbered, for close on 200 000 men responded to the Emperor's call. The invaders proved no match for the Ethiopians who in fighting at Gura between 7 and 9 March won another signal victory. Only a few hundred Egyptians survived the Ethiopian assault. They left behind them 16 cannon, and 12 000 or 13 000 Remington rifles, besides much ammunition and other supplies.[133]

The Ethiopian victories at Gundat and Gura destroyed Egyptian dreams of empire. Ismāʿīl, who had lost over 20 000 men, besides most of his artillery and other weapons, and with his country facing economic collapse, had to abandon his expansionist aims. He soon went bankrupt and was deposed in June 1879. Discontent had meanwhile spread among his army, largely on acccount of the arrogant incapacity of the Turkish and Circassian commanders who had led the Egyptian soldiers to disaster. Defeat in Ethiopia thus sowed seeds which bore bitter fruit for the Khedive, and it was significant that one of the Egyptian colonels at Massawa during the débâcle, ʿUrābī Pasha, emerged as the leader of Egypt's first nationalist rebellion.

Ethiopia, though the victor, also suffered from the fighting. As early as 1873 a British traveller, A. E. De Cosson, observed that Hamasén had been 'depopulated' as a result of the ravages of the Egyptians, and that Asmara 'was almost deserted'.[134] Yohannes, for his part, sought to minimize such miseries and, as Colonel William Dye, an American with the Egyptian army, admitted, ordered that though cereals might be taken by his soldiers, 'herds and clothing must be spared'.[135] The campaigns of 1875–6, followed by the depradations of an Egyptian-backed chieftain, Ras Walda Mikaʿél, nevertheless led to much devastation.[136] A British observer, A. B. Wylde, subsequently noted that Mikaʿél had 'turned the Hamasén plateau, formerly known as the plain of the thousand villages ... into a howling wilderness of ruined houses, with a few half-starved peasantry.'[137]

The victories over Egypt nevertheless enhanced the prestige, and strength, of Yohannes who, thanks to the supplies he had seized, became the first well-armed ruler of his country since the advent of guns over three centuries earlier. The end of the fighting left him free to proceed with unification. He marched south to Wallo to settle accounts with Menelik. The ruler of Shoa, who was dependent on supplies passing through

133. On the Egyptian campaigns see W. Mc. E. Dye, 1880, *passim*; G. B. Hill, 1881, pp. 205–6; G. Rohlfs, 1885, pp. 44–54; A. B. Wylde, 1901, pp. 26–81; M. Chaîne, 1913, p. 8; J. de Coursac, 1926, pp. 322–4 and *passim*; A. Bizzoni, 1897, pp. 60–4; J. S. Trimingham, 1952, pp. 121–2; Zewde Gabre-Sellassie, 1975, pp. 59–63.

134. E. A. De Cosson, 1877, Vol. I, p. 50.

135. W. Mc.E. Dye, 1880, p. 292.

136. ibid., p. 652.

137. A. B. Wylde, 1901, p. 28.

Egyptian-occupied territories, had failed to support Yohannes in his time of need, and had carried out an expedition to Bagemder and Gojam, well into the Emperor's sphere of interest, while carrying on friendly correspondence with the Khedive.[138]

War between the rulers of Tigré and Shoa, the two most powerful sections of Christian Ethiopia, seemed imminent. Menelik at first thought of suing for peace, but, on learning of the harsh conditions demanded by Yohannes, mobilized his men in January 1878. The prospect of conflict was, however, frightening to many on both sides who felt that it would be only of advantage to their common enemies. Yohannes, though the stronger of the two, was short of supplies, and would be operating in hostile territory against a by no means negligible army: the outcome was uncertain, but the large number of firearms suggested the likelihood of heavy casualties. Many a monk and member of the clergy travelled between the camps, urging on both monarchs the undesirability of shedding Christian blood.

Yohannes, convinced of the advantages of compromise, agreed in February to open talks with Menelik. An accord, negotiated by one of the Emperor's priests, was concluded in March. Its terms, though never published, seem to have covered the following points:[139]

1 Menelik renounced the title of Emperor.
2 Yohannes recognized Menelik's independence, subject to the payment of tax.
3 Yohannes consented to crown Menelik as king of Shoa and Wallo, and accepted the right of Menelik's descendants to succeed as rulers of those provinces.
4 Each ruler promised to help the other in time of need.
5 Menelik agreed that within two years the route between Zeila and Shoa would be closed to Europeans.

Yohannes then crowned his erstwhile enemy with pomp and splendour. On the one hand, this act symbolized the *de jure* paramountcy of Yohannes, but on the other was an expression of Menelik's *de facto* independence.[140]

The two rulers subsequently met at Boru Méda, in Wallo, to discuss religious controversies within the Ethiopian Orthodox Church, and the desirability of converting Muslims and traditionalists, particularly on the periphery of the country where loyalty was uncertain. It was agreed that they should be given three and five years respectively to embrace

138. On suggestions that Menelik was actually conspiring with the Egyptians against Yohannes, see H. G. Marcus, 1975, pp. 38–43; and Zewde Gabre-Sellassie, 1975, pp. 55–9, 61, 65, 260–2.

139. G. Massala, 1892, Vol. 11, pp. 5–23; A. Cecchi, 1886–7, Vol. 1, pp. 422–3; T. Waldmeier, 1886, pp. 133–4; Guèbrè Sellassié, 1930–2, Vol. I, pp. 138–48. For a recent discussion of the Tigré–Shoa agreement, see Zewde Gabre-Sellassie, 1975, pp. 93–4.

140. G. Massala, 1892, Vol. 11, p. 60.

Christianity, and that all non-Christian government officials should be baptised.[141] The two principal chiefs of Wallo, Imām Muḥammad 'Alī and Imām Abba Watta, were accordingly christened Mika'él and Hayla Maryam, and given the rank of Ras and Dajazamach.[142] Their followers, and many others, were also converted, and numerous mosques and sanctuaries of traditional religions destroyed. A large number of such conversions were, however, nominal. The Italian missionary Massala saw converts going straight from the church where they had been christened to the mosque to have their baptism removed,[143] while not a few were referred to as 'Christians by day, Muslims by night'. Other Muslims fled the country, though in certain areas where non-Christians were denied the right to own land baptisms enabled Muslims to acquire land, which they retained even after their return to Islam.[144] Another result of the Boru Méda agreement was the expulsion of Roman Catholic missionaries from Shoa in 1879. Yohannes had long been opposed to missionaries of any kind.[145] Their main value was seen in the provision of technical skills, but Menelik offset any detrimental consequences of their departure by employing other foreigners, among them a Swiss craftsman, Alfred Ilg, who served as both a technician and a diplomatic adviser.[146]

Peace negotiations between Egypt and Yohannes had meanwhile been entrusted by Khedive Ismā'īl to Colonel Charles George Gordon, a British officer serving as Egyptian governor of the Sudan. Gordon, who recognized in his diary that his employer had 'stolen' territory from Ethiopia, and had treated her 'very badly and unjustly',[147] travelled on a futile mission[148] to Dabra Tabor to meet Yohannes in October 1879. The Emperor, he found, was intransigent in his demand for the 'retrocession' of the frontier districts of Bogos, Matamma and the Shanqella country, and also wanted access to the sea.[149] Insistent on the righteousness of his case, he upbraided the Englishman as a Christian serving a Muslim government. He wrote an angry letter to Khedive Tawfiḳ observing that Egypt had behaved like a 'robber', adding, 'You want peace, but you prevent the Abyssinian merchants to go to Massawa. You have taken land not your own'.[150] Gordon,

141. G. Rohlfs, 1885, pp. 149–56; A. Oppel, 1887, p. 307; Guèbrè Sellassié, 1930–2, Vol. 1, pp. 145–56; Zewde Gabre-Sellassie, 1975, pp. 95–6.

142. Guèbrè Sellassié, 1930–2, Vol. 1, pp. 155–6; J. S. Trimingham, 1952, pp. 24, 122.

143. G. Massala, 1892, Vol. II, p. 78.

144. Zewde Gabre-Sellassie, 1975, p. 97; R. Perini, 1905, p. 344; R. K. P. Pankhurst, 1968, p. 147.

145. G. Bianchi, 1886, p. 86. On Yohannes's attitude to missionaries see also Zewde Gabre-Sellassie, 1975, pp. 98–9.

146. C. Keller, 1918; W. Loepfe, 1974; R. K. P. Pankhurst, 1967, pp. 29–42.

147. G. B. Hill, 1881, pp. 403, 405, 406. See also p. 304.

148. Zewde Gabre-Sellassie, 1975, pp. 111–17.

149. ibid., pp. 412–14.

150. ibid., p. 420.

whose instructions precluded any cession of territory, found the interview embarrassing. Irritated by the close surveillance under which the Emperor placed him, he despaired of leaving the country, and later wrote in the memoirs of one of Téwodros's prisoners that had been lucky to get out alive. He observed in the memoirs that Emperor Yohannes talked 'like the Old Testament' and was 'rapidly going mad',[151] but to his sister he remarked that 'Johannes, oddly enough, is like myself – a religious fanatic. He has a mission; and will fulfil it, and that mission is to Christianize all Musselmans'.[152]

Yohannes had by then solid achievements to his credit. Having staved off the invasion by Egypt, and created a greater measure of unity than had existed for most of Téwodros's reign, he enabled his people to enter an unprecedented period of peace. A. B. Wylde, an acute observer, notes that Ethiopia after the Egyptian defeat 'enjoyed the blessings of tranquility and good crops' and 'improved with rapid strides'.[153]

Ethiopia, peaceful and prosperous at the end of our period, was, however, on the eve of major tribulations. The rise of the Sudanese Mahdī, Muḥammad Aḥmad, who was to announce his mission in 1881, meant the emergence of a dynamic new power which was soon to overrun the west of the empire and ravage Gondar, while the Italian seizure of Massawa in 1885, which began the European scramble for Africa in this part of the continent, was to be followed in less than half a decade by a great rinderpest epidemic and subsequent famine, which was once again to reduce the entire region to destitution and misery.

Global overview

Though Yohannes dominated the stage at the end of our period, and he was the ruler of the most powerful polity in the area and the only one significantly involved in international relations, his realm embraced only a fraction of the territory covered by this chapter. His empire, which was based on Tigré, nevertheless extended over virtually the entire Christian highlands. Ras Adal Tasama (later King Takla Haymanot) of Gojam and King (later Emperor) Menelik of Shoa had both been obliged to recognize his imperial authority. The Muslim leaders of Wallo, by now officially converted to Christianity, also indirectly accepted his overlordship. Further east however, the Muslim sultanate of Awsa was independent. The lowlands to the north-west and north-east of Tigré were under the control of the Egyptians, for Yohannes, despite his victories over them, had been unable either to reverse all their recent encroachments or accomplish his cherished ambition of gaining access to the sea. Egyptian rule was, however, to come

151. ibid., pp. 421–2, 424.
152. C. Gordon, 1902, p. 155.
153. A. B. Wylde, 1901, p. 30.

to an end in less than half a decade, though the area would then fall into the hands not of the rulers of Ethiopia, but of a colonial power, Italy.

The lands to the west, south and east were not yet incorporated within the Ethiopian state, for though Menelik had already made himself master of parts of Guragé, his major expeditions to the south were several years away. In the south-west of the country a cluster of small independent states still existed. They included the old kingdom of Kaffa, Janjero and Walamo, as well as several small Oromo monarchies: Jimma, whose last and most famous king, Abba Jifar II, had just ascended the throne, and Léka where Moroda, a local chief, was consolidating his power, besides Limmu, Goma, Guma, Géra and some other lesser political entities. The Oromo, as well as other groups to the south, in Arussi, Borana and elsewhere, likewise had a separate political existence.

To the south-east, Harar, once an independent city state, was under the occupation of Egypt, though this was soon to come to an end and Menelik would gain control of the town. Along the Gulf of Aden coast the Somali ports were also under Egyptian domination but this too was soon to terminate and be replaced by that of the three colonial powers, Britain, France and Italy. The remaining Somali ports, on the Atlantic coast, in Majerteyn to the north and Benadir to the south, were under the suzerainty of Oman and Zanzibar respectively. Around 1870, a dispute between the Majerteyn sultan, Oman Maḥmūd and his father-in-law, Yūsuf ʿAlī led to a split in the sultanate and the founding by Yūsuf ʿAlī of the new Sultanate of Hobya (Obbia) further south.[154] Along the lower Shebelle river, the development of commercial agriculture in the cultivation of grain, sesame, orchella and cotton, contributed to the prosperity of the Geledi sultanate up until the 1880s.[155] But Omani domination was soon to give way to Italian colonialism. Foreign influence in the Somali region was, however, limited to the coast, and the majority of the Somali who lived in the interior were, like many of the Oromo, entirely free of external authorities, and lived under the control of their local clans.

154. M. Pirone, 1961, p. 88.
155. L. V. Cassanelli, 1982, pp. 161–78.

16

Madagascar 1800–80

P. M. MUTIBWA
with a contribution by
F. V. ESOAVELOMANDROSO

Introduction

The history of Madagascar between 1800 and 1880 is characterized by two major trends which provide guidelines for our discussion. The first was the political evolution of the country and the diplomatic interaction between Madagascar and foreign powers, particularly Britain and France. Second, major changes took place in the social organization of the country, particularly in the religious, administrative and economic fields. Political evolution consisted mainly of the consolidation of the Merina monarchy and the expansion of its authority to the rest of the island. The diplomatic relations that this monarchy maintained with both Britain and France became a cornerstone of the country's development. The changes that were effected in administration, particularly in the establishment of law and order, facilitated economic development. This was also a major factor in Madagascar's efforts to modernize itself and to resist foreign domination. The embracing of foreign religions was viewed as part of this process of modernization.

A brief description of the country and its people may be necessary here. There are some eighteen ethnic groups in Madagascar of which the largest and, as it turned out, the most important in the nineteenth century, are the Merina who live on the central plateau of the island. This central plateau, known as Imerina (the country which one sees from afar), was the home of the Merina among whom there was a privileged class who came to rule the greater part of the island before it was colonized by the French. It is difficult to say what the population of Madagascar was during the period under review, but the British consul in Madagascar estimated it to be 5 million in 1865, of whom about 800 000 were Merina.[1] All the Malagasy groups speak the same language and have, with few exceptions, similar customs and religious traditions. Thus, despite the existence of regional

1. Public Record Office, Kew, England, Foreign Office, (hereinafter FO) 48/10, Pakenham to Russell, 31 January 1865.

differences, the Malagasy were, and have remained, one people, with one profound cultural and ethnic unity.[2]

The rulers of Imerina established their seat in Antananarivo, and it was from here that a line of able and often popular monarchs ruled the greater part of the island. The term 'government of the kingdom of Madagascar' will be used here to refer to this government in Antananarivo which, by 1880, was in control, despite spasmodic rebellions here and there of over two-thirds of the entire island. Hence, in spite of the importance of the history of different provinces and regions,[3] the discussion of the political, social, economic and administrative evolution of Madagascar turns mainly on the history of the central plateau as the focus or the heart of the rest of the island.

The era of Andrianampoinimerina (1792–1810)

It is difficult to appreciate the history of Madagascar in the nineteenth century without an examination of how Andrianampoinimerina, the founder of the Merina kingdom, came to power and consolidated his position on the central plateau. He reunified the Merina kingdom and expanded it. Furthermore, he reinforced the cohesiveness of the population as an essential factor in the policy of territorial expansion.

Around 1780 there existed in Central Imerina only three or four small kingdoms, all of which were locked in internecine civil wars. In about 1785 Ramboasalama, the nephew of the King of Ambohimanga, one of the small kingdoms, expelled his uncle and proclaimed himself king under the name of Andrianampoinimerina.[4] He then started to consolidate his position in Imerina, using diplomatic as well as military means. He liquidated the kings of Antananarivo and Ambohidratrimo who, although they had concluded peace with him, had continued to defy him.[5] In 1791 or 1792 Andrianampoinimerina moved his capital to Antananarivo and started to build the political and social structures of the new kingdom. It has since remained the capital of both Imerina and Madagascar.

The second part of Andrianampoinimerina's reign, roughly from 1800, featured expansion beyond Imerina, thus beginning the long and difficult task of uniting all the eighteen or so ethnic groups in Madagascar. He felt a strong desire to conquer the rest of the island, and on his deathbed he is

2. H. Deschamps, 1951, p. 53, has remarked that 'The unity of the Malagasy language is remarkable. From one end to another of the island, it is the same grammar, the same syntax and, for the great majority, the same words'.

3. The University of Madagascar, Department of History is pioneering work on the history of the regions, and is beginning thus to deepen our knowledge of the internal history of Madagascar.

4. For a short portrait of King Andrianampoinimerina, see H. Deschamps, 1967; A. Delivré, 1974.

5. R. W. Rabemananjara, 1952, p. 53.

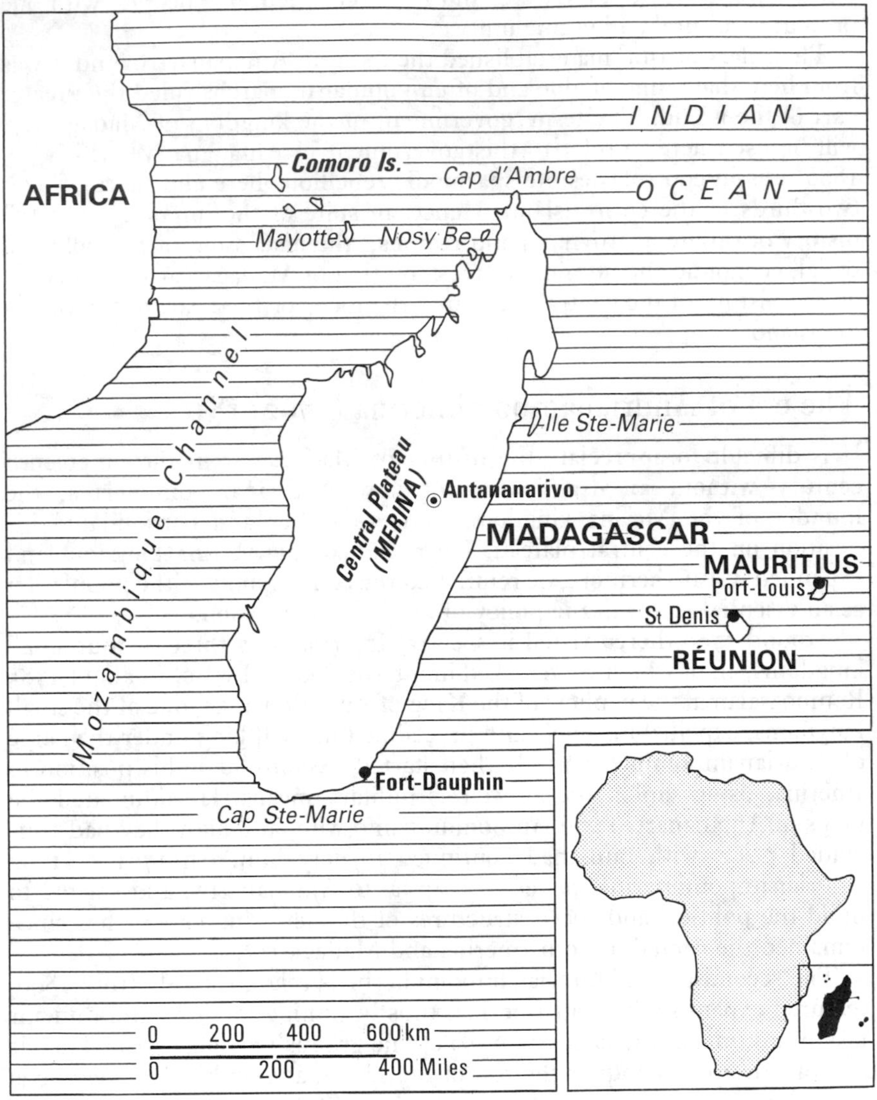

FIG. 16.1 *Madagascar and its neighbours (after P. M. Mutibwa)*

PLATE 16.1 *A view of Antananarivo in the 1850s*

reported to have told Radama, his son and successor, that 'the sea is my frontier'.[6] First he conquered portions of territories which were traditionally Merina, then occupied by neighbouring peoples such as the Bezanozano and the Sihanaka in the east.[7] Although he brought these people under his suzerainty, some of them, particularly the Bezanozano, continued to resist. He used force in consolidating his power in Imerina, but he also tried to present himself to his adversaries as a ruler whose only desire was peace and unity.

His expansion to the south was at first intended mainly to protect the Merina who had emigrated there. The Betsileo were already under Merina hegemony, and the Merina troops did not encounter great difficulties in moving further south to the Ankaratra Mountain and to the region of Faratsiho.[8] In the west, however, Andrianampoinimerina found, as his successors were also to find, that the Sakalava were a difficult nut to crush. In fact, all attempts to subdue them totally failed. It is true that he sometimes succeeded in establishing friendly relations with them; but quite often the Sakalava invaded Imerina, carrying the incursions almost to Antananarivo itself. The most important of the Sakalava kingdoms were

6. Lit. 'The sea is the limit of my rice paddy'. He linked the cultivation of rice to the struggle against famine and gave directives for the development of the plains of Betsimitatatra.

7. See J. Valette, 1971, p. 327ff.

8. ibid., p. 328. See also, J. Rainihifina, 1975. For the Merina emigration to Andrantsay and Voromahery (northern border of Betsileo), see D. Rasamuel, 1980; E. Fauroux, 1970, p. 83; J. Y. Marchal, 1967, pp. 241–80, and J. Dez, 1967, pp. 657–702.

Menabe and Boina, which between them formed an impregnable barrier to Merina expansion to the west. The fiercest resistance however came from the Ambongo. It should be added also that the Maroseranana Sakalava dynasty constituted the only real alternative to the Merina rulers since it it had extended its hegemony over the western part of the island before the nineteenth century and had concluded alliances with some of the kingdoms of the eastern part, for example the Betsimisaraka.[9] Nevertheless, by the time of his death in 1810, Andrianampoinimerina had made Imerina a force to reckon with throughout the island of Madagascar.

The great modernizer: King Radama I (1810–28)

Few rulers in Madagascar's history have become as legendary as Radama I, who succeeded to the throne in 1810 at the age of about 18. He is regarded, as indeed he saw himself, as the 'Napoleon' of Madagascar.

At the announcement of Andrianampoinimerina's death, some of the people he had conquered revolted. It thus became Radama's first task to subdue these rebels, particularly the Bezanozano of Ambotomanga, many of whom fled to the east. Although Radama succeeded in consolidating his position in Imerina, what he desired most was to reach the sea, as his father had directed him to do on his deathbed. Without direct access to the sea, the Merina felt hemmed in by their neighbours, who even raided them for slaves. Merina traders, increasingly anxious to trade at the ports of Tamatave and Majunga directly with Europeans, especially the British in the Mascarene Islands, were forced instead to exchange their handicrafts, rice, beef and other agricultural produce for European salt and ammunition through Bezanozano, Sihanaka and Sakalava intermediaries. Radama saw territorial expansion as part of the heritage of the Maroseranana that he had taken over and, above all, as a filial duty to respect the wishes of his ancestors and fulfil the predictions of soothsayers.[10]

It was to the east – towards the increasingly important port of Tamatave – that Radama's eyes were first focused. However, the political situation in the surrounding Betsimisaraka area called for intervention. The confederation organized in the eighteenth century by Ratsimilaho had broken up into a multitude of rival principalities at war one with another, and riddled with internal challengers, generally opposed to the authority of the *filoha* (ruling chiefs), who invited Radama to intervene. In the midst of this political chaos, Jean René, a *métis*, seized control of Tamatave in 1812.[11] It was largely Radama's desire to establish a route to this eastern port that dictated his diplomatic contacts with Sir Robert Townsend Farquhar, the Governor of Mauritius. His desire to reach the sea coincided with Farquhar's desire –

9. C. Guillain, 1845, p. 376.
10. H. Deschamps, 1960, p. 154. See also J. M. Filliot, 1974, p. 273.
11. H. Decary (ed.), 1939.

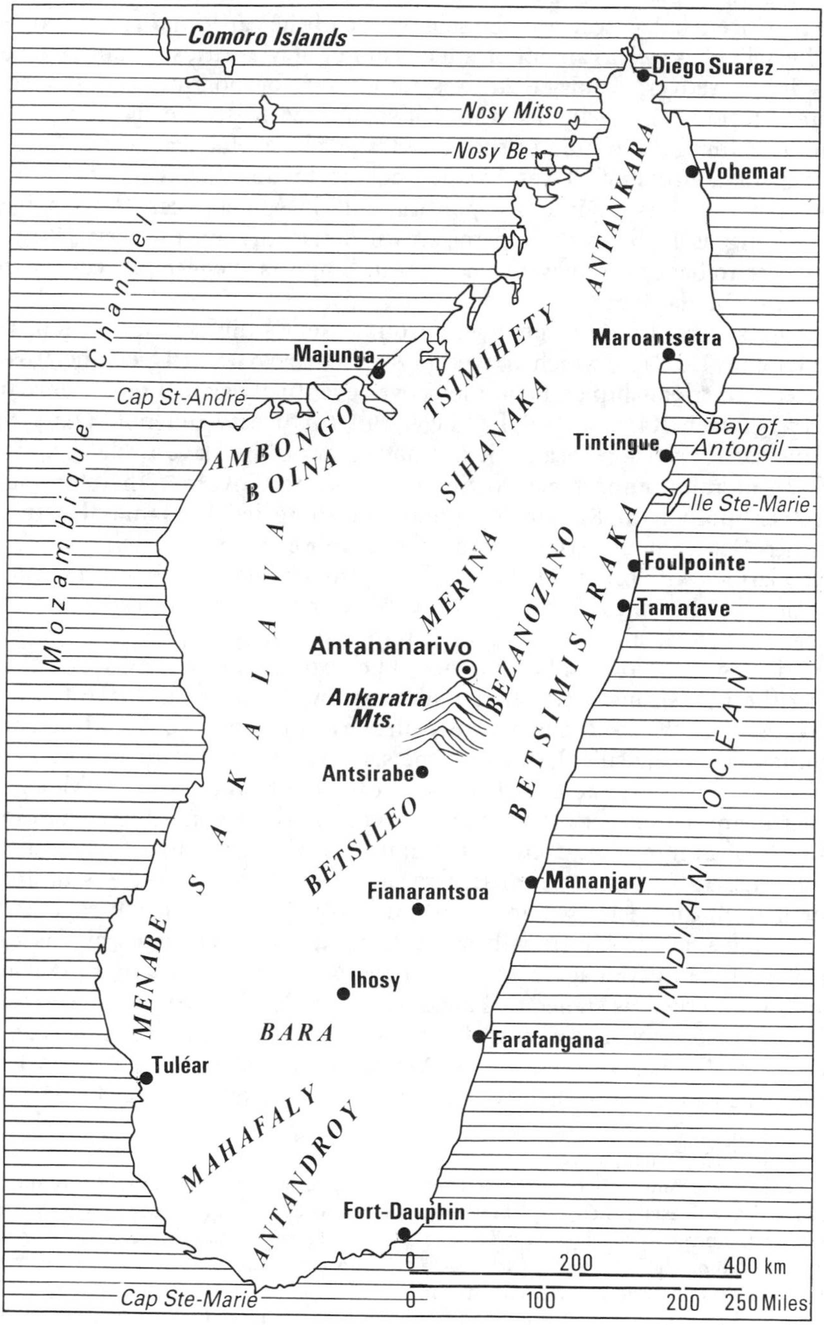

FIG. 16.2 *Madagascar, 1800–80 (after P. M. Mutibwa)*

and that of England – to control Madagascar, or at least to influence events there, since Madagascar was the sole source of the cattle and rice imported to Mauritius as well as an important consumer of Mauritius's manufactured goods. Moreover, Madagascar was important for political and strategic considerations. In particular, the British wanted to secure the support of the ruler for the abolition of the slave trade, since Madagascar was one of the main sources of slaves in the region. It was Sir Robert's desire, therefore, to pursue an active political role in Madagascar. This policy, coinciding as it did with Radama's own determination to expand to the east, was to have, as one writer has put it, 'important consequences for the future of Madagascar'.[12]

After several friendly contacts, Farquhar sent a diplomatic mission, led by Captain Le Sage, which arrived in Antananarivo on 21 December 1816. A treaty of friendship and commerce was eventually signed on 4 February 1817 between Radama and Le Sage. But this treaty did not satisfy the Mauritian Governor because it did not mention the slave trade, a matter of considerable importance to Sir Robert. The Governor therefore sent another mission to Radama's capital, this time led by James Hastie, a former Sergeant at Arms in India and more experienced in handling negotiations with oriental rulers.[13] Hastie brought along with him a number of gifts for the king, including horses, a compass, a map of the world and a chiming clock, all of which greatly impressed the young king and helped Hastie to win his love and confidence. The negotiations, however, stumbled over the British insistence that Radama should outlaw the slave trade in Madagascar. When Radama argued that by doing this he would be committing economic suicide because the slave trade was the major source of his revenue, Hastie had a ready answer: the British would pay the Malagasy ruler an annual sum of 1000 dollars in gold, 1000 dollars in silver, a hundred barrels of gunpowder, 100 English muskets with 100 flints, 400 soldiers' uniforms, 12 sergeants' swords, 600 pieces of cloth, a full-dress uniform for himself and 2 horses as compensation.[14] Radama considered that he had made a fair deal, especially since the treaty also recognized him as king of the whole of Madagascar. The Anglo–Malagasy Treaty of Friendship and Commerce was signed at Tamatave on 23 October 1817. James Hastie, the successful negotiator, was dispatched to Madagascar again in 1820 to act as the British Resident in the Malagasy capital. However, when Farquhar was in Britain on leave, his successor, Major General Gage John

12. J. Valette, 1971, p. 331.

13. H. Deschamps, 1960, p. 154. The first contact between Radama I and the Mauritian authorities was established early in 1816 when Sir Robert Farquhar sent Jacques Chardenoux (a former French slave-trader settled in Mauritius) to Antananarivo to pay a courtesy call on the king and to gather as much information as possible about the country, its people and its resources. See M. Brown, 1978, p. 137.

14. ibid., p. 143, n. 10. For internal sources, see L. Munthe, C. Ravoajanahary and S. Ayache, 1976.

Hall, refused to pay the subsidies stipulated in the treaty. This led to the breakdown of relations between the British and the Merina court, and allowed the French to retain a foothold in the Merina capital during a period of British dominance.[15] Radama was clearly upset by the British failure to fulfil the terms of the 1817 Treaty, but he was soon persuaded to forget the past in order to pursue his long-term interests, which he saw clearly as resting on the alliance between his country and Britain. He therefore accepted Hastie's apologies for the mistakes of Hall (who was recalled) and he accordingly renewed the treaty on 11 October 1820. In a separate document, Radama also allowed British missionaries to work in Madagascar.

Following this agreement, on 3 December 1820, David Jones of the London Missionary Society (LMS) arrived in Antananarivo. Radama welcomed British missionaries for they brought with them not only education (although tied to Christianity) but also technical assistance.[16] Radama wrote to the LMS asking them 'to send as many missionaries as they could, provided that they included craftsmen such as weavers and carpenters as well as men of religion'.[17] The missionaries opened the first school in Anatananarivo on 8 December 1820 with three pupils, young nephews of the king; and because of the tremendous personal encouragement which Radama gave to the missionaries, the LMS were able to boast of some 23 schools and about 2300 pupils by 1829. The missionaries reduced the Malagasy language to written form, using the Latin alphabet, and translated the Bible into it.

In this endeavour, several missionaries such as Jones, Bevan and Griffiths made significant contributions and they relied on the assistance and co-operation of able Malagasy converts. The missionary societies paid particular attention to printing and publishing. Thus, through the schools, Bible classes and the dissemination of printed material, education assisted not only proselytization but also literacy and the evolution of the Malagasy language and literature as an instrument of island-wide national integration. By 1827, more than 4000 Malagasy could read and write in their own language.[18] In the field of technical education, the British missionaries also made significant contributions. They sent some young Malagasy either to England or Mauritius for technical education; and at home introduced many technical skills and ideas such as carpentry, building, tannery, the art of modern tin-plating and weaving. The most outstanding missionary who assisted the Malagasy in technical education was James Cameron; he arrived in Antananarivo in 1826 and, except for the few years he spent in

15. M. Brown, 1978, p. 144.
16. V. Belrose-Huyghes, 1978b.
17. M. Brown, 1978, p. 155. See also, V. Belrose-Huyghes, 1978b, and J. Valette, 1962. For foreign influence on architecture see V. Belrose-Huyghes, 1975.
18. H. Deschamps, 1960, p. 161; V. Belrose-Huyghes, 1977; L. Munthe, 1969, p. 244; F. Raison, 1977.

exile, remained there until his death in 1875. One of the reasons why the missionaries were so successful was the role played by missionary wives in facilitating contact with Malagasy households, especially the aristocratic ladies, to whom they offered the rudiments of household instruction and provided services such as those of seamstresses.[19]

The most important technical assistance that Radama required was a modernized standing army on the British model. He recruited an army of about 15 000 men, equipped with good English guns from the Napoleonic Wars and even some light cannon. They were trained mainly by English instructors, the most important being Hastie and Brady. The resulting army was much better and more effective than those of his adversaries on the island, To sustain professional spirit, Radama I introduced a system of army ranks within the army, based on numbers of 'honours', one honour for a private, and up to ten honours for a general. The army became an important instrument not only in the conquest of other territories on the island but also in the maintenance of law and order in the conquered territories.

The submission of the coastal people in the east began in 1817 when, at the head of 30 000 soldiers, Radama descended upon Tamatave, securing on the way the submission of the Bezanozano. He concluded a peace pact with Jean René who had been in control of the town, and, from then on, the gateway to the outside world was secured. Radama returned to Tamatave in 1823 with an even bigger army, and on this occasion he secured recognition of his authority from the Betsimisaraka. He visited other territories on the eastern coast such as Foulpointe, Bay of Antongil, Vohemar and the Antankara territory. On his way back to the capital, in 1824, he passed through the country of the Tsimihety, where he established a post at Mandritasara, and that of the Sihanaka; both peoples recognized his authority. Meanwhile, Jean René, who had become Radama's agent at Tamatave, was carrying out a similar exercise in the regions south of Tamatave. Fort Dauphin in the extreme south-east of the island was reached in 1825, thereby further strengthening Radama's claim to be master of the whole eastern coast of Madagascar.[20]

It was in the west, in the Sakalava country, that Radama, like his predecessor, encountered the greatest difficulties. In 1820 he dispatched a large army against the king of Menabe, without success. In 1821, accompanied by Hastie, Radama returned to Menabe at the head of an army of some 70 000 soldiers, including a thousand professionals. This, too, failed to conquer the territory. In 1822, he returned with a well-armed and carefully prepared expedition of some 13 000 men which at last defeated the Menabe and established some fortified posts in their country. But the

19. V. Belrose-Huyghes, 1978a.

20. For more details, see H. Deschamps, 1960, pp. 151–61, to which this account is indebted.

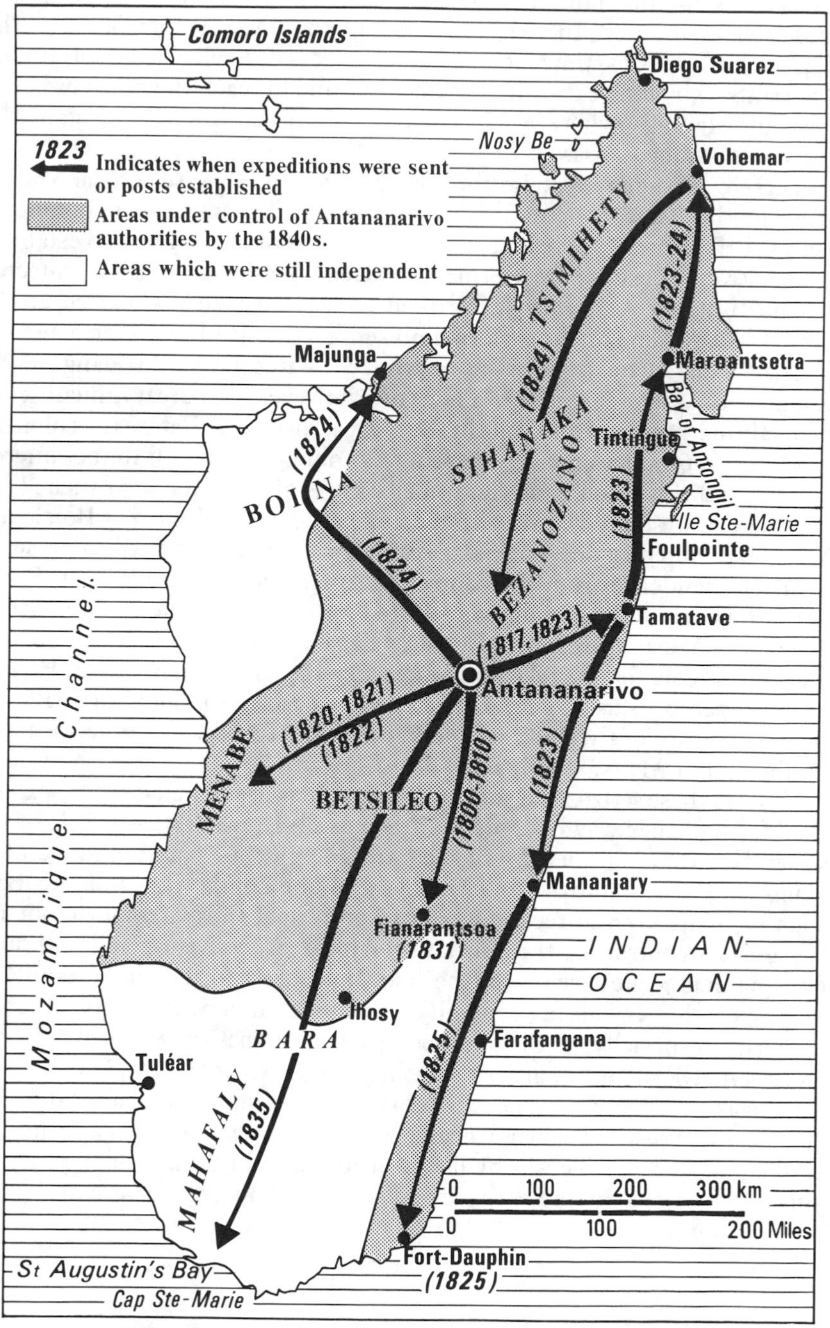

FIG. 16.3 *The expansion of the Merina kingdom, 1810–40 (after P. M. Mutibwa)*

victory was of limited duration because the Sakalava in the north continued to defy his authority. In 1824 he launched an attack against Boina in the north-west and this time he was more successful. The ruler of Boina, Andriantsoli, made peace and Radama was able to reach the north-western town of Majunga where a Merina post was established, but again the success was short-lived.

These campaigns illustrate the strengths and weaknesses of the Merina army in the contest for national integration. They were usually able to defeat rival armies. Thereafter, the usual means of control was to establish administrative posts where Merina *voanjo* (colonists) were settled, protected by the building of a *rova*, a fortified area similar to the palace at the capital and symbolizing the Merina presence. Also, Radama often arranged marriages of alliance, as in his marriage to Rosalimo, the daughter of Ramitraho, king of Menabe.[21] The army, however, had great difficulties in maintaining supplies from Imerina over great distances. Before the colonists were able to produce enough, the army was obliged to live off the conquered regions and this often provoked rebellion. As soon as Radama turned his back on the west and returned to Antananarivo, the Sakalava of Boina and Menabe revolted again. The Sakalava people were determined to preserve their independence from the control of Antananarivo. Similarly in Boina the Antalaotra trading group constituted a further obstacle to integration. They were Muslims, regarded by the Malagasy as foreigners.[22] This created grave problems for the Malagasy government, particularly as the French were prepared to use some of the rebellious Sakalava chiefs to challenge the sovereignty of the Merina rulers over some territories in the west and north-west of Madagascar.

Despite these setbacks, Radama I's campaigns had enabled him to extend the Merina hegemony over most of the island. By 1828, two-thirds of the whole island was under Merina control. Only the remote and desolate plains of the Antandroy and Mahafaly in the south-west and the Bara country, apart from a precarious Merina outpost at Ihosy, remained outside Radama I's control. In the Sakalava territory, as we have noted, although Radama had conquered Menabe and Boina territories and established outposts, the Sakalava generally remained independent of Merina authority, especially in the southern part of Boina known as Ambongo. But even if Radama's authority on the island was not complete, at least there was no effective challenge to his title as King of Madagascar.[23] But these campaigns had taken a heavy toll on Radama's energy and health, further weakened as he was by heavy drinking and licentious living. On 27 July 1828 he died at the early age of 36, thus bringing a successful reign to an abrupt end.

21. C. Guillain, 1845.
22. G. Rantoandro, 1981; M. Rasoamiaramanana, 1981.
23. M. Brown, 1978, p. 150.

Ranavalona I (1828–61): a period of reaction or stabilization?

Queen Ranavalona I was the cousin and first wife of Radama I and came to the throne with the assistance of the nobles and army chiefs whom Radama had removed from influential positions.[24] This meant that the new regime would attempt to remove Radama's close associates and replace them with men who had not accepted, or been party to, the policies pursued by the late king. The Queen's first chief advisers were Rainimahary and Andriamihaja; but these two men were eliminated one after the other and in the end the most important men who emerged to share power with the Queen were Rainiharo and Rainijohary. The former came from the Tsimiamboholahy clan and the other from Tsimahafotsy, the two clans that had assisted Andrianampoinimerina to found the Merina kingdom at the end of the eighteenth century. They developed for the most part from commoners and laid the foundation of the Hova middle class, which, as a result of the support its members gave the monarchy, gradually built up economic, administrative and political power that came to rival and erode the power of the monarchy.

The cornerstone of Ranavalona's policy was to safeguard, as she saw it, Madagascar's independence from foreign influence, particularly as this affected national institutions, traditions and customs. This meant, in terms of foreign policy, the desire to disengage from British influence, particularly in political and religious fields. In December 1828 the Ranavalona's government told Robert Lyall, the new British Resident, that although they would not reintroduce the slave trade, they did not wish to continue with the treaty, nor did they consider his presence in their capital necessary any longer. Trade between Madagascar and the islands of Mauritius and Réunion was banned. General Brady, who had been naturalized as a Malagasy and given noble rank by Radama I, was forced into retirement in 1829. Madagascar's disillusionment with foreign powers was heightened when, in 1829, Charles X's government in France, desirous to raise its prestige at home, ordered the bombardment and occupation of Tintingue and Tamatave, following a series of misunderstandings with the Malagasy over the French presence at Tintingue, opposite the island of Sainte-Marie. The Malagasy repulsed the invaders at Foulpointe. The unprovoked attack was disavowed by Louis-Philippe, Charles X's successor, but it left deep wounds in the hearts of the Malagasy. French claims on Madagascar became a permanent feature of Franco–Malagasy relations for the rest of the century. This sometimes produced a pro-British reaction and it explains why, in spite of the policy of cultural independence, British missionaries were not expelled from the country for another six years.

24. See G. Ayache, 1966; A. Delivré, 1974, for the importance of oral tradition in her nomination, and the role of Rainimahary, Andrianampoinimerina's companion. There were a few executions, but Ranavalona was quickly accepted by the people as Queen.

PLATE 16.2 *Andrianampoinimerina, d. 1810*

PLATE 16.3 *King Radama I, 1810–28*

PLATE 16.4 *Queen Ranavalona I, 1828–61*

PLATE 16.5 *King Radama II, 1861–63*

PLATE 16.6 *Queen Rasoherina, 1863–68*

PLATE 16.7 *Queen Ranavalona II, 1868–83*

Malagasy leaders welcomed and appreciated the technical assistance that the British missionaries were offering; but what they wanted most was secular, not religious education. The attitude of Ranavalona was, therefore, not one of systematic rejection, though she was from the start obviously less enthusiastic about Christianity than her predecessor. What worried the new leaders most and eventually drove them into a struggle against the growing influence of Christianity was that it constituted a challenge to Malagasy traditions and institutions generally, and the monarchy in particular. Christian rituals competed with the ceremonies of the royal religion. By discouraging the worship of *sampimoanja-Kana* (*sampy*), the royal divinity guaranteeing the well-being of the state, Christianity shook the foundations of royal power. Its egalitarian principles were also in conflict with the traditional hierarchy of castes.[25] Christianity was changing the traditions of the country and turning the Malagasy into worshippers of Jesus Christ whom they regarded as the whitemen's ancestor. By 1830 there were about 200 converted Christians who were even prepared to die for their faith; the government could not remain indifferent to this 'new power which had arisen in the land'.[26] When the missionaries refused to offer education without being allowed to preach their religion, the breach with Ranavalona was unavoidable. Her first response was to forbid baptism in 1832. Three years later all her subjects were prohibited from becoming or remaining Christians. The preaching of Christianity was banned, but the ban did not apply to secular education. Explaining the reasons for her decision, Ranavalona told the British missionaries, whom she summoned to her palace on 26 February 1835, that:

> While she thanked them for the good services they had rendered to the country, and while they were at liberty to follow their own religious customs, she would not permit her subjects to depart from their old customs ... She gave full permission for the teaching of the arts or sciences but not religion.[27]

The first martyrs fell; Rasalama in August 1837 and Raqarilahy-Andriamazok in February 1838. The missionaries went into exile and this was followed by a period of fierce persecution of Malagasy Christians during which several hundreds perished in violent deaths. Nevertheless, far from dying out, Christianity seems to have had a new rebirth.

The religion spread underground, with clandestine meetings of Christian communities in caves (e.g. in the region of Fihaonana in the Vonizongo, north-west of Imerina) and in private homes, even in Antananarivo. A group of Christians fled to Britain where they prepared themselves for an eventual return as missionaries. The Jesuits, for their part, organized a mission to the Petites Îles (Nosy Be, Nosy Faly and Mayotte in the north-

25. M. Brown, 1977.
26. See W. E. Cousins, 1895, pp. 83ff.
27. Quoted from P. M. Mutibwa, 1974, pp. 26–7.

west and Sainte-Marie in the east) from where they tried to infiltrate to the mainland, especially the Bay of Faly, which they were forced to leave in 1857. This has been referred to by some writers as 'the darkest period of Ranavalona's reign',[28] and Ranavalona has earned such names as the 'Queen Mary of Madagascar', 'a modern Messalina or female Nero'. Even so, the Malagasy court was anxious not to break completely with Britain, so as to avoid confrontation with a hostile alliance of Britain and France.

The Malagasy leaders realized that the country needed contact with the outside world, to secure European manufactured goods, particularly guns and ammunition. They also wanted to buy luxury goods such as cloth and alcohol and to expand their exports, mainly cattle and rice, to Mauritius and Réunion in order to pay for the necessary imports. Queen Ranavalona therefore wanted to find a *modus vivendi* with the Europeans, to enable her country to develop without the fear of European antagonism and war. In pursuit of this policy, she and her advisers decided in 1836 to send an embassy to France and England and to negotiate fresh treaties of friendship and commerce, based on respect for Malagasy culture and independence and to secure recognition for Ranavalona I as Queen of Madagascar.[29] The Malagasy embassy – the first ever to be sent to Europe – consisted of six officers and two secretaries and was led by Andriantsitchaina.[30] Their stay in Paris was uneventful and they then crossed the Channel to London. They were accorded an audience by King William IV and Queen Adelaide, but their talks with Lord Palmerston were unsatisfactory. The British government insisted on the freedom of commerce and navigation, which ran counter to Madagascar's desire to control its own trade and allow traffic only through ports under the effective control of the central government.

The failure of the embassy to conclude any treaty with either France or England increased the suspicions of the Malagasy towards foreigners, and the fears were well founded. In 1845, an Anglo-French naval squadron attacked Tamatave on the orders of the French and British authorities in Réunion and Mauritius respectively. The pretext for this attack was the proclamation in May of a Malagasy law that obliged all foreigners to obey the laws of the land, with the implications, the British alleged, that they were liable to public works, could be enslaved and were subject to the ordeal of *tangena*. The Malagasy were flabbergasted by the attack. They succeeded in repulsing it, and the survivors of the Anglo-French force were obliged to evacuate Tamatave, leaving behind the corpses of their slain comrades, whose heads were cut off by the Malagasy and impaled on poles as a warning to other would-be invaders. Although this attack was

28. M. Brown, 1978, p. 177; A. Boudou, 1940–2; also P. Rabary, 1957, and J. T. Hardyman, 1977.

29. Yet another reason was that rumours were circulating at the time that England was about to attack Madagascar, moving from Islary Bay near St Augustin Bay where the Malagasy had seen some English ships. See R. E. P. Wastell, 1944, p. 25.

30. For more details, see J. Valette, 1960.

disowned by the French and British governments, the damage had already been done. Queen Ranavalona reacted by expelling all foreign traders and suspending overseas trade, especially the export of beef and rice to Mauritius and Réunion, although trade with the USA continued.

This reaction was typical of the Malagasy: if Europe would not co-operate with them, they would help themselves and rely on their own initiatives. The Queen and the Andafiavaratra clan in particular and the oligarchy in general could adopt this attitude of resistance to foreigners because, despite sporadic revolts, they were in control of the most important provinces, whose economy they controlled, including a monopoly on the beef trade. In this lies their determination to continue to promote Western education and establish industries to produce those goods which they needed but which could not now be imported from outside. In maintaining commercial contacts with the outside world, the Queen used the services of a French national called de Lastelle, who was established at Tamatave, and an American national called William Marks at Majunga. With the support of de Lastelle, sugar plantations were established on the eastern coast, and a factory was installed at Mahela producing sugar and rum.[31] The Queen engaged Jean Laborde, a French adventurer, who arrived in Antananarivo in 1832 'as a kind of general superintendent of works'. He

PLATE 16.8 *The Queen's palace in Antananarivo begun in 1839 by Jean Laborde at the request of Queen Ranavalona I*

31. F. Nicol, 1940.

first established a factory at Ilafy, 10 km north of Antananarivo before moving to Mantasoa, on the edge of the eastern forest in a region rich in running water but where it was difficult to get the Malagasy to work willingly. At Mantasoa, with official backing, he established an industrial complex employing some 20 000 workers. This produced various goods ranging from guns and cannon to glass and soap. Perhaps Laborde's greatest and most lasting creation was the wooden palace of the Queen, later enclosed in stone by Cameron, which now dominates Antananarivo. De Lastelle and Laborde became Malagasy citizens and were incorporated into the ruling oligarchy.[32]

Queen Ranavalona continued the expansion which Radama I had begun and consolidated her administration in the conquered territories. The equipment of her army necessitated the prosecution of external trade to obtain ammunition and the encouragement of gun production at Laborde's factory. She levied special taxes for the support of the wars. The town of Fianarantsoa was created in 1831 as a regional capital, and the province of Betsileo was reorganized. From Fianarantsoa expeditions were dispatched in the 1830s to the south, some of which, under the command of Rainiharo, crossed the Bara, the Mahafaly and the Masikoro countries. One of these reached the Bay of Saint-Augustin in 1835.[33] In the west and north, the Sakalava and the Antankara continued to resist the authority of the central government. When the government's forces defeated the Sakalava chiefs, Tsiomako and Tsimiharo, they and their supporters fled to the neighbouring islands of Nosy Be, Nosy Faly and Nosy Mitso from where they sent messages to the French authorities in Réunion, placing their territories under French protection. In 1841, Amiral de Hell, the Governor of Réunion, accepted these requests and the treaties between the French and the rebellious Sakalava chiefs-in-exile formed the basis of France's claims to the western territories of Madagascar.[34]

With the death in 1852 of Rainiharo, who had headed the government from the 1830s, a new generation of younger men came to power. It was led by Rainivoninahitriniony and his younger brother Rainilaiarivony (Rainiharo's two sons) who became prime minister and commander-in-chief of the army respectively. What is more this new generation of leaders had the support of Rakoto Radama, Queen Ranavalona's son, who had been designated Crown Prince. These young men, including Prince Rakoto, had received some education from the missionaries and they were more outward-looking than the old group of Rainiharo and his associates. It is true that Rainijohary, the man who had shared power with the late Rainiharo, was still around, still referred to as Chief Minister and was opposed to any change of policy; but the presence of the Crown Prince, who called

32. S. Ayache, 1977; O. Caillon-Filet, 1978.
33. H. Deschamps, 1960, p. 170; S. Rakotomahandry, 1981; R. Decary, 1966.
34. C. Guillain, 1845; R. Decary, 1960.

Jean Laborde, the French engineer, 'Mon Père', could not but ensure a reorientation of Ranavalona's policies. In 1853, the ban on trade between Madagascar and the islands of Réunion and Mauritius was lifted after the merchants of those two islands (especially Mauritius) had paid a compensation of 15 000 dollars to Ranavalona. The Queen opened her doors to some foreigners. In 1856 she allowed the Reverend W. Ellis of the LMS to visit Antananarivo, bringing letters from the British government professing friendship and amity towards Madagascar. Two Roman Catholic priests, Père Finaz and Père Weber, were smuggled into the capital, Finaz as secretary to a French businessman called Lambert and Weber as a companion of a doctor who was to care for Rainijohary's brother.[35]

Joseph Lambert arrived in Antananarivo in 1855. He was a trader-planter from Mauritius whose chartered vessel had dealt with Madagascar and who had rendered important service to Ranavalona earlier in the year by replenishing supplies to the garrison in Fort Dauphin, which was then blockaded by rebellious peoples in the south-east. It is therefore not surprising that he was made welcome at court. Acting through Laborde's influence on Rakoto Radama, Lambert induced the prince to grant him a charter. This gave him rights to exploit the country's mineral and agricultural resources. The prince is also alleged to have requested a French protectorate over Madagascar. But Emperor Napoleon III was too preoccupied with the Crimean War to pursue a policy in Madagascar which could only have antagonized England, France's ally; in the event, the protectorate proposal was rejected by Paris.

Although Ranavalona was becoming more and more friendly towards foreigners, the hopes of the French and the British lay in the Crown Prince, who had clearly demonstrated his pro-European tendencies. It was largely this consideration that induced Lambert, on his return to Antananarivo in 1857, to plan a coup d'état. He did this with the support of Laborde, de Lastelle and the Rainiharo clan and other Malagasy who favoured modernity, especially the clandestine Christian communities, whose members had developed fraternal relations among themselves and who were close to the prince. The object of the plot was to overthrow Ranavalona and put the prince on the throne, but it was discovered before it could materialize, and Lambert and de Lastelle were expelled from Madagascar.[36] This brought to a head rumours that had been circulating in Madagascar and even in Europe that France was about to invade Madagascar, rumours which even received credence in London.[37] Ranavalona was hurt and disappointed by the treason of her son and by the disloyalty of the two

35. A. Boudou, 1940–2.

36. A. Boudou, 1943.

37. Cowley to Ihouvenel, 'Note Verbale', 19 February 1860, Ministère des Affaires Etrangères, Archives (hereinafter MAE), Quai d'Orsay, Paris, *Madagascar Series*, Tome IV.

Frenchmen, whom she had also come to regard as her own sons. Aged and worried, Ranavalona lived in an unhappy isolation until her death on 18 August 1861, after having designated Rakoto Radama as her successor. Rainijohary and his 'conservative' supporters tried to organize the succession to the throne of Rambossalama, the queen's nephew; but the support of Rainivoninahitriniony and his younger brother Rainilaiarivony for Ranavalona's nominee, whose progressive ideas they in fact shared, was decisive and ensured the Crown Prince's peaceful accession to the throne as Radama II. Rainivoninahitriniony was confirmed as prime minister and Rainilairivony as the commander-in-chief of the army. Their family, the Andafiararatra, thus established 'a firm grip of the government which they were not to relinquish for the duration of the monarchy'.[38]

What can be said of Queen Ranavalona I's reign in the history of Madagascar? To the Europeans it was a reign of terror, as one modern writer has called it.[39] To many of the subject peoples brought under Merina hegemony, her rule was also regarded as exploitative and tyrannical. The revolts of the peoples of the south-east and the brutal repressions that followed were notorious. Raombana, a modern Malagasy historian, has described in graphic terms the consequent desolation. Some peoples, such as the Antanosy, emigrated west to the valley of Onilahi to escape Merina rule. Nevertheless considerable industrial development was achieved in her reign, education took real roots and the process of modernization in many fields was never to be reversed. What is more, to many of her subjects, Ranavalona was a symbol of Malagasy nationalism and a bastion against foreign influences that were detrimental to Malagasy culture and tradition.[40]

The open-door policy: King Radama II, 1861–63

The main events of this short-lived regime of an extremely pro-European sovereign centred on Radama's precipitous attempt to reverse all the policies of the previous regime as far as foreign policy was concerned. In this, in fact, largely lie the reasons for its equally unprecedented brevity.

Radama II's ambition was to modernize his country by attracting foreign traders, investors and missionaries to Madagascar. He enthusiastically allowed Christianity to be taught and the missionaries and the exiled Malagasy Christians were all asked to return to Madagascar. He welcomed back his old friends, Laborde and Lambert, and other Europeans. At the end of the year, he dispatched Lambert on a diplomatic mission to France and Britain to seek their recognition of him as king of Madagascar, a matter that was crucial to his plans for a free flow of commerce between Madagascar and the outside world.

38. M. Brown, 1978, p. 189.

39. ibid., p. 188.

40. S. Ayache, 1975; Raombana, 1980; M. Brown, 1978, pp. 167, 188. For the lasting influence of the British missionaries on this period, see B. A. Gow, 1979.

France and Britain were not slow to respond to the Malagasy ruler's accession to the throne. They agreed to send goodwill missions and to appoint consuls to reside at Antananarivo. The British government nominated Conolly Pakenham as its representative in Madagascar, and pledged to support Madagascar's independence.[41] The French government nominated Jean Laborde, Radama's great friend, who had lived in Madagascar since 1832, as their consul, no doubt hoping to capitalize on his great influence in and knowledge of the country. The French also recognized Radama as king of Madagascar, although in Emperor Napoleon III's letter to Radama II vague references were made to France's 'ancient rights' on the island. The French government, however, made it clear to their consul that they had no intention of taking over the island, nor did they wish to compete with Britain for special privileges there.[42]

Missionaries soon followed the European diplomatic representatives. The Catholic mission, led by Père Jouen, arrived in September 1861. The LMS missionaries arrived in April 1862, led by the Reverend W. Ellis, who had visited Antananarivo in 1856. The fact that Ellis arrived with a bundle of letters for Radama from the British government convinced the Malagasy leaders that the LMS was indeed an official arm of Britain and this partly explains why he enjoyed so much influence in the Malagasy capital.

The Europeans took the opportunity of the changed circumstances to negotiate new treaties of friendship and commerce. The French signed a treaty on 12 September 1862 and the British on 4 December 1862. The contents of these documents caused concern to the Malagasy nobility. Rainivoninahitriniony, the Prime Minister, and his colleagues were not happy because the traders stipulated, *inter alia*, that foreign nationals could purchase and own land in Madagascar, contrary to Malagasy traditions. Moreover, the treaties exempted foreign nationals from payment of import and export duties, which were the principal sources of revenue for Malagasy officials, who received no regular salaries from the government. In addition, in September 1862, Radama had ratified the Charter which he had granted to his friend Lambert in 1855, which permitted Lambert to exploit the mineral and agricultural resources in the north-western territories of Madagascar. Another concession, covering the region of Vohemar, was also granted to a British national from Mauritius called Caldwell.

The King's Council was unanimous in its opposition to the conclusion of these conventions, which gave so many privileges to foreigners. Moreover, on 28 September 1862, Commodore Dupré, the French negotiator, induced Radama to sign a secret treaty in which the king recognized

41. PRO, FO/48/9, Russell to Pakenham, 10 May 1862. For more details see P. M. Mutibwa, 1974, pp. 58ff.

42. MAE, *Madagascar V*, Thouvenel to Laborde, 24 April 1862; Emperor Napoleon II to Radama II, 22 April 1862.

French rights to some parts of the island.[43] Although the French government disavowed this secret convention, Radama's ministers came to know of it and this increased their distrust of their king, who appeared ready to sign documents indiscriminately even when they threatened national independence.

By December 1862, Radama appeared to have fulfilled his plans to open up his country to foreign influence. But those sixteen months had been an unprecedented period for his subjects. Too much had occurred in too short a period, and people had not had enough time to digest the many rapid changes of policies, which were so different from those pursued by his predecessor. The treaties and the charters he had signed had angered the men who had helped him succeed to the throne; and the influence of the missionaries and other foreigners was growing so fast that many of his influential officials were alarmed. There was such discontent at the new policies that during the *Ramanenjana* epidemic, those affected claimed that they were possessed by the spirit of the late Queen Ranavalona. The climax came when Radama decided to remove from power Rainivoninahitriniony, the Prime Minister; Rainilaiarivony his younger brother; and Rainijohary. All three were leading members of the two clans of Tsimiamboholahy and Tsimahafotsy which, as we have noted, had assisted Andrianampoinimerina to found the Merina kingdom. Radama's plan was to replace this oligarchy by his friends of younger days who called themselves *mena maso* (literally red eyes), led by nobles from Vakinisinaony, the area of the older capitals of Merina, who claimed seniority and superiority to the Avaradrano of Antananarivo.[44]

Above all, Radama appears to have had more confidence in foreigners than in the Malagasy in running his government. His mission to Europe to seek recognition was led not by Malagasy officials (as in 1836–7) but by Lambert, the French adventurer. He relied too much on Ellis for advice and, on the death of Rahaniraka in November 1862, Radama appointed William Marks, an American national, and Clement Laborde, the French Consul's son, as Secretaries of State for Foreign Affairs. In this, as also in his decision to rely on the *mena maso*, the two sons of Rainiharo and their supporters, including Rainijohary, realized that the king was set on eradicating them. They decided to act before they were destroyed. When Radama refused to surrender the *mena maso* – and even threatened to punish those who opposed his will – the Prime Minister's group decided to remove him from power. In the early hours of 12 May 1863 Radama was assassinated; strangled with a silken sash so as to avoid the shedding of royal blood, which was contrary to Malagasy tradition. As Mervyn Brown has succinctly commented:

43. MAE, *Madagascar V*, Dupré to Drouyn de Lhuys, 23 October 1862.

44. For the ethnic background of Radama's supporters, see S. Ellis, 1980.

Weakness of character was the main cause of Radama's downfall. His natural goodness, undoubted intelligence and excellent intentions were not matched by self-discipline, powers of application or good judgement; and he proved unable to cope with the opposition aroused in various quarters by his sharp reversal of nearly all his mother's policies.[45]

Madagascar's policies reviewed: 1863–8

Radama II's successor was his wife Ravodozakandriana who took the royal name of Rasoherina. She was Radama I's first cousin, and the succession was therefore still in Andrianampoinimerina's line. She was *invited* – the word needs emphasizing – to become Queen by the oligarchy which had overthrown her husband and which, from now on, was the effective ruler of the country. It is important to emphasize that Rainivoninahitriniony, Rainilaiarivony and their associates were not anti-European or against the modernization of their country. It is true that the 'conservative' faction, led by Rainijohary, was still there and pressing for a complete reversal of Radama II's policies; but the prime minister's pro-European group commanded a majority in the Queen's Council.[46] What the new rulers disliked was the manner in which Radama had gone about the pro-European policy; they felt that modernization should not be pushed forward at the expense of the survival of their traditions and independence.

The new government was in the hands of Rainivoninahitriniony until July 1864, when he was replaced by Rainilaiarivony, his younger brother, who was the commander-in-chief of the army. Rainilaiarivony was to remain in control of his country's destiny for almost the remainder of the century. The new government wanted to continue with Radama's foreign policy; but with important modifications. Lambert's and Caldwell's charters, which compromised the country's independence, were cancelled. The treaties with France and Britain were to be revised, so that the offending articles permitting foreign nationals to own land in Madagascar and exempting them from import and export duties could be removed. In regard to domestic policy, Christianity would continue to be taught, but the customs of the country which forbade foreigners to visit or preach in such towns

45. M. Brown, 1978, p. 195. Soon after Radama II's death, rumours started circulating that he was alive and they went on for more than two years. Many of the Europeans, including the Reverend W. Ellis of the LMS and Laborde, the French Consul in Madagascar, believed these rumours and tried to get in contact with the fallen king. A study has been made by Raymond Delval in which it is demonstrated that indeed Radama II had survived and had escaped to the western part of the island where, after failing to make a comeback, he lived as an ordinary person until he died in old age in the late nineteenth century. See R. Delval, 1964.

46. The discussion of the political alignment of the Queen's Council is based on Jean Laborde's account in Laborde to Drouyn de Lhuys, 25 May 1865, MAE, *Madagascar, VII.*

as Ambohimanga should be observed. Foreigners who wished to come to Madagascar and assist in development projects were welcome. The Malagasy government sent letters to the French and British authorities in Réunion and Mauritius respectively, explaining to them the events that had occurred in Madagascar and outlining the new government's policies. In November 1863 the government sent an embassy to Britain and France in order to explain Madagascar's new policy and seek the revision of the treaties of 1862. The embassy was led by Rainifiringia, accompanied by Rainavidriandraina.

Britain and France reacted differently to the overthrow of Radama II. Lord John Russell, the British Foreign Secretary appreciated Madagascar's difficulties in dealing with foreign governments; while he regretted that the new government had abrogated an international treaty, he accepted Madagascar's request for the revision of the old treaty and refused to be drawn into a quarrel with Madagascar over the cancellation of Caldwell's concession.[47] The British government therefore gave a friendly welcome to the Malagasy embassy when it arrived in London in March 1864. A new draft treaty, incorporating most of Madagascar's proposals, was agreed upon subject to further negotiation in Antananarivo after the envoy's return to Madagascar. When these negotiations eventually began in 1865, difficulties emerged over Britain's demands that its nationals should be able to own land in Madagascar and that the duties on imports and exports should be 5 per cent rather than 10 per cent as the Malagasy were proposing. But the Malagasy were adamant on these points and in the end the British government accepted all the Malagasy proposals. The treaty was signed, amid much rejoicing, in Antananarivo on 27 June 1865.

The French government's reaction was different. It refused to accept the policies of the new regime in Antananarivo. The French were greatly upset by Radama II's removal which, both in Paris and in St Denis, was attributed to the influence of British missionaries, especially Ellis. The French government therefore refused to accept the abrogation of their treaty of 1862 or of the Lambert Charter, both of which had been ratified by Emperor Napoleon III. The Lambert Charter had been constituted under the Emperor's own patronage and a company had already been formed to exploit the concessions. For the French, therefore, to accept the cancellation of the Charter or the treaty would have been a damaging blow. Rather, they broke off diplomatic relations in September 1863.[48]

In Paris, the French government was under heavy pressure to use armed aggression to enforce the treaty of 1862 and the Lambert Charter; but even so it refused to be drawn into an expedition against Madagascar. Instead, it proposed considering revision of the treaty *provided* Madagascar paid an

47. See Codore to Drouyn de Lhuys, 28 November 1863, MAE, *Madagascar, VI* and Russell to Cowley, 7 June 1864, PRO, FO/48/6.

48. See Pakenham to Russell, 30 September 1863, FO/48/10 in which the conduct of the French special envoy to Madagascar, Commodore Dupré, is well discussed.

indemnity of 1 200 000 francs (or 240 000 dollars) for the cancellation of the Charter. This was communicated to the Malagasy envoys while they were still in Europe. Their visit to Paris, in July 1864, was therefore fruitless. Emperor Napoleon III even refused to receive them. All that they obtained was a friendly but strongly worded sermon from Drouyn de Lhuys, the French Minister of Foreign Affairs, on the importance of observing international conventions and on his government's unequivocal demand for a speedy payment of the indemnity if friendly relations were to be restored between the two countries.

On their return to Madagascar, the ambassadors explained to their government the seriousness with which the French viewed the cancellation of the Lambert Charter and the treaty. Because of their great desire to disengage themselves from the obligations of these two conventions, the Malagasy agreed to pay the indemnity, particularly as the British government showed no inclination to intervene in the matter on Madagascar's behalf. The indemnity was paid at Tamatave on 1 January 1866 and negotiations began between the two countries for a new treaty. However, instead of simply accepting a version of the Anglo–Malagasy treaty of June 1865, as the Malagasy had expected, the French still demanded that their nationals should be able to purchase and own land in Madagascar. The Malagasy naturally rejected the French demands. The French government, finding itself in an embarrassing position, asked the British government to seek an amendment of its own treaty with Madagascar so as to enable British and French nationals to acquire land in Madagascar. But the French manoeuvres failed, for the British declined to amend a treaty that had already been ratified. In the end, the French had no alternative but to accept the text of the Anglo-Malagasy treaty as the basis for a new Franco-Malagasy treaty, in which it was stipulated that French nationals would not have the right to purchase and own land in Madagascar. This was signed on 8 August 1868 at Antananarivo.

The five years that followed Radama II's overthrow were eventful for Madagascar. The island had experienced great difficulties with France over the cancellation of the conventions that Radama II had concluded. It had impressed the Malagasy that while Britain remained friendly and undemanding, France had been unfriendly and hostile. There was even fear in Antananarivo at the time that the French might invade Madagascar. On the occasion of the signing of the Anglo-Malagasy treaty in 1865, the Malagasy government, according to the French Consul in Antananarivo, 'thanked all the English – that is the LMS missionaries resident in Antananarivo – for having kindly associated themselves with the government in order to obtain the modifications they had demanded.[49] This was seen as cementing the Anglo–Malagasy friendship, which continued for the rest of the century. On the other hand, as a result of France's unfriendly

49. Laborde to Drouyn de Lhuys, 29 June 1865, MAE, *Madagascar, VII.*

policies, Malagasy friendship with the French received a serious setback. The British had stolen a march upon the French, and in the context of Malagasy politics this was an important development in the history of Madagascar.

Internal developments, 1861–80

So far our discussion of the period under review has been largely political and diplomatic. It has touched on the political evolution of the country from 1800 to about 1880, and on the diplomatic interaction between Madagascar, on the one hand, and Britain and France on the other. It is now necessary to turn to the evolution of the country in the field of administration and socio-economic development, particularly since developments in these areas were to prove crucial in Madagascar's struggle for survival as an independent state during the period of the European Scramble.

One of the most important events that occurred in Madagascar in this period, which was to have a tremendous impact on later developments, was the conversion to Christianity, in February 1869, of Queen Ranavalona II and her Prime Minister and husband, Rainilaiarivony. The zeal with which the missionaries worked, after their return to Madagascar in 1861, clearly indicated that there would soon be a religious revolution in the country. country. In 1863 there were already about 5000 Christians in the Malagasy capital out of a total population of some 60 000 people. At the end of 1868, the LMS alone had 10 546 church members and 153 000 adherents throughout Madagascar.[50] The Christian group, many of whose members were among the leading officials in the government, could no longer be ignored. Persecution could not be used as a means of eliminating Christianity: it had been tried in the 1830s and 1840s and it had failed. By the 1870s, the persecution of Christians would have meant trying to eliminate the most influential part of the population. The LMS converts had found leader in Rainimaharavo, the Malagasy Foreign Minister and Rainilaiarivony's open rival for leadership, who also happened to be pro-British. In order to neutralize Rainimaharavo and avoid a radical Christian revolution that may even have led to the replacement of Queen Ranavalona II by Prince Rasata (an LMS protégé) Ranavalona and her Prime Minister decided to embrace Christianity.[51] This is not, of course, to suggest that they did not believe in what they professed; but it does explain why and how their conversion to Christianity occurred at the time it did.

The fact that the Malagasy leaders had embraced Protestantism, the Englishmen's religion, rather than Catholicism, was important for the future of Madagascar in many ways. The Malagasy tended to regard

50. See the Chronicle of the LMS and the Reports of the LMS for the 1860s and 1870s.
51. D. Ralibera, 1977.

Protestantism as the religion of rulers and associated it with power, the more so as outside Imerina and the Betsileo country Christianity flourished only at the fortified posts garrisoned by Merina colonists, where the governor was also often something of an evangelist. The Catholics were very active in the Betsileo country and among the subject peoples, who developed a kind of people's Christianity alongside the official religion. Furthermore, in reaction to authority, there was a revival of traditional religions, despite the public destruction of *sampy* that accompanied the spread of Christianity. The best-known priests of *sampy* became the leaders of opposition to royal authority in the last quarter of the nineteenth century.[52]

Conversion of the rulers of Madagascar to Protestantism had occurred soon after the conclusion of the Franco–Malagasy treaty of 1868, which had been preceded, as we have already seen, by quarrels and even threats of war from France. It was at a time when Britain appeared – and *posed* – as Madagascar's true friend and ally, and British missionaries in Madagascar were not slow to emphasize this time and again. Through men such as James Cameron, the LMS had given a great deal of technical assistance to the Malagasy, and Rainilaiarivony and his colleagues believed that by embracing the LMS's brand of Christianity they would further cement this friendship. In fact, by embracing Protestantism they would draw closer to Britain as allies who could be expected to take their side should difficulties occur again with the French. The French also saw the Malagasy leadership's acceptance of Protestantism as indicative of its commitment to the British cause; its members saw the Queen's conversion as a demonstration of Madagascar's rejection of French culture and influence on the island in favour of the British.

The British missionaries, now that they had won the religious war, exploited their new advantages in the capital to expand their activities throughout Madagascar. Even the Catholics, lacking direct political influence in the capital were not precluded from proselytization in other parts of the country.[53] As mentioned above, they dominated evangelization in the Betsileo country. Other missionary societies came in and, by the last quarter of the nineteenth century, outlines of a division of zones of influence began to emerge: the Norske Missionary Society in the Vakinankaratra, the SPG in the east, the FFMA in the west. With the contribution of the different societies and the close alliance between the British missionaries and the Malagasy government, much was achieved in the field of education, social change and medical services. Reference has already been made to the spread of literacy and a written literature. Many revolutionary changes flowed from this, such as the transition from the traditional lunar calendar to the Gregorian calendar introduced by the British missionaries in 1864.

52. M. Esoavelomandroso, 1978b; S. Ellis, 1980.
53. A. Boudou, 1940–3.

PLATE 16.9 *The palanquin of Queen Rasoherina in front of a venerated building of Andrianampoinimerina's reign. In the background the Protestant church built during the reigns of Rasoherina and Ranavalona II*

There was also missionary influence on architecture, especially with the feverish building of churches and other monuments to the martyrs in an effort to make Antananarivo replace Ambohimango as a sacred city.[54] It was because of the remarkable progress that the Malagasy people achieved, especially in education, in the period under review that they won the admiration of the 'civilized world'. This in turn contributed a great deal to a near social revolution in the country.

British missionaries had opened the first schools in Antananarivo in 1820. When Christianity was banned and the missionaries left the country, secular education was continued by the Malagasy boys who had been taught by the missionaries. With the return of the missionaries after 1861, the pace of development greatly increased, with the result that by 1880 there were over 40 000 pupils in mission and government schools and the prime minister decreed that 'all children over the age of seven must attend school.'[55] Compulsory school attendance was in fact written into the Code of 305 articles in 1881, and in 1882 government inspectors began examining the schools in Imerina. Secondary schools were opened in the 1870s although these did not really take off until after 1880. Many boys, including two of the prime minister's children, were sent abroad for further studies, particularly to Britain and France. The expansion of education was facilitated by the number of printing presses established by the missions, publishing books, magazines and newspapers. With educational expansion dominated by missionary influence, it is not surprising that technical education did not keep pace with literary education, since the missionaries were more interested in building congregations than public works. The level of literary education that the Malagasy had achieved was however clearly evident from their diplomatic correspondence, both in English and French.

Medical services began in Madagascar with the opening, in 1862, of a dispensary in Antananarivo by the LMS, and three years later a hospital was opened at Analakely in the centre of the capital. In 1875 the Malagasy government itself set up its own medical services, with paid personnel. By 1880, Madagascar had produced her first qualified doctors; Dr Andrianaly and Dr Rajaonah (a son-in-law of the prime minister) both of whom had spent nine years studying medicine at Edinburgh University.[56]

In the field of constitutional and administrative evolution in Madagascar since the time of Radama I, the most important change was the replacement of the Merina monarch as the ruler of the country by a Hova oligarchy, headed by the family of Rainiharo. Movement in the direction of a constitutional monarchy began in the 1820s when Queen Ranavalona I was

54. F. Raison, 1970, 1977, 1979.

55. M. Brown, 1978, p. 212. See also B. A. Gow, 1978, ch. 4 in which the educational and medical work of British missions is well and fully discussed.

56. V. Ramanankasina, n.d.

obliged to share power with Rainiharo and Rainijohary, two men from important Hova families that had assisted Andrianampoinimerina in founding the Merina kingdom at the end of the eighteenth century and had risen from lowly backgrounds to positions of power and influence. The traditional form of government in Imerina had been that of 'personal rule' by the sovereign who governed the kingdom as he saw fit and only consulted his advisers at his own discretion. After the death of Radama I, however, the power of the Merina monarchy was increasingly eroded through the rise of the Hova middle class. The Hova played a leading part in the foundation and consolidation of the expansionist kingdom. Over the years, they exploited their position to enrich themselves from the new commercial opportunities as well as from their entrenched positions in the army and administrative hierarchies. Although the Andriana class continued to play an important role in the country, real power and influence in the army and government now rested with the Hova class. The most important change occurred after the assassination of King Radama II in 1863, when the new Queen, Rasoherina, was recognized formally as a constitutional monarch and the power to rule passed into the hands of the Hova oligarchy, which had overthrown her husband. Before her coronation, Rasoherina was required by the prime minister and his supporters 'to sign a set of articles in which she agreed, among other things, not to drink alcohol, not to pass the death sentence without the advice of councillors, not to promulgate any new law without the consent of the Council which they dominated.'[57]

The powers of government were in fact initially shared by the two brothers, Rainivoninahitriniony and Rainilaiarivony, who became prime minister and commander-in-chief of the army respectively. When, in July 1864, Prime Minister Rainivoninahitriniony was overthrown and replaced by Rainilaiarivony, the latter became both the prime minister and the commander-in-chief of the army, this being the first time that the two offices were held by one and the same person.[58] When Rainilaiarivony then married the new queen, even though she was past fifty and fifteen years older than him, the new prime minister became the most powerful man in the land. Rainilaiarivony became the ruler, the uncrowned king, in fact, of Madagascar. And he continued to entrench his position when he also married the succeeding queen. The effect of all this was to shift the power from the sovereign and the Andriana group to the prime minister, who was the head of the Hova oligarchy.[59]

In order to improve the maintenance of law and order and the functioning of the administrative organs of the state, a Code of 101 articles was promulgated in 1868, from which date more articles were added every year until the final figure of 305 articles was promulgated in March 1881. The

57. B. A. Gow, 1979, p. 41.
58. M. Brown, 1978, pp. 199–200.
59. P. M. Mutibwa, 1974, p. 88; M. Brown, 1978, p. 207.

general theme of the Code was that the customs and traditions of the country would be allowed to continue as long as they did not obstruct innovation. The Code of 101 articles which was printed and circulated was severe in its application, but certainly an improvement on old customs in many ways. It reduced 'the number of offences punishable by death from eighteen to thirteen – one of wilful murder and the other twelve being various forms of revolt against the state.' It also abolished the concept of collective family responsibility, under which wives and children were punished for a man's crimes. The laws were not applied in the same form in the provinces, where punishment tended to be lighter. There was even a special code of 118 articles decreed in 1873 by Ranavalona II for the Betsileo country.[60]

In 1876 three High Courts were created where there had previously only been one; these tried all the different types of cases, each with thirteen judges, eleven of whom were officers of the palace. In the villages, magistrates and village heads (*sakaizambohitra*) were appointed to administer justice; indeed at the local level the *fokon'olona* was reorganized in such a way that the village heads obtained more responsibilities in maintaining law and order and in ensuring justice and a fair deal for all. In all cases, however, whether tried in village courts or in the three superior courts at the capital, the final decisions rested with the prime minister. This centralization, although it placed a great deal of responsibility on one man, did however enable the government in Antananarivo to know what was happening in the provinces.

In March of the same year, a more thorough reorganization of government machinery was undertaken with the creation of a cabinet system with eight ministries: namely, interior, foreign affairs, war, justice, legislation, commerce and industry, finance, and education. The creation of these ministries was part of the new Code of 305 Articles which became the basis of other legal systems administered in Madagascar for the rest of the century and even during colonial rule. It marked, as one scholar has put it, 'a further advance towards a more humane system, although many punishments remained harsh and the code retained its essentially Malagasy character.'[61] This was another demonstration of the Malagasy desire to pull their country into the modern age and join the 'comity of nations'.

The army, too, underwent some important changes. Radama I's reforms in the army had been discarded by his successors; but, in 1872, the prime minister revived policies for modernizing the Malagasy army. In particular, with the assistance of a British army instructor, the government embarked on recruiting, training and equipping an enlarged and professional army. Jean Laborde's factory at Mantasoa for manufacturing light weapons had

60. See M. Brown, 1978, pp. 214–15 to which the discussion which follows immediately here is greatly indebted. See also, E. Thebault, 1960.

61. M. Brown, 1978, p. 216.

PLATE 16.10 *Ranavalona II's encampment upon her return from Fianarantsoa, 1873*

ceased operation when Laborde left the country. The government now resorted to importing arms from Europe, particularly from England and the USA. But this was expensive for the government, which had little revenue and very little foreign exchange. Arrangements had to be made, therefore, to manufacture smaller arms at home.

In 1876, further reforms were introduced in the army. From then on soldiers received an annual medical examination, the purchase of 'honours' and of release from military service was prohibited, and an end was made to the abuse of the system of aides-de-camp. In 1879 compulsory military service was introduced for a period of five years. Each of the six provinces of Imerina was called upon to produce 5000 troops, making a fairly formidable army of 30 000 professional soldiers. In the 1870s, well-planned expeditions were sent to suppress rebellions among the Sakalava (particularly of Menabe) and the Bara in the south. The expedition, which was sent to the Bara in 1873, was successful and at last brought that region under the control of the central government in Antananarivo. But as the 1870s gave way to the 1880s, it became increasingly clear that rather than suppressing mere rebellions on the island, the Malagasy army was going to be required for the defence of the country against French intervention.

In order to improve its image abroad, the Malagasy government banned the traffic in liquor, particularly rum. In fact, in 1863, believing that the consumption of alcohol had been responsible for Radama II's misconduct, the new government had decreed that the sovereign should not drink strong liquor. Customs such as *tangena* (or trial by ordeal) were abolished during Radama II's reign. The slave trade remained outlawed in Madagascar, although some foreign traders, particularly British and French nationals, continued in defiance of this law to trade slaves especially on the western coast of the island. In 1877 the Malagasy government also freed the Makoa, or *Masombiky* as they were referred to by the Merina, that is, all the slaves or descendants of the slaves who had been brought into Madagascar from the African mainland. Short of the abolition of slavery itself, the decree of 1877, which meant a great economic loss to the owners of the estimated 150 000 slaves who were freed, constituted a major social revolution and an indication of the country's determination to modernize itself.[62]

Economic development[63]

Prior to Madagascar's involvement in international trade, especially before the 1860s when Europeans started arriving in Madagascar in great numbers, the Malagasy had a self-sufficient economy. The bulk of the people were engaged in agriculture, primarily for the needs of their families, rice being the main food, especially on the central plateau of the island. The Malagasy had developed the planting of rice to such a high degree of specialization that one observer remarked 'that in few things is the industry and ingenuity of the Malagasy shown more than in the cultivation of rice.'[64] Besides agriculture, the economy of Madagascar depended on the rearing of cattle, particularly among the Sakalava in the west and the people in the south of the island. Sheep and pigs reared on the central plateau, and fish, formed major food items among the Malagasy. The Merina were unable to control the trade on the west coast: in the southern part, they were virtually absent,

PLATE 16.11 *Iron-smelting and smithing in Madagascar in the 1850s*

62. See PRO, FO/48/34, *Extracts from Report by Rear-Admiral W. Core-Jones.*
63. See P. M. Mutibwa, 1972. Much of the account which follows here owes a lot to this article.
64. Quoted in ibid. See also, H. Florent, 1979; G. Rantoandro, 1981; M. Rasoamiaramanana, 1974, 1981.

and in the north-western part, they had to compete with the Antalaotra. On the eastern coast, however, they installed and controlled an efficient commercial network.

The Malagasy were experts in two main industries, spinning and weaving on the one hand, and mining and metallurgy, especially iron, on the other. They made cloth, and produced a variety of metal articles for their own use. These provided the basis for the technical education received from Europeans. We have already referred to the goods that were made at Laborde's factory at Mantasoa, about 35 km south-east of Antananarivo. Alfred Grandidier, the famous nineteenth-century French explorer of Madagascar, informs us that at Mantasoa:

> Laborde forged iron and made pure steel; cement, cannons and mortars; all sorts of arms and ammunition; tannery; glasses and earthenware; pottery; pots and plates; bricks and tiles; soap of all colours; candles, paper and ink; potash, alum; sulphuric acids; and, after 1843, raised Chinese silk-worms.[65]

Many of these products ceased to be manufactured after Laborde left Madagascar in the late 1850s, but some of the men with whom he had worked were able to continue producing some of the goods necessary for their livelihood. What killed local industry in Madagascar was the importation of cheaper materials such as cloth, shoes and earthenware, from Europe and the USA.

King Radama's accession to the throne in 1810 saw the beginning of Madagascar's intensive involvement in international trade. The slave trade was a major feature of this trade, but with the conclusion of the Anglo–Malagasy Treaty in 1847, it was banned and was never carried out again in those regions where the Malagasy government's authority was effective. Slaves continued to be imported into Madagascar on the western coast and the north-west territories from the African mainland, under cover of contract labour. This trade was largely in the hands of the Antalaotra and the Indians, sometimes with the connivance of Merina officials.[66] At the same time, some slaves were exported from Madagascar to Réunion, Mauritius, the USA and the West Indies, especially from those areas outside the effective control of the Antananarivo authorities. The other important exports were rice and bullocks, while a variety of goods mostly cloth, guns, rum and machinery were imported. The trade in beef provided half of the government's customs revenue. Besides direct trade with Europe and the USA, Madagascar traded with Britain through Mauritius, Zanzibar[67] and the Seychelles and with France through the island of Réunion. The Malagasy trade was absolutely vital for the French island colony of

65. Quoted in P. M. Mutibwa, 1972.
66. M. Rasoamiaramanana, 1981; G. Campbell, 1981.
67. H. Kellenbenz, 1981.

PLATE 16.12 *Female slaves drawing water and pounding rice in Madagascar in the 1850s*

colony of Réunion, which obtained almost all its cattle and rice, not to mention slaves, from Madagascar. That was partly why the French settlers in Réunion and the small traders in Marseilles regarded Madagascar as their rightful sphere of influence.

Madagascar's international trade was based on treaties of friendship and commerce. We have noted the 1862 treaties with Britain and France which were reviewed in 1865 and 1868 respectively. The first treaty with the USA came in 1867, with the arrival of an American consul in Antananarivo. The Malagasy government also established embassies in Mauritius, Britain and France in order to facilitate trade.[68] The prime minister preferred to appoint as consuls leading traders in the capitals they were appointed to. For London, he chose Samuel Procter, who was head of a flourishing business with Madagascar. The appointment appears to have been made in 1862 when Radama II placed an order with Messrs Procter Bros of London for uniforms for Malagasy soldiers. For Paris, a well-known French trader with connections with Madagascar, Monsieur Hilarion Roux, was chosen in 1876 to be Madagascar's Consul General there. For Mauritius, the man appointed as Malagasy Consul was Hippolyte Lemiere, a member of the Mauritian Legislative Council and a leading trader there.[69] In 1881, to further encourage trade, the Ministry of Commerce and Industry,

68. See for example, Radama II to Lemiere, 25 September 1862, enclosed in Stenenson to Newcastle, 1 November 1862, PRO, CO 167/443, also quoted in P. M. Mutibwa, 1972.
69. P. M. Mutibwa, 1972.

generally known as the Ministry 'for the encouragement of Industrial Arts and Manufactures' was created.

In international trade, the Malagasy rulers encouraged both private and state enterprise. Senior government officials with enough capital established businesses and carried out a lucrative trade with Mauritius, Réunion and even Europe. Among the most active was Rainilaiarivony, the prime minister himself. Rainilaiarivony's agent in Mauritius was Consul Lemiere with whom he maintained a personal bank account which he used to purchase luxurious goods, mostly clothes, from Mauritius and Europe. The role of individuals was, however, only supplementary to that of the state. As we have already noted, it was the government in Antananarivo itself that established trading relations with foreign powers and foreign nationals, through the conclusion of treaties, the establishment of consulates abroad, and the granting of concessions to foreign capitalists for the development of mineral and other natural resources of the country. Malagasy traditions and the state's constitution forbade the outright grant of land to foreigners, but the government was willing to lease land on which foreigners could establish plantations or capital mineral resources. The first concession was granted in 1855 by Radama (while he was still a prince) to Joseph Lambert, a French adventurer, which was confirmed in the form of a treaty in September 1862. Although this concession was soon cancelled, it became government policy especially in the 1880s to grant similar concessions for the economic development of the country, though with more caution to avoid any terms or conditions that might threaten the independence of the country. In fact, the Code of 305 Articles promulgated in March 1881 forbade the sale of land, under pain of death, to any foreigners.

Conclusion

In our discussion we have noted the modernizing efforts deployed by the Malagasy to establish firm bases for the development of their country. This process began with the accession of King Radama I, and was consolidated in the first half of the nineteenth century. The return of foreigners after 1861, and particularly the encouragement of foreign trade and cultural influences opened yet a new era for the Malagasy. The process of modernization involved embracing Christianity and instituting a series of reforms that were geared to mobilizing the human and natural resources of the country for greater development in the political, social and economic spheres. These reforms carried out by Malagasy leaders, particularly from the time of Radama II's accession to the throne in 1861, were crucial in the evolution of Madagascar. In view of the persistent argument that Africa was colonized because of its poverty and lack of development, it is noteworthy that at least Madagascar, during the period under review, established important reforms which, as a British admiral observed in March 1881, had made the Malagasy 'a race fit to govern their land; and the fact obviated the necessity for the intervention of any outside nation'.[70] However, when the Scramble came, such developments did not shield Madagascar from the pressures of foreign intervention; in some ways, modernity had weakened the Kingdom;[71] in other ways, the reforms also strengthened the resistance that the Malagasy were able to muster.

70. PRO, FO 48/34, *Extracts from Report of Rear-Admiral W. Gore-Jones.*
71. G. Jacob, 1977.

17 New trends in the Maghrib: Algeria, Tunisia and Libya

M. H. CHERIF

During the nineteenth century the Maghrib underwent several major upheavals. The most striking feature of these was the disappearance of the independent states that had made up this part of North Africa at the beginning of the century, under pressure from and to the advantage of the principal European powers. The regime of the deys in Algeria began to decline in 1830 under repeated attacks from the French forces; Libya and its Ḳāramānlī rulers fell under direct Ottoman domination again in 1835; Tunisia, under the beys, became a French protectorate in 1881; Libya was invaded by the Italians in 1911 and Morocco met with a similar fate at the hands of the French and the Spanish in 1912. Needless to say, these political events are not the only changes that took place; they either crowned or preceded far-reaching new trends affecting economic, social or even cultural patterns, for all these were profoundly disturbed during the nineteenth century.

It was during this period that there came to the fore the first signs of 'development' on the one hand (in the European capitalist countries) and of 'underdevelopment' on the other hand (in parts of the world such as the Maghrib, with which we are concerned here).[1] An abundance of contemporary literature has taught us that these two phenomena are intimately related. Accordingly, it would be futile to look for the causes of the problems of nineteenth-century North Africa in purely local circumstances and to attribute these difficulties, as has been done in the past, to one-sided considerations such as the 'archaic' nature of society, 'secular backwardness' and the 'defects' peculiar to the civilizations of North Africa – and not to those of Europe – in general.

At the beginning of the nineteenth century, the Maghrib still enjoyed a relatively well-balanced way of life and we propose to examine its foundations and assess its strengths and weaknesses. This equilibrium was suddenly brought to an end, in the aftermath of 1815, when European expansionism began to turn towards North Africa, which was so near and with which it had been linked for so long by warlike or peaceful contacts through privateering or trade. European influence made itself felt in the

1. E. J. Hobsbawm, 1977; L. Valensi, 1978.

Maghrib at different periods and in various ways, depending on local circumstances; in the short term, it gave rise to different situations according to the different circumstances of each country and, in the long term, to similar upheavals, leading to the same result, namely colonization.

At that time, the Maghrib was split up between a legally independent country, Morocco, ruled by the ʿAlawite dynasty, and Regencies, which were theoretically provinces of the Ottoman empire but actually enjoyed a large measure of autonomy: the country governed from Algiers by an elective dey, the country governed from Tunis, where the Ḥusaynid dynasty had reigned since 1705, and the Regency of Tripoli which had been in the hands of the Ḳāramānlī family since 1711. What were the common characteristics of these Ottoman Regencies and on what type of society did they impose their rule?

The Makhzen at the beginning of the nineteenth century[2]

In Algiers, Tunis and Tripoli the state – the Makhzen, as it was traditionally called – took the form of a politico-military structure that was marginal to the main body of the society subject to its rule. The men who held the reins of power thought of themselves as being different from their subjects: Turks, who were assimilated in varying degrees in the Regencies, and *sharīfs* in Morocco. Within these circles, the highest offices were assigned to *mamlūks*: former slaves of Christian origin who had been converted and suitably trained to serve at court or in the army. The mainstay of these regimes consisted of foreign military bodies, largely Turkish janissaries. The main instruments of control of the Muslim society were drawn from outside its ranks and from other countries: hard currencies (Spanish piastres, in particular) obtained by seaborne trading activities or by privateering; 'modern' weapons and specialists in their use for the army; writing paper and book-keeping techniques (applied by Jewish accountants) for the 'administrative' services. However rudimentary these instruments may appear to be in comparison with those then used in Europe, they proved to be highly efficient in societies that were unfamiliar with them. The Makhzen represented a half-way stage between European or Turkish 'modernity' and the 'traditionalism' of local societies. The Makhzen was able to dominate the local societies and exploit them to its own advantage, sharing the profit to some extent with the notables in the cities and European merchant capitalists, for it was the latter who supplied the money, weapons, paper, etc. and carried away the produce from the countryside. Exploitation of this kind was responsible, to a large extent, for perpetuating the 'archaic' state of inland rural societies, if not for their actual decline.[3]

2. A. Laroui, 1970, pp. 244–67; M. H. Chérif, 1977.
3. These issues have been further explored in M. H. Chérif, 1979a.

PLATE 17.1 *The interior of the Ketchawa mosque in Algiers in 1833, (built in 1794)*

There was no lack of local support for the Makhzen in pre-colonial times: it could enlist the services of warlike groups (*'makhzen'*) and rely on the allegiance of notables in the cities (who provided *ḳā'id*s or governors, *lazzām* or tax farmers, *wakīl* or stewards, etc.), as well as on the co-operation of the prominent families in rural areas from which the *shaykhs* or local community leaders were drawn. It also had valuable allies in religious leaders: *'ulamā'* (scholars) in the cities, *murābiṭs* (holy men) and heads of brotherhoods (both in the cities and in the countryside) preached obedience to the government and thus helped to legitimize its power. The extent to which such local support was given determined the nature of the regime and, in fact, its chances of survival. In Algiers, the ascendancy of the Turkish janissaries (at least up to 1817), and that of the deys of Levantine origin, held in check any move towards an even partially integrated type of government, whereas in Tunis the beys, while continuing to call themselves 'Turks', had been assimilated since the mid-seventeenth century into the country which they governed. The same had been true of the Ḳāramānlī in Tripoli since 1711.

Urban society

Generally speaking, the same pattern of human relationships – characterized by the dominant sense of family or lineal interdependence, and the same Muslim culture – prevailed throughout the Maghrib. However, urban society tended to be more firmly established in the 'Tunisian' region, 'tribal' life was more common in Libya, rural communities predominated in Algeria and the mountain Berbers carried more weight everywhere in Morocco. Thus the Maghrib was already a heterogeneous society in which, roughly speaking, townsmen (*h'adhar*), sedentary villagers, 'tribal' groups and highlanders, especially mountain Berbers, could be distinguished.

The city is known to be an integral part of Islamic culture: accordingly, a string of cities stretched across the whole breadth of the Maghrib from Rabat and Fez in the west to Benghazi and Tripoli in the east, including Tlemcen, Algiers and Constantine in the Regency of Algiers and Tunis, Susa and Ḳayrawān in the Regency of Tunis.[4] Although these cities never accounted for more than 10 to 15 per cent of the population of the Maghrib, they constituted the focal points of the most lucrative and important activities: trade and handicrafts, some of which were developed on an all but capitalist scale, as in the case of the manufacturing of the fez – or felt cap – in Tunis;[5] religious teaching, culture, general education and religious law, based upon the study of books and written documents; and the performance of political, administrative and military functions, since the power of the Makhzen was concentrated in the towns and was more diluted in the countryside. Town life was therefore associated with a monetary economy, a culture based upon the written word, and consciousness of

4. L. Valensi, 1969a, pp. 50–61; P. Bourdieu, 1970, pp. 54–7; J. Berque, 1978, pp. 115–17, 221–30, 398–401, 434–40; R. Gallissot and L. Valensi, 1968; D. Sari, 1970, pp. 3–12, 32–56.

5. L. Valensi, 1969b, pp. 376–400.

PLATE 17.2 *A Ḳur᾿ānic school in Algiers in 1830*

in human relationships, as opposed to the lineal and theoretically egalitarian patterns of rural society. These features appear to be sufficiently distinctive to set urban society apart from rural society, despite a common kinship basis.[6]

Given such a variety of advantages, was urban society capable of evolving and leading the rest of the country along the road to radical changes, as was the case in contemporary Europe?[7] This question hinges on the nature of the urban 'middle class', on its strength and more especially its weaknesses. The latter was, in fact, quite substantial. Most of the methods and techniques employed in the urban areas continued to be the 'traditional' ones, giving poor quantitative and qualitative results. The town's economic impact on the countryside was very limited because of the importance of the subsistence economy and the resistance to change displayed by the rural – and especially the 'tribal' – communities. The competition encountered from European merchant capitalists was also very fierce: they even succeeded in taking over the organization and supervision of communications by sea between the various Muslim countries. Thus, those of the middle class who engaged in trade and handicrafts had difficulty in developing their activities on autonomous lines: they had to accept the somewhat paralyzing protection of the Makhzen whenever their business interests expanded beyond a particular point. It was usual to enter into a commercial partnership with some high-ranking person, for example, the Jews Bacri and Busnach with the dey of Algiers, and the Djerban merchant, Hadjdj Yūnis bin Yūnis, with the Tunisian prime minister, in about 1800. Internally, the urban 'middle class' had a preference for investing its assets in tax-farming (*lizma*).[8] Hampered as it was in its own development, the middle class could not act as a leavening agent for the transformation of society as a whole.

Rural society

A clear distinction was made by contemporary observers between the city-dweller (*h'adharī*) and the country-dweller (*badawī*). What were the criteria for such a distinction? On the one hand, there was a complex city culture based upon the written word, whereas in the rural areas there persisted an oral, repetitive tradition; in religious matters, the instruction in law dispensed by the *'ālim* ('scholar') in the city contrasted with the teachings of

6. L. Valensi, 1977, insists on the homogeneity of the Maghrebian society, characterized by the dominance of patrilineal kinship relationships. On the contrary, I have stressed the differences of the urban communities, and have explored details in several works, in particular M. H. Chérif, 1979b, esp. pp. 235–77.

7. R. Gallissot and L. Valensi, 1968, pp. 58–60; L. Valensi, 1978, pp. 574–86; A. Laroui, 1970, pp. 244–67; J. C. Vatin, 1974, pp. 104–10.

8. M. H. Chérif, forthcoming.

the *marabout* and the triumph of 'audio-visual' worship in the countryside.[9] In material matters, a monetary system and its concomitant activities were the life-blood of the cities, whereas a subsistence economy and the poorly developed means of production, as regards both human and technological resources were characteristic of the rural areas. From the social point of view, city-dwellers were becoming more rank-conscious and at the same time more individualistic, but country people abided by the undisputed rules of lineal or, to be more specific, patrilineal structures: this meant that human groups identified themselves in terms of their kinship ties – sometimes more mythical than real – with an eponymous ancestor ('son of ...'). Beduin society formed a pattern of juxtaposed 'segments', either allied or opposed to each other in accordance with certain rules dictated not so much by blood ties as by the natural environment or the necessity to maintain an overall equilibrium.[10] The lineal principle implied egalitarianism, in theory, between 'brothers' and 'cousins' who, in some instances, might be enemies; the collective ownership of land; and mutual dependence and assistance in work. Decisions were taken by a *shaykh* or leader, etymologically, 'the elder', who was 'elected' or, to be more accurate, chosen by heads of families at each level in the subdivision of the group.

What interpretation can be placed on this oversimplified description of the way in which Beduin or rural society was organized? Those who support the segmentation theory consider this to be merely a model, without any real material foundation, a purely 'structural' and mythical reconstitution of a factual situation. Everything is accounted for in terms of lineage and genealogy, whether the context be communal life, village or even urban society.[11] This interpretation has, not surprisingly, been criticized. It is objected to on the grounds that it attaches too little importance to material explanations of social organization, preferring the biological origins of the basic groupings rather than the results of adaptation to a very real natural environment; and analysing rural communities without reference to the Islamic or Makhzen background, thus overlooking the factor of historical development and so on.[12]

The present writer will merely point out that, while 'segmentary' features are quite pronounced in remote areas and among isolated communities, they nevertheless became blurred or disappeared altogether in rural areas exposed to the influence of towns or market centres. Such areas included the flat country surrounding towns within a radius of some ten to thirty kilometres, according to our estimates,[13] oases on the main caravan routes, certain regions specializing in a highly marketable commodity, such as corn

9. E. Gellner, 1969, pp. 7–8.
10. E. Gellner, 1973, pp. 59–66.
11. Cf. notes 6, 9 and 10 above.
12. A. Laroui, 1977, pp. 174–8; L. Ben Salem, 1982.
13. M.H. Chérif, 1979b.

in the cereal-growing *mulk* (property), or edible oil in the Tunisian Sahel, etc. The influence of the towns made itself felt in the economy through the currency of tangible assets, the system of land tenure requiring proof of encumbrance-free land ownership in conformity with written laws, and social relations implying some degree of subordination and exploitation: the *khammās* or 'fifth-share' tenant farmer was a familiar figure in these zones.[14] Even though the genealogical factor continued to be of fundamental importance, and small family holdings were very common in these 'open' sectors, the latter indisputably displayed features that were unknown in the 'tribal' or mountainous regions.

Because of their great diversity, their comparative isolation and their use of an inefficient 'traditional' technology, the North African communities and the Makhzen that dominated them, thanks partly to means imported from abroad, undoubtedly had many weaknesses, but they succeeded, all the same, in maintaining an equilibrium that was to be irremediably disturbed after 1815 with the fresh onslaught of European fleets and profiteers.

The European offensive

With the end of the Napoleonic Wars in 1815, the European offensive, relying on forces that became increasingly irresistible, was launched in the Maghrib and soon afterwards throughout the rest of the world. Initially, market considerations were the most decisive factor. As production grew in the Maghrib to keep pace with the rate of industrialization in Europe, prices fell accordingly and the terms of trade deteriorated. Under the harsh economic conditions of the times, competition became progressively fiercer and European policies for expansion overseas became more aggressive.[15] As early as 1816, the British fleet under Lord Exmouth was despatched to North Africa and this was repeated in 1819 under Admiral Freemantle with the co-operation of the French naval division of Admiral Jurien, in order to notify the 'Barbary' powers of the ban that had been placed on privateering by a concerted decision of the European nations. This ostensibly noble purpose, however, concealed rapacious intentions, since substantial commercial privileges were demanded by the French, especially on behalf of their countrymen living in Provence, and by the British on behalf of their Italian and Spanish clients, who were in competition with the French. This marked the beginning of an ultimately highly successful policy aimed at securing the submission of the North African countries to Europe's ever-growing economic and political demands.[16] Instructions given to the new French consul who was sent to Tunis at the head of a squadron in 1824 stressed 'the necessity of establishing relations with this

14. S. Bargaoui, 1982.
15. R. Schnerb, 1957, pp. 44–5; M. H. Chérif, 1970.
16. A. Laroui, 1970, pp. 275 ff.

inferior power [the Regency] which are more in keeping with the dignity and interests of the kingdom [of France]'.[17] European, and particularly French trade, derived the greatest benefit from this 'necessity', since it was enabled to expand rapidly by exceptionally advantageous facilities provided by a system that was revoltingly unfair. Even the shadiest European deals were sure to succeed thanks to the influence of the relevant consul. 'If there were no Barbary pirates, they would have to be invented', exclaimed one of the French merchants established in Tunis.[18] Another factor that came into play was the sense of 'national honour', for various aspirations could be satisfied or failures compensated for with only a minimum of risk in the Maghrib. It is common knowledge that the Algiers expedition in 1830 was decided on by a declining regime, intent upon restoring its prestige and strengthening its positions within France itself.

Concurrently with trading activities, business transactions of all kinds expanded, especially in the field of moneylending or usury. To quote but one example: the bey of Tunis, being short of money, got into the habit of selling locally produced oil, over which he had a trading monopoly, in advance to European merchants: the poor crop in 1828 caused a shortage of oil whereupon the merchants demanded and obtained a refund of the money they had advanced at the price for oil prevailing at the time in Marseilles.[19] This was by no means the end of the bey's difficulties. In the 1830s, the burden of the debts that continued to be incurred fell partly on a few highly placed persons, such as the prime minister, who was completely ruined in this way, and partly on the producers of the Sahel oil, who had to part with over two million francs between 1832 and 1845.[20] With consummate skill, the merchants induced the bey to insist that the sums he advanced to his subjects be repaid in money and not in oil, so that they alone would enjoy the profits from trading in this commodity. They eventually took the place of the bey in the practice of making pre-harvest loans to oil producers and, from 1838 onwards, a number of producers who were unable to settle their debts suffered a distraint upon their goods.[21]

The lending process, which started in this way, never ceased to gain ground. Around 1860, when there was plenty of capital in Europe and interest rates were falling, while the states of the Maghrib which were still independent at the time were embarking upon 'reforms' suggested by foreign consuls and advisers, European penetration developed on new lines, for it tended to turn from trade towards finance. Algeria was opened up

17. Quai d'Orsay Archives, Consular Correspondence, Tunis, Vol. 44, 'Instructions to the French Consul-general in Tunis', 28 November 1823.

18. ibid., Vol. 48, letter of 10 August 1830 (Discussions of the French 'nation' in Tunis).

19. M.H. Chérif, 1970, pp. 741–2; K. Chater, 1984, pp. 335–8.

20. Archives générales du Gouvernement tunisien, registres no. 2348, 2349, 2433, etc. . . ., cited by I. Saādoui in a 1980 research paper on Tunisian foreign trade in the first half of the nineteenth century.

21. ibid., and L. Valensi, 1977, p. 343.

for capitalist ventures or 'kid-glove colonization', as it was called, in the fields of agriculture, banking, public works, mining, and so on.[22]

The trend was more pronounced in Tunisia, where the country's financial resources were first exploited and then brought entirely under European control within the space of ten years, between about 1859 and 1869. Having committed themselves to a vast programme of 'modernization' and public works on the advice of the French and British consuls, the bey's ministers embarked upon a rash programme of expenditure to acquire in Europe, at exorbitant prices, obsolete military or naval equipment such as out-of-date guns, purchased in 1865, and engaging foreign contractors to carry out very costly public works of doubtful utility such as the rebuilding of the Roman aqueduct at Carthage, or the construction of consular residences for the representatives of European powers as from 1859,[23] and so on. The bey inevitably fell more and more deeply into debt, borrowing initially from local financial brokers and agents, especially Jews from Leghorn operating under European protection. By 1862, they already held claims amounting to almost 28 million francs in respect of loans raised by the government at usurious rates of interest.[24]

From 1863 onwards, the bey turned to foreign lenders, whose terms were theoretically more reasonable than those of local creditors, and loans authorized by the French government began to be floated on the Paris market. However, lucrative commissions, bribes, speculation or downright swindles serving the interests of European sharks like the Jewish bankers of German origin, Erlanger and Oppenheim, the manager of the Comptoir d'Escompte, Pinard, etc., and unscrupulous representatives of the bey such as the prime minister, Mustafā Khaznadār, made drastic inroads upon the sums borrowed actually received by the beylik.[25] These loans rapidly increased the national debt: approximately 100 million francs at the beginning of 1866 and 160 million in February 1870, as against an annual revenue of about 10 to 15 million francs.[26] Faced with a critical economic situation – poor harvests from 1866 to 1870, and even a famine and an epidemic in 1867 – the bey's government was soon bankrupt. On 5 July 1869 France, Britain and Italy compelled the bey to accept an international financial commission. This took control of all the revenue of the Tunisian state so as to ensure that the national debt would be repaid in annual instalments fixed at a figure of 6.5 million francs.[27] The years from 1870 to 1881 brought Tunisia some respite on the political scene owing to the absence of interference from France after her defeat and the honest and

22. A. Rey-Goldzeiguer, 1977, pp. 583–606.
23. A. Ibn Abī-Dhiyāf, 1963–4, Vol. 4, pp. 261–4; J. Ganiage, 1959, pp. 190–2.
24. J. Ganiage, 1959, p. 195.
25. ibid., pp. 203–16 and M. Bdira, 1978, pp. 121–4.
26. J. Ganiage, 1959, pp. 335–402.
27. ibid.

enlightened management of public affairs by Khayruddīn, who was prime minister from 1873 to 1877. Capitalist penetration continued, however, through the operations of banking establishments: The London Bank of Tunis, in partnership with Baring, Glynn, Mills, etc., from 1873 to 1876; the Société Marseillaise de Crédit, backed by the Crédit Industriel and, in association with the Péreire brothers, the Comptoir d'Escompte and the Banque des Pays-Bas, etc., especially from 1877 to 1881. Acting through subsidiaries or in association with certain industrial concerns such as the Société des Batignolles, capitalist consortia extorted profitable concessions from the defenceless bey: banks with special privileges, railway lines, mines, ports and vast estates.[28] Because of the role it played in the construction of basic installations and even in the field of production, capitalism was opening the way for direct colonization. Since vested interests had to be defended, the spokesmen of capitalism called for, and justified in advance, political intervention, namely the military expedition that speedily resulted in the establishment of the French protectorate in Tunisia on 12 May 1881.

In Algeria, the European penetration took a slightly different turn, due to the early conquest of the country in 1830. In addition to the inevitable arrival of capitalist commercial and banking interests, the colonists looked hungrily on Algerian land and made their claims to the authorities. The authorities obliged them in different ways: by confiscating land (particularly following major revolts such as that of 1871),[29] by billeting soldiers on unwilling rural communities, the most flagrant instance being the military ordinances and circulars of the 1840s,[30] and by encouraging the parcelling of 'collective' lands and the commandeering of property, e.g. by the law of 26 January 1873.[31] The few attempts made to protect the property of the local inhabitants – communal groups in particular – such as the Senatus Consultum of 1863, marked time in the face of the pressure of 'settler' circles. In 1882 European interests had already taken over 1 073 000 ha of land (1 337 000 ha by 1890), most of which was in the Tell region,[32] with obvious consequences for the indigenous population.

Factors of change

The age-old equilibrium of the way of life in the Maghrib was disturbed by European penetration in its various forms, the effects of which were felt either directly or indirectly in the commercial or financial fields. What were

28. ibid., pp. 421–6, 463–71, 564–88, 600–8 and 640–61.
29. C. R. Ageron, 1968, Vol. 1, pp. 24–36.
30. C. A. Julien, 1964; A. Rey-Goldzeiguer, 1977, p. 139.
31. C. R. Ageron, 1968, Vol. 1, pp. 78–88.
32. ibid., pp. 94–102.

the main instruments of change and on what lines did this transformation take place? What impact did European pressure have on the various categories of the local population?

The first of the factors of change was the seaborne trade conducted by European merchants or, in some rare cases, by their local agents or allies. It gradually weakened, and eventually superseded, the traditional long-distance caravan or even maritime trade with the Levant,[33] with the exception of the trans-Saharan transport system in Libya, which regained momentum around 1845 and held its own until after 1880.[34] Within the Maghrib itself, European manufactured goods (textiles, metallurgical products and military imported equipment right down to buttons for gaiters and food items such as sugar, tea and coffee quickly found customers among wealthy people in the Maghrib, and in due course among broader social classes. The volume of imports increased much faster than that of exports, and the resulting drain on financial resources had manifold consequences, particularly as regards foreign exchange.[35] Secondly, manufactured goods from Europe began to compete with the equivalent articles produced by craftsmen and eventually ousted them from local or foreign markets depending on well-to-do customers. A typical case is that of the Tunisian fez which, up to 1861–2, accounted for an annual export of about 3 million francs. By 1864–5, the value of these exports had been halved; by 1869–70, it had dropped to 850 000 francs; and it sank to its lowest level of 250 000 francs per annum in 1875–8.[36] It is true that European competition chiefly affected the production of high-quality handicraft goods and long-distance trading, but small tradesmen, such as retailers, were also harmed by the loss of well-to-do customers, foreign exchange disorders, the inescapable mesh of taxes, and in short, a process of general pauperization.

This process, coupled with the introduction of a monetary system into the economy calculated to benefit a minority, encouraged a tendency to resort to moneylenders, and usurers. Apart from the beylik's reliance on borrowed money already mentioned, usury wrought havoc everywhere, even in the remotest rural areas. Letters exchanged between the *ḳāʿid*s (provincial governors) of Tunisia refer again and again to the question of unpaid debts, owed usually to European merchants but also to some local notables. Notarial registers, which were preserved from 1875 onwards in Tunisia, abound with records of transactions between humble peasants and local money-lenders, most of whom were Jews.[37] The situation was probably worse in Algeria where, in the words of General Martimprey,

33. L. Valensi, 1969, pp. 70–83; N. Saïdouni, n.d., pp. 39–40.
34. J.L. Miège, 1975.
35. M.H. Chérif, 1970, pp. 728–9; L. Valensi, 1978, p. 583.
36. P. Pennec, 1964, p. 257.
37. S. Bargaoui, 1983, pp. 353–7.

deputy governor of Algeria in 1860, 'unfortunately, it is only too true that the spread of usury ... has been a consequence of French occupation'. Revolts and the ensuing repression, the disruption of rural life and traditional social patterns, the introduction of a monetary economy and the appearance of profiteers of every kind, even in the depths of the countryside; all these factors, combined with the ravages of a harsh climate and the crushing burden of taxation, contributed to the development of usury, one of the 'seven plagues' of Algeria in colonial times.[38]

Owing to the difficulties encountered by the state in Tunisia and in Morocco and by the colonial administration in Algeria, the tax system became oppressive and insatiable. Spurred on by necessity, the bey of Tunis as early as 1820 instituted a kind of monopoly on the oil trade, oil being the main export.

He had to give up this monopoly under the terms of the treaty imposed by France after the capture of Algiers in August 1830, but he instituted other monopolies, increased the number of indirect taxes and extended the tax-farming system in the 1840s.[39] He revised the rate and basis of assessment of the long-established taxes on production and introduced a poll tax (*iʿāna* or *majba*) in 1856.[40] The great uprising in Tunisia in 1864 was caused by the decision to double the rate of the *majba*. A few years later Morocco was faced with the same financial difficulties as those of Tunisia and resorted to the same disastrous expedients for dealing with them.[41] In Algeria, the indigenous population was compelled to pay the traditional 'Arab taxes' as well as new 'French taxes' (particularly the iniquitous communal taxes described by Jules Ferry in 1892 as 'a flagrant exploitation of the native people'). It also had to pay indirect taxes and the cash equivalent of the various statutory labour obligations, besides having to shoulder the burden of heavy war reparations following every revolt: for instance, the reparation demanded after the uprising of 1871 swallowed up about 70 per cent of the total value of the land owned by the Kabyles.[42]

In the new circumstances created by the disruption of the old economic and social patterns and the fleecing of the local population by the tax system and extortionate interest rates, the recurring climatic crises – which seem to have occurred more often in the nineteenth century than in the eighteenth century – took on catastrophic proportions. The crisis of 1866–9 in Tunisia and Algeria, and that of 1878–81 in Morocco reduced the

38. C.R. Ageron, 1968, Vol. 1, pp. 370–2, 383–6; A. Rey-Golzeiguer, 1977, pp. 171–2, 484–5.

39. Ibn Abī-Dhiyāf, 1963–4, Vol. 4, pp. 43–8, 55–6, 80–3, 144–56; L. C. Brown, 1974, pp. 134–7, 340–9; K. Chater, 1984, pp. 553–60.

40. Ibn Abī-Dhiyāf, 1963–4, Vol. 4, pp. 203–8; J. Ganiage, 1959, pp. 101–2.

41. J.L. Miège, 1961–3, Vol. 2, pp. 225–43; G. Ayache, 1979, pp. 97–138.

42. C.R. Ageron, 1968, Vol. 1, pp. 249–65, quoting Jules Ferry, p. 452.

population and had the effect of irremediably weakening the economy and the indigenous social structure.[43]

Beneficiaries of the crisis

As elsewhere, the situation that prevailed in the Maghrtib in the nineteenth century produced its breed of profiteers. First of all, there were the European settlers, whose numerical strength stood at 164 000 in 1855, 245 000 in 1872 and 375 000 in 1882 in Algeria.[44] In Tunisia, they numbered about 11 000 in 1856, 14 000 in 1870 and 19 000 in 1881.[45] In Libya, the figures remained fairly low until the early years of the twentieth century. Although most of the Europeans in Algeria and Tunisia were of humble origin, they enjoyed, nonetheless, a very privileged status by comparison with the majority of local people. The same was true of a Jewish minority, which succeeded in playing a role, in some capacity or another, within the European capitalist network and took advantage of their position as intermediaries between these networks and the indigenous population.[46] There were some, though fewer, Muslims who succeeded in playing a similar role: those who became consular agents, brokers and, more frequently, business associates of European trading concerns who sought at the earliest opportunity to escape from the control of the Muslim authorities so as to benefit from the protection of the European consuls in Tunisia, Libya and Morocco.[47] Much better known were the high-ranking servants of the Makhzen, who misused their positions in order to build up huge fortunes thanks to the confusion prevailing in their troubled countries: for example, Mustafā Khaznadār, the Tunisian prime minister from 1837 to 1873, accumulated a sum amounting, at a conservative estimate, to some 25 million francs, the greater part of which was invested in France.[48]

The colonial officials in Algeria and the weakened authority of the bey in Tunisia had to rely, in rural areas, on certain influential persons who exercised a kind of 'feudal' power over the communities within their jurisdiction, for example Muḳrānī in Algeria, until he rebelled and died in 1871,[49] and ʿAlī bin Khalīfa in south-eastern Tunisia from 1840 to 1881,

43. L. Valensi, 1977, pp. 307, 315; J. Poncet, 1954, pp. 316–23; A. Rey-Goldzeiguer, 1977, pp. 441–93.

44. C. R. Ageron, 1979, pp. 118–19.

45. J. Ganiage, 1959, pp. 44–5; A. Mahjoubi, 1977, p. 33, n. 84.

46. J. Ganiage, 1959, pp. 312–13; A. Laroui, 1977, pp. 310–14.

47. On the question of the status of 'infidel' accorded to some Muslims, for a favourable view, see Ibn Abī-Dhiyāf, 1963–4, Vol. 4, pp. 117–18; J. Ganiage, 1959; pp. 181–2; for Morocco, see A. Laroui, 1977, pp. 251–4, 314–15; B. Brignon et al., 1967, pp. 291, 294.

48. J. Ganiage, 1959, pp. 426–36.

49. M. Lacheraf, 1978, pp. 53–60; For Muḳrānī, see A. Rey-Goldzeiguer, 1977, p. 775.

before he decided in that year to head the resistance movement against France which subsequently led to his exile in Libya.[50] The same kind of trend seems to explain the rise of a number of religious families who monopolized, from generation to generation, the key positions either within the learned Islamic communities enjoying a semi-official status, especially in Tunisia,[51] or among the various Islamic brotherhoods in Algeria and Morocco.[52]

The victims of the crisis

Countless individuals suffered from the combined consequences of the numerous factors already referred to: poor harvests, the effects of the integration of the Maghrib into the world market, crippling taxation and, in the case of Algeria, the devastation wreaked by the colonial war and the harshness of the law of the conqueror, who alienated some of the country's best land to a foreign minority. This state of affairs became immediately apparent in the widespread pauperization of the population and the disruption of traditional social structures, so that economic and demographic disaster was inevitable during a crisis such as the one that lasted from 1866 to 1869.[53]

What were the reactions of the victims? First of all, they expressed the 'fatalistic' resignation which, in the eyes of all European observers of Muslim society in the nineteenth century, could not be too forcefully condemned. In 1892, Masqueray wrote with reference to the Muslims in Algeria: 'Resignation is even stronger than anger in this astonishing world of Islam' or, more appropriately, 'in this new confederation of paupers'.[54] This attitude, like the will to fight that had existed in the past, seems to have contributed quite naturally to reinforcing the positions of local saints and brotherhoods as the few bastions of resistance in a disintegrating society.[55] In the very first years of the nineteenth century, there were distinct signs of a reactivation of the brotherhood system. This trend probably bore some relation to the serious events that were unsettling the established order in certain parts of the world at that time and which affected the Maghrib itself: it was apparent among the Darḳāwiyya masses, who rebelled against Turkish rule in the early 1800s; among the Tijāniyya notables, who laid emphasis on meditation and were inclined to compromise with the authorities, even the French after 1830; and among the Ḳādirīyya

50. A. Kraīem, 1983, pp. 145–58.

51. The monopolistic tendencies of the great religious families was accentuated from the 1860s onwards, no doubt arising from the crisis in the regime. See A. H. Green, 1978, pp. 93–5.

52. Cf. notes 55 and 56, below.

53. Cf. note 43 above.

54. Cited by C. R. Ageron, 1968, Vol. 1, p. 128.

55. J. Berque, 1978, pp. 423–9.

and Raḥmāniyya, who led, from time to time, the struggle against the occupying power. The phenomenon has been particularly well observed, not to say highlighted, in Algeria, where the destruction of the scholarly and urban aspects of Islamic life and, more generally, of the traditional fabric of society, is said to have caused the mass of the Muslim population to turn once more for inspiration to the *zāwiya*s (sanctuaries) and brotherhoods.[56] In nineteenth-century Tunisia too, it seems to the present writer that the brotherhoods gave proof of fresh vitality after a long period of comparative apathy and that certain saints or representatives of brotherhoods played a prominent role at that time.[57] The trend was even more pronounced in Morocco, the land where *zāwiya*s and brotherhoods flourished most.

At the opposite end of the Maghrib, on the borders of Egypt, the Sanūsiyya was founded in 1843 and, within about sixty years, had built up an organization that exercised effective religious and political power not only in Cyrenaica, but also well beyond its boundaries, in the Sudan, the Sahara and elsewhere: by 1900, it had established as many as 146 lodges.[58] Although no research has been done specifically on the connection between European aggression and the growing influence of *marabouts* and brotherhoods, the present writer has no hesitation in saying that there was a relation of cause and effect between the two phenomena.

As another consequence of European penetration or conquest, revolts broke out more and more frequently and on an ever-increasing scale in the Maghrib in the nineteenth century. Individual acts of banditry, theft, arson or wilful damage to forests, performed either as an elementary form of resistance or as a means of survival, became everyday incidents in the countryside, especially in times of crisis, as in Tunisia during the 1860s.[59] Local rebellions also proliferated, not only in occupied Algeria up to 1881 when the last major rising occurred in the south Oran district[60] but also in Morocco and in Tunisia where, in the aftermath of 1815, they once more became common occurrences, after a respite of more than fifty years. Some of the more broadly based revolts roused to action the inhabitants of vast regions, or even of an entire country. There were, for example, the uprisings of Libyan rural communities and mountain folk against the Ottoman occupying authorities, during which the legendary heroes Ghūma al-

56. C.R. Ageron, 1968, Vol. 1, pp. 293–301; Y. Turin, 1971, pp. 110–15, 129–45.

57. L.C. Brown, 1974, pp. 174–83; A. Ben Achour, 1977, pp. 218–22; A.H. Green, 1978, pp. 65–7 (see also notes 40, 41, 42, 43, 44, in particular).

58. E. Evans-Pritchard, 1949.

59. Several references to the rural unrest are to be found in Correspondence from the *Ḳaʿid*s (provincial governors) in the Archives générales du Gouvernement tunisien; M.H. Chérif, 1980.

60. M. Lacheraf, 1978, pp. 69–87; Proceedings of the Colloquium held in Algiers in February 1982, on the theme of armed resistance in Algeria in the nineteenth century (forthcoming).

Maḥmūdī and ʿAbd al-Djalīl won fame and a rudimentary ʿArab' consciousness began to find expression in the struggle against the Turks in the 1830s and 1840s;[61] the insurrection of all the Tunisian peoples, who formed a league in 1864 when the tax burden was increased in order to pay the bey's foreign debts; the flare-up in Kabylia and the neighbouring regions in Algeria, in 1871, which was caused by the news of the establishment of the civilian government well-disposed towards the European settlers, and which took advantage of the defeat inflicted on France by Prussia. All these great endeavours failed, owing as much to the firepower of the regular armies as to the inherent lack of cohesion between the insurgent peoples.

Furthermore, the attempts at reform undertaken in various fields in order to restore an equilibrium that had been dangerously disturbed proved to be equally ineffective. These attempts will be studied below within the context of the situation prevailing in each state in the Maghrib.

Algeria

The countries of the Maghrib fell under direct European domination at different points in time: Algeria in 1830, Tunisia in 1881, Libya in 1911 and Morocco in 1912. Needless to say, the fact that they were not all colonized at the same time should not be regarded as a mere historical accident, but as the result of the varying degrees of resistance encountered within each country.

Of all the regimes in the Maghrib, the Regency of Algiers was most successful in preserving its non-indigenous features at the beginning of the nineteenth century, at least as far as Algiers itself and the central government were concerned. The government remained exclusively in the hands of the Turks, who continued longer than elsewhere to enjoy the privileges of a dominant 'caste'. This distinctive characteristic of Algeria is attributable to its more rural nature by comparison with the other countries in the Maghrib: here, the segmentation of society was more pronounced than elsewhere, the 'middle class' (*baldī*), which could have assimilated the conquerors, was weaker and urban culture was less developed.

Can it be said, then, that the Algerian political regime was opposed to change? Seemingly not. Throughout the eighteenth century, a kind of limited oligarchy – invariably of Turkish origin – consolidated its position at the expense of the turbulent militia of janissaries: it chose the dey from within its own ranks and conferred greater stability upon the central institutions. It is clear that the trend was towards a gradual decline in the power of the purely military and alien element to the advantage of the 'political' fraction of the ruling class. The process culminated in the 'revolution' of ʿAlī Khūdja, who dealt ruthlessly with the militia, in 1817,

61. Archives générales du Gouvernement tunisien, box 184, files 1020–1023: see in particular letter from Ghūma to the Bey of Tunis, 10 dū l-ḳiʿda 1271 (end of July 1855), (file 184–1020).

and drew support from certain sections of the local population, such as the *kologlus* (people of mixed Turkish and Arab blood) and the *Zwāwa* Kabyles.[62] This was exactly the turn which events had taken in Tunisia and Tripoli, but in Algeria the trend developed a hundred years later. Changes occurred earlier in the eastern or western provinces (*beyliks*). Ever since the eighteenth century, the beys had been compelled to rely on predominantly 'Arab' armed forces and to practise a skilful policy of forming alliances with local notables.[63] This was one of the reasons why the resistance to French occupation was more prolonged and more stubborn in those provinces than in Algiers and its region.

Despite these signs of change, the 'Algerian' regime, as a whole, retained until practically the end of its existence its non-indigenous character, which generated contradictions and sharp conflicts. Serious uprisings, under religious leadership provided by the brotherhoods, shook the western part of the country from 1803 to 1805 and a large area in Kabylia in 1814–15.[64] A kind of 'national' reaction was taking shape before the French conquest and it foreshadowed ʿAbd al-Ḳādir's iminent enterprise.

The decision to launch the Algiers expedition was based on reasons pertaining to French domestic politics but had little to do with the real economic and social needs of France at that time. This accounts for the hesitations and contradictions of French policy in the years after the French victory. Plans were made, in particular, for the limited occupation of certain coastal areas around the main towns, while the hinterland was to be left to rulers brought in from abroad, Tunisian princes were proposed in 1830 and 1831; or chosen after negotiation with those who really controlled the country, for example, Aḥmad, the Bey of Constantine in 1832 and the Amīr ʿAbd al-Ḳādir.[65]

Unlike his rival in Constantine, who perpetuated and perfected the Turkish, or *kologlu*, system of government in the province of Constantine from 1830 to 1837;[66] and *marabouts* with their age-old traditions such as Bū-Maʿza, active in the Wādī Chelif region from 1845 to 1847, and the 'Sultan' of Wargla, another 'political' *mahdī*, prominent in south-eastern Algeria from 1851 to 1853;[67] ʿAbd al-Ḳādir attempted to set up a true 'national' state and to kindle the spark of a sense of 'Arab nationality' according to the testimony provided even by his enemies.[68] He was born in 1808 in a *marabout* family and was always, first and foremost, a scholar

62. P. Boyer, 1970a, pp. 121–3; 1970b, p. 92.
63. P. Boyer, 1970b, pp. 87–8; A. Laroui, 1970, pp. 248–9.
64. P. Boyer, 1970a, pp. 119–21; N. Saīdouni, n.d., pp. 59–61.
65. On the Amīr ʿAbd al-Ḳādir, we have an impressive bibliography; see for example, M. Lacheraf, 1978; A. Saʿdallah, 1983, Vol. 2, pp. 40–6; R. Gallissot, 1965, pp. 339–68; C.R. Ageron, 1977, pp. 19–49.
66. A. Temimi, 1978.
67. A. Rey, 1978, pp. 197–221.
68. Cf. note 65 above.

(*ʿālim*) and a reformer in the sense in which the term was understood at the time: he taught that a return to the fountainhead of faith was the prerequisite for a regeneration of the *ʿumma* (Islamic community). In the prevailing state of anarchy, communal chiefs and *marabouts* from the Oran district elected him as sole leader of the resistance movement in November 1832.

Through sheer strength of personality, by diplomacy or by force, he succeeded in uniting under his leadership the inhabitants of two-thirds of Algeria in 1839 when he was at the height of his power. Accordingly, the French authorities, under Desmichels in 1834 and Bugeaud in 1837, having decided to set limits to the French occupation, reached an agreement with him and recognized his authority over the Algerian hinterland in exchange, admittedly, for his recognition of the French occupation of the coastal regions. The French even helped him at one time to repulse his opponents. ʿAbd al-Ḳādir gradually worked out a state structure which although not centralized at least performed a unifying function and took account both of Ḳurʾānic principles as regards taxation and justice and of local realities, harmonizing 'administrative' and military organization with the prevailing social conditions. Bugeaud, by whom ʿAbd al Ḳādir was defeated, personally acknowledged that: 'The organization devised by the Emir, based as it was on a perfect knowledge of every part of the territory, of inter-ethnic relations and of the interests of the various sections of the population – in short, on a profound understanding of human and material problems, seemed to me to be worth preserving'. This outline of a 'national' state, together with the intertwined religious and patriotic sentiments to which it appealed, explain the vigour and persistence of the resistance movement led by the '*amīr* of the faithful' from 1832 to 1847. However, the enormous disparity between his forces and those of his enemies (Bugeaud mobilized over a hundred thousand soldiers against him), the scorched earth policy applied by the French and, above all, the divided state of Algerian society at that time, eventually got the better of the indomitable *amīr*: having been hounded across Algeria, he sought refuge in Morocco but finally gave himself up to the French at the end of 1847.

Colonial society and its institutions were gradually established as countless difficulties were overcome after a good deal of trial and error. Algeria was placed under the authority of a governor-general and divided into a 'civilian territory', where the Europeans lived and French institutions developed, and 'military territories', where the Muslim communities were subject to the discretionary powers of the army. Under the Second Empire, concurrently with the expansion of capitalist colonization, efforts were made to consolidate the power of prominent leaders of the indigenous population with a view to obtaining their support in the administration of the 'military territories', for example, the famous 'Arab kingdom' experiment. However, the Emperor's good intentions came to naught when the economy collapsed, in so far as Muslim society was concerned, in 1867–9 and the French army was decisively defeated in 1870.[69]

This defeat and, more particularly, the threat of an extension of civilian rule, which was tantamount to the ascendancy of the European settlers, triggered off a major insurrection in Kabylia and the neighbouring regions in 1871. It was headed by 'feudal lords' like Muḳrānī and other leading members of certain brotherhoods, especially those of the Raḥmāniyya. The revolt was crushed with great bloodshed and was followed by the economic ruin of the communities involved. About 800 000 people had to pay reparations amounting to more than 70 per cent of the value of their land.[70] This marked the beginning of the years when the settlers held the reins of power and the Muslim population experienced the darkest period of the 'colonial night'. Having been reduced to poverty, deprived of many of its social and cultural traditions and subjected to a special administrative system of great severity, the indigenous population could at last be exploited quite openly for the benefit of the European minority, from the ranks of which were drawn practically all the members of representative bodies at the communal, departmental and central government levels. Before 1891, Muslim interests were defended only by a small group of people who belonged mostly to the Société pour la protection des Indigènes founded in 1881.[71]

Tunisia

As Tunisia was the country most open to foreign influence and most centralized in political terms, it was also the first to experiment with Western-style reforms and to suffer the worst disaster, second only to the one experienced by Algeria.

A relatively active 'middle class' had regular foreign commercial contacts, particularly with the Levantine countries, while members of the ruling class who engaged in foreign trade dealt mainly with European merchants. The pressure of these different commercial interests and the power of the local notables soon influenced the political system, which gradually attenuated its military and alien features as it developed into a kind of 'semi-national monarchy', following a trend that had begun even before the beginning of the eighteenth century. Without renouncing its allegiance to the Ottoman empire or dispensing with the services of the janissaries and *mamlūk*s who continued to be two of the pillars of the beylik structure, the regime extended its network of allies and supporters among the local population so as to broaden and stabilize the basis of its authority. It

69. A. Rey-Goldzeiguer, 1977, pp. 545–7, 686–8.
70. See note 29 above.
71. C. R. Ageron has devoted his monumental thesis (1968) to this period and this work has drawn heavily on it. The Société pour la protection des Indigènes is discussed in Vol. 1, pp. 414 ff.

undoubtedly reached the peak of its power under the rule of Ḥammūda Pashā, from 1782 to 1814.[72]

Immediately after peace had been restored in Europe, the leading Christian powers demanded and easily obtained from the Bey of Tunis a promise to abolish privateering and to open up his country to trade and other forms of European enterprise. Mention has already been made of the harmful economic and financial consequences of this decision for Tunisia. In addition, a military threat arose in each of the neighbouring countries in the 1830s, when Tripoli became an outpost of the Ottoman empire in 1835 and when Constantine came under French rule in 1837. Following the example of Muḥammad ʿAlī of Egypt and Maḥmūd II of Turkey, Aḥmad, the Bey of Tunis (1837–55) also decided to borrow from Europe. Moreover, he was pressured into taking this path – for different, but equally prejudicial reasons – by both the Ottoman sultan and the consuls of the great powers.[73]

He immediately launched a bold policy of introducing reforms which, however, were carried out too hastily and without taking account of the country's human and financial resources. A new army (*nizāmī*) was organized on the lines of a Western army, with similar weapons, techniques and methods, even imitating the details of uniforms and parade drill. It was manned by conscripts and its officers were trained at an 'école polytechnique' founded for this purpose at Le Bardo. To meet the needs of the new army, Aḥmad Bey set up modern factories for the production of guns, gunpowder, cloth and footwear. The ensuing financial problems soon led him to undertake a complete overhaul of the old tax system and of the administrative services; at one point, even a bank of issue was established. Apart from purely utilitarian measures, Aḥmad Bey took a number of decisions that went against local traditions, although not against the letter of Ḳurʾānic law. In 1846, he decreed the abolition of slavery in his provinces, one year before the same decision was taken by Turkey and two years before it was taken by the French in Algeria. He was the first head of a non-European state to set foot in Europe when he undertook an official visit to France in 1847. Furthermore, he set in motion a trend towards the 'nationalization' of the state by reducing the privileges of the Turks, not only within the army but even among the *ʿulamāʾ*, so that the Turkish and indigenous members of that group were placed on an equal footing; he thus appealed directly to the 'patriotism of the sons of Tunisia'.

The programme of reforms was ambitious, as we have seen, but the results fell far short of expectations. Within the regular army, recruitment, training, equipment and discipline left much to be desired. Most of the factories, built at great expense, never became operational. It was symbolic

72. M.H. Chérif, 1978.

73. A. Ibn Abī-Dhiyāf, 1963–4, Vol. 4, pp. 9–182; L.C. Brown, 1974; K. Chater, 1984, pp. 483–583.

PLATE 17.3 *Members of the Tunisian nizāmī (army) in European-style uniforms*

of the fruitless endeavours of Aḥmad Bey that a large frigate built in a dock at La Goulette was never able to put to sea because the access channel was too narrow. Worst of all, these costly innovations quickly exhausted the beylik's financial resources: hence the increase in taxation, the recourse to ruinous expedients such as seventy tax-farming concessions granted to the unscrupulous, but all-powerful Maḥmūd bin 'Ayyād, and the ensuing unpopularity of the reforms and of the regime itself.[74]

It is pointless to dwell here on the causes of Aḥmad Bey's failure, since the same experiments in modernization undertaken in Egypt, Turkey and, later, in Morocco, produced the same negative results. Broadly speaking, it can be said that the reforms were ill-adapted to the human environment which they were supposed to change. Furthermore, it was not in the interests of the advanced countries of Europe to see these reforms come to fruition, for the attempts to introduce them were regarded simply as an opportunity for obtaining profitable contracts for Europeans and their business associates in the Maghrib.

On the death of Aḥmad Bey in 1855, the situation in Tunisia was very serious. The reforms had produced few tangible results, apart from sowing the seeds of a nation-state and promoting the formation, at the bey's court, of a group of people favourably disposed towards modernization; but they had increased the danger of foreign intervention and accentuated internal

74. ibid.

weaknesses. These were exploited by the European consuls and profiteers, together with their local allies, most of whom were Jews who enjoyed the protection of influential foreigners or of prominent courtiers.

By 1856–7, the European powers brought greater pressure to bear in favour of 'reforms' which were to pave the way specifically for the development of capitalist enterprise. On 10 September 1857, Aḥmad Bey's successor, Muḥammad Bey, was compelled by the British and French consuls, under threat of armed force, to adopt the Fundamental Pact or *'ahd al-amān*. In addition to asserting the security of the life and property of the inhabitants of the Regency in general, the text granted rights and safeguards to non-Muslim minorities in particular, including the right of foreigners to own property and the unrestricted right to pursue any occupation and proclaimed the freedom of trade.[75] The Pact was only a preamble to a more detailed constitution, which was rapidly drawn up and came into force on 24 April 1861. As the first of its kind in the Muslim Arab world, this document laid down the principle of the separation of the executive, legislative and judicial powers, thereby establishing a constitutional system of government. Furthermore, a municipal council was set up in Tunis in 1858, ministries and administrative services were reorganized and a printing house was founded in Tunis that included among its publications a weekly newspaper.[76]

As was to be expected, these reforms met with the same fate as those that had been introduced previously by Aḥmad Bey, since they were not adapted to the social conditions and psychological attitudes prevailing at the time, and were inspired by foreign models. In the meantime, even greater facilities were provided for the activities of European firms. Foreign trade expanded rapidly; the volume of goods imported by the Tunisian government significantly increased – the flow of supplies from France being ensured by the Rothschild company; the British secured land concessions, the right to set up a bank with special privileges and the right to construct a railway line, ventures which collapsed soon after they were launched. The French undertook to supply military equipment and obtained major public works contracts to which we have already referred.[77] The Regency's level of expenditure rose at an alarming rate, whereas its revenue had been reduced by the abolition of monopolies (in accordance with one of the provisions of the Fundamental Pact) and by the granting of privileges to Europeans: it soon started to sink into debt. In order to meet running expenses and cope with the servicing of the government debts, the bey Muḥammad al-Ṣādiḳ decided to double the rate of the poll tax at the end of 1863.

This sparked off the 1864 insurrection, which was supported by virtually

75. A. Ibn Abī-Dhiyāf, 1963–4, Vol. 4, pp. 240–4.
76. J. Ganiage, 1959, pp. 76–88.
77. See note 23 above.

all the ethnic groups and some of the sedentary farmers, who were united by the determination to fight against the arbitrary imposition of taxes and the disastrous reform policy. For three or four months, the insurgents displayed exemplary discipline in their campaign against the beylik and its servants, but the bey's promises and the intrigues of his court soon undermined the unity and determination of the rebels. One by one, the groups laid down their arms and the farming regions were subjected to severe repressive measures from which they never recovered.[78]

The financial situation of the beylik became all the more precarious when the country had to contend with poor harvests from 1866 to 1870 and even a terrible famine, combined with a cholera epidemic in 1867. Bankruptcy was inevitable. On 5 July 1869, an International Financial Commission was set up in Tunis in order to exercise control over the revenue of the beylik and ensure the repayment of the national debt in annual instalments amounting to some 6.5 million francs.[79]

Various drastic measures succeeded, to some extent, in improving the situation, especially as France, which was the chief power interested in occupying Tunisia, lost much prestige as a result of its defeat in 1870. In 1873, Mustafā Khaznadār, a venal individual who had governed since 1837, was replaced by Khāyr al-dīn, a statesman of great integrity and perspicacity.[80] He undertook, through practical and deliberately limited measures, to revive economic activity, particularly agriculture; to organize the administrative services more efficiently; to raise standards of conduct among government servants, and to promote modern educational methods. He was responsible notably for founding Sadiki College, which was to play a leading role in the cultural and even political life of Tunisia in colonial times. He was aided, furthermore, by the very favourable agricultural conditions that prevailed between 1873 and 1875. However, with the return of lean years and the restoration of French prestige in Tunisia as from 1876, he was faced with ever-increasing difficulties, until he fell from power in July 1877. This event heralded a relapse into incompetence and chaos and the country slid into the downward path towards disaster. Nothing could be more symptomatic of those sad times than the political success of Mustafā ibn Ismāʿīl, the bey's former minion and favourite, who was all-powerful until the French forces entered Tunisia, and the protectorate treaty imposed on the bey was signed on 12 May 1881.[81]

Libya

Libya, which formed part of the Ottoman empire, being dominated by the Sahara Desert to a larger extent than any other country in the Maghrib, was

78. J. Ganiage, 1959, pp. 267–70; B. Slama, 1967.
79. See note 27 above.
80. V. M. Bayram, 1885, Vol. 2, pp. 46–93; G. S. van Kriecken, 1976, pp. 161–272.
81. V. M. Bayram, 1885, pp. 97–115; J. Ganiage, 1959, pp. 476–91.

less avidly coveted by the Europeans before 1880 and therefore preserved its specific identity and economic life the longest, as is demonstrated by the vitality of the caravan trade up to about 1903 (Tripoli) and even 1911 (Benghazi).

Around 1800 Libya comprised one real city, Tripoli, and a few other towns on the coast, including Benghazi and Darna, as well as some located in oases (e.g. Ghadāmes, Murzuk and Awdjīla). A mere handful of peasants (*hawāra*) cultivated the little arable land to be found between Misrata and Zwara, while the overwhelming majority of the population led nomadic lives inland, either as shepherds covering small and fairly regular circuits (*'urūba'*), or as cameleers covering sometimes vast and highly irregular circuits (*bawādi*).

Paradoxically, the most powerful communities were those that lived deep in the desert. At all periods the government of the country in Tripoli had to come to an arrangement with the desert powers in order for peace to prevail. On the coast, long-distance trade, regional trade, handicrafts and, up to 1815, privateering were sources of revenue to the urban middle class, made up of large families prominent in the military (*karāghla*), trade (*tudjdjār*) and religious studies (*'ulamā'*) who had formed the mainstay of the local *Ḳāramānlī* dynasty from 1710.[82]

Following a particularly serious power struggle, the dynasty recovered its position in 1794, in the reign of Yūsuf Ḳāramānlī. He revived trans-Saharan trade and revived maritime pillage, which led to a war with the USA from 1801 to 1805.[83] Yūsuf emerged triumphant. However, the ban placed on privateering by the European powers in 1815 and the accompanying policing of the seas created financial difficulties. The tax levy that followed met with resistance, resulting finally in Yūsuf's abdication in 1832.[84] At the beginning of his reign, two coalitions of nomads, headed respectively by the Maḥamid (*'urūba*) and the Awlād Sulaymān (*bawādi*), resisted the central authority's attempt to extend its power in Tripolitania, especially after the *bawādi* had occupied the key points of the Fezzān in 1804. But with the help of the Meghara, who headed a coalition of nomads allied to the Ḳāramānlī, this resistance was crushed in 1812 and the future chiefs of the two coalitions, Ghūma and 'Abd al-Djalīl, were brought up at court. However, in 1830, taking advantage of the power crisis, they resumed leadership of the Maḥamid and the Awlād Sulaymān, became independent and, when the dynasty came to an end in 1835, dominated the Fezzān and Tripolitania all the way to Benghazi.[85]

The power crisis was resolved when the Porte resumed direct control of Libya. This switch was of immediate benefit to the middle class, especially

82. A. Barbar, 1980, pp. 33–43, 96–121.

83. K. Folayan, 1972, pp. 261–70.

84. E. Rossi, 1968, pp. 259–94.

85. D. Cordell, 1972, pp. 12–21; G. F. Lyon, 1821, pp. 54–6; G. Nachtigal, 1967, Vol. 1, pp. 19–22.

the *karāghla*, in particular through the granting of tax relief, as the new authorities needed their support.[86] For the Ottomans had to contend with the coalitions of nomads. Their military operations were unsuccessful. Finally the Turks managed to form an alliance with another ʿ*urūba* nomadic group, headed by Tarhuna, and above all to sow discord and distrust between Ghūma and ʿAbd al-Djalīl. The Awlād Sulaymān were finally defeated in 1842 and driven back towards Chad. Weakened by the famine of 1856, the Maḥamid in their turn submitted after Ghūma's death in 1858.[87] The Ottomans now ruled over the whole of Tripolitania and part of the Fezzān. In the meantime a similar situation was developing in Barḳa (Cyrenaica), where the Sanūsiyya, a religious brotherhood bent on bringing the population back to the true faith and converting the Tubu, had been founded in 1843. It rapidly carved out a prominent place for itself through its success in organizing a major caravan route from Barḳa to Wadai and, above all, by effectively settling disputes between the various nomadic communities. The Turks began treating with the order in 1856 and secured its services as intermediary between themselves and the nomad population.[88]

Being eventually obliged to establish their direct or indirect authority, the Ottoman rulers, after 1860, began to introduce their *tanzimat* – but cautiously, because their authority continued to be challenged in the Fezzān and in Ghāt by the Tuareg and because it was necessary to avoid offending the urban middle class so as to be able to secure the support of at least one section of it for each reform. Steps were gradually taken to introduce judicial reforms from 1865 onwards, schools (1869), a municipal government (1872), administrative reforms (1864 and 1875), hospitals and a central market (1880). Starting in 1870, centres for the distribution of food in times of shortage were also established. Serious famines occurred in 1870–1, 1881–9, 1892, 1897, 1907, 1908 and 1910. The last measure was the only one to the advantage of the masses (*al-ʿamma*); all the other reforms benefited only the middle class, mainly traders, and had the effect of increasing the tax burden of the ordinary people. Their social and economic effects remained fairly limited, however. Despite the growing volume of imported European goods after 1850, the economy remained healthy. Local industry stood up well to competition, and a balanced budget continued to be ensured thanks to esparto exports.[89]

But the continual food shortage from 1881 to 1889 was the first sign of far-reaching change. Exports suffered. In addition, the market price of

86. A. Barbar, 1980, p. 25.

87. A. J. Cachia, 1975, pp. 30–6; N. Slousch, 1908, pp. 58–84, 211–32, 433–53; D. Cordell, 1972, pp. 21–7; E. Rossi, 1968, pp. 297–312.

88. A. Barbar, 1980, pp. 121–7; D. Cordell, 1977, pp. 21–36; E. E. Evans-Pritchard, 1949; N. Ziadeh, 1958.

89. A. Barbar, 1980, pp. 25–33, 54–63, 71–80; A. J. Cachia, 1975, pp. 36–42, 68–93, 125–33; E. Rossi, 1968, pp. 312–52.

PLATE 17.4 *The tomb of Hasanain Pas̲h̲a, founder of the Sanūsiyya*

esparto collapsed, the volume of imported foodstuffs increased and from 1892 onwards the balance of trade showed a deficit. This deficit assumed huge proportions and became permanent after 1897. For, from that time onwards, the food requirements of the masses changed. Imported tea, sugar, flour and tobacco were widely consumed in large quantities. Then the income from Saharan trade dried up. Borno ceased to be a source of trade in 1895; Kano in 1903.[90] The Sanūsiyya was also in difficulty in Barḳa and after 1901 was weakened by its military operations in Chad. The order became a big landowner in 1902 to make up for the losses foreseen on the trans-Saharan trade, thereby alienating some of its supporters. Lastly, the order was unsuccessful in holding its own against rival orders proselytizing in the region. Around 1910 the Sanūsiyya had fewer settlements than in 1853.[91]

Under these circumstances, the wealthy European firms that had been established in Tripoli, and also in Benghazi, found it easy to work themselves into good positions. The society was undergoing a process of radical change; the old patterns had been disrupted. This situation led directly to the attempted Italian conquest of 1911 and to the war that lasted from 1911 to 1932.[92]

90. A. Barbar, 1980, pp. 139–44.
91. A. Barbar, 1980, pp. 128–31.
92. A. Barbar, 1980, pp. 139–82

The trans-Saharan trade

The trans-Saharan trade was still flourishing at the beginning of the nineteenth century, both in the west (from Timbuktu to Tafilālet and from Goulimime to Taodeni) and in the centre (from Tunis and Tripoli to Ghadāmes), and Sudanese exports still consisted of slaves and gold. Around the 1840s, trade that relied on the use of the western routes declined while trade by way of the routes of the central Sahara thrived, especially between Tripoli and Kano and between Tripoli and Borno. In addition, a new direct link between Wadaī and Barḳa, discovered in 1809 or 1810, became a major caravan route after 1850.[93] During the latter half of the century the slave trade went into a slow decline, although along the Borno route it continued longer and along the Wadaī route it even increased and went on doing so after 1900.[94] Ivory exports, which were fairly stable, peaked around 1877. The place of slaves as items of trade was taken first by ostrich feathers, mainly from 1878 to 1883, and then by hides, especially goatskins. To these were added fabrics dyed with indigo, from the Hausa country a small quantity of gold and a few other sundry articles. English cotton goods

PLATE 17.5 *Upper-class Algerian women with a black slave attendant*

93. Regarding this question, see C. W. Newbury, 1966; J. L. Miège, 1961–3, Vol. 3, pp. 371–447; M. Johnson, 1976; D. Cordell, 1977; S. Baier, 1974; 1977.

94. D. Cordell, 1977, p. 35.

were the main item to be carried southwards. In 1860 they represented some 70 per cent of the value of imports. Other imports consisted of North African woollen garments from Tripolitania, Austro-Hungarian textiles, woollen goods and carpets, ironmongery, medicines, devotional articles, perfumes, jewellery, silks, pearls and above all, weapons and ammunition. In addition, there was a constant demand for salt from the Sahara, dates from oases and cereals from the Sahel.[95]

Trans-Saharan trade did not undergo a decline until Atlantic shipping and overland transport (railways) in West Africa began to constitute competitive alternatives. Political developments played a secondary though important role. The fortunes of Wadai account for the importance of the Wadai–Barḳa route as early as 1850. In 1895 trade by way of the Tripoli–Borno route suffered from the operations conducted by Rabeh, and the disruptions caused mainly by the French conquests in West Africa had their repercussions. But trade went into an irreversible decline in 1903 when caravans became more expensive than rail and ship combined.[96] In the east, the isolated position of Wadai and Barḳa enabled it to survive until 1911, even after the British regained control over the Sudan in 1898, no doubt because of the blockading of Dārfūr. It was then, after 1900, that traditional patterns of life in the Sahara were destroyed, shortly before the final invasion of the last extensive territories that had not yet been colonized.

Conclusion

Sooner or later, and with varying degrees of violence, each of the countries of the Maghrib was subjected to the same process, one which led from autonomy to dependence. It is therefore useless to seek the reason for this collapse at the local level in the errors committed by a particular ruler or in the unscrupulous behaviour of a particular European agent. A single external factor, namely the expansion of Western capitalism, sealed the fate of the Maghrib, just as it sealed the fate of the rest of the non-European world. In about 1885, this expansion was described by Jules Ferry, one of the promoters of colonization, as 'an irresistible movement [that is] impelling the great powers to embark upon the conquest of new lands', 'the peremptory demonstration and inescapable law of an economic system common to the whole of Europe'.[97]

However, it may have been due to certain local conditions, or to an accidental event of historic importance in the case of Algeria, that there were marked discrepancies in the rate at which the various countries of the Maghrib were reduced to a state of dependence, as well as considerable differences regarding the methods used for that purpose and the reactions

95. See note 93 above, and A. Barbar, 1980, pp. 64–76.
96. A. Barbar, 1980, p. 140, gives figures.
97. Cited by L. Bergeron, 1968, t. VIII, p. 319.

of the population. Algeria was crushed by force of arms even before the middle of the century and was the country where the European assault was most ruthless and most traumatic for the traditional society and culture. Tunisia, on the other hand, was penetrated gradually as the capitalist system itself developed, and the government attempted to react by implementing a policy of modernistic reforms. Although it proved to be ineffective and ruinous at the time, this policy nevertheless laid down valuable foundations for the future, the emergence of a modernistic social elite, the first steps towards the creation of a nation-state, etc. Libya where direct Turkish rule was re-established in 1835, was thereby protected for some time from European ambitions, which were also discouraged by its poverty and remoteness. Can it be said that the specific conditions experienced by the countries of the Maghrib during the nineteenth century had repercussions throughout the colonial period and even beyond? The present writer has no doubt that this was the case.

18 Morocco from the beginning of the nineteenth century to 1880

A. LAROUI

After the long and glorious reign of Mawlāy Ismā'īl (1672–1727) Morocco went through a period of anarchy that wrecked the economy, disturbed the social structure and destroyed the army. Sultan Muḥammad III (1757–90) gradually took things in hand and laid the foundations of 'modern' Morocco, a process consolidated by his son Sulaymān (1792–1822). He made the Makhzen (government) conform more closely to the *sharī'a* (Islamic law) and gave it a more distinctly urban basis. He governed directly the sedentary farming and arboricultural regions of Haouz and Dir, as well as Gharb, a swampy region good for subsistence farming; through the great *ḳā'ids* (*ḳabīla* chieftains) and the *shaykh*s of the *zāwiya* (masters of religious orders) he governed indirectly the mountain and desert regions, thus making a distinction between a domain of sovereignty and a domain of suzerainty, customarily called *bilād al-makhzen* and *bilād al-sibā*, although this places them in too systematic an opposition.

Morocco was then reorganized on a restrictive basis. Certain groups profiteering from the privileges of the Makhzen were removed from power; naturally they attempted to regain their position, by resorting to rebellion, if necessary. Conscious of its youthful strength, the Europe of the Congress of Vienna made its pressure felt, particularly after the taking of Algiers by the French in 1830. The Makhzen had two problems to solve simultaneously: strengthening itself to stand against the foreign danger, and broadening its territorial and political base. The dual reform encountered colonial manoeuvring and domestic opposition. In spite of the strong personality of Sultan 'Abd al-Raḥmān (1822–59), the intelligence of Muḥammad IV (1859–73), and the prestige of Ḥasan I (1873–94), the essential aim, to escape foreign control, was not definitively achieved, although in 1880 Morocco still presented the façade of a stable state. But the major achievement of this period, which saw heavier European pressure and an active policy of reform, was undeniably the implanting of a traditionalistic and highly sensitive sense of Moroccan community, which gave Morocco a special position in north-western Africa.

PLATE 18.1 *Sultan ʿAbd al-Raḥmān (1822–59) in 1832*

The politico-social structure

The noteworthy political institution of nineteenth-century Morocco was the *bayʿa* (investiture contract), deliberately modelled directly on that by which the Prophet Muḥammad had set up the first Muslim community of Medina, and which Morocco alone preserved in its original purity.[1]

1. A. Ibn Zaīdān, 1961–2, Vol. 1, pp. 8–35.

A written contract binding the sultan and the various groups of the population, and a process of legitimizing political authority, which is thus no longer based on force alone, *the bayʿa* strengthened the Moroccan people's feeling of belonging to an intangible national community unaffected by political and military changes. At each change of reign army commanders, representatives of the urban classes, *ḳāʿid*s and *shaykh*s of *zāwiya*s sent their oaths of allegiance to court. All written in approximately the same style, these oaths defined the rights and duties of the sultan and of the people. The duty of the former was dual: to defend the land[2] against foreign enemies and to maintain peace at home. In return, the people owed him complete obedience, as long as he did not transgress the law and custom of Islam, complying with the orders of the Makhzen, paying the legal taxes, providing armed contingents in time of peace and rallying to the colours in time of war. The ritual formula appears as follows, taken from the *bayʿa* of the inhabitants of Rabat sent to ʿAbd al-Raḥmān: 'We swear before God and his angels to heed and to carry out the orders of the Imam, in so far as they are lawful and within our capacity ... the bargain being concluded, we obey as God has commanded us to do and the Sultan respects our rights and those of all his other subjects, as God has ordered him.'[3]

To carry out his duties the sultan had a Makhzen composed essentially of an army and a bureaucracy.

Until the post-1885 military reforms, the Moroccan army consisted of three groups, of varying origin and efficiency: The *bwakher* (classical: *ʿabid al-Bukhārī*) represented the few hundred slave troops remaining from the 50 000 who had made up Mawlāy Ismāʿīl's black guards; the *gīsh* (classical: *jaīsh*), numbering no more than 9000, were composed of contingents from certain communities (Cheraga, Oulad Jami', Oudaya, Cherarda) that farmed state lands for their own benefit and in the nineteenth century were settled around Fez and in the suburbs of Rabat and Larache; The *nuaib* (classical: *nawa'ib*, plural of *nā'iba*) were temporary troops provided by other communities, notably those of Haouz and Dir, at the sovereign's demand. As conceived by Muḥammad III, this army was a police force to maintain domestic order. That is why troops trained in the European style, the *ʿaskarī*, were created after the defeat of Isly at the hands of the French.[4]

The bureaucracy was composed of viziers and secretaries of the ministries

2. Contrary to general ideas, Morocco's territory was clearly defined from the sixteenth century on. The wars of the Saʿadian and ʿAlawite sovereigns against the Turks of Algiers ended with a recognized frontier between the two parties. In the Sahara, Shārifian sovereignty extended to the oases whose sedentary inhabitants signed the *bayʿa* and to the boundaries of the grazing zones of the nomadic groups that did likewise. The nineteenth-century sultan's dealings with the European Powers show clearly that the Makhzen had a precise concept of what was Moroccan territory.

3. A. Ibn Zaīdān, 1929–33, Vol. 5, pp. 9–15.

4. J. Erckmann, 1885.

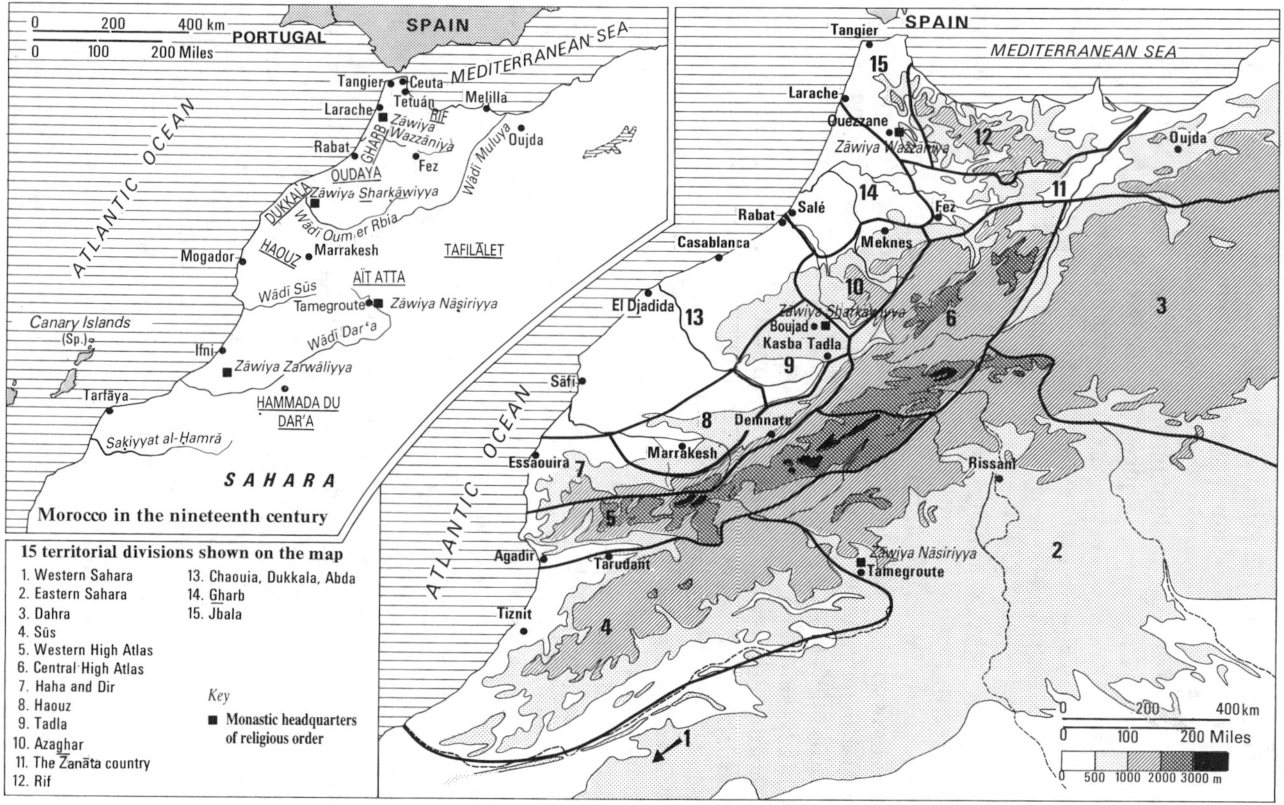

FIG. 18.1 *The historical regions of Morocco in the nineteenth century* (*Source:* Origines sociales et culturelles du nationalisme marocain *by A. Laroui, 1977*)

(*kuttāb*) grouped into departments known as *banīka* in Morocco. This bureaucracy carried on the Andalusian tradition, maintained by the instruction proferred at Ḳarāwiyyīn University at Fez and an elaborate system of co-optation. Also, a number of the viziers and secretaries were of Andalusian origin. From the middle of the nineteenth century a new type of Makhzen official appeared, to meet the needs stemming from expanded relations with Europe. These were the *umanā* (plural of *amīn*, customs inspector) and *tulba* (plural of *tālib*, advanced student), less versed in rhetoric and history, but more familiar with European languages and financial problems.[5]

The Moroccan state, which was based on Islamic orthodoxy, had as its legal source of income receipts from the state lands, the *zakāt* (a tax on commercial capital and farm produce), the proceeds of which were to be spent for specifically defined purposes, and the taxes on foreign trade; all other tax income, including the tithe (*'ushur*), descendant of the *kharādj*, were of dubious legality.[6]

With his hands tied in the field of taxation, the sultan was forced to limit his spending to a strict minimum. Muḥammad III contented himself with revenue from the customs and the *zakāt* from the Haouz region and Crown farmland (*'azīb*). He had nevertheless maintained a tax on imported fabrics, leather and sulphur. After obtaining authorization from a few *'ulamā'*, he later instituted town dues and a tax on markets and on weights and measures.[7] The merchants and craftsmen resented these and forced Sultan Sulaymān to remove them on his accession to the throne. To make up the losses to the Treasury, aggravated by his decision to discourage trade with Europe, the sovereign engaged in more and more tours of rural areas, in order to derive the maximum revenue from the *zakāt* and tithe, which naturally led to lively discontent on the part of the rural population. In 1850 his successor, 'Abd al-Raḥmān, had to revive the tax on leather and then another on cattle sold in the *sūḳ*s. In 1860, following its defeat by Spain, Morocco had to pay compensation of 100 million francs, the equivalent of twenty times the Moroccan budget of the time.[8] Tax reform was imperative. In spite of Sultan Muḥammad IV's urgent appeal, the *'ulamā'* nevertheless clung to the orthodox point of view.[9] All through the nineteenth century the problem of taxes remained central to Morocco's history and was never resolved satisfactorily. Experience impelled the Makhzen to limit its responsibilities, in order to keep expenditures down to the level of available income, rather than raising the latter in order to be able to achieve desirable

5. A. Ibn Zaīdān, 1961–2, Vol. 1, pp. 46ff.

6. In Muslim law *kharādj* is justified by conquest. But most *'ulamā'* consider that Morocco's inhabitants embraced Islam voluntarily. See P. Śaran and J. Burton-Page, 1965.

7. A. al-Nāṣirī, 1954–6, Vol. 9, p. 61. It is thought that these various taxes brought in three million francs, which was enough to pay the costs of the army and bureaucracy.

8. J. L. Miège, 1961–3, Vol. 2, p. 362.

9. M. Dāwud, 1956–70, Vol. 5, pp. 97–9.

be able to achieve desirable goals. However, with increasing European pressure, overall reform became increasingly urgent; there was no longer any question of being satisfied with what was possible.

Between the army and bureaucracy on the one hand and the urban and rural population on the other there were intermediate bodies that, while enjoying some autonomy, were part of the Makhzen, in the broader sense.[10] As spokesmen for social classes or regional groups, they energetically defended traditional rights against the sultan; being responsible to him, they carried out the Makhzen's orders; taking account of local habits and practices.

The clerical class was made up of the *'ulamā'* teachers, *ḳāḍīs*, *muftīs*, *nādhirs* of the *ḥabūs* (administrators of the religious foundations), and *muḥtasibs* (officers in charge of the markets). This essentially urban administration, which strictly applied the commandments of *sharī'a*, was theoretically under the supervision of the sultan-imām, but it enjoyed unquestionable autonomy.[11] The sovereign could alter neither the content nor the form of education, which was the Ḳarāwiyyīn's prerogative; nor could he disregard the views of other *'ulamā'* when making appointments to the posts just mentioned; nor could he turn towards his own coffers the income of the *ḥabūs*; nor could he veto the decrees of the *muḥtasib*. *Sharī'a*, a veritable constitution governing social life, was under the custody of the *'ulamā'* and any open attempt to change it was out of the question, even when it came from the sultan.[12]

The *shurafā* (*sharīfs*), direct descendants of the Prophet Muḥammad, formed a kind of religious aristocracy distributed throughout Morocco's town and countryside. Three times, under sultans Ismā'īl, Muḥammad III and Sulaymān, a census was taken of the *shurafā*, for they enjoyed special legal status and social prestige.[13] They had the privilege of being judged by their own *naḳib* (officials). As descendants of the founder of the state of Islam, they possessed rights over the public treasury and were thus exempt from several taxes as well as receiving numerous gifts from the sultan.[14] As descendants of the Messenger of God, they were endowed in the public eye with a special blessing (*baraka*), usually dormant, but in favourable conditions capable of being transformed into supernatural power. Hence their role as miracle-workers and arbitrators, services for which they were paid, and to which the sultan himself did not hesitate to resort on occasion.

The *zāwiyas*, social groups with a religious basis, took a number of

10. There is a distinction between Makhzen in the strict sense of the government and Makhzen in the broader sense of the country's political and religious elite. It is the latter meaning that is understood when speaking of Makhzanīya and Makhzen families.

11. Duties to *sharī'a* are distinguished from duties to the Makhzen. See Muḥammad b. Ja'afar al-Kattānī, 1899, Vol. 3, p. 5.

12. A. Ibn Zaīdān, 1961–2, Vol. 2, pp. 163–88.

13. E. Lévi-Provençal, 1922.

14. al-Mahdī al-Wazzānī, 1900, Vol. 2, p. 92.

forms in nineteenth-century Morocco, two of them of great importance: (a) the *zāwiya*-brotherhood, such as the Tijāniyya or Darḳāwiyya, without distinction as to social class, wealth, occupation or ethnic origin; they thus played a powerful role in horizontal integration; (b) the *zāwiya* principality, whose chief was delegated virtually complete authority over his fief, such as the Wazzāniyya in the north, the Sharḳāwiyya at Tadla, the Nāsiriyya in the south-west or the Zarwāliyya in the Anti-Atlas. Each *zāwiya* attempted to be both at the same time and sometimes succeeded, as witness the Nāsiriyya; it could assume another form, but in every case it was a school of social discipline and an outpost of Makhzen authority, in spite of its apparent independence.[15] This role was especially visible in the towns, where *zāwiya* and corporation (*hinta*) had the same members and pursued the same aims.

The *ḳabīla* chieftains had widely variable status. To the Makhzen the *ḳabīla* was essentially an administrative and fiscal concept, applied equally to a region (Doukkala), a mountain canton (Beni Ouriaghel), a nomad confederation (Aït Atta) or a transplanted community of soldier-shepherds (Cherarda). In every case authority was delegated to a *ḳā'id* appointed by a *dahir* (decree) after the approval of the people of the district. The *ḳā'id* was of course both the sultan's representative and the spokesman of the people of the district, one of the two roles unfailingly predominating, depending on the distance from the central government and the region's wealth. Facing this *ḳā'id* there was always the *'amil* (governor), who collected taxes and raised the troop levies. In certain favourable circumstances one person could combine the two roles, but they were nevertheless separate functions. Kaidal families grew up – there were two per *ḳabīla* – the one on the Makhzen's side, the other favouring local interests; whether in power or out of power, these families formed part of the country's administrative elite.[16]

These intermediate bodies, urban or rural, based on individual ties or kinship, were in the final analysis cogs in the sultan's government. In defending *sharī'*a the *'ulamā'* were strengthening the legitimacy of the sultan-imām, since Islam is primarily a political community. The *shurafā* acted as mediators between central government and local chieftains in times of trouble, serious or fleeting. The *zāwiya shaykh* governed distant and unproductive regions on behalf of the sultan or maintained peace in strategic regions.[17] When a *zāwiya* set itself up against the sovereign for political reasons, he destroyed it. The same may be said of the *ḳabīla* chieftains. They were granted broad autonomy when fighting foreigners,

15. E. Michaux-Bellaire, 1921.

16. R. Montagne, 1930, is a classic book, but should be read critically, for the Makhzen documents themselves oblige us to alter many accepted notions about the concept of the *ḳabīla*.

17. A. G. P. Martin, 1923 (on the rôle of the *Zāwiya* Wazzāniyya zāwiyas in Tūwāt); P. Durand, 1930, pp. 65–77 (on the rôle of the *zāwiya* Sharḳāwiyya *Zāwiya* in the Tadla).

as in the Rīf where the Spaniards at Ceuta or Melilla were continually under siege, or when their region was mountainous or desert, but if they claimed complete independence by disobeying the sultan's commands or failing to apply *sharīʿa*, they were declared in a state of *siba*, that is, guilty of breaking without justification the *bayʿa* (contract); they could be reduced by force or diplomacy, in a whirlwind campaign or by a slow process of attrition, depending on the military forces at the sovereign's disposal, but the sovereignty of the sultan and *sharīʿa* was never surrendered.[18]

Morocco's socio-political system, as reorganized by Muḥammad III, marked a return to Islamic orthodoxy. In recognizing the autonomy of the intermediate bodies and limiting the ambitions of the central government, it had reinforced the idea of a Moroccan state, by encouraging each occupational, social or ethnic group to voice its claims inside the Makhzen. However, this system contained its own contradictions; it manifestly wavered between two ideals: the one, the rule of *sharīʿa* and direct government, would have been welcomed by the *ʿulamāʾ* and the merchants; the other, more to the liking of the local chiefs, would have had the sultan merely as a unifying symbol, possessing only the authority delegated to him by those chiefs. This system was the result of the changed power relationship between Morocco and Europe arising during the mercantile era. Before it stabilized it had to cope with even stronger European pressure; its contradictions came into the open after Morocco's military defeats, by France in 1844 and then by Spain in 1860.

The Makhzen's reforms in response to the European offensive

The colonial powers' policies in regard to Morocco will be analysed elsewhere.[19] Here we shall only recall that until 1880 there was a European consensus to maintain the status quo in the empire of Morocco. No territorial expansion by France from its Algerian base or by Spain from Ceuta or Melilla; no commercial privileges for British goods. In spite of several concessions extorted by France and Spain after the wars of 1844 and 1859–60 these principles were reaffirmed at the 1880 Madrid Conference and remained in effect until the end of the nineteenth century.[20]

18. The colonial powers interpreted the concept of *siba* according to the requirements of their expansionist policy. It is now to be understood in its original framework and not in relation to European law of the period.

19. See Chapter 19 below.

20. Bugeaud's forces attacked the Moroccan army at Isly near Oujda on 14 August 1844; the French navy shelled Mogador on the 15th after bombarding Tangier on the 6th. The Treaty of Tangier, signed on 19 September, ended the war, but the Lalla Marnia convention of 18 March 1845 did not settle the border dispute, due to French ambitions in the Sahara. In the autumn of 1859 the Spanish organized a European army at Ceuta; after a few skirmishes at Cabo Negro they entered Tetuán on 6 February 1860. By the treaty of 20

Nevertheless, the demands of the European powers ran absolutely counter to the sultan's authority. During the conquest of Algeria, the sultan could not maintain the neutrality counselled by England and simple common sense, for Muslim common law imposed on him the obligation to assist neighbouring Muslims abandoned by their legitimate sovereign, in this case the Ottoman ruler.[21] In 1859 men of the Rīf destroyed a building constructed by the Spaniards of Ceuta outside the town walls and tore up the flag flying over it. Madrid demanded that the twelve men it considered responsible be handed over. The sultan could not comply, for he would then have been guilty of a deliberate breach of his *bay'a* oath.[22] In matters of trade, in which Britain was particularly concerned, the sultan could not by a simple stroke of the pen free exports, grant European rights of property ownership, or oblige the *ḳāḍīs* to accept the evidence of non-Muslims, for on all these points the prohibition of religious law was uncompromising.[23] Thus the sultan found himself in an unenviable position, torn between the demands of the Europeans and the arrogant opposition of the *'ulamā'*; to the former he was an obscurantist, to the latter an innovator. Hence the ambiguity of the reforms.

In the nineteenth century both the Makhzen and the European consuls were agreed that the army should be reinforced and the government reorganized to ensure safety, order and justice for all. The problem lay in the legal framework: should it be *shrarī'a*, or new legislation of European inspiration? The opposition between the two could not be peacefully resolved. The Makhzen did carry out a reform, but one that was limited and thus unsatisfactory in European eyes.

Muḥammad IV lived through the two defeats of Isly and Tetuán, the latter when already sultan, the former while still heir-apparent and commander-in-chief of the army, which explains the moves he took to introduce military reforms from 1845 on. To break through the prevailing traditionalism, he commissioned from a well-known *'alim* a work that would justify reform on traditional grounds.[24]

He brought in Tunisians who had served in the Ottoman army to organize regiments trained in European style, the *'askarī*: initially they amounted to only some 500 men. With the help of renegade Europeans, the best-known being the Frenchman de Saulty, who had taken the Muslim name of 'Abd al-Raḥmān al-'Alī, he set up at Fez an engineering school (*madrasat al-Muhandisīn*) to train surveyors, topographers, cartographers and artillerymen. For it he commissioned a Maltese writer to translate various treatises on geometry, supervising the work directly himself. Via

November 1861 Spain obtained an enlargement of the boundaries of Ceuta and Melilla, commercial concessions and a fishing port in the south, which was sited at Ifni in 1883.

21. A. Tasūlī, n.d.
22. A. al-Nāṣirī, 1954–6, Vol. 4; J. L. Miège, 1961–3, Vol. 2, pp. 360–2.
23. A. Tasūli, n.d., Ch. 1, section 4.
24. M. al-Khardūdī, n.d.

his Gibraltar representative he asked the Pasha of Egypt to send him scientific books translated from the European languages. Sultan ʿAbd al-Raḥmān let his son have his way but assumed no responsibility for this reform, the immediate benefits of which he could not see. Once sultan, Muḥammad IV would undoubtedly have pursued this reform more vigorously, if the 1859–60 war had not raised a labyrinth of financial problems for him. None the less, he decided to send a group of *Bwakher* to Egypt for artillery training. After 1870 there were regular missions sent to Gibraltar for two-year training courses. Ḥasan I carried on his father's policy, under more favourable conditions. He set up a regular recruiting system: each town of the empire had to supply 500 recruits, each port 200, each region 2000; this produced an army of 25 000 soldiers. In 1877 he asked France to obtain officers to instruct his artillery groups. In 1880, 180 commissioned and non-commissioned officers returned home from abroad and were formed into the *harraba* regiment under a British commanding officer, Major Maclean. Later, Ḥasan I sent other military missions to Belgium, Germany and Italy. With this reorganized army he could reassert his sovereignty over distant regions like Sūs and Tafilālet, which were coveted by several European Powers.[25]

C. John Drummond Hay, Her Britannic Majesty's Minister at Tangier from 1839 to 1886, was as ardent in his defence of the sultan's sovereignty and territory as in his demands that the country be opened to international trade.[26] He used his immense prestige with Sultan ʿAbd al-Raḥmān to get him to accept the Treaty of Friendship, Trade and Navigation of 9 December 1856. This laid down the following principles: freedom of trade, an end to all public or private monopolies, guaranteed safety of property and person, the opening of consulates throughout the country, exemption of foreign traders and their Moroccan associates from all taxes and duties except customs duties and anchorage and pilotage fees.[27]

Opening Morocco to European trade had several unfortunate consequences: the first was a severe monetary crisis. In the eighteenth century the *dinār*, a gold coin, had completely vanished: Morocco's monetary system became bimetallic, based on silver and bronze. The legal silver coins were the Spanish peseta and douro and the French franc and écu; douro and écu were called rials. The bronze coins, minted in Morocco, were the *ukia* (ounce) and *mūzūna*. The *mithkāl* served as the unit of account: it was worth 10 ounces, and the ounce was worth 4 *mūzūna*. As trade relations with Europe expanded, silver coins became rarer and the more common bronze coins became devalued. By mid-century they had dropped to one-fourth their original value, with the consequences that are well known in all inflations: rising prices, impoverishment of the

25. J. L. Miège, 1961–3, Vol. 1, p. 208. See particularly M. al-Mannūnī, 1973, p. 55.
26. J. D. Hay, 1896.
27. See the text in P. L. Rivière, 1924–5, Vol. 1, pp. 36–42.

PLATE 18.2 *Sultan Ḥasan I (1873–94)*

population, government finances in difficulty, concentration of property in the hands of a minority. The Makhzen attempted to respond, with authoritarian measures in 1852, 1862, 1869 and 1877, each time hoping to return to a parity level already exceeded. The sultan could only benefit from these revaluations if he demanded payment to him in silver coins, while he himself was able to settle his debts in rials or ounces at will. But the foreign merchants reduced the state's income from customs duties by paying in devalued ounces, while the sultan had to pay his foreign debts in Spanish piastres and French écus, which he bought at high rates. The currency measures thus had the end-result of accentuating the treasury's difficulties. At the end of our period Ḥasan I decided to mint a new silver coin (the Ḥasan rial, worth five francs) but without withdrawing the bronze coin; the latter continued to decline in value (by 1881 the rial was worth 14 *mithkāl* instead of 10) and it brought down the new coins with it.[28]

The Makhzen's spending was continuing to rise because of reform measures and the many debts and reparations to European states and merchants. Fiscal reform was imperative. But the sultan was not free to undertake it without consulting the *ʿulamāʾ*, since this was a matter of common law. Earlier, the *ʿulamāʾ* had several times declared illegal the taxes on commercial transactions known under the generic term *mukūs* (pl. of *maks*), when they were not temporary and spent on specific purposes; any land tax was also unacceptable to them, since Moroccans were independent and full owners of their land.[29] In July 1860, Muḥammad IV asked the *ʿulamāʾ* to tell him how to pay the war reparations that would enable him to recover Tetuán, which was occupied by the Spanish, and to prevent other towns from falling into their hands. The *ʿulamāʾ* remained true to their orthodox position, holding that only an extraordinary, that is temporary, tax, affecting all inhabitants equally and levied directly – i.e., not farmed out to third parties – would be legal, although the sultan had been careful to explain to them that circumstances did not permit him to put such a measure into effect.[30] Overruling their objections, he instituted indirect taxes that incited sullen and tenacious opposition from the urban population. When his successor was proclaimed in 1873, the craftsmen demanded abolition of these *mukūs* as the price of signing the *bayʿa*, and Ḥasan I had to reduce the rebellious town-dwellers by force. Later he introduced, on an experimental basis, the *tertib*, a fixed-rate tax on land collected by special categories of *umanā* (customs collectors). Without consulting *ʿulamāʾ*, of whose adverse views in the matter he was already aware, he began by levying it in the Haouz, the kingdom's best-governed

28. J.L. Miège, 1961–3, Vol. 2, pp. 388–9; Vol. 3, pp. 97–107, 434–7. See also G. Ayache, 1958, pp. 271–310. At the beginning of the century 10 ounces were worth 5 pesetas; in 1845 they were worth 3.25 pesetas and in 1874 only one peseta. Figures from al-Nāṣirī. 1954–6, Vol. 9, p. 208.

29. al-Mahdī al-Wazzānī, 1900, Vol. 3, p. 92.

30. M. Dāwud, 1956–70, Vol. 5, pp. 99–100.

PLATE 18.3 *Silver rial minted in Paris in 1881 for Ḥasan I*

district. But he quickly let it lapse, for reasons not yet clear but which undoubtedly had to do with public opinion and the opposition of certain army leaders. Without financial resources the Makhzen was obliged to restrict its ambitions for reform, keeping its regular expenses down to the lowest possible level.

After 1856 the number of European traders installed in Morocco rose steadily. In response to their complaints the Makhzen launched on a programme of government reform. In 1861 a corps of customs inspectors, the *umanā*, was set up. Recruited from traders, government officials and notaries, and relatively well paid, they were installed in the eight ports open to foreign trade; at their side they had Spanish inspectors responsible for vetting customs receipts, 60 per cent of which were destined for war reparation payments. These *umanā*, several of whom had made fortunes abroad (Gibraltar, Marseilles, Manchester, Genoa), helped to rationalize Morocco's bureaucracy and were very influential under Muḥammad IV and Ḥasan I. Another group also enjoyed increasing prestige: the *tulba*, who had been sent to Europe for training and to learn foreign languages. Between 1874 and 1888 there were eight missions, totalling 350 individuals, taking the road towards the principal countries of Europe. On their return home these young men were used in the tax division of the Department of the Mint of the celebrated *makina* at Fez (an armaments factory organized by Italians), which was reorganized in 1886, and in the Ministry of Foreign Affairs (*wizīrat al-bar*).[31]

But the European traders' real goal was to restrict the *ḳāḍī*s' authority.[32] They would rather be judged by the governor (*ḳā'id* or *'amil*), while hoping to be one day under the jurisdiction of a joint tribunal applying a legal code of Western inspiration. On the pretext that it had been a moderating influence on Spain in 1860, France brought Muḥammed IV to accept the convention of 19 August 1863, which granted judiciary privileges both to foreign merchants and their Moroccan associates. Instead of being under the authority of the *ḳāḍī*, they were to be judged by the governor, in the presence of the European consul concerned. While the number of their Moroccan associates remained low (200 per *ḳabīla* around 1870), the situation, while offensive to the sultan, was nevertheless bearable. But the consuls soon conferred the status of *samsār* (trade middleman) on any one, Jew or Muslim, who wished to evade the *ḳāḍī*'s jurisdiction and who could afford to pay for the title.[33] Seeing its authority undermined by this illegal protection, arising from a tendentious interpretation of the 1863 convention, the Makhzen protested unendingly and finally won Britain over to its viewpoint. A twelve-nation international conference was held at Madrid in July 1880 to put an end to the practice. The number of those entitled to protection was strictly limited: henceforth each trader had to be satisfied with two *samsār*s; only they personally and those members of their family living under their roofs could claim the protection of the foreign country. In return for this limitation, however, the property rights of the Europeans established in the ports were recognized, something which the sultan viewed with an unfavourable eye.

The consequence of European pressure was thus a reform of Morocco's army, government, monetary and tax system. However, the scope of this reform was restricted both by foreign obstacles and by domestic problems. The Europeans were happy about measures guaranteeing them security and favouring their trade operations, but they did not – particularly the French and Spanish – want the Makhzen to become so strong as to be able

31. J.L. Miège, 1961–3, Vol. 4, pp. 397–408.

32. 'To penetrate Morocco peacefully, it is first necessary to de-Muslimize it'. G. Maura, 1911, p. 197.

33. J.D. Hay, 1896, pp. 321–3.

to oppose their aims successfully.[34] In addition, the sultan was not free to tamper with education, the judiciary or religious institutions, given the intransigence of the *ʿulamāʾ*. This limitation of the field open to reform, further limited by scanty financial resources, had an unexpected result: instead of becoming strong and independent, the sultan was gradually tied more closely to Europe with each successive reform of his country. For, as foreign relations expanded, the number of foreign traders grew and there were more incidents calling forth heavy fines or territorial concessions or entailing a loss of prestige.[35]

The people saw a cause-and-effect relationship between admission of the foreigners, the ensuing reforms and their own poverty. Public opinion became more and more incensed against the foreigners, for economic, psychological and religious reasons.

Popular reactions

Morocco's farm production depended – and still depends – on the vagaries of climate; now it had to cope with the growing demand of the European exporters. The result was a series of famines that had severe effects on the urban and rural population: 1850, 1857, 1867 and particularly the terrible years of 1878 and 1881, when 12–15 per cent of the inhabitants of the towns are estimated to have survived on public charity and 64 000 Moroccans had to emigrate.[36] Outside the ramparts of the towns there were already rising quarters of *nualas* similar to the slums and shantytowns of the twentieth century. Unable to pay their taxes or repay their debts to European traders, many crop and livestock farmers left their lands; this drift to the towns affected about one-third of the agricultural land in the south and around the coastal towns. The Makhzen suffered doubly from the consequences of this situation. First, receipts from the *zakāt* declined; second, the Europeans demanded that it pay the debts of private individuals, particularly when the debtors were *ḳāʿid*s. What is more, illegal low-price transactions were taking place between foreigners, via the intermediary of the *samsār*s and with the blessing of unscrupulous *ḳāḍī*s; and tax revenue on the property in question was accordingly forfeited. The sultan attempted to stem this disastrous tide. In a series of measures from 1873 to 1883, he banned Europeans from the rural *sūḳ*s, required *ḳāʿid*s to keep their own property separate from that of persons under their jurisdiction and restricted the number of *ḳāḍī*s and notaries entitled to authenticate the promissory notes covering these sales.[37] If the rural population was becoming impover-

34. J. Caillé, 1951, p. 121.

35. 'After the reforms Turkey and Egypt became richer but much less independent', said Sultan Muḥammad IV to the French Minister Tissot. See J. D. Hay, 1896, pp. 288–9.

36. J. L. Miège, 1961–3, Vol. 3, pp. 367, 444.

37. A. Ibn Zaīdān, 1961–2, Vol. 1, pp. 364–6; Vol. 2, pp. 48–51, 129–31.

ished, the urban population was in no better state. Everyone was affected by the rise in price of the basic necessities: grains, wool, hides. Imported goods (cloth, candles, matches, sugar) were cheap, but they represented severe competition for the craftsmen who were the backbone of the urban economy. Government employees, whether paid by the Makhzen, *ḥabūs* or even the population themselves, were suffering from the evils of devaluation: between 1845 and 1874, their wages in real terms dropped to one-tenth of their original value.[38] The only ones to escape this general pauperization were the merchants and associates of European traders, who were able to get hold of silver coins. Their capital automatically rose in value; they paid ridiculously low prices for their purchases of buildings and property and they lent money at usurious levels to the rural population and even to members of the Makhzen. The way they were enriching themselves, which appeared even worse because of its contrast with the general poverty, was felt as another evil consequence of opening the country to foreign business.

The Moroccan people were sensitive to more than these merely economic aspects: they resented as well, and perhaps above all, the decline in the authority of the *ḳāḍī*, the sultan and, in the last analysis, Islam itself. Each colonial power laid much stress on respect for its flag. If one of its citizens was killed, its consul cared little whether there had been provocation or whether it was intentional homicide or not; he demanded the execution of the guilty person (where this was uncertain, execution of all those present at the incident), monetary reparations to the victim's family, the dismissal of agents he considered insufficiently zealous in the matter, an official government apology, and protection for the flag.[39]

Under conditions like these, officials did not know how to act. If they rejected the consul's complaints and the affair turned out badly for the sultan, they were the ones to suffer the consequences; on the other hand, if they agreed to flout custom, which left the decision in the hands of the central authority, and were diligent about the case and then the result was a popular uprising, they again bore the responsibility. Their prestige was constantly eroded, to the detriment of the public order that the Europeans claimed to need.[40]

The *ḳāḍī* and *muḥtasib* were particular victims of this situation contrary to the letter of *sharīʿa*. Hence their fierce opposition to protection. With Britain's active backing, the British Jew and philanthropist Sir Moses Montefiore visited Morocco following which Sultan Muḥammad IV issued the *dahir* of 5 February 1864: it ordered Moroccan officials to treat Jews' affairs with speed and justice, threatening them with grave sanctions if they did not comply. 'As soon as the Jews had the *dahir*, they made copies of

38. See note 28 above.
39. G. Ayache, 1965, pp. 159–204.
40. A. Ibn Zaīdān, 1929–33, Vol. 2, p. 374.

it which they distributed in all the towns; they acted together to make themselves independent of all authority, particularly that of the ports', says the historian al-Nāṣirī.[41] The *'ulamā'* saw this decree as a blow aimed at *sharī'a* and the reaction was so violent that Muḥammad IV had to back down. Muslim protégés aroused even greater hostility. At the Friday prayers in the mosques the *'ulamā'* presented numerous pamphlets urging the sultan to take severe reprisals against them. 'If you do not,' one of these *'ulamā'* said, 'doubt will be sown in the minds of the ignorant, who will begin to think ill of Islam and to believe that the religion of the infidels is superior to it'.[42]

When the sultan failed to follow their advice, because he did not want to create problems with the European powers, they turned to the people for support. The same *'alim* just cited said on this subject: 'The duty of every believer is to refrain from frequenting these protégés, inviting them, sharing their food, tying himself to them in friendship or marriage'.[43] Since the majority of these Muslim protégés were wealthy merchants, the *'ulamā'*s campaign, which was supported by the urban working class, took on the aspect of an attack by the religious aristocracy against a new elite emerging thanks to the unprecedented conditions created by the opening up of the country.

If the reforms were a consequence of foreign pressure, they were in turn the cause of violent xenophobia. Their net effect on everyday life was adverse and the Moroccans naturally associated them with the Europeans' daily more pervasive presence. 'The reason for price rises and famine is cohabitation with the Europeans', said al-Nāṣirī.[44] Everyone wished to reduce contact with the foreigners to an absolute minimum; more, the ideal became a return to life of earlier times. All classes turned to a romantic ideology that beautified the past and resurrected tradition (*ihyā' al-sunna*). To restrict the Europeans' sphere of operations, the sultan dragged out every negotiation, which irritated the consuls and aroused cries of obstruction. 'We must discuss, discuss and discuss again, only good can come of it', Ḥasan I advised one of his representatives at Tangier.[45] The clerical orders demanded strict application of *sharī'a* in all areas of social life and gave the word reform a very special meaning. It was, in the *'ulamā'*'s view, not so much a matter of changing institutions, which was impossible in any event, but of returning to the code of the elders (*salaf*), those who set the Muslims their examples of greatness and justice. In opposition to the concept of *nidhām*, reorganization of their army, bureaucracy and daily life, they set up the notion of *iṣlāḥ*, personal moral and religious renewal. This was the

41. A. al-Naṣīrī, 1954–6, Vol. 9, p. 114.
42. M. al-Mannūnī, 1973, p. 256.
43. ibid.
44. A. al-Naṣīrī, 1954–6, Vol. 9, p. 208.
45. A. Ibn Zaīdān, 1929–33, Vol. 2, p. 376.

movement called *salafism* (Muslim fundamentalism).[46] The urban man-in-the-street thought back with nostalgia to the good old days when food and goods were cheap, and when personal needs and the Makhzen's requirements were limited. For those who appeared to him clearly responsible for the current difficulties, he nourished a mixture of fear, admiration, scorn and hatred. The people's xenophobia, the *'ulamā'*'s *salafism* and the Makhzen's conservatism were expressions of their experience: the decadence of their earlier society when confronted with nineteenth-century liberal capitalism. Morocco's political and religious elite was violently anti-liberal at the time. 'There is no possible doubt whatever that liberty as the Europeans understand it is an innovation of atheistic libertines, since it denies the rights of God, parents, and even human nature itself'.[47] The positive value of the dialectic by which Moroccan society was being modernized, subjected to and at the same time reacting against European influences, was not perceived by those involved. They failed to see in it promise of a different future; they felt only the submerging of a past that time had gilded over – a past when the people were prosperous, the *'ulamā'* were heeded, the Makhzen was obeyed, and the sultan was independent.

Conclusion

In 1880 the grave five-year agricultural crisis was coming to an end. The Makhzen was paying the last instalment of the war reparations to Spain and the loan from the British banks. The Spanish inspectors, whose presence was a continual source of friction and a painful reminder of the defeat of 1860, were soon to quit Morocco's ports, and the *mūkūs* would soon be abolished.[48] The Madrid Conference, the first session of which ended on 3 July 1880 with the signature of the international convention for the protection of Morocco, seemed to be a relative victory for Britain and Morocco. France, which had not completely recovered from the defeat of 1870, had not succeeded in imposing its views, in spite of tactical support from Germany.[49] The latter country soon after entered in force on the Moroccan scene to oppose British commercial interests and thwart French political designs. Morocco's territory was protected against the machinations of the French at Tūwāt, the English at Tarfāya and the Spanish at Saḳiyyat al-Ḥamrā.[50] In short, Ḥasan I, reigning over what was sometimes called the Caliphate of the West, to distinguish it from the Ottoman empire, appeared as a great sultan, both at home and abroad.

The social contradictions born of the intensified contacts with Europe

46. See A. Merad, 1965.
47. A. al-Naṣīrī, 1954–6, Vol. 9, pp. 114–15.
48. ibid., p. 147. Town dues were abolished in December 1885. The people impatiently awaited the removal of the other taxes as well.
49. J. L. Miège, 1961–3, Vol. 3, pp. 263–92.
50. ibid., p. 357; see also A. Ibn Zaīdān, 1929–33, Vol. 2, pp. 333–5.

were at work, but at the time they seemed controllable. With the patronage of a country like Britain – or failing that, Germany – Morocco seemed to be on the path to successful regeneration. In any event, that was the belief of Moroccans in the twentieth century. Independent of its actual achievements, the reign of Ḥasan I became a new golden age. The reforms undertaken were considered adequate to give birth to a strong, modern and independent Morocco, had there not been the manoeuvres of France and Spain. The reformism of the Makhzen, the *salafism* of the *ʿulamāʾ* and the anti-Europeanism of the rural population combined to give rise to the activist ideology of twentieth-century nationalism.

There remains the task of objectively evaluating the results of this policy of reform. What must be stressed is that it took place entirely within the framework bequeathed by Muḥammad III, who himself had had to cope with an abrupt change in the power relationship between Morocco and Europe. In fact, a thorough understanding of the circumstances determining Muḥammad III's choices must be the foundation for any rational judgement of the evolution of Morocco's society in the nineteenth century.

19

New patterns of European intervention in the Maghrib

N. IVANOV

Commercial expansion and the struggle for control over the world's trade routes were among the most marked characteristics of European colonialism in the eighteenth and early nineteenth centuries. The 'Holy War' at sea, which Algeria, Tunisia, Tripolitania and Morocco had been waging for a long time, was a source of grave anxiety to European traders and shipowners. At the beginning of the nineteenth century, Europe still went in fear of the corsairs of the Maghrib. If Neapolitan sailing ships were making for the coast and caught sight of a Tunisian or Tripolitanian flag, their crews were quick to make their escape. The merchants of Marseilles, Leghorn and other major European trading ports used to take full advantage of such displays of panic to get the better of their competitors, and especially 'Tunis-ach-chattra' (Tunisia-the-crafty) which entered the broad Mediterranean arena during the Napoleonic Wars. In 1800, Tunisian ships arrived in Malta and in 1809 in Leghorn. The dey's government in Algeria did very profitable business selling wheat. The trade and shipping conditions laid down by the Maghribian states aroused intense annoyance in Europe. Algeria, Tunisia and Tripolitania levied tribute and obliged friendly countries to pay for the free passage of their ships on the basis of peace and maritime navigation treaties. Many conflicts arose on account of delayed payments and other violations of the treaties, so that relations between the Maghrib and Europe became increasingly strained.[1]

The bourgeoisie of the Mediterranean states of Europe supported the Maltese and Neapolitan pirates who cruelly harried the Muslim merchant ships. As soon as the Napoleonic Wars ended, the European bourgeoisie managed to organize massive naval expeditions against the Maghrib. Under cover of the struggle against piracy, Britain, France, the Netherlands, Austria and the USA directed their squadrons towards the North African coast. American ships were the first to appear off Algiers, in 1815. They were followed by an Anglo-Dutch squadron under the command of Lord Exmouth and Van Cappellen at the beginning of 1816. After 'sanctions' had been imposed on Tripoli and Tunis, the squadron fiercely bombarded Algiers (27 August 1816), pouring 34 000 shells into the town. In 1819, an

1. For further details see N. A. Ivanov, 1976, chs 3 and 4.

Anglo–French squadron reappeared off the North African coast, thereby forcing the regents in Tunis, Algiers and Tripoli to declare an end to piracy. In 1825, the British again bombarded Algiers. On 20 October 1827, at the battle of Navarino, the remains of the Tunisian and Algerian fleets and Egyptian and Turkish vessels were destroyed by a united Anglo–French–Russian squadron. In 1829, the Austrians set fire to the Moroccan ships which, on Mawlāy ʻAbd al-Raḥmān's orders, tried to revive the Holy War. The Maghribian countries lost the war at sea, which opened wide the gates to an intensive commercial expansion of the European states. After the destruction of the Maghribian fleet, these states secured the monopoly of the flag and, in fact, took over the Tunisian and Tripolitanian trade with Europe.

Morocco and Algeria each tried to defend its own position, which led to a subsequent deterioration of their relations with the maritime powers. The refusal on the part of the dey's government to grant special rights and privileges to the French merchants, who called for the establishment of a 'capitulation system' in Algeria and, in particular, the dey's refusal to recognize that France alone was competent to solve the monetary claims between the two countries led to the declaration of a French naval blockade of Algeria in 1827. As for Morocco, its government decided to do without the outside world and closed the country to foreigners. In 1822, there were only five Moroccan ports open to Europeans where carefully supervised trading could be conducted.

European pressure on traditional society

The growth of European trade in Tunis and Tripoli, its usurious character and the process of inflation in the economy of those countries were the prime cause of their financial difficulties.[2] In 1824, the regents in Tunis signed the first debtor's bills; those in Tripolitania – the Ḳāramānlīs – merely followed their example. Several ministers in those countries fell into debt. And so it is not surprising that towards the end of the 1820s Tunis and Tripoli began to give up all political resistance to Europe. By 1827 they were no longer refusing the foreign consuls anything and by degrees fell into line with their policy. The first one-sided treaties imposed on those countries reflected the special nature of the relations of Tunis and Tripoli with the European powers. Under the Franco–Tunisian Treaty of 8 August 1830, Tunis confirmed all previous peace, trade and shipping treaties; declared France to be the most favoured nation; gave up in advance all dues and tributes levied on European countries; accepted the principle of free trade, and extended the capitulation rights granted to foreigners. A similar treaty was signed between France and Tripolitania on 11 August 1830.

2. M. H. Chérif, 1970; E. Rossi, 1968, pp. 282ff.

All these treaties strengthened the French position in North Africa considerably. Tunisia was quickly turned into a semi-vassal of France, whose greatest rival, Britain, was seriously worried and did its best to ensure the success of the Turkish expedition to Tripolitania in 1835. In May of that year, the Turks invaded Tripoli and, after dethroning the Ḳāramānlī dynasty, proclaimed the re-establishment of Ottoman power on 1 June 1835. In 1835–6, Turkish garrisons were stationed in several coastal towns in Tripolitania and Cyrenaica. However, the Turks met with serious difficulties in their conquest of some of the inland regions. From 1835 to 1858, the Turks were desperately engaged in crushing rebellions of the indigenous population: the latter produced some remarkable leaders; among them Ghūma al-Maḥmūdī acquired the greatest renown as an uncompromising enemy of the Turks and died sword in hand in March 1858.

As the pacification proceeded, the Turks introduced reforms into the country, trying to establish administrative and legal organization along European lines. The governor, 'Uthmān Amīn Pasha (1842–7), reorganized the administration, system of justice, taxation laws, etc. in accordance with the principles of the Tanzimāt. In 1851, a mixed court of justice was established in Tripoli and this at once strengthened the position of foreigners. All that, together with reforms that undermined the foundations of traditional society, caused dismay and gave rise to protests among the indigenous population, especially the nomadic groups and peasants. 'Turks and Europeans,' Sīdī Muḥammad al-Mahdī, son of the founder of the Sanūsī order used to say, 'are people tarred with the same brush'.[3]

In Tunisia, reforms were begun in 1830 and continued by Aḥmad Bey (1837–55), an ardent admirer of Muḥammad 'Alī. The regents of Tunis, in an attempt to overcome military and technological underdevelopment, disbanded the militia composed of janissaries and laid the foundations of a regular army and an armaments industry by importing machinery and equipment from Europe.

Following the example of Egypt, government monopolies were established, leading to the nationalization of the economy. A State Bank was founded (1847) and fiduciary currency was put into circulation. In 1841, Aḥmad Bey prohibited the sale of slaves and abolished all forms of slavery in Tunisia. In 1838, a military college and a polytechnic school were established; Tunisians began to study foreign languages, to go abroad for their studies and to translate the works of European authors.

Wishing to flatter the foreign consuls, the authorities in Tunis and Tripoli encouraged the activities of the Christian missionaries. The Franciscans opened the first boys' school in Tripoli in 1816, followed by a girls' school in 1846. In 1845, Abbé Bourgade founded the Collège Saint-Louis and a few primary schools in Tunisia; he also set up an Arab printing press in Tunis. In 1826, the first performances of the Leghorn theatre took

3. E. Rossi, 1968, p. 327.

place.[4] In 1838, the first Tunisian newspaper appeared in Italian; a number of Italian immigrants settled in the country, including some in search of political asylum, as, for example, Garibaldi (in 1835 and again in 1849).

Many contacts with Europeans contributed towards the intellectual awakening of the country and provided the basis for Westernization among the ruling elite. Influenced by the military uniform, government circles in Tunis and Tripoli adopted European dress, manners and way of life. No trace remained of the old anti-European phobia. In 1845–6, the Tunisian authorities organized lavish receptions in honour of the Duc de Montpensier and the Prince de Joinville, sons of King Louis-Philippe. In November 1846, Aḥmad Bey paid a visit to France, thereby breaking away from all the age-old prejudice.

In contrast with their rulers, the people in general, who bore the full burden of building palaces, factories and barracks, were discontented with Westernization and the growth of foreign influence. They regarded their rulers as turncoats and continued to follow the traditional way of life. The attitude of the Algerian and Moroccan rulers was the same, as both these countries remained unaffected by Western influences which, at the time, were spreading throughout most of the Muslim states.

The conquest of Algeria

Algeria paid a heavy price for its government's inertia. Ḥuṣayn Dey, having done everything to embitter relations with France, did nothing to strengthen the country's defences. In the eyes of Algerian patriots, this was tantamount to treason and pointed to the corruption of the regime.[5]

Algeria was not in the least prepared for war. The enemy had been expected for the past three years, but when the French ships were sighted on 14 June 1830 in Sīdi-Farrudj Bay (Sidi-Ferruch in French accounts), it came as a complete surprise. The French managed to land an expeditionary force consisting of 37 500 men led by General de Bourmont. It was not until 19 June 1830 that the bulk of Ḥuṣayn Dey's army (composed of janissaries and *makhzen*) under Ibrāhīm Agha, reinforced by militia from Kabylia – a total of 40 000 men – attacked the French at Staoueli. This battle ended in the complete defeat of Ibrāhīm Agha, and revealed all the shortcomings of the military and technical organization of Ḥuṣayn Dey's army, which had nothing to oppose the French with save the courage of its soldiers. A second attempt to stop the enemy's advance (the battle of Sīdī Khalef of 24 June) again turned into a defeat for Ibrāhīm Agha. On 29 June the French, having gained possession of the coast of Bouzarea, began laying siege to the fort known as Sultan Calassi (le fort de l'Empereur)

4. S. Pantucek, 1969, p. 47; T. A. Pontintseva, 1977; J. M. Landau, 1958.

5. Opinions of this sort are particularly apparent in the account by M. al-Kadir, 1903; and the most characteristic extracts are given by A. Benachenbour, 1966.

that protected Algiers on the landward side. The assault was launched on 4 July. 'It was a cruel fight between military skill and desperation,' wrote Colonel Bogdanovitch, 'finally military skill prevailed: the thick walls of the castle collapsed; the canons defending it were put out of action; many a brave Turk perished under a hail of bullets and bombs; the remnants of the garrison fled towards the city; but instead of finding there the safety expected, they fell under the bullets of the artillery fired at them from the Kasbah on the dey's orders'.[6]

On 5 July 1830, Ḥuṣayn Dey signed an act of capitulation and surrendered Algiers. He was allowed – as were all the members of the Dīwān and the janissaries – to leave the country with their families and belongings. The supreme authority passed into the hands of the French military command. But the latter was entirely lacking in administrative organization, and had no clear idea of what needed to be done. It is curious to note that the Comte de Bourmont, who won his Field Marshal's baton for defeating the dey's army, ordered his engineers to prepare two projects simultaneously: the first, to widen and deepen the port of Algiers; the second, to fill it up. The Polignac Government entered into negotiations with a view to placing Algiers directly under Turkish administration.[7] After the July Revolution (1830), plans for dividing up the country were produced: to the French were assigned the city of Algiers and a number of coastal centres, while the provinces of Oran and Constantine were brought under the beys of Tunis. The total number of men in the army of occupation was reduced to 9300. However, the treaties with Tunisia, signed by General Clauzel on 18 December 1830, were not ratified by the French government and the French generals continued to act at their own risk. After arranging for some increase in the military drafts, they occupied Oran (1831), Bône (1832) and Bougie (1834).

The waverings of the French government finally ended in a decision in favour of the bourgeoisie of Marseilles and the army of occupation which, intoxicated by easy victories, had pillaged the country shamelessly and refused to give up the 'spoils of victory'. The decree of 22 July 1834 establishing a governor-generalship of French possessions in North Africa signified a refusal to evacuate Algiers, and the idea of a 'limited occupation' was officially adopted up to 1840. Its interpretation in practice depended entirely on the will and personal inclinations of the many French generals who governed the country from 1830 to 1841. In most cases they were in

6. M. N. Bogdanovitch, 1849, p. 54.

7. In 1830, after the defeat of the dey's army, the Ottoman empire insisted on the maintenance of Algeria's territorial integrity under the sultan's orders and refused to recognize the French conquest. However, after losing its army and meeting with financial disaster during the war with Russia in 1828–9, Turkey was unable to do anything except utter protests. It should be noted that in trying to make contact with the Porte over the Algerian question, the French government wished first of all to obtain Russia's consent. For materials from the French diplomatic archives, see C. R. Ageron, 1964, p. 9.

favour of a system of 'indirect government', and this was instituted by signing treaties with the indigenous chiefs (peace, recognition of vassalage, freedom to trade, payment of tribute). To establish liaison with the French commanders, 'Arab bureaux' were organized that gradually became the principal link in indirect government. Only in the coastal towns, where the French garrisons were continually establishing themselves, did a civil administrative system begin to take shape; this system was naturally a reproduction of the principles and standards of public administration in the metropolis. Little by little it acquired legal status.In 1845, the whole of Algeria was divided up into 'Arab territory' in which the *sharī'a* (Islamic legal system) and the system of indirect government prevailed, and 'civil territory' in which the French system of justice and administration was officially recognized. In particular, under a statute of 28 September 1847, 'civil territory' was made subject to the law of 1837 on communes.

The resistance in Algeria

The occupation of the coastal areas left the social structures of Algerian society unchanged. The traditional chiefs, who were very often the representatives of the old ruling class, retained, as before, control over the local authorities. Ḥuṣayn Dey's capitulation and the confusion into which the old form of administration had fallen created a political vacuum. A 'period of anarchy' (1830–4) set in when various local centres and communities no longer recognized any authority. Except for certain classes of the well-to-do urban population and a few politically minded chiefs, the country looked with hatred on the French occupation. The bulk of the population, and particularly the peasants and nomads, were determined to defend their personality and independence. However, the absence of any centralized authority or common centre made it inevitable that this struggle should be at the local level and that passive forms of resistance that were not well co-ordinated should very often predominate. To start with, resistance took the form of a refusal to recognize the occupation, faithfulness to Islam, the blockading of occupied towns and regions and attacks on French detachments and fortified posts, the assassination of certain Europeans, and summary justice meted out to traitors and renegades, often turning into a large-scale massacre.

As the struggle proceeded, two main centres of resistance were formed, one in the east, the other in the west. In the east, Aḥmad Dey, the former governor of Constantine, assumed leadership. He relied upon what was left of the janissaries and on the *makhzen* communities in eastern Algeria; he modelled his policy on that of the Porte and attempted to restore the dey system. Claiming to be the successor of Ḥuṣayn Dey, he checked the decay of the administration, consolidated the machinery of state and reinforced the army. In the early days, he represented the main threat to the French.

In the west of the country, ʿAbd al-Ḳādir, son of a *marabout* of S̲h̲ārifian origin, headed the revolt, relying politically upon Moroccan support. In his proclamations he promised to put an end to anarchy, to uphold the *s̲h̲arīʿa* and to lead a Holy War against the French. In October 1831, he was proclaimed *amīr* and installed in the residence of the beys at Mascara. On 27 November 1832, the Assembly of *ʿulamāʾ* and representatives of the Beduin groups in western Algeria recognized him as governor. Through his energy, determination and courage and his successes in the armed struggle against the French, especially the victory won at Macta on 26 June 1835, ʿAbd al-Ḳādir consolidated his authority. On two occasions, under the Desmichels Treaty (27 February 1834) and that of Tafna (30 May 1837), the French recognized him as sole governor of the whole of central and western Algeria with the exception of the coastal enclaves. As a convinced upholder of Islam, a fervent admirer of Muḥammad ʿAlī, and as a poet and thinker, ʿAbd al-Ḳādir aspired not only to regenerate Algeria but also to reform it. In the bitter struggle against the beys of Oran and Titeri (former janissaries), *kologlus* and the *makhzen* communities serving under them, and against the partisans of Aḥmad Bey and the Tijāniyya brotherhood whose stronghold was Ḳsār Ain-Mahdī (captured in 1838), ʿAbd al-Ḳādir created a unified and centralized state of Arab *s̲h̲arīf*s, which encompassed two-thirds of contemporary Algerian territory. Here he put an end to anarchy and disorder and set up a well-co-ordinated legal and administrative system on the basis of local rule by caliphs, *agha*s and *ḳāʾid*s, which ensured a rigid discipline. In 1838, he undertook the formation of a regular army which, two years later, numbered 10 000 men. Following Muḥammad ʿAlī's example, he introduced a state-administered economy, established a system of monopolies, founded arms factories and built fortresses for defending the country against subversive elements and the foreign enemy.[8]

To begin with, the Algerians met with success by taking skilful advantage of the wavering policy in Paris and the inability of the French generals to counter guerrilla tactics effectively. Up to 1837, they warded off all attempts by the French to penetrate into the beleaguered towns. Some setbacks met with in the west (the evacuation of Mascara, the loss of Tlemcen, defeat on the banks of the Sikkak in July 1836) were offset by the resounding victory of 23–24 November 1836 at Constantine, where the troops of Aḥmad Bey and the defenders of the town led by Ben Aissa utterly defeated Marshal Clauzel's corps of 7400 men. However, this victory was rendered practically useless owing to the dispersed character of the resistance. After concluding the Treaty of Tafna, the French had a free hand in the west and, after careful preparations, they undertook a decisive campaign against Aḥmad Bey in 1837. On 13 October 1837, they seized Constantine, which

8. See A. Benachenbour, 1966, p. 69ff, for a detailed analysis of state political and military structures under ʿAbd al-Ḳādir.

PLATE 19.1 *'Abd al-Ḳādir*

meant the collapse of the rampart shielding organized resistance in the east. Aḥmad Bey fled to the mountains, whence he harried the French and the puppet government set up in the east until 1843.

With the fall of Constantine, the main part of the struggle centred in the west. In answer to the provocative march-past of French troops at the 'Iron Gates' (Bibāns), 'Abd al-Ḳādir declared a *djihād* and ransacked the immediate neighbourhood of Algiers. However, he was forced to swing to

PLATE 19.2 *Infantry of 'Abd al-Ḳādir*

PLATE 19.3 *Cavalry of 'Abd al- Ḳādir*

the defensive after his defeat at Wādī al-Alleug on 31 December 1839. In 1840–1, he relinquished Mascara, Saida, Mēdēa, Taza, Boghar, Bū-Saāda, and finally Takdempt, and in 1842 set up a nomad capital known as his *smala*. His rout by the troops of the Duc d'Aumale on 15 May 1843 led to the disintegration of the whole administrative and military system which he had set up. He withdrew to Morocco with a group of followers. Flattering promises, gold offered by French agents, the part played by certain religious leaders in disseminating the *fatwā* of the '*ulamā*' in Ḳayrawān and Cairo condemning the 'absurd resistance' and the unnecessary cruelty displayed by the *amīr* himself – all these separate factors were not, however, ultimately responsible for 'Abd-al-Ḳādir's defeat: supreme importance must be ascribed to the 'scorched earth' tactics employed by Marshal Bugeaud, who ordered the fields to be burnt, the flocks and herds driven off, and the grain silos and water points seized.

'Abd al-Ḳādir's attempts to rekindle the struggle from his base in Morocco led to the Franco–Moroccan war. The Moroccan catastrophe at the battle of Isly of 14 August 1844 and the bombardment of Tangier and Mogador by the French fleet led Mawlāy 'Abd al-Raḥmān to abandon his support of 'Abd al-Ḳādir and to make peace with France. The sultan denounced 'Abd al-Ḳādir as a 'kāfir' and even started hostilities against him. In 1845, the Taibiyya brotherhood announced the arrival of the Mahdī Muḥammad ben 'Abdallah, widely known by his nickname of Bū Maza (the man with the goat), and proclaimed the *djihād*. Very quickly the revolt spread to the Dahra, then to the Ouarsenis and the Cheliff valley. Simultaneously, small mobile detachments of 'Abd al-Ḳādir's forces

PLATE 19.4 *The Franco-Moroccan war: the Battle of Isly, 1844*

appeared in the steppes, fighting side by side with their erstwhile enemies, the Dergawa *marabouts*, against the French. The crushing of this poorly organized and isolated rebellion was marked by exceptional displays of cruelty. There was, for example, the case of Colonel Pélissier, who caused hundreds of Algerians who had found shelter in caves in the mountains to be suffocated with smoke. It was not until 1847 that Bū Maza and later on ʿAbd al-Ḳādir laid down their arms and surrendered to the victors.

In 1848–9, the last pockets of resistance were wiped out in the Aurès and in the Mzāb, where Aḥmad Bey and the *marabout* Bū Ziyan were leading the struggle. In 1852, after heavy fighting, the French occupied Lag͟hwāt and in 1854 Tuggurt. In 1856, a delegation of Saharan Tuareg came to Algiers and proclaimed their loyalty to France, promising Tuareg support as far south as Timbuktu. In the northern part of the country, the hillmen of Kabylia were the last to submit. In the years following 1851, under the leadership of Bū Bag͟hla, they obstinately opposed French ambitions to penetrate into the mountains of Greater and Lesser Kabylia. It was not until 1857, after a desperate struggle against the troops of General Randon, that they ceased to resist. The entire country passed under the control of the French military command and became a conglomeration of French communes and vassal territories under the protection of the 'Arab bureaux'.

PLATE 19.5 *Surrender of ʿAbd al-Ḳādir*

Colonization and financial servitude

The threat of a general uprising prevented the French government from colonizing the inland regions of Algeria. Bugeaud's experiments in colonization, together with the expansion of immigration under the Second Republic (1848–51) and the Ministry for Algeria in Paris (1858–60), met with the uncompromising resistance of the army, which was responsible for the country's security. The policy of assimilation on the part of the Republicans who, in 1848, proclaimed Algeria to be an integral part of France and divided up the country's 'civil territory' into departments, 'arrondissements' and communes with French administrators in charge, was halted under the Second Empire. Furthermore, in 1852, Napoleon III abrogated the representation of Europeans in Algeria in the French parliament and in 1860, after his visit to Algeria, condemned for good the policy of assimilation. The 'romantic' attitude of the army officers triumphed over the 'mercantile' attitude of the colonists. Instead of siding with the colonists, Napoleon III decided to ally himself with the traditional chiefs (the 'feudal lords') and declared Algeria to be an 'Arab kingdom'. The 'civil territory' was strictly limited (10 160 sq km in 1866 or 2.5 per cent of the total territory of northern Algeria, containing 8 per cent of the Muslim population). Beyond these limits, all power remained in the hands of the military and the traditional Muslim administrative authorities, acting under the supervision of the 'Arab bureaux'. It was Napoleon III's idea that European emigrants should only settle in the town and practise trade and technical occupations. Under a Senate decree of 1863, the land was reserved for the Algerian communities, who held it in accordance with traditional principles.[9] It was only what was held to be 'surplus' land that passed to the state and could be granted to concessionaire companies or individuals. In industry and trade, unrestricted private enterprise was the rule. The monopolies current in the time of the deys and ʿAbd al-Ḳādir were completely abolished. In modernizing the administrative and legal structure inherited from ʿAbd al-Ḳādir, the authorities reorganized the Muslim system of justice (1854); this reform was backed by the setting up of mixed Franco–Muslim courts and of the Muslim high council of justice. The champions of the 'Arab kingdom' took an interest in Muslim religious observances, encouraged the building of mosques, the pilgrimage to Mecca, and so on. Under the Senate decree of 1865, Algerians had the right to join the French army and the administration. Lastly, in 1869, a draft constitution for Algeria was prepared,[10] providing for the country's autonomy and Muslim representatives in all elected assemblies.

The administrative, legal and economic reforms carried out in Tunisia and Tripolitania in the mid-nineteenth century were similar in content. In Tunisia, the liberal group led by Kh̲āyr al-Dīn Pas̲h̲a (1826–89), supported by the powers, succeeded in producing, on 9 September 1857, the *ʿAhd al-Amān* (Fundamental Pact) – a reform manifesto reproducing the main principles of the Tanzimāt. As a result of this, the monopolies were abolished and private enterprise was established (October 1851) and the municipality was reorganized (1860). On 23 April 1861, the Constitution was promulgated; it made ministers responsible to a representative assembly, the Supreme Council. In Tripolitania, in 1865, under the governorship of Maḥmūd Nedim Pas̲h̲a, a new administrative reform was introduced and commercial, civil and criminal courts were established.

9. Fierce discussions have raged around the characteristics of traditional social structures in pre-capitalist Algerian society. That among Soviet historians on the nature of pre-capitalist societies in Asia and Africa received an unexpected follow-up during discussions concerning the form of Asian production in 1962, in Paris, under the auspices of the Centre for Marxist Studies and Research. An article by A. Djeghloul (1975, 1976) has become one of the recent echoes of that discussion. During the international symposia held at Kichinev (1973) and Bucharest (1974), a more insightful conception, to my mind, of 'oriental feudalism' was put forward. Basing himself on the 'social pluristructuration' theory, R. G. Landa, 1976, pp. 49–55, 109–20, proposed his own solution to the problem. The work by M. M. Kovalevskii, edited by F. B. Miller, 1879, has lost none of its importance for the study of communal society in Kabylia. An analysis of the various forms of farming contract can be found in the work of L. Milliot, 1911. One of the latest general works, which takes stock of the various contributions on the subject based on French sources, is that of J. Ruedy, 1967.

10. See C. R. Ageron, 1964, pp. 32–8 and 1972, pp. 60ff for a criticism of certain traditional tenets appearing in French historiography.

Through these reforms, the necessary conditions for the development of private enterprise in Algeria, Tunisia and Tripolitania were created, and the abolition of customs barriers between Algeria and France (1851) opened the markets of these countries to foreign goods. It was all plain sailing for big capital, banks, concessionaires and real-estate companies. In Algeria, the Banque de l'Algérie was opened in 1851, followed by the Société coloniale de crédit agricole (1863) and other banks. In Tunisia, the first attempts by the British to found the Bank of Tunisia (1853) were countered by the French, and it was not until 1873 that the British succeeded in opening the London Bank of Tunisia. The Société franco-tunisienne de crédit was started with French capital (1879). In Tripolitania, the first banks made their appearance in 1880. Banks, concession-holders and companies were closely linked together. In Algeria, the authorities accorded them special advantages, notably in the case of the giant Compagnie génevoise (1853, 20 000 ha), the 'Société générale algérienne' (1864, 100 000 ha) and many others. In Tunisia, the British were the first to obtain a concession (Djedeida, 7000 ha) in 1856. They were followed by the French (Sīdī Ṯabet Estates, in 1886) and the Italians (Società anonima commerciale, industriale ed agricola per la Tunisia, in 1870). These began by mining lead, exporting esparto grass and experimenting with growing such crops as cotton, tobacco and potatoes. In 1857, in Algeria and in 1859 in Tunisia, the building of railways was started. The foreign companies modernized the ports, set up telegraph lines, built roads and breakwaters, and under them town planning, particularly along the coast, was begun.

The setting up of an economic infrastructure, which facilitated the 'development' of North Africa by foreign capital, was reinforced by a sort of 'cultural' infrastructure connected with the study of natural resources and the training of Europeanized personnel. In Algeria, the first Franco–Arab secondary school was opened in 1857, followed by a teacher training school in 1865. In Tunisia, in addition to the Saint-Louis secondary school the 'Sadikiya' national secondary school was established in 1875; the curricula of the 'Zitouna' were updated. At Tripoli, the first day school in which foreign languages were taught was opened in 1858. An Arab press made its appearance, such as the government papers *al-Moubachir* in Algeria (1847), *Ar-Raid at-Tunisi* in Tunisia (1860) and *Taraboulous al-Gharb* at Tripoli (1866).[11]

Whereas in Algeria the development of the country by foreign capital was begun after the occupation, in Tunisia and Tripolitania it preceded the conquest. The colonial subjection of these countries went hand in hand with the compliance and even complicity of the indigenous chiefs; their modernization, which weighed heavily on their budgets, was largely carried out through foreign loans. They were made to accept extremely harsh

11. For the first newspaper in Arabic in North Africa, see F. di Tarazi, 1913 and C. Sourian-Hoeberechts, 1969.

terms and were systematically robbed by the local officials and European contractors. Moreover, these loans led to an extravagant increase in foreign debts. When, in 1869, Tunisia's foreign debt rose to twelve times the amount of its national revenue, the government declared itself bankrupt and approved the setting up of an international financial commission, which took over control of the state finances. Although the country retained the trappings of independence, it was, in fact, turned into a semi-colony of the Euopean powers.

Morocco, which managed to resist foreign pressure longer than the other North African countries, finally submitted to the same fate. The Anglo–Moroccan treaty of 1856 'opened' the country to foreign capital. The Hispano–Moroccan War[12] of 1859–60 ended with the onerous Treaty of Tetuān (26 April 1860) by which Spain enlarged her enclaves, obtained a huge indemnity and, most important of all, managed to extend the capitulation rights and privileges of her nationals. Similar treaties paving the way for the country's colonial subjection were concluded with France (on 19 August 1863) and other European states.

The 'discovery' of Tunisia, Tripolitania and Morocco, and the conquest of Algeria, were accompanied by the settlement in those countries of a large number of foreigners (Europeans and Levantines), who acted as the agents of big capital. They represented foreign firms, went in for trade (not being averse to indulging in contraband, usury and various kinds of corrupt practices), and bought houses, gardens and real estate. By 1856 they enjoyed extraterritorial rights in Tunisia, at Tripoli and in Morocco and were subject only to the consuls of their respective countries.[13]

The European colonists in Algeria were in a still more privileged position. Throughout the civil territory, they had their own administrative and legal system and formed a closed society hostile to the indigenous population. By 1856 the birth rate exceeded the death rate. 'These signs,' writes C. R. Ageron, 'made it clear that a colony of settlers had been founded'.[14] The intrigues of the immigrants kept pace with the increase in their numbers: they decided they must put an end to the 'military regime', 'retrieve' the land that had been 'relinquished' by the Senate decree of 1863, establish the system of private ownership of land everywhere and generalize the civil administration system.

12. E. Szymanski, 1965, pp. 54–64. For the distressing financial consequences of the war see G. Ayache, 1958.

13. An excellent selection of materials concerning the privileges of Europeans in Morocco is found in J. L. Miège, 1961–3, Vols. 1–4.

14. C. R. Ageron, 1964, p. 28.

The reaction of traditional society

The ambitions of the colonists and omnipotence of the foreign tycoons, the very fact of the immigrants' increasing penetration in every sphere of national life aggravated the indigenous population of North Africa. Liberals[15] like Khāyr al-Dīn, Ḥuṣayn, Kabadu, and Muḥammad Bayram in Tunisia and Koussantini in Algeria, who suffered at the sight of their countries' misfortunes and at the same time understood the need for reforms, were alone and cut off from the people. Napoleon III's 'civilizing policy' in Algeria, and the reforms in Tunisia and Tripolitania, met with incomprehension from the majority of the population, if not open hostility. It interpreted them as yet another stage in colonial subjection, like having to renounce the *sharīʿa* and Muslim personal identity. These reforms aroused particular animosity among the *marabouts* and the rural population. The peasants and nomads regarded the Europeanized Muslims as turncoats and refused to place any confidence in them. The folklore poetry[16] shows that the common run of Muslims were heartbroken at the collapse of the patriarchal past, felt themselves to be strangers in the 'century of dishonour', 'without faith or law', and turned away from those who, according to the poet Mohand-ou-Mhand (1845–1906), had once been lions and were now under the yoke.

At the beginning of the 1860s, the bitter struggle against the foreigner was widely supported among the people in nearly every Muslim country. Active propaganda for a pan-Muslim *djihād* was started. It was precisely at this time that the power of the Sanūsiyya brotherhood, which revered the assassination of Europeans as an act of the highest devotion, began to be felt. It is not surprising that under these circumstances all difficulties and even chance incidents were used as pretexts for displays of mass action. The relatively limited rebellions in the Aurès (1859) and the Hodna (1860) and the disturbances in Tunis (1862) were the forerunners of the major national uprisings of the 1860s and early 1870s. They spread quickly and confusedly like some uncontrolled outburst of the people's wrath. Barbarous looting, assassinations, the seemingly absurd destruction of telegraph poles, post offices and of anything European testified to the tremendous force of the hidden desire for vengeance. As a rule these insurrections were not strictly organized. There were sometimes nominal leaders who were not in complete control of the situation. It was only the participation of the religious brotherhoods that united them in a Holy War for the triumph of the Faith.

The first rebellion of this kind broke out in Tunisia; it started in March

15. A. Hourani, 1962, gives the characteristics and peculiarities of Arab liberal thought in the nineteenth century.

16. For interesting material reflecting the struggle of the Algerian people in their poetry, see A. Memmi, 1963.

1864 and spread throughout the country. Its leader was 'Alī ben Guedahem (the 'People's Bey') and it was ideologically motivated by the Tijāniyya brotherhood. It was only the isolation of rebels, who, according to J. Ganiage, 'could not make up their minds to win'[17] that enabled the bey's government to save the capital, destroy the '*shartiyas*' (communes, elected rebellious bodies dealing with local affairs), and in April 1865 to stamp out the last pockets of resistance.

The rebellion of the Ouled Sīdī Shaykh, linked with the religious Dergawa brotherhood, was of a similar nature. It broke out in April 1864, spread over vast areas of the High Plateaux and towards autumn reached the region of Oran, the Dahra and other localities in western Algeria. Only after bringing reinforcements from overseas were the French able, in 1865, to crush the detachments of rebels led by the legendary Si Sliman.

The promulgation of the civil regime of 9 March 1870 and the fall of the Second Empire were the signal for the most widespread rebellion in eastern Algeria. In the autumn of 1870 the first '*shartiyas*' were organized, but it was not until January 1871 that the initial battles took place. The rebellion spread to most of the region of Constantine, Greater Kabylia and a few places in the west. On 8 April 1871 Shaykh al-Ḥaddād, chief of the Raḥmāniyya brotherhood, declared the *djihād*. The *bachagha* Al-Maḳrani became the military leader of the revolt and, after his death, his brother Bū-Mezrag took his place. It was not until January 1872 that the French seized the rebel's bases and became masters of the situation.

The stamping out of these insurrections was accompanied by wholesale repression, followed by fines, confiscations of land and disarmament of the communities. The European colonists, far from making common cause with the insurgents, in many cases took part in the armed struggle against the Muslims. It should be noted that the immigrants, who were fighting for democratic and socialist revolutionary ideals – which they did in brilliant fashion during the Algiers Commune of 1870–1 – were at the same time opposed to the national aspirations of the North African Muslims.

Towards an imperialist policy

The crushing of the uprisings of the 1860s and early 1870s opened the way to an unrestricted colonization of North Africa. Moreover, the changes taking place in Europe, and in particular the dominant role played by capitalist enterprise, fostered colonial expansion. By degrees it took on the character of a purely imperialistic struggle for dividing up the world, and for the monopoly of sources of raw materials and other natural resources.

The 'golden age' of colonization started in Algeria.[18] On 24 October 1870, the military governor-general was replaced by a 'civil governor of

17. J. Ganiage, 1959, p. 251.
18. See C. R. Ageron, 1968, Vol. 1.

the three departments of Algeria'. Within a few years the European colonists had turned into a privileged dominant social class of 'citizens' – a 'white minority' – enjoying all civil and political rights. The indigenous population, referred to as 'subjects', was deprived of rights and governed by rules based on the so-called 'native code' (decrees of 1874), instituting the 'regime for the native population', which lasted until 1936. New landed property laws (the Ollivier decree of 1870 and, more particularly, the statute of 26 July 1873) established the principle of private property and the free transfer of land to the colonists. French capital investment increased considerably and trade and other economic ties with the metropolis expanded.

Towards the end of the nineteenth century a similar situation obtained in Tunisia. The destinies of the country were decided at the Congress of Berlin in 1878 where, after considerable diplomatic skirmishing, Bismarck 'returned' it to France.[19] Attempts by Khāyr al-Dīn, the prime minister (1873–7), to 'cover' Tunisia's independence with the fiction of Ottoman sovereignty were unsuccessful. On 24 April 1881 French troops crossed the frontier; on 12 May, under threat of deposition, the bey was forced to sign the Treaty of Bardo, and on 8 June 1883, after all resistance had been crushed, he also signed the Convention of Al-Marsa which provided the legal basis of the colonial regime for the Protectorate.

Tripolitania and Morocco succeeded in postponing a European occupation. The chief claimant as regards Tripoli was Italy, which had been watching the struggle for Tunisia anxiously in the years preceding 1881, but it was only at the beginning of the 1880s that it began pressing its claims.[20] In 1884–5, the Italian High Command prepared plans for war. However, owing to a lack of agreement among the imperialist powers, their execution had to be postponed.[21] For the same reason, Morocco was able to avoid foreign occupation until the end of the nineteenth century. However, its attempts to curtail the privileges and high-handedness of foreigners suffered a setback. At a conference of the European powers and the USA, held in Madrid in 1880, Moroccan sovereignty was once again subjected to restrictions and it was announced that no changes could be made in the administration of the country without the prior consent of the powers that attended the conference.

In the Muslim world, the carving up and occupation of the greater part of North Africa were regarded as a fresh outrage against Islam. The struggle of the North African fighters for the Faith met with support (in most cases

19. See J. Ganiage, 1959, pp. 701–58 for various aspects of the Great Powers' struggle for Tunisia.

20. E. de Leone, 1960, pp. 301ff. The general atmosphere of Italian activity is described in the notes of the Russian traveller, A. V. Elisseev, who visited Tripolitania in 1894. See A. V. Elisseev, 1896, p. 79.

21. For the main features of the diplomatic struggle that preceded the conquest of Libya, see V. L. Loutskii, 1965, pp. 269–72 and the English translation, V. Lutsky, 1969.

moral support only) in Istanbul and in other countries of the East.[22] Relying on this support, new attempts were made in Algeria and Tunisia to arrest colonization by force of arms: these were the uprisings led by Bū Amāma in Algeria, in 1881, and by ʿAlī bin Khalīfa in Tunisia in 1881–3. Despite the tenacity and heroism displayed by the rebels, these uprisings failed to attain their objective. In point of fact, they had already become rearguard actions, the last-ditch attempts of a traditional society to defend the avenues of its idiosyncratic development on the basis of ancient moral and social structures, already undermined during the foreign conquest and the development of colonial capitalism.

22. For data on this question, see A. Martel, 1965, pp. 228ff. For the relations between the Porte and the Sanūsiyya, see N. A. Ziadeh, 1958, pp. 61ff. And for the attempts by ʿAbd al-Ḥamīd II to co-ordinate and direct the anti-foreigner demonstrations in the Arab countries, especially in Egypt, see H. Adali, 1968, pp. 54ff.

20 The Sahara in the nineteenth century

S. BAIER

The reconstruction of Saharan history should take account of events at two levels, first the ebb and flow in the lives of Saharan nomads and inhabitants of oases – seasonal migration to and from pasture, the formation of new alliances and the break-up of others, the rise and fall of leaders, the story of raid and counter-raid, the epics of gallant warriors and noblewomen, and the life and times of merchants, holy men, and scholars.[1] Superimposed upon these local histories is the second level, with its larger patterns of historical change. In the nineteenth century the Sahara, remote though it was, came into increasingly close contact with the world economy. By the close of the century European economic penetration had affected the lives of many people, and the European conquest of the desert, though far from complete, had produced fundamental change in the nature of relationships between the Sahara and the outside world.

The paucity of data for history at either level presents both problems and challenges and points to the need for research in Ottoman, French, Italian, Egyptian, and Moroccan archives and in private collections. By the nineteenth century European interest in the desert increased because European powers viewed it as a commercial avenue to the Sudan, and European sources provide data that give some notion of historical processes. All written accounts, whether in European languages, Turkish, or Arabic, need to be filled out with oral histories, which have been collected only in a piecemeal fashion. For example, the Tuareg of the central Sahara have been well researched, but for other groups very little historical material exists. In some Saharan societies the lack of depth in genealogies and the absence of local Arabic historical writings present the historian with problems that may never be solved.

This chapter will survey the history of the Sahara in the nineteenth century by focusing on the camel nomads, the inhabitants of the desert who lived from their herds. In good times wealth in camels conferred awesome military power on their owners by giving them the ability to mount lightning raids on oasis dwellers and sedentary agriculturalists, and

1. The author would like to thank Charles Stewart for reading a draft of this chapter and making a number of helpful suggestions for revision.

then to escape into the wilderness with impunity. This military advantage allowed them to raid for slaves, as they often did along the southern shore of the desert, the Sahel; or to dominate sedentary agriculturalists living in oases or in the Sahel by demanding tribute in return for protection. Although nomads could enslave, destroy date palms or standing crops, steal grain stores, and disrupt trade, more often their goal was to control and appropriate the production of agriculturalists, not to annihilate them. The nomads are therefore the proper focus for much social and economic history, as well as key actors in political, military, and religious change.

Society and environment

Pastoral nomadism is of course a complete and perfect adaptation to the arid environment of the desert. But within the deceptively simple framework implied by the word desert, as defined by low rainfall, there exists a rich variety of climate and landform that has shaped the societies of the Sahara.

At the risk of simplification it may be said that the desert is subject to two rainfall regimes, with the southern desert receiving precipitation in the summer and the northern desert in the winter, and some overlap of the two along the Atlantic coast. Little rain falls, and even that is extremely unevenly distributed in time and space, so that in the most arid parts of the desert some locations may not have had rain for ten years or more. The desert is driest in the central portions and especially in the eastern central desert, in present-day Egypt and eastern Libya. Three 'bridges' of higher than average rainfall traverse the central, dry portions of the desert from north to south, the first joining Senegal to Morocco slightly inland from the drier Atlantic coast, the second connecting the Niger bend to Algeria, and the third following the high ground bordering on the Red Sea. Not surprisingly, population is concentrated in relatively well-watered portions of the desert, and caravaneers have usually avoided the most arid regions of Egypt and Libya. Precipitation increases with altitude up to a certain height, and the landform of the Sahara has as many nuances as does its climate. After rains, formerly dry river beds or *wādīs* may flow for hundreds of kilometres, and for great distances just under the surface of the sand. In some cases irrigated agriculture is possible because of the high water table. In areas of dunes called *ergs* the sand itself holds great quantities of moisture; dunes absorb almost all rainfall and give off very little water to underground aquifers. In addition, the sand loses moisture to the atmosphere very slowly, since drifting exposes only the windward surface of the dunes.[2]

Herders and their animals can live in the desert only if they move from place to place to take advantage of scattered and short-lived pasture. But in the desert fringes a variety of human adaptations to the environment

2. J. Dubief, 1973, pp. 125–30.

are possible, including various degrees of dependence on agriculture and various mixes of animals in the herds. In the Sahel, cattle nomads lived in symbiotic relationships with sedentary agriculturalists, and some camel nomads divided the labour of their families between herding and farming. Others sacrificed crop yields to the needs of the herds by sowing crops, leaving with the herds to search for pasture, and returning to harvest the meagre returns of the fields. In the central, dry parts of the desert, nomadic pastoralists kept several kinds of animals, but they relied heavily on the camel because of its adaptation to aridity. Camels needed various kinds of pasture to do well and therefore had to be taken periodically from *ergs* to rocky ground (*regs*). This necessity, as well as the search for pasture, determined the amplitude of movements of camel nomads.[3] Those whose territory included adjacent areas of rocky and sandy ground, such as the Chaamba, migrated shorter distances than those without both kinds of terrain, such as the Regibat, despite other similarities in their respective territories.

The arid environment has encouraged the evolution of similar uncentralized political systems among most nomadic people, systems that balance the need for dispersal in the search for pasture with the necessity of unified action in the face of an outside threat. These societies, which have been described in the anthropological literature as segmentary lineage systems, place each person in a series of widening and overlapping descent groups that are larger the more distant an ancestor is chosen as a point of reference.[4] Genealogy can be used to divide a society into x number of maximal segments, each of which is in turn divided into y number of segments and z number of clans, on down through intermediate levels to the extended family. Societies organized according to descent may resolve internal conflict without recourse to central authority if the power of segments at an appropriate level in the genealogical structure is in balance, and the history of these societies often exhibits this mechanism in operation. But history also demonstrates that segments may unite to face an outside threat, and that military exigency may even give rise to something resembling central authority. Sedentary or semi-sedentary people have often assimilated non-kin who migrated to their territory, and in these societies residence in the same territory may replace kinship as a principle of association. Even societies that are organized according to descent may have leaders or councils at various levels in the segmentary structure or distributed throughout it; wealthy men may attract followers who are not kin; or alliances may contradict or partially offset the notion of kinship as a determinant of allegiance.

Another similarity among Saharan people was hierarchical social struc-

3. A. Cauneille, 1968, pp. 108–9.
4. D. M. Hart, 1967; E. Gellner, 1973, pp. 18–19; 1969, pp. 35–69; E. E. Evans-Pritchard, 1949, pp. 29–61.

ture, a consequence of the power of warriors to concentrate wealth so as to reinforce their own position of dominance. A common pattern was that lineages of aristocratic warriors controlled groups of free but politically subordinate people, the descendants of conquered nomads. People of lower status, slaves or the descendants of slaves, worked as servants, herders, artisans, trade specialists, or farmers.

Changing relations with the outside world

Desert nomads lived in a world of their own, but they were not immune from influences from the outside. For one thing they were so specialized in animal husbandry that to obtain grain and other items they depended not only on plunder and tribute, but also on peaceful trade with sedentary states. Another factor was that their military advantage of mobility did not extend far beyond the desert fringe. More fertile regions supported larger populations, and these thickly settled areas could muster enough defenders to offset the advantage that the less numerous nomads enjoyed in their own realm.

At the beginning of the nineteenth century the style of interaction between nomads and sedentary states differed greatly at the northern and southern edges of the desert. In West and Central Africa a principal for sedentary rulers was to keep the nomads at a safe distance, a problem mitigated somewhat in North Africa by geographical barriers such as the Atlas and other mountain ranges. South of the desert the best strategy was to involve nomads in the economy of the fertile areas by giving them a stake in desert-edge commerce, urban growth, and agriculture, and by using nomadic contingents in armies fighting other sedentary states. It was also prudent, as in China, to use one group of nomads as 'hired guns' to keep others at bay. The same principles applied north of the desert, but in the nineteenth century the Ottoman regencies and the sultanate of Morocco showed considerable skill in maintaining balances of power among nomads and sparing themselves direct confrontations.[5] A principal difference was their wealth relative to sub-Saharan states, which facilitated ruling through favoured groups and allowed North African rulers to support small but well-armed forces which might intervene from time to time in the affairs of nomads. In addition, Maghribi authorities enjoyed prestige as the spiritual as well as temporal rulers of Muslim states, or their representatives, a status that enabled skilful or revered sultans or governors to use diplomacy to maximize the effect of their small armed contingents.

The advance of the Ottomans in Cyrenaica and Tripolitania and the French in Algeria marked a turning point in relationships between Saharan societies and outsiders. The French and Ottoman advances southward into the desert had similar timing in the early stages and derived from analogous

5. E. Gellner, 1978.

strategic considerations, namely the desire to control and tax trans-Saharan trade and to prevent other powers from annexing the hinterland of footholds near the Mediterranean. Despite the similar speed of the advance, the style of the two powers differed greatly.[6] Since Ottoman governors had fewer means at their disposal than the French, their relations with nomads in the hinterland of their domains in Tripolitania and Cyrenaica were far more discreet. Their knowledge of the structure of local politics enabled them to exploit the changing pattern of feuds, warfare between groups, and alliances. They drew upon a long experience of governing segmentary societies and carrying on diplomatic relations with those they could not govern, and they were also accorded legitimacy and status as representatives of the political centre of the Muslim world.

In 1835, the Ottomans took direct control of Tripolitania and Cyrenaica from the semi-autonomous Ḳāramānlī dynasty in an effort to block the inroads of French influence from Egypt. A series of incidents in Ottoman efforts to extend their control of the desert in Tripolitania and Cyrenaica illustrate the character of their government. In theory a *kaimakam* resided in Djalo, and it was his duty to oversee efforts to collect taxes levied on the date palms of Djalo and Awdjīla and to maintain order in the surrounding desert. But by 1869 the *kaimakam* spent most of the time in Benghazi, and so a tax collector, who visited the oasis once a year, was the only regular Ottoman representative in the interior. In return for the tax they paid, oasis dwellers of Awdjīla asked for protection from the nomadic Zuwaya, who were interfering with the flow of trans-Saharan trade and attempting to extend control over the oasis. J. P. Mason recorded an oral tradition telling of the visit of an Ottoman official to Awdjīla to make peace with the Zuwaya, whom the Ottomans had apparently been fighting. In 1856, the *kaimakam* of Benghazi ruled through the shaykh of the Bara'asa, a Beduin group, which he supported with fifty armed soldiers.[7] The influence of the Ottoman government never reached very far into the Cyrenaican desert, and by the later decades of the century the Sanūsiyya, a *ṣūfī ṭarīḳa* (brotherhood) founded in the 1840s, had become the effective government in the interior.[8]

Even the limited ability of the Ottomans to tax date production or interfere in the affairs of nomads met with resistance. The Ottoman governor, 'Alī Askar who arrived in Tripoli in 1838, encountered three resistance leaders in the Tripolitanian hinterland, and the experience of one of these leaders, 'Abd al-Djalīl of the Awlād Sulaymān, a nomadic group of the Fezzān and the Syrte, is instructive. The Pasha first negotiated

6. A. Martel, 1965, Vol. 1, pp. 101–32. For the role of the British in blocking French advances towards Ghadāmes, see A. A. Boahen, 1964, pp. 132–212.

7. For a general history of Tripolitania, see L. C. Féraud, 1927. For Awdjīla history, see J. P. Mason, 1971, pp. 200–6; 1976.

8. D. D. Cordell, 1977a; and E. E. Evans-Pritchard, 1949, *passim.*

with ʿAbd al-Dj̱alīl, recognizing him as the legitimate ruler of his domains in return for a promise not to disrupt trade between Tripoli and the interior. But ʿAbd al-Dj̱alīl proved too powerful for Ottoman purposes when he initiated contacts with commercial interests in Tunisia and Egypt, demonstrating that he had at least the potential to threaten the prosperity of Tripoli. ʿAlī Askar used diplomatic contacts to discredit ʿAbd al-Dj̱alīl in the eyes of his allies, who recognized the threat posed by a concentration of power. On three critical occasions when ʿAbd al-Dj̱alīl faced Ottoman forces on the battlefield in 1840 and 1841, he was deserted and turned upon by former allies. In the final fight, ʿAbd al-Dj̱alīl was killed and his forces nearly wiped out, but the defeated Awlād Sulaymān fled south along the caravan route from the Fezzān to Borno. Previously ʿAbd al-Dj̱alīl had formed marriage alliances with important families in Borno as part of a strategy of building a commercial empire that would have included contacts in the Sudanese kingdom. Capitalizing on these alliances, surviving Awlād Sulaymān took up positions on the nomadic frontier of Borno, where they were of use to the Borno ruler to block the depredations of the Tuareg. But in 1850 the Awlād Sulaymān were soundly defeated by these nomadic foes. Twice in a decade they had nearly been annihilated, but they survived to become the scourge of trade and of neighbouring nomads and agricultural people. They augmented their numbers by assimilating slaves taken in raids and by calling on their former *soff* allies from the Syrte and the Fezzān.[9]

The experience of the Awlād Sulaymān demonstrates that even the limited military resources of the Ottoman pas̱ha of Tripoli could produce disruption among nomads, and it shows that the ability of the Ottomans to manipulate segmentary politics and to shift *soff* alliances was an important skill. The French, on the other hand, had no so such advantage and relied almost entirely on the force of arms. The first obstacle to the expansion of the French in Algeria was the state formed by ʿAbd al-Ḳādir, but after defeating him in 1847 they turned their attention towards the desert, and in the 1850s under General Randon they took an interest in re-establishing commercial relations between Algeria and the Western Sudan. To provide security for the trade they hoped to promote, they established outposts at Géryville and Lag̱hwāt in 1852, Wargla in 1853, and Tuggurt in 1854. In the west, military expansion south of Géryville halted with the revolt of the Awlād Sīdī S̱hayḵh, which lasted intermittently for nearly twenty years, and suffered other temporary setbacks with the Franco-Prussian war of 1870 and a serious uprising in the Kabylia Mountains in 1871. Renewed

9. For a general account of resistance in the Tripolitanian hinterland, see A. Martel, 1965, pp. 103–6; for a detailed history of the Awlād Sulaymān, on which the above account is based, see D. D. Cordell, 1972, pp. 11–45. In this instance *soff* refers to a pact between the Awlād Sulaymān and another Beduin group; but *soff* alliances, like *leff* alliances in Morocco, might also unite groups within a *ḳabīla* and in some cases partially replace or contradict relations of descent.

interest in trans-Saharan commerce and ill-considered plans for a trans-Saharan railway spurred further penetration into the desert in the 1870s. The southern portion of the Algerian desert remained beyond French control, and the advance south of Wargla was halted when Ahaggar Tuareg massacred the second Flatters expedition in 1881, demonstrating that the occupation of Tuareg country could prove costly indeed. After 1890, the French had the approval of the British for further Saharan conquest, and the final phase began in 1899 with the occupation of In Ṣalāḥ. The last serious resistance was put down in 1902 with the defeat of the Ahaggar. In these final operations the French turned to the new expedient of recruiting nomadic people en masse into their service as irregulars, and this allowed them to combine the mobility and local knowledge of nomads with the vastly superior firepower of the French army. In the defeat of the Ahaggar in 1902 the French took advantage of long-standing animosity between Chaamba and Tuareg; in the final battle a single French officer led a force composed entirely of well-trained and heavily-armed Chaamba mounted on their best camels.[10]

Unlike the French, the Moroccan central government, despite economic reforms in the second half of the nineteenth century, did not have the means to finance an army capable of extending effective occupation beyond the Atlas mountains to the pre-Saharan fringe. Nor could the Moroccans stand up to the French army, which exerted pressure on the frontier with Algeria and sometimes pursued dissident groups into Moroccan territory. The pre-Saharan fringe of Morocco belonged to the *bilād al-sibā*, or land of dissidence, but this translation obscures long-standing and important economic, religious and social ties between *sibā* and Makhzen, the territory where the sultan could collect taxes and exert his authority. Morocco enjoyed the informal protection of the British, who controlled the lion's share of Moroccan import-export trade, and British interest in Morocco helped to postpone the French takeover. In efforts to protect their territory beyond the Atlas, Moroccan sultans took care to throw into relief existing political and diplomatic ties with the south-east. Even if Moroccan sultans could not tax or control nomadic groups beyond the Atlas, they could enter into local politics by throwing their weight behind one faction or another, by mediating disputes, or by capitalizing on their prestige as religious leaders. The religious influence of the Moroccan sultan extended as far as the Niger bend; the Kunta *shaykh* Aḥmad al-Bekkai, leader of the Ḳādirīyya in the Sudan, recognized Mawlāy ʿAbd al-Raḥmān as *imām* of all Muslims and carried on diplomatic correspondence with the Moroccan crown.[11]

10. A. Bernard, 1906, pp. 16–110. For the Moroccan–Algerian border region, see R. E. Dunn, 1977, pp. 137–75. For the conquest of the Tuareg, see J. Keenan, 1977, pp. 72–85.

11. R.E. Dunn, 1972, pp. 106–7; 1977, pp. 31–9, 137–75; E. Burke III, 1972, pp. 176–8; 1976, pp. 1–40; J.M. Abun-Nasr, 1975, pp. 284–303. On the Kunta, see A. Zebadia, 1974; A. A. Batran, 1974.

The real significance of the French occupation of the Algerian desert was that it was a phenomenon of an entirely new order. It was far more permanent than the occasional expeditions of the Moroccan sultan into the desert, journeys whose main purpose was to make and renew acquaintances with important local people. It also contrasted sharply with the infrequent visits of Ottoman officials to the oases of Cyrenaica and with the Ottoman policy of leaving the nomads to themselves except for occasional attempts to tip the balance in disputes between groups. For the first time, nomads had to contend with an army of occupation that was armed with modern weapons and staffed with local guides and irregulars who knew the desert. The French army administered nomads through the *Bureaux arabes*, an elite group of officers, some of whom spoke Arabic. These officers gathered intelligence on Muslim leaders and brotherhoods, dispensed justice, and ruled their charges through appointed chiefs. While it would not be advisable to overstate the degree of control that the French actually had in the early years in the desert, it is necessary to point out that the French occupation was far more complete than sedentary states on the periphery of the Sahara had ever even attempted. It was also very expensive, especially in relation to the ability of marginal land in the desert and desert fringe to produce a surplus. Historians have explored the impoverishment of the Muslim population as a result of losses of land and livestock, and the revolts that were caused by the French policy of *cantonnement*. It would, however, be instructive to assess to what extent Saharan people, as opposed to Algerians in general, had to pay for the occupation of the desert, but this will have to await further research.[12]

While it is not possible to give a full account of resistance to the French in the Algerian Sahara, a history of this resistance would benefit from the framework worked out by Ross Dunn for responses to the French in the pre-Saharan fringe of Morocco. This conceptual framework draws attention to the uncertain nature of alliance groups in nomadic societies, and the extreme unpredictability of the French invasion. The French could destroy standing crops, palm plantations, irrigation works, and livestock. On the other hand, they established conditions for permanent peace on their terms, a peace which might nonetheless promote expanded trade. Above all, according to Dunn, the arrival of the French created a new degree of uncertainty in the life of nomads and oasis dwellers:

> In short, their coming added to the extreme caprices of nature a whole new set of economic uncertainties. Consequently, every tribe and *qsar*, indeed every group, large or small, with shared interests in resources, was obliged to weigh its response to the French army against the effects, for better or worse, on its economic well-being. The crisis produced not an adjournment, but an intensification of the struggle

12. C.-R. Ageron, 1968, Vol. I, pp. 3–56, 239–65, 367–93; Vol. II, pp. 737–858; A. Bernard and N. Lacroix, 1906, pp. 122–6.

> to outwit the environment, as cooperating groups and individuals sought simultaneously to protect their vital resources and to avoid unconditional submission to the advancing army.[13]

Dunn observes that the ideology of kinship could form a basis for military unity in the face of an ephemeral outside threat. But it was of little value 'in circumstances where survival depended essentially upon the ability of groups with shared resources to reconcile their politics to their economic interests through a fragmented, contradictory process of attack, compromise, and evasion'.[14] Although this conclusion is intended for the Dawi Mani, it might well apply to the history of many other Saharan societies.

Unity in resistance was of course possible despite the uncertainties of the environment and the fission inherent in nomadic society, and religion provided the framework for most large-scale movements. In the normal course of desert life *ṣūfī ṭarīḳa*, with their *zāwiya*s or centres of learning, which drew followers and attracted students, performed valuable political services by dispensing justice and mediating disputes between factions, segments, or whole peoples. The need for education and the arbitration of disputes won respect for *ṣūfī* saints and leaders and earned them reputations as scholars, mystics, and jurists. In a crisis it was natural that the orders and their respected leaders would be thrust into political and military roles. Before the French conquest the Darḳāwiyya channelled opposition to Ottoman rule among the Kabyles and south of Oran. Similarly, resistance to the French coalesced around religious leaders and their orders, as for example the movement led by ʿAbd al-Ḳādir, the revolt of Awlād Sīdī S̲h̲ayk̲h̲, and resistance organized by the Sanūsiyya in Libya, Chad, and Niger after 1900.[15]

In another case unusual economic circumstances resulting from the French push into the desert in the 1850s and 1860s helped bring about unified action among the Ahaggar Tuareg. Cut off from northern markets, Ahaggar transformed the basis of their economy. Because of relative stability under the leadership of the *amenukal* al-Hadjdj Aḥmed (1830–77), it was possible to extend cultivation in Ahaggar with the labour of servile agriculturalists. The attack on the Flatters mission in 1881 occurred during a severe drought in 1880–3. Later, as the French occupied the oases of the central Sahara, Ahaggar responded by using pastures in what is today north-western Niger and by caravan trade with the southern desert fringe. They took salt from the *sebkhra* or salt plain at Amadror, along with dates and small quantities of imported British cotton goods, to Damergu, at the northernmost limit of sedentary agriculture on the Tripoli–Kano route

13. R. E. Dunn, 1977, p. 225.
14. ibid.
15. C.-R. Ageron, 1968, Vol. 1, pp. 62–6; J. A. Abun-Nasr, 1975, pp. 240–6; B. G. Martin, 1976, pp. 36–67.

north of Zinder. The unity of the Ahaggar confederation, which facilitated these economic adjustments, was without doubt the product of conflict with neighbours. In the 1870s, the Ahaggar had mounted a serious challenge to the Ajjer Tuareg to their east and north, which was growing rich with the boom conditions in Tripoli–Kano trade during that decade, and they faced hostile Tuareg groups in other directions, such as the Oulliminden to the south-west and certain Aïr Tuareg to the south-east.[16]

A full account of resistance would also call attention to the mobility of camel nomads and their ability to migrate with their herds from one end of the Sahara to the other as long as they were willing to take up a life fraught with danger and uncertainty. A case in point is the fifty years' odyssey of the Djeramna, who first ran afoul of the French in 1881 near Géryville during the revolt of the Awlād Sīdī Shaykh, an uprising sparked by land shortage, news of the massacre of the Flatters expedition, and the departure of French troops to help in the Tunisian campaign. When Bū Amāma, the leader of the uprising, was deserted by his partisans, the Djeramna left to join the Ahaggar Tuareg. In 1889, they took part in a raid led by the Chaamba on the Tripoli–Kano road south of Ghadāmes; somewhat later they were reported to have taken part in a raid in the Fezzān and another in southern Tunisia. With the collapse of Tuareg resistance they retreated to the Tripolitanian highlands bordering on southern Tunisia and Algeria and their raids became an issue in territorial rivalry between the French and the Turks. In 1925, they finally returned to surrender at Géryville nearly fifty years after having left on their wanderings.[17]

Desert trade and the nomads

Changes in European military technology accelerated in the latter half of the nineteenth century, with the result that European forces, armed with the latest weapons, faced opponents with outdated arms. Technological change did not only permit the conquest of the desert; it also transformed the economic life of the Sahara, as the manufacture of cheap products permitted a new phase of European penetration. Trade with Europe had existed before, but the nineteenth century witnessed a massive increase in the scale of this trade with varying effects depending on the structure of Saharan regional economies. For example, the cotton goods industry of Morocco, which had trans-Atlas outlets, succumbed after 1860 to the competition of Manchester cotton goods, while the woollen textile industry of southern Tunisia fared much better and continued to feed products into trans-Saharan networks.[18] On the fringe of the Sahara various groups

16. J. Keenan, 1977, pp. 63–85, 139–40; 1972, pp. 345–56; J. Dubief, 1947, pp. 15–16; G. Gardel, 1961, pp. 126, 144–56.

17. P. Boyer, 1971.

18. K. Brown, 1976, p. 9; A. Martel, 1965, Vol. 1, p. 125.

involved themselves in exports of primary products. For example north of the Senegal basin increased exports of gum arabic allowed a *zāwīya* lineage, whose members specialized in Islamic scholarship and the mediation of disputes and organized trading caravans to *escales* on the Senegal river to gain in power and influence.[19] In the area north of the Sokoto caliphate the rise of exports of ostrich feathers and tanned goat skins in the last thirty years of the century forced nomadic ruling classes to adjust to the new-found ability of peasants and servile agriculturalists to earn income from collecting and selling these products.[20] European economic penetration also affected the tastes of consumers, so that the custom of drinking heavily sugared tea spread during the century.

PLATE 20.1 *Desert-edge trade: 'Moors' trading gum at the* escale *of Bakel on the Senegal River*

A major mechanism of closer contact with the world economy was trans-Saharan trade, which for centuries had involved Saharan merchants, guides, transporters, and suppliers of commodities as diverse as food, goat skins to serve as water containers, and exports such as ostrich feathers for the European market. In the first place the people of the northern oases such as Tafilālet, Mzab, Ghadāmes, the Fezzān, Awdjīla, and Sīwa played a pivotal role in organizing and financing trade. Perhaps because of the strategic location of these oases and because the oases relied heavily on the trade of dates for grain from zones of rainfall agriculture farther north, oasis dwellers, with their long histories of trade, moved naturally into trans-Saharan commerce over the centuries as opportunities opened up. Nomadic

19. C. C. Stewart and E. K. Stewart, 1973, pp. 86–97, 119–20, 151–3.
20. S. Baier, 1977.

groups such as the Ahaggar and Kel-Ewey Tuareg, the Tubu, and the Zuwaya of the central Sahara (a Beduin group not to be confused with *zāwiya* clerical lineages in Mauritania) traded small quantities of slaves and other products on their own account, but they could not match the scale of sedentary merchants from the northern oases, who had financial backing from middlemen in Mediterranean ports and ultimately from Europe, especially when prices and conditions on the routes were favourable. Consequently the main role of camel nomads was to provide transport animals, guides, and military escorts for caravans, and they also ran freight delivery services for merchants who were unable to or preferred not to accompany caravans.[21] Most groups of Saharan nomads had a major stake in the trade that passed through their territory: Regibat on the route to western Morocco; Aït Khabbash (a segment of the Aït Atta) on the Tafilālet–Tūwāt road; Chaamba on the routes north of Tūwāt; Tuareg on the Tripoli–Kano route; Tubu on the Borno–Fezzān road; Mujabra and Zuwaya for traffic between Benghazi and Wadai; Kabābīsh on the Darb al-Arbaʿīn (forty-day road) between Dārfūr and the lower Nile.

PLATE 20.2 *The* ḳaṣba (*citadel*) *of Murzuk in the Fezzan in 1869*

A major dynamic of nineteenth-century desert history was the ebb and flow of trade on these routes. Much further research will be necessary before the detail or even an outline of this process can be completed, but

21. On trans-Saharan trade through Tripoli, see M. El-Hachaichi, 1912, pp. 200–2; H. Méhier de Mathuisieulx, 1904, pp. 20–34; T. S. Jago, 1902. For arrangements between merchants and Tuareg lineages for transport, escorts and deliveries, see M. Brulard, 1958, pp. 202–15.

shifts in trade can be presumed to have affected the constant themes in desert history of migration and warfare. Control of a trade route, with the revenue it brought from tools and services, was a considerable prize and was subject to challenge from nomadic rivals. The concentration of wealth in lineages, segments, or whole ethnic groups often upset the normal course of affairs in local politics, which depended on roughly equal distribution of power among segments at a given level in the structure. Wealthy groups were likely to maintain their positions, but an element of instability came from the ease with which even large caravans fell prey to raiders lying in ambush. Finally, the decline of a once-active trade route required readjustment. The paucity of historical material on this issue does not permit conclusions. Some groups, such as the Chaamba, responded to a decline in the trade they carried by increasing their commitment to desert-edge regional trade or by raiding wealthy neighbours; others, such as the Kābābīsh of the desert Nile, who took the decline of the forty-day route in their stride by turning to nearly exclusive reliance on animal husbandry, seem to have adjusted more easily.[22]

A prominent overall pattern in the shifting location and volume of trade through the desert was the movement of trade away from the French in Algeria, a major irony because it so thoroughly frustrated imperial economic objectives. In the early days of the French occupation, trade picked up; after 1833, caravan traffic between Fez and Tlemcen began again, and British products imported through the Moroccan port of Tetuān entered western Algeria. Trade between Tetouān and ʿAbd al-Ḳādir's domains increased after 1837 and especially after 1839 when the need for arms assured a lively commerce. But trade declined after the fall of ʿAbd al-Ḳādir's state, a result in part of the prohibitive import duties on trans-Saharan products in transit from the Western Sudan, and restrictions on goods entering Algeria from neighbouring territories. The French tried to remedy both situations in the 1850s and 1860s, but trade failed to respond.[23] Another factor was the collapse of Algerian demand for slaves; while this is often cited as an explanation for Algerian commercial difficulties, it needs to be re-evaluated in the light of recent evidence that the Algerian slave trade was never important compared with other North African receiving areas.[24] A final consideration was that Algerian territory did not offer an advantage in terms of security for caravans, since at any given time hostility between the French and one or another group in Saharan Algeria threatened the safety of commerce.

The route west of Algeria prospered until the late 1870s, when it began its final decline, and it shifted westward in Morocco during the course of the nineteenth century. As the importance of Figuig, located near the

22. Y. Tégnier, 1939, pp. 108ff.; T. Asad, 1966, pp. 79–88.
23. J.-L. Miège, 1961–3, Vol. 2, pp. 158–63; Vol. 3, pp. 74–5.
24. R. A. Austen, 1979.

PLATE 20.3 *Oasis Society: women in the Murzuk market, 1869*

Algerian border, declined, Abū Am, situated about 240km south-west of Figuig, prospered, and Abū Am took over most of the slave trade entering Morocco. Most other commerce shifted even farther west towards the Atlantic coast, a consequence of the founding of the port of Mogador, which from its strategic location took over an increasing share of trans-Saharan trade after the 1840s.[25] A way station for the route to Mogador grew up at Tindūf, the site of an ancient *ḳsār*, when an alliance centring on the Tadjakant was victorious over the Regibat at mid-century. An enlarged alliance defended the oasis until 1884 when Regibat won out once more.[26] Declining trade was without doubt a factor in this struggle; trade to Mogador reached a peak in 1878 but began its final downward slide thereafter. It ended altogether shortly after the arrival of the French in Timbuktu in 1894 and the opening of a combination of river and overland routes between Timbuktu and St-Louis at the mouth of the Senegal.[27]

25. R. E. Dunn, 1977, pp. 107–12; 1971.
26. A. Pigeot, 1956, pp. 85–94; A. Laugel, 1959, pp. 301–10.
27. J.-L. Miège, 1961–3, Vol. 4, pp. 380–5.

PLATE 20.4 *Minaret of the Agades mosque*

Trade on the route between Tripoli and Kano increased after mid-century, especially after the success of Ottoman efforts to keep peace south of Ghadāmes after 1850. The next thirty years represent the golden age of commerce on this route, and a boom in ostrich feather exports in the 1870s pushed the value of trade to what must have been a record high. Trade suffered a temporary decline during the depression of the 1880s but recovered with rising exports of tanned goat skins in the 1890s. Adjdjer Tuareg ran caravans between Ghadāmes and Iferuan, a resting place in the Aïr Mountains, and Tuareg of the Kel-Ewey confederation carried trade between Iferuan and Kano. Both groups encountered challenges from their neighbours; in the north the Adjdjer beat off attacks from Chaamba and from Ahaggar Tuareg, and in the south Kel-Ewey encountered a challenge from the Imezureg of Damergu, a semi-sedentary Tuareg group with a localized power base and the ability to profit from the taxation of the ostrich feather trade from their area. Tripoli–Kano trade lasted longer than trade to Mogador because Kano was better protected from competing maritime routes, but cheap maritime freight rates combined with growing insecurity on the desert portions of the route to bring about a sharp decline in trade after 1900. The British in Nigeria sought to deflect Tripoli–Kano trade towards the port of Lagos, while the French in Niger attempted to keep the desert route open. The final blow to the old route occurred when the railway arrived in Kano in 1911.[28]

By the turn of the century the Benghazi–Wadai route was more vital than any other. This direct route between Cyrenaica and Wadai had been discovered early in the century, and Wadai sultans, whose state had grown increasingly powerful after the mid-eighteenth century, were anxious to promote a route which bypassed Borno to the west and Dārfūr to the east. From 1860 the fortunes of the trade route were intertwined with those of the Sanūsiyya, a Muslim brotherhood that spread among the Beduin of Cyrenaica after 1843 and later extended southward along the trade route. The success of the order had a great impact on trade, since a single organization spanned the entire length of the route, providing merchants with a common legal, social, and commercial framework and even a postal system. The leaders of the order strove to promote trade by maintaining peace along the route, and to this end they mediated disputes between lineages, segments, or whole ethnic groups and often successfully appealed for the return of merchandise stolen in raids on caravans. Trade in turn benefited the leadership of the Sanūsiyya by bringing revenue from tolls, payment for storage space, and gifts from merchants, as well as lending an element of unity to far-flung Sanūsī domains.[29]

Benghazi–Wadai trade lasted past the turn of the century because of the Sanūsiyya and because the route served areas more remote than the southern termini of Tripoli–Kano trade. The easternmost route, the Darb al-Arbaʿīn, declined after mid-century with the rise of Benghazi–Wadaī trade and the formation of the far-ranging trade empire of the Djallāba.

28. M. Johnson, 1976a; S. Baier, 1977, pp. 39–45; C. W. Newbury, 1966; S. Baier, 1980, chaps 3 and 4.
29. D. D. Cordell, 1977.

After 1885, the Mahdist state in the Sudan disrupted the Darb al-Arbaʿīn and the Nile routes as well.

The trans-Saharan slave trade also affected the lives of nomadic people in a variety of ways. Saharan societies near the West African Sahel raided Sudanese populations for slaves, and occasional trans-Saharan slave raids have been recorded, as in the case of the Awlād Sulaymān before they moved to the Chad basin and the Banū Muḥammad in the early twentieth century. Nomads traded some slaves on their own account, just as they handled small quantities of other trans-Saharan products, but by and large they were transporters rather than financiers. Transit trade in slaves probably brought nomads less revenue than other forms of commerce, because merchants did not have to pay for transport, but they did pay tolls.

Perhaps the most important impact of the slave trade on Saharan societies was the ready supply of slave labour, which became an important factor during times of expansion, especially on the desert edge, where labour could be used not only for herding but also in agriculture and artisan occupations. A case in point is that of the Kel-Ewey Tuareg, who expanded their economy during the nineteenth century, a time of good climate in the region, achieved prosperity from trans-Saharan trade and salt trade, and made growing investments in the entire region centring on the corridor from the Aïr to Kano. Little information is available on the evolution of systems of social stratification in the desert except among other Tuareg groups. The new reliance on agriculture based on servile labour in Ahaggar has been mentioned, and among the Kel-Gress and the Tuareg of the Imannen emphasis shifted from the use of slave labour in herding to the collection of tribute from sedentary agriculturalists. This reorientation came about when desert warriors arrived in areas of the Sahel where agriculture was possible and demanded tribute from local cultivators, or raided for slaves, who in times merged with the sedentary tribute-paying population.[30] Another case of economic expansion also suggests that there was a need for additional slave labour, namely the imperialism of the Aït Atta, a group that had been on the move in the pre-Saharan fringe of Morocco since the seventeenth century. In the nineteenth century, the Aït Kabbash, a segment of the Ait Atta, led the desert vanguard of this expansion by extending their influence over trade between Tafilālet and Tūwāt and extorting protection money from the inhabitants of Tūwāt.[31]

Little is known about the volume of the slave trade across the desert, but Ralph Austen has compiled preliminary estimates, based on a wide variety of sources, and these offer some surprises. According to Austen, the commerce in human beings, far from declining in the nineteenth century, was actually on the rise; a greater volume of trade reached receiving

30. P.E. Lovejoy and S. Baier, 1975; S. Baier and P.E. Lovejoy, 1977. On sedentarization and tribute, see P. Bonte, 1976; H. Guillaume, 1976.

31. R.E. Dunn, 1972.

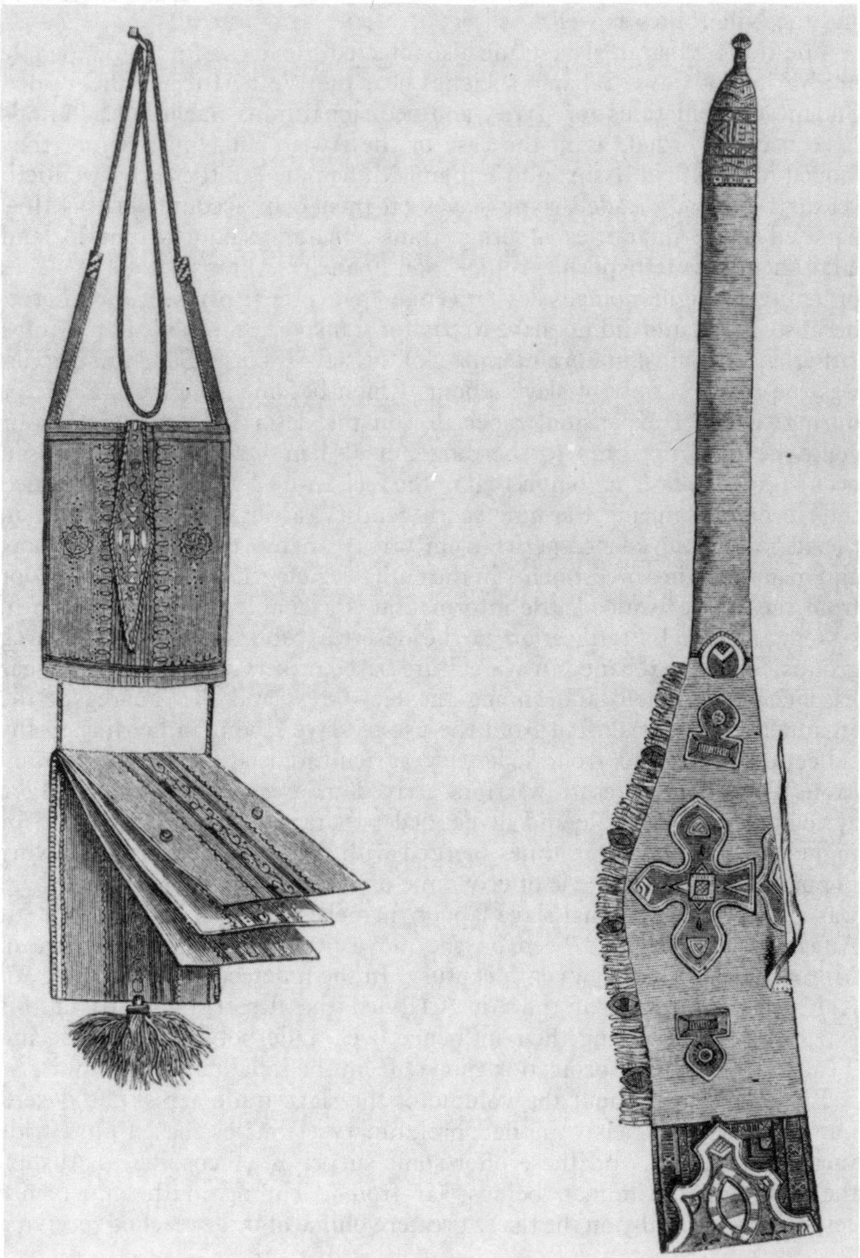

PLATE 20.5 *Tuareg leather goods on sale in Timbuktu in the 1850s*

areas in North Africa and the Middle East than in any previous century. Austen's figures show that between 1800 and 1880 something in the order of half a million slaves entered Egypt, and a quarter of a million were taken to Morocco. Few entered Algeria after the French conquest, but Algeria had never been as important a market as other areas.[32] In Libya, the Benghazi–Wadai route continued to provide slaves to Egypt and other areas in the Middle East into the late nineteenth century, because this route was less easily monitored by European abolitionists than the Tripoli–Kano route. Farther east the Nile routes continued to carry slaves even into the early twentieth century.[33]

The firearms trade into and across the desert also continued, despite attempts by European powers to stop it. At Tripoli, and especially at Benghazi, a lively firearms trade was reported in the early 1880s, and many smuggled rifles, especially eighteen-shot Winchester repeaters, were imported for use by caravan escorts. But some of these modern weapons must have reached other nomadic groups as well, allowing them to mount successful raids because firepower added to the tactical advantages of surprise that raiding parties already enjoyed.[34] The penetration of modern repeaters into the desert seems to have been greatest along the Benghazi–Wadai route, but other areas were affected as well; Joseph Smaldone has assembled evidence to show that a turning point in the spread of firearms occurred among Ahaggar Tuareg in the 1890s. To the north-west, in Morocco, contraband sales of the 1860 model single-shot Remington breechloader were so great that by the end of the century it had become the basic rifle for many groups throughout the country, including pre-Saharan nomads. Although the evidence is far from complete, increased insecurity on the Tripoli–Kano route after 1898 may have been due to the spread of firearms to raiders.[35]

The region surrounding the southern terminus of the Tripoli–Kano trade route provides an example of the economic, political, and religious influence of desert people on the Sudan. In the savanna, the nineteenth century marked the culmination of a process in which the centralization of state structures, Islamization, and economic growth were closely intertwined. The *djihād* of the early nineteenth century, although only a final stage in this longer process, resulted in the formation of the Sokoto caliphate, a large state which promoted economic growth in its centre near Kano, Katsina, and Zaria (and around its secondary centre in the Sokoto-Rima valley) and relocated population from beyond its borders towards the centre through slave-raiding. In the centre of the region, rich farmland

32. R. A. Austen, 1979.

33. J. P. Mason, 1971, p. 267. For the slave trade from equatorial Africa towards Egypt, see D. D. Cordell, 1977b.

34. P. Bettoli, 1882, p. 267.

35. J. P. Smaldone, 1971, pp. 161–2; 1977, pp. 100–1; H. J. Fisher and V. Rowland, 1971, pp. 233–4, 240.

permitted production for the market on slave estates or by peasants, and this surplus production encouraged the growth of urban centres and craft production.[36] Kano and neighbouring towns developed a cottage textile industry which supplied cloth to a large area of the Central Sudan and Tuareg country to the north. Economic growth in the desert, especially in the corridor between Zinder and the Aïr massif, which was dominated by Kel-Ewey Tuareg, complemented the development of the savanna. Tuareg traded dates and salt from Bilma and Fachi, animals, and animal products for grain and manufactured articles from the Sudan. The Kel-Ewey and their allies maintained an elaborate commercial network in the savanna that included urban centres of craftsmen and trade specialists, most of servile origin, and rural estates worked by slaves or their descendants. These estates, located throughout the Sahel and savanna, provided a proportion of the grain needed by desert nomads, served as resting places for transhumant Tuareg during the dry season, and functioned as places of refuge during drought.[37]

Although peaceful economic exchange was the predominant mode of interaction between Tuareg and their sedentary neighbours, at least in the Kano–Aïr corridor, the economic strength of the noble Tuareg rested on their possession of camels and firearms and their mobility. Tuareg could be powerful allies of sedentary states, valued as much for their aid in military campaigns against enemies as for their economic potential, as was the case in relations between Damagaram, a state formed north of the Caliphate in the early nineteenth century and increasingly powerful and troublesome by the end. Tuareg could, on the other hand, be devastating enemies, as witnessed by the destruction they wrought in Borno in the early nineteenth century.

The southern Sahara also served as a reservoir of Islamic learning that had a continuing impact on the savanna over the centuries, and particularly during the nineteenth century.[38] A number of desert-edge regions, including the Central Sudan, the Senegal basin, the interior delta of the Niger, and the Chad basin, supplied grain to neighbouring desert people, and these economic ties fostered the exchange of ideas. Characteristic of southern Saharan societies was a division into warrior and saintly lineages, the first aspiring to warfare and politics, the second having an ideology of pacificism, experience in commerce, and a shared intellectual tradition. Like the segmentary structure itself, the bipartite division was a model of society rather than a description of reality, so that only the holiest of holy men actually refrained from fighting, and warrior lineages engaged in commerce, though they were less specialized in this activity than the clerical

36. P.E. Lovejoy and S. Baier, 1975; P.E. Lovejoy, 1978; Smaldone, 1977, pp. 39–68 and *passim*.
37. P.E. Lovejoy and S. Baier, 1975, pp. 564–71.
38. C.C. Stewart, 1976a.

lineages. Nevertheless the *zāwiya* clerical lineages of Mauritania, Kunta clerics of the Niger bend and the *inislimin* among the Tuareg mastered the two politically useful sciences of *fiḳh* (jurisprudence) and *taṣawwuf* (mysticism). Like the Sanūsiyya or Moroccan clerical lineages, they performed the valuable function of mediation and arbitration, and their activities had economic, political, and scholarly aspects. They maintained and developed Islamic scholarship over the centuries and their influence extended south of the desert where Saharan scholarship affected both the quietist tradition and the spread of Islam by militant reformers.

Conclusion

The nineteenth century was a time of dramatic change in the desert. The French occupation of Algeria shattered the economic unity of North Africa by deflecting trans-Saharan trade to routes east and west of Algeria and by disrupting east–west caravan traffic along the northern fringe of the desert. The advance of the French army was a direct and immediate manifestation of the impact of Europe, a presence more remote if no less real elsewhere because of the shifting volume and composition of trans-Saharan trade. By the end of the century trans-Saharan trade, with the revenue and ready supply of labour it brought, had all but collapsed. The importance of this trade in the lives of nomads suggests the need for further research on the effects of shifts in commerce and its decline: what was the effect of the formation of the state ruled by ʿAbd al-Ḳādir astride a major east–west route? How precisely did desert people react to shifts in commerce? How did declining trade affect resistance? The French occupation of the desert also introduced a new military factor in the relationship between desert people and the outside world. The mobility of nomads allowed a number of options in resistance that might coalesce around Muslim leaders and religious orders, but the arid environment often limited the freedom of groups or individuals with shared resources by presenting them with a choice between resistance and survival. Another subject for further research is the uneven and dissimilar effect of European economic penetration on the regional economies at the fringe of the desert in pre-Saharan Morocco which was dominated by Ait Atta expansion; in coastal Morocco where trans-Atlas and trans-Saharan economic links were shaken to their foundations; in Algeria where the activities of the French were predominant; north of the Senegal basin where gum exports increased the stakes in competition among Moorish groups; north of the Niger bend; in the Sokoto caliphate where economic strength must be seen in light of the end of the Atlantic slave trade as well as Islamization and centralization within the region; in the Chad basin; and to the east where the expansion of Wadai transformed both the desert to its north and the forest to its south. The history of each of these regions raises a series of questions on issues such as change in social stratification, similarities and differences in response to the French army, and the direction of reorientation in regional economies. Another task for researchers is, as Charles Stewart has suggested, to provide detail on religious ties between the southern Sahara and West and Central Africa seen within the theme of religious, political, and economic unity in these desert-edge regions.[39]

A theme that runs throughout Saharan history is the all-pervasive influence of climate, as the pressures of drought or overpopulation drove nomads from arid regions and attracted them to more fertile land on the desert margins or towards higher and better-watered land. Existing climatic data permit only the most general conclusions about the nineteenth century: little more can be said than that the century did not witness catastrophes such as those of the middle seventeenth and eighteenth centuries or the Sahelian droughts of 1911–14 and 1969–73; that the early nineteenth century, despite the absence of severe drought except in the Chad basin in the 1830s, was drier on the average than the period 1600–1800; and that moist conditions returned between 1870 and 1895 but deteriorated towards the end of the century and culminated in the drought of the early twentieth century.[40] These general statements obviously mask a plethora of local and regional variation. Detailed data on climate would permit a better understanding of many aspects of human activity, and especially relationships between scarcity and warfare, migration, and social stratification, but unfortunately data at this level of detail are almost non-existent.

39. C. C. Stewart, 1976a, pp. 81–5. For a study of desert–savanna economic links north of the middle Niger, see R. Roberts, 1978.

40. S. E. Nicholson, 1976; forthcoming.

21 The nineteenth-century Islamic revolutions in West Africa

A. BATRAN

The setting for the drama that was to unfold in nineteenth-century West Africa was that corridor known to classical Arab geographers and historians as Bilād al-Sūdān (Land of the black people). Hemmed in between an ever-encroaching Sahara in the north and an unfriendly climate in the south, the region's historical importance, prosperity and stability depended to a large extent on a delicate balance maintained between the environment, man and animals; between settled agriculturists and pastoral nomads; between town dwellers and rural populations; between free men and those of servile status; and between Muslims and those who adhered to their traditional beliefs. Furthermore, the region had become, since ancient times, an international market where local merchandise and foreign imports were exchanged. Again, Bilād al-Sūdān represented an area of tremendous human mobility and population mixing exemplified by the spread of the Fulbe (Fulani, Peul) whose original homeland was in Futa Toro, over a wide canvas extending from Lake Chad and the Cameroon in the east to the Atlantic Ocean in the west. It was the region where great states and empires rose and fell, a region that represented the earliest *dār al-Islām* (abode of Islam) in West Africa. It was the stage that witnessed, after a long gestation – a long period of teaching and preaching, and ultimately of violent outbursts – the birth of three caliphates: the Sokoto caliphate in northern Nigeria, the Hamdullahi caliphate in Massina, and the Tijāniyya caliphate in the Senegambia and Massina.

The religious background of the reform movements

The nineteenth-century West African *djihād* movements were basically religious drives towards the realization of the basic teachings and practices that had characterized Islam in its early days. And since Islam is a comprehensive religion concerned with every aspect of society, the religious, social, economic, and political motivations of the *djihād* cannot be separated. Hence, the nineteenth-century Islamic revolutions expressed a variety of deep-seated concerns that were reflected in a situation of crisis in the Sudanic milieu.

The West African revolutionaries, S͟hayk͟h (Shehu) ʿUt͟hmān dan Fodio

(Usman ibn Fudī), Seku Ahmadu (Shaykh Aḥmad Lobbo) and al-Hadjdj ʿUmar, were men of religion. They were scholastic giants and charismatic leaders whose lives and actions followed closely the example of Muḥammad and the dictates of the *sharīʿa*.[1] Their call for reconstruction and reform (*tadjdīd*) and their ultimate recourse to militant action, they sincerely believed, were ordained by Allah, foretold by the Prophet, sanctioned by the spiritual forefathers, and had precedents in past and contemporary times. Accordingly, they perceived themselves to be the chosen instruments to execute the Divine will.

The proponents of *djihād* drew upon several Ḳu'rānic verses, Prophetic traditions (*ḥadīth*), and the consensus of the jurists (*idjmāʿ*) to emphasize the obligation of *djihād* and the abundant rewards awaiting the *mudjahidūn* in the hereafter.[2] It is important to note that in West Africa, as elsewhere in *dār al-Islām*, *djihād* had assumed *ṣūfī* (mystical) overtones involving self-mortification and a strict code of moral behaviour. The *mudjahidūn* were fully expected to lead an exemplary life and to practise what they preached.

Furthermore, Muḥammad's prophecy that 'Allah will send to this *umma* (Muslim community) at the beginning of every hundred years he who will renew her religion for her' was all too well known in the Western Sudan. Indeed, the whole eschatological tradition, bequeathed by earlier generations, had a profound influence on the programmes and actions of the *djihād* leadership. The popular appeal of this tradition and the frenzied passions it is apt to unleash are universally acknowledged; for the messianic figure embodied the hopes and aspirations of the masses, and provided what they believed to be a sure way out of a crisis. The expected deliverer is said to have been commissioned by Allah to promote vigorously by the tongue (preaching and teaching) and, if necessary, by hand (*djihād*) the Ḳu'rānic injunction of *amr bil-maʿruf wal-nahi ʿan al-munkar* (commanding the good and prohibiting the evil). He was to erase unbelief, injustice and oppression; he was to build a better world and attain, for the *umma*, a satisfying religion.

1. There are several general works on the nineteenth-century West African Islamic revolutions, for example. J. R. Willis, 1967; M. Last, 1974, pp. 1–24; H. F. C. Smith, 1961; B. Martin, 1976, pp. 13–35, 68–98; M. Hiskett, 1976. On the *djihād* of Shaykh ʿUthmān dan Fodio, see M. Last, 1967)a); H. A. S. Johnston, 1967; F. H. el-Masri, 1963, 1979; M. Hiskett, 1973. For Seku Ahmadu's movement see: W. A. Brown, 1969; A. H. Ba and S. Daget, 1962. On the *djihād* of al-Hadjdj ʿUmar, see: J. R. Willis, 1970, forthcoming; O. Jah, 1973; M. A. Tyam, 1961: B. O. Oloruntimehin, 1972(a).

2. Ḳurʿān II: 126: 'Fighting is enjoined on you, though it is disliked by you; and it may be that you dislike a thing while it is good for you, and it may be that you love a thing while it is evil for you; and Allah knows while you know not.' Ḳurʿān II: 193: 'And fight them until there is no persecution, and religion is only for Allah. But if they desist then there should be no hostility except against oppressors.' Also the *ḥadīth*: 'Whoso among you sees anything blameworthy shall alter it with the hand: if he cannot do this, he shall do it with the tongue; if he cannot do this, he shall do it at heart; this is the least that religion demands'.

Nowhere in *dār al-Islām* did the concept of *tadjdīd* have a more profound effect than in nineteenth-century West Africa. In that century, the Muslims in West Africa anxiously awaited the advent of the *mudjaddid* (reformer/renewer).[3] It is claimed that Muḥammad had prophesied that twelve caliphs (*mudjaddidūn*) would follow him. Thereafter, a period of anarchy heralding the end of the world would prevail. Local traditions proudly maintain that the Prophet had honoured Takrūr (West Africa) with the last two *mudjaddidūn*. It was generally believed in the Western Sudan that the first ten reformers had already appeared in the Muslim East (five in Medina, two in Egypt, one in Syria, and two in Iraq) and that Askia al-Muḥammad, the great Songhay monarch (1493–1528), was designated the eleventh. The twelfth and last *mudjaddid*, so it was said, was to make his appearance in the Western Sudan during the thirteenth century of the Hidjra, i.e. between 1785 and 1881.[4] This millennial climate was exploited by the nineteenth-century West African *djihād* leaders to their own advantage. That both Shaykh ʿUthmān dan Fodio and Seku Ahmadu claimed to be the *mudjaddid* of the fateful thirteenth century of the Hidjra had already been noted.[5] Although al-ʿHadjdj ʿUmar never took the title of either *mudjaddid* or *mahdī*, he nonetheless assumed a Tijāni–ṣūfī variation, that of *Khalīfat Khatim al-Awlyya*ʿ (successor of the Seal of Saints, that is, Aḥmad al-Tijāni, founder of the Tijāniyya *ṭarīḳa*).[6]

The legitimacy and righteousness of the *djihād* were further strengthened by the claim that the three men were each entrusted with the Divine mission by the Prophet and the founder of the *ṭarīḳa* (*ṣūfī* order or brotherhood) to which he belonged. Such claims presented convincing proof of the sincerity of the leadership and countered the anticipated anti-*djihād* charges levelled by sceptics and detractors, the so-called *ʿulamāʾ al-sūʿ* (time-serving and evil scholars). Shaykh ʿUthmān assured his audience that he was ordered to carry out the *djihād* by the founder of the Ḳādirīyya *ṭarīḳa* himself, ʿAbd al-Ḳādir al-djilani (d. 1166), in the presence of the Prophet, his Companions, and all the notable saints. This mystical vision was experienced by Shaykh ʿUthmān in 1794, ten years before the commencement of his *djihād*:

> When I reached forty years, five months and some days, God drew me to Him, and I found the Lord of djinns and men, our Lord Muḥammad ... With him were the Companions, and the prophets, and the saints. Then they welcomed me, and sat me down in their midst. Then ... our Lord ʿAbdal-Ḳādir al-Djilani brought a green

3. J. R. Willis, 1967; A. A. Batran, 1983; M. A. al-Hajj, 1967.
4. ibid.
5. J. R. Willis, 1967; A. A. Batran, 1983, pp. 32–9; al-Naqar, 1972, pp. 77–8; W. A. Brown, 1969, p. 21.
6. O. Jah, 1973, p. 4, pp. 123 *et seq.* According to J. R. Willis, forthcoming, and B. Martin, 1963, al-Hadjdj ʿUmar's followers claimed for him the title of *mahdī* and that of *wazīr al-mahdī*.

> robe ... and a turban! ... The Messenger of God clasped them to his bosom for a time ... ʿAbdal-Ḳādir al-Djilani sat me down, and clothed me and enturbaned me. Then he addressed me as 'Imam of the saints' and commanded me to do what is approved of and forbade me to do what is disapproved of; and he girded me with the Sword of Truth [Sayf al-Haḳ] to unsheath against the enemies of God.[7]

It is claimed that al-Hadjdj ʿUmar was ordered by his spiritual mentor, Muḥammad al-Ghali of Mecca to bring about reform in the Western Sudan.[8] Later, when the violent clash with his adversaries became inevitable, al-Hadjdj ʿUmar began to be gripped by mystical visions instructing him to undertake the *djihād*:

> Previously I had only been authorized by Muḥammad and shaykh al-Tidjāni to summon the unbelievers to Islam and to guide them down the correct path ... then I was instructed to execute the *djihād* ... I received this permission through a Divine voice which said to me: 'you are now permitted to conduct *djihād*'. This took place in the evening of 21st of Dhul-Qa'da, in the year 1268 [6 September 1852].[9]

Rooted deeply in orthodoxy and *ṣūfī* thought, the nineteenth-century West African *djihād*s were not, however, an isolated phenomenon: they were the latest manifestations of a long tradition of reform in Bilād al-Sūdān that aimed at the revolutionary realization of equity and justice promised by Islam but denied by oppressive, compromising, and iniquitous regimes.

Attempts have been made to find a common origin for the West African Islamic revolutions in the *djihād* of Naṣīr al-Dīn (d. 1677),[10] in the Almoravid movement of the eleventh century,[11] and even in the Khāridjite revolution in North Africa in the eighth century.[12] It has, however, been correctly argued that such a chronological approach 'suggests ... somewhat simplistic causal links' with these early outbursts of militancy rather than direct descent.[13] While it cannot be denied that the leaders of the West African *djihād*s were aware of these successful movements and even of other less successful attempts,[14] it seems more likely that they drew immediate inspiration from contemporary sources closer to home. Before them were the achievements of their own ancestors, the Torodbe, in Bundu, Futa

7. M. Hiskett, 1973, p. 66.
8. J. R. Willis, forthcoming, ch. 6; O. Jah, 1973, pp. 131–2.
9. ibid.
10. P. D. Curtin, 1971.
11. M. A. al-Hajj, 1964, p. 58.
12. O. Jah. 1973, pp. 62–4.
13. C. C. Stewart, 1976a, p. 91.
14. See F. H. el-Masri, 1979, p. 32, where it is reported that Shaykh ʿUthmān made references to the unsuccessful, indeed disastrous *djihād* of Aḥmad ibn Abu Mahalli of Tafilālet in the early seventeenth century.

Jallon and Futa Toro, the peaceful reform endeavours of Shaykh al-Mukhtār al-Kunti and Muḥammad ibn ʿAbd al-Karīm al-Maghīlī, the *ṣūfī* reaction to the outbreak of Wahhābī fundamentalism in Arabia, as well as, in the case of Shaykh Ahmadu and al-Hadjdj ʿUmar, the precedent of Shaykh ʿUthmān's *djihād* in Hausaland.

The *djihād* leaders traced their roots back to the holiest region in Bilād al-Sūdān, the celebrated Takrūr (Futa Toro), where the earliest Islamic state in West Africa is said to have emerged.[15] Most important is that they all belonged to that 'society' of *ʿulamā*ʾ (scholars) known as the Torodbe. J. R. Willis informs us that the Torodbe were an eclectic group of Muslims drawn from diverse ethnic groups throughout the Western and Central Sudan.[16] Torodbe 'society', he adds, comprised groups of individuals of Fulbe, Wolof, Mande, Hausa, Berber, slave and caste origin. Nevertheless, the Torodbe were identified with the Fulbe. They spoke the Fulbe language (Fulfulde), intermarried with them, and accompanied the Fulbe in their endless migrations. Throughout the Western Sudan, Torodbe became synonymous with Fulbe. In fact, the Torodbe constituted the scholarly faction of the Fulbe.

Islam was the Torodbe way of life; it was the means of their spiritual and material sustenance. The Torodbe shared their preoccupation with Islam with the neighbouring scholastic clans, the *zawāyā*, of the Western Sahara.[17] But, while each *zawāyā* clan stood out as a separate ethnic unit whose members were related by blood, the Torodbe 'shook the sense of ethnic differences ... to establish a society open to all individuals inclined to embrace their customs and beliefs.'[18] This social amalgam of clerics and students could still boast of having given birth to scholastic dynasties (*bayt al-ʿilm*), such as the Toronkawa of Shaykh ʿUthmān, the Bari of Shaykh Ahmadu, and al-Hadjdj ʿUmar's family, the Tall. Further still, the Torodbe could proudly point to a distinguished past: to the Torodbe *djihād* of Mālik Sī in the closing decades of the seventeenth century, of Karamoko Ibrāhīm Mūsa and Ibrāhīm Sori in the middle of the eighteenth century, of Sulaymān Baal in the 1770s, and to the resultant formation of the Torodbe imamates of Bundu, Futa Jallon, and Futa Toro. It was to this background of historical vintage that al-Hadjdj ʿUmar reached out to awaken the dormant *djihād* spirit among the Banu Toro (sons of Futa Toro). Reminding them that *djihād* was their cherished tradition, al-Hadjdj ʿUmar said:

> Banu Toro are the same as our first ancestors; painstaking and strong, and the best of men, and upright. Banu Toro ... return to your

15. J. R. Willis, 1978, pp. 195–6; forthcoming, ch. 2; B. Martin, 1976, pp. 15–16; J. S. Trimingham, 1962, pp. 161–2.
16. J. R. Willis, forthcoming, ch. 1; 1978, pp. 196 *et seq.*
17. On the Zawāyā see, for example, J. R. Willis, 1979b, pp. 3–12; C. C. Stewart, 1976(a); H. T. Norris, 1968; A. A. Batran, 1972.
18. J. R. Willis, forthcoming, ch. 3.

> inheritance: the *djihād* against the enemies of Allah ... Mount Sinai is your place of origin because of the *djihād* ... Banu Toro, ... become like your ancestors.[19]

The Torodbe revolutionary tradition was further underlined in a poem attributed to Muḥammad Bello, son and successor of Shaykh ʿUthmān dan Fodio. The poem, if at all authentic, would have been written by Bello before 1837, when he died. The poem opens with a lengthy introduction in praise of al-Hadjdj ʿUmar, Bello's son-in-law. Thereafter, it recounts the 'glorious' exploits of the Banu Toro (the Torodbe). It is said that al-Hadjdj ʿUmar included the poem in his propaganda messages to the dignitaries of Futa Toro. ʿUmar's intentions were obviously to impress upon the readers that the Fodio family fully supported his (Torodbe) *djihād*:

> These [Banu Toro/Torodbe] are my people; the origin of my clan; ... for the support of Islam they are in league; ... of them are some who excelled in the religious sciences ... and those who defended themselves against the wickedness of the enemy and declared *djihād*.[20]

The West African *djihād* leaders had yet another fountain of inspiration in the 'quietiest' reform model of Shaykh al-Mukhtār al-Kunti (1729–1811). From around 1750 until the time of his death in 1811, al-Kunti held the mantle of the Ḳādirīyya *ṭarīḳa* in West Africa; he was its founding father and spiritual director.[21] It was with the 'pen' and not the 'sword' that al-Kunti exercised unparalleled influence in the Western Sudan. Both Shaykh ʿUthmān and Shaykh Ahmadu considered him their spiritual guide in the Ḳādirī Way. His legal opinions on religious matters were often referred to by the *djihād* and his name was invoked by them to shore up and legitimize revolutionary action. Muḥammad Bello asserts that when al-Kunti heard of Shaykh ʿUthmān's *djihād* he blessed it and predicted its success. 'Usman ibn Fudi,' he is reported to have said, 'is one of the accomplished saints; his *djihād* is just.'[22] With these words, al-Kunti cast the weight of his enormous prestige behind the Torodbe leader. Although al-Hadjdj ʿUmar was of a different *ṣūfī* persuasion, he nonetheless held al-Kunti in high esteem and was equally influenced by the latter's opinions.[23]

The reformers were also influenced by the radical ideas of the itinerant Maghribian scholar Muḥammad ibn ʿAbd al-Karīm al-Maghīlī (d. 1503–6).[24] They relied heavily on his judgements to distinguish between *dār al-Islām* and *dār al-Ḥarb* (abode of war/infidels), to define the state of *kufr* (unbelief), and to identify *ʿulamāʾ al-suʿ*. According to al-Maghīlī:

19. J. R. Willis, 1970, pp. 98–100.
20. ibid., pp. 97–8.
21. A. A. Batran, 1973, 1974, 1979.
22. A. A. Batran, 1973, pp. 349–50.
23. J. R. Willis, 1979c, p. 181.
24. M. Hiskett, 1962, pp. 578 *et seq.*; M. A. al-Hajj, 1964, pp. 53 et seq., J. R. Willis, 1970, pp. 38–42 and 148–51.

> The inhabitants of any land reflect the true religious sentiments of the ruler. If the ruler is Muslim, his land is *Bilād al-Islām*, if the ruler is *kāfir* (infidel), his land is *Bilād al-Kufr* and flight from it to another is obligatory.[25]

Al-Maghīlī's ruling with regard to the syncretic rulers and *'ulamā' al-sū'* was clear: they were unbelievers, and *djihād* against them was obligatory on Muslims. Such rulers and scholars, he said, 'have covered truth with falsehood in a way that makes a number of ignorant Muslims go astray.'[26]

West African Muslims were by no means closed to influences from the outside. Religious and political developments in the Muslim East, particularly those that directly affected the birthplace of Islam, Arabia, had their repercussions throughout *dāral-Islām*. One such event was the reaction of Eastern *ṣūfīsm* to the capture of Mecca (1803) and Medina (1805) by the Wahhābī fundamentalists.

Notwithstanding the rejection of some of the Wahhābī doctrines by a large segment of Muslims, the Wahhābī revolution had naturally served as a catalyst for militant action in the world of Islam. Moreoever, by their condemnation of *ṣūfī* beliefs and practices, the Wahhābīs provoked a vigorous *ṣūfī* revival spearheaded by the Khalwatiyya *ṭarīḳa* and the renowned *ṣufī* teacher, Aḥmad ibn Idrīs al-Fasi (d. 1837).[27] Part of that *ṣūfī* revival was the birth of the Tijāniyya order which al-Hadjdj 'Umar espoused and cultivated in West Africa in his capacity as Khalīfa of Aḥmad al-Tijāni. It is claimed that during his sojourn in Cairo, al-Hadjdj 'Umar came directly under the influence of Khalwati shaykhs.[28] It is also argued that the *djihād* of Shaykh 'Uthmān was linked to the Khalwati *ṣūfī* reformism through the agency of his mentor, Djibril ibn 'Umar.[29]

If the West African *djihāds* were thus considered within the context of the wider Islamic militant and quietist reform movements, there were undoubtedly 'familial' ties between the three of them. Indeed, the *djihād* of Shaykh 'Uthmān, launched in 1804, reactivated the revolutionary religious fervour that was fermenting underneath the surface in the Western Sudan. The Sokoto *djihād* literature 'calling upon Muslims to overthrow compromising and pagan authorities, or at least to withdraw from political rule of such authorities, and poetic epics in Fulfulde celebrating the exploits of the Fudis and the *mudjahidūn* in Hausaland', were widely spread in Bilād

25. M. A. al-Hajj, 1964, p. 50; J. R. Willis, 1970, p. 38.
26. M. A. al-Hajj, 1964, p. 56.
27. J. O. Voll, 1969, pp. 90–103; B. G. Martin, 1972, pp. 302–3. Reaction to the Wahābī anti-ṣūfism was very strong in Western Sudan. Shaykh al-Mukhtār al-Kunti issued a *fetwa* declaring that *hadjdj* was not obligatory on Muslims under the prevailing conditions in Arabia. See U. al-Naqar, 1972, pp. 47–8; A. A. Batran, 1972, pp. 186–9.
28. M. Hiskett, 1976, pp. 161–2.
29. B. G. Martin, 1976, pp. 24–5. Is is said that Djibril ibn 'Umar had tried unsuccessfully to raise the *djihād* in the region of Aïr. See F. H. El-Masri, 1963, pp. 438–9.

al-Sūdān.[30] Fulbe *mudjahidūn* from the Niger Bend are reported to have participated in the *djihād* of Shaykh ʿUthmān and to have carried the revolutionary spirit with them back to their respective homelands. Unsubstantiated claims not only make Shaykh Ahmadu a former student of Shaykh ʿUthmān, but also an active campaigner in the latter's *djihād*.[31] In addition, Shaykh Ahmadu is said to have received the support and blessings of the leaders of the Sokoto *djihād*. It is also reported that Shaykh ʿUthmān had personally furnished Shaykh Ahmadu with a flag to display before his marching *mudjahidūn*.[32] Furthermore, Shaykh Ahmadu corresponded with Abdullahi dan Fodio, brother and successor of Shaykh ʿUthmān, seeking his legal opinion in regard to the status of the Massina Muslim scholars who opposed his *djihād*. Apart from Shaykh Ahmadu's *djihād*, the northern regions of Massina witnessed between 1816 and 1823 the outbreak of at least three Sokoto-inspired movements. The first was led by a Hausa scholar, Malam Saʿid and was directed against the Tuareg in the Guimbala. Saʿid's forces were however vanquished. Subsequently, Malam Saʿid disappeared from the region and presumably returned to Hausaland. The two other *djihād* leaders, al-Faḳih al-Ḥusayn Koita and Alfa Aḥmad Alfaka, were of local Fulbe origin. Koita's movement broke out in the Fittuga, while that of Alfaka was centred in the Farimaka. Shaykh Ahmadu, who saw in the two movements a direct threat to his young *dina* (caliphate), moved quickly to defeat Koita and to incorporate Alfaka as an agent of Hamdullahi.[33] The third *djihād* leader, al-Hadjdj ʿUmar, had an extended stay in the Sokoto caliphate that lasted for more than six years. He visited Sokoto twice on his outward and return journeys from the pilgrimage. While in Sokoto, al-Hadjdj ʿUmar continued his preaching and mediating activities and initiated followers into the Tijāniyya brotherhood.

The motivating forces underlying the reform movements

The establishment of a truly Islamic society and the extension of the frontiers of *dār al-Islām* were thus the objectives of the leaders of the West African *djihād*s. Islam, they believed, provided the ideal framework for the organization of the community as well as a means of salvation in the world to come. But the translation of these beliefs into reality depended on their ability to win over a following committed to their cause and strong enough to bring about the desired changes.

As heirs to a rich tradition of scholasticism, the future reformers had their education in the 'academies' of illustrious professors within their own localities and even in distant lands. There, they received intensive training

30. W. A. Brown, 1969, pp. 66–7; U. al-Naqar, 1972, p. 51.

31. J. S. Trimingham, 1962, p. 177. It would appear that Shaykh Ahmadu had never travelled outside Massina.

32. U. al-Naqar, 1972, p. 51; W. A. Brown, 1969, pp. 17, 22.

33. W. A. Brown, 1969, pp. 66–7.

in the exoteric as well as the esoteric sciences, and emerged as accomplished scholars and *ṣūfī* shaykhs dedicated to teaching and preaching and to the spread of their respective *ṣūfī* brotherhoods. Students who joined the peripatetic '*Zāwiya*' of Shaykh 'Uthmān and Shaykh Ahmadu were initiated into the Ḳādirīyya, while those taught by al-Hadjdj 'Umar received the *Tijāni wird*. It was this body of faithful initiates that constituted the nucleus of the *mudjahidūn*. Thoroughly reared in the secrets of the Mystical Way (*asrar al-Tāriḳ*), they faithfully upheld the ideals of their masters. Their absolute and blind obedience to their spiritual guides, the result of their *ṣūfī* training, made of them a potentially explosive force, ever eager to answer the calls of their shaykhs and to fight and die as martyrs for them. For, in their eyes, the shaykhs were spiritually and intellectually superior to all other '*ulamā*'. They were the favourite saints of Allah, the possessors of the *baraka* (Divine blessing and miraculous powers), and the only link between the disciples and the founders of the *ṭarīḳa*s. Indeed, they were the awaited saviours and liberators of the thirteenth century of the Hidjra.

Islam in the nineteenth-century Western Sudan undoubtedly fell far short of the ideals of the reformers and their committed followers. The reformers complained of the pervasiveness of non-Islamic practices among rulers and subjects alike. They condemned the injustices and oppression perpetrated by the ruling dynasties and accused them of mixing Islam with traditional religious customs (*takhliṭ*), and even outright unbelief. They assailed the '*ulamā*' for tolerating, indeed endorsing the debased state into which Islam had sunk. Among the most disturbing factors – of particular relevance to al-Hadjdj 'Umar – was the aggressive French (infidel) military and economic expansion into Futa Toro and the neighbouring countries.

Most, if not all, of these complaints are evidently legitimate. Islamic influences and literacy in Arabic permeated Bilād al-Sūdān mainly through the agency of local Muslim traders and scholars.[34] The success that these proselytizers had ought not to conceal the fact that the converts did not altogether abandon their religious inheritance. Indeed, such non-violent proselytization produced, as it was bound to, a *rapprochement* between Islam and traditional African beliefs. This mixed or syncretic Islam was practised by members of the ruling class and their converted subjects. In Hausaland, Massina and the Senegambia, West African rulers not only exhibited a commitment to Islam, but also had intimate relationships with the Muslim trading and scholarly communities. The Muslim scholars, literate in Arabic and reputedly in possession of potent 'magical' powers, became especially useful as political and administrative functionaries in the royal courts. Muslim traders, with their intimate historical connection with the international trade in gold, salt, slaves and other items, were an important source of wealth. Hence, the Muslim party welcomed the patronage and protection of the ruling dynasties. Understandably, it tolerated the

34. See, for example, N. Levtzion, 1973, pp. 183–99; J. S. Trimingham, 1969.

excessive un-Islamic indulgences of the rulers and was even prepared to defend them.

To the reformers, true Islam offered no room for compromise. Hence, the whole range of *bid'a* (innovations, i.e. traditional religious practices grafted onto Islam) had to be stemmed. This was first attempted by preaching; by calling upon Muslims to return to pure, unadulterated Islam. Eventually, preaching undermined the 'constitutional' establishments as the reformers aimed their venom at the rulers and the court scholars. They scourged the *'ulamā'* for their moral laxity, unscrupulous opportunism, ignorance and corruption of Islam. They condemned such things as the oppression and corruption of the rulers, their abuse of power, their imposition of uncanonical and brutal taxation on their subjects and their 'raising of the flag of the worldly kingdom higher than the banner of Islam'.[35] Al-Hadjdj 'Umar warned, 'Be it known to every sensible man in every epoch of human history that those who involve themselves in worldly affairs (*mukibbin 'ala ad-dunya*), such as the infidel dogs, treacherous kings, and the corrupt *'ulamā'*, are subject to humiliation and disappointment in this world and in the hereafter.'[36] That such words preached revolution is obvious. The reaction of the authorities to the menacing storm came quickly. They tried to nip the impending revolution in the bud.

Predictably, the reformers considered such attempts to be acts of unbelief, and their perpetrators infidels. And since it was ordained that 'if the ruler is infidel, his land is *Bilād al-Kufr*', the Western Sudan now represented *dār al-Ḥarb*, the conquest and incorporation of which into *dār al-Islām* was obligatory on Muslims. Within a few years, the *mudjahidūn* and their allies swept away the authority of the *sarki*s of the Hausa states, that of the *ardo*s of Massina and the *fama*s of Segu and Kaarta, as well as the authority of the *almami*s of Bundu, Futa Jallon, and Futa Toro. Hausaland was consequently transformed into a caliphate under the leadership of *amīr al-mu'minīn* (Commander of the Believers) 'Uthmān dan Fodio; Massina became a *dina* (caliphate) with Shaykh Aḥmad Lobbo, now holding the title of *amīr- al-mu'minīn*, as its ruler; and the Senegambia and Massina were in turn united as the Tijāniyya caliphate under the authority of *Khalīfat Khatim al-Awlyya'*, al-Hadjdj 'Umar.

The *mudjahidūn* who humbled the mighty powers of Bilād al-Sūdān were of different social and ethnic backgrounds. They came from the Fulbe, the Hausa, the Mande, the Wolof, and the Tuareg; from nomadic pastoralists, semi-settled and settled communities; from the ranks of literate *'ulamā'* and *murīd*s (*ṣūfī* disciples), and the illiterate societies; and from caste groups, and manumitted and bonded slaves. Each group had its particular grievances, and all shared the dream of great advantages accruing to them if the *status quo* was changed.

35. M. A. al-Hajj, 1964, p. 50.
36. O. Jah, 1973, p. 184.

At the core of the *mudjahidūn* were the students (*murīds/talībs*) who followed the *shaykhs* in their preaching tours (*siyaḥa*) and accompanied them in their forced emigration (*ḥidjra*) from the land of *kufr*. Together with the independent or self-supporting scholars who joined the camps of the *shaykhs*, they constituted the *djamaʿa* (the Community of the Faithful). Driven by religious zeal and guided by the visions of the *shaykhs*, the *djamaʿa* became the staunchest strugglers in the path of Allah (*mudjahidūn fi sabil Allah*). Certainly, the religious fervour that the reformers had ignited did spread to some Muslim elements outside the immediate *djamaʿa* who, spellbound by the charisma of the *shaykhs*, threw in their lot with the reformers. But these 'insiders', the vanguard of reform, were by no means numerically or militarily superior to the armies that the West African rulers had under their command. Hence, victory was made possible only after the ranks of the *djamaʿa* had been swollen by 'outsiders' who, doubtless, formed the majority of the fighting forces. These 'outsiders' were certainly syncretists (*mukhalliṭūn*), but their participation in the *djihād* decidedly closed the socio-religious gap that had separated them from the *djamaʿa*. The imperfects were now brought into the fold of the *mudjahidūn* whose ultimate reward was paradise.

The bulk of the 'insiders', and perhaps the 'outsiders' as well, were Fulbe in origin. The reformers themselves had close ties with the Fulbe and the leadership of the caliphates was Fulbe dominated. This preponderant Fulbe influence in the reform movements has led some to conclude that the *djihād* was a series of ethnic wars designed to foster Fulbe domination over their host countries. To be sure, some Fulbe had joined the *djihād* out of a sense of ethnic solidarity. However, it is evident that large numbers of Fulbe fought on the side of the anti-*djihād* forces. Again, the *djihād*s of Shaykh Ahmadu Lobbo and al-Hadjdj ʿUmar were in large part directed against Fulbe political leadership in Massina and the Senegambia.

The Fulbe diaspora from Futa Toro predated the *djihād* by some four or five centuries. Wherever they went, the Fulbe, largely cattle herders, lived outside the confines of urban centres and agriculturalist societies. Their seasonal search for water and pastures, however, took them into settled agricultural areas in the south, and Tuareg regions in the north.[37] In the dry season the Fulbe were forced to graze their cattle on farmlands. This seasonal pressure on the agriculturalists, particularly at the time when crops were still being harvested, aroused tension between the agriculturalist communities and the pastoral Fulbe. Further still, by coming within reach of the urban-based authorities, the Fulbe were subjected to taxation, and to restrictions on the movements of their herds and use of water sources.[38] The Fulbe were also forced to pay fines for damages that their cattle caused to crops. During the wet seasons, the Fulbe moved their herds to drier

37. W. A. Brown, 1969, p. 60; M. Last, 1967, pp. lxii–lxiii; M. Hiskett, 1976, p. 138.
38. M. Last, 1967; pp. lxii-lxxiv; M. Hiskett, 1976, p. 138.

areas in the north where they competed with the Tuareg for water sources. It was during that time that the cattle of the Fulbe bore the brunt of Tuareg raids.[39] Moreover, Tuareg depredations and pressure on the nomadic Fulbe increased whenever drought or famine struck the Sahel. The Fulbe had long chafed at the restrictions, the taxes, the fines, and the constant threat to their herds. The *djihād* offered them a welcome alternative: freedom from the burden of taxes and fines, and security from Tuareg pillage.

Besides, the Fulbe of Massina and Senegambia had other complaints. In about the middle of the eighteenth century, the Bambara of Segu succeeded in extending their suzerainty over the Fulbe of Massina. The *fama*s of Segu did not, however, administer Massina directly. They relied on the local ruling dynasties, the *arma* (descendants of the Moroccan conquerors of Songhay) to oversee the towns of Jenne, Timbuktu and Sungojo, and the Fulbe Dikko warlords to govern the rest of the Niger Bend on their behalf. The *fama*s exacted an annual tribute from the Fulbe, said to have consisted of '100 boys, 100 girls, 100 male horses, 100 female horses, a measure of gold', and a large number of cattle.[40] Moreover, the herds of the Fulbe became fair game for the Bambara overlords and the Dikko, who habitually raided Fulbe camps. The *arma* joined in the forays. It is said that on one occasion (1810–11), the Bambara spent some four months in Massina pillaging Fulbe cattle and seizing large quantities of rice from the farmers. The enslavement of the Fulbe and the plundering of their cattle, as well as the unrestrained use of violence against them by the Bambara and the local authorities were among the major factors behind the Fulbe alliance with Shaykh Ahmadu.

Apparently, Shaykh Aḥmadu's *djihād* was one of a series of Fulbe-inspired attempts to overthrow Bambara hegemony in the region. The nationalist struggle was championed by the Fulbe leaders, Hammadi Badejio and his son, Golajio. In 1815–16, only two years before Shaykh Ahmadu began his *djihād*, Golajio had captured the region of Kunari from the Bambara. Shaykh Ahmadu quickly allied himself to these patriotic forces. The coalition won a resounding victory against the Dikko and the Bambara at the battle of Nukuma.[41]

The Fulbe of the Senegambia fared no better than their kinsmen elsewhere. They too suffered from the ravages and the harsh rule of the Torodbe *almami*s whom they had helped put in power a century or two earlier. For by the middle of the nineteenth century, the *almami*s turned into oppressive hereditary oligarchies that preyed on their subjects. Furthermore, the *almami*s entered into economic and political partnership with the French whom they allowed to construct fortified posts along the valley

39. W. A. Brown, 1969, pp. 35–6; M. Last, 1967, p. lxiii.

40. W. A. Brown, 1969, p. 182, n. 25.

41. ibid., *passim*. Nukuma was the decisive battle that resulted in the establishment of the Hamdullahi caliphate.

of the Senegal river. The military presence of the French and their growing authority in the area were strongly resented by the pious among the Fulbe who considered them (as Christians) to be *ahl adh-dhimma* (protected people) to be tolerated provided they paid the prescribed *djizya* (poll tax or tribute) and exercised no influence in *dār al-Islām*.[42] The refusal of the French to pay the *djizya*, or any other tax for that matter, was considered incompatible with their status as tributaries under Muslim law. It is thus not surprising that the Fulbe of Futa Toro responded enthusiastically to the appeal of al-Hadjdj 'Umar to join his *djihād* against the corrupt local rulers and the 'infidel' French. Throughout the different phases of the *djihād*, Futa Toro, 'Umar's home area, continued to furnish the bulk of the Tijāni *mudjahidūn*.

Similarly, the reformers drew substantial support from the immense slave population and caste groups that existed in Bilād al-Sūdan. The nineteenth-century Sudanic aristocracy, that is the ruling dynasties and the scholarly and trading communities, depended to a large extent on the toil of and trade in these servile groups for its wealth and prestige. The endogamous caste clans were employed in socially inferior artisanal occupations, such as blacksmithing, fishing, weaving and tanning. Slaves were employed in farming, herding, domestic services, and in fighting (as warriors and bodyguards).

It would appear that the enormous pool of slaves that had existed in the Western Sudan increased greatly on the eve of the *djihād* as a result of the availability of firearms, and the dramatic expansion in the export of slaves to the European merchants on the coast.[43] The aristocracy in the region preyed on peasants and pastoralists, and on Muslims and non-Muslims alike. The fear of loss of freedom, and the violence that accompanied slave-raiding drove scores of would-be victims to seek refuge with the *shaykh*s. Muslim and non-Muslim slaves likewise sought redemption by joining the *djihād* and becoming members of the new society. Consequently, slaves constituted a considerable proportion of the *mudjahidūn* and the flock of students and initiates that had gathered around the reformers. Both Shaykh Ahmadu and al-Hadjdj 'Umar successfully appealed to slaves to fight on their side. Shaykh Ahmadu is said to have announced, 'All you *machube* [slaves] who came to me today are liberated. All the *machube* will find paradise with me.'[44] It is not without significance that Shaykh Ahmadu made his stand against the Bambara and the Dikko at the Sebera, a region that was densely populated with slaves and caste groups.

The indebtedness of the reformers to the servile groups was boundless.

42. J. R. Willis, 1970, pp. 160 *et seq.*; O. Jah, pp. 152–3, 179–81, 205 *et seq.*

43. J. R. Willis, 1978, pp. 208–10; W. A. Brown, 1969, pp. 114–15, 124–5; M. Hiskett, 1976, pp. 138–9; P. E. Lovejoy, 1983, pp. 188–99. It was estimated that by the middle of the nineteenth century the slave population in Futa Jallon was almost half the total population of the region.

44. W. A. Brown, 1969, pp. 188–9, footnote no. 52.

Consequently, they rewarded them abundantly. Slaves were manumitted, and were endowed with the legal share of the booty. A few of them filled prestigious positions in the administration. Hence, one meets in the caliphates 'with the strange paradox of the lowest orders of humanity ascending to the highest offices of state'.[45]

The Community of the Faithful in *dār al-Hidjra*

The teaching and preaching of the reformers had continued for several decades before the authorities detected any sign of danger. But once the teachers turned into political agitators, the rulers and their *'ulamā'* were quick to expel them from their midst, to restrict their activities, and to harass their followers.[46] The inevitable violent confrontation took place following the expulsion of the shaykhs and their retinue from their centres of Degel in Hausaland, Kuby in Massina, and Jugunku in Futa Jallon, and their subsequent settlement in *dār al-Hidjra*. There, in Gudu (1804), Nukuma (1816–17) and Dinguiraye (1849), the *djama'a* took its definite shape. Far removed from the immediate attention of the authorities, the *djama'a* now prepared itself for the imminent eruption. Arms were collected and stored, defences were erected, and 'Uthmān dan Fodio and Shaykh Ahmadu Lobbo assumed the title of *amīr al-mu'minīn*. Al-Hadjdj 'Umar, it must be remembered, had already been appointed *Khalīfat Khatim al-Awlyya'*.

A continuous stream of a whole population of refugees, either responding to the appeals of the shaykhs or fleeing from persecution, made its way to dār al-Hidjra. Teachers and their students, slaves and free men, and peasants and nomads milled around the leaders of the *djihāds*. The atmosphere inside the settlements was one of great religious intensity and expectations. Students were instructed in Islamic sciences, particularly *ṣūfism*, and were initiated into the Ḳādirīyya and Tijāniyya *ṣūfī* orders. It is to be expected that there was endless discussion of the events that led to the *hidjra* (emigration) and its parallelism with the *hidjra* of the Prophet from Mecca to Medina (622), as well as of war preparations.

The *hidjra* was certainly the most critical phase in the careers of the reformers. It was, however, by no means self-imposed, nor was it, as most scholars would have us believe, deliberately undertaken to legitimize the *djihād*.[47] Again, the *hidjra* was not, as is generally argued, a fundamental prerequisite for the West African reform movements, for the revolts would have erupted even if the *hidjra* had never taken place. To be sure, the

45. J.R. Willis, forthcoming, ch. 3.

46. A.A. Batran, 1974, p. 49.

47. O. Jah, 1973, pp. 180–5, maintains that it was not certain whether al-Hadjdj 'Umar had left Jugunku voluntarily or had been forcibly expelled. None the less, he argues that the Almami of Futa Jallon did decide to expel 'Umar and that the Almami could have made conditions too difficult for the Shaykh and his *djama'a* to remain in Jugunku.

drama began to unfold several years before the *hidjra*. Quoting the *Tazyyn al-Warakat* of Abdullahi dan Fodio, F.H. el-Masri explained that preparations for the Sokoto *djihād*, particularly the collection of arms, had begun since 1797.[48] By that time, the *djihād* had developed an almost unstoppable momentum; it had certainly matured in the mind of Shaykh ʿUthmān:

> Arms had been collected since 1797 when the community had demanded to break with unbelievers and wage a *djihād* but Dan Fodio asked them rather to arm themselves. He himself turned to prayer and sought the intercession of his Shaykh, ʿAbdal-Ḳādir al-Djaylani to let him see Hausaland ruled by Islamic law.[49]

Equally, al-Hadjdj ʿUmar's activities (recruitment of followers, agitation, and the collection of arms) before his *hidjra* to Dinguiraye (1849) had sufficiently alarmed the authorities in Massina, Segu, and throughout the Senegambia, to either detain him, plot his assassination, or deny him passage through their territories. ʿUmar's choice of Jugunku, his first academic centre, according to Willis, was not accidental, for its geographical location 'afforded [the Shaykh] a convenient place from which he could venture into an active trade in arms and armaments'.[50] Stripped of its post-*djihād* pious trappings, the *hidjra*, or more correctly the forced exile of the reformers, still proved to be invaluable. It removed the *djamʿa* from immediate danger and afforded the time to prepare for the inevitable confrontation.

Undoubtedly, the reformers had an overwhelming advantage over their adversaries. They profoundly believed in the sacredness of their mission; and they were able to articulate the grievances and frustrations of the masses. Above all, they had the unflinching loyalty of the *djamaʿa*, for *ṣūfī* education stressed complete and blind obedience to the person of *Shaykh al-Ṭarīḳa*. According to the *ṣūfīs*:

> The *murīd* [disciple/initiated] is he who has no wish other than the wish of his shaikh. He must lose himself in his shaikh to such an extent that nothing of himself is left for him. He is [to be] like the corpse between [sic] the hands of the mortician, or the pen between the fingers of the copyist.[51]

The reformers had yet another asset in their personal religious charisma. As spiritual guides of *ṣūfī* brotherhoods, they were recognized as saints and possessors of the Divine *baraka*. These powers, so their followers believed, enabled the *shaykhs* to relieve natural disasters such as drought and famine, to fertilize the land, animals and women, to smite their enemies, etc. Stories

48. F.H. El-Masri, 1978, p. 23.
49. ibid.
50. J.R. Willis, 1970, p. 90.
51. A.A. Batran, 1974, p. 49.

about the *shaykhs*' miracles were widely circulated and believed. In a society that nurtured a strong belief in the existence of supernatural forces, the reputed efficacious 'magical' powers of the *shaykhs* contributed immeasurably to their popularity.[52] And the numerous unsuccessful attempts on their lives were strong proof of their Divine protection. Moreover, their intellectual superiority, their ascetic life style, and their distance from the 'corrupt' rulers, underscored the confidence that the masses had in them.

The reformers did not hastily plunge their followers into reckless adventurism. Their retaliation to provocations came after thorough preparation and at a time chosen by them. Shaykh 'Uthmān, for example, warned against adventurism for 'it only results in failure and drags weak Muslims into perdition'.[53] Hence, their conquest of such large areas was a testimony to their careful planning. They certainly won their victories 'despite the strength of their opponents', for there is no conclusive evidence to support the commonly held view that dynastic rivalries, and an alleged general decline in the power of the Sudanic states were major factors in the success of the *djihāds*.[54]

It is interesting to note that while the *djihāds* of Shaykh 'Uthmān and Shaykh Ahmadu were mainly restricted to their home regions of Hausaland and Massina, al-Hadjdj 'Umar's movement, launched from the eastern borderline of Futa Jallon, aimed at the conquest of the whole of the Western Sudan. 'Umar was never able to secure his homeland, Futa Toro, for by that time the French were well entrenched in the area. He did, however, attack the French positions at Medina (Médine) (1857) and Matam (1858–9) but his forces were repulsed with heavy losses. Subsequently, he turned his attention towards the east to devour Segu (1861) and the caliphate of Hamdullahi (1862).

It is not difficult to imagine how far east al-Hadjdj 'Umar contemplated extending his caliphate. His objective was simply to establish the authority of *Khalīfat Khatim al-Awlyya'* over the entire Bilād al-Sūdān.[55] His 'international' conquests were made possible by the fact that his forces were more broadly based than those of Shaykh 'Uthmān and Shaykh Ahmadu. They were drawn from all the regions; and were composed of largely well-trained and well-equipped Tijāni affiliates whom al-Hadjdj 'Umar had personally initiated during his extensive travels throughout the Western Sudan. His eastern drive however came to an end following his tragic death in Massina (1864).

52. M. Last, 1967, pp. 3–13; W. A. Brown, 1969, pp. 48, 116, 123; O. Jah, 1973 pp. 237 *et seq.*

53. F. H. El-Masri, 1978, p. 22.

54. M. Hiskett, 1976, p. 139.

55. O. Jah, 1973, *passim.*

Some consequences of the *djihād*s

It was for the first and perhaps the last time that such huge territories in Bilād al-Sūdān were transformed into centralized Islamic theocracies. But the degree of centralization differed from one caliphate to the other. It would appear that it was only in Hamdullahi (1818–62), with its small area, its small homogeneous population, and its good communications, that a high degree of centralization was achieved. As a result, Shaykh Ahmadu and his successors were able to apply the *sharī'a* to an extent that was not possible in the other caliphates.

The supreme offices of *amīr al-mu'minīn* (al-Hadjdj 'Umar's son and successor, Aḥmad, assumed that title as well) and that of *Shaykh al-Ṭarīḳa* were vested in the descendants of the reformers who resided in the capital cities. The caliphates were divided into *imarat* (emirates), each governed by a top-ranking *mudjahīd*. Most of the *amīr*s (provincial governors) were scholars, but clan leaders and freed slaves (al-Hadjdj 'Umar is said to have entertained a preference for slaves) were to be found among them. In later years appointment to high-ranking positions depended, to a large extent, on blood ties to the caliphal line or to prestigious *mudjahidūn*.

In general, traditional power and social standing were transferred to a new elite, the *mudjahidūn*. Since the Fulbe had formed the backbone of the fighters, they thus became the aristocrats *par excellence* of the Western Sudan. They filled most of the administrative positions, and many of them were settled on land alienated during the course of the *djihād*. Fulbe and other landowners depended on slave labour to farm their agricultural holdings.[56] It seems that the proportion of slaves to freemen in the caliphates remained at the high level it had reached in pre-*djihād* days. Slaves who had participated in the *djihād* were freed, but those who had not gone over to the *shaykh*s were re-enslaved. More slaves were secured in raids across frontiers and in rebellions. The legal status of captured slaves was spelt out in the *fatwā* (legal opinion) of al-Maghīlī:

> As for one you find in their [unbelievers'] hands, as a slave, who claims to be a free-born Muslim, his word is to be accepted until proof is established to confirm that he is a slave ... Any person you leave from among them, because he claims that he is a free-born Muslim, then it becomes evident to you that he was unbeliever, enslave him again.[57]

All individuals and groups within the caliphates were afforded protection and security. The southern movements of pastoral groups were regulated to minimize tension between them and the peasant communities. Northern frontiers and pastures were constantly watched to restrain Tuareg raids.

56. M. Last, 1974, p. 28; P. E. Lovejoy, 1983, pp. 188–99. According to Last, the settlement of the pastoral Fulbe was more intensive in Sokoto than in the other caliphates.
57. F. H. El-Masri (ed.), 1979, p. 119.

And slave-raiding within the communities was stopped. *Sharīʿa* courts were established and *ḳādīs* (judges) were appointed by the caliphs and the *amīrs*. Many un-Islamic practices were banned. For example prohibition on drinking of alcohol was strictly enforced; the hated taxes of the discredited regimes were replaced by the canonical *zakāt* (tithe), *kharadj* (land tax), and *djizya*; the number of wives was restricted to four, etc.[58] Taxes were allocated and collected by the *amīrs* who, more often than not, levied them arbitrarily.

The revolutions achieved their greatest success in the fields of education and conversion. Schools were founded throughout the caliphates, and a large number of missionaries penetrated unconverted areas. A cadre of *Ṣūfī* teachers emerged. Some teachers settled in the newly founded cultural and learning centres such as Sokoto, Gwandu, Hamdullahi and Segu, as well as in other towns and villages. Other teachers pursued the traditionally honoured *siyaha*. But most teachers, especially those in the outlying districts, had to wrestle with the eternal problem of *takhliṭ*. Many traditional norms were eventually tolerated. Indeed once the initial zeal had subsided, some of the original ideals slowly bowed to pragmatism and the passage of time. The sheer size of the caliphates and the dominant presence of the 'imperfect outsiders' within the *djamaʿa* made compromises unavoidable. It must be remembered that although the declared objective of the reformers was the realization of an ideal Islam, most of the *mudjahidūn* espoused more mundane motives. Nonetheless, the *djihād* resulted in the entrenchment of Islam and the two rival *ṣūfī* brotherhoods, the Ḳādirīyya and the Tijāniyya, in West Africa. The Torodbe Islamic revolutionary tradition was kept alive by a new generation of *djihād* leaders such as Maba Diakhou of the Gambia (*c.* 1809–67), Maḥmadu Lamin of Senegambia (1885–8), and Samori Ture of Guinea (1879–98) who rose in the name of Islam against the foreign invaders and their local allies but were finally overwhelmed by the might of the European war machine.[59]

58. A. G. Hopkins, 1973, p. 144, states that the ban on alcohol raised the demand in Hausaland for kola, a stimulant that was not prohibited by Muslim law.

59. I. Hrbek, 1979; C. A. Quinn, 1979; Y. Person, 1979.

22 The Sokoto caliphate and Borno

M. LAST

Introduction

The Sokoto caliphate and Borno are part of a single region, in which for most of the nineteenth century the caliphate was the dominant partner. But also within that region were other states and peoples whose contribution, willingly made or not, was very considerable. In this chapter I will, however, outline only the political structures and general developments within the caliphate and Borno in the belief that these largely determined the shape of the region's common history.

In the past fifteen years almost every state in the region has been the subject of at least one, more or less detailed, historical study, and almost without exception these studies have been confined to political developments. More recently religious and now economic themes have been taken up, but despite the quantity of material available there are still large gaps both in our data and in our understanding. This chapter does not attempt a synthesis of all these studies; it is meant instead to suggest a framework for understanding the history of the region in the years 1820 to 1880 and for opening some further avenues for research.

The emphasis here is put on the period 1820–80, the period when relatively stable government had been re-established following the fighting, the famines and the dislocation of civil society during the period of wars known as the *djihād*. But by way of introduction, the period *c.*1775–1820 will be summarized in three sections: the first, *c.*1775–95, when the expression of discontent among the Muslim reformist party in such states as Gobir was both peaceful and successful; the second, *c.*1795–1810, when the clash of interests and ideas pushed the various parties involved in state affairs into a full-scale war; and the third, *c.*1810–20, when the new governments sought to cope with the consequences of war, in some cases trying out new methods of administration, in others trying out new sites for settlement. The real achievement of the administrations after *c.*1820 was their success in bringing back to the region a stability that was the foundation for an unprecedented economic boom: a period of growth on a scale not seen in the region since perhaps the fifteenth or sixteenth centuries.

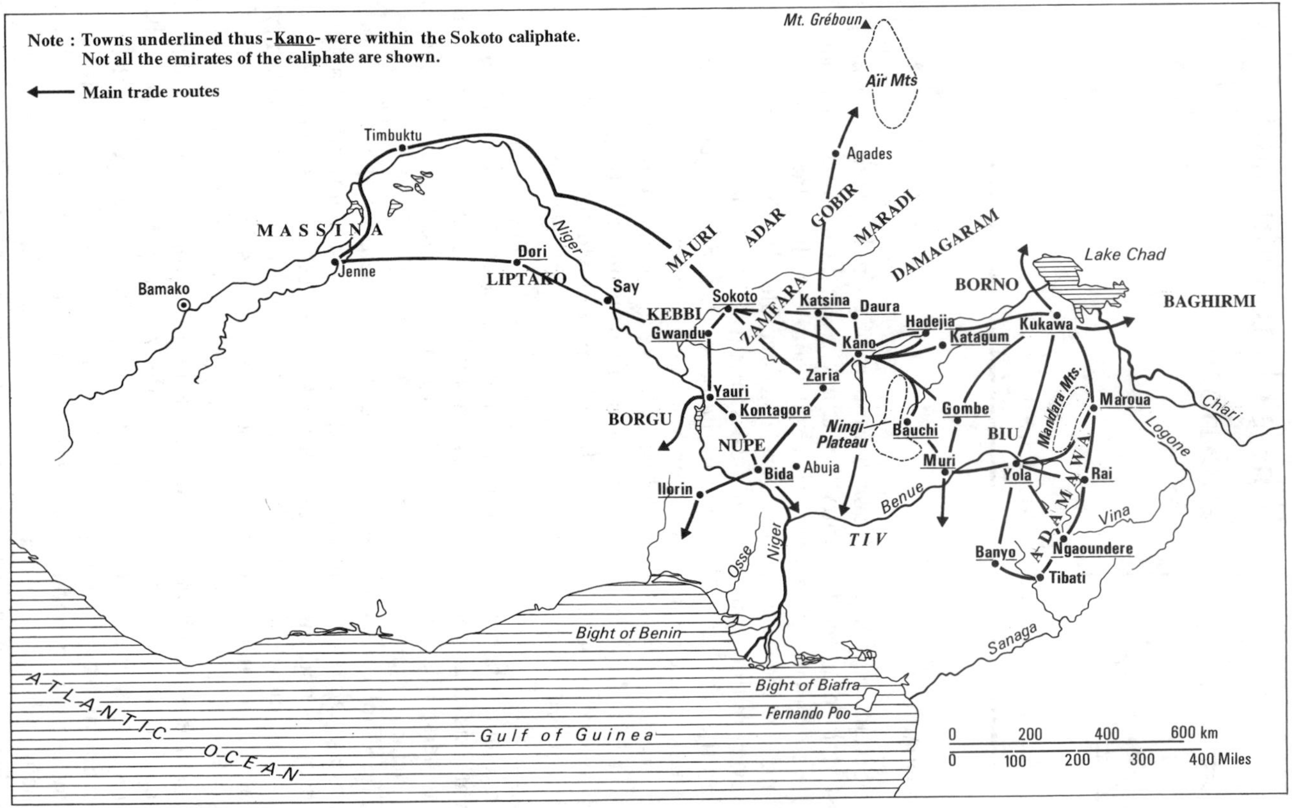

FIG. 22.1 *The Sokoto caliphate and Borno and their neighbours (after M. Last)*

The social cost of this success was the loss of much local autonomy, both political and economic, as well as the loss of a particular style of life: though these losses were resisted, the full history of this resistance has yet to be written.

*c.*1775–95: the opening door to reform

The areas where the Muslim reform party was strongest and won the most notable successes were not in Borno itself but in the Hausa states and Nupe which had once been part of a wider Borno 'caliphate'. In the context of urban politics, rulers mainly in favour of religious reform came to power for example in Nupe (the Etsu Jibril), in Kano (the Sarki Alwali), in Zaria (the Sarki Isḥāḳ) and in Katsina (the Sarki Gozo); even in Gobir, Kebbi and Zamfara where Shaykh 'Uthmān dan Fodio (Usman dan Fodio) was preaching reform to an increasing following, the sultans in the region (such as Bawa Jan Gwarzo at Alkalawa) were prepared to come to a political agreement with the reformers. It was, however, in the countryside where the reform movement was most radical and was achieving spectacular success. Led initially (but rashly) by al-Hadjdj Jibril al-Aqdasi (from Agades) but developed with great skill by Shaykh 'Uthmān, the reform movement was at first primarily concerned with spreading better Islamic education and practice throughout the rural areas, while the Shaykh (like other scholars elsewhere in the region) acted as tutor and adviser to the sultans in his area. After *c.*1788, however, the movement sought to establish autonomous communities of its own, mainly on the margins of Hausa states, and to claim for Muslims living in existing settlements the rights of an autonomous 'caste'.[1]

The shift away from a strategy of reforming the state to a strategy of autonomy within or outside the state paralleled political developments in other contexts. The Gobir state had largely ceased to pay tribute to Borno (and had perhaps forfeited thereby some of its formal Islamic legitimacy in the eyes of the reformers); similarly, the sultanate of Mandara, immediately to the south of Borno, had successfully fought for its independence from Borno, *c.*1781, while even within Borno the local ruler of Daya was ready to try and assert his autonomy.[2] At a time of political fragmentation the reformers, it seems, recognized that their successes in getting reform-

1. For an extended study of the life of Shaykh 'Uthmān, see M. Hiskett, 1973. A contemporary account is in U. F. Malumfashi, 1973. For a new analysis of the movement within its wider West African context, see M. Last (1988).

2. On Mandara, see B. M. Barkindo, 1980. On eighteenth-century Borno, see J. E. Lavers, 1980, pp. 206–9. Daya finally revolted, it is thought, about 1805, cf. S. W. Koelle, 1854, pp. 212–23. The broader reasons for the decline of Borno on the one hand, and the increasing acceptance of Islam in rural areas on the other, are complex and much debated. Economic factors include the shift in eighteenth-century trade away from a northern to a more southern orientation, and a consequent increase in the importance of rural producer-traders and their struggle for a free market.

minded sultans appointed could only be temporary, and that the better solution – having their own autonomous communities and their rights as an autonomous 'caste' – was likely to be longer lasting, if more dangerous to attain. But as a strategy it has two other advantages: first, it was a solution used earlier not only in Borno but elsewhere in West Africa; secondly, and more importantly, it paralleled the experience of the Prophet at Mecca.

*c.*1795–1810: the military confrontation

One consequence of claiming, and getting, special rights within the Muslim state for Muslims of a particular persuasion (the reformers were distinguished by the name 'Kadirawa' in Hausa on account of their membership of the Ḳādirīyya brotherhood) was that local government officials were thus deprived of their authority to adjudicate and tax all their subjects. As increasing numbers (including slaves) claimed the new privileged status, political authorities at the local level rejected many of the new claims and used military force to reimpose their authority. In the turmoil slaves escaped and made their way to freedom in the newly autonomous communities, which refused to return them, on the grounds that they were Muslims, to their owners. The measures the government took to restore order and recoup its lossses only exacerbated the rift between rural and urban society: officials were apt to raid markets and confiscate people's produce and livestock. More significantly, attacks, possibly as reprisals, were launched against Fulbe (Fulani, Peul) pastoralists, to enslave them and seize their cattle, on the assumption that the reformers (a large proportion of whom spoke the Fulbe language, Fulfulde) would thus be forced to call off their activities. With hindsight it was arguably the most fateful decision of the war: it drove the pastoralists into the reformers' camp and so enabled the reformers in the long run to withstand disastrous setbacks, with the result that the reformers and their pastoralist allies eventually won the war; it gave the pastoralist military faction an unintended influence in the post-*djihād* state, and so altered considerably the way the new state came to be administered; finally, it reinforced the stereotype that the *djihād* was merely a Fellata (Fulbe) war, as the Borno scholars called it; and consequently gave substance to the jibe that the caliphate was a 'Fulbe empire'.[3]

Formal war was declared in 1804 after Shaykh 'Uthmān made the *hidjra* with his community from Degel to Gudu where the Shaykh was then elected *imām* of the new 'state'. By the beginning of 1806 war flags had been distributed regionally and commanders formally appointed for each

3. For contemporary accusations that the djihād was a Fulbe affair, see the letters from Borno quoted in M. Bello, 1951, and the letter from the scholar 'Abd al-Salām quoted in M. Bello, 1970, Vol. 1, pp. 18–35. Much of the detailed campaigning in the *djihād* is known only for the Sokoto area, from contemporary documents: for summaries based on these, see M. Hiskett, 1973; M. Last, 1967.

area. Within each of the Hausa states, the reformers' strategy was for units to continue to operate locally and then unite for a concerted attack on the state capital. Thus the Shaykh's forces operated independently of, for example, their allies in Kano, while within Kano each unit fought its own separate campaign. A disaster in one battle did not therefore endanger the whole movement, but decentralization of command was to have important political consequences later.

The reformers, using guerrilla tactics and weaponry, were relatively secure in the countryside; their main losses, they said, came not from fighting, but from famine and epidemic disease. But on at least two occasions the Shaykh's army came near to being wiped out (Tsuntsua, 1804; Alwassa, 1805), and these losses, of scholars and students especially, made the Shaykh more than ever dependent on pastoralist support. Furthermore, because of the famine, more and more Tuareg were being forced south to buy or seize food, and they were now in competition with the reformers and their pastoralist allies for scarce pasture and grain. Until now, (*c.*1804), the reformers, amongst whom were a number of Tuareg scholars and who counted the Sultan of Agades as an ally, had been able to prevent serious clashes with the Tuareg.

To bring the war to a quick end it was necessary, however, to capture, and hold, the sultan's palace in each of the states. For the war was about 'kingship' and not, at this stage, much about territory. Only in Borno was the authority of the *mai* strong enough to survive the loss of his capital, Birni Ngazargamo; in part because the reformers were themselves unable to hold onto the capital once they had captured it (in the end the site was simply abandoned). Militarily, kingship was symbolized, and defended, by heavy cavalry, of which the state had the effective monopoly. The reformers' bowmen and spearmen with their superior morale and a few horsemen, and so long as they chose their ground, might be able tactically to defeat in battle the rather ineffective state cavalry sent against them. But to win the war, the reformers needed their own cavalry, and some of the military organization it required. 'Guerrillas' had to become government.

By January 1809, all the main Hausa states had capitulated and their sultans had fled into exile, after four years of intermittent campaigning. The hardest fighting had been endured by the Shaykh's forces in Gobir. The success of the outnumbered, out-equipped Muslim reformers, first in battle and then in their final series of triumphs in state after state during 1807 and 1808 seemed to them to be both a miracle and proof of the rightness of their cause; the parallel, again, with the Prophet's success at the battle of Badr only confirmed it.

*c.*1810–20: the aftermath of war

After the four years of fighting, famine and epidemics, the main problem was reconstruction. For some of the defeated – the *mai* of Borno, for example, or the ex-sultans of the Hausa states – the task was to instal themselves in places of exile, reassemble their courts and build up their armies again in order to recover their lost kingdoms. The most successful were the *mai*s of Borno, the least so were perhaps the ex-sultans of Kano, whilst others merely came to terms with the new regime. In some areas, such as Nupe, the war was not yet over, in other areas, such as Ọyọ, it had scarcely begun.

For the victorious Muslim reformers, reconstruction was complicated by the need to keep precisely to Islamic law. Initially Shaykh ʿUthmān had been very strict in his interpretation of what was legal and illegal for a proper Muslim, but after 1810 he gradually altered his position, tolerating practices (such as the use of music) he had earlier condemned.[4] Nonetheless the concern of all the *djihād* leaders – Shaykh ʿUthmān, his brother ʿAbdullāh and the Shaykh's son Muḥammad Bello – was to appoint at all levels of the administration men with both the education to understand Islamic law and the personal authority to implement it. But casualties among scholars and students had been especially high during the war, and even in Sokoto at this time there were not enough learned men to post as local *amīr*s, judges and *imām*s to the rural areas. Elsewhere in the caliphate the shortage in this early period was even more acute, despite the Shaykh's policy of sending students back to their home areas. Inevitably the shortfall was made good by appointing kinsmen who could be supervised from the centre.

A stop-gap solution to the shortage of personnel was to employ former officials of the previous regime. Initially some were given territorial or judicial posts – in Kano, they were known as Hausawa – but their loyalty to the new government soon came under suspicion, and many at the local level were replaced. Similarly there was a problem over whether to allow traders from formerly 'enemy areas' to come and buy in the markets of the caliphate. From early on, this cross-frontier trade seems to have been regarded with suspicion, and Hausa traders who had stayed behind, or local Hausa officials who wanted to restore an economy based on trading, found themselves in a difficult position.

Given the inexperience of the new administration and the potential for distrust, the burden of supervising the caliphal government was initially enormous. A great number of complaints and disputes from all over the caliphate came to the Shaykh for arbitration. First there were the disputes among military commanders and among scholars over who should be allocated what territory to administer. But in practice a number of such disputes were resolved either by force or by the aggrieved party setting himself up independently of his rival and owing allegiance to the Shaykh direct. A second group of problems consisted of claims arising out of misconduct by the *djihād* armies during the war: cases of wrongful enslave-

4. For a fuller examination of this shift in attitude, see F. H. El-Masri, 1978, pp. 13–33.

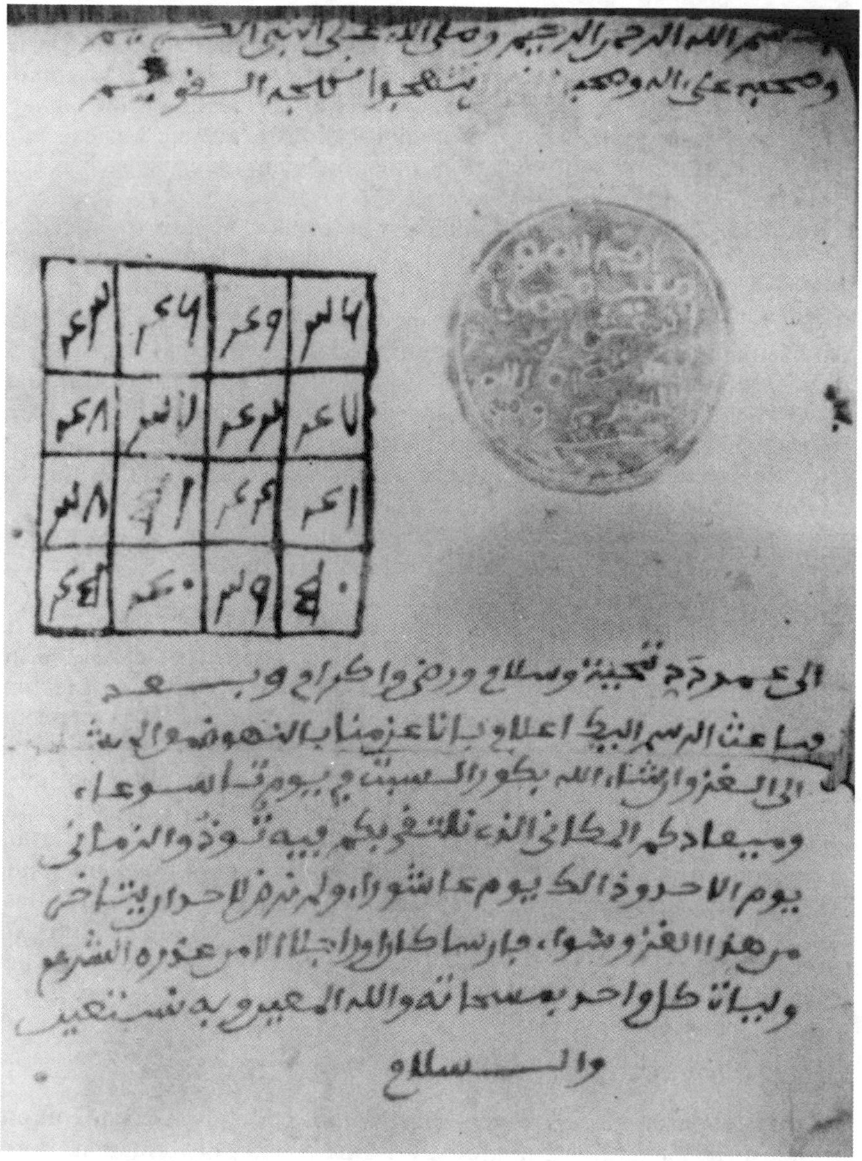

PLATE 22.1 *A letter from Muḥammad Bello, Caliph of Sokoto, 1817–37, to ʿUmar Dadi of Kanoma giving details of the rendez-vous for a campaign*

ment or wrongful seizure of property or land. A third group were problems among disillusioned scholars, caused in part by the Shaykh's earlier espousal of millenarian ideas, about which after 1810 he changed his mind.[5] Nonetheless at least one new claimant to Mahdist leadership came forward and attracted support away from the new caliphate, and he was executed by staking. But there continued to be other dissident scholars, such as Dan Buya or those with ʿAbd al-Salām.

Inevitably the number and complexity of disputes became too much for the Shaykh, who now retired to teach and write: he fell ill *c.*1815 and died two years later. As five years earlier, in 1812, the task of arbitrating disputes had been divided between ʿAbdullāh dan Fodio and the Shaykh's son Muḥammad Bello, there was no dramatic shift in policy at the Shaykh's death. One reason for the number of disputes lay in the structure of emirate government in this early period, in which the pattern of decentralized military command had been carried over from the days of *djihād*. The *amīr*, though the original appointee and 'flag-bearer', was still only the first among equals; in some cases there was more than one 'flag-bearer' in a territory, while in other cases the original appointee proved too weak to assert his authority. By 1820, some of the older 'flag-bearers' had died, or a modus vivendi had been reached.

Finally, at this early period, the areas under the full control of the reformers were relatively restricted. In Sokoto itself, the settled, secure zone was perhaps as small as a strip 40 km wide was 65 km long, stretching south from Sokoto. Similarly in Kano, Katsina, Daura and Zaria the secure hinterland was limited, and it is probable that in emirates like Bauchi the situation, territorially, was even more precarious. But the important point is that by 1820 there was no *other* viable government with any semblance of legitimacy or widespread support that could rival the new administration. The problem, then, was to extend the administration to the countryside, and incorporate the rural areas into the caliphate. In Borno, by contrast, the problem for the *mai*s was to use their existing ties to the countryside to reorganize the state in order to preserve its autonomy vis-à-vis the new caliphate.

The Sokoto caliphate: 1820–80

In 1820 the Sokoto caliphate was composed of some seven major emirates with a further ten large emirates still in the process of formation. Borno too was re-established after the retreat from its capital and the loss of extensive areas in the west and south. In order to understand the changes implied by the terms 'caliphate' and 'emirate', let us briefly and very schematically recapitulate the old political system the reformers had replaced.

5. For a detailed examination of Mahdism, see M. A. al-Hajj, 1973.

The most notable feature of the old system was the role of the king, known variously as *mai, sarki, etsu, alafin*. Before the shifts in power in the late eighteenth century, the king had ritual functions and a role that required a certain seclusion from the public; the palace was more sacred than a mere house. The king was more or less above politics, a symbol of great authority in whose name all acts were done; he represented the state. A number of men and women who as slaves or eunuchs were without kin or heirs were servants dedicated to the palace and the king's person; they formed one section of the administration. Another section was formed by large independent households with hereditary claims to titles, the holders of which thus had their own followings of men. A third section was the family of the king, particularly the king's mother or sister, his brothers and sons. The composition of councils and bodies responsible for rituals or for military leadership varied in detail from state to state, often with the palace slaves and the free office-holders divided into orders through which individuals could move by promotion. Political competition was limited to the offices *under* the king. As far as we know there were in the late eighteenth century trends for kings to take a more active part in politics, to become more exclusively Muslim and to promote reforms on the lines of Islamic government.[6] Economically, it seems that it was a period of rising levels of consumption (particularly of cotton cloth) and demand for slaves; and there was a need to regulate the expanding market and protect it. The effects of these changes reverberated down to the trading, farming and pastoral communities in the countryside, as those involved in political competition sought to strengthen their hold on their bases of power; as a consequence of which the *djihād* found widespread support among the victims of these changes.

The Muslim reformers (who included at least one of the last, reforming Hausa kings) had a very different blueprint to institute. The role of the king was replaced by an *amīr* neither whose person nor whose palace was sacred. Allāh, and not the state personified by the king, was the source of authority. Consequently the *amīr* was chosen not for any inherited quality of sacredness but for his personal piety towards Allāh. The *amīr* was the first among equals; his companions as a group were to share power under the *amīr*'s leadership. As a result, the role of palace slave-officials was to be reduced to that of personal servants and the formal office of queen mother or sister was eliminated. The *amīr* was part of the political process, and his office was theoretically open to any suitably pious candidate. A minimal bureaucracy of ministers, judges, inspectors, police and *imāms* was established as prescribed by the blueprint; and the regulations of the *sharīʿa* law, following the Māliki school of interpretation, were to order

6. For a reconstruction of the pre-*djihād* state of Borno, see J. E. Lavers, 1980, pp. 187–209; N. M. Alkali, 1978. For a pre-*djihād* Hausa state see A. Hassan and A. S. Naibi, 1962; M. G. Smith, 1960; Y. B. Usman, 1981.

relations between persons and between groups. The changes were designed to limit and formalize the political processes, to prevent gross manipulation of previously unwritten rules as well as to curtail the growth of palace-centred government. It was intended to do away with the ambiguity of a Muslim wielding ritual authority based on local, traditional religious belief, and replace it with an authority derived solely from Allāh, an authority not only acceptable to the Muslim community but also accountable to it. The blueprint's detail is most conveniently set out by ʿAbdullāh dan Fodio in his book to guide the Kano community on their new constitution, *Ḍiyaʾ al-ḥukkam*.[7] But as problems arose, Muḥammad Bello and subsequent caliphs wrote letters to the various leaders of nascent communities, outlining the crucial elements of the new system and adding some practical details. From one viewpoint, the political and intellectual history of the nineteenth century can be seen as an extended exercise in trying to implement or modify the reformers' blueprint. From another viewpoint (also implied in the blueprint), it is a history of the development and purposeful integration of the rural economies of the region, and their closer linking with first the Mediterranean and later the Atlantic economies. To these reformers' concerns, there was also added a distinctive sense of urgency and seriousness if the community was to be rebuilt, materially and spiritually, in time for the expected coming of the Mahdī.

The office of caliph

One of the most important innovations the reformers instituted was the office of caliph. In the eighteenth century the Hausa states and their neighbours were autonomous political units. Borno had exercised a degree of suzerainty over the states at various times in the past, and had used the term caliph; its *mai* even in the eighteenth century was the most senior, probably the most powerful ruler in the area. Under the new system the emirates were clearly under the suzerainty of the caliph at Sokoto, from whom authority to govern in specific areas emanated. With its explicit basis in Islamic constitutional practice, the caliph was formally above any local or ethnic identity in a way no previous suzerain had been; and in recognition of the otherworldly source of his authority, the role of caliph was to be demonstrably different from that of previous rulers – without ceremony or ritualization, without ostentatious wealth.

When Shaykh ʿUthmān dan Fodio died in April 1817, the lands of the caliph had already been divided up and administered in two main blocs.

7. For a recent study of ʿAbdullāh dan Fodio's ideas and their context, see A. A. A. Hamid, 1980. For a general study of caliphal policies and practice, see M. M. Tukur, 1977. Many of the traditional, pre-*djihād* titles were later introduced, including in some emirates, titles for important women of the ruling family (e.g. *madaki* in Kano, *inna* at Sokoto). The study of women's roles and organizations in the nineteenth century is only just beginning: cf. J. Boyd, 1982.

The division into quadrants is common enough: Wadai and Borno had probably used it and the symbolic maps of Hausa towns employ a similar conception. The fourfold division resolves into two pairs, each with a senior and two junior partners. With Bello's succession in 1817 to the office of caliph, the pattern was changed. Before 1817 the caliph Shaykh ʿUthmān had two officials to whom he delegated all responsibility – his brother ʿAbdullāh as vizier, and his son Muḥammad Bello as *amīr al-Sūdān* (*ʿAmīr* of the Blacks'). After 1817 the caliph (now Muḥammad Bello) left full responsibility for the western emirates delegated as before to his uncle ʿAbdullāh, now known simply as 'the *amīr*'; but he kept for himself full responsibility for the eastern emirates, delegating only executive duties to his friend and servant Gidado, who was now to be known as the vizier.

As responsibility included retaining the taxes derived from the area, it was appropriate that the richer emirates should fall within the caliph's sphere. For the eastern emirates, particularly Kano and Zaria in the early period, were able to underwrite the caliphal economy. Without these payments it would have been difficult to develop the caliphal capital and its hinterland, or even maintain an appropriate level of generosity for visitors. Captives as well as clothes and other items were sent regularly, but captives in particular were crucial both for expanding the area under cultivation around Sokoto and its outlying villages (for the area had not been a centre of cultivation before), and for putting up adequate defences such as high mud walls and flat-roofed, fireproof houses and building permanent mosques for the new settlements.[8]

The relationship between Sokoto and Gwandu is too complex to detail here, and in part depended on the personal characters of the *amīr*s at any given time. But there was something of the dual organization so common in West Africa, by which Gwandu had the role of uncle and represented ritual authority (the *amīr*s of Gwandu were notable for their piety) while at Sokoto the caliph had the role of the active nephew, in charge of affairs with ultimate political authority. Such a relationship seems to have held between ʿAbdullāh and Bello, and between Khalīl and ʿAlī; it forestalled any conflict and justified Gwandu's relative lack of interest in expanding its control over its subordinate emirates.

The relationship between the other *amīr*s and the caliph during the period 1820–45 was imbued more with the equality of former comrades-in-arms and fellow students than with the formality of superior and inferior. In particular, Yakubu of Bauchi, a veteran of the early community and not a Fulbe like the others, had a special, almost avuncular, link with the caliphs after Bello's death. There was inevitably a considerable degree of autonomy as each *amīr* consolidated his territorial position; but it is hard

8. The date when the remittances to Sokoto started, and their value, is not precisely known. In *c.*1850 the amount demanded was sharply increased. Cf. M. G. Smith, 1960, pp. 154, 157.

to be sure if certain appointments within an emirate (such as Kano) were not being vetted or recommended by the caliph in the same way as Shaykh ʿUthmān had carefully controlled appointments during the *djihād* by the strict allocation of flags.

The caliphal administration

With Muḥammad Bello now acting in three capacities, as caliph, as head of the eastern emirates and as head of the Sokoto hinterland, it was necessary to establish a caliphal administration. In the first of these capacities, Muḥammad Bello was engaged in writing books and letters of advice, while in his role as local commander-in-chief he took charge of the military defence of Sokoto. Furthermore, the caliph did not usually travel beyond Sokoto or Zamfara. The caliphal administration was largely responsible, then, for the supervision of the eastern emirates, and in particular for maintaining the revenue on which the caliphate depended.

For his administration, the caliph could call on five groups: his household retainers, mostly slaves or eunuchs, whose duties included for example looking after the stables; his erstwhile companions-in-arms, who now acted as advisers and special messengers; the immediate family and kin of his father the Shaykh; the leaders of local Fulbe clans; and finally the families who comprised his father's old community and formed the scholar class in the capital. These last were given judicial or religious responsibilities in the new administration or were allocated minor territorial posts, while the major territorial responsibilities within Sokoto fell to the clan leaders and the caliph's kinsmen. The caliph's advisers, given titles like *waziri, magajin gari, magajin rafi, galadima,* were the caliph's links with the emirates, the majority of which came under the waziri's office. These officials themselves had private household officials of their own and occupied distinct quarters in the town, but initially they had a relatively minor role in the territorial administration of the Sokoto hinterland or in Sokoto local politics. They were overshadowed by the *sarkin yaki* or the scholarly relatives and descendants of the Shaykh. But in the course of the century, as they became large and wealthy lineages in their own right, they played an increasingly central role in Sokoto politics and particularly in the election of the caliph.

A major task of the caliphal administration was to appoint or sanction the appointment of the *amīr*s, and to resolve any disputes over succession. The caliph's delegate (such as the *waziri*) installed the new *amīr*, having the appropriate letter with the caliphal seal ready and the space for the *amīr*'s name left blank. The following year, the new *amīr* would come in person to Sokoto to salute the caliph. As interregna were apt to be periods of licensed lawlessness, it was important that there be less than a week's delay in appointing a legitimate ruler. The caliph's delegates therefore in some instances had considerable responsibility. Extending out of this capacity to appoint (or dismiss), the caliph and his delegates acted as mediators in the event of a major dispute involving an *amīr*: they were the last court of appeal. Inevitably, as the office of the vizierate grew, the range of problems that came into the *waziri*'s orbit increased particularly as the *waziri*, with his own personal delegates permanently resident in the two major emirates of Kano and Zaria, was the sole travelling delegate of the caliph.[9]

A further function of the caliphal administration was to receive or collect the gifts, tax or tribute that was destined for the treasury at Sokoto. Payments were made at least twice a year, coinciding with the two festivals of the Muslim year, though collection undoubtedly occurred in the emirates after the harvest irrespective of the date on which the festivals fell. What percentage of the total revenue collected in an emirate went to Sokoto is not known. In addition, the caliph was an heir to part of an *amīr*'s wealth on his death; and received a present on an *amīr*'s accession. The caliph also received a share of the booty from a campaign in any of the emirates, though the amount seems to have depended on the local ruler and on how strongly the caliph's delegate pressed for it. Given the informal nature of much of these payments, it is not surprising that the caliphal administration was often seen as grasping. As the political connections and importance of the vizierate itself increased, so did the *waziri* require more presents to redistribute in order to maintain his place in the system. In the course of the century, when the *waziri* took on a greater role in Sokoto's internal politics, the vizierate had to build up its own economic base comparable to the resources of the other notables who, unlike the *waziri*, had territories to administer directly. Equally, the caliph's requirements increased as the century wore on and the international standing of the caliphate developed. The relative poverty of the Sokoto hinterland, its higher than average population of scholars and students, few farmers, many pastoralists – all of whom escaped any taxation other than *zakāt* (alms) – made Sokoto a burden on the other emirates. Originally, it had seemed beneficial that the new community grew up in a virtual no-man's-land, where the temptations of materialism were largely absent. But it made the caliph dependent on the continued good will of the emirates, and on the ability of the caliphal administration to ensure that goodwill.

One problem was the very size of the caliphate and the time taken in travelling the great distances involved. One contemporary calculated the caliphate as four months' journey from west to east and two months' journey from north to south. Although it was possible for a runner to take a message the six hundred and fifty kilometres from Sokoto to Bauchi in eight days, the normal travelling speed of officials like the vizier was some twenty-five kilometres a day. Another factor was the relative lack of military coercion involved.

9. For a detailed study of the vizierate, see M. Last, 1967a.

Military and diplomatic activities

The caliphate did not maintain a standing army. Indeed compared with states of similar size the Sokoto caliphate was in no sense a military machine.[10] Its annual mobilization was often little more than an exercise to demonstrate loyalty, to threaten opposition and police the frontier. After the initial campaigns to set up a frontier, the caliphate never acted in concert to conquer more territory; nor indeed were there any plans or ambitions for doing so. The area under caliphal rule did indeed expand piecemeal through the initiative of individual *amīr*s and freelance commanders, particularly in the south and east, but this expansion was as much a product of local emirate politics as caliphal policy. Apart from an ideological commitment to *djihād*, the only permanent caliphal requirement which might prompt military action in the emirates was the need to meet the continual deficit in the Sokoto budget. Thus, though the caliph was often involved in campaigns within the Sokoto–Zamfara region, he did not campaign outside it. For the occasional major campaigns in the eastern emirates the vizier (or on two occasions the *amīr* of Bauchi) led the Sokoto forces.

The army was not a professional force, nor was it based on squads of slave soldiers. Levies were drawn by each official from his household and from villages under his jurisdiction. Weapons and mounts were not usually provided by the state, nor were soldiers recompensed except by a share of the booty. It was a duty to serve, but not usually compulsory, though doubtless there were as many perils in staying behind to defend the village against marauders and wild animals. Campaigns were fought in the dry season, usually about harvest time at the earliest (though volunteers would be short then), with the aim of destroying the enemies' crops. In practice rainy season warfare was impracticable, not only because of pressure from other work or the nature of the terrain, but also because rain on leather shields or bow strings was disastrous. Late dry-season campaigning was restricted by shortages of water for horses and men, but surprise atttacks by small bands were feasible any time.

Regiments were variously armed, with a few men mounted on horses or camels; the majority were armed with spears, bows and swords. Certain peoples specialized in archery, particularly with arrows poisoned to make up for the lack of penetrating power; others specialized in barbed spears. Swords were less common and, unless made of particularly good local iron

10. Specific studies on military affairs are: J. P. Smaldone, 1977; R. C. C. Law, 1980 (but cf. R. Harris, 1982, pp. 81–5). The outline presented here, particularly in putting less emphasis on the military's role, differs somewhat from the analysis in these two books. J. Boyd has kindly drawn my attention to the formation of a special caliphal bodyguard first formed *c.*1850 as much, it seems, for external as for internal security (Alhaji Junaidu, 1957, p. 54). No study has been made of strictly palace formations and security, though references are frequent.

or of imported steel, were seen as a potential liability. Guns did not become available in any significant quantity until towards the end of the period; then they tended to be the weapon of privately maintained, semi-professional (and therefore slave) forces, but their comparative lack of practice prevented them from being formidable. As in the eighteenth-century states, the most effective weapon of the caliphate was its cavalry. Initially the reformers in the *djihād* had lacked horses or camels and were thus at a disadvantage against the Tuareg or the forces of the Gobir states. But cavalry had little success, not merely against the determined soldiery of the *djihād*, but also against walled towns or mountainous strongholds. The history of the caliphate's major campaigns records many defeats as well as victories, and smaller, wholly mounted contingents were probably much more effective. There was, therefore, a tactic quite distinct from the set-pieces battles known as *daga* and which resulted in high casualties – the common raid, *hari*, on the civilian population. Given the heterogeneous, highly mobile character of Hausa society, with its traders, slaves and refugees, it was easy to plant spies and infiltrators in an unwary community and take the place by surprise.

In short, the caliphate did not introduce any new strategy or military technology, nor did it possess any overwhelming advantage beyond the size of its potential resources; and these were never mobilized all at once. Guerrilla warfare, brought about by the displacement of peoples after the *djihād*, by food shortages due to the dislocation of agriculture, or simply by the profits to be made from the sale of captives, plagued the caliphate for much of the century. Too much can be made of the insecurity, but at least in some areas the expectation of becoming a slave at some period in one's life was high.[11] Ransoms could be arranged, prisoners freed, a captive might even escape, but if, as often happened, the whole family or village was broken up in a raid, there was little to return to. Trade was seemingly not much affected by warfare, though certain areas might get cut off. Trading expeditions were armed, while for some traders their staple was to supply armies with horses and weapons in return for prisoners to take away and resell at some distance from their home.

Given the military limitations, diplomacy was an important aspect of caliphal policy.[12] The caliphs appear to have handled most of the diplomatic correspondence themselves. No state visits by the caliph took place, nor was any senior member of the caliph's staff sent on embassies overseas. Instead passing scholars, pilgrims and traders acted as bearers of messages, and brought news of political developments abroad. Correspondence was

11. A vivid, personal account of one such capture (*c.*1850), is in A. H. M. Kirk-Greene and P. Newman (eds), 1971, pp. 29–101.

12. For general accounts of diplomacy, see R. A. Adeleye, 1970; M. Minna, 1982. Belief in the imminent ending of the world is likely to have made diplomatic relations with other states appear of secondary importance, and this may account for the paucity of diplomatic records in the Sokoto archives.

exchanged with Morocco, Tripoli and Britain, and was preserved: but no doubt much more important exchanges were conveyed orally or have been lost. But Muḥammad Bello's interest in external relations was as much intellectual as commercial or political. Keen and able to keep up with developments, ideas and inventions in North Africa and the world beyond, he was concerned to bring the caliphate more fully into the metropolitan Muslim world. At the same time, with his concern for the world's approaching end and the possibility of having to migrate east to Mecca, he tried to ensure that the road be kept open, and appointed a distant kinsman of the Shaykh to oversee the Baghirmi section of the route.

Diplomacy was also important in the caliphate's relations in the north and west. On the northern front, relations with the Tuareg were as ambiguous as the political situation was fluid. The sultan of Agades was an early ally, with his claims over the settled if not the nomad population of the area. There were allies, too, among the various *shaykh*s and traders; one *shaykh* in particular, Muḥammad Djailani, attempted to raise a *djihād*, an attempt that seems to have been temporarily more successful than Djibrīl b. ʿUmar's in the late eighteenth century.[13] But the noble segments of Tuareg clans (particularly the Ulemiden), with their vassals, proved strong enough to prevent the formation of a powerful Muslim specialist class. In consequence the caliphate had no organized network of *shaykh*s similar to that of the Kunta at Timbuktu on which to draw for help. The attempt by the caliph at Sokoto to organize such a network among the Tuareg and to take on the role of mediator in Tuareg affairs met with only limited success. Instead Tuareg scholars and their supporters could take refuge at Sokoto.

Relations with the Kunta *shaykh*s at Timbuktu, however, were cordial. As the leading Muslim centre in the west, the Sokoto scholars tended to look more in that direction than to Borno. Poems and visits were exchanged; the Sokoto scholars took their Ḳādirī *wird* and some *salasil* from the Kunta, and in the controversy over the Tijāniyya, the Kunta at Timbuktu were the bastion of Ḳādirī orthodoxy.[14]

The new caliphate at Massina, however, posed problems both for the Kunta *shaykh*s and for Sokoto. The exact details and sequence of Sokoto–Massina relations is not yet clear, but it is difficult not to see it as inextricably bound up with the more local problems of Kunta–Massina hostilities.[15] Although the Sokoto caliphate could claim the allegiance of areas up to the borders of Massina beyond Liptako, Gwandu had no effective presence with which to claim Massina itself. The major obstacle to an effective western policy was the evident uncontrollability of the Argungu–Mauri–

13. On the *djihād* of Muḥammad Djailani, see H. T. Norris, 1975, ch. 11; cf. D. Hamani in Y. B. Usman (ed.), 1979, pp. 392–407.

14. On the Kunta, see A. Zebadia, 1974.

15. On Massina, see W. A. Brown, 1969; and C. C. Stewart in Y. B. Usman (ed.), 1979, pp. 408–29.

Zaberma axis; but an equal obstacle was perhaps Gwandu's unwillingness to organize itself militarily. Unlike Sokoto, it had little regular support from Yauri, Nupe or Ilọrin, all of which suffered a degree of civil disturbance lacking in the eastern emirates. The *amīr* at Gwandu might mediate and advise; indeed the *amīr* even went in person to Nupe, but neither the base for an effective force nor the means of sustaining it were available to Gwandu, at least not until late in the nineteenth century.

Finally, on the frontier with Borno, whose western territories had become the embryo emirates of Hadejia, Katagum, Missau and Gombe, the initial failure to reach a compromise (in the celebrated correspondence between Muḥammad Bello and *Shaykh* al-Kanēmi during the *djihād*) set the tone for the rest of the century. Mediation was rejected during the three years of Borno invasions into eastern Kano between 1824 and 1826, and no formal, public peace was made between the two states. Organized hostilities simply lapsed, without diplomacy or a decisive victory. In consequence no 'gifts', the crucial symbol of international relations, passed in either direction.

More successful was the mixture of diplomacy and force that resulted in truces (for example with Kebbi: the Lafiyar Togo 1866–74) or treaties with smaller neighbouring communities to which the caliphate offered protection (*amana*) in return for a tax. In some areas the tax, assessed collectively, stipulated captives as well as goods such as mats, and so was similar to the contributions of some emirates. But we do not know how the rate per head differed from the rate of tax on Muslims within the caliphate.

But diplomacy and warfare aside, the commonest instrument of policy in inter-state relations was economic. Military destruction of crops or grain stores was only one aspect. Particular groups, such as the Tuareg, might be refused access to markets, to certain commodities (like grain) or to wells. Given the local annual variations in rainfall, such bans could be very effective. Less effective were embargoes on the export or import of items such as horses, weapons, salt or types of cloth, while an indiscriminate blockade of towns or areas was difficult to sustain, not least because smuggling offered high profits. But the disruption in the normal flow of caliphal trade caused for example by Ningi and Mbutawa raids was serious enough to require a remedy. Indeed their own experience of severe food shortages and the interruption of the grain trade during the *djihād* had made men like Muḥammad Bello acutely aware of the importance of encouraging traders by keeping roads open, establishing markets and enforcing the laws regulating fair trading. In consequence, as the caliphal economy became relatively more efficient and neighbouring peoples depended more heavily on caliphal trade and traders, economic policy was increasingly a more effective instrument of power than warfare.

The emirates: political structure

To consider the development of each emirate separately is beyond the scope of this chapter. Here I will compare the emirates in order to show the basic differences, and then offer some generalizations on society in the emirates.

Despite the initially very wide criteria of eligibility, all emirates but one normally had *amīr*s appointed on principles of heredity and seniority from a single lineage; but in some, appointments eventually alternated between two or more branches of a 'royal' lineage. Only in Zaria did the office of *amīr* rotate round three totally distinct lineages.

The role and distribution of offices under the *amīr* did not follow a single pattern, but broadly the political structures of the emirates fell into two types, each of which consisted of two sub-types:

(1) Those emirates that were established with the support of large cohesive groups; some of the major government functions and territories were distributed among members of these groups or among those associated with them, and the descendants of the early office-holders maintained their rights in the office and in the property associated with it. These emirates ('lineage-based') divide into two sub-types:

- (1a) those such as Zaria and Kano where the major office-holders (including the *amīr*'s kin) reside in the capital and form the *amīr*'s council while using delegates of their own to control the territories allocated to the office.
- (1b) those such as Sokoto and Katagum where the office-holders with territorial responsibilities (including the *amīr*'s kin) reside outside the capital; the *amīr*'s council consists of advisers appointed personally and not linked particularly to specific pressure groups; these advisers act as intermediaries between the *amīr* and the powerful office-holders outside the capital.

(2) Those emirates (and they form a small minority) which were *not* established with the support of one or more large groups but relied instead on a heterogeneous band of individuals attached to the *amīr* either as friends or as slaves. No office-holding dynasties developed, nor therefore did permanent offices with official property (with the exception, of course, of the *amīr*'s). These emirates ('clientage-based') subdivide into two:

- (2a) an emirate such as Hadejia where power was concentrated in the *amīr* at the capital, with usually a large slave component in the administration; the *amīr*'s council was informal with no balance of power between separate interest groups.
- (2b) an emirate such as Ilọrin, Nupe or al-Kanēmi's administration in the state of Borno, where there was, however

short-lived, a dyarchy in which the traditional ruler maintained his court at the same time as the 'Mallam' (in Nupe and Ilọrin) and the 'Shaykh' (in Borno) ran a centralized, client-based administration of his own.

The emirates of type 2 usually experienced civil war. Those with a dyarchy eliminated early the traditional ruler, in Ilọrin and Nupe by the 1830s, in Borno by 1846. But peace did not necessarily follow. Civil war between claimants within the *amīr*'s dynasty broke out in Nupe, Hadejia and Borno, and neither Nupe nor Hadejia established stable governments until *c.*1860. Nupe then developed a political structure of type 1a (like Zaria, but with the office of *amīr* rotating round *related* lineages), while Hadejia and Borno continued to maintain a client-based government dependent on an *amīr* wielding supreme power and backed by a large body of royal slaves.

The emirates of type 1 are more numerous and so more varied. Centralized or decentralized residence is a quick but superficial criterion for distinguishing between these emirates. Decentralized residence implies a category of intermediaries at the capital, who at the outset might be seen as 'clients' of the *amīr*. But they, given the lineage idiom of the political system, developed lineages of their own; in consequence, the *amīr* created a further category of clients from those unable to develop lineages, namely palace slaves, but they played a minor role. Centralized residence, in contrast, implied no such category of intermediaries between office-holder and *amīr*, but in time the *amīr* developed a palace slave retinue to act as his personal agents, and they played an important role in government. Centralized residence also implied that the office-holder could have charge of a number of widely dispersed towns, villages or peoples (thus preventing any territorial blocs of power), whereas decentralized residence usually meant that the office-holder's headquarters were within an area that owed allegiance to him as a whole, with only a few, if any, villages likely to owe extra-territorial allegiance to another office.

Residence as a criterion cannot be applied too strictly. Many emirates modified their residence rules for various offices in the course of the century (for example, the office of Madaki of Bauchi was transferred back to the capital from Wase early in the century); many offices had more than one residence and the exact allocation of time spent in which place is not known, nor is it known how often an office-holder outside the capital might ride in for important meetings. Finally, the relative importance of offices could change, so that in an emirate like Bauchi, power under the *amīr* seems in the course of the century to have oscillated between offices at the centre and offices in some of the territories. But residence does reflect conditions early in the history of each emirate, and draws attention to important economic and political differences between the emirates.

Politically emirates of type 1b (that is, with territorial office-holders residing outside the capital) were responding to the basic requirement of the *djihād*, which was to establish and maintain frontier posts within which the new emirate's economy might be rebuilt. Lacking their own towns, and lacking concentrated, settled populations on which to base themselves, these emirates were militarily very precarious. Much of the manpower and time in the early decades went in constructing strongholds (the classical Islamic term, *ribāṭ*, was used for these, whose occupants were known as *murābiṭūn*) and in organizing adequate agriculture in the face of attacks or threats of attack. In addition, when pastoralists had to be settled or some non-Muslim group was to be incorporated into the emirate, these had to be helped in reorienting themselves to the occupations and rules of Muslim life in the *ribaṭ*s. The problems encountered are vividly recorded in the books and letters sent by the reform leaders to each other.

Economically these emirates were chronically short of labour. Trade routes were not yet well established and protected; and the risk of attack from displaced or hostile populations made for a shortage of land safe for farming. In sum, the precariousness of some emirates in the early period should not be underestimated; nor, therefore, should one overestimate the formal nature of government or political organization. Given this basic fluidity, the danger both initially and throughout the century was that a powerful office-holder would seek complete autonomy and appeal to Sokoto for recognition as an independent emirate. In such cases diplomacy was not always able to prevent armed conflict breaking out.

In the course of the century, the trend was for offices at the capital to become more powerful than all but one or two territorially based offices. In consequence those office-holders outside who sought to maintain their position (especially members of the *amīr*'s own lineage with claims to inherit) tended to reside more in the capital. The trend is associated with the growing population and security of the frontiers, with the gradual absorption of previously distinct groups into the more homogeneous society of the caliphate and with the formalization of the office of *amīr* as the sole source of power in the emirate.

Emirates of type 1a, with office-holders resident at the capital, had markedly different experiences in the early period of the caliphate. Only in Kano and Zaria were conditions favourable for a large urban 'court' since not only was the city ready built, but so was the economy, with agricultural production and trade networks well established. Defence too was less of a problem. Existing towns might be renamed *ribāṭ*s but the large settled population was not in itself rebellious while the deposed kings of Kano and Zaria posed little threat from their distant places of exile.

The economic strength of these emirates made them indispensable to the caliphate's finances, and, if the *amīr* gained sole control in any of them, it might possibly tempt him to rival the caliph. In consequence, the aim both of the caliphal administration and of the groups excluded from the office of *amīr*, was to prevent an excessive concentration of power. In Zaria the problem was solved by rotating the office of *amīr* and other positions round three distinct lineages, by the caliph's readiness to depose an *amīr*, and finally by relatively short periods in office (the longest period, fourteen years, was enjoyed by only two *amīrs*). The cost of this solution was a sometimes ineffective *amīr*. In Kano, by contrast, a protracted civil war which followed the accession of the second *amīr*, Ibrāhīm Dabo, and the *amīr*'s long reign of 27 years (1819–46) both ruled out rotation of offices as a remedy for undue concentration of power. Instead, the territorial strength of the major office-holders and their independence as councillors and 'kingmakers' were guaranteed – but only with partial success, since a second 27-year reign (by Dabo's son, the fourth *amīr* ʿAbdullāh) resulted in a further concentration of offices and resources in his family. Sokoto had no adequate reason nor possibly the ability to depose the *amīr* in Kano. There was, then, a rapid narrowing down of those eligible for office (since eligibility to hold office depended on one's father having held office); and the cost of being excluded from office was the relative impoverishment and loss of status for oneself, one's descendants and dependents. Competition amongst members of the 'royal' lineage therefore was serious, and gave rise to two years of bitter civil war in 1893–5. The concentration of office-holders at the capital not only increased the costs of maintaining there a rapidly growing, aristocratic ruling class (a cost that perhaps only Kano or Zaria could initially have afforded), but also heightened the risk of eventual conflict at the centre of the emirate. In contrast, the civil wars at the end of the century in emirates of type 1b – Gombe, Katagum – were centrifugal. Paradoxically, in Bauchi decentralization was necessary again in order to forestall centrifugal revolts, but by further diminishing the value of offices available to the *amīr*'s kin at the centre (where after a period of centralization the palace administration with its personal advisers and slave officials had grown relatively strong), decentralization only heightened competition for the sole remaining, really important office, that of *amīr*. The consequence was a disastrous war within and around the capital *c.*1881–2.

In the case of Katsina, the original, rather limited lineage-based centralization gave way, in the face of militarism, to an increasingly autocratic palace government. These changes occurred without civil strife, in part because there had always been considerable autonomy in outlying districts, the growing prosperity of which made office at the capital less important.

So far only the upper levels of the administrative system have been discussed. Administration at the 'grass roots' was more uniform (and similar to that found elsewhere in West Africa). The smallest units, households or camps, were grouped into larger units, defined by a territory or by kinship. Generally pastoralists, Tuareg or Fulbe, were more organized through links of kinship than were agriculturalists, and in consequence retained their own *ardo'en* or *tambura* as leaders. Their cohesion gave them a political strength that the more fragmented agriculturalists did not have, but this superior strength relative to the rest of the population did not last into the second half of the century.

In larger, long-settled towns and villages ward representatives could be co-ordinated by one of their number, known as the *mai gari*, *magaji*, *dagaci* or *mukoshi*. The links between these representatives of the local population and the upper levels of the administration were in the hands of *jakadu*, servants or agents of the office-holder allocated the responsibility for that section of the population. Similarly, messengers linked the office-holder to his *amīr*. The function of the administration was primarily tax collection, but this was as much a political as an economic act; to pay was also a symbolic act of submission, to refuse payment was a token of rebellion. As a necessary part of tax collection, the administration gathered political information, ratified appointments; collected shares of inheritance, took charge of and dispatched the property of strangers who died en route; organized the arrest of a criminal or a runaway slave, forwarded defendants in civil cases, arranged the release of someone wrongfully detained or someone to be ransomed; took intractable cases for mediation by the office-holder or themselves answered charges of oppression by complainants at the *amīr*'s personal court; and in time of war organized the recruitment of people for campaigns. Some indication of the administrative work in the late nineteenth century has been preserved in the correspondence which has been kept by descendants of officials in Sokoto, Gombe and Bauchi.

Social structure

Society in the caliphate broadly divided into two: the office-oriented, comprising the title-holders, their kinsmen, scholars, clients and their household slaves; and those who were not office-oriented, but were occupied in farming, trading and all the various craft occupations that characterized the complex, productive economy of the caliphate, along with their slaves. The boundary between the two was never clear-cut, and allowed for movement both ways. In particular, scholars and slaves could be associated with either category. But attitudes of scholars, for example, were by no means uniformly in favour of the office-oriented, resulting in an ideal of office-shunning piety that drew its inspiration from the founder of the caliphate, the Shaykh ʿUthmān dan Fodio.

A distinctive feature of the office-oriented was their relative immobility. If they left the emirate where they had rights to office, these rights were not transferred to their place of exile, though they might retain their title as a courtesy. By comparison, ordinary people were free to move from emirate to emirate, and did so if they felt excessively oppressed. As slaves could not easily move of their own accord without being taken as runaways, free commoners (*talakawa*) dominated trade, transport and all crafts requiring journeymen, if necessary taking their slaves with them as assistants or porters.

A further distinctive feature of the office-oriented was their concern for genealogies, for dynastic marriage alliances and relatively strict rules of patrilineal inheritance. By contrast, commoners maintained a generalized identity with a particular area or ethnic group by facial marks and distinctive traditions but they ignored the minute detail of genealogy. Though commoners usually continued in their father's occupations, there was no rigid caste-like system as elsewhere in West Africa. Furthermore, whereas wives of the major office-holders were kept in purdah, dominating large polygynous households staffed with concubines and servants, the wives of others were not so restricted and, in most parts of the caliphate, participated in trade, in producing goods for sale and in agriculture.

The proportion of the population that could be categorized as 'office-oriented' cannot be realistically estimated. Estimates have, however, been made of the proportion of slaves to free men – ranging from 1:4 to 1:2 – but it is not clear how these proportions were calculated. The number of slaves within the office-oriented segment of society probably increased overall as the century wore on; certainly the importance of the position which some of them held increased, as the value was recognized of having personally loyal, politically non-competitive officials in the *amīr*'s government. In the countryside, however, the changes in the proportion of slaves to free are not known but the number of slaves probably grew in the course of the century. Captives were seen as a solution to the chronic shortage of manpower, particularly in underpopulated areas like Sokoto where the emirate was founded in an area marginal to the old states of the region. Similarly, areas of great plains, such as Bauchi, had need of men to work the land. The percentage of captives re-exported for sale on the Atlantic coast or in North Africa is not known; but restrictions were in force over whom one could sell for export, and the trade itself declined in the second half of the century.[16]

Slaves were allowed to own property and to have time to work for themselves, and could expect to have the chance of redeeming themselves. Owners did not always have enough work for them to do, and were prepared to let slaves rent back their own labour. In addition, there was the possibility that an owner would emancipate a slave for services rendered or to celebrate an occasion or some success for which Allāh was to be thanked. Again, the number of freedmen, let alone the variable rate of their emancipation, is not known.

Women slaves could marry other slaves, and their children tended to become part of their owner's household, though still of slave status. But

16. No detailed study of slavery in all its different forms in the Sokoto caliphate has so far been published, but several studies examine the problem for a particular place and period. For example, on Kano, see P. Hill, 1977, ch. XIII; on Zaria, J. S. Hogendorn, 1977; on Adamawa, P. Burnham, in J. L. Watson (ed.), 1980; and on the trade generally, D. C. Tambo, 1976.

women slaves could also have children by free men, in which case their children were free and they themselves would be free on their owner's death. As men of royal households before they formally married commonly took concubines, many eldest sons were sons of concubines. Islamic law does not recognize, as for example Fulbe pastoral practice did, a distinction between sons of free wives and sons of concubines for purposes of inheritance. Consequently a number of *amīr*s were sons of concubines: indeed a concubine mother was seen to be a necessary qualification for a 'real' *amīr*, presumably because the *amīr* could not be influenced by maternal kin. Islamic law also does not recognize the common West African distinction between slaves born in captivity and those born free, by which the former, as children of slaves, were not normally sold away from their natal home. Although in certain areas or amongst certain classes the distinction remained valid (the Hausa term, *cucenawa*, is the same as that used in Borno and Fezzān where it is equivalent to Haratin), the only formal ban the reformers of the *djihād* appear to have recognized was on the export of these Muslim slaves, particularly to Christian states. That is, the slaves were by birth members not of a particular lineage but of Muslim society. But the change also implies that slaves had become more marketable and so more widely distributed.

Slaves did not pay tax. But like sons or wives working in *gandu* (that is, for the head of their household), alongside whom slaves usually worked, they contributed about three-quarters of their working time to their owner; but unlike sons, they could not expect to inherit and become in their turn the head of a household – they were forever 'sons'; in slave villages, owned either by the state or by families, slaves had their own households and worked under their headman; superficially such settlements were no different from free villages.

If slaves paid no tax, nor did many of their owners. Exactly who did pay what at a particular time is not known. Sokoto, for example, was exempt from *Kurdin kasa*, the general land tax also known as *haraji* (*Kharadj*). Fulani pastoralists paid a tax (*jangali*) on their herds (though for some it was officially referred to as *djizya*, for others it was *zakāt*, alms). Hausa farmers each paid about 2500 cowries per annum, *c.*1850, in Kano, while in Zaria a hoe tax was levied (presumably because women played a larger part in farming there); a higher rate of tax was paid by Maguzawa (non-Muslim Hausa) in Kano possibly for the same reason. Otherwise higher rates applied to all non-Muslim communities as part of their tributary status within the Muslim state. Traders, certain crafts (such as dyers) and certain luxury crops paid taxes, a levy in effect on dry-season work. In addition, there would be annual gifts to pay on occasions of celebration or mourning; there would be alms; and doubtless some requisitioning of food whenever an army went by. It is obviously impossible to calculate tax rates, which will in any case have varied very widely. But, to risk a guess and a generalization, the percentage of annual income taken in the basic agricultural tax seems relatively low, equivalent in labour time to contributing perhaps rather less than a day's work a week throughout the farming season.

Office-holders paid much of their tax in the form of inheritance levies, in taxes on their accession to office and in a series of gifts due on the appointment of an *amīr* or caliph. Their own income was derived from a share of the taxes they collected, from a share of the booty and from gifts, but their maintenance was probably provided largely by surpluses from farms manned by slaves and belonging some to the office, some to the lineage.

Consumption by the office-oriented segment of society was, compared to some states, not very conspicuous. Apart from horses and clothes, the most obvious signs of wealth were the number of men in attendance 'doing nothing' and the amount of charity dispensed. Food was therefore needed in large quantities but apart from extra spices, meat, honey and kola, the food was not particularly elaborate. Nor were there expensive accoutrements of office, even for the caliph – no thrones or stools of gold, no crowns or precious jewels, not even an extravagance like Asante cloth (instead, plain white was the approved symbol of high office).

There were, however, large variations in wealth, not only between official households and commoners but also between commoners. An obvious indicator is the way slaves were distributed throughout the population, with some farmers (and some slaves) owning a hundred or more; but prices were low enough for most households probably to own one or two. Pastoral Fulbe, for example, used them for help in herding; Maguzawa absorbed them into their families. But wealth was not a very permanent asset: a ransom payment plus the escape of one's slaves might ruin a farming family, like that of Baba of Karo, within a few years.[17] So, too, could the loss of a caravan. Furthermore, with wealth divided between all a man's sons and with wealthy men tending to have more wives and consequently more sons, fortunes among commoners were rarely preserved over generations. Finally the ethos of the caliphate, as shown in the writings of its founders and in the popular, vernacular poetry of its scholars, was sceptical about the ultimate value of great wealth and its consumption.

I would suggest, therefore, that:

(1) The level of tax generally on free men was acceptably low; and the levy on slaves' production, while very much higher, was not insupportable, being probably not more than what a son would contribute to his father's *gandu*.

(2) The level of consumption by official households was relatively low, even though in some areas, such as Sokoto, the number of consumers may have been high.

(3) Due to the comparatively high population density of the caliphate

17. M. Smith, 1954. Baba is of course referring to events that happened after 1880.

(in contrast, say, to earlier centuries), the ratio of tax receivers to taxpayers overall remained sufficiently low that a little tax paid by a large number added up to a substantial sum, a sum quite adequate not only to support the administrative machinery but also to finance the kinds of conspicuous consumption that made for social distinctions in the caliphate.

(4) Finally, though profits from long-distance trade were not the main source of revenue, there was the potentially considerable income derived from the export of captives with which to make up for any shortfall in revenue. But the exporters' demand for captives did not prevent the settlement of captives in large numbers within the caliphate. Otherwise, the caliphate lacked the sort of monopolies other states had, over gold or salt mines for example, or over specific crops like kola or oil palms; it lacked, too, a monopoly over licences to trade, over transport, over a sole 'port of entry'. It lacked, I suggest, even a monopoly of force. If this general analysis of the caliphate's economy – characterized by a low degree of exploitation and control – is correct, then it suggests enough of a potential surplus in wealth and labour-time to create the boom in the caliphate's trade and production in the second half of the nineteenth century

The economic foundation for this expansion lay in the agricultural infrastructure built up under the caliphate. It was made possible by a considerable investment in labour, initially largely imported in the form of captives. Land was cleared and its fertility increased over the years by careful drainage, crop rotation and manuring by the herds already in the possession of the new settlers. Cattle tracks were fenced; wells were built to save water-carrying; the *ribāṭ*s, newly walled, gave greater protection. But it also seems probable that agriculture became relatively more efficient, as the sophisticated division of labour-time and the provision of incentives for private production became the norm, and as iron became plentiful enough for agricultural tools to be designed and widely used for specific tasks. In Sokoto, irrigation with the shaduf was introduced, while another technical innovation was a small sugar plantation and refinery, on, it seems, a Brazilian model. I suggest that the improved output from agriculture made possible an increase in the acreage under such cash crops as cotton, onions, groundnuts (processed, for example, into snacks) and this in turn resulted in a gradual expansion of activity not only by craftsmen but also by farmers doubling as transporters and traders. Though the evidence and dating for some of these improvements is still uncertain, the general agricultural investment in the early caliphate is too considerable to be overlooked.

Changes in the Sokoto caliphate, 1820–80

At a number of points in this chapter, trends and developments have been mentioned. At this stage, it might be useful to summarize the changes, dividing the period 1820–80 into three phases: the first – 1820–45 – a period of establishment; the second – 1845–55 – a decade of transition and disquiet; the third – 1855–80 – a period of economic expansion.

1820–45

Two requirements dominated this period. First, the need for military security against attacks by peoples defeated or displaced in the course of establishing the caliphate. Second, the need not merely to rebuild an agricultural economy dislocated by war and brigandage but also to establish from scratch agricultural and military settlements manned by people for many of whom such a settlement was a new experience.

To achieve success required leaders of considerable charisma, as well as an esprit de corps derived for some from their common faith as Muslims, for others from a common pride in being Fulbe. There was, too, an urgency, arising in part from expectations that the world's end was imminent, in part from the very precariousness of life in some of the emirates in this period.

The history of the period, then, is often a chronicle of campaigns, of the foundation of this *ribāṭ* or the submission of that town, accompanied by reports of deaths or the number of prisoners taken. It is a period free of famine, in contrast to the epidemics, locusts and starvation which marked the *dj̲ihād*. It is a period, too, of internal political stability, with embryonic administrations and posts (usually given the old Hausa titles) allocated to men whose exact biographies and characters are scarcely known.

Kano, Zaria and Katsina stand out as exceptions in this period, carrying over intact the developed infrastructure of the former Hausa states. Their trade was, however, affected by hostilities with Borno and with the Tuareg and Hausa to the north. Both Kano and Zaria had a change of *amīr*, Kano in 1819, Zaria in 1821, which resulted in political reorganization. In Zaria, despite threats of violence, it was carried out peacefully. In Kano the *amīr* had to put down a widespread revolt led by his own *galadima*; in addition he had to drive out the Muslim leader Dan Tunku, the eventual *amīr* of Kazaure.

Towards the end of the period, most emirates were securely established, the most notable exception being Nupe. Capitals had been built (with the further exception of Hadejia), and trade, according to European reports on the Niger, was well established, despite the uncertainties in Nupe and some inflation. The caliphal administration had been active, intervening in Zaria to determine appointments within the emirate, while on the frontiers, by *c.*1840, threat of invasion had greatly diminished.

The intellectual history of this period is to be found in the continuing stream of books, poetry and letters written by the caliph Muḥammad Bello in Arabic on a wide range of subjects, from constitutional advice to mysticism and medicine. But he was not alone in writing: there were histories by his vizier Gidado, poetry by his sister Asma', and numbers of other works by the family or students of the Shaykh. There were visits and exchanges of letters and poems, stressing the Ḳādirī links, from the Kunta *shaykh*s at Timbuktu and from Kamr al-Din. There was the visit too of al-Hadjdj 'Umar, who introduced instead the Tijāni *wird* and won over some scholars in Sokoto and elsewhere during his stay of some eight years. Throughout the period the inspiration of the *djihād* continued to sustain scholarship, and scholars continued to take important roles in the government of most emirates. Typical, perhaps, was the *amīr* of Kano, Ibrāhīm Dabo, who found time to write a book on the practice of mysticism and yet was pragmatic enough to reinstitute, with the caliph Muḥammad Bello's permission, some pre-*djihād* Hausa symbols and practices in order to make himself an effective ruler of Hausa subjects. But above all there was the expansion of education in both towns and villages. No figures for the nineteenth century are available, though there were reckoned to be some 40 000 mallams in 1920 (almost certainly more, therefore, in 1900 before the emigration), and we know that large numbers of scholars and students died in the *djihād*, their deaths due not only to war but also to disease and starvation.[18] If one factor making the expansion possible was the contribution made in the primary stages of Ḳur'ānic education by women teachers in the large households, another was the widespread copying of textbooks now made possible by a seemingly better supply and lower cost of paper.

1845–55

These ten years were an interlude of great change; they mark a watershed, but one in which the efforts to build up a stable state on Islamic principles were called temporarily into question. A principal cause for these changes was simply old age. The reformers who had led the *djihād* were old men by the 1840s, and one by one they died or retired after some thirty years of leadership. Buba Yero of Gombe, 1841; Atiku in Sokoto, 1842; Yakubu of Bauchi, 1845; Sambo of Hadejia, 1845; Dan Kawa of Katagum, 1846; Ibrāhīm Dabo of Kano, 1846; Adama of Adamawa (Fombina), 1848. The eastern emirates were particularly affected, but in the west the *amīr*'s authority was successfully overthrown in Yauri 1844–8, and replaced by a mercenary general in Nupe, 1847–56.

Militarily there were renewed dangers and setbacks. Between 1843 and 1844 there was a major revolt in western Katsina, led from Maradi by

18. The 1921 census counted some 34 903 mallams as 'teachers', but classified some 46 000 as being occupied in the profession of mallam – the two categories being recognized, of course, as overlapping. The figures must naturally be treated with caution. C. K. Meek, 1925, Vol. 2, pp. 218, 226, 256–7.

refugee Katsinawa, but it was defeated by combined forces from six emirates; the rebel area was so severely punished by the *amīr* of Katsina that the caliph had to remove him from office. Much more serious were the Zaberma-Kebbi-Gobir uprisings that threatened Sokoto and Gwandu for some six years between 1849 and 1854, and the rebellion in Hadejia by Bukhari in which the Sokoto forces were defeated. The autonomy of Hadejia, which lasted some fifteen years (1848–63), resulted in devastation and famine over wide areas, and whole populations were enslaved. The first famine for some decades in Kano had occurred in 1847, so that the effect of Bukhari's wars was to prolong starvation in eastern Kano for several years.

Finally, there were intellectual and religious movements that set off emigrations during this decade. The publication of al-Hadjdj ʿUmar's book in 1845 added fuel to the controversy over the Tijāniyya brotherhood, and in particular over the caliph Muḥammad Bello's interest in it – a point which brought lengthy rebuttals from the viziers of Sokoto.[19] But the *amīr* of Gwandu's chief minister and a distinguished scholar from the days of the djihād, Modibbo Raji, resigned his post *c.*1850 and, announcing openly his previously covert allegiance to the Tijāniyya, emigrated east to Adamawa. Others joined him from Kano, while Zaria too became a centre for Tijāni scholars. One 'royal' lineage, the Mallawa, became identified with the Tijāniyya but the only nineteenth-century Tijāniyya *amīr* of Zaria, Sidi ʿAbd al-Ḳadīr, was deposed after nine months, in December 1854. Possibly connected (or confused) with this movement, Mallam Hamza and fifteen scholars withdrew from Kano in protest, finally settling in Ningi whence they were later to organize a state to raid very effectively into Kano and Bauchi. In still another incident, linked in part, no doubt, to the economic conditions in eastern Kano, a certain Ibrāhīm Sharīf al-Dīn, *c.*1855 gathered large numbers from Kano and the eastern emirates for a popular Mahdist emigration east, only to be massacred in Baghirmi.

Despite this list of changes there were of course stable points. Indeed it is the stability of the system that is perhaps more remarkable. Throughout the period the two senior caliphal leaders, the *amīr* of Gwandu Khalīl (1833–58, but he retired from campaigning in 1849) and the caliph, the young ʿAli b. Bello (1842–59), remained in office, as did a number of the young new appointments in the eastern emirates. We know an unusual amount about the general conditions of this decade from the journals of the traveller Heinrich Barth, who was in the area for some four years (1851–5). He reports a sense of insecurity, but nothing in his account suggests the sort of disorder that might be inferred from the list of changes I gave above. But Barth's Hausa servant Dorugu, who was enslaved on the

19. ʿUmar al-Futi, 1845. On the controversy, see M. Last, 1967a, pp. 215–19. For somewhat divergent accounts of the career of al-Hadjdj ʿUmar, see J. R. Willis, 1970, and O, Jah, 1973.

borders of Daura and Damagaram at this time, provides an eyewitness account of the effects of raids and famines on the lives of farmers and their families.[20]

It is perhaps simplistic to speak of the interlude as marking the handing over of power from one generation to the next, not only within the caliphate but also in the states opposed to the caliphate, such as Borno or Maradi. But most of those on either side of the frontier who were *amīrs in c.*1855 had a further 15–20 years in office, and together they effectively constituted a new generation. It is worth noting that of other states dramatically reformed at the turn of the century the caliphate and its neighbours were not alone in experiencing a critical period *c.*1850: Egypt, France, Austria, Germany, Italy are obvious examples. As in these countries, so in the caliphate. I think the most important feature of the decade was the intellectual disquiet which seemed to question the validity of the state in the state's own, spiritual terms. Exactly why the disquiet became open, and exactly what was the reaction of the caliphal scholarly establishment has still to be researched in detail; but the nature of the dispute and the disputants has ensured the survival of at least some documentary evidence. I suspect that these years marked a parting of the ways for the community of scholars, some to opt out of government for ever, others to try and maintain an Islamic administration. Fifty years later, on the arrival of Christian colonial over-rule, a similar problem caused a similar parting – but the issues were clearer then.

1855–80

The most notable result of the previous decade was to make a modus vivendi an acceptable policy both for the caliphate and for many of its opponents. By 1863, when the rebel *amīr* Bukhari died, Hadejia automatically returned to the caliphate. Even the Nupe civil wars were resolved by 1859. Though Nupe became for the first time a stable political entity, it was at the expense of the area to the north where a new emirate, Kontagora, was being carved out of the borderlands of Yauri, Nupe and Zaria. Kontagora attracted the footloose adventurers, many of 'royal' blood, whose ambitions could not be met within the framework of the established emirates. Other areas attracted such men, most notably the southern Zaria–Bauchi borders and the semi-autonomous emirates of Adamawa in the east. Not all emigrants were pilgrims; but nor were they all warriors. The floating population of the caliphate, drawn both from within and across the frontiers, turned its hand now not only to soldiering but also to porterage and trade, to hunting for ivory or, later, to rubber-tapping. All such men, whatever their origin, tend to be labelled 'Hausa', a term that now signified that they belonged not to an ethnic group but to the wider

20. H. Barth, 1857. The autobiography of Dorugu is reprinted in A. H. M. Kirk-Greene and P. Newman (eds), 1971, pp. 29–101.

society of the caliphate, with its diffuse, complex economy and its lingua franca.[21]

Two features of this period stand out in the histories of the emirates. First is the relative peace and stability of the region. Raids and attacks continued, but they were not invasions that might seriously endanger, let alone topple, the caliphate. Similarly campaigns by the *amīrs* continued, but the situation was effectively a stalemate. The opponents of the caliphate had themselves by now established stable political systems. After 1880, however, the crises were to recur again.

The second important feature is the economic expansion of the caliphate. The evidence for this is (1) the settlement of new areas of land, the establishment of new villages and the continuing immigration of labour, free or captive; (2) the increasing number of Hausa-based traders and transporters on the main trade routes and in the main items of trade, thus implying a shift of traders into Hausa towns from elsewhere; (3) the expansion of 'Hausa' traders into new areas far beyond the caliphate's frontiers and concomitantly the extension of the cowrie as currency to new areas; (4) the increasing exports of finished cloth and other goods to other areas of the Western Sudan, as well as exports of materials such as ivory or shea-butter oil to Europe; and increasing imports of popular luxuries such as kola, and a range of European products. The added demand for labour, not merely in production but in transporting and packing, was seemingly easily met: for example, Michael Mason calculates that it required 1500 pots to hold a mere 25 tons of shea oil, yet Nupe's exports of oil were able to rise during the eight years 1871–8 from 120 tons to 1500 tons.[22]

Inflation accompanied the economic expansion. Not only, however, do the social effects of inflation elude precision, but the actual details, let alone the local variations, are hard to discover. Exchange rates tabled by Marion Johnson suggest that the cowrie was devalued from 2500 to the silver dollar *c.*1855 to 5000 *c.*1890.[23] Taxes rose, it seems, from figures given by M. G. Smith, at approximately the same rate, while on the basis of prices given by Barth and later travellers the cost of living at least for the well-to-do rose twice as fast.[24] If the general trend is correct, the implication is that the middle income 'gentry' without access to state revenue, to the export

21. On the Hausa diaspora, see M. Adamu, 1978.

22. M. Mason, 1970, ch. 3. On cloth, see P. Shea, 1974/77.

23. M. Johnson, 1970.

24. Any assessment of the rise in the cost of living for particular groups is very difficult indeed. Whereas it is possible from the data in H. Barth, 1857, to reconstruct the prices of a 'basket' of goods, travellers' accounts in the 1880s and 1890s are less comprehensive and less precise: cf. for example, P. Staudinger, 1889; P.L. Monteil, 1895; C.H. Robinson, 1896. Sharp local and seasonal fluctuations, heightened perhaps in Monteil's case by the size of the traveller's entourage itself or, in Robinson's case, by the Kano civil war, are further complications. For Kano, cf. M. G. Smith (forthcoming).

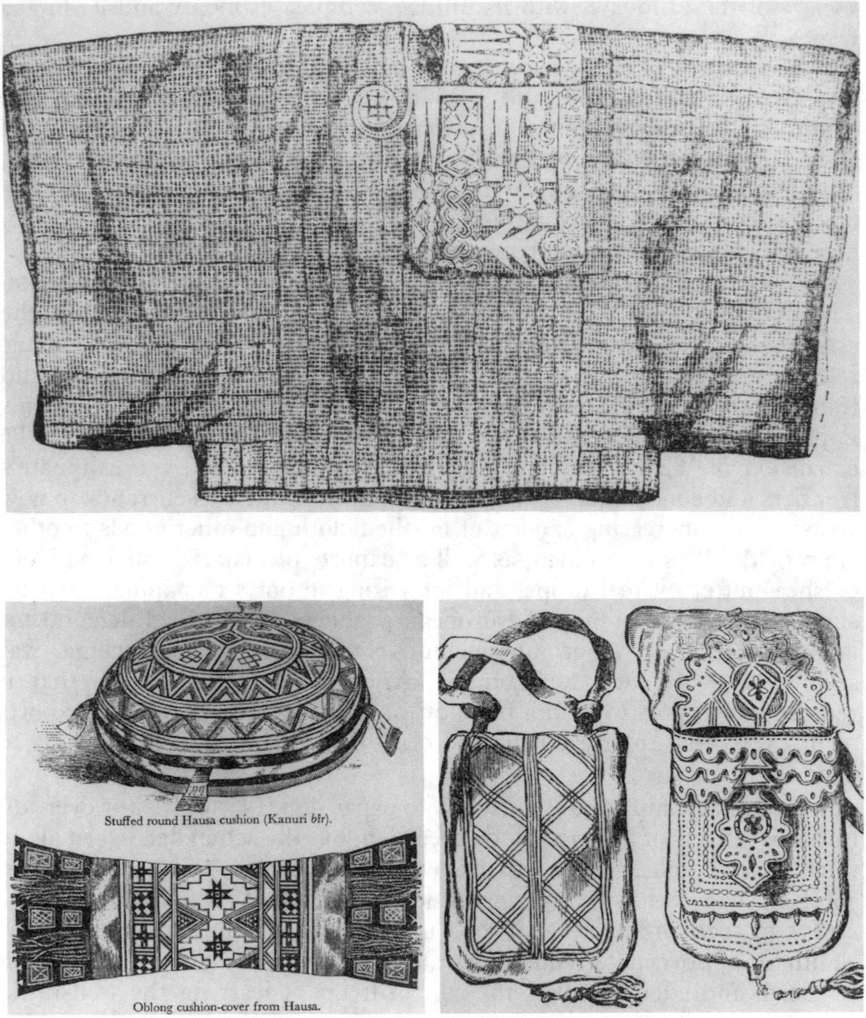
Stuffed round Hausa cushion (Kanuri *bīr*).
Oblong cushion-cover from Hausa.

PLATE 22.2 *Hausa craft goods collected by Gustav Nachtigal in 1870*

of captives or to specialized long-distance trade, will have gradually seen their standard of living fall closer to that of primary producers – the farmers and craftsmen, slave or free, who probably benefited a little from the inflation. Such a development would both increase competition for office and add fuel to millenarian ideas always smouldering in the caliphate, enough to prompt the emigrations and civil conflicts that marked the last two decades of the century. These crises emphasized a fundamental problem of the later caliphate – the danger that the increase, in numbers or expectations, of the officials, their kin and their dependents would continue despite any recession in the economy.

Intellectually the significant development of this period was the increasing use of Hausa instead of Arabic or Fulfulde in books and poetry. Translations were made by members of the Shaykh's family of some of the early *djihād* poetry, which suggests that there was seen to be a demand for the ideas and records of the *djihād* reformers among a wider public for whom Hausa in Arabic script was more accessible than Arabic.[25] Original compositions were fewer than in previous periods, or at least less has survived. Otherwise, there is some indication of tension between government and scholars in Adamawa, where there was an attempt to control what books scholars might teach – the ban was presumably aimed at the Tijāni scholars – but this was rescinded under the next *amīr*, Sanda, who included scholars in his council. As the thirteenth Islamic century came to a close (AH 1300 = 1883), there may well have been millenarian expectations, but these did not have political expression till *c.*1883, in Kano under Liman Yamusa, on the Borno frontier under Djibrīl Gaini, and under Hayatu, a great-grandson of the *Shaykh*, in Adamawa. Elsewhere it was quiet, as presumably individuals in the west migrated to join these eastern foci, ready for the projected final pilgrimage. But this was not in fact to occur until 1903.

Borno, 1820–80

The history of the Sokoto caliphate and that of its opponents and neighbours are inextricably linked. The effect of the caliphate on its smaller neighbours was to make them adopt political institutions that could cope with the pressures from outside; and these institutions often mirrored those of the Muslim states. Chiefs or 'big men' arose in societies where previously there had been no unified organization, but the histories of the many different peoples involved has not yet been analysed, and may never be. The seismic shock wave, with the caliphate as the epicentre, was felt in areas quite remote from the frontiers, as the need to pay the agreed indemnities resulted in raids or payments exacted in turn from the tributary's weaker neighbours. But the relationship was not simply one of war. Trade had been organized for centuries despite the small scale of the peoples and economies involved. The caliphate's trade simply permeated, expanded and shifted these trade routes, as had the trade of other dominant states before, irrespective of frontiers.

Indeed 'frontiers' is a difficult term to use; it applied, it seems, more to rights of taxation than to any limitation on movement. 'Enemy' is another such difficult term. It was possible, for example, for Siddiku, the *amīr* of

25. On this movement, see B. Sa'id, 1978.

Katsina, to defeat an invasion from Maradi; then, on being deposed by Sokoto because of the severity of his punishment of Maradi's allies, himself to seek refuge in Maradi and with them to invade Sokoto's dependents in Zamfara; finally he returned to Sokoto to retire. It was normal, too, for a rebel against an emirate to take refuge in a neighbouring emirate without causing friction between the two. It was not unusual for Hausa traders to supply the enemy in a war, and to follow behind any raiding army, ready to buy up its captives and to sell weapons and horses in return.

In short, identities based on local nationalism or on ethnic origin served, when relevant, to order relations *between* groups, not to isolate them. The caliphate and the surrounding states and peoples therefore formed a social and economic region in which, not surprisingly, political events in one state could be almost immediately echoed in another and in which the broad direction and timing of these events were similar.

The history of Borno provides an example of this interdependence. Borno was the most important opponent and neighbour of the caliphate, and the state whose hegemony the caliphate took over; political developments in one state were of great significance for the other. At the same time, Borno stands in strong contrast to the caliphate, representing an alternative solution that Shaykh ʿUthmān had once been ready to try.

The details of Shaykh ʿUthmān dan Fodio's *djihād* and its immediate effects on Borno are outside the scope of this chapter.[26] Suffice it to say that the state of Borno opposed the attacks made against its peoples and as a result temporarily lost its capital to the *mudjahidūn*, and lost permanently a large area of its territory. In order to turn back both the ideological and military attack, the *mai* of Borno sought weapons similar to those of Sokoto: the *shaykh* he employed (al-Hadjdj Muḥammad al-Amīn al-Kānāmī) was a scholar of some note, acquainted with the politics of the Mediterranean world and with connections in the Fezzān; locally he had links with Shuwa Arab pastoralists as well as a more personal following of Kanēmbu. In short, he could represent the established international order in opposition to the 'Fellata' reformers.

After al-Kānāmī's military victories, the *mai* appointed him as a semi-autonomous chief, resident locally at Ngurno, in the manner of a viceroy like the traditional *galadima* at Nguru. He was given or accepted no formal Borno title; though *waziri* is what he was called in one later account, such a title could imply not only his acceptance of the political system, but also his subordination within it.[27] Furthermore, his role was larger, combining military command and territorial control, than any office before him. He took more personal charge of his territory than could the *mai* in his; al-

26. For some of the details of the *djihād*, see L. Brenner, 1973, pp. 26–47. The main contemporary text is that of M. Bello, 1951 or 1964.

27. Cf, the document translated by H. R. Palmer, 1928, Vol. 2, p. 119; the occasion is the restoration of Dunama as *mai* and the 'deposition' of Ngileroma.

PLATE 22.3 *Shaykh Muḥammad al-Amān al-Kānāmī*

Kānāmī appointed his own slaves to govern towns; he expanded his chiefdom at the same time by absorbing under his direct rule the previously semi-autonomous chiefdoms that lay within his general sphere. Furthermore, he maintained a standing army of Kanēmbu spearmen beside his headquarters, while on the frontier he posted slave commanders rather in the manner of Sokoto's *murābiṭūn*. His council consisted of some six friends, some of whom he had known since childhood. Having at first a comparatively small and thinly populated area under his control and consequently little revenue, he depended more on trade and the export of captives than on fiefs, into which he encouraged different groups to immigrate. He did not maintain a large court; instead slave officials, lacking extended families of their own, not only gave him undivided loyalty but also absorbed less revenue.

By contrast the *mai*, who still had his court, had a much reduced territory with which to maintain and reward them; in addition he could not, or did not, take over a semi-autonomous chiefdom such as Marte which was in his sphere. But he did have the traditional authority derived from his dynasty's right to the throne and from the stability and sense of identity that such continuity represented.

The first period: 1820–45, the Borno dyarchy

In 1820, the state of Borno effectively had two sometimes overlapping political zones dividing the country: Shaykh al-Kānāmī and his councillors (now at Kukawa), extending their territory to the south, east and west; and the *mai* and his courtiers at Birni Kafela, in charge of the rest of Borno. Al-Kānāmī's position had in the year 1820 been greatly strengthened if not formalized. Mai Dunama had died in battle against Baghirmi and al-Kānāmī had supervised the accession of Dunama's young son Ibrāhīm. From this time al-Kānāmī took the title Shaykh; and on his seal he used AH 1235 (i.e. 1819–20 of the Christian era) as the year of his own accession to power, or at least as the year he wished to commemorate.

Conventionally, the history of Borno is narrated as if al-Kānāmī had supreme power from this time on. The conventional view may well be correct, but the evidence is not conclusive: it derives in part from eyewitness accounts of two British envoys, Denham and Clapperton.[28] Their reports are so biased in favour of al-Kānāmī and against the *mai* Ibrāhīm that they can scarcely be taken seriously as objective political analyses.[29] As a guest of al-Kānāmī, as a friend of the North African traders frequenting

28. D. Denham and H. Clapperton, 1826.

29. L. Brenner 1973, pp. 21–2, 46–7, quote Denham and Clapperton's passages about al-Kānāmī and *mai* Ibrāhīm and makes clear their bias. Most of the data in this section are derived from Brenner's study and from J. E. Lavers, 1977, Vol. 7, pp. 45–71. I am very grateful to Lavers for his comments on this section; he does not, of course, agree with all the interpretation suggested here.

PLATE PLATE 22.4 One of Shaykh al-Kānāmī's Kanēmbu spearmen

al-Kānāmī's court and travelling under the protection of a Tripoli envoy who negotiated with al-Kānāmī, Denham shows considerable prejudice against the *mai*, whose court he rarely visited and scarcely understood.

Retrospectively, al-Kānāmī's accession to sole power may well seem to have occurred from an early period. But at the time it was probably not as clear-cut. *Mai* Ibrāhīm still had a considerable court: 260–300 were in attendance at the morning levée when Denham was there, and many of these will have been fief-holders with their own followings. Al-Kānāmī himself had to forward, as would any fiefholder, a proportion of the revenue he received from his fiefs – half, Denham says. Among those who continued to support the *mai* were groups who particularly resented the newcomers – for example, the Sugurti Kanēmbu, the Black Shuwa, already established scholars like M. ʿAbdullāh of Yale Garua or M. Fanami of the Manga. It was also to be expected that traditional title-holders like the *galadima* or the *martema* would oppose an extension of al-Kānāmī's power. To these one might add the Kanuri clans, each with their *chima jilibe*, but it is impossible, from the published histories, to work out the extent to which, in the early period, these clan leaders were still being appointed by the *mai*, or even remained loyal to him. Nor is it clear how rapidly the territorial leaders (*chima chidibe*) came to be appointed by al-Kānāmī, though the later complaints at the extension of 'Shuwa rule' (to Gazir province by 1842) suggest it was not necessarily very rapid nor complete. Indeed the division of authority between territorial and associational officials could easily be adapted to the kind of dyarchy I suggest. Therefore while we do not know in detail which *chima*s stayed at the *mai*'s court in Birni Kafela, I think the assumption must be that the majority of the 'Kanuri aristocracy' were there – even if at the same time they may have kept a younger kinsman in Kukawa as well.

If we assume that *mai* Ibrāhīm was not the farcical figure Denham depicts, but rather the head of a still powerful court, then the activities of al-Kānāmī make better sense. As a kind of 'super-*galadima*', or viceroy, he was given charge of frontier areas not only in the south-west (the *galadima* had charge of the west), but also in the south. He had the right to raise an army; he also had the charge of North Africans in Borno and the conduct of foreign relations that that implied. His western policy (1824–30) was concerned less with an attack on the caliphate itself than with the re-establishment in Nguderi of a western Borno to which the *galadima* had no claim. Al-Kānāmī's western Borno was probably intended to include some of the eastern emirates (if not Kano) but in this he failed. He did, however, drive out Muḥammad Manga (who followed Sokoto's leadership), and by penetrating as far as Kano demonstrated the military capability of Borno in the frontier area. He furthermore helped to re-establish Gumel as a client state of his, winning over the Manga after defeating them. The *galadima*, thus encircled, fled to Sokoto but returned to submit to al-Kānāmī and accepted from him a very much reduced territory. By 1830, then, al-Kānāmī had his own state of western Borno, governed by slave *kachellas* and containing a variety of peoples without any marked loyalty to the *mai*.

This western 'sub-state' was supplemented by a similar area in the south, consisting mainly of Kotoko towns and the marches of Baghirmi, and again ruled by slaves. Initially, 1818–24, al-Kānāmī had tried with North African help to establish a large south-eastern protectorate over Kanēm with Baghirmi as a vassal, but this proved impossible. The frontier wars that enabled this expansion certainly drew a free army of cavalry from Birni Kafela, men who responded to the same sort of opportunities that attracted freelance volunteers from Sokoto for campaigns in Zaria or Bauchi. Meanwhile the bulk of Borno proper, east of Lake Chad, still followed the traditional Kanuri authorities, owing allegiance to the *mai*.

There is no reason to suppose the arrangement did not work well; the *mai* commanding the majority of Kanuri Borno and drawing revenue from it; al-Kānāmī commanding the frontier zones to the west and south, employing Borno cavalry and sending on to the *mai* the *mai*'s share of the revenue. Al-Kānāmī made no attempt to outshine the *mai*'s court. Indeed in some respects they were following the ancient pattern of a traditional royal city separated by some miles from the strictly Muslim trading town, with its residences for foreigners. And for foreigners like Denham and his friends, all the activity seemed to take place in Kukawa.

Very little has been recorded of the activities of *mai* Ibrāhīm's court, not least because few survived the dynasty's destruction in 1846. Al-Hadjdj ʿUmar, during his visit to Borno, did convert one notable member of the *mai*'s family to the Tijāniyya and so incurred the enmity of either the *mai* or al-Kānāmī – we do not know which, but conventionally it is assumed to be the latter.[30]

One reason, I believe, for the success of the arrangement between the *mai* and al-Kānāmī was al-Kānāmī's notable lack of dogmatism or ambition. Al-Kānāmī does not seem to have had a vision of a new Borno. There are no books or letters by him in which reforms are proposed. He did not share the millenarian expectations or the urgent commitment of the Sokoto leaders, nor did he attract around him men with a similar sense of mission. He himself is diffident about his reasons for staying on in Borno; his interests were not parochial and his loyalties were not 'tribalistic'. The lack of ideology, and the lack of the confidence and dynamism that an ideology can inspire, is in strong contrast to Sokoto. There was no poetry in praise of 'martyrs' in Borno. In so far as he was breaking the monopoly the *mai* had of loyalty, al-Kānāmī offered little to replace it beyond a personal loyalty to himself, a common opposition to the 'Fellata' (Fulbe) of Sokoto and a commitment to the wider Islamic world of which he felt himself a part. Al-Kānāmī could use the *mai*'s authority as an institution around which to rally Borno and which was larger than mere sectional interests; similarly the *mai* could use al-Kānāmī precisely because al-Kānāmī did not share the reformist zeal that would have destroyed traditional Borno. Even had he so wished, al-Kānāmī probably did not have enough support to overthrow the *mai*, nor could he push through any fundamental reforms so long as he relied on the *mai* for Borno unity. His embassy, in the 1830s, to the Ottoman Porte (which implies that he repudiated the *mai*'s traditional claim to be caliph) seems to have made no difference at the time. The problem for Borno came when the state had neither the overarching traditional institutions nor a strong ideological commitment; at this point

30. U. al-Naqar, 1972, pp. 72–4, 144.

(but not, I suggest, before), analysis of Borno politics can use the language of patron–client relations and speak of personal advantage as the main motivation.

The interdependence between *mai* Ibrāhīm and al-Kānāmī proved personal to them. On al-Kānāmī's death in 1837, the relationship between *mai* and *Shaykh* came up for renegotiation, and the evidence suggests that it was al-Kānāmī's three Shuwa advisers rather than his son ʿUmar who not so much negotiated as dictated terms to the *mai*. The *mai* quite properly, I suggest, ordered ʿUmar to come and be installed in his father's place; the Kukawa advisers instead threatened to attack Birni Kafela if the *mai* did not pay homage to the new *Shaykh*. There is no report of such a visit by the *mai* to Kukawa before, and the symbolic importance of this act cannot be underestimated. As a natural consequence, the new *Shaykh* added injury to insult and forwarded less revenue to the *mai* than had his father. Thus ʿUmar's councillors jeopardized some twenty years of co-operation with the *mai*, and lost their own lives as a result. Furthermore, it cost the life of al-Kānāmī's oldest councillor, al-Hadjdj Sudani, who may have wished to support ʿUmar's brother ʿAbd al-Raḥmān for the office of *Shaykh*. The accession then divided not only Shaykh ʿUmar against *mai* Ibrāhīm, but also, eventually, Shaykh ʿUmar against his brother.

Borno 1845–55: a period of transition

If the years 1845–55 were difficult for the Sokoto caliphate, Borno by comparison suffered considerably more, not only by way of invasion, civil war and execution, but also in fundamental changes to the political system. The office of *mai* was abolished, his court disbanded; the separate, unostentatious court of the *Shaykh* with its special international connections disappeared too. By amalgamating the two offices, *mai* and *Shaykh*, ʿUmar established a new style of politics that distinguished it not only from the preceding regimes in Borno but also from the Sokoto caliphate.

Briefly what happened in this decade was this. With his traditional authority so seriously called into question, in 1846 *mai* Ibrāhīm encouraged the Sultan of Wadai to invade Borno. In this he repeated the error his father had made twenty-seven years before, when Dunama had called in the Sultan of Baghirmi to destroy al-Kānāmī and had lost his own life instead. In the invasion two of ʿUmar's chief councillors, M. Tirab and Aḥmed Gonimi, were killed in battle against the Wadai army; ʿUmar executed *mai* Ibrāhīm after the battle and subsequently defeated and killed his successor *mai* ʿAlī.

The new vizier, al-Hadjdj Bashir, became Shaykh ʿUmar's favourite at the expense of ʿAbd al-Raḥmān. In 1853 ʿAbd al-Raḥmān forced the deposition of ʿUmar and Bashir was killed; the following year ʿAbd al-Raḥmān was deposed in his turn, and executed. ʿUmar, reinstated, then continued to rule for the next twenty-six years, until his death in 1881.

It is not, I suggest, merely a coincidence that the same decade proved critical for both the Sokoto caliphate and Borno. In general terms, of course, the *djihād* in which both states were involved brought into power men of approximately similar ages; in which case problems of succession were likely to affect both states simultaneously. But, in addition, the pressure on Borno from the caliphate had diminished: ideologically the concerns of the 1840s were more about millenarian pilgrimages and the Tijāniyya than about *djihād*, while militarily there was detente despite occasional limited campaigns along the frontiers. One could argue that the very lack of tension allowed internal rivalries to surface: the court at Kukawa no longer needed the *mai* as a symbol of Borno unity; there was even no need for unity within Kukawa itself. This set off a chain reaction: civil war in Borno encouraged Bukhari's rebellion against Sokoto; the confusion on Borno's western frontier led Bashir to overreach himself and ʿAbd al-Raḥmān to risk deposing ʿUmar. On a popular level, the effect of the events of this decade was shown by the support given to the millenarian leader Ibrāhīm Sharīf al-Dīn as he passed through Borno on his way east in 1856. But a striking aspect of these events was the inability, or unwillingness, of either state to take advantage of the other's disorders, and the rapid return to normality after 1855.

The second period, 1855–80: the Borno Shaykhdom

The second period saw Borno as a unitary state. ʿUmar, though retaining the title *shaykh* and his headquarters at Kukawa, took on a more formal, distant role as head of state, with an enlarged court. As part of the new formality, he had a first minister to whom he gave considerable authority, but the *shaykh* had all power centralized in his hands and delegated it to whomever he chose. As before, the court consisted of members of the *shaykh*'s family, free notables and slave officials (even the names of al-Kānāmī's councillors were preserved as new titles), but the slave component, which included a royal slave army of *c.*3000 men, was more powerful than previously, though still dependent for office solely on the favour of the *shaykh*. Sons of slaves did occasionally inherit their father's position, but slaves had no lineages with claims to particular office or to wealth. Therefore an increase in the slave component in government affected the process of selection among the free candidates for office: for a free notable an inherited title did not necessarily carry with it specific functions or power. In consequence there was no formal 'balance of power' maintained over time, and there were no traditionally powerful lineages with bases of their own; in many cases the most influential men had no formal titles. Advancement was through clientage within a hierarchy of patron–client relations headed by the *shaykh*. By comparison with Sokoto, competition was open, unrestricted by rights of birth or rank.

If this analysis of Borno politics in terms of patron–clientage is correct (and it is the analysis of R. Cohen and L. Brenner), such a system had its origins in al-Kānāmī's use of slaves and a few friends to run his early administration.[31] Because of the country's divided loyalty, with the older lineages probably following the *mai*, the *Shaykh* did not take over a hereditary administration; and the deaths of al-Kānāmī's councillors in the disorders of 1846–54 cut short any development in that direction. Members of the *mai*'s administration too were discredited after 1846. It is difficult to see, then, what other form of political recruitment Shaykh ʿUmar could have used at the time. It may however be an anachronism to treat patron–clientage as the traditional Borno system, or even as the dominant system in the early nineteenth century. Al-Kānāmī's councillors primarily were not his clients but his partners, with a considerable degree of independence – thus their crucial role in the events following al-Kānāmī's death. Ministerial dynasties were then still a possible development. I would suggest, after all, that there *was* a marked political change after the period 1845–55, but one made easier by simply extending over the whole political spectrum the principle al-Kānāmī used in his appointment of slave officials.

As important as these political trends were the changes in the economy which had to support the political structure. As suggested earlier, the salient fact of the period is the expansion of both the trade and the production of the Sokoto caliphate, with vacant land being settled within the frontiers and 'Hausa' traders pushing into areas far beyond. In such conditions not only did the Hausa-based traders come into Borno, but Borno-based traders increasingly moved their centre of operation to Hausaland. The political and ideological détente between the two states permitted this; indeed the embargoes of the early part of the nineteenth century were exceptional when seen against the long tradition of Borno's western trade. But it does seem that Borno, in competition with the trade centres of the caliphate, had increasingly less to offer. An old staple like natron (sodium carbonate) was still exported, though it probably faced greater competition from other kinds of salt from elsewhere. Another staple export, captives, seems gradually to have declined; though it is possible that captives were increasingly used for work in Borno, the productive base of the Borno economy does not appear to have expanded at the rate the caliphate's expanded. Other exports or re-exports mentioned, like hides, skins, ivory or ostrich feathers, also passed along Hausa trade routes, and new sources of supply – e.g., ivory from Adamawa – were explored under the protection of the caliphate. In brief, it seems that Borno was being drawn into the caliphate's economy as a supplier of raw materials and as a consumer of luxuries, with less profit accruing to those in power than before. One symbol of this shift is the fact that Borno had at last become part of the west African cowrie currency zone by 1850; another is the difficulty traders had in collecting debts in the capital – perhaps the volume

31. L. Brenner and R. Cohen, 1974, pp. 109–10; 1988.

PLATE 22.5 *Embroidered Borno woman's blouse made in the 1870s*

of trade could no longer carry such overheads – and North African traders became wary of coming to Borno. The Saharan trade had been an important element in al-Kānāmī's policies, and to this end Borno had regained control in the 1840s of Zinder, a major port of entry. But this advantage was no longer a sufficient weapon in the economic competition with the caliphate.

If these factors are added up – the increase in numbers, slaves and free, at court; the inflation in prices of luxury goods; an inadequate base in production for export; the diminishing role of Borno as the major trade centre – it is less surprising that trade debts proved harder to repay, or that, in 1883, it would become necessary to levy a tax expropriating half of every taxpayer's property. If the expropriation reflects taxpayers' regular inability to pay the annual tax, one might infer that the countryside by now was producing little surplus. We know, however, nothing in detail of what was happening in rural areas between 1855 and 1880, except that no farmers' revolts occurred until the millenarian movements of the 1880s.

It may be true that Borno was stagnating under Shaykh ʿUmar's inadequate leadership, but a deeper reason may be Borno's relation to the caliphate's expanding economy. If this is the case, Borno provides an interesting instance of the effects of the caliphate on a peripheral state, and a model for comparing the experiences of other states on the economic periphery. Politically, the alternatives open to Shaykh ʿUmar and his administration seem limited in hindsight: opportunities for real territorial expansion were limited in the west and south by the caliphate's own expansion and in the east by Baghirmi and Wadai; even Damagaram on the north-west proved difficult to keep under Borno control. Another solution might have been to reduce the numbers at court and to decentralize the administration, but this would have been to reverse the trend of decades and undermine the politics of clientage; it also involved territorial expansion or migration. In the event the stability under Shaykh 'Umar gave way to a third solution – political violence and the elimination of rivals; but this lies outside the scope of this chapter.

Conclusion

Despite the obvious, gross differences in area and population, the comparison of Borno with the Sokoto caliphate illuminates the factors making for the different histories of the two states. In the simplest, most personal terms, the initial contrast can be summarised as follows:

(1) Al-Kānāmī had a ritually important, if not militarily strong, *mai* with whom to share power; Sokoto under Muḥammad Bello had no such alternative traditional ruler.

(2) Al-Kānāmī had not the same widespread or numerous family and clan connections to give him the powerful support which Muḥammad Bello had.

(3) In consequence al-Kānāmī relied on slaves and friends, centralizing control in his own hands; Muḥammad Bello had to delegate authority and decentralize power to his fellow *mudjahidūn* and *murābiṭūn*, who tended to form lineages or local interest groups.

(4) In order to unite Borno after its defeats, al-Kānāmī had to rely on traditional loyalty to the *mai*, on his own charisma, on self-interest and shared opposition to 'Fellata', whereas Muḥammad Bello, after the spectacular success of the *djihād*, had the strong, millenarian commitment to Islam with which to unite his widely dispersed *amīr*s.

(5) To make up for its curtailed revenue, Borno depended on the export of captives, a trade stimulated in part by Borno's special North African connections: for Sokoto, with its wider sources of revenue, the demand was to import captives, a demand stimulated by the various lineages and gentry requiring labour for farm and craft production – in the long run to the great advantage of the Sokoto economy.

The tension between the two states in the first period was a further, potent factor in dictating the ideological and political responses of the two states. Conversely the relative relaxation of tension contributed indirectly to the disorders of 1845–55 and their containment.

In the second period, when competition was economic rather than political, Borno tended to develop a political system in which clientage and individual advancement were important principles, whereas the Sokoto government developed groups with corporate interests and kept an Islamic, if no longer strongly millenarian, commitment with which to limit those interests and provide a moral yardstick. The relative dynamism and the greater natural wealth of the caliphate tended to drain Borno economically, though the détente may also have opened greater opportunities for Borno farmers and traders to supply the expanding market of the caliphate. Whereas in Borno it was the people in the capital who were most affected by the economic decline, in Sokoto the pious 'gentry' seem to have been pressured most by the changing nature of the caliphate.

23 Massina and the Torodbe (Tukuloor) empire until 1878

M. LY-TALL

Massina

As indicated in Chapters 21 and 22 above, the late eighteenth and early nineteenth centuries were marked all over West Africa by the emergence of a social category hitherto dominated by sedentarized peoples, the nomadic Fulbe (Fulani, Peul). Their numbers had increased constantly since the fifteenth century as a result of successive waves of migration and, at the same time, their economic importance had been growing continuously since gold had ceased to be the motor of the West African economy.

One after the other, in Futa Jallon and Futa Toro, inspired by the Islamic ideas of justice and equality, they shook off the rule of the sedentarized peoples. In the early nineteenth century, the movement spread to Hausaland and from there to Liptako and Massina. Already, in the closing years of the eighteenth century, in the reign of the Fama of Segu, Ngolo Jara (Diarra) (1766–90), a first attempt by the Fulbe in the inland Niger delta to free themselves had ended in failure.[1] But Bambara pressure in the inland Niger delta reached its height in the early nineteenth century, under Da Monzon (1808–27), making life for the Fulbe very insecure.

The Muslim revolution in Massina: the reign of Seku Ahmadu (Shaykh Aḥmad Lobbo)

The insecure situation of the Fulbe in the inland Niger delta just before the outbreak of the revolution

The power of Segu had been constantly expanding over all the neighbouring countries since the reign of Ngolo Zara. Under Monzon Jara

1. Ngola Zara waged a merciless war on the Fulbe for eight years. Many of them took refuge in Wasulu; see E. Mage, 1868, p. 401. See also L. Tauxier, 1942, p. 90. For the regnal dates of the Fama of Segu we have generally adopted those suggested by Tauxier, who made a critical and comparative study of the question. We are aware that these dates are only very approximate.

(Diarra) (1790–1808), it extended as far as Bundu in the west and the Dogon country in the east.[2] Under Da Monzon, the exactions of the Segu *tonzons* in the Fulbe encampments were constantly increasing. At the same time, in Muslim centres such as Jenne, Islam, having adapted itself to customary practices and the demands of trade, had lost all its vitality.[3] But since the second half of the eighteenth century, the successes of the Muslim-Fulbe revolutions in Futa Jallon and Futa Toro had opened up new prospects for the whole of the Islamic community in West Africa. Not far away from Massina, in Sokoto and Liptako, the traditional chieftaincies had just been overthrown, between 1804 and 1810. Many Fulbe from the inland Niger delta had taken part in this movement. On their return home, they helped spread the new revolutionary ideas.

The beginnings of the Muslim revolution in the inland Niger delta

Between 1815 and 1818, several marabouts endeavoured to exploit the revolutionary atmosphere prevailing in the delta area to shake off the Bambara yoke. The first to do so was a mallam who had come from Sokoto in 1815, Ibn Saʿīd, who succeeded in winning over the whole of the province of Gimballa but failed to win over the other Fulbe and above all the Tuareg. At the very same time, in Farimake, another marabout, Ahmadu Alfaka Kujajo, was preaching the holy war. All of them claimed allegiance to ʿUthmān dan Fodio (Usman dan Fodio).[4] But the two aspirants who had most success were Ahmadu Hammadi Bubu Sangare of Runde Siru and al-Ḥusayn Koita from the province of Fittuga.[5] The former finally emerged as the leader of the *djihād* in Massina.

Seku Ahmadu (Shaykh Aḥmad Lobbo), founder of the dina *of Massina*

Born in about 1773 at Malangal in the province of Massina, Seku Ahmadu (Shaykh Aḥmad Lobbo) was noted for his piety, honesty and humility, all qualities that made him a first-rate leader of men. He was from a modest social background and he had received a rather ordinary theological training.[6] It was not until he was aged about 22 that he began to study deeply at the feet of a leading mystic in Jenne, Kabara Farma. His reputation for holiness and his preaching in favour of a return to pure Islam rapidly attracted round him a host of *tālib*s (followers) already convinced by the ideas emanating from Sokoto. In 1816, he pledged allegiance to ʿUthmān

2. L. Tauxier, 1942, p. 101. In 1796, all the countries between the Niger, Kaarta and Bundu were devastated, while the nearest countries (Beledugu, Dedugu, Fuladugu) were subjugated.
3. C. Monteil, 1932, pp. 52–4.
4. H. Diallo, 1979, p. 138 and F. B. S. Diarah, 1982, pp. 97–8.
5. H. Diallo, 1979, p. 140.
6. F. B. S. Diarah, 1982, p. 84.

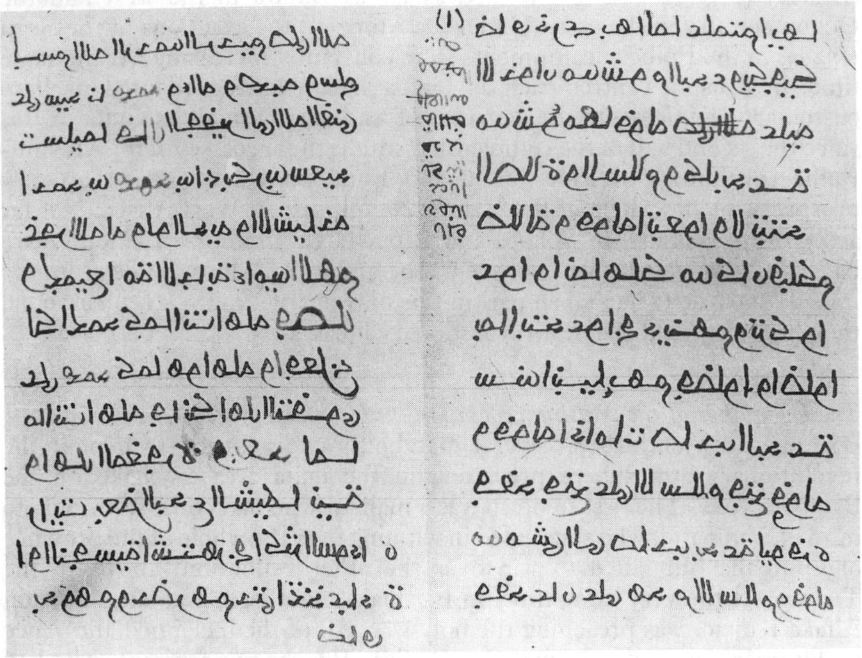

PLATE 23.1 *The opening pages of* al-Idtirar *said to be the only book written by Seku Ahmadu (Shaykh Aḥmad Lobbo)*

dan Fodio who sent him a flag and awarded him the title of Shaykh.[7] At the same time he received several books on Muslim law from Sokoto.[8]

The movement broke out in 1818 in the shape of a revolt organized by Seku Ahmadu against the exactions of the dynasty of the Ardo'en and their Segu allies.[9] The Fama of Segu, underestimating the scale of the movement, requested one of his columns that was going into Gimballa for a police operation to 'punish the marabout and his supporters on his way through'.[10]

7. In West African languages this word becomes Shehu, Seku or Sheku, whence Seku Ahmadu, Sheku 'Umar.

8. According to some sources, he received four books dealing with government, the behaviour of princes and teachings on the subject of justice and on difficult passages in the Ḳu'rān; see H. Diallo, 1979, p. 138. In addition to this allegiance to the leader of the Sokoto *djihād*, at least in its early stages, Seku Ahmadu was strongly helped by his manipulation of the *Ta'rīkh al-Fattāsh* to pass himself off as the twelfth caliph, whose coming had been predicted to Askiya Muḥammad at the time of his pilgrimage to Mecca (see M. Ly-Tall, 1972). The belief of the oppressed peoples of the nineteenth century in a Madhī had already been skilfully exploited by 'Uthmān dan Fodio in Hausaland.

9. See A. H. Ba, and J. Daget, 1962, pp. 29–31.

10. C. Monteil, 1932, p. 103.

The defeat of the Segu army at Nukuma precipitated a coming together of the majority of Fulbe around the man who henceforth appeared as their protector against Bambara tyranny. At the same time, the Jenne marabouts, who had from the first demonstrated great hostility to Seku Ahmadu, were put down in 1819 after a long siege. The Fulbe were converted *en masse*, and, thanks to a remarkable spirit of organization, Massina rapidly established itself as a powerful Muslim state at the very gates of Segu. There was implacable war between the two neighbours during the reign of Da Monzon. It was still raging quite strongly in March 1828 when René Caillé reached Jenne and reported that 'Seku Ahmadu, the chief of the land of Jenne, is still waging a fierce war against the Bambara of Segu whom he wants to win over to the banner of the Prophet. But these Bambara are warlike and are resisting him'.[11] It only ended long after the French traveller had left, when the combatants were exhausted after a terrible famine in the area.[12] The Bambara finally came to terms with reality and accepted the presence of a Muslim state on their borders.

But Seku Ahmadu had to face up to resistance from another quarter, of a more insidious kind, from the Fulbe of Fittuga where another marabout, al-Ḥusayn Koita, was leading a movement which also had the aim of launching a *djihād* in the inland Niger delta area. Fittuga was situated on the route linking Timbuktu to Gwandu and was a vitally important trading centre for the Kunta and Sokoto. Muḥammad Bello, Shaykh 'Uthmān's successor, gave all the more support to al-Ḥusayn Koita's movement because Seku Ahmadu had taken advantage of the succession crisis that broke out after the death of Shaykh 'Uthmān to renounce his allegiance to Sokoto. Backed by the Kunta and by Muḥammad Bello, Fittuga held out against Seku Ahmadu until 1823, when it was subjugated and its leader executed.[13] The way was now open for the conquest of Timbuktu.

Since the break-up of the Songhay empire, no durable political authority had been able to establish itself in Timbuktu. Sometimes, under the influence of the Arma, sometimes under that of the Bambara or the Tuareg, Timbuktu had succeeded in maintaining the prosperity of its trade thanks to the protection of the Kunta, a 'Moorish tribe' that had imposed its authority there in the second half of the eighteenth century. They were skilful traders, and had become the protectors of all the routes linking the various regions of the Sahara to Timbuktu. At the same time, they enjoyed great religious authority throughout the region since one of them, Shaykh al-Mukhtār al-Kunti (1729/30–1811), had introduced the Ḳādiriyya brotherhood there at the beginning of the nineteenth century. His grandson, al-Mukhtār al-Saghir, responded to the appeal from the traders and political

11. R. Caillé, 1830, Vol. 2, p. 214.
12. L. Faidherbe, 1863, p. 11.
13. H. Diallo, 1979, pp. 138–42.

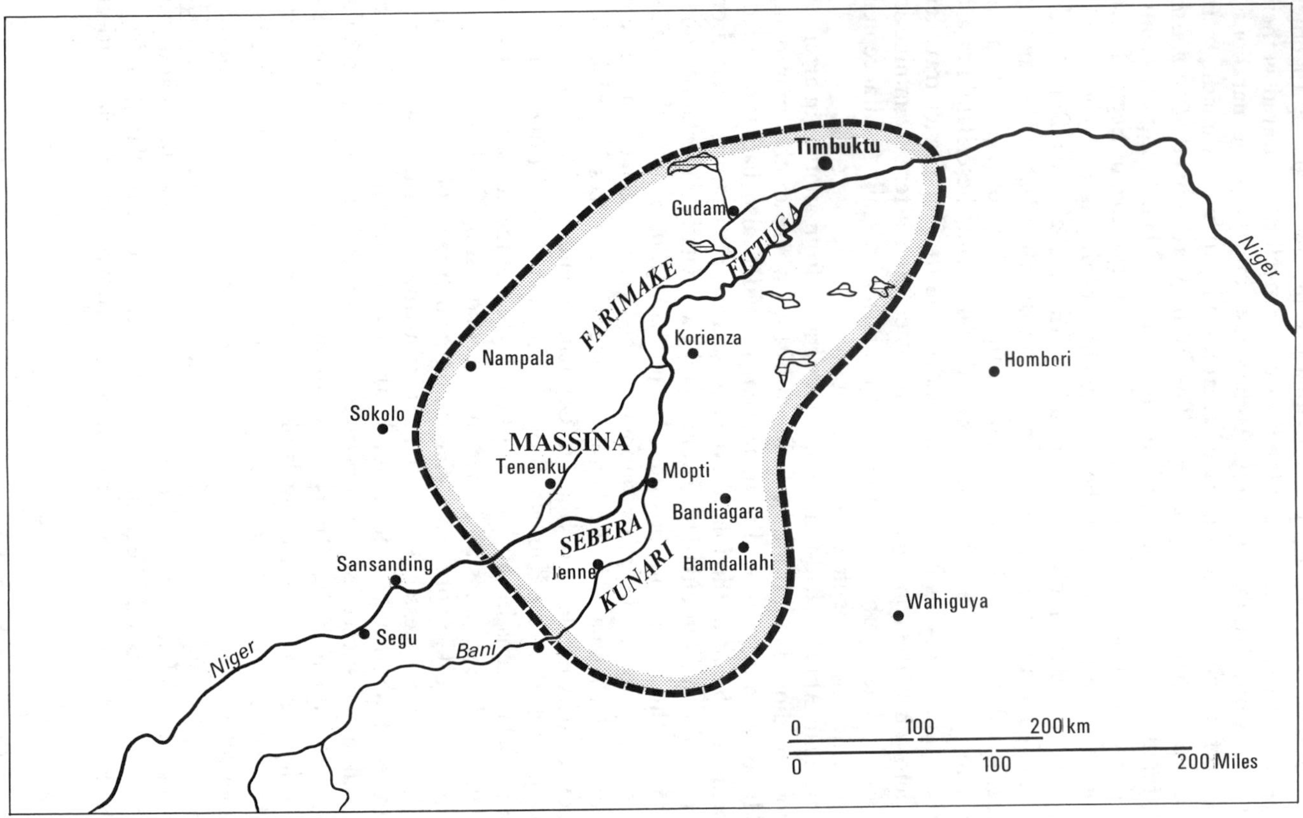

FIG. 23.1 *Massina at its apogee, 1830 (after M. Ly-Tall)*

leaders of Timbuktu and in 1826 went to the help of the famous city besieged by the troops of Massina:

> In 1826, the Fulbe of Massina seized Timbuktu and almost ruined its trade forever, the exactions of the conquerors extending not only to the idolatrous peoples (Mande, Mossi, Songhay) but also to their merchant coreligionist in Twāt and Ghadāmès. These latter, finding themselves oppressed, called in Shaykh al-Mukhtār from Azuad: he was the elder brother of al-Bekkai, of the Kunta tribe, a highly influential man among the Berber peoples, and they entrusted their interests to him.[14]

The Kunta leader failed to prevent the taking of the town and its occupation by a military garrison until the death of Seku Ahmadu.[15] When this happened in 1845, Massina's authority extended from Jenne to Timbuktu and from the region of Napala to Dogon country.[16] In a reign lasting twenty-seven years, Seku Ahmadu had also provided the new theocratic state, called the *dina* (religion), with firmly based religious and administrative structures.

The institutions of the dina

As in the Islamic states of Futa Jallon, Futa Toro and the Sokoto caliphate, all areas of the life of the state were henceforth to be governed by Muslim law. A grand council of forty members appointed by Seku Ahmadu assisted him in all areas of the exercise of power. To be a member of this illustrious assembly it was necessary to be married, to lead a blameless life, to boast a good education and to be 40 years old. Two of the grand councillors at the same time constituted Seku Ahmadu's privy council and with him considered all state business before submitting it to the grand council.

Justice in the first instance was everywhere dispensed by *ḳādi*s. The supreme judicial body was in theory the grand council; but after the early years, when he did not always manage to impose his views on some old marabouts more learned than himself,[17] Seku Ahmadu eventually got the grand council to accept all his opinions. Several stories reported by A. H. Bâ and J. Daget tend to show that Seku Ahmadu did not always respect the relatively democratic institutions he had himself set up. Thus he set his face against the grand council's decision to abolish castes:

> The marabouts on the Grand Council, on the strength of the verse in the Ḳu'rān: 'all believers are brothers', had proposed the abolition of castes. Next day Seku Ahmadu had lizards, frogs, fish, chickens and mutton cooked all together, offered the dish to the marabouts and

14. J. Ancelle, 1887, p. 114; see also H. Barth, 1863, Vol. 4, pp. 32–3, P. Marty, 1920–1, Vol. 1, p. 75; A. Raffenel, 1856, Vol. 2, pp. 352–3.
15. L. Faidherbe, 1863, p. 11; M. Delafosse, 1972, Vol. 2, pp. 236–9.
16. M. Delafosse, 1972, Vol. 2, pp. 236–7; see also L. Faidherbe, 1966, p. 51.
17. A. H. Ba and J. Daget, 1962, p. 62.

invited them to eat. 'What,' they cried, 'would you have us eat such a mixture?' 'Is a single one of all these meats forbidden by the Ḳu'rān?' retorted Seku Ahmadu. 'No, but although the Book may not forbid it, it disgusts us to eat lizard and frog and mix these meats with those we are used to eating.' 'Likewise, although the Book does not forbid it, it disgusts me to mix together nobles and caste people and abolish the barrier by which we customarily separate them.'[18]

Punishments were very severe. Ahmadu Hammadi Samba Bubakari, known as Hambarbe Samata, who acted as public prosecutor, was extremely strict; 'he always had within reach his law book, his Ḳu'rān, his sword and a whip. Throughout all the time the *dina* was at Nukuma he dispensed justice on the spot, and himself carried out the sentence then and there.'[19]

Taxes and levies were collected with the same stringency by officials who were paid partly out of the fruits of their labour. In addition to the ordinary dues provided for by Islam (*zakāt*, *mudu* and *usuru*), the grand council introduced the *pabé* or war-contribution for those who could not physically take part, and for the non-Islamized countries.[20] In addition, large estates were cultivated by captives on behalf of the *dina*. The province of Massina produced large quantities of rice, millet and various vegetables.[21] On the other hand, trade suffered severely from the constant state of war with the neighbouring Bambara. Jenne, the great trading centre of the area, was no longer in contact with Bure, and its markets were no longer frequented by the Moors:

> This war is doing a great deal of harm to Jenne's trade because it cuts off any sort of communication with Yamina and Sansanding, Bamako and Bure, from where the gold that is traded throughout the interior comes ... The traders and merchants of Jenne are suffering greatly from this war; but they are afraid to complain openly. I think myself that they would gain little from doing so anyway. Several blacks have told me that since it has broken out the Moors had been leaving this trade centre to go to Sansanding.[22]

Administratively the country was divided into five military provinces entrusted to relatives or faithful disciples of Seku Ahmadu. In Jenne, 'Uthmān Bukhari Hammadun Sangaré, his first disciple, watched trade on the Niger and the border area between the Niger and the Bani; he bore the title of Amiru Mangal.[23] From Tenenku, the chief of Massina province, Bori Hamsala, a nephew of Seku Ahmadu, watched the western border.

18. A.H. Ba and J. Daget, 1962, pp. 67–8. On the often personal nature of Seku Ahmadu's power, see also C. Monteil, 1932, pp. 108, 112–13.
19. A. H. Ba and Daget, J. 1962, p. 65.
20. ibid., 67 and 280.
21. R. Caillé, 1830, Vol. 2, pp. 217–18.
22. R. Caillé, 1830, Vol. 2, pp. 214–15.
23. He was the commander-in-chief of the army.

The chief of Fakala, Alfa Samba Futa, was responsible for watching the right bank of the Bani. Finally, the chiefs of Hayré, Nabbé and Dundé watched, respectively, the eastern border and the lake area.

Hamdallahi, the new capital established *c.*1820, was the seat of the central government. Nukuma, in the middle of the floodplain, was too vulnerable at times of high water. Seku Ahmadu preferred a more easily defended site 25km south-, south-east of the present town of Mopti, in a contact zone between the areas liable to flooding and the areas above the flood line. Building work took three years. The mosque, built by masons from Jenne, and Seku Ahmadu's palace were the most impressive buildings in the city. The residential area, which had about eighteen districts, was surrounded by a protective wall pierced by four gates. Policing was carried out by seven marabouts assisted by a large number of mounted men who criss-crossed the districts in small groups. The town was said to be very tidy.[24]

PLATE 23.2 *Ruins of a defensive tower of the* tata *(fortress) at Hamdallahi*

Life at Hamdallahi was governed by extreme austerity. There were strict rules about how the various classes of society spent their time. Anyone found on the streets after the evening prayer, for example, had to establish his identity and, if married, was taken to court; in town, people on horseback might not, on pain of severe penalties, glance into the compounds they

24. A.H. Ba and J. Daget, 1962, pp. 43–50; see also F.B.S. Diarah, 1982, pp. 122–39 ff.

PLATE 23.3 *Tomb of Seku Ahmadu at Hamdallahi*

were passing; both the young and elderly widows had to be kept in seclusion so that old men should not be reminded of their youth; and so on.

But Seku Ahmadu's prime achievement was unquestionably his campaign to sedentarize the Fulbe. In addition to laying out Hamdallahi, he had many farming and stock-breeding villages built. This latter activity naturally attracted the organizers' full attention. Grazing areas and transhumance were meticulously regulated, here again by a sort of paramilitary organization.[25] All these institutions only bore fruit under Seku Ahmadu's son, Ahmadu Seku.

The reign of Ahmadu Seku (1845–53)

Ahmadu Seku's reign is regarded in Massina as the most peaceful and prosperous, in contradistinction to his father's wartorn one and Ahmadu's Seku's own son's, which was deeply marked by the war with al-Hadjdj ʿUmar.[26] But the beginning was not easy. The first difficulties arose at the time of the succession. Seku Ahmadu died on 19 March 1845, and according to Massina traditions, the only criteria for the appointment of a new head of the *dina* were supposed to be learning and piety. Though the supporters of dynastic succession by Seku Ahmadu's family managed to appease the ambitions of his nephew Balobbo by giving him the post of commander-in-chief of the army, there remained other persons such as Alfa Nuhum

25. A. H. Ba and J. Daget, 1962, pp. 81–103; see also N. Waïgalo, 1977, pp. 8–9.
26. I. Barry, 1975, pp. 24–5.

Tayru and al-Hadjdj Mody Seydu who were not of the dead leader's family but met the required conditions better than his eldest son.[27] Ahmadu Seku's nomination thus led to some discontent.

Among the youth the strictness of the *dina* was becoming increasingly unbearable. So when the new leader made known his intention to pursue his father's policy unchanged, lampoons were recited throughout Hamdallahi against 'these old turbanned marabouts, ever ready to enforce Islamic laws strictly and without the slightest concession'.[28]

In addition to these domestic difficulties, when Seku Ahmadu's death was announced the Saro Bambara and the Tuareg of the Timbuktu area rose in revolt: 'When Seku Ahmadu's death was announced, Massina was overcome with grief; but drums of joy resounded in Bambara country, and the same Tuareg [i.e. those of Lake Gossi], at once organized feasts to thank heaven for ridding them of their most powerful enemy'.[29] While repression in Saro, Balobbo's mother's homeland, was never very violent, it was most energetically prosecuted against the Tuareg by the same Balobbo, who was said to be anxious to take the opportunity to show the grand council how wrong it had been to prefer his cousin to himself as successor to Seku Ahmadu.[30]

Taking advantage of the succession crisis at Hamdallahi, the Tuareg of the Timbuktu area had got rid of Sansirfi, the representative of the central power there, and proclaimed their independence. At the beginning of 1846 Balobbo marched against them. Taken by surprise, they were cut down by the Fulbe lancers near Lake Gossi. They then asked the Kunta family to intercede on their behalf. Shaykh Sidi al-Mukhtār having died shortly after Seku Ahmadu, his brother Shaykh Sidi al-Bekkai started negotiations with Massina. Promoted illegally to the title of Shaykh al-Kunti, Sidi al-Bekkai was determined to do everything he could to gain effective control of affairs in Timbuktu.[31] Despite the opposition of the leaders in Hamdallahi, he went there in 1847; he secured the disbandment of the military garrison in Timbuktu but failed to prevent Sansirfi taking up his post again. After the Tuareg, the Monimpe Bambara were the second great target of Hamdallahi under Ahmadu Seku. But the closing years of his reign were fairly peaceful and, by and large, Seku Ahmadu's successor, combining firmness and diplomacy, managed to maintain the frontiers of the kingdom intact and re-establish a certain entente in the interior. On his death in February

27. ibid., p. 15.
28. I. Barry, 1975, p. 21; see also A. H. Ba and J. Daget, 1962, p. 259.
29. I. Barry, 1975, p. 21.
30. A. H. Ba and J. Daget, 1962, pp. 258, 266–7.
31. He had just ousted his elder brother Shaykh Sidi Hammada from the title of Shaykh al-Kunti, which was his by right. Barth, albeit his friend, mentioned among his character traits that of stopping at nothing to gain his ends (H. Barth, 1863, Vol. 4, pp. 86–7). See also A. H. Ba and J. Daget, 1962, p. 274.

1853, however, both the domestic and the foreign difficulties arose again in heightened form.

Ahmadu mo Ahmadu, last ruler of Massina (1853–62)

Ahmadu mo Ahmadu's reign began with a major succession crisis, involving the various members of Seku Ahmadu's family. The custom had already been established of selecting the head of the *dina* from among the descendants of Seku Ahmadu. Balobbo, admittedly a prestigious military leader, knew that he did not meet all the requirements, particularly that of learning, to be chosen. So he intrigued with the young Ahmadu mo Ahmadu, the dead ruler's son,[32] and managed to get him nominated as ruler, hoping of course to keep him in leading reins,[33] thus sowing the seeds of discord in Massina. The candidate who met all the requirements for election, Abdulaye Seku, the dead ruler's brother, did not admit defeat:

> He decided with the support of the Kunta and the armies of Kunari and Haïré to march on Hamdallahi, to which he laid siege. The capital was split between supporters of Ahmadu mo Ahmadu and Abdulaye Seku. Feelings ran high, and the collision could come at any time; but the worst was avoided thanks to the aged Adya's intervention with her son, Abdulaye Seku.[34] But from then on Massina was split into hostile camps, which waged cold war on each other.[35]

Ahmadu mo Ahmadu's reign only deepened these divisions. He lacked both the education and the political breadth of his predecessors. When he came to power he made radical changes in the very foundations of the *dina*: the venerable marabouts were replaced by young men of his own age and liberalized outlook.[36] Forty years after the foundation of the *dina*, Ibrahima Barry tells us, enthusiasm had declined; 'rivalries, intrigues and self-seeking got the upper hand again';[37] and the same author reports an anecdote which is indicative of the atmosphere that prevailed among the Massina ruling class. One of the members of Balobbo's conspiracy, who had been arrested by al-Hadjdj 'Umar, said one day to his gaoler, who was making fun of him, 'Whatever punishment I suffer [he was to be shot], I prefer it to being ruled by the baby'. The baby was Ahmadu mo Ahmadu.[38]

32. Different informants put his age between 18 and 24.

33. I. Barry, 1975, pp. 29–30; N. Waïgalo, 1977, pp. 1–2; see also A. H. Ba and J. Daget, 1962, p. 286.

34. She was also the deceased's mother and Ahmadu mo Ahmadu's grandmother. She was said to have a soft spot for her grandson.

35. N. Waïgalo, 1977, p. 2.

36. I. Barry, 1975, pp. 32, 36, 38–41; N. Waïgalo, 1970, p. 34. See also F. B. S. Diarah, 1982, pp. 321–32.

37. I. Barry, 1975, p. 42.

38. ibid. On the internal divisions within Massina during Ahmadu mo Ahmadu's reign, see also E. Mage, 1868, p. 263, and al-Hadjdj 'Umar Tal, 1983, pp. 52–3.

It is easy to understand that Massina, sapped by these internal divisions, could not put up effective resistance to al-Hadjdj ʿUmar's movement.

The Torodbe (Tukuloor) empire

In both the Western and the Central Sudan the slave trade, by upsetting the traditional foundations of society, had created a situation of permanent crisis and helped states to spring up on all sides whose viability depended on a continuation of the trade. In Futa Jallon, Futa Toro, Sokoto and Massina, where there was a sizeable Muslim community, Islam's reaction to this situation took the form of a national revolution led by the most oppressed people of the age, the Fulbe. Slavery was not abolished, but was governed by legal provisions, namely the Ḳu'rān. West of the Niger, between Massina, Futa Jallon and Futa Toro, a myriad of little states more or less dependent on Segu or Kaarta still escaped Muslim law. Disunited and a prey to internal divisions, they were to fail to offer effective resistance to the militant proselytism of an infant Muslim sect, the Tijāniyya.[39]

Al-Hadjdj ʿUmar's *djihād* and the birth of the Muslim empire of Segu (1852–62)

After the successes of the eighteenth and early nineteenth century, Islamization was marking time on all sides. The new theocracies were also riven by succession crises; and in the case of the Western Sudan there was also the danger posed by French power, a resolute enemy of the Muslim religion. Thus in Futa Toro, in the first half of the nineteenth century, Islam was threatened from within, from the east and from the west. Al-Hadjdj ʿUmar's movement was a reaction to this situation.

Outline of ʿUmar Saidu's life

ʿUmar Saidu (al-Hadjdj ʿUmar) was born in about 1796[40] at Halwar, in Toro, the province closest to the French colony of Saint-Louis. He came from a family that had played an active part in the great Muslim revolution of the late eighteenth century, and his whole childhood was steeped in Islamic culture. Through his exceptional intelligence and perspicacity he

39. From the name of its founder, Aḥmad al-Tijāni (1737–1815). This brotherhood was born in southern Algeria in about 1782. It spread rapidly throughout North Africa and especially in Morocco, where the *zāwiya* of Fez became the biggest centre. It was relatively more liberal in nature and its basic principles were more simple than those of the other brotherhoods. It was first introduced south of the Sahara by the Ida or ʿAlī but it only became widespread there through Sheku ʿUmar.

40. According to Futa traditions he was born on the eve of the battle of Bungowi, which Almami Abdul Kadri fought in 1796 to convert the Damel of Kajor, Amari Ngone Ndella, to Islam. It was ʿUmar's imminent birth that stopped his father, Saidu ʿUthmān, a disciple of Sulaymān Bal, taking part in that battle. See, among others, M. Kamara, 1975, p. 154, and F. Dumont, 1974, p. 4.

very early assimilated and mastered all the Islamic sciences. He soon rejected the old Ḳādirīyya sect,[41] under cover of which what can only be described as fiefs controlled by marabouts had grown up all over Senegambia. After initiation into the infant Tijāni sect he left Futa in 1826 to go and master the principles of the new brotherhood at its source. He was not to return to his native village until early 1847.[42]

Twenty years of travelling, including three in the Holy Places of Islam, gave him knowledge unique in black Africa at that time and great experience both of the Muslim countries visited and of the non-Islamized states. He came back with the title of Grand Caliph of the Tijāniyya,[43] with the mission of completing the Islamization of black Africa.

In Sokoto, where he stayed from 1830 to 1838,[44] he studied the principles of the holy war at the feet of Muḥammad Bello. His vast learning and strong personality made him one of the leading figures in the Muslim state of Sokoto. In 1838, recalled by his own people, he started homewards. Futa Toro, weakened by the increasingly frequent incursions of the periodic raids of the Massassi into its eastern provinces, could no longer be a firm base for the launching of a *djihād*. Al-Hadjdj ʿUmar accordingly settled down in Futa Jallon, where the Tijāniyya had many adherents and where (within the Ḳādirīyya itself), he knew that he could count on the support of the Alfaya, who were keen supporters of militant Islam.[45] Despite the hostility of the Soriyya party in power, al-Hadjdj ʿUmar made Jugunku his prime operational base from which recruitment and the purchase of arms were stepped up. At the same time in his most famous book, the *Rimah*, he perfected the ideological instrument of his campaign.[46] On his return from the campaign of exposition and recruitment in Futa Toro in 1847, he speeded up the preparations and transferred his capital to Dinguiraye in Jalonkadugu, whose ruler, Gimba Sacko, was soon to regret having given him asylum. Convinced nevertheless of his military superiority,

41. The Ḳādirīyya is one of the oldest brotherhoods south of the Sahara, where it was introduced by the Kunta.

42. F. Carrère and P. Holle, 1855, p. 194.

43. That is, supreme head of the brotherhood in the land of the blacks.

44. These are the dates accepted by the historians of Ahmadu Bello University, Zaria, Nigeria, according to a letter dated 24 December 1981 from the then head of the department, Madhī Adamu.

45. See al-Hadjdj ʿUmar Tal, nd (b), p. 9; T. Diallo, 1972, pp. 37, 38, 148–50. On the other hand the Soriyya, descended from the military leader Ibrahima Sori Mawdo (who owed his enthronement solely to the continual pressure brought to bear on the new state by the Djalonke and Fulbe), were political rather than religious.

46. In it, using simple language that brought it within the reach of his compatriots, he developed the main theses of the Tijāniyya, enriched by his personal experience and comments by many scholars of this new brotherhood. Reproduced in quantity, it was circulated throughout all of sub-Saharan Africa and even beyond. F. Dumont, 1974, pp. 64–5, tells us that the *Rimah* is to this day 'the book par excellence of literate Tijāni, from the lowliest marabout to the most exalted guide'.

Gimba Sacko launched his troops against Dinguiraye. He was driven back and, after several successes over small neighbouring villages, the *mudjahidūn*[47] captured the redoubtable fortress of Tamba, capital of Jalonkadugu in 1852.

The launching of the djihād

Between the middle of the eighteenth and the middle of the nineteenth centuries, the Massassi coming from Segu country had established in Kaarta a state whose influence was felt from Bakhunu to Gajaga. Its power rested on a formidable professional army, made up essentially of crown captives wholly devoted to their masters. They were always in the forefront, and it was they who took the responsibility for making breaches in the enemy camps. Their leader played a prominent role at the court of the *fama*,[48] especially at succession times. He ran the country's affairs between the death of a *fama* and the enthronement of the heir-presumptive.[49] The second factor which added to the strength of the Kaarta forces was their cavalry, almost entirely composed of Massassi. Finally, a degree of mastery of the making of gunpowder made this army one of the most feared in the Upper Senegal area.

Power was organized into a sort of absolute monarchy in which succession was collateral in the Kurubari (Kulibali) family. Speedy and strict justice enabled this state to intervene very effectively, while a judiciously deployed system of endogamy enabled the Massassi to strengthen their power through carefully chosen marriage alliances. They had rapidly become the main arbiters of all the wars in Senegambia.[50] Their support was often sought to settle disputes between one country and another, which gave them the opportunity to make profitable raids. Being far better trained in the art of war than their neighbours, they also exacted a heavy tribute for these services. Thus, one by one, all the small chieftaincies of the area, Bundu, Xaso, Gajaga, were destabilized. Their pressure was felt as far away as the eastern provinces of Futa Toro.[51]

This was the position until the civil war which erupted in Kaarta in 1843 between the Massassi and the Jawara (Diawara). After the Massassi had reached the country in the middle of the eighteenth century, they had acted as the protectors of the Jawara, whom they found settled there. But, once in control of the country, they soon began to behave as veritable masters and to drive the Jawara southwards; the Jawara were henceforth

47. Name given in Islam to fighters for the faith.
48. The title of the Bambara kings.
49. A. Raffenel, 1856, Vol. 2, p. 387.
50. A. Ba, recording of 10 and 11 February 1982. See also F. Carrère and P. Holle, 1855, p. 181 and E. Mage, 1868, p. 97.
51. The slaves obtained in these wars and raids were sold to the authorities in Saint-Louis or the Gambia of which they had become the main suppliers.

subjected to heavy taxes and all sorts of harassments.[52] In 1843, the Jawara, driven out of Nioro, their capital, rose in revolt, plunging Kaarta into a civil war which was to last seven years. The Massassi won the war in 1850, but they were henceforth weakened and divided.[53]

The western Massassi (those in the Koniakary area) had been unwilling to take part in the war against the Jawara which, according to them, had been declared by Mamadi Kandia, the last Kurubari king, for personal reasons.[54] The latter, to revenge himself, left them to face the Muslim army alone. After the capture of Koniakary, the Massassi assembled at Yeliman to defend the old royal capital, but in vain: it was destroyed in February 1855, which led to the surrender of Mamadi Kandia and all the Kaarta chiefs (those of the Jawara, the Kagoro and the Bakhunu Fulbe). On 11 April 1855, the *mudjahidūn* made their triumphal entry into Nioro, and the Massassi were subjected to the rules of Islam.

These produced such upheavals in their everyday life that revolts soon broke out on all sides, keeping the Muslim troops on the alert until 1856. The repression was extremely violent: Mamadi Kandia and a great many Massassi were put to death. Those who escaped withdrew towards the borders of Segu.

Al-Hadjdj ʿUmar left Alfa ʿUmar Thierno Bayla in charge of the province and went towards Khasso, which the French had withdrawn from his sphere of influence by setting up a confederation there headed by their friend Diuka Sambala of Medina (Médine). Besieging this town in the spring of 1857 was the most difficult action the Muslim army had to undertake. Despite being menaced by French artillery fire, the Muslims fought with a determination that compelled the admiration of their adversaries. Much was at stake: for the Futanke, the wiping out of many years of humiliation and annoyance imposed by the new French policy in Senegal. It was no accident that the general who attracted most notice at Medina was Mamadu Kuro, the headman of Ngano, a village that had been destroyed in 1854 by French troops.

The whole ideological base of the *djihād* rested on Divine protection: thus it is understandable that the disciples of al-Hadjdj ʿUmar, Muhamadu Aliu Tyam and Thierno Abdul,[55] tried to explain the failure at Medina by the indiscipline of the *talīb*s or on the grounds that it was not their master's mission to fight the whites. The length of the siege, the successive reinforcements sent to Medina and the fury with which the *mudjahidūn*

52. A. Raffenel, 1846, pp. 298–301; 1856, Vol 1, p. 337.

53. A. Ba, recordings of 10, 11 and 15 February 1982; F. Carrère and P. Holle, 1855, p. 184.

54. The excuse for the war was the assassination of a Jawara prince by Mamadi Kandia's son; but the underlying reason was that the Jawara had had enough of Bambara rule, which with its arrogance and exorbitant tributes and, to crown it all, expulsion from Nioro had become unbearable, according to the Bambara *dieli* as reported by D. S. Diallo, 1977, p. 10.

55. E. Mage's main informant about the life of al-Hadjdj ʿUmar.

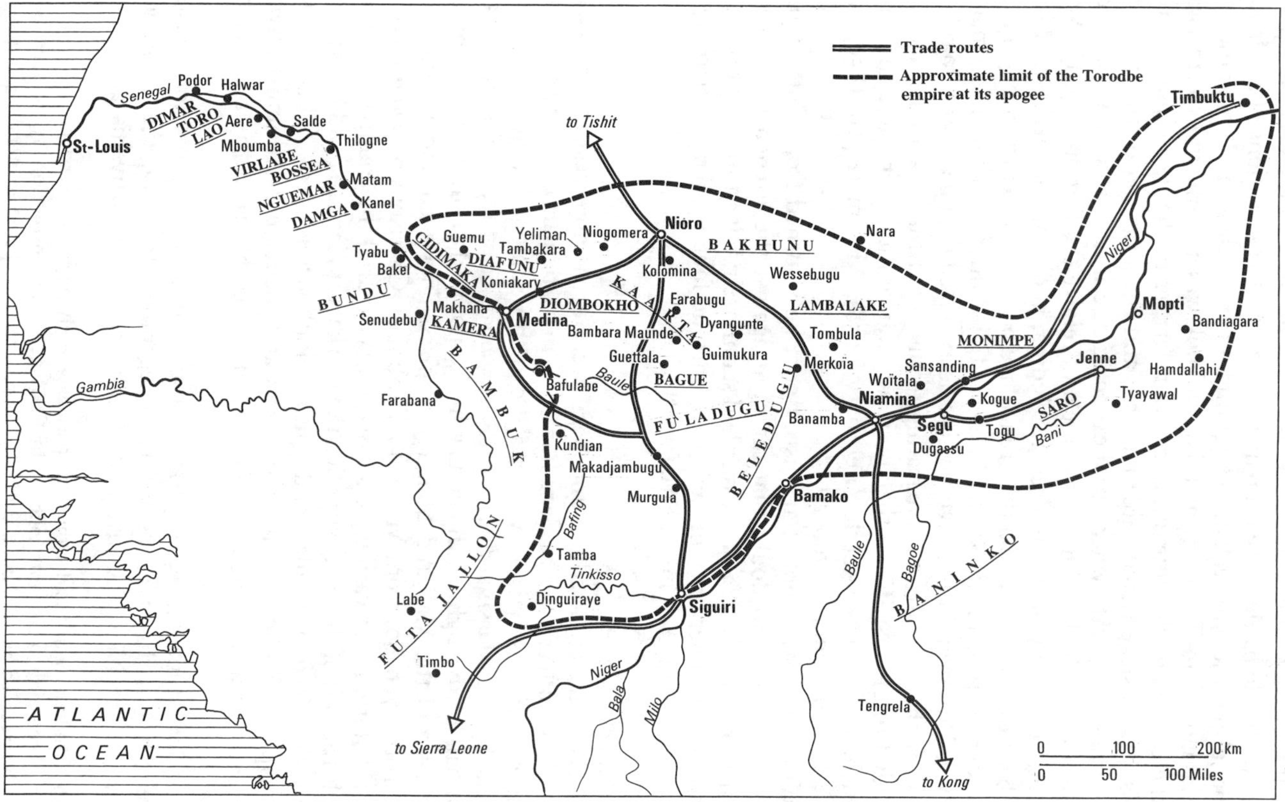

FIG. 23.2 *The Torodbe empire at its apogee (after M. Ly-Tall)*

fought certainly show that 'Umar agreed. Moreover in the earliest reports we have on the battle there is no mention of these reservations of al-Hadjdj 'Umar about the outbreak of the fighting. On the other hand we know that Muhamadu Aliu Tyam throughout his book was at pains to explain away all the defeats of the Muslim army by referring to the indiscipline of the *talībs*.[56] The siege lasted three months, and the situation of the besieged was almost desperate when an unexpected rise in the water level allowed Governor Faidherbe himself to come and relieve the fort on 18 July 1857.

Futa lost many of its children at Medina, and some of the best. It had just been demonstrated that the French had become masters of Senegambia. In order to rebuild his strength, al-Hadjdj 'Umar continued his march towards Bundu and Futa. Everywhere he exhorted the inhabitants to refuse to live with the whites by emigrating to the new Muslim state he had just founded to the east. From then on it was war to the bitter end against the French, at Ndium-in-Ferlo (February 1858), Matam (April 1859) and Arundu and Gemu (October 1859).

With a following put at at least 40 000, he returned from Futa in July 1859.[57] There is no doubt that the fight against the French was not the primary task that al-Hadjdj 'Umar had set himself; but although thoroughly aware of the superiority of their weaponry he fought them tenaciously at Medina, Gemu, Ndium and Matam.[58]

The march on Segu

The Bambara of Beledugu and Segu were even more resistant to Islam than those of Kaarta. The Segu Bambara, in particular, had resisted several centuries of proselytism by Marka, Bozo and Somono marabouts and the *djihād* by the Massina *dina*. The Segu *fanga*, or state, established in the first half of the eighteenth century in the political vacuum created by the break-up of the Mali and Songhay empires, flourished under Ngolo Jara (Diarra) (1766–90) from Mande to Timbuktu. Garrisons of *tonjon*s (crown slaves) stationed at various strategic points ensured the country's security, while the rest of the army supplied the markets at Kangaba and Sansanding with slaves from regular raids into neighbouring areas. This was the principal source of revenue of the *fama* and the *tonjon*s. Administratively, the country was divided into five provinces, each headed by a son of the *fama*.

Under Monzon, Ngolo Jara's son and successor (1790–1808), Segu's strength was displayed as far as Senegambia. In 1796, the whole area between the Niger, Kaarta and Bundu was ravaged by his armies; the

56. Modern traditions, for the same reasons, merely repeat this version.

57. According to accounts collected by E. Mage at Segu in 1864, many contingents had already preceded him to Nioro. But these figures are not to be taken literally.

58. Everywhere in West Africa it was the French who were the aggressors, not the ones being attacked. They took the initiative of fighting chiefs who were hampering their economic interests.

immediate neighbours, Beledugu, Dedugu and Fuladugu, were subjugated.[59]

With the reign of Da Monzon (1808–27), a long decline began, marked in particular by the emancipation of the Fulbe and the birth on the eastern borders of Segu of an increasingly threatening Muslim state, the *dina* of Hamdallahi. Thus, when al-Hadjdj ʿUmar visited it in about 1839, on his return from Mecca, it was a country in crisis. The reigning *fama*, Cefolo, was very ill, almost dying. The power struggle was already under way within the royal family. One of the claimants to the throne, Torokoro Mari, even agreed to be converted by the Tukuloor marabout in prison, in exchange for his blessings and prayers.[60] An alliance sealed between them was to enable Segu to be peacefully Islamized when the time was ripe.

But in 1859, Torokoro Mari, whose prayers had been heard and who had been reigning for six years, was denounced and put to death by the *tonjons*.[61] Al-Hadjdj ʿUmar, who returned from Futa in September 1859, decided to march on the Bambara capital. He left Nioro on 12 September 1859 and went towards Segu, preaching and converting as he went. In Beledugu, on 20 November 1859, the redoubtable citadel of Merkoia in which all the fugitives from Kaarta had taken refuge put up a ferocious resistance to this advance of Islam; and for the first time the *mudjahidūn* were obliged to use the two cannon captured from the French in 1858. From then on his progress slowed down. On 25 May 1860 he reached the Niger at Niamina. From there on the Muslim army was in Segu territory.

In the Bambara capital ʿAlī Monzon Jara had in 1859 replaced Torokoro Mari, who was regarded as too favourable to the Muslims; he was invested only after swearing to defend Segu against any intrusion by Islam.[62] Hence (despite his Muslim first name) he could not have sincerely embraced this religion, as the leaders of Massina were later to argue. He gathered a powerful army together at Woïtala, under the command of his own son. The battle that was joined in this village is said to have been one of the bloodiest of the *djihād*. It was only on 9 September 1859, after four days of fighting, that this stronghold was taken, opening the way for the march on Segu.

The only salvation remaining for ʿAlī Monzon was alliance with his erstwhile enemies, the leaders of Massina. Since the Islamic revolution in this country, Hamadallahi and Segu had always been at war. All attempts by the various leaders of Massina to subjugate Segu had ended in failure.[63] Taking advantage even of the succession crises in Massina, the Bambara had several times carried the war there.[64] The leader of Hamdallahi, like

59. L. Tauxier, 1942, p. 101.
60. A. Koné, 1978, p. 62.
61. ibid.; see also E. Mage, 1868, pp. 234–46.
62. E. Mage, 1868, p. 246.
63. E. Delafosse, 1972, Vol. 2, p. 293.
64. I. Barry, 1975, p. 27.

that of Segu, was all the more inclined to let bygones be bygones because al-Hadjdj ʿUmar, by his presence in the Niger basin, was challenging both his political and his religious hegemony. But in the throes of deep-seated crises neither of them was able to offer effective resistance to ʿUmar's better-organized and better-equipped army. On 9 March 1861, the Muslim army entered Segu. ʿAlī Jara was forewarned, and had just enough time to save his skin by taking refuge in Massina.

The war with Massina

From Sokoto to Jugunku the Tukuloor pilgrim, with this impressive retinue, his many belongings and his scarcely veiled intention to wage war against the infidels, certainly perturbed the existing rulers, both traditionalist and otherwise. The Muslims were split between three main areas of influence: Futa Toro in the north-west, Futa Jallon in the south-west, and Massina in the east. Inside this triangle, except for Bundu, was a mass of traditionalist societies, into which, when conditions were propitious, the Muslims sent expeditions ostensibly directed towards holy war, but whose ulterior motive was often in fact to obtain slaves.[65] Nevertheless the Muslim rulers, after the successes of the early years, were everywhere somewhat on the defensive. This was particularly so in the case of the ruler of Massina in his relations with his non-Muslim neighbours.

Al-Hadjdj ʿUmar was inevitably perceived as a dangerous rival. After his victory over the Massassi in April 1855, he announced the 'good news' to a number of Muslim rulers, including that of Massina; the latter's reply, calling on him to go back home, certainly did not augur well for future relations between the two Muslim leaders of the Western Sudan.[66] In the following year, in August 1856, a Massina army moved to confront al-Hadjdj ʿUmar. The battle of Kasakary marks the outbreak of a war that was to last until 1864.

Nevertheless the two Muslim leaders were to try by means of several letters to find a solution to their differences. But it was virtually a dialogue of the deaf; ʿUmar relied on his wide Islamic learning to demonstrate to the ruler of Massina that so far from opposing him he should combine with him to fight against the infidels; Ahmadu mo Ahmadu for his part countered with arguments that were more political in nature, drawing attention to the fact that the whole area from Segu to Kaarta came under his influence.[67]

After ʿUmar's army had entered Sansanding in October 1860, the com-

65. This phenomenon occurred also in Hausaland, where the Muslim rulers took care not to Islamize everyone so as not to deprive themselves of reservoirs of slaves.

66. Ahmadu mo Ahmadu of Massina considered that all the non-Muslim countries between the Niger and Kaarta were in his sphere of influence.

67. On this exchange of letters between ʿUmar and Ahmadu mo Ahmadu, see the recent translation and annotation in al-Hadjdj ʿUmar Tal, 1983; there is also interesting information in F. Dumont, 1974, F. B. S. Diarah, 1982, and M. al-Hafiz al-Tidjāni, 1983.

bined forces of Segu and Massina came and pitched camp before this town. This confrontation lasted two months, neither of the parties being willing to be the first to start fighting. But in this very tense atmosphere a small incident in February 1860 was enough to bring about the clash.[68]

Thus we see that until the last moment 'Umar does not seem to have wanted war.[69] After all, he had himself condemned in very violent terms the armed conflict between the rulers of Borno and Sokoto. The suggestion he made to the ruler of Massina, who had not succeeded in converting the Bambara of Segu,[70] that he should combine with him, must have been quite sincere. But it was also difficult for Ahmadu mo Ahmadu to agree to this suggestion, as this would have meant acknowledging his supremacy. Despite the exhange of many letters, war was thus almost inevitable, given that both sides dug in their heels.[71] The alliance between Massina and Segu gave 'Umar the legal grounds for fighting Ahmadu mo Ahmadu.

After a stay of a year in the Bambara capital, 'Umar marched on Massina in April 1862. Hamdallahi was occupied in the following month. Ahmadu mo Ahmadu died from wounds sustained during the battle of Tyayawal (10 May 1862).[72] Balobbo, who had never renounced the throne of Massina, surrendered fairly readily, hoping in this way to achieve his own ends. But 'Umar never left those who had fought against him in power. Believing that with Ahmadu mo Ahmadu's death he had achieved the much desired unity with Massina, he left all the country's high officials in post;[73] but in January

68. According to F. Dumont, 1974, p. 126, the Massinanke fired at supporters of 'Umar while they were bathing. According to Mage, shots were exchanged between the fishermen of the two camps. By the time 'Umar had been told, and tried to restrain his troops, they had already begun to cross the river: E. Mage, 1868, p. 106.

69. According to all our informants in Futa he did not want it: O. Bâ, nd., p. 109, verso; Tapsiru Ahmadu Abdul Niagane, recording of 3 May 1981; Al-Hajj Ahmadu Ibrahima Datt, recording of 4 May 1981. When the great *djihād* was launched in June 1854, Kaarta and Segu were the only objectives al-Hadjdj 'Umar was aiming at, according to M. A. Tyam, 1935, p. 45. Likewise as regards Massina traditions, N. Waïgalo, 1977, p. 6, tells us that the purpose of Ahmadu Haïmut of Hayre's mission was to avoid war and seek the support of the ruler of Massina in the pursuit of the *djihād* towards Mossi country.

70. On Sheku 'Umar's approach some well-timed conversions were made, but did not affect the basic problem: the Bambara of Segu remained deeply attached to their religion. The many idols found in Segu were to be put on display at Hamdallahi: M. A. Tyam, 1935, pp. 183–4. On the religion of the Bambara before 'Umar's *djihād*, see E. Mage, 1988; M. Delafosse, 1972; L. Tauxier, 1942; C. Monteil, 1977; and al-Hadjdj 'Umar Tal, 1983.

71. For details of these letters, see F. Dumont, 1974, pp. 141–82 and al-Hadjdj 'Umar Tal, 1983.

72. Tyayawal is a wood in a marshy area near Sofara. It was there that the last great clash between the armies of Ahmadu mo Ahmadu and 'Umar took place. The Massinanke defended themselves stubbornly, but some military chiefs of Massina are said to have deliberately avoided being at Tyayawal (N. Waigalo, 1977, p. 32). Above all, 'Umar's army excelled that of Massina both in armaments and in organization. Individual acts of valour were unduly important among the Fulbe.

73. N. Waigalo, 1977, p. 33.

1863 he placed it under his son Ahmadu, intending himself to 'continue operations against the infidels at the head of his troops, swollen by the addition of those of Massina'.[74] Disappointed, Balobbo turned towards Timbuktu in March 1863; he knew that in Sīdī Aḥmād al-Bekkai he would find a resolute opponent of 'Umar. When he learned of this, 'Umar had him arrested, together with many of his followers.

The Timbuktu–Massina coalition and the end of al-Hadjdj 'Umar

We have seen that Timbuktu nominally came under Hamdallahi. In actual fact power there was in the hands of the Kunta, whose chief, Sīdī Aḥmād al-Bekkai, was especially jealous of the degree of religious supremacy that he enjoyed throughout the Niger basin. The advance of 'Umar's army was bound to worry him. In 1860 he made contact with the Bambara and offered them his moral support.[75] Two years later, in 1862, while he was making peace proposals to 'Umar, he was simultaneously offering to help the revolt that was simmering at Hamdallahi.[76] Balobbo and his supporters, who had escaped, organized the revolt with his help. First at Mani Mani and then in Kunari the coalition partners inflicted severe defeats on 'Umar's army; it lost its best generals, Alfa 'Umar Thierno Bayla and Alfa 'Uthmān, in May and June 1863.[77] After an eight months' siege, the rest of the army attempted a break-out on 7 February 1864. 'Umar was pursued and took refuge in the cave at Degembere, where he died on 14 February 1864 a few hours before the arrival of reinforcements under his nephew, Tijāni Alfa. The latter, furiously angry, pursued the struggle relentlessly against the coalition partners, who were no longer in agreement (each wanting power for himself). One by one, they were all defeated. In February 1865[78] the moving spirit of the coalition, Sīdī al-Bekkai, was killed in a clash at Sare Dina, in Sebera. Tijāni became the master of Massina and Timbuktu. This was to become the most important province of the empire, after Kaarta and Segu.

The political, economic and social structure of the Torodbe (Tukuloor) empire

Al-Hadjdj 'Umar and the army of the mudjahidūn

With the occupation of Massina al-Hadjdj 'Umar's empire reached its maximum extent, stretching from Gidimaka to Timbuktu and from Dinguiraye to the Sahara.[79] This vast territory took the form not so much of a

74. E. Mage, 1868, p. 268.

75. In 1860, he sent a letter to this effect to 'Alī Monzon; C. Gerresch, 1976, p. 894.

76. C. Gerresch, 1976, p. 895. Not all the Kunta family shared Sidi Aḥmād al-Bekkai's views: a large part of it preferred al-Hadjdj 'Umar (C. Gerresch, 1976, p. 893).

77. M. A. Tyam, 1935, pp. 190–2, notes 1092 and 1110.

78. E. Mage, 1868, p. 450.

79. E. Mage, 1868, p. 113, gives Medina and Tengrela as the western borders; Dinguiraye and Gidimaka seem nearer to the facts.

centralized state as of a set of strong points, from which a political-cum-religious administration went out to consolidate the spread of Islam. Al-Hadjdj ʿUmar, on whose prestige this whole edifice rested, saw himself only as a *mudjahīd*, a fighter for the faith. He did not concern himself much with organization or administration, but contented himself with appointing *talību*s in each of the newly converted places, choosing them in general according to the criterion of education and morality.[80] These *talību*s were responsible for the task of organization. ʿUmar himself was first and foremost a mystic,[81] convinced that he had been entrusted with a Divine mission, namely to complete the Islamization of the blacks. In the execution of this task nothing stopped him, neither the hostility of Muslim rulers nor the fierce resistance of some non-Muslim rulers. Like the Prophet, whose heir he was convinced he was, obstacles in his path, far from discouraging him, strengthened him in his determination: 'the heir inherits everything possessed by him whose heir he is'.[82]

In physical terms the only eyewitness description we have of him is that of Paul Holle, who says that he saw him in August 1847 at Bakel: he describes him as 'a man with a striking face, on which were depicted a lively intelligence and an impression of meditation and calculation'.[83] He was brilliantly seconded by the greatest of his generals, Alfa 'Umar Thierno Bayla Wan, with whom he used to say he always had a complete identity of views.[84] The second closest person to him was Abdulaye Hausa, who had followed him from Sokoto. Generally speaking, despite the personal ascendancy he had over his companions (which was reinforced by Tijāniyya doctrine about relations between the Shaykh and his disciples), he associated the *talību*s with all major decisions. Moreover it could not have been otherwise in these Torodbe-dominated circles, where everyone was full of his own importance. It was during his spiritual retreats that he perfected most of his plans, drawing extensively on the experience of the Prophet Muḥammad and of the Apostles of Islam who had preceded him. Then he would submit them for approval to the council of the *talību*s.[85] After all, it was very important for the success of the *djihād* to have the continuous support of these disciples, who had left their families and homeland to

80. As F. Dumont, 1974, p. 121, so well shows, he was an anti-Sultan. It is significant that it should have been an Islamicist who first stressed this fundamental feature of ʿUmar's. It is a pity that the latter's many writings have not yet been translated.

81. He was often in *Khalwa*. All his major decisions were taken after one of his spiritual retreats.

82. al-Hadjdj ʿUmar Tal, nd (b).

83. F. Carrère and P. Holle, 1855, pp. 191–2.

84. Tapsiru Ahmadu Abdul Niagane, recording of 3 May 1981.

85. M. A. Tyam shows us him often in *Khalwa*. This same author tells us of several cases of disobedience by the *talību*s, but always to explain a failure. So we do not know how much credence to give to these various accounts; their very number is enough to suggest that some of them are true.

follow him. So he spared no effort to keep them attached to him, both by demonstrations of his supernatural powers and by distribution of goods. Traditions have preserved the image of him as a very generous man.[86] He paid particular attention to the upkeep of the army.

It was in Hausaland that al-Hadjdj ʿUmar recruited the first members of this army, and it continued to grow from Sokoto to Dinguiraye. It was multi-ethnic, and included contingents from Futa Toro, Hausaland, Futa Jallon, Khasso, Kaarta and Segu. The first-named were far the most numerous: from Jugunku until the departure from Nioro in 1859 Futa Toro continued to supply the army of the *djihād* with manpower.[87]

The *djihād* army comprised four battalions, each organized around a contingent from Futa: the Toro battalion included Toro, Bundu, Gidimaka and part of Futa Jallon; the Yirlabe battalion included the Yirlabe, the Habbiyabe, Khasso, Diafunu, Bakhunu and the Wolarbe Fulbe; the Ngenar battalion included the Ngenar, the Bosseyabe, the Jawara and the Massassi; and lastly the Murgula battalion included the Madinka and part of Futa Jallon. Al-Hadjdj ʿUmar's guard was provided by a large predominantly Hausa group.[88] Each battalion had its own flag (black for the Yirlabe, red and white for the Torodbe).

The armaments consisted mainly of trade rifles and swords; a few privileged individuals had double-barrelled rifles. A large party of blacksmiths followed the army and kept it supplied with ball.[89] In July 1858, at Ndium-in-Ferlo, followers of ʿUmar captured two out-of-order mountain guns from the fleeing Captain Cornu, and they were repaired by the army engineer, Samba Ndiaye. They were to play an important part in the Beledugu and Segu campaigns. But what gave the *mudjahidūn* their strength was above all their faith and a well-thought out strategy. Al-Hadjdj ʿUmar regularly told them about the promises of enjoyment in this world and the next held out to fighters for the faith.[90] On the eve of difficult battles we see him redoubling his activity. Drawing on the Ḳu'rān and the main writings about the life of the Prophet Muḥammad and his Caliphs, he urged his men to brave all difficulties. Thus at Yagine:

86. Goods were distributed at Nioro before leaving for Medina, and at Segu before leaving for Massina.

87. Every time he needed to rebuild his army it was to Futa Toro that he sent his emissaries; in 1849 to prepare the attack on Tamba, in 1853 before the great *djihād* and in 1855 after the very costly battle of Yeliman: M. A. Tyam, 1935, pp. 43, 44, 47. The trend was to continue under his son Ahmadu. He himself carried out a big tour there in 1858–9 before marching on Segu, and brought back from it more than 40 000 people counting both civilians and soldiers.

88. O. Ba, nd, p. 78 verso. We note that the Sofa did not yet exist as a battalion.

89. E. Mage has given us details of Ahmadu's munitions on the eve of the battle of Toghu: 4200kg of local powder, 15–20kg of European powder, nine large bags of gun flints and 150 000 ball: E. Mage, 1868, p. 415.

90. According to the traditions he preached every night; see O. Ba, nd, p. 86.

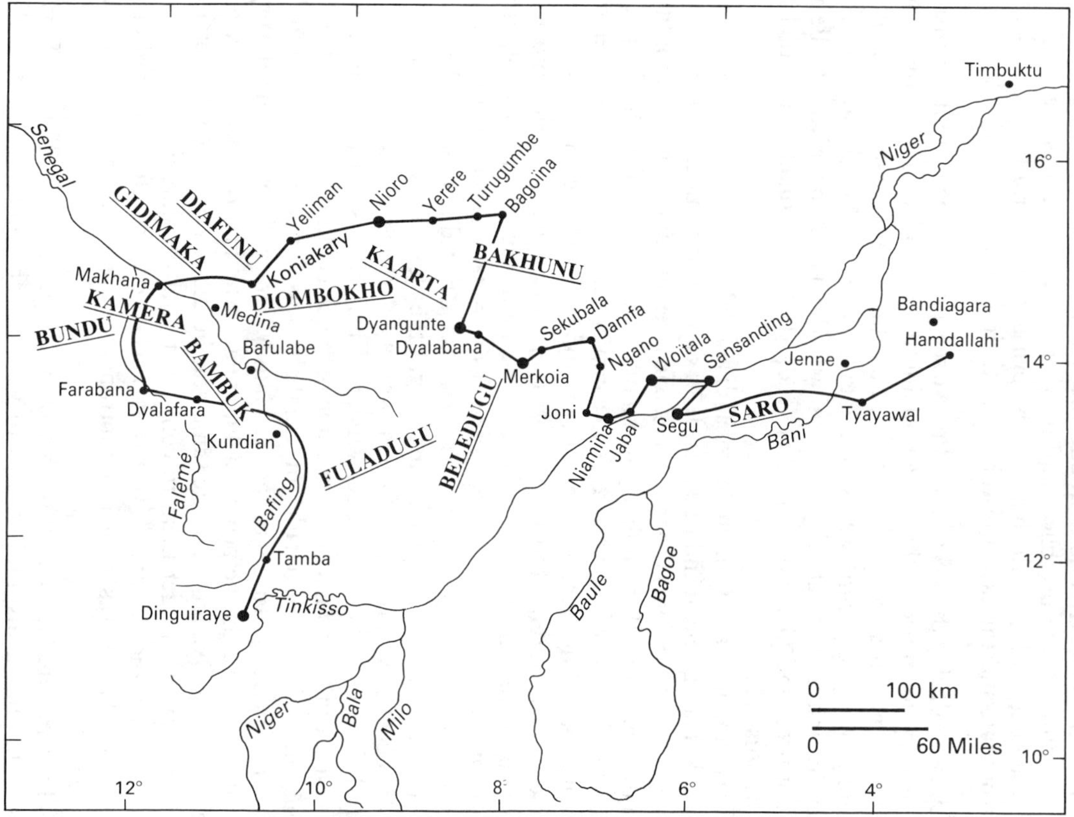

FIG. 23.3 *From Dinguiraye to Hamdallahi (after M. Ly-Tall)*

> the Differentiator ordered the criers to summon the army; the army formed up; the Shaykh harangued, the learned one who is not wrong ... There the One and Only overjoyed the *talibs*; he drew their attention to the promises of reward and the threats of eternal punishment; the traditions about the Prophet and the sayings were expounded. He preached, and filled their hearts with aspirations for the next world; so much so that he pricked this world for them like a bubble, and the next world became their goal.[91]

Likewise during the siege of Medina we see him pouring forth inexhaustible energy to improve the morale of his troops and to assure them of divine protection and paradise. And when, to denigrate him, Paul Holle said to a very young *talib* who was dying: 'Poor boy, why was not your Al Aghi the first into the attack this morning?', the dying boy, giving Holle a look of profound pity, cried out 'My God, My God, I thank you. I die! I see paradise ...'

This fanatical army often faced a disunited enemy. This was so in Bambuk, Kaarta, Segu and Massina. It was also clearly superior in military strategy: e.g. diversionary manoeuvres, encirclement of the enemy, rapidity of movement and all the military techniques that had enabled the Prophet and his caliphs in a few short years to conquer vast territories. Even terror became a strategic weapon: the massacre of men and the enslavement of women and children[92] broke the morale of threatened countries and led some to surrender without a fight. When approaching a country, the procedure was always the same: emissaries were sent to the chief to invite him to convert; if he acquiesced, his head was shaved and he was handed a string of prayer beads (*satala*) and taught the elementary rules of Islam. The procedure was the same for his subjects. A *talib* and a small garrison were left to consolidate this conversion. This recourse to peaceful conversion saved them many battles, some of which could have been difficult. Thus the redoubtable citadel of Farabana was invested without much resistance in 1854. In 1856, too, al-Hadjdj 'Umar showed himself very conciliatory towards the people of Farabugu, who had revolted; and after the capture of Dyangunte in the same year he did not hesitate to negotiate with the Kamori to get them to conform to the Muslim rules about the possessions of the defeated.[93] It was only when people refused to embrace Islam that battle was joined. Unfortunately this was what most often happened.

The commanding general of this army was Alfa 'Umar Thierno Bayla Wan. One day a dispute arose as to who was the more attached to Al-

91. M. A. Tyam, 1935, pp. 56–7.

92. Muslim law allows the killing in battle only of those capable of bearing arms. Women and, by analogy, children under 15, were spared.

93. M. A. Tyam, 1935, pp. 81, 82, 98, 100, 124–6. He was to show the same spirit in Gidimaka and Diafunu.

Hadjdj 'Umar, Alfa 'Umar Thierno Bayla or Abdulaye Hausa. Some said the former, others the latter. To settle the matter the two parties went to 'Umar himself, who said to them, 'If someone came along with a sword and offered a choice between cutting off his head or 'Umar's, Abdulaye Hausa would choose his own. If I have something very important to undertake, you will find that whatever I have decided Alfa 'Umar is of the same opinion as me'.[94] Alfa 'Umar Thierno Bayla was the linchpin of the *djihād*; Al-Hadjdj 'Umar could be said to have been only its brain.

Other military leaders have remained very famous in the memory of the Futanke; for instance, Alfa 'Umar Thierno Molle Ly, one of the first companions, who died at Merkoïa; Alfa 'Uthmān, who died in Massina; and Mamadu Hamat Kuro Wan, one of the bravest. The latter came from the village of Ngano (near Kanel), which had suffered particularly under the exactions of the new interventionist policy of the authorities at Saint-Louis; he joined al-Hadjdj 'Umar with his whole village at Farabana in 1854. He was one of the fiercest opponents of the French. It was he, braving the cannon balls, who managed to scale the fort at Medina and plant the Muslim flag on it. He was cut down by a machine-gun immediately afterwards.

Despite its courage and organization this army was not immune from the great failing of all African armies of the time, that of being dependent on war booty. While Muslim law did admittedly introduce some order into its distribution, the fact remained that booty occupied too important a place in the fighting not to influence the way it was conducted. Al-Hadjdj 'Umar's personality, and the care he took to share out booty regularly and fairly, maintained the cohesion of the army until his death. The same was no longer true under Ahmadu. But the army played a very important role in the system; in particular, the allegiance of the various provinces of the empire depended on it.

The administration of the provinces: a decentralized administration

The provinces, as we have seen, were dotted with fortified centres from which Islam was to radiate outwards. The most important were Dinguiraye, Kundian, Nioro, Koniakary, Dyangunte, Diala, Farabugu, Murgula and Segu. Dinguiraye, Nioro, Koniakary and Segu were effectively regional capitals.

On the borders of Futa Jallon and the Mande countries, Dinguiraye was the first historic province of the empire. It was long to shelter all al-Hadjdj 'Umar's family, under the headship of his son Mohammadu Habibu (grandson of Muḥammad Bello). The fortress of Kundian in Bambuk also theoretically came under it. Built in 1858 under the direct supervision of

94. Tapsiru Ahmadu Abdul Niagane, recording of 3 May 1981.

al-Hadjdj ʿUmar himself, this fort was to keep all the Mande countries in order.[95] Mage was impressed by it, and tells us 'that it would present great difficulties to an attacking regular force'. The administration there was under the dual control of a Django freedman assisted by a *talib* Racine Tall, a cousin of al-Hadjdj ʿUmar.

Nioro was the biggest province under al-Hadjdj ʿUmar. It had many fortresses, the most important being those of Farabugu, Dyangunte and Nioro itself. A big Fulbe and Torodbe colony occupied most of the villages from which the Massassi had been driven out. As the colonial power became more oppressive, the influx of immigrants from Futa increased. The temporary administration set up in 1857 under the general direction of Alfa ʿUmar Thierno Bayla was noticeably remodelled in 1859 to meet the needs of the Segu campaign.[96] Massassi resistance having been finally broken, Sheku left Nioro with many district chiefs. All that remained in Kaarta were civilians protected by small garrisons. At Dyangunte, Thierno Bubacar Sire Ly replaced Abdulaye Hausa; at Farabugu and Nioro the freedmen Dandangura and Mustafa succeeded Khalidu Elimane Demba and Alfa ʿUmar Thierno Bayla.

Diombokho was the province nearest to Medina and Bakel. The *tata* (fortress) of Koniakary[97] built in January 1857, was to protect Diombokho against both the French and their ally Diuka Sambala. In 1866 the head of the *talib*s Thierno Musa,[98] the instigator of the local convention signed in 1860 with the commander of Bakel, gave Mage a warm welcome; the military governor, San Mody, on the other hand, did not hide his hostility.

Nioro was too near the French; and we know that al-Hadjdj ʿUmar particularly hated living with them. This is certainly the explanation of the importance that Segu took on in the Torodbe empire, whose capital it was to be under Ahmadu. Before 1864 it was a provincial capital like the others, governed from April 1862 by ʿUmar's eldest son. He was assisted by certain of his father's old companions, such as Thierno Abdul Segu, Thierno Ahmadu and Samba Ndiaye, the chief engineer of most of the fortifications in the empire.[99] But the most influential people at court were undoubtedly

95. E. Mage, who was at Kundian in 1863, describes the fort as 'a square of 60 metres, four to eight metres high and 1.50 metres thick at the base, flanked by 16 towers', 1868, pp. 82–3.

96. The following is how this administration stood in 1857 according to ʿOmar Ba, nd, p. 96, verso: Thierno Djubairu Bubu Haruna in Diafunu, Thierno Ahmadu Umakala in Kaniarene, Modi Mamadu Pakao at Niogomera, Sulayman Baba Raki at Diala, Kalidu Elimane Dema at Farabugu, ʿUmar Mamadu Lamine at Gemukura, Abdulaye Hausa at Dyangunte and Abdulaye ʿAlī in Bakhunu. See also B. O. Oloruntimehin, 1972, p. 92.

97. Built entirely of stone, it was two metres thick and several metres high; the remains, which withstood Archinard's artillery, are impressive to this day.

98. He succeeded Thierno Djibi in this post in 1859.

99. E. Mage, 1868, p. 222.

Baba Ulibo and Bobbo, respectively viceroy and diplomatic adviser.[100] For the defence of the town and its environs, when ʿUmar left for Massina, he had only 1500 *ṭālib*s and a contingent of Jawara and Massassi *sofas* under the overall command of Thierno Alassane Bâ. Ahmadu thus had to organize everything in this province, where, like everywhere else, al-Hadjdj ʿUmar had done no more than pass through.[101] In February 1863 this vast territory was theoretically enlarged by the addition of Massina. But the revolt that broke out there in the following month stopped this being put into effect at all: and when after ʿUmar's death, Tijāni Alfa reconquered Massina, it was for his own benefit.

In all these Muslim fortresses in newly converted areas, where hostility to Islam was overt, the administration was always dual, with a religious head to continue Islamization under the protection of a military governor. In each of them ʿUmar had a house, and part of his family lived there. Thus he did not think of himself as having a fixed residence like temporal rulers.

As in Futo Toro, each of the provinces was organized as an independent unit: al-Hadjdj ʿUmar was merely the spiritual head of the whole empire. The system was very efficient if we are to believe the testimony of Mage, who visited most of the provinces between 1863 and 1866. Despite the existence of some areas of dissidence (it could hardly have been otherwise, considering the amount of upheaval the new government brought about in the ancestral habits of the peoples involved), the French traveller was struck by the order and security that reigned throughout.[102]

In all the provinces justice was dispensed according to Ḳu'rānic law by *ḳāḍī*s in the case of civil offences; crimes and political offences were brought before the religious head of the provincial capital. Thus at Segu, Mage tells us that the two great judicial authorities were the *ḳāḍī* and Ahmadu himself, and there was no appeal against their judgements. Punishments were the same as in all the Muslim countries: floggings were the commonest, and spared nobody, not even high officials of the empire.[103]

100. The latter was from Hausaland, and played a very important role in the negotiations between Mage and Ahmadu. He was the most anti-French of Ahmadu's associates. The former was the son of Ulibo Bâ, who had followed ʿUmar from Nioro; he, on the other hand, was pro-French.

101. He stayed a year at Segu, using the time mainly to write his book. the *Bayān Mawaḳa*.

102. He could not resist comparing this situation with the one that prevailed, for instance, in Khasso: it was characterized, according to him, by complete disorder and insecurity, due to the repeated raids organized by Diuku Sambala into the neighbouring countries: E. Mage, 1868, p. 86.

103. ibid., p. 344.

The economy and finances of the empire

The objective al-Hadjdj 'Umar set himself left little room for the economic development of the conquered territories. The wealth accumulated since Sokoto and the war booty taken from the vanquished peoples was more than enough to keep the war machine going, and it was only to stop with his death. The economic demands of constant warfare thus rebounded upon the provincial authorities.

The consequences of a decade of wars were particularly disastrous for the economies of the conquered countries. But not all the provinces were affected in the same way. Agriculture, which had suffered most from the *djihād*, seems to have picked up in 1863–4. The Madinka countries that Mage travelled through were especially rich in cotton. In the province of Kita, the villages were surrounded by fields of tobacco, vegetables, water melons and shea trees.[104] At Guettala, in Bague, the Kagoro, freed from the excessive pressure of the Massassi, had begun to work much harder: '[They] told me that they were happy, that they were not being pillaged any more, that the country was peaceful, that everyone was working because the marabout al-Hadjdj 'Umar had ordered it to be so'.[105]

In Kaarta and Dyangunte, Mage spoke of a veritable plenty (a good millet harvest at Bambara Muntan and Madiaga). But it was above all the village of Dyangunte itself that impressed the French traveller with its abundance of rice, millet, maize, groundnuts, cotton, beans, tomatoes, onions and tobacco: 'At night my men were given plenty of couscous, and I was given about six litres of milk; we ate all the better because Fahmara was being given presents'.[106]

Even cattle, which had constituted a large part of the booty of the *djihād*, were still plentiful in Kaarta.[107] The province of Segu itself was no less prosperous: agriculture there was quite diversified[108] and many herds of livestock supplied the traditional trade towards Bure.

In the Central Sudan, the state of war had never completely halted trade, since all the belligerents got something out of it. The main caravan routes linking the Central Sudan to the north and the south remained busy. Many caravans transported salt and livestock from Nioro to Bure, whence they would bring back gold and slaves.[109] Nioro, Koniakary, Kita, Banamba, Niamina and Segu were major staging-posts for this trade, which ended traditionally at Bakel, Medina, Freetown, Bathurst or among the Moors. But since the war with the French, links between Medina and Bakel had

104. E. Mage, 1868, pp. 89–100.
105. ibid., p. 116.
106. ibid., pp. 137–8.
107. ibid., p. 123.
108. ibid., pp. 148, 156, 161, 165.
109. ibid., pp. 105–23.

been suspended.[110] One of the aims of Mage's journey was to negotiate the re-establishment of this trade. But since the theocratic revolution in Massina, towns such as Niamina and Sansanding had gone into decline. Sansanding, Timbuktu's entrepôt, had also been the leading slave market in the region. The kings of Segu and the Cisse chiefs of the town had grown very rich on this slave trade.[111] When he occupied it in September 1860, al-Hadjdj 'Umar suppressed the various taxes paid to one or other of them (thus turning Bubu Cisse into an implacable opponent) and replaced them with Muslim taxes. But in March 1863, just when Sīdī Aḥmad al-Bekkai's emissaries were endeavouring to raise the whole of Segu and Massina, Ahmadu was unwise enough to impose a special tax on the town. The wealthy Soninke city joined the rebellion and rapidly became its nerve centre.

After each victory all the possessions of the vanquished were seized and divided into five parts, one of which went to the state and the other four to the fighters. Considerable reserves of gold, livestock and goods of all kinds were built up at Dinguiraye, Nioro and Segu. Al-Hadjdj 'Umar periodically carried out a substantial distribution from them to his *talibs*,[112] he himself lived entirely off his own possessions. The *zakāt*, or tithe, was levied in kind on Muslims only; it went to meet the many demands for hospitality, and to help the needy and orphans.[113] The *mudu*, or annual alms, was required of every Muslim on the feast of Ramadān; it went to the ecclesiastical officials (imāms, *ḳāḍīs*, lawyers and Ḳu'rān readers) and also to the needy. The *usuru* was initially paid only by caravans, at the rate of one-tenth of the value of the merchandise; later it was extended to stockbreeders, at the rate of one head of cattle for every thirty.[114]

While the arrangements for and destination of these various kinds of revenue were always fully observed under the leader of the *djihād*, under Ahmadu they were a frequent cause of revolts.[115] There was also muted opposition from the *talibs*, who reproached al-Hadjdj 'Umar's successor with being less generous than his father.

*A society dominated by the talib*s

Al-Hadjdj 'Umar's *talib*s were of all races and from all countries.[116] They came from the most varied social backgrounds. Princes as well as former

110. ibid., p. 120.
111. ibid., p. 526.
112. This happened when leaving Nioro in 1859, and when leaving Segu in 1862.
113. A considerable proportion went towards the maintenance of families of soldiers killed in the *djihād*.
114. B. O. Oloruntimehin, 1972, p. 177.
115. Such as that of the Soninke community of Sansanding in 1863 which, according to E. Mage, 1868, p. 275, was caused by the levying of too heavy a special contribution.
116. E. Mage, 1868, pp. 78–344.

slaves were to be met among the closest companions. We have seen that one of 'Umar's objectives was to democratize society by resisting the domination of the traditional aristocracy.

Hence throughout the empire the old aristocracy of birth was supplanted by a new political-cum-religious elite, recruited on the basis of its knowledge and practice of Islam. In all the provincial capitals and all the large villages this new elite was present in greater or lesser numbers to help the newly converted inhabitants to familiarize themselves with the rites of their new religion. Thus at Dyangunte in February 1864 there were 540 of them, from all walks of life: some even spoke a little French, which would suggest that they came from Saint-Louis. Under the direction of Thierno Bubacar Sire Ly they spent much of their time in a shed near the mosque, reading, writing or teaching the Ku'rān.[117] They monopolized all the senior posts in the empire. Thus under Ahmadu they were soon to elevate themselves into a fractious aristocracy. Ahmadu, who had neither the religious nor the military stature of 'Umar, found it difficult to assert his authority over his father's former companions; and this quite naturally led him to rely on the *sofas*.

This social category, whose functions were more military than religious, consisted of the mass of the conquered peoples, enrolled in the army of the *djihād*. Newly converted to Islam, they had but a rudimentary knowledge of it.[118] Under 'Umar they formed part of the Ngenar battalion; but after the bulk of the army had left for Massina, Ahmadu himself had to build up an army: the immigrants from Futa preferred to remain in Kaarta, which was nearer to their own country, and all that was left for him were the volunteers from the subjugated countries. They were organized in an independent battalion; and Ahmadu even gave them some junior posts in the administration, in order to reduce the influence of the *talīb*s. This rivalry between the *talīb*s and the *sofas* was one of the difficulties 'Umar's successor was to face throughout his reign.

The problems of the succession to al-Hadjdj 'Umar: Ahmadu's attempts to continue his father's work

A difficult succession: the first years of Ahmadu's government (1862–9)
After the disaster at Degembere, Ahmadu, the eldest of al-Hadjdj 'Umar's sons, found himself at the head of an enormous and very decentralized empire organized around four provinces as different as Dinguiraye, headed by Mohamadu Habibu Thierno Musa, and Segu, which he himself headed. Each of these provincial heads had periodically to account to him for his

117. E. Mage, 1868, p. 141.
118. The difference between the *sofas* and the *talīb*s was largely one of level of education. Well-educated former slaves became *talīb*s.

PLATE 23.4 *Entrance of Ahmadu's palace in Segu-Sikoro*

stewardship.[119] But while the first year of his installation at Segu went off without problems, in 1863 a plot was discovered simultaneously at Segu and Hamdallahi. The cutting of communications with Massina at the end of May put Ahmadu in a difficult situation, isolated with a handful of men (1,500 *tal̄ib*s) in a hostile country. To cope with this situation he had special taxes levied, which only increased the unrest. The rich Soninke city of Sansanding broke into open rebellion in December 1863; and despite reinforcements of more than 2000 men sent from Nioro, Ahmadu did not succeed in re-establishing his authority in Sansanding. It is true that this new contingent of Torodbe immigrants recently arrived in Nioro had left Futa more to escape French power than to wage the *dj̲ihād*. Not being among those who had been carefully indoctrinated by al-Hadj̲dj̲ ʿUmar himself, they were more interested in worldly goods. When they were masters of Sansanding, thirst for booty lost them their victory.[120]

Ahmadu thus found himself at the head of two kinds of *tal̄ib*s: his father's former companions, who were motivated more by faith but regarded him

119. It is beyond doubt that ʿUmar left the entire succession to his eldest son. E. Mage, 1868, p. 113, gathered this information at Segu barely a year after final confirmation of this nomination, when it was uncertain whether even Ahmadu was aware of his death. B. O. Oloruntimehin's hypothesis casting doubt on ʿUmar's decision is therefore unacceptable.

120. See E. Mage, 1868, p. 279.

as a child,[121] and the new *talibs*, less disinterested and less well-disciplined. Unfortunately for him, he played a third card, that of the volunteers from the subjugated countries, the *sofas*.[122]

Ahmadu, who was highly educated, had been trained by al-Hadjdj ʿUmar himself who, Mohamadu Aliu Tyam says, gave him everything. But in spite of outstanding intelligence and greaty piety he never managed to assert himself as his father had done. He was less energetic, as Mage describes him:

> At first sight I thought Ahmadu was nineteen or twenty; in fact he was thirty. Seated, he looked small; actually he is tall and well built. His face is very sweet, his expression calm, and he looks intelligent. He held a string of beads in his hand, which he told, muttering, during breaks in the conversation. In front of him on his goatskin were an Arabic book and his sandals, and also his sword.[123]

The first years of his reign were somewhat difficult. Despite a large garrison stationed at Niamina to maintain communications with Nioro, and another at Tenengu, revolt rumbled throughout the region. Until 1866, victories were indecisive: the most stubborn resistance came from Beledugu. At times the road to Nioro was even cut. The revolt by Beledugu, together with that by Sansanding, supported by Mari Jara (Diarra), kept people on edge until 1869. Agriculture and even trade suffered greatly from the revolts. Villages such as Tombula, whose prosperity had struck Mage in 1863, were nothing but ruins two years later. But the situation was far from desperate. In 1866, the French emissary, whom no weakness in the Segu regime escaped, thought that Ahmadu would eventually re-establish his authority, if not over the whole empire, at least over the whole of Segu province. This in fact happened in 1869.

But while he was struggling with Bambara resistance, Ahmadu was less able to concern himself with the other parts of the empire. Though Mustafa, from Nioro, accounted to him fairly regularly for his stewardship (many emissaries from Nioro came to Segu while Mage was there), the same was not true of his cousin Tijāni Alfa, who after subjugating Massina administered it in an entirely independent fashion. He said that he too was ʿUmar's legitimate successor, and exhibited some relics of him to justify his statement. He managed to play cleverly on the hatred the Habe nursed towards their former Fulbe masters. A great military leader as well as a great religious leader, he perpetuated his uncle's religious fervour at Bandiagara, his new capital: 'At Bandiagara the day is spent in prayers, and the town is like a great monastery, with Tijāni as the abbot. No shouting, no singing, no music or dancing'.[124]

121. E. Mage, 1868, p. 318.
122. On Ahmadu's difficulties with his father's *talibs*, see ibid., pp. 222–305.
123. ibid., p. 214.
124. Report by Lieutenant-Commander Caron, quoted in Y. Saint-Martin, 1970, p. 103.

But the fiercest opposition to Ahmadu came from his brother Mohammadu Habibu, who had kept his distance since their father's death.[125] Another brother, Mukhtār, had set himself up in Koniakary on his own initiative, and by agreement with Habibu aspired to replace Mustafa (who had remained loyal to Ahmadu) at Nioro. By 1869, peace having returned to the Segu region, Ahmadu left his brother Ajibu there and started for Kaarta, whence Mustafa had just warned him of the threat to Nioro from his brothers Mohammadu Habibu and Mukhtār, where many *talībs* had already been won over to their side. Both grandsons of Muḥammad Bello through their mother, they added to this illustrious maternal ancestry great intelligence and considerable generosity and *savoir-faire*.[126]

Ahmadu strengthens his authority (1869–78)

Ahmadu for his part could not let a hostile chief establish himself in Nioro, which was vital to Segu. In late 1869 he arrived in Kaarta. Around the same time a Moroccan *sharīf* of the Alawite dynasty conferred on him the important religious title of *amīr al-mu'minīn*, i.e. commander of the faithful. Henceforth he could assert himself over all his other brothers. For four years, he carried on a bitter struggle against all those who had stayed in Kaarta and supported Habibu and Mukhtār in their demand for the sharing of their father's inheritance. At the same time he strengthened his authority in Gidimaka and the Khassonke territory of Logo[127] and suppressed some Bambara and Soninke centres of rebellion.

In 1874 he was at the height of his power.[128] But though he emerged victorious from this fratricidal war, unrest was to persist for a long time in Kaarta. The *talībs* disapproved of the chaining up of Habibu and Mukhtār. Ahmadu was therefore compelled to behave with more conciliation towards his other brothers, and to take more account of their demands for a share in the administration of the empire created by the father of them all. Thus Mustafa was confirmed in the command of Nioro, to which Ahmadu had appointed him in March 1873. He became the ruler of the whole of Kaarta, having under him his brothers Seidu at Dinguiraye, Bassiru at Koniakary, Daye at Diala and Nuru in Diafunu. Once a year, on the feast of *tabaski*, they were all to meet at Segu and agree among themselves.[129] At Segu itself Ahmadu strengthened his administration. His informal council, which

125. Relations between the two brothers seemed good before Habibu learned that his father had left everything to Ahmadu. Thus in February 1864 Mage travelled in the company of some Soninke traders one of whom had been entrusted by Habibu with lavish presents to take to Ahmadu: E. Mage, 1868, p. 108.

126. B.O. Oloruntimehin, 1972, p. 179.

127. The chiefs of Logo never accepted the French-imposed suzerainty of Diuka Sambala.

128. Y. Saint-Martin, 1967, p. 150.

129. This system never worked properly, and in 1884 Ahmadu went back again to Kaarta to oppose his dissident brothers.

PLATE 23.5 *Ahmadu receiving visitors in the palace court*

included religious and military figures such as Thierno Alassane Bâ, Thierno Abdul Khadri Bâ, Baba Ulibo and Bobbo, was enlarged by the inclusion of some of his relatives such as Seidu Jeliya and Muḥammad Jeliya. In the cantons the system of administration was in general maintained: Ahmadu merely replaced the recalcitrant chiefs with their more well-disposed relatives and appointed supervisory staff for them. Fortified Torodbe villages set up on all sides reinforced security in these subjugated areas.[130]

Together with the resumption of the traditional commercial exchanges with the French trading posts of the upper Senegal,[131] trade developed with the English trading posts, leading to some diversification of the economy.[132] The Hausa trade and the kola-nut trade also expanded. Freed from interference from the French, who since 1866 had concerned themselves rather with the Southern Rivers, a new balance thus took shape in the Central Sudan. But the process was abruptly halted in 1878 by the French intervention in Logo.

130. Archives of ex-French West Africa, *Notice sur le cercle du Ségou*, 1 G320/I 1904, pp. 15–16.

131. Ahmadu had suspended trading relations throughout his struggle with his brothers.

132. B. O. Oloruntimehin, 1972, p. 207, notes the despatch of an English mission under the Governor of the Gambia himself to Segu in May 1876.

Conclusion

By 1878 Ahmadu had overcome all the obstacles that had faced him after his father's death. Admittedly the Bambara, especially those of Beledugu, had not yet given up defending their ancestral beliefs. But they no longer represented a serious danger to the consolidation of the empire.[133] The many garrisons, formidable for the period, and the universal vocation of Islam, would eventually have brought about national cohesion in this large grouping. The policy of co-operation with all races and social categories initiated by al-Hadjdj 'Umar himself was in general continued by his children and all the Torodbe, thus creating the conditions for cultural integration. It is significant in this connection that the former French colonial territory of Soudan which covered the former Torodbe empire, was one of the West African states that had very few problems of ethnic rivalry. Granted that peoples conditioned by several centuries of belief in their traditional religions were obviously put off by the violence with which Islam was imposed, nevertheless the ground was already prepared for more peaceful methods of proselytization. Both in Senegambia (which the colonial power believed it had cleansed of his influence) and in the Central Sudan, most of the great religious leaders to emerge after al-Hadjdj 'Umar were in one way or another to lay claim to his mantle.

133. Y. Saint-Martin, 1970, p. 119.

24 States and peoples of Senegambia and Upper Guinea

Y. PERSON*

Whether there is a unity running through the history of the peoples of the west coast of Africa from the Senegal to the Bandama[1] seems doubtful, although in the prelude to the colonial period from the legal ending of the slave trade at the beginning of the century to the eve of the great colonial conquest, the history of the region does have a certain homogeneity. The region thus defined covers very different culture areas. The only obvious unifying factor is European influence all along the coast, and the formation of the earliest colonial enclaves, which is dealt with elsewhere. This chapter must necessarily be conceived from the viewpoint of the African peoples and it will therefore, be arranged geographically to deal in turn with the major cultural areas: that is Senegambia, Upper Guinea and the Futa Jallon, the Kru country, the southern Mande and, lastly, the Mande from the upper Niger to the Bandama.

Senegambia

Senegambia[2] is the only region where the old Western Sudanic cultural area (characterized by large states with a substantial Muslim minority) made contact with the Atlantic coast, that is, a zone where the corrosive power of Europe had been at work for centuries, mainly through the slave trade to the Americas. The Sudanese and Muslim character of these societies made them more stable than those of the Gulf of Guinea, but they were nevertheless deeply affected by changes in the external demand for their products and people. The slave trade from this region had been declining since the 1760s, with a brief increase in the 1780s. Neither the legal abolition of the British slave trade in 1808 nor the effective enforcement of the French anti-slave-trade legislation in 1831 made much

1. Upper Guinea proper runs from the Gambia to Cape Palmas. But the ethnic boundary between two profoundly contrasting worlds, that of the Kru and the Akan, lies farther east on the Bandama. This is the one adopted here.

2. For the Wolof, see O. Ba, 1976; B. Barry, 1972; L. G. Colvin, 1981, 1982, and V. Monteil, 1966. For the Sereer, pending the theses of J. Boulegue and M. Gueye, see M. A. Klein, 1968. For Gambia see C. A. Quinn, 1972.

* deceased in December 1982.

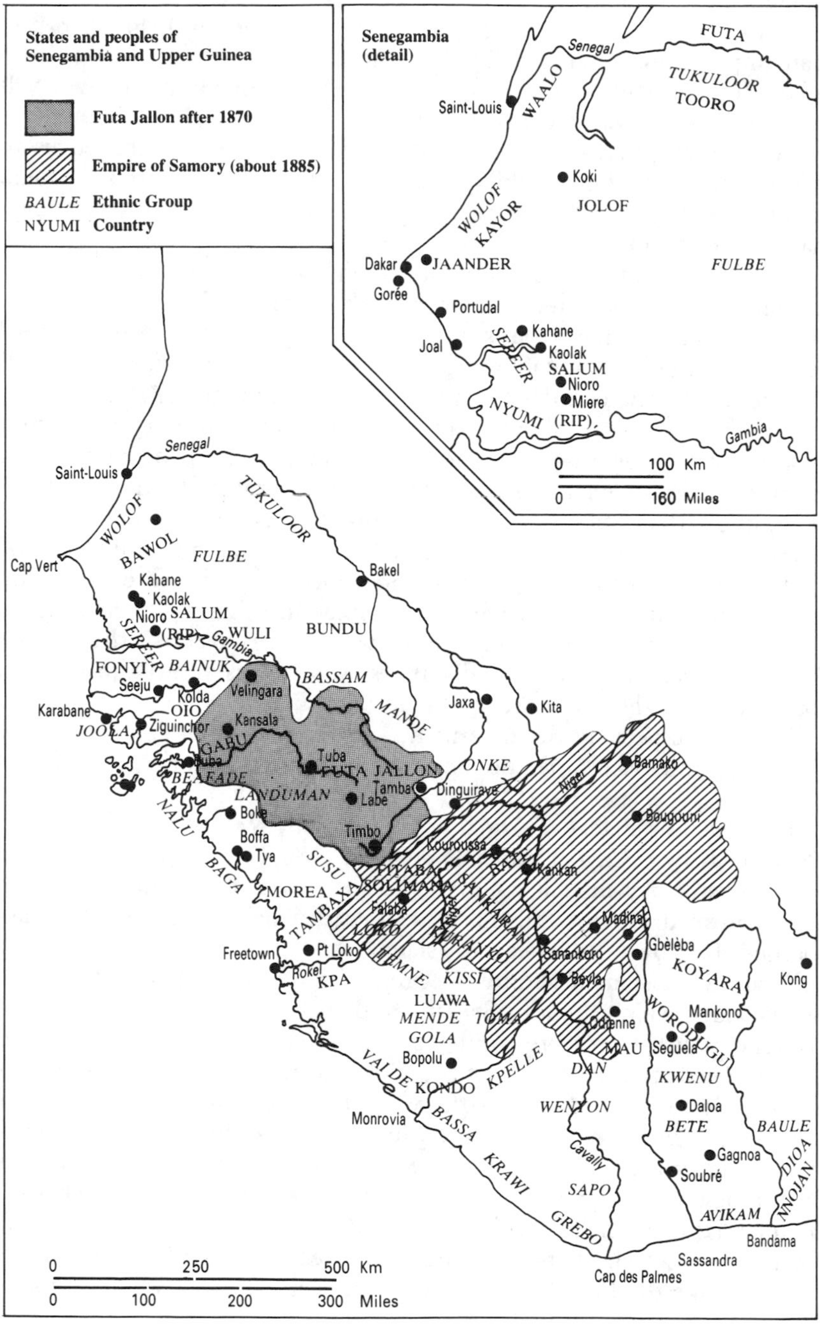

FIG. 24.1 *States and populations of Senegambia and Upper Guinea (after Y. Person)*

difference to a trade that was already declining but nevertheless continued in a small way in various disguised or illegal forms until the 1850s. The more important economic change was the enormous increases in the prices offered for Senegambian products. By the 1830s, the annual average value of gum exports was already more than five times the value of slave exports at their peak, and alongside the revived gum trade were remarkable increases in the export of gold, hides, ivory, and beeswax, with the groundnuts that were to be the major export by mid-century also beginning to make an appearance.[3]

These changes in foreign trade made enormous differences in the local economies as well, shifting income from those who had once profited from the slave trade to new groups who were in a position to profit from the new production. From the late eighteenth century, and for reasons that were at least partially independent of the European factor, Islam began to gain a new dynamism. The peasantry began to convert *en masse*, partly as a form of protest against the aristocracy that was seeking to profit from the new economic currents by raiding the peasantry rather than protecting it. Senegambian societies thus found themselves caught between two new forces, a newly aggressive Islam and the new economic influences of a world economy being overturned and remade by the forces of industrialization. The old political and social structures, failing to reform, were to find themselves incapable of dealing with the serious crisis that overtook them. The resulting political disorders were to last until the European conquests brought a new order.

This was especially the case in the north, with the Wolof and Sereer kingdoms, and these two nationalities had a distinct historical tradition and unity.

The crushing defeat of Almami Abdul Ḳādir Kan of Futa Toro by the Damel of Kayor (Cayor), Amari Ngone, in 1786, re-established the powers of the aristocracy in that country and in Waalo. But, while the princes moved toward a more and more overt traditionalist religion, the masses speeded their own conversion to Islam.

Waalo was also damaged by the proximity of the French trading post at Saint-Louis, which fell into British hands between 1809 and 1817. It was also under direct pressure from the Trarza Moors, to whom it had been forced to cede the right bank of the river and whose frequent incursions it was unable to resist. This was the weakened, disturbed country in which the new relationships with Europe uneasily took shape. The clandestine slave trade was not important further north than Portuguese Guinea. When the French re-occupied Saint-Louis and Gorée (1817), a new basis for commercial relationships had to be found. Gum, hides, and beeswax were commodities which any peasant could produce. The French on the Senegal, however, like the British further south in Sierra Leone, wanted to set up

3. P. D. Curtin, 1975, 1981.

European-run plantations as a substitute for the West Indian plantations. This was the aim of the great agricultural colonization scheme based mainly on cotton and sponsored by Governor Schmaltz and Baron Roger at the expense of Waalo from 1819 to 1827. The enterprise failed because of technical mistakes, shortage of manpower, opposition from traders and the hostility of the Africans. Thereafter, a purely commercial policy was adopted in which the Saint-Louis merchants had to adapt to the growing influence of the great export houses, above all those of Bordeaux. During the high-water season on the Senegal river, the traders went to the landing places on both banks of the river, the Mauritanian and the Senegalese, and upstream as far as Bakel, in Gadiaga.

For a time, the French increased 'customs' paid to the Wolof aristocracy, but this only aggravated the succession wars normal in this political system. From 1827 to 1840, strife was continual between the Tejek (Teedyekk) and Jos (Dyoos) matrilineages, represented mainly by Brak Fara Penda Adam Salt (1827–40), and Brak Xerfi Xari Daaro (1830–5). But the ordinary people did not support either. In 1830, when the whole system seemed on the point of collapse, a man of caste, the blacksmith, Diile of Kayor, became head of the Muslim opposition to the aristocracy. In a few weeks, he conquered the whole country in the name of an egalitarian Islam, and the traditional system seemed to have been destroyed, but the French governor of Saint-Louis intervened militarily, defeated Diile, seized him and had him publicly hanged.

After this, the French refused to intervene again in the factional struggle, though the Trarza did regularly cross the river and ravage Waalo. Weary of war, some leading figures formed a Moorish party, and in 1833 married the young leader Njambot (Ndyömböt) of the Tejek clan, to Muḥammad al-Ḥabīb, *amīr* of the Trarza. This did not restore peace; the governor of Saint-Louis, furious at finding himself surrounded by the Moors, henceforth gave all his support to the Jos. The Tejek (Teedyekk) won the day, however, and on the death of Njambot in 1846, control of the country passed to her sister, Ndate Yalla, under cover of a phantom Brak, Mo Mboj Maalik (1840–55).

This disorder on the outskirts of Saint-Louis became intolerable, once France adopted an imperialist stance. Governor Faidherbe's first act was the complete annexation of Waalo in three military campaigns from January to June 1855. The country was divided into five cantons, but despite the depopulation the ending of the old kingdom was unpopular. The French tried in vain to use Leon Jop Sidia, the French-educated heir of the Braks, as a figurehead and they ended by deporting him to Gabon. It was in this country, however, from 1855 to 1880, that the French were to perfect the methods of administration and conquest that were to prove their worth a little later throughout West Africa.

Kayor, which was much richer and more populous than Waalo, and further from Saint-Louis, at first put up stiffer resistance. From the middle of the eighteenth century, moreover, until 1855, it was connected by a personal link to the half-Sereer kingdom of Bawol (Baol). Here, too, the upsurge of Islam around the centre of Koki threatened the traditional aristocracy. Despite the royal victory in 1786, many Muslims fled to Cape Verde, where they set up a Muslim Lebu 'republic'. The Damels had no outlet to the coast other than the difficult port of Rufisque. The neighbouring province of Jaander (Diander) was thoroughly Islamized and therefore not reliable. But, after the suppression of the northern Muslims in 1837, the reign of Maisa Tneda Joor (1832–55) was peaceful.

Then the final crisis began. The French, previously cooped up on the island of Gorée, occupied Dakar in 1857, and soon took steps to link it to Saint-Louis by telegraph. Kayor was thus caught in a pincer movement, and sank into disorder during the short reigns of Makodu (1859–61) and Majoojoo (1861–4). But in 1862, the party of resistance to the Damel got the young Laat Joor Ngone Latir Jop (Lat-Dior) elected. Driven out by the French, he took refuge with Maba, the Islamic leader of Salum, and went over to Islam in its Tijāni form. This, the brotherhood of Al-Hadjdj 'Umar Tal, and various associated Islamic paths, was to spread very rapidly in a country which had previously known only the Ḳādirīyya. This diversity was the precursor of the marabout phenomenon, which was to characterize the region in the colonial period, and to become a feature of African resistance. The European crisis of 1867, and still more the disaster of 1870, led France to retrench overseas. Laat Joor, back in Kayor as the cantonal head, took the title of Damel, and at once set about completing the Islamization of the country in order to restore unity between the aristocracy and the people. He prevaricated with France, determined not to give ground on essentials. In 1875, with French assistance, he drove the Tukuloor Marabout Amadu Sheku out of Jolof and installed his relative Albury Njay there.

As early as 1850, the cultivation of groundnuts had been spreading throughout Senegambia, which was thus made dependent on the world economy. This situation was to be reinforced in 1879 by the plan for a railway line from Dakar to Saint-Louis to which Laat Joor agreed in principle. He realized, however, that he was losing his country; and, in 1881, he made an about-turn and prohibited the project, preferring hopeless resistance to submission. His death in 1886, after a long guerrilla war, marked the end of the kingdom and the establishment of the colonial order.

Jolof, also faced with the upsurge of Islam, did not so directly experience the impact of Europe, being poor and isolated in the hinterland. Its history goes hand in hand with that of Kayor, but Albury managed to prolong his resistance, now active, now passive, until 1890. Refusing to accept submission, he then joined up with Ahmadu of Segu, son of al-Hadjdj 'Umar, and went with him to the borders of Sokoto, where, about 1900, he met his death in one of the last areas of free Africa.

The Sereer had had stable kingdoms from the fourteenth century onward, with a social organization very similar to that of the Wolof, in spite of a different language (much nearer to Fulfulde than to Wolof) and with their own remarkable mixed agricultural–pastoral system of agriculture. Siin (Sine), purely Sereer, was untouched by Islam until the time of French rule. Salum, while more powerful, was less homogeneous. In the eighteenth century it was expanded militarily, extending its territory as far as the Gambia. But these eastern lands were peopled mainly by Wolof and Mandinka. The Buur of Salum expanded to the south into the old Mandinka kingdoms of Nyumi and Baadibu (Rip). Minority Islam was everywhere present in either its Wolof–Tukuloor form or its Mandinka form. The only purely Sereer traditionalist area was the province around the capital, Kahane, near Kaolak.

The cultivation of groundnuts started very early here, exported both through the Gambia and the Petite Côte (Joal, Portudal), where Catholic missions appeared very early, in 1849. They hoped to take advantage of the absence of Islam and the presence of a long-established Portuguese–African community which had only just then given up using Portuguese Creole.

As on the lower Senegal, the traditionalist aristocracy, both Sereer and Mandinka, were in a difficult situation, caught between the demands of the Europeans and a rebellious Islam which organized the peasants and the minorities against them. The dynamism of the Tijāniyya was an additional factor, al-Hadjdj ʻUmar having visited the country in about 1847, before starting his own war. One of his disciples, Maaba Jaaxu (Maba), a Tukuloor marabout settled among the Wolof communities of Baadibu, was to overthrow the old order. He called his house, Nioro, in honour of his master.

A similar 'Marabout War' had already been raging since 1845 in Kombo, around Banjul, south of the river. In 1859, Faidherbe and the Governor of the Gambia, Benjamin d'Arcy, launched a converging drive against Salum and Baadibu, occupying Kaolak. In 1861, Maba rallied the Muslims of Baadibu, which he soon mastered. He then entered the Nyumi civil war, in a limited way, so as not to displease the British. Having rallied the Muslims of eastern Salum, he launched an attack on that state in 1862, and the Buur, Samba Laobe Fal, could not stand against him in spite of French support. From there, in 1865, with the support of Laat Joor, he conquered part of Bawol and the whole of Jolof. Kayor, threatening the French, reacted by burning down Nioro, in Baadibu, after an indecisive battle.

The end came, however, from another quarter. In July 1867, Maba invaded Siin, but in this homogeneous country without Muslims he came up against a real national resistance from the Sereer. He was defeated and killed by the Bur Kumba Ndofen Juuf (Diouf) (1853–71).

Maba's disunited empire was soon weakened in quarrels among his successors, making possible a reconstruction of Salum, where the intervention of the French from Kaolak became more and more direct. But

PLATE 24.1 *Coastal chiefs of the Mandinka in Gambia in 1805*

Namur Ndari, Maba's successor, extended his influence over Niani and Wuli, further up the Gambia, though his interventions south of the river were unsuccessful. The French had no difficulty in occupying the region in 1887.

Upper Guinea and Futa Jallon

The Gambia river, navigable over hundreds of kilometres, had for centuries provided the outlet to the sea for the gold mines in the Joola countries of the upper Senegal and upper Niger. Further south it was a different world, that of Upper Guinea, where decentralized farming peoples, speaking mostly West Atlantic languages, had long occupied the sea coast. From Monrovia to the Gambia, the Sudanic zone only began to have contacts with the sea coast in the eighteenth century. This region was also one of the earliest centres of European influence in Guinea-Bissau, home of Creole culture, and later Sierra Leone and Liberia. Like Senegambia, this region was important for the slave trade in the sixteenth century, though, in the eighteenth century, its role declined.

Outside the coastal area, the two most important peoples were the Mandinka and the Fulbe (Fulani, Peul). The Mandinka empire of Kaabu (Gabu) dated back to the thirteenth century and had been independent of old Mali since the sixteenth. The Fulbe had been in the area since at least the fifteenth century but had founded the Muslim state of Futa Jallon only after 1727.

At the beginning of the nineteenth century, Portuguese influence was in decline, but the clandestine slave trade was to continue for quite a time on both sides of the anti-slavery centre of Sierra Leone. Mandinka Kaabu had trouble maintaining its influence as far as the southern shores of the Gambia, and failed altogether with its former vassals the Baïnuk, on the coast. The Foa (Balanta), non-centralized peasants, destroyed the Baïnuk capital in 1830, and most of the survivors joined the Mandinka or else the Joola (Dyula), the hardy 'anarchic' traditionalist rice-growers who occupied the whole coastal area to the north. In the east, the Fulbe of Futa Jallon dominated the Mandinka as far as the Gambia in Kantora. In Kaabu and its dependencies, a Fulbe minority was growing increasingly impatient with its subordinate position.

At this period, the French set up trading posts in the Casamance, at Karabane in 1836 and then at Seeju (Sediou) in 1838. The groundnut trade soon grew, with predictable economic and social consequences.[4]

But the overthrow of the old order began in 1859, when Futa Jallon, and in particular the great Alfa Mo Labe, Yaya Maudo, began a decisive

4. For the Casamance, see C. Roche, 1976; F. A. Leary, 1969. For Guinea-Bissau and Kaabu, A. Teixeira da Mota, 1954; M. Mane, 1974–5; A. Carreira, 1947; J. Vellez Caroço, 1948.

struggle against Kaabu, whose king, Yargi Sayon, was killed. The old empire collapsed in 1867 with the fall of Kansala in what was to be Portuguese Guinea, the Almami Umaru of Timbo having come to reinforce Alfa Mo Labe. Among the Mandinka vassal kingdoms, Brasu soon succumbed at the hands of Alfa Moola, but Oio kept its freedom until the Portuguese conquest in 1905.

The fall of Kaabu had major repercussions; the Fulbe rebelled against their Mandinka masters as far as the banks of the Gambia. In 1869, Alfa Moolo, a person of obscure origins, organized the kingdom of Fuladugu, from Kolda to Velingara, upstream from Seeju. He vaguely recognized the authority of Timbo, and set in train a policy of systematic Fulanization of his subjects. Until his death in 1881, this neo-Muslim ruler was the scourge of the Mandinka.

The Mandinka tried to rally near Seeju, under Sunkari Kamara, whose opposition to trade soon set the French against him. His revolt against French influence in 1873, since the Balanba and Musa Moola's Fulbe joined against him, was doomed to failure. Sunkari had to submit but, in 1882, flung himself into a last vain revolt that marked the end of his career.

The Mandinka on the banks of the Gambia regrouped more effectively around a religious leader of Jaxaanke (Dyakhanke) origin from the upper Senegal, the famous Fode Kaba Dumbuya. Starting in 1875, he turned himself into a war leader, to resist Alfa Moola, with the support of Maba's people. Alfa Moola, however, drove him back westwards, and from 1878 onwards Fode Kaba maintained himself by dominating the Joola (Dyula) of Fonyi, whom he partly converted to Islam.

The resistance of the Mandinka in the Casamance, caught between the Fulbe and the French, was effective in the end, for they succeeded in preserving their nationality by turning *en masse* to Islam under the influence of Sunkari and Fode Kaba. But when Musa Moolo, son of Alfa Moolo, went over to the French side in 1883, this gave the Fulbe a certain advantage. Playing on Anglo–French rivalries, Fode Kaba managed to maintain his position on the frontier of the Gambia until he was eliminated in 1901. The armed resistance of 'anarchists' like the Joola was to continue until 1913, and even after the First World War.

From the Gambia to Sierra Leone, the history of the whole area was dominated from the beginning of the eighteenth century on by the development of the great Fulbe state of Futa Jallon.[5] Thanks to it, long-distance trade carrying Sudanic influences found its way to the coast and there linked up with the Europeans. Until the beginning of the eighteenth century, trade had percolated through a world of decentralized societies only with difficulty. Now, regular caravan routes came down from the

5. On Futa Jallon, see the thesis by T. Diallo, 1973. The major texts in Fulbe have been published by A. I. Sow, 1966, 1968. A summary of this information, made in 1966, can be found in Y. Person, 1974. On the Fulbe, see J. Mendes Moreira, 1948; W. Derman, 1973.

upper Niger across the High Plateau of the Futa to the Portuguese trading posts on the Rio Geba (Bissau and Buba), to the Rio Nuñez and the Rio Pongos, where the French built Boke in 1866 and Boffa in 1867, and finally to Sierra Leone. There, too, groundnuts appeared, although at the limit of their natural habitat. This was the famous 'Côte des Rivières' of the nineteenth-century French travellers. The English called it 'the northern rivers' on account of its position relative to Sierra Leone. Because of its deep indentations and inaccessible anchorages it was also one of the regions where the clandestine slave trade continued until the middle of the century.

This persistence is also explained by the proximity of Futa Jallon. This great Fulbe state, very greedy for slaves, raided for them, and imported a large number from the hinterland or took them from among the coastal minority peoples. Some were then made available for export.

At the beginning of the nineteenth century, Fulbe society in Futa Jallon seemed relatively stable. The victors in the holy war had set up a new aristocracy, which had established itself at the head of an extremely rigid and hierarchical society. At the level both of the state, of the nine largely independent provinces (*diwal*) that composed it, and of the 'parishes' (*missidi*, each comprising a 'noble' village and many farming hamlets), a haughty, self-confident class was in command. The defeated subjects, especially former Jallonke (Yalunka), had been oppressed to the point of losing their language, and their ranks had been swollen by imported slaves. Making up at least three-quarters of the population, they were closely supervised and harshly exploited. Between the strata of this harsh society, there were marginals, outcasts virtually without the law: in particular, poor Fulbe lineages that had not managed to seize estates during the war eked out their existence on meagre herds in the gaps between *missidi*. On the credit side, there was a remarkable spread of Islamic culture, accompanied by (as was rare in sub-Saharan Africa) frequent use of Fulfulde in written form. Though highly cultured, the aristocracy marked itself off by stockbreeding and warfare and also by certain forms of adventurous trade. The cultural tradition that underlay the political structure remained alive, and was localized in the *diwal* of Fugumba, whose marabouts decided political disputes by consecrating the *almamis* ('imāms' – successive rulers of the state).

But the Fulbe did not monopolize religion; they even entrusted a prestigious role to outsiders regarded as neutral. These were an ethnic minority with whom we are already familiar, namely the Jaxaanke (Dyakhanke), who had, since the sixteenth century, covered first the Gambia and then the Futa and the Rivers with their commercial ventures. These western Joola (Dyula) were first and foremost men of religion, and in principle non-violent. In the Futa, in addition to long-distance trade, they had become the masters of religious culture since founding Tuba, near Labe, in about 1810. The aristocracy encouraged them because of their political neutrality, and their influence extended from Kankan in the upper Niger basin to the European trading posts of Sierra Leone.

The power of Futa Jallon rested on military force, on the hordes of white-robed horsemen that came down from the high sandstone plateau to raid and then return. But this force depended on the political unity of the state, and the conflicts of the late eighteenth century almost ended it. In order to survive, in 1799, the aristocracy limited the damage by compromise. The two great families, Alfaya and Soriya, would each designate an *almami* at the same time, and the two would reign, in rotation, at Timbo,

PLATE 24.2 *View of Timbo, capital of the Futa Jallon, c. 1815.*

alternating every two years. This famous compromise obviously did not always work well and led to countless conflicts, but in the main it was effective. Civil wars were, in fact, a built-in feature and a normal way of achieving power, and the rules merely limited the amount of violence. This itself avoided the break-up of the kingdom: the split between the two parties was reproduced at the level of every *diwal* and *missidi*. Thus, although the great northern *diwal* of Labe, dominated by the Jallo (Diallo), was alone more powerful than all the rest of the Futa it never occurred to it to break away.

These divisions were deep for all that, and limited the Fulbe's ability to pursue aggressive policies. Indeed, the territory of the Futa as constituted at the beginning of the nineteenth century, never extended further, the great exception being Labe. Those of the Jallonke who had not been enslaved reorganized themselves in the east and south with their backs to the Mandinka, whose culture they increasingly assimilated. The result was the kingdom of Tamba, which closed the Niger route and dominated the Bouré gold mines; and thus too Solimana was organized around the fortress of Falaba and closed the route to the south for the Fulbe. This route was blocked also by Farana, set up by the Mandinka of Sankaran astride the Niger fords.

The only exception to this freezing of frontiers at the beginning of the nineteenth century was Labe, which at the beginning of the century did not extend northwards beyond the upper reaches of the Rio Grande. In 1810–20, however, it thrust beyond and soon reached the upper Gambia, where it dominated the Mandinka of Kantora. This expansion, which meant actual genocide for various traditionalist groups of people of the Tanda or Badiar family (Chapi, Pakesi and Bassari), was the work of the powerful Alfa Molabe, reinforced by the *almamis* themselves, who called the whole Futa to arms as for a crusade. This was the case particularly with Umaru, the Soriya *almami* from 1840 until his death in 1869, who made up for his defeats at the hands of the Hubbu by wars in the north. We have seen that this expansion finally triumphed with the destruction in 1867 of the Mandinka empire of Kaabu and, at least temporarily, the adherence of Alfa Moolo's new Fulbe state of Fuladugu.

While Labe was developing in the north, the factional war around Timbo was only a sterile, bloody game for the first half of the century. The details are well known, and it is pointless to go over them again here. After the interminable war at the beginning of the century between Abdulay Babemba (Alfaya) and Abdul Gadiri (Soriya), Abdulay's son, Bubakar Maudo, remained in power for twelve years (1827–39) in violation of the rule of rotation. The civil war was in full swing in 1844 when al-Hadjdj ʿUmar, returning from his famous pilgrimage, came to live near Futa. From then on, the system was to work more or less properly, but this cannot be explained solely by the prestige of the Tijāniyya marabout, who in any case left the Futa in about 1847. The fact is that in the middle of the century, the Futa aristocracy put its quarrels aside, for it had to face a new danger: the revolt of the Hubbu.

Hubbu rassul allāh, those who love God, seems to have been a religious sect of extremist puritan members of the Ḳādirīyya who split off from the Fulbe aristocracy, which mainly joined the Tijāniyya under the influence of al-Hadjdj ʿUmar, though the Fulbe also feared ʿUmar's radicalism and ordered him to leave the country. This was certainly how the Hubbu founder, Modi Mamadu Jue (Dyue), a noted scholar who had studied in Mauritania under Shaykh Sidia, saw things. Although the basic research has not been done, the hypothesis can be put forward that this religious upsurge allowed outcasts from Fulbe society to organize their protests. The Hubbu seem to have comprised marginal Fulbe, excluded from the partition, and serfs of Jallonke origin or recently imported slaves. The movement broke out all over the Futa in 1849; but it was mostly suppressed.

The rebels took refuge in the outlying areas, in the coastal zone or towards the upper Niger. They then entrenched themselves in Fitaba under the personal leadership of Jue and then of his son Abal and thenceforth constituted a serious threat which the *almamis* never succeeded in eliminating. Despite their small numbers, they attracted marginal elements from all quarters and created in their fortress, Boketto, an atmosphere of feverish mysticism. They were formidable fighters, and must have aroused some response in the Fulbe conscience, for the *almamis* had difficulty in mobilizing forces against them. The Hubbu twice burnt Timbo and all attacks launched against Boketto failed. In 1871, the Alfaya *almami*, Ibrāhīm Sori Dara, met his death trying to take Boketto. Eventually the Fulbe had to appeal to Samori – whose march to the sea the Hubbu were obstructing – before this focus of opposition was crushed in 1884.

The alliance with Samori, who arrived on their borders in 1879, was to prove profitable for the Fulbe of Futa, who sold him cattle in exchange for slaves. Even with the Hubbu threat diminished, this society could still only maintain its divided balance, and it offered but weak resistance to the colonial conquest.

By superseding a fragmented political structure, the formation of Futa Jallon had opened up a huge area for Sudanic trade to reach the sea coast, even though security remained only relative and the Fulbe aristocracy had odd ideas about the protection of caravans. René Caillé, who crossed the country from Boke to the Niger, bore witness to this in 1827.

The opening up of the coast to Sudanic influences was radically to change the civilization of the lowland peoples, especially since many of them had to accept the political authority of Futa Jallon.[6]

To the north-west the Fulbe dominated much of what is now Guinea-Bissau, and this domain was further extended after the fall of Kansala (1867). Further south they controlled the upper navigable point on the Rio Nuñez by imposing their sway on the Landuman of Boke through whom contact was made with the Europeans. Although they had massacred Fulbe traders in 1840, the Landuman were unable to free themselves, and fell into a long civil war from 1844 to 1849. In 1856, Faidherbe brought them into the colonial era prematurely by building a fort.

On the sea, the Beafade in Guinea-Bissau and the Nalu on the Rio Nuñez escaped the authority of the Fulbe in their marshy lands, but hardly interfered with trade with the Europeans. The Nalu lineage of the Tawela claims Mandinka origin, although their culture shows nothing of Mandinka

6. The history of the coastal area has been very unevenly studied, what is now the Republic of Guinea being neglected. The confused old book by W. Arcin, 1911, is still used. For Sierra Leone, see C. Fyfe, 1962; O. Goerg, 1980; J. S. Trimingham, and C. Fyfe, 1960; A. M. Howard, 1976. For the period preceding our own there is a very interesting summary by W. Rodney, 1970, reviewed by Y. Person, 1971. See also Unesco, *General History of Africa*, Vols 3 and 4.

influence. They distinguished themselves by King Dina Salifu's ambivalent resistance to French authority.

Further south, on the Rio Pongos, among the Susu who bordered on Boffa, the authority of Timbo was strongest. Close relations of the Mandinka, the Susu then had a culture strongly marked by the coastal and forest area influences, especially from the Baga, relatives of the Temne, whom they had assimilated. They had suffered heavily from the slave trade, and European influences show among them in many racially mixed families descended from American and British slave-traders. Thanks to them, the clandestine slave trade did not readily die out. Situated as they were at the border line from Futa Jallon, however, the Susu were infiltrated by Islam; and their culture was Sudanized at an increasing rate during the colonial period. Those on the Rio Pongos constituted the kingdom of Tya, which was dominated by the Damba (Kati) clan. The 'mulatto war' that began in 1865 ended in the defeat of the pro-slavery, pro-Fulbe party: some Lightburn Timbo had just resigned themselves to this when the French occupation took place in 1868.

Further south, the authority of the Futa did not extend as far as the sea, but Sudanic influence was nonetheless profound. Since the mid-eighteenth century, Morea (Melakori) had been dominated by a lineage of the Ture clan, which had come from Kankan as traders and been linguistically assimilated to the Susu whilst still remaining strictly Muslim.[7] The *almamis* of this small state maintained their sway with the help of the Jallonke of Solimana. From 1865 onwards, they were rent by interminable civil war between the pro-Islamic party of *Almami* Bokari and the 'Maliguistes' of Maliki Gheli. The establishment of the French not far away at Benty in 1869 did not improve the situation, for the conflict was to become a feature of Anglo-French frontier rivalry. It provoked the intervention of the Temne of Satan Lahay and the Susu of Karimu, chief of Tambaxa and a great enemy of the English. Samori himself joined in after 1884, and the matter was only settled after the Anglo-French boundary delimitation of 1889.

The case of Morea well illustrates the socio-cultural phenomenon that had been at work on the Rivers Coast since the eighteenth century. Peoples speaking various languages and living in coastal agricultural civilizations had in the sixteenth century been subjected to northern influence through the agency of the Somba invasion, but had absorbed it. Thereafter, with the arrival of Sudanic traders on the coast, these old cultures were radically changed. Mandinka and Fulbe lineages settled everywhere, became politically dominant and introduced new ideas of politics. Egalitarian, relatively unstratified societies thus came to accept organization into warrior chiefdoms and semi-centralized states. These peoples nevertheless retained

7. For the southern Susu, and particularly the Morea crisis, see Y. Person, 1965–75, Vol 2.

their cultural identities: the newcomers, few in number, were completely assimilated linguistically. This phenomenon covered essentially southern Susu country and the domains of the Limba, Loko, and Temne. It stopped short abruptly at Sierra Leone, that is, on the verge of the forest lands of the south, which had mainly stayed closed to the Sudanic trade routes. But major social effects extended well beyond that. Thus, from the Temne to the Kpelle of Liberia social and political life was dominated by great initiation societies, the best known of which, that for men, was often called Poron (compare the *Poro* of the Senufo).[8] Hence, this was a basic social phenomenon transcending the borders of the historical areas just defined.

The Loko, the advance guard of the Mende, were isolated between the Temne and the Limba with their backs to the sea. They managed to survive under the rule of a lineage of Mandinka origin which gave them a great leader, Pa-Koba, ally of Samori.[9]

After 1787, the Temne, speaking a West Atlantic language close to Baga and Landuman, had to give up Sierra Leone to the British colony which served as base for the anti-slavery patrol and where the Creole (Krio) ethnicity soon came into being. Their main centre was Port Loko, terminus of the caravans from the Futa and upper Niger, where the Susu had taken power at the end of the eighteenth century. In 1818, Islamized Temne drove out the Susu, and their leader, the *alkali,* in 1825, made an alliance with the British. The north of Temne country was dominated by Kambia, where the Satan Lahay family reigned; despite its complete assimilation it claimed descent from the Ture of Bate (Kankan). South of the Rokel, the Yoni, who formed the advance guard of the Temne, felt themselves isolated as the Freetown trade grew around them, while the expansion of the Kpa Mende closed the south to them. They flung themselves into long wars to free themselves, and the problem was resolved by the British army in 1886.

South of the Rokel, however, we are in a different region, where the thickness of the forest had prevented the maintenance of links with the Sudan, though such links had been initiated in the sixteenth century. The slave trade, on the other hand, had been keenly pursued on the coast and survived in its clandestine form until 1845 despite the proximity of Freetown and Monrovia. The history of the interior only becomes structured and clear to us in the middle of the century, when a trading network run by Sierra Leone Creoles made its way there and began to integrate the region into the world market: but the network did not link up with the termini of the tracks to the Sudan, as in the northern sector. This new field of force led to an increase in local conflicts, and gave them new directions.

South of the Temne, the eighteenth century saw a great southern Mande

8. See K. Little, 1954, 1965, 1966.

9. For the Loko and some of the Temne, see Y. Person, 1968–75, Vol. 2. For the Mende, see K. Little, 1954.

people, the Mende, near kin of the Toma, strongly resume their expansion. They got closer to the sea by absorbing the Bulom, who were thus separated for good from the Kissi. The Mende formed great warrior chiefdoms, relatively centralized, and their women played an exceptional political role. Their advance guard, the Kpa Mende who, because of their war with the Yoni, went into alliance with the British, were governed about 1880 by the famous Madam Yoko. In the extreme east of the Mende domain the great Luawa chiefdom was, at the end of the century, the domain of a powerful conqueror of Kissi origin, Kai-Lundu, whose army of mercenaries faced up to the advance guards of Samori and raided deep into Kpelle and Toma country in what is now Liberia.[10]

The advance of the Mende separated two closely related Mande peoples, the Kono, hemmed in in the then unprospected diamond-bearing mountains of the interior, and the Vai, established on the coast on what is now the Sierra Leone–Liberia border since the mid-fifteenth century at the latest. The latter maintained quite sizable chiefdoms derived from the Somba 'empire' of the sixteenth century, and played an active part in the growth of the slave trade that characterized the area in the eighteenth century. It is therefore not surprising that they should have helped the clandestine slave trade, whose most prominent representative in their area was the Spaniard Pedro Blanco, until about 1845. These dubious relationships with the outside world caused the Vai culture to change considerably but they also brought out the Vai's creative initiative. In about 1818, just how is not clear, they invented one of the few typically African scripts.[11]

But since the eighteenth century, the Vai and their eastern neighbours, the De of Monrovia, who are Kru-speaking, had been bottled up on the coast by the extremely vigorous expansion of a people from the interior,[12] the Gola, speakers of a West Atlantic language like the Kissi. Under pressure in the north from the Mende and their kinsmen, they left their homeland of Kongaba and fanned out towards the sea. At the beginning of the nineteenth century, their advance guard came into contact with the Kpelle and interposed themselves between the coastal peoples and the route to the Sudan.

We have reached the line of the Saint-Paul river, which links the coast of Monrovia to the Konyan highlands and marks the boundary of the

10. For the career of Kai-Lundu and his mercenaries the Tyogbufey, see Y. Person 1968–75, Vol. 2, which contained a bibliography complete up to 1970. K.C. Wylie, 1970–1 needs to be added.

11. For another view, see A. Jones, 1981; Y. Person, 1982. On the Vai script, see P. Hair, 1963.

12. The historical bibliography of the Liberian state is not given here. For the Gola, see the remarkable articles by W.L. Azevedo, 1969–71. On the Kpelle, see most recently R.M. Fulton, 1968. For a general account, see G. Schwab and G.W. Harley, 1947 (with bibliography to that date).

Sudanic world of the Mandinka of the region. In general, the forest barrier was unbroken south of the Rokel (and the Futa Jallon link of the upper Niger to the coast at Sierra Leone), as far as the Bandama or even the Comoé river, much further east. Here at the Saint-Paul, however, we find an isolated opening between the savanna and the sea, which determined the location of the Vai and the subsequent siting of Monrovia. It was opened up by the great Somba invasion in the sixteenth century, but then fell into disuse. In the eighteenth century, when the slave trade finally developed from Sierra Leone to the Kru coast, this outlet for slaves from the interior saw renewed activity. Thus, at the end of the century, an influx of Mandinka coming down from Konyan gave rise to the warrior state of Kondo around the chiefdom of Bopolu. Determined to keep the route open, the Bopolu chiefs organized a confederacy of Toma (Loma), Kpelle (Guerze), Vai, De, and Gola chiefdoms on the lower Saint-Paul. Soon after 1820, Bopolu, became the capital of Sau Boso, the famous soldier of fortune, who, like the Vai, became an ally of the founders of Liberia. After 1830, however, his power was threatened by the Gola chief, Jenkins, and, after his death in 1836, the hegemony of Kondo collapsed.[13] The Liberians had to deal with the hostile but now dominant Gola, and it was this in particular that lay behind Anderson's journey as far as Konyan in 1869. The Samorians stepped in to re-open the route after 1885, and it was not until 1898 that part of the Gola rallied to the Monrovia government.

The Kru bloc

The last coastal sector we have to consider, that from Monrovia to the Bandama, forms the frontage to the vast forest mass inhabited by the peoples of the Kru family.[14] Forest farmers, hunters, but also remarkable seamen, the Kru are distinguished by their physical anthropology (absence of sickle-cells) and the tone languages they speak, which are so singular that they cannot be classified with any known group.

At this time, no communication was possible between the sea and the savanna west of the Bandama, whose valley had in any case been closed by the Baule at the beginning of the eighteenth century. The rivers were hardly navigable. In this overgrown country, communities had no tradition of political centralization or long-distance trade, only a relay trade passing goods between contiguous peoples. Hence, this country's history is one of small groups continually splitting up to occupy the ground, of their cultural and technical interchanges, and of their relationships with Europe's sea-borne trade during recent centuries. The name Kru seems to be a corruption

13. On Bopolu and Kondo, see S. E. Holsoe, 1967.

14. The Kru coast is beginning to be rather more studied, see G. E. Brooks, 1972; C. Behrens, 1974; R. W. Davis, 1976. For the interior the situation is improving, see G. Schroeder and D. Siebel, 1974; A. Schwartz, 1973: Schwartz's thesis on the 'Kru' of the Tabu area (Ivory Coast) is expected; E. Terray, 1969.

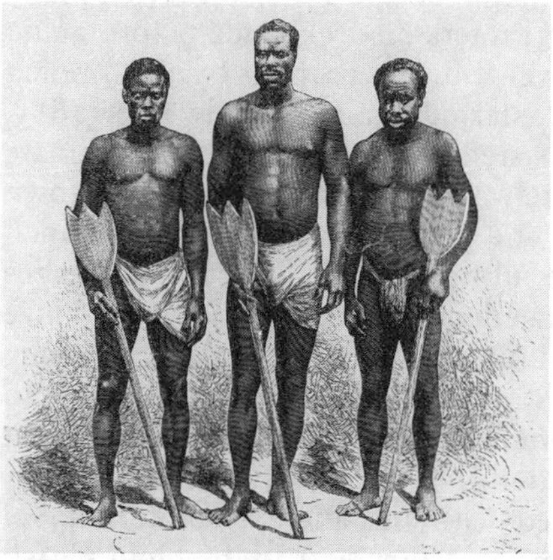

PLATE 24.3 *Kru canoemen*

PLATE 24.4 *Kru houses*

of Krawi, the name of one of the coastal ethnicities in the western group between the Bassa and the Grebo. This name was extended to the whole of the language family whose best-known member it was. Despite the great homogeneity of the Kru, two sub-families can be distinguished, one on each side of the Sassandra, the Bete–Dida group to the east and the Bakwe group to the west. We shall be concerned primarily with the latter.

At the beginning of the nineteenth century, an east-west movement of Wenyon lineages (Kran and Gere) had been going on for centuries in the sparsely inhabited lands of the interior. Having fanned out from the Sassandra to the Cavally across the Guiglo and Toulepleu plateau, it came to an end about the middle of the century when its advance guard came up against the Gio (Dan), solidly established on the upper Cestos, while, on their left, those who called themselves the Sapo moved towards the sea near the mouth of the Sina, cutting the Krawi almost in two. Groups from the same area, settled downstream on the Cavally, became integrated with the Grebo, whose coastal section had come from the east by sea and been stabilized since at least 1701.

The most spectacular and best-known changes, however, took place on the sea coast. The distinction between peasants and sailors, or 'bushmen' and 'fishmen' was of long standing; but the volume of the slave trade in the eighteenth century in this hitherto relatively spared area stengthened the position of the 'bushmen'. However, the famous group of 'five Kru towns' which seem to have come fairly recently (about the sixteenth century) from the interior, played a special role in the slave trade. Among them, the two communities – peasants and sailors – were closely integrated. This district round the Setta-Kru, which formed the heart of Krawi country, forged special links with Sierra Leone, which brought a new impetus for culture change. It seems that, from the 1780s onwards, many boats used to take on 'fishmen' as interpreters or deckhands before going on into the Gulf of Guinea. This movement, interrupted by the French Revolution and the Napoleonic Wars, started again strongly after 1815, when the clandestine slave trade co-existed with the incipient legitimate trade. The Kru soon established themselves in large numbers in Freetown and then in Monrovia as labourers and woodcutters. They remained cohesive, but adopted aspects of Creole culture as well. The coastal lineages ('fishmen' or 'Krumen') used their connections with the interior to mobilize labour. Throughout the nineteenth century, ships rarely sailed east along the coast without taking on 'Krumen', and this activity gradually spread as far as the Sassandra. It changed somewhat in nature but not in extent after 1850, when steam largely replaced sail.

European activity became integrated with the ancient community of coastal fishermen which stretched from the Krawi east to the Gold Coast; it was symbolized by the worship of the famous 'Big Devil' of Hedie, near the mouth of the Cavally, which drew people from as far as the Alladian country on the Ivory Coast. Sailing ships usually dropped south away from the coast on their westward, return voyages to avoid contrary winds and current, but this caused no problem for the Krumen, who landed far to the east with their pay. They found little difficulty in returning home. The problem did not arise at all in the time of the steamships, since these came back the same way along the coast.

After 1821, the coastal fringe came more or less under the authority of the government of Liberia. This is outside the scope of this chapter. But it is worth noting that the culture change begun at Freetown was to become more pronounced in some areas under the influence of Protestant missions, especially among the Grebo, who began writing their language and came close to achieving national consciousness. In 1871, having heard of the Fante Confederation on the Gold Coast, they set up a constitution for a 'Kingdom of the Grebo' which the Liberians were unable to reduce militarily until 1910. One of the inspirers of Grebo nationalism was the future Prophet Harris, famous on the Ivory Coast.[15]

Beyond the Sassandra, concentrations of people in Kru territory were to be found among the Bete of Gagnoa and some of the Dida, in areas that had been somewhat compressed by the northward expansion of forest-fringe peoples like some southern Mande, the Guro, or the Baule, whose political structures beyond the Bandama had been strengthened by an Akan minority in the eighteenth century. This pressure, and the establishment of other Akan – the Avikam – the advance guard of the Nnajan (Alladian), at the mouth of the Bandama, had hemmed in the Dida, and settled Baule lineages among them.

At the same time, the line of the Sassandra remained within Kru

15. On Harris, see G. M. Haliburton, 1971.

domains: some boats moved on its reaches, and the east–west movement of lineages from Soubré or Gagnoa to the sea coast indicates that the influence of European trade was spreading. These lineages reinforced the Neyo people at the mouth of the river, whose culture began to change through contact with European ships, especially ones from Liverpool. Violent incidents, however, showed that these coastal people were the descendants of those who had long ago earned the area the name 'Côte des Males Gens'.

The world of the southern Mande

Between the savannas of Guinea and the coastal peoples lay the belt of southern Mande peoples: Mende, Toma, Kpelle (Guerze), Dan (Yakouba) and Kwenu (Guro), to mention only the main ones.[16] Living in the savanna bordering on the forest, or in the depths of the great forest itself, they put out their advance guards towards the Atlantic coast. Though they came from the borders of the savanna, these peoples' culture nevertheless had many traits in common with that of the Rivers, and even with the Kru. In the absence of centralized state structure, their political life was dominated by secret initiation societies, which, among other things, produced striking masks.

The history of these transitional peoples is inseparable from that of the coastal peoples, with whom they always mixed. But it cannot be tackled without taking account of the southern Mandinka who bordered them to the north and had for centuries driven them back and infiltrated their populations and influenced their cultures, unaware of the distant kinship between all Mande languages.

The southern Mandinka (leaving aside the Kono and Vai) were those of the upper Niger, stretching from the borders of Futa Jallon to the Bandama, where they met the Senufo and Baule. They clearly belonged to the Sudanic world of the savanna country. This southern part of the savanna was never part of the empire of Mali; but at the beginning of the nineteenth century the southern Mandinka (who had centuries earlier ousted or assimilated southern Mende or Voltaics there), covered the area with a loose fabric of peasantry whose economic life was articulated by a long-distance trade network which conveyed the kola nuts of the southern forests towards the line of the Niger. These east–west routes inevitably ended in an area of large broker villages in contact with the 'forest people'. Thanks to their regular contacts with these 'barbarians', peddlers and caravans had an

16. For the southern Mandinka as a whole, I venture to refer to my thesis, which contains a virtually complete bibliography up to 1970, and even a little beyond: Y. Person, 1968–75, Vols 2 and 3. The general index is in Volume 3. This piece of work set out to give a general account of the area in the nineteenth century, not merely a view of Samori. For the latter's career, there is a full account in Y. Person, 1972. To place Samori's early days in a wider context, see Y. Person, 1974.

assured supply of kola. Major crafts, particularly weaving, were connected with these activities.

From east to west, each sector of the forest fringe was linked with a staging area farther north: the Sankaran and Kuranko were in contact with the Kissi, the Toron and Konyan of Beyla with the Toma and Kpelle, Odienne country (Kabadugu) and the Mau of Touba with the Dan and, lastly, the Worodugu of Seguela and the Koyara of Monkono with the Guro. René Caillé has given a good description of this remarkably speculative trade; for kola nuts do not keep long, and their price fluctuates wildly.

In this generally traditionalist society dominated by a warrior aristocracy, Islam was a necessary and ubiquitous minority, naturally connected with this trading network. In the south, however, the network ran up against the impenetrable wall of the forest from which the kola came. Indeed, the remarkable feature of the area until the colonial conquest was its isolation from the sea, accessible only in the west, from the upper Niger to Futa Jallon and the Rivers or Sierra Leone, and to a lesser extent from Konyan to Cape Mount (Monrovia area). Even these routes had only become important in the eighteenth century, with the expansion of the slave trade. In the east, the Bandama had once provided an outlet for Worodugu, and, further away, for the Kong area; but this outlet had been closed by the Baule in about 1720, and from then on it meant going to the Comoe or to Kumasi to find an outlet to the sea. The country of the southern Mandinka was thus a dead end, and it traditionally looked towards the Niger and the Sudan from which its culture came.

In the eighteenth century in the far west of this region, the village of Kankan on the Milo developed into a major trading centre, taking advantage of the Futa Jallon outlet to the sea, thus becoming a counterpart of Kong on the Comoé. Kankan was admirably situated at the upstream end of the navigable reach to Bamako, and at the meeting point of the shortest routes from the forest in Kissi country and from the sea through Futa Jallon or Sierra Leone. It was the centre for the famous Maninka Mori, or Muslim Mandinka, whose culture permeated the whole world of the Joola (Dyula) from poor peddlers to rich merchants who worked the southern routes. The Kaba who dominated Kankan were a political, religious, and commercial family all at the same time, although in the religious field they had competition from the Sherifu. Mamadu Sanusi Kaba, who was in charge of the town for a long time (roughly from 1810 to 1850) had kept up the alliance with Timbo and done relatively little fighting, except against the Jallonke of Tamba, who several times closed the Segu route to trade. But al-Hadjdj ʿUmar had visited the town in about 1845 on his return from Mecca, and the Kaba he had converted helped him, in 1851, at the beginning of his Holy War, to destroy the Jallonke kingdom of Tamba. Alfa Mamadu Kaba next sought to impose control over his traditionalist neighbours by armed force, but Kankan, isolated as it was, was not strong enough. The Kaba met serious reverses, and the town suffered a commercial blockade. This explains why, in 1874, they appealed for help from the new Muslim conqueror who was organizing the southern lands, Samori Ture.

Actually the disruption of the old order among the southern Mandinka had started south of Kankan, in Toron and Konyan, before al-Hadjdj 'Umar's visit. The most likely explanation is that the opening up in the eighteenth century of the routes to the Côte des Rivières had increased the size and importance of the Muslim trader element. The export of slaves produced by local wars was to continue until the middle of the nineteenth century for the clandestine export trade, and until the colonial conquest for use in Futa Jallon. Next, the need to import cloth and European arms became well-established. Essential as it was to society as a whole, the growing Joola minority became aware, through Islam, of the holy wars and Muslim theocracies in the north. The influence of the Futa came in through Kankan, and the kola-nut caravans went up as far as Shehu Ahmadu's Massina. The time came when the Joola and Muslim elements would no longer accept the place assigned them by society as a whole, while the society, ossified by tradition, was unable to reform. There followed a series of localized conflicts, from the north-western Ivory Coast to the upper Niger. But the resistance remained insurmountable. What was needed if the movement was to become general was the emergence of a local man obviously anxious to change, without destroying, the society from which he came, but sufficiently open to the outside world to promote new methods. This is what Samori did; and I have suggested calling the movement as a whole the Joola Revolution. It would, however, be the second such revolution, if the same name is used for the rise of the empire of Kong at the beginning of the eighteenth century.

The first movement began in about 1835, far to the south, on the borders of Toron and Konyan, and not far from the Toma producers of kola. The person responsible was Moriule Sise, a religious man from the Kankan area but brought up in Futa, who gathered around him adventurers from all quarters in the new town of Madina (Toron). After a period of destructive radicalism, he was killed in 1845, and his state almost collapsed.When it was reconstructed by his sons, Sere-Burlay (Abdulaye) (1845–59) and Sere Brema (Ibrahima) (1859–81), the need for compromise with the local people and some respect for their institutions had become clearer to all. But their role still remained precarious and unstable. Though at one time they greatly extended their authority to the south across the Upper Konyan as far as the forest fringes of Kpelle country, they never managed to link up with Kankan to the north. Here, in Sabadugu, a great traditionalist war leader, Nantenen-Famudu Kuruma, organized resistance to the two Muslim powers, and placed himself between them (Lower Toron).

But in the upper valley of the Milo straddling Toron and Konyan, another Joola lineage stock, the Berete, organized a local hegemony which closed the west to the Sise in the name of the Konate traditionalists. The Sise twice defeated them, but this only paved the way for Samori.

Moriule had been killed by Vakaba Ture, a young Joola from the Odienne area who had initially fought under him but had come to defend his mother's village. The Odienne area had been occupied since the eighteenth century by a traditionalist military state, Nafana, which had driven back the Senufo to protect the Joola. Vakaba managed to mobilize the Muslims and get himself accepted by many traditionalists and so he destroyed Nafana and built Kabadugu (or Kabasarana) on its ruins. Better based, this new kingdom turned out to be much stronger and more stable than the Sise domain. It extended in particular along the east–west kola trade routes to the gates of Touba. Vakaba died in 1857; his son, Vamuktar (1858–75), was the most warlike sovereign of the family. He twice encouraged his cousin, Bunu Mameri, to carve out a new kingdom for the Ture on the northern routes in the area of Wasulu on Bougouni (Mali) (1868–70 and 1873–5). The intervention of the Sise and the reaction of the Wasulunke thwarted this grand design, which ended in Vamuktar's death.

Kabadugu then underwent a serious crisis; many of the vassal cantons revolted on the accession of Vakaba's last son, Mangbe Amadu (1875–94). One of his chief generals, Vakuru Bamba, seceded and established a small military state towards Touba, which he was later to extend towards Seguela and Mankono. Amadu spent several years imposing his authority by force of arms, and it is understandable that a weakened Kabadugu unhesitatingly joined Samori when he appeared on its frontiers in 1881. This submission was sealed by marriages, and turned out to be sincere and lasting.

Space does not permit us here to deal with secondary 'Joola' movements like those of Fode Drame Sulemani Savane on the forest fringes in Kissi country, or Hedi Mori in the Koyara of Mankono (Ivory Coast). All were connected in various ways with Islam and the world of trade. Despite their diversity, they clearly demonstrate that this minority no longer accepted the place it traditionally occupied and was capable of disrupting society as a whole. They provide the framework needed for understanding Samori, who brought this movement to its peak by eliminating or winning over all his rivals, and particularly by making the disruption he imposed acceptable or even desirable to the Mandinka as a whole, including the traditionalists with whom he had close connections.

Samori Ture came from lower Konyan, that is, from the upper Milo valley on the borders of Toron. His ancestors were Muslim peddlers from the Kankan area. Isolated in a traditionalist environment into which they married, they had gradually reverted to traditional religious practices as they settled down as weavers, cultivators, and stockbreeders. Samori, born about 1830 at Manyambaladugu, counted among his ancestors more Kamara or Konate – traditionalist peasants – than Muslim traders.

Reverting to trade to escape from his father's authority, Samori found his vocation as a warrior when he joined the Sise to free his mother, who had been captured during the war with the Berete (1848). The Berete then called upon his talents when he fell out with the masters of Madina (1859–

61). But eventually, in 1861, Samori found himself alone and hunted, and thus had to begin his personal career utterly on his own.

There is no need to give a further account of these events, which have recently been the subject of several publications. Samori succeeded in winning over the traditionalists of lower Toron, his relations on his mother's side. They felt helpless in the face of the Muslim conquerors who were rising up on all sides, and appealed to the military talents of this brilliant 'nephew'. He was, in fact, to protect them until the French invasion, whilst also eroding their freedom somewhat. In return, they gave him the wherewithal to conquer his first domain. His style of leadership, with the changes he imposed on Mandinka society by ending the internal conflicts, opening the trade routes and emancipating the Joola Muslims without enslaving the traditionalists, soon brought a rush of followers and support. The pump being thus primed, expansion proceeded with increasing speed from 1871 to 1881, and was near its peak when the unforeseen invasion by the French changed the character of the movement.

Supported by most of the Kamara, and subjugating the others, Samori, with his base at Sanankoro, first made himself master of the upper Milo, accepted as such by the Sise whom he soon called in against the Berete. The Berete having been eliminated, Sere-Brema became concerned about the new power; but Samori avoided conflict by taking refuge in the forest among the Toma. He came back in 1867 with new forces, taking advantage of the Sise's involvement in Wasulu, where they were exhausting their strength against the Ture.

Samori then carefully organized and armed his forces, abandoning upper Konyan to the traditionalist Kamara of Saxajiigi, whom he did not fight, he claimed, because they were his kin. In 1871, he marched due north, eliminating the hegemony of traditionalist Nantenen-Famudu, against which the Sise had finally failed. There, in newly conquered territory at Bissandugu, he set up his capital, to show that he was creating his own empire independently of his relations and the country of his birth.

The Sise dared not react, and Samori then made an alliance with Kankan, in the name of Islam, whose commercial blockade he had broken, retaining for himself authority over the defeated. He made himself master of the rich upper Niger valley from the frontiers of Futa Jallon and Kurussa to Siguiri and the Bure, and thus suddenly found himself at the head of an empire definitely larger than those of his predecessors and neighbours. Its size was already creating organizational problems, which he tackled by modelling his administration on the Tukuloor empire, whose neighbour he now was but towards which he soon conceived a muted hostility. It was foreseeable that he would have to try to eliminate it if he wished to continue his expansion in the north.

But this over-rapid expansion soon provoked a serious crisis. In 1878, the Sise drove Samori out of Sankaran and set out to reconquer the west as far as Sierra Leone in order to encircle and circumscribe the conqueror's domains. Kankan, under the influence of the Tukuloor, broke away from him. Then, in 1879, Samori turned on his two Muslim neighbours simultaneously. Taking advantage of their scattered forces, he eliminated them in two brilliant campaigns (December 1879 to April 1881). Kankan eventually submitted again, some of the Kaba fleeing to Segu whence they were to come back with the French. The Sise were now prisoners and Madina destroyed, its population being transferred to Bissandugu. Odienne also came over, opening the way to the upper Ivory Coast (modern Côte d'Ivoire).

It was there at Gbèlèba that Samori spent the rainy season of 1881, when the Senegalese lieutenant Alakamessa came to bring him the challenge of the French, then marching towards the Niger. The French commander of Kita ordered Samori not to attack Kenyeran, where the Kankan were holding out. The military confrontation which was to begin in early 1882 lasted with intervals of peace until 1896, but cannot be pursued here since it is outside the scope of this volume, both chronologically and from the point of view of subject matter.

By 1881, Samori's empire was established. It was a military hegemony that changed Mandinka society without destroying it. The Muslim traders had a more important place, but the traditionalists kept their freedom. The sovereign who, in about 1868, took the title of *faama* connoting a military leader, adopted that of *almami* on the model of Futa Jallon only in 1884. This shows the growth of Muslim influence after the annexation of Kankan; but the identity crisis which resulted from it cannot be dealt with here. It was connected with the beginning of the war with France.

In 1880–1, the new empire, though run by an Islamized military class, could not be regarded as a Muslim state. Samori was not a cultured Muslim, though he belatedly made remarkable efforts to educate himself. He had set up a system of military control of the territory, sometimes modelling himself on some of the achievements of the Fulbe and Tukuloor, but without their religious emphasis. Samori, who was a brilliant empiricist, had managed in twenty years to give this society a new equilibrium more favourable to the Joola, thus solving the crisis it had been going through for half a century. Here we leave him, at the moment when, his triumph achieved, he found himself suddenly confronted by the French invasion that was to give a new direction to the end of his career. It was no longer a question of rebuilding an African society on African lines in response to an African crisis, but of trying to repel the foreign invasion, and, insofar as that was impossible, of surviving as long as he could.

Conclusion

The only factor common to the area in question during the period preceding the colonial conquest of Africa was really the advance of European influence. The latter was, of course, strong on the coast. The clandestine slave trade persisted there until the middle of the century; but the major fact was the appearance of new African products, palm oil and groundnuts, which allowed European products hitherto reserved for the aristocracy to spread among the masses. The coastal area thus became part of the world market, and economically dependent, long before military conquest and political domination became realities.

These influences were much weaker in the interior, where Sudanic tradition linked to Islam persisted. But it was the growth of trade with the outside world that explains the Joola revolution. Without knowing it, it was to some extent in response to the impact of the outside world that Samori built the empire that was to succeed in delaying the coming of the colonial conquest for twenty years.

25 States and peoples of the Niger Bend and the Volta

K. ARHIN and J. KI-ZERBO

The nineteenth century was undoubtedly a period of major upheavals of various kinds for the countries of the Niger Bend and the Volta. Political and institutional disintegration affected the centralized state systems in particular, and more specifically those that constituted empires such as Asante (Ashanti), Kong, and the Mossi and Bambara kingdoms. What is more, this disruption stemmed from internal tensions, but also, increasingly, from external causes, particularly notable changes in trade flows.

Peoples migrated, especially non-centralized groups. These 'Völkerwanderungen' have in many cases given shape to the ethnic distribution map as it still stands today. There were economic changes that marked the end of one era and heralded another, the colonial period. These changes were often the cause and sometimes the result of the political changes. The Islamic and Christian religions spread rapidly, fostered by Islamic hegemonies at work in the Sahel or by the advance of European colonization. All these processes contributed to the vigorous reshaping of the physiognomy of this region, weakening it and facilitating or even bringing about the establishment of the colonial system.

Political and institutional upheavals

During the eighteenth century, the countries of the basin of the Volta and the Niger Bend were seats of political power extending beyond the region, supplanting the vast empire of Gao, which fell in the late sixteenth century, or trying to exploit the new economic and political conditions brought about on the Gold Coast by the slave trade. However, during the nineteenth century, new conditions led to the disintegration of the great kingdoms and gave rise to migratory movements among the peoples not integrated by centralized powers.

The Asante system: its rise and decline

In the eighteenth century the Asante dynasties carved a vast empire for themselves in the heart of the forest and south of the Black Volta river bend.[1] Thanks to Osei Tutu, the founder, Opoku Ware and Osei Kodjo, this kingdom was highly integrated, with its nucleus around Kumasi and the Golden Stool (*sikadwa*). It wielded undisputed economic and political power over the coast and over the dependent kingdoms to the north. Towards the centre, kingdoms associated with the Oyoko clan from Kumasi gradually became subjugated and tributary on account of structural reforms carried out by Osei Kodjo, first, in the kingdom of Kumasi, and then at the expense of the neighbouring Akan kingdoms: Mampong, Nsuta, Dwaben, Bekwai, Kokofu, Bono, as also Denkyira, Ahafo, Sefwi, Adansi, etc. In this region, the Kumasihene (king of Kumasi) became the Asantehene. From this base, the Asante dynasty held political and economic sway over the coastal kingdoms (Wassa, Nzima, Twifu, Akwamu, Akyem, Akuapem, Ga and Adangbe), and more especially the coastal strip of the Fante chieftaincies. Similarly, to the north, the kingdoms of Gyaman, Gonja, Dagomba and Mamprusi came under the sway of Asante, sanctioned by a yearly tribute (*ayibuade*) of two thousand slaves, especially after the 1794 treaty.

The nineteenth century was to start with the reign of one of the greatest of the Asantehenes, Osei Bonsu (1801–24), whose victorious armies pushed through to the coast in a series of campaigns (1807, 1811 and 1814). The British, who at the time were caught up in the Napoleonic Wars and had no clear policy for their Gold Coast settlements, could not but recognize, through the President of the Council of Merchants, Colonel Torrane, and his successors, the reality of the suzerainty, or even sovereignty, of Asante over all the coastal peoples.

Asante took advantage of this acquiescence to put down a Gonja rebellion, and then the Gyaman (Abron) rebellion, in the north. However, after gaining time by transferring responsibility for the trading posts to the London Company of Merchants and by sending envoys to the Asantehene's court (Bowdich and Dupuis) with draft treaties which remained practically a dead letter, the British Crown took direct responsibility for the forts in 1821, putting them under the authority of the Governor of Sierra Leone, Sir Charles MacCarthy. During a bold drive on Kumasi, disaster befell Sir Charles at Nsamanku (1824), where he fell to Asante forces.[2] Spurred on by this exploit, the Asante resumed their drive towards the coast but were crushed at Dodowa (1826) by a broad coalition of coastal peoples under the aegis of the British. The bell had tolled for the power of Asante.

The following period (1826–74) was marked by a few indecisive victories of the Asante troops and, above all, by peaceful administration on the coast under Governor George Maclean (1830–43) and the remarkable attempts of the Fante and other coastal peoples to acquire true autonomy in the face of Kumasi threats and European encroachments.

1. See Unesco, *General History of Africa*, Vol. 5, ch. 12.
2. On MacCarthy's campaign, see A. A. Boahen, 1974, pp. 188–9.

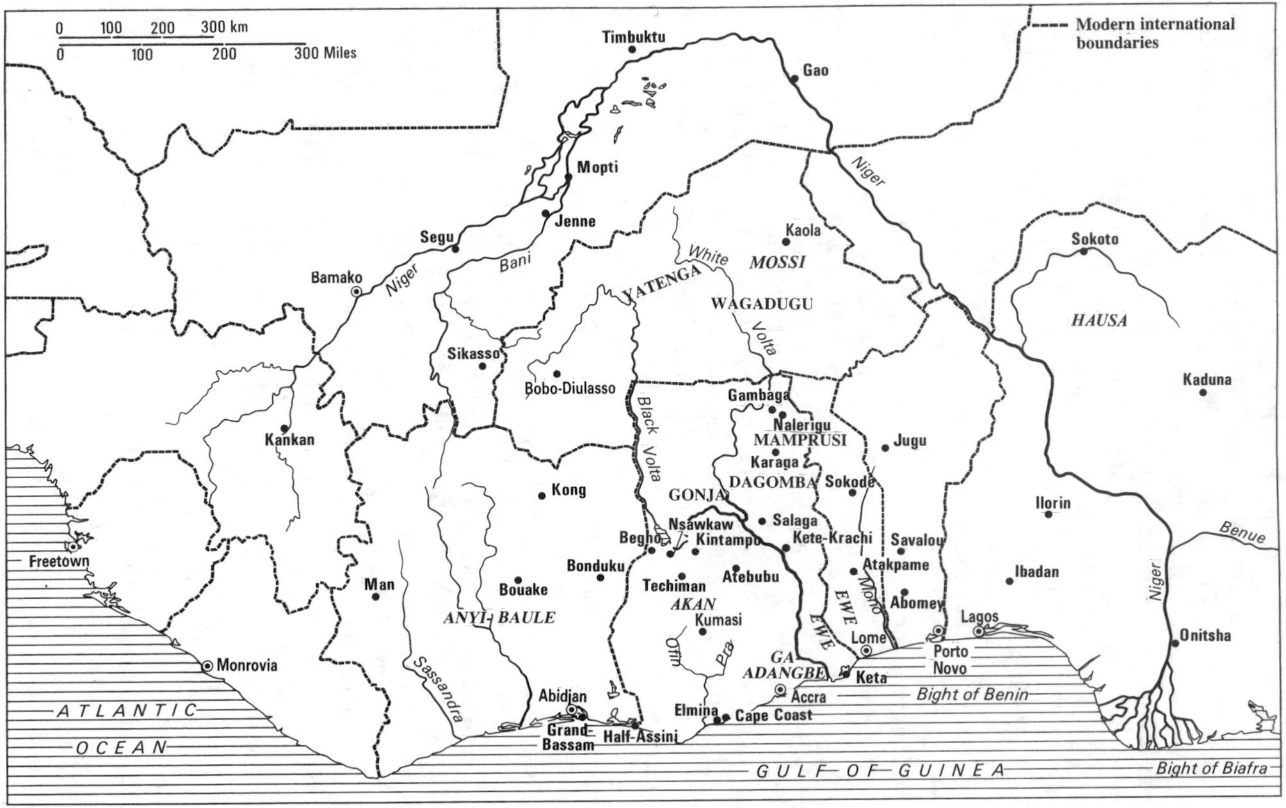

FIG. 25.1 *West Africa: some of the peoples and towns mentioned in the text (after K. Arhin)*

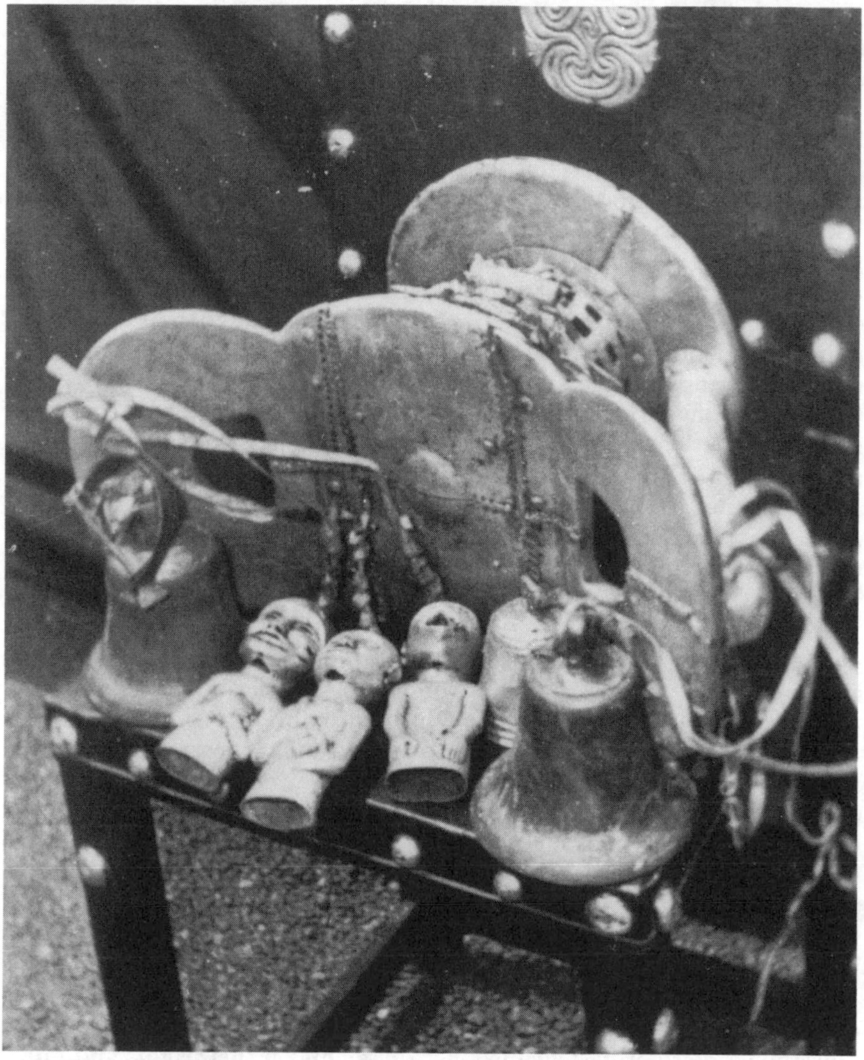

PLATE 25.1 *The Golden Stool of Asante*

Maclean's career[3] blossomed after the new retreat of the British government, which, caught up between its embarrassing allies on the coast and the fighting spirit of Asante, felt that the Gold Coast was too expensive in terms of money and human lives despite the British victory at Dodowa. Maclean, President of the Council of Merchants that provided the local administration of the forts, could therefore give free reign to his business

3. For Maclean's career, see G. E. Metcalfe, 1962.

acumen and knowledge of people, often disregarding official instructions from London, where a committee of merchants once again had charge of the forts. He had a twofold objective: to keep Asante at bay and to bring the coastal peoples under his control. He therefore had a tripartite Fante–British–Asante treaty signed whereby the parties recognized the independence of the coastal countries south of the Pra river, agreed to bring any conflict before the British party and undertook to keep trade routes open. Maclean tried gradually to acquaint the Fante with English legal principles through a hierarchy of courts ranging from the chiefs' courts to those over which he himself presided. Local militias posted at the chiefs' courts helped to apply the new laws, whilst the introduction of cowries for minor transactions and the encouragement of the production of palm oil started to change the economic structure.

However, the British government decided to resume direct control of the coastal settlements in 1843 and to govern them by a legal convention among the chiefs recognizing British law (the Bond of 1844).[4] In 1858 the administration of the Gold Coast, which, apart from the forts, was a protectorate rather than a colony, was separated from Sierra Leone. The Gold Coast was granted its own governor, who presided over the legislative and executive councils.

In accordance with the general principle that local populations should defray the costs of measures calculated to enhance their material, social and intellectual progress, a poll tax of one shilling per head was instituted in 1852 and generally accepted, though only very briefly.[5] In fact, resistance to the tax soon became very strong, not so much because the officials responsible for tax collection were supplanting the chiefs, but because only 8 per cent of the revenue was used for schools and roads, most of it being used to pay the host of civil servants on administrative duties. Despite subsequent attempts at reform and punitive expeditions, Governor Pine was forced to abandon the tax in 1864.

This was the first resistance movement of a purely social and national, that is to say non-ethnic, character. It was very quickly followed, moreover, by an action[6] of much greater scope since it was political in nature. As early as 1864, the chiefs on the Gold Coast sent a register of grievances to Governor Pine to protest against encroachments on their rights and interests, giving specific examples, such as imprisonment by mere civil servants, to show how their dignity had been flouted.[7] Shortly afterwards, Aggrey, the 'king' of Cape Coast, went even further. On the advice of a talented lawyer, Charles Bannerman, he protested against the fact that the inhabi-

4. Lord Stanley to Lt Governor H. W. Hill, 16 December 1843, document no. 124 in G. E. Metcalfe (ed.), 1964.
5. Poll Tax Ordinance, 19 April 1852, document no. 181 in G. E. Metcalfe (ed.), 1964.
6. Cf. A. A. Boahen, 1974, p. 239.
7. Document no. 243 in G. E. Metcalfe (ed.), 1964.

tants of his territory were treated as British subjects, demanded that the relationships between the chiefs and the governor be clarified and queried the fact that he received no share of the fiscal revenue.[8] Lastly, Aggrey threatened to raise a local militia to ensure the security of his territory. He was deported to Sierra Leone.

However, the movement gained momentum, inspired by African intellectuals whom the Colonial Office described even in 1855 as a half-civilized intermediary class with ideas acquired from missionaries and others. They pressed for emancipation, telling the Africans: 'You are not British subjects, therefore you are not bound to obedience. You have a right to share power in your own country. Only by uniting will you gain access to your rights'. Such were the ideas of James Africanus Horton, a Sierra Leonean, Joseph Smith, Henry Barnes, T. Hughes, F. L. Grant and R. J. Ghartey. Under the circumstances the coastal chiefs were very open to such arguments. They dreaded being attacked again by the Asante and were determined to contribute to their own defence, but they disapproved of the flabby attitude of the Dutch to Kumasi and its coastal ally, Elmina. They therefore opposed the exchange of forts that the British contemplated with the Dutch in order to make their respective territories homogeneous. However, they were also afraid of being abandoned by the British, who pressed them to unite against Asante in defence of the coast, but did not intend to give them the means to do so. Two experiments in self-government were therefore tried on the western and the eastern parts of the coast.

In the west, the Mankessim assembly, comprising Fante chiefs but also delegates from Denkyira, Wassa, Twifu and Assin, drafted three constitutions in succession.[9] The first came in 1868; the second, signed and sealed by thirty-one chiefs and kings in November 1871, instituted a king-president elected by his peers to preside over the national assembly made up of the chiefs. The representative assembly, for its part, made up of delegations of two members (a chief and a learned person) from each kingdom, was presided over by the vice-president, who also presided over the executive council. In 1872, however, this constitution was amended in order to make the legitimacy of the confederation subject to recognition by the British government, which was further required to provide half of the budget of the confederation and, failing that, to assume all its responsibilities by converting the Gold Coast into a colony. The confederation had of course become operational in three years, raising an army of 15 000 men, setting up institutions and officials, including the supreme court, and levying a tax of which two-thirds went to the confederation and one-third to the member chieftaincies.

To the east, around Accra, it inspired a similar confederation, but a very

8. Carnavon to Blackhall, 23 February 1867, document no. 258, in ibid.

9. Quassie (Kwassi); Edoo *et al* to Sir A. F. Kennedy, 24 November 1871, document no. 278 in ibid.

timid one in the face of the power of the chiefs in that region. Moreover the autonomist movement in the west was already dying out by 1872, for in that year the Dutch finally sold their forts and left the Gold Coast, thus removing one reason for fear on the part of the confederated chiefs – whose army, incidentally, was not successful in forcing a decision against Fort Elmina, and whose financial resources remained inadequate. Above all, however, the British did their utmost to repress intellectuals and divide the chiefs until the Fante Confederation collapsed.

Although short-lived, the Fante Confederation was of great significance. It was the last gasp of protest on the Gold Coast against creeping colonialism. It attempted to recapture the Fante unity that had been destroyed by the decisive influences of the European presence. It foreshadowed the role that the educated elite would in future assume in the affairs of the Gold Coast: that of providing guidance for the non-literate traditional leaders of the peoples. It thus indicated the way in which the colonial situation, in providing education, was also providing the instrument of its own ultimate destruction. This was the basis of the antagonism that the colonial governments thereafter showed to the educated elite.

In 1872 the Asante sent an invasion force south to enforce what they regarded as their ancient right to Elmina and to revive their claims to Assin, Denkyira and Akyem. Having suppressed the Confederation and bought out the Dutch in 1872, the British decided to organize a response that would settle the Asante question once and for all. In 1874 they despatched a strong army under General Wolseley which captured and burnt Kumasi. In the same year, the Treaty of Fomena, under which Asante definitively renounced all its rights on the Gold Coast was imposed on the Asantehene, Kofi Karikari.

Asante was further weakened in 1875 by its war with Dwaben, which was defeated, its inhabitants seeking refuge in the British protectorate. Now Dwaben was one of the most valiant and faithful central Asante towns. After its defeat, anarchy took over in Kumasi and in the tributary countries to the north despite the policy of consolidation followed by Asantehene Kwaku Dwa III, called Prempeh (the Fat). He was arrested by ruse in 1896 at the time of the rush for colonial territory and deported.

The unrivalled power of Asante during the eighteenth and early nineteenth centuries had of course been ultimately due to its favourable intermediary position between two poles, that is, the Niger Bend and the coast of the Gulf of Guinea, but also to its leaders' skill in political and administrative organization.[10] During the early nineteenth century, this system reached a high degree of perfection and efficiency, which alone justified its growing expansion until it engulfed the Fante states. The great Asante kingdom then comprised three types of territorial unit.

First, there was the central group of Asante chiefdoms, long united

10. See Unesco, *General History of Africa*, Vol. 5.

under the authority of the Asantehene by the same language, geographical contiguity, a vast network of family ties and affinities, a century of common military activities and pride in their spectacular achievements. In addition, and fundamentally, there was the mystical bond of belief in the protecting power of the Golden Stool of the Asante and the spirits of the Asantehene's ancestors.[11] Membership in the union took the following tangible forms: participation by chiefs of member states in the enthronement of the head of state of Kumasi, the Asante sovereign, and the swearing of an oath of allegiance to him; attendance at the general assembly (*nhyiamu*) of chiefs at which major political matters (such as war, peace and treaties) were discussed, and acceptance of the great Asante oath as the supreme instrument of justice for all of the Asantehene's territories.[12]

These integrative institutions constituted the fundamental bases of the state machinery. They were to be found in all the Akan states as well as in Asante, which meant that the idea of the legitimacy of power through conquest had replaced that of political identity established through kinship and religion. The second category of states in this vast empire was therefore the Akan states bordering Asante territory. The peoples of these states understood the meaning of these institutions. They were expected to live under the Asantehene's authority so as to derive the same benefits from these institutions as the Asante peoples.

The third category of states included geographically and culturally distant peoples such as the Dagomba, the Mamprusi and the Gonja. They were viewed by the Asante authorities primarily as having to contribute to the economic development of the metropolis. These non-Akan states to the north were subjected to military and political control because of their economic resources. They also supplied, in the form of tribute, a large part of the manpower used in Asante wars and agriculture.[13] This significant distinction has been contested on the grounds that economic and political motivations existed in all the Asante wars. In a similar vein, references have been made to the presence of Asante representatives in all types of states and also to the introduction of substantial Asante features into the Dagomba army or interventions by the Asantehene in Gonja and Dagomba succession disputes.[14]

It is obvious nevertheless that the mandates of the Asante regional commissioners varied according to the situation. In the Akan regions they had to ensure that disputes were settled by enforcing observance of the Asantehene's oath so as to emphasize his sovereignty over these territories. The collection of taxes in these regions, seen by contemporary European

11. Cf. R. S. Rattray, 1929, pp. 398–409; K. A. Busia, 1951; I. Wilks, 1975, ch. 2.
12. I. Wilks, 1975; J. M. Sarbah, 1906; K. A. Busia, 1951, p. 78; R. S. Rattray, 1929, pp. 388–9.
13. T. E. Bowdich, 1819, pp. 320–1.
14. J. K. Fynn, 1974. I. Wilks, 1975, pp. 42–60, rejects this classification.

observers as a form of exploitation, was no problem for the Asantehene, since Asante states themselves had to bear the same burdens.[15] The real problem was territorial sovereignty. In non-Akan regions, the commissioners strove to strengthen the terms of the 'treaty' between the Asantehene and the Dagomba, for example,[16] concerning the tribute. On the other hand, we have no evidence confirming the presence of Gonja or Dagomba contingents in the Asante army or of payment by these countries of the Asante war tax (*apeatoo*). The settlement of the Gonja and Dagomba succession disputes must therefore be considered as a political act with economic motives: peace in these territories guaranteed payment of the tribute, as well as the introduction of Asante institutions into the Dagomba army. An old Asante source declared on this subject: *Na yene wonom nko nhyiamu* ('We did not hold council with them').

PLATE 25.2 *The Exchequer Court, Kumasi, 1817*

However, with the Akan states the problem was essentially one of sovereignty. There is no doubt about the economic aspect of the Asante conquests in the south but it is clear that, in the early nineteenth century, the Asante were mainly interested in political domination over the other Akan peoples on whom they sought to impose their own central institutions. First of all, the tribute extorted from the vanquished peoples gradually

15. B. Cruickshank, 1853, Vol. 2, p. 143.
16. T.E. Bowdich, 1819, p. 235.

became a war tax (*apeatoo*).[17] Then, the great Asante oath, the *Ntam Kesie*, deemed to be the supreme instrument of justice, was instituted among the other Akan peoples and their own local oaths were subordinated to it.[18] At a later stage, the main Akan leaders in the surrounding areas were required to attend the annual ceremony of the *Odwira*, at which they had to pay homage to their suzerain, the Asantehene.[19] Lastly, contingents from all the Akan states fought as Asante forces in Asante wars inside and outside the empire. The problem of sovereignty led to frequent clashes between the Asante and the other Akan, or the Europeans. The closing of the trade routes leading to Accra, decreed by the Akyem and the Akuapem was the cause of wars with the Asantehene since he considered it mainly as an act of rebellion and a rejection of the political domination of the Asante. Asante attacks on the Fante were inspired by this same desire for political hegemony.

PLATE 25.3 *The first day of the Odwira festival in Kumasi, 1817*

As proof of sovereignty, the Asantehene referred to documents binding the signatories to pay rent for Cape Coast Castle and Fort Anomabo, which he said he had acquired during the conquest of Fante territory in 1807.[20] After the defeat of Gyaman in 1818, the Asantehene declared that the people of Kommenda and Cape Coast should pay the *aseda*, a levy of gratitude, to express joy at the victory of their lord and master.[21] In 1822, the Asantehene's commissioners went so far as to demand the trial and punishment of a police sergeant at Fort Anomabo because he did not react

17. T. E. Bowdich, 1819, p. 320.
18. Cf. Major Chisholm to Sir Charles MacCarthy, 30 September 1822, document no. 56 in G. E. Metcalfe (ed.), 1964.
19. J. M. Sarbah, 1906.
20. T. E. Bowdich, 1819, pp. 47, 68.
21. The Governor and the Council to the African Committee, 11 January 1819, document no. 39 in G. E. Metcalfe (ed.), 1964; see also the Governor and the Council to the committee, 22 March 1819, document no. 110 in ibid.

properly when an Asante tradesman uttered the Asantehene's oath before him.[22]

The Mossi states

The Mossi territory, which had undergone remarkable development since the sixteenth century, reaching its zenith in the eighteenth,[23] was by the beginning of the nineteenth century in a state of decomposition leading to paralysis from within and disintegration from without of the two main kingdoms of Wagadugu and Yatenga. Only the Busuma kingdom benefited from this *débâcle*, extending and consolidating its influence.

Two examples will suffice to illustrate the gravity of the decadence into which the powerful kingdom of Wagadugu had fallen: the Busuma war and the Lallé war.

The expanding Busuma kingdom clashed at the beginning of the century with the kingdom of Wagadugu, then headed by Mogho Naaba Dulugu. It was by intervening in the internal disputes of Salmatenga (in the Kaya region) that Naaba Piga of Busuma succeeded in gaining control over this chieftaincy. But when he gave refuge to an exile from the kingdom of Wagadugu, he was invaded by Naaba Dulugu's forces and had to seek refuge at Mane, which was itself at war with the chief of Zitenga, under the protection of Wagadugu. It was therefore a circular war in the course of which many princes, unhappy about the campaign against Mane, defected and Naaba Dulugu of Wagadugu was mortally wounded. Naaba Piga's successor, feeling that the chief of Mane was responsible for Naaba Dulugu's death, forced the Naaba of Mane to poison himself, while Dulugu's successor, Naaba Sawadogho, forced the chief of Zitenga, his own brother, who had dared to contest his throne, to commit suicide.

Fifty years later, Wagadugu, allied with Boulsa, was again to attack Busuma, allied with Pisila. Although harassed, Naaba Ligidi of Busuma was nevertheless to make a successful raid with his cavalry on the capital of the Mogho Naaba, at Wagadugu, causing considerable material damage and loss of life.[24]

Moreover, the wars between Busuma and the kingdom of Riziam enabled Busuma, not without difficulty, to annex the chieftaincies of Salmatenga

22. See document no. 63, in ibid. K. A. Busia, 1951, p. 78, defines an oath as a stereotyped expression with a very obscure allusion to a tragic event in the history of the political community to which the oath refers, the chief of which is said to possess the oath. By recalling the event in question, the oath is supposed to disturb the spirits of the dead ancestors of the royal line, who must then be appeased by sacrifices. This is why an oath must be uttered only according to the prescribed rules as a legal instrument binding a party in a conflict to appear before the court of the leader to whom the oath was made, or as a means of appealing to a higher court; cf. R. S. Rattray, 1929, pp. 76, 102–4, 315 ff.

23. See Unesco, *General History of Africa*, Vol. 5, ch. 12.

24. Y. Tiendrebeogo, 1964, pp. 57–8.

and Pikutenga. In these operations, Naaba Koabgha of Riziam enlisted the assistance of a Fulbe (Fulani, Peul) chief in Jelgoji.

In 1881, Naaba Ligidi of Busuma launched an expedition against Koala, to the north of the Gulmancé territory, bordering the Fulbe kingdom of Dori and the Mossi territory. The Busuma troops took the fortified village of Koala with great difficulty. The amīr of Dori was awaiting its defeat in order to seize it, but Naaba Ligidi did not help the Fulbe in this aim.[25] At his death in 1890, Naaba Ligidi had extended the Busuma kingdom to the utmost. At the price of many clashes, he had made it preponderant on the border of the Fulbe and Gulmancé country.

Whereas to the east of Wagadugu, Busuma was taking the land, to the west the ruler of Lallé, a powerful chieftaincy adjacent to Gurunsi territory, was also in open rebellion. This war, which was to smoulder for a long time and flare up fifty years later, was to draw an increasing number of peoples into the maelstrom until the French conquest.

It started under Naaba Karfo (1842–9) of Wagadugu, sparked off by a trivial incident, which illustrates the degree of decay of the Mossi system at the time. The situation was considerably worsened by the fact that the Naaba of Wagadugu was opposed by one of his most powerful vassals, allied with his principal 'minister', the Widi Naba.[26] This was a formidable coalition since it brought together two generally antagonistic social groups: a nobleman at the head of territorial troops and the most eminent representative of the 'bureaucratic' caste, a commoner by birth, but a member of the sovereign's entourage who handled major affairs of state. During this civil war, which spelt the end of the kingdom of Wagadugu, Naaba Wobgho of Lallé, whose territory to the east ran too far into loyalist territories, increasingly sought support from the western areas mainly inhabited by the Gurunsi, whose services were heavily called upon, whilst the Mogho Naaba succeeded by ruse in securing the death of his rebel 'minister'.

Under Mogho Naaba Sanem of Wagadugu (1871–89), however, the conflict with Naaba Wobgho of Lallé was resumed with greater vigour. It continued under the next Mogho Naaba of Wagadugu, also called Wobgho, (1889–97). In the first battle the royalist forces were routed. War-weary, the Mogho Naaba, unable to put down the rebellion, turned to Zamberma (Zabarima) mercenaries in order to win the battle decisively.

The Zamberma had left their country (present-day Niger) to escape the exactions of the Fulbe.[27] They entered the services of the Ya Na (the king of Yendi), Na Abdulai, as slave-hunters. They marched under the orders of Alfa Hano, later under Gazari, and, finally, under Babato. Having fallen out with the Ya Na, they set about gaining control of the relatively highly

25. P. Delmond, 1953, p. 39.
26. Y. Tiendrebeogo, 1964, pp. 48–9.
27. M. Izard, 1970, Vol. 1, pp. 183 ff.

populated and fertile Gurunsi country, which they exploited. When Mogho Naaba Wobgho recruited them against Lallé, they advanced into Mossi territory, giving no quarter to anyone. The 'chiefs' faithful to the Mogho Naaba opposed them and blocked their passage, as at Saponé, where they were crushed, and as at Kayao. The Mogho Naaba's army itself inflicted heavy losses on them, and the *tapsoba* (general-in-chief) only allowed them to pass, unwillingly, after receiving orders from Wagadugu. It was after many bloody clashes that the Zamberma, weakened, reached the rebellious province of Lallé, where they were pushed back into the marshes and cut down. Only remnants of this intervention party were to reach Leo.[28] By a macabre quirk of fate the European conquest forced the Mogho Naaba of Wagadugu to flee from the French into British territory in 1897, whilst his vassal and namesake Wobgbo of Lallé was defeated by the French and executed at Wagadugu.

In the northern Mossi lands, the preponderance of Yatenga was patent but, during the nineteenth century, decadence was also obvious. Apart from a few operations for the purposes of extension and integration, as in the kingdoms of Yako and Tatenga (Riziam), Yatenga interventions during this period were reactions to external threats, a typical example being the Jelgoji operations, and an unending civil war among the pretenders to the throne, most of whom were not to survive long enough even to be enthroned.

The two main attempts at integration by conquest were those of the Naaba Tuguri (1806–22) against Yako.[29] However, the overlord of that kingdom, situated between the Mogho Naaba of Wagadugu and the Naaba of Yatenga, was more under the influence of the former. Naaba Silem of Yako, deposed by Naaba Tuguri of Yatenga, regained control a year later, undoubtedly with the assistance of his great neighbour in Wagadugu.

The action against Riziam could not but yield results. In fact that kingdom, whose capital Sabcé was not in the centre but in the southern region, had brought all its efforts to bear on that side, particularly against the powerful Busuma Naabas. The north, which was connected to the southern region solely via a narrow sparsely populated corridor was no longer closely related to the southern base of the kingdom. On the other hand, from the reign of Naaba Kango onwards this northern region was under the influence and pressure of Yatenga. The campaigns of Naaba Totebalbo (1834–50) and Naaba Yemde (1850–77) led to the outright annexation of the Titao and Toulfé territory, which further isolated the Rumba chiefdom of Mengao from the Toulfé chiefdom. A warlord, originally a slave, was posted at Titao. Under the surveillance of the chief of Kosouka, the master of Zitenga in Tikaré was under strict control, which

28. Y. Tiendrebeogo, 1964, pp. 70–1.
29. See D. Nacanabo, 1982.

PLATE 25.4 *Mossi masked figures – probably 'earth priests' representing aboriginal authority, early 20th century*

PLATE 25.5 *Mogho Nqaaba Sanem being greeted by his subjects, 1888*

was to make him draw closer to his 'brother', the Naaba of Datenga, and even to the king of Riziam.

Moreover, the extremely hard campaigns in Riziam, a rugged country, had cost Yatenga dearly, including the life of Naaba Totebalbo. Gains in the campaigns against Jelgoji were also quite costly. The frontier with the Massina empire was by then more clearly defined of course, but the Mossi interventions had strengthened the will of Jelgoji to be independent of Yatenga.[30]

The seeds of anarchy and civil war had already been sown in the election at the beginning of the nineteenth century of Naaba Tuguri against the will of his numerous brothers. Rivals frequently replaced each other in quick succession, ruling alternately or even simultaneously, each with his own clan and capital. Such was the case of Naaba Wobgho and Naaba Nyambemogho on the one hand, and Naaba Korogho and Naaba Ragongo on the other. The princes raised their troops from among the San (Samo) people in Gomboro (archers) and/or the Fulbe in Tiou (horsemen) in order to dictate political decisions through force of arms.[31]

All in all, Yatenga's historical development tended in the direction of the outside world in the nineteenth century, as it did in the eighteenth, except that the challenges and dangers became much more serious. Under Naaba Baogho (1885–94), supported by the sons of Sagha (except the Tuguri clan), fratricide struggles broke out. The sons of Sagha were splitting up in turn into the Totebalbo clan and the Yemde clan. They finally agreed to install Naaba Baogho, but this was immediately challenged by the sons of Tuguri, an ideal opportunity for French intervention.[32]

The western and southern Volta plateaux

In this region, lineage groups and clans that for the most part lacked centralized power stood up rather well to the upheavals of the time. The area had witnessed for centuries the penetration of the Joola (Dyula) and the Marka who, through intermarriage with the indigenous peoples, had evolved new cultural, social and economic groups, one prototype being the Bobo-Joola people. A purely theoretical line should not, however, be drawn between peoples with centralized power and the others. In fact, centralization can take non-political forms, such as the *poro* society of the Senufo, a very large-scale religious community that determined social hierarchy. It is therefore in no way surprising that peoples with little political hierarchy should have weathered the turmoil of the nineteenth century differently from societies with more elaborate political structures. Such observations help us to understand the turbulent history of the

30. M. Izard, 1970, Vol. 2, p. 350.
31. ibid., pp. 331–3.
32. J. Ki-Zerbo, 1953. The fratricidal wars between 'sons of Tuguri' and the 'sons of Sagha' provided the occasion for French intervention.

Voltaic groups in this region during the nineteenth-century: invasions, preventive attacks, resistance, adaptation and intermarriage. Generally, while more or less vigorously rejecting attempts at domination on the part of the Mande, Mossi, Zerma, Marka and Fulbe groups, the more sedentary, indigenous peoples became used to their presence and economic activity, moving when political pressure or economic exaction became too great. We can only give a few examples here.

Gwiriko and Kenedugu are both offshoots of the power of the Kong Wattara.[33] Towards the end of the nineteenth century they were to be replaced as a result of the eastward drift of another Joola empire, that of Samori Ture.[34] Gwiriko,[35] formed in the eighteenth century around Bobo Diulasso and the northern loop of the Black Volta, flourished by dint of quelled revolts between the successive hegemonies of the Niger Bend (Segu, Massina, the Tukuloor empire) and the kingdoms of the Central Mossi plateau. But after Maghan Ulé Wattara (1749–1809) and his son, Diori Wattara, the empire collapsed on all sides, on account of secessionist resistance by subjected peoples or the emigration of small groups also trying their luck. Tiéfo, Bobo Joola, Bolon, etc., shook off the yoke. Bako Moru (1839–51) halted the *débâcle* for a time by forming an alliance with Tiéfo and Bobo Joola to crush the Kenedugu forces at Uléni where the future king, Tieba, was to be captured and sold as a slave.

After him, decadence set in again and a family of Marka marabouts from Jenne built up a fiefdom for themselves around Boromo under the orders of Mamadu Karantao, bringing together the Marka, Mossi and Dagari-Joola. The indigenous Kô were driven out of Boromo. Then, in defiance of the authority of the Wattara, he moved on to conquer Bwamu (territory of the Bwaba) and founded Wahabu. His son, Karamoko Moktar, continued his work in Bwamu and in the Dagari and Wiile territory, though not without difficulties and some failures.

What Karamoko Moktar tried to do from southern Gwiriko, the Kenedugu did from the north. They were a distant Kong offshoot under the Traoré, a Joola-influenced, that is, Islamized, Senufo group which became organized in the eighteenth century around Sikasso. Between 1850 and 1860, Laula founded the power of the Traoré on the small Senufo chieftaincies. Their authority was to be confirmed from 1875 onwards by King Tieba, an ally of the French. After drawing closer to the Kiembagha of Korogho and victoriously repelling a siege laid by Samori against his strongly built fortress at Sikasso, Tieba too suffered defeat in 1890 at Sinematiali.

33. For the development of the empire of Kong, see Unesco, *General History of Africa*, Vol. 5, ch. 12.

34. See Ch. 24, above.

35. See Unesco, *General History of Africa*, Vol. 5, ch. 12.

The peoples to the south-west of what is now Burkina Faso lived through this period under a similar climate of pressure, instability and conflict. Ethnic migrations were the rule in this region. The Pwa, Sissala, Gan, Dyan, Birifor, Dagara and Dagara-Joola followed, jostled and repelled one another, intermarried, gathered together and separated in this area, especially during the first decades of the nineteenth century.

Of course these were not human tidal waves.[36] M. Père, quoting her oral sources, mentions small groups, sometimes comprising several units, setting out as scouts 'to see if the place is good', to be joined by others on 'seeing that it was good'. The remarkable point here is that the closest family ties were maintained among these ethnic groups despite their diversity in the strictest sense of the term. For example, they all belonged to the four great matriarchies and bore matronymics.[37] They all spoke Voltaic languages that were frequently very close to each other. They had the same cultural, funerary, matrimonial and initiation customs, dispersed settlement patterns, similar social structures, identical agricultural methods (intensive on alluvial or domestic soils, extensive elsewhere), etc. Yet, there were enough differences in all these respects to make each group cling fiercely to its own identity.

The Kulango, Teese, Gan, Pwa and Dyan were already there at the dawn of the nineteenth century. Then came the Lobi, by far the most numerous. They came over the Black Volta from present-day Ghana in two groups at the end of the eighteenth century. To the north were the Nako (Lobi plainsmen) and, to the south, Lobi mountain-dwellers. They pushed out the Dyan, Gan and Teese without major clashes, through the continuous arrival of pioneer migrants from overpopulated areas who settled at the expense of the scattered peoples, although there were some localized conflicts in marginal areas of friction. Then came the Birifor, from the same origin, along three main routes, settling between the Dagara-Wiile and Lobi, between the Dyan and the Pwa, and in the heart of Lobi country. They constitute the prototype of the mixed breed, akin to the Lobi in terms of culture and to the Dagara in terms of language, and frequently trilingual. Finally, the Dagara in turn crossed the Black Volta from east (left bank) to west (right bank). They can be divided into two groups: the Dagara Wiile, who settled in the north-west, and the Dagara Lobir, who settled along the river banks. All these peoples were to spend most of their time establishing themselves or defending themselves, not so much from their immediate neighbours, but from Joola contingents from all quarters, who held them to ransom without succeeding in subjugating them.

36. Cf. H. Guilhem and J. Hébert, 1961, pp. 87 ff.

37. M. Père, 1982. The matronymics were Hien/Da/Kambou-Kambiré/Sib-Sou-Palé.

Other peoples

These remarks also apply to other non-centralized Voltaic peoples such as the Gurunsi, the Bisa and the Samo (Sanan) in the nineteenth century. We have already seen how the Zamberma pillaged the Gurunsi, who, even under normal circumstances, paid a heavy tribute to the neighbouring Mossi kingdoms while markedly merging with them over the centuries. The Bisa not only maintained their positions to the south-west of the Moaga bloc, but seem to have spread further afield during this period. 'Far from being pushed back by the Mossi, the Bisa seem ... to have gained ground at the expense of their neighbours. This would make the Bisa chiefdom of Garango very recent.'[38]

As for the San (Samo) country to the north, bordering Yatenga, far from being conquered, it was repeatedly used as a withdrawal base and 'sanctuary' in the course of Yatenga's unending dynastic struggles during the period under study. These and other peoples were to be reckoned with, as were the recently settled Marka (Dafing) chiefdoms, such as Lanfiera. In short, the achievements of non-centralized peoples at the end of the nineteenth century were not negligible. In 1885, a coalition comprising the Bwaga, Ko and Gurunsi, similar to coalitions which rose elsewhere against Kong, Bobo or Sikasso, inflicted a resounding defeat on the Zamberma. These African village democracies, which practised traditional religion, were endowed with remarkable vitality, which was to be brilliantly asserted against the colonizers but has not been sufficiently stressed by historians to date.

The eastern regions of the Volta plateaux

Here in the north, Jelgoji and Liptako constituted a border region between the new powers of Massina and Sokoto on one side and the ageing Yatenga on the other. Liptako did best out of this situation, pushing the formerly dominant Gulmanceba further south.

Early in the century Fulbe groups and camps were to be found there, under the domination of the Fulbe *ardo* in the Niger Bend, or of the Gulmanceba chiefs further south. In Jelgoji, at the same time, the Jelgoɓe Fulbe were subjects of the Jalluɓe, whom they served as herdsmen, in a region inhabited by Kurumba, who in turn were tributaries of the Jalluɓe. The Jelgoɓe revolted against the latter, and ultimately succeeded in becoming independent of them, perhaps with the support of Yatenga. They simultaneously shook off the yoke of the indigenous inhabitants led by the Konfe aristocracy under the *ayo* (king) of Lurum, whose capital was Mengao, and founded the principalities of Jiibo and Barbulle. In Liptako, the Ferrobe Fulbe, who also had come from Massina, had settled in Weedu under the leadership of Birmali Sala Paté and lived there as subjects of the

38. M. Izard, 1970, Vol. 2, p. 226.

Gulmanceba of Kaola until about 1810. But then the success of the *djihād* in Sokoto came to be perceived by these Fulbe as significant for both Islam and the Fulbe and they rose in an ethnic and religious revolt against their Gulmanceba masters, who had retained their traditional religion.[39] Accordingly, Brahima Saidu Diandikko sent a delegation to Sokoto to seek Shaykh 'Uthmān's blessing. He returned with a standard that conferred legitimacy on his struggle against the Gulmanceba. Harassment and extortion on the part of the Gulmanceba overlords provided the Fulbe with a *casus belli*. Heifers had been killed, milk had been wantonly spilled or given to dogs to drink, a Fulbe woman had been bound, her head shaven, legacies had been confiscated; all these actions were contrary to Islam and the 'Fulbe way'.

Brahima Saidu, who had been nothing more than the *jooro* (village headman) of Weedu, a post to which he had been appointed by the Gulmancé chief of Kaola, became an *amiiru* (*amīr*) and launched a holy war, which ended with the Gulmanceba being pushed southward, although extensive regions of mixed population remained. However, the other Fulbe clans (the Tukuloor and the Waakambe) objected to the growing power of Brahima Saidu. They sent a delegation to complain to Shaykh 'Uthmān, who replied that while it was undoubtedly 'preferable to leave power to him to whom God has destined it', he did not see why they themselves had not declared a holy war, inasmuch as they had been established in that 'pagan' environment longer than had the Ferrobe.[40] Sokoto always put its political and religious influence behind the new dynasty and intervened on occasions, as for example in 1890, to settle disputes between rival claimants to the emirate. In return, the amīr of Dori provided Sokoto with little enough: no military assistance was sent, and the yearly tribute in kind (grain, livestock, slaves and cloth) could not be supplied, as often as not, because of the unsafe condition of the roads, especially after the empire was divided up and Dori became subject to the rule of Gwandu. Specifically, the Kebbi rising, and subsequently Arewa and the Zamberma, constituted a formidable barrier. The *djihād* of Massina on the other hand, had little impact on the chieftaincies of Jiibo and Barbulle, where the influence of the traditional religions prevailed. In addition, although Jiibo and Barbulle paid tribute to Hamdallahi until 1858, they did not regard themselves as subject to the rule of Massina,[41] perhaps because the latter had no local representative. In practice, at any rate, they enjoyed autonomy. The tribute thus represented an act of deference. It may also have been intended to anticipate any possible attempt at conquest. From the standpoint of Massina, the tribute was presumably the practical expression of its suzerainty, which it would have liked to strengthen. An opportunity presented

39. H. Diallo, 1979, p. 97 ff.
40. ibid., p. 107.
41. ibid., p. 118.

itself in 1858,[42] in connection with a dispute over the succession in Barbulle. Hamdallahi sent out a force under the command of al-Hadjdj Modi to intervene in the issue, and the forces of Jiibo, Barbulle and Tongomayel, which had finally reconciled their difference, were crushed. Yatenga and Datenga, becoming uneasy, responded to the appeal of Jelgoji. At Pobé Mengao they combined to inflict a stinging defeat on the Massinankobé. The latter returned in force with Ba Lobbo. In the meantime, however, the grasping and arrogant behaviour of the Mossi victors had exasperated the Fulbe to such an extent that they had risen in revolt, massacred the Mossi and gone back to being on good terms with Massina.

In point of fact, both in Jiibo and in Barbulle several families were locked in a struggle for power, and as a result tended to seek the support of Yatenga whenever their rivals were allied with Massina. Another factor was the internal struggle between local chiefs and the simmering resistance of the indigenous Kurumba. By the end of the century the latter, under the principality of Aribinda, had become enough of a threat to provoke a coalition between Jelgoji and Liptako.

The Tuareg also had to be reckoned with. As early as 1804 the Udallan Tuareg had settled in the region that bears their name and began exacting tribute from the Gulmaceba and the Songhay. Both Sori Hamma (1832–61) and subsequently Bokar Sori (1890–2) were defeated at their hands and had to fortify Dori with palisades. The Tuareg had been pushed eastward as a result of the consolidation of the empire of Massina, and had settled along the Béli river.

The political organization of Liptako represented an attempt to maintain a balance between the clans, and this was reflected in its very structures. Power was transmitted through patrilineal descent from Saidu, the father of that Brahima who had led the *djihād*. However, the Ferrobe eventually decided or agreed that their antagonists, the Torodbe, should constitute the electoral college that designated the *amīr*. The college investigated each candidate's personal qualities, such as justice and piety, as well as the services he had rendered, the extent of his matrimonial alliances, and the like, and finally gave a decision. By means of this participation, the Torodbe, even though they were debarred from wielding power themselves, were placed in a position where they could in a sense decide among the Ferrobe claimants, and this served to integrate them into the system.[43]

Once the new *amīr* had been tentatively selected, he was subjected to an interview and asked trick questions. Then animals were sacrificed to the genii and to a sacred snake. A new traditional drum was made, to be included among the symbols of power granted by the Sokoto council.[44] The new *amīr*'s head was swathed in a turban by one of the Torodbe in

42. A. H. Ba and J. Daget, 1962; M. Izard, 1970, Vol. 2, pp. 334 ff.
43. H. Diallo, 1979, pp. 155 ff.
44. ibid., p. 161.

the presence of the chief *imām* and the *ḳāḍī*, and facing the standard he swore to respect the customs and principles of Islam and to maintain the welfare of his people. This was a ritual of political and religious renewal of cosmic dimensions, designed to appease supernatural forces of all descriptions. The religious authorities were appointed by the *ḳāḍī* of Dori and were invested with judicial power as courts of appeal. In addition, there was a network of village *imāms*, headed by the chief *imām* of Dori.

The local power structure was also designed to provide a place for the older Fulbe clans which could not aspire to the office of *amīr*: the *jooro* (village headmen) were selected from the ranks of the heads of families of more ancient lineage. Jelgoji had a similar system for incorporating all clans within a single structure: the chief was elected by an electoral college made up of aged notables of Sadaabé descent, i.e. representatives of the people who had been dominant in the region before the arrival of the Jelgoɓé, whereas only a member of the latter could actually be chief. In practice, the chief was invariably a member of the Nyorgo family. The insignia of the office was a staff (symbolizing stock-breeding) hung with various kinds of agricultural products. Here again, the material prosperity of the new chief's reign was secured by means of sacrifices carried out by the indigenous Kurumba.

The Bambara kingdoms of Segu and Kaarta

After reaching their full flowering in the course of the eighteenth century, the kingdoms of Segu and Kaarta lingered on in a way that exhibited the most negative aspects of their policies: acts of aggression that were regarded as acts of bravery, raids carried out with no attempt at organization, fratricidal warfare between kingdoms and within individual kingdoms. For example, the Massassi of Kaarta, who were of royal blood, regarded the rulers of Segu, at any rate from the time of the successors of Denkoro, son of Biton Kurubari (Kulibali), as military chiefs of slave origin, in other words as mere professional warriors. The more populous kingdom of Segu was the stronger of the two, and the kings of Segu hated the Massassi, who treated them with utter contempt. This situation accounts for the persistent assaults carried out by Segu against Kaarta. The latter was usually defeated but never conquered.[45]

This period was also characterized by the increasing prominence of the *tonjons* (a nation of freedmen who had become notable warriors) as they took advantage of their strength. For example, in the course of a war between Torokoro Mari (1854–6) and his brother Kégué Mari before Massala, the *tonjons* who had been enlisted by both brothers decided to use blank ammunition.[46] When Torokoro expressed astonishment that no one had been hurt among the ranks of either besiegers or besieged, one of

45. L. Tauxier, 1942, p. 143.
46. ibid., p. 99.

*tonjon*s told him bluntly, 'We have had enough of your fratricidal wars. They must cease!' The action was broken off forthwith.

In the kingdom of Segu, Monzon Jara (Diarra) (*c* 1790–1808) won renown by his campaigns against not only Kaarta and Massina but also against the Dogon and the Mossi. Da Monzon (1808–27), his successor, was defeated by Seku Ahmadu Barri of Massina while coming to the assistance of his own vassal, the *ardo* Dicko, who was a non-Muslim Fulbe. This experience taught him that the main enemy was not the 'fellow' kingdom of Kaarta. Da Monzon was a fierce and unscrupulous man.[47] His successor, Tyefolo (1827–39), made the mistake of having a pilgrim returning from Mecca put in chains: he proved to be no ordinary pilgrim, but al-Hadjdj 'Umar, who was never to forget his humiliation, even though he was released at the instance of Muslim notables, including the Torodbe, Thierno Abdul.

PLATE 25.6 *Bambara house types, 1887*

The years of anarchy that followed Tyefolo's reign were marked by the epic and legendary figure of Bakari Dyan, a chief of the Ferrobe Fulbe ('Fulbe' freed to serve the state, though they were not all Fulbe by any means). Bakari Dyan not only successfully resisted the attacks launched by

47. In this connection, cf. the episode of Mama Dyetoura, 'the most handsome of men' in the opinion of Da Monzon's wives. Da Monzon, mad with jealousy, succeeded in eliminating Mama Dyetoura by treachery. See V. Monteil, 1977, pp. 92 ff.

Massina, killing the redoubtable Blissi himself, but captured many villages, to the gratification of the people of Segu. His successors were unremarkable, until ʿAlī Monzon Jara, who was defeated and slain by al-Hadjdj ʿUmar. However, Bambara resistance continued under elected chiefs operating from Bani on the right bank.

The kingdom of Kaarta's centre of gravity shifted between the Senegal and Niger basins. Whereas Desse Koro, early in the century, took advantage of unsettled conditions in Segu to seize Nyamina, Mussa Kura Bo, his successor, allied himself with Bundu against ʿAbd al-Ḳādir of Futa Toro, who was to be defeated and killed in 1807. Moussa Koura Bo also operated against the Kagoro of Beledugu and against the Mandinka. Under Bodian Moriba the Great (1815–38) an alliance was entered into with Upper Galam against the *almami* of Bundu, allied with Khasso. The Khaartanke won a decisive victory in that area in 1818, while Moriba's son ravaged Fuladuu in the Kita region.

In the face of Fulbe and Tukuloor expansionism, Naniemiba (1839–41) and Kirango Bâ (1841–44) of Segu finally negotiated a reconciliation with Nyaralen Gran (1832–43) and Mamadi Kandia (1843–54), who in any case had their hands full with their war against the Jawara (Diawara). It was too late: all of them, including Massina's Fulbe adversary, were to be swept away in the *djihād* led by al-Hadjdj ʿUmar.

Summary

Thus, in the centre and the north of the region covered in this chapter, existing political structures went into in a state of increasingly rapid decline in the nineteenth century and in some cases came to be dominated by new forces which had arisen mainly as a result of the Sokoto *djihād*. These took advantage of the internal decay of the existing structures to establish themselves, before being swept away in their turn by foreign powers that were even more formidable.

There can be no single explanation for this kind of decline, such as might be offered if it were seen solely in terms of external influences, or as part of a predisposition towards colonization. There is no doubt that, as a result of processes which had come into operation some time before, kingdoms and peoples that had not adopted centralized systems of government were about to reach a turning point in their history as regards both their internal affairs and the external influences to which they were subject.

In turn, the Mossi, Bambara and Joola kingdoms had attempted to gain control of an area including both the fringes of the desert and the edges of the forest. Although none of them achieved this on any lasting basis, in each case the high point of their power coincided with their maximum north–south extension, even though the nucleus of the Bambara empire of Segu kept more closely to its west–east axis of the valley of the Niger. However, during the nineteenth century, political instability and population movements were widespread. Brutal massacres and secessionist movements were led by the very people who were supposed to represent authority, such as the Tondyon of Segu and the ministers of the court of Wagadugu. Some notable exceptions notwithstanding, the frequency and extent of these conflicts grew and the tendency towards social dislocation was undoubtedly linked with the growing opportunities available to the peripheral powers and the rebels to obtain arms and use them to challenge the reigning chiefs.

In addition, the captives which these kingdoms needed as a form of currency with which to buy rare goods and the instruments of war were being carried off at a rate which was becoming less and less compatible with the survival of the societies concerned, especially when they were seized from peoples already subject to tribute, since that depleted the reserves of the dominant powers. Due to a by no means unusual time-lag, European decisions to abolish the slave trade did not prevent it from reaching a paroxysm in the course of the nineteenth century in a number of countries on the Niger Bend and in the upper basin of the various affluents of the Volta. Emancipation by the state and reintegration into lineage groups did little to reduce the destructive effects of this scourge, which was not to abate until the end of the nineteenth century. In fact, those countries whose economies had been kept going by the 'ports of the desert' at the end of the caravan routes were now enclosed and isolated, being separated from the coast by other states, at a time when basic trading patterns were collapsing. In such circumstances they were bound, slowly but inexorably, to fall into decline.

In these circumstances, as often happens in periods of crisis, social divisions were exacerbated, transforming the relatively egalitarian structures that had been characteristic of the societies of the Sahel during their period of ascendancy. Another factor was the evolution of the religious movements which, after the tolerance towards traditional cults shown during the preceding centuries, had adopted a more intransigent attitude as a result of the *djihād*, which had triumphed in Liptako and had swept through the Bambara states. Even the Yarsé of the Mossi country, previously so flexible in both religious and political affairs, began to take up much more rigid positions and engaged in proselytism. However, the Islamic successor states were themselves ephemeral, for they were victims of the same objective conditions that had already doomed the autonomous development of the African states.

However, it should not be forgotten that, behind the disruption and dislocation of external state structures during this period, many peoples, throughout all these upheavals, which sometimes involved tragic movements of population, were tenaciously continuing to work and ensure the survival of society. This reminds us that, despite the convulsions of the societies to which they belonged, whether endogenous or caused by external factors, the ordinary people were far from prostrate, as is shown by their remarkable ability to rise to the major challenges of the period, such as the intrusion of colonialism.

Socio-economic tensions

Production and trade

During this period, to an even greater extent than is the case today, the basis of economic activity was agriculture. While statistics are lacking, we may safely estimate that 99 per cent of the population of the region in question was engaged in agriculture, especially the sedentary indigenous peoples. The small minority engaged in trade, apart from artisans, consisted mainly of groups sprung from peoples for whom commerce was a way of life, or peoples interested in conquest; some peoples, like the Joola, combined the two activities. In general terms, we may say that the coastal regions essentially imported gold and slaves and supplied European products, while the Sahel imported kola nuts and obtained weapons from the coast and exported, for the most part, salt, livestock and slaves. Between the coast and the Sahel there were intermediate savanna regions that supplied slaves and livestock, including donkeys for trade and horses for war and for princely courts, but also cereals and gold.

The abolition of the slave trade by Britain in 1807 introduced an element of structural imbalance into this situation, especially in the south, where surveillance was instituted earliest and maintained most strictly, although domestic slavery was tolerated.[48] During the second half of the nineteenth century slavery expanded very substantially, especially in the Niger bend. This was because the cost of weapons increased steadily, so that progressively greater numbers of slaves had to be offered in exchange. It is not surprising, then, to find entire groups, such as the Zamberma, specializing in the extraction of this 'black ore'. The main sources of supply, however, were not only the great *djihād* conducted by the Muslim leaders of the north and the conflicts in M̄ossi territory. The trade was also fed from a host of channels that sluiced off slaves from peoples belonging to hundreds of chieftaincies, from the territories of the Tuareg to the areas bordering the trading posts on the coast. During the final decades of the nineteenth century, war broke out in virtually every decade and in virtually every region, and war meant captives. These victims were for the most part from sedentary agricultural communities, which served as a veritable breeding stock for the trade. Hence the underpopulated areas to be found in regions that were literally drained of their inhabitants. Tribute exacted in the form of captives was extremely heavy in many instances. When indigenous peoples took action to organize their own defence, they were frequently used as mercenaries in wars elsewhere, as in the case of some

48. A. A. Boahen, 1974, p. 179.

of the Gurunsi who fought in the ranks of the Zamberma, and the Samo (Sanan) who took part in the dynastic wars of Yatenga.

Trade channels

The southern part of the region with which we are here concerned was, as we have observed, the scene of a desperate struggle by the Asante to control the European trading posts on the coast, which were of crucial importance to its survival: only if it held them could it maintain control of both ends of the trade channel. The abolition of the slave trade, which accounted for nine-tenths of the Gold Coast's exports at the beginning of the century, abruptly altered the economic situation. By 1840, however, palm oil had already succeeded the slave trade as the coast's leading export product, a development that was largely due to Maclean's policy. Palm oil was followed in the 1870s and 1880s by rubber, and both laid the foundations of structural changes in the economies of the southern Gold Coast.

While Asante and Voltaic gold moved southward for the most part, kola nuts moved northward. The more westerly routes through Kong and Buna, however, were steadily abandoned in favour of the north-eastern routes through the Dagomba and Hausa country, as Thomas Bowdich reports. Trade in the north was further stimulated by the abolition of the slave trade on the coast, the fact that the routes to the Fante country were closed from time to time, and the political stability of Hausaland and Borno after the *djihād* led by ʿU͟thmān dan Fodio. Thus it came about that luxury products from Europe moved down through North Africa, the Fezzān and the Hausa country, or even on occasion up via the Dahomey coast to Kano and onward to the Niger Bend. Silks and carpets from Turkey and Tripoli, natron from Borno, and Hausa textiles, were exchanged for kola nuts, gold, cotton materials from Dagomba, Mossi and Mande, shea butter and livestock from the Sudanese Sahel.

This accounts for the tremendous expansion of Salaga in the state of Gonja during this period.[49] That city assumed the role formerly played by Gbuipe in Gonja. Salaga was the point of departure for Yendi, Sansanne Mango and beyond, as far as the Volta, Hausa or Yoruba territories. Dupuis tells us that Salaga was twice the size of Kumasi, with a population of 400 000. Its prosperity was to continue until the collapse of Asante power, when the trade routes shifted towards Kintampo. As far as transactions were concerned, barter was the general rule, although gold dust might be used for larger deals, and also cowries, which Maclean decreed should be legal tender on the coast. At Logofiela, J. B. Kietegha discovered heaps of cowries side by side with fragments of earthenware jars, which it has proved

49. K. Arhin, 1979, ch. 3.

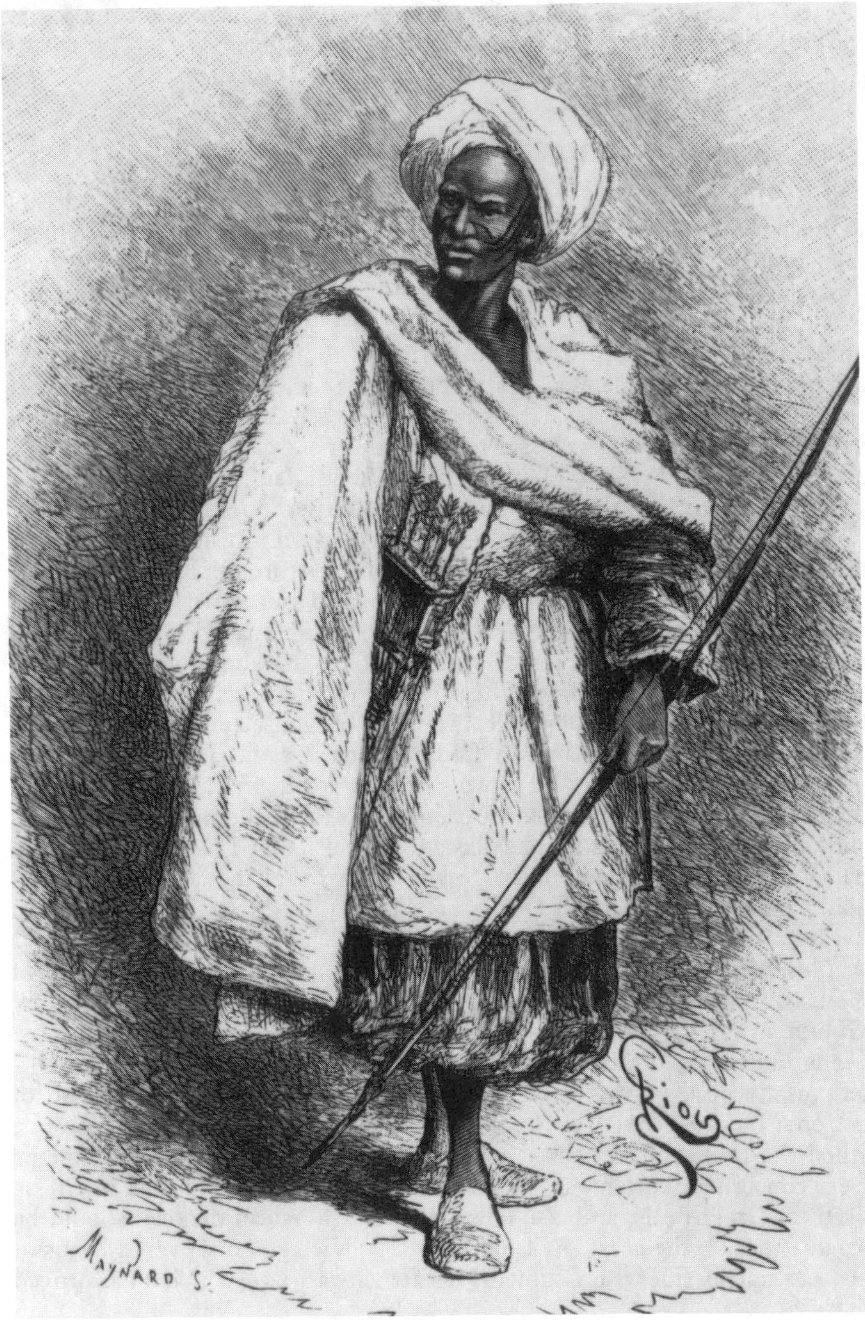

PLATE 25.7 *A Mossi merchant, 1888*

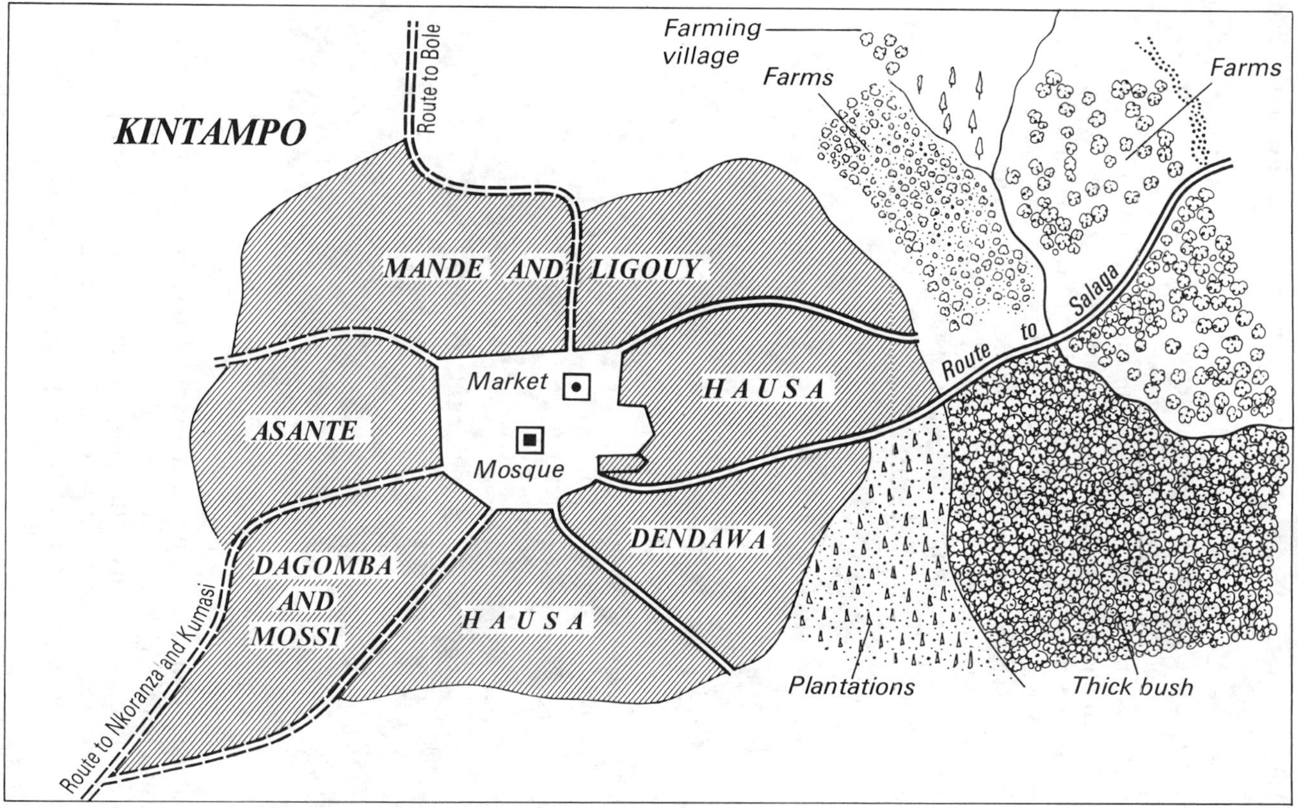

FIG. 25.2 *Kintampo: a trading town in the Gold Coast hinterland (after L. G. Singer, 1892)*

feasible to reconstitute, and which have been dug out of sites in the Pura region.[50]

Besides the Asante and Lobi gold, the left bank of the upper Black Volta witnessed, especially in the nineteenth century, an extraordinary concentration of gold diggers of various origins: Dyan, Dagara, Bobo-Joola, Bwaba and Mossi, in addition to the indigenous Gurunsi. Using only crude implements (picks, hoes, earthenware jars, calabashes and pans), they extracted the gold. As only men could 'see the gold and kill it', the system of division of labour in force assigned men the tasks of prospecting, digging, and crushing quartz, while women were responsible for ore-carrying and washing operations. By the end of the century, the proportion of slaves among such communities was substantial (sixty per family in the village of Pura).[51] The noteworthy feature here is that these were family

PLATE 25.8 *Salaga in 1888*

or individual enterprises, unrelated to any centralized state. The Zamberma invasion led the peasantry in some villages in the gold-bearing district to conceal their implements in the hills and go on to a war footing; captured men were sold for 100 000 cowries, and women captives for double that sum. In some respects, evidently, gold production and slave-hunting were

50. Small cowries, which were preferred to large ones, were exchanged for the latter at the rate of 10 000 small to 11 000 large. This led to the appearance of currency exchange operators, who made a profit of 10 per cent; cf. J. B. Kietegha, 1983, p. 185.

51. ibid.

incompatible. Armed raiding groups, however, naturally preferred slaves, since they were much more profitable[52] and in addition were also used in washing the gold. During the first half of the nineteenth century, as much as 50 kg of gold may have been produced annually in the Pura region alone.[53]

Whereas this gold was carried mainly to the Sahara and Morocco, gold from Lobi went out to the Gold Coast or Liberia. Part of the gold was hoarded in the form of dust or nuggets in bamboo stalks or pieces of cloth, hidden in attics, or buried in earthenware pots. It was carried via local and regional trade routes, sometimes to Bobo, San, Jenne and Mopti, sometimes to Kong and Asante, sometimes to Gaoua (Lobi) or Salaga via Wessa and Wa, and sometimes to Wagadugu and onward to Puytenga, Tenkodogo and Salaga. In local trade it was used to purchase salt, kola nuts, *boubous* (loose ankle-length robes), slaves, livestock and grain. According to L. G. Binger, bar salt from the desert was much more highly regarded than other kinds. It came from Taoudeni by way of Timbuktu, Mopti, Jenne, Bla and San, subsequently being distributed throughout the Sahel and the savanna country. The same was true of the salt that reached Segu by way of Adrar and Tichit. Sea salt from the coast and salt collected from the river saltpan at Daboya was carried as far as Kong. In the Volta region of the Sahel, the chiefs of Jiibo developed a cunning technique for accumulating slaves. If a slave killed someone and then gave himself up to the chief, he would be acquitted and would become the property of the latter; in cases of theft, if the thief was rich the chief would strip him of his wealth.[54] By the end of the century, the population of Dori included 50 000 free men and 50 000 captives. Yet the careful and observant traveller, Heinrich Barth, who passed through the region in 1853, says nothing about slaves in his account. This points to a substantial increase in slave-trading in the region during the second half of the century.

The network of routes spreading out from Dori is enough in itself to convey some idea of how open the Sahel was to trade from all sides. As the legislation of the empire of Massina, with its heavy taxes and its ban on tobacco, was very burdensome for Timbuktu, the merchants diverted their trade to Gao, controlled as it was by the Moors and Tuareg of whom there were so many in Dori. While the route from Kayes to Dori by way of Bamako and Bandiagara was held by the Joola, the route from Sokoto to Dori by way of Sansanne Mango was dominated by the Hausa, and the one from Wahiguya to Dori via Yako and Kaya, or from Wagadugu to Dori via Zitenga and Puytenga, was used by the Mossi. Goods imported into Dori included tobacco, matting, livestock and salt from the north,

52. To the slave-dealers, slaves are said to have been ninety times as profitable as gold, according to V. Kachinsky, quoted in ibid., p. 155.

53. J. Sagatzky, 1940, folio 5.

54. H. Diallo, 1979, p. 169.

which were exchanged for lengths of cotton, Hausa turbans and European manufactured products. Loincloths and *boubous* came from the Hausa country to be traded for livestock and salt. The slaves, lengths of cloth, worked copper and donkeys of Mossi country were exchanged for kola nuts from Asante, salt, and livestock. In return for their Guinea cloth and hardware, traders from the Joola lands took home salt and livestock. In Jiibo, which was full to overflowing with Yarse traders from Wahiguya, barter was the universal rule, whereas cowries were used in Dori. In the latter town, as a result of their activity, traders found themselves associated with the aristocratic clans, with which in some instances they were also allied by marriage. However, they inhabited their own quarters of the town, and were kept out of political life.

In the aggregate, while the activity of the traders was marginal in relation to the economy as a whole, it had a strong qualitative influence on the lives of all. To realize this, we need only recall the importance of border communities such as Begho, Kafaba, Kintampo and Atebubu, in which composite societies rapidly grew up. Gonja, Joola, Hausa, Dagomba, Asante, Fulbe, Yoruba, Dendi, Borno, Bariba, Kulango, Gurunsi and others flocked into Salaga.[55] The place became a true microcosm, in which the division of labour was carried further than was the case in the more homogeneous indigenous society: there were landowners, tenants, brokers and a variety of craftsmen.[56]

Social change

Social change arises naturally in periods of upheaval. This was true of the lands lying in the Niger Bend and the Volta basin in the nineteenth century. While we have few documents on this aspect of the historical process, it appears that social changes were greater in centralized states than in societies in which administration was decentralized, greater in the coastal regions than in the lands of the interior, and greater in Islamized areas than elsewhere. While sedentary societies that did not have a centralized power structure were the most affected by the convulsions of the time, they took refuge in fidelity to their traditional code of life as an antidote to their trials.

The situation of slaves and caste members was much worse in centralized states. The most radical upheaval was undoubtedly the one that occurred in the Fulbe groups: originally nomads under the domination of the Gulmanceba, within a few years after the *djihād* they in turn had become overlords ruling indigenous peoples, or peoples whom they had reduced to the level of commoners, captives and serfs (*bellah* or *remaibe*), condemned to the tasks of cultivation and herding. In addition, there were artisans and *griots*. It was a meticulously stratified society in which every individual had

55. L. G. Binger, quoted in M. Johnson, nd, SAL/19/1.
56. K. Arhin, 1979, ch. 3.

and knew his place. Over and above one-fifth of all plunder taken in raids,[57] the *amīr* of Liptako received gifts and a tribute on harvests that was known as the *zakāt*. Similarly, the chiefs of Jiibo received gifts at 'salutations' and levied a tax on salt for which traders were liable. Aristocrats were sometimes attended by hundreds of dependants. While the conditions of slaves improved with seniority (*rimaibe* could own property), the status of captives was to raise problems in Liptako. 'Uthmān dan Fodio himself advised the *amīr* to free slaves who had taken part in the struggle against the Gulmanceba. Furthermore in 1861 the Amīr Seeku Saalu was confronted by a slave uprising touched off by the marabout Abdul Kadiri, who aspired to seize power. The *amīr* was able to retrieve the situation only by agreeing to manumissions.

Artisans were denied the rights enjoyed by freemen and nobles, and were reduced to endogamy. While a noble could marry slave girls, he could not marry a blacksmith's daughter.[58] And yet, like the *griot*, whose verbal magic consolidated the power of the rulers and even gave him a very small share of it, the blacksmith was feared because of the magical nature of his work. He was also a mediator in conflicts between individuals and families. However, there was no shortage of subjects of tension.[59]

In the Mossi kingdom of Wagadugu, slaves were made into eunuchs in sufficiently large numbers for it to be feasible to export them northward. In Asante, the quantity of human livestock obtained by the payment of tribute was so great that when the slave trade was abolished, the Asantehene stated that he could not feed the 20 000 captives whom he had on his hands, adding, 'unless I kill or sell them, they will grow strong and kill my people'.[60]

It appears, however, that social relations between slaves and their owners were marked by less hostility in societies not having a central power structure. We are told that in the village of Pura, slaves were fed 'just like everyone else'. M. Père tells us that in the Lobi country, each submatriclan was divided into two groups: the true-born Weya, and the Dea, who were of captive origin. The latter category included people who had been adopted because they had been found at the door one morning, seeking refuge from famine or raiding. Both categories, however, were fully integrated within

57. According to strict orthodoxy, it was the *ḳāḍī* who should have received this; cf. H. Diallo, 1979, p. 274.

58. This continued to be the case in Yatenga until well into the twentieth century.

59. It is related that if a village headman was ordered to supply a horse and for the purpose took a horse belonging to a blacksmith, all the blacksmiths of Liptako, with one accord, would bring their anvils and set them down before the *amiiru*, saying, 'The land is yours, but our iron belongs to us. We shall make no more hoes, picks or lances. If the people wish, let them farm no more'. Eventually the *amiiru* would come to an agreement with the blacksmiths and give them back their horse, whereupon they would return to their villages. H. Diallo, 1979, p. 186.

60. J. Dupuis, quoted in A. Boahen, 1974, p. 179.

the social structure as sources of production and progeny. Accordingly, a slave lived in the same hut as his master, whom he addressed as 'father'; he was a member of the same kin group as the latter and was subject to the same rituals and taboos and engaged in the same work; his owner gave him a wife, he possessed a field, and was entitled to accumulate cowries to the point of buying his freedom or purchasing another man to replace him. What was required of him was that he remain in the same village as his master.[61] Here we see a clear indication of a deliberate policy of using slavery as a means of strengthening clan or territorial groups.

Other types of tension became more accentuated in the centralized states during this period, namely Asante, the Bambara kingdoms, Yatenga, the kingdom of Wagadugu and Gwiriko: all of these witnessed rivalry between the lordly or noble class and the ruler. Such a rivalry occurred in the kingdom of Wagadugu, where Mogho Naaba Karfo (1842–9) decided to distribute to the poor among the common people the property that he had confiscated from the wealthy. In dispensing justice, he was accessible to noble and commoner alike. It is highly likely that this social policy was a factor in the great rebellion of the princes that broke out in his reign at the instigation of the most important of his ministers, the Widi Naaba.

Lastly, we may mention the coastal lands, where the driving forces of trade and education were producing a qualitatively new type of social stratification. Once the basis of commercial activity had shifted from the slave trade to the exchange of palm oil, rubber, ivory and gold for European products, a new merchant class emerged, operating with stocks of trade goods advanced by European companies, whose agents they actually were. Thus began the careers of a number of great merchants with establishments in the coastal centres. At a lower level, swarms of petty dealers who played the role of door-to-door salesmen to the suppliers gravitated around the great merchants, on whom they were dependent.[62] The Asante merchants who, for their part, controlled the supply of products from the interior of Africa, namely the *akonkofo*, also constituted a factor to be reckoned with.[63]

In much the same way, in the field of education new categories, or even entire social classes, came into being along the coast. At the top of the hierarchy stood the descendants of the great merchant families, such as the Bannermans of the Gold Coast who, since the early years of the century, had been educated in Europe or at Fourah Bay College (founded in 1827) in Sierra Leone. These people were regarded as 'English gentlemen', and behaved accordingly. They were accepted in European circles and rose to positions of responsibility as magistrates, commanders of forts and the like. At the other end of the scale were the great mass of persons known ironically as 'Cape Coast scholars', who had received only rudimentary education.

61. M. Père, 1982, pp. 214 et seq.
62. B. Cruickshank, 1853, Vol. 2, pp. 30–94.
63. I. Wilks, 1975, pp. 699–705.

They were employed as clerks at wretched wages or, unemployed, were reduced to travelling about through the bush as brokers for English or African merchants. They were regarded with contempt as caricatures of English civilization, living as parasites on illiterate chiefs and their peoples. Between these two extremes stood those Africans who, without becoming highly learned, had nevertheless received a sufficiently good education to be able to become independent merchants or managers in the coastal towns.[64] In this way the bases for subsequent social contradictions were laid. Nevertheless, it should be noted that it was the cooperation between the educated entrepreneurial class that made the Fante Confederation possible.

Religious change

In this region the nineteenth century was a period of rapid advance for Islam in the north and centre, while Christianity was reintroduced in the south. More than ever these two religions were associated with the prestige of education, in the form of the ability to write, and with a much wider world than the one bounded by local horizons.

In the northern part of the region the wide influence of the *djihāds* led by eminent men (ʿUthmān Dan Fodio of Sokoto, Seku Ahmadu of Massina and al-Hadjdj ʿUmar Tal) produced powerful and lasting effects, as, for example, the *djihād* and the emirate of Liptako.

Even the Bambara and Mossi kingdoms were carried along in the wake of this uprush of Islamic proselytizing activity, or at any rate influenced by it. The Bambara and the Mossi have usually been termed 'ramparts against the expansion of Islam', but if this cliché was ever true, it certainly was not so in the nineteenth century, when Islam was a powerful force not only at the top of the social order in these kingdoms, but in every part of society. We need look no further than the kingdom of Segu under Monzon Jara early in the century; here, the ruler's mother, Makoro, made use of the services of marabouts from Segu Sikoro and Tegu to bring about a reconciliation between the king and his brother Nyanakoro Da. Monzon Jara's successor asked a learned marabout who was a friend of his for a talisman that would bring him victory. Torokoro Mari (1854–6) turned over one of his sons to al-Hadjdj ʿUmar and asked the latter to bring him up; to be sure, this induced the monarch's warriors to abandon their allegiance and drown him, explaining to his successor, 'We killed your brother because he wanted to compel us to become Muslims, and because he was squandering the state's resources by showering gifts on marabouts'.[65] In the Mossi kingdoms, the only Muslims up to that point had been the Yarsé, but early in the nineteenth century the Mogho-Naaba openly

64. P. Foster, 1965, pp. 68–9.
65. V. Monteil, 1977, p. 100.

embraced the Islamic faith and in their turn these established nuclei of missionary activity.

Naaba Dulugu of Wagadugu erected a mosque and treated the *imām* as an important person at his court. Nevertheless, as though seeking to avoid an excessively abrupt change, he exiled his son, the future Naaba Sawadogo, and deposed Pwanda, the headman of Kombissiri. These two zealots then retired to Basan-Warga and turned it into a religious base. When Naaba Sawadogo acceded to the throne, he reinstated the headman of Kombissiri, which in its turn became a hotbed of the faith, and sent his own son to the Ḳu'rān school in Sarabatenga Yarsé.

Under Naaba Karfo, the rebel Naaba Wobgho of Lallé went to the *imām* of Wagadugu and asked him to intercede on his behalf with the king. Lastly, Naaba Kutu had received an authentic Ḳu'rānic education. Abandoning the attempt to reconcile his religion with traditional ritual, he turned the practice of the latter over to his ministers, along with the administration of customary justice. He built a mosque at the eastern gate of his palace (the gate which was for women and prisoners of war), performed the duties prescribed by Islam and sent one of his sons to the Ḳu'rān school. On the other hand, he helped Naaba Peogho of Bulsa to suppress a rebellion of Muslim origin that had been fomented by the Fulbe Modibo Mamadu from Futa Jallon. The latter, who bore the title of *wālī* (or saint), disappointed at the Naaba's attitude to his efforts to make converts, unhesitatingly stirred up an insurrection, which was supported by Yarsé, Maransé (Sonrai) and Fulbe in particular. He was compelled to flee and his *talībs* (followers) were slaughtered.[66] In point of fact, as the Mossi engaged in trade in ever-growing numbers, they inevitably found themselves caught up in the process of Islamization as well. That process had been under way for a long time in the western part of the Volta basin and was continuing under the auspices of Kong, Gwiriko, Bobo Diulasso, and subsequently, for a short time, Samori Ture. The religion spread in the rather unreceptive Bwa, San, Gurunsi or Lobi environments thanks to Joola traders or Marka (Dafing) marabouts such as those of Wahabu and Lanfiera.

In the centre of the region under consideration, it was in the nineteenth century that Islam became the leading religion of Dagomba and Mamprusi, as also in Sansanne Mango. *Imāms* were religious and political figures. In Asante, Osei Kwame (1777–1801) was sympathetic to Islam; conceivably he may have been deposed for that reason. Osei Bonsu, for his part, declared, 'the book [Ḳu'rān] is strong and I like it, because it is the book of the great God'. Bowdich speaks of a thousand or so Muslims in Kumasi under the leadership of Muḥammad al-Ghamba, known as Baba, who was the son of the *imām* of Mamprusi and made good use of his position as a member of the royal council. Muslim traders from the Arab world, of course, flocked into the capital, and amulets prepared by marabouts,

66. Cf. G. Chéron, 1924, p. 653; J. Withers-Gill, 1924; N. Levtzion, 1968, p. 170.

especially battle tunics, sold for high prices.[67] Undoubtedly it is important not to exaggerate the impact of Islam on the traditional religious system of the Asante empire, which in practice was largely identified with the political structure. Nevertheless, its influence was at work, and it did its utmost to keep princes from succumbing to the Christian religion and its missionaries, as was also the case in Buganda at almost the same period.

While Christianity was to make its appearance in Timbuktu only at the end of the century with the arrival of the White Fathers, it had returned to the Gold Coast in the southern part of the region long before. The evangelical Basel Mission, followed by the Bremen Mission, were established by 1828 throughout the entire south-eastern part of the Gold Coast (on the Akuapim scarp, in Accra, Akyem, Ada, and the Ewe-speaking Keta and Peki areas). They opened model farms and technical schools.[68] Methodist missionaries, under the leadership of George Maclean, concentrated their efforts on the western coast, with Cape Coast as a base. Thomas Birch Freeman, a man of great ability, strove tirelessly to found Methodist schools throughout the interior as far as the Asante country and along the coast as far as Yorubaland.[69]

Freeman was inspired by the ideals of the Society for the Abolition of the Slave Trade and for the Civilization of Africa, the objectives of which included studying the leading languages and reducing the most important of them to writing; introducing the printing press and local paper manufacture; investigating the climates of different districts; introducing the science of medicine; building roads and canals for transport and an effective drainage system for the sake of sanitation; sharing with the Africans the most up-to-date agricultural knowledge; providing them with equipment and seed of good quality, and also advising on the best crops to produce for the world market.[70] Like the Basel Mission, they established model farms in the Cape Coast district. They admitted girls who often numbered up to three out of ten in their schools.[71] Even more impressively, with a view to removing the language barrier to evangelization, as early as the eighteenth century they had translated the basic works of Christianity into Ga. In 1875 the Reverend J. G. Christaller published a Twi grammar, and his dictionary of the Akan languages, first published in 1881, is still the best available.[72]

Despite the efforts of Christianity and Islam in the region, traditional religion continued to command the allegiance of a large majority of the

67. Cf. A. Boahen, 1974, pp. 191–4.
68. H. W. Debrunner, 1967, chs 6 and 7.
69. See T. B. Freeman, 1843.
70. H. W. Debrunner, 1967, p. 104.
71. Testimony of the Reverend J. Beecham, Proceedings of the Special Committee on Dr Madden's report, 1842, in G. Metcalfe (ed.), 1964, p. 176.
72. J. G. Christaller, 1875, 1933.

PLATE 25.8 *A Basel mission carpentry workshop in Christiansborg (Accra). Engraving from a photographic original, probably ca. 1870*

population, and in many instances survived within the new religions as well.

Conclusion

On the whole, the peoples of the lands of the Niger Bend and the Volta basin, thanks to their fratricidal internecine conflicts throughout the entire nineteenth century, paved the way for aggression from without; indeed, they invited such intervention on occasion to settle their differences. It may be suggested, however, that the seeds of that process were present in the economic contradictions touched off centuries earlier by the slave trade. Migrations and the settlement of new population groups, social tensions and even political and religious expansion are intelligible only with reference to this major phenomenon that had dominated the preceding centuries and of which the nineteenth century was at once the paroxysm and the culmination. In that sense, here as elsewhere in Africa the nineteenth century does indeed mark the end of a very long period.

26 Dahomey, Yorubaland, Borgu and Benin in the nineteenth century

A. I. ASIWAJU

The Mono–Niger area as the unit of analysis

The area covered by this chapter is the region bounded in the west by the Mono river (the present-day Benin–Togo border), in the east and north by the Niger and in the south by the Bight of Benin (Atlantic Ocean). It is mostly an undulating plain with a general rise from the coast towards the interior, where the highest altitudes are in the Atacora and Kukuru hills. The vegetation is, on the whole, open. The really dense rain-forest types are encountered principally in the south-east – that is in the area of the ancient Benin kingdom, now embraced within the Bendel state of Nigeria and to a lesser extent along the main river valleys.

The area includes a substantial part of the famous 'gap' described in West African geography: the extension of the savanna belt of the western and central Sudanic zone through the forest zone to communicate directly with the sea. The whole of the ancient Fon kingdom of Dahomey and the western half of Yorubaland as well as Borgu are located within this 'gap'. Drainage is assured by several rivers, among them the Niger, the Benin, the Ọwena, Ọṣun, Ogun, Yewa, Wẹmẹ (Ouémé on French maps), the Ọpara, the Zou and the Mono.

There are four main distinct, though evidently interrelated culture areas, comprising the Aja in the west, the Yoruba in the centre, the Borgu (pronounced Bohu) in the north and the Edo in the east. As is to be expected, each of these main culture areas is subdivided in terms of such sub-cultural traits as dialect, ecology and specific occupation. The Aja-speaking peoples[1] are in three principal sub-groups, made up of the Fon who dominated the ancient kingdom of Dahomey; the Gun of the Wẹmẹ river valley and the Porto Novo-Badagry region astride the southern end of the present-day border between Nigeria and the People's Republic of Benin (former French Dahomey); and the Ewe between the Cufo and Mono rivers in the south-western parts of the Benin Republic with the bulk of their kinsmen in the adjacent areas of southern Togo and south-

1. A. I. Asiwaju, 1979.

eastern Ghana. North and east of the Fon, concentrated on the Agbome (Abomey) plateau are the Mahi in Paouignan, Savalu, Wese, Dassa-zoume, Jaluku and Kọvẹ (Covè). This group also shares observable Aja sub-cultural traits and memories of ancestral interconnections.

The Yoruba (Nago in French ethnographic literature) culture area is by far the most extensive in the Mono–Niger region.[2] It embraces the area of the present-day Ogun, Lagos Ọyọ, and Ondo states of Nigeria and nearly a half of Kwara State, as well as the adjacent parts of the eastern Benin Republic and central Togo further west. There are numerous sub-groups ranging from the small-size category, illustrated by the Ifẹ, organized into a single kingdom, or the Ẹkiti type organized into several autonomous monarchies. Within the Nigerian region, the main Yoruba sub-groups are the Ọyọ (the most numerous single sub-group, with land and people shared between the Ọyọ and Kwara states); Ibarapa astride the boundary between the Ọyọ and Ogun states; the Ifẹ and Ijẹṣa located within Ọyọ State; the Ijẹbu shared between the Ogun and Lagos states, the Ẹgba and Ẹgbado in Ogun State; the Ondo, Ikale, Ẹkiti, Ọwọ and Akoko in Ondo State; and the Awori and related Ẹgbado sub-groups in Lagos State. Straddling the Nigeria–Benin international boundary are, from north to south, the Ṣabẹ (Savé), the Ketu, the Ọhọri (Holli), the Ifọnyin and the Anago sub-groups. To this already long list must be added the Ana, Fẹ (Ifẹ) and Mayinbiri (Manigri) in the middle latitudes of the Benin Republic and the Atakpame area of Togo.

Like Yorubaland, Borgu is today an internationally partitioned culture area.[3] Busa and Illo (two of the three main traditional power centres) are situated mostly in the area of the present-day Borgu local government area of Kwara State and adjacent parts of the Sokoto State of Nigeria, while Nikki, the third and territorially the largest traditional state, was split by the present-day Nigeria–Benin border such that Nikki and the western half of the traditional state were located on the Benin side of the border and the rest of the area of the kingdom on what became the Nigerian side of the border.

The sub-cultural divisions more or less reflect the traditional socio-political sub-groupings and levels of differentiation. As Marjorie Stewart has correctly observed, Borgu emerged, presumably late in the fifteenth century, as a conglomerate of politically independent states with the main power centres in Busa, Nikki and Illo. The early formation of these states would appear to have resulted from the merger of an incoming group, most probably Mande-speaking from Mali, and some pre-existing people to form a new state and distinctive culture. This view has some support in the traditions of origin of the Borgu states and appears borne out by the fact that there are two major languages spoken in Borgu: Batonu (also

2. D. Forde, 1951; J. Bertho, 1949; E. G. Parrinder, 1947, 1955; P. Mercier, 1950.
3. O. Bagodo, 1979; M. Stewart, forthcoming

PLATE 26.1 *Carving of a warrior on the shoulders of a* babalawo *(medicine man) from north-eastern Yorubaland (probably) carved between 1850 and 1875*

referred to variously as Baruba, Bariba, Barba), a Voltaic language spoken by the vast majority of the masses, and Boko (also called Zugwenu), a south-eastern division of the Mande languages spoken by the ruling class, or the *Wasạngari*.

Each of these two main languages is divided into several distinct dialects. Boko, for example, is spoken in four main dialects; Boko-Busa (Bisagwe), spoken at Busa and Wawa; Boko-Nikki in Nikki, Segbana and Kandi in the Benin Republic and Nikki-related chiefdoms such as Yeshikera, Kaiama, Sandiru, Ilesa Bariba, Aliyara and Okuta in Nigeria; and Tienga or Kienga spoken in Illo, Dekala and northern Aliyara District. The linguistic unity of Borgu is achieved through bilingualism, which bridges the gap between the masses and their traditional ruling classes. The cultural unity, indicated in language use, is cemented by the traditions of common origin of the kingdoms and the common acknowledgement of Busa as the ancestral home of all Borgu rulers.

The fourth major culture area of the region is that of the Edo-speaking people of the Benin kingdom.[4] These include not only the Edo of Benin City and metropolitan area. There are also the linguistically and historically related Ishan (Esan) Ivbiosakan and Akoko Edo in the north and the Itsekiri, Urhobo and Isoko to the south and south-east.

These four major culture areas were not isolated zones. Indeed, by the beginning of the nineteenth century, the extent of the cultural or ethnic interpenetrations had been such as to indicate the evolution of a single discernible culture complex of which the Yoruba, the Aja, the Borgu and the Edo can be regarded as sub-systems. Quite apart from the ideology of unity, emphasized in traditions of common origin, which seeks to link at least the traditional ruling classes in the four cultural sub-units, there were observable linguistic and other cultural as well as economic and political factors of inter-group relations in the region concerned. These linkages, emphasized in several studies,[5] point to successive migrations and resultant population movements and counter-movements which continued into the nineteenth century until formally discouraged by the establishment of territorially structured European colonial states characterized by exclusive borders. The history of the region from the Mono to the Niger is therefore best conceived as an account of the interpenetration, not only between and among the Aja, the Yoruba, the Bariba and the Edo, but also between them individually and severally and such neighbours as the Nupe, the Jukun, the Kanuri, the Gbari, the Hausa and the Fulbe (Fulani) to the north; the Ewe, the Ga, the Adangbe, the Krobo and the Fante to the west; and the

4. R. E. Bradbury, 1957; A. F. C. Ryder, 1969.

5. The Kisra traditions of origin link the Yoruba with Borgu, Ife is the accepted ancestral home of all Yoruba and Benin monarchs, and the Aja also claim remote origin from Ife. See F. de Medeiros, 1984; I. A. Akinjogbin and G. O. Ekemode (eds), 1976.

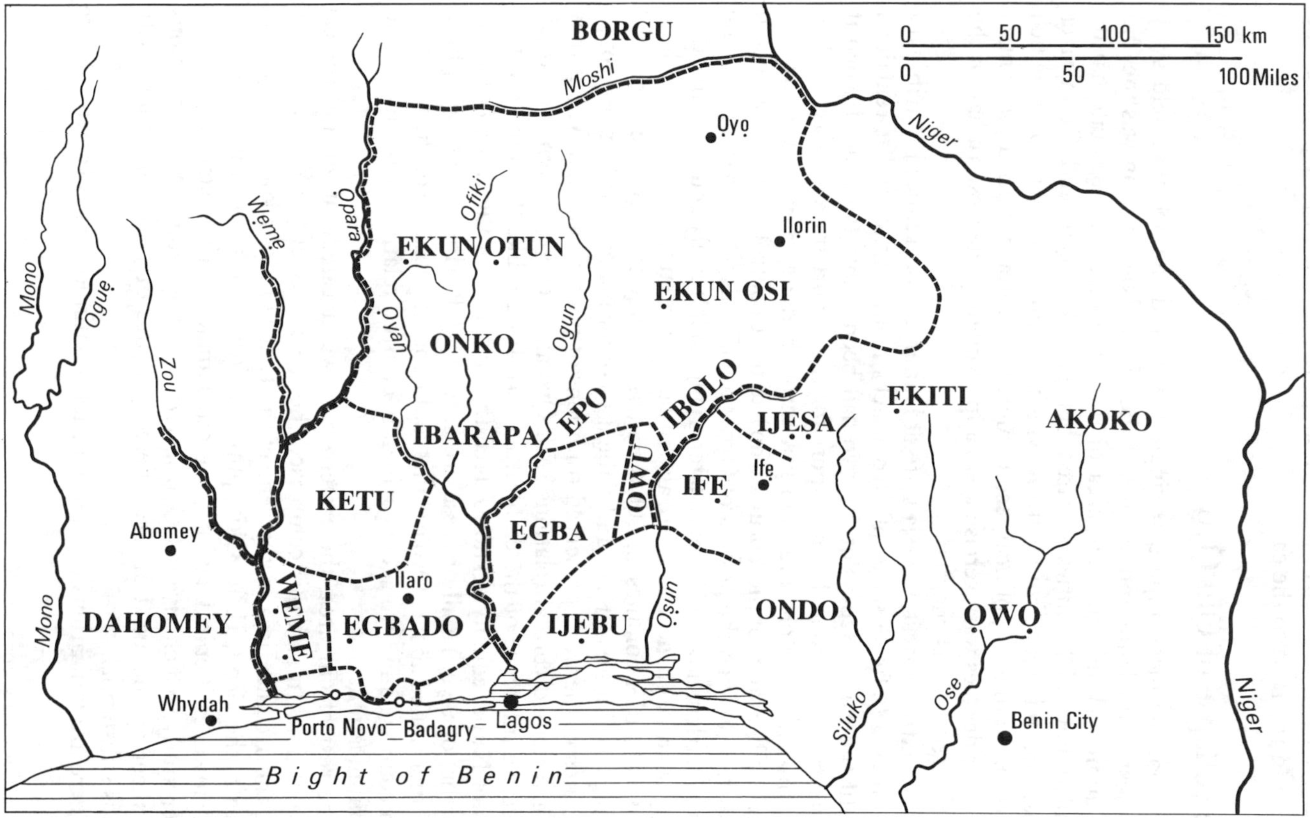

FIG. 26.1 *Yoruba-Aja country showing the Old Oyo Empire (early nineteenth century)*
Source: J. F. Ade Ajayi and M Crowder (eds.), *History of West Africa*, Longman, 1974, p. 131

Ijo, the Itsekiri, the Isoko, the Urhobo, the western Igbo, the Igala, the Igbira and the Basa to the east.

The collapse of Old Ọyọ

In *c.* 1800, the most important single power and the one that held sway over most of the lands and peoples of the Mono–Niger region was the Old Ọyọ empire.[6] While the core area of this renowned Yoruba state hardly extended beyond localities situated between the Ọṣun and Ogun river basins, the territory from within which tribute came and over which discernible military, political, economic and cultural influence or control of varying degrees was exercised was approximately the western half of the area covered by this chapter.

In the extreme west, the Aja state of Dahomey was reduced to tributary status in 1748 after a series of Ọyọ attacks from *c.* 1740, and it remained so until the early 1820s; Porto Novo had been similarly reduced when it was secured by Ọyọ as its main port for the export trade in slaves.[7] The route linking this port and Ọyọ ran through the areas of the Ẹgba and Ẹgbado sub-groups of the Yoruba who had to be controlled by Ọyọ imperial authorities through the posting of Ọyọ state officials (*ajẹlẹ*) to such strategic Ẹgbado settlements as Ilaro and, later, Ijanna. Culturally and economically, the Ẹgba and Ẹgbado areas were also intensely penetrated by the Ọyọ: there were Ọyọ settler colonies and Ọyọ traders actively engaged in commercial activities in the area.[8] Ketu and Ṣabẹ, two other major Yoruba sub-groups and states in the west, preserved traditions of political autonomy, but they also maintained cordial relations with Ọyọ and benefited from the overall protective influence of the empire. Eastern Borgu, like the south-western parts of Nupe, equally acknowledged the authority of the *alafin* (king and emperor) of Ọyọ. In all of these areas, which fell within the geographical 'gap' mentioned above, Ọyọ cavalry could operate because of the relatively open country, and Ọyọ agents evidently enjoyed relatively easy access and communication.

The rest of our area, the eastern half, was located within the tropical forest region. In part this comprised the remainder of the Yoruba culture area, the Ifẹ and Ijẹṣa in the centre; the Ekiti, Ondo, Akoko and Ọwọ in the east; the Ijẹbu, Ikale, Okiti-pupa and Awori to the south. There was also, however, Benin kingdom, the other major African state in the area under study, which rivalled Ọyọ in terms of the extent of its hegemony and sheer splendour. But, even here, evidence of vital connections with Ọyọ is substantial.

There are indications of a more or less continuous involvement of Ọyọ

6. R. C. C. Law, 1977.
7. P. Morton-Williams, 1964.
8. H. Clapperton, 1829; R. Lander, 1830.

PLATE 26.2 *The Gateway of the Ijebu Yoruba town of Ipara, c. 1855. (Church mission of Gleaver 1855)*

in the history of Ifẹ, Ijeṣa, Ekiti, Ondo and Ijẹbu. In addition to traditions recorded by Samuel Johnson,[9] there is the view expressed by S. A. Akintoye that 'at various times and to varying degrees, the Ekiti, Ijẹṣa and Igbomina also came under Ọyọ influence'.[10] While there is no evidence to support Peter Morton-Williams's suggestion that the Ekiti, Ijẹṣa and Akoko might have served as 'slave reservoirs' for the Ọyọ empire,[11] there are convincing proofs of Ọyọ military pressures on the Ijẹṣa which the Ijẹṣa successfully repulsed. The foundation of Ẹdẹ by Ọyọ and of Oṣogbo by the Ijẹṣa has been explained in terms of the need for the two Yoruba states to establish military outposts to keep a watch on each other. The subsequent relations between these two neighbouring communities constituted a measure of the eventual interpenetration of the two Yoruba sub-cultures.

Ọyọ–Benin relations are even more impressively recorded.[12] The ruling dynasties in both claim common origin not only from Ifẹ but even from the same founder, Ọranyan. Both, therefore, maintained ritual links with Ifẹ. This fraternal feeling would appear to have been sustained by the minimal opportunities for friction between the two states; Ọyọ power was

9. S. Johnson, 1921.
10. S. A. Akintoye, 1971, pp. 29–30.
11. ibid., P. Morton-Williams, 1964.
12. J. F. A. Ajayi in J. F. A. Ajayi and M. Crowder (eds), 1974.

based on cavalry forces and confined more or less to the relatively open country to the west and north-west of the area under study, while Benin military tactics were only suited to operations in the proverbial 'evergreen forest' of the eastern half. Because of this difference in ecology, the trading activities of the two states were also complementary.

The main point of outlining these details is to make it clear that Old Ọyọ was so much at the centre of the history of the entire region from the Mono to the Niger that its collapse in the third decade of the nineteenth century was bound to produce socio-political vibrations not just in Yorubaland but also in Dahomey, Borgu and in the area of the Benin kingdom. As J. F. A. Ajayi put it, the 'collapse of the Old Ọyọ empire ... had important consequences for the Aja-speaking peoples to the west as well as for the Benin empire to the east.'[13] It marked the beginning of a more or less continuous period of warfare and generalized insecurity in the region under review. The inevitable adverse effects on European trade along the coast of the Bight of Benin created local conditions favourable to rival interventions by Britain, France and, eventually, Germany in the politics of the region.

It is impossible and perhaps unnecessary[14] to recount here details of the collapse of the Ọyọ empire. Suffice it to point out that as in the case of other similarly well-established and long-lived states, this was not a sudden affair. The signs of decline were already visible in the eighteenth century; and they steadily intensified in the first two decades of the nineteenth.

Internal factors which manifested themselves so clearly in the struggle for power between successive *alafins* and the lineage chiefs, beginning in the second half of the eighteenth century, became progressively complicated by the effects of externally based stimuli deriving from the decline of the overseas slave trade and, more significantly,the southward extension of the *djihād* of 'Uthmān dan Fodio.

Already in the eighteenth century, paradoxically also the era of Ọyọ's greatest expansion and the zenith of its power, the empire had begun to show itself to be a deteriorating structure and militarily and territorially vulnerable. The rebellion which the Ẹgba successfully staged under Liṣabi, their legendary hero, in *c.* 1774, was followed by the defeat of the Ọyọ army by Borgu and Nupe in 1783 and 1791 respectively. The collapse of the empire in *c.* 1835 followed a period of complete deterioration of the internal political situation featuring a series of short-lived and largely unsuccessful *alafin*s including Aole and Maku and ending in a protracted interregnum of close to two decades.

The revolt of Afonja, the *arẹ-ọna-hakanfo*, or commander-in-chief of

13. J. F. A. Ajayi, p. 129.

14. For further details see J. F. A. Ajayi, 1974; R. Law, 1977; J. F. A. Ajayi and S. A. Akintoye, 1980; I. A. Akinjogbin, 1965.

the Ọyọ army, who with the assistance of the Muslims among the Ọyọ Yoruba tried to declare himself an independent ruler at Ilọrin, ushered in the last phase. The *Djama'a*, the troops that Afonja's Yoruba Muslim supporters gathered in his support soon became a force beyond his own control. Al-Ṣāliḥ Alimi, the Fulbe itinerant Muslim teacher and mystic whom Afonja had allied with to prosecute his successful revolt against the *alafin*'s authority, gained control of the *Djama'a* and Afonja was eventually liquidated by the force. It was Alimi's son and successor, Abdul Salaam, who established Ilọrin's independence vis-à-vis Ọyọ. After he had obtained the blessing of the Sokoto caliphate and become the first amīr of Ilọrin, he turned Ilọrin from its former status as 'a rebellious province of Ọyọ into a frontier post of the Fulani jihād.'[15]

The effects of the collapse of Ọyọ were felt most sharply in the western half of the area, where the impact of the empire had been greatest and most direct. In the main there was a situation of generalized warfare and attendant insecurity for more or less the whole of the remainder of the century. This had the ultimate effect of disrupting trade on the coast and encouraging the intervention of Europeans in the politics of the interior. Here again, this is an aspect of history that has been well researched and for which there are readily available publications. What is required here, therefore, is a summary.

The *djihād* of 'Uthmān dan Fodio, which was extended to Ilọrin as a result of the crisis in Old Ọyọ, spread in other directions, including Borgu and the closely related north-western Yoruba state of Ṣabẹ and the adjacent Aja-speaking area.[16] There are also indications of raiding activities in northern Ẹgbado communities by elements locally perceived as supporters of the Fulbe *djihād*.[17] The Fulbe menace produced a situation in which the Borgu states characteristically closed ranks against common external enemies. An alliance between Borgu and Ọyọ resulted in a desperate but ill-fated attempt to confront the Fulbe in the Eleduwẹ War of 1836. The threat of continued expansion of the Sokoto caliphate into central Yorubaland south of Ilọrin was not stemmed until its decisive defeat at Oṣogbo in 1840.

More devastating, however, than these *djihād* wars were the ones that the Yoruba fought among themselves. These may be subdivided into three major phases; the Owu War of *c.* 1820–5, the Ijaye War of 1860–5, and the sixteen-year Ekitiparapọ or Kiriji War of 1877–93.[18] The Owu War was principally a conflict over the control of Apomu market between the Ifẹ allied with Ijẹbu on the one hand and the Owu allegedly supported by their Ẹgba neighbours on the other. The Ifẹ-Ijẹbu allies were assisted by

15. J. F. A. Ajayi, 1974, p. 144.
16. D. Ross, 1967.
17. A. I. Asiwaju, 1976.
18. J. F. A. Ajayi and R. S. Smith, 1964; S. A. Akintoye, 1971; B. Awe, 1964.

Ọyọ warriors who formed part of the large number of refugees who had been moving southwards following the troubles in Old Ọyọ.

The Owu war led to the destruction of Owu and the displacement of the entire original Ẹgba communities from the historical Ẹgba forest to

PLATE 26.3 *A view of Ibadan in 1854 with the Church Missionary Society compound in the foreground*

territories to the south and west. The foundation of Ibadan as a camp dominated by the victorious warriors at Owu in *c.* 1829 and of Abẹokuta as an Ẹgba refugee camp in *c.* 1830 has been credited to the aftermath of this war. The establishment of Ijaye under Kurumi and the re-establishment of the Ọyọ empire with a new capital at Agọ-Ọja (the present-day Ọyọ, some 50 km north of Ibadan) by Alafin Atiba were also events of the late 1820s and early 1830s. The new settlements rapidly grew into new power bases in Yorubaland, each vying for recognition and succession to the political leadership which had been rendered vacant, as it were, by the disappearance of Old Ọyọ. The Ijaye War, a contest mainly between Ijaye allied with Abẹokuta on the one hand and Ibadan on the other is best understood as a major example of this struggle for leadership. Although the destruction of Ijaye in 1862 marked the climax, the ripple effects continued until the final battles in Ikorodu in 1865.[19] The Ekitiparapọ, as the name denotes, was a grand anti-Ibadan alliance of the Ekiti, the Ijẹṣa and the Igbomina, whom Ibadan had conquered and integrated into its emergent empire following the victory over Ijaye.[20]

19. J. F. A. Ajayi and R. S. Smith, 1964, p. 120.
20. B. Awe, 1964.

The rise of Dahomey as an autonomous kingdom in the early 1820s and, thereafter, its frequent incursions into Yorubaland in the remaining years of the nineteenth century up to the French conquest in 1892 were all direct effects of the disappearance of Old Ọyọ.[21] With an area of jurisdiction extending from the Wẹmẹ river in the east to the Cufo river in the west and from the Atlantic Ocean to latitude 7°N, the kingdom of Dahomey in *c.* 1800 approximated to the southern third of the present-day People's Republic of Benin.

Although independence from Ọyọ had been the policy of all Dahomey monarchs, beginning with Kpengla (1774–89), it was not until the opening years of the reign of Gezo (1818–58) that the Ọyọ imperial yoke was repudiated. In spite of occasional disruptions and violence in the Agbome court, as can be illustrated by the regicide of Agonglo (Kpengla's son and successor) in 1797 and the deposition of Adandozan (1797–1818) in favour of Gezo (his junior brother), Dahomey in contrast to Old Ọyọ in the eighteenth and nineteenth centuries was remarkable for the appreciably long reigns of its kings.

Political stability was further guaranteed by the successful operation of the highly centralized administration for which the kingdom is well known. The European anti-slave trade movement hit the state's economy, based as it was almost solely on the slave trade. However, Gezo's economic policy was to continue to respond to the demand for slaves from Portuguese dealers while at the same time responding to the stimulus of the export trade in palm oil as the ultimate substitute for slave exports.[22] These signs of the relative political and economic strength of Dahomey were becoming visible at the same time as symptoms of advanced decline were becoming increasingly apparent in Old Ọyọ. It was the combination of these factors that ostensibly encouraged Gezo to stage a unilateral declaration of independence in the early 1820s.

It has been customary to state that Ọyọ responded to this development by sending an expeditionary force under one Balogun Ajanaku but that the Ọyọ army was routed by Dahomey. The truth, rather, seems to be that Ọyọ in the 1820s was hardly in any position to send any worthwhile army to deal with a rebellion in a place as distant as Dahomey. Research has, in fact, shown that rather than being an official Ọyọ army, the force that Ajanaku led against Dahomey in the early 1820s was more probably a joint Ṣabẹ-Ketu affair.[23] It was made up of Yoruba and Mahi troops and Ajanaku himself, although often described as a *balogun* (warlord) of Ọyọ, has been more reliably reported by local Fon traditions to have been an indigene of Sabe. This military initiative fell within the familiar pattern of military

21. D. Ross, 1967; K. Folayan, 1967; S. O. Biobaku, 1957.

22. For a recent study of the economic policy of the autonomous kingdom of Dahomey, see E. Soumoni, 1983.

23. D. Ross, 1967, pp. 37–40.

alliances which Yoruba and related communities, who had enjoyed the protection of Old Ọyọ vis-à-vis Dahomey, came to form to defend themselves and conduct pre-emptive attacks against their common enemy once Ọyọ was no more.[24] In any case, Ajanaku's men were defeated and he himself was captured and executed by Gezo.

Thus began the series of systematic invasions of Yorubaland by Dahomey. Motivated by considerations of state security and by the insatiable demand for slaves for export, for labour for both cash crop and subsistence agriculture for the state and for the purpose of human sacrifice at the well-known annual customs, the invasion affected not only the Yoruba west of the Ogun river. Equally affected were the Aja and Manhi communities and states east of the Wẹmẹ river, including Porto Novo.[25]

While the invasion of the Mahi immediately north of Agbome and of Porto Novo in the south-east was carried out in the 1820s, in the 1830s the concentration was on such Ẹgbado towns as Ijanna and Refurefu, which were razed to the ground in 1831 and 1836 respectively. Ijanna, as noted above, was the residence of the Ọyọ imperial agent and the main centre for collecting and forwarding tributes from the Ẹgbado and neighbouring area. In the 1840s and again in the 1880s, Okeọdan and Ṣabẹ were ravaged. Also in the latter decade, the kingdom of Ketu, which began to be harassed in the late 1870s, was finally destroyed in 1886, four years after Imẹkọ, the one other major town within the kingdom, had been burnt down.

In the 1850s and 1860s, an important target was the new Ẹgba-Yoruba state of Abẹokuta whose rise was viewed in Agbome as a threat to the independence of Dahomey. This danger became real with Ẹgba military activities and associated political expansion into the areas of western Yorubaland where Dahomey was also conducting its raids. The clash between the two in the Awori town of Ado-Odo in 1844 and the eventual defeat of Dahomey, sowed the seeds of future acrimony between the two. Although the two direct attacks that Dahomey conducted against Abẹokuta in 1851 and 1864 met with resounding failure, the punitive expedition against Ẹgbado allies of the Ẹgba led to the destruction of Iṣaga in 1862 and the attendant devastation of the surrounding area. Dahomeyan raids against the Yoruba in the upper reaches of the Ogun river continued into the late 1880s and early 1890s and were, in fact, not terminated until the defeat of the Fon kingdom by the French in 1892.

The Dahomey wars of the nineteenth century, like the other wars of the period, were not necessarily inter-ethnic conflicts. This point is easily proved not only by the Dahomey invasion of Aja communities in the Wẹmẹ river valley but also by the devastating war against Porto Novo in the late 1880s and early 1890s following the breakdown of an accord that was

24. Other similar alliances in the nineteenth century included the one between Ketu and Ohori, and between Okeọdan and Ipokia. See A.I. Asiwaju, 1976.

25. A. I. Asiwaju, 1979; T. Moulero, 1966.

reached shortly after the invasions of the 1820s and that had for decades thereafter guaranteed peaceful relations between the two Aja states and their satellites.

The nineteenth-century wars in the western half of the area from the Mono to the Niger produced far-reaching population shifts and demographic changes. First was the massive enslavement and shipment of Yoruba and related Aja populations to the Americas and, when intercepted by anti-slavery squadrons, Sierra Leone. Within the affected West African localities themselves, socio-political changes of revolutionary character also took place, occasioned by the massive movements of population.[26] In Yorubaland, the wars led to large-scale destruction of pre-nineteenth century settlements, the foundation of a whole series of new towns and considerable enlargement of existing ones. In the area of Old Ọyọ, which exemplified the huge loss of population involved, established towns including the ancient Ọyọ city itself, Igboho, Ikoyi, Igbọn, Irẹsa and Oje were destroyed. Beyond that, other Yoruba towns destroyed included Ṣabẹ, Ketu, Owu and a whole series of Ẹgba and related Rẹmọ communities. This created the phenomenon of 'ruined cities' noted by travellers in nineteenth-century Yorubaland. There was a general movement of population from the troubled interior in the north towards the south. New settlements included Ibadan, Abẹokuta, Ṣagamu, Oke-Ọdan and Aiyede. The coast and its immediate hinterland, which in *c.* 1800 was generally sparsely populated, became an area of teeming population at the close of the period.

In the Aja-speaking area, the general direction of population movement was south-eastward. In the nineteenth century, Aja refugees from the Wẹmẹ river valley and the Porto Novo region swelled the ranks of related communities that had earlier settled in the adjacent parts of the present-day Lagos State and Ogun State of Nigeria following the Dahomeyan conquest of the coastal Aja states of Allada and Whydah in 1724 and 1727 respectively.[27] This extension of the Aja culture area eastwards was a significant contribution of the nineteenth-century wars to ethnic interpenetration in the area under study.

The wars and their social effects culminated in the development of a new society; and this gave rise to the need to fashion new methods and styles of government. The new situation made for the emergence of warriors as the dominant class and the eclipsing of the pre-existing monarchical class. This is particularly true of the Yoruba area where the *ọba*s lost control to the *balogun*s or warlords. The experiments with military dictatorship in Ijaiye under Kurumi, federalism in Abẹokuta under Ṣodẹkẹ and constitutional monarchy in Ẹpẹ under Kosọkọ illustrate the efforts in nineteenth-century Yorubaland to fashion new constitutions appropriate for

26. P. Verger, 1955, pp. 3–11; C. Fyfe, 1962, pp. 292–3.
27. A. I. Asiwaju, 1979.

the political management of the new society generated by the wars.[28] The eventual adoption in the twentieth century of the Yoruba-style *ọba*-ship institution by some of the Aja communities within the Nigerian region exemplified the continuing nature of this cultural adaptation process.[29]

The decline of the Benin kingdom

Because of the unique strength of its monarchy and the resistance of its centralized institutions, Benin was spared the Ọyọ experience of actual collapse before the era of European conquest. However, the kingdom could not be said to have escaped the destructive influences of the nineteenth century.[30]

By *c.* 1800 the kingdom consisted of the area approximating more or less to the eastern half of the Mono–Niger region east of a line drawn north–south from Ọtun in Ekiti to the coast. The area embraced the eastern Yoruba states of Ẹkiti, Ondo and Ọwọ, the western Igbo communities west of the Niger delta; the Urhobo, Itsekiri and the Ijọ in the south. Although the Edo of Benin City and the metropolitan area constituted the core of the kingdom, the other Edo-speaking peoples such as the Esan and the northern Edo in the north-east and the Urhobo and Isoko to the south-east may be considered the immediate outer ring of the area of jurisdiction of the Bini monarch. Further afield, Benin influence, if not suzerainty, was acknowledged all along the Atlantic coast as far west as Lagos and beyond. As with the Itsekiri, there was a widely acknowledged dynastic relationship between Benin and the ruling elites in most Awori-Yoruba and related Anago chiefdoms where (as in Ẹkiti, Ọwọ and Ondo) there is still visible evidence of the Benin impact on titles and court ceremonials.[31]

Benin is usually portrayed as having been in continuous decline in the eighteenth and nineteenth centuries. However, while recent research has shown that this decline was far from being continuous and was often punctuated by periods of revival and territorial expansion, there seems little doubt that in the three or four decades immediately preceding the loss of independence, the Benin kingdom underwent radical contraction because of a three-sided assault on its territory. The Fulbe *djihād*, which had knocked Old Ọyọ off its feet, also penetrated the northern and north-eastern part of the Benin kingdom. While the Fulbe, based in Nupe, forced such northern Edo groups as the Esan and Ivbiosakon to pay tribute to the emir of Bida and to be accessible for Islamic proselytization, the *Djama'a* from Ilọrin raided into the northern Ẹkiti states. The Fulbe menace was aggravated by the eastward expansion of Ibadan, whose wars of conquest were again carried into the Benin domains in eastern Yoru-

28. G. O. Oguntomisin, 1979; J. A. Atanda, 1984.
29. A. I. Asiwaju, 1979, pp. 22–3.
30. R. E. Bradbury, 1967; O. Ikime, 1980b.
31. A. I. Asiwaju, 1976, pp. 18–19.

PLATE 26.4 *Shrine altar in the king's compound, Benin*

baland. The fact that Benin was unable to send assistance to these harassed vassal states was demonstration enough of the evil days that had beset this famous West African forest state.

Finally, there was the menace posed by European penetration, both through Lagos, the most important centre in the area of Benin influence along the coast, and up the Niger river in the south-east. The Benin kingdom began to feel the embarrassment of this development when its trading privileges in the coastal trade, especially its control over the commerce on the Benin river in the western Niger delta, came to be challenged by European traders, mostly British, and the African middlemen, especially the Itsekiri and the Ijọ. The eclipse of the Benin port of Ughoton demonstrated quite painfully to Benin that the days of its near monopoly of coastal trade had ended.

The coastal trade encouraged the spirit of political autonomy among the Itsekiri. This eventually led to a situation of war between the Olu of Warri and the *ọba* of Benin, and the new wealth also nourished political conflicts within the Warri kingdom itself. There was, for example, so much rivalry and acrimony, so many succession disputes, protest migrations and the setting up of autonomous and rival power centres that for the rest of the century no generally acceptable successor could be found for the stool of the Olu of Warri when Akengbua, the incumbent from 1809, died in 1848. As with the Itsekiri kingdom, Agbor, whose monarchy had also been organized on the Benin model and operated as a Benin dependency, grew steadily into an autonomous state again largely under the influence of the new coastal trade. Ovonramwen, the last Oba of independent Benin, was determined to reinvigorate the kingdom and this policy included an expedition against Agbor with a view to re-asserting Benin authority there. The effort was, however, belated; the Benin expeditionary force against Agbor was just taking position at Obadan when the British expeditionary force against Benin itself was reported to be nearing the gate of the capital in 1897.[32]

PLATE 26.5 *A view of Benin city at the time of the British invasion, 1897*

While the kingdom faced assaults from outside, the metropolis itself was far from calm. The obaship experienced considerable instability largely as a result of succession disputes. Although Ọba Osemwede, who died in 1851, was succeeded by Adolo, this was not before the eruption of a violent succession scuffle. The intensification of human sacrifice in Benin City from the late 1880s has been interpreted by some as evidence of the desperation of the rulers seeking ritual solution to the political problem of an imminent collapse. Ọba Ovonranwen is reported to have faced the active opposition of Orokhorho, his own brother, and such leading chiefs as the Eriko, Oburaye, Obazelu and Osia. These chiefs had to be executed as part of the *ọba's* determination to strengthen his own position and achieve a revival of the kingdom. The anti-European mood in Benin in the 1890s

32. O. Ikime, 1980b.

before the British conquest must be measured against this desperate internal situation.

The growth of European interest

In discussing the growth of European interest in the area of West Africa under review, it is useful to distinguish between two phases: that of freedom of movement for the European powers involved up to 1861 when Lagos was annexed to the British Crown, and the succeeding era of international rivalry between France and Britain with Germany entering the competition in the 1880s. This latter phase terminated only with the partition of the area between Britain and France in 1889. In all this, however, the point to emphasize is that the pattern of European activities at any particular time in the region was as much in response to the European metropolitan demands as to the stimulus of the local situation.

In the earlier phase European traders, explorers or travellers and Christian missionaries operated in Africa without much concern for the national identities of the individual agents. A famous German explorer like Heinrich Barth served 'an official British expedition', while a British explorer of the calibre of H. M. Stanley was in the service of King Leopold of Belgium. Major Christian missionary bodies such as the Church Missionary Society (CMS) of the Church of England and the Lyons-based Société des Missions Africaines (SMA) of the Roman Catholic Church each employed a mix of European nationals. Father Boghero, who led the SMA in an effort to re-introduce Roman Catholic Christianity to West Africa in the nineteenth century, was an Italian. The pioneer SMA Fathers in most parts of the area which became Nigeria were French, just as it was such British missionaries as Thomas Birch Freeman of the Methodists and Samuel Ajayi Crowther of the CMS who pioneered the work of Christian missions in what was to become French Dahomey (present-day People's Republic of Benin).[33] British, French, German and Portuguese traders set up businesses adjacent to one another and, as the case of Badagry clearly demonstrated, there were residential quarters for diverse European nationals in the major ports all along the coast of the Bight of Benin.

Traders moved back and forth between the coastal ports in search of the most favourable terms of trade, and according to the varying fortunes of the ports and the states whose economies came to depend increasingly on the coastal trade.

This flexibility in the composition and activities of the different categories of Europeans harmonized with a similar flexibility in the pre-existing local African situation characterized, as we have seen, more by a historically and culturally interlocking pattern and networks than by any rigidly structured

33. A. O. Makozi and G. J. A. Ojo, 1982; E. G. Parrinder, 1967.

differentiations. The movement of European traders, travellers and missionaries was dictated largely by the abolitionist movement.

It was realized that the slave trade could only be effectively stopped at the source of supply in the African interior. European exploration of the interior, illustrated in the area under study by the works of Mungo Park, Hugh Clapperton and the Lander brothers, was aimed at collecting both scientific and intelligence information primarily for the use of the abolitionist movement. Missionaries normally followed or accompanied the explorers for the same reason. Of course, the new trend was also influenced by the ambition of European traders to reach interior markets directly rather than continue to treat with the middlemen along the coast.

All these European activities had to reckon with the local African situation in which they operated. The European explorers, missionaries and traders were obliged to operate within the pre-existing transportation and communication systems, and the pattern of geographical and ethnographical inter-relationships. Mungo Park met his death in a canoe accident on the Niger, an age-old traditional transportation system, on the rapids at a point near Busa in Borgu. In their search for the source of the Niger river Hugh Clapperton and the Landers used an ancient overland route that connected different sub-groups of the Yoruba and their Aja-speaking neighbours. This route also linked Yorubaland with Borgu, Hausaland, Borno and beyond. The Christian missionary journeys across the wide expanse of Yorubaland from north to south and east to west and between Yorubaland and Dahomey were made possible because the necessary interconnecting routes already existed.

Because the lands and peoples were so interwoven, developments in one part always had effects and implications in other parts. European abolitionists found, for example, that to stop the slave trade and the wars in the interior, they had to reckon not just with the coastal rulers but also with the different power bases in the interior. Both British and French abolitionist missions from different parts of the Lower Guinea coast commonly had to visit Dahomey kings at Agbome in the first half of the century. To mediate in the Dahomey–Yoruba wars, visits had to be arranged to both Abẹokuta and Agbome. Similarly, British peacemakers involved in resolving aspects of nineteenth-century Yoruba warfare had to travel virtually throughout the length and breadth of the culture area.

Unfortunately, the European approach was divisive, tending towards politically structured differentiation. This was already noticeable in the late 1840s and early 1850s. The appointment in 1849 of John Beecroft as British Consul for the Bights of Benin and Bonny (formerly Biafra) signalled the dawn of a new era. British interests came to be specifically protected vis-à-vis the interest of other European nationals; British interests were also advanced against those of Africans. We have already drawn attention to the penetration of the Benin kingdom from the Niger delta and the resultant whittling down of Benin's trading hinterland to the extent of the eventual abandonment of Ughoton, Benin's traditional port. Further west, suspicion of British political intentions grew in 1851 when Lagos was bombarded by the anti-slave trade squadron.

The events that marked the real turning point, however, were the formal annexation of Lagos to the British Crown in 1861 and a British naval action against Porto Novo later the same year.[34] These two British actions naturally sensitized the French, who had considerable commercial interests in Whydah and Porto Novo. Encouraged by Porto Novo itself, a French protectorate was declared over this coastal Aja state in 1863 to check further British advance along the coast to the west. Both the British and the French soon discovered the obvious: that the real value of Lagos or Porto Novo was to be measured in terms of the trade with the hinterland in the Yoruba and Aja interior which the two ports shared. This involvement of both Britain and France in the trade and politics of Lagos and Porto Novo respectively sparked off a spell of dramatic rivalry between the two powers in a bid to control Yorubaland, especially the western parts, and the adjacent Aja-speaking communities. In this Anglo-French rivalry, western Yorubaland became the main theatre because of the positive response of the local peoples, who saw in the European interventions the solution to the problem of the continuous invasion of their area by their more powerful neighbours.

Thus as early as the 1860s, at a time when the French and British governments were generally opposed to colonial acquisitions in Africa, the special circumstances of this particular African locality had already involved the two most active European nations in a struggle for territorial possession. The Anglo-French convention of August 1863 actually agreed on a partition of the area between the two powers, with the Yewa river, about 20 km west of what became the border in 1889, as the agreed boundary. The French and British declarations of protectorates in the area between 1862 and 1863 did not enjoy official ratification and had to be abandoned in the 1870s. But the struggle was resumed again in the 1880s, partly because of the entry of Germany into the race and partly because of renewed invasions by Dahomey which increased the determination of the rulers of Porto Novo and the states of western Yorubaland to seek protection from the French or the British. The French conquest of Dahomey in 1892, the Anglo-French Partition of Borgu in 1895, the extension of British rule over the rest of Yorubaland and their conquest of Benin in 1897 must be seen as the logical conclusion of the Anglo-French rivalry of the 1860s, itself provoked by the pre-existing unities of the hinterland of the ports the European powers tried to control on the coast.

34. C. W. Newbury, 1961; A. I. Asiwaju, 1976.

Socio-economic change and institutional adaptation

In spite of their dramatic character, the wars of the nineteenth century and the resultant European intervention in the politics of the Mono–Niger region must not be stressed at the expense of the more far-reaching though subtle changes going on within the societies themselves. First were the effects of the massive population movements, both within and beyond the region, to which we have drawn attention. The forced migrations furthered the interpenetration and mixing of the ethnic and sub-ethnic groups. They led to the growth of new settlements within the region as well as an increased influx of slaves and the resultant rise in the population of Africans in the Americas notably in Bahia in Brazil. This influx of slaves from this region into the New World eventually became an important factor in modernizing the Mono–Niger area when the 'Saros' and 'Amaros' (Brazilians) returned and Christian missionaries arrived.

As noted above, there was a marked west–east trend in the migration of Aja-speaking peoples, especially in the second half of the nineteenth century when Dahomey renewed its invasion of Gun and Yoruba states and communities east of the Wẹmẹ river valley. This led not only to an increase in the size of existing eastern Aja settlements such as Badagry, Ajido and Koga; it also brought about the creation of numerous new settlements in the western and south-western parts of the area of the present-day Lagos State and Ogun State of Nigeria.[35]

A similar colonization movement was in evidence further east. In Yorubaland, for example, there was a remarkable interpenetration and mixing of the several sub-ethnic groups. Here the most spectacular effect was produced by the Ọyọ, whose diaspora began in the first two decades of the century when the forces of instability were unleashed on the capital of the old empire. By 1830, the main centres in which Ọyọ migrants settled had included Ibadan, Ijaye and present-day Ọyọ town, north of Ibadan. However, it was Ibadan imperialist expansion between the 1840s and 1860s that led to the full flowering of the Ọyọ diaspora. As a result, several Ọyọ communities moving in from the north-west were established among the Igbomina, Ijẹṣa, Ẹkiti, Akoko, Ondo, Ikalẹ and Ilajẹ sub-culture areas of eastern and south-eastern Yorubaland.[36] Conversely, eastern Yoruba groups such as the Ẹkiti and Ijẹṣa came as captives or freedmen to Ibadan and several other settlements in Ọṣun, Ijẹbu and the Ẹgba areas in the west and south. In Borgu the Fulbe *djihād* brought about a population movement southwards into the Yoruba culture area comparable with that of the late sixteenth century when the fall of Songhay caused a similar pressure by the Mande from the north.[37] The nineteenth-century movements streng-

35. A. I. Asiwaju, 1979.
36. S. A. Akintoye, 1971, pp. 213ff.
37. T. Moulero, 1964; A. I. Asiwaju, 1973.

thened the existing network of interpenetration between Borgu and such north-western Yoruba communities as the Ọyọ, Ṣabẹ and Ketu.

The mixing of ethnic and sub-ethnic groups resulted in considerable mutual exchange of ideas and material culture. We have already observed that the twentieth-century development that allowed the Aja in the area of the present-day Badagry local government area of Lagos State in Nigeria to adopt the Yoruba *ọba*-ship institution must be traced to the nineteenth-century and pre-nineteenth century migrations and resultant adoption of Yoruba institutions by the Aja. Similarly, Ọyọ cultural influences found in eastern Yorubaland – worship of Ṣango, the spread of the men's loom, shoulder sling drums – must be considered not so much as evidence of Ọyọ hegemony before 1800 as of the nineteenth-century diaspora of the Ọyọ following the fall of the empire.[38]

A similar influence from Benin, especially on court ceremonials, regalia and chieftaincy titles in Ọwọ, Ẹkiti, Akoko, Ondo, Ijẹṣa – as among the Awori astride the present-day Nigeria–Benin border – showed the widespread effect of the theme of inter-group penetration and commensurate institutional adaptation. That such Benin cultural influence on the Yoruba has its demographic dimension is clearly reflected in traditions of Benin settlements in the Yoruba areas in question. The socio-political impact of Benin on other Edo-speaking peoples as well as the Itsekiri, the Urhobo, and the Isoko to the east and north of Benin has been much more systematically studied.[39]

Above all, the nineteenth century witnessed the foundation of the modern settlement pattern in which location along or close to the coast conferred great advantages: witness, for example, the heightened status of Warri vis-à-vis Benin, Lagos vis-à-vis the rest of Yorubaland, Porto Novo, Whydah and, most spectacular of all, Cotonou on the Aja coast. The period also anticipated the new society of the later colonial and post-colonial period, characterized by a closer association, if not integration, within the Western European economy and culture.

The new changes resulted from a combination of factors, including the nineteenth-century wars which, as in Yorubaland, had the effect of rendering the coastal areas relatively safe and attractive to migration from the hinterlands in which most of the fighting took place; the sea-borne trade which was rendered permanent by the transition from slave to 'legitimate' trade, thereby conferring a definite economic advantage on the coastal regions; and the steady growth of European interest, which enlarged the traditional role of selected coastal towns such as Lagos, Porto Novo and eventually Cotonou to take on new and increasing responsibilities not only as ports but also as political capitals of emergent colonial states and their independent African successors.

38. J. F. A. Ajayi, 1974.
39. S. A. Akintoye, 1969; A. I. Asiwaju, 1976.

In all these changes, however, the economic factor would appear to have been the most dominant, especially with reference to the European presence. Trade, above all, brought the European to Africa and has remained the most important consideration for his continued stay. The nineteenth century was especially critical because of the change in the established pattern brought about by the abolition of the export trade in slaves, which had dominated transactions for over three centuries. Known in European records of the pre-abolition era as 'the Slave Coast', this area of West Africa was among those most involved in the slave trade; and the relatively smooth transition to 'legitimate' trade must ultimately be credited to the adaptive capacity of the indigenous societies.

In this regard, there is, perhaps, no better illustration than the case of Dahomey, traditionally considered to be the most persistent slave-raiding and slave-trading state in West Africa. Although the British anti-slave trade squadron had succeeded in stamping out the overseas trade in slaves along the coast of Porto Novo by 1851, Whydah, the Dahomey port, did not really cease to export slaves until the abolition of slavery in Brazil in 1888.[40] This Dahomey indulgence turned the Aja coast, especially the stretch between the Wẹmẹ and the Mono into favourable spots for the settlement of Portuguese (mostly Brazilian) slavers, who had been chased out of such ports as Lagos and Badagry where the British anti-slave trade measures took effect much earlier. Dahomey continued with the slave trade for as long as there were customers.

Indeed, the Dahomey authorities could not appreciate the demand which several British and French abolitionist delegations made on them to stop the trade, given the willingness of the Brazil-based Portuguese dealers to continue transacting the business in Dahomey ports.

Nevertheless, Dahomey realized that changes were taking place. Its adjustment to changing times was noticeable from the mid-century when, under the influence of a French trading firm, Victor Régis, King Gezo (*c*. 1818–58) of Dahomey was persuaded to intensify the trade in palm oil, first as a supplement to the export of slaves and eventually as the dominant factor in the state's export economy.[41] The transition from slave to 'legitimate' trade meant a corresponding increase in the need to retain war captives as labour for the maintenance and expansion of the palm oil industry. Slaves also came to be used more for transporting goods from the interior to the coast and vice-versa than as commodities for export. By the time of the French conquest of 1892–4, the foundation of Dahomey's new economy – the monoculture of palm produce – had already been laid. Developments in Dahomey mirrored those in other parts of the Mono–Niger region where, as in Yorubaland, war captives who otherwise would

40. E. Soumoni, 1983; P. Verger, 1976.
41. E. Soumoni, 1983.

PLATE 26.6 *Statue of a standing man probably representing King Gezo 1818–58*

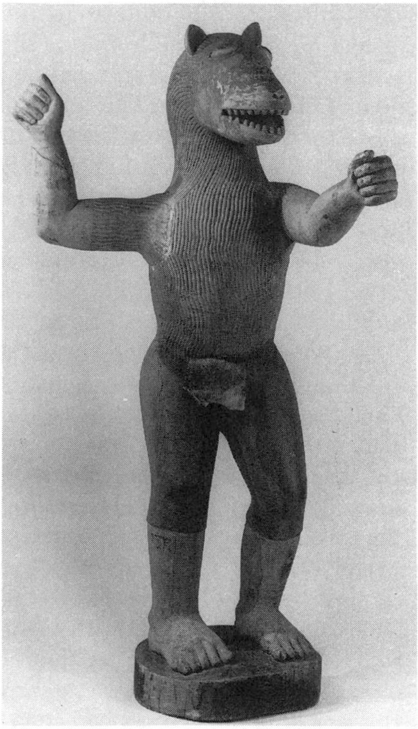

PLATE 26.7 *King Glélé (1858–89) symbolically represented as a lion*

have been sold for export overseas came to be used extensively as labour on farm plantations, or for transporting trade goods to and from the coast.

The abolitionist movement produced other far-reaching consequences for the area; of these, perhaps the most significant were those concerned with the modernization process. In this regard, obviously the most important single factor was the return of liberated slaves, 'Saros' from Sierra Leone and the 'Amaros' or 'Brazilians' mostly from Bahia but also from Cuba and other parts of the West Indies. Apart from being the factor that originally attracted European Christian missionaries, whose role in the Gulf of Guinea as modernizers is well known,[42] the liberated Africans initially played the critical role of the first-generation middle class. Having been subjected to what has been described as 'the hard school of slavery',[43] the liberated Africans returning from Sierra Leone were 'already fashioned

42. J. E. A. Ajayi, 1965; E. A. Ayandele, 1966.
43. A. B. Aderibigbe, 1959, p. 174.

elites' with a considerable attachment to cultural models of contemporary Victorian England, while among their Brazilian counterparts were artisans, traders, mechanics and 'trained cultivators of the soil'. Among them were pioneers not only in the Christian ministry, as illustrated by such celebrities as Bishop Samuel Ajayi Crowther and Reverend James Johnson (otherwise known as Holy Johnson) in the Nigerian region, but also many other less famous individuals who worked on African languages, printing, publishing, building and other occupations.

Although they first settled along the coast in such locations as Whydah, Agwe, Porto Novo, Badagry and Lagos, their influence and impact spread far into the Yoruba and Aja hinterlands and beyond. Indeed in Yorubaland, Abẹokuta rather than Lagos was the centre for the diaspora of the 'Saros', and Brazilian architecture, a major feature of the Brazilian presence in nineteenth century Lagos, was known to have spread also to Ijẹbu Ode, Ibadan and Ileṣa. There was no formal division or partition between Saros and Brazilians as to where either or both could settle on the Gulf of Benin: some Saros lived and worked in Porto Novo and further west[44] while in the Lagos Colony British policy especially under Alfred Moloney (Governor on several occasions between 1878 and 1890) was expressly favourable to the settlement of 'Brazilians'. Nevertheless, cultural and historical factors dictated a differentiation with regards to areas of actual concentration and overall impact. Thus, the predominantly Protestant anglophone Saros came to be more characteristic of the area east of the Wẹmẹ river valley which, by the close of our period, had emerged as the zone of Anglo-Saxon colonial influence and eventual control.

In the west, the predominantly Catholic and lusophone Brazilian Africans initially found a more congenial cultural environment in Porto Novo and Whydah, where they had been preceded by an older 'Brazilian' community founded by Brazilian Portuguese slavers who had to withdraw entirely to the Aja coast in consequence of the British anti-slave trade naval action further east. The eventual substitution of French for Portuguese control of the area of the Gulf of Benin west of the Wẹmẹ still left a residue of Latin culture sufficient to make Brazilians prefer this to the eastern coast, where Latin cultural influence was destined for eventual extinction. Consequently, it was in the area that eventually became French Dahomey – that is the western parts of the region under discussion – that Brazilian Africans made their greatest impact. Not only did they co-operate with the French in the latter's successful bid to conquer Dahomey and create their new colony: Brazilians also ranked first and foremost in the colony in taking full advantage of French colonial education, thus making them a crucial factor in the growth of Dahomey as the 'Quartier Latin of French West Africa'.[45]

44. P. Verger, 1976, pp. 536–7.
45. D. d'Almeida, 1973, Chs 1 and 2.

However, this dichotomy in the locational focus of the impact of Saros and Brazilians must not be interpreted as contradictory to the overall development of the Mono–Niger region as an integral whole. Strong feelings of community based on specific kinship ties and general historical and cultural affinities among descendants of the da Silvas, the d'Almeidas, the Dos Regos, the de Souzas, the Pedros, the Martins, the Pereiras and so on, whether in Lagos, Whydah, Agwe or Porto Novo, warn against such interpretations. Indeed, the continuous recognition to this day of the relationship between West African Brazilian families and their original Brazilian bases, particularly those in the state of Bahia, makes the Brazilian connection an illustrious example of the essential unity not only of the history of Africa but also of the vital communication between the continent and the black diaspora.

27 The Niger delta and the Cameroon region

E. J. ALAGOA *with contributions on the Cameroon by* **L. Z. ELANGO** *and on Gabon by* **M. METEGUE N'NAH**

Introduction

This study deals with that portion of coastland in the Bight of Benin and the Bight of Bonny, formerly called Biafra, lying between the estuary of the Benin river on the west and the estuary of the Ogowe basin to the east. The greater part of the coastal region from the west comprising the creeks and swamplands of the Niger delta, is occupied by the Ijọ, although the small Itsekiri kingdom in the western extremity of the Niger delta also exercised influence over wide areas of the delta. To the immediate western hinterland of this region was the dominating polity of Benin and various groups related to that kingdom by political or cultural affiliation. The great Igbo hinterland lies astride the north of the Niger delta, spreading across both shores of the Niger river on its lower course. Igboland is most extensive to the east of the Niger, spreading to the northern reaches of the Cross river basin.

East of the Niger delta lies the Cross river, whose estuary was dominated in the nineteenth century by the Efik state of Calabar. The rest of the Cross river valley was and is populated mostly by various Ibibio groups, and in the northern sectors by various Bantu-related groups. The fourth sub-region is that of the Cameroon coast and its hinterland to the east of the Cross river valley. The fifth sub-region is the basin of the Ogowe and the surrounding regions of Equatorial Guinea and Gabon.

All the peoples of the region were related from prehistoric times, being all members of the Niger-Congo linguistic family.[1] The Igbo and other peoples of the Niger delta periphery were of the Kwa sub-family, while the peoples of the Cross river valley and most of the peoples of what is now Cameroon and Equatorial Guinea belonged together to the Bantu. The Ijo of the Niger delta formed a distinct sub-family.

Early relationships evidenced by linguistic similarities and attested by traditions of origin and migrations were reinforced by contact through

1. J.H. Greenberg, 1966.

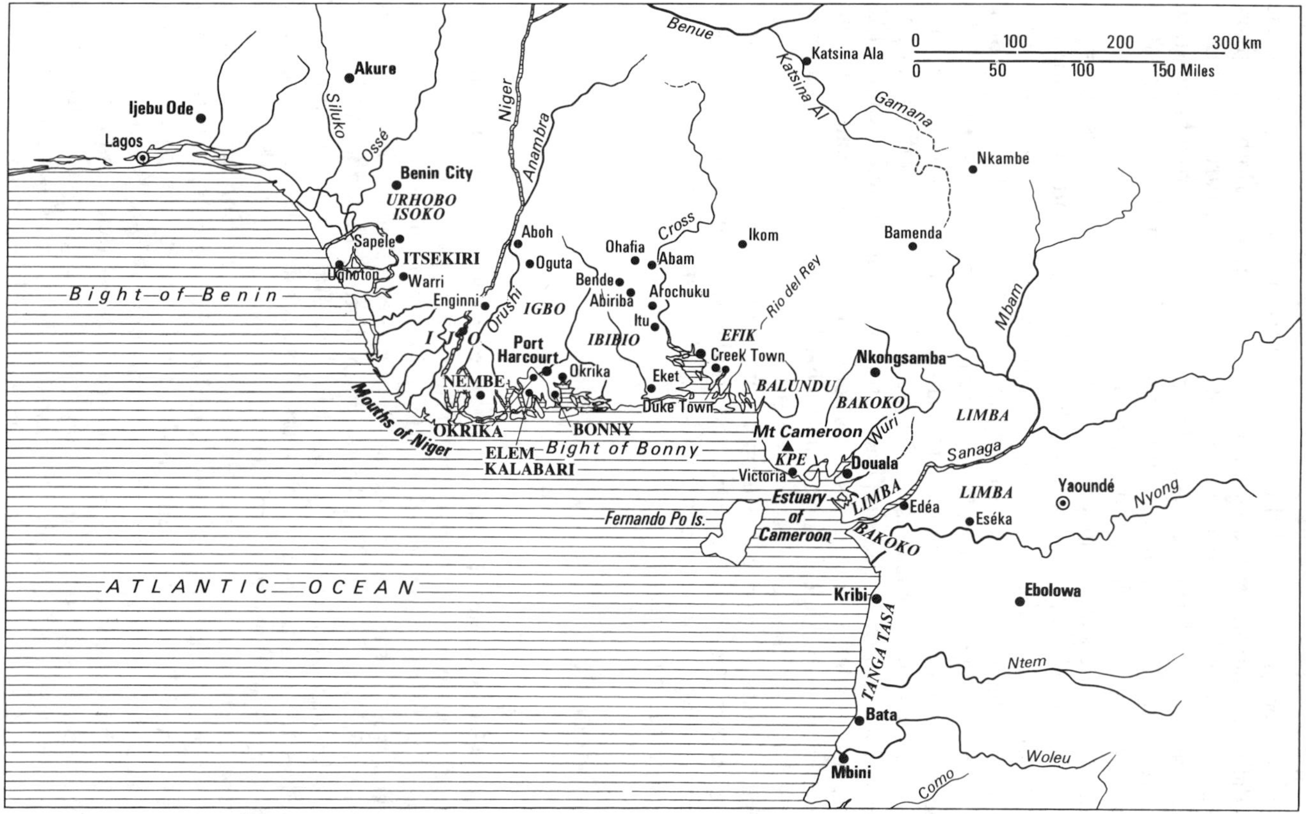

FIG. 27.1 *Niger delta and the Cameroons in the nineteenth century (after E. J. Alagoa)*

trade in the nineteenth century.[2] Trade routes established before the nineteenth century traversed the Niger delta from east to west, and to the hinterland, to join other routes stretching to the north. Both the Niger, the Cross river and other major rivers of the region were arteries of trade linking peoples along their courses, and receiving goods brought down to them from inland routes such as those passing from the Cross river valley to the Cameroon hinterland and south to the coast.

European traders along the coast, and gradually up the rivers, made use of the long-established centres of trade on the coast, and received goods brought down from the hinterland. Accordingly, the European presence on the coast became another unifying factor in the history of the region, presenting common problems and stimuli to change. Thus, each of the communities in the region underwent changes or adaptations in their social, political or cultural structures in the face of the external influences and challenge of European intrusion. The factors of European activity included: (1) the slave trade and the effects of its abolition in the nineteenth century; (2) the change to trade in local produce in place of slaves, sometimes referred to as legitimate trade; (3) the entry of Christian missionaries into the region, and (4) the onset of European imperialism and colonial conquest. These factors then, must be analysed in the study of each of the sub-regions in order to obtain a general idea of the history of the whole region in the nineteenth century.

The Niger delta

The western delta

The Itsekiri kingdom of Warri (Ode Itsekiri) was the most important political and commercial centre within the western delta from the fifteenth century to the early nineteenth century. The more numerous Ijọ to the east and west of the Itsekiri did not develop centralized polities of a size to offer effective competition. In the immediate hinterland, the Urhobo and Isoko were also largely organized in decentralized communities, and served as the producers and suppliers of slaves and, later, palm oil and palm kernels to the Itsekiri middlemen. However, up to the nineteenth century, the Itsekiri kingdom itself was known to the European visitors as merely a 'principality' of the Benin kingdom. Accordingly, early traders to the western delta usually went up the Benin river to the port of Gwato (Ughoton) where they dealt with the agents of the *ọba* of Benin.

From about the late seventeenth century, direct Benin influence began to fade in the western delta, and European traders began to use ports within the Niger delta on the Benin, Escravos, and Forcados estuaries. By the beginning of the nineteenth century, several Itsekiri chiefs had moved from

2. E. J. Alagoa, 1970; R. Harris, 1972; E. M. Chilver, 1961.

PLATE 27.1 *An Itsekiri village on the Benin river in the 1890s*

Warri (Ode Itsekiri) to establish trading posts on the Benin estuary, and soon the Benin port of Gwato (Ughoton) ceased to be a centre of the overseas trade. Throughout the nineteenth century, then, the Itsekiri were the effective leaders in the trade of the western delta, and Benin had to receive supplies of European goods through them.[3] Benin tried to maintain political dominance over the Itsekiri kingdom, and demanded a form of tribute in trade goods from the Olu of Warri, on pain of the closure of the hinterland trade routes. However, Olu Akengbuwa was able to defy the *ọba* of Benin, to the extent of giving asylum to a dissident Benin chief. But when Akengbuwa died in 1848, his subjects believed him a victim of the *ọba*'s curse, which was also thought to have kept the Itsekiri without a ruler from 1848 to 1936.

Olu Akengbuwa used agents called 'Governors of the River' stationed at the estuary of the Benin river to collect duties from the European traders, and fix prices for produce. At the beginning of the nineteenth century, the most senior chiefs such as the *iyatsere* (war captain) and the *uwangue* (chief spokesman and custodian of the regalia) served as governors of the river. But in the 1840s, Akengbuwa appointed his own sons. Accordingly, after 1848, there was no clear procedure for appointment to this office and the British consuls and traders intervened in the numerous disputes. Thus they installed Diare in 1851, and removed his successor, Tsanomi in 1879 for his attempts to force the British traders to pay fair prices for palm oil.

3. P. C. Lloyd, 1963; O. Ikime, 1968; A. F. C. Ryder, 1961.

Nana Olomu, the last and best known governor of the Benin river (1884–94) had to fight a violent war with British marines before being captured and exiled to Calabar in 1894 as one of the victims of the British imperial conquest of Nigeria.

PLATE 27.2 *Nana Olomu of Itsekiri*

The Ijọ of the western delta were in control of most of the waterways. Since they could not gain direct contact with the visiting European traders, they resorted to piracy and harassment of Itsekiri and European vessels. But some Ijọ communities carried on internal trade with the Itsekiri and others. The Itsekiri supplied clay pots to such Ijọ communities as the Gbaramatu and Bassan, and also sold salt to traders from the eastern delta who took it up the Niger. The Egbema and Olodiama Ijọ in the forest region on the upper reaches of the Benin river also made canoes and collected dyewoods for sale in the lagoon areas to the west in the Ijẹbu country, and as far as Lagos (Eko). They obtained local cloth in exchange from the Ijẹbu. Other Ijọ exchanged dried fish and salt, which was manufactured by the Itsekiri, with the Urhobo, Isoko, and Igbo groups along the periphery of the Niger delta and along the lower Niger.

In the nineteenth century, the western delta did not become as important as the eastern delta as a centre for the overseas trade in slaves, palm oil and palm kernels. Thus, in the 1840s there were only two British firms trading at the ports of Bobi and Jakpa followed by three others in the following decade. The first British consul to the Bights of Benin and Bonny in 1849, John Beecroft, settled at Fernando Po, close to the Cameroon coast and the eastern Niger delta. It was only in 1891 that a vice-consul was sent to the inland port of Sapele in the western delta to monitor the penetration of the Nigerian hinterland in this area. By this time, the scramble for African territories had started, and Nana Olomu had to fight to try to stop them. The missionaries followed the flag in the western delta.

The eastern delta

The Ijọ groups in the eastern delta developed state institutions based on a number of cities or population centres, such as Nembe, Bonny, Elem Kalabari, and Okrika.[4] These states, named city-states by K. O. Dike,[5] had developed their peculiar institutions from a common model of the decentralized Ijọ communities of the western and central delta in response to a variety of challenges: (1) different ecological conditions of the mangrove swamps of the eastern delta; (2) the long-distance trade with the Igbo hinterland, exchanging fish and salt for yams, slaves and other produce; and (3) trade with the western delta in salt, pottery, cassava products and canoes.

In these states, the operation of the internal long-distance trade as well as the Atlantic slave trade was in the hands of the political leaders, the kings or *amanyanabo*, and the House Heads (leaders of the lineage-type political units or *wari*, of which the cities were composed). The open criteria for advancement within the House system made for easy recruitment of new members from slaves or refugees.

4. R. Horton, 1969; E. J. Alagoa, 1971a.
5. K. O. Dike, 1956.

This pre-nineteenth-century baseline of the eastern delta states is important for a proper understanding of the effects on them of the increasing impact of European influence and intervention in the nineteenth century. It is the differences in the baseline that determined the differences in the effects of the similar external influences on the delta states and on Calabar and the Cameroon coast.

The decision to abolish the slave trade by Britain in 1807 was an important factor for change. Efforts to effect stoppage of the trade led to new activities by British traders, consuls, and naval officers, resulting in new relationships with the delta states. First, it led to an increased British presence in the Bight of Bonny. For example, in 1827 a naval squadron was stationed at Fernando Po, and in 1849, the first British consul, John Beecroft, was appointed for the entire territories of the Bights of Benin and Bonny. The Court of Mixed Commissions was also set up at Freetown, Sierra Leone, to try the captains of captured slave ships, and to set free the slaves of condemned slavers. For the delta states, these developments meant the demonstration of British power in their waters, bringing the era of gunboat diplomacy in which the British consuls used naval power to negotiate favourable conditions for British traders, missionaries, and explorers. In practice, the consuls, especially after 1850, continued and stepped up a policy started in the 1830s by Edward Nicolls, Governor of Fernando Po, of signing treaties with the local chiefs.[6] These treaties stipulated the stoppage of the slave trade by the rulers; the adoption of 'legitimate trade', that is, trade in goods other than slaves; laid down regulations for the conduct of legitimate trade; specified the sums of customs duties or *comey* to be paid by the traders, as well as subsidies that the British government was to pay the local rulers for their agreement to give up the slave trade.

These British activities on the coast gradually eroded the power of the local rulers, especially when the consuls and naval officers assisted the British traders to set up their own judicial systems over and above the law of the local states, the so-called Courts of Equity, composed mainly of British traders with the participation of a few local House Heads or chiefs. These courts were, naturally, under the control of the British, and not of the local rulers.

In addition to the British consuls and naval officers on the coast, British traders and missionaries tried to get into the hinterland, for example, by sponsoring voyages of exploration. Many decades of British efforts to discover the course and sources of the Niger river were crowned with success when Richard and John Lander were brought from Aboh to Nembe (Brass) by its ruler, King Boy Amain, in 1830. Once the estuaries of the many rivers of the Niger delta were shown to be the entrance to the great Niger river, British interest was greatly increased in the area as a highway

6. G. I. Jones, 1963, pp. 221–42: E. J. Alagoa and A. Fombo, 1972, pp. 90–121.

into the rich interior of Nigeria and West Africa. British traders, such as Macgregor Laird, as well as humanitarians and missionaries tried to move up the delta into the hinterland between the 1830s and 1850s.

In the eastern delta itself, the Church Missionary Society under the leadership of the Nigerian ex-slave, Bishop Samuel Ajayi Crowther, established missions at Bonny in 1864, at Twon-Brass in the Nembe kingdom in 1868, at Elem Kalabari (New Calabar in the documents) in 1874, and at Okrika in 1880. Both at Bonny and Nembe, the rulers invited the missionaries for a number of reasons. Some wished to have the missionaries establish schools in which their children could learn to read, write and speak English in order to carry on their commercial relations with British firms. It was also believed that permission for the missionaries would lead to better relations with the British government, represented by the consuls and naval officers, and serve to strengthen them against neighbouring states in internal power struggles. These same reasons sometimes led to the missionaries being rejected in other parts of the eastern delta. Thus, once the Church Missionary Society was established at Bonny, Jaja of Opobo, who had broken away from Bonny in 1869 to form his state of Opobo, would have nothing to do with that mission. The establishment of Christian missions was, however, resisted by powerful interests within each of the delta states, and Christianity constituted a factor of social instability in the nineteenth century. Dike considered that Christianity turned the slaves into revolutionaries who created upheavals in these states; but recent research has discovered other social and political factors to explain the problems of the delta states in the nineteenth century.[7]

The roots of the social problems in the delta states may be traced to the difficulties the ruling groups faced in changing from an economy based on the slave trade to one based on palm produce. Those settlements established during the slave trade were unaware of the strength of the external forces behind the abolitionist movement, and could not wholly commit themselves to a new and difficult trade commodity. A switch meant changing old trade habits and methods, and dealing with a new set of white traders. Internally too, it was more difficult to process palm oil, and to crack the palm nuts to obtain the kernels than to organize slave supply. For the delta merchants, it meant having to penetrate deeper into the hinterland to the centres of production, and the use of a larger labour force and canoes. It was a situation with the potential for making the old established leaders bankrupt, and encouraging the rise of new enterprising ones. Three major developments flowed from this: first, the new trade led to an increase in the internal slave trade to supply the manpower requirements of the delta states; second, the growth of new Houses and Heads resulted in the disturbance of the

7. K. O. Dike, 1956, especially ch. V, pp. 153–65; E. J. Alagoa, 1971b; G. I. Jones, 1963, pp. 121–32, 160–1.

PLATE 27.3 *King Jaja of Opobo*

internal political balance (Dike's slave revolts) and, third, competition for the hinterland markets led to several wars between the delta states.

The introduction of slaves into the delta communities had begun long before the nineteenth century, and each of the states already had procedures for integrating the new recruits into the community. The numbers required to be integrated increased in the nineteenth century but, in most of the states, new and more drastic methods were used to acculturate purchased slaves. In almost every delta state, a new slave had his hair ritually shaved, in the manner of a new-born baby, to symbolize his rebirth into the community. From thenceforth, he became the child of a senior member of the purchasing chief's household. Such a slave thus acquired the full rights of membership of a House unit, and could rise in the hierarchy according to his ability, even to be its Head. Membership of the mask-dancing society of *Ekine* or *Sekiapu* quickly acculturated such men in the folklore and language. In some states, such as Elem Kalabari, there were vigilante groups known as *Koronogbo*, which terrorized persons who did not acculturate fully or quickly. In such circumstances, slaves did not have the corporate and separate identity or suffer such discrimination as to dispose them to seek to revolt, or to be able to do so successfully.

However, the recruitment of slave manpower for the palm-oil trade swelled the households of minor chiefs, who eventually broke off from their parent Houses. The expansion of some Houses by the formation of branches was sometimes at the expense of older Houses whose members passed over to more prosperous Houses through debts and other means. This situation of competition for trade and manpower produced rapid changes in the local balance of wealth and political power. Even within the older Houses, the leadership changed. Thus, in the crucial decades of the 1860s and 1870s, the two royal factions of Anna Pepple and Manilla Pepple in the kingdom of Bonny were led by Jaja and Oko Jumbo, both of slave origin. It was the struggle for power within the state of Bonny in the 1860s that resulted in the foundation of the new state of Opobo in 1869 with Jaja as its *amanyanabo* or king. It may be noted also that the reigning king of Bonny, George Pepple (1866–88) was unable to stop the factions drifting to war.

The crisis in Elem Kalabari in 1882–84 was similar to that at Bonny. Two factions, both derived from the royal line, struggled for leadership. The Amakiri faction won, and the Barboy or Will Braide group were obliged to move to the new town of Bakana. But even the victorious group had to move out of Elem Kalabari, whose location was dangerously close to the rival state of Bonny. Two additional towns were founded from the dispersal of Elem Kalabari: Buguma where Amakiri, the paramount ruler of the Kalabari resided, and Abonnema, both closer to the hinterland markets.

In the other two eastern delta states of Nembe and Okrika, no major disruptions of the political system occurred. The only recorded internal disturbance of the nineteenth century at Nembe was at the funeral of King Ockiya in 1879, when the Christians and the traditionalists fought over who should conduct rites over his body. A compromise was reached, and each group performed their rites separately. There was no division into factions of slaves and free. In north Nembe and Okrika, major political crises had occurred in the eighteenth century in which new dynasties had come into power, the Mingi in Nembe, and the Ado in Okrika. They were still in control in the nineteenth century, and no powerful opposition developed. It may be noted also that these two states did not carry on the overseas trade at the same high level as Bonny and Elem Kalabari.

The kingdom of Elem Kalabari tended to be the pivot of the balance of power in the eastern Niger delta. It fought against Nembe to its west, Bonny to its south-east, and Okrika to the east in the mid and late nineteenth century. These other states tended to form alliances from time to time, although Okrika appears to have resented a position of apparent dependence on Bonny through whose coastal port Okrika exported its produce. Elem Kalabari, however, had an ally, at least against Bonny, after Jaja established himself at Opobo, in 1869. For the rest of the century, Opobo tried to keep Bonny out of its traditional markets in the Imo river valley. This made it even more urgent for Bonny to seek other markets up the New Calabar river in the Obiatubo area claimed by Elem Kalabari, and through Kalabari territory to the lower Niger north of Nembe. The Kalabari also moved up the Engenni and Orashi rivers in territory previously under the control of Nembe.

The British consuls on the coast tried to use these inter-state wars as a lever to obtain an opening for their own traders and missionaries to move into the hinterland. The consuls served as mediators between the states in the making of peace treaties. Thus, consular-mediated treaties were signed between Bonny and Elem Kalabari (New Calabar) in 1871, Opobo and Bonny in 1873, Bonny and Elem Kalabari in 1879, Elem Kalabari and Okrika in 1871, Nembe and Elem Kalabari in 1871. The inter-state wars did not weaken the resolve of each of the states to keep European traders from encroaching on their spheres of trade or in the maintenance of their sovereignty. The British had clashed with King William Pepple of Bonny as early as 1854, when they exiled him to Fernando Po, Ascension, Sierra Leone and London. They used disturbances caused by local feuds as an excuse. In 1887 they could find no such excuse when they removed Jaja of Opobo for his opposition to direct British trade in the Imo river valley. The rulers of Nembe (Brass), lying on the main Nun estuary of the Niger, were involved in quarrels between exploring and trading British expeditions and local peoples from the 1830s when British citizens got killed or shot at. The final showdown came in 1895, when the Nembe attacked the major depot of the Royal Niger Company at the port of Akassa and destroyed it. This was in protest against the Company's attempt to establish monopoly trade all the way up from Akassa in the delta to Lokoja at the Niger–Benue confluence. Also in 1898, King Ibanichuka of Okrika was seized by the British consul for his refusal to take orders from the new British Protectorate government of Southern Nigeria. King Koko of Nembe managed to escape capture by hiding in remote villages in his kingdom.

By the end of the nineteenth century, then, the British had taken over political control of the eastern Niger delta and, for the first two or three decades of the twentieth century, the states could not crown new kings. However, the loss of sovereignty did not mean the final dissolution of these states or their basic cultural and social structures and values.

The Igbo hinterland

Igboland would appear to have been characterized for a long time by its comparatively dense population, and its organization into small-scale political units. These characteristics made it particularly vulnerable to the destructive effects of the slave trade, since there were no large states able to protect their citizens. Rather, the various Igbo communities would appear to have engaged in inter-group wars, raids, and kidnappings for slaves to sell to the delta states and the Efik of Calabar, who served as middlemen. That is, although Igboland provided most of the slaves sold at the ports of Bonny, and Elem Kalabari, in the Niger delta, and at Calabar on the Cross river estuary, the Igbo did not come into direct contact with the Europeans before the nineteenth century. Also, the Igbo country was not reached by visiting Europeans until the closing years of the nineteenth century and the beginning of the twentieth century. And these initial contacts took place along such river routes as the Niger, the Imo, and the Cross river. Thus the communities at the market centres on the rivers at which the coastal middlemen met hinterland traders became better known than others. The Aro who controlled the internal trade routes and some of the markets at which the coastal middlemen purchased slaves and, later, palm oil and palm kernels became notorious for their abilities both as traders and as the operators of a well-reputed oracle. Similarly, the Ndoki towns of Akwette and Ohombele on the Imo river served as the markets for Bonny and Opobo. On the Niger, the states of Aboh, Osomari, Oguta, Asaba, and Onitsha provided market centres which were the foci for external influences and contacts.

Although the Atlantic slave trade was formally abolished by the British in 1807, it lingered on on the coast till about 1850. And for the rest of the century, the internal trade for slaves among the coastal peoples increased because of the demands of the palm-oil trade. Similar demands for man-power in the production of palm oil and palm kernels, as for crop farming and ritual services, encouraged the continuance of the internal slave trade within Igboland.[8] Accordingly, the slave trade and slavery must be considered an important factor for social change in Igboland for most of the nineteenth century.

The predominantly disruptive character of the slave trade may be shown in different ways. First, the manner in which slaves were procured tended to destroy social and political structures. Social outcasts, offenders against the law, were sold into slavery. A few persons were sold in times of famine or for debt. But the majority of slaves were apparently taken by kidnapping, raiding and wars. The oracle of the Aro is also known to have sold persons it adjudged guilty. But the Aro trade network throughout most of Igboland also obtained many of its slaves through the raids of its mercenary allies, the Abam, Ohaffia, Abiriba, and Edda. Accordingly, the extensive influence exercised by the Aro over Igboland through its oracle did not become an integrative force.[9] The element of violence inherent in Aro addiction to the slave trade thus distinguished their influence from the earlier ritual influence of the Nri people over wide areas of Igboland.

In the economic sphere also, the disruption to normal agricultural activities must have been considerable. In addition, as was the case in the trade between the coastal middlemen and the Europeans, what the Igbo obtained for the slaves taken out was never commensurate with the total loss sustained as a result of the slave trade. Slaves were paid for with salt, fish, spirits, firearms, hats and beads, as well as iron, copper, and brass

8. W. R. G. Horton, 1954; E. Isichei, 1973.
9. F. I. Ekejiuba, 1972; S. Ottenberg, 1958.

bars. The metal bars were turned into pewters, ritual bells, state swords, leg-rings, and other ornaments. But these supplies replaced local industries, and the Awka smiths turned their backs on local sources of metal. Importation of salt and cloth also undermined local industries.

The first direct reports of the Igbo hinterland were taken to Europe by Richard and John Lander in 1830, when they passed through Onitsha, Asaba, and Aboh to the Niger delta. They were followed by other British explorers and traders and missionaries in 1841 and 1854. In 1856, Macgregor Laird established the first trading station at Onitsha, and in 1879, the United African Company was formed out of the many rival British firms attempting to trade along the Niger valley. It received a royal charter in 1886 as the Royal Niger Company with powers of government. It established one of its main depots in Igboland at Asaba, complete with constabulary and trading station. Missionary activities among the Niger Igbo had been started as early as 1856 at Onitsha under the leadership of Ajayi Crowther and other freed slaves from Sierra Leone, some of them of Igbo origin, and belonging to the Church Missionary Society. However, the Catholic Society of African Missions (SMA), from Lyons, established rival stations on the west bank of the Niger from the 1880s; first at Asaba, and later at Isele-Uku, and Ibusa.

Thus, the first inroads into Igboland were made by the traders and missionaries, along the Niger. These first intrusions were resisted by the Igbo.[10] Among the western Igbo, resistance took the form of violent outbreaks organized by the *ekumeku* secret societies between 1898 and 1911. First, the Royal Niger Company, and then the British Protectorate government after 1900, crushed every manifestation of resistance with brutal severity. The most spectacular effort by the British was the Aro Expedition of 1900 which covered 15 500 sq km of Igbo territory, using four units from Unwana, Itu, Akwete, and Oguta, all converging on Bende and Arochuku. This represented the formal conquest of Igboland, and a sort of anti-climax, since the Aro system the British had come to confront militarily proved to be only a group of religious experts and traders working together. No military force came out to oppose the British. The Aro challenge to British authority had been indirect, commercial and ideological.

All current studies of the British conquest of Igboland through the defeat of the oracle-based structure of the Aro, and of the secret-society style opposition of the *ekumuku*, in the Asaba hinterland, suggest that, thereafter, Igbo society was left wide open to the entrance of foreign influences. For example, it is stated that conversion to Christianity became a 'mass movement', and a 'dramatic' phenomenon. According to F.K. Ekechi, 'the most bewildering mass movement of the 1900s has been partly attributed to Igbo attempts to circumvent various forms of British overrule';

10. F.K. Ekechi, 1972; P.A. Igbafe, 1971.

while Simon Ottenberg believes that the Igbo have been particularly receptive to change because of their social structures, attitudes, and history.[11] However, there is no evidence that the Igbo have, in fact, discarded their traditional culture and religion for Christianity to a much greater extent than other comparable groups in Nigeria and the rest of Africa.

The Cross river basin

The Efik state of Calabar at the estuary of the Cross river dominated the trade along the Cross river basin. Along the coast, its trade area met that of the delta state of Opobo in the Ibeno and Qua-Iboe river basins. However, the largest ethnic group in the basin was the Ibibio, who also constituted the majority of slaves exported from this part of the coast. Produce from the upper Cross river valley and from the Igbo country to the north-west reached the Efik traders through the Aro, who dominated the Ibibio market town of Itu. Some of the groups on the upper Cross river also tried to share in the proceeds of the trade with the Efik, through their ability to disrupt trade or charge tolls. Thus the Itu, Umon, and Akunakuna, among others, always had some quarrel or other with the trading houses of Calabar. Some of the groups in the upper Cross river also carried on direct trade contacts with peoples of the northern Cameroon region. Ikom was one such centre of trade with the Cameroon as well as with the Igbo to the west and Calabar to the south.

Although the trade of Calabar was similar to that of the delta states in slaves and later in palm oil and palm kernels, its history was different because of its different environment and social structures. The two major communities of Duke Town and Creek Town of which the Efik state was composed, were based on firm land as against the delta swamp environment of their western neighbours. Accordingly, Calabar had farm settlements of slaves who supplied some of its agricultural needs, and even some export commodities such as palm oil. The social structure of Calabar also did not encourage the integration of slaves into the political system. Although the domestic or city slaves took part in the overseas trade and sometimes became rich and influential, the *Ekpe* secret society of Calabar kept them out of the higher grades in which lay the power of the state. This contrasted with the open *Ekine* or *Sekiapu* society of the delta states which was a positive agent of acculturation and integration of slaves into the culture and full life of the community.

The external agents of change represented by the European traders, consuls, and missionaries exercised greater influence in Calabar. The traders were, at first, not permitted to establish stations on land, and had to live in hulks (roofed-over ships) moored permanently on the river as

11. F.K. Ekechi, 1972, p. xiii; S. Ottenberg, 1959.

houseboats and offices. They tried to exercise some influence through the trusts or credits they gave to Efik traders; and sometimes used economic sanctions by collectively suspending trade with any defaulting Efik merchant. But when, in the nineteenth century, the Efik began to quarrel among themselves, the traders came in as arbitrators and kingmakers.

Missionaries of the Church of Scotland Mission reached Calabar in 1846. They formed a little self-governing colony of five to six white missionaries, teachers, staff, and converts, at Duke Town and Creek Town. The mission station served as a sanctuary for refugees from the community. But the missionaries also watched the local scene, and reported developments to the British consul, or tried to exercise moral influence and to intervene in other ways.

Since the Cross river estuary was so accessible to the British Preventive Naval Squadron at Fernando Po, it was comparatively easy to stop the slave trade at Calabar. In 1842, an abolition treaty was signed and an annual subsidy was agreed to be paid to the rulers of Calabar. From 1842, British influence in Calabar gradually increased until 1891 when a Protectorate administration was established there.[12]

The *obong* of Calabar

One reason for British intervention in Calabar was the weakness of the *obong*, king of Calabar, deriving from the comparative newness of the institution of kingship in Calabar. Eighteenth-century visitors to the Niger delta and the Cross river mention single kings for the delta states, but referred to 'kings' for Calabar. Some of these political leaders were possibly lineage heads, or *Ekpe* titleholders. The position of *obong* or king only began to be established from the beginning of the nineteenth century. Duke Ephraim (Efiom) (*c.* 1800–34) emerged first as paramount leader in Duke Town, and the most powerful ruler on the Cross river. Eyo Honesty I of Creek Town (d. 1820), occupied a similar position in Creek Town. Both men established their position over others of similar lineage connections because of their superior wealth acquired from the overseas trade.

There were a number of other elements of weakness in the monarchical institutions in Calabar in addition to its newness. First was the presence of two competing kings at Duke Town and Creek Town. Second was the competition for the office between several political leaders and members of the Ekpe society. Such competition led to arbitration by the British consul, traders, or missionaries. Third, and most serious, the office of *obong* became identified in the nineteenth century with the external trade. He had few traditional functions or authority, all his activities being concerned with the external trade. Thus, the *obong* collected the *comey* dues from the foreign traders, granted rights of mooring and trade to the supercargoes, and set in motion the traditional judicial processes when approached. The

12. D. Forde (ed.), 1956; A. J. H. Latham, 1973; K. K. Nair, 1972.

internal powers of making laws and enforcing them lay with the leaders of the *Ekpe* secret society. Accordingly, the main function of the *obong* in the nineteenth century was to stand between the local communities and the whitemen, who were therefore interested in who was appointed to the office.

The relative powers of the kings of Duke Town and Creek Town fluctuated in the first half of the nineteenth century. Duke Ephraim of Duke Town (1800–34) was not only the richest chief on the river, but also held the highest *Ekpe* title of Eyamba. He received the largest share of *comey*, dividing the remainder among the other chiefs. After the death of Duke Ephraim, Eyo Honesty II of Creek Town (1836–58) became the most influential trader. By 1852 he was receiving two-thirds of the *comey*, while the ruler of Duke Town received only a third. In spite of wealth and trade, the kings of Duke Town generally succeeded in keeping the most important *Ekpe* title of *eyamba* outside the reach of the leaders of Creek Town, who held the second highest title of *obunko*.

Succession disputes for the leadership of Duke Town and Creek Town presented a serious problem for the political system on the Cross river. The Eyo lineage achieved an early dominance in Creek Town that it maintained for the rest of the century. The rival lineage of Akabom migrated to found the settlement of Cobham Town. The position was different in Duke Town. When Duke Ephraim died in 1834, he was succeeded, not by his son or a member of his lineage, but by Eyamba V, that is, the fifth holder of the *eyamba* title of the *Ekpe* society. At the death of Eyamba V in 1847, there was a dispute between the lineages of Eyamba and Duke Ephraim. The British set up a third candidate, Archibong I. At the death of Archibong I in 1852, the traders and the consul recognized Ephraim Duke. Thenceforward, disputes arose between the Duke, Eyamba, and Archibong lineages. Accordingly, each used various means including the techniques of witchcraft accusations and trial by ordeal using *esere* bean poison against its rivals.[13]

The *Ekpe* society and the Bloodmen

The *Ekpe* society of Calabar was an adaptation of a cult of the leopard present among many forest groups in the Cross river valley and in parts of the Cameroon. It was played as a masquerade by the young men, wearing hooded raffia costumes, while women and non-members shut themselves up in their houses. But the main function of the members was to hold weekly meetings at which social questions were discussed.

The *Ekpe* society, which, in the hinterland village communities, comprised all elders, became an exclusive secret organization in the large commercial community of Calabar. It also became increasingly stratified into grades, rising from five recorded in 1828 to ten in 1840 and eleven in

13. A. J. H. Latham, 1972.

1858. Slaves were originally excluded from *Ekpe*, but third-generation slaves born within the homes of members came to be admitted into the lower grades. But since the grades were attained by payment of prescribed fees, the highest grades were monopolized by the rich free nobility, the highest two by the political heads of Duke Town and Creek Town.

Ekpe was the effective law-making and enforcing authority in Calabar in the nineteenth century, and was utilized for the purpose by the foreign visitors as well. Thus, in 1850, the missionaries, supercargoes, and consul pressed the leaders of Calabar to enact an *Ekpe* law against human sacrifice at the deaths of rulers. *Ekpe* may be considered to have been an asset in the political system of Calabar in that it united all the free men of wealth and influence in a common organization. But its discrimination against the large body of men of slave origin and the poor led to the social disturbances of the mid-nineteenth century, which Dike has referred to as slave revolts.

The association of plantation slaves known as the Bloodmen came into being specifically as a pressure group to prevent the sacrifice of slaves at the deaths of kings and lineage heads. Such an organization of slaves on a blood oath was possible in Calabar because of their concentration in plantations, and because of the common disabilities they suffered. However, the association did not become a revolt for the emancipation of slaves, or even for the seizure of political power from the *Ekpe*. All the association achieved was to come into Calabar from the plantations in a body each time a notable man was ill or died, and there was danger of slaves being sacrificed or made to take poison ordeal. Their agitation led to the 1850–1 *Ekpe* law against human sacrifice, and King Archibong I considered it necessary to secure their support in the faction fights over the office of *obong*.

The social and political history of Calabar, then, was similar to that of the delta states in the types of external pressures to which the system was subject, but different in the specific internal resolution of the problems. *Ekpe*, the position of the monarchy, and the Bloodmen, were unique phenomena in the situation at Calabar.

The Cameroon coast and its hinterland[14]

The Cameroon coast, including a number of rocky offshore islands, is generally characterized by a maze of mangrove swamps, creeks and inlets, immediately behind which lies the tropical rain forest. It is inhabited by three main clusters of the north-western Bantu, namely, the Kpe-Mboko, the Duala-Limba, and the Tanga-Yasa,[15] with numerous clans and sub-clans. These peoples, whose traditions suggest common origins and affini-

14. This section is the summary of a contribution by Dr Lovett Z. Elango of the History Department, University of Yaoundé, Cameroon.
15. E. Ardener, 1956, p. 39.

ties, are basically agriculturists, fishermen, and hunters. They bartered fish for food at markets. They were generally organized under autonomous villages, but sometimes as among the Bubi, Duala, and Isuwu, there were petty paramount chiefs. Among the Duala, Isuwu, and others, the most prestigious secret society was the *Jengu*, based on the veneration of water spirits.[16]

As in the case of the Niger delta peoples, these north-western Bantu communities were subjected to pressure in the nineteenth century from Christian missionaries, European traders and imperialists. The greatest pressure came from the abolitionists[17] because, by the beginning of the nineteenth century, each of the communities included a lower class of slaves and the attempt to abolish the institution of slavery created for them a critical economic problem in terms both of finding substitute products such as palm oil and palm kernels in place of slaves and of finding adequate labour to produce and transport these products.

The Duala of the Cameroon were probably on the coast from as early as the sixteenth century, but established themselves as a centralized state when they conquered and absorbed other Bantu groups from about 1706 onwards.[18] They had a paramount chief, but as early as 1792 English traders on the Cameroon river intervened in a succession dispute. They imposed on the Duala the candidate of the junior lineage, known as King Bell. In 1814 Akwa, the more popular candidate of the senior lineage, declared his independence. For most of the nineteenth century, therefore, the Duala were divided into two main groups, the Bell and Akwa, and Duala politics revolved around Kings Bell and Akwa. These rival groups were each further subdivided into 'towns' or wards. But in order to preserve their ethnic solidarity in the face of this tendency to fission, the Duala created the new institution of *ngondo*. This was a council of Duala notables, comprising representatives of all the councils of the various Duala villages.[19]

Located on the western spur of Mount Cameroon and on the Bimbia river, a tributary of the Cameroon river, was the Isuwu trading polity of Bimbia. Bimbia, composed of three villages ruled by lineage heads assisted by a council of chiefs, had been known as a minor trading centre from at least the mid-seventeenth century. The power and prestige of these men, as of Bimbia itself, resided in their middleman position in the overseas trade. The leading chiefs of Bimbia also derived status and support from their membership of *Jengu*.

The richest and best known of the Bimbia merchant princes was Bile, known to the Europeans as King William. His mother was of the Bimbia

16. R. Bureau, 1962, pp. 107–38.
17. L. Z. Elango, 1974.
18. E. Mveng, 1963.
19. V. T. Levine, 1971.

PLATE 27.4 *King Bell's house in the 1840s*

ruling family, but Bile had lived in the home of his Duala father in the Cameroon river in his childhood. Driven to Bimbia by his paternal kinsmen, he attached himself to his senior maternal uncle, who employed him as his emissary in his dealings with the Europeans because of his previous experience from the Cameroon river. Bile acquired wealth, new experience, and influence, and was chosen as the logical successor to his uncle. In 1833, Bile was able to convince the British representative in Fernando Po, Colonel Nicolls, to recognize him as king of the entire coastal region from Bimbia to Rio del Rey, including its offshore Bubi islands, in return for ceding the same region to Britain as a protectorate. Although the British rejected the voluntary cession, Bile retained the title of king until his death in 1879. The separate polities of Duala and Bimbia thus developed ties in the nineteenth century. Cultural ties were reinforced by *Jengu* solidarity, as well as by King William's part-Duala ancestry. In commerce, Bimbia and Bell Town traders co-operated in developing the trade of the Rio del Rey area. They developed two major routes. First was the coastal route through the creeks linking the two areas, much as is still the case today. Some Bimbia and Duala traders resided at different villages along the route to receive goods for exchange with the local people. Second was the overland route which served as an alternative when stormy weather and rough seas made the creek route unsafe. This route round Mount Cameroon also tapped the resources of ivory. The network of internal trade routes of the hinterland Bimbia and Bell Town trade zones overlapped with that of the Efik traders of Calabar and the Cross river around Rio del Rey.

The commercial unity of the Cameroon–Bimbia–Rio del Rey region was further enhanced by the links established by each of the sub-sections of the region with the Bamenda grasslands in the interior.[20] Thus, many of the slaves reaching the coast between 1820 and the 1840s came from the Bamenda 'grassfields' and reached Bimbia and the Cameroon river via the Rio del Rey region. But by the mid-nineteenth century, Bell Town and Bimbia traders, working together, had begun to compete successfully though peacefully with the leading traders of the Rio del Rey.

The slaves who arrived at the coast in the 1840s, mostly captives from the Bali–Chamba raids in the Bamenda grasslands, represented a critical element in the transition of coastal societies from slave-trading to legitimate commerce. In the Cameroon river and Bimbia, as in Calabar and the Niger delta, slaves were used in producing palm oil and palm kernels and other commodities of legitimate commerce. At Bimbia and the Cameroon river, an important variation was the well-organized system by which Kings William and Bell hired out some of their slaves to the West African Company at Fernando Po. The system assumed the nature of indenture, and provided an additional source of wealth for both monarchs. But the system was open to abuses, and led to British parliamentary investigation. King William was moved to protest not only against the company's failure to pay his men but also their maltreatment.

British interest in the abolition of the slave trade and the establishment of legitimate trade led to treaties and the gradual loss of the sovereignty of the local rulers. Although the treaty of 1833 between Nicolls and King William was rejected, British agents concluded treaties between 1840 and 1844 that provided them with the legal basis for intervention in local politics. Such interventions often involved the use of British gunboats to bully chiefs who violated the terms of these treaties, or to collect trade debts owed to Europeans. In 1852 John Beecroft even presided at the election of a new chief of Akwa Town. Sometimes British intervention and arbitration was invited by local rulers: for example, by King William to establish his authority over Bimbia and Rio del Rey. But the more frequent excuse for British intervention arose from the disputes between European and local traders over the repayment of credit or 'trust'. In 1856, the system of arbitration and settlement of disputes between Africans and Europeans was institutionalized in a Court of Equity established at Duala.

The missionaries represented an important element of foreign influence. In 1843, Joseph Merrick, a West Indian mulatto, was sent to Fernando Po by the British Baptist Mission Society. In the same year he established a mission at Bell Town, and in 1844, at Bimbia.[21] He and his colleagues

20. E. M. Chilver, 1961.
21. S. N. Gwei, 1966.

gradually built churches, schools, carpenters' workshops and, at Bimbia, a printing press. Local opposition was soon aroused by efforts at mass conversion. Conflicts with the missionaries became intensified in the 1850s because of smallpox epidemics, inter-ethnic wars and famines, and the British had to intervene to protect the missionaries and their converts. When the Spanish governor proclaimed Catholicism as the official religion of Fernando Po in 1858, the position of the Baptists became untenable at Clarence. Accordingly, Alfred Saker built a new settlement at Ambas Bay which he named Victoria, in June 1858. But local opposition to the Baptists continued to be high, especially as many of the Anglo–West Indian settlers at Victoria also traded in competition with the Bimbia population.

In the 1860s and 1870s there was a decline in the trade of the Cameroon coast which produced a feeling of insecurity among the rulers and restless insubordination among the sub-chiefs. This led to appeals to Queen Victoria for protection. It was in these circumstances that the Germans annexed the Cameroon in July 1884. Resistance to German annexation broke out almost immediately, with some measure of British support locally. The resistance stiffened even more when the chiefs realized that the Germans were determined to push inland, thereby destroying their middleman monopoly. The resistance and attempts at pacification ended only with the outbreak of the First World War.[22] The British, for their part, were unable to reverse the situation. Only Victoria remained a British foothold, but even here, the missionaries were unable to withstand German harassment. Victoria was formally transferred to Germany on 28 March 1887. The Germans wasted no time in moving up into the Bamenda grasslands to secure control of the hinterland trade, and divert it from going on to Calabar as it had begun to do.

The Ogowe basin and surrounding regions[23]

To the south of Cameroon, the Ogowe basin and surrounding regions (the Woleu, Noya and Como basins to the north and the Nyanga basin to the south) correspond more or less to the modern territories of Equatorial Guinea and Gabon. Covered largely by equatorial forest, this vast area, bordering on the Congo basin to the south and east, has been inhabited by man since time immemorial, as testified by the remains of stone tools discovered during archaeological excavations conducted at various sites in Gabon some twenty years ago.

As yet, however, we know nothing about the physical characteristics or the mores and way of life of these first inhabitants of the region. They may have been the ancestors of the Pygmies, who are found scattered today in small groups in the forest, where they live by hunting and fishing, using

22. R. Joseph, 1974; H. R. Rudin, 1938.

23. This section is based on a contribution by Nicolas Metegue N'Nah, Head of the Department of History, University of Libreville.

their catch to trade by barter with the neighbouring Bantu-speaking peoples.

These Bantu-speaking peoples had by the nineteenth century formed a large number of political entities of varying sizes: village-states (Fang, Kele, Seke, Benga); confederations (Mpongwe, Gisir, Punu, Obamba); and kingdoms (Nkomi, Orungu, Galwa from 1860 on).[24] Within these political entities, the different peoples engaged in a range of activities, nomadic agriculture, hunting, fishing and crafts. These crafts were distinguished above all by the quality of the goods produced, as for example the ironware manufactured by the Fang, who were considered by European travellers in the nineteenth century to be the best ironsmiths of the region, and the fabrics woven by the peoples of the Upper Ngunyi (Gisir, Apindji and Mitsogo in particular). The products of these economic activities served as the basis for extensive trading among the different communities. For example, a vigorous trade in cassava flour and dried fish was carried on between the Mpongwe confederation, in the Como estuary, and the Orungu kingdom in the Ogowe delta; the famous *bongo* cloth produced by the weavers in the hinterland was transported from the upper Ngunyi to the coast by way of the Ogowe and the Rembo-Nkomi; finally, from the Atlantic seaboard convoys laden with bales of locally produced salt set out regularly for the interior. After the arrival of the Portuguese on the coast in 1471, trading was intensified to the point of becoming the main activity of the coastal peoples in the seventeenth, eighteenth and nineteenth centuries, cheap European goods – guns, alcoholic beverages, fabrics, cheap glassware, trinkets – being bartered for slaves, ivory, palm oil, rubber, ebony and redwood.

This development of commercial activity on the coast had major consequences. First, it triggered off the migration of certain peoples such as the Fang who, preceded by the Kele, moved away from the area embracing northern Gabon, southern Cameroon and the eastern region of Equatorial Guinea, where they had long been settled, towards the coast, and pushed on to Eliva Nkomi (Fernan-Vaz lagoon), which they reached at the end of the nineteenth century. Second, this was the root cause of a profound transformation of indigenous societies. The old social structure, characterized by blood ties and by the emergence in each clan of three social classes, namely, pure-bloods (*fumu* in Punu, *awo-ntche* in Omyene, *atem bo bayong* in Fang), half-castes (*awoga* in Omyene, *mintobe* in Fang) and slaves, began to be replaced by another social stratification based on wealth in which, alongside a middle and a lower class, a merchant upper middle class or bourgeoisie composed essentially of chiefs and notables, who exercised a monopoly on big business, featured prominently.

At the beginning of the nineteenth century, this social evolution, which

24. Cf. N. Metegue N'Nah, 1979. N.B. It should be pointed out that, until the seventeenth century, the Tyo and Vili kingdoms included vast areas of present-day Gabon.

PLATE 27.5 *The Ogowe River Trader, Ouassengo, with ivory tusks and female members of his household*

was not very noticeable among the peoples of the interior, was more pronounced on the coast. There, commencing in 1839,[25] treaties were signed which led to the establishment of the French trading post of Gabon, of which Libreville, founded in 1849 at the mouth of the Como, became the chief town. A large number of missions of exploration set off from this station, extending French territorial claims far into the interior of the country and making Gabon the European gateway to Central Africa. Journeys were undertaken by Paul Belloni du Chaillu (1856–9 and 1863–5), Serval and Griffon du Bellay (1862), Aymes (1867), Alfred Marche and the Marquis de Compiègne (1873–4), Pierre Savorgnan de Brazza (1875–8, 1879–82 and 1883–5), Paul Crampel (1888–9), and Fourneau and Dolisie (1889). To the north, the French fell foul of the Spanish, who launched several expeditions from Fernando Po into Rio Muni, notably those led by Nicolas Manterola and Guillemar de Aragon (1845), Manuel Iradier, Ossorio and Montes de Oca (1884).

While the exploration of the country by Europeans progressed, and

25. N.B. The first treaty authorizing colonial occupation to be signed in the region in question was concluded on 9 February 1839 by Bouet-Willaumez and Antchuwe Kowe Rapontyombo, alias 'King Denis'.

PLATE 27.6 *Antchuwe Kowe Rapontyombo ('King Denis'), an Ogowe river ruler, with his senior wife*

despite the resistance which the indigenous peoples put up, treaties were concluded with certain chiefs, and European traders and missionaries settled in the different regions. By 1882 there were in the Ogowe basin and surrounding regions over ninety commercial establishments belonging largely to English companies (John Holt, Hatton and Cookson), German companies (Woermann, Schulze, Lübke, Küderling), a Spanish company (Transatlantica) and a French company (Dubarry Frères). In addition, there were over twenty missionary stations and about the same number of denominational schools.

However, despite the deep inroads made by Western influences, the indigenous societies were able to retain their identity. For it must be pointed out that, towards the end of the nineteenth century, vast regions were still all but unaffected by these alien influences. Even where, as on the coast, such influences were already very powerful, they ran up against various forms of diehard opposition from the local cultures. Thus the large-scale effort to evangelize the local populations had to contend with such widespread indigenous cults as *Bwiti, Bieri* and *Ombwiri*, and social customs such as polygamy.

Conclusion

The nineteenth century, then, saw the gradual infiltration of British influence over much of the region, with French and eventually also, German influence in the Cameroons region. However, it is clear that the hinterland parts of the region were outside the direct influence of Europe to the end of our period. But even the coastal areas, which were in direct contact with European traders long before the nineteenth century, were not easily conquered, and their internal history was determined by local factors, and often by relations with other neighbouring polities. Thus, although all the coastal communities in the region took part in the same overseas trade, each developed different institutions to contain its impact, deriving solutions to similar problems from separate internal histories and cultures. The *wari* or House institution of the delta states was not the same as that of the Efik of the Cross river, who also adapted the *Ekpe* of hinterland groups to new functions. In similar circumstances, the Cameroon coastal groups developed *Jengu*, which differed from the *Ekpe* secret society of the Efik, as well as from the open *Ekine* or *Sekiapu* masquerade society of the delta states, or the *Bwiti, Bieri* and *Ombwiri* of the Ogowe basin and Gabon.

Further, important as was the overseas trade in slaves and later palm oil and palm kernels to the development of these communities, it must be borne in mind that the internal trade routes and exchange of local produce between groups constituted the basic economic mainstay of the majority of the people throughout the nineteenth century. In political developments even along the coast, internal cultural factors were still pre-eminent: the Itsekiri of the western delta still considered the curse of the *ọba* of Benin a potent determinant of history, in spite of the practical sovereignty and great success in the overseas trade won by the kingdom of Warri by the nineteenth century.

In sum then, the great attention given to the external factors of European overseas trade, Christian missionary activities and colonial conquest should not obscure the essential primacy of internal factors in the historical development of the peoples between the Niger delta and the Ogowe basin in the nineteenth century. The effects of the external factors were by no means immediately overwhelming, and the communities continued to enjoy autonomy in most aspects of their life. This essential autonomy from the burgeoning impact of the external Western world was to continue throughout the colonial period so that these communities did not get all the elements of their culture, institutions and identity completely swept away.

28 The African diaspora

F. W. KNIGHT *with contributions by*
Y. TALIB *and* P. D. CURTIN

Introduction

The remarkable mass migration of Africans to the Americas, the Middle East and Europe under the aegis of the trans-Atlantic and other branches of the slave trade constitutes one of the major events of African and world history.[1] This emigration, largely involuntary on the part of the participants, lasted for centuries, leaving residual communities of varying sizes scattered about in Europe, the Middle East and the Americas.[2]

The exodus into Asia Minor and the Levantine Mediterranean world is the oldest sector of the African diaspora and lasted longest. It probably began several centuries before the Christian era, and reached its apogee during the period of Muslim ascendancy after the seventh century. Most Africans arrived via the trans-Saharan slave routes, but a number also migrated as free individuals, scholars, teachers, traders and pilgrims to the holy cities of Mecca and Medina. Since the Mediterranean world did not practise an extensive plantation economy, the volume of sub-Saharan Africans fed into the system remained relatively low, probably not exceeding several hundreds per year. Within the Ottoman empire large numbers of Africans were employed as soldiers and sailors, eunuchs, concubines, administrators and, in cases such as Abū'l-Misk Kāfūr of Egypt (*d.* 968), could even become the effective ruler of the state. Within Muslim states, Africans did not inherit their status as slaves, and in some cases could maintain a cohesive culture interacting with that of their hosts.

1. J. M. McPherson, L.B. Holland *et al.*, 1971, provides a good starting-point for any study of the African diaspora. Since its publication, there has been a veritable explosion of excellent monographs, especially on the Afro-American theme, e.g., D. B. Davis, 1975; R. W. Fogel and S. L. Engerman, 1974; H. G. Gutman, 1975; E. D. Genovese, 1974; S. L. Engerman and E. D. Genovese (eds), 1975; G. M. Hall, 1971; D. W. Cohen and J. P. Greene (eds), 1972; H. Hoetink, 1973; R. Anstey, 1975; J. Palacios Preciados, 1973; R. Sheridan, 1973; R. S. Dunn, 1972; C. A. Palmer, 1976, 1981; R. Bean, 1975; H. Klein, 1978; L. Rout, 1976; F. P. Bowser, 1974; W. Dean, 1976; B. W. Higman, 1976; M. Craton, 1978; O. Patterson, 1982; T. Berlin and R. Hoffman (eds), 1983; P. D. Curtin, 1979.
2. See R. David, 1970, pp. 33–50; L. Bugner, 1980; M. Moreno Fraginals, 1977.

Africans followed the spread of Islam by land and sea into India and the Far East. As late as the 1520s and 1530s, some 5000 African soldiers served with the troops of Sultan Bahadur of Gujerat, while additional Africans served in his navy. More Africans were found in the armies and administration of the Sultan of Delhi, as well as in Bengal and the Deccan. Indeed, the expansion of the Ottoman empire into south-eastern Europe brought Africans along with it to serve as soldiers and bureaucrats.

The African contact with Europe was a continuation of Mediterranean commercial and military activity. By the fifteenth century a small trade in

PLATE 28.1 *Figure of a negroid man with an Indonesian kris at his back waistband, probably from what is now Vietnam and probably dating from the seventeenth century*

African slaves flourished in the Mediterranean and substantial numbers of Africans were found in Sicily, Cyprus and Crete, as well as on the southern Iberian coast. Seville had a black population of about five thousand in the early sixteenth century, and substantial numbers of Africans lived in Málaga, Huelva, Cadiz and Lisbon. Direct maritime links between Europe and Africa increased the black populations and, by the late eighteenth century, France had a black population of approximately 2000, and England nearly 15 000. Though minuscule compared with the flood of Africans imported to the Americas at that time, these small concentrations were sufficient to warrant official concern in both countries. A royal decree in France banned inter-racial marriages in 1777; while the celebrated Mansfield Judgement in England in 1772 declared that Africans could not be enslaved in England.

It was, however, in the Americas that the African diaspora was most pronounced. Africans and their descendants, generally called Afro-Americans, played a prominent part in the development of every society in the New World, from the discovery of the region by the Europeans in the late fifteenth century until modern times. Regardless of the number of Africans that arrived in any particular country, the overall impact of Africa remained inescapable and profound.

Africans and Afro-Americans, both as slaves and as free persons, helped subdue the vast wildernesses everywhere throughout the Americas from Alaska to Argentina. They crossed the mighty rivers with the first explorers of the New World. They helped conquer and subordinate the indigenous inhabitants and the sophisticated civilizations of Mexico and Peru. They actively participated in forging the new communities which formed the bases for the later heterogenous and polyphonous societies. They helped build the new cities of the Iberians – Santo Domingo in 1496; Mexico City and Havana in 1522; Pernambuco and Lima in 1535; Buenos Aires and Valparaiso in 1536; Bahia in 1549; and Rio de Janeiro in 1565. They also helped build the port cities of the English settlers in the seventeenth and early eighteenth centuries: Boston, New York, Philadelphia, Jamestown and Charleston.

Like all the other immigrant groups – largely free persons – that came to the Americas between the sixteenth and the nineteenth centuries, the Africans performed every type of task, and fulfilled every social role. They were pioneers and conquistadors, pirates and bucaneers, gauchos, llaneros, bandeirantes, slave-owners, merchants, servants and slaves. They featured more prominently in some occupations than in others, and they were legally excluded from those of highest social status. After the seventeenth century, however, Africans constituted the only legal slaves in the Americas, thus rendering an enduring social stigma to the African population in American societies.[3] Before the final abolition of the slave system in Brazil in 1888,

3. D.B. Davis, 1966, pp. 223–61.

the majority of Africans in the Americas were slaves, performing the greater proportion of manual and physically demanding, often debilitating, tasks without which the colonies, possessions, and nations could not have been an economic success.

The long, important and varied association with the evolution of the modern American societies enabled the Africans to make an indelible imprint on the languages, cultures, economies, and ethnic composition of almost every community in the New World.[4] The greatest impact occurred in the plantation zones, among those communities that developed along the Atlantic and Caribbean coastlands from the south-eastern USA to the north-eastern part of Brazil, and along the Pacific coastlands of Colombia, Ecuador and Peru.

The Middle East and south-east Asia[5]

Ethiopians were highly prized in Arabia and India on account of their intelligence and appearance. The slaves exported from Ethiopia in the nineteenth century to various parts of Asia were mostly children, ranging in age from 8 to 16 years. Some were captives taken in the wars waged by the southern Ethiopian kingdom of Shoa on the Oromo ('Galla') peoples along its borders. The slaves were carried in caravans of several hundreds and transported to the Ethiopian coast for shipment at the ports of Berbera, Zeila, Tajura, Assab, Obock and Massawa, from where they were ferried across the Red Sea to the ports of Jeddah, Mocha, and Hoideida. Buyers came from several towns in the Yemen and the Ḥidjāz. There were also seaborne traders from the Hadramawt, Zanzibar, Ōman, India and the Persian Gulf. This trade was largely in Arab hands backed by Indian financiers from the Gujarat (Banians).[6]

The major source of supply of slaves to Asia was, however, eastern Africa. As pointed out by J. B. Kelly,[7] the slave trade from Zanzibar was virtually a monopoly of the Muscat Arabs and their rulers who derived their revenue mostly from the custom duties levied on the trade. In the early nineteenth century, Muscat was the greatest clearing house of the traffic to the Gulf, Persia, Iraḳ and India, but as the century wore on its dominance was to be challenged by the port of Sur to the southward. The majority of the slaves landed at Muscat were sold within Oman itself. The

4. Special number of *Daedalus* (*Journal of the American Academy of Arts and Sciences*), **103**, 2, 1974 entitled 'Slavery, Colonialism and Racism'; S. W. Mintz, 1971; B. Nuñez, 1980; R. M. Levine, 1980; N. Sanchez-Albornoz, 1974.

5. The need for further work has already been pointed out by B. A. Ogot, 1979, p. 175. For Turkish archives see C. Orhanlu, 1972 and 1976–7, pp. 145–56. For early anthropological work, see R. Skene, 1917; G. Pesente, 1912, 1929; D. C. Philliot and R. F. Azoo, 1906–7.

6. R. H. K. Darkwah, 1975, p. 168; J. B. Kelly, 1968, pp. 417–18.

7. J. B. Kelly, 1968, pp. 413–14.

PLATE 28.2 *The slave trade from East Africa in the 1850s, as seen by Sir Richard Burton*

rest were bought by agents from the Trucial Coast, notably the Ḳawāsim, for resale on the coast or in the markets of Persia, Iraḳ, Bahrain, Kuwait, Hasa and Nadj. From Muscat and Sur, slaves were also conveyed to the ports of Sindh̲, Kutch, Kathiawar and the Bombay Presidency, in Bahraini, Kuwaiti and Indian bottoms. Those intended for the Persian market were landed at Bushire as well as brought across the Gulf to Lingah from Sharjah. It is important to note that, in the early nineteenth century, slaves were rarely brought all the way across Arabia from the Red Sea for sale on the Gulf Coast. Basra was the chief market for slaves carried up the Gulf.

British and Dutch slavers also participated in this lucrative trade. Slaves largely from the island of Madagascar – 'Kāfirs'[8] as they were called – were imported into the Bombay and Madras Presidencies as well as the infant British settlements on the west coast of Sumatra to meet the labour needs of their respective factories.[9] It must be emphasized here that the nineteenth century witnessed not only population movements of Africans, but also of Malays, Indians, and Chinese, either as slaves or indentured labourers

8. *Kāfir* in Arabic means infidel, impious wretch, one who does not recognize the blessings of God. It also means to cover up, to conceal, deny. It has become an appellation usually applied by Arabs to all non-Muslims and hence to particular groups of people. It was widely used in India and the Malay Archipelago to describe non-Christian and non-Muslim African slaves. See H. Yule and A. C. Burnell, 1886, pp. 141–2.

9. H. Dodwell (ed.), 1920, pp. 100, 104, 135, 159–60, 188, 202, 223; F. W. Mees (ed.), 1928, p. 76.

throughout the Indian Ocean area. This interaction of peoples of varied backgrounds merits further study.[10]

The annual pilgrimage to Mecca also played an important, albeit a seasonal, role in the involuntary and voluntary movements of Africans to the Middle East. Many West African pilgrims reached Mecca via the Cairo caravan or by way of the Red Sea ports of Suākin and Massawa, thereby constituting small diaspora communities.[11] Ever since the time of the great Malian King, Mansa Mūsā, such wealthy African pilgrims were 'accompanied by a number of slaves, some of whom [they sell] on the way as a kind of traveller's cheque – to pay the expenses of [their] journey'.[12] Therefore it was no accident that Mecca emerged as the chief market in the Arabian peninsula. Not only African slaves were brought thither for resale, but also Circassians, Malays, Indians and Central Asians. They were then distributed by individual buyers throughout the Muslim world.[13]

A small number of Africans stayed back in the holy cities of western Arabia in pursuit of higher religious studies. West Africans of the Mālikite school of law predominated.[14] Those from East Africa sat at the feet of their Shāfiʿite professors in the North Yemeni towns of Zabid and Beit al-Fakīh and the celebrated religious centres of the Hadramawt – Tarim, ʿAinat, Seiwun and Gaidun.[15]

As in previous centuries African slave labour was indispensable in the social, economic and political spheres of many Asian societies. In areas dominated by British and Dutch colonial powers, especially in India and the Malay archipelago, slaves, including Africans, provided the base of a plantation economy similar to that found in the Americas. In the Middle East, especially in Arabia, a large number of African slaves were variously employed in domestic capacities as chambermaids, sailors, soldiers, administrators, shop assistants and the like. In the rural areas they worked as agricultural labourers, water carriers, camel drivers and shepherds. As mentioned above, Ethiopians, as contrasted to Nubians, Sudanese and East Africans, were much favoured and did lighter work.[16] J. L. Burckhardt, the Victorian traveller, observed that, alongside their bonded compatriots,

10. Not all members of these diaspora communities were slaves, a number were political exiles. Leaders of abortive anti-colonial revolts in Indonesia, for example, were sent to the Dutch penal settlement on Sri Lanka and to the Cape Colony. On estimates of the number of slaves that were shipped to Asia see B. A. Ogot, 1979, p. 177. For varying figures see J. B. Kelly, 1968, pp. 414–16; W. Wilburn, 1813, Vol. 1, pp. 35, 60.

11. For recent studies on West African pilgrims see U. al-Naqar, 1972, and J. S. Berks, 1978.

12. B. Lewis, 1971, p. 37.

13. For details on the Mecca slave market see C. S. Hurgronje, 1970, pp. 14–15; R. Burton, 1964, Vol. 1, p. 252. On the redistribution of African slaves see R. Winstedt, 1958, p. 53, W. Ochsenwald, 1980, pp. 115–26.

14. C. S. Hurgronje, 1970, p. 182.

15. See *Majalah al-Rabitah al-ʾAlawi*, 1350 AH, Vol. 4, pp. 30–1.

16. C. S. Hurgronje, 1970, pp. 11, 13.

poor African pilgrims largely from West Africa – known locally as 'Tekrourys' – served during their sojourn as porters, dockers, streetsweepers, firewood-fetchers, makers of pots, mats and baskets, and brewers of an intoxicating drink called 'bouza'.[17]

In India, the African slave undertook a number of menial tasks which Indians either could not (because of caste restrictions) or would not perform, or for which the British deemed themselves to be unsuited. In the princely states, slaves, especially Africans, served primarily as domestics – concubines, eunuchs, water carriers, barbers, personal guards, stableboys, etc. We are informed that the king of Oudh (in what is now Uttar Pradesh) was supplied in the early nineteenth century with many Ethiopian male and female slaves and paid princely sums for them. Upon purchase they were all converted to Islam. We are also told that 'the rich and aristocratic Muslims, especially those who lived in cities like Patna and Calcutta, used to own besides male and female slaves, a large number of Habshi [Ethiopian] eunuchs'.[18] As in earlier periods, African slaves were considered to be luxury and prestige commodities. An owner's social status was measured by the number of his slaves, who constituted an important part of his retinue and an ostentatious way of displaying wealth and power.

In the Bengal, Bombay and Madras Presidencies, in addition to carrying out obvious domestic tasks slaves, notably from Madagascar, also played vital economic and military roles in the development of these infant British colonies. British East India Company records for the late eighteenth and early nineteeenth centuries testify to the arduous work they carried out in the building of fortifications (eg. Fort St David in South India) as soldiers, sailors, dockers, and agricultural labourers.[19]

In the Malay Archipelago, especially on the west coast of Sumatra, such as the British settlement of Benkulen,[20] African slaves worked in a variety of ways as soldiers, trained mechanics, masons and carpenters, in addition to gathering and transporting pepper. The least-favoured were those who laboured under atrocious conditions in the Dutch gold mines, especially at Salida.[21]

The assimilation of peoples of African origin into the local Asian populations was not as widespread as is often assumed, despite the time-honoured custom of concubinage.[22] Traits of a 'closed mode of slavery'

17. J. L. Burckhardt, 1829, pp. 258–75, 382.

18. A. K. Chattopadhyay, 1977, pp. 29, 40–1.

19. H. Dodwell (ed.), 1920, pp. 104, 135.

20. W. F. Mees (ed.), 1920 (Court to Fort Marlborough, 25 February 1773). Slaves also laboured in the sugar and arrack industry.

21. See J. Paulus (ed.), 1917–21, Vol. 1, pp. 806–11.

22. See the propaganda line summed up in C. Doughty, 1926, Vol. 1, pp. 554–5, 'In those Africans there is no resentment that they have been made slaves – they are often captives of their own wars – even though cruel men-stealers rent them from their parentage. The patrons who paid their price have adopted them into their households, the males are

similar to those of the slave systems in the Americas were often visible. It was inconceivable, for example, that an African, either as a slave or a freed man, would be accepted into the kinship system of his owner. Africans were 'maintained as separate ethnic groups that reproduced themselves either by natural processes or by constant recruitments'. Formidable social barriers were erected to prevent them entering the mainstream of society. Not only were they not assimilated but were 'kept at arm's length by virtue of the stigma attached to their status of slave'.[23]

In the valleys and towns of south-western Arabia are still to be found many diverse groups of peoples of African origin – the Akhdam, Subyan, Hujūr and the Gabart.[24] They do the most menial of jobs as scavengers and sweepers, work considered polluting and unclean by the Arab inhabitants. They are virtually considered as outcasts and obliged to live in their separate quarters. The lot of poor African pilgrims in the Ḥidjāz was hardly any better. It was reported that most of them were found living together in some of the huts of the public place called 'El Menakh' in the holy city of Medina.[25] According to H. R. Dickson,[26] no true Arab would marry a freed slave woman, as it constituted a blot on the badge of honour and blood of the group. Many Sidis were reported in Bombay as living in their own quarter near the city prison.[27] The British East India Company slaves on the island of Sumatra were forced to inhabit 'a small village near the sea' away from the Malay settlements and the fort.[28]

circumcised and – that which enfranchises their souls, even in the long passion of homesickness – God has visited them in their mishap, they can say, "it was His Grace" since they are thereby entered into the saving religion. This therefore, they think is the better country'. Contrast the picture of cruelty, discrimination, escapes and revolts so apparent in the documents; see D. Lombardi, 1971, p. 237; A. K. Chattopadhyay, 1977, pp. 42, 45, 53; C. Colomb, 1873, pp. 101–2; H. R. Dickson, 1941, p. 502, on Arab attitudes on the handling of domestic slaves; and D. C. Philliot and R. F. Azoo, 1906–7, pp. 431, 434, on prejudices shown against Africans in the Hadramawt. On the islands of Negrais, at the mouth of the Bassein river in Lower Burma, a settlement established by the Government of Fort St George in India, owing to the 'unconciliating and perverse disposition' of its superintendent, a state of unceasing fervent prevailed. 'Caffre slaves who had been introduced for the purpose of cultivating the land rose against their masters, and seizing on the boats belonging to the island effected their escape.' See M. Symes, 1800, p. 10.

23. See the analysis in M. Finley, 1976, pp. 819–21.

24. R. B. Serjeant, 1966, pp. 28–33.

25. J. L. Burckhardt, 1829, p. 382.

26. H. R. Dickson, 1941, p. 503.

27. The Gazeteer of Bombay City and Island, 1910, Vol. 2, p. 262.

28. J. Bastin, 1965, p. 43. In the British Indian Empire the slaveowner was by law given full power over his property. It was held quite proper to seek to recover fugitive slaves. It was illegal on the part of anyone to 'harbour such runaways as knowingly to receive any stolen property'. The slave who absconded was open to punishment, usually by flogging. Many advertisements appeared in the Indian press of the period offering rewards for the return of runaways and warnings against their employment. See A. K. Chattopadhyay, 1977, p. 57. In the Middle East, cases of runaway slaves were common, and dated back as

PLATE 28.3 *Black servant and eunuch with the child of their master in East India in the nineteenth century*

It is interesting to note that these disparate African diaspora communities were well organized, and kept alive their own national traditions. C. S. Hurgronje[29] observed that the Nubians of Mecca were superficial Muslims and spoke little Arabic and 'from Thursday afternoon to Friday morning they hold festival, regaling themselves with their national music with song and dance. Each community of such Negroes has its own Shaykh who settles disputes by his judicial sentences, and by his side stands an officer called nagib with a stick to carry out sentences.'

The diaspora in Europe

Although the African diaspora took place mainly through the slave trade, Africans also found their way into the outer world as free people independent of the slave trade, or as a new phase of life after a period of slavery in the tropical Americas. Indeed, Africans had been present in Western Europe from Classical Antiquity onwards, though the numbers only became substantial from about the fifteenth century on, when black Africans, first as slaves and then as freedmen, began to appear in southern Spain and Portugal, arriving at first by way of the trans-Saharan trade to North Africa. Then, as the direct maritime trade from Europe began to open in the second half of the century, still larger numbers of Africans appeared in Europe.[30]

Many were slaves at first, especially in Portugal, the only significant slave-trading European power till nearly the middle of the seventeenth century. Over time, however, many found their way into the broader European society, though often at the bottom of the social hierarchy, since their social condition was assimilated to that of their fellow Africans who did most of the physical labour in the tropical colonies. Their legal status was also ambiguous. The law, in northern Europe generally, no longer recognized the status of slave, though European colonial laws did. From 1685, residence in France was held to confer freedom, and the same was true of England after the notable judicial decision of Lord Mansfield in 1772 already noted. In both situations, however, slaves from the colonies were still slaves *de facto*; in many instances until the European powers abolished slavery in the colonies themselves, in 1834 for Britain, 1848 for France, and 1888 for Brazil.

In spite of their ambiguous legal status, free Africans were present in Western Europe in considerable numbers from at least the mid-eighteenth century on. Estimates vary, but by 1800 they would have numbered several thousand in each of Spain, Portugal, France, or Britain; and in Spain or Portugal they would have been more numerous in an earlier period. The

far as it has been ascertained to tenth-century Iraq. For details see C. Pellat, 1953, pp. 233–4. For Sumatra see J. Bastin. op. cit., p. 89.

29. C. S. Hurgronje, 1970, pp. 11–12. See also M. b. Hashim, 1350 AH, pp. 42–3.

30. A. C. de C. M. Saunders, 1982.

numbers were small in any case, compared with total European populations, but the African immigrants tended to be concentrated in the main cities, particularly in the port towns, so that their presence was more visible than their numbers would suggest.[31] It goes without saying that, for any period before the 1840s, far more people of tropical African descent would have been found in Europe than Europeans in tropical Africa.

This community of Africans in Europe was also concentrated in certain occupations, especially domestic service, this being partly a carry-over from the occupational status of Africans who came by way of West Indian slavery, partly a reflection of the European fad for exotic servants. African sailors were also common by this time in the merchant service, though more so in Portugal than in France or Britain. Another significant, if smaller, group was made up of students, who began to arrive in Europe in significant numbers by the middle of the eighteenth century and, in increasing numbers, throughout the nineteenth century. In an era in which commercial contact between Europe and Africa was increasing, it was an obvious advantage to African traders to be literate in a Western language and to have some acquaintance with European accounting practices. Many of these students therefore came to Europe through the good offices of European slave-traders operating in Africa and studied under their care in the principal slave-trade ports like Liverpool or Nantes.

Still another peculiarity of the African communities in Europe was the fact that they were overwhelmingly male. This fact had two important implications. The African community was not self-sustaining. It had to be, and was, constantly replenished from overseas. This is not to say that the Africans had no sexual relations with European women, but the products of these relationships tended to be culturally European rather than African. After a few generations, the African physical appearance tended to disappear into the general European genetic pool.

Some Africans also found their way into Eastern Europe, in spite of a more attenuated maritime contact with tropical Africa itself. There, the main line of entry was by way of the Ottoman slave trade, which was not mainly a trade in North Africans, but included sub-Saharan Africans drawn across the Sahara to Ottoman-associated ports like Tripoli, or brought north down the Nile from what is now the southern Sudan.[32] In a few instances, small pockets of African culture persisted in parts of the Ottoman empire into the twentieth century, such as a small Hausa-speaking community in what is now Yugoslavia.

31. P. D. Curtin, 1967, esp. pp. 3–16; W. Rodney, 1975; W. B. Cohen, 1980, especially pp. 110–52.

32. E. R. Toledano, 1982.

The western diaspora: background to the nineteenth century

Compared with Europe and Asia, the African diaspora in the Americas was enormous. The Afro-American population at the beginning of the nineteenth century, including both the free and the enslaved, has been estimated at approximately 8.5 million. Of this number more than 2 million, or nearly 25 per cent, lived in the USA, the majority by far living in the so-called 'Slave States' along the Atlantic seaboard from Delaware to Florida, with small concentrations throughout the northern and interior states east of the Mississippi river, especially in large cities like New York, Boston and Philadelphia. In 1810, about 2 million Africans and Afro-Americans were in the Antillean islands of the Caribbean Sea. Slightly more than 1 million were in the English Caribbean islands of Jamaica, St Kitts, Antigua, Nevis, Anguilla, St Lucia, St Vincent, Barbados, Grenada and Trinidad. Haiti, formerly the flourishing French sugar colony of Saint-Domingue, had about 450 000. Cuba had 400 000; Puerto Rico, 280 000. Brazil had 2.5 million, and mainland Spanish America had a combined total of about 1.3 million. Most Afro-Americans in Puerto Rico were free, as were the great majority of the 400 000 in Mexico; 400 000 in Venezuela; 200 000 in Colombia; 50 000 in Ecuador; and 30 000 each in Chile and Argentina.[33]

The general conditions in which the African and Afro-American population found itself during the nineteenth century, therefore, depended on a large number of factors. The proportion of the non-white population in the society was one factor. The ratio of slave to free was another. The profile of the trade, the way each colony developed and socio-economic changes from time to time also affected the black experience in the Americas. This black experience throughout the Americas varied considerably, and should not be considered to be a single, undeviating common form for all colonies and all places. Afro-American society responded to local conditions everywhere, although patterns can be traced which illustrate a uniformity or basic similarity from the USA to Brazil.[34]

The basic divisions in Afro-American society and culture stemmed less from the imperial boundaries which affected the evolution of the American societies than from their fortuitous circumstances of location, crop culture and socio-economic structures. Throughout the Americas, Africans – slaves as well as free – living and working in cities seemed to enjoy a wider contact,

33. The population figures, rounded and adjusted in some cases, are taken from J. H. Franklin, 1969, pp. 120, 145–9, 171, 174, 186; F. Tannenbaum, 1946, pp. 8–14; R. Conrad, 1972, p. 283; J. V. Lombardi, 1971, p. 35; P. D. Curtin, 1969, p. 22; G. Aguirre de Beltran, 1972, pp. 233–4; F. P. Bowser, 1974, p. 333; D. W. Cohen and J. P. Greene, 1972, pp. 4, 10, 14.

34. M. Harris, 1964; H. Hoetink, 1973; R. B. Toplin (ed.), 1974, and 1981; P. Villiers, 1982.

more opportunities for upward social mobility and greater opportunities for liberty than those held in large gangs on rural plantations, *haciendas*, and *ingenios*. And this generalization seemed valid across the conventional imperial divisions. Also, with the exception of the USA, life expectancy under slavery was considerably less than in the free society, with the consequence that all the American slave societies south of the Rio Bravo (called the Rio Grande in the USA) suffered an absolute decline among the non-free sector of the population.[35]

Latin Americans had a longer social experience with the institution of slavery and its concomitant social effects than their fellow colonists in British or French America. Apart from their Iberian frontier experience, Spanish and Portuguese colonists used Africans as slaves for more than a hundred years before the English and French established their slave colonies in Barbados, Jamaica, Plymouth, Virginia, the Carolinas, Louisiana and Saint-Domingue.[36]

Yet, by the nineteenth century, the differences between the slave systems in the western hemisphere were more differences of degree than fundamental differences of kind. In all systems manumission from the status of slavery was relatively rare; women benefited more from the laws than men; family integrity remained fragile; and colour and origin constituted major factors in status considerations.

One dismal reflection of the general condition of the Afro-American population during its centuries of the American experience can be deduced from the astonishing fact that the overall population of 8.5 million Africans and Afro-Americans existing in the Americas at the beginning of the nineteenth century almost certainly represented less than the number of Africans transported to the Americas after 1600.[37]

The single largest American importer of African slaves was Brazil. During the course of the slave trade, Brazil received approximately 38 per cent of all Africans introduced to the New World. The region which today comprises Latin America and the Caribbean altogether absorbed 86 per cent of the trade; with 36 per cent ending up in the Caribbean islands. But the history of the African in the New World cannot be appreciated merely by considering the gross figures for the trade, like some bulk cargo carried and left in the various states of the Americas. A more meaningful sense of the varying impact and varied possibilities for social development is gleaned

35. P. D. Curtin, 1969; S. L. Engerman and E. D. Genovese (eds), 1975.

36. L. Hanke, 1970; M. Crahan and F. W. Knight (eds), 1979.

37. Estimates of the number of Africans who came to the Americas by way of the slave trade vary from as low as 3.5 million to a high of 25 million. P. D. Curtin, 1969, gives the best overall profile of volume flow, suggesting almost 10 million. Curtin's figures have been modified somewhat by a recent synthesis using the very large amount of new data that have appeared since 1969, yielding an addition of 2 to 3 per cent. See, J. E. Inikori, 1976a; E. Vila Vilar, 1977a, pp. 267–80; S. L. Engerman and E. D. Genovese (eds), 1975, pp. 3–128; H. A. Gemery and J. S. Hogendorn (eds), 1979, and, especially, P. E. Lovejoy, 1982.

by looking at the relative participation of these various regions century by century. Differences in the date of entry into the trans-Atlantic trade, and fluctuations in the volume of acceptances played some part in the demographic and cultural forms which eventually emerged in the Americas by the late nineteenth century.

Before 1600, the Americas were truly the hegemonic preserve of the Iberians, and so the Spanish and the Portuguese divided the Africans who came to the New World during that time, with the Spanish getting about 60 per cent, or more than 125 000.[38] Those Africans helped maintain social viability, while the new diseases introduced by the incoming Europeans and Africans decimated the local indigenous Indian populations, especially in the highlands of Mexico and Peru.[39] Considering the later history of the African in the New World, it is interesting to note that at the end of the sixteenth century, Africans in general considered themselves superior to the local Indians, and treated them with the same arrogance and condescension that their fellow Spanish did in Spanish America.[40]

About a million and a half Africans came to the Americas during the seventeenth century. Of this number, 41 per cent went to Brazil, 35 per cent went to the fledgling British, Dutch and French colonies (mainly in the circum-Caribbean region), and 22 per cent went to Spanish America. This was the period in which the fully organized, highly capitalized trans-Atlantic slave trade began. The annual average importation rate rose from about 1800 Africans during the sixteenth century, to more than 17 000. The declining relative participation of the Spanish reflected the demographic recovery of the mainland Indian populations. But the slack in the Spanish sector was more than compensated for by the increasing demand for labourers in the expanding Brazilian sugar zones of the north-east, and the developing socio-economic complex based on sugar production in the eastern Caribbean islands.

The eighteenth century constituted the apogee of the African migration to the Americas. Both the plantation societies in the Americas and the slave trade which supplied the manpower needs reached their fullest maturity. Between 1700 and 1810 more than half of all the Africans ever to come to the New World arrived: perhaps far more than 6 million Africans. In demographic terms, it was probably the period of the greatest reciprocal impact between Africa and the wider world, with established commercial contacts across the Indian Ocean as well as with Europe and the Americas.

Of the staggering number of eighteenth-century imports, Brazil received 31.3 per cent, or more than 1.8 million Africans. The British Caribbean got 23.2 per cent – about 1.4 million slaves – with more than 600 000 going

38. P. D. Curtin, 1969; E. Vila Vilar, 1973, 1977b; J. Palacios Preciados, 1973.

39. W. M. Denevan, 1976; E. Wolf, 1959, pp. 194–6; C. Gibson, 1967, pp. 140–59; A. W. Crosby, 1972.

40. J. Lockhart, 1968, pp. 171–98.

to the principal sugar-producing island of Jamaica. The French Antilles received 22.3 per cent, or more than 1.3 million, with their premier plantation colony of Saint-Domingue on the western part of Hispaniola getting nearly 800 000 slaves. Spanish America imported 9.6 per cent, or more than 600 000, with the majority going to their Caribbean islands of Cuba and Puerto Rico and the eastern part of Hispaniola, their coastal colonies on the northern fringe of South America, and the interior of Peru via the Rio de la Plata region. The Dutch and the Danish Caribbean got 5.8 per cent, or approximately 450 000; and the USA – which until 1776 comprised the colonies of British North America – took in about 5.8 per cent, or somewhat less than 400 000 Africans.[41]

TABLE 28.1 *Slave imports, 1700–1810*

Region	*Approximate percentage of all Africans**	*Approximate number of Africans*
Brazil	31.3	1 800 000
British Caribbean	23.2	1 400 000
French Antilles	22.3	1 300 000
Spanish America	9.6	600 000
Dutch and Danish Antilles	8.0	450 000
British North America–USA	5.8	350 000
TOTAL		5 900 000

* Does not add up to 100 per cent because of rounding off of figures.

The eighteenth century, then, represented the period *par excellence* of the growth of the plantation slave society in the New World. The classical examples were the sugar, indigo, coffee and spice plantations of the Caribbean region and Brazil, and the rice and cotton plantations booming in the southern and south-western part of the USA after 1790. The agricultural revolution in the Americas flourished during the period and the local export economies expanded and stabilized.[42] Besides, the local societies had attained by the end of the century a form of rigidity, self-assurance and maturity which were to influence their attitudes and ways of life in the later nineteenth century. These attitudes fashioned the pattern of inclusion or exclusion of all later immigrants to the Americas, as well as definitively freezing the profile of all groups in the local societies. Not surprisingly, the very time when the American colonies of the Europeans were breaking

41. These figures are based on adjustments of those published in P. D. Curtin, 1969, 1976.

42. R. Davis, 1973.

away from their metropoles in the name of freedom, they were busily circumscribing ever more sharply the freedom, expectations and legal privileges of their non-white population. With the eighteenth century began the most dismal period of depression and exploitation of the Africans in the New World.[43]

The abolitionist period

Nevertheless, by 1810 the tide had begun to change inexorably for the American slave society. The institutions of slavery slowly crumbled from within and without. The curious combination of political freedom which gave white Americans a greater voice in their internal affairs, economic self-interest, humanitarianism, imperial incompatibility, and the unquenchable thirst for liberty on the part of the enslaved, ultimately destroyed the American slave system.[44] The political independence of the USA after 1776, Haiti after 1804, the mainland Spanish colonies after 1825, and Brazil after 1822, gave a different complexion to the political dimension of the system of slavery and the slave trade, and had repercussions outside the parochial boundaries of each empire, colony and state.

The loss of the British North American colonies in 1783 and the termination of the British slave trade in 1808 affected slavery and the African in profound ways. The largest and most efficient supplier removed itself from the market, and began an intensive campaign to persuade other European states to follow its example. The British anti-slavery campaign sharply reduced the number of Africans taken to the Americas during the nineteenth century, although the total remains high. Before the trade ended in 1870, the pattern returned to that which prevailed during its first century.[45] The Spanish and Portuguese colonies again became the major importers. Of the nearly 2 million Africans who arrived in the New World during this period, more than 1.1 million (or about 60 per cent) went to Brazil. More than 600 000 (about 31.9 per cent) went to the Spanish Antilles, with the greater proportion by far going to Cuba. The rest went to the French Caribbean, with a small number entering the USA.

The trans-Atlantic slave trade, and therefore the migration of Africans, responded to the expanding demands for a labour force to develop the agricultural potential of the new-found lands as well as the supply conditions for Africans in Africa.[46] Most Africans consequently entered plantation agricultural complexes in the Americas.

But since the plantation complex varied throughout the Americas the socializing forces within which the Africans and their descendants would

43. F. W. Knight, 1974; R. B. Toplin (ed.), 1974.
44. I. Berlin and R. Hoffman (eds), 1983.
45. H. Hoetink, 1979, pp. 20–40.
46. H. S. Klein (ed.), 1978, pp. 239–45; S. Miers and I. Kopytoff (eds), 1977, pp. 3–78.

mould their own American culture likewise varied. Throughout the Americas, therefore, the amalgam of cultures would demonstrate great variety.

Certainly this can be seen in the modifications which took place in the worship of Shango, perhaps the most widely distributed African religious form in the New World.[47] While the Nigerian – more specifically, the Yoruba – origin was never in doubt, the forms of Shango varied considerably from Cuba, to Trinidad, to Haiti, to Brazil. In Cuba, in particular, the cult became quite Catholicized, and the originally male African Shango became female, while other forms of the ritual as well as the symbols were transposed and, in some cases, transformed. What held true for the worship of Shango also followed in other aspects of community life and organization. It became increasingly more difficult for creole Africans to maintain their original social forms in the New World, however great their numbers, owing to the development of a structure which had stabilized by the nineteenth century, and to which they were forced to become a part, and to make necessary adaption.

The inescapable reality for Africans coming to the New World in the nineteenth century meant that at the very time when they were affecting the pattern of cultural transmission – as they had always done – they themselves were enormously affected by the profound changes that slavery and the slave trade had wrought on Africa, the Americas, and Europe. These changes naturally affected, in turn, the culture of these three areas, and contributed to a sharper distinction and discrimination of each region's peculiar culture.[48]

Part of this reality, of course, was the bewildering variation in the situation in which an arriving African could find himself. In the Caribbean, the Africans formed the majority of the population. The phenotype was self-evidently black. In the USA on the other hand, black phenotypes were a minority of the national population, however concentrated they might have been in some individual states. In parts of Latin America such as Ecuador, Chile and Argentina, the blacks had virtually disappeared genetically among the American Indian and European groups, illustrating a broad spectrum of biological intermixture.[49]

Nor did the demographic evolution of the regions follow the logical pattern of relative participation in the trans-Atlantic slave trade. The Afro-American components of American societies did not necessarily correspond to the proportion of Africans imported during the centuries of the slave trade. Brazil, for example, imported about 4 million slaves during the course of the trade, a figure which, as we have noted, was approximately

47. W. R. Bascom, 1972; R. G. Hamilton, 1970, pp. 356–73; M. Schuler, 1980, pp. 30–44; G. E. Simpson, 1978, pp. 75–82, and 190–2.
48. H. L. Shapiro, 1953.
49. G. R. Andrews, 1980.

38 per cent of the trans-Atlantic trade.[50] At the end of slavery in 1890, Brazil had an Afro-American population of about 4 million, which comprised 33 per cent of the local Brazilian population and about 36 per cent of the total Afro-American population of the western hemisphere. The Caribbean region imported approximately 5 million slaves, or 43 per cent of the trade, and when the last Caribbean island to abolish slavery – Cuba – did so in 1886, the region had a mere 3 million Afro-Americans, which, while they averaged about 60 per cent of the local regional population, accounted for only 18 per cent of the total Afro-Americans in the hemisphere. The USA received about 0.5 million Africans from the trade, or about 4.5 per cent, but had an Afro-American population of about 4.5 million at the end of slavery there in 1865. This group formed only 7.0 per cent of the local population, but was 40.5 per cent of all the Afro-Americans in the western hemisphere.

TABLE 28.2 *Slave imports and nineteenth-century populations*

Region	*Slaves (millions)*	*Percentage of trade*	*Afro-American population* (millions)	*Percentages of population* Local	Hemisphere
Brazil	4.0	38.0	4.0 (1890)	33.0	36.0
Caribbean	5.0	43.0	2.2 (1886)	60.0	18.0
USA	0.5	4.5	4.5 (1865)	7.0	40.0

The figures in Table 28.2 demonstrate quite unequivocally a marked variation in the ability of regional black populations to expand during the period of the slave trade and slavery. In general, with the exception of the USA, Afro-American populations either stagnated, or failed to expand naturally. In Latin America and the Caribbean, the slave populations declined at the astonishing rate of 2.0 to 4.0 per cent per annum, resulting in an overall slave population at the end of slavery which was far less than the total number of slaves imported to the colonies, a decline which could not be made up by the normal healthy growth of the free population.

A few examples illustrate the general pattern. During the eighteenth century alone, Jamaica imported more than 600 000 slaves. In 1838, at the end of slavery, the slave population was less than 250 000 and the entire black population under 350 000. Saint-Domingue imported more than 800 000 slaves during the eighteenth century, yet the slave population numbered a mere 480 000 in 1790 on the eve of the revolution there. The total non-white population numbered half a million. Between 1810 and 1870 Cuba imported about 600 000 African slaves. In 1810, the free non-white population of Cuba numbered about 114 000 individuals. By 1880 the

50. Slave importation figures based on P. D. Curtin, 1969; Afro-American populations derived from D. W. Cohen and J. P. Greene (eds), 1972, pp. 4–14.

slave population was estimated at merely 200 000 and the free non-white population slightly more than 269 000 persons.

The drastic decline of the American slave populations (except in the case of the USA) provides the most serious indictment of the system of slavery which failed dismally either to create an inherently viable and self-reproducing society or to provide an efficient and reliable labour supply. Moreover, the legacies of slavery permanently retarded the abilities of the Afro-American population to compete effectively in those political, economic and social structures where they did not form the overwhelming majority of the population.

The impact of Africa

When the American slave systems disintegrated during the nineteenth century, the basic institutional forms and social attitudes of the societies had already been established. In general American societies were hostile to Africans and African culture.

Nevertheless, the impact of Africa was inescapable in many aspects of American society: phenotype, language, music, religion, cuisine, art, agriculture and architecture. In some cases, the influences from Africa were strong enough and pervasive enough to forge a genuine Afro-American culture competing with, and sometimes complementing the European-derived culture.

In the USA the political structure imposed a rigid dichotomy between black and white in the population, relegating any individual with any degree of African ancestry to the category of black.[51] By contrast, throughout the rest of the hemisphere a three-tiered social categorization prevailed, corresponding to the dominant groups of black, mixed, and white. The relatively small number of white persons at the top of the social pyramid in most societies afforded the dominant African majorities the opportunity to impose their values and their cultures on the rest of the society.

Within the three-tiered structure each caste had its own set of legal rights and social privileges based on a combination of wealth, colour and occupation. In the sugar and plantation-based economic zones of Brazil, the Caribbean, and the lowlands of Mexico, Colombia and Peru, the rights of slaves as well as free persons of colour tended to be circumscribed in direct proportion to the overall demands of their labour. In the coffee, cattle and fishing areas of south-eastern Brazil, Puerto Rico, eastern Cuba, and the interior provinces of Venezuela and Argentina, social mobility tended to be greater, social distances shorter, and internal class and caste distinctions more relaxed and less formal than in the plantation zones. Meanwhile, in the towns and cities like Buenos Aires, Lima, São Paulo, Caracas, Havana, Vera Cruz, Puebla and Mexico City, Africans enjoyed

51. L. Foner, 1970; W. Jordan, 1968; P. Mason, 1970.

considerable freedom from restraint, and often competed for some of the occupations performed by other free members of the society. These social arrangements affected but did not determine the relationship between Afro-Americans and the rest of the population in the later nineteenth century and the twentieth century.

While slavery persisted, the majority of Africans and Afro-Americans served either as agricultural field hands, or in domestic service. Nevertheless, about 20 per cent were sailors, curers, artisans, muleteers, nursemaids, wetnurses, merchants, property owners (including property in slaves), shopkeepers, mining and sugar experts, and vendors of fish, condiments and ground provisions. Indeed, in the later eighteenth century Edward Long was complaining that a substantial proportion of the currency in Jamaica was in the hands of this sector of the population, and that they monopolized the transportation systems overland as well as along the coast.[52]

This situation did not change very much after slavery was abolished, although the number of peasant farmers of African descent increased sharply in the Caribbean. Occupation and biological heritage could and did increase class and caste mobility both during and after slavery. An individual or a family could work their way outward and often upward from slavery to freedom, or from free black to mulatto (especially in Brazil and Spanish America), or from mulatto to white (an exceptional achievement requiring a considerable amount of money) when the indices of race were more strongly cultural than biological. By the later eighteenth century some Spanish American planters and merchants, doubtful of their status, bought certificates from the Crown, called *limpieza de sangre,* which certified that they had no Moorish or Jewish ancestors in at least the preceding four generations. Ultimately, however, internal social mobility and the general quality of life depended on the immediate circumstances of the community: on factors of demography, economy, law, social and political philosophy, and degree of cultural pluralism. For the less stable or mature the society, the more the Africans and Afro-Americans influenced the structure and carved a niche for themselves and their descendants.

Where they could – and where they had no other recourse – Africans and Afro-Americans adjusted to the conditions in which they found themselves. In a milieu of cultural symbiosis, Africans contributed almost as much to the rest of the society as they accepted from it. Of course, the more they needed and the less they found, the more they became creative – as the *patois* speech pattern of the previously French eastern Caribbean islands and the *papiamento* of the previously Dutch Antilles reveal. Creativity became especially necessary where a small number of Europeans lived among a large number of Africans as was the case in many colonies of exploitation such as Jamaica, Barbados, Trinidad and Saint-Domingue. Where the European population failed to comprise a critical mass, the

52. E. Long, 1774.

Africans had to build a society from a diverse collectivity of individuals who had little more in common than their skin colour and their servility. The adoption of their customs and behaviour by the non-African sector indicated the measure of their success.

Africans did not always conform to the society into which they were thrust. For centuries *marronage*, or the flight from the slave system, existed as an integral aspect of slavery.[53] In Brazil, the north-east witnessed the establishment of the *quilombo* of Palmares which lasted almost a century and which was eliminated only with the largest military force ever mounted in the Americas by the Portuguese and Brazilians. Maroon towns existed for equally long periods in Esmeraldas in Ecuador and in parts of the Blue Mountains and the Cockpit Country of Jamaica. *Marronage* manifested not only the wish to be free, it was an eloquent and visible condemnation of the system of slavery by Africans.

By the time African slavery was eliminated in the Americas, the position of the African sector had worsened dramatically from what it had been a century before. The political and economic reconstruction that followed the Civil War in the USA accompanied a movement of legal discrimination and social and economic exclusion of the non-white sector, characterized by segregated institutions, lynchings, and overtly racist societies and organizations, which combined until the middle of the twentieth century.[54] The general conditions experienced by black Americans then compared with those prevailing today in a more extreme way in South Africa.

In the USA Afro-Americans formed a small minority, relatively powerless in political terms. By contrast, in Haiti they controlled the state after the revolution of 1789, and, throughout the nineteenth century, African cultural revival became the strongest social cement for that impoverished, isolated country, especially exemplified in the syncretic religious practice of *vodun*. Elsewhere, in places like Cuba, Jamaica, Barbados, and Brazil, a small number of Afro-Americans attained positions of social prestige and political power. The long, bitter and difficult wars in Cuba between 1868 and 1898 made Afro-Cubans such as Antonio Maceo and Máximo Gomez national heroes and international figures in the struggle for political independence. Nevertheless, as late as 1912 Cuba still experienced a major racial war, and hostility to Afro-Cubans did not diminish until the Revolution led by Fidel Castro in 1959.

Afro-American accomplishments both at the individual and at the collective level were outstanding during the nineteenth century. Despite the diverging paths of Africa and the Americas, despite their monumental legal and social disabilities, despite their enormous economic handicaps, despite the aggressive antagonism of white Americans, the Africans created successful communities throughout the Americas. They established edu-

53. Y. Debbasch, 1961–2; M. Schuler, 1970; R. Price, 1973.
54. G. Myrdal, 1944.

PLATE 28.4 *Toussaint L'Ouverture, leader of the Saint-Domingue revolution and father of independent Haiti*

cational institutions such as the Mico Colleges in Antigua and Jamaica, Codrington College in Barbados, and a number of colleges in the USA: Virginia Union University (1864), Atlanta University and Fisk University (1865) and the Hampton Institute and Howard University in 1867. Afro-

Americans have played a significant role in American technological innovation. Benjamin Banneker, from Maryland, a mathematician and almanac publisher, assisted in the surveying of the District of Columbia. Between 1835 and 1836, Henry Blair, a slave from Maryland, patented two corn harvesters. In the 1850s Benjamin Montgomery, a slave owned by Jefferson Davis, the President of the Confederate States of the South, invented a propeller for boats. Norbert Rilleux, born in New Orleans and educated in Paris, invented in 1846 the vacuum evaporation pan which considerably advanced the process of sugar refining. In 1852, Elijah McKoy invented the cup which allowed machines to be lubricated while in operation. Jan Matzeliger, born in Dutch Guiana, invented the lasting machine which revolutionized the shoe industry of New England. George Washington Carver, the agricultural chemist from Tuskegee Institute, invented more than three hundred products from the peanut, thereby reinvigorating the agricultural economy of many parts of the South.[55]

The diaspora was cruel and difficult for the transported Africans. Involuntarily dislocated and transferred to strange lands, placed in the most onerous servility, and often associated with hostile people, these Africans demonstrated heroic patience, perseverance, adaptability and creativity. Eventually they became an unavoidable part of most American societies. Through civil and international wars, through prosperity and depression, and all types of political change, Africans worked, fought, and eventually established themselves within the several nations in the Americas as well as Europe.

The diaspora and Africa

But the thought of Africa remained a constant theme, pursued with varying degrees of seriousness by both white and black Americans. In the USA, the idea of the repatriation of Africans had been mentioned occasionally throughout the eighteenth century, most notably in 1777, when Thomas Jefferson sponsored a report in a committee of the Virginia legislature. Repatriation began in earnest after 1815, however, when a small group of thirty-eight black Americans led by Paul Cuffe returned to Africa. By 1830, Liberia had become the focus for a general colony of repatriated Africans, mostly ex-slaves, sponsored by the American Colonization Society with the financial support of the Federal as well as many State governments. By 1860, only about 15 000 settlers had returned to Africa. After the Civil War, less than 2000 settlers made the trip, despite the rapid deterioration of the conditions of life for Afro-Americans in the USA.

Two other sources provided returning immigrants. The first came from the unknown number of maroons and Africans taken from confiscated slave ships during the nineteenth century, and shipped back to Africa by the

55. J.H. Franklin, 1969, p. 197.

British in their zealous attempt to terminate the trade in slaves and replace it by 'legitimate' trade. The second source of African returnees came from an even smaller number of missionaries recruited in the Caribbean and southern states of the USA, principally by the Moravians and Presbyterians, to assist in the propagation of the Christian Gospel in West Africa. The most well-known example of this is perhaps the Basel Mission enterprise among the Akwapim hills of Ghana in the 1830s and 1840s, and their decision in 1843 to use Jamaicans as substitutes for German and Swiss missionaries whose mortality in the field proved too high for evangelical efficacy.

While Africans who came to the New World can be numbered in millions, their descendants who returned to Africa amounted to only a few thousands.[56] Many reasons account for this, not the least of which was the significant lack of support to establish the type of transportation system which had previously facilitated the westward trans-Atlantic flow. Repatriation during the nineteenth century offered few material rewards for Europeans or non-Europeans. But by 1900, the divergence between Africa and the Americas had become too great. Persons of African descent became caught up in the self-consciousness of the age which produced the type of xenophobic nationalism that all but destroyed the appeal of Africa. Moreover, the interest in Africa after the end of the slave trade grew from national lusts for power and wealth – and Afro-Americans lacked both political power and the wealth needed to stimulate their own interest, or influence those who were partitioning Africa into colonial spheres. The Afro-American view became focused more on the new developments within their hemisphere. Internal and inter-regional migrations and the quest to establish the good life against new deleterious challenges absorbed their attention. The African connection faded, but did not die. The return-to-Africa movement found individual promoters who could occasionally infuse the movement with new appeal. In 1897, Henry Sylvester Williams, a Trinidadian-born lawyer living in London, founded the Pan-African Association, whose later membership would include George Padmore, Kwame Nkrumah and C. L. R. James. In the 1920s Marcus Garvey founded the Universal Negro Improvement Association, a movement designed to spur African decolonization and unite all Africans wherever they were found. Garvey's organization had branches in Canada, the USA, the Caribbean, Latin America and Africa.[57] By the time that Garvey's organization collapsed in 1927, Africa, and especially the Ethiopian question, had already begun to assume paramount importance in world affairs.

56. T. Shick, 1980.
57. T. Martin, 1976; E. D. Cronon, 1962; R. A. Hill (ed.), 1983.

29 Conclusion: Africa on the eve of the European conquest

J. F. A. AJAYI

Introduction

The aim of this concluding chapter is to highlight the main trends of African historical evolution at the end of the third quarter of the nineteenth century, particularly in the decade 1875–85, which saw the rising tide of European interest culminate in a scramble for territory, the Berlin West African Conference, the partition and the eventual conquest of Africa. A panoramic view of Africa on the eve of the European conquest suggests discernible, predominant trends in spite of the diverse varieties of states, peoples and polities, and seemingly divergent tendencies. A predominant trend would appear to have been the determined effort on the part of various African leaders to strengthen their power and their capacity to defend African territories and interests. These efforts were, however, systematically undermined and eventually subverted by the European presence.

As the chapters in this volume have shown, the nineteenth century in Africa was a period of rapid and sometimes contradictory changes. Up to the third quarter of the century, the most far-reaching and widespread of the changes had their origin in internal factors. Other changes were much affected or even initiated by European commercial, missionary or consular activities operating on the coast and, especially after 1850, increasingly penetrating into the interior. Some of the movements for change, such as the efforts of some rulers to unify Ethiopia and reform its institutions, were local in their impact. Others, like the activities of the ambitious khedives of Egypt in the Nile valley had repercussions throughout a whole region. The Mfecane had begun as a local affair, but soon spread over the whole of Southern, Central and parts of East Africa and, even on the eve of the European conquest, the history of these areas was still largely the history of the states that had resulted from it or were very much affected by it.[1]

The *djihād* movements of Islamic reformation covered the whole of the

1. See Chapter 10, above.

Sudanic zone of West Africa, and the eastern Sahara up to Cyrenaica, and spread south to the borders of the forest region as their impact reached Senegambia and the Voltaic regions, the southern Mandinka, northern Yoruba and the Edo-speaking peoples. As the European demand for palm oil, peanuts, ivory, sisal and rubber grew and the internal network of long-distance trade routes responded to these demands, trade became a major factor affecting access to firearms and the acquisition of wealth, and hence the rise and fall of states over wide areas of Africa. As a consequence of this expanding European trade and the activities of European and American missionaries, Christianity and European ideas of social and political organization also became factors of change over a wide area stretching from Sierra Leone to Southern Africa and Madagascar.

What stands out most prominently in these different movements is the efforts of various African leaders in the nineteenth century in different parts of the continent to reform their societies. Some of the efforts were inspired by the heritage of cultures in Africa, others by reformist ideas in Islam. In most cases, the leaders were only too ready to take advantage of opportunities offered by the expanding scope of trade and the activities of Europeans, whether traders or missionaries, hunters of game or hunters of concessions. Another feature that stands out just as prominently was how these efforts of African leaders to reform were systematically being undermined by the very activities of European traders, missionaries and hunters that African leaders tried to exploit.

It is remarkable how little attention so far has been paid to this feature of the nineteenth century: of internal efforts at reform systematically being aborted by external intervention. Because of the assumption that colonialism and integration into the world economy were necessary conditions of modernization, most historians have failed to notice how much the nineteenth century represented an African effort at self-development and to what extent European conquest and colonialism was a subversion of that effort.

Political structures

This effort at self-development was perhaps most prominent in the realm of political structures and state power. The grand lesson of the slave trade era long driven home in West and Central Africa, and being learnt in East Africa in the course of the nineteenth century, was that the way to survive and perhaps even profit from the slave trade was to strengthen the structures and military basis of state power.

At the beginning of the nineteenth century, as we have noted in most parts of Africa, 'the political and economic structures ... seemed to have a certain fragility about them. There appears to have been a perpetual ebb and flow in the frontiers of the state systems, and in the rise and fall of administrative centres.'[2] The state made minimum demands on people in the payment of homage, tribute and military service in return for protection. In most cases, the day-to-day life of the people largely revolved around a network of kinship, religious, judicial and economic institutions that often cut across state frontiers. Only in the Maghrib and Egypt had the operation of Islamic law over several centuries produced political structures with an appreciable level of durability. Elsewhere in Africa, tremendous effort had to be invested in the nineteenth century to evolve new and potentially more durable political structures. In the intense political rivalries that resulted, some of the effort was no doubt counterproductive and in some places the first visible result was disintegration of empires and decentralization, if not fragmentation, of authority. In the words of K. Arhin and J. Ki-Zerbo describing the Voltaic regions:

> During the nineteenth century, political instability and population movements were widespread. Brutal massacres and secessionist movements were led by the very people who were supposed to represent authority . . . Some notable exceptions notwithstanding, the frequency and extent of these conflicts grew and the tendency towards social dislocation was undoubtedly linked with the growing opportunities available to the peripheral powers and the rebels to obtain arms and use them to challenge the reigning chiefs.[3]

Notable examples of this tendency were the initial impact of the Mfecane, and the impact of trade and the Chokwe and Ovimbundu expansion on the Luba and Lunda state systems.[4] Several states and empires disappeared. And yet even more noticeable were the many new centres of power that emerged, experimenting with new administrative structures, generally tending towards a more effective exercise of power by the ruler, clearer definition of his jurisdiction, greater control of officials who owed their positions to his favour rather than their own hereditary rights, improved tax systems and the like.[5]

Some historians have described these reformist movements as the activities of African 'proto-nationalists and empire builders' engaged in a kind of African Scramble which in part provoked, or at least helps to explain, the European Scramble.[6] In fact, these reformist activities were not a sudden or fitful movement in any way comparable with the European Scramble. The search for more stable political structures had been going on throughout the nineteenth century and indeed before then as part of the general evolution of the peoples. Perhaps there was a quickening of the pace, and changes hitherto associated with the rise of states like Old Ọyọ

2. See Chapter 1, p.5, above.
3. See Chapter 25, pp. 684–5, above.
4. Chapters 4, 5 and 11 above.
5. See T. C. McCaskie, 1980.
6. See for example R. Robinson, 1985.

in the seventeenth century or Asante, Dahomey, Futa Jallon, Futa Toro and Bondu in the eighteenth century became more general in the nineteenth century. Certainly there seems to have been a more determined effort to institutionalize political change in more permanent structures sustained by new military, social and economic systems.

Of the major states that survived from the eighteenth century, few could have done so without major internal reform. This was because the intense political rivalry and the need to control the expanding scope of commercial relations created such new challenges that each state either tried to reform and expand at the expense of its neighbours or faced disintegration and fragmentation. Few were allowed, like Benin, to merely contract and survive.[7] Most, like, for example, Asante, Dahomey and Buganda, had constantly to maintain and even improve on their efficiency largely in terms of the ability of the ruler to centralize power, weaken subordinates, extract more and more surpluses from them; monopolize major economic and stragetic resources; institutionalize a hierarchy of officials dependent on the ruler for appointment, advancement and discipline; and sustain these powers by the establishment and control of a standing military force, commanded by officials similarly dependent on the ruler. This veritable revolution was sometimes achieved without an obvious change of political system; sometimes, as in the case of Borno, it necessitated a change of dynasty.[8] Often there was a compromise as 'new men' were appointed to old chieftaincies and made to function in new bureaucratic ways, or new offices came to acquire something of the ethos of older traditional titles.

The Mfecane spread far and wide a new model of the northern Nguni state as revolutionized by Shaka. The new state involved basically the adaptation of the age-grade system to create what was virtually a standing army. This ranged far and wide to recruit young men into the army and women as wives, all at the disposal of the king to whom all resources belonged, including cattle and agricultural produce with which to sustain the army and an expanding court. It also involved acculturation of conquered peoples into the dominant culture, and an entirely new conception of the relationship between the ruler and the ruled.[9] The personality of the ruler and the quality of his leadership still seemed to have mattered more than the structures of the state, and the state was often rent apart by the family feuds of the royal lineage. But there is no doubt that for all the initial devastation and confusion created, the Mfecane succeeded in establishing several larger, more efficient and stronger states, with more durable structures than had existed previously. The new states also had more-clearly defined frontiers, if only because they made such demands on the ruled that there could be little doubt about the extent or limits of

7. See Chapter 26, above.
8. See Chapter 22, above.
9. See Chapter 5, above.

jurisdiction. The ruler might still exploit his headship of different religious cults but, increasingly, he was ceasing to be merely a ritual leader. His managerial, administrative and military capabilities as effective and executive head of the state machine became more important than the network of kinship and ritual connections, though in some cases these continued to be important as ideology and source of legitimization.

In the case of Ethiopia, the aim of reform was not to create a new state or strengthen an existing one, but to revive an ancient one, an ancient Coptic Christian-dominated empire that had disintegrated into several competing chieftaincies under pressure from both the Muslim Oromo and European Christians. The struggle was for one or the other of the competitors to claim and assert the authority of the emperor, re-establish its alliance with the Church, reform and equip it and use it to bring other rival powers, Christian and Muslim alike, under obedience to the emperor. The historic traditions of the empire and the number and relative strengths of the competitors left no wide margin for the emperors, Téwodros II and Yohannes IV, to manoeuvre in creating the revived state. And the task of creating new structures could not even begin until military superiority had been achieved. The two emperors succeeded to a considerable extent, one after the other, enough to revive national consciousness but not enough to monopolize economic or strategic resources, or totally curb the ambitions of subordinate powers wishing to collaborate with enemies from Egypt in the north or European invaders from the coast.[10]

There was a similar factor of nostalgia in the effort of the khedives of Egypt to consolidate their rule into a strong national hereditary monarchy and to expand the powers of Egypt in the Nile valley and revive, or at least rival, the ancient glories of the pharaohs or of the Egypt of the Fāṭimid caliphs. Muḥammad ʿAlī's aim was to decimate and undermine the Mamluks, establish a new hierarchy of officials and councils, reform agriculture and redistribute land so as to strengthen the ruler's control over land and agriculture, extract more surpluses so as to have funds to build a modern industrial economy, support a reformed army, and buy autonomy from the Ottomans.

Khedive Ismāʿīl revived and advanced this spirit of reform, employing Europeans to supervise abolitionist and commercial ventures in the Sudan, completing the cutting of the Suez Canal and constructing other canals and irrigation works, railways, communication systems and the like. His aim was, within the limitations of Ottoman overlordship, which European powers exploited to impose unfair treaties to entrench their interests, to buy European technology to modernize Egyptian structures and institutions.[11]

Ostensibly, the aim of the *djihād* movements was to recreate classical Islamic institutions of the time of the orthodox caliphs. In more practical

10. See Chapter 15, above. See above R. A. Caulk, 1972.
11. See Chapter 13, above.

terms, it was to create Islamic theocratic states in place of traditional societies ruled by Muslims and traditionalists. It was to instal rulers chosen for their learning and piety and dedicated to running the affairs of the state on the principles of the Ḳu'rān and Islamic laws, and committed to establishing truly Islamic institutions. By the 1870s, the successors of the founders in Sokoto had achieved a fair measure of success. Under the overall supervision of the caliph, the individual *amīrs* had certainly achieved more durable political structures than the Hausa rulers they had displaced. It is true that in many respects the rulers and the aristocratic classes around them had re-absorbed many of the Hausa nobility and privileges of fiefholders and merchant princes. However, the relative degree of peace that the caliphate enjoyed, the attention to markets, industries, crafts and trade routes, the power of judges and other officials and the control of *amīrs* over the officials, all ensured a higher degree of executive authority in the state.

Seku Ahmadu, who had succeeded al-Hadjdj 'Umar Tal shortly after Massina had been incorporated into the empire, had to battle both with internal dynastic rivalries and the hostility of the French, which further encouraged dissident groups from within. In spite of such difficulties and limitations, the empire had provided an overall framework of state, legal principles and administrative structures that united a wide range of peoples over the vast empire. State structures apart, the Tijāni order provided a faith and way of life that acted as a further bond of unity and loyalty to the ruler. The example of the Dinguiraye revolution encouraged many religious leaders to extend the *djihād* into other areas, to replace secular-minded Muslims and traditionalists with clerics seeking to establish Islamic theocracies. Thus, in the disintegrated empire of Jolof, the states of Kayor (Cayor) and Wolof came under the rule of clerics, and began to extend Islam as a factor of reform in Senegambia. Among the southern Mandinka where Muslims were in a minority, Samori Ture, a Joola (Dyula) warrior with a commercial background, sought to use Islam to unify his peoples irrespective of whether they were previously Muslim or traditionalists.[12] We find Islam serving the same purpose in Nupe and Ilọrin, where rulers embraced Islam with its tradition of literacy and pattern of political and social institutions not only to convert a traditional ritual kingship into an executive theocratic state, but also as a factor of conversion to facilitate expansion among non-Muslim peoples.

Christianity served a similar purpose, providing a cultural framework for creating a Creole society out of disparate groups of peoples settled in Freetown and surrounding villages, as in various settlements on the Liberian coast, or in Libreville, Freretown, and other freed slave settlements. In various places, missionaries seeking converts often received a warm welcome from African rulers who, although very jealous of their inde-

12. See Chapter 24, above.

pendence and not keen to have their people converted, saw in missionary activities a possible access route to European education which might teach literacy and technical skills such as carpentry, printing and, if possible, also the manufacture of guns and gunpowder. The rulers of Madagascar tried to balance British Protestants and French Catholics, then rejected both and sought to ban their religious activities, and ended up getting the court and the bureaucratic elite to become Protestant while Catholicism made significant progress in some of the provinces. The rulers tried to use European ideas in diplomacy, judicial reforms, military reorganization and in establishing a constitutional monarchy.[13] Similarly, beleaguered as they were by aggressive white racialism, a number of the new states in Southern Africa such as Moshoeshoe's kingdom of the Basuto accepted missionaries as their advisers and external champions, protected them and even promulgated laws to assist them in their work of conversion.[14] In the Fante states on the Gold Coast and at other important missionary centres, notably Abẹokuta in south-western Yorubaland, a number of Western-educated African leaders used their literacy and European contacts to get reforms carried out in the traditional state structures. These included the creation of chancelleries to be managed by literate Africans to control diplomatic relations with Europeans and guide the external relations of the states; the reform of tax systems by the introduction of regulated taxes in place of tolls and tribute; and the improvement of the judicial system by the introduction of record-keeping and putting enacted laws into writing.[15]

Military systems

Ultimately, the durability of political structures depended on the military. This was never more so than in the nineteenth century. Hitherto the network of kinship and cultic relationships probably mattered more than the military system. As long as the bulk of the army consisted of occasional levies of the mass of the population who brought their own arms and provisions to defend their villages when attacked, for short periods of the dry season, in between normal agricultural life, the army mattered more in relation to neighbours than in the structure of power within the state. Raising the levies depended on the political acumen of the ruler and he could rarely claim a monopoly of that. The emergence of a cavalry force created an elite in the army and generally also reflected the emergence of an aristocratic group whose members shared with the ruler access to the resources to buy and equip horses, and recruit and maintain horsemen and cavalry forces.

It is now clear that the barrel-loaded musket or the various types of

13. See Chapter 16, above.
14. See Chapter 7, above.
15. See A. Pallinder-Law, 1974; see also Chapter 3, above.

trade guns, Dane guns, etc., whether imported or locally manufactured had, up to the middle of the nineteenth century, made little difference to and the structures of the state in Africa. It could succeed for a while in the hands of disciplined troops against people unused to firearms: such as the Egyptian soldiers in the southern Sudan in the 1840s. It was, however, no match for a disciplined cavalry force armed with spears or poisoned arrows, which could withstand the first volley and rush the musketeers before they could reload. Shaka's *impis* showed the superiority of the short stabbing spear in the hands of such disciplined soldiers. Ẹgba warriors in Abẹokuta acquired European armaments, including some cannons, which helped in resisting the Dahomey invasions, but they were no match in the 1860s for the better-disciplined Ibadan soldiers who fought mostly with locally manufactured weapons. Similarly Téwodros won victories over those with advantages of musket firepower through surprise attacks and forced marches with troops travelling light.[16]

The major revolution of the nineteenth century in warfare was the rise of the professional warrior. The intense political rivalries and the frequency of wars left a few people more or less permanently under arms and the professional warrior emerged as a regular part of society. Usually, there was no large standing army as such. War was a kind of enterprise, or a feature of the enterprise in search of political power and control of economic resources. The warrior was often an entrepreneur who, having amassed some wealth from trading, was in a position to attract followers or to recruit or capture slaves to serve in his private army. With this he pursued his interest in search of political and economic power, either independently or as part of the resources available for the use of a state. If successful, he thus acquired title to an office which he used to integrate himself into a political system. Sometimes, a ruler like Moshoeshoe was himself the most successful entrepreneur in amassing the necessary resources to organize clients and recruits into an army, thus leaving other lesser entrepreneurs little choice but to accept integration on his own terms.[17]

Shaka established the model of the king as war leader. He alone constituted the age regiments and organized their training, discipline, provisioning, and equipment as professional warriors. He redesigned the war implements, and depended on local manufactures for such equipment. The army became the core of the state. Many a general seceded with portions of the army under his command, roamed over wide expanses of territory as he recruited more followers, acquired cattle and women, and eventually used his troops to impose his rule over different communities of people, thus creating a kingdom. The main advantage of such professional warriors

16. See the discussions in two special numbers of the *Journal of African History* (Vol. 12, nos. 2 and 4, 1971) entitled 'Papers on firearms in sub-Saharan Africa'. See also J. P. Smaldone, 1972; R. A. Caulk, 1972.

17. B. Awe, 1973; Chapter 5, above.

was not so much their armament as discipline, training and provisioning. Even where they had to live off the field, the requisitioning was organized and did not degenerate into looting. The most successful of such standing armies in Africa in the nineteenth century depended on local resources for their training, equipment and generalship. This was in contrast with those that sought to model themselves on European armies in terms of uniforms, barrack life, drilling and titles. In the case of Madagascar, reforms even went as far as the purchase of rank, and other early nineteenth-century European practices.

Because of the powerful example of European armies, European muskets spread in Africa and many of the new armies began to adopt them, some because of their firepower (e.g. Enfield rifles), others because of their noise and the effectiveness of a row of musketeers making enough loud reports to frighten an approaching line of cavalry into confusion. Many an African ruler sought after cannons and artillery. However, on account of the weight and amount of gunpowder these weapons consumed, rulers tried to get them manufactured locally, with very indifferent success. By the 1870s more-sophisticated guns began to be imported: breechloaders, repeater rifles, machine guns, and artillery, the ultimate development being the Maxim gun, which Europeans managed to monopolize. Some African rulers, like the Ẹgba chiefs, used European cannon more for psychological warfare than for genuinely military purposes. The argument here is that the importation of European guns had been considered desirable by many rulers even before the nineteenth century. It was, however, not clear until the third quarter of the century, when more effective guns began to be imported, that European armaments could be said to be making a significant difference to warfare in Africa. Imported European guns were by then establishing an undisputed superiority and their importation became a critical factor in war. Consequently also, the search for their acquisition became an essential feature of commerce, diplomacy and statecraft.

The revolution created by the growing importance of European armaments can be illustrated by the difference in the experience of emperors Téwodros and Yohannes in Ethiopia. Téwodros tried to get European technicians to manufacture cannons and gunpowder locally, but he proved that, even without such armaments, he could defeat armies better equipped with muskets. Yohannes and, to an even greater degree, Menelik after him, realized that the emperor would succeed in his task of subjugating his enemies in Tigre and the coastal plains only to the extent that he could use his position to acquire more and better European guns than they had. Similarly, rulers not only in North Africa but also in the Sahara and the Sudan, through trade and diplomacy, began to stockpile European guns, mostly from North Africa but also from the trade to the coast both of West and East Africa. The rulers of Madagascar did the same. In Central and East Africa, commerce was dominated by the hunt for ivory, which further encouraged the importation of firearms and the militarization of society.

One major effect of this growing importance of European firearms was the relative decline of cavalry as the elite and striking force in areas where it had been important and its replacement by a European-style armed infantry. In the forest areas and in places influenced by Nguni warfare, the traditional elite was already the infantry. Here the main trends of the nineteenth century were the training and increasing professionalism and subsequent introduction of European armaments to this infantry. In the widespread movement of peoples, such as followed the Mfecane or the collapse of the Old Ọyọ empire, sometimes a people in a scrubland area hitherto depending on cavalry moved into a more forested area where cavalry warfare was difficult, and this further encouraged the decline of cavalries. Some of the states in direct confrontation with European settlers, having a tradition of mounted riflemen, bred ponies for fast movement, organized importation of European arms and created new armies that for a while had the balance of power on their side. In much of the rest of Africa and especially the Sudan, where for centuries the cavalry had been the core and the elite of the armies, trained, professional foot soldiers armed with rifles rose to become the elite force. The cavalry was beginning to be relegated to the second line of defence and reserve. This sharpened the revolution in the military systems in Africa and had important social and economic implications that all helped to strengthen the ruler as the chief executive of the state.

Social and economic transformation

Evidence has been accumulated to show that the nineteenth century witnessed major social transformations in Africa, especially in the nature of slavery and through the rise of both a warrior class and a politically powerful merchant class. These facilitated, partly caused, and were also in part the result of the changes we have noted above in the political structures and military systems. More than that, there was a growing demand for labour outside the customary bounds of the household unit, the village community or age grade associations. While the various societies remained resistant to freemen selling their labour, the predominant tendency in the nineteenth century was towards expansion of the scale of slave labour, an increase in the areas in which enforced labour was used, and a greater use of migrant labour. The general trend in the third quarter of the nineteenth century was for increased slaveholding in general, even in rural areas, an increase in the number of slaves held within each household, and an increase in the use of slaves in production under quasi-capitalist conditions, thus making their lives harsher than ever before.[18]

With the intensification of political rivalries from the very beginning of the century, it became usual to press disputes over land, cattle, and even

18. G. M. McSheffrey, 1983.

doctrinal differences to the point of completely destroying the enemy as an identifiable entity. Whole communities were incorporated into existing polities or dispersed and the bulk of the young men and women taken away as captives. Such captives were used to satisfy the increasing demand for labour in agriculture, craft production and mining and also as warriors in the emerging professional armies. The new state structures and military systems diminished the importance of the old aristocracies, whose members had depended on the accumulation of wives and extended families for their social, economic and political support, but they also created new bureaucratic groups that needed to be freed from normal agricultural duties. These new aristocracies depended not on large kinship groups as such, but on large households of clients and captives who maintained increasingly large farms to provision the household as well as groups of warriors at the battlefront. They were also deployed to produce goods for the local markets and for long-distance trade, so as to acquire the wealth necessary to attract more clients and buy imported arms and ammunition.

With the effective end of the Atlantic slave trade and the increased demand for gold, palm oil, palm kernels and peanuts from western Africa, sugar cane from Mauritius, Réunion and the Mascarene Islands in the Indian Ocean, as well as ivory and cloves from East and Central Africa, there was an increased demand for captives not only to produce these goods, but also to transport them by headload or by canoes down to the coast. Plantation slavery emerged, either in the form of slave settlements in the rural areas managed according to customary law on the Guinea coast, or Islamic law in the Muslim areas, or approximating to American-type plantations in the Indian Ocean islands. With the increased use of people of slave origin as warriors and in administrative positions at various courts, it has been estimated that in many parts of Africa slave populations could range between 25 and 50 per cent of the total population.[19] Although there were examples of slave revolts, and the particular example of the Lozi who threw off their Kololo overlords,[20] generally the slave populations did not form a distinct class. The bulk performed menial jobs, largely as agricultural labourers. However the substantial groups of warriors and domestic slaves, and the significant few who rose to positions of trust and power as successful warriors, traders or administrators, and the variations in their fortunes and life styles, made combination as a class of slaves very difficult. Only in places like Old Calabar, where the slaves were permanently alienated, with little inclination to integrate them culturally, and with a tradition of competition among the ruling elite to show off wealth by the number of slaves killed in funeral ceremonies,[21] did the slaves in the agricultural villages combine in a secret cult to demand improved conditions. Elsewhere,

19. See also Chapter 25, above.
20. W. G. Clarence-Smith, 1979b.
21. K. K. Nair, 1972, p. 48. See also Chapter 27, above.

the prevalent ethos was acculturation and integration into the society through individual households. While the degree of integration was clearly limited – as witnessed by the number anxious to be redeemed or, having been emancipated by colonial laws, who were anxious to return to their original homes – it was real enough to suggest that the dynamics of change in most of the African communities was the tension of age and sex within each household, and of status and competition for power between the lineages and kinship groups, rather than between broad classes in society.

It is not so easy to define the effects of the expanding scope of commercial activities on social formations in quantitative terms. That the number and the importance of merchants increased cannot be doubted. What is not clear is the extent to which a merchant or capitalist class may be said to have emerged. The tradition of long-distance trading with caravan centres and organization for security, provisioning, credit facilities, transportation and so on was already well established in North and West Africa and was developing rapidly in Central and East Africa in the nineteenth century. These developments occurred in Islamic areas where book-keeping was in Arabic, as well as in the old slave-trading parts of West Africa where the languages of commerce were European languages, and in areas of East Africa where Swahili was expanding as the language of commerce. There is evidence that in parts of the coastal areas of West Africa slave labour was beginning to be supplemented by expanding older forms of enforced labour, where money is loaned in return for a 'hostage' whose labour served partly as interest on the loan and partly as a guarantee that the loan would eventually be repaid. It was indicative of the increasing importance of the groups of merchants and of banking services that this type of enforced labour was greatly expanded in scope. It is said that by the 1870s on the Gold Coast, the system began to rival slave labour in significance, slavery being the method of recruiting labour from outside the immediate community, and the system of 'hostages' for recruiting labour from within the community itself.[22] Yet, outside of the North African coastal cities, a distinct merchant class was slow in evolving. In the areas influenced by Christianity and European ideas, a group of merchants similar to the Victorian middle class began to emerge. But even in those places, apart from Sierra Leone and Liberia, such merchants seeking influence and power within the traditional states did so largely by obtaining chieftaincy titles within the evolving state structures. In many parts of the Sudan and Senegambia, the dominant merchants were closely connected with Muslim religious leaders, and there was not a distinct merchant class but rather a clerical merchant class. In other places there was no clear division between the merchants and the warriors and the ruling elite. Many of those who started life by going on trading ventures as young men, grew prosperous enough to organize others to go on such ventures and with such wealth

22. G. M. McSheffrey, 1983.

bought rights to traditional decision-making offices while they managed their farms, supervised their cattle and other property, and organized their paramilitary body of clients and supporters.

Already by the 1870s, in Southern Africa the demand of the commercial farmers, mostly Boers but also a few Britons, was creating an insatiable demand for labour. While the Cape Colony had relied on emancipated slaves, 'apprentices' and migrants such as the Mfengu fleeing from the Mfecane, white farmers in Natal, Orange Free State and Transvaal relied more on neighbouring Africans rendered landless and restricted in movement by the Pass Laws. By the time the diamond fields of Griqualand West had added their own demands for labour, it had become necessary also to organize migrant labour from further afield. Although officially there was no slavery or 'hostage' system in South Africa, the basis of a worse system of proletarianization was already laid: African states were deliberately deprived of the best land, creating landless peoples who had no choice but to work under harsh conditions set by their ruthless rivals. Thus the grim struggle between the white colonies and the African states with the partisan arbitration of the British overlords was no longer only about land and cattle but also about the total supremacy that would confer power to extract labour by force. It was a struggle that could not be resolved by federation in an 'informal empire'. However, while this became increasingly clear to all the groups of Europeans – settlers, colonial officials and imperial overlords – the leaders of the different African states failed to appreciate how much the rules of the game were changing by the third quarter of the nineteenth century.

The changing balance of power

The 1870s saw major changes not only in the internal structures of African states, but also in the roles and capabilities of Europeans in Africa. By 1870, the effects of the Industrial Revolution on state structures and warfare in Europe were becoming manifest. It was becoming clear how rapidly the gap in the relative balance of power between European nations and African states was widening. In that year, Germany and Italy emerged as unified and fortified states and their citizens were soon demanding more effective involvement in the competition for African resources. In 1870–1, Bismarck sealed the unification of Germany by defeating France in a war that introduced new military technologies, especially in improved armaments and new standards of training and tactics. These developments were soon making their impact felt in Africa, especially in the importation of improved guns. Following their defeat, the French promoted a strategy for revival that involved seeking an empire in Africa either for its intrinsic value, to boost morale, or both. They developed a new policy of aggressively extending and defending French interests in Africa generally, through commercial and missionary agents and, specifically, by consolidating their positions in

Algeria and Senegambia. The revolt in Kabylia was fiercely suppressed. The opportunity was taken to confiscate many hectares of Arab agricultural and grazing land, distributing these to European settlers and forcing the landless Arabs to provide cheap labour. The settlers – French, Spanish, Italian, Maltese and Greek, Christian and Jew – were designated French *citizens* and were therefore in a privileged position over the Arabs, who were deemed to be French *subjects*.

The general effect of these developments was to intensify the competition among the Europeans. Partly in response to the French forward policy, the British showed no less eagerness to consolidate and defend their positions. The discovery of diamonds in 1869–70 in Griqualand West in South Africa, and the prospects of finding gold in large quantities, began to raise the fever of competition and alter the basis of the relationship between Europeans in Africa and between them and the Africans. Various European activities, hitherto pursued seemingly for their own sake or for humanitarian purposes, began to be re-evaluated from the point of view of their contribution to various European national interests. Explorers were no longer expected merely to satisfy scientific curiosity but were also encouraged to gather strategic intelligence and trade secrets. Missionaries were not just individual servants of God obeying a divine call to evangelize but were regarded as organized national agents of acculturation, part of whose objective was to weaken the cultural and commercial exclusivity of their hosts. Traders were not just seeking profit, but were preparing the way for their own nations to establish control. Thus the widespread collaboration between Africans and Europeans, seemingly to utilize European ideas and European technologies for nation-building in the revolutionary situation of the nineteenth century began to be seen as subversive, contributing directly to the systematic abortion of the efforts of African leaders to reform and modernize their societies.

In the same vein, African rulers generally viewed the activities of abolitionists as negative. In many cases, with the ending of the Atlantic slave trade, and after resisting and stalling, they began to co-operate to the extent that alternative trade in agricultural produce, gold, ivory and other commodities came to replace the slave trade and there was no interference with the holding of slaves and other sources of enforced labour. There was thus a basis for co-operation. As noted above, increased use of slaves was the basis of that co-operation. The Europeans recognized this, but in the 1870s, while not abandoning that position, began to use emancipation as a potential factor for weakening the economic base of African states. It should be specifically noted in this connection that most of the armies the Europeans were raising were manned by emancipated African slaves loyal to their redeemers, who armed and commanded them.

Similarly, most African leaders were very suspicious of European missionaries. Eventually many welcomed missionaries if they played down the factor of conversion and emphasized education. Many rulers welcomed the opportunity for some of their slaves, or even their sons, to acquire the skills of reading and writing as a key to the white man's knowledge, and as a basis of commercial relations. The missionaries were even more welcome when they taught new technologies such as the printing of books, house-building, mechanized farming, vaccination, and the like. They were also sometimes called upon to teach techniques for making guns, gunpowder and other strategic goods, or at least to assist with their importation. By the 1870s, it was becoming clearer that the process of acculturation was weakening the identity of the host states, and their resolve to maintain their independence. Missionary activities also became a factor of division conditioning some African states to support particular European nationals and others to oppose.

Perhaps the most subversive of the European activities was trade. Trade provided a basis for co-operation between Africans and Europeans, as both had a mutual interest in promoting its expansion. African rulers had to regulate trade for strategic reasons and to ensure that the African state and African merchants derived as much advantage from it as possible. European traders, of course, also owed it to themselves to negotiate for trading terms that allowed them to make as much profit as possible. In North Africa, they had exploited the weaknesses of the Ottoman emperor to secure excessive privileges for European nationals by treaty, in return for helping to prop up the Ottoman overlordship, thus weakening the ability of North African rulers to regulate trade in their own domains. The Europeans also reserved the right to help themselves to parts of the Ottoman empire whenever it suited the concert of European powers: France defeated the Bey of Algiers in 1830 and laid claims to the whole beylik, and in 1878 claimed Tunisia, just as Britain was to claim Egypt in 1882.

In the 1870s, free trade was the slogan by which Europeans fought against the right of African rulers to regulate trade.[23] In the name of free trade, they sought more and more privileges for European traders. They encouraged African rulers to borrow heavily from European banks and dubious European adventurers. They manipulated servicing of the loans to acquire rights to the produce and to customs duties years in advance. They signed one-sided agreements for the collection of debts and enforced these and other privileges of European traders to weaken the economies of the states and even more the control of the rulers over the economy. In Egypt and Tunisia, they forced on the rulers international debt commissions which greatly undermined the autonomy of the rulers, provoked riots, hindered reform and directly led to the loss of independence with little or no fighting involved. But free trade was only a slogan to give the

23. The clearest statement of this was in the General Act of the Berlin Conference where free trade was proclaimed on the Congo and the Niger as a prelude to the monopolistic policies of Leopold's International African Association and of the Royal Niger Company.

European traders control of the economy so that they could begin to exclude not only African traders but also other European nationals.

The reason for the new confidence and aggressiveness of the Europeans from the 1870s onwards was to be found in the maturing phase of capitalism as manifested in new guns which tilted the balance of power in favour of European-led armies. The change was not sudden, and the Europeans themselves did not exaggerate their advantage. Up to 1871, perhaps largely because of its proximity to France, the French engaged as many as 110 000 troops in the war in Algeria. With the notable exception of the Anglo–Boer War of 1899–1902 in which the British committed an even larger force, no other power could afford so large a force in Africa. The British employed as many as 12 000, mostly Indian troops, in the invasion of Ethiopia in 1868 but only 2500 British troops under Sir Garnet Wolseley when Asante was invaded and Kumasi sacked. Thereafter, the Europeans preferred to depend more on recruiting and training emancipated slaves. Several African armies – such as the Zulu *impis*, the Dahomean Amazons, and the Zanzibari *baluchis* – were well known for their training and discipline. There were also African generals who could match European generalship and often had the advantage of better knowledge of the terrain. Europeans always managed to recruit not only enough African troops of their own but also allies. The military intelligence and information gathered from traders and missionaries always provided a basis for recruiting such allies. However, the critical factor that bred the new confidence and kept the morale of European officers and their African rank-and-file high was the knowledge that as long as they retained superiority both in the quality and quantity of arms, though they might lose a battle or two, they would ultimately win the war.

The legacy of wars

We may conclude that by the 1870s the efforts at fundamental reconstruction of society in different parts of the continent had produced major changes which, for all the divergent tendencies, may be said on the whole to have strengthened the capacity of Africans to defend themselves and their interests. It is clear also that at the same time the European presence was undermining those structures and constituted a grave threat to African security. This was the more so because the success of the African leaders had been achieved at the cost of what may be called the legacy of wars.

There had emerged larger, stronger states with a tendency towards the concentration of executive power in individuals and specific title holders directly responsible to the ruler, and officials gaining office more by merit, achievement and favour of the ruler than by hereditary rights. In the process of achieving such stronger states with a more effective concentration of executive power, weaker states had disappeared. Various groups in danger of losing power and various vested interests adversely affected had fought back and wars had become endemic. The more the Europeans perceived this growth of African state power, the more they were determined to frustrate it, and they were able to exploit this legacy of wars to create divisions and provide opportunities for intervention.

The states that emerged had evolved more durable political institutions that were generally more effective than ever before in exacting the demands of the ruler on the ruled. This, as we have noted above, implied a clearer delimitation of jurisdiction and a clearer definition of frontiers. Perhaps it also heightened the consciousness of the value of land. At any rate, wars became more ruthless and more total than hitherto. They were usually fought not merely to establish the relative authorities of competing rulers, but affected the fortunes of society as a whole: the victor not infrequently took the bulk of able-bodied persons among the vanquished as captives, seized land and cattle and sometimes annexed the whole community with a subsequent loss of their identity.

It should be emphasized that, to a considerable extent, the nineteenth-century wars, while strengthening state power, did so at the expense of other forms of solidarity. The intensity of political rivalries and economic competition involved in the wars was such that little respect was shown for what we would now call ethnicity: cultural affinities in sharing a common language, common myths of origin and the network of kinship and religious interrelationships which in the past had usually transcended the frontiers of state power. While this decline of ethnicity was probably not new, it became more general than ever before in the nineteenth century. In the conflicts and processes of state formation associated with the Mfecane or the Yoruba, Asante, or Maasai wars of the nineteenth century, it is clear that the factor of state power was far more important than that of ethnicity. Indeed, when we consider the extent of the wars, the diverse movements of people associated with the slave trade and the processes of state formation and state reconstruction going on, it is ironic that the old anthropological notion of the 'tribe' as a static biological organism was ever thought to apply to African peoples on the eve of the colonial conquest. On the contrary, the new state structures, which were not based on ethnicity, had become more important than ethnic solidarity in determining the response of various African peoples to the European challenge.

The European strategy towards growing state power in Africa, was initially to emphasize strong national interests. European missionaries, traders, explorers and consular agents, who had previously tended to act separately and often at loggerheads, began to consolidate behind national interests. The situation early in the century when German explorers and missionaries were sponsored by British institutions, or French and British traders co-operated at the court of Zanzibar, became increasingly difficult in the 1870s. This strategy was, however, ineffective, as African rulers began to realize that all European nationals ultimately served the same interests, whether missionaries or traders or explorers. What was more, they were also quite adept at playing off one European power against another. It was this that dictated the new tactics of the Europeans.

As noted above, the critical factor in the changing balance of power in Africa in the 1870s was not the troops, nor their training and discipline or generalship, but the quality and quantity of the guns available to the respective sides. The ultimate answer in the contest for power in Africa therefore depended on the monopolization of arms and ammunition. This was not easy to achieve as long as Europeans pursued national interests and African rulers could play off one power against another. Moreover, in the essential search for allies, Europeans had to use the supply of quality guns to bargain for treaties, concessions, neutrality or active participation in wars against rival African states. It therefore became essential to regulate their Scramble on the basis of international agreements and, in particular, to limit the supply of arms and ammunition. The most intense rivalry was between the British and the French. The British tried to secure their interests by also playing the role of protectors of Portuguese interests. This gave Bismarck the opportunity to play the role of an interested broker by convening an International Conference in Berlin. This Conference in turn gave King Leopold his chance to seek for international support for his ambitions on the Congo by proclaiming free trade and humanitarian anti-slavery ambitions.[24] This prepared the way for the Brussels Act which banned the supply of arms to African rulers in the name of an anti-slavery campaign.

The truth was that by linking the limitation of arms with the anti-slavery campaign, the British were able to exempt the 'self-governing' settlers in South Africa from the operations of the Brussels Act. By this device also, while constantly fighting African states and negotiating various treaties and conventions with African rulers, they could pretend that, by owning slaves and dealing in slaves, African states enjoyed no recognition in international law. It was thus possible to pretend in the General Act of the Berlin Conference of 1885 and the Brussels Act of 1889 that in international law Africa was a *terra nullius* and only European powers and settlers had interests there that had to be protected.

In other words, while European powers were dealing with individual African states, recognizing them, befriending some and fighting others in Africa, in Europe they closed ranks along racial lines and formed a cartel to regulate the flow of essential arms to the Africans. African leaders had no answer to this strategy. The competition for power in Africa had been drawn into the international politics of the Concert of Europe where African diplomatic skills were at a grave disadvantage. It is doubtful whether African leaders realized until too late how great was the danger that threatened them. They were used to thinking that the European base was far away and that, in the final analysis, they had the advantage of numbers.

24. See the General Act of the Berlin Conference, and also S. Miers, 1971.

They continued to act as if they could play off one European power against another. In South Africa, they even believed that they could appeal to the Queen of England and her direct representatives to carry out treaty obligations against the wishes of Anglo-Boer settlers and fortune seekers. Far from any notion of forging a pan-African solidarity similar to that pursued by the Europeans, each African state acted as seemed best in its own individual interest.

It appears that, if any factor is to be singled out, the basic explanation for this was to be found not only in the diplomatic abilities of the European strategists, but also in the legacy of wars that was part of the revolutionary situation of nineteenth-century Africa. It was the intensity of the rivalries and the bitterness of the wars that made African rulers slow to realize that tackling the European threat should have taken precedence over their inter-state rivalries, and that they should have united to face it.

Members of the International Scientific Committee for the Drafting of a General History of Africa

The dates cited below refer to dates of membership.

Professor J. F. A. Ajayi
(Nigeria), from 1971
Editor Volume VI

Professor F. A. Albuquerque Mourao
(Brazil), from 1975

Professor A. A. Boahen
(Ghana), from 1971
Editor Volume VII

H. E. Boubou Hama
(Niger), 1971–8 (resigned in 1978; deceased 1982)

Dr (Mrs) Mutumba M. Bull
(Zambia), from 1971

Professor D. Chanaiwa
(Zimbabwe), from 1975

Professor P. D. Curtin
(USA), from 1975

Professor J. Devisse
(France), from 1971

Professor M. Difuila
(Angola), from 1978

The late Professor Cheikh Anta Diop
(Senegal), 1971–86; deceased 1986

Professor H. Djait
(Tunisia), from 1975

Professor J. D. Fage
(UK), 1971–81 (resigned)

H. E. M. El Fasi
(Morocco), from 1971
Editor Volume III

Professor J. L. Franco
(Cuba), from 1971; deceased 1989

The late Mr M. H. I. Galaal
(Somalia), 1971–81; deceased 1981

Professor Dr V. L. Grottanelli
(Italy), from 1971

Professor E. Haberland
(Federal Republic of Germany), from 1971

Dr Aklilu Habte
(Ethiopia), from 1971

H. E. A. Hampate Ba
(Mali), 1971–8 (resigned)

Dr I. S. El-Hareir
(Libya), from 1978

Dr I. Hrbek
(Czechoslovakia), from 1971
Assistant Editor Volume III

Dr (Mrs) A. Jones
(Liberia), from 1971

The late Abbé Alexis Kagame
(Rwanda), 1971–81; deceased 1981

Professor I. N. Kimambo
(Tanzania), from 1971

Professor J. Ki-Zerbo
(Burkina Faso), from 1971
Editor Volume I

Mr D. Laya
(Niger), from 1979

Dr A. Letnev
(USSR), from 1971

Dr G. Mokhtar
(Egypt), from 1971
Editor Volume II

Professor P. Mutibwa
(Uganda), from 1975

Professor D. T. Niane
(Senegal), from 1971
Editor Volume IV

Professor L. D. Ngcongco
(Botswana), from 1971

Professor T. Obenga
(People's Republic of the Congo),
from 1975

Professor B. A. Ogot
(Kenya), from 1971
Editor Volume V

Professor C. Ravoajanahary
(Madagascar), from 1971

The late Professor W. Rodney
(Guyana), 1979–80; deceased 1980

The late Professor M. Shibeika
(Sudan), 1971–80; deceased 1980

Professor Y. A. Talib
(Singapore), from 1975

The late Professor A. Teixeira da Mota
(Portugal), 1978–82; deceased 1982

Mgr T. Tshibangu
(Zaïre), from 1971

Professor J. Vansina
(Belgium), from 1971

The late Rt Hon. Dr E. Williams
(Trinidad and Tobago), 1976–8;
resigned 1978; deceased 1980

Professor A. A. Mazrui
(Kenya)
Editor Volume VIII, not a
member of the Committee

Professor C. Wondji
(Ivory Coast)
Assistant Editor Volume VIII, not
a member of the Committee

Secretariat of the International
Scientific Committee
A. Gatera, Division of Cultural Studies and
Policies
1, rue Miollis, 75015 Paris

Biographies of authors

CHAPTER 1 J. J. Ade Ajayi (Nigeria): specialist in nineteenth century West African history; author of numerous publications and journal articles on African history; former Vice-Chancellor, University of Lagos; Professor of History, University of Ibadan.

CHAPTER 2 I. Wallerstein (U.S.A): specialist in African sociology and world-economic systems; author of various publications and articles; formerly Professor of Sociology, University College of Dar-es-Salaam, Columbia University, New York and McGill University, Montreal; Director of the Fernand Braudel Center for the Study of Economies, Historical Systems, and Civilizations, SUNY, Binghamton.

CHAPTER 3 A. Adu Boahen (Ghana): specialist in West African colonial history; author of numerous publications and articles on African history; former Professor and Head of the Department of History, University of Ghana.

CHAPTER 4 S. Daget (France): specialist in the African slave trade in the nineteenth century; author of numerous publications and articles on the African slave trade; Professor of History, University of Nantes.

CHAPTER 5 L. D. Ngcongco (Botswana): specialist in Southern African history; has published various studies on Botswana in pre-colonial times; formerly Director, National Institute of Development, Research and Documentation; Professor and Head, Department of History, University of Botswana.

CHAPTER 6 E. K. Mashingaidze (Zimbabwe): specialist in Southern African history; former lecturer, National University of Lesotho and former Zimbabwean Ambassador to the United Nations; Permanent Secretary in Harare.

CHAPTER 7 N. M. Bhebe (Zimbabwe): specialist in Southern African history; author of various works on the Ndebele; former lecturer, University of Swaziland; Senior lecturer, University of Zimbabwe.

CHAPTER 8 A. F. Isaacman (U.S.A): specialist in African history; author of several works on the social history of Mozambique in the nineteenth- and twentieth-centuries; Professor of History, University of Minnesota.

CHAPTER 9 A. I. Salim (Kenya): specialist in East African history; author of many articles on the Swahili-speaking peoples; Professor and currently Chairman, Department of History, University of Nairobi.

CHAPTER 10 I. N. Kimambo (Tanzania): specialist in East African history; author of several publications on the pre-colonial history of Tanzanian peoples; formerly Chief Academic Officer, currently Professor, Department of History, University of Dar es-Salaam.

CHAPTER 11 D. W. Cohen (U.S.A.): specialist in African historical anthropology applying the techniques of anthropology and social history to explore historical problems of the Lakes Region in the nineteenth century; with interest in the anthropologies and histories which Africans have themselves produced outside the academic guilds; Professor of History and Anthropology, The Johns Hopkins University, Baltimore.

CHAPTER 12 J. L. Vellut (Belgium): specialist in Central African history; author of several publications and articles on Congo, Zaire and Angola; Professor of History, University of Louvain.

CHAPTER 13 A. Abdel-Malek (Egypt): specialist in Arab-world sociology and social philosophy; author of numerous publications and articles on the Arab and Afro-Asian world, political and social theory; Directeur de recherche, Centre National de la Recherche Scientifique, Paris; Project Coordinator, now General Editor (SCA-NST), The United Nations University, Tokyo; writer and columnist, Cairo.

CHAPTER 14 H. A. Ibrahim (Sudan): specialist in nineteenth and twentieth century history of Egypt and the Sudan; author of numerous publications and articles; Professor of History and Dean, Faculty of Arts, University of Khartoum.

B. A. Ogot (Kenya): specialist in African history, pioneer in the techniques of oral history; author of many publications on East African history; former Director of the International Louis Leakey Memorial Institute; Professor of History, Kenyatta University, Nairobi.

CHAPTER 15 R. Pankhurst (U.K.): specialist in Ethiopian history; author of several publications on Ethiopian history and culture; former Director of the Institute of Ethiopian Studies, Addis Ababa; Professor of Ethiopian Studies, Institute of Ethiopian Studies, Addis Ababa.

CHAPTER 16 P. W. Mutibwa (Uganda): specialist and author of several publications on the history of Madagascar in the nineteenth century; Research Professor of History, Makerere University, Kampala.

F. V. Esoavelomandroso (Madagascar): specialist in the eighteenth and nineteenth century history of Madagascar; Professor of History, Faculté des Lettres, University of Antananarivo.

CHAPTER 17 M. H. Cherif (Tunisia): specialist in North-African social and political history; author of several articles on North-African history; University Professor and Dean, Faculté des sciences humaines et sociales, Tunis.

CHAPTER 18 A. Laroui (Morocco): specialist in the history of the Maghrib; author of several works on the history of Morocco and on nineteenth century history of North Africa; Professor of Contemporary History, University of Rabat.

CHAPTER 19 N. A. Ivanov (USSR): specialist in mediaeval and contemporary North African history; author of several publications on contemporary North African history; Chargé de recherches, Institute of Oriental Studies, USSR Academy of Sciences, Moscow.

CHAPTER 20 S. Baier (U.S.A.): specialist in West African economic history and in particular the history of the Sahel in West Africa; author of many publications on the Sahelian economies; formerly Assistant-Director of the Boston University African Studies Center; currently Senior Software Engineer at Access Technology, Natick, Massachusetts.

CHAPTER 21 A. A. Batran (Sudan): specialist in the history of Islam in Africa; author of works and articles on Religious Brotherhoods Sufism and the Evolution of Scholarship in West and North Africa; Professor of African History, Howard University, Washington DC.

CHAPTER 22 D. M. Last (U.K.): specialist in African history and sociology; author of several works on the history and culture of the Hausa, and intellectual life in the Western Sudan; Reader in Social Anthropology, University College, London.

CHAPTER 23 M. Ly-Tall (Mali): specialist in the history of Mali; has published works on the Mali Empire and life of al-Hadjdj Umar Tall: Maître-Assistant, IFAN, University of Dakar.

CHAPTER 24 Y. Person (France): specialist in the history of Africa, particularly the Mandingo world; has published many works on the history of Africa; Professor of History, University of Paris I, Panthéon-Sorbonne; deceased.

CHAPTER 25 K. Arhin (Ghana): specialist in social anthropology, especially the history and culture of the Akan; has published many works on the Asante; Professor of African Studies, Institute of African Studies, University of Ghana.

J. Ki-Zerbo (Burkina Faso): specialist in African history and methodology; author of a number of works dealing with Black Africa and its history; Professor of History, University of Dakar.

CHAPTER 26 A. I. Asiwaju (Nigeria): specialist in African history; author of several works on the Yoruba- and Aja-speaking peoples and the impact of colonial boundaries on African peoples; Professor of History, University of Lagos.

CHAPTER 27 E. J. Alagoa (Nigeria): specialist in African history and methodology; author of various studies of the Ijo, the techniques of oral history and archaeology; Professor of History, University of Port Harcourt.

L. Z. Elango (Cameroon): specialist in the history of Cameroon; Lecturer, Department of History, University of Yaoundé.

M. Metegue N'Nah (Gabon): specialist in the history of Central Africa; Head, Department of History, University of Libreville.

CHAPTER 28 F. W. Knight (Jamaica): specialist in the history of the African Diaspora; author of several publications on Cuba, the Slave society and the African Diaspora; Professor of History, The Johns Hopkins University, Baltimore.

Y. A. Talib (Singapore): specialist in Islam, the Malay world and the Middle East, particularly South-West Arabia; author of several works on the subject; Head, Department of Malay Studies, National University of Singapore.

P. D. Curtin (U.S.A.): specialist and author of numerous publications on African history and the history of the slave trade; Professor of History, The Johns Hopkins University, Baltimore.

CHAPTER 29 J. F. Ade Ajayi (Nigeria).

Bibliography

Abbreviations and list of periodicals

AHS African Historical Studies (became *IJAHS* in 1972); Boston University, African Studies Center
BCEHSAOF Bulletin du Comité d'Etudes Historiques et Scientifiques de l'Afrique occidentale française, Dakar
BIFAN Bulletin de l'Institut Français (later *Fondamental*) *de l'Afrique Noire*, Dakar
BSOAS Bulletin of the School of Oriental and African Studies, London
CEA Cahiers d'Etudes Africaines, Paris: Mouton
CJAS Canadian Journal of African Studies, Canadian Association of African Studies, Department of Geography, Carleton University, Ottawa
CUP Cambridge University Press
EALB East African Literature Bureau, Nairobi
EAPH East African Publishing House, Nairobi
HA History in Africa: A Journal of Method, Waltham, Massachusetts
HMSO Her (His) Majesty's Stationery Office, London
HUP Harvard University Press
IAI International African Institute, London
IFAN Institut Français (later Fondamental) de l'Afrique Noire, Dakar
IJAHS International Journal of African Historical Studies, Boston University, African Studies Center
IRSH Institut de Recherches Humaines, Niamey
IUP Ibadan University Press
JAH Journal of African History, Cambridge: CUP
JHSN Journal of the Historical Society of Nigeria, Ibadan
JHUP Johns Hopkins University Press, Baltimore
JICH Journal of Imperial and Commonwealth History, Institute of Commonwealth Studies, London
JRAI Journal of the Royal Anthropological Institute, London
JSAS Journal of Southern African Studies, London: OUP
KUP Khartoum University Press
MUP Manchester University Press
NEA Nouvelles Editions Africaines, Dakar
NUP Northwestern University Press
OUP Oxford University Press
PUF Presses Universitaires de France, Paris
PUP Princeton University Press
RFHOM Revue française d'Histoire d'Outre-mer, Paris
ROMM Revue de l'Occident Musulman et de la Méditerranée, Aix-en-Provence
SFHOM Société française d'Histoire d'Outre-mer, Paris
SNR Sudan Notes and Records, Khartoum
SOAS School of Oriental and African Studies, University of London
SUP Stanford University Press
TAJH Transafrican Journal of History, Nairobi: EAPH
THSG Transactions of the Historical Society of Ghana, Legon
TNR Tanzania Notes and Records, Dar es Salaam
UCP University of California Press
UJ Uganda Journal, Kampala
UPP University of Pennsylvania Press
UWP University of Wisconsin Press
YUP Yale University Press

Bibliography

Abbadie, A. d' (1868a) *L'Abyssinie et le roi Théodore* (Paris).
Abbadie, A. d' (1868b) *Douze ans dans la Haute-Ethiopie* (Paris).

Abdallah, Yohanna B. (1973) *The Yaos. Chiikala cha Wayao* (ed. and tr. by Meredith Sanderson, 2nd edn, London: Frank Cass).

Abd al-Malik, A. (1962) *Egypte. Société militaire* (Paris).

Abd al-Malik, A. (1969) *Idéologie et renaissance nationale: l'Egypte moderne* (Paris: Anthropos).

Abir, M. (1965) 'The emergence and consolidation of the monarchies of Enarea and Jimma in the first half of the nineteenth century', *JAH*, **6**, 2, pp. 205–19.

Abir, M. (1968) *Ethiopia. The Era of the Princes. The Challenge of Islam and the Reunification of the Christian Empire 1769–1855* (London: Longman).

Abir, M. (1977) 'Modernisation, reaction and Muhammad Ali's "Empire" ', *Middle Eastern Studies*, 13, 3, pp. 295–313.

Abitbol, M. (1979) *Tombouctou et les Arma de la conquête marocaine du Soudan nigérien en 1591 à l'hégémonie de l'Empire du Maçina en 1833* (Paris: Maisonneuve & Larose).

Abraham, D. P. (1966) 'The roles of Chaminuka and the Mhondoro cults in Shona political history', in E. Stokes and R. Brown (eds), pp. 28–42.

Abubakar, S. (1970) *The Lamibe of Fombina: A Political History of Adamawa 1809–1901* (Zaria: Ahmadu Bello University Press).

Abun-Nasr, J. M. (1962) 'Some aspects of the Umari branch of the Tijanniyya', *JAH*, **3**, 2, pp. 329–31.

Abun-Nasr, J. M. (1971) *A History of the Maghrib* (Cambridge: CUP).

Abun-Nasr, J. M. (1975) *A History of the Maghrib* (2nd edn, Cambridge: CUP).

Acocks, J. P. H. (1953) *Veld Types of South Africa* (Pretoria: Department of Agriculture).

Adams, Charles C. (1933) *Islam and Modernism in Egypt, a Study of the Modern Reform Movement Inaugurated by Muhammad* 'Abduh (London: OUP).

Adamu, M. (1978) *The Hausa Factor in West African History* (Zaria: Ahmadu Bello University Press).

Adamu, M. (1979) 'The delivery of slaves from the central Sudan to the Bight of Benin in the eighteenth and nineteenth centuries', in H. A. Gemery and J. S. Hogendorn (eds), pp. 163–80.

Addis Hiwet (1975) *Ethiopia: From Autocracy to Revolution* (London: Review of African Political Economy).

Aderibigbe, A. B. (1959) 'The expansion of the Lagos Protectorate 1861–1900', (PhD thesis: University of London).

Afawarq-Garba Yasus (1901) *Daqmawi Menilek* (Rome).

Agar-Hamilton, J. A. I. (1928) *The Native Policy of the Voortrekkers: An Essay on the History of the Interior of South Africa, 1836–1858.* (Cape Town: Miller).

Ageron, C.-R. (1964) *Histoire de l'Algérie contemporaire, 1830–1964* (Paris: PUF).

Ageron, C.-R. (1968) *Les Algériens musulmans et la France, 1871–1919*, (2 vols, Paris: Faculté des Lettres et Sciences Humaines, Sorbonne).

Ageron, C.-R. (1972) *Politiques coloniales au Maghreb* (Paris: PUF).

Ageron, C.-R. (1977) 'Abdel-Kader', in *Les Africains* (Paris: Jeune Afrique) **1**, pp. 19–49.

Ageron, C.-R. (1979) *De l'insurrection de 1871 au déclenchement de la guerre de libération (1954). Histoire de l'Algérie contemporaine*, **2** (Paris: PUF).

Aguirre Beltran, G. (1972) *La población negra de México* (2nd edn, Mexico City: Fondo de Cultura Económica).

Ahmed, J. M. (1966) *The Intellectual Origins of Egyptian Nationalism* (London: OUP).

Ajayi, J. F. A. (1969) *Christian Missions in Nigeria, 1841–1891. The Making of a New Elite* (Evanston: NUP).

Ajayi, J. F. A. (1974) 'The aftermath of the collapse of Old Oyo', in J. F. A. Ajayi and M. Crowder (eds), pp. 129–66.

Ajayi, J. F. A. and Crowder, M. (eds) (1974) *History of West Africa*, Vol. 2 (London: Longman).

Ajayi, J. F. A. and Crowder, M. (eds) (1988) *History of West Africa*, Vol. 2 (2nd edn, London: Longman).

Ajayi, J. F. A. and Oloruntimehin, B. O. (1976) 'West Africa in the anti-slave trade era', in J. E. Flint (ed.), pp. 200–21.

Ajayi, J. F. A. and Smith, R. S. (1964) *Yoruba Warfare in the Nineteenth Century* (Cambridge: CUP).

Akinjogbin, I. A. (1965) 'The prelude to the Yoruba civil wars of the nineteenth century', *Odu*, **2**, 2, pp. 81–6.

Akinjogbin, I. A. (1967) *Dahomey and Its Neighbours, 1708–1818* (Cambridge: CUP).

Akinjogbin, I. A. and Ekemode, G. O. (eds) (1976) *Proceedings of the Conference on Yoruba Civilization Held at the University of Ife, Nigeria, 26–31 July 1976.*

Akintoye, S. A. (1969) 'The north-eastern districts of the Yoruba country and the Benin kingdom', *JHSN*, **4**, 4, pp. 539–53.

Akintoye, S. A. (1971) *Revolution and Power Politics in Yorubaland, 1840–1893* (London: Longman).
Alagoa, E. J. (1964) *The Small Brave City State: A History of Nembe-Brass in the Niger Delta* (Madison: University of Wisconsin Press).
Alagoa, E. J. (1970) 'Long-distance trade and states in the Niger Delta', *JAH*, **11**, 3, pp. 319–29.
Alagoa, E. J. (1971a) 'The development of institutions in the states of the Eastern Niger Delta', *JAH*, **12**, 2, pp. 269–78.
Alagoa, E. J. (1971b) 'Nineteenth-century revolutions in the states of the eastern Niger Delta and Calabar', *JHSN*, 5, pp. 565–73.
Alagoa, E. J. and Fombo, A. (1972) *A Chronicle of Grand Bonny* (Ibadan: IUP).
Ali, A. I. M. (1972) *The British, the Slave Trade and Slavery in the Sudan, 1820–1881* (Khartoum: KUP).
Allen, J. de Vere (ed.) (1977) *Al-Inkishafi. Catechism of a Soul* (Nairobi, Kampala and Dar es Salaam: EALB).
Alpers, E. A. (1967) *The East African Slave Trade* (Historical Association of Tanzania, Paper no. 3, Nairobi: EAPH).
Alpers, E. A. (1969) 'Trade, state and society among the Yao in the nineteenth century', *JAH*, **10**, 3, pp. 405–20.
Alpers, E. A. (1972) 'Towards a history of the expansion of Islam in East Africa: the matrilineal peoples of the southern interior', in T. O. Ranger and I. Kimambo (eds), pp. 172–96.
Alpers, E. A. (1974) 'The nineteenth century: prelude to colonialism', in B. A. Ogot (ed.), pp. 229–48.
Alpers, E. A. (1975) *Ivory and Slaves in East Central Africa* (London: Heinemann).
Alpers, E. A. (1976) 'Gujarat and the trade of East Africa, *c*.1500–1800', *IJAHS*, **9**, 1, pp. 22–44.
Amulree, Lord (1970) 'Prince Alamayou of Ethiopia', *Ethiopia Observer*, **13**, pp. 8–15.
Ancelle, J. (1887) *Les explorations au Sénégal et dans les contrées voisines* (Paris: Maisonneuve).
Andrews, G. R. (1980) *The Afro-Argentines of Buenos Aires 1800–1900* (Madison: UWP).
Anonymous (nd) 'Histoire des Bahunde' (unpublished manuscript, Bukavu, Zaire, CELA-White Fathers' Language Institute).
Anstey, R. (1975) *The Atlantic Slave Trade and British Abolition, 1760–1810* (London:Macmillan).
Arcin, A. (1911) *Histoire de la Guinée Française* (Paris: Chalamel).
Ardener, E. (1956) *Coastal Bantu of the Cameroons* (London: IAI).
Arhin, K. (1967) 'The structure of Greater Ashanti (1700–1824)', *JAH*, **8**, 1, pp. 65–85.
Arhin, K. (1970) 'Aspects of the Ashanti northern trade in the nineteenth century', *Africa*, **40**, 4, pp. 363–73.
Arhin, K. (1979) *West African Traders in Ghana in the Nineteenth and Twentieth Centuries* (London: Longman).
Arnot, F. S. (1889) *Garenganze or Seven Years' Pioneer Mission Work in Central Africa* (London: Hawkins).
Asad, T. (1966) 'A note on the history of the Kababish tribe', *SNR*, **47**, pp. 79–87.
Asiegbu, J. U. J. (1969) *Slavery and the Politics of Liberation, 1787–1861: A Study of Liberated African Emigration and British Anti-Slavery Policy* (London: Longmans Green).
Asiwaju, A. I. (1973) 'A note on the history of Sabe: an ancient Yoruba kingdom', *Lagos Notes and Records*, **4**, pp. 17–29.
Asiwaju, A. I. (1976) *Western Yorubaland Under European Rule, 1889–1945: A Comparative Analysis of French and British Colonialism* (London: Longman).
Asiwaju, A. I. (1979) 'The Aja-speaking peoples of Nigeria: a note on their origins, settlement and cultural adaptation up to 1945', *Africa*, **49**, 1, pp. 15–28.
Atmore, A. and Marks, S. (1974) 'The imperial factor in South Africa in the nineteenth century: towards a reassessment', *JICH*, **3**, 1, pp. 105–39.
Austen, R. A. (1970) 'The abolition of the overseas slave trade: a distorted theme in West African history', *JHSN*, **5**, 2, pp. 257–74.
Austen, R. A. (1979) 'The trans-Saharan slave trade: a tentative census', in H. A. Gemery and J. S. Hogendorn (eds), pp. 23–76.
Awe, B. (1964) 'The rise of Ibadan as a Yoruba power, 1851–1893' (DPhil thesis, Oxford University).
Awe, B. (1973) 'Militarism and economic development in nineteenth century Yoruba country: the Ibadan example', *JAH*, 14, 1, pp. 65–78.
Ayache, G. (1958) 'Aspects de la crise financière au Maroc après l'expédition espagnole de 1860', *Revue historique*, **220**, 2, pp. 271–310.
Ayache, G. (1965) 'La crise des relations germano-marocaines, 1894–1897', *Hespéris-Tamuda*, **6**, pp. 159–204.
Ayache, G. (1979) *Etudes d'histoire marocaine* (Rabat: SMER).

Ayache, S. (1963) *L'accession au trône (1828) de Ranavalona I: à travers le témoignage de Raombana (1854)* (Tananarive: Imprimerie Nationale).
Ayache, S. (1975) 'Esquisse pour le portrait d'une reine: Ranavalona Ière', *Omaly sy Anio*, **1–2**, pp. 251–70.
Ayache, S. (1977) 'Jean Laborde vu par les témoins malgaches', *Omaly sy Anio*, **5–6**, pp. 191–222.
Ayandele, E. A. (1966) *The Missionary Impact on Modern Nigeria 1842–1914: A political and Social Analysis* (London: Longmans Green).
Ayliff, J. and Whiteside, J. (1962) *History of the Abambo, Generally known as Fingos*, (1st edn, 1912, Cape Town).
d'Azevedo, W. L. (1969–71) 'A tribal reaction to nationalism', *Liberian Studies Journal*, **1**, 2, pp. 1–21; **2**, 1, pp. 43–63; **2**, 2, pp. 99–115; **3**, 1, pp. 1–19.

Ba, A. H. and Daget, J. (1962) *L'Empire peul du Macina (1818–1853)* (Paris: Mouton).
Ba, O. (1976) *La pénétration française au Cayor, 1854–1861* (Dakar: Oumar Ba).
Ba, O. (nd) *El Hadj Oumar Tal* (unpublished ms).
Baer, G. (1961) 'The village shaykh in modern Egypt', in U. Heyd (ed.) *Studies in Islamic History and Civilization* (Jerusalem: Hebrew University).
Baer, G. (1962) *A History of Landownership in Modern Egypt 1800–1950* (London: OUP).
Baeta, C. G. (ed.) (1968) *Christianity in Tropical Africa* (London: OUP).
Bagodo, O. (1979) 'Le royaume Borgu Wassangari de Nikki dans la première moitié du XIXe siècle: essai d'histoire politique' (Mémoire de Maitrise d'Histoire, Université Nationale du Benin, Abomey-Calavi).
Baier, S. (1977) 'Trans-Saharan trade and the Sahel: Damergu 1870–1930', *JAH*, **18**, 1, pp. 37–60.
Baier, S. (1980) *An Economic History of Central Niger* (Oxford: Clarendon Press).
Baier, S. and Lovejoy, P. E. (1977) 'The Tuareg of the Central Sudan: gradations of servility at the desert edge (Niger and Nigeria)', in S. Miers and I. Kopytoff (eds), pp. 391–411.
Bain, A. G. (1949) *Journal of Andrew Geddes Bain* (Cape Town: Van Riebeeck Society).
Baker, S. W. (1879) *Ismailia* (2nd edn, London: Macmillan).
al-Barawi, R. and Eleish, M. H. (1944) *Al-tatawwor al-iqtisadi fī Misr fī'l-asr al-ḥadīth* (Cairo: Maktabat al-Nahdah al-Misriyyah).
Barbar, A. (1980) 'The Tarabulus (Libyan) resistance to the Italian invasion: 1911–1920' (PhD thesis, University of Wisconsin, Madison).
Bargaoui, S. (1982) 'Al milkiya wa alaḳāt el- 'amal fī nāh'iyati Tūnis fī awākhir al-karn al-tāsa' 'ashar wa bidāyat al-ḳarn al 'ishrīn' (Thèse de doctorat de 3ème cycle, Université de Tunis).
Bargaoui, S. (1983) 'Le phénomène de l'usure dans la Tunisie de 1881', in *Réactions à l'occupation française de la Tunisie en 1881* (Tunis: CNUDST).
Barkindo, B. M. (ed.) (1978) *Studies in the History of Kano* (Ibadan: Heinemann).
Barnes, J. A. (1951) *Marriage in a Changing Society: A Study in Structural Change among the Fort Jameson Ngoni* (London: OUP).
Barrett, D. B. (1968) *Schism and Renewal in Africa* (Nairobi: OUP).
Barry, B. (1972) *Le royaume du Waalo. Le Sénégal avant la conquête* (Paris: Maspero).
Bartels, F. L. (1965) *The Roots of Ghana Methodism* (Cambridge: CUP).
Barth, H. (1857) *Travels and Discoveries in North and Central Africa* (5 vols, London: Longman, Brown, Green, Longmans and Roberts).
Barth, H. (1863) *Voyages et découvertes dans l'Afrique septentrionale et centrale pendant les années 1849 à 1855* (4 vols, Paris: Bohné).
Bascom, W. R. (1972) *Shango in the New World* (Austin: University of Texas Press).
Bastin, John (1965) *The British in West Sumatra, 1685–1825* (University of Malaya Press: Kuala Lumpur).
Bastin, J. (1977) *A History of Modern Southeast Asia* (2nd edn, London: Prentice-Hall).
Bathurst, R. C. (1967) 'The Ya'rubi Dynasty of Oman', (DPhil. thesis, Oxford University).
Batran, A. A. (1972) 'Sidi al-Mukhtar al-Kunti and the recrudescence of Islam in the Western Sahara and the Middle Niger' (PhD thesis, University of Birmingham).
Batran, A. A. (1973) 'An introductory note on the impact of Sidi al-Mukhtar al-Kunti (1729–1811) on west African Islam in the 18th and 19th centuries', *JHSN*, **6**, 4, pp. 347–52.
Batran, A. A. (1974) 'The Qadiriyya-Mukhtariyya Brotherhood in West Africa: the concept of Tasawwuf in the writings of Sidi al-Mukhtar al-Kunti', *TAJH*, **4**, 1/2, pp. 41–70.
Batran, A. A. (1983) *Islam and Revolution in Africa: A Study in Arab-Islamic Affairs* (Brattleboro: Center for Arab and Islamic Studies).
Bayram, V. M. (1885) *Gafwat al-i'tibār* (Cairo).

Bazin, J. and Terray, E. (1982) *Guerres de lignages et guerres d'États en Afrique* (Paris: Archives contemporaines).
Bdira, M. (1978) *Relations internationales et sous-développement: La Tunisie, 1857–1864* (Uppsala: Acta Univers. Upsal.).
Beach, D. (1977) 'The Shona economy: branches of production', in R. Palmer and N. Parsons (eds), pp. 37–65.
Beach, D. (1980) *The Shona and Zimbabwe, 900–1850* (New York: Macmillan).
Beachey, R. W. (1967) 'The East African ivory trade in the nineteenth century,' *JAH*, **8**, 2, pp. 269–90.
Bean, R. (1975) *The British Trans-Atlantic Slave Trade, 1650–1775* (New York: Arne Press).
Beemer, H. (1937) 'The development of the military organisation in Swaziland', *Africa*, **10**, pp. 55–74.
Behrens, C. (1974) *Les Kroumen de la côte occidentale d'Afrique* (Bordeaux CNRS, centre d'études de géographie Tropicale, Talence).
Beke, C. T. (1867) *The British Captives in Abyssinia* (2nd edn, London: Longman, Green, Reader & Dyer).
Bello, M. (1951) *Infaq al-Maisur* (ed. C. E. J. Whitting, London: Luzac).
Bello, M. (1964) *Infaq al-Maisur* (ed. 'Ali 'Abd al- 'Azim, Cairo).
Belrose-Huyghes, V. (1975) 'Un exemple de syncrétisme esthétique au XIXe siècle: le Rova de Tananarive d'Andrianjaka à Radama Ier', *Omaly sy Anio*, **1–2**, pp. 273–307.
Belrose-Huyghes, V. (1977) 'Considération sur l'introduction de l'imprimerie à Madagascar', *Omaly sy Anio*, **5–6**, pp. 89–105.
Belrose-Huyghes, V. (1978a) 'Le contact missionnaire au féminin: Madagascar et la LMS, 1795–1835', *Omaly sy Anio*, **7–8**, pp. 83–131.
Belrose-Huyghes, V. (1978b) 'Historique de la pénétration protestante à Madagascar jusqu'en 1829' (Thèse de 3ème cycle, Paris–Antananarivo).
Benachenhour, A. (1966) *L'Etat algérien en 1830. Ses institutions sous l'émir Abd-el-Kader* (Algiers).
Benedict, B. (1965) *Mauritius: Problems of a Plural Society* (New York: Praeger).
Bennett, N. R. (1968) 'The Arab impact', in B. A. Ogot and J. A. Kieran (eds), pp. 216–37.
Bennett, N. R. (1974) 'The Arab impact', in B. A. Ogot (ed.), pp. 210–28.
Bennett, N. R. (1978) *A History of the Arab State of Zanzibar* (London: Methuen).
Bennett, N. R. (1981) *Mirambo of Tanganyika, 1840–1884* (New York: OUP).
Ben Salem, L. (1982) 'Intérêt des analyses en termes de segmentarité pour l'étude des sociétés du Maghreb', *ROMM*, **33**, pp. 113–35.
Berger, I. (1981) *Religion and Resistance in East African Kingdoms in the Precolonial Period* (Tervuren: Musée Royale de l'Afrique Centrale).
Berlin, I. and Hoffman, R. (eds) (1983) *Slavery and Freedom in the Age of the American Revolution* (Charlottesville: University Press of Virginia).
Bernard, A. (1906) *La pénétration saharienne (Algiers: Imprimerie Algérienne).*
Bernard, A. and Lacroix, N. (1906) *L'évolution du nomadisme en Algérie* (Paris: Challamel).
Berntsen, J. L. (1979) 'Pastoralism, raiding and prophets: Maasailand in the nineteenth century' (PhD thesis, University of Wisconsin, Madison).
Berque, J. (1978) *L'intérieur du Maghreb, XVe–XIXe siècle* (Paris: Gallimard).
Bertho, J. (1949) 'La parenté des Yoruba aux peuplades du Dahomey et du Togo', *Africa*, **19**, pp. 121–32.
Bethell, L. (1970) *The Abolition of the Brazilian Slave Trade. Britain, Brazil and the Slave Trade Question, 1807–1869* (Cambridge: CUP).
Bettoli, P. (1882) 'Tripoli commerciale', *L'Esploratore*, **6**.
Bhila, H. H. K. (1972) 'Trade and the survival of an African polity: the external relations of Manyika from the sixteenth to the early nineteenth century', *Rhodesia History*, **3**, pp. 11–28.
Bianchi, G. (1886) *Alla terra dei Galla: narrazione della Spedizione Bianchi in Africa nel 1879–80* (Milan: Treves).
Bieber, F. J. (1920–3) *Kaffa: ein altkuschilisches Volkstum in Inner Afrika* (Munster: W. Aschendorffsche Verlagsbuchhandlung).
Binger, L.-G. (1892) *Du Niger au golfe de Guinée par le pays de Kong et le Mossi (1887–1889)* (2 vols, Paris: Hachette).
Biobaku, S. O. (1957) *The Egba and Their Neighbours* (Oxford: Clarendon Press).
Bird, J. (ed.) (1888) *The Annals of Natal 1495–1845* (2 vols, Pietermaritzburg: Davis).
Birks, J. S. (1978) *Across the Savannahs to Mecca: The Overland Pilgrimage Route from West Africa* (London: Hurst).
Birmingham, D. (1976) 'The forest and the savanna of Central Africa', in J. E. Flint (ed.), pp. 222–69.

Bizzoni, A. (1897) *L'Eritrea nel passato e nel presente* (Milan: Sonzogno).
Blanc, H. (1868) *A Narrative of Captivity in Abyssinia* (London: Smith, Elder).
Boahen, A. A. (1964) *Britain, the Sahara, and the Western Sudan, 1788–1861* (Oxford: Clarendon Press).
Boahen, A. A. (1966) *Topics in West African History* (London: Longman).
Boahen, A. A. (1974) 'Politics in Ghana, 1800–1874', in J. F. A. Ajayi and M. Crowder (eds), pp. 167–261.
Boahen, A. A. (1975) *Ghana: Evolution and Change in the Nineteenth and Twentieth Centuries* (London: Longman).
Bogdanovitch, M. N. (1849) *Algirija v novejchee vrenja* (St Petersburg).
Bonner, P. (1983) *Kings, Commoners and Concessionaires: The Evolution and Dissolution of the Nineteenth-Century Swazi State* (Cambridge: CUP).
Bonté, P. (1976) 'Structures de classe et structures sociales chez les Kel Gress', *ROMM*, **21**, pp. 141–62.
Bontinck, F. (1974) 'La double traversée de l'Afrique par trois Arabes de Zanzibar (1845–1860)', *Etudes d'Histoire africaine*, **6**, pp. 5–53.
Bosworth, C. E., Van Donzel, E., Lewis, B., Pellat, C. (eds) (1978) *The Encyclopedia of Islam*, new edn., Vol. 4 (Leiden/London: Brill/Luzac).
Botte, R. (1982) 'La guerre interne au Burundi', in J. Bazin and E. Terray (eds).pp 269–317.
Boudou, A. (1940–2) *Les jésuites à Madagascar aux XIXe siècle.* (Paris: Beauchesne).
Boudou, A. (1943) 'Le complot de 1857', in *Collection de Documents conçernant Madagascar et les pays voisins* (Paris: Académie Malgache).
Bouët-Willaumez, E. (1846) *Description nautique des côtes de l'Afrique occidentale comprises entre le Sénégal et l'Equateur* (Paris: Imprimerie Nationale).
Bouët-Willaumez, E. (1848) *Commerce et traite des noirs aux côtes occidentales d'Afrique* (Paris: Imprimerie Nationale).
Boulard, M. (1958) 'Aperçu sur le commerce caravanier Tripolitaine–Ghet–Niger vers la fin du XIVe siècle', *Bulletin de Liaison Saharienne*, **9**, pp. 202–15.
Bourdieu, P. (1970) *Sociologie de l'Algérie* (3rd edn, Paris: PUF).
Bowdich, T. E. (1819) *A Mission from Cape Coast Castle to Ashantee* (London: John Murray).
Bowring, J. (1840) *Report on Egypt and Candia* Cmd Paper, (London).
Bowser, F. P. (1974) *The African Slave in Colonial Peru, 1524–1650* (Stanford: SUP).
Boyd, J. (1982) 'The contribution of Nana Asma'u Fodio to the jihadist movement of Shehu Dan Fodio from 1820 to 1865' (MPhil thesis, North London Polytechnic).
Boyer, P. (1970a) 'Des pachas triennaux à la révolution d'Ali Khodja Dey (1571–1817)', *Revue Historique*, **244**, 495, pp. 99–124.
Boyer, P. (1970b) 'Le problème kouloughli dans la Régence d'Alger', *ROMM*, **numéro spécial,** pp. 79–94.
Boyer, P. (1971) 'L'Odyssée d'une tribu saharienne: les Djerama, 1881–1929', *ROMM*, **10**, pp. 27–54.
Brasseur, P. (1975a) 'A la recherche d'un absolu missionnaire Mgr Truffet, vicaire apostolique des Deux-Guinées (1812–1847)', *CEA*, **15**, 2, pp. 259–85.
Brasseur, P. (1975b) 'Missions catholiques et administration française sur la côte d'Afrique', *RFHOM*, **62**, 3, pp. 415–46.
Bréhier, L. (1901) *L'Egypte de 1798 à 1900* (Paris: Combet).
Brelsford, W. V. (1956) *The Tribes of Northern Rhodesia* (Lusaka).
Brenner, L. (1973) *The Shehus of Kukawa* (Oxford: Clarendon Press).
Brenner, L. and Cohen, R. (1988) '*Bonno in the 19th century*' in J. F. A. Ajayi and M. Crowder (eds), *History of West Africa*, Vol. 2 (2nd edn, London, Longman)
Bridge, H. (1845) *Journal of an African Cruiser* (London: Wiley & Putnam).
Brignon, J. et al. (1967) *Histoire du Maroc* (Paris: Hatier).
Broadbent, S. (1865) *A Narrative of the First Introduction of Christianity amongst the Barolong Tribe of Bechuanas, South Africa* (London: Wesleyan Mission House).
Brookes, E. H. (1974) *White Rule in Southern Africa 1830–1910* (Pietermaritzburg: University of Natal Press).
Brookes, E. H. and Webb, C. de B. (1965) *A History of Natal* (Pietermaritzburg: University of Natal Press).
Brooks, G. E. (1972) *The Kru Mariner in the Nineteenth Century* (Newark, Delaware: University of Delaware).
Brooks, G. E. (1975) 'Peanuts and colonialism: consequences of the commercialization of peanuts in West Africa, 1830–70', *JAH*, **16**, 1, pp. 29–54.
Brown, K. (1976) *People of Salé: Tradition and Change in a Moroccan City, 1830–1930* (Cambridge, Mass.: HUP).

Brown, L. C. (1974) *The Tunisia of Ahmad Bey, 1837–1855* (Princeton: PUP).
Brown, M. (1977) 'Ranavalona I and the missionaries 1828–40', *Omaly sy Anio*, **5–6**, pp. 191–222.
Brown, M. (1978) *Madagascar Rediscovered: A History from Early Times to Independence* (London: Damien Tunnacliffe).
Brown, W. A. (1968) 'Towards a chronology of the caliphate of Hamdullahi (Māsina)', *CEA*, **7**, 31, pp. 428–43.
Brown, W. A. (1969) 'The caliphate of Hamdullahi, *c.*1818–1864: A study in African history and traditions' (PhD thesis, University of Wisconsin, Madison).
Brownlee, C. (1896) *Reminiscences of Kaffir Life and History, and Other Papers* (Lovedale: Lovedale Mission Press).
Brunschwig, H. (1963) *L'Avènement de l'Afrique Noire* (Paris: Colin).
Bryant, A. T. (1929) *Olden Times in Zululand and Natal* (London: Longmans, Green).
Bryant, A. T. (1964) *A History of the Zulu and Neighbouring Tribes* (Cape Town: C. Strvik).
Bugner, L. (ed.) (1980) *The Image of the Black in Western Art* (New York: William Morrow).
Bull, M. M. (1972) 'Lewanika's achievement', *JAH*, **13**, 4, pp. 463–72.
Bundy, C. (1979) *The Rise and Fall of the South African Peasantry* (Berkeley: UCP).
Burckhardt, J. L. (1829) *Travels in Arabia* (London: H. Colburn).
Bureau, R. (1962) 'Ethno-sociologie religieuse des Duala et apparentés', *Recherches et Etudes Camerounaises*, **7/8**, pp. 1–372.
Burke III, E. (1972) 'The image of the Moroccan state in French ethnological literature: a new look at the origins of Lyautey's Berber policy', in E. Gellner and C. Micaud (eds).
Burke III, E. (1976) *Prelude to the Protectorate in Morocco: Precolonial Protest and Resistance 1860–1912* (Chicago: Chicago University Press).
Burman, S. (1981) *Chiefdom Politics and Alien Law: Basutuland under Cape Rule, 1871–1884* (New York: Africana Publishing).
Burton, R. F. (1860) *The Lake Regions of Central Africa* (2 vols, London: Longman, Green, Longman & Roberts).
Burton, R. F. (1872) *Zanzibar; City, Island and Coast* (2 vols, London: Tinsley Brothers).
Burton, R. F. (1894) *First Footsteps in East Africa* (London: Tylston & Arnold).
Burton, R. F. (1964) *Pilgrimage to al-Madinah and Meccah* (2 vols, London: Dover).
Busia, K. A. (1951) *The Position of the Chief in the Modern Political System of Ashanti* (London: OUP).
Butler, G. (1974) *The 1820 Settlers. An Illustrated Commentary* (Cape Town: Human & Rousseau).

Cachia, A. J. (1975) *Libya Under the Second Ottoman Occupation, 1835–1911* (Tripoli).
Caillé, J. (1951) *Charles Jagerschmidt, chargé d'affaires de France au Maroc (1820–1894)* (Paris: Larose).
Caillé, R. (1830) *Journal d'un voyage à Tombuctou et à Jenné dans l'Afrique Centrale* (3 vols, Paris: Imprimerie Royale).
Caillon-Fillet, O. (1978) 'Jean Laborde et l'Océan Indien' (thèse de 3e cycle, Université de Aix-en-Provence).
Cameron, V. L. (1877) *Across Africa* (2 vols, 4th edn, London: Daldy, Isbister).
Campbell, G. (1981) 'Madagascar and the slave trade, 1850–1895', *JAH*, **22**, 2, pp. 203–28.
Caplan, G. L. (1970) *The Elites of Barotseland 1878–1969* (Berkeley: UCP).
Carreira, A. (1947) *Mandingas da Guiné Portuguesa* (Bissau: Centro do Estudos da Guiné Portuguesa. Memórias no 4).
Carrère, F. and Holle, P. (1855) *De la Sénégambie française* (Paris: Librairie de Firmin Didot Frères, Fils & Cie).
Casalis, E. (1861) *The Basutos* (London: Nisbet).
Cassanelli, L. V. (1982) *The Shaping of Somali Society* (Philadelphia: UPP).
Caulk, R. A. (1966) 'The origins and development of the foreign policy of Menilek II, 1865–96' (PhD thesis, University of London).
Caulk, R. A. (1972) 'Firearms and princely power in Ethiopia in the nineteenth century', *JAH*, **13**, 4, pp. 591–608.
Cauneille, A. (1968) *Les Chaamba (leur nomadisme): évolution de la tribu durant l'administration française* (Paris: CNRS).
Cecchi, A. (1886–7) *Da Zeila alle frontiere del Caffa* (Rome: Loescher).
Cerulli, E. (1942) 'Gli Emiri di Harar dal secolo XVI, alla conquista egiziana', *Rassegna di Studi Etiopici*, **2**.
Cerulli, E. (1943–47) *Etiopi in Palestina* (Rome: Libreria dello Stato).
Cerulli, E. (1957–64) *Somalia. Scritti vari editi ed inediti* (3 vols, Rome: Amministrazione Fiducitaria Italiana di Somalia).

Chaine, M. (1913) 'Histoire du règne de Iohannès IV, roi d'Ethiopie (1868–1889)', *Revue Sémitique*, **21**, pp. 178–91.

Chamberlin, C. (1979) 'Bulk exports, trade tiers, regulation, and development: an economic approach to the study of West Africa's "Legitimate Trade"', *Journal of Economic History*, **39**, 2, pp. 419–38.

Chater, K. (1984) *Dépendance et mutations précoloniales. La Régence de Tunis de 1815 à 1857* (Tunis: Publications de l'Université de Tunis).

Chattopadhyay, A. K. (1977) *Slavery in the Bengal Presidency, 1772–1843* (London).

Chaudhuri, K. N. (1966) 'India's foreign trade and the cessation of the East India Company's trading activities, 1828–40', *Economic History Review*, 2nd ser., **19**, 2, pp. 345–63.

Chérif, M. H. (1970) 'Expansion européenne et difficultés tunisiennes de 1815 à 1830', *Annales ESC*, **25**, 3, pp. 714–45.

Chérif, M. H. (1977) 'Pays du Maghreb en voie de stabilisation', in A. Soboul et al. *Le siècle des Lumières. L'essor/1715–1750* (Paris: PUF), Vol. 2, pp. 907–21.

Chérif, M. H. (1978) 'H'ammuda Pacha Bey et l'affermissement de l'antonomie tunisienne', in *Les Africains* (Paris: Jeune Afrique), Vol. 7, pp. 99–127.

Chérif, M. H. (1979a) 'Pouvoir et société dans la Tunisie de H'usayn bin Ali, 1705–1740' (Thèse de doctorat d'Etat, Université de Paris, Sorbonne).

Chérif, M. H. (1979b) 'Propriété des oliviers au Sahel dee débuts du XVIIe à ceux du XIXe siècle', in *Actes du Premier Congrès d'Histoire et de la Civilisation du Maghreb* (Tunis: Centre d'Etudes et de Recherches Economiques et Sociales) Vol. 2, pp. 209–52.

Chérif, M. H. (1980) 'Les mouvements paysans dans la Tunisie du XIXe siècle', *ROMM*, **30**, pp. 21–55.

Chérif, M. H. (forthcoming) 'Al-lizma wal-lazzāma bi-Tūnis fī l-ḳarn al-t͟hāmin as͟har', *Cahiers de Tunisie*.

Chéron, G. (1924) 'Contributions à l'histoire du Mossi: traditions relatives au cercle de Kaya', *BCEHSAOF*, **7**, 4, pp. 634–91.

Childs, G. M. (1970) 'The chronology of the Ovimbundu Kingdom', *JAH*, **11**, 2, pp. 241—57.

Chilver, E. M. (1961) 'Nineteenth century trade in the Bamenda Grassfields, Southern Cameroons', *Afrika und Übersee*, 14.

Chittick, H. N. and Rotberg, R. I. (1975) *East Africa and the Orient: Cultural Synthesis in Pre-colonial Times.* (New York: Africana Publishing).

Chrétien, J. P. (1981) 'Le commerce du sel de l'Uvinza au XIXe siècle: de la cueillette au monopole capitaliste', in *Le sol, la parole et l'écrit. Mélanges en hommage à Raymond Mauny* (2 vols, Paris: SFHOM), Vol. 2, pp. 919–40.

Christaller, J. G. (1875) *A Grammar of the Asante and Fante Languages* (Basel: Basel Evangelical Missionary Society).

Christaller, J. G. (1933) *Dictionary of the Asante and Fante Language* (2nd edn, first edn 1881, Basel: Basel Evangelical Missionary Society).

Clapperton, H. (1829) *Journal of a Second Expedition into the Interior of Africa* (London: Murray).

Clarence-Smith, W. G. (1979a) *Slaves, Peasants and Capitalists in Southern Angola, 1840–1926* (Cambridge: CUP).

Clarence-Smith, W. G. (1979b) 'Slaves, commoners and landlords in Bulozi *c.*1875 to 1906', *JAH*, **20**, 2, pp. 219–34.

Clarence-Smith, W. G. and Moorsom, R. (1975) 'Underdevelopment and class formation in Ovamboland, 1845–1915', *JAH*, **16**, 3, pp. 365–81.

Cohen, D. W. (1977) *Womunafu's Bunafu: A Study of Authority in a Nineteenth Century African Community* (Princeton: PUP).

Cohen, D. W. (1983) 'Food production and food exchange in the pre-colonial lakes plateau region of East Africa', in R. I. Rotberg (ed.) *Imperialism, Colonialism, and Hunger: East and Central Africa* (Lexington, Mass.: Lexington).

Cohen, D. W. (forthcoming) *Busoga, 1700–1900.*

Cohen, D. W. and Greene, J. P. (eds) (1972) *Neither Slave nor Free: The freedmen of African Descent in the Slave Societies of the New World* (Baltimore: JHUP).

Cohen, R. and Brenner, L. (1974) 'Bornu in the nineteenth century', in J. F. A. Ajayi and M. Crowder (eds), pp. 93–128.

Cohen, W. B. (1980) *The French Encounter with Africans: White Responses to Blacks, 1530–1880* (Bloomington: Indiana University Press).

Coleman, J. S. (1958) *Nigeria: Background to Nationalism* (Berkeley & Los Angeles: UCP).

Collins, R. O. (1975) *The Southern Sudan in Historical Perspective* (Tel Aviv, University of Tel-Aviv Students Association).

Collins, R. O. and Tignor, R. L. (1967) *Egypt and the Sudan* (Englewood Cliffs, NJ: Prentice-Hall).

Colomb, P. H. (1873) *Slave-Catching in the Indian Ocean* (London: Longmans, Green).

Colvin, L. G. (1974) 'Islam and the state of Kajoor: a case of successful resistance to jihad', *JAH*, **15**, 4, pp. 587–606.

Colvin, L. G. (1981) *Historical Dictionary of Senegal* (Metuchen, NJ: Scarecrow Press).

Colvin, L. G. (1982) *Kajor and the French. A Study of Diplomacy from the Slave Trade through the Conquest* (New York: Nok).

Combes, E. and Tamasier, M. (1838) *Voyage en Abyssinie, dans le pays des Galla, de Choa et d'Ifat* (4 vols, Paris: L. Dessessart).

Conrad, R. (1972) *The Destruction of Brazilian Slavery, 1850–1888* (Berkeley: UCP).

Conti Rossini, C. (1921) 'L'editto di ras Gugsa sui feudi', *Rassegna Coloniale*, **1**.

Conti Rossini, C. (1947) 'Nuovi documenti per la storia d'Abissinia nel secolo XIX', *Atti del Accademia Nazionale dei Lincei*, **2**.

Cooper, F. (1977) *Plantation Slavery on the East Coast of Africa* (New Haven and London: YUP).

Coquery-Vidrovitch, C. (1971) 'De la traite des esclaves à l'exportation de l'huile de palme et des palmistes au Dahomey: XIXe siècle', in C. Meillassoux, (ed.), pp. 107–23.

Coquery-Vidrovitch, C. (1972) 'Research on an African mode of production', in M. A. Klein and G. W. Johnson (eds), pp. 33–52.

Coquery-Vidrovitch, C. (1976) 'La mise en dépendance de l'Afrique noire: essai de périodisation historique', *CEA*, **16**, 1–2, pp. 7–58.

Coquery-Vidrovitch, C. and Moniot, H. (1974) *L'Afrique noire de 1800 à nos jours* (Paris: PUF).

Cordell, D. D. (1972) 'The Awlad as Sulayman' (MA dissertation, University of Wisconsin, Madison).

Cordell, D. D. (1977a) 'Eastern Libya, Wadai and the Sanūsīya: A ṭariqa and a trade route', *JAH*, **18**, 1, pp. 21–36.

Cordell, D. D. (1977b) 'Dar al-Kuti: a history of the slave trade and state formation on the Islamic frontier in northern Equatorial Africa (Central African Republic and Chad) in the nineteenth and early twentieth centuries' (PhD thesis, University of Wisconsin).

Cornevin, R. (1962) *Histoire du Dahomey* (Paris: Berger-Levrault).

Corwin, A. F. (1967) *Spain and the Abolition of Slavery in Cuba, 1817–1886* (Austin and London: University of Texas Press).

Coupland, R. (1933) *The British Anti-Slavery Movement* (Oxford: Clarendon Press).

Coupland, R. (1938) *East Africa and its Invaders* (Oxford: Clarendon Press).

Coupland, R. (1939) *The Exploitation of East Africa, 1856–1890* (London: Faber).

Coursac, J. de (1926) *Une page de l'histoire d'Ethiopie. Le règne de Yohannès* (Romans).

Cousins, W. E. (1895) *Madagascar of Today: A Sketch of the Island* (London: Religious Tract Society).

Crabitès, P. (1933) *Gordon, the Sudan and Slavery* (London: Routledge).

Crahan, M. and Knight, F. W. (eds) (1979) *Africa and the Caribbean, the Legacies of a Link* (Baltimore: JHUP).

Craton, M. (1978) *Searching for the Invisible Man: Slaves and Plantation Life in Jamaica* (Cambridge, Mass: HUP).

Craton, M. (ed.) (1979) *Roots and Branches: Current Directions in Slave Studies* (Oxford: Pergamon).

Cronon, E. D. (1962) *Black Moses: The Study of Marcus Garvey* (Madison: UWP).

Crosby Jr, A. W. (1972) *The Columbian Exchange: Biological and Cultural Consequences of 1492* (Westport, Conn.: Greenwood Press).

Crouchley, A. E. (1937) 'The development of commerce in the reign of Mohammad Ali', *L'Egypte contemporaine*, 28.

Crouchley, A. E. (1938) *The Economic Development of Modern Egypt* (London: Longmans, Green).

Crummey, D. (1969) 'Tēwodros as reformer and modernizer', *JAH*, **10**, 3, pp. 457–69.

Crummey, D. (1971) 'The violence of Téwodros', *Journal of Ethiopian Studies*, **9**, 2, pp. 107–25.

Crummey, D. (1972) *Priests and Politicians: Protestant and Catholic Missions in Orthodox Ethiopia, 1830–1868* (Oxford: Clarendon Press).

Cummings, R. (1975) 'Aspects of human porterage with special reference to the Akamba of Kenya' (PhD thesis, University of California at Los Angeles).

Cunnison, Ian (1959) *The Luapula Peoples of Northern Rhodesia* (Manchester: MUP).

Cunnison, Ian (1966) 'Kazembe and the Arabs to 1870', in E. Stokes and R. Brown (eds), pp. 226–37.

Curtin, P. D. (ed.) (1967) *Africa Remembered* (Madison: UWP).

Curtin, P. D. (1969) *The Atlantic Slave Trade: A Census* (Madison: UWP).

Curtin, P. D. (1971) 'Jihad in West Africa: early phases and inter-relations in Mauritania and Senegal', *JAH*, **12**, 1, pp. 11–24.

Curtin, P. D. (1975) *Economic Change in Pre-Colonial Africa: Senegambia in the Era of the Slave Trade* (Madison: UWP).

Curtin, P. D. (1976) 'Measuring the Atlantic slave trade once again: a comment', *JAH*, 17, 4, pp. 595–605.
Curtin, P. D. (1979) 'The African diaspora', in M. Craton (ed.), pp. 1–17.
Curtin, P. D. (1981) 'The abolition of the slave trade from Senegambia', in D. Eltis and J. Walvin (eds), pp. 83–97.
Curtin, P. D., Feierman, S., Thompson, L. and Vansina, J. (1978) *African History* (Boston: Little, Brown).
Cuypers, J. B. (1970) *L'alimentation chez les Shi* (Tervuren: Musée royal de l'Afrique centrale).

Dachs, A. (1972) 'Politics of collaboration: imperialism in practice', in B. Pachai (ed.) *The Early History of Malawi* (London: Longman), pp. 283–92.
Daget, S. (1973) 'Les mots esclave, nègre, Noir et les jugements de valeur sur la traite négrière dans la littérature abolitionniste française, de 1770 à 1845', *RFHOM*, **60**, 4, pp. 511–48.
Daget, S. (1975) 'Long cours et négriers nantais du trafic illégal (1814–1833)', *RFHOM*, **62**, 1–2, pp. 90–134.
Daget, S. (1979) 'British repression of the illegal French slave trade: some considerations', in H. A. Gemery and J. S. Hogendorn (eds), pp. 419–42.
Daget, S. (1980) 'Rôle et contribution des états-côtiers dans l'évolution des rapports entre Africains et Européens du XVe au XIXe siècle', *Annales de l'Université d'Abidjan* sér. *D.* (*Lettres*), **13**, pp. 311–36.
Daget, S. (1983) *Catalogue analytique des armements français soupçonnés de participation au trafic négrier illégal, 1814–1867* (Paris: SFHOM).
D'Almeida, D. (1973) 'Le Dahomey et l'administration coloniale française' (Diplôme des Sciences Economiques et Sociales, Viè section, Université de Paris, Sorbonne).
Darkwah, R. H. (1975) *Shewa, Menilek and the Ethiopian Empire, 1813–1889* (London: Heinemann).
Davenport, T. R. H. (1969) 'The consolidation of a new society: the Cape Colony', in M. Wilson and L. Thompson, (eds), pp. 272–333.
Davenport, T. R. H. (1978) *South Africa: A Modern History* (2nd edn, London: Macmillan).
David, R. (1970) 'Negro contributions to the exploration of the globe', in J. S. Roucek and T. Kiernan (eds) *The Negro Impact on Western Civilization* (New York: Philosophical Library).
Davis, D. B. (1966) *The Problem of Slavery in Western Culture* (Ithaca: Cornell University Press).
Davis, D. B. (1975) *The Problem of Slavery in the Age of Revolution, 1770–1823* (Ithaca: Cornell University Press).
Davis, R. (1973) *The Rise of the Atlantic Economies* (Ithaca: Cornell University Press).
Davis, R. W. (1976) *Ethnolinguistic Studies on the Kru Coast, Liberia* (Newark, Delaware: Liberian Studies Association).
De Cosson, E. A. (1877) *The Cradle of the Blue Nile* (London).
De Kiewiet, C. W. (1937) *The Imperial Factor in South Africa* (Cambridge: CUP).
De Kiewiet, C. W. (1968) *A History of South Africa, Social and Economic* (London: OUP).
Dean, W. (1976) *Rio Claro: A Brazilian Plantation System, 1820–1920* (Stanford: SUP).
Debbasch, Y. (1961–2) 'Le marronage: essai sur la désertion de l'esclavage antillais', *L'Année Sociologique*.
Debrunner, H. W. (1967) *A History of Christianity in Ghana* (Accra: Waterville).
Decary, R. (ed.) (1939) *Les Voyages du lieutenant de vaisseau Frappaz dans les mers des Indes* (Tananarive: Académie malgache).
Decary, R. (1960) *L'île Nosy Bé de Madagascar: histoire d'une colonisation* (Paris).
Degler, C. (1971) *Neither Black nor White: Slavery and Race Relations in Brazil and the United States* (New York: Macmillan).
Delafosse, M. (1972) *Haut-Sénégal-Niger* (2 vols, Paris: Maisonneuve & Larose).
Delius, P. (1980) 'Migrant labour and the Pedi, 1840–80', in S. Marks and A. Atmore (eds), pp. 293–312.
Delivré, A. (1974) *L'Histoire des rois d'Imerina, Interprétation d'une tradition orale* (Paris: Klincksieck).
Delmond, P. (1953) 'Dans la Boucle du Niger. Dori, ville peul', in *Mélanges ethnologiques* (Mémoires d'IFAN, **23**, Dakar: IFAN), pp. 9–109.
Delval, R. (1964) *Radama II: Prince de la Renaissance Malgache, 1861–1863* (Paris: Editions de l'Ecole).
Denevan, W. M. (ed.) (1976) *The Native Population of the Americas in 1492* (Madison: UWP).
Deng, F. M. (1978) *Africans of Two Worlds* (New Haven & London: YUP).
Denis, P. (1961) *Histoire des Mangbetu et des Matshaga jusqu'a l'arrivée des Belges* (Tervuren: Musée royal de l'Afrique centrale).
Denoon, D. (1973) *Southern Africa since 1800* (New York: Praeger).

Derman, W. (1973) *Serfs, Peasants, and Socialists* (Berkeley & Los Angeles: UCP).
Derricourt, R. (1974) 'Settlements in the Transkei and Ciskei before the Mfecane', in C. Saunders and R. Derricourt (eds), pp. 39–82.
Deschamps, H. (1951) *Madagascar, Comores, Terres australes* (Paris: Berger-Levrault).
Deschamps, H. (1960) *Histoire de Madagascar* (Paris: Berger-Levrault).
Deschamps, H. (1965) *Quinze ans de Gabon: Les débuts de l'etablissement français 1839–1853* (Paris: SFHOM).
Dez, J. (1967) 'Le Vakinankaratra, esquisse d'une histoire régionale', *Bulletin de Madagascar*, **256**, pp. 657–702.
Diallo, D. S. (1977) 'Origines de la guerre civile au Kaarta sous le règne de Mamary Kandia (1842–1855)', *Notes Africaines*, **53**, pp. 9–10.
Diallo, H. (1979) *Le Jelgooji et le Liptako.*
Diallo, T. (1972) *Les institutions politiques du Fouta Djalon au XIXe siècle* (*Fifi Laamu Alsilaamaaku Fuuta Jallo*) (Dakar: IFAN, Initiations et Etudes Africaines, **28**).
Diarah, F. B. S. (1982) 'L'organisation politique du Maçina (Diina) 1818–1862' (Thèse de 3e cycle, Université de Paris I).
Dias, J. R. (1981) 'Famine and disease in the history of Angola *c.*1830–1930', *JAH*, **22**, 3, pp. 349–79.
Dickson, H. R. (1941) *The Arab of the Desert* (London: Allen & Unwin).
Dike, K. O. (1956) *Trade and Politics in the Niger Delta, 1830–1885: An Introduction to the Economic and Political History of Nigeria* (Oxford: Clarendon Press).
Djeghloul, A. (1976) 'La formation sociale algérienne à la veille de la colonisation', *La Pensée*, **185**, pp. 61–81.
Djirdjis, F. (1958) *Dirāsāt fi tārīkh Miṣr al-siyāsī mundhou-'l 'aṣr al-Mamlūkī* (Cairo: Al-Dar al-Micriyyahli'-l-Kotob).
Dodwell, H. H. (ed.) (1920) *Records of Fort St. George: Calendar of Madras Despatches* (Madras: Government Press).
Dodwell, H. H. (1931) *The Founder of Modern Egypt; a Study of Muhammad 'Ali* (Cambridge: CUP).
Doughty, C. (1926) *Travels in Arabia Deserta* (London: Cape).
Douin, G. (1933–41) *Histoire du règne de Khédive Ismaïl* (3 vols, Rome: Société Royale de Géographie d'Egypte).
Drachoussoff, V. (1947) 'Essai sur l'agriculture indigène au Bas-Congo', *Bulletin agricole du Congo belge et du Ruanda-Urundi.*
Drake, B. K. (1976) 'Continuity and flexibility in Liverpool's trade with Africa and the Caribbean', *Business History*, **18**, 1, pp. 85–97.
Drescher, S. (1976) 'Le "déclin" du système esclavagiste britannique et l'abolition de la traite', *Annales ESC*, **31**, 2, pp. 414–35.
Drescher, S. (1977) *Econocide. British Slavery in the Era of Abolition* (Pittsburgh: Pittsburgh University Press).
Dubief, J. (1973) 'Les pluies, les crues et leurs effets au Sahara', in *Maghreb et Sahara: études geographiques offertes à Jean Despois* (Paris: Société de Géographie), pp. 125–30.
Dufton, H. (1867) *Narrative of a Journey through Abyssinia in 1862–3* (London: Chapman & Hall).
Dugmore, R. H. (1958) *The Reminiscences of an Albany Settler* (ed. by E. Van der Riet and L. A. Hewson, Cape Town: Grocott & Sherry).
Dumett, R. E. (1971) 'The rubber trade of the Gold Coast and Asante in the nineteenth century: African innovation and market responsiveness', *JAH*, **12**, 1, pp. 79–101.
Duminy, A. and Ballard, C. (eds) (1981) *The Anglo-Zulu War: New Perspectives* (Pietermaritzburg: University of Natal Press).
Dumont, F. (1974) *L'Anti-Sultan ou Al-Hajj Omar Tal du Fouta, Combattant de la foi* (Dakar and Abidjan: NEA).
Dunn, R. E. (1971) 'The trade of Tafilalt: commercial change in south-east Morocco on the eve of the Protectorate', *AHS*, **4**, 2, pp. 271–304.
Dunn, R. E. (1972) 'Berber imperialism: the Ait Atta expansion in southeast Morocco', in E. Gellner and C. Micaud (eds), pp. 85–107.
Dunn, R. E. (1977) *Resistance in the Desert: Moroccan Responses to French Imperialism*, 1881–1912 (London: Croom Helm).
Dunn, R. S. (1972) *Sugar and Slaves: The Rise of the Planter Class in the English West Indies, 1624–1713* (Chapel Hill: University of North Carolina Press).
Dupre, G. and Massala, A. (1975) 'Marchés et pouvoir chez les Beembe', *Annales ESC*, **30**, 6, pp. 1447–76.
Dupuis, J. (1824) *Journal of a Residence in Ashantee* (London: Henry Colburn).

Durand, P. (1930) 'Boujad, ville sainte', *Renseignements Coloniaux*, February 1980, pp. 65–77.
Dye, W. McE. (1880) *Moslem Egypt and Christian Abyssinia* (New York: Atkin & Prout).

Echard, N. (1975) 'L'expérience du passé: histoire de la société paysanne hausa de L'Ader', *Etudes nigériennes,* Niamey (IRSH). **36**.
Ehrensaft, P. (1972) 'The political economy of informal empire in pre-colonial Nigeria, 1807–1884', *CJAS*, **6**, 3, pp. 451–90.
Ekechi, F. K. (1972) *Missionary Enterprise and Rivalry in Igboland 1857–1914* (London: Frank Cass).
Ekejiuba, F. I. (1972) 'The Aro systems of trade in the nineteenth century', *Ikenga*, **1**, 1, pp. 11–26; **1**, 2, pp. 10–21.
Ekman, E. (1975) 'Sweden, the slave trade and slavery', *RFHOM*, 62, 226–7, pp. 221–31.
Elango, L. Z. (1974) 'Bimbia and British in the nineteenth century, 1833–1879. A study in Anglo-Bimbian trade and diplomatic relations' (unpublished PhD, Boston University).
Elisseev, A. V. (1896) *Po belu svetu. Otcherki i Kartiny iz poutechestvii pe trjom tchastjam starogo sveta* (St Petersburg: Sejkin).
Ellenbergsr, D. and MacGregor, J. (1912) *A History of the Basuto, Ancient and Modern* (London).
Ellis, S. (1980) 'Resistance or collaboration: the Menalamba in the kingdom of Imerina, 1895–1899' (DPhil thesis, Oxford University).
Ellis, W. (1838) *History of Madagascar* (2 vols, London: Fisher).
Ellis, W. (1858) *Three Visits to Madagascar During the Years 1853–1854–1856* (London: Murray).
Ellis, W. (1867) *Madagascar Revisited: Describing the Events of a New Reign and the Revolution which followed* (London: Murray).
Ellis, W. (nd, preface 1869) *The Marty Church: A Narrative of the Introduction, Progress and Triumph of Christianity in Madagascar* (London: Snow).
Eltis, D. (1977) 'The export of slaves from Africa, 1821–1843', *Journal of Economic History*, **37**, 2, pp. 409–33.
Eltis, D. (1979) 'The direction and fluctuation of the transatlantic slave trade, 1821–1843: a revision of the 1845 Parliamentary Paper', in H. A. Gemery and J. S. Hogendorn (eds), pp. 273–302.
Eltis, D. and Walvin, J. (eds) (1981) *The Abolition of the Atlantic Slave Trade. Origins and Effects in Europe, Africa and the Americas* (Madison: UWP).
Engerman, S. L. and Genovese, E. D. (eds) (1975) *Race and Slavery in the Western Hemisphere: Quantitative Studies* (Princeton: PUP).
Erckmann, J. (1885) *Le Maroc moderne* (Paris: Challamel).
Esoavelomandroso, M. (1978a) 'Notes sur l'enseignement sous Ranavalona Ière: l'instruction réservée à l'élite', *Ambario*, **2–3**, pp. 283–90.
Esoavelomandroso, M. (1978b) 'Religion et politique: l'évangélisation du pays betsimisarka à la fin du XIXe siècle,' *Omaly sy Anio*, **7–8**, pp. 7–42.
Estermann, C. (1956–61) *Etnografia do sudoeste de Angola* (3 vols, Lisbon: Junta de Investigaçoês do Ultramar).
Etherington, N. A. (1979) 'Labour supply and the genesis of South African confederation in the 1870s', *JAH,* **20,** 2, pp. 235–53.
Etherington, N. A. (1981) 'Anglo-Zulu relations, 1856–78', in A. Duminy and C. Ballard (eds), pp. 13–52.
Evans-Pritchard, E. E. (1949) *The Sanusi of Cyrenaica* (London: OUP).

Fage, J. D. (1959) *An Introduction to the History of West Africa* (2nd edn, Cambridge: CUP).
Fage, J. D. (1975) 'The effect of the export slave trade on African population', in R. P. Moss and R. J. Rathbone (eds), *The Population Factor in African Studies* (London: University of London Press), pp. 15–23.
Fahmy, M. (1954) *La révolution de l'industrie en Egypte et ses conséquences sociales au XIXe siècle (1800–1850)*, (Leiden: Brill).
Faidherbe, L. (1863) *L'Avenir du Sahara et du Soudan* (Paris: Librairie Challamel Aine).
Fantahun Birhane (1973) 'Gojjam 1800–1855' (fourth-year student essay, Haile Sellassie I University, Addis Ababa).
Farsy, A. S. (1942) *Seyyid Said bin Sultan* (Zanzibar: Mwongozi Printing Press).
Fauroux, E. (1970) 'Le royaume d'Ambohidranandriana', *Taloka*, **3**, pp. 55–83.
Feierman, S. (1974) *The Shambaa Kingdom: A History* (Madison: UWP).
Feo Cardoso, J. C. (1825) *Memorias contendo a biographia do vice almirante Luiz da Motta Feo e Torres* (Paris: Fantin).
Féraud, L. C. (1927) *Annales tripolitaines* (Tunis/Paris: Tournier/Vuibert).

Ferrandi, U. (1903) *Seconda spedizione Bòttego. Lugh, emporio commerciale sul Giuba* (Rome: Società geografica italiana).
Ferret, P. V. and Galinier, J. G. (1847–8) *Voyage en Abyssinie* (Paris: Paulin).
Filliot, J. M. (1974) *La traite des esclaves vers les Mascareignes au XVIIIe siècle* (Paris: ORSTOM).
Finley, M. I. (1976) 'A peculiar institution', *Times Literary Supplement*, **3877**, pp. 819–21.
Fisher, H. J. and Rowland, V. (1971) 'Firearms in the Central Sudan', *JAH*, **12**, 3, pp. 215–39.
Flint, E. (1970) 'Trade and politics in Barotseland during the Kololo period', *JAH*, **11**, 1, pp. 71–86.
Flint, J. E. (1963) 'The wider background to partition and colonial occupation', in R. Oliver and G. Mathew (eds), pp. 352–90.
Flint, J. E. (1974) 'Economic change in West Africa in the nineteenth century', in J. F. A. Ajayi and M. Crowder (eds), pp. 380–401.
Flint, J. E. (ed.) (1976) *The Cambridge History of Africa, Vol. 5, from c.1790 to c.1870* (Cambridge: CUP).
Florent, H. (1979) *Le gouvernement de Tamatave de 1864 à 1882. Développement economique* (Tananarive: TER, Département d'histoire).
Fogel, R. W. and Engerman, S. L. (1974) *Time on the Cross: The Economics of American Negro Slavery* (2 vols, Boston: Little, Brown).
Folayan, K. (1967) 'The Egbado and Yoruba-Aja power politics, 1832–1894' (MA thesis, University of Ibadan).
Folayan, K. (1972) 'Tripoli and the war with the USA, 1801–5', *JAH*, **13**, 2, pp. 261–70.
Foner, L. (1970) 'The free people of color in Louisiana and St Dominique: a comparative portrait of two three-caste slave societies', *Journal of Social History*, **3**, 4, pp. 406–30.
Forde, D. (1951) *The Yoruba-speaking Peoples of South-Western Nigeria* (London: IAI).
Forde, D. (ed.) (1956) *Efik Traders of Old Calabar* (London: OUP).
Forde, D. (ed.) (1967) *West Africa. Kingdoms in the Nineteenth Century* (London: OUP).
Forde, D. and Jones, G. I. (1950) *The Ibo and Ibibio-speaking Peoples of South-Eastern Nigeria* (London: IAI).
Foster, P. (1965) *Education and Social Change in Ghana* (London: Routledge, Kegan Paul).
Franklin, J. H. (1969) *From Slavery to Freedom: A History of Negro-Americans* (3rd edn, New York: Knopf).
Freeman, R. A. (1898) *Travels and Life in Ashanti and Jaman* (London: Constable).
Freeman, T. B. (1843) *Journal of Two Visits to the Kingdom of Ashantee in Western Africa* (London: Mason).
Freeman-Greenville, G. S. P. (1962) *The East African Coast: Select Documents* (Oxford: Clarendon Press).
Freeman-Greenville, G. S. P. (1963) 'The coast, 1498–1840', in R. Oliver and G. Mathew (eds), pp. 129–68.
Freeman-Greenville, G. S. P. (1965) *The French At Kilwa Island* (Oxford: Clarendon Press).
Freund, W. M. (1974) 'Thoughts on the study of the history of the Cape eastern frontier zone', in C. Saunders and R. Derricourt (eds), pp. 83–99.
Frost, J. (1974) 'A history of the Shilluk of the southern Sudan' (PhD thesis, University of California, Santa Barbara).
Fulton, R. M. (1968) 'The Kpelle traditional political system', *Liberian Studies Journal*, **1**, 1, pp. 1–19.
Fyfe, C. (1962) *A History of Sierra Leone* (Oxford: Clarendon Press).
Fyfe, C. (1963) *Sierra Leone Inheritance* ((London: OUP).
Fyfe, C. (1972) *Africanus Horton, 1835–1883* (New York: OUP).
Fyfe, C. (ed.) (1978) *African Studies since 1945: A Tribute to Basil Davidson* (London: Longman).
Fyle, C. M. (1981) *The History of Sierra Leone: A Concise Introduction* (London: Evans).
Fynn, H. (1888) in J. Bird (ed.) *Annals of Natal 1495–1845* (2 vols, Pietermaritzburg: Davis).
Fynn, J. K. (1974) 'The structure of Greater Ashanti: another view', *THSG*, **15**, 1, pp. 1–22.

Gabira Madihin Kidana (1972) 'Yohannes IV: religious aspects of his internal policy' (fourth-year student essay Haile Sellassie I University, Addis Ababa).
Galbraith, J. S. (1970) 'Myth of the "Little England" era', in A. G. L. Shaw (ed.) *Great Britain and the Colonies, 1815–1865* (London: Methuen), pp. 27–45.
Gallagher, J. and Robinson, R. (1953) 'The imperialism of free trade', *Economic History Review*, **6**, 1.
Gallisot, R. (1965) 'Abdelkader et la nationalité algérienne', *Revue Historique*, **89**, 2, pp. 339–68.
Gallisot, R. and Valensi, L. (1968) 'Le Maghreb précolonial: mode de production archaïque ou mode de production féodal', *La Pensée*, **142**, pp. 57–93.
Ganiage, J. (1959) *Les origines du protectorat français en Tunisie (1861–1881)* (Paris: PUF).

Gann, L. (1972) 'The end of the slave trade in British Central Africa: 1889–1912', in M. Klein and G. W. Johnson (eds).
Gann, L. H. and Duignan, P. (eds) (1969) *Colonialism in Africa, 1870–1960, Vol. 1: The History and Politics of Colonialism 1870–1914* (Cambridge: CUP).
Gann, L. H. and Duignan, P. (eds) (1970) *Colonialism in Africa, 1870–1960, Vol. 2: The History and Politics of Colonialism 1914–1960* (Cambridge: CUP).
Gardel, G. (1961) *Les Touareg Ajjer* (Algiers: Baconnier).
Gbadamosi, T. G. (1979) *The Growth of Islam among the Yoruba* (London: Longman).
Gellner, E. (1969) *Saints of the Atlas* (London: Weidenfeld & Nicolson).
Gellner, E. (1972) 'Religious and political organisation of the Berbers of the central High Atlas', in E. Gellner and C. Micaud (eds), pp. 59–66.
Gellner, E. (1978) 'Review of C. L. Brown, *The Tunisia of Ahmed Bey, 1837–1855*', *Middle Eastern Studies*, **14**, 1, pp. 127–30.
Gellner, E. and Micaud, C. (eds) (1972) *Arabs and Berbers. From Tribe to Nation in North Africa* (London: Duckworth).
Gemery, H. A. and Hogendorn, J. S. (eds) (1979) *The Uncommon Market. Essays in the Economic History of the Atlantic Slave Trade* (New York: Academic Press).
Genovese, E. D. (1968) *Economie politique de l'esclavage* (Paris: Maspero).
Genovese, E. D. (1974) *Roll, Jordan, Roll: The World the Slaves Made* (New York: Pantheon).
Gerresch, C. (1976) 'Une lettre d'Ahmed al-Bakkay de Tombouctou à Al-Hajj Umar', *BIFAN* (*B*), **28**, pp. 890–903.
Ghurbāl, M. S. (1928) *The Beginnings of the Egyptian Question and the Rise of Mehemet Ali: A Study in the Diplomacy of the Napoleonic Era based on Researches in the British and French Archives* (London: Routledge, Kegan Paul).
Ghurbāl, M. S. (1944) *Mohammad- 'Ali al-Kabir* (Cairo: Dar Ihya al-Kotob al- 'Arabiyyah).
Gibb, H. A. R. and Bowen, H. (1950) *Islamic Society and the West* (London: OUP).
Gibson, C. (1967) *Spain in America* (New York: Harper).
Girard, S. (1873) *Souvenir d'un voyage en Abyssinie* (Paris).
Girault, L. (1959) 'Essai sur les religions des Dagara', *BIFAN*, **21**, pp. 329–56.
Gluckman, M. (1963) 'The rise of a Zulu empire', *Scientific American*, **202**.
Gobat, S. (1834) *Journal of a Three Years' Residence in Abyssinia* (London: Hatchard and Son).
Godelier, M. (1975) 'Modes of production, kinship and demographic structure', in M. Bloch (ed.), *Marxist Analysis and Social Anthropology* (London: Malaby), pp. 3–29.
Goerg, O. (1980) 'La destruction d'un réseau d'échange précolonial: l'exemple de la Guinée', *JAH*, **21**, 4, pp. 467–84.
Good, C. M. (1972) 'Salt, trade and disease: aspects of development in Africa's northern great lakes region', *IJAHS*, **5**, 4, pp. 543–86.
Goodfellow, C. F. (1966) *Great Britain and South African Confederation 1870–1881* (Cape Town: OUP).
Gordon, C. G. (1902) *Letters of General C. G. Gordon to his sister M. A. Gordon* London: Macmillan and Co; New York: The MacMillan Company
Gourou, P. (1955) *La densité de la population rurale au Congo belge* (Brussels: ARSC).
Gourou, P. (1971) 'Favourable or hostile physical environments', in *Leçons de géographie tropicale*, (The Hague-Paris: Mouton), pp. 89–90.
Gow, B. A. (1979) *Madagascar and the Protestant Impact: The Work of the British Missions, 1818–95* (London: Longman).
Gran, P. (1979) *Islamic Roots of Capitalism: Egypt 1760–1840* (Austin & London: University of Texas Press).
Grandidier, A. and Grandidier, G. (eds) (1942) *Histoire Physique, Naturelle et Politique de Madagascar* (36 vols, Paris: Imprimerie Nationale).
Gray, J. M. (1947) 'Ahmed b. Ibrahim – the first Arab to reach Buganda', *UJ*, **11**, pp. 80–97.
Gray, J. M. (1957) 'Trading expeditions from the coast to Lakes Tanganyika and Victoria before 1857', *TNR*, **2**, pp. 226–47.
Gray, J. M. (1962) *History of Zanzibar from the Middle Ages to 1856* (London: OUP).
Gray, J. M. (1963) 'Zanzibar and the coastal belt, 1840–1884', in R. Oliver and G. Mathew (eds), pp. 212–51.
Gray, R. (1965) 'Eclipse maps', *JAH*, **6**, 3, pp. 251–62.
Gray, R. (1970) *A History of the Southern Sudan, 1839–1889* (Oxford: Clarendon Press).
Gray, R. and Birmingham, D. (eds) (1970) *Pre-colonial African Trade: Essays on Trade in Central and Eastern Africa before 1900* (London: OUP).
Great Britain, House of Commons (1868) *Correspondence respecting Abyssinia 1846–1868* (London).

Green, A. H. (1978) *The Tunisian Ulama, 1873–1915* (Leyden: Brill).

Green, W. A. (1974) 'The West Indies and British West African policy in the nineteenth century: a corrective comment', *JAH*, **15**, 2, pp. 247–59.

Green-Pedersen, S. E. (1975) 'The history of the Danish slave trade, 1733–1807', *RFHOM*, **62**, 226–7, pp. 196–220.

Greenberg, J. H. (1966) *Languages of Africa* (Bloomington: Indiana University Press).

Greenfield, R. (1965) *Ethiopia: A New Political History* (London: Pall Mall).

Groves, C. P. (1954) *The Planting of Christianity in Africa*, Vol. 2 (London: Lutterworth).

Guèbrè Sellassié, G. (1930–2) *Chronique du règne de Ménélik II, roi des rois d'Ethiopie* (Paris: Maisonneuve).

Guilhem, H. and Hebert, J. (1961) *Précis d'Histoire de la Haute-Volta* (Paris: Ligel).

Guillain, C. (1845) *Documents sur l'histoire, la géographie et le commerce de la partie occidentale de Madagascar* (2 vols, Paris: Imprimerie Royale).

Guillain, C. (1856) *Documents sur l'histoire, la géographie et le commerce de l'Afrique Occidentale* (2 vols, Paris: Bertrand).

Guillaume, H. (1976) 'Les liens de dépendance à l'époque précoloniale, chez les Touaregs de l'Imannen (Niger)', *ROMM*, **21**, pp. 111–29.

Gulliver, P. H. (1955) 'A history of the Songea Ngoni', *TNR*, **41**, pp. 16 30.

Gulliver, P. H. (1963) *Social Control in an African Society: A Study of the Arusha Agricultural Maasai of Northern Tanganyika* (London: Routledge, Kegan Paul).

Gutman, H. G. (1975) *Slavery and the Numbers Game. A Critique of Time on the Cross* (Urbana: University of Illinois Press).

Guy, J. (1977) 'Ecological factors in the rise of Shaka and the Zulu kingdom', (paper read at the Conference on Southern African History, National University of Lesotho, 1–6 August 1977).

Guy, J. (1980) *The Destruction of the Zulu Kingdom. The Civil War in Zululand 1879–1884* (London: Longman).

Guy, J. (1981) 'The role of colonial officials in the destruction of the Zulu kingdom', in A. Duminy and C. Ballard (eds), pp. 148–69.

Gwei, S. N. (1966) *History of the British Baptist Mission in Cameroons with beginnings in Fernando Po 1841–1866* (unpublished mémoire de maîtrise, Séminaire de théologie baptiste, Rushlikon-Zurich).

al-Hachaichi, M. (1912) *Voyage au pays senoussiya* (Paris: Challamel).

Hafkin, N. (1973) 'Trade, society and politics in northern Mozambique' (PhD thesis, Boston University).

Hair, P. (1963) 'Notes on the discovery of the Vai script', *Sierra Leone Language Review*, **2**.

al-Hajj, M. A. (1964) 'The Fulani concept of jihad', *Odu*, **1**, pp. 45–58.

al-Hajj, M. A. (1967) 'The 13th century in Muslim escatology: Mahdist expectations in the Sokoto caliphate', *Research Bulletin, Centre for Arabic Documentation* (Ibadan), **3**, 2, pp. 100–15.

Haliburton, G. M. (1971) *The Prophet Harris* (London: Longman).

Hall, G. M. (1971) *Social Control in Slave Plantation Societies: A Comparison of St Domingue and Cuba* (Baltimore: JHUP).

Hamani, D. (1975) *Contribution à l'étude de l'histoire des états Hausa: l'Adar précolonial* (Niamey: IRSH).

Hamani, D. (1979) 'Adar, the Touareg and Sokoto', in Y. B. Usman (ed.) *Studies in the History of the Sokoto Caliphate* (Sokoto: State History Bureau), pp. 392–407.

Hamid, A. A. A. (1980) 'Abdullah b. Fudi as an exegetist' (PhD thesis, Ahmadu Bello University, Zaria).

Hamilton Jr, R. G. (1970) 'The present state of African cults in Bahia', *Journal of Social History*, **3**, 4, pp. 356–73.

Hammond, R. J. (1966) *Portugal and Africa, 1815–1910* (Stanford: SUP).

Hammond, R. J. (1969) 'Uneconomic imperialism: Portugal in Africa before 1910', in L. H. Gann and P. Duignan (eds), pp. 352–82.

Hancock, W. K. (1942) *Survey of British Commonwealth Affairs, Vol. 2: Problems of Economic Policy, 1918–39* (London: OUP).

Hanke, L. (1970) *Aristotle and the American Indians: A Study in Race Prejudice in the Modern World* (Bloomington: Indiana University Press).

Hardyman, J. T. (1977) 'Malagasy refugees to Britain, 1838–41', *Omaly sy Anio*, **5–6**, pp. 141–89.

Harries, L. (1961) *Swahili Poetry* (Oxford: Clarendon Press).

Harries, P. (1981) 'Slavery, social incorporation and surplus extraction: the nature of free and unfree labour in south-east Africa', *JAH*, **22**, 3, pp. 309–30.

Harris, M. (1964) *Patterns of Race in the Americas* (New York: Walker).

Harris, R. (1972) 'The history of trade at Ikom, Eastern Nigeria', *Africa*, **63**, 2, pp. 122–39.

Harris, R. (1982) 'The horse in West African history', *Africa*, **52**, 1, pp. 81–5.
Harris, W. C. (1844) *The Highlands of Ethiopia* (London: Longman).
Hart, D. M. (1966) 'Segmentary system and the role of "five-fifths" in tribal Morocco', *ROMM*, **3**, pp. 65–95.
Hart, D. M. (1970) 'Conflicting models of Berber tribal structure in the Moroccan Rif: the segmentary alliance systems of the Aith Waryachar', *ROMM*, **7**, pp. 93–100.
Hartwig, G. W. (1970) 'The Victoria Nyanza as a trade route in the nineteenth century', *JAH*, **11**, 4, pp. 535–52.
Hartwig, G. W. (1976) *The Art of Survival in East Africa: The Kerebe and Long-Distance Trade, 1800–1895* (New York: Africana Publishing).
Hartwig, G. W. (1978) 'Social consequences of epidemic diseases: the nineteenth century in eastern Africa', in G. W. Hartwig and K. D. Patterson (eds), pp. 25–42.
Hartwig, G. W. and Patterson, K. D. (eds) (1978) *Disease in African History* (Durham, N. C.: Duke University Press).
Hasan, Y. F. (1967) *The Arabs and the Sudan* (Edinburgh: Edinburgh University Press).
Hassan, A. and Naibi, A. S. (1962) *A Chronicle of Abuja* (Lagos: African Universities Press).
al-Haṭṭāb, A. (1935) 'Dirasāt tārikhiyya iḳtiṣadiyya li 'aṣr Muḥammad 'Ali i: al-iḥtikār wa'l-nizām al-zirā 'ī', *Madjallat Koulliyat Ādāb al Ḳāhira*, **3**, 1935.
Hay, J. D. (1896) *A Memoir* (London: Murray).
Hay, M. J. (1975) 'Economic change in late nineteenth century Kowe, western Kenya', *Hadith*, **5**, pp. 90–107.
Hebert, J. et al. (1976) *Esquisse monographique du pays dagara* (Diebougou: roneo).
Hedges, D. (1978) 'Trade and politics in southern Mozambique and Zululand in the eighteenth and early nineteenth centuries' (PhD thesis, University of London).
Herold, J. C. (1962) *Bonaparte en Egypte* (Paris: Plon).
Herskovits, M. J. (1938) *Dahomey, an Ancient West African Kingdom* (New York: J. J. Augustin).
Hertslet, E. (1894) *The Map of Africa by Treaty* (2 vols, London: Harrison).
Hichens, W. (ed.) (1939) *Al-Inkishafi: The Soul's Awakening* (London: Sheldon Press).
Higman, B. W. (1976) *Slave Economy and Society in Jamaica 1807–1832* (New York: CUP).
Hill, G. B. (1887) *Colonel Gordon in Central Africa* (London).
Hill, P. (1977) *Population, Prosperity and Poverty. Rural Kano 1900 and 1970* (Cambridge: CUP).
Hill R. (1965) *Sudan Transport* (London: OUP).
Hill, R. (1966) *Egypt in the Sudan* (London: OUP).
Hill, R.A. (ed.) (1983) *The Marcus Garvey and Universal Negro Improvement Association Papers*, Vols 1 and 2 (Berkeley: UCP).
Hiskett, M. (1962) 'An Islamic tradition of reform in the Western Sudan from the sixteenth to the eighteenth century', *BSOAS*, **25**, pp. 577–96.
Hiskett, M. (1973) *The Sword of Truth* (New York: OUP).
Hiskett, M. (1975) *A History of Hausa Islamic Verse* (London: SOAS).
Hiskett, M. (1976) 'The nineteenth-century jihads in West Africa', in J. E. Flint (ed.), pp. 125–69.
Hitchcock, R. and Smith, M. R. (eds) (1982) *Settlement in Botswana* (London: Heinemann).
Hobsbawm, E. J. (1977) *Industry and Empire* (new edn, Harmondsworth: Penguin).
Hodgkin, T. (1956) *Nationalism in Colonial Africa* (London: Muller).
Hoetink, H. (1973) *Slavery and Race Relations in the Americas: Comparative Notes on their Nature and Nexus* (New York: Harper & Row).
Hoetink, H. (1979) 'The cultural links', in M. Crahan and F. W. Knight (eds).
Hogendorn, J. S. (1977) 'The economics of slave use on two "plantations" in the Zaria emirate of the Sokoto caliphate', *IJAHS*, **10**, 3, pp. 369–83.
Holland, T. J. and Hozier, H. M. (1870) *Record of the Expedition to Abyssinia* (London: HMSO).
Holsoe, S. E. (1967) 'The cassava-leaf people: an ethno-historical study of the Vai people with a particular emphasis on the Tewo chiefdom' (PhD thesis, Boston University).
Holt, P. M. (1970) *The Mahdist State in the Sudan 1881–1898* (2nd edn, Oxford: Clarendon Press).
Holt, P. M. (1973) *Studies in the History of the Near East* (London: OUP).
Holt, P. M. (1976) 'Egypt and the Nile Valley', in J. E. Flint (ed.), pp. 13–50.
Hopkins, A. G. (1970) 'The creation of a colonial monetary system: the origins of the West African Currency Board', *African Historical Studies*, **3**, 1, pp. 101–32.
Hopkins, A. G. (1973) *An Economic History of West Africa* (London: Longman).
Hopkins, A. G. (1980) 'Africa's Age of Improvement', *HA*, **7**, pp. 141–60.
Hopkins, T. K. and Wallerstein, I. (1982) 'Structural transformations of the world-economy', in T. K. Hopkins, I. Wallerstein, et al., *World-Systems Analysis: Theory and Methodology* (Beverly Hills: Sage), pp. 104–20.

Horton, J. A. (1969) *West African Countries and Peoples* (ed. by G. Shepperson, Edinburgh: Edinburgh University Press).
Horton, R. (1954) 'The ohu system of slavery in a northern Ibo village-group', *Africa*, **24**, 4, pp. 311–6.
Horton, R. (1969) 'From fishing village to city-state: a social history of New Calabar', in M. Douglas and P. Kaberry (eds) *Man in Africa* (London: Tavistock), pp. 37–58.
Hourani, A. (1962) *Arabic Thought in the Liberal Age 1798–1939* (London: OUP).
Howard, A. M. (1976) 'The relevance of spatial analysis for African economic history: the Sierra Leone–Guinea system', *JAH*, **17**, 3, pp. 365–88.
Hozier, H. M. (1869) *The British Expedition to Abyssinia* (London: Macmillan).
Hrbek, I. (1968) 'Towards a periodisation of African history', in T. O. Ranger (ed.), pp. 37–52.
Hrbek, I. (1979) 'The early period of Maḥmadu Lamin's activities', in J. R. Willis (ed.), pp. 211–32.
Hughes, A. J. B. (1956) *Kin, Caste and Nation amongst the Rhodesian Ndebele* (Rhodes-Livingstone Papers, **25**, Manchester: MUP).
Hulstaert, G. (1976) *Proverbes Mongo*, no. 49, Relations commerciales de l'Equateur, *Enquêtes et documents d'histoire africaine* (Louvain: mimeograph).
Ḥumayda, B. K. (1973) 'Malamiḥ nin Ta'rikh al-Sūdān fī 'ahd al-Kidiwi Ismā'īl, 1863–1879' (PhD thesis, University of Khartoum).
Hunt, D. R. (1937) 'An account of the Bapedi', *Bantu Studies*, **5**.
Huntingford, G. W. B. (1955) *The Galla of Ethiopia: The Kingdoms of Kafa and Janjero* (London: IAI).
Hurgronje, J. S. (1970) *Mekka in the Latter Part of the 19th Century: Daily Life, Customs and Learning of the Moslims of the East-Indian Archipelago* (Leiden: Brill).

Ibn Abī-Dhiyāf, A. (1963–4) *Ith'āf ahl al-zamān bi-akhbar muluk Tunis wa'ahb al-aman* (Tunis: SEACI).
Ibn Zaīdān (1929–33) *Ithar A'lām al-Nās bi-Jamāl Akhbār Hādirat Maknās* (5 vols, Rabat).
Ibn Zaīdān (1961–2) *Al-'Izz wa al-Sawla fī Ma'ālim Nudhum al-Dawla* (2 vols, Rabat).
Ibrāhīm, H. A. (1973) *Muḥammad 'Alī fī" al-Sūdān: dirāsah li-aḥdāf alfatḥ al-Turkī-al-Miṣrī* (Khartoum: KUP).
Ibrāhīm, H. A. (1980a) *Muḥammad 'Alī fī al Sūdān 1838–1839* (Khartoum).
Ibrāhīm, H. A. (1980b) *Rihlat Muḥammad 'Alī ila al-Sūdān 1838–9* (Khartoum).
Inikori, J. E. (1977) 'The import of firearms into West Africa, 1750–1807: a quantitative analysis', *JAH*, **18**, 3, pp. 339–68.
Inikori, J. E. (ed.) (1982a) *Forced Migration. The Impact of the Export Slave Trade on African Societies* (London: Hutchinson).
Inikori, J. E. (1982b) 'Introduction', in J. E. Inikori: (ed.), pp. 13–60.
Inskeep, R. R. (1969) 'The archaeological background', in M. Wilson and L. Thompson (eds) Vol. I, pp. 1–39.
Isaacman, A. (1972a) *The Africanization of a European Institution; the Zambezi Prazos, 1750–1902* (Madison: UWP).
Isaacman, A. (1972b) 'The origin, formation and early history of the Chikunda of South-Central Africa', *JAH*, **13**, 3, pp. 443–62.
Isaacman, A. (1973) 'Madzi-Manga, Mhondoro and the use of oral traditions – a chapter in Barue religious and political history', *JAH*, **14**, 3, pp. 395–409.
Isaacman, A. (1976) *The Tradition of Resistance in Mozambique: Anti-Colonial Activity in the Zambesi Valley 1850–1921* (Berkeley: UCP).
Isaacman, A. and Isaacman, B. (1977) 'Resistance and collaboration in Southern and Central Africa, *c.* 1850–1920', *IJAHS*, **10**, 1, pp. 31–62.
Isenberg, C. W. and Krapf, J. L. (1843) *Journals ... detailing their Proceedings in the Kingdom of Shoa* (London: Seeley, Burnside & Seeley).
Isichei, E. (1973) *The Ibo people and the Europeans: The Genesis of a Relationship to 1906* (London: Faber).
Issawi, C. P. (1963) *Egypt in Revolution, an Economic Analysis* (London: OUP).
Issawi, C. P. (1966) *Economic History of the Middle East 1800–1914; a Book of Readings* (Chicago: University of Chicago Press).
Italy, Ministero degli Affari Esteri (1906) *Trattati, convenzioni, accordi, protocolli ed altri documenti dll' Africa* (Rome).
Ivanov, N. A. (1976) 'Tunisia' and 'Libya', in V. G. Solodovnikov (ed.) *Istorija natsionalno-osvoboditelnoi bordy narodov Afriki v Novoe uremja* (Moscow: Naouka).
Izard, M. (1970) *Introduction à l'histoire des royaumes Mossi* (2 vols, Recherches Voltaiques, **12**, Paris/Ouagadougou: CNRS/CVRS).

al-Jabri, M. A. (nd) *Fi Sha'n Allah* (Cairo).
Jackson, K. A. (1972) 'An ethnohistorical study of the oral traditions of the Akamba of Kenya' (PhD thesis, University of California, Los Angeles).
Jacob, G. (1977) 'Influences occidentales en Imerina et déséquilibres économiques avant la conquête française', *Omaly sy Anio*, **5–6**, pp. 223–31.
Jacobs, A. H. (1965) 'The traditional political organization of the pastoral Massai' (DPhil thesis, Oxford University).
Jaenen, C. J. (1966) 'Theodore II and British intervention in Ethiopia', *Canadian Journal of History*, **1**, 2, pp. 26–56.
Jago, T. S. (1902) 'Report on the trade and economy of the Vilayet of Tripoli in Northern Africa in the past forty years', in Great Britain, *House of Commons Sessional Papers*, Vol. 103.
Jah, O. (1973) 'Sufism and nineteenth century jihad movements: a case study of al-Hajj Umar al-Futi's philosophy of jihad and its sufi bases' (PhD thesis, McGill University).
Jakobsson, S. (1972) *Am I not a Man and a Brother? British Missions and the Abolition of the Slavery in West Africa and the West Indies, 1756–1838* (Uppsala: Gleerup).
Jésman, C. (1958) *The Russians in Ethiopia. An Essay in Futility* (London: Chatto & Windus).
Jésman, C. (1966) 'The tragedy of Magdala: a historical study', *Ethiopia Observer*, **10**.
Johnson, M. (1970) 'The cowrie currencies of West Africa', *JAH* , **11**, 1, pp. 17–49; 3, pp. 331–53.
Johnson, M. (1976a) 'Calico caravans: the Tripoli-Kano trade after 1880', *JAH*, **17**, 1, pp. 95–117.
Johnson, M. (1976b) 'The economic foundations of an Islamic theocracy – the case of Masina', *JAH*, **17**, 4, pp. 481–95.
Johnson, M. (nd) *Salaga Papers* (2 vols, Legon: Institute of African Studies).
Johnson, S. (1921) *History of the Yorubas* (London: Routledge).
Johnston, C. (1844) *Travels in Southern Abyssinia* (London: J. Madden and Co).
Johnston, H. H. (1902) *The Uganda Protectorate* (London: Hutchinson and Co).
Johnston, H. A. S. (1967) *The Fulani Empire of Sokoto* (London: OUP).
Jones, A. (1981) 'Who were the Vai?', *JAH*, **22**, 2, pp. 159–78.
Jones, G. I. (1963) *The Trading States of the Oil Rivers: a Study of Political Development in Eastern Nigeria* (London: OUP).
Jordan, W. (1968) *White over Black: American Attitudes Towards the Negro, 1550–1812* (Chapel Hill: University of North Carolina Press).
Joseph, R. A. (1974) 'Settlers, strikers and *Sans-Travail*: the Douala riots of September 1945', *JAH* , **15**, 4, pp. 669–87.
Julien, C. A. (1964) *Histoire de l'Algérie contemporaine*, Vol. 1, *La conquête et les débuts de la colonisation* (Paris: Presses Universitaire de France).
Julien, C. A. (1967) *Les Africains* (Paris: Jeune Afrique).
July, R. (1967) *The Origins of Modern African Thought* (New York: Praeger).
Juneidu, Alhaji (1957) *Tarihin Fulani* (Zaria).

Kachinsky, V. (1935) *Les aspects historiques et sociaux de la question de l'or du Togo* (Paris).
al-Kadir (1903) *Tuhfat as-airfī maathir al-amīr Abd-al-Kadir* (Alexandria).
Kagame, A. (1961) *L'histoire des armées bovines dans l'ancien Rwanda* (Brussels: Académie Royale des Science d'Outre-Mer).
Kagame, A. (1963) *Les Milices du Rwanda précolonial* (Brussels: Académie Royale des Science d'Outre-Mer).
Kamara, M. (1975) *La vie d'El Hadji Omar* (trans. by Amar Samb, Dakar: Editions Hilal).
Kamuhangire, E. M. (1972a) 'Migration, settlement and state formation in the south-western Uganda salt lakes region, 1500–1800' (seminar paper Makerere University).
Kamuhangire, E. M. (1972b) 'Pre-colonial trade in south-western Uganda' (seminar paper Makerere University).
Kamuhangire, E. M. (1976) 'The precolonial economic and social history of East Africa, with special reference to the south-western Uganda salt lakes region', *Hadith*, **5**, pp. 66–89.
Kanya-Forster, A. S. (1969) *The Conquest of the Western Sudan* (Cambridge: CUP).
Kaplow, S. B. (1977) 'The mudfish and the crocodile: underdevelopment of a West African bourgeoisie', *Science and Society*, **41**, pp. 313–33.
Kaplow, S. B. (1978) 'Primitive accumulation and traditional social relations on the nineteenth century Gold Coast', *CJAS*, **12**, 1, pp. 19–36.
al-Kardūdī, M. (nd) *Kash al-Ghumma bi-Bayān anna Harb al-Nidhām haqq 'alā al-Umma* (Fez).
Kasirye, J. (1959) *Abateregga Ku Namulondo ya Buganda* (London).
Kasozi, A. B. (1974) 'The spread of Islam in Uganda, 1844–1945' (PhD thesis, University of California, Santa Cruz).

Katzen, M. F. (1969) 'White settlers and the origin of a new society, 1652–1778', in M. Wilson and L. Thompson (eds), pp. 187–232.
Keenan, J. (1972) 'Social change among the Tuareg', in E.Gellner and C. Micaud (eds), pp. 345–60.
Keenan, J. (1977) *The Tuareg: People of Ahaggar* (London: Allen Lane).
Kellenbenz, H. (1981) 'Zanzibar et Madagascar dans le commerce allemand, 1840–1880', *Colloque de Majunga sur l'histoire et la culture du nord-ouest.*
Kelly, J. B. (1968) *Britain and the Persian Gulf, 1795–1880.* (Oxford: Clarendon Press).
Kenny, M. (1979) 'Pre-colonial trade in eastern Lake Victoria', *Azania*, **14**, pp. 97–107.
Kent, R. K. (1962) *From Madagascar to the Malagasy Republic* (London: Thames and Hudson).
Kevalevskii, M. M. (1879) *Obchinnoje zemlevladejije pritahiny, khod i posledstvija ege razlogenija* (Moscow).
Khallaf, H. (1962) *Al-tagdid fi'l-iqticad al-Micri al-hadith* (Cairo: 'Issa al-Babi al-Hababi & Co).
Khankī, G. (1948) 'Ibrāhīm bāshā', *Al-kitāb*, **6**.
Kietegha, J. B. (1983) *L'or de la Volta Noire* (Paris: Karthala).
Kimambo, I. N. (1969) *A Political History of the Pare of Tanzania c. 1500–1900* (Nairobi: EAPH).
Kimambo, I. N. (1970) 'The economic history of the Kamba 1850–1950', *Hadith*, **2**, pp. 79–103.
Kimambo, I. N. (1974) 'The Eastern Bantu peoples', in B. A. Ogot (ed.), pp. 195–209.
Kimambo, I. N. and Temu, C. W.. (eds) (1969) *A History of Tanzania* (Nairobi: EAPH).
Kimble, D. (1963) *A Political History of the Gold Coast* (Oxford: Clarendon Press).
Kistner, W. (1952) 'The anti-slavery agitation against the Transvaal Republic, 1852–1868', in *Archives Year Book for South African History* (Pretoria: Ministry of Education, Arts and Science), **2**, pp. 193–225.
Kittler, G. D. (1961) *The White Fathers* (New York: Image Books).
Kiwanuka, M. S. N. (1967) *Mutesa of Uganda* (Nairobi: EAPH).
Kiwanuka, S. N. (1972) *A History of Buganda* (London: Longman).
Ki-Zerbo, J. (1953) 'La pénétration française dans les pays de la Haute-Volta' (pre-doctoral dissertation, Université de Paris).
Kjekshus, H. (1977) *Ecology Control and Economic Development in East African History* (London: Heinemann).
Klein, H. S. (1972) 'The Portuguese slave trade from Angola in the eighteenth century', *Journal of Economic History*, **32**, 4, pp. 894–918.
Klein, H. S. (1976) 'The Cuban slave trade in a period of transition 1790–1843', *RFHOM*, **62**, 226–7, pp. 67–89.
Klein, H. S. (ed.) (1978) *The Middle Passage. Comparative Studies in the Atlantic Slave Trade* (Princeton: PUP).
Klein, M. A. (1968) *Islam and Imperialism in Senegal Sine-Saloum, 1847–1914* (Stanford: SUP).
Klein, M. A. (1972) 'Social and economic factors in the Muslim revolution in Senegambia', *JAH*, **13**, 3, pp. 419–41.
Klein, M. A. (1975) 'The study of slavery in Africa', *JAH*, **19**, 4, pp. 599–609.
Klein, M. A. and Johnson, G. W. (eds) (1972) *Perspectives on the African Past* (Boston: Boston University Press).
Knight, F. W. (1970) *Slave Society in Cuba during the Nineteenth Century* (Madison: UWP).
Knight, F. W. (1974) *The African Dimension in Latin America and the Caribbean: An Historical Dictionary and Bibliography* (Metuchen, NJ: Scarecrow Press).
Kolmodin, J. (1912–15) *Traditions de Tsazzega et Hazzega* (3 vols, Rome: C. de Luigi).
Koné, A. (1978) 'La prise de Segu et la fin d'El Hadj Omar', *Notes Africaines*, **159**, pp. 61–3.
Kraiem, A. (1983) 'Ali ben Khalifa', in *Réactions à L'occupation française de la Tunisie en 1881* (Tunis: CNUDST), pp. 145–58.
Krapf, J. L. (1860) *Travels, Researches and Missionary Labors during an Eighteen Years' Residence in Eastern Africa.* (Boston: Ticknor & Fields).
Kriecken, G. S. van (1976) *Khayr al-din et la Tunisie (1850–1881)* (Leiden: Brill).
Kuper, H. (1947) *An African Aristocracy: Rank among the Swazi of Bechuanaland* (London: OUP).
Kuper, L. (1971) 'African nationalism in South Africa, 1910–1964', in M. Wilson and L. Thompson (eds), pp. 424–76.

Lacheraf, M. (1978) *L'Algérie, nation et société* (2nd edn, Algiers: SNED).
Laitin, D. D. (1982) 'The international economy and state formation among the Yoruba in the nineteenth century', *International Organization*, **26**, 4, pp. 657–714.
Lancaster, C. S. (1974) 'Ethnic identity, history and "tribe" in the middle Zambesi valley', *American Ethnologist*, **1**, pp. 707–30.

Landa, R. G. (1976) *Borba algirskogo naroda protiv europejskoi kolonisatsii, 1830–1918* (Moscow: Naouka).
Landau, J. M. (1953) *Parliaments and Parties in Egypt* (Tel Aviv: Israel Publishing House).
Landau, J. M. (1958) *Studies in the Arab Theater and Cinema* (Philadelphia: University of Pennsylvania Press).
Lander, R. (1830) *Records of Captain Clapperton's Last Expedition* (London: Colburn & Bentley).
Landes, David S. (1958) *Bankers and Pashas: International Finance and Economic Imperialism in Egypt* (London: Heinemann).
Langworthy, H. W. (1971) 'Conflict among rulers in the history of Undi's Chewa kingdom', *TAJH*, 1, pp. 1–24.
Langworthy, H. W. (1972) *Zambia Before 1890* (London: Longman).
Langworthy, H. W. (nd) 'Swahili influence in the area between Lake Malawi and the Luangwa river' (unpublished manuscript).
Laroui, A. (1970) *L'histoire du Maghreb. Un essai de synthèse* (Paris: Maspero).
Laroui, A. (1975) *L'histoire du Maghreb*, Vol. 2 (Paris: Maspero).
Laroui, A. (1977) *Les origines sociales et culturelles du nationalisme marocain (1830–1912)* (Paris: Maspero).
Last, M. (1967a) *The Sokoto Caliphate* (London: Longman).
Last, M. (1967b) 'A note on the attitudes to the supernatural in the Sokoto jihad', *JHSN*, **4**, 1, pp. 3–13.
Last, M. (1974) 'Reform in West Africa: the jihad movements of the nineteenth century', in J. F. A. Ajayi and M. Crowder (eds), pp. 1–29.
Last, M. (1988) 'Reform in West Africa: the jihad movements of the nineteenth century' in J. F. A. Ajayi and M. Crowder (eds) *History of West Africa*, Vol. 2, (new edn, London: Longman).
Last, M. and al-Hajj, M. A. (1965) 'Attempts at defining a Muslim in 19th century Hausaland and Bornu', *JHSN*, **3**, 2, pp. 231–40.
Latham, A. J. H. (1972) 'Witchcraft accusations and economic tension in pre-colonial Old Calabar', *JAH*, **13**, 2, pp. 249–60.
Latham, A. J. H. (1973) *Old Calabar, 1600–1891. The Impact of the International Economy upon a Traditional Society* (Oxford: Clarendon Press).
Latham, A. J. H. (1978) 'Price fluctuations in the early palm oil trade', *JAH*, **19**, 2, pp. 213–18.
Laugel, A. (1959) 'Les Tadjakant, caravaniers du désert', *Bulletin de Liaison Saharienne*, **10**, 6, pp. 301–10.
Lavers, J. E. (1977) 'El-Kanemi (1775–1837)', in C. A. Julien (ed.) *Les Africains* (Paris: Editions Jeune Afrique), Vol. 7, pp. 45–71.
Lavers, J. E. (1980) 'Kanem and Borno to 1808', in O. Ikime (ed.) *Groundwork of Nigeria History* (Ibadan: Heinemann),, pp. 187–209.
Law, R. (1977) *The Oyo Empire, c. 1600–c. 1836: A West African Imperialism in the Era of the Atlantic Slave Trade* (Oxford: Clarendon Press).
Law, R. (1980) *The Horse in West African History* (London: IAI).
Leary, F. A. (1969) 'Islam, politics, and colonialism. A political history of Islam in the Casamance region of Senegal (1850–1919)' (PhD thesis, Northwestern University).
Lebel, P. (1974) 'Oral traditions and chronicles on Guragé immigration', *Journal of Ethiopian Studies*, **12**, 2, pp. 95–106.
Lefèbvre, T. (1845–54) *Voyage en Abyssinie* (6 vols, Paris: A. Bertrand).
Lihīta, M. F. (1944) *Tarīkh Miṣr al-iḳtiṣādī fi'l-'uṣūrr al-ḥadītha* (Cairo: Maktabat al-Nabdah al-Micriyyah).
Lejean, G. (1865) *Théodore II: Le nouvel empire d'Abyssinie* (Paris: Amyot).
Lejean, G. (1872) *Voyage en Abyssinie* (Paris: Hachette).
Leone, E. de (1882) *The Khedive's Egypt* (2nd edn, London).
Leone, E. de (1965) *La colonizzazione dell'Africa del Nord (Algeria, Tunisia, Morocco, Libia)* (Padua: CEDAM).
Lesseps, F. de (1869) *Egypte et Turquie* (Paris: Plon).
Leveen, P. E. (1971) 'British slave trade suppression policies, 1821–1865: impact and implications' (PhD thesis, University of Chicago).
Lévi-Provençal, E. (1922) *Les historiens des Chorfa: essai sur la littérature historique et biographique au Maroc du XVIe au XIXe siècle* (Paris: Larose).
Levine, D. N. (1965) *Wax and Gold: Tradition and Innovation in Ethiopian Culture* (Chicago and London: University of Chicago Press).
Levine, D. N. (1974) *Greater Ethiopia. The Evolution of a Multiethnic Society* (Chicago and London: University of Chicago Press).

Levine, R. M. (1980) *Race and Ethnic Relations in Latin America and the Caribbean: An Historical Dictionary and Bibliography* (Metuchen, NJ: Scarecrow Press).
Levine, V. T. (1971) *The Cameroon Federal Republic* (Ithaca: Cornell University Press).
Levtzion, N. (1968) *Muslims and Chiefs in West Africa* (Oxford: Clarendon Press).
Lewis, B. (1971) 'Hadjdj', in B. Lewis, V. L. Ménage, C. Pellat and J. Schacht (eds), pp. 37–8.
Lewis, B., Ménage, V. L., Pellat, C. and Schacht, J. (eds) (1971) *The Encyclopedia of Islam*, Vol. 3 (new edn, Leiden/London: Brill/Luzac).
Lewis, B., Pellat, C. and Schacht, J. (eds) (1965) *The Encyclopedia of Islam*, Vol. 2 (new edn, Leiden/London: Brill/Luzac).
Lewis, H. S. (1965) *A Galla Monarchy: Jimma Abba Jifar, Ethiopia, 1830–1932* (Madison: UWP).
Lewis, I. M. (1955) *Peoples of the Horn of Africa* (London: IAI).
Lewis, I. M. (1965) *The Modern History of Somaliland* (London: OUP).
Liesegang, G. (1967) 'Beitrage zur Geschichte des Reiches der Gaza Nguni im sudlichen Mocambique' (PhD thesis, University of Cologne).
Liesegang, G. (nd) 'Famines and smallpox in southeastern Africa' (unpublished manuscript).
Linant de Bellefonds, A. (1872–3) *Mémoires sur les principaux travaux d'utilité publiqwue exécutés en Egypte, depuis la plus haute Antiquité jusqu'à nos jours* (Paris).
Lindblom, G. (1920) *The Akamba in British East Africa* (2nd edn, Uppsala: Appelbergs).
Little, K. (1951) *The Mende of Sierra Leone* (London: Routledge & Kegan Paul).
Little, K. (1965–6) 'The political function of the Poro', *Africa*, **35**, 4, pp. 349–65; **36**, 1, pp. 62–72.
Little, K. (1970) *The Mende of Sierra Leone* (London: Routledge & Kegan Paul).
Livingstone, D. (1857) *Missionary Travels and Researches in South Africa* (London: Murray).
Lloyd, C. (1949) *The Navy and the Slave Trade. The Suppression of the African Slave Trade in the Nineteenth Century* (London: Longman).
Lloyd, P. C. (1963) 'The Itsekiri in the nineteenth century: an outline social history', *JAH*, **4**, 2, pp. 207–31.
Lobato, A. (1948) *Historia da Fundaçāo de Lourenço Marques* (Lisbon: Edições da Revista "Lusitania").
Lockhart, J. (1968) *Spanish Peru, 1532–1560: A Colonial Society* (Madison: UWP).
Loepfe, W. (1974) *Alfred Ilg und die äthiopische Eisenbahn* (Zurich: Atlantis).
Lombardi, D. (1971) 'Un 'expert' Saxon dans les mines d'or de Sumatra au XVIIe siècle', *Archipel*, 2, pp. 225–42.
Long, Edward (1774) *The History of Jamaica*, (3 vols, London: Lowndes).
Loutskii, V. L. (1965) *Novaja istorija arabskih stran* (Moscow: Naouka).
Lovejoy, P. E. (1974) 'Interregional monetary flows in the precolonial trade of Nigeria', *JAH*, **15**, 4, pp. 563–85.
Lovejoy, P. E. (1978) 'Plantations in the economy of the Sokoto caliphate', *JAH*, **19**, 3, pp. 341–68.
Lovejoy, P. E. (1982) 'The volume of the Atlantic slave trade: a synthesis', *JAH*, **23**, 3, pp. 473–501.
Lovejoy, P. E. (1983) *Transformations in Slavery: A History of Slavery in Africa* (Cambridge: CUP).
Lovejoy, P. E. and Baier, S. (1975) 'The desert-side economy of the Central Sudan', *IJAHS*, **8**, 4, pp. 553–83.
Low, D. A. (1963) 'The northern interior, 1840–84', in R. Oliver and G. Mathew (eds), pp. 297–331.
Lutsky, V. (1965) *Modern History of the Arab Countries* (Moscow: Progress Publishers).
Ly, M. (1972) 'Quelques remarques sur le *Tarikh el Fettach*', *BIFAN* (B), **34**, 3, pp. 471–93.
Lye, W. F. (1967) 'The Difaqane: the Mfecane in the southern Sotho area, 1822–24', *JAH*, **8**, 1, pp. 107–31.
Lye, W. F. (1969) 'The distribution of the Sotho peoples after the Difaqane', in L. Thompson (ed.), pp. 190–206.
Lye, W. F. (ed.) (1975) *Andrew Smith's Journal of his expedition into the interior of South Africa 1834–36* (Cape Town: Balkem).
Lynch, H. (1967) *Edward Wilmot Blyden, Pan-Negro Patriot, 1832–1912* (London: OUP).
Lyon, G. F. (1821) *A Narrative of Travels in Northern Africa in the years 1818, 1819 and 1820* (London: Murray).

Mage, E. (1868) *Voyage au Soudan Occidental (1863–1866)* (Paris: Hachette).
Magubane, B. M. (1979) *The Political Economy of Race and Class in South Africa* (New York: Monthly Review Press).
Mahjoubi, A. (1977) *L'établissement du Protectorat français en Tunisie* (Tunis: Publications de l'Université).
Mainga, M. (1973) *Bulozi Under the Luyana Kings: Political Evolution and State Formation in Pre-colonial Zambia* (London: Longman).

Makozi, A. O. and Ojo, G. J. A. (eds) (1982) *The History of the Catholic Church in Nigeria* (London: Macmillan).
Malaisse, F. et al (1972) 'The miombo ecosystem: a preliminary study', in P. Golley and F. Golley (eds), *Tropical Ecology* (Athens, Georgia: University of Georgia Press), pp. 363–405.
Malortie, Baron de (1882) Egypt: *Native Rulers and Foreign Interference* (London: Ridgway).
Malumfashi, U. F. (1973) 'The life and ideas of Shaikh Uthman dan Fodio, being an edition, translation and analysis of Rawd al-jinan and al-Kashf wa 'l-hayan' (MA thesis, Bayero University, Kano).
Mandala, E. (1979) 'The Kololo interlude in Southern Africa, 1861–1891' (MA thesis, University of Malawi).
Mane, M. (1974–5) *Contribution à l'histoire du Kaabu, des origines au XIXe siècle* (Dakar, Mémoire de l'Université de Dakar).
Mangestu Lamma (1959) *Mashafa Tizita* (Addis Ababa).
Manning, P. (1979) 'The slave trade in the Bight of Benin, 1640–1890', in H. A. Gemery and J. S. Hogendorn (eds), pp. 107–41.
Marchal, J. Y. (1967) 'Contribution à l'étude historique du Vakinankaratra, évolution du peuplement dans la Cuvette d'Ambohimanambola, sous-préfecture de Batafo', *Bulletin de Madagascar*, **250**, pp. 241–80.
Marcus, H. G. (1975) *The Life and Times of Menilek II, 1844–1913* (Oxford: Clarendon Press).
Markham, C. R. (1869) *A History of the Abyssinian Expedition* (London: Prideaux).
Marks, S. (1967a) 'The rise of the Zulu kingdom', in R. Oliver (ed.), pp. 85–91.
Marks, S. (1967b) 'The Nguni, the Natalians and their history', *JAH*, **8**, 3, pp. 529–40.
Marks, S. and Atmore, A. (eds) (1980) *Economy and Society in Pre-industrial South Africa* (London: Longman).
Marshall, J. P. (1968) *Problems of Empire: Britain and India, 1757–1813* (London: Allen & Unwin).
Martel, A. (1965) *Les confins saharo-tripolitains de la Tunisie, 1818–1911* (Paris: PUF).
Martin, B. G. (1963) 'A mahdist document from Futa Jallon', *BIFAN* (B), **25**, 1–2, pp. 47–57.
Martin, B. G. (1972) 'A short history of the Khalwati order of dervishes', in N. Keddie (ed.) *Scholars, Saints and Sufis* (Berkeley: UCP), pp. 275–305.
Martin, B. G. (1976) *Muslim Brotherhoods in Nineteenth Century Africa* (Cambridge: CUP).
Martin, T. (1976) *Race First: The Ideological and Organizational Struggles of Marcus Garvey and the Universal Negro Improvement Association* (Westport, Conn.: Greenwood Press).
Marty, P. (1920–1) *Etudes sur l'Islam et les Tribus du Soudan* (4 vols, Paris: Leroux).
Mason, J. P. (1971) 'The social history and anthropology of the Arabized Berbers of Augila oasis in the Libyan Sahara Desert' (PhD thesis, Boston University).
Mason, J. P. (1978) 'Desert strongmen in the East Libyan Sahara (*c.* 1820): a reconstruction of local power in the region of the Augila oasis', *Revue d'histoire maghrébine*, **6**, pp. 180–8.
Mason, M. (1970) 'The Nupe Kingdom in the nineteenth century; a political history' (PhD thesis, University of Birmingham).
Mason, P. (1970) *Race Relations* (London: OUP).
Mason, R. J. (1973) 'The first Early Iron-Age in South Africa: Broederstroom 24/73', *South African Journal of Science*, **69**.
al Masri, F. H. (1963) 'The life of Shehu Usman dan Fodio before the jihad', *JHSN*, **2**, 4, pp. 435–48.
al Masri, F. H. (ed. and trans.) (1978) *Bōyan Wujūb al-Hijra 'ala'l-Ibed* by 'Uthman Ibn Fūdī (Khartoum: KUP).
Massaia. (1921–30) *I miei trentacinque anni di missione nell' alta Etiopia* (Rome: Coop tipografrica Manuzio (12 vol.).
Matsebula, J. S. M. (1972) *A History of Swaziland* (Cape Town: Longman).
Matthews, T. I. (1981) 'Portuguese, Chikunda and the people of the Gwembe valley: the impact of the "Lower Zambezi Complex" on Southern Zambia', *JAH*, **22**, 1, 23–42.
Maura y Gamazo, G. (1911) *La question marocaine du point de vue espagnol* (Paris: Challamel).
Maxwell, W. E. (1932) 'The law relating to slavery among the Malays', *Journal of the Malayan Branch of the Royal Asiatic Society*, **10**, 1.
M'Bokolo, E. (1981) *Noirs et blancs en Afrique équatoriale: Les sociétés côtières et la pénétration française (vers 1820–1874)* (Paris: Mouton).
McCall, D. F. and Bennett, N. R. (eds) (1971) *Aspects of West African Islam* (Boston: Boston University African Studies Center).
McCarthy, M. (1983) *Social Change and the Growth of British Power in the Gold Coast: the Fante states 1807–1874* (Lanham, Md: University Press of America).
McCaskie, T. C. (1980) 'Office, land and subjects in the history of the Manwere *fekuo* of Kumase: an essay in the political economy of the Asante state', *JAH*, **21**, 2, pp. 189–208.

McCoan, J. C. (1887) *Egypt as it is* (London: Cassell).
McGaffey, W. (1970) *Custom and Government in the Lower Congo* (Berkeley and Los Angeles: UCP).
McKay, W. F. (1975) 'A precolonial history of the southern Kenya coast' (PhD thesis, Boston University).
McPherson, J. M., Holland, L. B., et al. (1971) *Blacks in America: Bibliographical Essays* (New York: Doubleday).
McSheffrey, G. M. (1983) 'Slavery, indentured servitude, legitimate trade and the impact of abolition in the Gold Coast, 1874–1901', *JAH*, **24**, 3, pp. 349–68.
Mears, W. G. A. (1970) *Wesleyan Baralong Mission in Trans-Orangia, 1821–1884* (2nd edn, Cape Town: Struik).
Medeiros, F. de (1984) 'Peuples du golfe du Benin Aja-ewe', in *Colloque de Cotonou* (Paris: Karthala).
Meek, C. K. (1925) *The Northern Tribes of Nigeria* (2 vols, London: OUP).
Méhier de Mathuisieulx, H. (1904) 'Une mission en Tripolitanie', *Renseignements Coloniaux*, January 1904, pp. 20–34.
Meillassoux, C. (1971a) 'Introduction', in C. Meillassoux (ed.), (London: OUP), pp. 3–86.
Meillassoux, C. (ed.) (1971b) *The Development of Indigenous Trade and Markets in West Africa* (London: OUP).
Meillassoux, C. (1974) 'From reproduction to production. A Marxist approach to economic anthropology', *Economy and Society*, **3**, pp. 315–45.
Meillassoux, C. (1975) *L'esclavage en Afrique précoloniale* (Paris: Maspero).
Meillassoux, C. (1981) *Maidens, Meal and Money* (Cambridge: CUP).
Memmi, A. (1963) *La poésie algérienne de 1830 à nos jours (Approches socio-historiques)* (Paris: Mouton).
Mendes Moreira, J. (1948) *Fulas do Cabu* (Bissau: Centro de Estudos da Guiné Portuguesa).
Merad, A. (1978) 'Iṣlāḥ', in C. E. Bosworth, E. Van Donzel, B. Lewis and C. Pellat (eds), pp. 141–63.
Mercer, P. (1971) 'Shilluk trade and politics from the mid-seventeenth century to 1861', *JAH*, **12**, 3, pp. 407–26.
Mercier, P. (1950) 'Notice sur le peuplement Yoruba du Dahomey-Togo', *Etudes Dahoméennes*, **4**, pp. 29–40.
Metcalfe, G. E. (1962) *Maclean of the Gold Coast* (London: OUP).
Metcalfe, G. E. (1964) *Great Britain and Ghana: Documents of Ghana History, 1807–1957* (London: Nelson).
Metegue N'Nah, N. (1979) *Economies et sociétés au Gabon dans la première moitié du XIXe siècle* (Paris: L'Harmattan).
Meyer-Heiselberg, R. (1967) *Notes from the Liberated African Department in the Archives at Fourah Bay College, Freetown, Sierra Leone* (Uppsala: Scandinavian Institute of African Studies).
Michailidis, G. (1950) 'Le désert et la civilisation égyptienne', *Cahiers d'Histoire Egyptienne.*
Michaux-Bellaire, E. (1921) 'Essai sur l'histoire des confréries religieuses, *Hespéris*, **1**, pp. 141–58.
Middleton, J. and Campbell, J. (1965) *Zanzibar: Its Society and Its Politics* (London: OUP).
Miège, J. L. (1961–3) *Le Maroc et l'Europe (1830–1894)* (4 vols, Paris: PUF).
Miège, J. L. (1975) 'La Libye et le commerce transsaharien au XIXe siècle', *ROMM*, **19**, pp. 135–68.
Miers, S. (1971) 'Notes on the arms trade and government policy in Southern Africa between 1870 and 1890', *JAH*, **12**, 4, pp. 571–8.
Miers, S. (1975) *Britain and the Ending of the Slave Trade* (London: Longman).
Miers, S. and Kopytoff, I. (eds) (1977) *Slavery in Africa: Historical and Anthropological Perspectives* (Madison: UWP).
Miller, J. C. (1973) 'Slaves, slavers and social change in nineteenth century Kasanje', in F. W. Heimer (ed.) *Social Change in Angola* (Munich: Weltforum Verlag), pp. 9–29.
Milliot, L. (1911) *L'Association agricole chez les Musulmans du Maghreb, (Maroc, Algérie, Tunisie)* (Paris: Rousseau).
Minna, M. (1982) 'Sultan Muhammad Bello and his intellectual contribution to the Sokoto Caliphate', (PhD thesis, London University).
Mintz, S. W. (1971) 'Towards an Afro-American history', *UNESCO Journal of World History*, **13**, 2, pp. 317–32.
Moffat, R. (1945) *The Matebele Journals* (ed. J. P. R. Wallis, 2 vols, London: Chatto & Windus).
Moffat, R. and Moffat, M. (1951) *Apprenticeship at Kuruman* (ed. I. Schapera, London: Chatto & Windus).
Mondon-Vidailhet, F. M. C. (1905) *Chronique de Theodoros II* (Paris: Bibliothēque Nationale).
Montagne, R. (1930) *Les Berbères et le Makhzen dans le sud du Maroc* (Paris).
Monteil, C. (1932) *Une cité soudanaise, Djenne, métropole du Delta central du Niger* (Paris: Société d'Editions géographiques, maritimes et coloniales).

Monteil, P. L. (1894) *De Saint-Louis à Tripoli par le Tchad* (Paris: Alcan).
Monteil, V. (1966) *Esquisses Sénégalaises* (Dakar: IFAN).
Monteil, V. (1977) *Les Bambara de Segou et de Kaarta* (1st edn, 1924, Paris: Maisonneuve).
Moreno Fraginals, M. (ed.) (1977) *Africa en America Latina* (Mexico: UNESCO).
Moreno, M. (1942) 'La cronaca di re Teodoro attribuita al dabtàrà "Zaneb"', *Rassegna di Studi Etiopici*, 2, pp. 143–80.
Morgan, M. (1969) 'Continuities and traditions in Ethiopian history. An investigation of the reign of Tewodros', *Ethiopia Observer*, 12.
Morton-Williams, P. (1964) 'The Oyo Yoruba and the Atlantic trade, 1670–1830', *JHSN*, 3, 1.
Moulero, T. (1964) 'Histoire et légende de Chabi', *Etudes Dahoméennes*, 2, pp. 51–93.
Moursy, M. K. (1914) *De l'étendue du droit de propriété, étude historique, juridique et comparée* (Paris: Recueil Sirey).
Mouser, B. L. (1973) 'Traders, coasters and conflict in the Rio Pongo from 1790–1808', *JAH*, 14, 1, pp. 45–64.
Mouser, B. L. (1975) 'Landlords – strangers: a process of accommodation and assimilation', *IJAHS*, 8, 3, pp. 425–40.
Moyer, R. A. (1974) 'The Mfengu, self-defence and the Cape frontier wars', in C. Saunders and R. Derricourt (eds), pp. 101–26.
Mudenge, S. I. (1974) 'The role of foreign trade in the Rozvi empire: a reappraisal', *JAH*, 15, 3, pp. 373–91.
Muller, C. F. J. (ed.) (1974) *Five Hundred Years: A History of South Africa* (2nd edn, Pretoria and Cape Town: University of South Africa).
Munro, J. F. (1976) *Africa and the International Economy* (London: Dent).
Munthe, L. (1969) *La Bible à Madagascar, les deux premières traductions du Nouveau Testament malgache* (Oslo: Egede Instututtet).
Munthe, L., Ravoajanahary, C. and Ayache, S. (1976) 'Radama Ier et les Anglais: les négociations de 1817 d'après les sources malgaches', *Omaly sy Anio*, 3–4, pp. 9–104.
Murray, D. R. (1971) 'Statistics of the slave trade to Cuba, 1790–1867', *Journal of Latin American Studies*, 3, 2, pp. 131–49.
Mustafa, A. A. (1965) *Micr wa'l-mas'alah al-Micriyyah* (Cairo: Dar al-Ma'aref).
Mutibwa, P. M. (1972) 'Trade and economic development in nineteenth-century Madagascar', *TAJH*, 2, 1, pp. 32–63.
Mutibwa, P. M. (1974) *The Malagasy and the Europeans: Madagascar's Foreign Relations, 1861–1895* (London: Longman).
Mveng, E. (1963) *Histoire du Cameroun* (Paris: Présence Africaine).
Mworoha, E. (1977) *Peuples et rois de l'Afrique des lacs* (Dakar: NEA).
Myatt, F. (1970) *The March to Magdala* (London: Leo Cooper).
Myrdal, G. (1944) *An American Dilemma* (2 vols, New York: Harper and Row).

Nacanabo, D. (1982) 'Le royaume maagha de Yako' (doctoral thesis, Université de Paris).
Nachtigal, G. (1967) *Sahara und Sudan, Ergebnisse Sechsjahriger Reisen in Afrika* (Graz).
Nair, K. K. (1972) *Politics and Society in South Eastern Nigeria 1841–1906: A Study of Power, Diplomacy and Commerce in Old Calabar* (London: Frank Cass).
al-Naqar, U. (1972) *The Pilgrimage Tradition in West Africa: An Historical Study with Special Reference to the Nineteenth Century* (Khartoum: KUP).
Nardin, J. C. (1965) 'Le Libéria et l'opinion publique en France, 1821–1847', *CAE*, 6, 1, pp. 96–144.
al-Naṣīrī, A. (1954–56) Al-Istiqṣā li-Akhbār Duwal al-Maghrib al-Aqṣā, 9 vol. (Casablanca).
Nayenga, F. P. B. (1976) 'An economic history of the lacustrine states of Busoga, Uganda, 1750–1939' (PhD thesis, University of Michigan).
Needham, D. E. (1974) *From Iron Age to Independence: History of Central Africa* (London: Longman).
Neumark, S. D. (1954) *Foreign Trade and Economic Development in Africa: A Historical Perspective* (Stanford: Food Research Institute).
Newbury, C. W. (1961) *The Western Slave Coast and Its Rulers: European Trade and Administration Among the Yoruba and Adja-Speaking Peoples of South-Western Nigeria, Southern Dahomey and Togo* (Oxford: Clarendon Press).
Newbury, C. W. (1966) *North African and Western Sudan trade in the nineteenth century: a re-evaluation, JAH*, 7, 2, pp. 233–46.
Newbury, C. W. (1968) 'The protectionist revival in French colonial trade: the case of Senegal', *Economic History Review*, 21, 2, pp. 337–48.
Newbury, C. W. (1972) 'Credit in early nineteenth century West African trade', *JAH*, 13, 1, pp. 81–95.

Newbury, D. S. (1975) 'Rwabugiri and Ijwi' *Etudes d'Histoire Africaine*, **7**, pp. 155–73.
Newbury, D. S. (1980) 'Lake Kivu regional trade during the nineteenth century', *Journal des Africanistes*, **50**, 2, pp. 6–30.
Newbury, D. S. (nd) 'Lake Kivu regional trade during the nineteenth century' (unpublished paper).
Newbury, M. C. (1975) 'The cohesion of oppression: a century of clientship in Kinyaga, Rwanda' (PhD thesis, University of Wisconsin).
Newitt, M. D. D. (1973a) *Portuguese Settlement on the Zambesi, Exploration, Land Tenure and Colonial Rule in East Africa*, (London: Longman).
Newitt, M. D. D. (1973b) 'Angoche, the slave trade and the Portuguese *c*. 1844–1910', *JAH*, **13**, 4, pp. 659–73.
Ngcongco, L. (1982a) 'Impact of the Difaqane on Tswana states', in R. Hitchcock and M. R. Smith (eds), pp. 161–71.
Ngcongco, L. (1982b) 'Precolonial migration in south-eastern Botswana' in R. Hitchcock and M. R. Smith (eds), pp. 23–9.
Nicholls, C. S. (1971) *The Swahili Coast: Politics, Diplomacy and Trade on the East African Littoral, 1798–1856* (London: Allen & Unwin).
Nicholson, S. E. (1976) 'A climatic chronology for Africa: synthesis of geological, historical and meteorological information and data' (PhD thesis, University of Wisconsin).
Nicholson, S. E. (forthcoming) 'Saharan climates in historic times', in H. Faure and M. E. J. Williams (eds) *The Sahara and the Nile*.
Nicol, F. (1940) 'Les traitants français de la côte est de Madagascar, de Ranavalona I à Radama II', *Mémoire de l'Académie Malgache*, **33**.
Nöldeke, T. (1892) *Sketches from Eastern History* (London & Edinburgh: A. & C. Black).
Norris, H. T. (1968) *Shinqiti Folk Literature and Song* (Oxford: Clarendon Press).
Norris, H. T. (1975) *The Tuaregs* (Warminster: Aris & Philips).
Northrup, D. (1976) 'The compatibility of the slave and palm oil trades in the Bight of Biafra', *JAH* , **17**, 3, pp. 352–64.
Nuñez, B. (1980) *Dictionary of Afro-Latin American Civilization* (Westport, Conn.: Greenwood Press).
Nwani, O. A. (1975) 'The quantity theory in the early monetary system of West Africa with particular emphasis on Nigeria, 1850–1895', *Journal of Political Economy*, **83**, 1, pp. 185–93.

Ochsenwald, W. (1980) 'Muslim–European conflict in the Hijaz: the slave trade controversy, 1840–1895', *Middle Eastern Studies*, **16**, 1, pp. 115–26.
Oded, A. (1974) *Islam in Uganda* (New York: Halsted Press).
Ogot, B. A. (1967) *A History of the Southern Luo People, 1500–1900* (Nairobi: EAPH).
Ogot, B. A. (1968) 'Kenya under the British, 1895 to 1963', in B. A. Ogot and J. A. Kieran (eds), pp. 255–89.
Ogot, B. A. (ed.), (1974) *Zamani: A Survey of East African History* (2nd edn, Nairobi: EAPH).
Ogot, B. A. (ed.) (1976) *Kenya Before 1900* (Nairobi: EAPH).
Ogot, B. A. (1979) 'Population movements between East Africa, the Horn of Africa and the neighbouring countries', in *The African Slave Trade from the Fifteenth to the Nineteenth Century* (Unesco, General History of Africa, Studies and Documents, **2**, Paris), pp. 175–82.
Ogot, B. A. and Kieran, J. A. (eds) (1968) *Zamani: A Survey of East African History* (Nairobi: EAPH).
Olaniyan, R. (1974) 'British desires for legitimate trade in West Africa, 1860–1874: 1, the Imperial dilemma', *Odu*, **9**, pp. 23–44.
Oliveira Martins, F. A. (ed.) (1952) 'Hermenegildo Capelo e Roberto Ivens, vol. II', in *Diarios da viagem de Angola a contra-costa* (Lisbon), pp. 366–83.
Oliver, R. (1952) *The Missionary Factor in East Africa* (London: Longmans, Green).
Oliver, R. (ed.) (1967) *The Middle Age of African History* (London: OUP).
Oliver, R. (1965) *The Missionary Factor in East Africa* (2nd edn, London: Longman).
Oliver, R. and Fage, J. D. (1962) *A Short History of Africa* (Harmondsworth: Penguin).
Oliver, R. and Mathew, G. (eds) (1963) *A History of East Africa, Vol. 1* (Oxford: Clarendon Press).
Oloruntimehin, B. O. (1972a) *The Segu Tukulor Empire* (London: Longman).
Oloruntimehin, B. O. (1972b) 'The impact of the abolition movement on the social and political development of West Africa in the nineteenth and twentieth centuries', *Ibadan*, **7**, 1, pp. 33–58.
Omer-Cooper, J. D. (1966) *The Zulu Aftermath, A Nineteenth Century Revolution in Bantu Africa* (London: Longman).
Omer-Cooper, J. D. (1969) 'Aspects of political change in the nineteenth century Mfecane', in L. Thompson (ed.), pp. 207–29.
Omer-Cooper, J. D. (1976a) 'The Nguni outburst', in J. E. Flint (ed.), pp. 319–52.

Omer-Cooper, J. D. (1976b) 'Colonial South Africa and its frontiers', in J. E. Flint (ed.), pp. 353–92.

Onneken, A. (1956) *Die Konigskultur Kaffas und der verwandten Konigreiche* (Frankfurt).

Oppel, A. (1887) 'Die religiosen Verhaltnisse von Afrika', *Zeitschrift der Gesselschaft fur Erdkunde zu Berlin*, **21**.

Orhanlu, C. (1972) 'Turkish archival sources about Ethiopia', *IV Congresso Internazionale di Studi Etiopici* (Rome).

Orhanlu, C. (1976–7) 'Turkish language publications and records about Africa' [in Turkish], *Tarih Institusu Dergisi*, **7–8**, pp. 145–56.

Ottenberg, S. (1958) 'Ibo oracles and intergroup relations', *Southwestern Journal of Anthropology*, **14**, 3, pp. 295–317.

Ottenberg, S. (1959) 'Ibo receptivity to change', in W. R. Bascom and M. J. Herskovits (eds), *Continuity and Change in African Culture* (Chicago: University of Chicago Press), pp. 130–43.

Packard, R. M. (1981) *Chiefship and Cosmology: An Historical Study of Political Competition* (Bloomington: Indiana University Press).

Page, M. E. (1974) 'The Manyena hordes of Tippu Tip: a case study in social stratification and the slave trade in East Africa', *IJAHS*, **7**, 1, pp. 69–84.

Palacios Preciados, J. (1973) *La Trata de Negros por Cartagena de Indias, 1650–1750* (Tunja, Colombia: Universidad Pedagogica y Technologica).

Pallinder-Law, A. (1974) 'Aborted modernization in West Africa? The case of Abeokuta', *JAH*, **15**, 1, pp. 65–82.

Palmer, C. A. (1976) *Slaves of the White God: Blacks in Mexico, 1570–1650* (Cambridge, Mass: HUP).

Palmer, C. A. (1981) *Human Cargoes: The British Slave Trade to Spanish America, 1700–1739* (Urbana: University of Illinois Press).

Palmer, H. R. (1928) *Sudanese Memoirs* (Lagos: Government Printer).

Palmer, R. and Parsons, N. (eds) (1977a) *The Roots of Rural Poverty in Central and Southern Africa* (London: Heinemann).

Palmer, R. and Parsons, N. (1977b) 'Introduction: historical background', in R. Palmer and N. Parsons (eds), pp. 1–32.

Pankhurst, R. K. P. (1961) *An Introduction to the Economic History of Ethiopia from early times to 1800* (London: Lalibela House).

Pankhurst, R. K. P. (1964) 'Ethiopia and the Red Sea and Gulf of Aden ports in the nineteenth and twentieth centuries', *Ethiopia Observer*, **8**.

Pankhurst, R. K. P. (1966a) 'The Emperor Theodore and the question of foreign artisans in Ethiopia' in *Boston University Papers in African History*, Vol. 2 (Boston: African Studies Centre, Boston University).

Pankhurst, R. K. P. (1966b) 'The Saint-Simonians and Ethiopia', *in Proceedings of the Third International Conference of Ethiopian Studies* (Addis Ababa: Haile Sellassie I university, Institute of Ethiopian Studies).

Pankhurst, R. K. P. (1966c) *State and Land in Ethiopian History* (Addis Ababa: Haile Sellassie I University, Institute of Ethiopian Studies).

Pankhurst, R. K. P. (1967) 'Menilek and the utilisation of foreign skills', *Journal of Ethiopian Studies*, **5**, 1, pp. 29–42.

Pankhurst, R. K. P. (1968) *Economic History of Ethiopia 1800–1935* (Addis Ababa: Haile Sellassie I University, Institute of Ethiopian Studies).

Pankhurst, R. K. P. (1972) 'Yohannes Kotzika, the Greeks and British intervention against Emperor Tewodros in 1867–8', *Abba Salama*, **3**, pp. 87–117.

Pankhurst, R. K. P. (1973a) 'Popular opposition in Britain to British intervention against Emperor Tewodros of Ethiopia (1867–1868)', *Ethiopia Observer*, **14**, pp. 141–203.

Pankhurst, R. K. P. (1973b) 'The library of Emperor Tewodros at Maqdala (Magdala)', *BSOAS*, **36**, pp. 17–42.

Pankhurst, R. K. P. (1974) 'Tewodros. The question of a Greco-Romanian or Russian hermit or adventurer in nineteenth century Ethiopia', *Abba Salama*, **5**, pp. 136–59.

Pantucek, S. (1969) *Tounisskaja literatoura. Krathii etcherk* (Moscow: Nauka).

Parkinson, C. N. (1937) *Trade in the Eastern Seas, 1793–1813* (Cambridge: CUP).

Parkyns, M. (1854) *Life in Abyssinia* (New York: Appleton).

Parrinder, E. G. (1947) 'The Yoruba-speaking peoples of Dahomey', *Africa*, **17**, pp. 122–48.

Parrinder, E. G. (1955) 'Some western Yoruba towns', *Odu*, **2**, pp. 4–10.

Parrinder, E. G. (1967) *Story of Ketu* (Ibadan: IUP).

Patterson, O. (1982) *Slavery and Social Death: A Comparative Study* (Cambridge, Mass.: HUP).

Paulus, J. (ed.) (1917–21) *Encyclopaedie van Nederlandsch-Indië* ('s-Gravenhage: Nijhoff/Leiden: Brill).

Pellat, C. (1953) *Le milieu baṣrien et le formation de Ǧahiẓ* (Paris).

Pennec, P. (1964) *Les transformations des corps de métiers de Tunis* (Tunis: ISEA-AM).

Père, M. (1982) *Les deux bouches. Les sociétés du rameau Lobi entre la tradition et le changement* (Paris: TI).

Perini, R. (1905) *Di qua del Mareb* (Florence).

Person, Y. (1968–75) *Samori, unu Révolution Dyula* (3 vols, Dakar: IFAN).

Person, Y. (1971) 'Ethnic movements and acculturation in Upper Guinea since the fifteenth century', *IJAHS*, 4, pp. 669–89.

Person, Y. (1972) 'Samori and resistance to the French', in R. Rotberg and A. Mazrui (eds), *Protest and Power in Black Africa* (New York: OUP), pp. 80–112.

Person, Y. (1974) 'The Atlantic Coast and the northern savannas, 1800–1880', in J. F. A. Ajayi and M. Crowder (eds), pp. 262–307.

Person, Y. (1979) 'Samori and Islam', in J. R. Willis (ed.), pp. 259–77.

Person, Y. (1981) 'Communication: who were the Vai?', *JAH* 23, 1, p. 133.

Pesenti, G. (1912) *Di alcumni canti arabici e somalici.*

Pesenti, G. (1929) *Canti sacri e profani, danze e ritmi degli Arabi, dei Somali e dei Suahili* (Milan: L'Eroica).

Peterson, J. (1969) *Province of Freedom. A History of Sierra Leone, 1787–1870* (London: Faber).

Petherick, J. and Petherick, K. (1869) *Travels in Central Africa and Exploration of the Western Tributaries* (London).

Philliot, D. C. and Azoo, R. F. (1906–7) 'Some Arab folk tales from the Hadramout', *Journal of the Royal Asiatic Society of Bengal*, pp. 399–439.

Phillipson, D. W. (1969) 'Early iron-using peoples of Southern Africa', in L. Thompson (ed.), pp. 24–49.

Phiri, K. M. (1975) 'Chewa history in Central Malawi and the use of oral traditions, 1600–1920' (PhD thesis, University of Wisconsin).

Pigeot, A. (1956) 'Les français à Tindouf', *Bulletin de Liaison Saharienne* 7, 23, pp. 85–94.

Pirone, M. (1961) *Appunti di Storia dell'Africa* (Rome: Edizioni Rioerche).

Plowden, W. C. (1868) *Travels in Abyssinia and the Galla Country* (London: Longmans, Green).

Porter, A. (1963) *Creoledom: A Study of the Development of Freetown Society* (London: OUP).

Porter, D. H. (1970) *The Abolition of the Slave Trade in England, 1784–1807* (New York: Archon).

Price, R. (1973) *Maroon Societies* (New York: Doubleday-Anchor).

Priestley, M. (1969) *West African Trade and Coast Society, A Family Study* (London: OUP).

Prins, A. H. (1962) *The Swahili-Speaking Peoples of Zanzibar and the East African Coast* (London: IAI).

Prins, A. H. (1971) *Didemic Lamu: Social Stratification and Spatial Structure in a Muslim Maritime Town* (Groningen).

Quinn, C. A. (1972) *Mandingo Kingdoms of the Senegambia: Traditionalism, Islam and European Expansion* (London: OUP).

Quinn, C. A. (1979) 'Maba Diakhou and the Gambian jihād, 1850–1890', in J. R. Willis (ed.), pp. 233–58.

Rabary, Le pasteur (1957) *Ny Maritiora Malagasy* (Tananarive: Imprimerie Luthérienne).

al-Rafe'i, A.-R. (1948a) *Al-thawrah al-'Arabiyyah* (Cairo).

al-Rafe'i, A.-R. (1948b) *Asr Isma'il* (2nd edn, Cairo: Mataba at al-Nahdah al-Micriyyah).

al-Rafe'i, A.-R. (1948c) *Micr wa'l-Soudan fi awa'el 'ahd al-ihtilal (tarikh Migr al-qawmi min sanat 1882 ila sanat 1892)* (2nd edn, Cairo: Maktabat al-Nahdah al-Micriyyah).

al-Rafeʿī A.-R. (1951) *'Asr Mohammad-Alī* (3rd edn, Cairo: Maktabat al-Nahdah al-Micriyyah).

Raffenel, A. (1856) *Nouveau voyage dans le pays des nègres* (2 vols, Paris: N. Chaix).

Rainihifina, J. (1975) *Lovantsaina, I, Tantara betsileo* (2nd edn, Fianarantsoa).

Raison, F. (1970) 'Un tournant dans l'histoire religieuse merina du XIXe siècle: la fondation des temples protestants à Tananarive entre 1861 et 1869', *Annales de l'Université de Madagascar* (série Lettres et Sciences humaines), 11, pp. 11–56.

Raison, F. (1977) 'L'échange inégal de la langue, la pénétration des techniques linguistiques dans une civilisation de l'oral (Imerina au début du XIXe siècle)', *Annales ESC*, 32, 4, pp. 639–69.

Raison, F. (1979) 'Temps de l'astrologie, temps de l'histoire: le premier almanach de LMS en Imerina, 1864', *Omaly sy Anio*, 9, pp. 41–78.

Rakotomahandry, S. (1981) *L'armée royale sous Ranavalona Ière, aspects sociaux et économiques. Essai de description statistique* (Tananarive: TER Département d'histoire).

Ralibera, D. (1977) 'Recherches sur la conversion de Ranavalona II', *Omaly sy Anio*, **7–8**, pp. 7–42.

Ramanakasina, V. (nd) *Medicine and Doctors in the Anglo-Malagasy Civilisation* (Tananarive: TER, Département des Langues Vivantes).

Ranger, T. O. (1963) 'The last days of the empire of the Mwene Mutapa' (unpublished paper presented at the History of Central African Peoples Conference, Lusaka).

Ranger, T. O. (ed.) (1968) *Emerging Themes of African History* (Nairobi: EAPH).

Ranger, T. O. (1973) 'Territorial cults in the history of Central Africa', *JAH*, **14**, 4, pp. 581–98.

Ranger, T. O. (1975) *Dance and Society in Eastern Africa 1890–1970: The Beni Ngoma* (London: Heinemann).

Ranger, T. O. and Kimambo, I. (eds) (1972) *The Historical Study of African Religion* (Berkeley: UCP).

Rangley, W. H. J. (1959) 'The Makololo of Dr Livingstone', *Nyasaland Journal*, **12**, pp. 59–98.

Rantoandro, G. (1981) 'Une communauté mercantile du Nord-Ouest: les Antalaotra', *Colloque sur l'histoire et la culture du nord-ouest, Majunga*.

Raombaha (1980) *Histoires I* (edn and French trans. by S. Ayache, Fianarantosa).

Rasamuel, D. (1980) *Traditions orales et archéologie de la basse Sahatorendrika: Etude de sources concernant le peuplement* (2 vols, TER, Département d'histoire).

Rasmussen, R. K. (1977) *Mzilikazi of the Ndebele* (London: Heinemann).

Rasoamioraramanana, M. (1974) *Aspects économiques et sociaux de la vie à Majunga 1862–1881* (TER, Département d'histoire).

Rasoamioraramanana, M. (1981a) 'Un grand port de l'Ouest: Majunga (1862–1881)', *Recherches, Pédagogie, Culture*, Jan 1981, pp. 78–9.

Rasoamioraramanana, M. (1981b) 'Pouvoir merina et esclavage dans le Boina dans la deuxième moitié du XIXe siècle, 1862–1883', *Colloque sur l'histoire et la culture du nord-ouest, Majunga*.

Rassam, H. (1869) *Narrative of the British Mission to Theodore, King of Abyssinia* (London: Murray).

Ravisse, P. (1896) (Ismail Pacha, Khedive d'Egypte (1830–1895), extract from the *Revue d'Egypte* (Cairo).

Redmayne, A. (1968a) 'Mkwawa and the Hehe wars', *JAH*, **9**, 3, pp. 409–36.

Redmayne, A. (1968b) 'The Hehe', in A. D. Roberts (ed.), pp. 37–58.

Renault, F. (1976) *Libération d'esclaves et nouvelle servitude* (Abidjan-Dakar: NEA).

Renault, F. and Daget, S. (1980) 'La traite des esclaves en Afrique', *Etudes Scientifiques* (Cairo).

Rennie, J. K. (1966) 'The Ngoni states and European intrusion', in E. Stokes and R. Brown (eds), pp. 302–31.

Revoil, G. (1885) 'Voyage chez les Benadirs, les Comalis et les Bayouns en 1882–1883', *Le Tour du Monde*, **49**.

Rey, A. (1978) 'Mohammed Bin 'Abdallah ou le combat du chérif de Ouergla', in *Les Africains*, Vol. 12 (Paris: Jeune Afrique).

Rey-Goldzeiguer, A. (1977) *Le royaume arabe* (Paris).

Reynolds, B. (1968) *The Material Culture of the Peoples of the Gwembe Valley* (Manchester: MUP).

Reynolds, E. (1974a) *Trade and Economic Change on the Gold Coast, 1807–1874* (London: Longman).

Reynolds, E. (1974b) 'The rise and fall of an African merchant class on the Gold Coast, 1830–1874', *CEA*, **14**, 2, pp. 253–64.

Reynolds, E. (1975) 'Economic imperialism: the case of the Gold Coast', *Journal of Economic History*, . **35**, 1, pp. 94–116.

Richards, A. R. (1977) 'Primitive accumulation in Egypt, 1798–1882', *Review*, **1**, 2, pp. 3–49.

Ritter, E. A. (1955) *Shaka Zulu* (London: Longman).

Rivière, P. L. (1924–5) *Traités, codes et lois du Maroc* (Paris: Recueil Sirey).

Rivlin, H. A. B. (1961) *The Agricultural Policy of Muhammad 'Ali in Egypt* (Cambridge, Mass.: HUP).

Roberts, A. D. (ed.) (1968) *Tanzania before 1900* (Nairobi: EAPH).

Roberts, A. D. (1969) 'Political change in the nineteenth century', in I. N. Kimambo and A. J. Temu (eds), pp. 57–84.

Roberts, A. D. (1970a) 'Pre-colonial trade in Zambia', *African Social Research*, **10**, pp. 715–46.

Roberts, A. D. (1970b) 'Nyamwezi trade', in R. Gray and D. Birmingham (eds), pp. 39–74.

Roberts, A. D. (1973) *A History of the Bemba* (Madison: UWP).

Roberts, R. (1978) 'The Maraka and the economy of the middle Niger valley, 1790–1908' (PhD thesis, University of Toronto).

Roberts, R. (1980) 'Long distance trade and production: Sinsani in the nineteenth century', *JAH*, **21**, 2, pp. 169–88.

Robertson, A. F. (1978) *Community of Strangers: A Journal of Discovery in Uganda* (London: Scolar Press).
Robinson, C. H. (1895) *Hausaland* (London: Sampson Low Marston).
Robinson, R. (1985) 'The Berlin Conference of 1884–85 and the Scramble for Africa', in *Proceedings of the Conference on the Berlin West African Conference* (Berlin, February 1985, edited by the German Historical Institute, London).
Robinson, R. and Gallagher, J. (1961) *Africa and the Victorians: The Official Mind of Imperialism* (London: Macmillan).
Roche, C. (1976) *Conquête et résistance des peuples de la Casamance* (Dakar: NEA).
Rochet d'Héricourt, C. F. X. (1841) *Voyage sur la côte orientale de la mer Rouge, dans le pays d'Adal et le royaume de Choa* (Paris: Bertrand).
Rochet d'Héricourt, C. F. X. (1846) *Second voyage sur les deux rives de la mer Rouge, dans le pays des Adels et le royaume de Choa* (Paris: Bertrand).
Rodney, W. (1970) *A History of the Upper Guinea Coast 1545–1800* (Oxford: Clarendon Press).
Rodney, W. (1972) *How Europe Underdeveloped Africa* (London: Bogle l'Ouverture).
Rodney, W. (1975) 'Africa in Europe and the Americas' in R. Gray (ed.) *The Cambridge History of Africa, Vol 4, From c. 1600 to c. 1790* (Cambridge: CUP), pp. 578–622.
Rohlfs, G. (1883) *Meine Mission nach Abessyinien auf Begfehl Sr. Maj. des deutschen Kaisers, im Winter 1880–81* (Leipzig).
Roncek, J. S. and Kiernan, T. (eds) (1970) *The Negro Impact on Western Civilization* (New York: Philosophical Library).
Ronen, D. (1971) 'On the African role in the trans-Atlantic slave trade in Dahomey', *CEA*, 11, 1, pp. 5–13.
Ross, D. (1967) 'The rise of the autonomous kingdom of Dahomey, 1818–1894' (PhD thesis, University of London).
Rossi, E. (1968) *Storia di Tripoli e della Tripolitania* (Rome: Istituto per l'Oriente).
Roux, E. (1964) *Time Longer than Rope* (2nd edn, Madison: UWP).
Rout, L. B. (1976) *The African Experience in Spanish America, 1502 to the Present Day* (Cambridge: CUP).
Rowley, H. (1867) *The Story of the Universities' Mission to Central Africa* (London: Saunders, Otley).
Rubenson, S. (1966) *King of Kings: Tewodros of Ethiopia* (Nairobi: OUP).
Rudin, H. R. (1938) *Germans in the Cameroons, 1884–1914* (New Haven: YUP).
Ruedy, J. (1967) *Land Policy in Colonial Algeria. The Origins of the Rural Public Domain* (Berkeley and Los Angeles: UCP).
Russel, S. (1884) *Une mission en Abyssinie et dans la mer Rouge* (Paris: Plon, Nourrit).
Ryder, A. F. C. (1961) 'Missionary activities in the kingdom of Warri to the early nineteenth century', *JHSN*, 2, 2, pp. 251–7.

Sabry, M. (1930) *L'Empire égyptien sous Mohamed-Ali et la question d'Orient (1811–1849)* (Paris: Paul Geuthner).
Sabry, M. (1933) *L'empire égyptien sous Ismail et l'ingérence anglo-française (1863–1879)* (Paris: Paul Geuthner).
Sa'dallah, A. (1983) *Al h'araka al wat'aniya al-jazā'iriya* (3rd edn, Algiers: SNED).
Sagatzky, J. (1940) 'Problèmes d'organisation de l'industrie aurifère dans l'ex-Haute Volta, II, domaine politique' (unpublished manuscript, Abidjan, 23 July 1940).
Saīdouni, N. (nd) *Al-niz'ām al-mālī li-l Jazā ir.*
Saint-Martin, Y. (1967) *L'empire toucouleur et la France, un demi-siècle de relations diplomatiques (1846–1893)* (Dakar: Publications de la Faculté de lettres et sciences humaines).
Salim, A. I. (1973) *The Swahili-Speaking Peoples of Kenya's Coast, 1895–1965* (Nairobi: EAPH).
Salt, H. (1814) *A Voyage to Abyssinia* (London: Rivington).
Sammarco, A. (1935) *Précis de l'histoire d'Egypte par divers historiens et archéologues, Vol. 4: Les règnes de 'Abbas, de Sa'id et d'Ismail (1848–1879)* (Rome: Istituto Poligrafico del Stato).
Sanchez-Albornoz, N. (1974) *The Population of Latin America: A History* (Berkeley: UCP).
Sanders, P. (1975) *Moshoeshoe: Chief of the Sotho* (London: Heinemann).
Santi, P. and Hill, R. (eds) (1980) *The Europeans in the Sudan 1834–1878* (Oxford: Clarendon Press).
Saran, P. and Burton-Page, J. (1965) 'Ḍarībah' in B. Lewis, C. Pellat and J. Schacht (eds), pp. 142–58.
Sarbah, J. M. (1906) *Fanti National Constitution* (London: Clowes).
Sari, D. (1970) *Les villes précoloniales de l'Algérie occidentale* (Algiers: SNED).
Saunders, A. C. de C. M. (1982) *A Social History of Black Slaves and Freedmen in Portugal, 1441–1555* (Cambridge: CUP).

Saunders, C. and Derricourt, R. (eds) (1974) *Beyond the Cape Frontier. Studies in the History of the Transkei and Ciskei* (London: Longman).
Schnapper, B. (1961) *La politique et le commerce français dans le golfe de Guinée de 1838 à 1871* (Paris and The Hague: Mouton).
Schnapper, B. (1959) 'La fin du régime de l'Exclusif: Le commerce étranger dans les possessions françaises d'Afrique tropicale (1817–1870)', *Annales Africaines*, pp. 149–99.
Schnerb, R. (1957) *Le XIXe siècle. L'apogée de l'expansion européene (1815–1914)* (Paris: PUF).
Schoffeleers, M. (1972a) 'The history and political role of the M'bona cult among the Mang'anja' in T. O. Ranger and I. Kimambo (eds), pp. 73–94.
Schoffeleers, M. (1972b) 'The Gisumphi and M'bona cults in Malawi: a comparative history', (unpublished paper presented at the Conference on Religious History, Lusaka).
Schroder, G. and Siebel, D. (1974) *Ethnographic Survey of Southwestern Liberia: The Liberian Kran and the Sapo* (Newark: University of Delaware, Department of Anthropology).
Schuler, M. (1970) 'Ethnic slave rebellions in the Caribbean and the Guianas', *Journal of Social History* 3, 4.
Schuler, M. (1980) *Alas, Alas Kongo: A Social History of Indentured African Immigration into Jamaica, 1841–1865* (Baltimore: JHUP).
Schwab, G. and Harley, G. W. (1947) *Tribes of the Liberian Hinterland* (Cambridge, Mass.: HUP).
Schwartz, A. (1973) *Mise en place des populations Guere et Wobe* (Abidjan: duplicated).
Schweinfurth, G. (1873) *The Heart of Africa* (London: Low, Marston, Low & Searle).
Scott, E. P. (1978) 'Subsistence, markets and rural development in Hausaland', *Journal of Developing Areas*, 12, 4, pp. 449–70.
Seddon, D. (1978) 'Economic anthropology or political economy? (I): Approaches to the analysis of pre-capitalist formation in the Maghreb', in J. Clammer (ed.), *The New Economic Anthropology* (London: Macmillan), pp. 61–109.
Selous, F. (1893) *Travels and Adventures in South-East Africa* (London: Ward).
Serjeant, R. B. (1966) 'South Arabia and Ethiopia – African elements in the South Arabian population', *Proceedings of the 3rd International Conference of Ethiopian Studies* Vol. I, pp. 25–33.
Shack, W. A. (1966) *The Gurage* (London: OUP).
Shapiro, H. L. (1953) *Race Mixture* (Paris: UNESCO).
al-Sharqāwī, M. (1958) *Misr fi'l-qarn al-'thamen 'ashar* (3 vols, Cairo).
Shea, P. J. (1974) 'Economies of scale and the dyeing industry of precolonial Kano', *Kano Studies*, ns, 1, 2, pp. 55–61.
Shea, P. J. (1978) 'Approaching the study of production in rural Kano', in B. M. Barkindo (ed.).
Shea, P. J. (forthcoming) *Black Cloth*.
Shepherd, A. F. (1868) *The Campaign in Abyssinia* (Bombay 'Times of India' Office).
Shepperson, G. (1968) 'Ethiopianism: past and present', in C. G. Baeta (ed.), pp. 249–68.
Shepperson, G. and Price, T. (1958) *Independent African: John Chilembwe and the Origins, Setting and Significance of the Nyasaland Native Uprising of 1915* (Edinburgh: Edinburgh University Press).
Shepstone, T. (1888) 'The early history of the Zulu-Kafir race of south-eastern Africa', in J. Bird (ed.), *The Annals of Natal, 1495–1845* (2 vols, Pietermaritzburg: Davis), pp. xxx–xxx.
Sheridan, R. (1974) *Sugar and Slavery: An Economic History of the British West Indies, 1623–1775* (Baltimore: John Hopkins University Press).
Sheriff, A. M. H. (1971) 'The rise of a commercial empire: an aspect of the economic history of Zanzibar, 1780–1873' (PhD thesis, University of London).
Sheriff, A. M. H. (1980) 'Tanzanian societies at the time of partition', in M. H. Y. Kaniki (ed.), *Tanzania Under Colonial Rule* (London: Longman), pp. 11–50.
Shibayka, M. (1957) *Al-Sudan fi Qarn* (Cairo).
Shorter, A. (1969) *Nyungu-ya-Mawe* (Nairobi: EAPH).
Shorter, A. (1972) *Chiefship in Western Tanzania: A Political History of the Kimbu* (Oxford: Clarendon Press).
Shuqayr, N. (1967) *Jughrà fiyat-wa-Tārikh al Sūdān* (Beirut).
Shukri, M. F. (1937) *Khedive Ismail and Slavery in the Sudan, 1863–1879* (Cairo).
Shukri, M. F. (1946) *Misr wal Sayada ala al-Sudan* (Cairo).
Shukri, M. F. (1948) *Al-Ḥukm al-Miṣrī fil Sūdān 1820–1885* (Cairo).
Shukri, M. F. (1958) *Misr wal Sudan, Ta rikh Wahdat, Waoil Nil al-Siyasis il Qarn al-Tesi-a Ashar* (Cairo).
Sillery, A. (1952) *The Bechuanaland Protectorate* (Cape Town: OUP).
Sillery, A. (1954) *Sechele* (Cape Town: OUP).
Simpson, G. E. (1978) *Black Religions in the New World* (New York: Columbia University Press).
Skene, R. (1917) 'Arab-Swahili dances and ceremonies', *JRAI*, 47, pp. 413–34.

Skinner, E. P. (1964) *The Mossi of Upper Volta: The Political Development of a Sudanese People* (Stanford: SUP).
Slama, B. (1967) *L'insurrection de 1864 en Tunisie* (Tunis: Maison tunisienne de l'édition).
Slousch, N. (1908) 'La Tripolitaine sous la domination des Karamanli', *Revue du Monde Musulman*, 6, pp. 58–84, 211–32, 433–53.
Smaldone, J. P. (1971) 'The firearms trade in the Central Sudan in the nineteenth century', in D. F. McCall and N. R. Bennett (eds).
Smaldone, J. P. (1972) 'Firearms in the Central Sudan: a revaluation', *JAH*, 13, 4, pp. 591–608.
Smaldone, J. P. (1977) *Warfare in the Sokoto Caliphate* (Cambridge: CUP).
Smith, A. (1963) 'The southern section of the interior, 1840–84', in R. Oliver and G. Mathew (eds), pp. 253–96.
Smith, A. K. (1969) 'The trade of Delagoa Bay as a factor in Nguni politics 1750–1835', in L. Thompson (ed.), pp. 171–89.
Smith, A. K. (1973) 'The peoples of Southern Mozambique: an historical survey', *JAH*, 14, 4, pp. 565–80.
Smith, E. W. (1956) 'Sebetwane and the Makalolo', *African Studies*, 15, 2, pp. 49–74.
Smith, H. F. C. (1961) 'A neglected theme of West African history; the Islamic revolutions of the 19th century', *JHSN*, 2, 2, pp. 169–85.
Smith, I. R. (1972) *The Emin Pasha Relief Expedition 1886–90* (Oxford: Clarendon Press).
Smith, M. G. (1960) *Government in Zazzau* (London: OUP).
Smith, M. G. (1978) *The Affairs of Daura* (Berkeley: UCP).
Soleillet, P. (1887) *Voyage à Segou, 1878–1879* (Paris: Challamel).
Soumoni, E. (1983) 'Trade and politics in Dahomey 1841–1892, with particular reference to the House of Regis' (PhD thesis, University of Ife).
Sourian-Hoebrechts, C. (1969) *La presse maghrebine Libye, Tunisie, Algérie; èvolution historique, situation en 1965, organisation et problèmes actvels* (Paris: Editions du Centre National de la Recherche Scientifique).
Sousberghe, L. de (1961) *Deux palabres d'esclaves chez les Pende* (Brussels: ARSC).
Sow, A. I. (1966) *La femme, la vache et la foi* (Paris: Julliard).
Sow, A. I. (1968) *Chroniques et récits du Fuuta Jallon* (Paris: Klincksieck).
Spear, T. (1972) 'Zwangendaba's Ngoni 1821–1890: a political and social history of a migration' (Occasional Paper No. 4 of the African Studies Program, University of Wisconsin, Madison).
Spear, T. (1974) 'The Kaya complex: a history of the Mijikenda peoples of the Kenya coast to 1900'. (PhD thesis, University of Wisconsin).
Spear, T. (1981) *Kenya's Past: An Introduction to Historical Method in Africa* (London: Longman).
Spitzer, L. (1974) *The Creoles of Sierra Leone* (Madison: UWP).
Stamm, A. (1972) 'La société créole à Saint-Paul de Loanda dans les années 1838–1848', *RFHOM*, 217, pp. 578–610.
Stanley, H. M. (1872) *How I Found Livingstone* (London: Sampson, Low, Marston, Low & Searle).
Stanley, H. M. (1874) *Coomassie and Magdala* (London: Sampson, Low, Marston, Low & Searle).
Stanley, H. M. (1878) *Through the Dark Continent* (2 vols, London: Low, Marston, Searle & Rivington).
Staudenraus, P. J. (1961) *The African Colonization Movement, 1816–1863* (New York: Columbia University Press).
Staudinger, P. (1889) *Im Herzen der Haussa Länder* (Berlin: Landsberger).
Stefaniszyn, B. and de Santana, H. (1960) 'The rise of the Chikunda condottieri', *Northern Rhodesian Journal*, 4, pp. 361–8.
Stengers, J. (1962) 'L'impérialisme colonial de la fin du XIXe siècle; mythe ou réalité', *JAH*, 3, 3, pp. 469–91.
Stevenson-Hamilton, J. (1929) *The Low-Veld: Its Wild Life and its People* (London: Cassell).
Stewart, C. C. (1976a) 'Southern Saharan scholarship and the *Bilād al-Sūdān*', *JAH*, 17, 1, pp. 73–93.
Stewart, C. C. (1976b) 'Frontier disputes and problems of legitimation: Sokoto–Masina relations, 1817–1837', *JAH*, 17, 4, pp. 495–514.
Stewart, C. C. and Stewart, E. K. (1973) *Islam and the Social Order in Mauritania: A Case Study from the Nineteenth Century* (Oxford: Clarendon Press).
Stewart, M. (forthcoming) 'The Borgu people of Nigeria and Benin: the disruptive effect of partition on tradition and political and economic relations', *JHSN*.
Stitz, V. (1974) *Studien zur Kulturgeographie Zentraläthiopiens* (Bonn: Dümmlers).
Stokes, E. and Brown, R. (eds) (1966) *The Zambezian Past: Studies in Central African History* (Manchester: MUP).
Sundkler, B. G. (1961) *Bantu Prophets in South Africa* (2nd edn, London: OUP).

Swai, B. (1984) 'Precolonial states and European merchant capital in Eastern Africa', in A. Salim (ed.), *State Formation in Eastern Africa* (London: Heinemann), pp. 15–35.
Symes, M. (1800) *An Account of an Embassy to the Kingdom of Ava* (London: Bulmer).
Szymanski, E. (1965) 'La guerre hispano-marocaine 1859–1860', *Rocznik orientalistyczny*, **2**, pp. 54–64.

Tagher, J. (1949) 'Bibliographie analytique et critique des publications françaises et anglaises relatives à l'histoire du règne de Mohammad Ali', *Cahiers d'histoire égyptienne* , **2**, pp. 128–235.
al-Ṭahṭāwī, R. R. (1869) *Manāhedj al-albāb al-Miṣriyya fi mabāhedj al-ādāb al-* 'aṣriyya.
Takla Yasus (nd) *Tarika Nagast Za Ityopiya* ms in the Institute of Ethiopian Studies Library, Addis Ababa).
Tal, Al-Hajj 'Uumar (nd[a]) *Les Rimah* (trans. Maurice Puech, Dakar, Diplômes d'Etudes Supérieures).
Tal, Al-Hajj 'Uumar (nd[b]) *Safinat al-saada* (trans. M. Gueye).
Tal, Al-Hajj 'Umar (1983) *Bayān Mawaḳa* (trans. S. M. Mahibou and J. L. Triaud, (Paris: Editions du CNRS).
Tambo, D. C. (1976) 'The Sokoto caliphate slave trade in the nineteenth century', *IJAHS*, **9**, 2, pp. 187–217.
Tannenbaum, F. (1946) *Slave and Citizen* (New York: Vintage).
Tasūlī, A. (nd) *Jawāb 'alā su'āl al-Amīr 'Abd al-Qādir* (Fez).
Tedeschi, S. (1874) L'emirato di Harar Secondo un documento inedito', *Accademia Nazionale dei Lincei, Atti del IV Congresso Internazionale di Studi Etiopici* (Rome).
Tégnier, Y. (1939) *Les petit-fils de Touameur. Les Chaamba sous le régime français, leur transformation* (Paris: Editions Domat-Montchrestien).
Teixeira Da Mota, A. (1954) *Guiné Portuguesa* (2 vols, Lisbon: Agência Geral do Ultramar).
Temini, A. (1978) *Le beylik de Constantine et Hadj Ahmed Bey (1830–1837)* (Tunis: Publications de la RHM).
Temperley, H. (1972) *British Anti-Slavery, 1823–1870* (London: Longman).
Terray, E. (1969) *L'organisation sociale des Dida de Côte d'Ivoire* (*Dijon, Imprimerie Darantiére*).
Terray, E. (1972) *Marxism and 'Primitive' Societies* (New York: Monthly Review Press).
Theal, G. M. (1891) *History of South Africa, 1795–1834* (London: Swan, Sonnenschein).
Theal, G. M. (1900) *History of South Africa: The Republics and Native Territories from 1854 to 1872* (London: Swan, Sonnenschein).
Thebault, E. (1960) *Code des 305 articles* (Etudes malgaches, Tananarive: Centre de Droit Privé).
Thiers, H. (1867) *L'Egypte ancienne et moderne à l'Exposition Universelle* (Paris: Dramard–Baudry).
Thomas, R. and Bean, R. (1974) 'The fishers of men: the profits of the slave trade', *Journal of Economic History*, **34**, 4, pp. 885–914.
Thompson, L. (1969a) 'Co-operation and conflict: the Zulu kingdom and Natal', in M. Wilson and L. Thompson (eds), pp. 334–90.
Thompson, L. (1969b) 'Co-operation and conflict: the High Veld', in M. Wilson and L. Thompson (eds), pp. 391–446.
Thompson, L. (ed.) (1969c) *African Societies in Southern Africa* (London: Heinemann).
Thompson, L. (1971a) 'The subjection of the African chiefdoms, 1870–1898', in M. Wilson and L. Thompson (eds), pp. 245–86.
Thompson, L. (1971b) 'The compromise of Union', in M. Wilson and L. Thompson (eds), pp. 325–64.
Thompson, L. (1975) *Survival in Two Worlds: Moshoeshoe of Lesotho 1786–1870* (Oxford: Clarendon Press).
Thompson, V. and Adloff, R. (1965) *The Malagasy Republic: Madagascar Today* (Stanford: SUP).
Thomson, J. (1885) *Through Masai Land* (London: Low, Marston, Searle & Rivington).
Thornton, J. (1977) 'Demography and history in the kingdom of Kongo, 1550–1750', *JAH*, **18**, 4, pp. 507–30.
Tiendrebeogo, Y. (1964) *Histoire et coutumes royales des Mossi de Ouagadougou* (Ouagadougou: Naba).
Toledano, E. (1982) *The Ottoman Slave Trade and Its Suppression, 1840–1890* (Princeton: PUP).
Tonnoir, R. (1970) *Giribuma. Contribution à l'histoire et à la petite histoire du Congo équatorial* (Tervuren: Musée royal de l'Afrique centrale).
Toplin, R. B. (ed.) (1974) *Slavery and Race Relations in Latin America* (Westport, Conn.: Greenwood Press).
Toplin, R. B. (ed.) (1981) *Freedom and Prejudice: The Legacy of Slavery in the United States and Brazil* (Westport, Conn.: Greenwood Press).
Tosh, J. (1970) 'The northern interlacustrine region', in R. Gray and D. Birmingham (eds), pp. 103–18.

Tosh, J. (1978) 'Lango agriculture during the early colonial period: land and labour in a cash-crop economy', *JAH*, **19**, 3, pp. 415–39.

Tosh, J. (1980) 'The cash-crop revolution in tropical Africa: an agricultural reappraisal', *African Affairs*, **79**, 314, pp. 79–94.

Townsend, W. J. (1892) *Madagascar: Its Missionaries and Martyrs* (London: Partridge and Co).

Trapiols, S. (1964) 'The origins of the Cape franchise qualifications of 1853', *JAH*, **5**, 1, pp. 37–54.

Trimingham, J. S. (1952) *Islam in Ethiopia* (London: OUP).

Trimingham, J. S. (1962) *A History of Islam in West Africa* (London: OUP).

Trimingham, J. S. (1969) 'The expansion of Islam', in J. Kritzeck and I. M. Lewis (eds), *Islam in Africa* (New York: Van Nostrand-Reinhold Co), pp. 13–28.

Trimingham, J. S. and Fyfe, C. (1960) 'The early expansion of Islam in Sierra Leone', *Sierra Leone Bulletin of Religions*, **2**.

Tukur, M. M. (1977) 'Values and public affairs: the relevance of the Sokoto Caliphal experience to the transformation of the Nigerian polity' (PhD thesis, Ahmadu Bello University).

Turc, N. (1950) *Chronique d'Egypte, 1798–1804* (Cairo: G. Wiet).

Turyahikayo-Rugyeme, B. (1976) 'Markets in pre-colonial East Africa: the case of the Bakiga', *Current Anthropology*, **17**, 2, pp. 286–90.

Twaddle, M. (1966) 'The founding of Mbale', *UJ*, **30**, 1, pp. 25–38.

Tyam, M. A. (1935) *La vie d'El Hadj Omar, qacida en poular* (trans. H. Gaden, Paris: Institut d'Ethnologie).

Tyam, M. A. (1961) *La Vie d'El-Hadj Omar (Qacida en Poular)* (trans. H. Gaden, Paris).

Tylden, G. (1950) *Rise of the Basuto* (Cape Town: Juta and Co).

Tzadua, P. (1968) *The Petha Nagast, The Law of Kings* (Addis Ababa).

Ullendorff, E. (1960) *The Ethiopians* (London: OUP).

Unomah, A. C. (1972) 'Economic expansion and political change in Unyanyembe (*c.* 1840–1900)' (PhD thesis, University of Ibadan).

Unomah, A. C. and Webster, J. B. (1976) 'East Africa: the expansion of commerce', in J. E. Flint (ed.), pp. 270–318.

Uzoigwe, G. N. (1973) 'The slave trade and African society', *THSG*, **14**, 2, pp. 187–212.

Vail, H. L. (1972) 'Suggestions towards a reinterpreted Tumbuka history', in B. Pachai (ed.), *The Early History of Malawi* (Evanston: NUP).

Vail, H. L. (1977) 'Ecology and history: the example of Eastern Zambia', *JSAS*, **2**, pp. 129–55.

Valensi, L. (1969a) *Le Maghreb avant la prise d'Alger 1790–1830* (Paris: Flammarion).

Valensi, L. (1969b) 'Islam et capitalisme: production et commerce des chéchias en Tunisie et en France aux 18e et 19e siècles', *Revue d'histoire moderne et contemporaine*, **17**, pp. 376–400.

Valensi, L. (1977) *Fellahs tunisiens. L'économie rurale et la vie des campagnes aux 18e et 19e siècles* (Paris & The Hague: Mouton).

Valensi, L. (1978) 'Pays avancés et pays dominés', in L. Bergeron (ed.), *Inerties et révolutions 1730–1840* (Paris).

Valentia, G. (1809) *Voyages and Travels to India, Ceylon, the Red Sea, Abyssinia and Egypt* (London: W. Miller).

Valette, J. (1960) *Les Relations extérieures de Madagascar au XIXème siècle* (Tananarive: Imprimerie officielle).

Valette, J. (1962) *Etude sur le règne de Radama I* (Tananarive: Imprimerie nationale).

Valette, J. (1971) 'Madagascar', in H. Deschamps (ed.), *Histoire de l'Afrique Noire*, Vol. 2 (Paris).

Van Jaarsveld, F. A. (1961) *The Awakening of Afrikaner Nationalism 1868–1881* (Cape Town: Human & Rousseau).

Van Jaarsveld, F. A. (1975) *From Van Riebeeck to Vorster 1652–1947: An Introduction to the History of the Republic of South Africa* (Johannesburg: Perskor).

Van Warmelo, J. J. (1935) *A Preliminary Survey of the Bantu Tribes of South Africa* (Pretoria: Government Printer).

Vansina, J. (1966) *Kingdoms of the Savanna* (Madison: University of Wisconsin Press).

Vansina, J. (1973) *The Tio Kingdom of the Middle Congo, 1880–1892* (London: OUP).

Vansina, J. (1978) 'Finding food and the history of pre-colonial Equatorial Africa', *African Economic History*, 7, pp. 9–19.

Vatin, J. C. (1974) *L'Algérie politique. Histoire et société* (Paris: A. Colin).

Vellez Caroço, J. (1948) *Monjur, o Gabú e a sua história* (Bissau: Centro de Estudos de Guiné Portuguesa).

Vellut, J.-L. (1972) 'Notes sur le Lunda et la frontière luso-africaine (1700–1900)', *Etudes d'Histoire Africaine*, 3, pp. 61–166.
Vellut, J.-L. (1975) 'Le royaume de Cassange et les réseaux luso-africains (*ca.* 1750–1810)', *CAE*, 15, 1, pp. 117–36.
Verbeken, A. (1956) *Msiri, roi de Garenganze l'homme rouge du Katanga* (Brussels).
Verger, P. (1955) 'Yoruba influences in Brazil', *Odu*, I, 3.
Verger, P. (1968) *Flux et reflux de la traite des nègres entre le golfe de Bénin et Bahia de Todos los Santos, du XVIIe au XIXe siècle* (Paris: Mouton).
Verger, P. (1976) *Trade Relations between the Bight of Benin and Bahia* (Ibadan: Ibadan University Press).
Vila Vilar, E. (1973) 'Los asientos portuguesos y el contrabando de negros', *Anuario de Estudios Americanos*, 30, pp. 557–9.
Vila Vilar, E. (1977) 'The large-scale introduction of Africans into Vera Cruz and Cartagena', in V. Rubin and A. Tuden (eds), *Comparative Perspectives on Slavery in New World Plantation Societies* (New York: New York Academy of Sciences), pp. 267–80.
Villari, L. (1938) 'I "gulti" della regions di Axum', *Rassegna Economica dell' Africa Italiana*, 26.
Villiers, P. (1982) *Traite des noirs et navires négriers au XVIIe siècle* (Paris: Seigneurs).
Vis, H. L., Yourassowsky, C. and van der Borght, H. (1975) *A Nutritional Survey in the Republic of Rwanda* (Tervuren: Musée royal de l'Afrique centrale).
Voll, J. O. (1969) 'A history of the Khatmiyyah tariqa', (PhD thesis, Harvard University).

Wagner, R. (1980) 'Zoutpansberg: the dynamics of a hunting frontier, 1848–67', in S. Marks and A. Atmore (eds), pp. 313–49.
Wahidah, A. F. S. (1950) *Fi usul as-mas'alah al-Misriyyah* (Cairo: Matba' at Misr).
Waïgalo, N. (1977) Le Maçina de 1853 à 1896 (dissertation, Bamako).
Waldmeier, T. (1886) *The Autobiography of Theophilus Waldmeier* (London: Partridge).
Walker, E. A. (1957) *A History of Southern Africa* (3rd edn, London: Longmans, Green).
Wallace, D. M. (1883) *Egypt and the Egyptian Question* (London: Macmillan).
Wallerstein, I. (1970) 'The colonial era in Africa: changes in the social structure', in L. H. Gann and P. Duignan (eds), pp. 399–421.
Wallerstein, I. (1973) 'Africa in a capitalist world', *Issues*, 3, 3, pp. 1–11.
Wallerstein, I. (1974) *The Modern World-System: Vol. 1, Capitalist Agriculture and the Origins of the European World-Economy in the Sixteenth Century* (New York: Academic Press).
Wallerstein, I. (1976) 'The three stages of African involvement in the world-economy', in P. C. W. Gutkind and I. Wallerstein (eds), *The Political Economy of Contemporary Africa* (Beverly Hills: Sage), pp. 30–57.
Wallerstein, I. (1980) *The Modern World-System: Vol. 2, Mercantilism and the Consolidation of the European World-Economy, 1600–1750* (New York: Academic Press).
Wastell, R. E. P. (1944) 'British imperial policy in relation to Madagascar, 1810–1896' (PhD thesis, University of London).
Webb, C. de B. (1981) 'The origins of the war: problems of interpretation', in A. Duminy and C. Ballard (eds), pp. 1–12.
Weld, H. B. (1922) *The Royal Chronicle of Abyssinia* (Cambridge: CUP).
Were, G. S. (1967) *A History of the Abaluyia of Western Kenya c. 1500–1930* (Nairobi: EAPH).
Were, G. S. (1968) 'The Western Bantu peoples from AD 1300 to 1800', in B. A. Ogot and J. A. Kieran (eds), pp. 177–97.
Wheeler, D. L. (1964) 'A note on smallpox in Angola, 1670–1875', *Studia*, 13–14, pp. 351–62.
Wheeler, D. L. (1968) 'Gungunhana', in N. R. Bennett (ed.) *Leadership in Eastern Africa* (Boston: Boston University Press).
Wheeler, D. L. (1972) 'The first Portuguese colonial movement, 1835–1875', *Iberian Studies*, 1, 1, pp. 25–7.
Wheeler, D. L. and Pélissier, R. (1971) *Angola* (New York: Praeger).
Wilburn, W. (1813) *Oriental Commerce* (London).
Wilkins, K. St. C. (1870) *Reconnoitring in Abyssinia* (London).
Wilks, I. (1975) *Asante in the Nineteenth Century: The Structure and Evolution of a Political Order* (Cambridge: CUP).
Williams, E. (1944) *Capitalism and Slavery* (London: Deutsch).
Willis, J. R. (1967) 'Jihād fī sabīl Allāh – its doctrinal basis in Islam and some aspects of its evolution in nineteenth-century West Africa', *JAH*, 8, 3, pp. 395–415.
Willis, J. R. (1970) "Al-Ḥājj 'Umar Sa'id al-Fūtī al-Tūrī (*c.* 1794–1864) and the doctrinal basis of his Islamic reformist movement in the Western Sudan' (PhD thesis, University of London).

Willis, J. R. (1978) 'The Torodbe clerisy: a social view', *JAH*, **19**, 2, pp. 195–212.
Willis, J. R. (ed.) (1979a) *Studies in West African Islamic History: The Cultivators of Islam* (London: Cass).
Willis, J. R. (1979b) 'Introduction: reflections on the diffusion of Islam in West Africa', in J. R. Willis (ed.) (1979a), pp. 1–39.
Willis, J. R. (1979c) 'The writings of al-Ḥājj 'Umar al-Fūtī and Shaykh Mukhtār b. Wadī' at Allāh: literary themes, sources and influences', in J. R. Willis (ed.) (1979a), pp. 177–210.
Willis, J. R. (forthcoming) *The Umarian Jama'a.*
Wills, A. J. (1964) *An Introduction to the History of Central Africa* (London: OUP).
Wills, A. J. (1967) *An Introduction to the History of Central Africa* (2nd edn, London: OUP).
Wilson, A. (1972) 'Long-distance trade and the Luba Lomani empire', *JAH*, **13**, 4, pp. 575–89.
Wilson, M. (1958) 'The early history of the Transkei and Ciskei', *African Studies*, **18**, 4.
Wilson, M. (1969a) 'The Sotho, Venda, and Tsonga', in M. Wilson and L. Thompson (eds), pp. 131–82.
Wilson, M. (1969b) 'Co-operation and conflict: the Eastern Cape Frontier', in M. Wilson and L. Thompson (eds), pp. 233–71.
Wilson, M. (1971) 'The growth of peasant communities', in M. Wilson and L. Thompson (eds), pp. 49–103.
Wilson, M. and Thompson, L. (eds) (1969) *The Oxford History of South Africa. Vol. 1: South Africa to 1870* (Oxford: Clarendon Press).
Wilson, M. and Thompson, L. (eds) (1971) *The Oxford History of South Africa. Vol. 2: South Africa 1870–1966.* (Oxford: Clarendon Press).
Winstedt, R. (1958) *The Malays, a Cultural History* (5th edn, London: Routledge and Kegan Paul).
Withers-Gill, J. (1924) *The Moshi Tribe* (Accra: Government Printer).
Wolf, E. (1959) *Sons of the Shaking Earth* (Chicago: University of Chicago Press).
Wylde, A. B. (1901) *Modern Abyssinia* (London: Methuen).
Wylie, K. C. (1970–1) 'Notes on Kailundu's campaign into Liberia in 1889', *Liberian Studies Journal*, 3, 2, pp. 167–72.
Wylie, K. C. (1977) *The Political Kingdom of the Temne. Temne Government in Sierra Leone, 1825–1910*, (New York: Africana Publishing).

Ylvisaker, M. (1975) 'The political and economic relationship of the Lamu archipelago to the adjacent Kenya coast in the nineteenth century' (PhD thesis, Boston University).
Ylvisaker, M. (1983) *Lamu in the Nineteenth Century: Land, Trade and Politics* (Boston: Boston University Press).
Yoder, J. C. (1974) 'Fly and elephant parties: political polarization in Dahomey, 1840–1870', *JAH*, 15, 3, pp. 417–32.
Yule, H. and Burnell, A. C. (1886) *Hobson-Jobson: being a glossary of Anglo-Indian colloquial words and phrases* (London: John Murray).

Zebadia, A. (1974) 'The career and correspondence of Ahmed al-Bakkāy of Tombuctu: an historical study of his political and religious role from 1847 to 1866' (PhD thesis, University of London).
el-Zein, A. (1974) *Sacred Meadows: Structural Analysis of Religious Symbolism in an East African Town* (Evanston: NUP).
Zewde Gabre-Sellassie (1975) *Yohannes IV of Ethiopia* (Oxford: Clarendon Press).
Ziadeh, N. (1958) *Sanūsīyah: A Study of a Revivalist Movement in Islam* (Leiden: Brill).

Index

Notes:
1. Page references with n refer to footnotes where extra detail is given.
2. Sub-entries are in alphabetical order, except where chronological order is significant.
3. Individual places shown on maps have not been included in the page references.

Nine Nations, 220